A TREATISE

ON THE

LAW AND PRACTICE

OF

INJUNCTIONS IN EQUITY

BY

WILLIAM WILLIAMSON KERR,

OF LINCOLN'S INN, BARRISTER-AT-LAW.

EDITED, WITH NOTES AND REFERENCES TO AMERICAN CASES,

By WM. A. HERRICK.

BOSTON:

LITTLE, BROWN, AND COMPANY.

1871.

ADVERTISEMENT.

This Edition of Kerr on Injunctions in Equity is a reprint of the English edition with the author's *addenda et corrigenda* inserted in the proper places in the text and notes. The Editor has prefixed to the chapters and sections of the author a considerably minute analysis of the same, and made such notes and references to American cases as he thought would serve to make the work more acceptable to American lawyers. The English cases which have been reported since the publication of the English edition are added to the original notes and not distinguished from them.

SUMMARY OF CONTENTS.

THE FIGURES REFER TO THE STAR PAGING.

CHAPTER XXI.

CHAPTER XXII.

CHAPTER XXIII.

CHAPTER XXIV.

CHAPTER XXV.

CHAPTER XXVI.

CHAPTER XXVII.

CHAPTER XXVIII.

CHAPTER XXIX.

TABLE OF CASES CITED.

b

STATUTES REFERRED TO.

A TREATISE

ON THE

LAW AND PRACTICE OF INJUNCTIONS IN EQUITY.

A TREATISE

ON THE

LAW AND PRACTICE OF INJUNCTIONS IN EQUITY.

CHAPTER I.

THE NATURE AND THE LIMITS OF THE JURISDICTION OF THE
COURT OF CHANCERY.

1. Civil property is the subject-matter of the jurisdiction of the court of chancery.
2. Matters of a political character not within its jurisdiction.
3. Nor will the court interfere in favor of the laws of another country in conflict with the policy of its own.
4. Nor with the public duties of any department of government, foreign sovereignty, &c.
5. Jurisdiction is not entertained if the remedy at law is adequate. — Meaning of "concurrent" jurisdiction.
6. "Complete justice" comprises what in view of courts of equity. — Discretion of court.
7. Want of legal remedy does not necessarily create an equitable right.
8. Court of chancery is not deprived of its jurisdiction once assumed except by express statutory enactment.
9. The exercise of its jurisdiction is discretionary with the court.
10. Court of equity will not allow itself to be made the instrument of injustice.
11. *Lord Redesdale's* description and division of the jurisdiction of courts of equity.
12. This jurisdiction operates *in personam.*
13. This fact extends instead of contracting its powers.
14. Court has power to restrain a man from applying to parliament or foreign legislature.
15. Modes of relief in equity twofold, — remedial and preventive.

1. THE subject-matter of the jurisdiction of the court of chancery is civil property. The court is conversant only with questions of property and the maintenance of civil rights. Injury to property, whether actual or prospective, is the foundation on which the jurisdiction rests (*a*). The court has no jurisdiction in matters merely criminal or merely immoral, which do not affect any right to property.[1] If a charge be of a

---

(*a*) Att.-Gen. *v.* Sheffield Gas Co., 3 D. M. & G. 304, 320; Emperor of Austria *v.* Day, 3 D. F. & J. 217, 253.
[1] Burnett *v.* Craig, 30 Ala. 135;

Brandreth *v.* Lance, 8 Paige, 24. See also Kneedler *v.* Lane, 3 Grant's Cases, 523.

1

criminal nature, or an offence against the public peace, and does not touch the enjoyment of property, jurisdiction cannot be entertained. The court has no jurisdiction to restrain or prevent crime, or to enforce the performance of a moral duty, except so far as the same is concerned with rights to property; nor can it interfere on the ground of any criminal offence committed, or for the purpose of giving a better remedy in the case of a criminal offence, or for putting a stop to acts, which, if permitted, would lead to a breach of the public peace (b). The possible effect of the acts and conduct of one man on the reputation of another, is not a ground for the interference of the court, unless there be an injury to property (c). An in-
* 2   junction * cannot therefore be had to restrain the publication of a libel (d), or proceedings in a criminal matter (e). But if an act which is criminal touches also the enjoyment of property, the court has jurisdiction, but its interference is founded solely on the ground of injury to property (f). If a party, who might proceed by indictment, chooses to consider the matter not as an indictable offence, but thinks proper to go to a court of law for recompense in matter of damages, the case becomes a civil action, and the defendant is entitled to all equities which defendants have in general cases in actions for damages (g).

2. Nor do matters of a political character come within the jurisdiction of the court of chancery. The court will not interfere with the view of preventing revolution in a foreign country, or in favor either of the prerogative of a foreign sovereign or the political rights of his subjects, or in aid of the revenue laws of a foreign country. But if a case of injury to the property of a foreign sovereign or his government or his

---

(b) Ib. Mayor of York v. Pilkington, 2 Atk. 302; Gurtside v. Outram, 3 Jur. N. S. 40.

(c) Clarke v. Freeman, 11 Beav. 112; Cox v. Cox, 11 Ha. 124.

(d) Gee v. Pritchard, 2 Sw. 402; Martin v. Wright, 6 Sim. 297; Clarke v. Freeman, 11 Beav. 112. See Emperor of Austria v. Day, 3 D. F. & J. 217, 253.

(e) Holderstaffe v. Saunders, 6 Mod. 12; Montagu v. Dudman, 2 Ves. 396;

Macaulay v. Shackell, 1 Bligh, N. S. 96, 127. Comp. Turner v. Turner, 15 Jur. 218.

(f) Mayor of York v. Pilkington, 2 Atk. 302; Macaulay v. Shackell, 1 Bligh, N. S. 127; Att.-Gen. v. Sheffield Gas Co., 3 D. M. & G. 304, 320; Emperor of Austria v. Day, 3 D. F. & J. 217, 253.

(g) Macaulay v. Shackell, 1 Bligh, N. S. 96, 127.

subjects be made out, the court has jurisdiction to interfere at the suit of a foreign sovereign (h).[1]

3. Nor will the court interfere in favor of any laws of a foreign country which are in conflict with our own laws, on subjects of religion and morality (i). Where the courts of one country are called upon to enforce a contract entered into in another, it is not enough that the contract should be valid according to the laws of that country; for if any part of the contract is inconsistent either with the law or policy of the former, the contract will not be enforced even as to another part of it, which would not be open to objection, and may be the only part remaining to be performed (k).

4. * The court of chancery has no jurisdiction to   * 3 interfere with the public duties of any of the departments of government (m), or with the sovereign acts of a foreign government (n), or to make a decree against a foreign ambassador who does not submit to the jurisdiction (o).

5. Though the jurisdiction of the court of chancery is limited to matters which concern civil property, jurisdiction will not be entertained in all cases which touch the enjoyment of property. If the remedy to be had in the courts of ordinary jurisdiction is sufficient for the purposes of complete justice, the court of chancery will not entertain jurisdiction. The sufficiency or the inadequacy, as the case may be, of the powers of the courts of ordinary jurisdiction for effectuating the purposes of complete justice is the rule and measure which regulates the course of the court of chancery in assuming or declining

---

(h) Emperor of Austria v. Day, 3 D. F. & J. 217; United States v. Prioleau, 2 H. & M. 559; 2 L. R. Eq. 659. Comp. City of Berne v. Bank of England, 9 Ves. 347; Jones v. Garcia del Rio, T. & R. 299.

(i) Emperor of Austria v. Day, 3 D. F. & J. 217, 253.

(k) Hope v. Carnegie, 8 D. M. & G. 731; but see Quarrier v. Colston, 1 Ph. 151.

(m) Ellis v. Grey, 6 Sim. 214.

(n) Gladstone v. Ottoman Bank, 1 H. & M. 505.

(o) Gladstone v. Musurus Bey, ib. 495. See Service v. Casteneda, 2 Coll. 56.

[1] Where the jurisdiction of the court depends upon the party, it is the party named in the record. Therefore, where in a suit in equity to compel the conveyance of certain real estate, standing in the name of the respondent, he pleaded to the jurisdiction that he was, and was from the first, well known to the petitioners to be only the agent of the British government, a foreign sovereignty, not liable to suit; that he had no personal interest whatever in the matter of the suit, and that the British government was the sole party to be affected by it, the plea was overruled in demurrer. Sharp's Rifle Manf'g Co. v. Rowan, 34 Conn. 329. See Osborn v. Bank of the United States, 9 Wheat. 738; Irvine v. Lowry, 14 Peters, 293; Bonnafee v. Williams, 3 Howard, 574:

to assume jurisdiction (*p*). If the remedy given by those courts is clear, certain, sufficient, and coextensive with the requisitions of the case, the court of chancery will not entertain jurisdiction. If, on the other hand, it falls short of what is required for the purposes of complete justice, the court will step in and supply the defect (*q*). When it is said that the jurisdiction of equity is "concurrent" with that of another court, it merely means that the measure of relief in the other court is the measure of relief in equity, and that the only difference is in the form of proceedings. But when the aid of the court is sought on the ground of the insufficiency of the relief to be got in the other court, the principle of the interference is not that the court has concurrent jurisdiction which would only enable it to do the very thing which the other court might itself, but that the court does not enough (*r*).

6. In determining whether the remedy given by the courts of ordinary jurisdiction comes up to the requisitions of complete *justice, a court of equity does not exercise a mere arbitrary discretion (*s*). Complete justice, as understood by a court of equity, though originally founded on the principles of natural justice and reason, has by authority, decision, and statute long grown into a system, and assumed a technical consistency and shape, and must be contradistinguished from all considerations of discretion, fairness, and equal justice, in the popular sense of the word (*t*). The principles of equity are as fixed and certain as the principles upon which the courts of common law proceed (*u*). "There are certain fixed principles," said Lord Redesdale, in Bond *v.* Hopkins (*x*), "on which courts of equity act, which are well settled. The cases which occur are various, but they are all decided on fixed principles. Courts of equity have in these respects no more discretionary power than the courts of law. They decide new cases as they arise by the principles on which former cases have been decided, and may thus enlarge and

---

(*p*) Mit. Pl. 145; Att.-Gen. *v.* Sheffield Gas. Co., 3 D. M. & G. 304, 320.

(*q*) Lumley *v.* Wagner, 1 D. M. & G. 616; Hunt *v.* Hunt, 8 Jur. N. S. 86; Emperor of Austria *v.* Day, 3 D. F. & J. 253.

(*r*) Castelli *v.* Cook, 7 Ha. 89.

(*s*) 1 Ha. 138.

(*t*) 1 Coop. t. Cot. 120. See Gardiner *v.* Edwards, 5 Ves. 592; Grierson *v.* Eyre, 9 Ves. 341.

(*u*) Emperor of Austria *v.* Day, 3 D. F. & J. 217, 238, 254.

(*x*) 1 Sch. & Lef. 429.

illustrate the operation of those principles; but the principles are as fixed and certain as the principles on which the courts of common law proceed" (*y*). "The discretion of the court," said Lord Romilly, M.R., in Haywood *v.* Cope (*z*), "must be exercised according to fixed and settled rules. The discretion which is to be exercised here is to be governed by the rules of law and equity, which are not to oppose, but each in its turn to be subservient to the other. This discretion in some cases follows the law implicitly; in others it assists and advances the remedy; in others again it relieves against the abuses or alleviates the rigor of it; but in no case does it contradict or overturn the grounds and principles thereof, as has been sometimes ignorantly imputed to this court. That is a discretionary power which neither this nor any other court, not even the highest, acting in a judicial capacity, is by the constitution intrusted with." It is, however, the duty of the court to adapt its practice and course of proceeding, as far as possible, to the existing state of society, and to apply its jurisdiction to all those new * cases which, from the progress daily   * 5 making in the affairs of men, must continually arise, and not, from too strict an adherence to forms and rules, established under very different circumstances, decline to administer justice and to enforce the rights for which there is no other remedy (*a*). The jurisdiction of the court must not be narrowed to cases in which the jurisdiction has been exercised. The cases in which the jurisdiction has been exercised are merely examples, and must not be looked on as the measure of the jurisdiction (*b*).[1]

7. The mere want of a legal remedy does not create an equitable right or a remedy in equity (*c*). A court of equity will, in certain cases, supply a remedy, where, in consequence of

---

(*y*) See case of Queensberry Leases, 1 Bligh, 339, 501, per Lord Redesdale.

(*z*) 25 Beav. 151.

(*a*) Taylor *v.* Salmon, 4 M. & C. 134, 141.

(*b*) Slim *v.* Croucher, 1 D. F. & J. 518. See also Jenner *v.* Morris, 3 D. F. & J 55.

(*c*) Kirk *v.* Bromley Union, 2 Ph. 648.

[1] "The absence of a plain and adequate remedy at law affords the only test of equity jurisdiction, and the application of this principle to a particular case must depend altogether upon the character of the case, as disclosed in the pleadings;" but in order to be plain and adequate the remedy at law must be as practical and efficient to the ends of justice, and its prompt administration, as the remedy in equity. Boyce's Ex'rs *v.* Grundy, 3 Peters, 210; Watson *v.* Sutherland, 5 Wallace, 74.

the infirmity of legal process, there is neither a right nor a remedy at law, but only what the law in principle acknowledges to be a wrong (d). But it does not follow that because in any particular instance there is no legal remedy, therefore there must be an equitable one, unless there be an equitable right (e). Neither is a court of equity bound to find an equitable effect for any instrument, merely because the construction put upon it in a court of law leaves it inoperative (f). Circumstances must be shown bringing the case within the principle upon which the peculiar jurisdiction is founded (g). Where the will of the legislature is clearly pronounced with regard to all the circumstances which belong to a case, equity can neither take it up where the laws leave it, nor extend the remedy further than the law allows (h).[1]

8. It is an established principle of the court never to abandon a jurisdiction which it has once assumed. The enlargement of the limits of the jurisdiction of other courts or the creation of a new jurisdiction in other courts, whether by statutory enactment, or by an alteration of the rules of pleading, or by the adoption of equitable principles, does not oust
* 6   or displace * the jurisdiction of the court in matters originally within its cognizance, and in which relief was originally to be had in equity alone (i). Express statutory enactment can alone take away any part of the original jurisdiction of the court (k). If the case be one in which the court has never assumed jurisdiction, and there is a complete remedy

---

(d) 3 D. F. & J. 55, 254, per Turner, L. J.

(e) Wake v. Conyers, 1 Ed. 335; Serj. Maynard's case, 2 Freem. 2; Macleod v. Drummond, 14 Ves. 360.

(f) Gladstone v. Birley, 2 Mer. 401.

(g) Gardiner v. Edwards, 5 Ves. 592; Grierson v. Eyre, 9 Ves. 341; comp. Parkhurst v. Lowten, 2 Sw. 209.

(h) Heard v. Stanford, Ca. t. Talb. 174.

(i) Walmisley v. Child, 1 Ves. 341; Codd v. Wooden, 3 Bro. C. C. 72; Atkinson v. Leonard, ib. 218; Ex parte Greenway, 6 Ves. 812; Bromley v. Holland, 7 Ves. 19; Jackman v. Mitchell, 13 Ves. 581; Eyre v. Everett, 2 Russ. 382; Att.-Gen. v. Aspinall, 2 M. & C. 613; Williams v. Roberts, 8 Ha. 315;

Duke of Beaufort v. Need, 12 Cl. & Fin. 248, 258; Wright v. Maidstone, 1 K. & J. 709; Davies v. Stainbank, 6 D. M. & G. 696; Slim v. Croucher, 1 D. F. & J. 528; Stackhouse v. Countess of Jersey, 1 J. & H. 721; Barry v. Crosskey, 2 J. & H. 1; Jenner v. Morris, 3 D. F. & J. 45; Shepard v. Brown, 4 Giff. 208.

(k) Slim v. Croucher, 1 D. F. & J. 528.

[1] Where a statute has made provision for all the circumstances of a particular case, no relief can be afforded in equity, though the provisions of the statute may conflict with the notions of natural justice and equity entertained by a court of chancery. Glenn v. Fowler, 8 Gill & J. 340.

at law, the jurisdiction will not be entertained (*l*). The circumstance that a court of law may have assumed jurisdiction in matters not originally within its cognizance, does not alter the principle that a court of equity will not impeach the decision of a court of law after it has solemnly decided the subject of the suit (*m*).

9. The existence of the jurisdiction is never of itself a reason for its exercise. The court is in each case guided by its own discretion, and will not interfere unless it is satisfied that the case is one in which the jurisdiction can be properly and beneficially exercised, and ought in fact to be exercised (*n*).[1] The question for the court to consider where its interposition is sought in cases where a remedy may be had in the courts of ordinary jurisdiction, is whether the remedy there given is sufficient and adequate for the purposes of justice (*o*). It by no means follows that because a statute gives a court of law juris-

(*l*) Wright *v.* Lord Maidstone, 1 K. & J. 701.

(*m*) Thompson *v.* Dereham, 1 Ha. 379.

(*n*) Lumley *v.* Wagner, 1 D. M. & G. 616; Slim *v.* Croucher, 1 D. F. & J. 528.

(*o*) Hunt *v.* Hunt, 8 Jur. N. S. 86; Emperor of Austria *v.* Day, 3 D. F. & J. 217, 253.

[1] The granting, continuing, and dissolving of temporary injunctions rests in the discretion of the court of original jurisdiction; and therefore an appeal will not lie from an order dissolving such injunction by the court granting it. Van Dewater *v.* Kelsey, 1 N. Y. 533.

The granting of an execution is not *ex debito justitiæ* for any injury threatened or done to the estate or rights of a person; but the granting of it must always rest in sound discretion governed by the nature of the case. Hine *v.* Stephens, 33 Conn. 497 and cases cited; Grey *v.* Ohio and Pennsylvania Railroad, 1 Grant's Cases, 412; Cobb *v.* Smith, 16 Wis. 661; Jones *v.* Newark, 3 Stockton, 452; Reddall *v.* Bryan, 14 Md. 444.

And the granting and continuing of injunctions rests mainly on equitable grounds, and is not exercised for the mere purpose of protecting legal rights irrespective of the claim of the party to equitable relief. Hilles *v.* Parrish, 1 Mc-

Carter, 380; Kneedler *v.* Lane, 3 Grant's Cases, 523; State *v.* Judge, 16 La. An. 233. As to considerations which will determine the court in granting an injunction, see Real Del Monte, &c., Mining Co. *v.* Pond, &c., Mining Co., 23 Cal. 82; Wason *v.* Sanborn, 45 N. H. 169; Lewis *v.* Rough, 26 Ind. 398. The court may refuse an injunction if the proceedings are such as to show that a full disclosure of all the facts has not been made by the complainant. Canton Co. *v.* Northern, &c., R. Co., 21 Md. 383.

The necessity that the subject-matter should be capable of being clearly ascertained, is most obvious, in order that the mandate of the court may be certain, and without ambiguity, that what the defendant is commanded to do, or not to do, may be certain and definite. Wason *v.* Sanborn, 45 N. H. 169.

The trivial amount of damage already suffered by the plaintiff is no reason for refusing a perpetual injunction, where, without it, the adverse use might ripen into a right. Corning *v.* Troy, &c., Factory, 34 Barb. 485.

Where the defendant asserted a perpetual public easement in the lands of the plaintiff, and in assertion of his claim committed such acts upon the land, as in time, if not restrained, might afford a vindication of his claim, it was held, that a court of equity might properly grant an injunction. Carpenter *v.* Gwynn, 35 Barb. 395.

diction in certain matters, that therefore this court should decline to exercise the jurisdiction (*p*). The superior powers which a court of equity possesses, of adapting its decrees to the special circumstances of each particular case, of adjust-
* 7   ing cross equities, * of laying down the conduct to be observed by the several parties to the suit, of imposing terms, and generally of doing justice in the most minute detail, makes the interference of the court in matters of complex and intricate litigation so conducive to the interests of justice, that jurisdiction will be entertained in cases where the courts of ordinary jurisdiction are themselves able to give a remedy (*q*).

10. A court of equity will in no case allow itself to be made the instrument of injustice. In cases depending on legal titles equity follows the law: where, however, by the interposition of the court to prevent an act rightfully or wrongfully intended, a man has lost a remedy at law, the court will give him a remedy equivalent to that from which the interposition of the court has debarred him (*r*).

11. The general jurisdiction of the court of chancery has been divided by Lord Redesdale in his treatise on Pleading into two classes. The first class is where the court is called upon to decide the right to property; the other is where it is called upon to interfere without deciding upon any such right. The first of these classes has been subdivided by him into three sub-classes. 1st. Where the principle of the law gives a right, but the forms of law do not give a remedy, or cannot give the most complete remedy. In such cases the court will interfere and give those remedies which the ordinary courts would give, if their powers were equal to the purpose, or their modes of administering justice would reach the evil, and also to enforce the remedies attempted to be given by those courts where their effect is so defeated (*s*). 2d. Where the powers of the law are abused and exercised contrary to conscience. 3d. Where the law gives no right, but the principles of complete justice require the interference of the judicial power to prevent the

---

(*p*) Stewart *v.* Great Western Railway Co., 11 Jur. N. S. 628.
(*q*) Slim *v.* Croucher, 1 D. F. & J. 524; Barry *v.* Crosskey, 2 J. & H. 1.
(*r*) Pulteney *v.* Warren, 6 Ves. 73;
Brown *v.* Newall, 2 M. & C. 558, 572. See Shine *v.* Gough, 1 B. & B. 444.
(*s*) See Jenner *v.* Morris, 3 D. F. & J. 55.

recurrence of a wrong. With reference to the second of these classes into which the jurisdiction has been divided, courts of equity administer to the ends of justice : 1st, By removing impediments * to the fair decision of a question in other   * 8 courts ; 2dly, By providing for the safety of property in dispute pending litigation ; 3dly, By preserving property in danger of being dissipated or destroyed by those to whose care it is by law intrusted, or by persons having immediate but partial interests ; 4thly, By restraining the assertion of doubtful rights in a manner productive of irreparable injury ; 5thly, By preventing injury to those persons from the doubtful title of others ; 6thly, By putting a bound to vexatious and oppressive litigation, and to prevent multiplicity of suits ; 7thly, By preserving testimony and enforcing discovery (t). This description and division of the jurisdiction has been adopted and approved by Lord Justice Turner, and has been applied by him as the test by which the jurisdiction of the court must be considered as bounded. In a case which could not be brought within any of these subdivisions, he would not entertain jurisdiction, saying that the court cannot extend its jurisdiction under color of carrying out its principles (u).

12. The jurisdiction of the court of chancery over property is not immediate, but is carried into effect by means of personal decrees (x). The court being, from its original constitution, a court of conscience, persons are the objects to whom its decrees and orders are addressed. An immediate jurisdiction over things has been in certain cases conferred by statute ; but with these exceptions, and with that of the jurisdiction by writ of assistance in certain cases (y), the form and character of the original constitution of the jurisdiction has not been changed. Except in the case of infants, the court does not exercise any jurisdiction over persons where no claims or rights to property are concerned. The relation of persons to property is, in all cases, with the single exception of the case of infants, requisite to be shown as a foundation for the interference of the court, persons being the object and property the subject-

(t) Mitf. Pl. 133.
(u) Pennell v. Roy, 3 D. M. & G. 138. See 3 D. F. & J. 55, 254; per Turner, L. J.

(x) Houlditch v. Lord Donegal, 8 Bligh, 344.
(y) 1 Atk. 544; 1 Ves. 454; 3 Bligh, 165.

matter of the jurisdiction. The court has no jurisdiction, unless
the person to whom its orders are addressed is within
* 9   the reach of the * court or amenable to its jurisdiction.

The person must be not only within the reach of the
court as to locality, but he must bear such a character as shall
render him personally amenable to the jurisdiction (z).

13. The fact that the orders and decrees of the court operate
immediately upon persons has had the effect of giving the court
a very extensive jurisdiction instead of presenting an obstacle
to its powers, as might perhaps have been expected. As a consequence of the rule, the court may exercise jurisdiction quite
independently of the locality of the act to be done, provided
the person against whom relief is sought is within the reach
and amenable to the process of the court. In exercising the
jurisdiction, the court does not lay any claim to the exercise of
judicial or administrative rights in a foreign country, but proceeds solely on the circumstance of the person to whom the
order is addressed being within the reach of the court (a).

14. As a further consequence of the same rule, the court
has power, upon a proper case being made out, to restrain a
man from applying to Parliament (b), or to the legislature of
a foreign country (c). But the jurisdiction will only be exercised under very exceptional circumstances (d).[1] The court
cannot, however, restrain a man from applying for a grant to
a foreign sovereign, nor, after the grant is made, can the court
prevent a man from using the grant made by the same sovereign authority. The fact that the grant so made may be
inconsistent with a grant previously made by the same sovereign authority does not give a man any equity to apply to the
court (e).

(z) 5 H. L. 436.
(a) Houlditch v. Lord Donegal, 8
Bligh, 341; Lord Portarlington v. Soulby, 3 M. & K. 108; Carron Iron Co. v.
Maclaren, 5 H. L. 436; but see Norris
v. Chambres, 7 Jur. N. S. 689; see also
Cood v. Cood, 33 Beav. 314.

(b) Ware v. Grand Junction Railway
Co., 2 R. & M. 483; Heathcoate v. North
Staffordshire Railway Co., 2 Mac. & G.
109; Stockton and Hartlepool Railway
Co. v. Leeds and Thirsk Railway Co., 2
Ph. 666; comp. Att.-Gen. v. Manches-

ter and Leeds Railway Co., 1 Ra. Ca.
436.

(c) Bell v. Sierra Nevada Co., 1 D. F.
& J. 183.

(d) See also Lancaster and Carlisle
Railway Co. v. North Western Railway
Co., 2 K. & J. 293.

(e) Gladstone v. Ottoman Bank, 1 H.
& M. 505.

[1] It is held in Story v. Jersey City
and Bergen Point Plank Road Co., 1 C.
E. Green, 13, that the court has no
power to restrain a citizen from peti-

15. The relief afforded by courts of equity is of a twofold * character. It is either remedial or preventive.   * 10 The court either grants positive and affirmative relief, or restrains the doing of acts which are against equity and conscience.   In giving remedial relief, the court proceeds usually by decree.   Preventive relief is administered by injunction.   Relief by decree and relief by injunction are supplementary to each other in meeting and completing the requisitions of justice.   Whenever a man appears entitled to equitable relief, if it consists in restraining the commission or the continuance of some act of the defendant, a court of equity administers that relief by injunction (f).

tioning the legislature upon any subject   (f) See Eden on Inj. 2.
in which he is interested.

* 11   * CHAPTER II.

INJUNCTIONS IN GENERAL.

1. An injunction defined.
2. Distinction between interlocutory and perpetual injunctions.

1. AN injunction is a writ issuing by order and under seal of a court of equity. A writ of injunction may be described to be a judicial process whereby a party is required to do a particular thing or to refrain from doing a particular thing according to the exigency of the writ. The process, however, is rather preventive than restorative, though it is by no means confined to the former object. When commanding an act to be done, it issues after decree, and is in the nature of an execution to enforce the same; as, for instance, it may contain a direction to the party defendant to yield up or to quit or continue the possession of the land or other property which constitutes the subject-matter of the decree in favor of the other party (*a*).

2. Injunctions are either interlocutory or perpetual. Interlocutory injunctions are such as are to continue until the hearing of the cause upon the merits, or until discovery, if that be the object of the application, or generally until further order. Perpetual injunctions are such as form part of the decree made at the hearing upon the merits, whereby the defendant is perpetually inhibited from the assertion of a right or perpetually restrained from the commission of an act which would be contrary to equity and good conscience (*b*). The perpetual injunction is in effect a decree, and concludes a right. The interlocutory injunction is merely provisional in its nature, and does not conclude a right. The effect and object

* 12   of the interlocutory injunction is merely to preserve the property in dispute *in statu quo* until the hearing or further order. In interfering by interlocutory injunction, the

(*a*) Gilb. For. Rom., ch. 11, pp. 194, 195; Stribley *v.* Hawke, 3 Atk. 275; Huguenin *v.* Basley, 15 Ves. 180; Gray *v.* Stanford, 8 Ir. Eq. 678; Eden on

Inj., ch. 1, pp. 1, 2; Story Eq. Jur. 861, 862.

(*b*) Gilb. For. Rom. 194, 195.

court does not in general profess to anticipate the determination of the right, but merely gives it as its opinion that there is a substantial question to be tried, and that till the question is ripe for trial, a case has been made out for the preservation of the property in the mean time *in statu quo*. A man who comes to the court for an interlocutory injunction is not required to make out a case which will entitle him at all events to relief at the hearing. It is enough if he can show that he has a fair question to raise as to the existence of the right which he alleges, and can satisfy the court that the property should be preserved in its present actual condition, until such question can be disposed of (*c*).[1]

(*c*) Glascott *v.* Lang, 3 M. & C. 451, 455; Hilton *v.* Lord Granville, Cr. & Ph. 283, 292; Great Western Railway Co. *v.* Birmingham and Oxford Junction Railway Co., 2 Ph. 597, 603; Shrewsbury and Chester Railway Co. *v.* Shrewsbury and Birmingham Railway Co., 1 Sim. N. S. 410, 426; Dyke *v.* Taylor, 3 D. F. & J. 467; Walker *v.* Jones, 1 L. R. P. C. 50, 61.

[1] "Except to stay waste, and prevent some irreparable injury, the writ of injunction is only granted as ancillary, or in aid of some primary equity, which the plaintiff seeks, by his bill, to enforce." Scofield *v.* Bokkelen, 5 Jones Eq. 342.

An unlawful act will not be enjoined simply because unlawful. It must cause irreparable injury, for which there is no redress at law. Babcock *v.* New Jersey Stock Yard Co., 5 C. E. Green, 298. And irreparable injury is such as is not susceptible of compensation in damages. Richard's Appeal, 57 Penn. St. 105.

* 13   # *CHAPTER III.

INJUNCTIONS TO RESTRAIN PROCEEDINGS AT LAW.

1. A DEFENDANT to an action at law has often some equitable defence which a court of law cannot take cognizance of either by reason of want of jurisdiction, or from the infirmity of legal process. As it would be against conscience and good faith that the plaintiff at law should use the advantage of which he is thus possessed at law, a court of equity will restrain by injunction an action at law, where the right sought to be enforced by the action is subservient to an equitable claim which the defendant at law cannot set up there. The court interferes on the principle of preventing a legal right from being enforced in an inequitable manner, or for an inequitable purpose.[1] The

[1] To prevent an unfair use being made of the process of a court of law, in order to deprive another party of his just rights. Smithurst *v.* Edmunds, 1 McCarter, 408.

right to relief by injunction extends to all cases where actions at law have been commenced before the ordinary tribunals in respect of disputes which involve an equitable element. The ground for imposing the restraint is, that as the ordinary tribunals cannot adjudicate an equity, a part only of the dispute, and not the whole dispute, would be decided there. The court, therefore, interferes in order that the real question, and the whole matter in dispute between the parties may be determined (*a*). It is not, however, the course of the court to withdraw the consideration and decision of a case from a court of law, unless it can be shown to the satisfaction of the court that the case involves an equitable element. A man has no right to come to the court for relief, if he has a good defence at law and * cannot show a good equitable case (*b*).   * 14 The mere assertion of an equity is not sufficient. A case must be shown sufficient to satisfy the court that the question really involves an equitable element, and is a fit subject for investigation in a court of equity (*c*). The court must, before it interferes, be satisfied that there is an equity calling for its interference as clear as the legal right which it is called upon to control (*d*). It is not, however, necessary that a case should be made out which would entitle the plaintiff to relief, at all events at the hearing. It is enough if the court finds upon the pleadings and the evidence a case which makes the transaction a proper subject for investigation in a court of equity (*e*). The question for the court upon the interlocutory application is not the final merits of the case. When the case comes on to be heard, the final merits may be very different. But this consideration will not prevent the court from breaking in upon the proceedings at law, where from the merits to be gathered from the pleadings and conflicting affidavits there appears on the whole a case

(*a*) Jones *v.* Hughes, 1 Ha. 389 ; McFadden *v.* Jenkins, *ib.* 458 ; Thompson *v.* Dereham, *ib.* 379 ; Dawson *v.* Lawes, Kay, 281 ; Magnay *v.* Mines Royal Co., 3 Drew. 130 ; Buckland *v.* Gibbins, 32 L. J. Ch. 391. See Duncombe *v.* Greenacre, 2 D. F. & J. 509 ; Causton *v.* City Offices Co., 14 W. R. 977.

(*b*) Hardinge *v.* Webster, 1 Dr. & Sm. 101 ; Traill *v.* Baring, 33 L. J. Ch. 521.

(*c*) Meux *v.* Smith, 7 Jur. 821 ; Hardinge *v.* Webster, 1 Dr. & Sm. 101 ; Dyke *v.* Taylor, 3 D. F. & J. 473.

(*d*) Osborne *v.* Eales, 2 Moo. P. C. N. S. 125.

(*e*) Glascott *v.* Lang, 2 M. & C. 451, 455 ; Powell *v.* Lloyd, 1 Y. & J. 427 ; Meux *v.* Smith, 7 Jur. 821. See Cotesworth *v.* Stephens, 4 Ha. 185 ; Williams *v.* Roberts, 8 Ha. 315.

proper for the investigation of the court, and a fair question to be reserved till the hearing (*f*). The court deals with the injunction upon the evidence before it. If the court sees nothing to deprive the plaintiff of the equity to which the circumstances entitle him, it is bound to grant the injunction. If there be any new facts, the defendant may avail himself of them at the hearing, or on the motion to dissolve (*g*).

2. The writ of injunction by which proceedings at law are restrained, is not in the nature of a prohibition. In issuing injunctions, courts of equity claim no supremacy over the ordinary tribunals. An injunction is addressed only to the individual, and is not directed to the court.[1] Courts of equity in issuing the writ, not only do not deny, but in fact

* 15   admit, the * jurisdiction of the ordinary tribunals.[2] The

---

(*f*) Magnay *v.* Mines Royal Co., 3 Drew, 130.

(*g*) Espey *v.* Lake, 10 Ha. 260.

[1] Where a citizen of one state has attached in another state, personal property of a debtor, who resides in the first state, and who is insolvent under the laws of such state, it is the duty of the court of that state, in the exercise of a sound judicial discretion, to enjoin the creditor from proceeding with his suit, if thereby the property will come to the hands of the assignees in insolvency. Dehon *v.* Foster, 7 Allen, 57.

A state court has no power to enjoin proceedings in a court of the United States. Kendall *v.* Winsor, 6 R. I. 453.

But where parties were enjoined by the state court from prosecuting certain claims, and while the injunction was in force filed a bill in the United States court to foreclose a mortgage given to secure these claims, it was held that the state court had the right to punish them for proceeding in the United States court in violation of the injunction, but no right to order a dismissal of the proceedings. Hines *v.* Rawson, 40 Ga. 356.

And in Williams *v.* Ayrault, 31 Barb. 364, it is held, that an action cannot be maintained in the courts of one state to enjoin and restrain the prosecution of an action commenced and pending in a court of a sister state ; and this is said to be the settled rule in this country. But the contrary is held in Vermont. Bank of Bellows Falls *v.* R. & B. Railroad, 28 Vt. 470. See Story's Eq. Jur. §§ 899 and 900.

[2] One court will not restrain by injunction the proceedings previously instituted in another of co-ordinate chancery jurisdiction. The proper course is to apply to the court by petition for an order in the original suit. Platto *v.* Deuster, 22 Wis. 482.

"With the proceedings and determinations of inferior boards or tribunals of special jurisdiction, courts of equity will not interfere, unless it should become necessary to prevent a multiplicity of suits or irreparable injury, or unless the proceeding sought to be annulled or corrrected is valid upon its face, and the alleged invalidity consists in matters to be established by extrinsic evidence. In other cases the review and correction of the proceedings must be obtained by the writ of *certiorari*." Therefore, where a bill was filed to enjoin the enforcement of certain judgments rendered against the complainant by the mayor of St. Louis for the amount of alleged benefit to his property from the opening of a street in that city, and setting forth, as grounds of relief, want of authority in the mayor, and various defects and irregularities in the proceedings, a demurrer on the ground that a court of equity had no jurisdiction of the matter, and that the complainant had a plain, adequate, and complete remedy at law, was sustained. Ewing *v.* City of St. Louis, 5 Wallace, 413.

Crandall *v.* Bacon, 20 Wis. 639. Nor will a court of equity grant an injunction against a non-resident trustee of

[16]

injunction merely controls the party personally to whom it is addressed in the use he is attempting to make of the judgments of those tribunals, where the legal right which he is asserting at law is subservient to an equitable interest of which a court of law cannot take cognizance. The real object of the injunction is to prevent the judgment of the courts of law from being made an instrument of injustice (*h*).

3. It is the rule of the court, in the exercise of its jurisdiction to restrain by injunction actions at law, not to break in upon the proceedings at law more than is necessary for the purposes of justice (*i*), or to interfere, except it is satisfied that the exercise of the jurisdiction will be beneficial (*k*). If the defendant at law has a good defence at law, and the remedy at law is as perfect and complete as the remedy in equity, the court will not restrain the action (*l*).[1] Where, for instance, the

---

railway mortgage bonds, the purpose of which is to transfer a litigation pending in the courts of the State where such trustee resides into another forum for decision. Bellows Falls Bank *v.* Rutland & Bur. R.R. 28 Vt. 470.

And where relief is asked on the grounds of accident or mistake alone, there must be clear, explicit, and conclusive proof of the mistake to justify the interference of a court of equity. Katz *v.* Moore, 13 Md. 566. In this last case the court refused to restrain execution of a judgment at law upon the ground that the defendant had been discharged under the insolvent laws prior to its rendition, and that it was not entered subject to such discharge. The court say that, though the complainant may have been released from legal liability to pay his debts on which the judgment was rendered, yet his moral obligation is as strong as ever, and would be a sufficient consideration for a new promise to pay them, and fully sustained the judgment.

Where an attorney of the court in regular practice and perfectly responsible appears, and answers for the defendant in a suit at law, though without authority, execution of the judgment obtained against such defendant will not be enjoined in equity. Bunton *v.* Lyford, 37 N. H. 512; Cyphert *v.* McClune, 22 Penn. 195; Jackson *v.* Stewart, 6 Johns. 84; Denton *v.* Noyes, 6 *ib.* 300.

(*h*) Hill *v.* Turner, 1 Atk. 516; Harrison *v.* Gurney, 2 J. & W. 563; Lord Portarlington *v.* Soulby, 3 M. & K. 104; Bunbury *v.* Bunbury, 3 Jur. 644; Heathcoate *v.* North Staffordshire Railway Co., 2 Mac. & G. 109; Hunt *v.* Hunt, 8 Jur. N. S. 88.

(*i*) Bond *v.* Hopkins, 1 Sch. & Lef. 431.

(*k*) Lumley *v.* Wagner, 1 D. M. & G. 616; Slim *v.* Croucher, 1 D. F. & J. 528.

(*l*) Thrale *v.* Ross, 3 Bro. C. C. 56; Corporation of Arundel *v.* Holmes, 4 Beav. 325; Norris *v.* Day, 4 Y. & C. 475; Fox *v.* Hill, 2 D. & J. 356; Thiedemann *v.* Goldschmidt, 1 D. F. & J. 4; Hardinge *v.* Webster, 1 Dr. & Sm. 106. See Graves *v.* Houlditch, 2 Pri. 147.

[1] But not unless the remedy at law is adequate. Bissell *v.* Beckwith, 33 Conn. 357. And the neglect in such case of the defendant to object to the jurisdiction of the court of equity will not entitle the complainant to a preliminary injunction to restrain the proceeding at law; but when a final decree shall be made, the court by injunction may restrain any proceedings at law inconsistent with the rights of the parties as established by such decree. N. Y. Dry Dock Co. *v.* The Amer. Life Ins. and Trust Co., &c., 11 Paige, 384.

And the ground that an award was obtained by the fraud and corruption of the arbitrators, or that the matters upon which the award was made were not

2

illegality of an instrument, if it be illegal, is apparent on the face of the instrument, so that no lapse of time, or change of circumstances, can weaken the means of defence, whenever an action shall be brought upon it, the defendant will be left to that means of defence, and has no occasion to come to equity for relief (*m*). But if the illegality of an instrument is not apparent on the face of an instrument, but depends on evidence *dehors* the instrument, so that the means of defence is likely to fail from lapse of time, or change of circumstances (*n*), *16 or if the court is *satisfied that the exercise of the jurisdiction would, under the circumstances of the case, be beneficial and conducive to the interests of justice, it will interfere even in cases where there may be a good defence at law, and will order the instrument to be delivered up and cancelled (*o*). If an equitable case be made by the bill, it is not the course of the court in a matter originally belonging to it, to allow an action at law to proceed, unless it is satisfied that a court of law can do justice between the parties (*p*).

submitted, are defences to a suit at law upon such award, and so an injunction will not be granted against a suit on such award. Snediker *v.* Pearson, 2 Barb. Ch. 107.

And where the plaintiff had recovered judgment in an action of ejectment for a forfeiture by reason of non-payment of rent, the defendant was not allowed to show, in a suit in equity, brought to restrain the enforcement of the judgment, that the rent ought, under the stipulations of the lease, to have been reduced in amount, as the plaintiff could not have recovered without proving to the satisfaction of the jury that the exact amount demanded was due. Any failure in this respect would have been fatal to the action. Then was the time for the defendant to assert and prove such claim. Sheets *v.* Selden, 7 Wallace, 416.

Chancellor Kent says : " It is a settled principle, that a party will not be aided after a trial at law, unless he can impeach the justice of the verdict or report, by facts, or on grounds of which he could not have availed himself, or was prevented from doing it by fraud or accident, or the act of the opposite party unmixed with negligence or fault on his part." Duncan *v.* Lyon, 3 Johns.

Ch. 356 ; Floyd *v.* Jayne, 6 Johns. Ch. 479. And not in equity in such cases, probably, if the court at law had power to grant a new trial of the cause. See Hubbard *v.* Eastman, 47 N. H. 507, for an extended discussion of this subject.

(*m*) Gray *v.* Mathias, 5 Ves. 286 ; Simpson *v.* Lord Howden, 3 M. & C. 97 ; Fenn *v.* Craig, 3 Y. & C. 216 ; Jones *v.* Lane, *ib.* 281, 294 ; Williams *v.* Flight, 5 Beav. 41 ; Smyth *v.* Griffin, 14 L. J. Ch. 28 ; Heath *v.* Heath, 9 Ir Eq. 635 ; Anderson *v.* Dowling, 11 Ir. Eq. 590.

(*n*) Bromley *v.* Holland, 5 Ves. 617, 7 Ves. 19 ; Hayward *v.* Dimsdale, 17 Ves. 111 ; Grover *v.* Hugell, 3 Russ. 428 ; Lord Milltown *v.* Stuart, 3 M. & C. 18 ; Fenn *v* Craig, 3 Y & C. 216 ; Jones *v.* Lane, *ib.* 281, 294 ; Sismey *v.* Eley, 17 Sim. 1. See Thiedemann *v.* Goldschmidt, 1 D. F. & J. 4 ; Cooper *v.* Joel, *ib.* 242.

(*o*) Jervis *v* White, 7 Ves. 415 ; Hodgson *v.* Murray, 2 Sim 517, 3 Sim. 283. See Williams *v.* Roberts, 8 Ha. 315 ; Cooper *v.* Joel, 27 Beav. 313, 317 ; Stackhouse *v* Countess of Jersey, 1 J. & H. 731.

(*p*) Meux *v* Smith, 7 Jur. 825. See Thrale *v.* Ross, 3 Bro. C. C. 56.

The court may in such a case interfere by way of injunction, if necessary, and also by way of ordering the instrument to be delivered up (*q*). Whether or not it will interfere depends on the discretion of the court, according to the circumstances of the case. If the court is satisfied that the case is one which may be more satisfactorily tried at law, the action will be allowed to proceed (*r*).[1]

4. The court will not restrain by injunction an action at law, whenever an action at law ought not to be brought (*s*), nor will an injunction lie merely because the defendant at law cannot make out his case at law (*t*): nor is the fact that a court of law is miscarrying, or an Act of Parliament being abused, a ground for the interference of the court to restrain an action at law (*u*).[1]

5. The allegations in the bill must show an equitable case, and must be sufficient to sustain the injunction (*x*). The bill must allege the substance of the ground of relief (*y*), and must show *grounds on which the action at law   *17

(*q*) Traill *v.* Baring, 33 L. J. Ch. 521, 526. See Houlditch *v.* Nias, 8 Pri. 689; Fernihough *v.* Leader, 15 L. J. Ch. 458; Allen *v.* Davis, 20 L. J. Ch. 44; *infra.*

(*r*) Clarke *v.* Manning, 7 Beav. 162. See Mackintosh *v.* Wyatt, 3 Ha. 562.

(*s*) Cooper *v.* Joel, 1 D. F. & J. 240.

(*t*) Mangles *v.* Grand Dock Colliery Co., 10 Sim. 519.

(*u*) Lord Portsmouth *v.* Partridge, 8 W. R. 658.

(*x*) Cresy *v.* Beaven, 13 Sim. 99. See Glennie *v.* Imri, 3 Y. & C. 444.

(*y*) Nokes *v.* Fish, 3 Drew. 735.

[1] Where by mistake, accident, or fraud, judgment has been entered for an amount or in terms not intended, equity will, on clear proof, give relief. Katz *v.* Moore, •13 Md. 566. See also Blakesley *v.* Johnson, 13 Wis. 530; Tomkins *v.* Tomkins, 3 Stockt. 512; Wingate *v.* Haywood, 40 N. H. 437.

But it must appear clearly and unequivocally that the judgment at law was wrongfully and fraudulently obtained, without any negligence or fault of the party impeaching the judgment. Hungerford *v.* Sigerson, 20 How. U. S. 156; Johnson *v.* Lyon, 14 Iowa, 431; Wells *v.* Wall, 1 Oregon, 295; *ib.* 344; Lansing *v.* Eddy, 1 Johns. Ch. 49; Penny *v.* Morton, 4 Johns. Ch. 566;

Bartholomew *v.* Yaw, 9 Paige, 165; Thompson *v.* Berry, 17 Johns. 436.

Irregularity in the proceedings by which judgment was obtained, such as no service or defect of jurisdiction in the court, is not enough to warrant an injunction. It must appear that substantial injustice will be done if the judgment is enforced. Coon *v.* Jones, 10 Iowa, 131; Ableman *v.* Roth, 12 Wis. 81; Shricker *v.* Field, 9 Iowa, 366; Shedd *v.* Bank of Brattleboro', 32 Vt. 709; Gregory *v.* Ford, 14 Cal. 138. *Contra*, Bell *v.* Williams, 1 Head, Tenn. 229.

But a person in the quiet possession of real estate as owner, may obtain an injunction to restrain others from dispossessing him by means of process growing out of litigation to which he was not a party. Goodnough *v.* Sheppard, 28 Ill. 81.

When an attorney brings a suit without any authority from the plaintiff, and the defendant obtains a judgment for costs, a court of equity will restrain the enforcing such judgment by a perpetual injunction, if it be shown that the attorney is poor and unable to respond. Smyth *v.* Balch, 40 N. H. 363.

Equity will enjoin an inequitable use of a good judgment. Garlick *v.* McArthur, 6 Wis. 450.

may be sustained, otherwise it is demurrable (z).[1] The bill generally alleges that the plaintiff has no defence at law (a); but the allegation is not necessary if the bill show on its face an equitable case. Demurrer will lie, if the capacity of the plaintiff to defend the action successfully at law is stated in the bill (b).

6. The allegations in the bill must be supported by affidavits, so as to show on the face of the evidence that they are well founded (c).

7. An injunction to restrain proceedings at law may be obtained *ex parte*, or upon notice (d). If the application is *ex parte*, great caution is necessary in the exercise of the jurisdiction (e).

8. The jurisdiction of the court to restrain by injunction proceedings at law being founded on equitable principles, the general conduct of a man who seeks the aid of the court, must be fair and equitable in respect of the transaction in question. It is a rule of equity, that a man who seeks the assistance of the court must do justice as to the matters in respect of which that assistance is asked (f). He must be able to show that his own acts and dealings in the matter have been fair and consistent with equity (g). A man who has put himself in the wrong, or who has by his own conduct brought about the state of things of which he complains, cannot invoke the aid of the court (h). A man may by acquiescing in the acts

*18   done by another materially *affecting his own interest preclude himself from afterwards exercising his legal right to the property in relation to which such acquiescence

---

(z) Balls v. Margrave, 3 Beav. 284; Derbyshire, Staffordshire, and Warwickshire Railway Co. v. Serrell, 2 De G. & S. 353.

(a) Brown v. Newall, 2 M. & C. 558, 576.

(b) Davies v. Salisbury, 14 L. J. Ch. 153.

(c) See Magnay v. Mines Royal Co., 3 Drew. 130, 133; see further, *infra*.

(d) Jones v. Bassett, 2 Russ. 405; Brown v. Newall, 2 M. & C. 558; Maclaren v. Stainton, 16 Beav. 279; Fisher v. Baldwin, 22 L. J. Ch. 966.

(e) Jarmuth v. Simmons, cited Set.

on Decr. 877. See as to *ex parte* applications, *infra*.

(f) Gibson v. Goldsmid, 5 D. M. & G. 757, 765.

(g) Bateman v. Ramsay, Sau. & Sc. 459; Batty v. Chester, 5 Beav. 103; Williams v. Roberts, 8 Ha. 315. See Ewing v. Osbaldiston, 2 M. & C. 53; Reynell v. Sprye, 1 D. M. & G. 679; Rees v. Fernie, 13 W. R. 6.

(h) Lloyd v. London, Chatham, and Dover Railway, 2 D. J. & S. 568; Dutton v. Furness, 35 L. J. Ch. 468.

[1] Minturn v. Farmers' Loan and Trust Company, 3 Comstock, 498; Perrine v. Striker, 7 Paige, 598.

has occurred (*i*). If in his dealings either with the person against whom he seeks relief, or with third parties, he has acted in an unfair or inequitable manner, he cannot have relief (*k*).

9. Delay in making the application is not, as a general rule, material, but if the application is not made until near the period of the trial, the court may refuse to interfere, unless the delay is satisfactorily accounted for (*l*). Delay may, however, affect materially the question of costs. A man who allows the proceedings at law to run on, will be ordered, although successful in restraining the action, to pay the costs subsequent to the declaration (*m*).

10. If the court shall be of opinion that there is on the whole a fair question to be reserved for the hearing, and that the conduct of the party who makes the application is free from any taint of fraud or illegality, it has next to determine whether he shall be put upon terms as a condition of its interposition in his favor, and if so, upon what terms an injunction shall be granted (*n*). The terms on which an injunction is granted are in each case a question for the discretion of the court, but the general principle upon which the court proceeds is to put the party applying upon such terms as will enable the court to do justice to the party restrained in the event of his failing to make out his case at the hearing (*o*). If the question between the parties depends partly on a legal title,* and ⠀⠀ * 19 partly on an equity, which will only arise in the event of that title being decided in one way, and the circumstances are such that the party applying may admit the legal right of the other party, the action will be restrained only upon the terms of his giving judgment in the action, such judgment to

(*i*) Gerrard *v.* O'Reilly, 3 Dr. & War. 414; Gregory *v.* Wilson, 9 Ha. 683; Whitehead *v.* Bennett, 9 W. R. 627; Burke *v.* Prior, 15 Ir. Ch. 106. See further as to acquiescence, *infra*.

(*k*) Nicholson *v.* Hooper, 4 M. & C. 179; Pope *v.* Lord Duncannon, 9 Sim. 179; Edelsten *v.* Vick, 11 Ha. 86.

(*l*) Thorpe *v.* Hughes, 3 M. & C. 742; Stokes *v.* Wilson, 12 Sim. 91; North Eastern Railway Co. *v.* Martin, 2 Ph. 758; Scotson *v.* Gaury, 1 Ha. 99; Ma-

clure *v.* Ripley, 13 Jur. 353; South Eastern Railway *v.* Brogden, 3 Mac. & G. 22; Holme *v.* Brown, 9 Ha. App. 29; Anderson *v.* Noble, 1 Drew. 143; Lloyd *v.* Adams, 4 K. & J. 470.

(*m*) Watson *v.* Alcock, 4 D. M. & G. 242.

(*n*) Taft *v.* Harrison, 10 Ha. 489; Magnay *v.* Mines Royal Co., 3 Drew. 130.

(*o*) Sanxter *v.* Foster, Cr. & Ph. 302.

be dealt with as the court shall direct (p), and undertaking to obey such orders as the court may think proper to make (q). The court may sometimes require that judgment should be given without prejudice to any question that may afterwards arise (r).

11. If the circumstances are not such as to enable the party who makes the application to admit the legal right of the other party, the court will allow the action to proceed to verdict or to judgment, and will not interfere until after verdict or judgment, as the case may be (s).

12. In cases where the question at issue between the parties has reference to the payment of moneys, the mere giving judgment is not sufficient to secure the fund to the party who may be found entitled to it. The usual course, therefore, in such cases, is to grant the injunction only upon the terms of the payment into court by the plaintiff in equity of the amount for which the action is brought (t), and of all sums of
* 20   money which may * become due during the pendency of the suit (u). Reasonable time will be given for the payment of the moneys, according to the greatness of the sum or the distance of the party (x). Where money has thus been

---

(p) Jones v. Bassett, 2 Russ. 405; Drummond v. Pigou, 2 M. & K. 168; Fennings v. Humphery, 4 Beav. 1; Barnard v. Wallis, Cr. & Ph. 85; Weeks v. Taylor, 3 W. R. 47; Chilton v. Campbell, 20 Beav. 531; Waterlow v. Bacon, 2 L. R. Eq. 514. Where an injunction is granted on the terms of allowing an action to proceed to judgment, such judgment to be dealt with as the court shall direct, the court will not allow such judgment to be used for another or different purpose; Weeks v. Taylor, 3 W. R. 47. See ib. as to the meaning, where the court grants an injunction in terms of giving judgment in an action.

(q) Hannam v. South London Waterworks Co., 2 Mer. 61; Attwood v. Barham, 2 Russ. 186; Waterlow v. Bacon, 2 L. R. Eq. 514.

(r) Brennan v. Preston, 1 W. R. 115.

(s) Barnard v. Wallis, Cr. & Ph. 85; Playfair v. Birmingham, Bristol, &c., Railway Co., 9 L. J. Ch. N. S. 253; Mott v. Blackwall Railway Co., 2 Ph. 632; Mackintosh v. Wyatt, 3 Ha. 562;

John v. John, 1 L. T. N. S. 385. See Edwards v. Champion, 1 De G. & S. 75; Smith v. Earl of Effingham, 11 Beav. 82; Earl of Shrewsbury v. Trappes, 2 D. F. & J. 172.

(t) Kensington v. White, 3 Pri. 164; Solly v. Moore, 8 Pri. 631; Maitland v. Backhouse, 16 Sim. 58; Playfair v. Birmingham, Bristol, &c., Railway Co., 9 L. J. Ch. N. S. 253; Bentinck v. Willinck, 2 Ha. 1; Cotesworth v. Stevens, 4 Ha. 185; Powell v. Thomas, 6 Ha. 305; Cook v. Betham, 4 Jur. 957; Meux v. Smith, 7 Jur. 821; Lord Milltown v. Stewart, 3 M. & C. 24; Armitstead v. Durham, 11 Beav. 561; Taft v. Harrison, 10 Ha. 489; Chilton v. Campbell, 20 Beav. 533; Fisher v. Baldwin, 22 L. J. Ch. 966; Magnay v. Mines Royal Co., 3 Drew. 130. See as to form of order, Taft v. Harrison, 10 Ha. 489.

(u) Pyke v. Northwood, 1 Beav. 152; Fennings v. Humphery, 4 Beav. 1; Magnay v. Mines Royal Co., 3 Drew. 130.

(x) Eden on Inj. 113.

once paid in, the court will use great caution in parting with it
(*y*). The moneys will not be paid out to defendant before a
decree in the suit (*z*). If the injunction is dissolved, the
moneys will be retained in court, until the legal right has been
ascertained (*a*). The moneys paid in are only a security, and
not a payment. If it turns out that less is due to the defendant than the amount paid in, the balance will be restored to
the plaintiff (*b*).

If the legal right is denied, payment into court will not be
ordered until the cause shall be in a state in which the court
can come to a conclusion as to the rights of parties (*c*).

If the equitable case presented by the bill is such that the
court is satisfied, it must be sustained at the hearing, or if there
is no danger of the money being lost in the mean time, or if
no case has been made out which makes it the duty of the
court to take care that if the injunction turns out to be not
well founded the defendant in equity should not be injured,
payment into court will not be ordered (*d*).

13. An injunction is not confined to any point of the proceedings at law. It may, upon a proper case being made
out, be granted * at any stage of the action. Thus, an   * 21
injunction may be granted to stay trial (*e*); or, after
verdict, to stay judgment (*f*); or, after judgment, to stay
execution or proceedings under an execution (*g*), and pending
an appeal (*h*); or, if execution has been effected, to stay the
moneys in the hands of the sheriff (*i*); or, if part only of the

---

(*y*) Eden on Inj. 116.
(*z*) Marsack *v.* Farlow, Jac. 572.
(*a*) Furnival *v.* Bogle, 4 Russ. 142.
See Brown *v.* Newall, 2 M. & C. 558.
(*b*) Broughton *v.* Pitchford, 6 Madd.
295.
(*c*) Lord Milltown *v.* Stewart, 3 M.
& C. 24. See Bank of Turkey *v.* Ottoman Bank, 2 L. R. Eq. 366.
(*d*) Parnell *v.* Nesbitt, 2 Pri. 150;
Goddard *v.* Carlisle, 9 Pri. 169; Maitland *v.* Backhouse, 17 L. J. Ch. 121;
Espey *v.* Lake, 10 Ha. 266; Smith *v.*
Reese River Co., 2 L. R. Eq. 264. See
Allan *v.* Inman, 7 Jur. 433; Bentinck
v. Willinck, 2 Ha. 1; Playfair *v.* Birmingham, Bristol, &c., Railway Co., 9
L. J. Ch. N. S. 253.
(*e*) M'Fadden *v.* Jenkins, 1 Ha. 458,
1 Ph. 157.

(*f*) Turner *v.* Wright, 1 J. & W.
290; Jones *v.* Hughes, 1 Ha. 383.
(*g*) Codd *v.* Wooden, 3 Bro. C. C. 72;
Lady Arundell *v.* Phipps, 10 Ves. 144;
Rowe *v.* Wood, cited 2 Sw. 234; Hawkshaw *v.* Parkins, *ib.* 539; Jones *v.* Bassett, 2 Russ. 405; Newland *v.* Painter,
4 M. & C. 408; Algar *v.* Murrell, 6 Jur.
775; Espey *v.* Lake, 10 Ha. 260, Fisher
v. Baldwin, 22 L. J. Ch. 966. See Williams *v.* Roberts, 8 Ha. 315.
(*h*) Earl of Shrewsbury *v.* Trappes,
2 D. F. & J. 172.
(*i*) Whittingham *v.* Burgoyne, 3
Aust. 900; Hawkshaw *v.* Parkins, 2
Sw. 539; Franklyn *v.* Thomas, 3 Mer.
234; Farquharson *v.* Pitcher 2 Russ.
81.

judgment has been levied by *fi. fa.*, to restrain the suing of another *fi. fa.* or a *ca. sa.*, according to the exigency of the particular case (*k*); or to restrain process in outlawry (*l*); or to stay the issuing of a writ of possession after verdict in ejectment (*m*); or to stay the delivery up of possession after a writ of possession has been issued (*n*).[1]

14. The right to grant an injunction after judgment was at one time the subject of a violent contest between the courts of common law and courts of equity. It was alleged by the common-law judges that after verdict there was no power in chancery to enjoin against execution; and it was said that, if after judgment the chancellor granted an injunction and committed the plaintiff to the Fleet, the Court of King's Bench would discharge him by *habeas corpus*. The jurisdiction seems to have been assumed about the beginning of the reign of King Edward the Fourth, and was continued during the reign of King Henry the Eighth. In the reign of Henry the Eighth the assertion of this jurisdiction was one of the articles of impeachment against Cardinal Wolsey. The same opposi-
* 22 tion was continued * against Wolsey's successor, Sir Thomas More. In the reign of King James the First, under the chancellorship of Lord Ellesmere, a vehement discussion took place, in which Lord Coke came forward as the chief opponent of the jurisdiction. The case was referred to five of the most eminent lawyers of the time, who made an elaborate report in favor of the jurisdiction claimed. The King confirmed this decision, and the jurisdiction was fully established (*o*).

(*k*) 3 Wood. Lect. 406, 407, 1 Madd. Ch. Pr. 183. See Hawkshaw *v.* Parkins, 2 Sw. 539; Williams *v.* Roberts, 8 Ha. 315.

(*l*) Drummond *v.* Pigou, 2 M. & K. 168.

(*m*) Buckland *v.* Gibbins, 32 L. J. Ch. 391. See 1 H. & C. 736.

(*n*) Story Eq. Jur. 886, *infra*.

(*o*) 1 Ch. Rep. App. Crowley's case, 2 Sw. 22, n., 1 Wood. Lect. 398; 3 *ib*. 156; 1 Spence's Eq. Jur. p. 674.

[1] It is the ordinary course to restrain the *execution*, but allow the plaintiff to proceed to judgment at law; and it is only upon an averment in the bill, that

the plaintiff in equity believes the answer will afford discovery material to his defence at law, that an injunction *to stay the trial* ought to be granted. Williams *v.* Sadler, 4 Jones Eq. 378.

Where property attached upon a writ of mesne process was bailed for safekeeping by the sheriff, and the debt subsequently paid by the debtor, but not until after final judgment had been recovered against the bailee of the property attached, and the creditors nevertheless attempted to enforce the judgment against the bailee, it was held to be substantially the same as if the judgment against the bailee had been

15. Relief will not be given in equity after judgment, unless some special equitable grounds for the interference of the court can be shown (*p*). A defence which has been fully and fairly tried at law cannot be set up as a ground for relief in equity after judgment (*q*), even although it may be the opinion of the court that the defence ought to have been sustained at law (*r*). Nor can a man who, having a good defence at law, neglects to avail himself of it there (*s*), or who suffers judgment to go against him by neglect (*t*), come to a court of equity for relief. The mere fact of the discovery of fresh evidence since the verdict is not a sufficient ground for the interference of the court (*u*). Still less can an equity arise if the evidence might have been procured before the trial with ordinary care and diligence, or if the grievance complained of has been caused by a mistake in pleading, or the conduct of a cause, or by surprise (*x*).

16. * But if an equitable case can be made out, relief   * 23 will be given after verdict or judgment (*y*). The general principle upon which relief will be given has been thus stated by Chief Justice Marshall in Marine Insurance Company *v.* Hodgson (*z*). " It may be stated as a general principle,

---

paid; that, being merely collateral to the principal debt, must fall with it, and its collection was accordingly enjoined. Paddock *v.* Palmer, 19 Vt. 581. See also, to same point, Keighler *v.* Savage Manufac. Co., 12 Md. 388; and Shaw *v.* Dwight, 16 Barb. 536, where a prior execution creditor was restrained from levying on the debtor's land, where his debt had been paid, in order to prevent the second execution creditor from collecting his debt.

(*p*) Rowe *v.* Wood, cited 2 Sw. 234, n.; Protheroe *v.* Forman, *ib.* 229; O'Mahony *v.* Dickson, 2 Sch. & Lef. 400. See Countess of Gainsborough *v.* Gifford, 2 P. W. 424; Hankey *v.* Vernon, 2 Cox, 12; Bateman *v.* Willoe, 1 Sch. & Lef. 205.

(*q*) Harrison *v.* Nettleship, 2 M. & K. 423. See Larabrie *v.* Brown, 1 D. & J. 205.

(*r*) Marine Insurance Co. *v.* Hodgson, 7 Cranch (Amer.) 332; Bateman *v.* Willoe, 1 Sch. & Lef. 205. See Simpson *v.* Lord Howden, 8 M. & C. 97; Terrell *v.* Higgs, 1 D. & J. 388.

(*s*) Protheroe *v.* Forman, 2 Sw. 229; Bateman *v.* Willoe, 1 Sch. & Lef. 205.

(*t*) Williams *v.* Lee, 3 Atk. 223; Lansing *v.* Edge, 1 Johns. Ch. (Amer.) 49. Comp. Griffith *v.* Edwards, 2 Jur. N. S. 584.

(*u*) Sewell *v.* Freestun, 1 Ch. Ca. 65; Ware *v.* Horwood, 14 Ves. 31; Taylor *v.* Shepherd, 1 Y. & C. 271; Bullock *v.* Chapman, 2 De G. & S. 211. Comp. Hankey *v.* Vernon, 2 Cox, 12; Wilmot *v.* Leonard, 3 Sw. 682.

(*x*) Curtis *v.* Smallrige, 2 Freem. 178; Stephenson *v.* Wilson, 2 Vern. 325; Blackall *v.* Coombs, 2 P. W. 70; Richards *v.* Symes, 2 Atk. 319; Kemp *v.* Mackrell, 2 Ves. 579; Holworthy *v.* Mortlock, 1 Cox, 141; Bateman *v.* Willoe, 1 Sch. & Lef. 201; Field *v.* Beaumont, 3 Madd. 102, 1 Sw. 204; Griffith *v.* Edwards, 2 Jur. N. S. 584; Prince of Wales Assurance Co. *v.* Trulock, 4 W. R. 788, 820, 5 W. R. 14; Larabrie *v.* Brown, 1 D. & J. 205. Comp. O'Neill *v.* Browne, 9 Ir. Eq. 131.

(*y*) Protheroe *v.* Forman, 2 Sw. 229; Bateman *v.* Willoe, 1 Sch. & Lef. 205; Harrison *v.* Nettleship, 2 M. & K. 423; Billage *v.* Southee, 9 Ha. 535; Withall *v.* Tuckwell, 5 Jur. N. S. 929.

(*z*) 7 Cranch (Amer.) 336.

that any fact which clearly proves it against conscience to execute a judgment, and of which the injured party could not have availed himself at law, or of which he might have availed himself, but was prevented by fraud or accident, unmixed with any fault or negligence in himself or his agents, will authorize a court of equity to interfere by injunction to restrain the adverse party from availing himself of such judgment." Relief will accordingly be given where material facts have been discovered since the trial at law, which were fraudulently concealed, or could not by ordinary care and diligence have been discovered before the trial (*a*).[1] So also relief will be given after verdict or judgment where the plaintiff in equity is precluded by the technical process of law from having the judgment set aside, or further proceedings stayed at law, and where the enforcement of the judgment or any further proceedings under the verdict would be against equity (*b*).

* 24   So also * relief will be given against a judgment which has been obtained by fraud or collusion (*c*).[2] So also relief will be given against a judgment where the case set up involves an equitable element, or there is an equitable question to be settled before the case can be disposed of at law (*d*), or

(*a*) Countess of Gainsborough v. Gifford, 2 P. W. 424; Wilmot v. Leonard, 3 Sw. 682; Williams v. Lee, 3 Atk. 223; Bateman v. Willoe, 1 Sch. & Lef. 2)4; Jarvis v. Chandler, T. & R. 319. See Ayre's case, 25 Beav. 513.

(*b*) Bateman v. Willoe, 1 Sch. & Lef. 204; Jones v. Hughes, 1 Ha. 383; Williams v. Roberts, 8 Ha. 315; Buckland v. Gibbins, 32 L. J. Ch. 391; Griffith v. Edwards, 2 Jur. N. S. 584.

(*c*) Isaac v. Humpage, 1 Ves. Jr. 427; 3 Bro. C. C. 463; Rowe v. Wood, 2 Sw. 234, n.; Annesley v. Rookes, 3 Mer. 226, n.; O'Neill v. Browne, 9 Ir. Eq. 131; Taylor v. Hughes, 2 J. & L. 24; Bargate v. Shortridge, 5 H. L. 297.

(*d*) O'Connor v. Spaight, 1 Sch. & Lef. 305; Playfair v. Birmingham, Bristol, &c., Railway Co., 9 L. J. Ch. N. S. 253; Barnard v. Wallis, Cr. & Ph. 85; Pearce v. Gray, 2 Y. & C. C. C. 222; Billage v. Southee, 9 Ha. 539.

[1] And the fact that the vendor of land is insolvent, and has no title to the land, is sufficient ground for enjoining a judgment against the vendor on his note for the purchase-money, although the time for conveying the land may not have arrived. Kelly v. Kelly, 2 Duvall (Ky.), 363.

It is said in Skillman v. Holcomb, 1 Beasley, 131, that it would take a very strong case of *fraud, mistake, surprise,* or *accident,* to induce the court to interfere with the completion of a sale upon *an execution at law.* Interfering with the execution of its own process is a very different thing from interfering with the process of another and independent tribunal.

In ejectment cases, where no discovery is sought to aid a defence at law, and the title at law is admitted, an injunction will be granted upon terms only so as to leave the party to proceed to trial and judgment at law. Ham v. Schuyler, 2 Johns. Ch. 140.

[2] A judgment creditor will be restrained from enforcing his judgment against the land of a subsequent purchaser from his debtor, so long as there is other land of the debtor remaining unsold, sufficient to satisfy the judgment. Massie v. Wilson, 16 Iowa, 390.

where the equitable defence could not be made available at law (*e*). A man who has a good equitable as well as a good legal defence to an action at law, is not bound to go into evidence at law, but may permit the verdict to go against him at law, and come afterwards to the court for relief, relying on his equitable case (*f*).

17. Where ejectment has been brought against a tenant, the landlord may make himself defendant to the action, and then file his bill for an injunction, or he may file a bill for an injunction before he has been admitted to defend the action, making the tenant a party (*g*). But he cannot let the action go on against the tenant, and then come into equity for an injunction to stay execution (*h*). A tenant cannot maintain an injunction to restrain his landlord from levying a distress upon him till the result of a trial for ejectment, which is brought against him by other parties, because a tenant cannot be allowed to bring his landlord's title into dispute, even if lands have been demised to him which his landlord has no right to let (*i*). But where a lease has been granted of freehold and copyhold lands by a man who was only tenant for life of the freehold, but the two descriptions of land were intermixed and confused, the representatives of the tenant for life were restrained from taking out execution on a verdict found for them in ejectment till the hearing, as the ejectment did not inform the court either as to the locality of the freehold lands, or as to the other points which could not be decided till the hearing (*k*). In a case * where there were two defendants to an ejectment,   * 25 and one of them who was not a party to the suit refused to give judgment at law, the court would not restrain proceedings in ejectment (*l*).[1]

A man who is proceeding fairly to establish his legal right

(*e*) Farquharson *v.* Pitcher, 2 Russ. 81; Whyte *v.* O'Brien, 1 Sim. & St. 551; Jones *v.* Hughes, 1 Ha. 383; Ayre's case, 25 Beav. 513; Maw *v.* Ulyatt, 31 L. J. Ch. 33. See Williams *v.* Roberts, 8 Ha. 315.

(*f*) Billage *v.* Southee, 9 Ha. 539.

(*g*) Lawley *v.* Walden, 3 Sw. 142, n.; Moses *v.* Lewis, Jac. 502; Poole *v.* Marsh, 8 Sim. 528.

(*h*) Moses *v.* Lewis, Jac. 502.

(*i*) Homan *v.* Moore, 4 Pri. 5.

(*k*) Hardcastle *v.* Shafto, ·1 Anst. 184.

(*l*) Redmond *v.* Goodall, Jon. 814.

[1] In a bill for an injunction to restrain proceedings in ejectment, the staleness of the defendant's claim, which he is enforcing at law, is no ground for granting an injunction. It is the complainant's claim to which the equitable defence of a stale claim is applicable. Horner *v.* Jobs, 2 Beasley, 19.

by ejectment will not be interfered with by the court (*m*). The rule obtains with peculiar force where the person in possession has got possession by tortious means (*n*). If an equitable case be made to appear, the court will restrain the proceedings in the action (*o*), although there may be a question whether the party who makes the application would not be successful at law (*p*).

The 25 & 26 Vict. c. 42, by which a court of equity is required to determine every question of law and fact incident to the relief sought, does not apply to suits to recover or defend the possession of land under a legal title, or under a title which would have been legal but for the existence of some outstanding term, lease, or mortgage. In such cases the same relief only is to be given in equity, as would have been proper according to the rules and practice of the court, if the Act had not passed.

18. The powers given to courts of common law by the Common Law Procedure Act, 17 & 18 Vict. c. 125, s. 83, to entertain defences by plea upon equitable grounds do not interfere with the jurisdiction of the court to restrain actions at law. The powers given by the Act are permissive only, and not compulsory, and do not deprive the defendant at law of the right he had before the passing of the Act of coming to a court of equity, and taking the benefit of a defence of which he could not avail himself in a court of law (*q*). A party to an action at law, who may have an equitable defence, is not bound to plead it at law, but may come into equity for relief (*r*), or he * may resist the action on other grounds, and also

* 26

institute a suit for relief (*s*). He is not precluded from coming to the court, unless he has already set up his equitable defence at law (*t*). If he has not pleaded his equitable

(*m*) Lord Sefton *v.* Lord Salisbury, 33 L. T. 27.

(*n*) Grafton *v.* Griffin, 1 R. & M. 336.

(*o*) Attwood *v.* Barham, 2 Russ. 186; Jones *v.* Bassett, *ib.* 405; Pyke *v.* Northwood, 1 Beav. 152; Edgecumbe *v.* Carpenter, *ib.* 171.

(*p*) Crofts *v.* Middleton, 8 D. M. & G. 192.

(*q*) Gompertz *v.* Pooley, 4 Drew. 448; Walker *v.* Micklethwaite, 1 Dr. &

Sm. 54; Davies *v.* Stainbank, 6 D. M. & G. 696.

(*r*) *Ib.* Kingsford *v.* Swinford, 28 L. J. Ch. 413; Jenner *v.* Morris, 3 D. F. & J. 45; Stewart *v.* Great Western Railway Co., 2 D. J. & S. 319.

(*s*) Davies *v.* Stainbank, 6 D. M. & G. 696.

(*t*) Stewart *v.* Great Western Railway Co., 2 Dr. & Sm. 438, 2 D. J. & S. 319.

defence at law, he may, after judgment, come into equity for relief (*u*) : but if he has exercised his option, and has attempted the equitable defence in a court of law, and there is no reason why the court of law should not deal with the equitable plea as well as a court of equity, and give him the same relief as a court of equity, he cannot come to the court and ask for an injunction to restrain the action on the very ground that he has made the subject of his equitable plea (*x*). Nor can relief be had in equity, if the equitable defence has been rejected at law on the merits in a case where the court of law had full jurisdiction (*y*.) But if a court of law refuses to entertain jurisdiction on an equitable plea on the ground that it is not authorized to do so by statute (*z*) ; or if, from any reason, a court of law cannot give the same relief as a court of equity would (*a*) ; or if, from the way in which the pleadings are framed, the case cannot be heard in a court of law on the merits (*b*), the court will not refuse to entertain a bill to restrain the action, merely on the ground of the plaintiff in equity having pleaded an equitable plea to the action (*c*). A defendant who has pleaded unsuccessfully at law on an equitable plea, grounded not upon the laws and principles by which courts of equity are governed, but upon the course and practice of those courts, is not precluded * by the decision at law from filing a bill on   * 27 the same grounds to restrain the action (*d*). Where a man brings an action at law, and defendant sets up a release which is impeachable upon equitable grounds, the case does not come within the principle applicable to a party who has attempted an equitable plea at law (*e*).

Unless the plea is such that a court of equity would grant a

(*u*) Thornton *v.* M'Kewan, 1 H. & M. 525.

(*x*) Farebrother *v.* Welchman, 3 Drew. 122; Leuty *v.* Hillas, 4 Jur. N. S. 1166; Gompertz *v.* Pooley, 4 Drew. 452; Evans *v.* Brembridge, 8 D. M. & G. 109 ; Walker *v.* Micklethwaite, 1 Dr. & Sm. 54 ; Waterlow *v.* Bacon, 2 L. R. Eq. 514.

(*y*) Magnay *v.* Mines Royal Co., 3 Drew. 130 ; Terrell *v.* Higgs, 1 D. & J. 392.

(*z*) Magnay *v.* Mines Royal Co., 3 Drew. 130.

(*a*) Waterlow *v.* Bacon, 2 L. R. Eq. 514.

(*b*) Evans *v.* Brembridge, 8 D. M. & G. 109 ; Waterlow *v.* Bacon, 2 L. R. Eq. 514.

(*c*) Waterlow *v.* Bacon, 2 L. R. Eq. 514.

(*d*) Protheroe *v.* Phelps, 7 D.ˈM. & G. 735.

(*e*) Stewart *v.* Great Western Railway Co., 2 Dr. & Sm. 438, 2 D. J. & S. 319.

perpetual injunction, it cannot be made the subject of an equitable plea at law (f). An equitable plea will not be supported in a court of law, except where the plea, the decision, and the judgment of the court upon it will work out and complete all the equity that belongs to the matter to which the plea refers (g). If the case be one in which a court of equity would only give a qualified or conditional relief, the equitable defence cannot be allowed at law (h). The equitable defence allowed by the statute means such a defence as would in a court of equity be a complete answer to the plaintiff's claim, and would as such afford sufficient ground for a perpetual injunction granted absolutely and without conditions (i). A party to an action in a court of common law will not be allowed to plead on equitable grounds, matter which he has raised in a suit in equity instituted with reference to the matters in the action (k).

19. There are many cases in which the legal defence to a claim set up at law rests exclusively or in a great degree within the knowledge of the party advancing the claim. As it is against conscience that he should proceed in the assertion of his claim * without communicating the knowl-

* 28

edge he possesses, or should seek to keep from the court of law facts which the plaintiff in equity alleges to be necessary for his defence, and to be necessary for the court of law to know in order to a due performance of its duty, a court of equity will restrain the proceedings at law until a full discovery has been made of all that he is bound to disclose (l).

20. Injunctions to restrain proceedings at law until answer were formerly called common injunctions. They were granted

(f) Mines Royal Co. v. Magnay, 10 Exch. 489; Hyde v. Graham, 1 H. & C. 598.

(g) Clerk v. Laurie, 1 H. & N. 452; Wakley v. Froggatt, 2 H. & C. 669.

(h) Mines Royal Co. v. Magnay, 10 Exch. 489; Steele v. Haddock, ib. 643; Vorley v. Bennett, 1 C. B. N. S. 225; Wood v. Dwarris, 11 Exch. 493; Wodehouse v. Farebrother, 5 E. & B. 277; Solvency Mutual Guarantee Society v. Freeman, 7 H. & N. 17; Borrowman v. Rossell, 16 C. B. N. S. 58.

(i) Mines Royal Co. v. Magnay, 10 Exch. 489; Wood v. Copper Mines Co., 17 C. B. 561; Wake v. Harrop, 6 H. &

N. 770. See Waterlow v. Bacon, 2 L. R. Eq. 514.

(k) Schlumberger v. Lister, 2 El. & El. 855.

(l) Wynne v. Jackson, 2 Russ. 351; Lord Portarlington v. Soulby, 3 M. & K. 104; Glascott v. Copper Mines Co., 11 Sim. 305; Lord Milltown v. Stewart, 3 M. & C. 24; Thorpe v. Hughes, ib. 742; Barker v. Barr, 1 Beav. 374; Rawson v. Samuel, Cr. & Ph. 169; Pearce v. Creswick, 2 Ha. 286; Benyon v. Nettlefold, 3 Mac. & G. 94; Williams v. Roberts, 8 Ha. 329; Fitzgerald v. Bult, 9 Ha. App. 66.

as of course upon the default of the defendant either in not
appearing or in not putting in an answer to the bill in due time.
The abuses which arose from bills being filed ostensibly for the
purposes of discovery, but in reality for the purpose of delaying the plaintiff by means of the injunction, led to the enactment 15 & 16 Vict. c. 89, s. 58, whereby it was declared that
the rules of the court with respect to staying proceedings at
law shall be, so far as the nature of the case will admit, assimilated to the rules with respect to injunctions generally, and
that such injunctions may be granted on interlocutory application, supported by affidavit in like manner as other injunctions
are granted by the court. An order was also made that no
injunction to stay proceedings at law is to be granted, as of
course, for default of appearance or of answer to the bill (m).
The statute does not deprive a plaintiff in equity of his right
to discovery in aid of his defence to an action at law, but merely
requires him to verify his bill by affidavit so as to show that the
case is not a fictitious one (n). Nor has the court lost its jurisdiction in regard to discovery, because courts of law have had
jurisdiction in discovery given them (o).

21. The affidavits on which the application is founded
must show * that the answer is material to his defence   * 29
on the trial of the action, and that the facts stated in the
bill are, so far as they are within the knowledge of the plaintiff, true, and as to all other facts that he believes them to be
true (p). If these facts are shown by affidavit, the court will
not upon a conflict of affidavits determine whether the plaintiff in equity should have a discovery or not, but will, after
interrogatories have been filed, grant as of course an injunction
until discovery be given (q). The motion will not be granted
until after interrogatories have been filed (r). But after inter-

(m) Consol. Ord. 25.
(n) Senior v. Pritchard, 16 Beav.
476; Lovell v. Galloway, 17 Beav. 6,
19 Beav. 643; Harris v. Collett, 26
Beav. 222.
(o) Barry v. Crosskey, 2 J. & H. 1;
Shepard v. Brown, 4 Giff. 208.
(p) Mollett v. Enequist, 25 Beav.
609; Harris v. Collett, 26 Beav. 226.
See Barker v. Burr, 1 Beav. 374.
(q) Senior v. Pritchard, 16 Beav.

476; Lovell v. Galloway, 17 Beav. 6;
Harris v. Collett, 26 Beav. 226. See
Fox v. Hill, 2 D. & J. 354. Comp.
Magnay v. Mines Royal Co., 3 Drew.
133.
(r) Lovell v. Galloway, 1 W. R. 118;
Chilton v. Campbell, 20 Beav. 532;
Fuller v. Ingram, 5 Jur. N. S. 510; but
see Fitzgerald v. Bult, 9 Ha. App. 65.
See as to filing interrogatories, Lambert
v. Lomas, 9 Ha. App. 29.

rogatories have been filed, the plaintiff is at liberty to move at once for an injunction to stay proceedings at law without waiting for an answer (s). If, however, it appears from the pleadings, or upon the whole matter taken together, that the allegation that the matters sought to be discovered by the bill would be a material defence to the action, cannot possibly be true in fact, the court will not interfere (t).

22. The interrogatories are not required to be as formerly (u), a literal echo of the bill (v). Nor is it necessary that every interrogatory should be founded on a distinct allegation in the bill, unless the nature of the case requires it (x).

23. A bill which prays specifically discovery only should not contain a prayer for general relief. If the prayer for general relief be added to the bill, it cannot be treated as a bill for discovery (y). A bill praying relief and discovery, if bad for * the former, is bad for the discovery (z). A plain-
* 30
tiff at law who files a bill for discovery, should not pray for an injunction in the mean time to restrain the defendant from all proceedings at law against plaintiff in the action. This prayer for an injunction is a prayer for relief, and there-fore fatal to the bill as a bill for discovery (a). A man not a party to the record at law, should not be made a party to a bill for discovery in aid of a defence to an action (b).

24. With respect to costs, the course is to make the costs of the application for an injunction to restrain an action at law costs in the cause (c). If the plaintiff has delayed unreason-ably in applying to the court so that costs have been incurred at law, he will be ordered to submit to such order as the court will make with respect to the costs of proceedings in the court where the action is restrained (d). He may be required to make the same submission in cases where there does not

---

(s) Lloyd v. Adams, 4 K. & J. 471.
(t) White v. Steinwacks, 19 Ves. 83; Thorpe v. Hughes, 3 M. & C. 742; Ashby v. Jackson, 6 Beav. 336.
(u) See Mackleston v. Brown, 6 Ves. 52.
(v) Perry v. Turpin, Kay, App. 49, 18 Jur. 594.
(x) Marsh v. Keith, 1 Dr. & Sm. 342.
(y) Ambury v. Jones, 1 Younge, 200;

Angel v. Westcomb, 6 Sim. 30. See Mills v. Campbell, 2 Y. & C. 389.
(z) Jones v. Maund, 3 Y. & C. 347.
(a) Andrews v. Lupton, 13 L. J. Ch. 201.
(b) Irving v. Thompson, 9 Sim. 17.
(c) Maitland v. Backhouse, 17 L. J. Ch. 121.
(d) Cotesworth v. Stephens, 4 Ha. 185; Watson v. Alcock, 4 D. M. & G. 242.

appear to have been any unreasonable delay in filing the bill (e).

25. The costs of the motion for an injunction to restrain proceedings at law until discovery are (if unsuccessfully opposed) payable by the defendant, although he may get the costs of the suit generally (f). If the application is unopposed, he is allowed the costs of the discovery (g).

(e) Waterlow v. Bacon, 2 L. R. Eq. 514.
(f) Lovell v. Galloway, 19 Beav. 643.

(g) Harris v. Collett, 26 Beav. 222. See further as to the costs of discovery, Morg. and Dav. on Costs, 147–151.

* 31   *CHAPTER IV.

EQUITABLE GROUNDS FOR RELIEF AGAINST PROCEEDINGS AT LAW.

SECTION I. — FRAUD.

1. THE subject which most frequently calls for the interference of a court of equity is comprehended under the extensive head of fraud. The first province of a court of equity being to enforce truth in the dealings of men, the correction and prevention of fraud is one of the principles which lies at the very

[34]

root of the whole doctrine of equity (*h*). A court of equity has an undoubted jurisdiction to relieve against every species of fraud (*i*), with the single exception of fraud in obtaining the execution or setting up of a will (*k*).[1]

2. It is not easy to give a definition of what constitutes fraud in the extensive signification in which that term is used by a court of equity (*l*). Fraud is so various in form and color, that it is difficult, if not impossible, to confine it within the limits of any precise definition. The fertility of man's invention in devising new schemes of fraud is so great, that courts of equity have declined the hopeless attempt of embracing in one formula all its varieties of form and color, reserving to themselves the liberty to deal with it under whatever form it may present itself: as new devices of fraud are invented, they will be met by new corrections (*m*). The general principle, * however, on which relief is granted against   * 32 fraud is, that where there is fraud there is not that consent which is essential to the validity of a transaction (*n*).[2] Fraud in the sense of a court of equity may be said to include properly all acts, omissions, and concealments, which involve a breach of legal or equitable duty, trust, or confidence, justly reposed, and are injurious to another, or by which an undue or unconscientious advantage is taken of another (*o*). Fraud in all cases implies a wilful act on the part of any one whereby another is sought to be deprived by illegal or inequitable means of what he is entitled to either at law or in equity (*p*).

3. In many cases of fraud courts of common law have a concurrent jurisdiction with courts of equity. But there are many courses of conduct which a court of equity construes to be fraudulent which cannot be taken notice of by a court of

---

(*h*) Warden *v.* Jones, 23 Beav. 493; Green *v.* Nixon, *ib.* 530.

(*i*) Colt *v.* Wollaston, 2 P. Wms. 156; Stent *v.* Baylis, *ib.* 219; Franks *v.* Weaver, 10 Beav. 297; Glasse *v.* Marshall, 15 Sim. 76.

(*k*) Jones *v.* Gregory, 2 D. J. & S. 83.

(*l*) Green *v.* Nixon, 23 Beav. 530; Reynell *v.* Sprye, 1 D. M. & G. 691, *per* Lord Cranworth.

(*m*) Sawyer *v.* Vernon, 1 Vern. 387; Lawley *v.* Hooper, 3 Atk. 279; Webb *v.* Rorke, 2 Sch. & Lef. 666; Lord Hardwicke's letter to Lord Kaimes; Life of Lord Kaimes, vol. ii. p. 341.

(*n*) Bennett *v.* Vade, 2 Atk. 324.

(*o*) 1 Fonb. Eq. bk. i. ch. 2, § 3; Story, Eq. Jur. 187.

(*p*) Green *v.* Nixon, 23 Beav. 530.

[1] Jones *v.* Bolles, 9 Wallace, 364.

[2] Harner *v.* Fisher, 58 Penn. St. 453.

law (*q*), though it is not easy to define the distinction between that which a court of equity treats as a fraud, and that which is considered fraud at law (*r*).[1] The circumstance, however, that relief can be had at law does not exclude the jurisdiction of the court (*s*). The rule of the court is to assume jurisdiction in all cases where the interests of justice call for and require its interference (*t*). The question for the court always is whether the facts are such as to constitute that kind of fraud which a court of law would necessarily take cognizance of and treat as fraud entitling a man to relief in the same manner and to the same extent as a court of equity would do (*u*).

Although a man may have a good defence to an action
* 33   at law, he * is not precluded from proceeding in equity to restrain the action (*x*). If there be an equitable case stated by the bill, there is jurisdiction in the court to interfere by way of injunction, if necessary, and also by way of ordering the instrument to be delivered up (*y*). Thus, proceedings at law upon an overdue bill of exchange were restrained, though there was a good defence at law (*z*). So also proceedings at law upon instruments given for a gambling debt have been restrained (*a*).[2] Whether, however, or not, it will interfere,

(*q*) Trenchard *v.* Wanley, 2 P. Wms. 166; Butcher *v.* Butcher, 1 V. & B. 98; Clarke *v.* Manning, 7 Beav. 167.

(*r*) Traill *v.* Baring, 33 L. J. Ch. 521; Stewart *v.* Great Western Railway Co., 2 Dr. & Sm. 438.

(*s*) Willson *v.* Short, 6 Ha. 366, 379; Robson *v.* Earl of Devon, 4 Jur. N. S. 245, *per* Lord Cranworth.

(*t*) Chesterfield *v.* Jannsen, 2 Ves. 155; Evans *v.* Bicknell, 6 Ves. 182; Bartlett *v.* Salmon, 6 D. M. & G. 40; Green *v.* Nixon, 23 Beav. 530; Slim *v.* Croucher, 1 D. F. & J. 523; Barry *v.* Crookey, 2 J. & H. 1.

(*u*) Stewart *v.* Great Western Railway Co., 2 Dr. & Sm. 438, *per* Kindersley, V. C.

(*x*) Fernihough *v.* Leader, 15 L. J. Ch. 458; London Assurance Co. *v.* Moses, 11 L. T. 532.

(*y*) Traill *v.* Baring, 33 L. J. Ch. 527, *per* Turner, L. J.; Bennett *v.* Vade, 2 Atk. 324; Jervis *v.* White, 7 Ves. 412; Esdaile *v.* La Nauze, 1 Y. & C. 394; Lovell *v.* Hicks, 2 Y. & C. 48; Allan *v.* Inman, 7 Jur. 433; Lloyd *v.* Clarke, 6 Beav. 309; Blair *v.* Bromley,

16 L. J. Ch. 108; London Assurance Co. *v.* Moses, 11 L. T. 532; Ellis *v.* Cowne, 12 L. T. 211; Allen *v.* Davis, 20 L. J. Ch. 44; Llewellin *v.* Pace, 1 W. R. 28; Small *v.* Currie, 5 D. M. & G. 141; Bartlett *v.* Salmon, 6 D. M. & G. 33; Cooper *v.* Joel, 1 D. F. & J. 242; Smith *v.* Reese River Co., 2 L. R. Eq. 264.

(*z*) Hodgson *v.* Murray, 2 Sim. 517, 3 Sim. 283; Stackhouse *v.* Countess of Jersey, 1 J & H. 731.

(*a*) Lord Portarlington *v.* Soulby, 3 M. & K. 104; Lord Milltown *v.* Stewart, 3 M. & C. 24. See Cooper *v.* Joel, 1 D. F. & J. 242; but see Fox *v.* Hill, 2 D. & J. 356; Thiedemann *v.* Goldschmidt, 1 D. F. & J. 4.

[1] As to fraud in cases of wills, see Story Eq. Jur., § 184. Constructive fraud is a conclusion of law from ascertained facts, and a denial of fraud in the answer does not avail if it admits facts from which fraud necessarily follows. Sayre *v.* Fredericks, 1 C. E. Green, N. J. 205.

[2] See in this connection Story's Eq. Jur., § 304, Redfield's ed.

depends on the discretion of the court according to all the circumstances of the case. If the court is satisfied that the case is one which may be more satisfactorily tried at law, the action will be allowed to proceed (*b*).

4. The largest class of cases in which courts of justice are called upon to give relief against fraud is where there has been misrepresentation or *suggestio falsi*. If a man represents as true that which he knows to be false with the intent to induce another to deal in a matter of interest, and the latter, believing the representation to be true, or not knowing it to be false, acts upon the faith of it and suffers damage thereby, there is fraud to support an action of deceit at law or to be a ground for the rescission of the transaction in equity (*c*). It is not, however,* necessary in order to constitute fraud that a   * 34 man who makes a false representation should know it to be false. It is enough that it be false, if it be made recklessly without an honest belief in its truth, or without any reasonable ground for believing it to be true, and be made for a fraudulent or dishonest purpose (*d*). If a duty is cast upon a man to know the truth, and he makes a representation in such a way as to induce a reasonable man to believe that it is true, and is meant to be acted on, he cannot be heard to say, if the representation proves to be untrue, that he believed it to be true and made the misstatement through mistake, ignorance, or forgetfulness (*e*). The principle, indeed, goes further. It is a principle common to both law and equity, that if a man makes a false representation, and the representation is made in such a way or under such circumstances as to induce a reasonable man to believe that it is true, and is meant to be acted on, and the man to whom it has been made acts upon the faith of it, and thereby alters his condition to his prejudice,

---

(*b*) Clarke *v.* Manning, 7 Beav. 162. See Macintosh *v.* Wyatt, 3 Ha. 562.

(*c*) Evans *v.* Bicknell, 6 Ves. 174; Edwards *v.* M'Cleay, 3 Sw. 287; Attwood *v.* Small, 6 Cl. & Fin. 233; Crawshay *v.* Thornton, 4 M. & G. 387; Willson *v.* Short, 6 Ha. 366, 379; Gerhard *v.* Bates, 2 E. & B. 476; Jennings *v.* Broughton, 17 Beav. 234, 5 D. M. & G. 126.

(*d*) Taylor *v.* Ashton, 11 M. & W. 413; Ormrod *v.* Huth, 14 M. & W. 651;

Thom *v.* Bigland, 8 Exch. 725; Evans *v.* Edmunds, 13 C. B. 777, 786; Smith *v.* Reese River Silver Mining Co., 2 L. R. Eq. 264. See Higgins *v.* Samels, 2 J. & H. 460.

(*e*) Burrowes *v.* Lock, 10 Ves. 470; Moens *v.* Heyworth, 10 M. & W. 147; Hutton *v.* Rossiter, 7 D. M. & G. 9; Pulsford *v.* Richards, 17 Beav. 87, 95; Rawlins *v.* Wickham, 3 D. & J. 304; Slim *v.* Croucher, 1 D. F. & J. 523.

the former cannot afterwards be heard to say that what he said
was false, and to assert the real truth in place of the falsehood
which has so misled the other. It is not necessary that the
party making the representation should know it to be false, or
ought in the due discharge of his duty to have known the
truth. It is enough that the representation was made deliberately, and in such a way as to give the person to whom it was
made reasonable grounds for supposing that it was meant to
be acted on (f).[1] The principle does not, however, apply
either at law or in equity, although a representation may prove
to be false, if it was a fair and reasonable one under the
general circumstances of the case, and be * made innocently and in an honest belief of its truth, by a man upon
whom no duty is cast to know the truth (g). In considering
whether a man had reasonable ground to believe a representation to be true, the position in which he was placed, and the
sources from which he drew the information, must be taken
into consideration (h). Though, however, a man making a
representation may at the time believe it to be true, and have
made it innocently, yet if, after discovering it to be untrue,
he suffers the other party to continue in error, and to act
on the belief that no mistake has been made, this from the
time of the discovery becomes in the contemplation of a court
of equity a fraudulent misrepresentation, even though not so
originally (i).

5. To constitute a fraudulent representation, the representation need not be made in terms expressly stating the existence
of some fact which does not exist. If a statement be made by
a man in such terms as would naturally lead the person to
whom it is made to suppose the existence of a certain state of
facts, and if such statement be so made designedly and fraudu-

* 35

(f) Pickard v. Sears, 6 A. & E. 469;
Freeman v. Cooke, 2 Exch. 662; West
v. Jones, 1 Sim. N. S. 207; Jorden v.
Money, 5 H. L. 185, 210; Slim v.
Croucher, 1 D. F. & J. 518; Swan v.
North British Australasian Co., 2 H. &
C. 182.

(g) Ormrod v. Huth, 14 M. & W.
651; Gorsuch v. Cree, 29 L. J. C. B.
308; Evans v. Wyatt, 31 Beav. 217:
Hume v. Pocock, 1 L. R. Ch. Ap. 379;

Smith v. Reese River Silver Mining
Co., 2 L. R. Eq. 264.
(h) Cullen v. Johnston's Trustees, 3
Dec. of Court of Session, 3d series, p.
936.
(i) Reynell v. Sprye, 1 D. M. & G.
660, 709; Traill v. Baring, 33 L. J. Ch.
521.
[1] Lobdell v. Baker, 3 Met. 469;
Brown v. Castles, 11 Cush. 368; Tyler
v. Black, 13 Howard, U. S. 230; Moor-
head v. Eades, 3 Bush, (Ky.) 121.

lently, it is as much a fraudulent misrepresentation as if the statement of an untrue fact were made in express terms (*k*). A representation, though literally true, may, under the circumstances of the case, be a misrepresentation (*l*). There is a misrepresentation, if a statement is calculated to throw the person to whom it is made off his guard, although it may be literally true (*m*). A misrepresentation is usually by word; but it may be as well by acts or deeds as by words, by artifices to mislead as well as by actual assertions (*n*).[1]

* 6. Misrepresentation may consist as well in the con-　* 36 cealment of what is true, as in the assertion of what is false (*o*). But to amount to a misrepresentation, the concealment must be of something that the party concealing was under some legal or equitable obligation to disclose (*p*). If the fact is one which ought to have been disclosed, the fact that it may not have been disclosed through mistake, ignorance, or forgetfulness, cannot be taken into consideration. It is immaterial that the concealment may not have been wilful or with a view to private advantage (*q*).

7. But in order that a misrepresentation may support an action at law, or be a ground for relief in equity, it must be, in the language of the Roman law, a representation *dans locum contractui*. There must be the assertion of a fact, on which the party entering into the transaction relied, and in the absence

---

(*k*) Lowndes *v*. Lane, 2 Cox, 363; Walker *v*. Symonds, 3 Sw. 1, 73; Drysdale *v*. Mace, 5 D. M. & G. 103; Lee *v*. Jones, 17 C. B. N. S. 510, *per* Crompton, J.

(*l*) Lowndes *v*. Lane, 2 Cox, 363; Flint *v*. Woodin, 9 Ha. 618; Stanton *v*. Tattersall, 1 Sm. & G. 529.

(*m*) Edwards *v*. Wickwar, 1 L. R. Eq. 68. See Cullen *v*. Johnston's Trustees, 3 Dec. of Court of Session, 3d series, p. 936.

(*n*) Sibbald *v*. Hill, 2 Dow. 266; Lovell *v*. Hicks, 2 Y. & C. 46; Crawshay *v*. Thornton, 4 M. & G. 387; Burnes *v*. Pennell, 2 H. L. 497, 529.

(*o*) Tapp *v*. Lee, 3 B. & P. 371; Early *v*. Garrett, 4 M. & R. 690.

(*p*) Irvine *v*. Kirkpatrick, 7 Bell, Sc. Ap. 186; Turner *v*. Harvey, Jac. 169; Greenfield *v*. Edwards, 2 D. J. & S. 582, 598.

(*q*) Pusey *v*. Desbouverie, 3 P. Wms.

315; Bowles *v*. Stuart, 1 Sch. & Lef. 209; Willis *v*. Willis, 17 Sim. 218; Railton *v*. Matthews, 10 Cl. & Fin. 934.

[1] Where one sold commercial paper, and concealed the fact that the maker's check had been protested that day, it was held a fraud, though he believed him to be solvent. Brown *v*. Montgomery, 20 N. Y. 287. And where a person in good credit and solvent had been accustomed to have his checks, for the day, certified good by the teller of the bank in the morning, continued the same course after he became utterly insolvent, without disclosing the fact to the bank, it was such a fraud as rendered the transaction void as between the parties. Bank of the Republic *v*. Baxter, 31 Vt. 101. See also Paddock *v*. Strobridge, 29 Vt. 470, where this subject is discussed, and the authorities compared by Redfield, C. J.

of which it is reasonable to infer that he would not have entered
into it: or the suppression of a fact, the knowledge of which, it
is reasonable to infer, would have made him abstain from the
transaction altogether (r). The representation must be material in its nature, and a determining ground of the transaction (s). A representation goes for nothing, unless it is a
proximate and determining cause of the transaction (u). It is
not enough that it may have remotely or indirectly contributed
to it, or may have supplied a motive to the other party to enter
into it. The representation must be the very ground on which
the transaction has taken place. The transaction must be a
necessary and not merely an indirect result of the representation (x). It is not, however, necessary that the repre-
* 37   sentation * should be the sole cause of the transaction.

It is enough that it may have constituted a material
inducement. If any one of several statements, all in their
nature more or less capable of leading the party to whom they
are addressed to adopt a particular line of conduct, be untrue,
the whole transaction is considered as having been fraudulently obtained (y). A man who has made a false representation in respect of a material matter, must, in order to be able
to rely on the defence that the transaction was not entered
into on the faith of the representation, be able to prove to
demonstration that it was not relied on (z). It is not enough
for him to say that there were other representations by which
the transaction may have been induced (a): nor can he be
heard to say what the other party would have done had no
misrepresentation been made (b).

8. It is not, however, enough that there has been a misrepresentation, and that it may have conduced in some way to the

(r) Pulsford v. Richards, 17 Beav. 87, 96.

(s) Jennings v. Broughton, 5 D. M. & G. 126, 136.

(u) Barry v. Crosskey, 2 J. & H. 1; New Brunswick, &c., Railway Co. v. Conybeare, 9 H. L. 711; Barrett's case, 3 D. J. & S. 30.

(x) Burnes v. Pennell, 2 H. L. 497, 531; Nicoll's case, 3 D. & J. 387, 439; New Brunswick, &c., Railway Co. v. Conybeare, 9 H. L. 711.

(y) Reynell v. Sprye, 1 D. M. & G. 660; Jennings v. Broughton, 5 D. M. & G. 126; Clarke v. Dickson, 6 C. B. N. S. 453; Smith v. Kay, 7 H. L. 750, 775.

(z) Rawlins v. Wickham, 3 D. & J. 304; Nicoll's case, ib. 387; Smith v. Kay, 7 H. L. 750, 775; Kisch v. Central Venezuela Railway Co., 3 D. J. & S. 122.

(a) Nicoll's case, 3 D. & J. 387, 439.

(b) Reynell v. Sprye, 1 D. M. & G. 660; Smith v. Kay, 7 H. L. 750, 770; Traill v. Baring, 33 L. J. Ch. 521, 527.

transaction in question. It is necessary that it should have been made in relation to the transaction in question, and with a view to induce the other party to act in the way that occasions the injury (c). A representation which has been made some time before the date of the transaction is not sufficient, unless it can be shown to have been immediately connected with it (d). A representation, to be of any avail whatever, must, unless under special circumstances, have been made at the time of the treaty (e), and should not have relation to any * collateral matter, or other relation or dealing between   * 38 the parties (f).

9. A misrepresentation, to be of any avail whatever, must enure to the date of the transaction in question (g). If a man to whom a representation has been made knows at the time, or discovers before entering into a transaction that the representation is false (h), or resorts to other means of knowledge open to him, and chooses to judge for himself in the matter, he cannot avail himself of the fact that there has been misrepresentation, or say that he has acted on the faith of the representation (i).

10. A false statement, to amount to a misrepresentation against which relief may be had either at law or in equity, should be in respect of an ascertainable fact, as distinguished from a mere matter of opinion (k).[1] A representation which

(c) East India Co. v. Henchman, 1 Ves. Jr. 287 ; Dobell v. Stevens, 3 B. & C. 623 ; Harris v. Kemble, 5 Bligh, N. S. 730 ; Attwood v. Small, 6 Cl. & Fin. 232, 445 ; Irvine v. Kirkpatrick, 7 Bell, Sc. Ap. 186 ; Burnes v. Pennell, 2 H. L. 497, 529 ; Smith v. Kay, 7 H. L. 750, 775 ; Nicoll's case, 3 D. & J. 387, 440.

(d) Burnes v. Pennell, 2 H. L. 497, 530. See Maunsell v. Hedges, 4 H. L. 1060, per Lord St. Leonards ; Barrett's case, 2 D. J. & S. 30.

(e) Harris v. Kemble, 1 Sim. 122, per Sir J. Leach. See Wheelton v. Hardisty, El. Bl. & El. 246 ; Hotsom v. Browne, 9 C. B. N. S. 445 ; Smith v. Kay, 7 H. L. 750.

(f) Harris v. Kemble, 1 Sim. 122, 5 Bligh, N. S. 730 ; National Exchange Co. v. Drew, 2 Macq. 103.

(g) Irvine v. Kirkpatrick, 7 Bell, Sc. Ap. 186.

(h) Ib. ; Lord Brooke v. Round-

thwaite, 5 Ha. 298, 306 ; Nelson v. Stocker, 4 D. & J. 465.

(i) Lysney v. Selby, 2 Raym. 1118, 1120 ; Attwood v. Small, 6 Cl. & Fin. 232 ; Clapham v. Shilleto, 7 Beav 146 ; Vigers v. Pike, 8 Cl. & Fin. 562, 650 ; Jennings v. Broughton, 17 Beav. 234, 5 D. M. & G. 126 ; Robson v. Lord Devon, 4 Jur. N. S. 245 ; Fairbrother v. Gibson, 1 D. & J. 602.

(k) Lysney v. Selby, 2 Raym. 1118 ; Brunton v. Lister, 3 Atk. 386 ; Jennings v. Broughton, 5 D M. & G. 134.

[1] " A representation of what the law will or will not permit to be done, is one upon which the party to whom it is made has no right to rely ; and if he does so, it is his own folly. and he cannot ask the court to relieve him from the consequences. The truth or falsehood of such a representation can be tested by ordinary vigilance and attention. It is an opinion in regard to the

merely amounts to a matter of opinion or judgment, or is
vague and indefinite in its nature and terms, or is merely a
loose, conjectural, or exaggerated statement, goes for nothing,
though it may not be true, for a man is not justified in placing
reliance on it (*l*).   But there must be no material misstatement of a fact (*m*).   The representation of an actual state of
       things as existing is equivalent to the representation
* 39   of a fact (*n*).   As distinguished from * the representa-
       tion as to a fact, or as to the actual existence of a cer-
tain state of things, the representation as to an intention to
do, or to abstain from doing, something, is not a ground for
relief, either at law or in equity (*o*).

11. The allegation of misrepresentation may be effectually
met by proof that the party complaining was well aware and
cognizant of the real facts of the case, but the proof of knowledge must be clear and conclusive.[1]   A man who, by misrep-

law, and is always understood as such."
Fish *v.* Cleland, 33 Ill. 243, 5 Hill, 303.

In Pennsylvania it is settled that the
"false statement of a material matter
will not overthrow a bargain unless the
statement was the means of producing
it." Clark *v.* Everhart, 63 Penn. St.
350. But query whether such statement would be strictly material.

(*l*) Haycraft *v.* Creasy, 2 East, 92;
Lord Brooke *v.* Roundthwaite, 5 Ha.
298; Irvine *v.* Kirkpatrick, 7 Bell, Sc.
Ap. 186; Jennings *v.* Broughton, 5 D.
M. & G. 136; New Brunswick, &c.,
Railway Co. *v.* Conybeare, 9 H. L. 711;
Kisch *v.* Central Venezuela Railway
Co., 3 D. J. & S. 122; Denton *v.* Mac-
neil, 2 L. R. Eq. 352.

(*m*) Kisch *v.* Central Venezuela Railway Co., 3 D. J. & S. 122; Denton *v.*
Macneil, 2 L. R. Eq. 352.

(*n*) Piggott *v.* Stratton, John. 359, 1
D. F. & J. 49.

(*o*) Jorden *v.* Money, 5 H. L. 214.
See Maunsell *v.* Hedges, 4 H. L. 1039;
Warden *v.* Jones, 2 D. & J. 77, 85; Pig-
gott *v.* Stratton, John. 359, 1 D. F. &
J. 49; Laver *v.* Fielder, 32 Beav. 4.

[1] In Stephens *v.* Orman, 10 Fla. 9, it is
held, that where the complainant had
full opportunity to examine the subject-
matter of the contract, and did examine
it, and trusted to his own judgment,
and not to the representations of the
other party, he could not be relieved in
equity, though the defendant concealed

material facts. But Judge Redfield, in
commenting on this subject, says, it is
questionable how far the circumstance
that the facts were open to the inspection of both parties should excuse the
party for obtaining an unjust advantage
either by suppression of the truth or
suggestion of falsehood, unless the
other party is guilty of unwarrantable
disregard of the most obvious precau-
tions to secure his own interests.
Story's Eq. Jur., Redfield's ed., § 203 *f*,
note. In Moorhead *v.* Eades, 3 Bush,
(Ky.) it is held, that when a confiding
vendee had no fitting or reasonable
opportunity to examine sufficiently for
himself the lot of goods constituting
the stock of a retail store, and decide
on his own judgment, the positive assertion and assurance of the vendor, "that
the cost and carriage of the goods
amounted to three thousand five hundred dollars," when, as afterwards ascertained, the total value did not exceed
two thousand dollars, such assurance
and assertion, according to the circumstances, may be either actually or constructively fraudulent. When the vendor knew or believed that it was not
true, the affirmation was actually fraudulent; and even if he believed it to be
true, it might be constructively fraudulent; for, unless he knew it to be true,
his duty was in good faith to express
candidly his mere opinion, which ought
not to disarm the vendee, or lull his pru-

resentation or inaccurate statements, has misled another, cannot be heard to say that it was his duty to institute inquiries, but must, in order to be able to rely on the defence that he was acquainted with the facts of the case, be able to show clearly, and upon incontestable evidence, that he knew the representation to be untrue (p). It is not enough that there may be circumstances in the case, which, in the absence of the representation, might have been sufficient to put him on inquiry. The doctrine of notice has no application where a distinct representation has been made. A man to whom a particular and distinct representation has been made, is entitled to rely on the representation, and need not make any further inquiry, although there are circumstances in the case from which an inference inconsistent with the representation might be drawn (q). He is not bound to inquire, unless something has happened to excite suspicion (r). The effect of what would be otherwise notice, may be destroyed, not only by actual misrepresentation, but by any thing calculated to deceive, or even to lull suspicion, on a particular point (s).[1]

*12. The principle of law, that a man who makes a   *40 representation to another in such a way, or under such circumstances, as to induce him to believe that it is meant to be acted on, is liable as for a fraud, in the event of the representation proving to be false, and damage accruing thereby to

---

dent vigilance, and on which opinion he therefore acts at his peril; and therefore a positive affirmation, if untrue, was both reckless and deceptive. See also Watts v. Cummins, 59 Penn. St. 84.

(p) Dyer v. Hargrave, 10 Ves. 505; Vigers v. Pike, 8 Cl. & Fin. 562, 650; Willson v. Short, 6 Ha. 366, 375; Kisch v. Central Venezuela Railway Co., 3 D. J. & S. 122.

(q) Van v. Corpe, 3 M. & K. 269; Flight v. Barton, ib. 282; Willson v. Short, 6 Ha. 366, 377; Reynell v. Sprye, 1 D. M. & G. 660, 710; Kisch v. Central Venezuela Railway Co., 3 D. J. & S. 122; Smith v. Reese River Silver Mining Co., 2 L. R. Eq. 264.

(r) Rawlins v. Wickham, 3 D. & J. 304.

(s) Dykes v. Blake, 4 Bing. N. C. 463; Bartlett v. Salmon, 6 D. M. & G.

33; Darlington v. Hamilton, Kay, 550; Smith v. Harrison, 26 L. J. Ch. 412.

[1] In Maul v. Rider, 59 Penn St. 167, the question of notice is discussed. It is held that the record of a deed is notice only to those bound to search for it. It is not publication to the world at large. And in reference to constructive notice it is considered well settled, that whatever puts a party on inquiry amounts in judgment of law to notice, provided the inquiry becomes a duty, as in case of purchasers and creditors, and would lead to the knowledge of the requisite fact by the exercise of ordinary diligence and understanding. Notice of a general rumor of a conveyance is not considered actual or constructive notice. There must be some act; some declaration from an authentic source, which a person would be careless if he disregarded.

the party to whom it was made, though common to both law
and equity, is not so general in its application at law as in
equity. In equity, the principle is of universal application,
and is the foundation of a most salutary part of the jurisdiction. Whatever may be the circumstances or peculiarities of
the case, a court of equity will not permit a man who has so
conducted himself as to cause a reasonable man to believe in
the existence of a certain actual state of things, and to believe
that the representation so conveyed to his mind was meant to
be acted on, to derogate from an interest in which that other
has been induced to deal upon the faith of the representation,
by determining the state of things which he has so held forth
as the consideration for the change of his condition by the
other, or to enforce his legal right, if any, against him, unless
the latter has received the benefit which he contemplated at
the time he was induced to alter his condition (*t*). Where,
accordingly, a lessor, pending an agreement for a building
lease, represented to the intended lessee, that he could not
obstruct the sea-view from the houses to be built by the lessee,
pursuant to the proposed lease, because he himself was a lessee
under a lease for 999 years, containing covenants which restricted him from so doing; but after the building lease had
been*taken, and the houses built upon the faith of the representation, the lessor surrendered his 999 years' lease, and took
a new lease omitting the restrictive covenants, the court
restrained him, by injunction, from building so as to obstruct
the sea-view (*u*). So, also, where on one of two partners retiring from business, it was left to arbitration to determine what
was to be paid to the retiring partner for the good-will of the
business, and they, on the clear understanding of the
parties * that the retiring partner would not set up trade
in the same street, or in the vicinity, allowed him 500*l.*
as the share of the good-will, but the award was silent on
the subject; the court, nevertheless, upon parol evidence of
the understanding on which the award was made, restrained

* 41

(*t*) Major *v.* Major, 1 Drew. 165;　240; Dendy *v.* Cary, 9 Jur. N. S. 845;
Evans *v.* Bremridge, 2 K. & J. 174, 8 D.　Yeomans *v.* Williams, 1 L. R. Eq. 185.
M. & G. 100; Piggott *v.* Stratton, John.　　(*u*) Piggott *v.* Stratton, John. 359, 1
359, 1 D. F. & J. 49; Cooper *v.* Joel, *ib.*　D. F. & J. 33.

him from carrying on trade in the same street or the same vicinity (*x*).

13. The equitable doctrine of acquiescence is founded on the same principle. Parties who stand by without asserting their rights, and allow others to incur liabilities which they might not have incurred if those rights had been asserted, will not afterwards be permitted by a court of equity to set up those rights to the prejudice of those by whom such liabilities have been incurred (*y*). Where, for instance, a man builds a house upon land, supposing it to be his own, or believing that he has a good title, and the real owner, perceiving his mistake, abstains from setting him right, and leaves him to persevere in his error: or where a man, under an expectation created or encouraged by the owner of land, that he shall have a certain interest, takes possession of such land with the consent of the owner, and upon the faith of such promise or expectation, with the knowledge and without objection by him, lays out money on the land: in such cases a court of equity will not afterwards allow the real owner or the landlord, as the case may be, to assert his legal right against the other without at least making him a proper compensation for the moneys which he has expended (*z*). If the works on which the moneys have been expended are of a permanent character, or are works which point to permanence, the court will not allow them to be interfered with, even on payment of money, but will require the land-owner to be satisfied with a proper compensation in respect * of the land which has been so taken (*a*). The principle applies to companies as well as individuals (*b*).   * 42

14. The rule at law as to leave and license not being countermandable, cannot, perhaps, as far as it goes, be distinguished

---

(*x*) Harrison *v.* Gardiner, 2 Madd. 198.

(*y*) Hunsdon *v.* Cheyney, 2 Vern. 150; Raw *v.* Pote, *ib.* 239; Draper *v.* Borlase, *ib.* 369; Berrisford *v.* Millward, 2 Atk. 49; Nicholson *v.* Hooper, 4 M. & C. 179; Olliver *v.* King, 8 D. M. & G. 110; Davies *v.* Davies, 6 Jur. N. S. 1322.

(*z*) Dann *v.* Spurrier, 7 Ves. 235; Shannon *v.* Bradstreet, 1 Sch. & Lef. 52; Gregory *v.* Mighell, 18 Ves. 328;

Gerrard *v.* O'Reilly, 3 Dr. & War. 414; Laird *v.* Birkenhead Railway Co., John. 514; Harcourt *v.* White, 28 Beav. 303; Ramsden *v.* Dyson, 1 L. R. H. L. 129.

(*a*) Clavering *v.* Thomas, cited 5 Ves. 689; Duke of Beaufort *v.* Patrick, 17 Beav. 60; Somersetshire Canal Co. *v.* Harcourt, 2 D. & J. 596; Mold *v.* Wheatcroft, 27 Beav. 516. See Bell *v.* Midland Railway Co., 3 D. & J. 673.

(*b*) Hill *v.* South Staffordshire Railway Co., 11 Jur. N. S. 192.

from the equitable doctrine of acquiescence (c), but leave and license executed may be set up at law, as giving a right and title only in cases where moneys have been expended by a man upon his own land (d). No right or title can be acquired at law to an easement or other right over the land of another, although the license may have been executed and moneys have been expended upon the land of the licensee by his express permission. The license may be at any time countermanded at the will of the owner of the soil (e). But in equity the principle applies as well where a man has been induced or encouraged to expend moneys on the land of another, as where the expenditure has been on his own land (f). In order to justify the application of the principle it is indispensable that the party against whom encouragement or acquiescence is alleged should be fully apprised of his rights, and should by his conduct encourage the other party to alter his condition, and that the latter should act on the faith of the encouragement so held out (g).

15. The principle does not apply in favor of a stranger who builds on land knowing it to be the property of another, * 43   nor in * favor of a lessee who expends moneys with the knowledge of his landlord on the improvement of the estate. If a stranger builds on land knowing it to be the property of another, equity will not prevent the real owner from afterwards claiming the land with the benefit of all the expenditure on it. So also if a tenant being in possession of land, and knowing the nature and extent of his interest, lays out money in the hope and expectation of an extended term, or an allowance for them, then, if such hope or expectation has not been created or encouraged by the landlord, the tenant has

---

(c) Davies v. Marshall, 10 C. B. N. S. 711, per Willes, J.; but see Swaine v. Great Northern Railway Co., 9 Jur. N. S. 1196.

(d) Winter v. Brockwell, 8 East, 309; Hewlins v. Shippam, 5 B. & C. 221; Liggins v. Ince, 7 Bing. 682; Davies v. Marshall, 10 C. B. N. S. 711.

(e) Wallis v. Harrison, 4 M. & W. 538; Wood v. Leadbitter, 13 M. & W. 838; Davies v. Marshall, 10 C. B. N. S.

711; but see Blood v. Keller, 11 Ir. C. L. 124.

(f) Duke of Devonshire v. Eglin, 14 Beav. 530; Duke of Beaufort v. Patrick, 17 Beav. 60; White v. Wakley, 26 Beav. 20; Laird v. Birkenhead Railway Co., John. 500.

(g) Dann v. Spurrier, 7 Ves. 230; Marker v. Marker, 9 Ha. 16; Hooper v. Cook, 25 L. J. Ch. 467; Ramsden v. Dyson, 1 L. R. H. L. 129. See infra.

no equity to prevent the landlord from taking possession of the land and buildings, when the tenancy is determined (*h*).

16. The equitable doctrine with respect to the part performance of parol agreements is founded on the same principle. At law the express language of the statute of frauds prevails, and the doctrine as to the part performance of parol agreements has no place; but in equity it is a fraud in the eye of the court to set up the absence of an agreement, where possession has been given on the faith of an agreement. If a man has been permitted to take possession on the faith of an agreement, it is against equity that he should be treated as a trespasser, and turned out of possession on the ground that there is no agreement (*i*).[1]

17. Besides that kind of fraud which consists in misrepresentation, express or implied, there is another which will be presumed where parties to a transaction do not stand on the equal footing on which parties to a transaction should stand (*k*). The equitable rule is of universal application that where a man is not a free agent, or is from his state of mind, age, weakness, or other peculiar circumstances, not equal to protecting himself, the court will protect him (*l*).   The contracts accordingly of * idiots, lunatics, and other persons,   * 44 *non compotes mentis*, are generally deemed invalid (*m*).

So also if a man be drunk to the extent of complete intoxication so as to be no longer under the guide of reason, or is in a state of excitement from excessive drinking almost amount-

(*h*) Pilling *v.* Armitage, 12 Ves. 78; Clare Hall *v.* Harding, 6 Ha. 273; Ramsden *v.* Dyson, 1 L. R. H. L. 129.

(*i*) Mundy *v.* Jolliffe, 5 M. & C. 177; Wilson *v.* West Hartlepool Railway and Harbor Co., 2 D. J. & S. 475. See Bond *v.* Hopkins, 1 Sch. & Lef. 413, 433.

(*k*) Edwards *v.* Meyrick, 2 Ha. 60.

(*l*) Evans *v.* Llewellyn, 1 Cox, 340; Crowe *v.* Ballard, 1 Ves. Jr. 215; Baker *v.* Monk, 10 Jur. N. S. 691.

(*m*) Niell *v.* Morley, 9 Ves. 478; Selby *v.* Jackson, 6 Beav. 192; Molton *v.* Camroux, 4 Exch. 17; Jacobs *v.* Richards, 18 Beav. 300; Bevan *v.* M'Donnell, 10 Exch. 184; Campbell *v.* Hooper, 3 Sm. & G. 153. See as to *non compotes mentis*, Blachford *v.* Christian, 1 Knapp, 73; Ball *v.* Mannin, 3 Bligh,

N. S. 1; Manby *v.* Bewicke, 3 K. & J. 342.

[1] Neale *v.* Neales, 9 Wallace, 1; Swain *v.* Seamens, *ib.* 254. But in the absence of evidence of change of situation, or part performance creating an estoppel against the plea of the statute of frauds, the court will not reform a deed involving the specific enforcement of an oral agreement within the statute of frauds; or when the term sought to be added would so modify the instrument as to make it operate to convey an interest, or secure a right which can only be conveyed or secured through an instrument in writing, and for which no writing has ever existed. Glass *v.* Hulbert, 102 Mass. 24. See the elaborate opinion of Wells, J., in this case for a full examination of the subject.

ing to madness, any transaction which he may enter into while he is in that state is invalid. If, however, the degree of intoxication falls short of such complete intoxication, he cannot have relief, unless it appear that he was drawn in to drink by the contrivance of the other party, or that an unfair advantage was taken of his situation (*n*).

The principle which vitiates a contract with an incapacitated person extends in equity to cases where from the peculiar relation which subsists between the parties, or from the influence which the one party has acquired over the other, the freedom of action which is essential to the validity of a transaction is overcome, and the equal footing on which parties to a transaction should stand is destroyed (*o*).[1]

18. Transactions between parties, one of whom stands towards the other in a position of a fiduciary character, are watched by a court of equity with more than ordinary jealousy. The duty of a person who fills a fiduciary position being to protect the interests which are confided to his care, he may not avail himself of the influence which his position gives him for the purposes of his own benefit and to the prejudice of those interests which he is bound to protect. It is a rule of equity that no man can be permitted to take a benefit where he has a duty to perform which is inconsistent with his acceptance of the benefit. The rule does not go the length of avoiding all transactions between persons standing in a fiduciary *45 relation and * those towards whom they stand in such relation. All that a court of equity requires is that the confidence which has been reposed be not betrayed. A transaction between them will be supported, if it appear that the parties were, notwithstanding the relation, substantially at arm's length, and on an equal footing, and that nothing has

---

(*n*) Cory *v.* Cory, 1 Ves. 19; Cooke *v.* Clayworth, 18 Ves. 16; Lightfoot *v.* Heron, 3 Y. & C. 586; Nagle *v.* Baylor, 3 Dr. & War. 60; Gore *v.* Gibson, 13 M. & W. 623, 626; Molton *v.* Camroux, 4 Exch. 17, 19; Shaw *v.* Thackeray, 1 Sm. & G. 539.

(*o*) Edwards *v.* Meyrick, 2 Ha. 60; Barrett *v.* Hartley, 2 L. R. Eq. 789.

[1] See Hetrick's Appeal, 58 Penn. St. 477, where it is said, that when a man,

broken by years and standing alone, and too enfeebled in mind and body to be watchful of his own interests, or to penetrate the designs of others, contracts with an unsuitable or insolvent man for necessary support and assistance for life, and surrenders by deed all his property to him, a chancellor should take hold of the slightest circumstance to set aside the deed; also, Lavette *v.* Sage, 29 Conn. 577.

happened which might not have happened had no such relation existed.   The burden of proof lies in all cases upon the
party who fills the position of active confidence to show that
the transaction has been fair.   If he can show to the satisfaction of the court that he disclosed fairly and honestly all he
knew respecting the subject-matter of the transaction, and did
not seek to secure surreptitiously any advantage for himself,
and that the other party entered into the transaction voluntarily and deliberately, knowing its nature and effect, or that he
had competent and independent legal advice, the transaction
will be supported (*p*).   The principle applies between trustee
and *cestui que trust* (*q*) ; between solicitor and client (*r*) ; [1]
between principal and agent (*s*) ; between guardian and
ward (*t*) ; between parent and child (*u*),[2] (unless the
transaction *comes within the protection extended to   *46
agreements entered into to preserve the peace of
families (*x*) ; between partners (*y*) ; and in other relations

(*p*) Gibson *v.* Jeyes, 6 Ves. 266 ;
Giddings *v.* Giddings, 3 Russ. 241 ;
Hunter *v.* Atkins, 3 M. & K. 113 ;
Greenlaw *v.* King, 10 L. J. Ch. 129 ;
Edwards *v.* Meyrick, 2 Ha. 60 ; Hogh-
ton *v.* Hoghton, 15 Beav. 278 ; Smith
v. Kay, 7 H. L. 750 ; Rhodes *v.* Bate, 1
L. R. Ch. Ap. 252.

(*q*) Clark *v.* Esdaile, 2 Ed. 134 ; *Ex
parte* James, 8 Ves. 337 ; *Ex parte* Bennett, 10 Ves. 394 ; Gregory *v.* Gregory,
Coop. 201 ; Grover *v.* Hugell, 3 Russ.
428 ; Wedderburn *v.* Wedderburn, 4 M.
& C. 41 ; Knight *v.* Marjoribanks, 2
Mac. & G. 10 ; Aberdeen Railway Co.
v. Blaikie, 1 Macq. 461.

(*r*) Gibson *v.* Jeyes, 6 Ves. 277 ;
Montesquieu *v.* Sandys, 18 Ves. 302 ;
Edwards *v.* Meyrick, 2 Ha. 60 ; Cutts
v. Salmon, 21 L. J. Ch. 750 ; Holman
v. Loynes, 4 D. M. & G. 270 ; Hesse *v.*
Briant, 6 D. M. & G. 623 ; Savery *v.*
King, 5 H. L. 627 ; Tomson *v.* Judge, 3
Drew. 306.

(*s*) York Buildings Co. *v.* M'Kenzie,
3 Pat. Sc. Ap. 398, 3 Ross, L. C. Sc.
305 ; *Ex parte* Hughes, 6 Ves. 617 ;
Naylor *v.* Salmon, 4 M. & C. 134 ; Trevelyan *v.* Charter, 4 L. J. Ch. N. S.
209 ; Charter *v.* Trevelyan, 11 Cl. &
Fin. 714, 732 ; Murphy *v.* O'Shea, 2 J.
& L. 422, 425 ; Clarke *v.* Tipping, 9
Beav. 284 ; Lewis *v.* Hillman, 3 H. L.
607 ; Bentley *v.* Craven, 18 Beav. 75 ;

Tyrrell *v.* Bank of London, 10 H. L.
26 ; Rhodes *v.* Bate, 1 L. R. Ch. App.
252.

(*t*) Hylton *v.* Hylton, 2 Ves. 548 ;
Hatch *v.* Hatch, 9 Ves. 292 ; Dawson *v.*
Massey, 1 B. & B. 219 ; Maitland *v.*
Irving, 15 Sim. 437 ; Archer *v.* Hudson,
15 L. J. Ch. 211 ; Maitland *v.* Back-
house, 17 L. J. Ch. 121 ; Espey *v.* Lake,
10 Ha. 260 ; Prideaux *v.* Lonsdale, 1 D.
J. & S. 433.

(*u*) Hoghton *v.* Hoghton, 15 Beav.
278 ; Baker *v.* Bradley 7 D. M. & G.
597 ; Wright *v.* Vanderplank, 8 D. M.
& G. 135, 146 ; Jenner *v.* Jenner 2 D.
F. & J. 359.

(*x*) Tweddell *v.* Tweddell, T. & R. 1 ;
Bellamy *v.* Sabine, 2 Ph. 425 ; Cooke *v.*
Burtchaell, 2 Dr. & War 165 ; Hogh-
ton *v.* Hoghton, 15 Beav. 278, 305 ;
Baker *v.* Bradley, 7 D. M. & G. 597 ;
Dimsdale *v.* Dimsdale, 3 Drew. 556 ;
Jenner *v.* Jenner, 2 D. F. & J. 359 ;
Williams *v.* Williams, 2 L. R. Ch. App.
294.

(*y*) Bayne *v.* Ferguson, 5 Dow. 151 ;
Maddeford *v.* Austwick, 1 Sim. 89 ;
Chambers *v.* Howell, 11 Beav. 6 ; Cle-
ments *v.* Hall, 2 D. & J. 173 ; Perens *v.*
Johnson, 3 Sm. & G. 419.

[1] Brown *v.* Bulkley, 1 McCarter, 451.
[2] But not necessarily between son-in-
law and parent-in-law. Fish *v.* Cleland, 33 Ill. 242.

where mutual agencies, rights, and duties, are created between parties either by their own acts or by operation of
law (z). The principle applies equally to the case of third
persons who make themselves parties to transactions between
persons filling a fiduciary position, and those towards whom
they stand in such relation, or who take securities with notice
that they have been obtained by a person filling a position of a
fiduciary character, from a person towards whom he stood in
such relation (a).[1]

19. The principle applies, even after the actual relation has
come to a close, unless there is distinct evidence of the determination of the influence (b), in which case it will no longer
apply; but a man who has filled a position of a fiduciary character, cannot, after the termination of the relation, be permitted
to avail himself for his own benefit, and to the prejudice of the
party towards whom he stood in such relation, of any information which he may have acquired during the existence of the
relation (c). Nor does the rule apply where the trans-
*47 action is * totally disconnected with the relation and
concerns objects and things, and embraced in, or
affected by, or dependent upon, that relation (d).

20. The principle on which a court of equity acts in relieving against transactions, on the ground of inequality of footing
between the parties, is not confined to cases where a fiduciary
relation can be shown to exist, but extends to all the varieties
of relations in which dominion may be exercised by one man
over another, and applies to every case where influence is

(z) Greenlaw v. King, 10 L. J. Ch.
129; Giddings v. Giddings, 3 Rus. 241;
Waters v. Bailey, 2 Y. & C. C. C. 219;
Tanner v. Elworthy, 4 Beav. 487;
Smith v. Kay, 7 H. L. 750; Coulson v.
Alison, 2 D. F. & J. 521; Prideaux v.
Lonsdale, 1 D. J. & S. 433.

(a) Ardglasse v. Pitt, 1 Vern. 238;
Espey v. Lake, 10 Ha. 260; Berdoe v.
Dawson, 34 Beav. 603; Wyse v. Lam-
bert, 16 Ir. Ch. 379.

(b) Rhodes v. Bate, 1 L. R. Ch. App.
252. See Maitland v. Irving, 15 Sim.
437; Archer v. Hudson, 15 L. J. Ch.
211; Maitland v. Backhouse, 17 L. J.
Ch. 121; Hoghton v. Hoghton, 15 Beav.
300; Wright v. Vanderplank, 8 D. M.
& G. 135.

(c) Ex parte Lacey, 6 Ves. 627; Ex
parte Bennett, 10 Ves. 394; Wood v.
Downes, 18 Ves. 120; Trevelyan v.
Charter, 4 L. J. Ch. N. S. 209; Holman
v. Loynes, 4 D. M. & G. 270; Moss v.
Bainbrigge, 6 D. M. & G. 292. See
Austen v. Chambers, 6 Cl. & Fin. 1;
Carter v. Palmer, 8 Cl. & Fin. 657, 707.
Compare Johnson v. Fesenmeyer, 3 D.
& J. 13.

(d) Montesquieu v. Sandys, 18 Ves.
313; Jones v. Thomas, 2 Y. & C. 498;
Edwards v. Meyrick, 2 Ha. 60, 68.

[1] In reference to this subject generally, see Highberger v. Stiffler, 21 Md.
338.

acquired and abused, or where confidence is reposed and betrayed (*e*). If the confidence or the influence can be shown to exist, the rules of equity are just as applicable in the one case as in the other (*f*).

21. Mere inadequacy of consideration or inequality in a bargain is not a ground for relief, if the party was in a situation to judge for himself, and entered into the transaction deliberately and advisedly (*g*).[1] The fact that he may be an illiterate person, or of advanced age, or in distress, or in bad health, and may have had no independent legal advice, is immaterial if it appear that he was fully competent to form an independent judgment (*h*). But the case is otherwise if the inadequacy of consideration is of so gross a nature as to shock the conscience, and amounts to conclusive evidence of fraud (*i*); or if one of the parties to * the transaction was from age,　　*48 ignorance, weakness of mind, body, or disposition, unable to protect himself (*k*). If it appear that one of the parties to the transaction was, from any of these causes, unable to protect himself, and that he had no independent professional advice, the onus of proof rests on the party who seeks to uphold the transaction to show that the other party entered into the transaction voluntarily and deliberately, knowing its nature and effect, and that his consent was not obtained by reason of any influence exerted over him (*l*).

(*e*) Dent *v.* Bennett, 4 M. & C. 269; Cooke *v.* Lamotte, 15 Beav. 234; Billage *v.* Southee, 9 Ha. 534, 540; Smith *v.* Kay, 7 H. L. 750, 779; Coulson *v.* Allison, 2 D. F. & J. 521; Rhodes *v.* Bate, 1 L. R. Ch. App. 252.

(*f*) 7 H. L. 779, *per* Lord Kingsdown. See Norton *v.* Relly, 2 Eden, 286; Casborne *v.* Barsham, 2 Beav. 75; Boyse *v.* Russborough, 3 Jur. N. S. 373; Beanland *v.* Bradley, 2 Sm. & G. 339; Nottidge *v.* Prince, 2 Giff. 246; Harrison *v.* Guest, 6 D. M. & G. 424, 8 H. L. 481; Williams *v.* Bayly, 1 L. R. H. L. 200.

(*g*) Griffith *v.* Spratley, 1 Cox, 383; Copis *v.* Middleton, 2 Madd. 410; Wood *v.* Abrey, 3 Madd. 417.

(*h*) Hunter *v.* Atkins, 3 M. & K. 113; Knight *v.* Marjoribanks, 11 Beav. 322, 2 Mac. & G. 10; Richards *v.* Curlewis, 3 Eq. Rep. 278; Curzon *v.* Belworthy, 3 H. L. 742; Harrison *v.* Guest, 6 D. M. & G. 434; 8 H. L. 481.

(*i*) Heathcoate *v.* Paignon, 2 Bro. C. C. 173; Evans *v.* Llewellin, 1 Cox, 333; Griffith *v.* Spratley, *ib.* 383; Underhill *v.* Horwood, 10 Ves. 209, 219; Borell *v.* Dann, 2 Ha. 440, 450.

(*k*) Evans *v.* Llewellin, 1 Cox, 333; Griffith *v.* Robbins, 3 Madd. 191; Abearne *v.* Hogan, Dru. 310; Cooke *v.* Lamotte, 15 Beav. 234; Smith *v.* Kay, 7 H. L. 750; Rhodes *v.* Bate, 1 L. R. Ch. App. 252.

(*l*) Ardglasse *v.* Muschamp, 1 Vern. 236; Evans *v.* Llewellin, 1 Cox, 333; Griffith *v.* Robbins, 3 Madd. 191; Wood *v.* Abrey, *ib.* 417; Willan *v.* Willan, 2 Dow. 274; Dent *v.* Bennett, 4 M. & C. 273; Abearne *v.* Hogan, Dru. 310; Cooke *v.* Lamotte, 15 Beav. 234; Smith *v.* Kay, 7 H. L. 750; Rhodes *v.* Bate, 1 L. R. Ch. App. 252.

[1] See Howard *v.* Edgell, 17 Vt. 9; Erwin *v.* Parham, 12 How. U. S. 197.

[51]

22. The equitable rule being, that particular persons in contracts, and other acts, shall not only transact *bonâ fide* between themselves, but shall not transact *malâ fide* in respect to other persons who stand in such a relation to either as to be affected by the transaction, or the consequences of it, relief may be had in equity when a contract, or other act, is substantially a fraud upon the rights, interests, or intentions of third parties (*m*). Upon this principle relief may be had in equity against sales by expectant heirs of their expectancies (*n*), or by reversioners or remainder-men of their reversions or remainders (*o*). But it is open to much doubt whether the principle should be extended to the case of reversioners and remainder-men (*p*).

23. Other classes of transactions against which a ** 49* court of equity * will relieve, as being in fraud of third parties, are frauds upon marriage articles (*q*); frauds upon the marital rights (*r*); bonds given to marry the obligor upon the death of a parent, or person standing *in loco parentis*, from whom the obligee has expectations, and from whom the transaction is to be kept concealed (*s*); bonds given, or agreements made, as a reward for using influence over others in favor of the obligee (*t*); secret agreements made by creditors with their debtors to represent their debts less than they are,

---

(*m*) 2 Ves. 157, *per* Lord Hardwicke, Wallis *v.* Duke of Portland, 3 Ves. 502.

(*n*) Twisleton *v.* Griffiths, 1 P. W. 310; Cole *v.* Gibbons, 3 *ib.* 293; Peacock *v.* Evans, 16 Ves. 512; Gowland *v.* De Faria, 17 Ves. 20; King *v.* Hamlet, 2 M. & K. 456; Earl of Aldborough *v.* Trye, 7 Cl. & Fin. 436; Edwards *v.* Burt, 2 D. M. & G. 63; Salter *v.* Bradshaw, 26 Beav. 164; Bromley *v.* Smith, *ib.* 662; Talbot *v.* Staniforth, 1 J. & H. 484. Comp. Shelley *v.* Nash, 3 Madd. 232; Fox *v.* Wright, 6 Madd. 111.

(*o*) Davis *v.* Duke of Marlborough, 2 Sw. 151; Wood *v.* Abrey, 3 Madd. 417; Davies *v.* Cooper, 5 M. & C. 270; Edwards *v.* Burt, 2 D. M. & G. 55; Talbot *v.* Staniforth, 1 J. & H. 484; Roberts *v.* Foster, 29 Beav. 467; Perfect *v.* Lane, 3 D. F. & J. 369.

(*p*) Wood *v.* Abrey, 3 Madd. 417; Tottenham *v.* Emmett, 14 W. R. 3.

(*q*) Redman *v.* Redman, 1 Vern. 348; Gale *v.* Lindo, *ib.* 475; Lamlee *v.* Hanmam, 2 Vern. 499; Turton *v.* Benson, 1 P. Wms. 496; Neville *v.* Wilkinson, 1 Bro. C. C. 543; Scott *v.* Scott, 1 Cox, 366; Jones *v.* Martin, 5 Ves. 265, n.; Palmer *v.* Neave, 11 Ves. 165. See M'Neill *v.* Cahill, 2 Bligh, 228.

(*r*) Goddard *v.* Snow, 1 Russ. 485; St. George *v.* Wake, 1 M. & K. 610; England *v.* Downs, 2 Beav. 522; Taylor *v.* Pugh, 1 Ha. 608; Llewellin *v.* Cobbold, 1 Sm. & G. 376; Griggs *v.* Staplee, 2 De G. & S. 572; Wrigley *v.* Swainson, 3 De G. & S. 458; Downes *v.* Jennings, 32 Beav. 290; Chambers *v.* Crabbe, 34 Beav. 457.

(*s*) Woodhouse *v.* Shepley, 2 Atk. 535; Cock *v.* Richards, 10 Ves. 429.

(*t*) Debenham *v.* Ox, 1 Ves. 276. Comp. Beckley *v.* Newland, 2 P. Wms. 182; Harwood *v.* Tooke, 2 Sim. 192; Wethered *v.* Wethered, *ib.* 183.

in order to deceive third persons (u); secret agreements between a particular creditor and a debtor, upon a composition by the debtor with his creditors, whereby the former secures to himself an undue advantage over the rest of the creditors (x) ; agreements between a company, and a creditor of the company, that the latter shall recover judgment against the company, and take out execution against a particular shareholder of the company (y) ; and transactions in fraud of creditors (z).   Here, also, may be noticed those transactions which *are in fraud of Acts of Parliament, or other   *50 legal provisions; frauds upon powers (a); the cases in which a bond given to secure one object is oppressively used to compel another (b) ; and transactions which are void upon principles of public policy, such as gaming (c) or stock-jobbing (d) bonds; bonds to secure future cohabitation (e) ; instruments containing conditions contrary to good morals or domestic peace (f) ; transactions affected by champerty (g) ; marriage brokage bonds (h) ; place brokage bonds (i) ; bonds

---

(u) Neville v. Wilkinson, 1 Bro. C. C. 543 ; Eastabrook v. Scott, 3 Ves. 456. Ex parte Sadler, 15 Ves. 52 ; Dalbiac v. Dalbiac, 16 Ves. 125. See Vauxhall Bridge Co. v. Earl Spencer, 2 Madd. 356 ; Simpson v. Lord Howden, 1 Keen, 583 ; 3 M. & C. 97.

(x) Jackman v. Mitchell, 13 Ves. 581 ; Cullingworth v. Lloyd, 2 Beav. 385 ; Pfleger v. Browne, 28 Beav. 391 ; Mare v. Sandford, 1 Giff. 288 ; Wood v. Barker, 1 L. R. Eq. 139.

(y) Taylor v. Hughes, 2 J. & L. 24 ; Fernihough v. Leader, 15 L. J. Ch. 458 ; 4 Ra. Ca. 373 ; Horn v. Kilkenny, &c., Railway Co., 1 K. & J. 399 ; Bargate v. Shortridge, 5 H. L. 247. Comp. Green v. Nixon, 23 Beav. 530 ; Beck v. Dean, 3 Jur. N. S. 14.

(z) Holloway v. Millard, 1 Madd. 414 ; Harman v. Richards, 10 Ha. 81 ; Goldsmith v. Russell, 5 D. M. & G. 547 ; French v. French, 6 D. M. & G. 95 ; Thompson v. Webster, 4 Drew. 628 ; Fraser v. Thompson, 4 D. & J. 660.

(a) Sug. Pow. 609 ; Agassiz v. Squire, 18 Beav. 431 ; Beere v. Hoffmeister, 23 Beav. 101 ; Wellesley v. Earl of Mornington, 2 K. & J. 143.

(b) Durston v. Sandys, 1 Vern. 411 ; 2 Ch. Ca. 186 ; Peele v. Capel, 1 Str. 534 ; Hillyard v. Stapleton, 1 Eq. Ab.

86 ; Grey v. Hesketh, Amb. 268 ; Roy v. Duke of Beaufort, 2 Atk. 190.

(c) Blackwell v. Redman, 1 Ch. Rep. 48 ; Humphreys v. Rigby, 2 Freem. 223 ; Rawden v. Shadwell, Amb. 269 ; Graves v. Houlditch, 2 Pri. 147 ; Earl of Milltown v. Stewart, 3 M. & C. 18. Comp. Quarrier v. Colston, 1 Ph. 151.

(d) Bancroft v. Wentworth, 3 Bro. C. C. 11 ; Bullock v. Richardson, 11 Ves. 373.

(e) Whaley v. Norton, 1 Vern. 483 ; Priest v. Parrott, 2 Ves. 160 ; Franco v. Bolton, 3 Ves. 368.

(f) Tenant v. Braie, Toth. 78 ; Traiton v. Traiton, 1 Vern. 413 ; Brown v. Peck, 1 Eden, 140.

(g) Reynell v. Sprye, 1 D. M. & G. 660.

(h) Hall v. Potter, 3 Lev. 412 ; Law v. Law, For. 140, 142 ; Stribblehill v. Brett, 2 Vern. 445 ; Cole v. Gibson, 1 Ves. 503, 506, 507 ; Williamson v. Gihon, 2 Sch. & Lef. 357.

(i) Law v. Law, For. 140 ; 3 P. Wms. 391 ; Bellamy v. Burrow, For. 97 ; Debenham v. Ox, 1 Ves. 276 ; Morris v. M'Culloch, 2 Eden, 190 ; Hanington v. Du Chatel, 1 Bro. C. C. 124 ; Hartwell v. Hartwell, 4 Ves. 811 ; Osborne v. Williams, 18 Ves. 379.

or securities for compounding a felony (k) ; and simoniacal (l) and illegal insurance (m) bonds.[1]

The principles upon which the Court relieves against fraud apply to the case of a stranger who is privy to the fraud, or obtains a security with notice of the circumstances under which it has been obtained (n).[2]

24. When a party to an illegal or immoral contract *51 comes himself * to be relieved from that contract, or its obligations, he must distinctly and exclusively state such grounds of relief as the court can legally attend to. He should not accompany his claims to relief which may be legitimate, with claims and complaints which are contaminated with the original immoral purpose (p). But the court may often give its assistance to one who is a *particeps criminis* to an illegal transaction. The general rule is, that where parties are concerned in illegal agreements or transactions courts of equity, following the rule of law as to participators in a common crime, will not interfere, acting upon the known maxim

---

(k) Johnson v. Ogilby, 3 P. W. 279; Claridge v. Hoare, 14 Ves. 59; Williams v. Bayley, 1 L. R. H. L. 200.

(l) Lord Kircudbright v. Lady Kircudbright, 8 Ves. 51.

(m) *Ex parte* Mather, 3 Ves. 373; Knowles v. Haughton, 11 Ves. 168.

(n) East India Co. v. Henchman, 1 Ves. Jr. 287; Maitland v. Backhouse, 17 L. J. Ch. 121; Espey v. Lake, 10 Ha. 260.

(p) Batty v. Chester, 5 Beav. 103.
[1] The subject of fraud in voluntary conveyances is discussed in Beal v. Warren, 2 Gray, 447, by Thomas, J., and the conclusion reached, that conveyances are not avoided merely because they are voluntary, but because they are fraudulent; that a voluntary gift of real estate is valid, as against subsequent purchasers and all other persons, unless it was fraudulent at the time of its execution; that a subsequent conveyance for a valuable consideration is evidence, but by no means conclusive evidence, of fraud in the first voluntary conveyance; and that a voluntary gift made when the grantor is not indebted in good faith, and without intent to defraud future creditors or subsequent purchasers, is good, as against a subsequent purchaser for

valuable consideration with notice. Such is understood to be the construction practically adopted in this commonwealth, and which is, to use the words of Chancellor Kent, "the better American doctrine."

Upon the question of contracts void, because in restraint of trade, see Keeler v. Taylor, 53 Penn. St. 467, where it is held that the general rule is that all restraints of trade are bad if nothing more appear; and that contracts in restraint of trade, to be good at law, must be founded in a valuable consideration, be reasonable, and impose no general restraint on trade and industry; but equity will not enforce such contracts, although good at law, if their terms be at all hard, or even complex. Such decrees are of grace, not of right.

[2] The principal is liable for the fraud of his agent in the performance of the business which he expected him to do, and for that which he knows he has done if he persist in taking the benefit of the act. Fitzsimmons v. Joslin, 21 Vt. 129. See this case for an elaborate examination of the question, and authorities by Judge Redfield; also, Bennett v. Judson, 21 N. Y. 238.

in pari delicto potior est conditio possidentis (*q*). But in cases
where agreements or transactions are repudiated upon grounds
of public policy, the objection that the plaintiff is *particeps
criminis* will not prevail, the public interest requiring that
relief should be given (*r*). And the cases are numerous
in which money paid for an illegal purpose has been decreed
to be repaid (*s*). Another exception to the general rule is
where the delinquency, though attaching to both parties, is not
equal in degree ; for two parties may concur in an illegal act,
without being deemed to be in all respects *in pari delicto* (*t*).

25. A distinction, moreover, is taken in equity between
enforcing illegal contracts, and asserting title to money arising from an illegal contract. If the transaction alleged to be
illegal is completed and closed, so that it will not be in any
manner affected by what the court is asked to do, the party to
the transaction who has possessed himself of the moneys arising
out of the transaction, cannot be permitted to set up the illegality of the transaction against the otherwise clear title of the
other. One of two partners, or joint adventurers, therefore,
who has possessed himself of the property common to both,
cannot be permitted to retain it, by merely showing that
in realizing it some provisions * in an Act of Parlia-   * 52
ment, or in the fiscal law of a foreign state, may have
been violated (*u*).[1]

SECTION II. — MISTAKE.

1. Mistake a ground of equitable jurisdiction.
2. Relief may be had in equity in some cases against mistake in matter of law.
3. But not in cases of money paid under mistake of law with full knowledge of facts.
4. Mistake of fact a common ground of equitable interposition.
5. Equity will not relieve in cases of want of due diligence.
6. Rectification of instruments made when both parties were mistaken, and the form intended can be clearly shown.

(*q*) Osborne *v.* Williams, 18 Ves. 379; Reynell *v.* Sprye, 1 D. M. & G. 660.

(*r*) 9 Ves. 298. See Williams *v.* Bayley, 1 L. R. H. L. 200.

(*s*) Goldsmith *v.* Bruning, 1 Eq. Ab. 89 ; Morris *v.* M'Culloch, 2 Eden, 190; Osborne *v.* Williams, 18 Ves. 379.

(*t*) Osborne *v.* Williams, 18 Ves. 379 ; Reynell *v.* Sprye, 1 D. M. & G. 660.

(*u*) Sharp *v.* Taylor, 2 Ph. 801; M'Blair *v.* Gibbes, 17 How. (Amer.) 232. See also Nash *v.* Ash, 1 Eden, 378; Mince *v.* Peters, Harg. MSS. No. 112, p. 86 ; Watts *v.* Brooks, 3 Ves. 612; Knowles *v.* Haughton, 11 Ves. 168.

[1] As to the proof to establish fraud, see Story's Eq. Jur. § 190, and § 190 *a*, Redfield's Ed.

1. Mistake is another head of equitable jurisdiction, the principle being that when there is mistake there is not that consent which is essential to the validity of the contract. *Non videatur qui errant consentire* (*x*).

Mistake may be in matter of law, or in matter of fact.

2. It has been often said that mistake in law cannot be admitted as a ground for relief (*y*). But the proposition in its generality is not correct, for there cannot any longer be a doubt that relief may be had in equity against mistake in law, and that the rule, *nemini jus ignorare licet*, is not universally applicable in equity (*z*). The jurisdiction must, however, be exercised with extreme caution, and only in cases where, under the general circumstances of the case, the court is satisfied that it would be unfair, and against conscience in the party benefited by the mistake, to retain the advantage which he has acquired (*a*). According to Papinian, *juris ignorantia non prodest acquirire volentibus, suum vero potentibus non nocet.*[1]

3. There seems to be no good reason why the same principles should not apply to the case of the payment of money under * mistake of law; but it appears to be

* 53

(*x*) Dig. Lib. 50.
(*y*) Marshall *v.* Collett, 1 Y. & C. 232; Denys *v.* Shuckburgh, 4 Y. & C. 42; Midland Great Western Railway Co. of Ireland *v.* Johnson, 6 H. L. 798; Story Eq. Jur. 111.
(*z*) Naylor *v.* Winch, 1 Sim. & St. 564; Watson *v.* Marston, 4 D. M. & G. 230, 236; Stone *v.* Godfrey, 18 Jur. 162; 5 D. M. & G. 76, 90.
(*a*) See Pusey *v.* Desbouverie, 3 P. Wms. 320; Bingham *v.* Bingham, 1 Ves. 126; S. C. Belt, Sup. 81; Lansdowne *v.* Lansdowne, Mose, 364; 2 J. & W. 205, n.; M'Carthy *v.* Decaix, 2 R. & M. 614; Reynell *v.* Sprye, 8 Ha. 222, 255; Cox *v.* Bruton, 5 W. R. 544; Broughton *v.* Hutt, 3 D. & J. 501; Bentley *v.* Mackay, 31 L. J. Ch. 697; *Re* Saxon Life Assurance Co., 2 J. & H. 408; D'Aguesseau, vol. 9, p. 624, Toull. Cod. civ. Liv. iii., tit. iii., c. 2, § 62. Larombière Théorie des Oblig., vol. i. pp. 43, 57.
[1] Upon this subject Judge Redfield in Story's Eq. Jur. §§ 138 *a* and *e*, says the distinction between mistakes of law and of fact is one of expediency and policy rather than of principle; and after commenting upon the general rule that mistakes of the law will not be relieved, he continues: " With these important qualifications, which will exclude all cases where the law is doubtful at the time, or where there is no marked injustice done by allowing the contract to stand, or no undue advantage gained, or where other rights have intervened, or the parties cannot be placed in *statu quo*, the rule that an admitted or clearly established misapprehension of the law does create a basis for the interference of courts of equity, resting in discretion, and to be exercised only in the most unquestionable and flagrant cases, is certainly more in consonance with the exact moral sense, and will be found, we believe, not at variance with the best-considered and best-reasoned cases upon the point, both English and American." Oliver *v.* Ins. Co., 2 Curtis, 277; Hunt *v.* Rousmaniere, 8 Wheaton, 174; Wheeler *v.* Smith, 9 How. U. S. 55; Bank of U. S. *v.* Daniels, 12 Peters, 32; Crosier *v.* Acer, 7 Paige, 137; Evants *v.* Strode, 11 Ohio, 480; Mc-Naughten *v.* Partridge, *ib.* 223; Green *v.* Morris and Essex R. R., Beasley Ch. 165; Beardsley *v.* Knight, 10 Vt. 185.

clearly established in equity, as well as at law, that money paid under a mistake of law, with full knowledge of facts, is not recoverable, and that even a promise to pay upon a supposed liability and in ignorance of the law, will bind the party (b). But the rule is liable to a qualification, if a man to whom money has been paid, has been accessory to the error of the other party, or has got some one to misinform him of the law (c). If the law mistaken is the law of a foreign state, the mistake is regarded as a mistake of fact (d).

4. Mistake of fact is a common head of equitable interposition. The mistake may be common to both parties to the transaction (e), or it may be the mistake of one party alone. If the mistake is common to both parties to the transaction, the one not thinking he is selling what the other does not think he is buying, the transaction will be set aside (f). But if the parties are aware, although the mistake be common, that the quantity or quality is not ascertainable, or if the subject-matter of the contract is, from its nature, doubtful or uncertain, or of a speculative character, the mistake goes for nothing. A contract for the sale of a thing, the extent and value of which is understood to be unknown to both parties, or which is, from its nature or character, doubtful or uncertain, is valid and binding (g). Care, too, must be taken in distinguishing cases where both parties are under a mistake as to the subject-matter of a contract, from cases where there is no doubt as to its extent; but the one has in fact sold more than he thought he was selling, and the other has got more than he expected. In such cases relief cannot be had, if there has been no unfairness on * either side (h). If the mistake is of   * 54 one party alone, relief will not usually be given in

(b) Brisbane v. Dacres, 5 Taunt. 143; Goodman v. Sayers, 2 J. & W. 263; Currie v. Goold, 2 Madd. 163; Drewry v. Barnes, 3 Russ. 94; Great Western Railway Co. v. Cripps, 5 Ha. 91; Bate v. Hooper, 5 D. M. & G. 338; Stafford v. Stafford, 1 D. & J. 197.

(c) Dixon v. Monkland Canal Co., 5 Wills. & Sh. Sc. Ap. 451.

(d) Haven v. Foster, 9 Pick. (Amer.) 112. See Leslie v. Baillie, 2 Y. & C. C. C. 91.

(e) Calverley v. Williams, 1 Ves. Jr.

210; Hitchcock v. Giddings, 4 Pri. 136; Colyer v. Clay, 7 Beav. 188.

(f) Hitchcock v. Giddings, 4 Pri. 136; Colyer v. Clay, 7 Beav. 188. See Cochrane v. Willis, 1 L. R. Ch. App. 58.

(g) Mortimer v. Cupper, 1 Bro. C. C. 156; Ridgway v. Sneyd, Kay, 627; Baxendale v. Seale, 19 Beav. 601. See Davis v. Shepherd, 1 L. R. Ch. App. 410.

(h) Okill v. Whittaker, 1 De G. & S. 83; 2 Ph. 338.

equity, unless there is evidence to show that the other was aware of and perceived the mistake, but did not rectify it (*i*). But, even in cases where it does not appear that the other party was aware of the mistake, relief may be had in equity, if under the general circumstances of the case it appears to the court that the transaction should not be allowed to stand (*k*).

5. What is the nature or degree of mistake which is relievable in equity, as distinguished from mistake which is due to negligence, and, therefore, not relievable, cannot well be defined, so as to establish a general rule, but must, in a great measure, depend on the discretion of the court, under all the circumstances of the case. Though a court of equity will relieve against mistake, it will not assist a man whose condition is attributable only to that want of due diligence which may be fairly expected from a reasonable person (*l*). Parties, for instance, who having a good defence, or plain and complete remedy at law, have neglected to avail themselves of it there, cannot come to equity for relief (*m*). Nor has a purchaser, who is evicted by reason of a defect in title which his legal adviser has overlooked, an equity to recover his purchase-money (*n*).[1] Nor can relief be had against a forfeiture where a man who is charged with a legal obligation neglects to perform it (*o*).

6. If there is an error in the reduction of an instru-
*55   ment into * writing, so that the instrument fails through some mistake of the draftsman, either in point of fact or

---

(*i*) See Cocking *v.* Pratt, 1 Ves. 400: East India Co. *v.* Neave. 5 Ves. 173; East India Co. *v.* Donald, 9 Ves. 275; Hore *v.* Becher, 12 Sim. 465; Worsley *v.* Frank, 11 L. T 392; Broughton *v.* Hutt, 3 D. & J. 501.

(*k*) East India Co. *v.* Neave, 5 Ves. 173.

(*l*) Duke of Beaufort *v.* Neeld, 12 Cl. & Fin. 248, 286; Leuty *v.* Hillas, 2 D. & J. 110; Wild *v.* Hillas, 28 L. J. Ch. 170; Price *v.* Ley, 4 Giff. 235.

(*m*) Stephenson *v.* Wilson, 2 Vern. 325; Blackhall *v.* Coombs, 2 P. Wms. 70; Holworthy *v.* Mortlock, 1 Cox, 141; Hankey *v.* Vernon, 2 Cox, 12; Stevens *v.* Praed, 2 Ves. Jr. 519; Bateman *v.* Willoe, 1 Sch. & Lef. 201; Hare *v.* Horwood, 14 Ves. 31; Drewry *v.*

Barnes, 3 Russ. 94. See Marquis of Breadalbane *v.* Marquis of Chandos, 2 M. & C. 719.

(*n*) Urmston *v.* Pate, 3 Ves. 235, n. See Maynard *v.* Moseley, 3 Sw. 651; Cator *v.* Lord Pembroke, 1 Bro. C. C. 301; 2 Bro. C. C. 282; Thomas *v.* Powell, 2 Cox, 394.

(*o*) Gregory *v.* Wilson, 9 Ha. 683, 689.

[1] See to same point, Earle *v.* DeWitt, 6 Allen, 520. Where a party asks for an injunction to restrain another from an inequitable use of his legal title, he must show such facts as entitle him to rescind on the ground of mistake or fraud. Watts *v.* Cummins, 59 Penn. St. 84.

law, to represent the real agreement of the parties, or omits or contains stipulations contrary to the common intention of all the parties, the court will correct and reform the instrument so as to make it conformable to the real intent of the parties (p).[1] It makes no difference that the instrument may have been drawn up by the party who seeks relief (q). But an instrument will not be rectified unless upon the clearest evidence of the alleged mistake, and unless it can be shown, clearly and precisely, what is the form to which the instrument ought to be brought, and unless it appear, upon clear and satisfactory proof, that the intention of the parties to which the instrument is sought to be made conformable, continued concurrently in the minds of all the parties down to the time of its execution (r).[2] If the mistake be not common to all the parties (s), or if one of the parties knew of the mistake at the time he executed the deed, the instrument cannot be rectified. Rectification can only be had when both parties executed it under a mistake, and have done what neither of them intended (t).[3] Parol evidence is admissible to show what the intention of the parties really was (u).

SECTION III. — ACCIDENT.

1. Relief in equity in cases of accidental loss or destruction of instrument, but none from covenants which party has voluntarily entered into.
2. Nor in any case where accident has arisen from party's own gross negligence or fault.

(p) Beaumont v. Bramley, T. & R. 41; Cockerell v. Cholmeley, Taml. 435; Ashurst v. Mill, 7 Ha. 502; Barrow v. Barrow, 18 Beav. 529; Murray v. Parker, 19 Beav. 308; Wake v. Harrop, 1 H. & C. 202; Borrowman v. Rossell, 16 C. B. N. S. 58; Scholfield v. Lockwood, 32 Beav. 436; 33 L. J. Ch. 106.

(q) Ball v. Storie, 1 Sim. & St. 218.

(r) Lord Townshend v. Stangroom, 6 Ves. 334; Beaumont v. Bramley, T. & R. 41, 50; Cockerell v. Cholmeley, Taml. 435; Carpmael v. Powis, 10 Beav. 39; Sells v. Sells, 1 Dr. & Sm. 42; Fallon v. Robins, 16 Ir. Ch. 422.

(s) Sells v. Sells, 1 Dr. & Sm. 42.

(t) Eaton v. Bennett, 34 Beav. 196; Fallon v. Robins, 16 Ir. Ch. 422.

(u) Barrow v. Barrow, 18 Beav. 532;

Murray v. Parker, 19 Beav. 308; Lackersteen v. Lackersteen, 6 Jur N. S. 1111. See further on the subject of rectification and mistake, Pap. Jurid. Society, vol. 3, p. 173.

[1] Woodbury Sav. Bank v. Charter Oak Ins. Co., 31 Conn. 517; Longhurst v. Star Ins. Co., 19 Iowa, 364; Jordan v. Stevens, 51 Me. 78; Brown v. Lamphear, 35 Vt. 252; Canedy v. Morey, 13 Gray, 373.

[2] Stockbridge Iron Co. v. Hudson Iron Co., 102 Mass. 49; Nevius v. Dunlap, 33 N. Y. 676; Sawyer v. Hovey, 3 Allen, 331; Edwards's Appeal, 59 Penn. St. 220.

[3] Nevius v. Dunlap, 33 N. Y 676; Lyman v. United Ins. Co., 17 Johns. 373; Schettiger v. Hopple, 3 Grant's Cas. 54.

1. Accident is another head of equitable jurisdiction, the
usual instance of which is the relief given where a bond
* 56   or other * security has been burnt, lost, or accidentally
destroyed (x). There is, however, no equity under
the head of accident in favor of a man who, having entered
into an express or positive covenant to do a certain act, or perform a particular duty, fails to comply with the stipulation. A
man who, by express covenant, has bound himself to do a particular thing, is bound to do it if he can, and cannot come to
the court to supply that provision which he has omitted to make
for himself. It is immaterial that unforeseen events have occurred which impose on him an additional duty or burden, or
that he has been prevented by accident from deriving the full
benefit of the covenant or contract on his own side. A party
to a contract may, if he chooses, guard himself by providing
against contingencies. If he neglects to do so, he must put
up with a loss, if a loss occurs, for the presumption in equity
as well as at law is, that the purpose of the parties was according to the legal effect of the covenant (y). Thus, if a lessee
covenant to keep the demised premises in repair, he will be
bound in equity, as well as at law, to rebuild them, notwithstanding any inevitable accident by which they may be destroyed
or injured (z). So, also, if a lessee covenants to pay rent during the term, it must be paid, notwithstanding the premises are
burnt down, during the term; and this is equally true as to
the rent, although the lessee has covenanted to repair, except
in case of casualty by fire (a). The fact of the premises being
insured makes no difference, the tenant has no equity to compel
the landlord to expend the insurance money in rebuilding the
premises, or to restrain him from suing for the rent
* 57   until the premises are rebuilt (b). * So also the lessee

(x) Walmsley v. Child, 1 Ves. 341;
Atkinson v. Leonard, 3 Bro. C. C. 218;
Ex parte Greenway, 6 Ves. 812; Kemp
v. Pryor, 7 Ves. 249; East India Co. v.
Boddam, 9 Ves. 464; Mossop v. Eaden,
16 Ves. 430; Macartney v. Graham, 2
Sim. 285; Williams v. Flight, 5 Beav.
41; Crosse v. Bedingfield, 12 Sim. 35;
Cooke v. Darwin, 18 Beav. 60.

(y) Hillier v. Parkinson, 9 L. J. Ch.
156; Philipps v. Jones, 9 Sim. 519;

Gregory v. Wilson, 9 Ha. 683, 689,
infra.

(z) Bullock v. Dommitt, 6 T. R. 650;
Leeds v. Cheetham, 1 Sim. 146; Gregg
v. Coates, 23 Beav. 33; Clark v. Glasgow Assurance Co., 1 Macq. 668.

(a) Holtzapffel v. Baker, 18 Ves. 115;
Leeds v. Cheetham, 1 Sim. 146; Gregg
v. Coates, 23 Beav. 33. See Bayne v.
Walker, 6 Pat. Sc. App. 217; Poole v.
Adams, 33 L. J. Ch. 639.

(b) Leeds v. Cheetham, 1 Sim. 146.

of a coal-mine, who has covenanted to pay a certain rent, or to work a certain number of acres annually, and to pay a certain rent for that quantity, cannot have relief on the ground that the mine is nearly exhausted, or that he is prevented by accident from working it, except at a ruinous expense (c). The loss will fall upon the purchaser if the premises are deteriorated by fire, or other accident, after the date, but before the completion of the contract (d).

2. A court of equity will, in no case, grant a man relief on the ground of accident, where the accident has arisen from his own gross negligence or fault. On this account, a party coming for relief is bound to show that his title to relief is unmixed with any gross misconduct, or negligence, of himself or his agents (e).

SECTION IV. — ACCOUNT.

1. In cases of general account between principal and agent, principal may have account taken in equity.
2. Complicated accounts taken in equity, although the form of the account is purely legal.
3. Where subject is merely matter of set-off and capable of proof at law, account will not lie.
4. Jurisdiction entertained where account is so complex as not to be practically taken at law, though there be no reciprocity of receipts and payments.
5. An account stated between the parties and acknowledged, is a defence to bill for an account.
6. Stated account may be impeached. Reasons therefor and practice.
7. Same rule applies to cases of settled accounts.
8. Injunction sometimes granted to restrain an action for a matter of account proper to be taken in equity.

1. Another head of equitable jurisdiction is that of account. If an equitable case be shown by the bill, account may always be had in equity (f). The position which an agent fills to-

---

(c) Philipps v. Jones, 9 Sim. 519; Mellers v. Duke of Devonshire, 16 Beav. 252; Ridgway v. Sneyd, Kay, 627.

(d) Paine v. Mellor, 6 Ves. 349; Coles v. Trecothick, 9 Ves. 234; Ex parte Minor, 11 Ves. 559; Harford v. Purrier, 1 Madd. 532; Akhurst v. Jackson, 1 Sw. 85; Revell v. Hussey, 2 B. & B. 287.

(e) Marine Insurance Co. v. Hodgson, 7 Cranch (Amer.), 336.

(f) East India Co. v. Henchman, 1 Ves. Jr. 287; Waring v. Manchester, Sheffield, and Lincolnshire Railway Co., 7 Ha. 482; 2 H. & Tw. 239; Bliss v. Smith, 34 Beav. 508.

wards his employer being one of a fiduciary character, he is bound to keep regular accounts. If he neglects this duty, and is not ready to settle his accounts when called upon to do so, his employer has a right to have the accounts taken in equity (*g*). There may, however, be a difference when there is no general account between principal and agent, but only an agency in a single transaction (*h*). An agent, on the
*58   other hand, cannot * maintain a bill for an account against his principal, except the case be one of mutual accounts, or except there be such a complication of accounts as to render the interference of a court of equity necessary (*i*). An exception, however, is allowed in the case of a steward, the nature of whose employment is such that money is often paid in confidence without vouchers, embracing a variety of accounts with the tenants, so that it would not be possible to do justice without an account in equity (*k*). The relation of banker and customer does not partake of a fiduciary character, or bear any analogy to that of principal and agent, so that the mere existence of the relation is not a foundation for a bill for an account by the customer (*l*).

2. The jurisdiction of the court, by way of account, is not limited to cases which involve an equitable element, but extends to cases of complicated accounts, although the form of the account is purely legal, and the items constituting the account are purely legal. The jurisdiction is entertained, not on the ground of the absence of a remedy at law, but because the remedy at law is less complete than the remedy in equity. Whether or not it will interfere is, in each case, a matter for the discretion of the court. If a court of law is competent to deal with the case, the court will not interfere. If, on the other hand, the case is such that a court of law has no adequate means of dealing with the matter, the court will entertain

---

(*g*) Lord Chedworth *v.* Edwards, 8 Ves. 46; Pearse *v.* Green, 1 J. & W. 135; Mackenzie *v.* Johnston, 4 Madd. 373; Clarke *v.* Tipping, 9 Beav. 284; Hemmings *v.* Pugh, 4 Giff. 456; Smith *v.* Leveaux, 2 D. J. & S. 1. Comp. Farebrother *v.* Welchman, 3 Drew. 122.
(*h*) Navulshaw *v.* Brownrigg, 2 D.

M. & G. 446; Philipps *v.* Philipps, 9 Ha. 471; Barry *v.* Stevens, 31 Beav. 258; Makepeace *v.* Rogers, 34 L. J. Ch. 396.
(*i*) Smith *v.* Leveaux, 2 D. J. & S. 1.
(*k*) Dinwiddie *v.* Bailey, 6 Ves. 136; Allison *v.* Herring, 9 Sim. 583.
(*l*) Foley *v.* Hill, 1 Ph. 399; 2 H. L. 28.

jurisdiction (*m*).[1] In determining whether or not it will interfere, the court reserves to itself a large discretion, in the
exercise of which due regard must be had, not only to the
nature of the case, but to the conduct of the parties (*n*).

The Common Law * Procedure Act, 1854, has not   * 59
affected the jurisdiction of the court (*o*).

3. Where the subject is merely a matter of set-off and capable of proof at law, a bill for an account will not lie (*p*). The
right to an account is essentially different from the right to set-
off. The right to account is not, like the right to set-off, a right
to amalgamate cross demands for the purpose of enabling one
action or suit to suffice; but it assumes that the several demands have no independent existence, but have been so connected by the original contract or course of dealing that the
only thing which either party can claim is the ultimate balance.
The only right is that of taking the account. An account is
not confined to mere receipts and payments of money, although
it ordinarily occurs in that form. But it is applicable to any
dealings which have been treated as equivalent to receipts and
payments. An account will lie in respect of reciprocal delivery
of goods, provided that in the course of dealing between the
parties such deliveries have been treated as items in an
account, and not as creating mere cross demands, or it will lie
in respect of a claim for work done, and partially paid by
advances from time to time, so that a balance only of the price
is ultimately due (*q*). There cannot be an account of debts
one way and damages another (*r*).

(*m*) North Eastern Railway Co. *v.*
Martin, 2 Ph. 764; South Eastern Railway Co. *v.* Brogden, 3 Mac. & G. 23:
Foley *v.* Hill, 2 H. L. 37; Anderson *v.*
Noble, 1 Drew. 143; Scott *v.* Corporation of Liverpool, 3 D. & J. 358; Hill
v. South Staffordshire Railway Co., 11
Jur. N. S. 192; Bliss *v.* Smith, 34 Beav.
508.

(*n*) 2 Ph. 762, *per* Lord Cottenham;
Taff Vale Co. *v.* Nixon, 1 H. L. 122;
Hill *v.* South Staffordshire Railway
Co., 11 Jur. N. S. 192; Dabbs *v.* Nugent,
ib 943.

(*o*) Crosskey *v.* European and American Steam Shipping Co., 1 J. & H.
108; Shepard *v.* Brown, 4 Giff. 208.

(*p*) Dinwiddie *v.* Bailey, 6 Ves. 186;

Townrow *v.* Benson, 3 Madd. 203. See
Norris *v.* Day, 4 Y. & C. 475.

(*q*) Wells *v.* Cooper, cited 6 Ves.
139; 9 Ves. 473; O'Connor *v.* Spaight,
1 Sch. & Lef. 305; Ranger *v.* Great
Western Railway Co., 1 Ra. Ca. 1; 5
H. L. 91; Adams, Doct. Eq. 223.

(*r*) Glennie *v.* Imri, 3 Y. & C. 436.

[1] Chief Justice Marshall says: " In
all cases in which an action of account
would be the proper remedy at law, and
in all cases where a trustee is a party,
the jurisdiction of a court of equity is
undoubted. It is the appropriate tribunal. But in transactions not of this
peculiar character, great complexity
ought to exist in the accounts, or some
difficulty at law should interpose, some

4. In the case of mutual accounts, or accounts involving reciprocity of receipts and payments, or consisting of a series of transactions on one side and of payments on the other, and not merely payments by way of set-off, the jurisdiction of the court is exercised in the most ample manner without any limitation (s). But it is not necessary to make out a case of

* 60   mutual * accounts. If the account is not merely from the number of its items, but from its nature so complex that it cannot be properly or practically taken at law, jurisdiction will be entertained, although there be no reciprocity of receipts and payments (t). A bill for an account, for instance, will lie as between landlord and tenant, where, from the complication of the items, or the complexity of the title occasioned by the acts of the landlord, the account may be taken more properly in equity than at law (u).[1] If on the other hand the account is simple and the remedy at law free from embarrassment, the necessity for equitable interference does not exist, and jurisdiction will not be entertained (v). If the facts stated in the bill show that no practical difficulty exists in proceeding at law, a mere allegation that the accounts are intricate will not prevent a demurrer (x). The mere fact that the accounts are such as would not be taken in an action at law, but would be sent by a court of law to a reference, is not of itself a reason for a court of equity to entertain jurisdiction (y).

discovery should be required, in order to induce a court of chancery to exercise jurisdiction." Fowle v. Lawrason, 5 Peters, 502.

(s) Dinwiddie v. Bailey, 6 Ves. 140; Courtenay v. Godschall, 9 Ves. 473. See Philipps v. Philpps, 9 Ha. 473; Padwick v. Hurst, 18 Beav. 580; Fluker v. Taylor, 3 Drew. 183.

(t) Philipps v. Philipps, 9 Ha. 473; Padwick v. Hurst, 18 Beav. 580; Fluker v. Taylor, 3 Drew. 191; Taff Vale Co. v. Nixon, 1 H. L. 111; Ranger v. Great Western Railway Co., 5 H. L. 91; Scott v. Corporation of Liverpool, 3 D. & J. 358; Macintosh v. Great Western Railway Co., 3 Sm. & G. 146; 11 Jur. N. S. 681; Smith v. Leveaux, 2 D. J. & S. 1.

(u) O'Connor v. Spaight, 1 Sch. & Lef. 305; Nixon v. Robinson, 2 J. & L. 4; Kennington v. Houghton, 2 Y. & C.

C. C. 627. Comp. Aldis v. Fraser, 15 Beav. 221.

(v) Bliss v. Smith, 34 Beav. 508.

(x) Foley v. Hill, 2 H. L. 38; Bowles v. Orr, 1 Y. & C. 464; Darthez v. Clemens, 6 Beav. 165; Frietas v. Dos Santos, 1 Y. & J 576; Farebrother v. Welchman, 3 Drew. 122; Padwick v. Hurst, 18 Beav. 582.

(y) Philipps v. Philipps, 9 Ha. 473. See Farebrother v. Welchman, 3 Drew. 122. Comp. Crosskey v. European and American Steam Shipping Co., 1 J. & H. 108.

[1] It is held where two tenants in common of personal property have used the same in the prosecution of business, under an agreement as to the compensation of one of them, who was "to superintend the establishment," and who survives the other, the administrator of the deceased tenant in com-

5. An account stated between the parties in which the balance is set forth and acknowledged, may be pleaded or set up as a bar to a bill for account (z). The parties having themselves disposed of the matter, and struck the balance of their account, the necessity for equitable interference does not exist, for there is no difficulty in proceeding at law (a). An * account stated to be a sufficient defence to a bill for   * 61 an account must be in writing, but it is not necessary that it should be signed by the parties, if it can be shown to have been acquiesced in by them. The mere delivery of an account without evidence of contemporaneous or subsequent conduct, will not prove it to be a stated account, but an acceptance implied from circumstances will suffice (b). Between merchants at home an account has been considered as accepted where no objection was made thereto within two or three posts (c). Between merchants in different countries a similar rule prevails, and if any account is transmitted from one to another showing a balance due to himself, and the other keep it two years without objection, the rule is to consider it as allowed (d). So also accounts of companies laid before shareholders at a general meeting and approved by them are binding (e).

6. A stated account may, however, be impeached either wholly or in part on the ground of fraud, or if important errors are specified and proved, but a general allegation that it is erroneous will not suffice (f). If there be fraud the whole account will be opened, and a new account will be taken

---

mon may maintain a bill in equity to compel the survivor to exhibit an account of the transactions under said agreement, and of the manner in which the business was carried on. Field v. Craig, 8 Allen, 357.

(z) Willis v. Jernegan, 2 Atk. 252; Endo v. Caleham, You. 306. See M'Kellar v. Wallace, 8 Moo. P. C. 378.

(a) Dawson v. Dawson, 1 Atk. 1; Taylor v. Hayling, 1 Cox, 435; 2 Bro. C. C. 310; Hirst v. Peirse, 4 Pri. 339; Chambers v. Goldwin, 9 Ves. 263; Darthez v. Lee, 2 Y. & C. 5.

(b) Willis v. Jernegan, 2 Atk. 252; Irvine v. Young, 1 Sim. & St. 333; Att.-Gen. v. Brooksbank, 2 Y. & J.

37; Hunter v. Belcher, 2 D. J. & S. 195. See Clements v. Bowes, 1 Drew. 692; Davies v. Spurling, Taml. 199; Blagrave v. Routh, 8 D. M. & G. 620.

(c) Sherman v. Sherman, 2 Vern. 276.

(d) Tickel v. Short, 2 Ves. 238.

(e) See Stupart v. Arrowsmith, 3 Sm. & G. 176; Kent v. Jackson, 2 D. M. & G. 49; Ex parte Bignold, 22 Beav. 165.

(f) Clarke v. Tipping, 9 Beav. 282; Darthez v. Lee, 2 Y. & C. 5; Allfrey v. Allfrey, 1 Mac. & G. 87; M'Kellar v. Wallace, 8 Moo. P. C. 378; Blagrave v. Routh, 8 D. M. & G. 620.

5

without reference to that which has been stated (*g*). If there be no fraud, but errors are alleged and proved, the account will be allowed to stand with liberty to surcharge and falsify (*h*). This leaves it in full force as a stated account, except so far as it can be impugned by the opposing party. If he shows the omission of a credit which ought to have been allowed

* 62 that is a surcharge: *if he shows the insertion of an improper charge, that is a falsification (*i*). Error in law is a sufficient foundation for a decree to surcharge and falsify (*j*).

7. The same considerations apply *a fortiori* to the case of settled accounts. A settled account is conclusive between the parties, and cannot be opened unless there be fraud (*k*). If there be merely error, the rule is only to give liberty to surcharge and falsify (*l*). In regard to acquiescence in stated accounts, although it amounts to an admission of their correctness, it by no means establishes the fact that they have been settled, even although the acquiescence has been for some considerable time. There must be other ingredients in the case to justify the conclusion of a settlement (*m*).

A man against whom an action has been brought for a matter of account, or for that which is the result of an account, has a right on making out a proper case to ask a court of equity to have the account there taken and to give him an injunction to restrain the action until the account has been taken (*n*). But the court will not, on the mere ground that it could properly and beneficially have entertained jurisdiction had it been appealed to in the first instance, be always willing

(*g*) Wharton *v.* May, 5 Ves. 27. 48; M'Kellar *v.* Wallace, 8 Moo. P. C. 378; Coleman *v.* Mellersh, 2 Mac. & G. 309; Blagrave *v.* Routh, 8 D. M. & G. 620.

(*h*) Davies *v.* Spurling, Taml. 199, 1 R. & M. 64; Lawless *v.* Mansfield, 1 Dr. & War. 557; Blagrave *v.* Routh, 8 D. M. & G. 620.

(*i*) Pitt *v.* Cholmondeley. 2 Ves. 565; Millar *v.* Craig, 6 Beav 435; Jones *v.* Moffett, 3 J. & L. 636.

(*j*) Roberts *v.* Kuffin, 2 Atk. 112.

(*k*) Brownell *v.* Brownell, 2 Bro. C. C. 62; Taylor *v.* Hayling, *ib.* 310; Chambers *v.* Goldwin, 9 Ves. 265;

Coleman *v.* Mellersh, 2 Mac. & G. 309; Hunter *v.* Belcher, 2 D. J. & S. 195.

(*l*) Vernon *v.* Vawdry, 2 Atk. 119; Chambers *v.* Goldwin, 9 Ves. 265; Drew *v.* Power, 1 Sch. & Lef. 192; Coleman *v.* Mellersh, 2 Mac. & G. 309; Sellar *v.* Griffin, 32 Beav. 545.

(*m*) Lord Clancarty *v.* Latouche, 1 B. & B. 428; Irvine *v.* Young, 1 Sim. & St. 333; Hunter *v.* Belcher, 2 D. J. & S. 194. See Parkinson *v.* Hanbury, *ib.* 450. Parkinson *v.* Hanbury, reported on appeal, 2 L. R. App. Ca. 1.

(*n*) Anderson *v.* Noble, 1 Drew. 143.

to withdraw the proceedings by injunction from the jurisdiction of a court of law. If a court of law be first set in motion in the matter, the court will not be willing to interfere, although the matter is one which could be more conveniently disposed of in equity (*o*), unless the account is of such a nature that justice does not seem likely to be done in the matter at law (*p*). But * if the case made out is such that it cannot   * 63 in the opinion of the court be adequately tried at law, the court will interpose and withdraw the matter from the consideration of a court of law (*q*). It is not necessarily a fatal objection to a bill for an account and a motion to restrain an action that the bill is filed by some only of the defendants at law (*r*). Nor is it necessary that the plaintiff should submit to account (*s*).

SECTION V. — EQUITABLE SET-OFF.

1. Set-off is a head of equitable jurisdiction.
2. Set-off an equitable doctrine. Character of it.
3. But courts of equity follow the law in matters of set-off unless there is some intervening equity going beyond the statute.
4. To warrant set-off the debts must be mutual, due in same right, and liquidated.
5. Neither future liability nor cross demand, accrued or acquired subsequently to the establishment at law of the demand, can be set up by way of set-off.
6. Agreements, whether express or implied, may confer the right of equitable sets-off. Insolvency of one of parties sufficient ground for equitable set-off.
7. Assignee of chose in action takes subject to equitable right of set-off.

1. Set-off is another head of equitable jurisdiction. The right of set-off is that right, which exists between two persons, each of whom, under an independent contract, owes an ascertained amount to the other, to set off their respective debts, by way of mutual deduction, so that a person to whom the larger debt is due shall recover the residue only after such deduction.

(*o*) Norris *v.* Day, 4 Y. & C. 475; South Eastern Railway Co. *v.* Brogden, 3 Mac. & G. 23.

(*p*) *Ib.*; North Eastern Railway Co. *v.* Martin, 2 Ph. 762; Dabbs *v.* Nugent, 11 Jur. N. S. 943.

(*q*) O'Connor *v.* Spaight, 1 Sch. & Lef. 308; O'Mahony *v.* Dickson, 2 Sch. & Lef. 400; South Eastern Railway Co.

v. Brogden, 3 Mac. & G. 23; Crosskey *v.* European and American Steam Shipping Co., 1 J. & H. 108; Dabbs *v.* Nugent, 11 Jur. N. S. 943.

(*r*) Crosskey *v.* European and American Steam Co., 1 J. & H. 108.

(*s*) Clarke *v.* Tipping, 4 Beav. 588.

At common law there was no right of set-off (*t*). If the party suing for a debt were himself a debtor to the defendant, he might, nevertheless, recover in his action, and the defendant was driven to a cross-action for his own claim. To obviate this inconvenience, it was enacted, that where there are mutual debts between plaintiff and defendant, or if either party sue or be sued, as executor or administrator, where there are mutual debts as between testator, or intestate, and either party, one may be set off against the other (*u*), and in the court of bankruptcy a still wider remedy is given, and the right of set-off is extended to cases where mutual credit has been given by the bankrupt and any other person, although there may not be actual debts on either side (*x*).

* 64   * 2. Courts of equity were in possession of the doctrine of set-off long before the right of set-off was introduced into the statute-law, and it seems probable that the statutory rights have been founded on the equitable rules (*y*). The equitable doctrine of set-off is founded on the doctrine of compensation of the Roman law (*z*), but the compensation of the civil law is not in all respects the same as the set-off of our own law. A set-off does not, as compensation in the civil law, operate of course by mere operation of law as an extinguishment of one debt by another, but is a mere right which a man may avail himself of, or not, as he pleases. A set-off is a mere matter of defence. A man is not bound to make use of it. He may, if he pleases, satisfy the whole of his debt, and then resort to a cross-action to recover the moneys due to him (*a*).

3. Courts of equity now follow the law in matters of set-off unless there is some intervening equity going beyond the statute (*b*). If the cross-demands are of legal cognizance, the

---

(*t*) Wallis *v.* Bastard, 4 D. M. & G. 249, 256.

(*u*) 2 Geo. 2, c. 22, 8 Geo. 2, c. 24.

(*x*) 12 & 13 Vict. c. 106, s. 171; Smith, Merc. Law, 649 ; Rose *v.* Hart, 1 Smith, L. C. 251–269. See as to set-off under the Companies' Act, 1862; Smith and Fleming's case, 1 L. R. Ch. App. 538 ; Grissell's case, *ib.* 528.

(*y*) *Ex parte* Stephens, 11 Ves. 27 ; *Ex parte* Blagden, 19 Ves. 467 ; Free-

man *v.* Lomas, 9 Ha. 112, *per* L. J. Turner; Wallis *v.* Bastard, 4 D. M. & G. 249, 256.

(*z*) Barker *v.* Braham, 2 W. Bl. 869 ; Freeman *v.* Lomas, 9 Ha. 112.

(*a*) Laing *v.* Chatham, 1 Camp. 252 ; Wallis *v.* Bastard, 4 D. M. & G. 249, 256.

(*b*) Medlicott *v.* Bowes, 1 Ves. 207 ; *Ex parte* Stephens, 11 Ves. 27 ; Town-row *v.* Benson, 3 Madd. 207.

right of set-off is also legal (*c*). Unless one of the demands involves an equitable element, or sets up some equitable ground for impeaching the legal title to the other demand, or unless both demands be of equitable cognizance, there is no set-off in equity. The mere existence of cross-demands does not create an equity. But if one demand is legal, and the other equitable, there is set-off in equity if there would be set-off at law had both demands been legal. Equity, in other words, looks to the beneficial ownership of the debt (*d*). A demand, for instance, * which a man has in the name of his trustee,   * 65 against another, will be set off against a demand which the latter has against him (*e*). So, also, the assignee of a legal debt, not assignable at law, may come into equity to have the benefit of a set-off (*f*).

4. To warrant set-off there must be mutual debts. The debts must be due in the same right, and must be clearly ascertained, or liquidated. Cross-demands existing in different rights, cannot, except under very special circumstances, be set off against each other in equity (*g*). The liability to pay the one demand, and the right to receive the money in respect of the other demand, must be, at the same time, vested in the same person (*h*), the principle being, that one man's money shall not be applied to pay off another man's debt (*i*). A claim accordingly, against a man in a representative capacity, cannot be set off in a suit brought in an individual capacity. The demand in respect of which set-off is sought, must be due to and from the same person in the same capacity. An executor cannot set off, against the claim for a legacy, a debt due to

---

(*c*) Dinwiddie *v.* Bailey, 6 Ves. 139; Townrow *v.* Benson, 3 Madd. 207; Harvey *v.* Wood, 5 Madd. 459.

(*d*) Clark *v.* Cort, Cr. & Ph. 154; Rawson *v.* Samuel, *ib.* 179; Dodd *v.* Lydall, 1 Ha. 333; Freeman *v.* Lomas, 9 Ha. 109; Smith *v.* Parkes, 16 Beav. 115; Hunt *v.* Jessell, 18 Beav. 100; Agra and Masterman's Bank *v.* Hoffman, 34 L. J. Ch. 285. See Bousfield *v.* Lawford, 1 D. J. & S. 459.

(*e*) Cochrane *v.* Green, 9 C. B. N. S. 448. See Cavendish *v.* Geaves, 24 Beav. 163. Comp. Pratt *v.* Keith, 33 L. J. Ch. 530.

(*f*) Clark *v.* Cort, Cr. & Ph. 154. See Cavendish *v.* Geaves, 24 Beav. 163.

(*g*) Chapman *v.* Derby, 2 Vern. 117; Whitaker *v.* Rush, Amb. 407; Bishop *v.* Church, 3 Atk. 691; Medlicott *v.* Bowes, 1 Ves. 208; Jones *v.* Mossop, 3 Ha. 568; Gale *v.* Luttrell, 1 .Y. & J. 180; Lambarde *v.* Older, 17 Beav. 542; Freeman *v.* Lomas, 9 Ha. 112. See Baldwin *v.* Baldwin, 3 Ir. Ch. 388.

(*h*) Cherry *v.* Boultbee, 4 M. & C. 442.

(*i*) Jones *v.* Mossop, 3 Ha. 568, 574.

him, personally, from the legatee (*k*). Nor can a man set off
what is due to him as executor against a debt due from himself (*l*). Nor can a private debt due from a trustee be set off
against a debt owing to him in his character of trustee (*m*).
Nor can the creditor of an intestate, who has purchased part
of the intestate's goods from the administrator, set off the
        amount against a debt due to him from the intestate
* 66   at his decease (*n*). Nor * can a joint debt be set off
        against a separate debt, or a separate debt against a
joint debt, as where there is a separate debt due to or from a
partner and a joint debt due from or to the partnership (*o*).

5. The cross demand in respect of which the claim to set off
is made must be an ascertained sum (*p*). A future liability
cannot be set off against a sum actually due (*q*). Nor can a
cross-demand accrued or acquired subsequently to the establishment at law of the demand, be set up by way of set-off (*r*).
Where a tenant had a judgment at law against his landlord for
excessive distress, and the landlord had obtained damages
awarded to him under an arbitration clause in the lease for a
larger sum, the court would not restrain the tenant from taking
proceedings on the judgment against the landlord (*s*). The
mere pendency of an account out of which a claim may arise,
will not give the right of set-off in equity against an ascertained
sum. Where the application in equity is for an account of
transactions under a contract, and the action at law is for
damages for the breach of it, there is no set-off. The object
and the subject-matter being totally distinct, the fact that the
agreement has been the origin of both does not form any bond
of union for the purpose of supporting an injunction (*t*). So,

(*k*) Whitaker *v.* Rush, Amb. 407;
Medlicott *v.* Bowes, 1 Ves. 207; Freeman *v.* Lomas, 9 Ha. 109.

(*l*) Bishop *v.* Church, 3 Atk. 691.

(*m*) Pratt *v.* Keith, 33 L. J. Ch. 530.

(*n*) Lambarde *v.* Older, 17 Beav.
542. Comp. Stephens *v.* Venables, 30
Beav. 625. See Smee *v.* Baines, 29
Beav. 661.

(*o*) Addis *v.* Knight, 2 Mer. 122; *Ex
parte* Ross, Buck, 125; Watts *v.* Christie, 11 Beav. 546.

(*p*) Beasley *v.* D'Arcy, 2 Sch. & Lef.
403, n.; Wartnaby *v.* Shuttleworth, 1

Jur. 469; Rawson *v.* Samuel, Cr. &
Ph. 178; Jenner *v.* Morris, 11 W. R.
943.

(*q*) Jeffreys *v.* Agra and Masterman's
Bank, 2 L. R. Eq. 674.

(*r*) Whyte *v.* O'Brien, 1 Sim. & St.
551.

(*s*) Maw *v.* Ulyatt, 31 L. J. Ch. 83.
Comp. Hamp *v.* Jones, 9 L. J. Ch. N.
S. 258.

(*t*) Rawson *v.* Samuel, Cr. &. Ph. 178;
Dodd *v.* Lydall, 1 Ha. 337, 3 Mac. & G.
26, *per* Lord Truro. See Holford *v.*
Wortheman, 2 W. R. 51.

also, where a plaintiff brought an action at law against a defendant to recover moneys alleged to be due under a contract, and defendant had a verdict in the action with costs, the court would not restrain him from suing out execution on the judgment, notwithstanding a bill had been filed by the plaintiff for an account of transactions under the same contract (*u*).   Damages * cannot, except under special cir-   * 67
cumstances, be set off against an ascertained claim (*v*).
The fact that goods as delivered may be inferior in quality or quantity to the goods as ordered, does not give a right to set-off in equity (*x*).

6. Agreements, however, whether express or implied, may confer the right of equitable set-off, and slight circumstances may be sufficient to warrant the court in presuming such an agreement (*y*).   Thus the right was admitted in Downman *v.* Matthews (*z*), upon the course of dealing (*a*) ; in Jeffs *v.* Wood (*b*), upon the fact of the legatee having omitted to credit the executor with the goods supplied ; and in Jones *v.* Mossop (*c*), upon the objections as to the demand having been removed by the answer (*d*).   So also as between joint and separate debts an equity may arise to justify set-off where there are circumstances of fraud (*e*), or where the party seeking relief is only a surety for a debt really separate (*f*), or where there are a series of transactions in which joint credit is given with reference to the separate debt (*g*).   But although slight circumstances may be sufficient to warrant the court in presuming an agreement that one demand should be set off against another, there must be some evidence to warrant the court in presuming that there was such an agreement (*h*).   In some

(*u*) Fisher *v.* Baldwin, 11 Ha. 352 ; Phipps *v.* Child, 3 Drew. 713.   See Whalley *v.* Ramage, 8 L. T. N. S. 499.

(*v*) Rawson *v.* Samuel, Cr. & Ph. 179 ; Stimson *v.* Hall, 1 H. & N. 831 ; Atterbury *v.* Jarvie, 2 H. & N. 114.

(*x*) Glennie *v.* Imri, 3 Y. & C. 440.

(*y*) Taylor *v.* Okey, 13 Ves. 180 ; Freeman *v.* Lomas, 9 Ha. 109, 112 ; Wallis *v.* Bastard, 4 D. M. & G. 257. Comp. Hunt *v.* Jessell, 18 Beav. 100.

(*z*) Prec. Ch. 580.

(*a*) See Curson *v.* African Co., 1 Vern. 121 ; Peters *v.* Soame, 2 Vern. 428 ; Wilson *v.* Gabriel, 4 B. & S. 243.

(*b*) 2 P. Wms. 128.

(*c*) 3 Ha. 568.

(*d*) 9 Ha. 114, *per* Turner, L. J.   See Smee *v.* Baines, 29 Beav. 661.

(*e*) *Ex parte* Stephens, 11 Ves. 24.

(*f*) *Ex parte* Hanson, 12 Ves. 346, S. C. 18 Ves. 232.

(*g*) Vulliamy *v.* Noble, 3 Mer. 618.

(*h*) Baldwin *v.* Baldwin, 3 Ir. Ch. 388.

cases where there is a clear natural connection between the claim and the cross-claim, and both originate from one trans- • action, a court of equity will interfere to prevent the one party from enforcing his claim without allowing the claim of the other, although one of the claims may be unliquidated (*i*).

* 68   * Where a tenant owed a landlord rent, and the latter had committed a trespass on the land which rendered it of less value, and prevented the tenant to a certain extent from getting rent out of it, a claim for damage was allowed to be set off against the claim for rent (*k*). So, also, a client who had pledged an estate to his solicitor as a security for costs was held entitled on a bill for foreclosure against him to have made out a case of equitable set-off, by the allegation that the costs had been occasioned by the negligence or want of skill of the solicitor (*l*). So also if an agent having a title to an estate should allow his principal to expend money upon the estate without any notice of that title, he will not be permitted after a recovery at law in ejectment to maintain an action at law against the principal for mesne profits, but the court will require that to the extent of the improvements there shall be set-off allowed to the principal against the mesne profits (*m*). So also a man who advances money to a deserted wife to enable her to provide herself with necessaries, may set off such sum against a debt due by him to the husband (*n*). So also the insolvency of one of the parties is a sufficient ground for a court of equity to allow an equitable set-off (*o*).

7. The assignee of a chose in action takes subject to any equitable right of set-off, existing as against the assignor at the date of or before notice of the assignment to the person in whose hands the property in question lies (*p*).

(*i*) See O'Mahony *v.* Dickson, 2 Sch. & Lef. 408; South Eastern Railway Co. *v.* Brogden, 3 Mac. & G. 25, *per* Lord Truro; Stimson *v.* Hall, 1 H. & N. 831; Atterbury *v.* Jarvie, 2 H. & N. 114; Wilson *v.* Gabriel, 4 B. & S. 243.

(*k*) Beasley *v.* D'Arcy, 2 Sch. & Lef. 403, n. See Hamp *v.* Jones, 9 L. J. Ch. N. S. 258. Comp. Townrow *v.* Benson, 3 Madd. 203; Pratt *v.* Keith, 33 L. J. Ch. 530.

(*l*) Piggott *v.* Williams, 6 Madd. 95.

(*m*) Lord Cawdor *v.* Lewis, 1 Y. & C. 427, 433. See Monypenny *v.* Bristow, 2 R. & M. 117.

(*n*) Jenner *v.* Morris, 3 D. F. & J. 45.

(*o*) Chapman *v.* Derby, 2 Vern. 117; Hawkins *v.* Freeman, 2 Eq. Ca. Ab. 10; Lord Lanesborough *v.* Jones, 1 P. W. 325; Lindsay *v.* Jackson, 2 Paige (Amer.), 582; Bradley *v.* Angel, 3 Comst. (Amer.) 475.

(*p*) Cavendish *v.* Geaves, 24 Beav. 163; Ashworth's case, 10 W. R. 771;

*SECTION VI. — MARSHALLING SECURITIES.   * 69

1. Where a person has two funds to resort to, and another person has some rights in common with him in one of the funds, but no right in the other, the latter will be restrained from proceeding against that fund which is alone liable to his debt until the other is exhausted.

1. Where a person has two funds to resort to, and another person has some rights in common with him on one of the funds, but no right on the other, the latter has a right to restrain the former from proceeding against that fund which is alone liable to his debt, until the other be exhausted (q). The doctrine was much discussed in the cases respecting the estates of the American loyalists (r), which, being confiscated, subject to their debts, it was contended that a creditor ought to be restrained from pursuing the debtor personally here, till he had applied to make that property available to the payment of the debt. In several of the cases upon the subject, Lord Thurlow, Lord Kenyon, and Lord Rosslyn, expressed decided opinions in favor of the relief so prayed, upon the principle that if it appeared that there was in the hands of the creditor either possession of the estate in fact, or the clear means of effecting that possession, he ought to be called on so to do; or at least the court should interpose, the creditor not having the power of assigning to the debtor those means which he had of affecting the property. In the last of these cases, the bill was dismissed upon the particular circumstances, as it did not appear that the creditor had the means of making his demand effectual against the fund arising from confiscation (s). Lord Eldon, however, expressed his dissent from the principles of these opinions : his lordship thought that as it could not be contended that under such circumstances the personal liability of the debtor is taken away, so it could not be law that the remedies resulting out of that liability should be restrained by

Stephens *v.* Venables, 30 Beav. 625; Webster *v.* Webster, 31 Beav. 393; Wilson *v.* Gabriel, 4 B. & S. 243; Jeffryes *v.* Agra and Masterman's Bank, 2 L. R. Eq. 674.

(q) Lanoy *v.* Duke of Athol, 2 Atk. 446; Aldrich *v.* Cooper, 8 Ves. 388.

(r) Holditch *v.* Mist, 1 P. Wms. 694;

Wright *v.* Nutt, 1 H. B. 136, 3 Bro. C. C. 326; Kempe *v.* Antill, 2 Bro. C. C. 11; Peters *v.* Erving, 3 Bro. C. C. 52; Folliot *v.* Ogden, 1 H. B. 123, in error, 3 T. R. 726, and afterwards in the House of Lords, 4 Bro. P. C. ed. Toml. 111; Dudley *v.* Folliot, *ib.* 584.

(s) Wright *v.* Simpson, 6 Ves. 714.

confining the remedies to particular funds, or by confining
them altogether as to the person, till the creditor had recourse,
not to all the funds of the debtor, but to some of his
* 70   funds, which funds in the original constitution * of the
debt, and the transaction forming the relation of debtor
and creditor, the debtor did not propose, nor the creditor
receive, as the funds to be charged by the contract; that considering it as a pledge, if the effect of the contract was that
he should have all the remedies belonging to the nature of a
pledge, and also personal responsibility, it was questionable
whether the revolution would have operated to drive the creditor to the pledge, and compel him to give up the other remedy
at the instance of the debtor; but that the difficulty was much
enhanced when the pledge was not given to' the creditor by the
contract, but thrown to him by an act not his own.

SECTION VII.—SURETYSHIP.

1. Sureties who are discharged in equity from their liabilities
under instruments of suretyship, are entitled to the assistance

[74]

of a court of equity in restraining the creditor from proceeding against them at law (*t*). The adoption by courts of law of the equitable doctrines as to the discharge of sureties, does not affect the jurisdiction of the court (*u*).

2. The liability of a surety may not be extended beyond the terms of his obligation. To the extent, and in the manner, and under the circumstances pointed out in his obligation, he is bound, but no further (*v*). The creditor, or obligee, may not, without the assent of the surety, enter into any valid and binding agreement with the debtor, which varies materially the situation, or enlarges the risk of the surety (*x*), or affects substantially his rights and remedies against the debtor (*y*). If he enters into any such agreement, or by the omission of a duty, * or something which he has engaged to per-   * 71 form, and which formed a material inducement to the surety on entering into the obligation, increases the risk of the surety, the surety is discharged (*z*). The surety has a right to insist upon a literal performance of the engagement to which he has become a party, and to say that no obligation to which he has not given his assent, shall be forced on him (*a*). It is immaterial that he may sustain no injury by a change in the instrument, or even that it may be for his benefit. He has a right to stand on the very terms of his obligation, and if he does not assent to any variation of it, and a variation be made, it is fatal (*b*). If the engagement is altered in a single line, no matter whether it be altered for the benefit of the surety, or whether the alteration be innocently made, the surety has a right to say the contract is no longer that for which he engaged

(*t*) Hawksbaw *v.* Parkins, 2 Sw. 544; Samuel *v.* Howarth, 3 Mer. 272; Allan *v.* Inman, 7 Jur. 433; Small *v.* Currie, 5 D. M. & G. 141.

(*u*) *Ib.*
(*v*) Miller *v.* Stewart, 9 Wheat. (Amer.) 703; Bonser *v.* Cox, 13 L. J. Ch. 260; Evans *v.* Bremridge, 8 D. M. & G. 100, 2 K. & J. 174.

(*x*) Eyre *v.* Bartrop, 3 Madd. 221; Owen *v.* Homan, 3 Mac. & G. 378; Newton *v.* Charlton, 10 Ha. 649; Small *v.* Currie, 5 D. M. & G. 141; Bonar *v.* Macdonald, 3 H. L. 226; Pooley *v.* Harradine, 7 E. & B. 442; Guardians of Portsea Union *v.* Whillier, 2 El. & El. 765.

(*y*) Rees *v.* Berrington, 2 Ves. Jr. 540; Mayhew *v.* Crickett, 2 Sw. 185; M'Taggart *v.* Watson, 3 Cl. & Fin. 525, 10 Bligh, N. S. 618.

(*z*) Watts *v* Shuttleworth, 5 H. & N. 235; Watson *v.* Alcock, 4 D. M. & G. 242; Lawrence *v.* Walmsley, 12 C. B. N. S. 799.

(*a*) Whitcher *v.* Hall, 5 B. & C. 269; Bonser *v.* Cox, 13 L. J. Ch. 260; Calvert *v.* London Docks Co., 2 Keen, 638; Newton *v.* Charlton, 10 Ha. 648; Blest *v.* Brown, 8 Jur. N. S. 602.

(*b*) Samuel *v.* Howarth, 3 Mer. 272.

to be surety, and he is entitled to be relieved from the engagement (*c*). But where a man enters into a bond as surety for
the performance by another of two things which are separate
and distinct, a subsequent alteration of the contract as to one
of them, without the assent of the surety, does not release the
surety from his engagement as to the other (*d*).[1] In cases,
also, where a man becomes surety to a bond for the due performance of his duties by another, and new duties are afterwards imposed on the latter, a distinction is to be observed
between new duties which only affect the surety indirectly by
increasing the temptations of the principal debtor to be dishonest, and new duties, for the due performance of which the
surety himself, under his bond, would be liable, if the same
continued valid (*e*).

    3. Parties to an accommodation bill stand to one another in
the relation of principal and surety (*f*).

* 72   * 4. A surety has the right, at any time, to satisfy
the obligations by which he is bound, and upon satisfying it to have immediate recourse at law against the principal
debtor in the name of the creditor or obligee, or to come into
a court of equity to compel the creditor or obligee to take pro-

---

(*c*) Blest *v.* Brown, 8 Jur. N. S. 603, *per* Lord Westbury.

(*d*) Harrison *v.* Seymour, 1 L. R. C. P. 519.

(*e*) Skillett *v.* Fletcher, 1 L. R. C. P. 217. Comp. Bonar *v.* Macdonald, 3 H. L. 226.

(*f*) Bailey *v.* Edwards, 4 B. & S. 761 ; Ewin *v.* Lancaster, 6 B. & S. 571.

[1] In Seely *v.* People, 27 Ill. 173, it is held, that where a party executes a bond as surety with another, whose name appears to the bond, but which name has been forged, he will not be liable. This case, and the principles governing such cases are discussed, by Judge Redfield in 2 Amer. Law Reg. N. S. 344 ; and in York County M. F. Ins. Co. *v.* Brooks, 51 Maine, 506, it is held, that where a surety to a bond signs upon the assurance that the principal will also procure two other persons, specified and known to such surety, to sign the bond before he delivers the same, which he fails to do, but this is wholly unknown to the obligee at the time he accepts the bond, such surety is bound to perform the obligation.

The questions involved in this case are further discussed by Judge Redfield in a note to the same, 3 Amer. Law Reg. N. S. 402, who thinks that too many of the American cases, in striving to require good faith and diligence of the obligor or promisor, have quite too much overlooked the corresponding obliga-tions on the part of the obligee, and he sees no good reasons why the obligee, who, in accepting the bond, trusts to the representations of the principal obligor as to the execution of the instrument by the others, who are known to stand as mere sureties, should be any more entitled to screen himself from those representations prov-ing false, than should the obligor. The true rule in each case, he concludes, seems to be that each party may stand upon the *facts of the case* unless he has been guilty of *fraudulent miscon-duct.* See also Chouteau *v.* Suydam, 21 N. Y. 179 ; Passumpsic Bank *v.* Goss, 31 Vt. 315, and Dixon *v.* Dixon, *ib.* 450 ; Smith *v.* United States, 2 Wallace, 219. The authorities are largely collected in McCramer *v.* Thompson,, Iowa.

ceedings at law against the principal debtor. If the creditor or
obligee, without the consent of the surety, enters into any
binding agreement with the debtor, whereby the time for the
payment of the debt is enlarged, the surety is discharged from
the obligation, for the creditor or obligee, by disabling himself
from having immediate recourse against the principal debtor at
any time at the option of the surety, has deprived the surety of
the equity which he has a right to demand, and which the relation between the surety and the debtor requires (*g*).   The
surety is discharged, if time be given to a debtor by a valid
agreement which ties up the hands of the creditor, though it
be for a single day.   The principle is the same whether the
time be long or short.   The creditor must be in such a situation that when the surety comes to be substituted in his place
by paying the debt, he may have an immediate right of action
against the principal debtor (*h*).   The creditor or obligee has
no right to give time to the principal debtor, though it be clearly
for the benefit of the surety.   The surety has alone the right
to determine whether or not it is for his benefit (*i*).

5. An agreement, however, between the creditor and the
debtor, extending the time of payment, will not discharge the
surety, unless it be founded on a sufficient consideration, and
unless it be an agreement which the debtor can enforce against
the creditor (*k*).   Nor will the surety be discharged, if
the agreement * giving time be with a stranger to the   * 73
original instrument, and not with the debtor (*l*).   Nor
will an agreement giving time discharge the surety, if the
rights and remedies of the surety against the principal debtor
are, notwithstanding the arrangement, not affected (*m*), and
still less if they are, in fact, accelerated (*n*) by the agree-

---

(*g*) Bees *v.* Berrington, 2 Ves. Jr. 540;
Wright *v.* Simpson, 6 Ves. 714, 734;
Boultbee *v.* Stubbs, 18 Ves. 20 ; Oakeley
v. Pasheller, 4 Cl. & Fin. 207 ; McTaggart
v. Watson, 3 Cl. & Fin. 525 ; Newton *v.*
Chorlton, 10 Ha. 649 ; Small *v.* Currie,
5 D. M. & G. 141 ; Strong *v.* Foster, 17
C. B. 201 ; Pooley *v.* Harradine, 7 E. &
B. 442; Bailey *v.* Edwards, 4 B. & S.
761.

(*h*) Tucker *v.* Laing, 2 K. & J. 745.

(*i*) Samuel *v.* Howarth, 3 Mer. 272;
Calvert *v.* London Docks Co., 2 Keen,
638.

(*k*) Heath *v.* Key, 1 Y. & J. 434 ; Blake
v. White, 1 Y. & C. 420 ; Tucker *v.*
Laing, 2 K. & J. 745.

(*l*) Frazer *v.* Jordan, 8 E. & B. 303.

(*m*) Prendergast *v.* Devey, 6 Madd.
124; Boaler *v.* Mayor, 19 C. B. N. S.
76.

(*n*) Hulme *v.* Coles, 2 Sim. 12.

ment (*o*). Nor is a surety discharged when the indulgence is granted to the principal debtor, after final judgment signed, or a decree obtained against the surety (*p*), or against the principal debtor (*q*).

6. Nor will the surety be discharged, if in the agreement giving time there is an express and unqualified reservation by the creditor of his rights and remedies against the surety, or if the agreement is so worded as to show that it was intended only to apply to suits for the benefit of the creditor, and to except from its operation suits at the instance of the surety, and on his behalf, for no alteration in the position of the surety is produced (*r*). But if the creditor has so bound himself that he could not, without a breach of faith and contract, sue the debtor, or if the case is such that if the surety should call on him to sue, he would be bound to refuse, there is a discharge, although there may be an express proviso in the agreement, that in the event of the proposal not being carried out fully into effect, the surety should be liable as if the deed had not been made (*s*). The reservation by the creditor of his rights against the surety will not be held to be abandoned, unless a clear and positive intention to abandon it be proved (*t*).

7. If time be given by deed, the reservation of the right to proceed against the surety should appear on the face of the instrument itself (*u*), and should be clearly and unequiv-

* 74   ocally * expressed (*x*). In the case of instruments not under seal, it may be proved by parol evidence (*y*). The absence, however, of the reservation will not destroy any independent equity which may subsist between the parties (*z*).

8. If the creditor release or compound with the debtor without the concurrence of the surety, the surety is discharged,

(*o*) See Whitfield *v.* Hodges, 1 M. & W. 679 ; Bower *v.* Tierman, 3 Denio (Amer.), 378.

(*p*) Jenkins *v.* Robertson, 2 Drew. 351 ; Bray *v.* Manson, 8 M. & W. 668.

(*q*) Pole *v.* Ford, 2 Chitt. 125.

(*r*) Boultbee *v.* Stubbs, 18 Ves. 20 ; Webb *v.* Hewitt, 3 K. & J. 438 ; Davies *v.* Stainbank, 6 D. M. & G. 689 ; Owen *v.* Homan, 4 H. L. 997.

(*s*) Bailey *v.* Edwards, 4 B. & S. 761.

(*t*) Close *v.* Close, 4 D. M. & G. 176.

(*u*) *Ex parte* Glendinning, Buck, 517.

(*x*) Boultbee *v.* Stubbs, 18 Ves. 20.

(*y*) Wyke *v.* Rogers, 1 D. M. & G. 408.

(*z*) *Ex parte* Harvey, 4 D. M. & G. 881. See Atkins *v.* Revel, 1 D. F. & J. 365.

although he may have acted under a mistake, or for the benefit of the surety (*a*). But there is no discharge, if the surety has expressly agreed to continue liable, notwithstanding the creditor may enter into a composition with the principal debtor (*b*). The partner of a firm may release or compound with a debtor, so as to bind the firm, and discharge a surety both at law and in equity (*c*). A surety, however, who has by his conduct converted himself in relation to the debt for which he was surety, into a principal debtor, will lose the benefit of the doctrine that a release given to the principal debtor will release the surety (*d*). If an actual release be given for the debt, which is effectual and valid, either at law (*e*) or in equity (*f*), the creditor cannot reserve his rights against the surety, for the debt is gone. A surety will not be discharged by the creditor signing the certificate of the bankrupt debtor, after proving the debt, although the surety may have given him notice not to sign it (*g*); but the surety will be discharged, if the conduct of the creditor be such as to deprive him of the benefit of proof against the estate of the bankrupt (*h*).

9. A covenant not to sue does not operate as a release so as to *discharge a surety (*i*). A voluntary declara-   * 75
tion by a creditor that he intends to release his debtor from his debt, though not amounting to a release at law, may, nevertheless, be held in equity to be a representation which the creditor is bound to make good (*k*).

10. The taking of further security from the debtor will not, unless it be in lieu of the original security, have the effect of discharging the surety (*l*): nor will the surety be discharged,

<hr>

(*a*) *Ex parte* Smith, 3 Bro. C. C. 1; *Ex parte* Wilson, 11 Ves. 410 ; *Ex parte* Glendinning, Buck, 517 ; Bowmaker *v.* Moore, 7 Price, 223. See Lewis *v.* Jones, 4 B. & C. 506.

(*b*) Union Bank of Manchester *v.* Beech, 3 H. & C. 672.

(*c*) Hawkshaw *v.* Parkins, 2 Swanst. 539.

(*d*) Hall *v.* Hutchons, 3 M. & K. 426 ; Reade *v.* Lowndes, 23 Beav. 361. See Jones *v.* Beach, 2 D. M. & G. 886.

(*e*) Nicholson *v.* Revill, 4 A. & E. 675 ; Kearsley *v.* Cole, 16 M. & W.

128. Comp. Price *v.* Barker, 4 E. & B. 760.

(*f*) Webb *v.* Hewitt, 3 K. & J. 438. See Taylor *v.* Manners, 1 L. R. Ch. Ap. 48.

(*g*) Browne *v.* Carr, 2 Russ. 600. See Ratcliffe *v.* Gunson, 6 Madd. 193.

(*h*) Pledge *v.* Buss, John. 666.

(*i*) Willis *v.* De Castro, 4 C. B. N. S. 216.

(*k*) Yeomans *v.* Williams, 1 L. R. Eq. 184.

(*l*) Eyre *v.* Everett, 2 Russ. 381 ; Gordon *v.* Calvert, 4 Russ. 581 ; Newton

if there is a general understanding between the parties, that the giving additional security shall not affect the original security (*m*). But if the additional or further security be in lieu of the original security (*n*), or if the original security be merged in the additional security (*o*), the surety will be discharged. There is, however, no merger, if the additional or further security is for a different sum, payable at a different time and with different interest (*p*).

11. The creditor may assign the debt and all the securities for payment: the right of the assignee against the surety is not destroyed, because the fact of the assignment has not been communicated to him. The surety is not entitled to be informed who his creditor from time to time may be. The assignee takes subject to all the equities which attach to the creditor, at the same time that he acquires all the rights (*q*).

12. The rule is the same both at law and in equity, that there is no positive duty incumbent on the creditor to prosecute measures of active diligence against the principal debtor. Mere passive inactivity or neglect on his part to call the principal debtor to account in a reasonable time, and enforce payment, does not in the absence of a special stipulation in the instrument of suretyship, rendering activity on his part
* 76   * necessary, operate to discharge the surety (*r*). The same principle applies to the case of a surety who has guaranteed the honesty of a person employed or intrusted by another with money. The mere passive inactivity or neglect of the person to whom the guarantee is given to call the party whose honesty has been guaranteed to account within a reasonable time, does not, in the absence of a special stipulation rendering activity on his part necessary, operate to discharge the surety.[1] The surety is not entitled to be released from the

---

v. Charlton, 10 Ha. 649; Wyke *v.* Rogers, 1 D. M. & G. 413.

(*m*) Boaler *v.* Mayor, 19 C. B. N. S. 76.

(*n*) Clarke *v.* Henty, 3 Y. &. C. 187.
(*o*) Boaler *v.* Mayor, 19 C. B. N. S. 76.

(*p*) Boaler *v.* Mayor, 19 C. B. N. S. 76.

(*q*) Wheatley *v.* Bastow, 7 D. M. &

G. 280. See South *v.* Bloxam, 2 H. & M. 457.

(*r*) Wright *v.* Simpson, 6 Ves. 714; Trent Navigation ·Co. *v.* Harley, 10 East, 34; Eyre *v.* Everett, 2 Russ. 381; Newton *v.* Chorlton, 10 Ha. 651; Price *v.* Kirkham, 3 H. & C. 437.

[1] This is held to be the law in Pittsburg, Fort W. & C. Railroad Co. *v.* Shaeffer, 8 Amer. Law Reg. 110, how-

obligation, because the employer fails to use all means in his power to guard against the consequences of dishonesty. There must be some positive act done by him to the prejudice of the surety, or such a degree of negligence as to imply connivance and fraud (s).[1]   But the passive inactivity of the creditor may discharge the surety, if there be a stipulation in the instrument of suretyship that the creditor is on default to sue the surety without delay (t).   The case as to the effect of delay to sue in the case of bills of exchange, turns on a different principle. By mercantile usage a contract is implied in the holder to give notice of dishonor within a certain time, to the drawer or indorser who stands in the situation of surety for the acceptor (u).

13. A man who has become bound as surety for the honesty of another, for an indefinite period, cannot put an end to his liability by giving notice to the obligee of his intention to be no longer bound (x).

14. A creditor cannot be compelled in equity to resort in the first instance to the principal debtor, or to the securities which he holds for the debt before proceeding at law against the surety (y).   There may, however, be extreme cases in * which a court of equity would grant the surety relief,   * 77

ever prejudicial the forbearance of the creditor may be to the surety. This case also decides that the sureties of a railroad officer, charged with the receipt and disbursement of money, are within the rule ; and the company is not bound to dismiss the officer as soon as any default becomes known, and to give notice to the sureties that they may take measures to secure themselves by proceedings against the principal. And where an officer of a corporation violates his duty, knowledge on the part of other officers of the corporation of the default, or even connivance in it, does not discharge the sureties.

(s) McTaggart v. Watson, 3 Cl. & Fin. 525, 10 Bligh, N. S. 618 ; Creighton v. Rankin, 7 Cl. & Fin. 325 ; Dawson v. Lawes, Kay, 280 ; Black v. Ottoman Bank, 8 Jur. N. S. 801.

(t) Monutague v. Tidcombe, 2 Vern. 518 ; Bank of Ireland v. Beresford, 6

Dow. 233 ; Holl v. Hadley, 2 A. & E. 758.

(u) 8 Jur. N. S. 802, per Lord Kingsdown.

(x) Gordon v. Calvert, 4 Russ. 581.   See Bonser v. Cox, 6 Beav. 379.

(y) Ranelagh v. Hays, 1 Vern. 189, 2 Ch. Ca. 146.

[1] In New York it is settled that if a surety request the creditor to collect the debt from the principal, and the creditor refuse or neglect to do so at a time when it is collectible, and from a subsequent change of circumstances it becomes uncollectible, the surety is, by such conduct of the creditor, exonerated from his liability.   Remsen v. Beekman, 25 N. Y. 555.   It is also held in this case that a surety who, by arrangement between himself and the principal debtor, takes the primary liability upon himself, may, by subsequent arrange-

6

as, for instance, where the creditor has only to put out his hand to receive payment, or where the surety is under a disability which prevents him from obtaining, in his own person, the benefit of securities which have been set apart for the creditor (*z*).

15. A surety, upon satisfying the obligation in which he is bound, is entitled to the benefit of all securities, either of a legal or an equitable nature, which the creditor or obligee has or could have enforced against the principal debtor (*a*), and all persons claiming under him (*b*).[1] The creditor is under an obligation to preserve for the surety all the securities which he has taken from the principal debtor. If he parts with any of them, or if the full benefit of any of them is lost through his act or default, the surety is exonerated to the extent to which

---

ment with third parties, re-establish himself in the position and with the rights of a surety without the consent of the creditor. In Singer *v.* Troutman, 49 Barb. 182, it is held that the creditor must be requested to enforce the collection of the debt *by due process of law*, and that nothing short of that will exonerate the surety. And where the request was that the creditor should " push " the principal and " keep pushing him," it was held that these words had not the same legal significance as the words " prosecute or collect," and to give them this signification in such case not only must the creditor so understand them, but the surety should have meant and intended that. *Ib.*

(*z*) Wright *v.* Nutt, 1 H. Bl. 136, 3 Bro. C. C. 326 ; Cottin *v.* Blane, 2 Anst. 544. But see Wright *v.* Simpson, 6 Ves. 714.

(*a*) Wright *v.* Morley, 11 Ves. 12 ; Craythorne *v.* Swinburne, 14 Ves. 159 ; Copis *v.* Middleton, T. & R. 224 ; Mayhew *v.* Crickett, 2 Swanst. 185 ; Yonge *v.* Reynell, 9 Ha. 809 ; Lake *v.* Brutton, 8 D. M. & G. 440 ; Brandon *v.* Brandon, 3 D. & J. 524 ; Ewart *v.* Latta, 4 Macq. 983. Comp. Williams *v.* Owen, 13 Sim. 597 ; Farebrother *v.* Wodehouse, 23 Beav. 18.

(*b*) Drew *v.* Lockett, 32 Beav. 499. See Mercantile Law Amendment Act, 19 & 20 Vict. c. 97, s. 5.

[1] Hayes *v.* Ward, 4 Johns. Ch. 130 ; Lewis *v.* Palmer, 28 N. Y. 271, and cases cited. City Bank *v.* Young, 43 N. H. 457 ; Butler *v.* Birkey, 13 Ohio St. 514 ; Brown *v.* Ray, 18 N. H. 102, Parker, C. J. ; Schnitzel's Appeal, 49 Penn. St. 23 ; Hartwell *v.* Smith, 15 Ohio St. 202. A statute which prohibits the transfer of bank stock or the receipt of dividends thereon by any stockholder who may, at the time, be indebted to the bank, though intended mainly for the security of the bank, operates also incidentally in favor of the indorsers of such debtors. The right of a bank to prevent such transfer or payment becomes absolute as soon as any such debt becomes due and payable ; and the legal title to the stock remains in the bank for its own security until payment, and for the benefit of the sureties of a debtor, if there be any afterwards. Klopp *v.* Lebanon Bank, 46 Penn. St. 88. And " it is well settled by the authorities that the creditor has an equitable claim to the security, as well when the mortgage is given for mere indemnity as when the condition is added that the principal shall pay the debt." Chapman, J., in New Bedford Ins. for Savings *v.* Fairhaven Bank, 9 Allen, 178, citing Moses *v.* Murgatroyd, 1 Johns. Ch. 119 ; Phillips *v.* Thompson, 2 Johns. Ch. 418 ; Ten Eyck *v.* Holmes, 3 Sandf. Ch. 428 ; Riddle *v.* Bowman, 7 Fost. N. H. 236 ; Aldrich *v.* Martin, 4 R. I. 520.

he is prejudiced thereby (*c*). The rule applies where the benefit of a security is lost, through the neglect of the creditor in not perfecting the instrument in the proper way (*d*). The right of the surety is the same, whether he knew of the existence of the securities or not (*e*), or whether the securities were deposited with the creditor subsequently to the date of the instrument of suretyship (*f*). The surety is entitled to have the security in the same plight and condition in which it stood in the creditor's * hands (*g*). A surety,   * 78 however, for part of a debt is not entitled to the benefit of a security given by the debtor to the creditor at a different time in a distinct transaction for another part of the debt (*h*).

16. The rule is the same both at law and in equity, that the question whether a party to a written instrument is a principal or only a surety, must be ascertained from the terms of the instrument itself (*i*). But in equity, persons who appear on the face of an instrument as joint debtors, may, by an arrangement between themselves, create the relation of principal and surety to each other without the knowledge of the creditor. So long as the creditor is ignorant of the change, he will not be affected by it; but as soon as he receives notice of the relation, the rights of the surety are the same as they would have been if the existence of the relation had appeared on the face of the instrument. The knowledge by the creditor of the existence of the relation creates an equity dehors the instrument, which will affect him with the consequences of the relation. The mere notice of the existence of the relation is sufficient to affect him without any further acceptance on his part. The creditor is bound from the date of the receipt of the notice. If, having such notice, he gives time to the principal debtor, the surety is

(*c*) Mayhew *v.* Crickett, 2 Swanst. 191; Williams *v.* Price, 1 Sim. & St. 581; Capel *v.* Butler, 2 Sim. & St. 457; Newton *v.* Charlton, 10 Ha. 649; Wheatley *v.* Bastow, D. M. & G. 261; Pearl *v.* Deacon, 1 D. & J. 462. Comp. Watson *v.* Alcock, 4 D. M. & G. 242; Watts *v.* Shuttleworth, 5 H. & N. 235, 7 H. & N. 353.

(*d*) Strange *v.* Fooks, 4 Giff. 408.

(*e*) Mayhew *v.* Crickett, 2 Swanst.

191; Newton *v.* Charlton, 10 Ha. 649; Lake *v.* Brutton, 8 D. M. & G. 452; Pearl *v.* Deacon, 1 D. & J. 462; Watts *v.* Shuttleworth, 7 H. & N. 353.

(*f*) Lake *v.* Brutton, 8 D. M. & G. 440; Pledge *v.* Buss, John. 666.

(*g*) Pledge *v.* Buss, John. 666.

(*h*) Wade *v.* Coope, 2 Sim. 155.

(*i*) Hollier *v.* Eyre, 9 Cl. & Fin. 1.

discharged (*j*). Notice that some of the parties to an instrument are not primarily liable, is enough to fix the creditor with the consequences of the relation, although there was no notice who the parties were. If the effect of the agreement between the creditor and the principal debtor be to alter the position of the parties who should turn out to be sureties, it is as wilfully done, and as inequitable, as if he had express notice who those parties were (*k*). Parol evidence, dehors the instru-

* 79   ment, * is admissible to show that a party who appears on the face of the instrument as a principal is only a surety, and that the creditor had notice of the existence of the relation between the parties (*l*).

SECTION VIII. — PENALTIES AND FORFEITURES.

1. Courts of equity will relieve against penalties and forfeitures.
2. Most familiar cases, those of a penalty to a bond or instrument securing the payment of money.
3. Jurisdiction extends to all agreements where a stipulation is made in the event of non-performance which is in effect a penalty.
4. Practice when penalty is to secure the due performance of some collateral act.
5. Statute provisions.
6. Distinction between penalties and liquidated damages.
7. Clauses imposing a forfeiture distinguished from clauses which give a privilege in the event of prompt payment.
8. Relief may be had in equity against forfeiture for non-payment of rent.
9. Practice before and under the statute.
10. Relief as well where there is a proviso that lease shall be void, as where there is power of re-entry.
11. Practice where there is a breach of other covenants as well as non-payment of rent.
12. Compensation not a ground of relief against forfeiture, except in case of a simple money payment. No relief against forfeiture for breach of covenant, except in special cases.

(*j*) Oakley *v.* Pasheller, 4 Cl. & Fin. 207, 10 Bligh, N. S. 548; Davies *v.* Stainbank, 6 D. M. & G. 679; Pooley *v.* Harradine, 7 E. & B. 442; White *v.* Corbett, 1 El. & El. 692; Greenough *v.* M'Clelland, 2 El. & El. 424; Wythes *v.* Labouchere, 3 D. & J. 593; Taylor *v.* Burgess, 5 H. & N. 1; Bailey *v.* Edwards, 4 B. & S. 761; Ewin *v.* Lancaster, 6 B. & S. 571. Comp.

Ex parte Graham, 5 D. M. & G. 356.

(*k*) Bailey *v.* Edwards, 4 B. & S. 761, 772.

(*l*) Craythorne *v.* Swinburne, 14 Ves. 160, 170; Clarke *v.* Henty, 3 Y. & C. 187. See Pooley *v.* Harradine, 7 E. & B. 442; Ewin *v.* Lancaster, 6 B. & S. 571.

1. A court of equity will relieve against penalties and forfeitures.[1] At law, on the breach of a covenant secured by a penalty, the full penalty may be enforced without regard to the damage sustained. In equity, however, contracts being treated as matters for specific performance, the annexation of a penalty does not alter the character of the contract. Where the payment of money or the doing of any particular act is secured by a penalty, equity treats the penalty as being merely the means of securing the payment of the money, or the due performance of the act contracted to be done, and not as a sum of money actually intended to be paid (m). The contracting party may not on the one hand evade performance by paying the penalty, (n), nor on the other hand enforce the penalty to its full nominal extent. If the party seeks to enforce his legal right to the full penal sum named in the penalty, a court of equity will grant relief to the party in default, upon his making full compensation for the actual damage sustained through his default.

(m) Peachy v. Duke of Somerset, 1 Stra. 447; Sloman v. Walter, 1 Bro. C. C. 419; Errington v. Aynsley, 2 Bro. C. C. 341; Ranger v. Great Western Railway Co., 5 H. L. 94. See *infra.*
(n) Hobson v. Trevor, 2 P. Wms. 191; Chilliner v. Chilliner, 2 Ves. 528; Hardy v. Martin, 1 Cox, 26; French v. Macale, 2 Dr. & War. 284.
[1] But does not enforce either. Horsburg v. Baker, 1 Peters, 232; Livingston v. Tompkins, 4 Johns. Ch. 431.

The principle upon which the relief is granted is that the other party may receive by way of recompense all that he expected and desired (*o*).

2. The most familiar and perhaps the earliest instance in which equity gave relief against penalties, was in the case of a penalty to a bond or instrument securing the payment of money. The * payment of the principal sum, interest, and costs being full compensation for the damage sustained for the non-payment of money at the appointed time, or in the mode appointed, the jurisdiction of equity in granting relief in all cases of the sort has been long established (*p*). The circumstances of the case, however, may be such as not to justify an interference on the part of the court with the legal right of the plaintiff to enforce the full penal sum named in the bond, notwithstanding that it may greatly exceed the sum for which the bond was given as a security (*q*). If a party chooses by improper proceedings to prevent a creditor from having payment as soon as he ought, these proceedings shall not operate to the prejudice of the creditor, but he shall be considered as entitled to receive what is really the amount due, and notwithstanding there is a penalty in the bond, that shall not be the limitation of what shall be recovered by him (*r*).

3. The jurisdiction of the court in relieving against penalties is not limited to the case of bonds or instruments which in terms impose a penalty, but extends to all agreements where a stipulation is made in the event of non-performance, which is in effect a penalty. If, for instance, the condition of a bond be to pay a higher rate of interest, if the debt be not paid on a certain day, equity will consider such condition in the nature of a penalty, and will relieve against it (*s*). So also if a certain rate of interest be reserved in a mortgage deed, with an agreement that if it be not punctually paid the rate shall be increased, the larger interest is regarded as in the nature of a

(o) Peachy *v.* Duke of Somerset, 1 Stra. 447.

(p) Holles *v.* Wyse, 2 Vern. 289; Strode *v.* Parker, 2 Vern. 316; Walmsley *v.* Booth, Barnard, 481; Peachy *v.* Duke of Somerset, 1 Stra. 447; Aylett *v.* Dodd, 2 Atk. 238; Seton *v.* Slade, 7 Ves. 273; Davis *v.* West, 12 Ves. 475.

(q) Osborne *v.* Eales, 2 Moo. P. C. N. S. 125.

(r) Grant *v.* Grant, 3 Sim. 340. See Pulteney *v.* Warren, 6 Ves. 79; Clark *v.* Lord Abingdon, 17 Ves. 106.

(s) Holles *v.* Wyse, 2 Vern. 289; Strode *v.* Parker, *ib.* 316; Walmsley *v.* Booth, Barnard, 481.

penalty, and will be relieved against (*t*). So also in the case of an estate sold by auction, although there be a condition to forfeit the deposit if the purchase be not completed within a certain time, the court * will relieve against   * 81 forfeiture upon payment of interests and costs (*u*).

4. If the intent of the insertion of the penalty is not to secure the payment of money, but to secure the due performance of some collateral act or undertaking, the bill will be retained, and an issue *quantum damnificatus* directed, and relief will be granted upon the payment of the damages as assessed by a jury (*x*). In Thomas *v.* Archbishop of Canterbury (*y*), where an administratrix had entered into the usual administration bond to exhibit an inventory within a limited time, and the time having elapsed without an inventory having been exhibited, the court restrained a creditor from putting the bond in suit, putting the plaintiff, however, on terms (*z*).

5. Two statutes, 8 & 9 Will. 3, c. 11, s. 8, and 4 Anne, c. 16, ss. 12, 13, the former applying to penalties for non-performance of covenants, and the second to penalties for non-payment of money, have had the effect of diminishing the frequency of equitable interference in restraining actions upon penalties, but they do not affect the jurisdiction of the court.

6. Care must be taken in distinguishing cases of penalties strictly so called from those cases where a certain sum is agreed upon by the parties to be paid as the price of doing or refraining from doing a certain act. Parties to an agreement are at full liberty to agree that in case the one party shall do or omit to do a certain stipulated act, the other party shall receive a certain fixed sum as a conventional amount of damages sustained by such act or omission. The stipulation is part of the express contract between the parties, and is good and valid both at law and in equity. A court of equity will in such cases, neither on the one hand restrain the doing of the act, nor relieve

---

(*t*) Rose *v.* Rose, Amb. 331; Nicholls *v.* Maynard, 3 Atk. 519; Seton *v.* Slade, 7 Ves. 273.

(*u*) Vernon *v.* Stephens, 2 P. W. 66; Moss *v.* Matthews, 3 Ves. 279; Casson *v.* Roberts, 32 L. J. Ch. 105. See Lennon *v.* Napper, 2 Sch. & Lef. 685.

(*x*) Sloman *v.* Walter, 1 Bro. C. C. 418; Hardy *v.* Martin, 1 Cox, 26; Errington *v.* Aynsley, 2 Bro. C. C. 341.

(*y*) 1 Cox, 399.

(*z*) See Benson *v.* Gibson, 3 Atk. 396.

against the payment• of the full amount agreed to be
* 82   * paid, if the act be done or omitted to be done as the
case may be (a).[1]

7. Cases where a penalty or forfeiture is introduced for the
purpose of security must be distinguished from cases where
there is no stipulation for penalty or forfeiture, but a privilege
is conferred, provided money be paid within a stated time. The
party claiming the privilege must be able to show that the
money was paid accordingly (b). As in the case of interest
reserved on a loan at five per cent, with a proviso that four per
cent will be accepted if paid within a limited time after it
comes due (c); or in the case of a covenant for the renewal
of a lease on the payment of a certain fine at a stated period
(d); or in the case of a power as to repurchase on payment
of rents or moneys at stated periods (e); or in the case of an
agreement by a creditor to take less than his debt, so as the
money is paid at a certain day (f). On the same principle a
proviso that a sum due should be payable by instalments, provided they were punctually paid, but that in case of any default in paying them, the whole sum should be payable at once,
does not amount to a penalty (g). So also if a contract provides that the purchase-money shall be paid in the course of or
at the end of ten years, and that the interest for the first two
years shall be five per cent, and the interest for the next two
years shall be six per cent, and the interest for the next
two years shall be seven per cent, and so on, the contract is
good (h).

8. The equitable doctrine of relief against penalties has

(a) Small v. Fitzwilliam, Prec. Ch. 102; French v. Macale, 2 Dr. & War. 269; Ranger v. Great Western Railway Co., 5 H. L. 94. See infra.

(b) Rose v. Rose, Amb. 331; Davis v. Thomas, 1 R. & M. 506. Comp. Carroll v. O'Connor, 11 Ir. Eq. 200.

(c) Nicholls v. Maynard, 3 Atk. 519.
(d) 1 R. & M. 508, per Sir J. Leach, M. R.

(e) Barrell v. Sabine, 1 Vern. 268; Joy v. Birch, 4 Cl. & Fin. 57, 89; Davis v. Thomas, 1 R. & M. 506; Brooke v. Garrod, 2 D. & J. 562. See Lord Ranelagh v. Melton, 2 Dr. & Sm. 278.

(f) Sewell v. Musson, 1 Vern. 210; Ex parte Bennett, 2 Atk. 527; Ford v. Earl of Chesterfield, 19 Beav. 431. See M'Kenzie v. M'Kenzie, 16 Ves. 372; Thomson v. Hudson, 2 L. R. Ch. App. 256.

(g) Sterne v. Beck, 1 D. J. & S. 595. Comp. Carroll v. O'Connor, 11 Ir. Eq. 200.

(h) Herbert v. Salisbury and Yeovil Railway Co., 2 L. R. Eq. 221.
[1] Skinner v. Dayton, 2 John. Ch. 526. And as to liquidated damages and penalties, see Van Buren v. Digges, 11 How. U. S. 461.

been *extended to leases containing a clause of re-   * 83
entry on non-payment of the rent at the appointed time.

The jurisdiction has been long established upon the principle
that the right of entry is in the nature of a penalty to secure the
payment of the rent, and that the payment of rent with interest
and costs is a sufficient compensation for the damage sustained,
and is as beneficial to the landlord, if paid at any time, as it
would be if paid at the appointed day (*i*). The soundness of
the principle has been much questioned by Lord Eldon and
other judges, it being by no means true that a subsequent payment of the rent, interest, and costs, is an equivalent for
punctuality of payment (*k*) ; but the doctrine has received a
parliamentary recognition by statute 4 Geo. 2, c. 28, ss. 2–4.

9. Before the statute was passed, the tenant could not only
obtain an injunction to restrain the lessor from turning him
out of possession, but might, at an indefinite time after he was
ejected, have filed his bill, and been relieved against the effects
of the non-payment of rent (*l*). The statute, by the second
clause, limited the time within which the lessee might obtain
relief to applications made within six months after execution ;
and, by the third clause, enacted that no lessee should be entitled to have or continue an injunction against proceedings in
ejectment, unless he should pay into court, within forty days
after answer, the arrears and costs, whereupon, according to
the fourth clause, all proceedings in the action should cease,
and the lessee should, if relieved under the statute, hold the
demised lands without any new lease (*m*). These clauses
have been re-enacted, with a few immaterial variations, and
have been, in effect, superseded by the Common Law Procedure Act, 15 & 16 Vict. c. 76 (*n*). The provision in the third
clause for payments into court of the arrears of rent
and costs, applies only to the case where the * tenant   * 84
comes for an injunction by which his possession is to be

(*i*) Cary, 45; Descarlett *v.* Dennett,
9 Mod. 23; Wadman *v.* Calcraft, 10
Ves. 68; Davis *v.* West, 12 Ves. 475;
Keating *v.* Sparrow, 1 B. & B. 367;
Bowser *v.* Colby, 1 Ha. 130.

(*k*) Hill *v.* Barclay, 16 Ves. 405, 18
Ves. 61; Reynolds *v.* Pitt, 19 Ves. 140;
Doe *v.* Smith, 7 Price, 326.

(*l*) Bowser *v.* Colby, 1 Ha. 125.
(*m*) See Doe *v.* Lewis, 1 Burr. 619;
Hill *v.* Barclay, 18 Ves. 60; Doe *v.*
Smith, 7 Price, 326; Bowser *v.* Colby,
1 Ha. 140.

(*n*) Ss. 210–212. See Hughes *v.* Howard, 25 Beav. 575.

continued, and the landlord restrained from proceeding with his ejectment. In all these cases, if the injunction is granted, the court is bound by the statute to impose such terms for the security of the landlord. But if the landlord is actually in possession, undisturbed by the interposition of the court, and the first application which the tenant makes to the court for relief is made at the hearing of the cause, the statute does not then apply (o).

10. Relief will be given against forfeiture for non-payment of rent, as well where there is a proviso that upon non-payment of rent the lease shall be void, as where there is a power of re-entry (p).

11. If a lessor is proceeding at law, not merely on account of the non-payment of rent, but also for the breach of other covenants, with respect to which there exists no equitable ground of relief, and there has been clearly a breach of one or more of such other covenants, the court will not restrain him from recovering in ejectment for the non-payment of rent (q): but if it is doubtful whether there has been a breach of any of the covenants, other than that for the non-payment of rent, the lessor will be allowed to proceed on any other covenant, against the breach of which the court does not relieve, but will be restrained from proceeding at law on account of the non-payment of rent (r).

Though relief will almost always be given against the forfeiture of a lease for non-payment of rent, a case may exist in which a lessee shall have so dealt with the property of his landlord, or otherwise so acted as to deprive himself of the right to equitable interference (s).

12. It was formerly laid down, and in several cases it
* 85   has been * held, that relief might be given in equity, against forfeiture, if compensation could be made, even

---

(o) Bowser v. Colby, 1 Ha. 127.

(p) Bowser v. Colby, 1 Ha. 128, 129.

(q) Wadman v. Calcraft, 10 Ves. 67; Davis v. West, 12 Ves. 475; Lovat v. Lord Ranelagh, 3 V. & B. 29; Home v. Thompson, Sau. & Sc. 615; Bowser v. Colby, 1 Ha. 134; Nokes v. Gibbon, 3 Drew. 693; Bamford v. Creasy, 3 Giff. 681.

(r) Davis v. West, 12 Ves. 475; Lovat v. Lord Ranelagh, 3 V. & B. 29; Bowser v. Colby, 1 Ha. 109; Bamford v. Creasy, 3 Giff. 681.

(s) 1 Ha. 138, per Wigram, V. C.

although the act or omission were voluntary (*t*). In Sanders *v.* Pope (*u*), Lord Erskine gave relief against the breach of a covenant to lay out a certain specific sum in repairs, upon the principle that compensation might be made; and in the subsequent case of Davis *v.* West (*v*), he laid down the same doctrine, referring to his previous decision, and saying that in giving judgment in that case he felt himself bound by the authorities. But the principle upon which Lord Erskine proceeded in those cases has been disapproved by Lord Eldon and other judges, and may be looked on as expressly and distinctly overruled (*x*); and it may now be considered as clear and settled law, that relief will not be given against forfeiture for breach of covenant, upon the ground that compensation may be made, except when the breach of covenant has been the omission of a simple money payment, such as rent (*y*). In no other cases will relief be given against forfeiture for the breach of a covenant, unless under very special circumstances (*z*). If the contract between a landlord and tenant be so strict that the lessor may enter upon a breach of one of the covenants, the court cannot interfere to modify the contract (*a*). "It is," said Lord Lyndhurst, in Hillier *v.* Parkinson (*b*), "a very vulgar and general notion that it is the province of a court of equity to step in upon every occasion where the strict rule of law appears to bear hard upon individuals in particular cases. If it were to be held that equity is to relieve in any case where the strict rule of law may press hard upon individuals, it would be nothing more or less than a * system   *86 of *ex post facto* laws. The doctrine of equitable relief against breaches of covenant is a mischievous one, and has been exploded. That is not a province of a court of equity:

(*t*) Popham *v.* Bampfield, 1 Vern. 83; Hayward *v.* Angell, *ib.* 222; Rose *v.* Rose, Amb. 332; Northcote *v.* Duke, Amb. 513; Cage *v.* Russell, 2 Vent. 352; Wafer *v.* Mocatto, 9 Mod. 112; Hack *v.* Leonard, *ib.* 91.
(*u*) 12 Ves. 289.
(*v*) *Ib.* 475.
(*x*) Hill *v.* Barclay, 18 Ves. 56; Reynolds *v.* Pitt, 19 Ves. 140; Bracebridge *v.* Buckley, 2 Price, 200; Gregory *v.* Wilson, 9 Ha. 689.
(*y*) Nesbitt *v.* Tredennick, 1 B. & B. 29, 47; Keating *v.* Sparrow, *ib.* 367; Job *v.* Banister, 2 K. & J. 382; Bowser *v.* Colby, 1 Ha. 134; Elliott *v.* Turner, 13 Sim. 485.
(*z*) Winthrop *v.* Murray, 8 Ha. 214; Shearman *v.* Macgregor, 11 Ha. 106.
(*a*) Meek *v.* Carter, 4 Jur. N. S. 992.
(*b*) 9 L. J. Ch. 156.

where there is a breach of covenant which produces a forfeiture at law, that also works a forfeiture here."

It is not, however, every breach of a covenant that at law
would work a forfeiture: it must be a serious, wilful, deliberate breach (c): but if a man who knows that he is charged
with a legal obligation neglects to perform it, his neglect to do
so must, even in equity, be deemed to be wilful, and, if he persist in it, to be deliberate (d).

13. Relief, accordingly, will not be given against forfeiture
for breach of covenant to repair, or spend a specific sum in repairs (e). A tenant is not absolved from the performance of
the covenants in his lease by notice to quit (f). Nor is notice
by the landlord to repair necessary, unless there be a stipulation in the lease rendering it necessary (g). "If," said
Thompson, C. B. (h), "a man covenant to do an act within a
certain time, no demand is necessary ; and a neglect of performance is tantamount to a refusal in law." The fact that
large sums of money may have been expended upon the premises does not create an equity for the interference of the
court, if there has been in fact a breach of the covenant to
repair (i). A covenant to repair is not broken by allowing
the premises to go out of repair. A reasonable time will be
allowed for repairs: if they are repaired within a reasonable
time, there is no breach of the covenant (j).

In *Ex parte* Vaughan (k), relief was given against ejectment brought by the committee of a lunatic's estate, against a
　　　　tenant for breach of a covenant to repair, on the ground
* 87　　that the * breach was not one which a judicious land-
　　　　lord would have taken advantage of. The case can,
however, hardly be treated as an exception to the general rule,
for the court was not adjudicating between the hostile claims

---

(c) Rankin v. Lay, 2 D. F. & J. 73,
per Lord Campbell. See Parker v. Taswell, 2 D. & J. 570, *per* Lord Chelmsford.

(d) Gregory v. Wilson, 9 Ha. 689, *per*
Turner, L. J.

(e) Bracebridge v. Buckley, 2 Price,
200 ; Gregory v. Wilson, 9 Ha. 689;
See Bargent v. Thompson, 4 Giff. 475.

(f) Gregory v. Wilson, 9 Ha. 688.
(g) Bracebridge v. Buckley, 2 Price,
200.
(h) Ib. 213.
(i) Job v. Banister, 26 L. J. Ch. 125,
3 Jur. N. S. 93.
(j) Ib. See Gauge v. Lockwood, 2
F. & F. 115.
(k) T. & R. 436.

of landlord and tenant, but was acting in lunacy on behalf of the lunatic, and merely refused as a landlord, and acting on his behalf, to take advantage of the forfeiture.

14. Nor will relief be given in equity against forfeiture for breach of a covenant to keep premises insured (*l*), or to pay the premiums, and keep up a policy of insurance (*m*). The omission to insure is stronger against a tenant than the omission to repair, because, in the latter case, the landlord may, by exercising due vigilance, see to the observance of the covenant, but in the former case, where the lessee has undertaken to keep insured, the landlord must rely upon him for the fulfilment of his obligation (*n*). Insurance after the breach has been committed has no effect in curing the breach (*o*). In Green *v.* Bridges (*p*), the court would not restrain proceedings in ejectment for breach of a covenant to insure in a lease for 999 years, though it was clear the reversion was of no use to the lessor.

The court has been empowered by statute 22 & 23 Vict. c. 35, ss. 4–9, to give relief against the breach of a covenant to keep premises insured, where the breach has been committed through accident, mistake, or otherwise, without fraud or gross negligence. Relief may not, however, be given more than once in respect of the same covenant: nor can relief be given where a forfeiture under the covenant has been already waived out of court in favor of the person seeking relief. Relief may be given under the statute, for breaches of covenant in leases granted before the statute (*q*).

15. * Relief may, however, be given in equity against   * 88 forfeiture, if the covenant to insure has been performed substantially, though it may not have been literally performed. At law, a covenant by the lessee to insure in the name of the lessor only is not performed by an insurance in the joint

(*l*) White *v.* Warner, 2 Mer. 459; Reynolds *v.* Pitt, 19 Ves. 140; Rolfe *v.* Harris, 2 Pri. 207, n. ; Green *v.* Bridges, 4 Sim. 96; Elliott *v.* Turner, 13 Sim. 477; Gregory *v.* Wilson, 9 Ha. 683; Shearman *v.* Macgregor, 11 Ha. 106; Nokes *v.* Gibbon, 3 Drew. 681; Meek *v.* Carter, 4 Jur. N. S. 992.

(*m*) Winthorp *v.* Murray, 8 Ha. 214.
(*n*) White *v.* Warner, 2 Mer. 459.

(*o*) Reynolds *v.* Pitt, 19 Ves. 140; Green *v.* Bridges, 4 Sim. 96; Elliott *v.* Turner, 13 Sim. 477; Gregory *v.* Wilson, 9 Ha. 689; Nokes *v.* Gibbon, 3 Drew. 681; Meek *v.* Carter, 4 Jur. N. S. 992.

(*p*) 4 Sim. 96.
(*q*) Page *v.* Bennett, 2 Giff. 117, 6 Jur. N. S. 419.

names and the lessee, because the arrangement is not so beneficial to the landlord as the arrangement for which he had
stipulated (*q*). But in equity relief may be given against
forfeiture, where the manner in which the insurance has been
effected is not so beneficial to the lessor as that for which
he had stipulated, if the covenant has been on the whole
substantially complied with. In Rogers *v.* Tudor (*r*), there
was a covenant in a lease that the lessee should insure
in his own name, and the name of the lessor, in the Law
Fire Insurance Office, or such other office as the lessor should
fix on, and the lessee effected an insurance in his own name
alone, without any communication with the lessor, in the
Phœnix office ; but the court held that though this was not a
literal performance of the obligation, the covenant to insure
was substantially complied with, and that no forfeiture on
which ejectment could be brought had taken place (*s*).

16. Nor will relief be given in any equity against forfeiture
for the breach of covenants in a building lease. In Nokes *v.*
Gibbon (*t*), the court would not relieve against the breach of
covenants in a building lease, for the making of a road and
footway, and for the digging of drains. The plaintiff, in
equity, alleged in excuse that it would have been useless to
make the roadway until the other houses in the row were completed. But the court held this to be no excuse, and not to
furnish any equity on which the legal right could be interfered
with. So, also, where a builder had agreed to take land on a
building lease, and to erect houses thereon within a specified
time, the land-owner making him certain advances, and there
was a clause of forfeiture in default of the completion of the
houses within the time, the court would not relieve
* 89   against forfeiture, * the landlord having performed his
own part of the contract (*u*). The fact that the lessor
has the option of either insisting on the forfeiture, or carrying
on the buildings at the expense of the lessee, does not qualify
or abridge the right of forfeiture upon breach of the cove-

(*q*) Penniall *v.* Harbone, 11 Q. B.
396. See Havens *v.* Middleton, 10 Ha.
641.
(*r*) 6 Jur. N. S. 692.
(*s*) See Gregory *v.* Wilson, 9 Ha.

683 ; Lillie *v.* Legh, 3 D. & J. 204;
Leather Co. *v.* Brassey, 8 Jur. N. S.
425.
(*t*) 3 Drew. 681.
(*u*) Croft *v.* Goldsmid, 24 Beav. 312.

nants (v). Neither the omission of the workmen employed by the lessee to perform the works in the manner stipulated, nor false representations made by them to their employer that the works had been effectually executed, can afford any equitable ground for relief against the legal right (x).

17. Nor will relief be granted in equity against forfeiture for the breach of covenants in a farming lease, as to mode of cultivation, &c. (y). Where a lessee under a lease to build and cultivate the land, which should not be built upon, in a husbandlike manner, with a clause of forfeiture in case of breach of the covenants, had built, with the knowledge of the lessor, a factory on the land, which he was obliged to pull down in consequence of an indictment, and had paid part of the proceeds to the lessor, in pursuance of an agreement between them, the court held he had no equity for relief against forfeiture, and refused to restrain ejectment for the non-cultivation of the land after the buildings had been pulled down (z). In an American case, Dunkee v. Adams (a), the court would not relieve against forfeiture for breaches of a covenant, securing the performance of certain personal services for the comfort and convenience of the party claiming the forfeiture.

18. Nor will relief be given in equity against forfeiture for the breach of a covenant not to assign without license (b) ; but equitable arrangements charging the property comprised in a lease, but not accompanied with a change of possession, or other * alteration of the property, do not work a for-   * 90 feiture of a lease in equity, notwithstanding there is a clause in the lease against assignment (c).

19. Nor will equity relieve a lessee, who carries on a trade

(v) Ib.

(x) Nokes v. Gibbon, 3 Drew. 681. See as to the due completion of a building contract and the fair and proper exercise of the architect's discretion, and the account and penalties, Pawley v. Turnbull, 3 Giff. 70.

(y) Lovat v. Lord Ranelagh, 3 V. & B. 25. See Porrett v. Barnes, 2 L. J. Ch. 142.

(z) Hills v. Rowlands, 4 D. M. & G. 430. See Rankin v. Lay, 2 D. F. & J. 28–42.

73, as to construction of covenants in a farming lease.

(a) 20 Verm. (Amer.) 415.

(b) Wafer v. Mocatto, 9 Mod. 112 ; Hill v. Barclay, 18 Ves. 63 ; Lovat v. Lord Ranelagh, 3 V. & B. 24. See Burke v. Prior, 15 Ir. Ch. 106.

(c) Bowser v. Colby, 1 Ha. 138. See Gourlay v. Duke of Somerset, 1 V. & B. 73 ; Croft v. Lumley, 6 H. L. 672. See also Dumpor's case, 1 Smith, L. C. 28–42.

without license contrary to covenant (*d*), or a licensee who has violated the covenants contained in a deed of license (*e*). In Elliott *v.* Turner (*f*), the defendants had obtained a license from the plaintiff to use his invention, and had covenanted to render a full account of the quantities of goods sold by them under the license every half-year, &c., &c., and also to give notice of their intention to use the invention at any other place, &c., &c., and had also covenanted that in the event of wilful neglect and default the license might be revoked by the plaintiff. The defendants having violated the covenants in the deed of license, the plaintiff exercised his right to revoke the license, and the court restrained them from selling any more goods under the license, as they had by their acts forfeited the license. "Although," said Shadwell, V. C. (*g*), "it may be perfectly true that if the plaintiff instead of giving the notice of revocation, which by the terms of the license deed he was authorized to give, had brought an action against the defendants, he might not have recovered damages; yet I apprehend that according to the principles of a court of equity, that circumstance has nothing whatever to do with his right to determine the license." So, also, and upon the same principle, the court would not relieve a lessee who, contrary to covenant not to suffer persons to make use of a way over part of the lands demised, had put up a gate at the entrance of the close, and permitted any persons to pass over the way, requiring them to pay (*h*).

There is no sound distinction between the principles of the Court as to relieving against forfeitures in cases of covenants for perpetual renewal, and in ordinary cases (*i*).

* 91   20. * Relief against forfeiture is sometimes sought by a person who is in possession of premises under an agreement for a lease, and before any legal relation exists between him and the owner. The court is always anxious in such cases to create the relation in order that the question of

(*d*) Macher *v.* Foundling Hospital, 1 V. & B. 188.
(*e*) Elliott *v.* Turner, 13 Sim. 475.
(*f*) *Ib.*
(*g*) *Ib.* 488.
(*h*) Descarlett *v.* Dennett, 9 Mod. 23.

(*i*) Job *v.* Banister, 2 K. & J. 374; on appeal, 26 L. J. Ch. 125, 3 Jur. N. S. 93; Murphy *v.* Jackson, 7 Ir. Ch. 189. But see Earl of Ross *v.* Worsop, 1 Bro. P. C. 281.

forfeiture may be tried (*k*). The usual course is to decree specific performance of the agreement for the lease, and either to antedate it, or to prevent the lessee from setting up the date so as to defeat an action at law (*l*). The court will not, however, in general grant a specific performance of an agreement on which it is satisfied that forfeiture will be the consequence. But when parties set up the consequence of forfeiture as against the right to specific performance, the court must be well satisfied that forfeiture would follow upon the agreement being decreed to be specifically performed (*m*). The court will also look to the fact by whose act and by whose conduct that forfeiture would be entailed. The conduct of the party who resists specific performance, may have been such as to prevent him from setting up the case of forfeiture as an answer to the case of the other party for specific performance of the agreement (*n*).

21. Though the rule of a court of equity in refusing to relieve against forfeiture for breach of covenant is in all ordinary cases very strict, the intervention of circumstances of a special and peculiar nature may raise an equity for the interference of the court. Mere accidental neglect to perform the covenants is not a ground for relief. A man who is charged with a legal obligation, and neglects to perform it, cannot have relief against the consequences of his neglect (*o*); but a neglect or omission, which arises from unavoidable accident, surprise, or mistake, may sometimes be relieved against (*p*). Thus where a lessee * was prevented by the state of the weather from completing the repairs of the premises within the prescribed time, and no notice was given to him by the lessor that the repairs should be expedited, an action of ejectment was re- *92

(*k*) Gregory *v.* Wilson, 9 Ha. 683; Parker *v.* Taswell, 2 D. & J. 559.

(*l*) Pain *v.* Coombs, 1 D. & J. 34; Lillie *v.* Legh, 3 D. & J. 210; Ranken *v.* Lay, 2 D. F. & J. 72. See Parker *v.* Taswell, 2 D. & J. 559; Poyntz *v.* Fortune, 27 Beav. 393.

(*m*) Gourlay *v.* Duke of Somerset, 1 V. & B. 68; Lovat *v.* Lord Ranelagh, 3 V. & B. 29; Lewis *v.* Bond, 18 Beav. 87; Gregory *v.* Wilson, 9 Ha. 688; Helling *v.* Lumley, 28 L. J. Ch. 249.

(*n*) Helling *v.* Lumley, 28 L. J. Ch. 249.

(*o*) Gregory *v.* Wilson, 9 Ha. 689; *supra*, p. 55.

(*p*) Eaton *v.* Lyon, 3 Ves. 690; Hill *v.* Barclay, 18 Ves. 62; Reynolds *v.* Pitt, 19 Ves. 142; Hannam *v.* South London Waterworks Co., 2 Mer. 65, n.; Firman *v.* Lord Ormonde, Beat. 347; Gregory *v.* Wilson, 9 Ha. 689; Shearman *v.* Macgregor, 11 Ha. 106.

7

strained by injunction (*q*). So, also, relief will be given where the person who seeks to enforce the forfeiture has stood by, and has by his conduct encouraged the other party in laying out moneys on the property (*r*), or a case of fraud can be made out (*s*). In Hannam *v.* South London Waterworks Co. (*t*), there was neither fraud, neglect, or surprise, but relief was granted under the peculiar circumstances of the case (*u*).

22. The right to enforce a forfeiture for a breach of covenant may be lost by waiver or acquiescence. The acceptance of rents or moneys due after notice of a breach of covenant, is, at law, a waiver of any breach committed prior to the acceptance (*x*), and will be taken to be a regular payment, if the person receives it without making any objection (*y*). So, also, is the bringing an action for rent subsequently to a breach of covenant with full knowledge of its existence a waiver of a forfeiture (*z*). If the covenant be a continuing one, such as a covenant to keep insured (*a*), to repair (*b*), or not to underlet (*c*). The acceptance of rent or moneys due is a waiver only of the breaches previous to the receipt. The right of re-entry or for-
* 93   feiture, however, for * any subsequent breach of the covenant is not affected by the acceptance (*d*). Nor will the acceptance of rent or moneys due operate as a waiver, if the lessor or acceptor is ignorant of the act of forfeiture (*e*). Nor, where there is a covenant in a lease against carrying on certain trades, does the waiver of the covenant as to one trade operate as a waiver as to the others (*f*). But a breach of a covenant not to trade with him without the knowledge of the

(*q*) Bargent *v.* Thompson, 4 Giff. 475. See Bamford *v.* Creasy, 3 Giff. 675.

(*r*) Meek *v.* Carter, 4 Jur. N. S. 992; North Staffordshire, &c., &c., Steel Co. *v.* Camoys, 11 Jur. N. S. 555; Burke *v.* Prior, 15 Ir. Ch. 106; Shearman *v.* Macgregor, 11 Ha. 106. See Lennon *v.* Napper, 2 Sch. & Lef. 682.

(*s*) Waring *v.* Manchester, Sheffield, and Lincolnshire Railroad Co., 2 H. & Tw. 239.

(*t*) 2 Mer. 65, n.

(*u*) See also Earl of Ross *v.* Worsop, 1 Bro. P. C. 281.

(*x*) Algar *v.* Murrell, 6 Jur. 776; Doe *v.* Gladwin, 6 Q. B. 953; Gregory *v.* Wilson, 9 H. 688; Havens *v.* Middleton, 10 Ha. 645; Wing *v.* Harvey, 5 D. M. & G. 265; Bridges *v.* Longman, 24 Beav. 27.

(*y*) Norton *v.* Wood, 1 R. & M. 178; Wing *v.* Harvey, 5 D. M. & G. 265; Croft *v.* Lumley, 6 H. L. 672.

(*z*) Dendy *v.* Nicholl, 4 C. B. N. S. 376.

(*a*) Doe *v.* Peck, 1 B. & A. 428.

(*b*) Doe *v.* Jones, 5 Exch. 498; Martin *v.* Clue, 22 L. J. Q. B. 147.

(*c*) Doe *v.* Bliss, 4 Taunt. 735.

(*d*) Doe *v.* Peck, 1 B. & A. 428; Anderson *v.* Bailey, 1 Russ. 316; Gregory *v.* Wilson, 9 Ha. 683.

(*e*) Doe *v.* Harrison, 2 T. R. 425.

(*f*) Macher *v.* Foundling Hospital, 1 V. & B. 188.

lessor, and an enjoyment for twenty years, is evidence from which a jury may presume license as against the assignee of the lessor (*g*). The principle that a landlord who receives rent from a tenant after a breach of covenant in a lease which the landlord is, by a proviso in the lease, entitled to look on as a forfeiture, is precluded from insisting on the forfeiture, applies as between the owner of a patent and a licensee (*h*).

23. As courts of law, in questions of forfeiture for breach of covenant, regard the substantial and not the literal performance of the contract, a court of equity is not often called upon to interfere on the ground of waiver or acquiescence to control the legal right of a lessor, or other person entitled to enforce a forfeiture. There may, however, be cases in which a landlord has so dealt with a tenant as to have created an equity against himself sufficiently strong to control his legal right, but a strong case will be required for the purpose. There must be fraud, or such a degree of acquiescence, on the part of the landlord, as in the view of the court would make it a fraud in him afterwards to insist upon his legal right (*i*). The ultimate right which the court has to deal with, is the legal right, and a case must be made out which would justify the court in dealing with that right (*k*). In Hillier *v.* Parkinson (*l*), where a lessor had * waived breaches of covenant on   * 94 the part of his lessee, Lord Lyndhurst would not extend the benefit of the waiver to sub-lessees holding under the lessee, and refused to restrain the lessee from executing a judgment in ejectment against his sub-lessee.

24. But although relief in equity may be obtained against a forfeiture, where the person incurring it has been misled by the person legally entitled to insist upon it, relief will not be given against a subsequent forfeiture, where no such excuse can be alleged. Thus, although relief may be had against the forfeiture of a lease, during a period in which the landlord has

(*g*) Gibson *v.* Doeg, 2 H. & N. 615.
(*h*) Warwick *v.* Hooper, 3 Mac. & G. 60.
(*i*) Gregory *v.* Wilson, 9 Ha. 688, 690; Att.-Gen. *v.* Briggs, 1 Jur. N. S. 1084; Gerrard *v.* O'Reilly, 3 Dr. & War. 414; Johnstone *v.* Hall, 2 K. & J. 414;

Burke *v.* Prior, 15 Ir. Ch. 106. See Blennerhasset *v.* Day, 2 B. & B. 104; Meek *v.* Carter, 4 Jur. N. S. 992.
(*k*) Gregory *v.* Wilson, 9 Ha. 688, 690. See Wing *v.* Harvey, 5 D. M. & G. 265; Johnstone *v.* Hall, 2 K. & J. 414.
(*l*) 9 L. J. Ch. 156.

dealt with the tenant, so as to lead him to suppose the forfeiture would not be insisted on, if a subsequent forfeiture is incurred after such dealings have ceased, the prior transaction will raise no equity for relief (*m*).

25. If it be doubtful whether there has been a breach of covenant, and whether, if there has been a breach, there has not been a waiver of that breach, the court will, on restraining proceedings in ejectment, either direct an issue to try first whether there has been a forfeiture; and, secondly, if there has been a forfeiture, whether the lessor has not done any act to disentitle himself from taking proceedings, or will itself examine witnesses, *vivâ voce*, as to either or both of these facts (*n*).

A man who seeks relief in equity against a forfeiture should use due diligence in making the application (*o*).

26. In the deeds of settlement of companies, or other public undertakings, there is generally inserted a stipulation that the shares shall be forfeited in the event of the non-payment of calls at the times appointed. Punctual payment being necessary in order to accomplish the corporate objects, equity will not grant relief against forfeiture. Thus Sir William Grant, M. R., refused to relieve against a forfeiture under the by-law of an incorporated company for waterworks, which pro-
*95   vided that the *members receiving notice of default in paying a call should incur forfeiture by non-payment ten days after, although the non-payment arose from ignorance of the call, absence from town when the notice was sent, and other circumstances (*p*). But there is no inherent power in the directors, or a general meeting of the shareholders of a company, to declare a forfeiture of shares. If there is no clause in the deed of settlement, or the Act of Parliament, or the charter conferring on the directors a power of forfeiture, they have no power to do so; nor can the power be conferred on them by a

---

(*m*) Flattery *v.* Anderdon, 12 Ir. Eq. 218. See Meek *v.* Carter, 4 Jur. N. S. 992.

(*n*) Thompson *v.* Guyon, 5 Sim. 65; Algar *v.* Murrell, 6 Jur. 775; Nokes *v.* Gibbon, 3 Drew. 681.

(*o*) Home *v.* Thompson, Sau. & Sc.

615; Prendergast *v.* Turton, 1 Y. & C. C. C. 98; 13 L. J. Ch. N. S. 268. See Lennon *v.* Napper, 2 Sch. & Lef. 682.

(*p*) Sparks *v.* Liverpool Waterworks Co., 13 Ves. 433. See Naylor *v.* South Devon Railway Co., 1 De G. & Sm. 32.

majority of the shareholders. A company has no power to declare a forfeiture except it be authorized by the rules, or the deed of settlement (*q*). A forfeiture of shares is *strictissimi juris*. The power must, in order to be effectually exercised, be pursued with great exactness, and must be exercised with perfect *bona fides*, and the evidence to establish the right must be clear and distinct (*r*). The exercise of the power will be closely scanned by a court of equity. In Norman *v.* Mitchell (*s*) and Watson *v.* Eales (*t*), injunctions were granted to restrain the carrying into effect of declarations of forfeiture of shares. If, however, the declaration of forfeiture, though not strictly regular, has complied substantially with the requisitions of the deed of settlement, it will be held good (*u*).

The same rule of refusing relief applies to the case of government loans where the shares of the stock are agreed to be forfeited, in the event of the want of punctual compliance with the terms of the loan, as to the time, and mode, and place of payment (*v*).

27. The same principles apply to the case of a contractor who has agreed to execute the public works of a company, and has bound himself for the due performance of his contract by forfeitures, *and has subjected himself to the arbitrary decision of a person nominated by his employers as to his liability thereto (*x*).   * 96

28. Under the old law no relief could be had in equity against the forfeiture of the legal title to a ship, where the forms prescribed by the Ship Registry Act had not been complied with. The court had no jurisdiction to interfere with the legal title of the registered owner of a ship even in cases of fraud (*y*). The jurisdiction which the court did not possess under the old law was not given by the Merchant Shipping

---

(*q*) Hart *v.* Clark, 6 D. M. & G. 248; Barton's case, 4 D. & J. 46.

(*r*) Richmond's case, 4 K. & J. 305; Stubbs *v.* Lister, 1 Y. & C. C. C. 97; Clark *v.* Hart, 6 H. L. 633, 6 D. M. & G. 248.

(*s*) 5 D. M. & G. 648.

(*t*) 23 Beav. 294.

(*u*) Wollaston's case, 4 D. & J. 437. See further on the subject of the for-feiture of shares, Lindley on Partnership, pp. 616–621.

(*v*) Sparks *v.* Proprietors of Liverpool Waterworks, 13 Ves. 433.

(*x*) Ranger *v.* Great Western Railway Co., 2 Jur. 787, 1031.

(*y*) Follett *v.* Delany, 2 De G. & S. 235; Hughes *v.* Morris, 2 D. M. & G. 354; M'Calmont *v.* Rankin, *ib.* 413; Parr *v.* Applebee, 7 D. M. & G. 591.

Acts, 1854 and 1855, 17 & 18 Vict. c. 104, or 18 & 19 Vict. c. 91. An agreement to sell or mortgage a ship, which did not satisfy the condition prescribed by those acts, was held not to pass any interest or to constitute a contract which the court could specifically perform (z). But by the Merchant Shipping Act, 1862, 25 & 26 Vict. c. 68, s. 3, it was enacted that equities arising under contract or otherwise may be enforced against the owners or mortgagees of the ship in respect of their interest therein, in the same manner as equities may be enforced against them in respect of any other personal property (a). Though, however, the court had no jurisdiction under the old law to relieve against the forfeiture of the legal title to a ship, where the forms prescribed by the Registry Acts had not been complied with, equitable relief could be given as between two parties, one of whom had the better equity, where the form prescribed by the Registry Acts had been, as far as circumstances would admit, complied with, and could be fully complied with by the interposition of the court (b). Accordingly the owner of a vessel, who had made a mortgage of it, and had repossessed himself of the bill of sale, was restrained from obtaining the certificate of registry, and from doing any act to prevent the mortgagee from procuring his bill of sale to be indorsed on the certificate (c).

* 97　　29. * Where a penalty or forfeiture is imposed by act of Parliament upon the doing or omission to do a certain act, relief cannot be had in equity, but the court will see that the proceedings making the forfeiture have been regular and *bonâ fide* (d). The same principle applies to cases of forfeiture founded on the customs of manors, and the general customs of certain kinds of estates such as copyholds, for in all these cases the forfeiture is treated as properly founded upon some positive law or some customary regulations, which had their origin in sound policy, and ought to be enforced for

---

(z) Liverpool Borough Bank v. Turner, 1 J. & H. 159, 2 D. F. & J. 502.

(a) See Lacon v. Liffen, 4 Giff. 75; Stapleton v Haymen, 2 H. & C. 918.

(b) Thompson v. Smith, 1 Madd. 395.

(c) *Ib.*

(d) Nesbitt v. Tredennick, 1 B. & B. 29; Keating v. Sparrow, *ib.* 373, 374; Blennerhasset v. Day, 2 B. & B. 125; Hughes v. Howard, 25 Beav. 575.

the general benefit (*e*). A court of equity has, however, a concurrent jurisdiction with courts of law to relieve a copyholder against an illegal seizure of the copyhold property by the lord of the manor (*f*).

30. With respect to relief against forfeitures for breach of condition, the same considerations apply as are applicable to the case of forfeitures for breach of covenant. The general rule formerly was that a court of equity would interfere and relieve against the breach of a condition subsequent, provided it was a case admitting of compensation in damages (*g*). But according to the modern doctrine of equity, relief is confined to cases where the value of the thing, for enforcing which the forfeiture is imposed, can be fully and completely estimated and compensated (*h*), and generally the omission and consequent forfeiture should be the result of inevitable accident (*i*).[1] If the omission * is wilful, relief will be   *98 denied (*k*).[2] Nor will relief be given where the condition subsequent is followed by a limitation over to a third person in case the condition be not fulfilled, and there be a breach of it (*l*). Nor will forfeitures under a condition in law which do not admit of compensation, or forfeitures which may be considered as limitations of the estate, and which determine it, when they happen be relieved against (*m*). If therefore a tenant for life makes a greater estate than his own, or if a tenant by copy affect to convey a greater estate than by law he

---

(*e*) Peachy *v.* Duke of Somerset, 1 Str. 447, 453; Pre. Ch. 568, 570, 574; Cox *v.* Higford, 2 Vern. 664; but see Nash *v.* Earl of Derby, 2 Vern. 537; Thomas *v.* Porter, 1 Ch. Ca. 95; Hill *v.* Barclay, 18 Ves. 64.

(*f*) Litton's case, Cary, 8; Andrews *v.* Hulse, 4 K. & J. 392.

(*g*) Popham *v.* Bampfield, 1 Vern. 83; Hayward *v.* Angell, *ib.* 222; Northcote *v.* Duke, Amb. 512; Cage *v.* Russell, 2 Vent. 352.

(*h*) Hill *v.* Barclay, 18 Ves. 56; Bracebridge *v.* Buckley, 2 Pri. 200; Rolfe *v.* Harris, *ib.* 207, n. See Cage *v.* Russell, 2 Vent. 352; Woodman *v.* Blake, 2 Vern. 222; Barnardiston *v.* Fane, *ib.* 366; Grimston *v.* Lord Bruce, *ib.* 594.

(*i*) Hill *v.* Barclay, 18 Ves. 56; Bracebridge *v.* Buckley, 2 Pri. 200;

Rolfe *v.* Harris, *ib.* 207. n. Comp. Cage *v.* Russell, 2 Vent. 352, Barnardiston *v.* Fane, 2 Vern. 366; Grimston *v.* Lord Bruce, *ib.* 594.

(*k*) Bracebridge *v.* Buckley, 2 Pri. 200. Comp. Cage *v.* Russell, 2 Vent. 352. See *per* Lord Eldon, 19 Ves. 140.

(*l*) Simpson *v.* Vickers, 14 Ves. 341.

(*m*) Keating *v.* Sparrow, 1 B. & B. 373; Nesbitt *v.* Tredennick, *ib.* 29. See Peachy *v.* Duke of Somerset, 1 Str. 447.

[1] This subject is carefully discussed in Henry *v.* Tupper, 29 Vt. 358. See also Harris *v.* Troup, 8 Paige, 425; Dunklee *v.* Adams, 20 Vt. 415; Wells *v.* Smith, 2 Edw. Ch. 78; Livingston *v.* Tompkins, 4 John. Ch. 431.

[2] Dunklee *v.* Adams, 20 Vt. 415.

may, he forfeits his estate, and can have no relief in equity (n).

31. Conditions precedent must be literally performed. A court of equity will not vest an estate, where, by reason of the non-performance of a condition precedent, it will not vest at law. The court cannot relieve from the consequences of a condition precedent unperformed (o), unless the party who takes the estate on non-performance of the condition has used an indirect practice or contrivance to prevent its performance (p). Infancy is not allowed as an excuse for not performing a condition precedent (q).

32. There is no equity, except under very special circumstances, to restrain a man from committing a forfeiture. The court, for instance, would not restrain a man from forfeiting his life estate by not adopting the name and arms of a testator (r). The court has jurisdiction at the suit of a shareholder to restrain a company incorporated by letters patent or royal charter, from doing an act which would occasion a forfeiture of the charter (s).

---

* 99   * SECTION IX. — EQUITABLE ASSIGNMENT.

1. Assignment of chose in action valid in equity. What constitutes such assignment.
2. Assignment of future acquired property valid in equity.
3. Notice to debtor of assignment necessary as against subsequent *bonâ fide* purchasers.
4. Assignments by officers in the public service of pay and salaries not valid.

1. At common law, a possibility or chose in action is not assignable (t), but in equity, assignments of a mere possibility or chose in action for valuable consideration, are valid and

---

(n) Peachy v. Duke of Somerset, *ib.*
(o) Popham v. Bampfield, 1 Vern. 83; Cary v. Bertie, 2 Vern. 333; Harvey v. Aston, 1 Atk. 361; Reynish v. Martin, 3 Atk. 330; Scott v. Tyler, 2 Bro. C. C. 431.
(p) Cary v. Bertie, 2 Vern. 342.

(q) Cary v. Bertie, 2 Vern. 333. See Ledward v. Hassells, 2 K. & J. 370.
(r) Semple v. Holland, 33 Beav. 94.
(s) Rendall v. Crystal Palace Co., 4 K. & J. 326.
(t) 10 Co. Rep. 48.

binding (*u*), and will be protected by injunction (*x*). To constitute an equitable assignment, no particular form or words are necessary (*y*). Any order, writing, or act, which makes an appropriation of a fund amounts to an equitable assignment (*z*). An order by a debtor to his creditor upon a person owing money, or holding funds, or goods belonging to the giver of the order, directing such person to pay such moneys, or funds, or to deliver such goods to the creditor, operates in equity as an assignment of the moneys, funds, or goods to which the order refers (*a*). The consent of the party from whom the debt is due, or on whom the order is made to pay the moneys, or to deliver the goods, is not necessary (*b*). A mere mandate, however, by a principal to his agent, to pay over moneys to a creditor of the party giving the order, does not operate as an assignment, unless the order has been communicated to the creditor (*c*). Nor does a mere power of attorney, or authority to a person to receive money, and directing him to pay it to a creditor of the party giving the
* authority, amount to an equitable assignment (*d*).   * 100
Where, however, a creditor in whose behalf a stake has been deposited by the debtor with a third person, receives notice of that fact from the stakeholder, the notice will convert the stakeholder into an agent for, and a debtor to, the creditor (*e*).

2. At law, a deed which professes to assign property which

(*u*) *Anon.*, Freem. Ch. 144; Squib *v.* Wyn, 1 P. Wms. 381.

(*x*) L'Estrange *v.* L'Estrange, 13 Beav. 281; Knight *v.* Bulkeley, 27 L. J. Ch. 592; Lloyd *v.* Eagle, 28 L. J. Ch. 389; Webster *v.* Webster, 31 Beav. 393; Marsh *v.* Peacock, 9 Jur. N. S. 789.

(*y*) Row *v.* Dawson, 1 Ves. 331; Malcolm *v.* Scott, 3 Ha. 39, 52.

(*z*) Thompson *v.* Spiers, 13 Sim. 469; Burn *v.* Carvalho, 4 M. & C. 690; Cook *v.* Black, 1 Ha. 390; M'Fadden *v.* Jenkyns, *ib.* 458, 1 Ph. 153; Malcolm *v.* Scott, 3 Ha. 39, 52, 6 Ha. 576; Swayne *v.* Swayne, 11 Beav. 466; L'Estrange *v.* L'Estrange, 13 Beav. 281; Myers *v.* United Guarantee, &c., Co., 7 D. M. & G. 112; Lambe *v.* Orton, 1 De G. & Sm. 128.

(*a*) Burn *v.* Carvalho, 4 M. & C. 702;

Ex parte South, 3 Sw. 393; L'Estrange *v.* L'Estrange, 13 Beav. 281; Diplock *v.* Hammond, 2 Sm. & G. 141, 5 D. M. & G. 320; Rayner *v.* Harford, 27 L. J. Ch. 709; Riccard *v.* Prichard, 1 K. & J. 277; Jones *v.* Farrell, 1 D. & J. 208. See Rodick *v.* Gandell, 1 D. M. & G. 763, 778.

(*b*) Row *v.* Dawson, 1 Ves. 331; *Ex parte* South, 3 Sw. 392; Morrell *v.* Wootten, 16 Beav. 197.

(*c*) Scott *v.* Porcher, 3 Mer 652; Morrell *v.* Wootten, 16 Beav. 197. See L'Estrange *v.* L'Estrange, 13 Beav. 281; Glyn *v.* Hood, 1 Giff. 328 Webster *v.* Webster, 31 Beav. 393.

(*d*) Rodick *v.* Gandell, 1 D. M. & G. 763. See Bell *v.* North Western Railway Co., 15 Beav. 548; Holroyd *v.* Griffiths, 3 Drew. 428.

(*e*) Kirwan *v.* Daniel, 5 Ha. 500.

is not in existence at the time of the assignment, is void (*f*). But in equity, if a man agrees to assign property of which he is not possessed at the time, and afterwards becomes possessed of property answering the description in the agreement, the beneficial interest in the property passes to the assignee immediately on the acquisition of the property (*g*). If the assignment is by way of mortgage, and the assignor afterwards attempts to remove any part of such property, except for the purpose of substitution, the mortgagee is entitled to an injunction to restrain such removal (*h*). In order, however, that an agreement to assign after-acquired property may amount to an actual assignment, it must purport to confer an interest in the future chattels immediately by its own force, and without the necessity of a further act on the part of the assignee, upon the future chattels coming into existence (*i*).

3. As between the parties themselves, an equitable assignment is binding without more: notice to the person on whom the order is made, or in whose hands the property lies, is not necessary (*k*). But as against purchasers for value the title is not perfect, unless notice of the assignment be given to the debtor, or other person who is in possession of the fund or property in question (*l*), or unless, at least, every thing * 101   be done that can be * reasonably expected to be done, in order to bring the fact to his knowledge (*m*). An equitable assignment, not duly perfected by notice, will not prevail as against subsequent assignees for value, with notice to the person who is in possession of the fund or property to which the notice relates. If an assignee fail to give notice, and a

---

(*f*) Robinson *v.* Macdonnell, 5 M. & S. 228.

(*g*) Curtis *v.* Auber, 1 J. & W. 526; Metcalfe *v.* Archbishop of York, 1 M. & C. 547; Wellesley *v.* Wellesley, 4 M. & C. 579; Douglas *v.* Russell, 1 M. & K. 488; Langton *v.* Horton, 1 Ha. 549; Holroyd *v.* Marshall, 10 H. L. 191, 211; Brown *v.* Bateman, 36 L. J. C. P. 134.

(*h*) Holroyd *v.* Marshall, 10 H. L. 191, 211, *per* Lord Westbury.

(*i*) Reeve *v.* Whitmore, 33 L. J. Ch. 63. See Belding *v.* Read, 3 H. & C. 955.

(*k*) Cook *v.* Black, 1 Ha. 390; Rodick

v. Gandell, 1 D. M. & G. 763; Wheatley *v.* Bastow, 7 D. M. & G. 261, 278; Kinderley *v.* Jervis, 22 Beav. 1; Justice *v.* Wynne, 12 Ir. Ch. 289.

(*l*) Dearle *v.* Hall, 3 Russ. 1; Foster *v.* Blackstone, 1 M. & K. 297, S. C., as Foster *v.* Cockerell, 9 Bligh, 332; Gardner *v.* Lachlan, 4 M. & C. 129; Meux *v.* Bell, 1 Ha. 73; Stocks *v.* Dobson, 4 D. M. & G. 11. See as to notice of assignment of freight, Brown *v.* Tanner, 2 L. R. Eq. 806.

(*m*) Etty *v.* Bridges, 2 Y. & C. C. C. 486; Feltham *v.* Cooke, 1 De G. & S. 307; Langton *v.* Horton, 1 Ha. 549.

subsequent assignee give notice, and neither the assignee giving notice, nor the person in possession of the fund or property to which the notice relates has, at the time of such notice being given, notice of the prior assignment, the assignee giving such notice obtains priority, although he may have advanced his money without making any previous inquiry (*n*).

4. There are certain cases in which assignments of choses in action cannot, on grounds of public policy, be sustained in equity. The pay and salaries of public officers payable to them for the purpose of supporting the dignity of their office, or to assure a due discharge of their duties, and in contemplation of future services, such as the pay, half-pay, and commission of an officer in the army or navy (*o*), and the salaries of persons in the civil service (*p*), are accordingly not assignable (*q*). The same doctrine applies to the case of compensations granted to a * public officer on the abolition   * 102 of his office, who, by the terms of the grant, may be required to return to the public service (*r*). But a man who is under no continuing duty to render future services may assign a pension given to him entirely for past services, whether granted to him for life or merely during the pleasure of others (*s*). A pension, however, is not assignable which has been granted as a perpetual memorial for public services (*t*). A pension granted to an officer or other person in the army, or his widow, has been declared not assignable by 47 Geo. III.

(*n*) Dearle *v.* Hall, 3 Russ. 1; Loveridge *v.* Cooper, *ib.* 30; Foster *v.* Blackstone, 1 M. & K. 297, S. C.; Foster *v.* Cockerell, 9 Bligh, 332; Meux *v.* Bell, 1 Ha. 84; Browne *v.* Savage, 4 Drew. 639; Wilson *v.* Gabriel, 4 B. & S. 243. See as to questions arising between a particular and statutory assignee, Barr's Trust, 4 K. & J. 219; *Re Vickre*, 7 W. R. 542; *Re Combe*, *ib.* 609; Bartlett *v.* Bartlett, 1 D. & J. 127; Edwards *v.* Martin, 1 L. R. Eq. 125; Webb's Policy, 36 L. J. Ch. 349. See further as to notice, White *v.* Tudor, L. C. vol. ii. p. 672.

(*o*) Barwick *v.* Reade, 1 H. Bl. 627; Flarty *v.* Odlum, 3 T. R. 681; Stone *v.* Liddisdale, 3 Anst. 533; Lidderdale *v.* Duke of Montrose, 4 T. R. 248; Collyer *v.* Fallon, T. & R. 459.

(*p*) Cooper *v.* Reilly, 2 Sim. 560;

Palmer *v.* Bate, 6 Moo. 28, 2 B. & B. 673. See Hill *v.* Paul, 8 Cl. & Fin. 295. Comp. Arbuthnot *v.* Norton, 5 Moo. R. C. 219.

(*q*) See Davis *v.* Duke of Marlborough, 1 Sw. 74; Wells *v.* Foster, 8 M. & W. 149.

(*r*) Wells *v.* Foster, 8 M. & W. 149. See Spooner *v.* Payne, 1 D. M. & G. 383.

(*s*) Wells *v.* Foster, 8 M. & W. 149; Tunstall *v.* Boothby, 10 Sim. 542, 9 L. J. Ch. N. S. 294; Spooner *v.* Payne, 1 D. M. & G. 383; Lloyd *v.* Eagle, 28 L. J. Ch. 389. See Davis *v.* Duke of Marlborough, 1 Sw. 74; Alexander *v.* Duke of Wellington, 2 R. & M. 35; Hall *v.* Lack, 7 Jur. 527.

(*t*) Davis *v.* Duke of Marlborough, 1 Sw. 74. See Grenfell *v.* Dean and Canons of Windsor, 2 Beav. 544.

c. 25, s. 4. Where, therefore, an officer in the Royal Artillery had assigned for value a pension granted to him on his leaving the service, the court would not restrain from applying for or receiving the pension (*u*). The act does not apply to pensions granted to officers in the East India Company's service, who have retired before (*x*) or since (*y*) the passing of the East India Act, 1858 (*z*). Nor does the act apply to a pension for wounds; a pension of the sort is assignable (*a*).

An officer in the army, although he cannot assign or mortgage his commission, may charge the moneys to arise from the sale of it (*b*), or the difference received by him upon retiring on half-pay (*c*).

—

*103   *SECTION X.— THE PREVENTION OF VEXATIOUS LITIGATION.

Election between Suit and Action.

1. Court of equity will restrain unnecessary litigation. Practice.

Injunctions after the Court is in Possession of a Cause.

2. While court of equity has possession of a cause, neither party can proceed at law.
3. Illustrations of this rule.
4. Injunctions granted on motion during progress of suit.
5. Case of mortgagee, only exception to rule that party cannot proceed at law and in equity at same time.
6. Injunctions granted after presentation of a petition for winding up a company, and after filing trust deed under English Bankruptcy Act.
7. Court will not permit a decree to work injury to innocent persons not party to it.

Injunctions against Creditors after Decree for the Administration of Assets.

8. Injunctions granted against creditors after decree for the administration of assets.
9–14. Practice in such cases.
15. Creditor who has recovered judgment before decree, will not be deprived of the fruits of his superior diligence.
16. Executor may lose his right to an injunction.
17. Effect of pleas at law to actions against executors.
18. Practice in the different forms of judgment.
19. The same doctrine which obtains in the case of actions against executors will be acted on in the case of the heir.

(*u*) Lloyd *v.* Cheetham, 3 Giff, 171.
(*x*) Heald *v.* Hay, *ib.* 467.
(*y*) Carew *v.* Cooper, 4 Giff. 619.
(*z*) See as to the power of the Court of Bankruptcy to order part of the pay or pension of officers in the military or civil service to be paid to their assignees in bankruptcy, 24 & 25 Vict. c. 134, s. 134.

(*a*) Knight *v.* Bulkeley, 27 L. J. Ch. 592, 5 Jur. N. S. 817.
(*b*) L'Estrange *v.* L'Estrange, 13 Beav. 281; Webster *v.* Webster, 31 Beav. 393; Buller *v.* Plunkett, 1 J. & H. 441; Somerset *v.* Cox, 33 Beav. 634; Marsh *v.* Peacocke, 9 Jur. N. S. 789.
(*c*) Price *v.* Lovett, 15 Jur. 786. See Bere *v.* Havelock, 15 L. T. 473.

1. The prevention of unnecessary or vexatious litigation is part of the proper office of a court of equity. A court of equity will not permit a man or his estate to be harassed and vexed by undue litigation. The instituting of unnecessary litigation is regarded by the court as against equity and conscience.[1]

Election between Suit and Action.

In accordance with this principle, the court will not permit a man to proceed, both at law and in equity, at the same time

---

[1] Where a right has been repeatedly established at law, or where the same right is subject to be controverted by different persons, a court of equity may put an end to litigation by restraining suits at law and settling the whole controversy, or, if need be, by directing a single trial at law; but the court will not interfere to quiet the possession of a party, where there has been no trial of the right at law and where there is but one adverse claimant. Thompson *v.* Engle, 3 Green, Ch. 271.

in respect of the same demand, but will compel him to elect in which court he will proceed (d). If the court is satisfied that the action and the suit are for the same demand, an order for election is a matter of course (e). The court has a discretion to retain the suit, if the plaintiff proceed with the action. If, however, the proceeding at law is ancillary to that in equity, the court may allow the action to proceed, retaining the bill in the mean time (f).

An injunction should be inserted in the order to elect (g). It seems, however, to be a question whether the order does not operate as an injunction against proceedings in equity or at law from the time when it is served (h), and whether any proceedings, after serving the order, may not be considered as an election to abide by the suit in which it is taken (i).

Injunctions after the Court is in Possession of a Cause.

2. After election to sue in equity, or after a court of equity has been once in possession of a cause, in which it has full power to do justice, a party to the suit may not, whilst proceedings before the court are pending, resort to another tribunal in
*104 respect of * the same matter or the same demand (j).

The rule applies to a plaintiff as well as to a defendant. If a party who has legal rights comes to the court for its aid, he is bound to put his legal rights under the control of the court. After electing to proceed in equity, he may not without leave of the court proceed at law (k). The rule is as much applicable after decree as it is pending the suit, except of course in cases where the right at law arises on an instrument executed under the decree (l). If the court finds it desirable for any special reason to allow proceedings to go on before

---

(d) Consol. Ord. XLII. rr. 5–8; Gedge v. Duke of Montrose, 5 W. R. 537.

(e) Hogue v. Curtis, 1 J. & W. 449; Fennings v. Humphery, 4 Beav. 1. See also as to election, Barker v. Smark, 3 Beav. 64.

(f) Royle v. Wynne, Cr. & Ph. 252.

(g) Set. Decr., 948, 950.

(h) Carwick v. Young, 2 Sw. 243; Fennings v. Humphery, 4 Beav. 1, 7, 8.

(i) Ib.

(j) Mocher v. Reed, 1 Ba. & Be. 318; Wilson v. Wethererd, 2 Mer. 406; Frank v. Basnett, 2 M. & K. 618; Drummond v. Pigou, ib. 168; Glascott v. Lang, 3 M. & C. 457; Brenan v. Preston, 10 Ha. 339, 1 W. R. 172; Phelps v. Prothero, 7 D. M. & G. 734.

(k) Mocher v. Reed, 1 Ba. & Be. 319; Phelps v. Prothero, 7 D. M. & G. 722.

(l) Reynolds v. Nelson, 6 Madd. 290; Phelps v. Prothero, 7 D. M. & G. 722.

another tribunal, leave will be given, or the proceedings will be allowed to go on (*m*). In Bell *v.* O'Reilly (*n*), Lord Redesdale seems to have considered that the proceedings at law, whilst a suit in equity was pending, might be treated as a contempt (*o*).

3. In accordance with this principle, a man who has filed a bill for the specific performance of an agreement is bound, irrespectively of the 21 & 22 Vict. c. 27, to submit his claim for damages to the judgment of the court, and may not proceed at law otherwise than by leave of the court. The fact that the damages may have arisen, in part at least, after the institution of the suit, is unimportant, if there has been ample opportunity of bringing them under the consideration of the court (*p*). So also, and upon the same principle, a man against whom a decree had been made in a suit 'for specific performance was restrained from bringing an action at law against the plaintiff in equity in respect of the non-completion of the contract within the specified time (*q*). So, also, the court will restrain an action at law, the bringing of which is against the spirit, * although not within the   * 105 letter of a former injunction (*r*). Nor can an action for trespass be allowed to proceed after an interlocutory order for delivery up of possession has been obtained (*s*). Nor can a man at the same time file a bill for specific performance and bring an action for use and occupation (*t*). So, also, actions at law for the deposit will not be allowed to proceed pending a suit for specific performance (*u*). So, also, a purchaser of book debts, under the order of the court, being, as a condition of his purchase, entitled to have delivered to him a particular set of account books of which he was unable to obtain possession, was restrained from bringing an action at law to recover

---

(*m*) Frank *v.* Basnett, 2 M. & K. 618; Brenan *v.* Preston, 10 Ha. 339.

(*n*) 2 Sch. & Lef. 430.

(*o*) Mocher *v.* Reed, 1 Ba. & Be. 319. See Phelps *v.* Prothero, 7 D. M. & G. 734.

(*p*) Phelps *v.* Prothero, 7 D. M. & G. 722.

(*q*) Reynolds *v.* Nelson, 6 Madd. 290; Frank *v.* Basnett, 2 M. & K. 618.

(*r*) Brenan *v.* Preston, 1 W. R. 172.

(*s*) Gedge *v.* Duke of Montrose, 5 W. R. 537.

(*t*) Carrick *v.* Young, 4 Madd. 437; Ambrose *v.* Mott, 2 Ha. 649.

(*u*) Levy *v.* Lindo, 3 Mer. 82; Johnson *v.* Smart, 2 Giff. 155; Kell *v.* Nokes, 32 L. J. Ch. 785.

them, on the ground that equity had the matter within its jurisdiction (*x*). So, also, although a solicitor may originally bring an action to recover his costs for business done in a suit in equity, yet, if an order has been obtained for the taxation of the costs in a suit, the court will be held to have assumed jurisdiction in the matter, and will not allow him, after the taxing of the bill, to proceed with the action (*y*).

If the plaintiff has, by tortious means, got into possession of property pending a suit to establish his equitable title to it, the court will not stay proceedings at law against him for the recovery of possession (*z*).

4. The injunction will be granted on motion in the suit (*a*). After a decree has been completely carried into execution, the cause is out of court. A motion for an injunction cannot be made in the cause. Relief can only be granted on a new bill (*b*).

5. The case of a mortgagee is an exception to the * 106   rule that a * man may not proceed at law and in equity at the same time, in respect of the same demand, as long as any thing remains due on the mortgage security. A mortgagee may pursue all his remedies at once. He may proceed on his mortgage in equity, and upon his bond, or covenant, at law, at the same time. If he sues on his bond, or covenant, at law, and does not get fully paid, he may still go on and foreclose the mortgage (*c*).

The case of a mortgagee forms the only exception to the rule. The vendor of an estate, who has taken a bond for the purchase-money, may not at the same time sue in equity for enforcing the lien on the estate, and at law on the bond (*d*). The doctrine that a mortgagee may pursue all his remedies at once, is limited to cases in which the proceedings at law and

---

(*x*) Stubbs *v.* Sargon, 4 Beav. 90.

(*y*) *Re* Bellott, 4 Madd. 379; *Re* Dillon, 2 Sch. & Lef. 110; Walton *v.* Johnson, 2 Sim. 456; Barr *v.* Wiggins, 4 Sim. 125. See as to costs, Carwick *v.* Young, 2 Sw. 242; Royle *v.* Wynne, Cr. & Ph. 252; Simpson *v.* Sadd, 3 W. R. 191.

(*z*) Grafton *v.* Griffin, 1 R. & M. 336.

(*a*) Harrison *v.* Gurney, 2 J. & W.

563; Wedderburn *v.* Wedderburn, 2 Beav. 208.

(*b*) Ford *v.* Compton, 1 Cox, 296.

(*c*) School *v.* Sall, 1 Sch. & Lef. 176; Taylor *v.* Waters, 1 M. & C. 266; Pell *v.* Stephens, 2 M. & K. 339; Lockhart *v.* Hardy, 9 Beav. 349; Willes *v.* Levett, 1 De G. & S. 392; Cockell *v.* Bacon, 16 Beav. 158. See further, *post.*

(*d*) Barker *v.* Smark, 3 Beav. 64.

in equity are both in the same country, and the means of preventing a fraudulent use being made of the multifarious remedies are at hand (e).

6. The court may, at any time after the presentation of a petition for winding up a company, and before making an order for winding up the company, upon the application of any creditor of the company, restrain further proceedings in any action or proceeding against any contributory of the company, or against the company, upon such terms as the court thinks fit (f). And after an order for winding up has been made, no action, or other proceeding, shall be proceeded with against the company, except with the leave of the court (g). The authority of the court to restrain proceedings after a winding up petition has been presented being discretionary, it will not be exercised when a *bonâ fide* action has been prosecuted to judgment (h), or execution * has been perfected by *107 seizure (i), before a petition for winding up has been presented.

After notice of the filing and registration of a trust deed for creditors, or an inspectorship, or composition deed under the Bankruptcy Act, 1861 (k), a judgment creditor may not proceed to execution without leave of the court (l).

7. The court will not permit a decree to work injury to innocent persons not parties to it. Where a decree of the court had given relief to a person whose title was gone at law, the party relieved will not be permitted to take proceedings at law to evict tenants on the premises, they being protected by the decree (m).

(e) Beckford v. Kemble, 1 Sim. & St. 15. See Lord Cranstown v. Johnstone, 3 Ves. 182, 5 Ves. 277 ; Perry v. Barker, 8 Ves. 530, 13 Ves. 204.

(f) 25 & 26 Vict. c. 89, ss. 85, 201.

(g) Ib; ss. 87, 202; Re Waterloo Life Insurance Co., 31 Beav. 589 ; Re Keynsham Co., 33 Beav. 123; Re Life Association of England, 34 L. J. Ch. 64. See as to costs, ib., Marlborough Club, 1 L. R. Eq. 216.

(h) Re London Cotton Co., 2 L. R. Eq. 53.

(i) Ex parte Parry, Re Great Ship Co., 33 L. J. Ch. 245; Re Hill Pottery Co., 1 L. R. Eq. 649.

(k) 24 & 25 Vict. c. 134, ss. 192–197.

(l) Ib. s. 198. See Ex parte Banfield, Re Ellis, 12 Jur. N. S. 37.

(m) Shine v. Gough, 1 B. & B. 444; supra, p. 7.

8

Injunctions against Creditors after Decree for the Administration of Assets.

8. After a decree for the administration of assets, a court of equity will not permit a creditor to institute proceedings at law. The decree is in the nature of a judgment for all the creditors under which they may all come in and obtain payment. The court has, by its decree, the complete control of the estate, and distributes the assets ratably, on the principles of equality, giving effect, however, to any legal rights of preference which any creditor may possess. As courts of law do not take notice of a decree in equity, the court interferes by injunction for the purpose of establishing its decree. The court could not execute its own decree, if it were to permit courts of law to alter the course of payment. To allow a creditor, after such a decree, to institute proceedings for himself, would give rise to great inconvenience and injustice. It would disturb the general principles of distribution which the court is always anxious to enforce, and would leave executors exposed to actions at law after the assets had been taken *108   out of their hands (n). Until a decree has been *made, under which he may come in and prove his debt, a creditor will not be restrained from proceeding at law (o). But from the moment a decree has been made, under which he may come in and prove his debt, a creditor will not be permitted to institute proceedings at law (p). There must, however, be a decree in existence, under which the creditor has a present right to go in and prove his debt. A decree which is only contingently for the common benefit of the creditors, is not sufficient (q). The same principles apply to

(n) 5 H. L. 440, *per* Lord Cranworth; Bank of England *v.* Morrice, 2 Bro. P. C. 465; Paxton *v.* Douglas, 8 Ves. 520; Largan *v.* Bowen, 1 Sch. & Lef. 299; Clarke *v.* Ormonde, Jac. 123; Lee *v.* Park, 1 Keen, 719; Mason *v.* Bogg, 2 M. & C. 448; Pennell *v.* Roy, 3 D. M. & G. 137, 138. Comp. Cockerell *v.* Dickens, 3 Moo. P. C. 98.

(o) Rush *v.* Higgs, 4 Ves. 643; Perry *v.* Phelips, 10 Ves. 40; Largan *v.* Bowen, 1 Sch. & Lef. 296; Ranken *v.* Harwood, 2 Ph. 22; Arnold *v.* Bainbrigge, 2 D. F. & J. 92.

(p) Clarke *v.* Lord Ormonde, Jac. 122; Pennell *v.* Roy, 3 D. M. & G. 138.

(q) Ranken *v.* Harwood, 2 Ph. 22.

the case of a legatee suing for his legacy after a decree for administration (*r*).

9. A decree obtained by one executor for administration against his co-executors, is a decree for the common benefit of all (*s*). An administration order, made on summons under 15 & 16 Vict. c. 86, has the effect of a decree (*t*). But an order for preliminary accounts and inquiries only under Consol. Ord. XX. will not have the effect of a decree (*u*). An executor or administrator may, after obtaining, under 13 & 14 Vict. c. 35, s. 19, an order for an account of the debts and liabilities of a deceased person, and filing a report as therein specified, obtain an injunction to restrain proceedings at law against him by claimants on the estate of the deceased (*x*). The order may be obtained immediately after probate or letters of administration have been granted, and an injunction may be had immediately afterwards (*y*).

10. After notice of a decree for administration of assets, actions *at law of creditors, which stood for *109 trial at the time of the decree, will be restrained (*z*). A person who is in the character of a creditor will be restrained, after decree, from proceeding at law, although he sues for unascertained damages, as upon breaches of a covenant to repair (*a*).

11. After a decree for administration by the Chancery Court of Lancaster, the Lords Justices, as the court of appeal from that court, will restrain a creditor out of the jurisdiction of that court, from bringing an action in one of the superior courts of common law (*b*).

12. The remedy by injunction to restrain a creditor from proceeding at law after a decree for administration, was formerly not given, unless upon bill filed, but an alteration was introduced by Lord Rosslyn (*c*); and the rule is now fully

(*r*) Ratcliffe *v.* Winch, 16 Beav. 576; Molyneux *v.* Scott, 3 Ir. Ch. 291.

(*s*) Macrae *v.* Smith, 2 K. & J. 413.

(*t*) Ratcliffe *v.* Winch, 16 Beav. 576; Brooker *v.* Brooker, 3 Sm. & G. 475.

(*u*) Teague *v.* Richards, 11 Sim. 46; Garner *v.* Briggs, 4 Jur. N. S. 231. See Perry *v.* Phelips, 10 Ves. 40.

(*x*) Sec. 24.

(*y*) 23 & 24 Vict. c. 38, s. 14.

(*z*) Clarke *v.* Lord Ormonde, Jac. 122.

(*a*) Sutton *v.* Mashiter, 2 Sim. 513.

(*b*) 17 & 18 Vict. c. 82, s. 7; Downes *v.* Jackson, 14 W. R. 907.

(*c*) Cleverley *v.* Cleverley, cit. 8 Ves. 520.

established, that an injunction may be obtained upon motion in the suit in which the decree was made after notice given to the creditor (d). The same rule obtains after an order on administration summons (e), or an order under 13 & 14 Vict. c. 35, s. 19, or 23 & 24 Vict. c. 38, s. 14.

13. An injunction to restrain a creditor from proceeding at law, after a decree for administration, may be obtained either by the executor or administrator (f), or by another creditor (g), or by a legatee (h), or by the heir (i).

14. As the practice of granting injunctions in cases of this description might be liable to much abuse by a friendly creditor filing a bill and obtaining a decree, or by connivance between the executor and a creditor, it is the rule of the *110 court not to *grant an injunction restraining a creditor from proceeding at law after a decree, without requiring an affidavit from the executor as to what assets he has in his hands (k). If the affidavit is satisfactory, an injunction will be granted (l): if the affidavit is unsatisfactory, or there is no satisfactory explanation as to the state of the assets, an injunction will be refused (m), or the application will be ordered to stand over until a satisfactory statement has been made (n). If the executor admit assets, the affidavit is not required (o). The rule as to the necessity of an affidavit of assets does not, however, seem to be an absolute one (p). The rule obtains as well where the application is made by legatees, as where it is made by executors or creditors (q).

(d) 5 H. L. 440, per Lord Cranworth; Paxton v. Douglas, 8 Ves. 520; Perry v. Phelips, 10 Ves. 39; Clarke v. Lord Ormonde, Jac. 124.

(e) Gardner v. Garrett, 20 Beav. 469; Brooker v. Brooker, 3 Sm. & G. 475.

(f) Bank of England v. Morrice, 2 Bro. P. C. 465. Paxton v. Douglas, 8 Ves. 520; Vernon v. Thellusson, 1 Ph. 466; Golder v. Golder, 9 Ha. 276.

(g) Brooks v. Reynolds, 1 Bro. C. C. 183, 2 Swanst. 544, n.; Dyer v. Kearsley, 2 Mer. 482, n.; Price v. Evans, 4 Sim. 517.

(h) Clarke v. Lord Ormonde, Jac. 122.

(i) Martin v. Martin, 1 Ves. 211. See Rouse v. Jones, 1 Ph. 462.

(k) Cleverley v. Cleverley, cit. 8 Ves. 520, n.; Paxton v. Douglas, 8 Ves. 520; Gilpin v. Lady Southampton, 18 Ves. 469; Vernon v. Thellusson, 1 Ph. 471; Macrae v. Smith, 2 K. & J. 413; Lawton v. Lawton, 8 W. R. 458.

(l) Vernon v. Thellusson, 1 Ph. 471.

(m) Lee v. Park, 1 Keen, 714.

(n) Pepper v. Foster, 6 Ir. Eq. 384.

(o) Lawton v. Lawton, 8 W. R. 458.

(p) Drewry v. Thacker, 3 Swanst. 546; Ratcliffe v. Winch, 16 Beav. 576.

(q) Clarke v. Lord Ormonde, Jac. 125. See Perry v. Phelips, 10 Ves. 38; Brooks v. Reynolds, 1 Bro. C. C. 183; Jackson v. Leaf, 1 J. & W. 231.

15. Whether, in order to warrant the interference of the court, it is necessary that the decree should have been made before the judgment at law has been obtained, is a subject which has led to some discussion. In Drewry *v.* Thacker (*r*) an executor was protected under the following circumstances: The administratrix had given cognovits to two bond creditors, with stay of execution in the event of payment by instalments at certain times. After default had been made, and decree for administration had been obtained, and the plaintiff had received notice of the decree, the sheriff took in execution the intestate's goods in the hands of the administratrix. Thereupon Leach, V. C., ordered the sheriff to restore the goods on payment of costs, and ordered, further, that if upon the administration of the estate by the court there should be a deficiency of assets to pay the two bond creditors in full, they were to be at liberty to proceed at law against the administratrix, as if the sheriff had returned * *nulla bona præter* the   * 111 sums received by such bond creditors upon the administration of assets. A motion being made before Lord Eldon to discharge the order, he found considerable difficulty in dealing with it, and said he recollected a case in which the court had interfered so far. In the result he did not make any order, so that the order of Leach, V. C., was left undisturbed. His remarks, however, leave it to be inferred that he would hesitate before restraining execution upon a judgment obtained at law before a decree in a creditors' suit was made (*s*). In Egan *v.* Baldwin (*t*), a creditor who had recovered judgment before decree, was restrained from proceeding against the executor after decree. " By the decree," said Macmahon, M. R., " this court has taken possession of the assets of the testator, and deprived the executor of all control over them. The court, therefore, cannot permit him to be sent to jail for not paying out of the assets which are to be administered here. The form of the judgment is of no consequence, nor whether it was before or after decree. The only question is whether it is sought to be enforced after the court is, by the decree, in

(*r*) 3 Swanst. 529.
(*s*) Lee *v.* Park, 1 Keen, 722, *per* De G. & S. 723.
Lord Langdale ; Vincent *v.* Godson,
(*t*) 1 Hog. 190, 2 Moll. 532.

possession of the assets " (*u*). Notwithstanding his remarks in Drewry *v.* Thacker, Lord Eldon, in the subsequent case of Clarke *v.* Lord Ormonde (*x*), said, that " even if the creditor has got a judgment before the decree, though he may come in and prove as such, he must not take out execution." In Lee *v.* Park (*y*), Lord Langdale, adverting to this dictum of Lord Eldon, denied that such was the ordinary rule, and in the case before him refused, upon a review of all the circumstances of the case, to deprive creditors who had recovered judgment before the decree, of the benefit of the judgment (*z*). The general principle, as asserted by Lord Langdale, in Lee *v.* Park, has been confirmed by subsequent authorities; and it may be now considered as the settled rule of the court that a creditor who has been so diligent as to recover judgment at law against

his debtor, or the legal personal representatives of his
*112 debtor, before * a decree for administration, or a decree

in a creditors' suit has been made, will not, except under very special circumstances, be deprived of the benefit of the judgment (*a*). Thus where a creditor who had recovered judgment, and sued out a writ of *fi. fa.* thereupon in the lifetime of the debtor, and placed the writ in the hands of the sheriff the day after the debtor died, but did not proceed to levy under the *fi. fa.* on goods left by the debtor until after a decree had been made for administration of the assets, the court would not restrain him from proceeding to execution (*b*). " At the death of the testator," said Wigram, V. C. (*c*), " supposing the writ to have been in the hands of the sheriff, the judgment creditor had a dominion over the goods paramount to that of the executor. The circumstance that the writ was not put into the hands of the sheriff until the death of the debtor does not make any difference, because the writ, when put into the hands of the sheriff, took effect as from the teste of the writ, and was effectual by means of the proceedings had in the testator's lifetime." On appeal, Lord Cottenham refused

(*u*) 1 Hog. 190, 2 Moll. 532.
(*x*) Jac. 124.
(*y*) 1 Keen, 724.
(*z*) See Vernon *v.* Thellusson, 1 Ph. 466.
(*a*) Ranken *v.* Harwood, 5 Ha. 222;

Larkins *v.* Paxton, 2 Beav. 219; Dollond *v.* Johnson, 2 Sm. & G. 301 ; Fowler *v.* Roberts, 2 Giff. 227. See Nunn *v.* Barlow, 1 Sim. & St. 588.
(*b*) Ranken *v.* Harwood, 5 Ha. 215.
(*c*) *Ib.* 221.

the motion, upon the ground that, from the form of the decree, the creditor had no present right to go in and prove. He expressed no opinion as to whether the writ of execution sued out by the creditor gave him a right to the goods paramount to that of the executor (*d*). So, also, in Vincent *v.* Godson (*e*), the court would not restrain a creditor who had obtained judgment against the executor before a decree in a creditors' suit, but after the filing of the bill, from proceeding to execution on the judgment after the decree had been made. So, also, in Marriage *v.* Skiggs (*f*), where a bill-holder had recovered judgment under the Bills of Exchange Act, 18 & 19 Vict. c. 67, against the executors of the drawer before the bill was proved (no application having been made by them to plead), and had caused execution to be levied, but before sale (the executors having in the mean time proved the will) a creditor * obtained, on summons, an administration decree, the   * 113 court would not restrain further proceedings in the execution. " The money," said Knight Bruce, L. J. (*g*), " was in the hands of the sheriff, at the instance of the creditor, before the decree, and therefore the decree does not, in my opinion, prejudice the right of the plaintiff in the action." So also, in Fowler *v.* Roberts (*h*), a judgment creditor, who had recovered judgment before the decree, was held entitled to enforce his judgment under 17 & 18 Vict. c. 125, s. 61, the Common Law Procedure Act, 1854, against a debtor to the testator's estate.

16. But where, although the decree is prior in time to the judgment at law, the executor has so pleaded as to entitle the plaintiff at law to a judgment to recover his demand *de bonis propriis* (*i*), or has acted in such a manner as to make himself personally liable (*k*), the action against him will be allowed to

---

(*d*) Ranken *v.* Harwood, 5 Ha. 223, 2 Ph. 22.
(*e*) 3 De G. & S. 726.
(*f*) 4 D. & J. 4.
(*g*) Ib.
(*h*) 2 Giff. 227.
(*i*) Brook *v.* Skinner, 2 Mer. 481, n.; Terrewest *v.* Featherby, 2 Mer. 481; Clarke *v.* Lord Ormonde, Jac. 124; Drewry *v.* Thacker, 3 Swanst. 529; Lord *v.* Wormleighton, Jac. 148; Lee *v.*

Park, 1 Keen, 721; Belmore *v.* Belmore, 12 Ir. Eq. 493; Powell *v.* Powell, *ib.* 501; Molyneux *v.* Scott, 3 Ir. Ch. 291; Comp. Bookless *v.* Crummack, C. P. C. 125; Ratcliffe *v.* Winch, 16 Beav. 576.

(*k*) *Re* Higgins' Trust, 2 Giff. 562; Lucas *v.* Williams, 3 Giff. 150, 10 W. R. 606, 677; Molyneux *v.* Scott, 3 Ir. Ch. 291. See Sexton *v.* Smith, 3 De G. & S. 694.

proceed. If the executor has any equity against the action, he must restrain it in the usual way, by instituting a suit for that purpose, and cannot do so upon motion in the suit for administering the assets of the person of whom he is executor (*l*).

17. Some misapprehension has existed in courts of equity as to the effect of pleas at law to actions against executors. In two cases, Brook *v.* Skinner (*m*) and Terrewest *v.* Featherby (*n*), Lord Eldon assumed, incorrectly, that upon the plea of *plene administravit*, if the verdict be found for the plaintiff, the judgment would be *de bonis testatoris et si non de propriis*, and refused an injunction to restrain execution. In the subsequent case, however, of Lord *v.* Wormleighton (*o*), Lord Eldon
* 114   intimated * that he had a wrong notion upon the subject when those decisions were pronounced. And in Vernon *v.* Thellusson (*p*), Lord Lyndhurst considered it to be clear that upon the plea of *plene administravit*, if the verdict be found for the plaintiff, and the plea be falsified, the judgment would be *de bonis testatoris* only, and for a sum not exceeding the value of the goods found by the jury to have come to the hands of the executor (*q*). There are but two cases, according to Mr. Justice Williams (*r*), in which the judgment against an executor is *de bonis testatoris et si non de propriis*, viz., where he pleads a release to himself, or *ne unques executor*. In all other cases, without respect to the plea being false, or even false within the knowledge of the executor, the judgment for the debt or damages is *de bonis testatoris* merely, and for the costs only *de bonis testatoris et si non de propriis*. But as at law every judgment recovered against an executor (except a judgment of assets *in futuro*), whether by default, or demurrer, or upon verdict, whatever may be the nature of the plea, is conclusive on the executor that he has assets to satisfy it, whether the judgment be *de bonis testatoris et si non de propriis*, or *de bonis testatoris* merely, the executor is equally compellable to pay the debt and costs ultimately out of his own pocket, if the assets are deficient. The course of compelling

(*l*) Lucas *v.* Williams, 10 W. R. 606, 677.
(*m*) Cit. 2 Mer. 481.
(*n*) 2 Mer. 480.
(*o*) Jac. 150.
(*p*) 1 Ph. 466.
(*q*) See Williams on Executors, 1773.
(*r*) *Ib.* 1736.

payment is indeed different, for on the former judgment the creditor may have execution *de bonis propriis* forthwith, if no goods can be found by the sheriff, which are the testator's; whereas on the latter judgment, unless the sheriff return a *devastavit* to the *fi. fa.*, the creditor must proceed by *sci. fa.* inquiry, or by action of debt suggesting a *devastavit* (*s*). In all cases where the judgment would be *de bonis testatoris* only, equity will interfere after decree to protect the executor against actions at law, upon the principle, that as the executor would be entitled, in the event of the judgment being satisfied out of his own property, to fall back upon the assets and be satisfied out of them, the result would be that the assets would be withdrawn from the general fund which ought to be distributed by the court for the common * benefit of the * 115 creditors (*t*). The suffering judgment to go against them by default (*u*), the giving in a plea of confession for the judgment (*x*), the putting in pleas, which may be falsified, although done merely for the purpose of gaining time to apply to the court for an injunction (*y*), will not deprive executors of their right to the protection of the court. An executor who has pleaded according to the truth of the case is clearly entitled, when the assets are taken out of his hands and administered by the court, to all the protection which the court can give him against personal liability in respect of the judgment at law (*z*).

18. In Kent *v.* Pickering (*a*), a creditor who had, after the usual decree in a creditors' suit, recovered judgment *de bonis testatoris et si non de propriis* in an action brought against executors, was restrained from proceeding at law against the assets only; but the court would not interpose to protect the executors from any liability to which they might have subjected themselves personally. The same doctrine was stated and

---

(*s*) Williams on Executors, 1774.
(*t*) Vernon *v.* Thellusson, 1 Ph. 466; Belmore *v.* Belmore, 12 Ir. Eq. 493; Powell *v.* Powell, *ib.* 501; Molyneux *v.* Scott, 3 Ir. Ch. 291.
(*u*) Dyer *v.* Kearsley, 2 Mer. 482, n.; Belmore *v.* Belmore, 12 Ir. Eq. 493.
(*x*) Quin *v.* Bagnall, 1 Ir. Eq. 110. See Kirby *v.* Barton, 8 Beav. 45.

(*y*) Lord *v.* Wormleighton, Jac. 148; Fielden *v.* Fielden, 1 Sim. & St. 256; Lee *v.* Park, 1 Keen, 726; Kirby *v.* Barton, 8 Beav. 45; Vernon *v.* Thellusson, 1 Ph. 466.
(*z*) Gaunt *v.* Taylor, 2 Ha. 413.
(*a*) 5 Sim. 569.

acted on in Burles v. Popplewell (b). In the Executors and Administrators (c), Mr. Justice Williams considers that an injunction in the special form in which it was granted in Kent v. Pickering proceeded on an incorrect assumption of the nature of a judgment in that form, inasmuch as the creditor must have resorted, and have resorted in vain, to the assets before he can have recourse to the executor's property and person. In Vernon v. Thellusson (d), Lord Lyndhurst appears in some measure to concede that if the judgment in that case had been *de bonis testatoris et si non de propriis*, the principle upon which the injunction was granted would have been inapplicable.

But the soundness of the distinction seems to be doubt-
*116 ful. The better * opinion would seem to be, that whether the judgment be *de bonis propriis* or *de bonis testatoris et si non de propriis*, a court of equity will in either case restrain execution upon a judgment against executors prosecuted after notice of decree. At law, an executor being compellable to pay the debt whether the judgment be *de bonis testatoris* or *de bonis testatoris et si non de propriis*, there is no principle upon which the court should interfere in the one case and decline to interfere in the other. The protection of the assets is in either case the ground of the interference of the court. If the judgment is in the form *de bonis testatoris et si non*, as to the costs only, *de propriis* against the executor, the court will of course not interfere. Mr. Justice Williams suggests that the judgment in Kent v. Pickering may have been in that form (e).

19. The same doctrine which obtains in the case of actions against executors will be acted on in the case of the heir. In Price v. Evans (f), the heir of an intestate in an action by a bond creditor against him had pleaded a false plea, and Shadwell, V. C., after a decree obtained in a suit by another creditor for the administration of the assets, restrained the plaintiff at law from taking out execution against the assets but not from proceeding against the heir personally. But in Rouse v. Jones (g), an action being brought against the heir upon a bond by the ancestor, he pleaded *riens par descent*

(b) 10 Sim. 383.   (e) Williams on Executors, 1775.
(c) P. 1775.   (f) 4 Sim. 514.
(d) 1 Ph. 468.   (g) 1 Ph. 462.

præter, &c. The usual decree having been obtained in a creditors' suit for the administration of the real and personal estate
of the intestate, the heir moved for an injunction to restrain
further proceedings in the action. The Vice-Chancellor refused
the motion with costs ; but Lord Lyndhurst reversed the judgment and granted an injunction on the ground, that even if the
verdict were obtained by the plaintiff upon the plea, and judgment be entered up and execution issue thereupon, the debt
due to the plaintiff would in effect be satisfied out of the real
assets of the deceased, and that the fund which ought to be
applied for the general benefit of all the creditors would be to
that extent diminished.

20. * As, on the one hand, a court of equity will not   * 117
after a decree for administration permit a creditor to institute proceedings at law against the executors, so, on the
other hand, an executor may not after a decree for administration institute proceedings at law against creditors. In
Oldfield *v.* Cobbett (*h*), a creditor of the testator filed a bill
against the executor for administration, and obtained an injunction and receiver. The plaintiff was found a creditor, and
the cause was heard on further directions, but the injunction
and receiver were not continued. The executor afterwards
brought an action at law against the plaintiff for moneys due to
the testator ; but the court by injunction summarily restrained
the proceedings ; and subsequently (*i*) Lord Langdale determined that after the estate has been fully administered in a
court of equity, the defendant, the executor, cannot be permitted, without the leave of the court, to commence an action
to recover from the plaintiff in the suit a portion of the testator's property (*j*).

21. A creditor whose action at law is stayed is entitled to his
costs down to the time when he had notice of the decree, and
to the costs of the application (*k*). If the personal represent-

---

(*h*) 5 Beav. 132.
(*i*) 6 Beav. 515.
(*j*) See S. C. 20 Beav. 564.
(*k*) Paxton *v.* Douglas, 8 Ves. 520 ;
Goate *v.* Fryer, 2 Cox, 202 ; Dyer *v.*
Kearsley, 2 Mer. 483, n ; Clarke *v.* Lord
Ormonde, Jac. 124 ; Anon., 2 Sim. & St.

424 ; Bookless *v.* Crummack, Coop. C.
C. 125 ; Rouse *v.* Jones, 1 Ph. 462 ; Ver-
non *v.* Thellusson, *ib.* 466 ; West *v.*
Swinburne, 14 Jur. 360 ; Ratcliffe *v.*
Winch, 16 Beav. 576 ; Lawton *v.* Law-
ton, 8 W. R. 458.

ative admit assets, and does not dispute the debt, the costs are payable at once (*l*). If the executor admit assets, but disputes, or does not admit the debt, the order will be that immediately on the creditor establishing his debt, the costs be taxed and paid by the executor (*m*). If the executor do not admit assets, the costs will be added to the debt (*n*). It was formerly doubted whether the creditor was entitled to
* 118 the costs of the application * to restrain his action (*o*) ; but the point is now decided in favor of the creditor (*p*). But if the creditor had notice of the decree at the time he issued his writ or commenced his action, he will not be entitled to any costs either of the action or the motion (*q*). Mere notice of a decree is a sufficient ground for making a creditor pay the costs of a motion to restrain him, if he prosecutes his action after notice (*r*). On the other hand, it is the duty of the personal representative to apply at once to restrain the action (*s*). If he appears to or takes any step in the action after decree (*t*), or merely omits to apply to restrain the action (*u*), the creditor may set off his costs incurred at law before notice of the decree against costs which he is ordered to pay, on the motion to restrain him (*x*).

Interpleader.

22. The equity on which the right to support a bill of interpleader is founded, is that there is a conflict between two or more persons severally claiming the same debt, duty, or obli-

---

(*l*) White *v.* Leatherdale, 1 W. R. 405 ; Davey *v.* Plestow, 19 L. J. Ch. 491 ; Cole *v.* Burgess, Kay, App. 1 ; Canham *v.* Neale, 26 Beav. 266 ; West *v.* Swinburne, 14 Jur. 360.

(*m*) Davey *v.* Plestow, 19 L. J. Ch. 491. See Noble *v.* Brett, 24 Beav. 507, 509 ; *Re* Life Association of England, 34 L. J. Ch. 64 ; King *v.* King, 34 Beav. 10.

(*n*) Canham *v.* Neale, 26 Beav. 266 ; Lawton *v.* Lawton, 8 W. R. 458 ; West *v.* Swinburne, 14 Jur. 360. See Goate *v.* Fryer, 3 Bro. C. C. 23.

(*o*) Farlow *v.* Wilson, 11 Pri. 95 ; Curre *v.* Bowyer, 3 Madd. 456 ; Anon.,

2 Sim. & St. 424 ; Earl of Portarlington, *v.* Damer, 2 Ph. 263.

(*p*) White *v.* Leatherdale, 1 W. R. 405.

(*q*) Jones *v.* Brain, 2 Y. & C. C. C. 172 ; *Re* Keynsham Co., 33 Beav. 123. *Re* Life Association of England, 34 L. J. Ch. 64.

(*r*) Gardner *v.* Garrett, 20 Beav. 469. See Boston *v.* Richardson, 3 W. R. 432.

(*s*) Packwood *v.* Maddison, 1 Sim. & St. 232 ; Therry *v.* Henderson, 1 Y. & C. C. C. 481.

(*t*) Turner *v.* Connor, 15 Sim. 630.

(*u*) Bear *v.* Smith, 16 Jur. 708.

(*x*) Gardner *v.* Garrett, 20 Beav. 469.

gation by different or separate interests, and that the person who is liable to discharge the debt, duty, or obligation does not know which of the claimants is in fact entitled, but is threatened with double vexation by having two or more processes going on against him at the same time in respect of a subject-matter in which he claims no interest, and in relation to which he has not incurred any independent liability to either of the claimants. The protection of the court is therefore sought, on the most obvious equity, that the claimants should be put to interplead and settle the contest between themselves, without involving * the plaintiff in a dispute in which * 119 he is not interested to any greater extent than as a mere stakeholder (*y*).

23. The principle on which the jurisdiction is based was recognized at common law, and was applied where a chattel had come to a man's possession by accident, or by bailment, from both claimants jointly, or from those under whom both made title. The technical forms of pleading excluded the principle, except in these two cases; but in equity, where these forms did not exist, its operation was extended to all cases where the same things, debt, or obligation was the subject of both claims (*z*).

24. The right to maintain an interpleading suit is founded, not on the consideration that a man is subjected to double liability, but on the fact that he is threatened with double vexation in respect of one liability (*a*). He will not, therefore, be precluded from resorting to equity, though both the claims are legal (*b*). The necessity, however, for bills of interpleader where both the claims are legal is much diminished, although

(*y*) Langston *v.* Boylston, 2 Ves. Jr. 109; Martinius *v.* Hellmuth, Coop. 245; Stevenson *v.* Anderson, 2 V. & B. 407; Pearson *v.* Cardon, 4 Sim. 218, 2 R. & M. 609; Glyn *v.* Duesbury, 11 Sim. 147; Crawford *v.* Fisher, 1 Ha. 436; East and West India Dock Co. *v.* Littledale, 7 Ha. 60; Crawshay *v.* Thornton, 2 M. & C. 19; Jones *v.* Thomas, 2 Sm. & G. 190; Desborough *v.* Harris, 5 D. M. & G. 439, 455; Nelson *v.* Barter, 2 H. & M. 334, 33 L. J. Ch. 705.

(*z*) Mitf. Pl. 165; Crawshay *v.* Thornton, 2 M. & C. 21; Glyn *v.* Duesbury, 11 Sim. 147.

(*a*) Langston *v.* Boylston, 2 Ves. Jr. 109; Angell *v.* Hadden, 15 Ves. 246; Crawford *v.* Fisher, 1 Ha. 436; East and West India Dock Co. *v.* Littledale, 7 Ha. 60; Great Southern and Western Railway Co. *v.* Corry, 15 W. R. 651.

(*b*) Lowndes *v.* Cornford, 18 Ves. 299; Oriental Bank *v.* Nicholson, 3 Jur. N. S. 857.

the jurisdiction is unaffected (c) by the stat. 1 & 2 Will. 4, c. 58, which enables courts of law to give relief by interpleader on the application of a defendant in any action of assumpsit, debt, detinue, or trover, showing that he claims no interest, and that the right is claimed by, or supposed to belong to, some third party who has sued, or is expected to sue, and that the defendant does not collude with such third party, but is ready to bring into court or otherwise dispose of the subject-
*120   matter as the court shall direct (d). The * jurisdiction at law has been still further enlarged by 23 & 24 Vict. c. 126, s. 12 (e).

25. If one of the claims is legal, and another equitable, the statutes do not apply, and the jurisdiction is exclusive in equity. Thus, for instance, if a debt or other chose in action has been assigned, and a controversy arise between the assignor or his assignees in bankruptcy, and the assignee, respecting the title, a bill of interpleader may be brought to have the point settled to whom it shall be paid (f).

26. It is not necessary that an action or suit should have been actually commenced by either or any of the claimants against the party, either at law or in equity. It is sufficient that a claim is made against him, and that he is in danger of being molested by double vexation (g).

27. In order that interpleader may lie, it must appear that the same thing, debt, or duty be claimed by both parties against whom relief is asked.[1] When the subject in dispute has a bodily existence, no difficulty can arise; but where it is a chose

---

(c) See Oriental Bank v. Nicholson, ib.

(d) See also 1 & 2 Vict. c. 45, s. 2.

(e) See Best v. Hayes, 1 H. & C. 718; Tanner v. European Bank, 1 L. R. Exch. 261.

(f) Wright v. Ward, 4 Russ. 215; Langton v. Horton, 3 Beav. 464. See Paris v. Gilham, Coop. 56; Martinius v. Hellmuth, ib. 245; Lowndes v. Cornford, 18 Ves. 299; Morgan v. Marsack, 2 Mer. 107; Warington v. Wheatstone, Jac. 205; Crawford v. Fisher, 10 Sim. 479; Hamilton v. Marks, 5 De G. & S. 638; Diplock v. Hammond, 2 Sm. & G. 141; Jones v. Thomas, 186; Jones v. Farrell, 1 D. & J. 212.

(g) Langston v. Boylston, 2 Ves. Jr. 107; Stevenson v. Anderson, 2 V. & B. 407; Morgan v. Marsack, 2 Mer. 107; Angell v. Hadden, 15 Ves. 244, 16 Ves. 202; Fairbrother v. Prattent, Dan. 64, 5 Pri. 303.

[1] The jurisdiction of the court "is properly applied to cases where two or more persons severally claim the same thing under different titles, or in separate interests, from another person, who, not claiming any title or interest therein himself, and not knowing to which of the claimants he ought of right to render the debt or duty claimed, or to deliver the property in his custody, is either molested by an action or actions

in action which has no bodily existence, it becomes necessary to determine what constitutes identity. When the claims made by the defendants are the same in amount, that circumstance goes far to determine the identity. The amount, however, may not of itself be sufficient, for the amount may be the same, and yet the debt may be different. The question, therefore, as to the identity of the debt is sometimes a difficult one, and must, in each case, be determined by the original constitution and nature of the debt (*h*). Thus, where two debts were originally and substantially different in their nature, the one being due to one of * the defendants in respect   * 121 of acts done by him in his character of architect and surveyor to the plaintiff, and the other being due to the other in respect of work and labor done, it was held that a bill of interpleader could not be supported (*i*). So, also, where an auctioneer, by direction of the owner, had sold to two persons successively, and had received a deposit from each, it was held that the auctioneer could not support a bill of interpleader against the owner and the two purchasers, because, although there was one question in common between the purchasers, viz., which was to be the purchaser of the estate, their claims against the auctioneer were for two different things, viz., each for his own deposit. The bill, therefore, was dismissed as against the second purchaser, and it was decreed that the

brought against him, or fears that he may suffer injury from the conflicting claims of the parties. He therefore applies to a court of equity to protect him, not only from being compelled to pay or deliver the thing claimed to both the claimants, but also from the vexation attending upon the suits which are or possibly may be instituted against him." Story's Eq. Jur. § 806, citing Bell *v.* Hunt, 3 Barb. Ch. 391 ; Strange *v.* Bell, 11 Geo. 103 ; Atkinson *v.* Works, 1 Cowen, 691, 703 ; Badeau *v.* Rogers, 2 Paige, 209 ; Mohawk and Hudson Railroad Co. *v.* Clute, 4 Paige, 384, 392 ; Richards *v.* Salter, 6 Johns. Ch. 445. In a very late case, where the plaintiff, as administrator, held the proceeds of a policy of insurance upon the life of his intestate which were claimed by one having an assignment from the intestate of said

policy, the court held that a bill of interpleader would not lie, but the court would take jurisdiction as of a bill by the administrator seeking the instruction and protection of the court. Stevens *v.* Warren, 101 Mass. 564.

And where there are other grounds of equitable jurisdiction, however, as in those cases where the complainant is entitled to equitable relief against the legal owner of the property, if the legal title is in dispute, so that the complainant cannot ascertain to which of the parties to that controversy the property really belongs, he may file a bill in the nature of a bill of interpleader, and for relief, against both of the complainants. Mohawk and Hudson Railroad Co. *v.* Clute, 4 Paige, 392.

(*h*) Glyn *v.* Duesbury, 11 Sim. 148.
(*i*) *Ib.*

the seller and the first purchaser should interplead as to the first deposit (*k*).

28. The claims must be not only in respect of the same debt, duty, or thing, but must, moreover, be in reality conflicting claims (*l*).[1] A mere pretext of a conflicting claim, or the mere possibility that there may be two liabilities, is not sufficient to support a bill of interpleader (*m*). An act by a party entitled giving a color of title to another person is sufficient (*n*); yet the court is bound to see that there is, in fact, a question to be tried (*o*). Where the title of one of the parties is subordinate to that of the other, the claims cannot be conflicting, and there can be no interpleader (*p*). Thus a life insurance company was held not entitled to file a bill of interpleader against the assignee for value of a policy of insurance with notice, who had brought an action for the moneys, the insurer, who had subsequently to the notice become insolvent, and his provisional assignee, on the ground that the insolvent had no title, and that the title of the provisional assignee was not an adverse claim, but only a claim after the assignee for value was

* 122 satisfied (*q*). Nor can * there be interpleader where the title of one of the claimants is paramount to that of the other, and the possession of the stakeholder or person in whose hands the property in question lies is in law the possession of the latter. A tenant, for instance, cannot sustain a bill of interpleader against his landlord on the ground of ejectment brought by a stranger claiming under a paramount title, for it is a rule of law that a tenant cannot dispute the title of his landlord (*r*). Nor can an agent file a bill of interpleader against his principal and a person claiming under a paramount title, for it is a rule of law that an agent cannot dispute the

---

(*k*) Hoggart *v.* Cutts, Cr. & Ph. 197.

(*l*) Cochrane *v.* O'Brien, 2 J. & L. 380.

(*m*) *Ib.*

(*n*) East India Co. *v.* Edwards, 18 Ves. 576.

(*o*) Glynn *v.* Locke, 3 Dr. & War. 11; Cochrane *v.* O'Brien, 2 J. & L. 380.

(*p*) Desborough *v.* Harris, 5 D. M. & G. 439.

(*q*) *Ib.* Comp. Duke of Bolton *v.*

Williams, 4 Bro. C. C. 297, 2 Ves. Jr. 138.

(*r*) Dungey *v.* Angove, 3 Ves. Jr. 303; Cook *v.* Lord Rosslyn, 1 Giff. 167: Elliott *v.* Kempston, 15 Ir. Ch. 120. See Clark *v.* Byne, 13 Ves. 386; Crawshay *v.* Thornton, 2 M. & C. 1, 30.

[1] See Mohawk and Hudson Railroad Co. *v.* Clute, 4 Paige, 392; an authority upon this precise point, and where the subject is considerably discussed.

title under which he holds (s). A distinction has been taken upon this subject between the case of a mere private agent or bailee, and that of a public agent or bailee (t) ; but it seems doubtful whether the distinction can be maintained (u). The case is different where, after the tenancy or agency is created, the landlord or principal transfers his interest to, or creates an interest in, some other person (x). A tenant may file a bill of interpleader against his landlord who has vested an interest in some other person under a derivative title, or has affected the title by some act subsequently to the commencement of the tenancy (y). So, also, where the title of a claimant to a lien on funds or other property in the hands of an agent is derivative from the principal, and has been created by him since the commencement of the agency, interpleader by the agent will lie (z). In filing the bill in such cases, the tenant or * agent does not dispute the title of his landlord or prin-   * 123 cipal, but claims to know who is, in fact, the landlord or principal whose tenant or agent he ought to be considered to be (a). The equity of the tenant or agent arises from the act of the landlord or principal, who has by his own act created a privity between him and other claimants (b).

29. In a case before Sir J. Leach (c), he doubted whether a. bill of interpleader would lie at the suit of a captain of a trading vessel against a party claiming, not under, but paramount to, the bill of lading, on the ground that delivery, according to

---

(s) Nicholson v. Knowles, 5 Madd. 47; Pearson v. Cardon, 2 R. & M. 606; Smith v. Hammond, 6 Sim. 10; Cooper v. De Tastet, Taml. 177; Crawshay v. Thornton, 2 M. & C. 1; Watts v. Hammond, 3 Eq. R. 641.

(t) Cooper v. De Tastet, Taml. 177.

(u) Crawshay v. Thornton, 2 M. & C. 1, 22.

(x) Crawshay v. Thornton, 2 M. & C. 1, 21; Stuart v. Welch, 4 M. & C. 305.

(y) Dungey v. Angove, 2 Ves. Jr. 303; Cowtan v. Williams, 9 Ves. 107; Clark v. Byne, 13 Ves. 383; Angell v. Hadden, 15 Ves. 244, 16 Ves. 202, 2 Mer. 164; Townley v. Deare, 3 Beav. 213; Jew v. Wood, Cr. & Ph. 186; Rickard v. Hyde, 2 Ir. Eq. 299; Doran v. Everitt, ib. 28; Cook v. Rosslyn, 1 Giff. 171.

(z) Wright v. Ward, 4 Russ. 215, 220; Pearson v. Cardon, 2 R. & M. 609; Sieveking v. Behrens, 2 M. &. C. 581, 591, 592; Stuart v. Welch, 4 M. & C. 316; Masterman v. Lewin, 2 Ph. 182; Smith v. Hammond, 6 Sim. 10; Crawshay v. Thornton, 2 M. & C. 1; Watts v. Hammond, 3 Eq. R. 641; Oriental Bank Corporation v. Nicholson, 3 Jur. N. S. 858.

(a) Stuart v. Welch, 4 M. & C. 305.

(b) Ib. Crawshay v. Thornton, 2 M. & C. 1, 21. See Cowtan v. Williams, 9 Ves. 107; Clark v. Byne, 13 Ves. 383.

(c) Lowe v. Richardson, 3 Madd. 278.

the bill of lading, would fully justify the captain. But in a
later case (*d*), the same judge thought that such a bill would
lie, as the right of possession in chattels may be in one person,
and the right of property in another (*e*).

30. It is also essential, in order that interpleader may lie,
that the party seeking relief should not have acknowledged a
title in one of the claimants, or come under any engagement,
or be under any liabilities to either of them, independently of
such liability as might exist from the situation in which they
are placed with reference to the property in question. If he
has come under any personal obligation to either of the claimants in respect of the specific property in dispute, independently
of the question of title, so that the whole of the rights claimed
by the defendants cannot be properly determined by litigation
between them, it is not a proper case for interpleader (*f*).
*124 But * an acknowledgment of title through ignorance of
the title being disputed goes for nothing (*g*).

31. A court of law is not, it may be observed, governed by
the technical rules which govern courts of equity upon bills of
interpleader, and may, under the provisions of the Common
Law Procedure Act, 23 & 24 Vict. c. 126, s. 12, give relief,
although one of the parties has incurred a personal obligation
independently of the question of property, and the claims are
not identical (*h*).

32. A party seeking relief by interpleader, must claim no
personal interest in the property in dispute (*i*). Where, for
instance, an action is brought against an auctioneer for a
deposit, he cannot sustain a bill of interpleader if he insists
upon retaining either his own commission or the duty (*k*). So,

(*d*) Morley *v.* Thompson, *ib.* 564, ind.
(*e*) See Warington *v.* Wheatstone, Jac. 202.
(*f*) Crawshay *v.* Thornton, 2 M. & C. 1; Cooper *v.* De Tastet, Taml. 177; Pearson *v.* Cardon, 2 R. & M. 606; Cochrane *v.* O'Brien, 2 J. & L. 380; Desborough *v.* Harris, 5 D. M. & G. 439, 455, *per* Lord Cranworth. See Stuart *v.* Welch, 4 M. & C. 306; Jew *v.* Wood, Cr. & Ph. 193; Sablicich *v.* Russell, 2 L. R. Eq. 441; Nelson *v.* Barter, 2 H. & M. 334, 33 L. J. Ch. 705.

(*g*) Jew *v.* Wood, Cr. & Ph. 185. So also if an engagement has been entered into with either of the claimants through misrepresentation, interpleader will lie. Costello *v.* Martin, 1 Ir. Rep. Eq. 50.
(*h*) Best *v.* Hayes, 1 H. & C. 718.
(*i*) Langston *v.* Boylston, 2 Ves. Jr. 103; Angell *v.* Hadden, 15 Ves. 244; Moore *v.* Usher, 7 Sim. 384; Hoggart *v.* Cutts, Cr. & Ph. 204; Jacobson *v.* Blackhurst, 2 J. & H. 486.
(*k*) Mitchell *v.* Hayne, 2 Sim. & St. 63. See Slingsby *v.* Boulton, 1 V. & B. 334.

also, where an interpleader bill alleged that the interest on a sum secured by a policy is not due from the company by whom the bill was filed, it was held not sustainable (*l*). So, also, where the bill prayed that the defendants might interplead as to a sum smaller than the claim appearing in the bill to be made against them, it was held not sustainable (*m*). It follows, therefore, from these cases, that where a bill of interpleader is filed in respect of a sum of money on which interest is recoverable at law, the plaintiff ought by his bill to offer to pay the interest (*n*).

33. The Interpleader Act, 1 & 2 Will. 4, c. 58, s. 6, gives a sheriff a certain degree of protection in case of the execution of writs of *fi. fa.* when issued out of courts of law. The Act does not apply to the protection of sheriffs in the execution of writs of *fi. fa.* when issued out of the Court of Chancery (*o*). *But the court may, by analogy to the rule at law, assume the jurisdiction on a proper case being made out (*p*).   * 125

34. The court does not encourage parties to come for interpleader if there be any other mode by which the conflicting claims can be adjusted with safety to the stakeholder (*q*).[1] If the court sees that the continuance of an injunction in an interpleading suit in full force may have the effect of enabling a stranger to deprive the parties to the suit of the legal rights which they have already acquired, the injunction will be suspended so far as to allow proceedings at law to go to judgment (*r*). Nor will an interpleader bill be sustained if the stakeholder knows that there is no desire on the part of a claimant to harass him. If he knows that the various claimants are about to litigate the questions at issue among themselves,

---

(*l*) Bignold *v.* Audland, 11 Sim. 24.
(*m*) Diplock *v.* Hammond, 2 Sm. & G. 141. Comp. Hamilton *v.* Marks, 5 De G. & S. 638.
(*n*) Bignold *v.* Audland, 11 Sim. 24; Langton *v.* Horton, 3 Beav. 464.
(*o*) Rock *v.* Cook, 2 Ph. 691.
(*p*) Tufton *v.* Harding, 29 L. J. Ch. 225; Dutton *v.* Furniss, 35 L. J. Ch. 463.

(*q*) Sieveking *v.* Behrens, 2 M. & C. 581.
(*r*) *Ib.*
[1] There is no need of a bill of interpleader, where the holder of a fund is already a party to a suit in chancery, brought by one claimant against the other to settle the right to the fund. He may apply by petition for leave to pay the fund into court to abide the event of litigation between the parties. Badeau *v.* Rogers, 2 Paige, 209.

the fact that he may have been made a party to a bill by one
claimant against the other claimants does not give him an
equity (*s*). Nor will interpleader lie if the stakeholder or person in whose possession the subject-matter of the claim is
placed might without any peril have paid or delivered it over
to one of the parties (*t*). It is not, however, so absolutely
clear that a debt, the subject of an action upon which judgment has not been recovered, is protected from foreign attachment as to make it the duty of the debtor to disregard such
attachment, and pay the debt after judgment to the judgment
creditor or his assignees (*u*). If there be a case for interpleader, the stakeholder is not bound to accept an indemnity
from either of the claimants, although the claimant offering
such indemnity shows an apparent title to the property in dispute (*x*).

35. A stakeholder against whom judgment has been
* 126 recovered * at law is entitled to interpleader if he has
acted fairly and honestly in the matter, and has not
neglected his duty (*y*). But if the demand has been contested by him at law, and has been decided against him, interpleader will not lie (*z*). It is, however, no objection to a bill
of interpleader that it is filed after verdict at law, where the
effect of the action was merely to ascertain the quantum of
damage due on the claim (*a*).

36. A man who has wrongly pleaded to an action at law concurrently with his bill for interpleader, may nevertheless maintain the suit (*b*).

37. A party seeking relief by interpleader must use due diligence in making the application. Delay may be fatal to the

(*s*) Diplock *v.* Hammond, 2 Sm. & G.
146. See Warington *v.* Wheatstone,
Jac. 202.

(*t*) Desborough *v.* Harris, 5 D. M. &
G. 439 ; Myers *v.* United Guarantee, &c.,
Society, 7 D. M. & G. 112.

(*u*) Nelson *v.* Barter, 2 H. & M. 334,
33 L. J. Ch. 705.

(*x*) East and West India Dock Co. *v.*
Littledale, 7 Ha. 57. See as to interpleader by a master of a ship against

owners of goods part of the cargo,
Sablicich *v.* Russell, 2 L. R. Eq. 441.

(*y*) Nelson *v.* Barter, 2 H. & M. 334,
33 L. J. Ch. 705.

(*z*) Cornish *v.* Tanner, 1 Y. & J. 333 ;
Larabrie *v.* Brown, 1 D. & J. 205. See
Oriental Bank *v.* Nicholson, 3 Jur. N. S.
858.

(*a*) Hamilton *v.* Marks, 5 De G. & S.
638.

(*b*) Jacobson *v.* Blackhurst, 2 J. & H.
486.

bill (c). So long, however, as the course of proceedings taken by the different claimants is such as, if persevered in, will determine their respective rights as between themselves with-out the intervention of this court, delay is not material (d). A sheriff who seeks by interpleader protection against an action at law for the seizure of goods which are not the prop-erty of the person against whom the *fi. fa.* was issued must apply without delay, for a very slight delay will defeat his title (e).

38. A bill of interpleader cannot be maintained by a man who does not admit a title in two claimants, and does not show two claimants in existence capable of interpleading. (f). An interpleading bill never suggests a case (g); the plaintiff admits a title as against himself in all the defendants (h). If the bill does not show that each of the defendants whom it seeks to compel to interplead claims a right, and such a right as they may interplead for, both may demur: the one, because the bill * shows no claim of right against him;   * 127 the other, because the bill, showing no claim of right in the codefendant, shows no case of interpleader (i). If the plaintiff does not show a right to compel the defendants to interplead whatever rights they may claim, each defendant may demur (k). The introduction of a superfluous defendant is no ground of demurrer on the part of any other defend-ant (l).

39. The bill must state the situation of the plaintiff, and the conflicting claims upon him, and pray that the claimants may interplead, so that the court may adjudge to whom the debt, demand, or property belongs, and that he may be indemni-fied (m). The plaintiff is not bound to show the existence of an apparent title in each of the defendants who are claimants to

(c) Larabrie v. Brown, 1 D. & J. 205.

(d) Sieveking v. Behrens, 2 M. & C. 581.

(e) Tufton v. Harding, 29 L. J. Ch. 225.

(f) See Metcalf v. Hervey, 1 Ves. 248; Slingsby v. Boulton, 1 V. & B. 334; Darthez v. Winter, 2 Sim. & St. 536.

(g) Dungey v. Angove, 2 Ves. Jr. 311.

(h) Slingsby v. Boulton, 1 V. & B. 334; Moore v. Usher, 7 Sim. 384; Townley v. Deare, 3 Beav. 216.

(i) Mitf. Pl. 166.

(k) Ib. 168.

(l) Fairbrother v. Beale, 3 De G. & S. 637.

(m) Mitf. Pl. 59.

the property in dispute (*n*). It is enough that he is threatened with double vexation (*o*). The facts stated in the bill should show that there is a substantial question to be tried. The mere fact that a claim is made and a question raised cannot avail, unless it appears to the court that there is a real and substantial question to be tried (*p*). The bill must be framed so that the decree may embrace the whole of it (*q*). If any actions at law are brought against the plaintiff, he may pray that the claimant may be restrained from proceeding till the right is determined (*r*). An injunction is of course, if the case be a proper subject for interpleader (*s*). If any money be due from the plaintiff, he should bring it into court, or should at least offer to do so by his bill (*t*). The mere absence of the offer is not, however, a ground for demurrer (*u*). But the injunction is granted only on the terms of payment into court, and the order must be drawn up so as to make

* 128　the payment a condition * precedent (*x*). On payment

into court, or if there is in the bill an offer to pay into court, the plaintiff may move *ex parte* for an injunction immediately on the bill being filed, without waiting for the appearance of the defendants (*y*). If the defendants have appeared, they should be served with notice of motion for an injunction (*z*). An affidavit of merits is unnecessary (*a*). Though the defendant should allege that the plaintiff has so dealt with him as to render it an improper case for interpleader, an injunction will still be granted, unless the court is satisfied either that the allegation is true, or at least that whether it be so or not is a substantial question to be tried (*b*).

(*n*) East and West India Dock Co. *v.* Littledale, 2 Ha. 57.
(*o*) Ib.
(*p*) Jew *v.* Wood, Cr. & Ph. 185.
(*q*) Crawford *v.* Fisher, 1 Ha. 436; Hoggart *v.* Cutts, Cr. & Ph. 199.
(*r*) Mitf. Pl. 167.
(*s*) Crawshay *v.* Thornton, 2 M. &. C. 1, 19.
(*t*) East India Co. *v.* Edwards, 18 Ves. 376; Warington *v.* Wheatstone, Jac. 202; Bignold *v.* Audland, 11 Sim. 23.
(*u*) Sieveking *v.* Behrens, 2 M. & C. 581; Meux *v.* Bell, 6 Sim. 175.

(*x*) Sieveking *v.* Behrens, 2 M. & C. 581; Hoggart *v.* Cutts, Cr. & Ph. 199; Pauli *v.* Von Melle, 8 Sim. 327.
(*y*) Warington *v.* Wheatstone, Jac. 205; Vicary *v.* Widger, 1 Sim. 15; Sieveking *v.* Behrens, 2 M. & C. 581; Hoggart *v.* Cutts, Cr. & Ph. 199.
(*z*) Sieveking *v.* Behrens, 2 M. & C. 581.
(*a*) Walbank *v.* Sparks, 1 Sim. 385; Sedgwick *v.* Clegg, 4 Jur. 742; Wood *v.* Lyne, 4 De G. & S. 16; Hamilton *v.* Marks, 5 De G. & S. 642.
(*b*) Jew *v.* Wood, Cr. & Ph. 185.

The Crown may be a defendant to an interpleading suit (c).

40. Inasmuch as the sole ground on which the jurisdiction of the court in cases of interpleader is supported is the danger of injury to the plaintiff from the doubtful titles of the defendants, the court, in order to prevent its proceedings being made the instrument of delay, or being used collusively, requires the plaintiff to file an affidavit that there has been no collusion between him and any of the parties (d). He need not swear that it was filed at his own expense (e), nor, it seems, that it was filed without the knowledge of either of the defendants (f). The court will not determine the affidavit to be false upon a counter-affidavit (g). But if there is a suspicion of collusion, an inquiry will be directed, and evidence is, it seems, admissible to show that the plaintiff has entered into possession of the subject of the suit under an indemnity from one of the defendants (h). The more usual way is to annex the affidavit to the bill; but it is not necessary that it should be actually * annexed to the bill. It is enough if it accom- * 129 panies it (i). The affidavit should be made by the plaintiff. An affidavit by his solicitor is not in general sufficient (k). But if the plaintiff is abroad, leave may be given to his solicitor to make it (l). In a case where there were several plaintiffs residing in distant places, and appearing by one solicitor, leave was given to him to make the affidavit; but the court would not thereupon grant an injunction until the hearing, but only granted an interim order for a reasonable time, upon an understanding that the plaintiffs should themselves in the mean time make the requisite affidavits (m). If plaintiffs are copartners, and the affidavit is made by one or several of the partners, it should give a satisfactory explanation why all the other members of the firm do not join in

---

(c) Reid v. Stearn, 6 Jur. N. S. Ch. 267.

(d) Mitf. Pl. 60; Stevenson v. Anderson, 2 V. & B. 410; Warington v. Wheatstone, Jac. 205.

(e) Metcalf v. Hervey, 1 Ves. 248.

(f) Stevenson v. Anderson, 2 V & B. 410.

(g) Ib.

(h) Dungey v. Angove, 2 Ves. Jr. 311; Statham v. Hull, T. & R. 30.

(i) Shepherd v. Jones, 3 D. F. & J. 57.

(k) Wood v. Lyne, 4 De G. & S. 16.

(l) Larabrie v. Brown, 1 D. & J. 204. See Dan. Ch. Pr 1419.

(m) Nelson v. Barter, 2 H. & M. 334.

it (*n*). If made by the registered officer of a company on behalf of the company, the affidavit should state that, to the best of his belief and knowledge, the company does not collude with any of the defendants. The statement that he, the registered officer, who is merely the nominal plaintiff, does not collude is not sufficient (*o*). The want of the affidavit is a ground of demurrer (*p*). Objections to its form should be taken on demurrer when the court may give leave to amend, and not on motion to dissolve, an injunction (*q*). In a case where a bill was filed by the owner of an estate, subject to a rent-charge, against conflicting claimants, an affidavit of no collusion was not required (*r*).

41. If the plaintiff has parted with the possession of the property in dispute, a bill of interpleader cannot be sustained upon an undertaking to pay over the value of it to the party who shall be found entitled to it (*s*). Nor can the ** 130* benefit of this species * of suit be obtained upon motion in a cause to which the stakeholder is a defendant. Accordingly, where money in the funds was the subject of a suit to which the bank was a defendant, Lord Thurlow refused, upon the application of the bank, to make any order upon the litigating parties to restrain them from proceeding at law against the bank to compel a transfer. He said they must apply by bill (*t*).

42. An interpleader bill is not demurrable because some of the defendants are out of the jurisdiction ; but the plaintiff must use due diligence to get them all before the court in reasonable time. If he can show that he has done so, but has not succeeded, he will be decreed to give up the subject of dispute to the defendant who has appeared, and will be protected against the others by perpetual injunction (*u*). In a case where the subject was a policy on a cargo lost, an injunction

(*n*) Gibbs *v.* Gibbs, 5 W. R. 243. See Braith. 369.

(*o*) Bignold *v.* Audland, 11 Sim. 23; Hamilton *v.* Marks, 5 De G. & S. 638. See Braith. 369; Great Southern and Western Railway Co. *v.* Corry, 15 W. R. 651.

(*p*) Mitf. Pl. 60 ; Bignold *v.* Audland, 11 Sim. 23.

(*q*) Wood *v.* Lyne, 4 De G. & S. 16 ; Hamilton *v.* Marks, 5 De G. & S. 638.

(*r*) Vyvyan *v.* Vyvyan, 30 Beav. 65, 31 L. J. Ch. 158.

(*s*) Burnett *v.* Anderson, 1 Mer. 405.

(*t*) Birch *v.* Corbin, 1 Cox, 144.

(*u*) Stevenson *v.* Anderson, 2 V. & B. 407. See Central Railroad of Georgia *v.* Mitchell, 2 H. & M. 452.

was granted to stay proceedings at law, although botl defendants resided abroad (*x*). So also, though one of th defendants has not appeared to the bill, and the usual proces of contempt has been gone through (*y*), or if one of them doe not appear at the hearing, a decree will be made (*z*).

43. A defendant who has put in his answer may, if any dela shall occur on the part of the codefendants in putting in thei answers, move to dissolve the injunction, or to have the subjec of interpleader delivered up, as the case may be, on notice t the plaintiff and his codefendants (*a*). If the codefendant have put in their answers, an inquiry may be directed as to th respective titles (*b*). But such inquiry cannot be directe until they have put in their answers, or the bill is taken *pr confesso* against them (*c*). A defendant who seeks for further delay * must satisfy the court that the case can- *13: not be put in a course for determination without further delay (*d*).

44. The interpleading plaintiff proceeds with the suit in th usual way, sets down the cause, and brings it to a hearing (*e*) It is not necessary for the defendants to enter into evidenc against each other (*f*). If at the hearing the question betweei the defendants is ripe for decision, the court will decide it; bu if it is not ripe for decision, an inquiry will be directed (*g*) But the more usual way is to obtain the direction at an earlie stage (*h*). A defendant may show at the hearing that the cas is not one for interpleader (*i*).

45. If an interpleading bill has been properly instituted, an a case for interpleader is made out, the plaintiff is entitled, i

---

(*x*) Martinius *v.* Helmuth, Coop. 245.
(*y*) Fairbrother *v.* Prattent, Dan. 64, 5 Pri. 303. See Hyde *v.* Warren, 19 Ves. 322.
(*z*) Hodges *v.* Smith, 1 Cox, 357.
(*a*) Hyde *v.* Warren, 19 Ves. 321; Stevenson *v.* Anderson, 2 V. & B. 407; Townley *v.* Deare, 3 Beav. 216; Masterman *v.* Lewin, 2 Ph. 182; East and West India Dock Co. *v.* Littledale, 7 Ha. 57.
(*b*) Masterman *v.* Lewin, 2 Ph. 142; Townley *v.* Deare, 3 Beav. 216.
(*c*) Masterman *v.* Lewin, 2 Ph. 182;

East and West India Dock Co. *v.* Little dale, 7 Ha. 57.
(*d*) East and West India Dock Cc *v.* Littledale, 7 Ha. 57.
(*e*) Jones *v.* Gilham, Coop. 49.
(*f*) Thames and Medway Canal Cc *v.* Nash, 5 Sim. 280; Catherall *v.* Davies 1 Giff. 326.
(*g*) See Angell *v.* Hadden, 16 Ves 203; Townley *v.* Deare, 3 Beav. 216 Crawford *v.* Fisher, 1 Ha. 436, 441 Bruce *v.* Elwin, 9 Ha. 294, *ib.*
(*h*) Crawford *v.* Fisher, 1 Ha. 436 Townley *v.* Deare, 3 Beav. 216.
(*i*) Toulmin *v.* Reed, 14 Beav. 499

there be a fund in court, to have his cost paid out of it (*k*).
If there is no fund in court, costs will be given against the
party who occasioned the suit (*l*). Costs will not, however, be
allowed of any proceedings which may have been taken in the
suit that are productive of needless expense (*m*). If the case
for a bill fails, it will be dismissed with costs as against the
plaintiff (*n*), except the suit has been adopted by the defendants, in which case plaintiff will be allowed his costs (*o*). If
the case for interpleader is partly made out and partly fails,
the bill will be dismissed with costs as against the
* 132 defendant who is * successful, but without costs as
against the defendant who occasioned the suit (*p*).
The costs of the defendants do not necessarily follow the
result of the suit, but are in the discretion of the court (*q*).
Sometimes no costs will be given on either side (*r*). At other
times one defendant will be allowed his costs against another (*s*).
On dismissal of a bill, the court cannot decree costs as against
a defendant whose misconduct occasioned the suit (*t*).

Perpetual Injunction.

46. The jurisdiction by perpetual injunction is founded on
the equity of putting a bound to harassing and vexatious litigation. If the court is of opinion at the hearing that the plaintiff has established a case which entitles him to an injunction,

(*k*) Aldrich *v.* Thompson, 2 Bro. C.
C. 149; Hodges *v.* Smith, 1 Cox, 357;
Paris *v.* Gilham, Coop. 56; Cowtan *v.*
Williams, 9 Ves. 107; Campbell *v.*
Salomons, 1 Sim. & St. 462.

(*l*) Aldridge *v.* Mesner, 6 Ves. 419;
Glynn *v.* Locke, 3 Dr. & War. 11; Cochrane *v.* O'Brien, 2 J. & L. 380.

(*m*) Sieveking *v.* Behrens, 2 M. & C.
581; Crawford *v.* Fisher, 1 Ha. 436;
Symes *v.* Magnay, 20 Beav. 47; Hale
v. Saloon Omnibus Co., 4 Drew. 492;
Jacobson *v.* Blackhurst, 2 J. & H. 486.

(*n*) Cochrane *v.* O'Brien, 2 J. & L.
380; Cook *v.* Earl of Rosslyn, 1 Giff.
167.

(*o*) Myers *v.* United Guarantee Society, 7 D. M. & G. 112.

(*p*) Hoggart *v.* Cutts, Cr. & Ph. 197;
Cochrane *v.* O'Brien, 2 J. & L. 380;

Glynn *v.* Locke, 3 Dr. & War. 11; Desborough *v.* Harris, 5 D. M. & G. 439.

(*q*) Meux *v.* Bell, 1 Ha. 73, 98.

(*r*) *Ib.* See Cook *v.* Earl of Rosslyn,
1 Giff. 167.

(*s*) Cowtan *v.* Williams, 9 Ves. 107;
Mason *v.* Hamilton, 5 Sim. 19; Fenn
v. Edmunds, 5 Ha. 314; Jacobson *v.*
Blackhurst, 2 J. & H. 486.

(*t*) Cochrane *v.* O'Brien, 2 J. & L. 380.
See further on the subject, Morg. &
Davy on Costs, 152–155. See, as to
orders and decree in an interpleading
suit, Seton on Decrees, p. 962; Hodges
v. Smith, 1 Cox, 357; Hoggart *v.* Cutts,
Cr. & Ph. 197; Glynn *v.* Locke, 3 Dr.
& War. 25; Smith *v.* Hammond, 6 Sim.
12; Fenn *v.* Edmunds, 5 Ha. 314; Bruce
v. Elwin, 9 Ha. 294.

or if a bill praying for an injunction is taken *pro confesso,* a perpetual injunction will be decreed (*u*). Where, for instance, there has been a decree for the performance of trusts, a defendant will be perpetually enjoined from setting up a legal estate against that decree (*x*). So also where two trials had been had at bar under the direction of the court, and verdict for the plaintiff had been found in both, a perpetual injunction was granted (*y*). It may indeed be stated as a general rule that if an equitable case for restraining proceedings at law be presented to the court, a perpetual * injunction will be   * 133 granted whenever it is necessary for the purposes of complete justice (*z*). A perpetual injunction is in effect a decree. It is final, and need not be revived on the death of either of the parties in order to be kept on foot (*a*). As a general rule, an injunction can only be made perpetual at the hearing of the cause (*b*).

47. It has been said that the court will not bind the inheritance upon one verdict only (*c*). Lord Northington, however, in the case of Darlington *v.* Bowes (*d*), expressed great disapprobation of the rule, and inquired if there was any instance of a decree upon one verdict only, observing that he thought there were some old ones, and that if any could be found he would certainly refuse the application before him for a new trial, but as none was produced the order was made. There is a case before Lord Clarendon in which a decree was made upon one verdict, and though it was disapproved of by Lord Keeper North, (*e*) yet there is a note in Viner which supports

---

(*u*) Gilb. For. Rom. 194; Knight *v.* Adamson, 2 Freem. 106; Selby *v.* Selby, 2 Dick. 678.

(*x*) Acherley *v.* Vernon, 2 Eq. Ca. Ab. 527; Selby *v.* Selby, 2 Dick. 678; Askew *v.* Poulterers' Co., 2 Ves. 90.

(*y*) Leighton *v.* Leighton, 1 P. Wms. 671, 4 Bro. P. C. 378; Davies *v.* Evans, 4 De G. & S. 440.

(*z*) Blad *v.* Bamfield, 3 Sw. 604; Burrows *v.* Jemineau, 2 Eq. Ab. 524; Durston *v.* Sandys, 1 Vern. 411; Webber *v.* Farmer, 4 Bro. P. C. 170; Clerke *v.* Moore, *ib.* 723; Hanington *v.* Du Chatel, 1 Bro. C. C. 124; Wilde *v.* Ashley, 2 Jur. 679; Meux *v.* Smith, 7 Jur. 821; Taylor *v.* Hughes, 2 J. &

L. 24; Hudson *v.* Temple, 29 Beav. 536.

(*a*) Askew *v.* Townsend, 2 Dick. 471.

(*b*) Day *v.* Snee, 3 V. & B. 170. See *infra.*

(*c*) Fitton *v.* Lord Macclesfield, 1 Vern. 292; Edwin *v.* Thomas, 2 Vern. 75; Leighton *v.* Leighton, 1 P. Wms. 671; Lord Fauconberg *v.* Price, Amb. 210; Lord Sherborne *v.* Naper, cit. 4 Ves. 206; Bates *v.* Graves, 2 Ves. Jr. 287.

(*d*) 1 Eden, 270.

(*e*) Fitton *v.* Lord Macclesfield, 1 Vern. 292.

it (*f*). The same thing was done in Lowe *v.* Jolliffe (*g*). There had been a verdict in favor of a will in *dev. vel non,* and a decree in the cause in chancery establishing the trusts of the will, and they had under the same decree been carried into effect. The heir-at-law having afterwards made his will and died, his devisee brought ejectment, upon which the devisees under the first will filed a bill for an injunction to restrain him from proceeding at law, and a perpetual injunction was decreed upon the hearing. The sound doctrine on the subject would seem to be that no general rule should be laid down as *134 to whether a perpetual injunction *should or should not be granted after a single trial at law. The question should depend in all cases upon the fact whether the conscience of the court is satisfied as to the result of the trial, and not on the number of trials which may have taken place (*h*). A nonsuit at law is to be regarded in the same light as a verdict. Where a man had elected to be nonsuited, and there was reason to conclude that the action had failed on the merits, the court restrained him from proceeding further at law (*i*).

48. In many cases the courts of ordinary jurisdiction admit, at least for a certain time, of repeated attempts to litigate the same question. To put an end to the oppression occasioned by the abuse of this privilege, courts of equity have assumed jurisdiction by perpetual injunction. Thus, actions of ejectment being the usual mode of trying titles at common law, and judgments in these actions not being in any degree conclusive, courts of equity will interfere, and after repeated trials and satisfactory determinations of questions, grant perpetual injunctions to restrain further litigation (*k*). The leading case on the subject is that of the Earl of Bath *v.* Sherwin (*l*), where, after five verdicts in favor of the plaintiff, a bill was filed for a perpetual injunction. Lord Cowper, though satisfied of the vexatious nature of the litigation, yet being unwilling to inter-

(*f*) Wilson *v.* Story, 14 Vin. Ab. 431.
(*g*) Dick. 388.
(*h*) See Stace *v.* Mabbott, 2 Ves. 552; Thomas *v.* Jones, 1 Y. & C. C. C. 527; Dawson *v.* Paver, 5 Ha. 415, 4 Ra. Ca. 85; Bennett *v.* Duke of Manchester, 2 W. R. 644; Swinfen *v.* Swinfen, 27 Beav. 152; Boyse *v.* Russborough, 6 H. L. 43.
(*i*) Allen *v.* Davis, 20 L. J. Ch. 44; Llewellin *v.* Pace, 1 W. R. 28.
(*k*) Mitf. Pl. 167.
(*l*) Prec. Ch. 261, Gilb. Eq. Rep. 2.

pose in a case where the title was purely legal, refused to decree an injunction, but recommended it to the plaintiff as a case proper for the House of Lords, and on an appeal a perpetual injunction was decreed (*m*). Upon this authority a perpetual injunction was decreed in the case of Barefoot *v.* Fry (*n*), where the defendant had brought five ejectments, and had been nonsuited upon full evidence in three of them, and had verdicts against him in the other two (*o*).[1]

49. In cases where there is one general common right to be established against several or a number of distinct persons, * whether one person claims or defends a right   *135 against many, or many claim or defend a right against one, a court of equity will interpose in order to prevent multiplicity of suits, and instead of suffering parties to be harassed by a number of separate suits, each of which only decide the particular right in question between the plaintiff and the defendant to it, it will at once determine the right by a decree, having previously, if necessary, directed an issue for its information (*p*).[2] It is no objection to the bill that the plaintiffs may each claim a right against one defendant, or several defendants may each have a right to make a separate defence against the claim of one plaintiff, provided there be only one general question to be settled which pervades the whole. It is enough that there is one general question as between the one plaintiff and the several defendants, or the one defendant and the several plaintiffs (*q*). If the parties are so numerous that it is impracticable to bring them all before the court, a bill may be filed against some of the parties, provided so many persons are made parties that their interests shall be such as to lead to a fair and honest support of the common interest; and when a decree has been

(*m*) 4 Bro. P. C. 373.
(*n*) Bunb. 158.
(*o*) See Leighton *v.* Leighton, 1 P. Wms. 670.
(*p*) Teynham *v.* Herbert, 2 Atk. 484, Mitf. Pl. 169; Sheffield Waterworks *v.* Yeomans, 2 L. R. Ch. App. 8.
(*q*) Powell *v.* Powis, 1 Y. & J. 161; Lord Sefton *v.* Salisbury, 7 W. R. 272; Sheffield Waterworks *v.* Yeomans, 2 L. R. Ch. App. 8.
[1] A bill of peace to restrain a person from instituting ejectment suits against another, on the ground that such suits would be vexatious, cannot be maintained unless the title to the land in dispute has been fully and satisfactorily litigated at law; the institution of repeated ejectment suits, if the same are abandoned before trial, cannot furnish a foundation for the maintenance of a bill of peace to restrain vexatious litigation. Patterson *v.* McCamant, 28 Mis. 210.
[2] McRoberts *v.* Washburne, 10 Minn. 23.

obtained with respect to the individual whose interest is fully
and fairly established, the court on the footing of the former
decree will carry the benefit of it into execution against other
individuals who were not parties (r). Actions by individuals
which go merely to establish their own private right and not
the common or public right of all, cannot be accepted as binding the public right. The court must have such a clear finding of a jury as will enable it with satisfaction to itself to
make a declaration as to their right binding on them and all
other persons (s).

50. A bill of this nature may be brought by a lord against
tenants for an encroachment, or by tenants against the
* 136 lord for * disturbance (t) ; by a party in interest to
establish a toll due by custom (u) ; or his right to the
profits of a fair, there being several claimants (x). So also
where a right of fishery was claimed by a corporation throughout the course of a considerable river, and was opposed by the
lords of manors and riparian proprietors, a bill was entertained
to establish that right against the several opponents, and a demurrer was overruled (y). So also a bill of the sort will lie
to settle the amount of a general fine to be paid by all the
copyhold tenants of a manor. So also it will lie to establish a
right of common of the freehold tenants of a manor (z).

51. The claim to an exclusive right of fishery, set up against
the common right of the public, is one which, if clearly established in point of fact, would give a man a right to ask for the
interference of a court of equity, by perpetual injunction (a).
So also the owner of a ferry franchise may come to the court

(r) Weale v. West Middlesex Waterworks Co., 1 J. &. W. 358; Adair v.
New River Co., 11 Ves. 429; Allen v.
Donnelly, 5 Ir. Ch. 236. See Foxwell
v. Webster, 10 Jur. N. S. 137.

(s) Allen v. Donnelly, 5 Ir. Ch. 236.

(t) How v. Bromsgrove, 1 Vern. 22;
Weeks v. Staker, 2 Vern. 301; Arthing-
ton v. Fawkes, ib. 356. See Lord Bath
v. Sherwin, Prec. Ch. 261; Lord Teynham v. Herbert, 2 Atk. 484; Hanson
v. Gardiner, 7 Ves. 309; Powell v.
Powis, 1 Y. & J. 161.

(u) City of London v. Perkins, 3 Bro.
P. C. 602.

(x) Ewelme Hospital v. Andover, 1
Vern. 266.

(y) Mayor of York v. Pilkington, 1
Atk. 282. See Ashworth v. Browne,
10 Ir. Ch. 421.

(z) Middleton v. Jackson, 1 Ch. Rep.
18; Popham v. Lancaster, ib. 51; Cowper v. Clark, 3 P. W. 157; Powell v.
Powis, 1 Y. & J. 159.

(a) Allen v. Donnelly, 5 Ir. Ch.
236; Ashworth v. Browne, 10 Ir. Ch.
421.

to be quieted in his right (*b*). But, as a general rule, the court will not establish a decree or perpetual injunction for the enjoyment of a right in contradiction to the public right, as if a man claims an exclusive right to a highway, or to obstruct the navigation (*c*).

52. A bill of the sort cannot be maintained where a right is disputed between two persons only, and the decree cannot conclude any one except them (*d*).

A bill of peace will lie against the lord by one copyholder on behalf of himself and the other copyholders to have their rights of common ascertained, but one copyholder not suing on behalf of all cannot maintain the suit (*e*).

(*b*) Letton *v.* Gooden, 2 L. R. Eq. 123.

(*c*) Hilton *v.* Lord Scarborough, 2 Eq. Ca. Ab. 171, Mitf. Pl. 171. See Allen *v.* Donnelly, 5 Ir. Ch. 236.

(*d*) Lord Teynham *v.* Herbert, 2 Atk. 483 ; Cowper *v.* Clark, 3 P. W. 157 ; Welby *v.* Duke of Rutland, 2 Bro. P. C. 39.

(*e*) Philipps *v.* Hudson, 2 L. R. Ch. App. 243.

As to bringing suit to remove a cloud upon a title, see Scott *v.* Onderdonk, 14 N. Y. 9 ; N. Y. & N. Haven R. R. Co. *v.* Schuyler, 17 N. Y. 592; and Wood *v.* Seeley, 32 N. Y. 105, where the court say the jurisdiction is not confined to any particular class of instruments if the invalidity does not appear upon their face. "Whatever their character, if they are capable of being used as a means of vexation or annoyance, if they throw a cloud upon the title or disturb the tranquil enjoyment of property, then it is against conscience and equity that they should be kept outstanding and ought to be cancelled." Where one purchased land under a contract for a conveyance with warranty of title, when he had completed the payment of the purchase-money, and knew that it was subject to an incumbrance, it was held, that he could not maintain a bill in equity to compel the executor and heir of the vendor to remove the incumbrance or provide indemnity for the vendee. Refeld *v.* Woodfolk, 22 How. U. S. 318.

*CHAPTER V.

INJUNCTIONS AGAINST PROCEEDINGS AT LAW UPON AND IN RESPECT
OF FOREIGN JUDGMENTS.

1. Court of Chancery has jurisdiction to restrain persons from acting on judgments of foreign courts.

2. Judgments of foreign courts, whether *in rem* or *personam*, disregarded, if the court giving it had no jurisdiction, or the forms of the court were grossly abused.

1. THE Court of Chancery has jurisdiction to restrain persons from suing on, or from acting on, judgments delivered by foreign courts (*e*). If the proceedings in the foreign courts were *in rem*, the judgment is conclusive here, and binding upon persons who were not before the court. The judgment cannot be questioned, even upon the ground that the foreign court had proceeded upon an erroneous notion of the law of England. Unless a case of perverse or intended disregard of the law of England can be made out in a case properly subject to that law by the comity of nations, a foreign judgment *in rem* will not be disregarded here (*f*). If, however, the proceedings were *in personam*, they are not binding here upon persons who were not summoned or made parties to the suit (*g*). The court here will examine the judgment for the purpose of ascertaining the fact (*h*). But a foreign judgment *in personam* is conclusive here, if the court which pronounced it had jurisdiction over the subject-matter of the suit, and the person against whom it is sought to be enforced (*i*). The judgment cannot be impeached on the ground that it is erroneous on the

*138 merits (*k*). Defences which might *have been raised

(*e*) Bowles *v.* Orr, 1 Y. & C. 464; Simpson *v.* Fogo, 1 J. & H. 18, 1 H. & M. 195.

(*f*) Imri *v.* Castrique, 8 C. B. N. S. 405; Simpson *v.* Fogo, 1 H. & M. 195. See Cammell *v.* Sewell, 5 H. & N. 728.

(*g*) Buchanan *v.* Rucker, 9 East, 192; Bank of Australasia *v.* Nias, 16 Q. B. 717; Castrique *v.* Imri, 8 C. B. N. S. 1; Simpson *v.* Fogo, 1 J. & H. 18.

(*h*) Reimers *v.* Druce, 23 Beav. 146.

(*i*) Ricardo *v.* Garcias, 12 Cl. & Fin. 368; Sheehy *v.* Professional Life Assurance Co., 3 C. B. N. S. 597; Simpson *v.* Fogo, 1 H. & M. 195; Vanquelin *v.* Bouard, 38 L. J. C. B. 78.

(*k*) Bank of Australasia *v.* Nias, 16 Q. B. 717; De Cosse Brissac *v.* Rathbone, 6 H. & N. 301; Scott *v.* Pilkington, 2 B. & S. 11; Simpson *v.* Fogo, 1 H. & M. 195.

in the foreign court cannot be brought here for the purpose of setting aside the judgment (*l*). But the court here may examine the judgment with reference to any thing that appears on the face of it; and if it appears on the face of the judgment that it proceeded upon principles not recognized by natural justice (*m*) or the law of England (*n*), or that the foreign court, while professing to administer English law, had been, in fact, mistaken as to the law (*o*), the judgment will be disregarded (*p*). The reasons which are attached to the judgment are part of the record, and will be treated as an integral part of the judgment (*q*). If the judgment of the foreign court can be shown to have been founded upon a perverse or intended disregard of the law of England, in a case properly subject to that law by the comity of nations, the case is much stronger than where there has been merely a mistaken notion as to English law (*r*). In Simpson *v.* Fogo (*s*), a British ship had been duly mortgaged in England. Afterwards she went to New Orleans, and was attached by the creditors of the mortgagor. The mortgagee intervened in the suit, but the court wholly disregarded his title, the law of Louisiana not allowing of mortgages of chattels, and the ship was sold, under a decree of the court, to the defendant. The ship having been brought to England, the mortgagee filed his bill to restrain the vessel from leaving Liverpool without his consent, and generally to establish his claim. A demurrer to the bill was overruled (*t*).

The judgment of a foreign court, whether *in rem* or *personam*, will, it would seem, be disregarded here, if it can be * shown that the court which pronounced it had no juris-   * 139 diction in the matter (*u*), or that the judgment had been

---

(*l*) Vanquelin *v.* Bouard, 33 L. J. C. B. 78.

(*m*) Buchanan *v.* Rucker, 9 East, 192; Price *v.* Dewhurst, 8 Sim. 279; Paul *v.* Roy, 15 Beav. 440; Bank of Australasia *v.* Nias, 16 Q. B. 717; Sheehy *v.* Professional Life Assurance Co., 3 C. B. N. S. 597; Simpson *v.* Fogo, 1 H. & M. 195.

(*n*) Bank of Australasia *v.* Nias, 16 Q. B. 717.

(*o*) Novelli *v.* Rossi, 2 B. & Ad. 757; Reimers *v.* Druce, 23 Beav. 154; on appeal, 3 Jur. N. S. 229; Simpson *v.* Fogo, 1 H. & M. 195.

(*p*) See Scott *v.* Pilkington, 2 B. & S. 11.

(*q*) Reimers *v.* Druce, 23 Beav. 154; Simpson *v.* Fogo, 1 H. & M. 195.

(*r*) Simpson *v.* Fogo, *ib.*

(*s*) 1 J. & H. 18.

(*t*) See S. C. 1 H. & M. 195.

(*u*) See Havelock *v.* Rockwood, 8 T. R. 268; Bowles *v.* Orr, 1 Y. & C. 464; Castrique *v.* Imri, 8 C. B. N. S. 1.

obtained through any gross abuse of the forms of the court (x). In Bowles $v.$ Orr (y), proceedings upon a foreign judgment *in personam* were restrained upon the ground of fraud, but the authority of the case is doubtful (z). The principles upon which the courts of this country deal with foreign judgments are better and more satisfactory than they were at the time when the judgment in Bowles $v.$ Orr was delivered. Whatever may be the value of that case as an authority at the present day, it seems clear that the courts of this country will not interfere with foreign judgments on the ground of fraud, where the fraud might have been pleaded as a defence in the foreign court, and was not pleaded, or was, if pleaded, overruled (a).[1] The question, however, remains open how far the courts of this country will interfere with foreign judgments where evidence of fraud may have been discovered after the date of the judgment (b).

The court will not carry into effect the interlocutory decree of a foreign court (c).

(x) Imri $v.$ Castrique, 8 C. B. N. S. 405; Castrique $v.$ Behrens, 30 L. J. Q. B. 163. See 2 Smith, L. C. 684.

(y) 1 Y. & C. 464.

(z) See Castrique $v.$ Behrens, 30 L. J. Q. B. 163; Vanquelin $v.$ Bouard, 33 L. J. C. B. 78.

(a) *Ib.*

(b) See as to setting aside judgments obtained by fraud, Shedden $v.$ Patrick, 1 Macq. 535.

(c) Paul $v.$ Roy, 15 Beav. 436. See Ball $v.$ Storie, 1 Sim. & St. 210.

[1] "The only question of fraud which is open to examination in a court of equity as a ground for enjoining the judgment of any court having jurisdiction of the case, whether domestic or foreign, is such as intervened in the proceedings by which the judgment was obtained." Story's Eq. Jur., § 1582.

* CHAPTER VI.   * 140

INJUNCTIONS IN RESPECT OF AWARDS.

1. COURTS of equity have always exercised jurisdiction over awards (*d*), and still entertain the jurisdiction, except where it is excluded by statute (*e*).[1]

2. In cases where the submission to arbitration was by agreement between the parties, the only mode of obtaining relief formerly against an award which had been obtained under circumstances of fraud or corruption on the part of the arbitrator, was by bill in equity. But if the agreement or submission to arbitration be in writing, and contains a proviso that it may be made a rule of court, the case is now governed by statute 9 & 10 Will. 3, c. 15, and the jurisdiction of equity is excluded (*f*). If there be such a proviso in the agreement or submission to arbitration, it is immaterial that it may not have been actually made a rule of court until after the award has been made or until after bill filed (*g*). The court of chancery is one of the courts of record invested with summary jurisdiction under the statute (*h*). If there was no proviso in

___

(*d*) Greenhill *v.* Church, 3 Rep. Ch. 49; Harris *v.* Mitchell, 2 Vern. 485; Burton *v.* Knight, *ib.* 514.

(*e*) Hamilton *v.* Rankin, 3 De G. & S. 782; Harding *v.* Wickham, 2 J. &. H. 676; Newry and Enniskillen Railway Co. *v.* Ulster Railway Co., 8 D. M. & G. 487; Smith *v.* Whitmore, 1 H. & M. 576, 2 D. J. & S. 297.

(*f*) Heming *v.* Swinnerton, 2 Ph. 79; Smith *v.* Whitmore, 1 H. & M. 576, 2 D. J. & S. 297.

(*g*) Nichols *v.* Roe, 3 M. & K. 439; Heming *v.* Swinnerton, 2 Ph. 79.

(*h*) Heming *v.* Swinnerton, 2 Ph 79. See Dawson *v.* Sadler, 1 Sim. & St. 537.

[1] In cases of fraud, mistake or accident, courts of equity may, in virtue of their general jurisdiction, interfere to set aside awards upon the same principles, and for the same reasons, which justify their interference in regard to other matters, where there is no adequate remedy at law. Story's Eq. Jur., § 1451, citing Duncan *v.* Lyon, 3 Johns. Ch. 356.

the agreement or submission to arbitration, enabling the parties to make it a rule of court, the jurisdiction was, until a
recent period, exclusive in equity (*i*). But by the
*141 seventeenth clause of the Common *Law Procedure
Act, 17 & 18 Vict. c. 125, it is declared that every agreement or submission to arbitration by consent, whether by deed
or instrument in writing, may be made a rule of a court of
common law, unless a contrary intention appears. The mere
existence, however, of a power to make an agreement or submission to arbitration a rule of court is not tantamount to an
agreement that it shall be made so, nor does it of itself, and
independently of agreement, exclude the ordinary jurisdiction
of the court (*k*). If there be no proviso that it may be made
a rule of court, it does not become a rule of court under the
Common Law Procedure Act, unless it be actually made a rule
of court (*l*). A submission to arbitration, under the Lands
Clauses Act, may be made a rule of any of the superior courts
on the application of either of the parties (*m*).

3. Before the statute 9 & 10 Will. 3, c. 15, courts of law
were in the practice, upon consent of parties, of referring
causes to arbitration, either by rule of court, or by order of
a judge, or at *nisi prius*, and of making the submission at the
same time a rule of court. In such cases courts of equity
exercised a concurrent jurisdiction over the award made under
the reference with courts of law, and the statute of William
does not appear to have interfered with the jurisdiction (*n*).
Nor has the jurisdiction been excluded by the enlarged powers
conferred on courts of common law by the Common Law Procedure Act, 17 & 18 Vict. c. 125, ss. 3–16. It is, however,
the rule of the court not to interfere with an award made
under a reference at law, unless there be something in the circumstances of the case to show, or to make it appear, that a
court of law has not full power and jurisdiction to grant full

---

(*i*) —— *v.* Mills, 17 Ves. 419;
Goodman *v.* Sayers, 2 J. & W. 249;
See Smith *v.* Whitmore, 1 H. & M. 576,
2 D. J. & S. 297.

(*k*) Smith *v.* Whitmore, 2 D. J. & S.
308, *per* L. J. Turner.

(*l*) *Ib.*

(*m*) 8 Vict. c. 18, s. 36.
(*n*) Lord Lonsdale *v.* Littledale, 2
Ves. Jr. 451; Nichols *v.* Chalie, 14 Ves.
267; Nicholls *v.* Roe, 3 M. & K. 439;
Chuck *v.* Cremer, 2 Ph. 477; Harding
v. Wickham, 2 J. & H. 676.

and adequate relief. The fact that a court of common law has a power of remitting the award for reconsideration, has weight with the court of chancery when called upon to interfere (o).

4. *The court has no jurisdiction to interfere with   *142 an award made under the provisions of the Benefit Building Act, 10 Geo. 4, c. 56, s. 27, unless there be error on the face of it, or it be shown to have been corruptly obtained (p).

5. The court has jurisdiction to entertain discovery in aid of a compulsory reference to arbitration (q).

6. In cases where the submission is by mere agreement between the parties, it is revocable by either party at the peril of an action for breach of agreement, until the award is made, unless there is a proviso in the agreement that it may be made a rule of court (r), or unless it has been actually made a rule of court under the Common Law Procedure Act, 17 & 18 Vict. c. 128, s. 17. But if there is no proviso in the agreement that it may be made a rule of court, and the submission is revoked before an award is made, a court of equity will not restrain a party from proceeding to enforce the award, merely on the ground that the submission had been revoked, if there were no good grounds for the revocation (s). All references to arbitration, made in pursuance of any rule of court, or judge's order, or order at *nisi prius*, are like references to arbitration, containing a proviso that they may be made a rule of court, irrevocable without leave of the court or a judge (t). A reference to arbitration, under the provisions of the Lands Clauses Act, is irrevocable by either party, without the consent of the other, although the submission may not have been made a rule of court (u).

7. A public board, such as the Board of Trade or Railway

(o) Londonderry and Enniskillen Railway Co. v. Leishman, 12 Beav. 423; Harding v. Wickham, 2 J. & H. 676.

(p) Armitage v. Walker, 2 K. & J. 211. See Fleming v. Self, 3 D. M. & G. 997.

(q) British Empire Shipping Co. v. Somes, 3 K. & J. 433.

(r) 3 & 4 Will. 4, c. 42, s. 39. See *Re* Kyle, 2 Jur. 760.

(s) Pope v. Lord Duncannon, 9 Sim. 177. See Harcourt v. Ramsbottom, 1 J. & W. 505.

(t) 3 & 4 Will. 4, c. 42, s. 39.

(u) 8 Vict. c. 18, s. 25.

Commissioners, is not bound by the strict practice which arbitrators are bound to adopt (x).

8. There is no original jurisdiction in the court in the nature of a writ of prohibition to restrain an arbitrator from proceeding to make an award. The conduct of the parties may, however, found a sufficient ground for the interference
* 143   of the court prior * to the award (y). If the agreement for reference is impeached as containing terms which it would be beyond the power of the arbitrator to determine, and which, if determined by him, would render the award invalid, the court may restrain the arbitrator from acting, and the parties from proceeding, before him for an award under the agreement (z).[1]

9. An agreement to refer disputes to arbitration does not oust the superior courts of their jurisdiction, nor can parties agree between themselves to withdraw the decision from the determination of the ordinary tribunals (a). But a man may covenant that no right of action shall accrue till a third person has decided on any difference that may arise between himself and the other party to the covenant (b). Where provisions exist for the settlement of disputes by arbitration, the court

---

(x) Newry and Enniskillen Railway Co. v. Ulster Railway Co., 8 D M. & G. 487.

(y) Pickering v. Cape Town Railway Co., 1 L. R. Eq. 84.

(z) Maunsell v. Midland Great Western Railway Co. of Ireland, 1 H. & M. 133.

(a) Thompson v. Charnock, 8 T. R. 139 ; Street v. Rigby, 6 Ves. 815 ; Nichols v. Charlie, 14 Ves. 269 ; Benson v. Heathorn, 1 Y. & C. C. C. 326 ; Horton v. Sayer, 4 H. & N. 643 ; Lee v. Page, 30 L. J. Ch. 857 ; Pickering v. Cape Town Railway Co., 1 L. R. Eq. 84 ; but see Dimsdale v. Robertson, 2 J. & L. 58.

(b) Scott v. Avery, 5 H. L. 811; Scott v. Corporation of Liverpool, 3 D. & J. 357.

[1] Under a general submission, arbitrators have power to decide on the law and fact. Boston Water Power Co. v. Gray, 6 Met. 131 ; Fairchild v. Adams, 11 Cush. 549; Speer v. Bidwell, 44 Penn. St. 23 ; Cushman v. Wooster, 45 N. H. 410. " And they are not bound to award on mere dry principles of law ; but they make their award according to the principles of equity and good conscience." Story's Eq. Jur., § 1454. And the court will not correct a mere mistake of judgment on the part of the arbitrator. Vanderwerker v. Vermont Central Railroad, 27 Vt. 130. But if by the submission the award is to be in accordance with the law, and it appears upon its face that a legal question involved was not decided, it will be fatal to the award. Estes v. Mansfield, 6 Allen, 69.

As to what improprieties of conduct of the parties or arbitrators, will induce a court of equity to set aside the award, see Emerson v. Udall, 13 Vt. 477 ; Cutting v. Carter, 29 Vt. 72 ; Brown v. Evans, 6 Allen, 333 ; Fisk v. South Wilbraham Mnfg. Co., 7 Allen, 476 ; Cleland v. Hedly, 5 R. I. 163.

will withhold its interposition, until the remedy thus provided for has been resorted to (c).

10. Equity will not give relief against an award where there has been any laches on the part of the party making the application (d), or his conduct has been such as to destroy his right to resort to the court for relief (e).

(c) Shrewsbury and Birmingham Railway Co. v. Stour Valley Railway Co., 2 D. M. &. G. 866.

(d) Jones v. Bennett, 1 Bro. P. C. 528. See Eads v. Williams, 3 Eq. Rep. 244; Nichols v. Hancock, 7 D. M. & G. 300.

(e) Smith v. Whitmore, 1 H. & M. 576, 2 D. J. & S. 297. See Ormes v. Beadel, 2 D. F. & J. 333.

*144   * CHAPTER VII.

INJUNCTIONS AGAINST PROCEEDINGS AT LAW AGAINST OR BY THE
OFFICERS OF THE COURT.

1. Court of equity will not permit its officers to be proceeded against at law for acts done in the course of their office.
2. All actions at law against receivers will be restrained.
3. So in case of a sequestrator in possession.
4. But not of a sheriff acting under a writ of *fi. fa.* issued by the court.
5. Court of equity will restrain its officers from seeking redress in other courts.

1. THE court will not permit its officers to be proceeded against at law for acts done in the course of their office. A man who may have sustained injury in consequence of any order or proceeding of the court, or by reason of any thing which has occurred in the execution of its process, must apply to the court for redress, and not to a court of law (*f*). If the matter complained of involves a question of the jurisdiction of the court, or of the validity and propriety of its orders or process, the court will never allow such a question to be carried to a court of law (*g*); but if, the jurisdiction of the court and the validity of its order being fully admitted, redress is sought merely in respect of some irregularity or excess in the execution of the order, the court will at its discretion either itself give redress to the aggrieved party, or give him leave to proceed at law for damages, as justice and convenience may require (*h*).[1] In Walker *v.* Micklethwait (*i*), a sheriff having

(*f*) Bailey *v.* Devereaux, 1 Vern. 269; May *v.* Hook, 1 J. & W. 663, n.; Frowd *v.* Lawrence, *ib.* 655; Aston *v.* Heron, 2 M. & K. 396; Arrowsmith *v.* Hill, 2 Ph. 609.

(*g*) Aston *v.* Heron, 2 M. & K. 396; Walker *v.* Micklethwait, 1 Dr. & Sm. 51.

(*h*) Aston *v.* Heron, 2 M. & K. 396; *Ex parte* Clarke, 1 R. & M. 563; Chalie *v.* Pickering, 1 Keen, 749; Darley *v.* Nicholson, 2 Dr. & War. 86; Arrowsmith *v.* Hill, 2 Ph. 609; Bricknell

v. Stamford, 1 Beav. 368; Morrison *v.* Morrison, 10 Jur. 773; Randfield *v.* Randfield, 1 Dr. & Sm. 310; Whitehead *v.* Lynes, 34 Beav. 161; Goucher *v.* Clayton, 14 L. T. N. S. 494.

(*i*) 1 Dr. & Sm. 51.

[1] " Wherever the jurisdiction of the court, the title of its officers, or the validity of its process or of its orders, is disputed or attempted to be drawn in question by a suit instituted in another court against those who are acting under the orders or the process of the

[152]

ejected, under a writ of assistance issued in pursuance of an order of the court, a person from premises which had been sold under an order of the court, an action of trover against the sheriff was restrained, although the action sought damages for a trespass by the sheriff in taking chattels not included in the order. * " The action," said Kindersley, V. C. (k), *145 " proceeds on the footing that the proceedings in this court are entirely wrong, and that the plaintiff is still owner of the property which has been sold by order of the court, and from which he has been ejected by the order of the court." The injunction is always without prejudice to any application that the defendant may be advised to make to the court for compensation (l). The defendant must, however, pay the costs of the application and the action (m).

2. When the court has appointed a receiver, it will not allow the possession of that receiver to be disturbed by any

---

court of chancery, it is bound to interfere for their protection. In such cases the court has no choice; it cannot allow any proceedings of the kind to go on without abandoning its own jurisdiction. It must restrain of course; otherwise it permits its own orders to be rescinded, and its jurisdiction to be questioned, — its orders to be rescinded indirectly and not by the superior court of appeal; its jurisdiction to be questioned by courts of inferior or co-ordinate authority. But where the process of the court has been irregularly and illegally issued, and has been set aside by the court itself for such irregularity, or where an officer of this court, under color or pretence of executing its orders, has transcended his authority and interfered with the personal rights of others, — where the process or the orders of this court have furnished a mere pretext for doing wrong, — there are no considerations, either of principle or of practical convenience, which require the court, in every case, to draw to itself the consideration of the matter, to prevent all other tribunals from punishing the wrong-doer, and to exclude the injured party from access to all redress save that which its own jurisdiction can afford. Where process is set aside for irregularity, I believe all courts exercise the power of making it a condition of the order, that no suit shall be brought for acts done under such voidable process, if the court, in the exercise of its discretion, thinks proper to insert such a condition in its order. And this court, upon a summary application, may restrain the prosecution of any such suit, although it has not been made a condition of the order that no suit shall be brought. But as, upon such an application, this court may afford the injured person redress here, the party who wishes this court to take the matter into its own hands and restrain all proceedings elsewhere, should seek the aid of this court promptly, and before he has tried the chances of a litigation of the matter in another tribunal." Mackay v. Blackett, 9 Paige, 437.

(k) Ib.

(l) Frowd v. Lawrence, 1 J. & W. 655; Philipps v. Worth, 2 R. & M. 638; Brandon v. Brandon, 1 L. J. Ch. N. S. 172; Bricknell v. Stamford, 1 Beav. 368; Walker v. Micklethwait, 1 Dr. & Sm. 51. See as to the principle upon which damages are to be ascertained, Moore v. Moore, 25 Beav. 8; see also Darley v. Nicholson, 2 Dr. & War. 86.

(m) Walker v. Micklethwait, 1 Dr. & Sm. 51; but see Philipps v. Worth, 2 R. & M. 638; Bricknell v. Stamford, 1 Beav. 869.

person, however good his right may be (n). If a party claiming a right in the same subject-matter was in possession of the
right which he claims at the time the receiver was appointed,
the appointment of the receiver leaves him in such possession ;
if, on the other hand, the claimant was out of possession, he
must apply to the court for leave before he institutes any legal
proceedings affecting the possession which the receiver has
acquired (o).[1] A man who thinks he has a right paramount
to that of the receiver must, before he presumes to take any
steps of his own motion, apply to the court for leave to assert
his right against the receiver. The court will not allow the
first step in an action at law to be taken against a receiver by
anybody without an application to the court for leave (p) ; nor
will it allow payment to him to be intercepted, although the
order appointing him may have been perfectly erroneous (q).

It is not competent to the sheriff to impugn the order
*146 appointing *a receiver, or to seize property in his pos-
session (r) ; nor can a railway company proceed under
the Lands Clauses Act to take without the leave of the court
lands in the possession of a receiver (s) ; nor can a receiver
appointed to get in property, part of which he finds in the possession of another receiver, take proceedings to deprive the
latter of such possession without the authority of the court (t).
Whether the party proceeding at law did or did not know that
a receiver has been appointed over property, or however clear
the right of the claimant may be, the court will restrain the
prosecution of the claim, if it be instituted without leave (u).
In Turner v. Turner (x), the agents of the receiver in a cause,
acting under leave of the court, having taken forcible posses
sion of a house occupied by a servant of one of the defend-

(n) Evelyn v. Lewis, 3 Ha. 472;
Defries v. Creed, 34 L. J. Ch. 607.
(o) Evelyn v. Lewis, 3 Ha. 472.
See Randfield v. Randfield, 1 Dr. &
Sm. 310.
(p) Evelyn v. Lewis, 3 Ha. 472;
Hawkins v. Gathercole, 1 Drew. 12;
Ames v. Birkenhead Docks, 20 Beav.
353.
(q) Ames v. Birkenhead Docks, 20
Beav. 353.
(r) Russell v. East Anglian Railway
Co., 3 Mac. & G. 117

(s) Tink v. Rundle, 10 Beav. 318.
(t) Ward v. Swift, 6 Ha. 312.
(u) Evelyn v. Lewis, 3 Ha. 473.
(x) 15 Jur. 218.
[1] In matter of Merritt, 5 Paige, 125.
And the court appointing the receiver
has jurisdiction to restrain him from
prosecuting an unjust and vexatious
suit at law, in the name of a third
person without his consent, although
the persons applying for such relief are
not parties to the suit in which the
receiver was appointed. Ib.

ants, an order was made restraining that defendant from prosecuting an indictment against the agents.   An action against a person who professes to act under the authority of a receiver, will not be restrained, unless it be clear that he was acting under authority (*y*).   The court will always, on a proper application being made, take care to give a party who has a right paramount to that of the receiver the means of obtaining justice, and will even assist him in asserting that right and having the benefit of it (*z*).   Leave may be given to bring ejectment (*a*).

3. A sequestrator in possession is an officer of the court; his possession may not be disturbed without the leave of the court (*b*).   If a sequestrator has been forcibly dispossessed, an injunction to restore possession will be awarded, and the party * so dispossessing him will be committed   * 147 for contempt (*c*).   If a sequestrator finds a person in possession of the property, the court will order a writ of assistance to issue, unless the party submit to come in and be examined *pro interesse suo* (*d*).   Where a sequestrator obtains possession of property as belonging to the party against whom the process issued, and such property is claimed by a third person, the mode of trying the right is in the discretion of the court (*e*).

4. A sheriff acting under a writ of *fi. fa.* issued by the court is not an officer of the court.   The rules which apply to the protection of the officers of the court do not apply to him (*f*).

5. The court of chancery assumes in many cases jurisdiction over its own officers, as such, to restrain them from seek-

(*y*) Birch *v.* Oldis, Sau. & Sc. 146.
(*z*) *Ib.*; Hawkins *v.* Gathercole, 1 Drew. 12; Russell *v.* East Anglian Railway Co., 3 Mac. & G. 104; Ames *v.* Birkenhead Docks, 20 Beav. 353; Randfield *v.* Randfeld, 1 Dr. & Sm. 310.
(*a*) Brooks *v.* Greathead, 1 J. & W. 179; see also as to interference with the possession of a receiver, Broad *v.* Wickham, 4 Sim. 511; De Winton *v.* Mayor of Brecon, 28 Beav. 202; Lane *v.* Sterne, 3 Giff. 629.
(*b*) Angell *v.* Smith, 9 Ves. 336; Brooks *v.* Greathead, 1 J. & W. 178;

Kaye *v.* Cunninghame, 5 Madd. 406. See Rock *v.* Cook, 2 Ph. 691.
(*c*) Pelham *v.* Duchess of Newcastle, 3 Sw. 289, n.; Angell *v.* Smith, 9 Ves. 336.
(*d*) Empringham *v.* Short, 3 Ha. 461.
(*e*) *Ib.*; see also as to sequestration, Wilson *v* Metcalfe, 1 Beav. 263; Tatham *v.* Parker, 1 Sm. & G. 506; Knight *v.* Knight, 4 W. R. 771.
(*f*) Rock *v.* Cook, 2 Ph. 691; Try *v.* Try, 13 Beav. 422. See Tufton *v.* Harding, 29 L. J. Ch. 225. Comp. Russell *v.* East Anglian Railway Co., 3 Mac. & G. 104.

ing redress in any other courts. Thus a man, who had been employed as an auctioneer in a sale directed by the court, by the committees of a lunatic's estate, and had carried in his claim before the Master, was restrained from bringing an action at law against the committees, the claim arising in the course of an employment under a lunacy, and for the purpose of carrying into effect the directions of the court in the lunacy being properly, in the absence of any special agreement to the contrary, the subject of an inquiry before the Master (g). So also, where commissioners for the examination of witnesses brought actions against the solicitor for fees claimed by them in respect of their business as commissioners, the court said the case was not distinguishable from *Re* Weaver, and restrained them referring it to the Master to inquire what was due to them for their fees (h).

(g) *Re* Weaver, 2 M. & C. 441.
(h) Blundell *v.* Gladstone, 9 Sim. 455; Ambrose *v.* Dunmow Union, 8 Beav. 43. See Peters *v.* Beer, 14 Beav. 101.

* CHAPTER VIII.   * 148

INJUNCTIONS TO RESTRAIN PROCEEDINGS IN THE ADMIRALTY COURT,
THE LORD MAYOR'S COURT, THE PROBATE COURT, AND THE
COURTS OF A FOREIGN COUNTRY.

1. Court of equity has jurisdiction to restrain parties from proceeding in courts other
   than those of common law.
2. Extent to which it will act upon matters in admiralty courts.
3. Will not interfere, however, unless to do so would be a sound exercise of its discretion.
4-6. Will restrain proceedings in ecclesiastical courts.
7-9. And in Lord Mayor's Court, county courts, and special tribunals.
10. Will not in general interfere with proceedings in courts of bankruptcy.
11. May restrain persons in its jurisdiction from prosecuting suits in courts of foreign
    countries.
12. But will not destroy any priority to which, from the nature of his security, a creditor
    in a foreign country is entitled as against the assets there, according to the law of
    that country, although they come to be distributed here.
13. Where the court is in possession of a cause, and has power to do justice, it will
    restrain the parties from proceeding in courts of a foreign country.
14. Even though no decree has been obtained in this country, if a suit here is best cal-
    culated to do justice.
15. But if more conducive to substantial justice, the foreign proceedings will be allowed
    to go on.
16. Proceedings in respect to a contract made here, in a foreign court, not in accordance
    with the rules of English law will be restrained.
17. Action here may be restrained to await decision of foreign court.
18. Limits of the jurisdiction to restrain actions and suits in other countries.
19. If court is in full possession of cause, injunction will be granted on motion, otherwise
    on bill.

1. THE jurisdiction of the court of chancery by injunction
is not confined to the staying of proceedings in the courts of
common law.   The court has clear and undisputable jurisdiction, on a proper case being made out, to restrain persons from
instituting or prosecuting suits in other courts in this country
than the courts of common law.   The principles on which the
court interferes with proceedings in other courts are the same
as those upon which it interferes with proceedings before
courts of law.   If the question is one which may be more
satisfactorily and more completely settled in equity than by

[157]

the court in which proceedings have been taken or instituted, the court of chancery will interfere by injunction, and draw the matter within its own jurisdiction. If, on the other hand, the powers of the court in which proceedings have been taken or instituted are sufficient and adequate for the purposes of justice, the proceedings will be allowed to take their course. The court will not interfere with proceedings in other courts, unless to do so would be a sound exercise of its discretion. It is not necessary to induce the court to interfere with the proceedings in other courts, that it should find a case which would entitle the plaintiff to relief at all events. It is quite sufficient if the court finds upon the pleadings, and upon the evidence a case which makes the transaction a proper subject of investigation in a court of equity (i).

2. The court of admiralty acts to a certain extent * 149   upon equitable * principles, and possesses a certain equitable jurisdiction (j) ; but in many cases the powers of that court are insufficient for the purposes of justice. In cases of the sort the court of chancery will, if necessary, act as ancillary to it, as in the appointment of a receiver *pendente lite*, and in other cases (k), or will restrain proceedings in that court, and will draw the matter within its own jurisdiction. Thus proceedings in the admiralty court on a bottomry bond, alleged to have been executed fraudulently, were restrained, notwithstanding the admiralty court had the power of moderating the amount of the demand to be recovered on the bond (l). "The court of admiralty," said Lord Cottenham (m), "though it possesses a certain equitable jurisdiction, possesses no jurisdiction enabling it to exercise the power which this court exercises over the instrument itself for the purpose of setting aside that which ought never to have existed, so as to prevent any validity being given to an instrument which originated in fraud " (n). In a subsequent case the court carried the jurisdiction farther, and restrained pro-

---

(i) Glascott v. Lang, 3 M. & C. 451 ; Cotesworth v. Stephens, 4 Ha. 194 ; Pennell v. Roy, 3 D. M. & G. 126. See Duncombe v. Greenacre, 2 D. F. & J. 509 ; Sablicich v. Russell, 2 L. R. Eq. 441.

(j) See *Re* Victoria, 5 Jur. N. S. 204.
(k) Brenan v. Preston, 10 Ha. 335.
(l) Glascott v. Lang, 3 M. & C. 451.
(m) *Ib*. 457.
(n) See Dobson v. Lyall, *ib*. 453, n.

ceedings commenced in the admiralty court on a bottomry bond, given under circumstances affording great suspicion of fraud, on the ground that it did not appear that the admiralty court, though it had jurisdiction to determine the validity of the bond, and to raise all such questions as might be necessary to do complete justice, could investigate the matter so conveniently, directly, and effectually as the court of chancery could (*o*).

In Jarvis *v*. Chandler (*p*), proceedings on a sentence in the admiralty court were restrained, new evidence having been discovered at a period when, according to the practice of that court, it could not be received.

3. The court will not, however, interfere with proceedings in the admiralty court, unless to do so would be a sound exercise * of its discretion (*q*).   Thus Lord Hardwicke   * 150 refused to restrain the admiralty court from entertaining a suit respecting the legality of the capture of a vessel as prize, in a case where it was alleged that some of the papers were lost, and that the captain of the vessel had been forced by the captors to sign a note which, if produced, would have led certainly to his being cast in the suit.'   He said that to exercise jurisdiction in such a case would entirely defeat the Act of Parliament in relation to prizes, and that the court of admiralty could by its own rules put the case into a proper method of inquiry, and do full justice (*r*).   So also, in Nicholl *v*. Goodair (*s*), the court refused to restrain the registrar of the court of admiralty from paying over to a bankrupt, under a treasury warrant, the proceeds of a vessel which had been condemned as a droit of the crown.   The proceeds had not at the time of the application reached the hands of the registrar.   The court was of opinion that it could not interfere until an actual trust had been created by the payment of the moneys over to the registrar.   To interfere, in the manner sought by the motion, with an officer of the court of admiralty, would

(*o*) Duncan *v*. M'Calmont, 3 Beav. 415. See Castelli *v*. Cook, 7 Ha. 89; Hughes *v*. Morris, 13 Jur. 1065 ; Place *v*. Potts, 5 H. L. 383.
(*p*) T. & R. 319.
(*q*) Glascott *v*. Lang, 3 M. & C. 451,

455. See Brenan *v*. Preston, 1 W. R. 69.
(*r*) Anon., 3 Atk. 350. See also Sablicich *v*. Russell, 2 L. R. Eq. 441.
(*s*) 10 Ves. 155.

have been an act in derogation of the jurisdiction of that court.

By the 514th clause of the Merchant Shipping Act, 1854, 17 & 18 Vict. c. 104, power is given to the court of chancery to determine, at the suit of a ship-owner, the damage payable upon loss or damage to the ship and cargo, to distribute the amount ratably among the several claimants, and to stop all actions and suits pending in the court of admiralty, or any other court relating to the same subject-matter (*t*). In an application under the clause, the ship-owner must aver that he has incurred liability in respect of some damage (*u*). Even although an adverse claimant has obtained a definitive judgment of the court of admiralty condemning the ship, * 151 the * court has jurisdiction to restrain him from proceeding farther there (*x*). The court has no control, however, over the ship itself, and cannot prevent the party who has obtained such a judgment from proceeding to a sale of the ship, and retaining out of the proceeds such costs as he may be entitled to retain under the order of the admiralty court (*y*). The 65th section of the Act which empowers the court to issue an order prohibiting for a time to be named in the order any dealing with the ship, or share of the ship, does not deprive the court of chancery of its ordinary jurisdiction to protect property during litigation (*z*).

4. The court of chancery had also jurisdiction to restrain proceedings in the ecclesiastical court (*a*). In Hill *v.* Turner (*b*), a low woman who had entrapped an infant ward of court into a marriage was restrained from proceeding against him for restitution of conjugal rights and alimony (*c*). So also, where a legacy had been left to a woman, the court restrained her husband from suing for it, till he had made an adequate settlement on her (*d*). So also, the next of kin of

(*t*) See Hill *v.* Audus, 1 K. & J. 263; African Steam Ship Co. *v.* Swanzy, *ib.* 326, 2 K. & J. 660; Leycester *v.* Logan, 3 K. & J. 446, 4 K. & J. 726.

(*u*) Hill *v.* Audus, 1 K. & J. 263.

(*x*) Leycester *v.* Logan, 3 K. & J. 446.

(*y*) *Ib.*, S. C. 4 K. & J. 725.

(*z*) Orr *v.* Dickenson, John. 4.

(*a*) Anon., 1 Atk. 491, 3 Atk. 627, 629.

(*b*) 3 Atk. 516.

(*c*) See Hunt *v.* Hunt, 8 Jur. N. S. 85.

(*d*) Anon., 1 Atk. 491; Mealis *v.* Mealis, 5 Ves. 517, n., Dick. 373. See Duncombe *v.* Greenacre, 2 D. F. & J. 509.

an intestate were restrained from proceeding in the ecclesiastical court against the wife and executrix of an intestate to
compel distribution where she had an equitable claim against
his personal estate (*e*). So also a legatee was restrained
after a decree for the administration of assets from suing for
his legacy (*f*). Where a party had long acted under a will,
and had admitted the validity of the probate in proceedings in
the court of chancery and the House of Lords, and then
sought, without bringing forward any new evidence, to contro-
vert the validity of the will in the ecclesiastical court, an injunction was granted to restrain him from proceeding in that
court (*g*).

5. * The court would not entertain a bill of discovery　* 152
in aid of the jurisdiction of the ecclesiastical court,
because that court was fully capable of coming at the discovery
itself (*h*). But inasmuch as the court of probate, established
under 20 & 21 Vict. c. 77, has not the same power of compelling discovery which the old court possessed, and the
ancient jurisdiction of the court is not affected by that act,
the court will restrain a man from proceeding in the court of
probate to prove a will until he has made the necessary discovery (*i*).

6. The court has, however, no jurisdiction to interfere
against the granting probate of a will on the ground of the
will having been obtained by fraud or forgery. The court of
probate is competent to deal with the matter (*k*).

7. The court of chancery has also jurisdiction to restrain
by injunction proceedings in the Lord Mayor's Court, and will
interpose, where the circumstances of the case create an equity
for the interference of the court, or the question at stake is
one which may be more satisfactorily and expeditiously settled

---

(*e*) Backhouse *v.* Hunter, 1 Cox, 342.
(*f*) Stonehouse *v.* Stonehouse, Dick.
98; Smith *v.* Kempson, *ib.* 769. See
Duncombe *v.* Greenacre, 2 D. F. & J.
509.
(*g*) Sheffield *v.* Duchess of Buckingham, 1 Atk. 628. See Gascoyne *v.*
Chandler, 3 Swanst. 418, n.
(*h*) Dun *v.* Coates, 1 Atk. 288; Earl
of Derby *v.* Duke of Atholl, 1 Ves.
202, 205.

(*i*) Fuller *v.* Ingram, 28 L. J. Ch.
432.
(*k*) Archer *v.* Mosse, 2 Vern. 8; Nelson *v.* Oldfield, *ib.* 76; Plume *v.* Beale,
1 P. Wms. 388; Kerrick *v.* Bransby, 7
Bro. P. C. 437; Allen *v.* Macpherson,
1 H. L. 191; Hindson *v.* Weatherill, 1
Sm. & G. 604. See Boyse *v.* Bussbo-
rough, 6 H. L. 1.

in equity between all the parties. Thus parties were, under the circumstances of the case, restrained after a commission in bankruptcy from taking proceedings in foreign attachment in the Lord Mayor's Court (*l*). So also proceedings in foreign attachment in the same court were restrained on the ground that the matter could be more satisfactorily and expeditiously settled in the court of chancery (*m*). So also a creditor of an intestate will be restrained from taking proceedings in the Lord Mayor's Court after a decree for administration (*n*). So

*153   also an officer who had made an equitable assignment of moneys to arise from *the sale of his commission, was restrained from taking proceedings by foreign attachment in respect of them (*o*). In Hipkins *v.* Newton (*p*), an injunction was granted restraining moneys from being paid out of the Lord Mayor's Court.

8. The court of chancery has also jurisdiction to restrain by injunction proceedings in the county courts (*q*).

9. Where the legislature has constituted a tribunal for a special purpose, the court of chancery will not prevent persons who are entitled to do so from applying to that tribunal (*r*). No equity can be founded on an allegation that a court, legally constituted, is not properly competent to decide questions within its jurisdiction (*s*). But if a case of fraud can be shown, the court will entertain jurisdiction (*t*).

10. The court of chancery will not in general interfere with proceedings in the court of bankruptcy, for that court has, to a certain extent, an equitable jurisdiction, and is therefore capable of doing justice between the parties in matters of equity (*u*). But the court of chancery will interfere to re-

(*l*) Barker *v.* Goodair, 11 Ves. 78; Sieveking *v.* Behrens, 2 M. & C. 581. See Pennell *v.* Roy, 3 D. M. & G. 136.

(*m*) Cotesworth *v.* Stephens, 4 Ha. 194. See Anderson *v.* Kemshead, 16 Beav. 329; Mildred *v.* Neate, Dick. 279; Furnival *v.* Boyle, 4 Russ. 142.

(*n*) Redhead *v.* Welton, 30 L. J. Ch. 577.

(*o*) L'Estrange *v.* L'Estrange, 13 Beav. 281; Webster *v.* Webster, 31 Beav. 393.

(*p*) 9 L. J. Ch. 227.

(*q*) Ratcliffe *v.* Winch, 16 Beav. 576; Neighbour *v.* Brown, 26 L. J. Ch. 670.

In Trinick *v.* Bordfield, Toth. 182, an injunction was granted to restrain proceedings in the Stanneries Court.

(*r*) Harris *v.* Jose, 14 W. R. 303.

(*s*) Barnsley Canal Co. *v.* Twibell, 7 Beav. 19. See Bateman *v.* Boynton, 1 L. R. Ch. Ap. 359; Earl Beauchamp *v.* Darby, 1 W. N. 308.

(*t*) Earl Beauchamp *v.* Darby, 1 W. N. 308.

(*u*) Ex parte Stephens, 11 Ves. 27; Ex parte Hanson, 12 Ves. 347; Ex parte Roffey, 19 Ves. 469; Thompson *v.* Dereham, 1 Ha. 358, *infra*.

strain a man from taking proceedings, the effect of which may
be to afford a foundation for an adjudication in bankruptcy, or
from doing any act by means of, or in consequence of, which
an act of bankruptcy may be deemed to have been committed
by another, in a case where such a proceeding or such an act
would be contrary to equity (*x*). The mere allegation that
the proceedings in bankruptcy, with a view to making an
alleged debtor a bankrupt, are dictated purely by malice, and
that no debt is due, is not sufficient (*y*).

11. * The jurisdiction of the court of chancery in   * 154
restraining proceedings in other courts is not confined
to courts within this country. The court has clear and undoubted jurisdiction on a proper case being made out to restrain
persons within its jurisdiction from prosecuting suits in the
courts of foreign countries. In the exercise of the jurisdiction the court does not proceed upon any claim of right to
interfere with or control the course of proceedings in the
tribunals of a foreign country, or to prevent them from adjudicating on the right of parties when drawn in controversy,
and duly presented for their determination. The jurisdiction
is founded on the clear authority vested in courts of equity
over persons within the limits of their jurisdiction, and amenable to process to restrain them from doing acts which work
wrong and injury to others, and are therefore contrary to
equity and good conscience. As the order of the court in
such cases is pointed solely at the individual, and does not extend to the tribunal where the suit or proceeding is pending,
it is wholly immaterial that the party to whom it is addressed
is prosecuting his action in the courts of a foreign country (*z*).
If the circumstances of the case are such as to make it the
duty of the court to restrain a party from instituting or carrying on proceedings in a court here, they will also warrant it in

---

(*x*) Attwood *v.* Banks, 2 Beav. 192;
Perry *v.* Walker, 1 Y. & C. C. C. 672;
Pim *v.* Wilson, 2 Ph. 653, 656.   See
Mather *v.* Lay, 2 J. & H. 374.   Comp.
Re London and Eastern Banking Cor-
poration, 2 D. & J. 484.

(*y*) Pim *v.* Wilson, 2 Ph. 653, 656.

(*z*) Lord Cranstown *v.* Johnstone, 3
Ves. 182, 5 Ves. 277; Lord Portarling-
ton *v.* Soulby, 3 M. & K. 108; Bunbury
v. Bunbury, 3 Jur. 648; Carron Iron
Co. *v.* Maclaren, 5 H. L. 416, 436, *per*
Lord Cranworth.

restraining proceedings in a foreign country (*a*). Thus, in Lord Portarlington *v.* Soulby (*b*), the indorsee of a bill of exchangê was restrained from suing the plaintiff in the Irish courts upon the bill upon certain equitable grounds which would have warranted a similar injunction against any action in the courts of this country. Upon the same principle the rule which prevents a creditor from proceeding with an action at law for the recovery of his debt after a decree in an administration or creditor's suit, is applicable to the case of a

* 155 creditor proceeding in a foreign court (*c*). * If after a decree for administration, under which he may come in and prove his debt, and have complete relief, a creditor within the jurisdiction institutes proceedings abroad in respect of the same matter, the court of chancery considers that act as a vexatious harassing of the opposite party, and restrains the foreign proceedings (*d*). Thus, in Beauchamp *v.* Lord Huntley (*e*), a creditor who had come in under a decree and got relief against the English assets, was restrained from further prosecuting a suit in relation to the same estate in Ireland. So also, in Graham *v.* Maxwell (*f*), a creditor who had come in here under a decree in an administration suit, was restrained from proceeding with an action in Scotland, which he had commenced in ignorance of the decree (*g*). The court may, however, under the peculiar circumstances of the case, decline to exercise the jurisdiction, although the person whose proceedings are sought to be restrained has appeared and put in an answer (*h*).

12. The rule which prevents a creditor within the jurisdiction from taking proceedings abroad after a decree for administration here, does not destroy any priority to which, from the nature of his security, a creditor in a foreign country is entitled as against the assets there according to the law of

(*a*) 5 H. L. 439, *per* Lord Cranworth; Portarlington *v.* Soulby, 3 M. & K. 104. See Ainslie *v.* Sims, 23 L. J. Ch. 163.

(*b*) 3 M. & K. 104.
(*c*) Graham *v.* Maxwell, 1 Mac. & G. 71.
(*d*) 5 H. L. 437, *per* Lord Cranworth.

(*e*) Jac. 546.
(*f*) 1 Mac. & G. 71.
(*g*) 5 H. L. 455, *per* Lord St. Leonards. See, as to the costs, Beauchamp *v.* Lord Huntley, Jac. 546; Graham *v.* Maxwell, 1 Mac. & G. 71.
(*h*) Stainton *v.* Carron Iron Co., 21 Beav. 159, 161.

that country, although they come to be distributed here (*i*). Thus, in Cooke *v.* Gregson (*k*), it was held that in a creditor's suit for the administration of assets, a judgment creditor in Ireland was as against the proceeds of Irish property entitled to priority over simple contract creditors (*l*).

13. The principle upon which the court, after being in full possession of a cause in which it has full power to do justice, interferes to restrain a party to the suit from resorting to another tribunal in respect of the same matter or the same demand, applies also where the proceedings are instituted in a *foreign country (*m*). In Harrison *v.* Gur-   *156 ney (*n*), a decree had been obtained for the execution of the trusts of a deed for the benefit of creditors, and a receiver of real estates in England and Ireland had been appointed. Some of the trustees afterwards filed a bill in Ireland for executing the trusts of the same deed. Lord Eldon restrained them from prosecuting that suit, on the ground that it sought the same relief as might be had under the decree obtained in this country. So also, in Beckford *v.* Kemble (*o*), after a decree in this country for an account on a bill to redeem a West India mortgage, Sir John Leach would not suffer the mortgagee to prosecute a suit in Jamaica for foreclosing the same mortgage on the ground that full relief might be had under the decree in this country (*p*). So also, in Booth *v.* Leycester (*q*), a person was restrained from prosecuting a suit in Ireland after a decree in this country, the subject-matter of the suit being the same as that already adjudicated on in the court. So also, in Wedderburn *v.* Wedderburn (*r*), where parties who had in a suit here established their right against the defendant, and had obtained an order, instituted proceedings in Scotland against some of the defendants for the same demand, an injunction was obtained at the

(*i*) 5 H. L. 455, *per* Lord St. Leonards.
(*k*) 2 Drew. 286.
(*l*) See Preston *v.* Lord Melville, 8 Cl. & Fin. 1.
(*m*) Wedderburn *v.* Wedderburn, 2 Beav. 208, 4 M. & C. 585; Carron Iron Co. *v.* Maclaren, 5 H. L. 440.

(*n*) 2 J. & W. 563.
(*o*) 1 Sim. & St. 7.
(*p*) See Maclaren *v.* Stainton, 26 L. J. Ch. 332.
(*q*) 1 Keen, 579.
(*r*) 2 Beav. 208, 4 M. & C. 585.

Rolls against their proceedings in Scotland, and Lord Cottenham confirmed the order (*s*).

14. Even though no decree has been obtained in this country, yet if a suit instituted abroad does not appear so well calculated to answer the ends of justice as the suit here, the court will restrain the foreign action, imposing, however, terms which it considers reasonable for protecting the party whom it enjoins. Thus, in Bushby *v.* Munday (*t*), Bushby had given a bond to Munday to secure a gambling debt, and Munday assigned the bond to Clowes. He proceeded in Scotland against Bushby, who was a Scotchman, and a proprietor of real estate.

Bushby filed a bill here to have the bond set aside and *157 delivered *up. Upon a motion for an injunction to stay the proceedings in Scotland, Sir J. Leach granted the injunction, because he considered the validity of the bond could be better tried in the country where the courts judicially knew the law than in Scotland, where the courts could only learn the law as a matter of fact to be communicated by way of evidence; and, secondly, that the remedy here, if the obligor should make out his title, would be more complete than could be had in Scotland. He laid it down generally that where parties, defendants, are resident in England, and brought here by subpœna, this court has jurisdiction to act upon them personally with respect to the objects of the suit, as the ends of justice require, and with that view to order them to take or to omit to take any steps or proceedings in any other court of justice, whether in this or in a foreign country. He therefore restrained the assignee from going on with the Scotch action, putting the plaintiff on such terms in Scotland as would secure to him the preferable lien which he might acquire by his suit on the bond there, if he should ultimately establish any demand on the bond (*u*). So also, in Bunbury *v.* Bunbury (*x*), Lord Cottenham affirming a judgment of Lord Langdale (*y*), restrained parties from prosecuting proceedings at law in

---

(*s*) *Per* Lord St. Leonards, 5 H. L. 454.
(*t*) 5 Madd. 297.
(*u*) *Per* Lords Cranworth and St.

Leonards, 5 H. L. 438, 453. See also, *per* Lord Brougham, *ib.* 446.
(*x*) 3 Jur. 644.
(*y*) *Ib.* 1 Beav. 335.

Demerara to recover real estates there, which involved questions depending on the law of Holland, and also on the law of England, and further questions of account which could only be taken in this country. He laid it down as a principle that where part of the subject-matter is admitted necessarily to be within the jurisdiction, the court will take upon itself to determine the whole matter, though it involves questions of foreign law, more especially where the question of foreign law depends to some extent upon the determination of the court as to the English law. Upon granting the injunction, his lordship put the plaintiff on terms to submit and carry into effect any order which the court might think fit to make in respect of the proceedings in Demerara. So also, in Hope v. Carnegie (z), the court, after decree for administration, restrained one of the parties interested from * prosecuting pro-   * 158 ceedings in a foreign country in respect to real and personal estates situate there (a).

15. If, however, from any cause it appears likely to be more conducive to substantial justice, or if, upon the balance of convenience and inconvenience, it appears desirable that the foreign proceedings should be allowed to take their course, the court will allow them to proceed (b). If, for instance, the court desires to ascertain what the foreign law is, the proceedings will be allowed to go on (c). So also, if the proceedings in the foreign country are calculated to give a security against the property there, so as to answer the demand under the decree here (d), or are necessary in order to protect the property there against the demands of creditors who have not appeared to the suit here, and are not within the jurisdiction (e), the proceedings will to this extent be allowed to proceed. In Harrison v. Gurney (f), Lord Eldon restrained a suit for administration in Ireland on the ground that the same

(z) 1 L. R. Ch. Ap. 320.
(a) See, as to the jurisdiction of the Court of Session in Scotland to grant an interdict to restrain a party from taking proceedings in the courts of another country, Dawson's Trustees v. Maclean, 22 Dec. of Ct. of Session, 2d series, p. 685.
(b) See Wright v. Simpson, 6 Ves. 730; Pennell v. Roy, 3 D. M. & G. 140;

Transatlantic Co. v. Pietroni, John. 604.
(c) Elliott v. Lord Minto, 6 Madd. 16. But see Bunbury v. Bunbury, 3 Jur. 644.
(d) Wedderburn v. Wedderburn, 2 Beav. 208, 4 M. & C. 585; Carron Iron Co. v. Maclaren, 5 H. L. 454.
(e) Parnell v. Parnell, 7 Ir. Ch. 322.
(f) 2 J. & W. 563.

relief was sought as could be had under the decree obtained in this court, but he would not prevent a bill from being filed in Ireland for the mere purpose of calling on a receiver there to account for his receipts and payments (*g*). In Jones *v.* Geddes (*h*), where the Vice-Chancellor had granted an injunction against a heritable bond creditor, who was proceeding in Scotland against the assignees in bankruptcy of the obligor who had real estate in Scotland, Lord Lyndhurst dissolved the injunction upon a simple consideration of the convenience and inconvenience of the different courses to be adopted (*i*).

*159   16. *The right to land in a foreign country must be determined by the laws of that country. But a contract with respect to land in a foreign country entered into here between persons within the jurisdiction, must be governed and construed by the rules of English law. Proceedings in the foreign court in respect of the contract which are not in accordance with the rules of English law will be restrained (*k*).

17. If after a suit has been instituted in a foreign country, in which full justice can be had, and to which both parties have appeared, one of whom commences an action at law in this country in respect of the same subject-matter, the court may restrain the proceedings until the decision of the foreign court has been come to (*l*).

18. The jurisdiction of the court in restraining parties from instituting proceedings in foreign courts, is in general limited to the case of persons who are within the power or the reach of the court. The court will not, unless under very special circumstances, interfere with the right of a foreigner resident abroad, who has not sought relief under a decree, or appeared in a suit here, to recover his debt according to the laws of his own country. The circumstance that a foreigner resident abroad may have property within this country, or may have a

---

(*g*) *Per* Lord Cranworth, 5 H. L. 437.
(*h*) 1 Ph. 724.
(*i*) *Per* Lord St. Leonards, 4 H. L. 454. See Kennedy *v.* Cassilis, 2 Swanst. 13 ; Venning *v.* Lloyd, 1 D. F. & J. 193.

(*k*) Cood *v.* Cood, 33 Beav. 314. Comp. Norris *v.* Chambres, 3 D. F. & J. 583. See Lord Cranstown *v.* Johnstone, 3 Ves. 182, 5 Ves. 277.
(*l*) Transatlantic Co. *v.* Pietroni, John. 604.

house of agency here, does not give the court jurisdiction (*m*). There may be cases in which the court will restrain a foreigner domiciled in another country, from proceeding to obtain payment of debts according to the law of the country in which he is domiciled, but a very strong case indeed must be made out (*n*). The mere fact that a person who takes proceedings in a foreign court may be within the reach of the court is not a sufficient ground for the exercise of the jurisdiction. In interfering to restrain actions prosecuted in other countries, the court will be very cautious as to extending its jurisdiction under the color of carrying out its principles. * Where the case made out is simply one of * 160 interference by a stranger, though within its jurisdiction, with the property of another in a mode which is warranted by the law of a foreign country upon an assumption of right, that constitutes no foundation for the interference of the court, though it may happen that there is no foundation of right. To do so would be to assume a jurisdiction to prescribe the courts in which parties should bring their suits, without there being any thing to affect the conscience of the parties, upon the simple ground that the suits were such as in the opinion of this court ought not to be maintained, and thus to bring under the decision of the court the question whether suits in other courts could be maintained, — a question which it is for those courts and not for this court to determine (*o*). Where, therefore, a debtor became bankrupt in England, having real estate in Scotland, a creditor who had not proved under the bankruptcy was not restrained from proceeding in an action against the assignees in Scotland for the purpose of recovering out of the real estate there an amount equal to the dividend, which would have been payable on the debt (*p*).

In Wallace *v.* Campbell (*q*), the court would not restrain the agent of the administration in England from sending over money of the intestate to Madeira, the intestate's estate being

---

(*m*) Carron Iron Co. *v.* Maclaren, 5 H. L. 416 ; Sudlow *v.* Dutch-Rhenish Railway Co., 21 Beav. 43.

(*n*) Maclaren *v.* Stainton, 26 L. J. Ch. 332. See Ainslie *v.* Sims, 23 L. J. Ch. 163.

(*o*) 3 D. M. & G. 139, *per* L. J. Turner.

(*p*) Pennell *v.* Roy, 3 D. M. & G. 139.

(*q*) 4 Y. & C. 167.

the subject of a suit in Madeira. "The court," said Lord Abinger, C. B. (r), "will take for granted that the foreign court will do justice as well as the court here" (s).

19. If the court is in full possession of the cause, or a decree has been made, an injunction will be granted on motion in the suit (t). If the court is not in possession of the matter, a bill must be filed (u).

(r) 4 Y. & C. 167.
(s) See Wright v. Simpson, 6 Ves. 73; Pennell v. Roy, 3 D. M. & G. 140.
(t) Harrison v. Gurney, 2 J. & W. 563; Wedderburn v. Wedderburn, 2 Beav. 208, 4 M. & C. 585; Graham v. Maxwell, 1 Mac. & G. 71.
(u) See Portarlington v. Soulby, 3 M. & K. 108.

* CHAPTER IX.   * 161

INJUNCTIONS AGAINST EXECUTORS.

1. Cases in which executor or administrator will be restrained from getting in assets, and receiver appointed.
2. Will not be restrained from parting with assets unless a case of past or probable misapplication of them is made out.
3. Injunction and receiver may be had pending suit respecting probate.
4. By late statute probate court may appoint receiver.

1. IF an executor or administrator through misconduct (v), insolvency (x), or bankruptcy (y), is bringing the property of the deceased into danger, an injunction will be granted to restrain him from getting in the assets, and a receiver will be appointed. If, however, a testator has selected an insolvent debtor as his executor, with full knowledge of his insolvency, the court will not, on the bare fact of the insolvency alone, interfere and appoint a receiver (z). The circumstance that an executor is poor and in mean circumstances, is not a sufficient ground for the interference of the court (a), but an injunction will be granted where an executor or administrator is proved to be of bad character, drunken habits, and great poverty (b). A wife, an executrix, will be restrained from getting in the assets of the testator, and a receiver will be appointed if her husband is abroad and not amenable to the jurisdiction of the court, because, where the husband is out of the jurisdiction there is no remedy if the wife waste the assets (c); but if she has been deserted by her husband, and

---

(v) Rogers v. Rogers, 1 Anst. 174; Middleton v. Dodswell, 13 Ves. 266; Harrison v. Cockerell, 3 Mer. 1.

(x) Scott v. Becher, 4 Price, 346; Mansfield v. Shaw, 3 Madd. 100, n.

(y) Gladdon v. Stoneman, 1 Madd. 143.

(z) Stainton v. Carron Co., 18 Beav. 161. See Langley v. Hawke, 5 Madd. 46.

(a) Hawthornthwaite v. Russell, 2 Atk. 126, S. C. Barnard, Ch. 334; Anon., 12 Ves. 4; Howard v. Papera, 1 Madd. 142.

(b) Everett v. Prythergh, 12 Sim. 365. See King v. Abbotson, 7 L. J. Exch. Eq. N. S. 6.

(c) Taylor v. Allen, 2 Atk. 213.

obtained an order for the protection of her property under the
21st section of the Divorce and Matrimonial Causes Act, 20
& 21 Vict. c. 85, the court will not interfere (*d*). If
*162   the husband of a married woman, who has been * ap-
pointed executrix, is of unsound mind, the court will
not restrain her from taking out probate, but will restrain her,
if she takes out probate, from intermeddling with the estate (*e*).
A woman, administratrix of her husband, who has died intestate, leaving children, will only be restrained as to two-thirds
of the intestate's personal estate, as she is absolutely entitled
to the other third for her own use (*f*).

2. The court will not restrain an executor from parting with
the assets unless a case of past or probable misapplication of
them has been made out. Thus, where an annuity secured
by a warrant of attorney had been granted, the court would
not, at the suit of the annuitant, restrain the executor of the
grantor from paying simple contract debts before setting apart
a fund to answer the future payment of the annuity (*g*). So,
also, where the only assets of a testator consisted of a devised
real estate, which was liable to his bond for securing an annuity, and before the annuity had fallen into arrear the annuitant
instituted a suit, alleging waste, and sought to restrain the
executrix from selling or mortgaging the real estate, the court
refused to interfere (*h*). The principle upon which these
cases proceeded was, that until an annuity is actually due
there is no legal title, and the liability is only in contingency (*i*).
Where, however, the liability in future is certain, the case is
different, and the assets may not be parted with (*k*).

3. Pending a suit in the proper court for obtaining (*l*), recalling, or revoking (*m*) any probate, or grant of administra-

---

(*d*) Bathe *v.* Bank of England, 4 K.
& J. 564. See *Re* Rainsdon, 4 Drew.
447; Postgate *v.* Barnes, 9 Jur. N. S.
456.

(*e*) Yetts *v.* Palmer, 9 Jur. N. S.
954.

(*f*) Rogers *v.* Rogers, 1 Anst. 174.

(*g*) Read *v.* Blunt, 5 Sim. 567. See
King *v.* Malcott, 9 Ha. 692.

(*h*) Norman *v.* Johnson, 29 Beav. 77;
Burrell *v.* Delevante, 30 Beav. 553.

(*i*) *Ib.*

(*k*) King *v.* Malcott, 9 Ha. 692;
Atkinson *v.* Gray, 1 Sm. & G. 577;
Henderson *v.* Gilchrist, 17 Jur. 570;
Ex parte Robinson's Executors, 6 D.
M. & G. 578, *per* Knight Bruce, L. J.

(*l*) Atkinson *v.* Henshaw, 2 V. & B.
85; Watkins *v.* Brent, 1 M. & C. 102;
Rendall *v.* Rendall, 1 Ha. 154.

(*m*) Rutherford *v.* Douglas, 1 Sim.
& St. 111; Watkins *v.* Brent, 1 M. & C.
102; Connor *v.* Connor, 16 L. J. Ch.
371; Newton *v.* Ricketts, 11 Jur. 662.

tion, the court has jurisdiction to interfere and appoint a receiver. If no probate or administration has been granted, it is of course to grant an injunction and appoint a receiver, * unless a special case can be made out for not doing   * 163 so (n). But if probate or administration has been already granted, and the suit is for the purpose of recalling or revoking probate, the course of the court is not to interfere, unless in cases of fraud (o), or unless it can be shown that the legal right to receive the assets is being abused or in danger of being abused (p).

4. By a late Act, 20 & 21 Vict. c. 77, creating the court of probate, and transferring to that court the jurisdiction of the ecclesiastical court in matters of probate, that court has been empowered to appoint a receiver of the real estate of any person deceased pending a suit touching the validity of any will by which his real estate may be affected ; and it is declared that such receiver shall have such power to receive all rents and profits of such real estate, and such powers of letting and managing such real estate, as the court may direct, s. 71.   The act does not, in express terms, interfere with or affect the jurisdiction of the court of chancery.

(n) Rendall v. Rendall, 1 Ha. 154; Steer v. Steer, 2 Dr. & Sm. 311.   See Smith v. Aykwell, 3 Atk. 566.

(o) Dew v. Clarke, 1 Sim. & St. 114; Watkins v. Brent, 1 M. & C. 97 ; Dimes v. Steinberg, 2 Sm. & G. 85.

(p) Rendall v. Rendall, 1 Ha. 152; Connor v. Connor, 16 L. J. Ch. 371; Newton v. Ricketts, 11 Jur. 662; Devey v. Thornton, 9 Ha. 229; Cumming v. Fraser, 28 Beav. 614.   See Marr v. Littlewood, 2 M. & C. 454.

* 164   # *CHAPTER X.

INJUNCTIONS BETWEEN PARTNERS.

1. Court may enjoin a partner from doing acts inconsistent with the duties of a partner.
2. An injunction will not be refused simply because a dissolution of partnership is not sought.
3. Case of England v. Carling on this point.
4. But in case of partnerships determinable at will, it is doubtful whether an injunction will be granted if a dissolution be not prayed for.
5. Injunctions will be granted pending a suit for dissolution.
6. After dissolution either partner may in the absence of agreement carry on the business.
7. In case of express agreements after dissolution, injunction will be granted.
8. Disposition of the name or partnership style after dissolution — is an asset of partnership.
9. Disposition after decease of a partner.
10. On sale of business right to the name or style passes with it.
11. Court will not interfere in cases of mere disagreement between partners, but only when misconduct is such as to render it impossible for the business to be carried on in a proper manner.
12. Partnership property will be protected from creditors of a deceased or bankrupt partner.
13. Actions at law by one partner against another will be restrained.
14. And injunctions will be granted to restrain a man from holding out another as partner.
15. Partner who seeks relief must do equity.
16. Difference of principles on which a receiver is appointed and an injunction granted.

1. THE court of chancery has jurisdiction to restrain by injunction one or more members of a partnership firm from doing acts inconsistent with the terms of the partnership agreement, or with the duties of a partner.

2. An injunction will not be refused simply because a dissolution of partnership is not sought (q). " If," said Wigram, V. C., in Fairthorne v. Weston (r), " it were the rule of the court that a bill would in no case lie to compel a man to observe the covenants in a partnership deed unless the bill

---

(q) Miles v. Thomas, 9 Sim. 606; Fairthorne v. Weston, 3 Ha. 387.

(r) Miles v. Thomas, 9 Sim. 606; Fairthorne v. Weston, 3 Ha. 387.

seeks a dissolution of the partnership, it is obvious that a person fraudulently inclined might, of his own mere will and pleasure, compel his copartners to submit to the alternative of dissolving a partnership or ruin him by a continued violation of the partnership contract " (s). Where, accordingly, a member of a partnership firm who had been suffering from temporary insanity had recovered, but was excluded by his copartners from the management of the affairs of the partnership, they were restrained from preventing him from transacting the business of the partnership as a partner (t). So, also, disputes having arisen among the partners in a partnership firm, formed for twenty-one years and determinable on twelve months' notice by either party, one of the partners was restrained from excluding his copartner from the partnership business, and from obstructing or interfering with the plaintiff in the exercise or enjoyment of his right under the partnership articles (u), and from applying any of the *funds or effects of the partnership, otherwise than in   * 165 the ordinary course of business, though no dissolution was sought (x).

3. In England v. Carling (y), where a partnership had been entered into for a term of years which had not expired, one of the partners who insisted on the dissolution and retired from the partnership and entered into a new partnership, was restrained from carrying on business with his new partners, or any other person than his old copartners, until the expiration of the term ; and the new partners with whom he had entered into partnership were also restrained from carrying on business with him, or otherwise, in the name of the old firm, and from receiving or opening letters addressed to it, and from interfering with its property. The retired partners were also restrained from publishing or circulating any notice of the

---

(s) See Richardson v. Hastings, 7 Beav. 301.

(t) Anon., 2 K. & J. 441.

(u) Hall v. Hall, 12 Beav. 414, 3 Mac. & G. 79; Shrewsbury and Chester Railway Co. v. Shrewsbury and Birmingham Railway Co., 1 Sim. N. S. 423, per Lord Cranworth ; Warder v. Stillwell, 26 L. J. Ch. 373.

(x) Hall v. Hall, 12 Beav. 414, 3 Mac. & G. 79. See Goodman v. Whitecombe, 1 J. & W. 589 ; Hawkins v. Blackford, 1 L. J. Ch. 142; Taylor v. Davis, 4 L. J. Ch. N. S. 18 ; Gardner v. M'Cutcheon, 4 Beav. 534.

(y) 8 Beav. 129.

dissolution of the old firm, before the expiration of the term for which it had been entered into.

4. It is doubtful whether the court would interfere in the case of partnerships determinable at will if a dissolution is not prayed for; for, supposing the court to interfere, the defendant might immediately dissolve the partnership (z). It is, however, probable that the court would not decline to interfere where the act complained of might tend to the destruction of the partnership, or where its interference might be of service in preventing the doing of an illegal act (a). In Glassington v. Thwaites (b), the plaintiff, who was one of the proprietors of a morning newspaper, obtained an injunction against his copartners, who were also proprietors of another newspaper in which he had no interest, from publishing in the latter paper any information obtained at the expense of the former until it should have been published in the former. So in Morris v. Colman (c), one of the proprietors of a theatre was restrained from acting contrary to the articles of partnership by
*166 writing plays for other theatres. * Had these cases been partnerships at will, an injunction would not have been without value (d).

5. In a suit instituted for the purpose of having a partnership dissolved, or of having an account taken after a partnership has been dissolved, one or more of the partners will be restrained from doing any act which will impede the winding up of the concern. One partner, for example, will be restrained from carrying on the concern for any other purpose than winding up (e). In a suit for dissolution, a partner has been restrained from improperly interfering with or obstructing the partnership business (f); from accepting or negotiating bills for other than partnership purposes (g); from drawing, accepting, indorsing, or negotiating any bill of

---

(z) Peacock v. Peacock, 16 Ves. 49.
(a) Miles v. Thomas, 9 Sim. 608. See Blisset v. Daniel, 10 Ha. 493; Lindley on Part., 179.
(b) 1 Sim. & St. 124.
(c) 18 Ves. 437.
(d) See Lindley on Part., 842.

(e) De Tastet v. Bordenave, Jac. 516.
(f) Charlton v. Poulter, 19 Ves. 147, n.; Smith v. Jeyes, 4 Beav. 508.
(g) Williams v. Bingley, 2 Vern. 278, n.

exchange in the partnership name (h) ; from getting in debts due to the firm (l) ; from continuing to keep away from the firm a partnership book (m) ; and generally, on a dissolution, one partner will be restrained from doing an intentional serious damage to the property of the firm (n) ; so, also, a surviving partner will be restrained from improperly ejecting the representatives of his deceased copartner (o) ; and they, on the other hand, will be restrained from making any improper use of the partnership property, the legal estate of which may be in them (p). So a surviving partner will be restrained from disposing of, or getting in, the partnership assets, if he has already made any improper use of the moneys received by him (q).[1]

6. After the dissolution of a partnership any one of the partners * may, in the absence of express agree- * 167 ment, recommence business in the old line in the old neighborhood (r). Though a retiring partner may have assigned his interest and good-will in the business to his copartner, an agreement not to recommence business will not be implied (s), but a retiring partner may not recommence or carry on business in such a way as to lead people to suppose that he is the successor of the old firm (t). He has, however, a right to say, in the absence of express agreement, that he lately belonged to a certain firm, and may advertise the fact (u), or to advertise that he is no longer connected with the concern (v). An agreement by one partner not to carry

---

(h) Jervis v. White, 7 Ves. 413; Hood v. Aston, 1 Russ. 412. In Jervis v. White and Hood v. Aston, the injunction was extended to restrain indorsees for value with constructive notice from negotiating the securities.

(l) Read v. Bowers, 4 Bro. C. C. 440.

(m) Charlton v. Poulter, 19 Ves. 147, n. ; Taylor v. Davis, 7 L. J. Ch. N. S. 179 ; Greatrex v. Greatrex, 1 De G. & S. 692.

(n) Crockford v. Alexander, 15 Ves. 138; Marshall v. Watson, 25 Beav. 501 ; Turner v. Major, 3 Giff. 442.

(o) Elliott v. Brown, 3 Sw. 489, n.; Hawkins v. Hawkins, 4 Jur. N. S. 1045.

(p) Alder v. Fouracre, 3 Sw. 489.

(q) Hartz v. Schrader, 8 Ves. 317.

(r) Shackle v. Baker 14 Ves. 468 ; Cruttwell v. Lye, 17 Ves. 335 ; Harrison v. Gardner 2 Madd. 198 ; Kennedy v. Lee, 3 Mer. 455. See Davies v. Hodgson, 25 Beav. 177 : Churton v. Douglas, Johns. 174 ; Parsons v. Hayward, 31 L. J. Ch. 666.

(s) Ib.

(t) Churton v. Douglas, Johns. 174 ; Hunt v. Hancock, 15 L. T. 499.

(u) Clark v. Leach, 32 Beav. 14.

(v) Bradbury v. Dickens, 27 Beav. 53. See Marshall v. Watson, 25 Beav. 501. [1] Equity will enjoin one partner from violating the rights of his copartner, even when a dissolution of the partnership is not necessarily contemplated.

on business in opposition to his late copartners may be sometimes implied (*x*).

7. A retiring partner who has entered into an express
agreement not to carry on business will be restrained according to the terms of the covenant, provided the covenant be
reasonable in its terms. Injunctions accordingly have been
granted to enforce covenants not to carry on a business (*y*),
not to get in the debts of the firm (*z*), and not to divulge a
trade secret (*a*).

8. A name or partnership style is an asset of the partnership. If on a dissolution the partners choose to divide the
assets, each of them may, in the absence of express agreement,
carry on the business in the name of the old firm. But if one
of the partners by arrangement takes the whole concern at a
valuation, the name is an item in the valuation, and the retiring partner may not continue the use of it (*b*). In
* 168   Bradbury *v.* Dickens (*c*), * an author, who had been in
partnership with a publisher, was restrained, after dissolution, from advertising that a certain publication would be
discontinued, the right to use the name of the publication
being partnership assets (*d*).

9. The right to use the style of the partnership firm until
dissolution belongs *primâ facie*, in the absence of agreement,
to the surviving partner. A surviving partner will not be
restrained from continuing to carry on the business in the
name of himself and his deceased partner, unless to do so is
contrary to agreement (*e*). On the other hand, the representatives of a deceased partner will, in the absence of agreement,
be restrained, till the right be established at law, from using
the name of the partnership firm (*f*). In Evans *v.* Hughes (*g*),
a surviving partner was restrained from carrying on business

(*x*) Harrison *v.* Gardner, 2 Madd.
198. See Cooper *v.* Watson, 3 Doug.
414; Goslin *v.* Ryan, 10 L. T. 36;
Lindley on Part. 707.
   (*y*) Whittaker *v.* Rowe, 3 Beav. 383;
Turner *v.* Evans, 2 D. M. & G. 740;
Turner *v.* Major, 3 Giff. 443. See
infra.
   (*z*) Davis *v.* Amer, 3 Drew. 64.
   (*a*) Morison *v.* Mont, 9 Ha. 241. See
infra.

(*b*) Banks *v.* Gibson, 34 Beav. 566.
(*c*) 27 Beav. 53.
(*d*) See Marshall *v.* Watson, 25 Beav.
501.
   (*e*) Webster *v.* Webster, 3 Sw. 490,
n.; Lewis *v.* Langdon, 7 Sim. 425.
   (*f*) Lewis *v.* Langdon, 7 Sim. 425.
See Robertson *v.* Quiddington, 28 Beav.
536.
   (*g*) 18 Jur. 691.

for three months after the decease of the other partner, under any style except that of the old firm, there being a stipulation in the articles of partnership that the representatives of a deceased partner might elect to take his share.

10. If the whole of a partnership concern and the good-will of a business have been sold, the right to the name or partnership style, as a general rule, passes with it (*h*).

11. The court will not interfere in all cases of misconduct to grant an injunction against one partner at the suit of another. Mere disagreements, or quarrels arising from bad temper and improprieties of conduct, are not a sufficient ground for the interference of the court. Unless a partner is conducting himself so grossly as to render it impossible for the business to be carried on in a proper manner, the court will not interfere (*i*). When partners have agreed that the management of their affairs shall be intrusted to one or more of them exclusively, the court * will not interpose, * 169 unless he or they is or are acting illegally, or in breach of the trust reposed in them, or have become insolvent (*k*). The court will not interfere to restrain a partner from acting as such, merely because if he were known to be acting as partner the confidence of the public in the concern might be shaken (*l*). In Anderson *v.* Wallace (*m*), however, where a partnership firm was formed between several persons for the purpose of horsing a mail-coach, one of the partners was restrained from horsing it, on the ground that his horses were so bad as to imperil the business of the concern. When the articles of partnership provide that it should be lawful for the other partners, in certain events, to expel any one of their number, the power may be exercised without any reason being assigned for such expulsion, but it must be exercised in good faith, and not against the truth and honor of the contract (*n*).

(*h*) Banks *v.* Gibson, 34 Beav. 566. See, as to the meaning of "good-will," Austen *v.* Boys, 2 D. & J. 626.

(*i*) Marshall *v.* Coleman, 2 J. & W. 268; Hawkins *v.* Blachford, 1 L. J. Ch. 142; Smith *v.* Jeyes, 4 Beav. 503; Warder *v.* Stillwell, 26 L. J. Ch. 373; Anderson *v.* Anderson, 25 Beav. 190; Baxter *v.* West, 1 Dr. & Sm. 173.

(*k*) Marshall *v.* Colman, 2 J. & W.

268; Goodman *v.* Whitcombe, 1 J. & W. 589; Lawson *v.* Morgan, 1 Price, 303; Cofton *v.* Horner, 5 Price, 537; Waters *v.* Taylor, 15 Ves. 10; Glassington *v.* Thwaites, 1 Sim. & St. 125; Smith *v.* Jeyes, 4 Beav. 304; Roberts *v.* Eberhardt, Kay, 160.

(*l*) Anon., 2 K. & J. 441.

(*m*) 2 Moll. 540.

(*n*) Blisset *v.* Daniel, 10 Ha. 493.

12. The court will interfere by injunction to protect partners from the interference of persons claiming the share of a late copartner by reason of his bankruptcy (*o*), or under an execution (*p*), or by reason of his death (*q*).

13. If one partner sues another at law, the court will interfere by injunction, if having regard to the partnership accounts, or the state of the partnership business, it can be shown that the action ought not to have been brought (*r*).

14. An injunction will be granted to restrain a person from holding out another as a partner, against the wish and without the authority of that other (*s*). So also a company *170 was restrained *from advertising a certain person as their trustee without his authority (*t*). Upon the same principle, a company will be restrained from wrongfully retaining on the list of shareholders a person who has ceased to be one (*u*).

15. A partner in a patent will not be restrained from publishing a book containing an account of the invention (*x*). A partner who seeks to restrain his copartner from violating the terms of a partnership agreement, or his duties as a partner, must be able to show that he is able and willing to perform his own part of the agreement, and has fulfilled the duties incumbent on himself (*y*). However improper the conduct of his copartner may have been, a partner may, by his own acts, debar and preclude himself from relief in equity (*z*). Acquiescence in the act complained of may disentitle a partner to relief against his copartners (*a*).

16. It may be observed that the appointment of a receiver

<hr />

(*o*) Fraser *v.* Kershaw, 2 K. & J. 500; Allen *v.* Kilbre, 4 Madd. 464; Davidson *v.* Napier, 1 Sim. 297; Freeland *v.* Stansfield, 2 Sm. & G. 479; Francis *v.* Spittle, 9 L. J. Ch. N. S. 230.
(*p*) Bevan *v.* Lewis, 1 Sim. 376; Newell *v.* Townshend, 6 Sim. 419.
(*q*) Philipps *v.* Atkinson, 2 Bro. C. C. 272.
(*r*) See Gold *v.* Canham, 1 Ch. Ca. 311, 2 Sw. 326, n. See, as to restraining ejectment by one partner against another, Elliott *v.* Brown, 3 Sw. 389, n.; Hawkins *v.* Hawkins, 4 Jur. N. S. 1045.

(*s*) Routh *v.* Webster, 10 Beav. 561; Bullock *v.* Chapman, 2 De G. & S. 211; Troughton *v.* Hunter, 18 Beav. 470.
(*t*) Routh *v.* Webster, 10 Beav. 561.
(*u*) Bullock *v.* Chapman, 2 De G. & S. 215.
(*x*) Hawkins *v.* Blachford, 1 L. J. Ch. 142.
(*y*) Smith *v.* Fromont, 3 Sw. 330; Const *v.* Harris, T. & R. 524.
(*z*) Littlewood *v.* Caldwell, 11 Price, 97.
(*a*) Glassington *v.* Thwaites, 1 Sim. & St. 125.

in partnership cases always operates as an injunction, though the court in granting or refusing an order for a receiver does not act upon the same principles as when it grants or refuses an order for an injunction. The injunction only excludes from the management of the partnership affairs the person against whom it is granted, whilst the appointment of a receiver excludes all the partners equally, the court taking upon itself, through the receiver, the management of the partnership affairs. It therefore does not follow that because the court will grant an injunction, it will also appoint a receiver, or that because it refuses to appoint a receiver, it will also decline to interfere by injunction (b).

(b) Lindley on Partnership, 851, 852. See Evans v. Coventry, 5 D. M. & G. 911.

* CHAPTER XI.

INJUNCTIONS AGAINST TRUSTEES.

1. Court will enjoin a trustee from wanton exercise of his legal powers.
2. Jurisdiction rests not upon the irremediable nature of the mischief, but upon the breach of trust.
3. Doubtful if trustees can be restrained from assenting to bill in Parliament.
4. Court may look into the circumstances, and decide whether it ought or not to do that which the legislature has, *primâ facie*, commanded to be done.
5. One having interest in trust estate in common may sue on behalf of himself and others.
6. Trustee may file bill against cotrustee.
7. Voluntary settlements, when may be enforced.
8 & 9. And trusts for religious bodies.
10. Proper parties in such cases.
11 & 12. Trust deed for the appointment of a schoolmaster must be strictly followed. Removal of master.
13. But jurisdiction of court over schools as respects removal of schoolmaster does not apply to private schools.

1. A TRUSTEE may not use the powers which the trust confers on him at law, except for the legitimate purposes of the trust. If he attempt to do so, the court will restrain him by injunction from making a wanton exercise of his legal powers (c). The circumstance that the *cestui que trust* may have a good defence at law will not prevent the court from exercising jurisdiction (d).[1]

2. When the act complained of would, if done, be irremediable, the court will interfere as a matter of course (e). In Pechel v. Fowler (f), a case in the Exchequer, it is said to have been held that a *cestui que trust* could not restrain an imprudent sale by a trustee for sale, because, as he might proceed against the trustee for the consequential damage, the injury was not irreparable, but Sir John Leach, under similar circum-

(c) Balls v. Strutt, 1 Ha. 146; M'Fadden v. Jenkyns, 1 Ph. 153; Wiles v. Gresham, 1 Eq. Rep. 348.

(d) Balls v. Strutt, 1 Ha. 146.

(e) Re Chertsey Market, 6 Price, 279; Att.-Gen. v. Foundling Hospital, 2 Ves. Jr. 42; Reeve v. Parkins, 2 J. & W. 390.

(f) 2 Anst. 549.

[1] It seems that a court of equity will restrain by injunction a trustee from submitting to arbitration a question in which the *cestui que trusts* are alone interested, without their consent and against their will. Crum v. Moore's Adm'r, 1 McCarter, 436, in which the cases are largely cited.

stances, granted an injunction (*g*), and other authorities show that the jurisdiction rests, not upon the irremediable nature of the mischief, but upon the breach of trust (*h*).

3. It is doubtful whether a *cestui que trust* can have an injunction to restrain trustees from assenting to a bill in Parliament (*i*).

4. Although the words of an act of Parliament be imperative, and there is no qualification on the face of the section, the *inherent authority of the court to repress   *172 fraud and prevent unfair dealing, and to exercise a wholesome control over persons standing in the character of trustees, empowers the court to look into the circumstances, and to decide whether it ought or not to do that which the legislature has, *primâ facie*, commanded to be done (*k*). An injunction accordingly was granted, on a proper case being made out, to restrain the directors of a company from acting on an order for payment out of court to them of a sum of money, notwithstanding the words of the act under which the order was made were imperative (*l*).

5. A man who has a common interest with others in a trust fund, or trust estate, is entitled to sue on behalf of himself and the others, to the protection of the property by injunction (*m*).

6. A trustee may file a bill against his cotrustee to prevent a breach of trust. If a breach of trust be threatened by a trustee, it is the duty of a trustee to prevent it by injunction (*n*).

7. If a voluntary settlement be binding on the settlor, an injunction may be had to restrain the commission of any act by which the settlement may be defeated (*o*). A voluntary settlement of personal chattels is binding on the settlor, and cannot be defeated by a subsequent sale (*p*). But a voluntary settle-

---

(*g*) Anon., 6 Madd. 10.
(*h*) Webb *v.* Earl of Shaftesbury, 7 Ves. 487, 488; Att.-Gen. *v.* Corporation of Liverpool, 1 M. & C. 210; Att.-Gen. *v.* Aspinall, 2 M. & C. 613. Comp. Milligan *v.* Mitchell, 1 M. & K. 446.
(*i*) Parker *v.* River Dun Navigation Co., 1 De G. & S. 192.
(*k*) Goodman *v.* De Beauvoir, 4 Ra. Ca. 381, 384.

(*l*) Goodman *v.* De Beauvoir, 4 Ra. Ca. 381, 384.
(*m*) Scott *v.* Becher, 4 Pri. 346.
(*n*) *Re* Chertsey Market, 6 Price, 279.
(*o*) Mackenzie *v.* Mackenzie, 16 Ves. 372; Spottiswode *v.* Stockdale, Coop. 102.
(*p*) Bill *v.* Cureton, 2 M. & K. 503.

ment of real, copyhold, or leasehold estate may be defeated by a subsequent sale (q). A mere trust for the payment of debts, executed by a man behind the backs of his creditors, and without communicating with them, is not binding on the debtor. He may at any time revoke the authority given to the trustees, who are merely his agents. In a case where a man, having executed such a deed, afterwards varied the trusts of the deed, the court would not interfere at the suit of a creditor under the first deed to restrain the trustees from executing the subsequent trusts (r). The case, however, is differ-
*173   ent if the creditor is a party to the * arrangement (s), or if, though not a party to the arrangement, he has been told by the debtor that he may look to the property comprised in the deed for the payment of his demand (t).

8. A court of equity will enforce by injunction trust deeds for religious bodies, or for the purposes of education. If a living, or the right of electing the incumbent of a parish, is vested in trustees, or a particular body, and an improper appointment is made, the court will restrain by injunction the person so appointed, or any other person than the person properly appointed, from performing divine service in the church or chapel (u). So also, if a man be elected or appointed minister of a dissenting chapel, improperly, or not in the mode provided for by the deed of trust, the court will, on a proper application being made, restrain him by injunction from officiating as pastor or intermeddling with the services and disturbing a pastor duly elected in the performance of divine service (x). So also, if the minister or pastor of a chapel has

(q) Pulvertoft v. Pulvertoft, 18 Ves. 84.

(r) Walwynn v. Coutts, 3 Mer. 707, 3 Sim. 14; Bill v. Cureton, 2 M. & K. 511.

(s) M'Kinnon v. Stewart, 1 Sim. N. S. 76; Montefiore v. Brown, 7 H. L. 241.

(t) Acton v. Woodgate, 2 M. & K. 492; Brown v. Cavendish, 1 J. & L. 636; Harland v. Binks, 15 Q. B. 713; Siggers v. Evans, 5 E. & B. 367. See Synnot v. Simpson, 5 H. L. 121.

(u) Att.-Gen. v. Earl of Powis, Kay,

186; Att.-Gen. v. Bishop of Lichfield, 5 Ves. 825; Edenborough v. Archbishop of Canterbury, 2 Russ. 93; Att.-Gen. v. Cuming, 2 Y. & C. C. C. 139; Carter v. Cropley, 8 D. M. & G. 680. See Davies v. Banks, 5 L. J. Ch. N. S. 274; Att.-Gen. v. St. Cross Hospital, 18 Beav. 601, 8 D. M. & G. 38.

(x) Perry v. Shipway, 4 D. & J. 353. See Leslie v. Bernie, 2 Russ. 114; Spurgin v. White, 2 Giff. 473; Ward v. Hipwell, 8 Jur. N. S. 666. See, as to form of order, Stott v. Storey, Set. in Decr. 938.

been improperly dismissed, the court will restrain the governing body from hindering him in the discharge of the duties of his office (*y*).

9. If ministers of dissenting chapels hold tenets differing from those of the founders, they will be restrained by injunction from preaching, although elected by a majority of the trustees or the congregation, as it is not in their power to alter the designed objects of the institution (*z*). So also the court will, upon a * proper case being made out, * 174 restrain a chapel from being used or enjoyed by persons not contemplated by the deed of foundation, and will restrain the minister from admitting to communion persons not contemplated by the deed of foundation (*a*). But if the majority of the congregation, or the trustees, have the power of varying the trusts, or doctrines, the court will not interfere (*b*). In Milligan *v.* Mitchell (*c*), Lord Brougham would not extend the injunction to restrain the trustees from allowing persons not duly elected from officiating in the mean time.

10. In a suit instituted by parishioners for the purpose of setting aside the nomination of a clerk to the bishop by the trustees of the advowson, or instituted by the minister of a dissenting body to restrain the trustees from removing him, or by the trustees or the congregation to restrain a minister improperly elected from officiating, the Attorney-General should not be made a party. It is purely a case between trustee and *cestui que trust*, and the suit should be by bill, and not by information (*d*). So also the regulation of the establishment of a dissenting chapel, not possessing a fixed income, but supported only by voluntary contributions, is the proper subject of

(*y*) Daugars *v.* Rivaz, 28 Beav. 233; Att.-Gen. *v.* Daugars, 33 Beav. 621. Comp. Porter *v.* Clarke, 2 Sim. 520.
(*z*) Att.-Gen. *v.* Welsh, 4 Ha. 572; Att.-Gen. *v.* Gardner, 2 De G. & S. 102; Att.-Gen. *v.* Munro, *ib.* 122; Att.-Gen. *v.* Shore, 11 Sim. 592; Shore *v.* Att.-Gen., 9 Cl. & Fin. 355; Craigdallie *v.* Aikman, 1 Dow. 1; Milligan *v.* Mitchell, 1 M. & K. 446; Broom *v.* Summers, 11 Sim. 353; Att.-Gen. *v.* Murdock, 1 D. M. & G. 86. See Att.-Gen. *v.* Pearson, 3 Mer. 353; Att.-Gen. *v.* Hutton, Dru. 480.
(*a*) Att.-Gen. *v.* Gould, 28 Beav.

485. See Att.-Gen. *v.* Munro, 9 Jur. 461.
(*b*) Att.-Gen. *v.* Etheridge, 32 L. J. Ch. 161.
(*c*) 1 M. & K. 446.
(*d*) Att.-Gen. *v.* Forster, 10 Ves. 335; Att.-Gen. *v.* Newcombe, 14 Ves. 1; Davis *v.* Jenkins, 3 V. & B. 157; Milligan *v.* Mitchell, 1 M. & K. 446; Skinners' Co. *v.* Irish Society, 12 Cl. & Fin. 425; Att.-Gen. *v.* Cuming, 2 Y. & C. C. C. 139; Carter *v.* Cropley, 8 D. M. & G. 680; Daugars *v.* Rivaz, 28 Beav. 233.

a bill, and not of an information (*e*). An individual should
sue alone, where he alone is interested (*f*), but the suit must
be on behalf of himself and all others who possess an interest in common with him, when others are interested
with him (*g*). All who sue must, however, have an interest
in the subject-matter of the trust; mere strangers to the trust
cannot sue (*h*).

*175   11. * The mode set forth in the instrument or deed
of foundation, or the trust deed, with respect to the appointment or removal of a schoolmaster, must in all cases be
adhered to (*i*). If the founder of a school gives no directions
as to the appointment or election of a schoolmaster, and appoints no visitor, he and his heirs as patrons have the appointment; but if the founder appoints a visitor, then the visitor is
entitled to appoint a schoolmaster (*k*).

12. Where trustees of a grammar-school have by the foundation deed power to remove a schoolmaster at their discretion, they may remove him without assigning any reason, so
long as they do not act from corrupt or improper motives (*l*).
But if the powers given to trustees to remove a schoolmaster
are in the nature of trusts, the court of chancery will entertain jurisdiction, and prevent a corrupt or improper exercise of
them (*m*). Thus, where trustees, with powers to remove a
schoolmaster, deprived him of his office, from improper motives, because he had voted for a certain candidate at a particular election (*n*), or arbitrarily, without giving him an
opportunity to answer the charges against him (*o*), the court
declared such removals void. In Willis v. Childe (*p*), power
having been given to the trustees, under a scheme of the court
for the regulation of a grammar-school which had been

(*e*) Davis *v.* Jenkins, 3 V. & B. 151.

(*f*) Dummer *v.* Corporation of Chippenham, 14 Ves. 245; Whiston *v.* Dean
and Chapter of Rochester, 7 Ha. 532;
Daugars *v.* Rivaz, 28 Beav. 233.

(*g*) Evan *v.* Corporation of Avon,
29 Beav. 144; Lang *v.* Purves, 8 Jur.
N. S. 524.

(*h*) *Ib.*

(*i*) Town of Salop *v.* Att.-Gen., 2
Bro. P. C. 402.

(*k*) Att.-Gen. *v.* Lord Carrington, 4
De G. & S. 140.

(*l*) Reg. *v.* Darlington School, 6 Q.
B. 682; *Ex parte* Holland, *Re* Buxton
School, 11 Jur. 581.

(*m*) See Gibson *v.* Ross, 7 Cl. & Fin.
241.

(*n*) Dummer *v.* Corporation of Chippenham, 14 Ves. 245.

(*o*) *Re* Philipps' Charity, 9 Jur. 959;
Re Fremington School, 10 Jur. 512;
Willis *v.* Childe, 13 Beav. 117.

(*p*) *Ib.*

founded by King Edward the Sixth, to remove the school-master " upon such grounds as they shall in their discretion in the due exercise and execution of the powers and trusts reposed in them deem just," Lord Langdale, being of opinion that the scheme of regulation did not confer on the trustees a power to dismiss the master arbitrarily upon any grounds they might deem just, free from the control of the court, granted an injunction to restrain the trustees from enforcing the dismissal and ejecting the master. In the same case at law (q), the court of exchequer * had held that the *176 trustees had a discretionary power; but Lord Langdale, nevertheless, granted the injunction.

13. The jurisdiction of the court over public schools, as respects the removal of a schoolmaster, does not apply to schools maintained by private funds. The mere incorporation of the trustees of a private establishment does not subject them to the same rules as those which affect public establishments (r). Nor has the court jurisdiction where there is no trust, and the schoolmaster is only an officer of a corporation. If unjustly removed, he must appeal to the visitors (s).

(q) Doe *dem.* Willis *v.* Childe, 5 Exch. 891.

(r) Gibson *v.* Ross, 7 Cl. & Fin. 241.

(s) Att.-Gen. *v.* Magdalen College, 10 Beav. 402; Whiston *v.* Dean and Chapter of Rochester, 7 Ha. 532; Att.-Gen. *v.* Sherborne Hospital, 18 Beav. 256. As to the power of removing schoolmasters under the Charitable Trusts Acts, 1853 and 1860, see 16 & 17 Vict. c. 137, s. 22, and 23 & 24 Vict. c. 136, s. 14.

* 177   * CHAPTER XII.

INJUNCTIONS AGAINST THE DISCLOSURE OF CONFIDENTIAL COMMU-
NICATIONS, PAPERS, SECRETS, ETC., ETC.

1. Court will restrain the disclosure of confidential communications, papers, secrets, &c., &c.
2. Grounds of the rule which protects from disclosure confidential communications between solicitor and client.
3. Distinction between voluntary and involuntary communication by solicitor.
4. Illegal purpose prevents privilege.
5. Solicitor will be restrained from acting against his former client.
6. No distinction in this respect between one who declines to act and one who has been discharged.
7. Allegation of solicitor that he cannot communicate any thing to injure does not prevent injunction.
8. Injunction will issue notwithstanding acquiescence for some time in employment of solicitor.
9. But only when necessary for protection of client.
10. Principle not extended to cases arising under the practice of retainer.
11. Court will not restrain a party from divulging a trade secret unless he is under a contract or duty.

1. A COURT of equity will, in the exercise of its jurisdiction to correct abuse of confidence, restrain by injunction the disclosure of confidential communications, papers, and secrets. In all cases where a confidential relationship can be shown to exist, the court fastens an obligation on the conscience of the party who has derived any confidential communication through that relationship, and will enforce it against him in the same manner as it enforces against a party, to whom a benefit is given, the obligation of performing a promise on the faith of which the benefit has been conferred (*t*). Upon this principle, persons into whose possession, or to whose knowledge, papers, documents, copies of books, &c., have come in the course of their employment, whether as solicitors, agents, accountants, merchants' clerks, assistants, &c., will be restrained from making them public or communicating their contents to a

(*t*) Morison *v.* Moat, 9 Ha. 255. See Gartside *v.* Outram, 3 Jur. N. S. 40.

stranger (*u*). The obligation applies to persons who have acquired their information at second hand from them (*x*). The protection which is given by the court to all who have employed any person in a confidential way in their affairs does not, however, extend to cases where a fraudulent transaction has come to the knowledge of such other person in * the   * 178 course of his employment (*y*). " An employer," said Wood, V. C. (*z*), " can have no property in iniquitous secrets." Nor does the principle apply to cases where a man gets information of matters not connected with transactions in respect of which he has been engaged, and threatens to publish it (*a*).

2. The rule which protects from disclosure confidential communications between solicitor and client does not rest simply upon the confidence reposed by the client in the solicitor, for there is no such rule in other cases in which, at least, equal confidence is reposed ; in the cases, for instance, of the medical adviser and the patient, and of the clergyman and the prisoner. It rests not only upon the confidence itself, but upon the necessity of carrying it out. It is for the interests of justice that the most full, free, and complete communication should take place between a client and his solicitor, for if that did not take place, it would be impossible to conduct a suit or to obtain justice, or for a man to defend himself and to prevent an injustice (*b*). The privilege is not confined to litigation actually commenced or in contemplation, but extends to all communications which pass between them in the cause, and for the purposes of the business (*c*). A solicitor may not, after the determination of a suit, disclose any confidential communications made during its progress (*d*). The privilege does not terminate with the death of the client, but

(*u*) Beer *v.* Ward, Jac. 80 ; Yovatt *v.* Winyard, 1 J. & W. 394 ; Evitt *v.* Price, 1 Sim. 483 ; Abernethy *v.* Hutchinson, 3 L. J. Ch. 209 ; Tipping *v.* Clarke, 8 L. T. 554 ; Prince Albert *v.* Strange, 1 Mac. & G. 25 ; Lewis *v.* Smith, *ib.* 417 ; Williams *v.* Prince of Wales Life Assurance Co., 23 Beav. 340. See Greenough *v.* Gaskell, 1 M. & K. 98 ; Mayall *v.* Higby, 1 H. & C. 151.

(*x*) Tipping *v.* Clarke, 8 L. T. 554, 2 Ha. 393 ; Prince Albert *v.* Strange, 1 Mac. & G. 25 ; Lewis *v.* Smith, *ib.* 417 ; Russell *v.* Jackson, 9 Ha. 391.

(*y*) Gartside *v.* Outram, 3 Jur. N. S. 40.

(*z*) *Ib.*

(*a*) Tipping *v.* Clarke, 8 L. T. 554.

(*b*) Greenough *v.* Gaskell, 1 My. & K. 98 ; Russell *v.* Jackson, 9 Ha. 391 ; Ford *v.* Tennant, 32 Beav. 164.

(*c*) Herring *v.* Clobery, 1 Ph. 91. See Thompson *v.* Falk, 1 Drew. 25.

(*d*) Biggs *v.* Head, Sau. & Sc. 335.

belongs as well to persons claiming under the client as against parties claiming adverse to him ; but it does not belong to executors as against the next of kin, nor to one of two parties claiming under the client rather than to the other, but, following the legal interest, is subject to the trusts and incidents to which the legal interest is subject (*e*). The privilege is limited to communications of a solicitor with his client and those persons necessarily employed under the solicitor, and
*179   does * not extend to communications between a solicitor and third parties (*f*).

3. In the exercise of its jurisdiction by injunction the court draws a distinction between cases where a solicitor voluntarily makes a communication of what has come to his knowledge in the course of his professional employment and cases where he is required to disclose what he knows by giving evidence before a court of justice (*g*). In the one case the court will interfere by injunction (*h*). In the other case it will not interfere (*i*).

4. The existence of an illegal purpose will prevent any privilege from attaching to the communications between a solicitor and client (*k*).

5. With the further view to the protection of a client from the disclosure of confidential communications, the court will not permit a solicitor who has been employed by one party to a suit to act for another party to the same suit against his former client (*l*). So, also, a solicitor who had been employed by a client to conclude an agreement on his behalf was restrained from acting as the solicitor of a person who had filed a bill to set aside the agreement, and from communicating to him any information relating to the agreement which came to his knowledge when acting as his solicitor (*m*). His partner was also restrained from acting as solicitor in the suit, although

---

(*e*) Russell *v.* Jackson, 9 Ha. 391. See Parratt *v.* Parratt, 2 De G. & S. 262; Hutchinson *v.* Newark, 3 De G. & S. 727.
(*f*) Ford *v.* Tennant, 32 Beav. 164.
(*g*) Beer *v.* Ward, Jac. 77.
(*h*) Lewis *v.* Smith, 1 Mac. & G. 417.
(*i*) Beer *v.* Ward, Jac. 77.

(*k*) Follett *v.* Jeffreys, 1 Sim. N. S. 3; Russell *v.* Jackson, 9 Ha. 389; Charlton *v.* Coombs, 4 Giff. 372. See Gartside *v.* Outram, 3 Jur. N. S. 40.
(*l*) Cholmondeley, Earl, *v.* Clinton, 19 Ves. 261.
(*m*) Davies *v.* Clough, 8 Sim. 262, affirmed, *ib.* 269, n.

he had not joined the partnership till after the transaction relating to the agreement had taken place (*n*).

6. There is no distinction between the case of a solicitor who has been discharged and of one who declines to act. In neither case will he be permitted to act against his former principal (*o*). The privilege does not terminate with the death of the client, * but belongs after his death to   *180 parties claiming under him as against parties adversely to him (*p*). Thus a solicitor was restrained, at the suit of the representatives of a deceased client, from acting as a solicitor for a creditor in whose name he had filed a bill to raise the amount of a judgment debt out of the estate of the deceased, although the creditor had been the client of the solicitor before he became concerned for the deceased (*q*).

7. The allegation of a solicitor that it is not in his power to communicate any thing to his client which might injure the interest of his former client, or that he has not betrayed any confidence, will not prevent the injunction from issuing (*r*).

8. The injunction will issue, notwithstanding acquiescence for some time in the employment of the solicitor (*s*). The fact that the client may suffer material inconvenience cannot be taken into consideration (*t*). The injunction goes to restrain the client from employing the solicitor, as well as the solicitor from being employed (*u*).

9. The principle will not, however, be carried so far as to impose a restraint which is not, in the opinion of the court, necessary for the protection of the client. In Bricheno *v.* Thorp (*x*) the court would not restrain the defendants from employing as their solicitor a gentleman who had been a clerk of the plaintiff's in the cause, but had, on the expiration of the time of his service, become a solicitor on his own account.

10. The principle upon which a solicitor who has acted for

(*n*) *Ib.*
(*o*) Cholmondeley, Earl, *v.* Clinton, 19 Ves. 261 ; Hutchins *v.* Hutchins, 1 Hog. 315 ; Biggs *v.* Head, Sau. & Sc. 336 ; Hobhouse *v.* Hamilton, *ib.* 359, n.
(*p*) Fenwick *v.* Reed, 1 Mer. 114 ; Biggs *v.* Head, Sau. & Sc. 335. See Russell *v.* Jackson, 9 Ha. 391.
(*q*) Biggs *v.* Head, Sau. & Sc. 335.

(*r*) Biggs *v.* Head, Sau. & Sc.   35 ; Hobhouse *v.* Hamilton, *ib.* 359 Magawly *v.* Brady, *ib.* 365, n.
(*s*) Hobhouse *v.* Hamilton, S 1. & Sc. 359, n.
(*t*) *Ib.*
(*u*) Biggs *v.* Head, Sau. & Sc. 335 ; Hobhouse *v.* Hamilton, *ib.* 359, n.
(*x*) Jac. 303.

a party in a cause is restrained from acting afterwards for an opposing party in the same cause will not be extended to questions arising under the practice of retainer. A motion to restrain a counsel from acting as counsel for the plaintiff from whom he had received a retainer since his elevation to the rank of king's counsel, on the ground that he had drawn the answer to the bill on behalf of the defendants, was refused (y).

* 181   11. * The court will not restrain a person from divulging a trade secret (z) ; but if a man who has a trade secret employs persons under a contract, either express or implied, or under a duty express or implied, those persons cannot gain the knowledge of the secret and then set it up against their employer (a).[1] In Morison v. Moat (b), the plaintiffs were the inventors of a secret medicine, and had communicated the secret to the father of the defendant, whom they took into partnership in consideration of his devoting all his time to the manufacture of the medicine. Previously to the secret being communicated to him, he had entered into a bond never to divulge it, but, in violation of his bond, the defendant's father communicated it to the defendant. The court restrained him from selling the medicine under the name of the medicine prepared according to the secret recipe, inasmuch as it was by the use of the name that he was availing himself of the breach of faith on the part of his father. Parties, however, in possession of a trade secret, who take a man into partnership, or into their employment, without making any stipulation as to the trade secret, and permit him to acquire a full knowledge of the secret, will be considered to have waived their right to preserve the secret for their separate benefit (c).

(y) Baylis v. Grout, 2 M. & K. 317.
(z) Newberry v. James, 2 Mer. 451 ;
Williams v. Williams, 3 Mer. 160.
(a) Williams v. Williams, 3 Mer. 160;
Yovatt v. Winyard, 1 J. & W. 394;
Morison v. Moat, 9 Ha. 241, aff. 21 L.
J. Ch. 248.

(b) Ib.
(c) Ib.
[1] See Peabody v. Norfolk, 98 Mass. 452; in which the subject is fully discussed and injunction granted.

* CHAPTER XIII.   * 182

INJUNCTIONS AGAINST THE PUBLICATION OF MANUSCRIPTS, LET-
TERS, AND OTHER UNPUBLISHED MATTER.

1. Author has at common law an absolute property in his work before publication;
   after publication, right exists only by statute. Ground of equitable interference to
   prevent a wrong. What amounts to a publication.
2. How the right is transferred.
3. Right passes upon death of author to personal representatives.
4. Creditors of bankrupt author not entitled to publish.
5. Right of author not affected by character of work.
6. The purchaser of a manuscript may alter it as he thinks fit.
7. Writers of letters have the right to control publication.
8 & 9. This is upon the right of property, and the right descends to personal representatives.
10 & 11. Qualifications of the right of the author in letters.
12. Application for injunction should be made at once.
13. Right of publication belongs exclusively to writer.
14. Lecture reduced to writing subject to same rules as other manuscripts. Qualification
   in reference to oral lectures.
15. Statute provisions on this subject.

1. THE author or composer of a work of literature, science,
or art, has, at common law, an absolute property in his work
before publication (*d*). "The nature of the right of an author
in his work before publication," said C. J. Erle, in Jefferys *v.*
Boosey (*e*), "is analogous to the rights of ownership in other
personal property. If he choose to keep his writings private,
he has the remedies for wrongful abstraction of copies analogous to those of an owner of personalty. He may prevent
publication; he may require back the copies wrongfully made;
he may sue for damages if any are sustained; if the wrongful
copies have been published abroad, and the books imported for
sale without knowledge of the wrong, the author's right to his
composition would be recognized against the importer, and the
sale would be stopped. These rights would be enforced for an

(*d*) Jefferys *v.* Boosey, 4 H. L. Ca.   Lord Cottenham; Wheaton *v.* Peters,
979, *per* Lord St. Leonards; Prince   8 Peters (Amer.) 591.
Albert *v.* Strange, 1 Mac. & G. 42, *per*   (*e*) 4 H. L. Ca. 867.

alien as well as for a native author, in case his writings were copied wrongfully abroad and published. Again, if an author choose to impart his manuscript to others without general publication, he has all the rights for disposing of it incidental to personalty. He may make an assignment, either absolute or qualified, in any degree. He may lend, or let, or give, or sell, any of his composition, with or without liberty to transcribe, and if with liberty of transcribing, he may fix the number of transcripts which he permits. If he prints for private circulation only, he still has the same rights, and all these rights he may pass to his assignee (*f*). "Every man," said Mr.
183   Justice Yates, in Millar *v.* Taylor (*g*), "has a right to keep his own sentiments if he pleases; he has a right to judge whether he will make them public or commit them only to the sight of his friends. The manuscript is, in every sense, his own peculiar property, and no man can take it from him, or make any use of it which he has not authorized, without being guilty of a violation of his property; and as every author or proprietor of a manuscript has a right to determine whether he will publish it or not, he has a right to the first publication, and whoever deprives him of that privilege is guilty of a manifest wrong, and the court has a right to stop it." In restraining by injunction the publication of a manuscript or other unpublished matter, a court of equity exercises an original and independent jurisdiction, not for the protection of a merely legal right, but to prevent what the court considers and treats as a wrong, whether arising from a violation of an unquestionable right or from a breach of contract or confidence (*h*). The author or composer of an unpublished work is entitled to an injunction to restrain the publication, whether he does or does not intend to seek profit by future publication. It is in either case equally an interference with his property (*i*). The leading case on the subject is Prince Albert *v.* Strange (*k*). Her Majesty and the Prince Consort had made certain etchings, and had certain lithographs to be

---

(*f*) See Mayall *v.* Higby, 1 H. & C. 148.
(*g*) 4 Burr. 2379.

(*h*) Prince Albert *v.* Strange, 1 Mac. & G. 42, *per* Lord Cottenham.
(*i*) *Ib.* 2 Mer. 437, *per* Lord Eldon.
(*k*) 1 Mac. & G. 25.

struck off from them for their own use, and not for the purpose of publication : one of the impressions had been surreptitiously retained by one of the workmen employed in the operation, and had passed from his hands into the hands of a publisher, who declared his intention of publicly exhibiting the impression so improperly obtained, and also of selling a descriptive catalogue of the lithographs. Lord Cottenham restrained the publication of the catalogue as well as the exhibition of the impression, upon the ground that, as the etchings were the exclusive property of the plaintiff, no one had, without his consent, the right to make any use whatever of them, either by publishing a catalogue of them, or otherwise. The order directed * the copies of the impression and the catalogues to be delivered up (*l*). The exclusive   * 184

right which the author or composer of any work of literature, science, or art, has at common law in his work ceases upon publication. After publication the right exists only by statute (*m*). Unless the right be secured by statute, any man may, after publication, copy a work, whether for publication or otherwise (*n*). What amounts to a publication so as to defeat the common law right, is a question of some nicety. The publication of a work for private purposes and private circulation, and the gift of a few copies to friends, is not a publication (*o*). Nor is the allowing a manuscript play to be acted a publication (*p*). Nor is the exhibition of a picture at a public exhibition or gallery, where copying is expressly or impliedly forbidden, or the exhibition of a picture for the purpose of obtaining subscribers to an engraving, a publication (*q*). Nor is the delivery of a lecture to an audience of persons admitted upon the payment of a fee or reward, a publication (*r*). To

---

(*l*) See also Webb *v.* Rose, cit. 4 Burr. 2330, 2 Bro. P. C. 138; Forrester *v.* Waller, cit. 4 Burr. 2331, 2 Swanst. 426; Duke of Queensberry *v.* Shebbeare, 2 Eden, 329; Turner *v.* Robinson, 10 Ir. Ch. 121, 510; Mayall *v.* Higby, 1 H. & C. 148.

(*m*) Jefferys *v.* Boosey, 4 H. L. Ca. 815; Reade *v.* Conquest, 9 C. B. N. S. 755.

(*n*) See Magdalen College *v.* Ward, 1 Coo. C. C. t. Cot. 265; Turner *v.* Robinson, 10 Ir. Ch. 121, 510.

(*o*) White *v.* Geroch, 2 B. & Ald. 298; Prince Albert *v.* Strange, 2 De G. & Sm. 686, 1 Mac. & G. 42; Jefferys *v.* Boosey, 4 H. L. Ca. 815.

(*p*) Macklin *v.* Richardson, Amb. 694. See Morris *v.* Kelly, 1 J. & W. 481; Gee *v.* Pritchard, 2 Swanst. 416.

(*q*) Turner *v.* Robinson, 10 Ir. Ch. 121, 510. But see Dalglish *v.* Jarvie, 2 Mac. & G. 231.

(*r*) Abernethy *v.* Hutchinson, 3 L. J. Ch. 209, 1 H. & Tw. 28.

be a publication, there must be a publication of the thing itself, and not of a mere copy. The mere publication, for instance, of a bust is not a publication of the statue from which the bust is taken, nor is the publication of a wood engraving a publication of the picture from which it is taken (*s*).

2. The right to unpublished matter passes with the transfer of the subject (*t*) ; but the mere parting with the possession of a manuscript is not of itself sufficient proof of an *185 intent to part * with the ownership of the intellectual contents. Thus the giving of a manuscript copy of Lord Clarendon's History, to be used as the donor should think fit, was held not to authorize the publication (*u*) ; and the possession of letters by the person to whom they are addressed does not take away from the writer the right to publish them (*x*). In Mr. Southey's case, Lord Eldon seemed to think that the circumstance of a manuscript being left for a long time in the hands of a publisher without inquiry, authorized the inference that he had abandoned his own right as an author, and he refused upon this and other grounds to interfere until the establishment of the right at law (*y*). The opinion of Lord Eldon in this case is opposed to the authority of the Duke of Queensberry *v.* Shebbeare, and does not seem sound. The sound rule of law upon the subject appears to be that when consent is not proved, the negative is implied as a tacit condition (*z*). Most of the cases proceed upon this principle, In Folsom *v.* Marsh (*a*), Mr. Justice Story held that unless there be a most unequivocal dedication by him of his papers or letters, either to the public or to some other person, the author has the exclusive property therein.

3. The right in manuscripts or other unpublished matter passes to the legal personal representatives of the author or composer (*b*). The property descends to the personal repre-

(*s*) Turner *v.* Robinson, 10 Ir. Ch. 121.
(*t*) Turner *v.* Robinson, 10 Ir. Ch. 121, 510.
(*u*) Duke of Queensberry *v.* Shebbeare, 2 Eden, 329.
(*x*) Pope *v.* Curl, 2 Atk. 342.
(*y*) Southey *v.* Sherwood, 2 Mer. 438.

(*z*) Per Willes, J., in Millar *v.* Taylor, 4 Burr. 2330.
(*a*) 2 Story (Amer.) 100.
(*b*) Thompson *v.* Stanhope, Amb. 737 ; Burnett *v.* Chetwode, 2 Mer. 441, n. ; Duke of Queensberry *v.* Shebbeare, 2 Eden, 329 ; Dodsley *v.* M'Farquhar, Mor. Dict. of Dec. 19, 20, 8308.

sentatives, though they have not a copy of the manuscript (c). In Duke of Queensberry v. Shebbeare (d), the representatives of Lord Clarendon obtained an injunction to restrain the printing of an unpublished copy of his "History of the Rebellion," which had been given by a former representative of the author to a person under whom the defendant claimed, but not with the intention that he should publish. After the death of an author, * his personal representatives may publish   * 186 or assent to the publication of writings which he never intended to publish (e). If, however, he had expressly forbidden the publication, the court might perhaps interfere (f).

4. The right in an unpublished manuscript belongs exclusively to the author, and cannot be seized by the creditors to the effect of entitling them to publish it (g).

5. In several cases where an unpublished work appeared to be of an irreligious, seditious, or libellous character, Lord Eldon would not interfere, at the suit of the author, to restrain its publication, until the legal right had been established (h). The principle, however, on which these cases proceeded does not appear sound, and would not, there is good reason to believe, be followed at the present time. The right of an author in his manuscript before publication is an absolute and exclusive one, and cannot be affected by the nature of the contents. The nature and the character of a work are fit considerations for the court in determining whether it ought to be protected after publication under the statutory law of copyright, but should not be gone into where a man is illegally deprived of an absolute and exclusive right of property (i).

6. A man who agrees to write a manuscript in such a form for another, as to enable the latter to publish it as his own composition, has no just ground of complaint in a court of equity if the latter mutilates the manuscript. In the absence of a contract, express or implied, reserving to the author a

(c) Duke of Queensberry v. Shebbeare, 2 Eden, 329 ; Millar v. Taylor, 4 Burr. 2397, per Lord Mansfield.
(d) 2 Eden, 329.
(e) Dodsley v. M'Farquhar, Mor. Dict. of Dec. 19, 20, 8308.
(f) Ib.

(g) Bell, Com. on Scotch Law, p. 68 ; Curtis on Copyright, 85.
(h) Walcot v. Walker, 7 Ves. 2 ; Southey v. Sherwood, 2 Mer. 438 ; Lawrence v. Smith, Jac. 471 ; Murray v. Benbow, ib. 474, n.
(i) See Oliver v. Oliver, 11 C. B. N. S. 139.

qualified copyright, the owner of an unpublished manuscript may alter it as he thinks proper (*k*). The allegation that the reputation of the author may suffer in consequence of the mutilation of the manuscript is not a ground for the interference of the court (*l*).

7. The principles on which the respective rights in *187 letters addressed *by one correspondent to another depend are analogous to those which govern in the case of other manuscripts. The receiver of a letter has a right to the possession of it, and may take proceedings at law for the recovery of it if it be taken out of his possession (*m*), but he has no right to publish the letter without the consent of the writer. A man by sending a letter to another gives him a right to read and keep the letter, but does not give him the right to publish its contents to the world. The writer of the letter has a right to control the act of publication, and to decide whether or not there shall be a publication (*n*).

8. The right has been called a right of property : the expression is perhaps not quite satisfactory, but, on the other hand, is sufficiently descriptive of a right which, however incorporeal, involves many of the essential elements of property, and is, at least, positive and definite. The word property means a substantial right or legal interest, as distinguished from mere considerations of feeling (*o*) ; and it is upon this right alone, and not because letters are written in confidence, or because the publication of them may wound the feelings of the writer, that the jurisdiction of the court in cases of the sort is founded (*p*). It is immaterial whether or not the intended publication be for the purposes of profit ; the writer has

(*k*) Cox *v.* Cox, 11 Ha. 118.
(*l*) *Ib.* See Clarke *v.* Freeman, 11 Beav. 112.
(*m*) Oliver *v.* Oliver, 11 C. B. N. S. 139.
(*n*) Pope *v.* Curl, 2 Atk. 341 ; Thompson *v.* Stanhope, Amb. 739 ; Cadell *v.* Stewart, Mor. Dict. of Dec. vols. 19, 20, App., Lit. Prop. p. 13 ; Gee *v.* Pritchard, 2 Swanst. 422 ; Palin *v.* Gathercole, 1 Coll. 565 ; Folsom *v.*

Marsh, 2 Story (Amer.) 100; Boosey *v.* Jefferys, 6 Exch. 583, *per* Lord Campbell.
(*o*) Curtis on Copyright, 94. See Gee *v.* Pritchard, 2 Swanst. 422; Southey *v.* Sherwood, 2 Mer. 435 ; Folsom *v.* Marsh, 2 Story (Amer.) 100.
(*p*) Gee *v.* Pritchard, 2 Swanst. 426, *per* Lord Eldon. See Hoyt *v.* M'Kenzie, 3 Barb. (Amer.) 322.

in either case a right to an injunction to restrain the publication (*q*). The right descends to the legal personal representatives of the writer (*r*).

9. If the letters are returned to the writer by the receiver, the right of possession of them is then abandoned; if copies are kept, there can be no publication of them (*s*). The editor of a newspaper, * to whom letters are sent for in-   * 188 sertion in the paper, may not publish them if, before publication, the writer wishes to withdraw them (*t*). The receiver of a letter, though he 'may not publish it, may destroy it (*u*).

10. The right of the writer of a letter to restrain the person to whom it is addressed from publishing it is, however, not absolute, but is liable to qualification. The receiver of a letter may publish it when it is necessary for the purposes of justice publicly administered in the ordinary mode of proceeding, or to vindicate his character from an accusation publicly made by the writer (*x*).

11. The general right of property of a writer in a letter is liable to certain exceptions and qualifications. The letter of an agent or a servant, for instance, written on behalf of or by the direction of the principal or the master, is the property of the principal or the master, and not of the agent or servant: the latter has no such property in it as to entitle him to prevent its publication, although he swears it was written in his private capacity. The rule is the same even when the letter has been only apparently written on behalf of the principal or master (*y*). The government has a right to pub-

(*q*) Pope *v.* Curl, 2 Atk. 341; Gee *v.* Pritchard, 2 Swanst. 422. See Folsom *v.* Marsh, 2 Story (Amer.) 100.

(*r*) Thompson *v.* Stanhope, Amb. 739; Earl of Granard *v.* Dunkin, 1 Ba. & Be. 207.

(*s*) Thompson *v.* Stanhope, Amb. 739; Perceval *v.* Phipps, 2 V. & B. 25; Gee *v.* Pritchard, 2· Swanst. 413. See —— *v.* Eaton, cit. 2 V. & B. 23.

(*t*) Davis *v.* Miller, 17 Dec. of Court of Session, 2d series, 1166. See 1 Jur. N. S. App. 523.

(*u*) Gee *v.* Pritchard, 2 Swanst. 418, *per* Lord Eldon. When letters are written " without prejudice," although they cannot be used against the writer, there is nothing to prevent the writer himself using them. Williams *v.* Thomas, 2 Dr. & Sm. 29.

(*x*) Perceval *v.* Phipps, 2 V. & B. 25; Gee *v.* Pritchard, 2 Swanst. 413; Folsom *v.* Marsh, 2 Story (Amer.) 100. See Howard *v.* Gun, 32 Beav. 462. Comp. Palin *v.* Gathercole, 1 Coll. 569.

(*y*) Howard *v.* Gun, 32 Beav. 462. See Folsom *v.* Marsh, 2 Story (Amer.) 100. See, as to the right of a solicitor to copies of letters relating to his clients' business, *Re* Thomson, 20 Beav. 545.

lish or to withhold from principles of public policy, according to the exigencies of the public service, letters addressed to the public offices Letters of this sort stand upon principles analogous to that which gives a private individual the right to publish the letters of his agent, and does not extend to make such letters common property to be published by any person *189 who may see fit, without the sanction * of the government, nor to take away the property of the writer or his representatives (z).

12. The application for an injunction should be made before any expense has been incurred by the person sought to be restrained (a).

13. The right of publishing a letter belongs exclusively to the writer : the receiver has not such an interest in the letter as will enable him to prevent the publication (b).

14. If a lecture has been reduced into writing, either wholly or substantially, the author has a right of property in it as a literary composition in the same manner as in the case of other manuscripts. The admission of persons to hear such a lecture affords no presumption that the speaker intends to give them a right to publish the information they may acquire. But when a court of equity is called upon to restrain a publication on the ground that it is a piracy of a composition in writing, the writing must be produced for the purpose of comparing the composition with the alleged piratical publication (c). In relation to a lecture or address purely oral, of which the speaker has no manuscript or any other writing which is such in its nature as that, coupled with what is delivered orally, it may be taken that he has substantially a written composition, the common law has not gone the length of saying that he can, on the footing of property, have a remedy for an unauthorized publication (d). But it does not follow that because the information communicated by a lecture is not committed to writing, but orally delivered, it is therefore within the power of any person who hears it to publish it. When persons are admitted

(z) Folsom v. Marsh, 2 Story (Amer.) 100; Curtis on Copyright, 98.
(a) Thompson v. Stanhope, Amb. 739. See Gee v. Pritchard, 2 Swanst. 425.
(b) See Pope v. Curl, 2 Atk. 341.

(c) Abernethy v. Hutchinson, 3 L. J. Ch. 209 ; 1 H. & Tw. 28.
(d) Abernethy v. Hutchinson, 3 L. J. Ch. 209, 1 H. & Tw. 28; Curtis on Copyright, 101.

as pupils, or otherwise, to hear public lectures, it is upon the implied confidence and contract that they will not use any means to injure or to take away the exclusive right of the lecturer in his own lecture. The hearer may take notes for the purposes of his own information, but he *may *190 not publish them for profit (e). Accordingly, if a person attending such lectures either publishes them or furnishes another with the means of publishing them, a court of equity will restrain such a publication as a violation of trust and confidence, founded on contract or implied from circumstances (f).

15. The right of property in lectures, whether oral or written, has been, since the case of Abernethy v. Hutchinson, recognized by statute. The 5 & 6 Will. 4, c. 65, enacts that the author or assignee of lectures to be delivered in any school, seminary, institution, or other place, shall have the sole right to publish them. The third clause declares that no person allowed, for a certain fee, reward, or otherwise, to attend or be present at any place shall be deemed and taken to be licensed or to have leave to print, copy, and publish such lectures only by reason of having leave to attend them. But the fifth clause provides that the operation of the act is to be restricted to lectures of the delivery of which notice in writing shall have been given to two justices living within five miles of the place of delivery two days before the delivery thereof. And it is further provided that the act shall not extend to any lecture or lectures delivered in any university, or public school or college, or on any public foundation, or by any individual, in virtue of, or according to, any gift, endowment, or foundation.

(e) Abernethy v. Hutchinson, 3 L. J. Ch. 209, 1 H. & Tw. 28; Curtis on Copyright, 102.　　　　　(f) Ib.

* 191   * CHAPTER XIV.

INJUNCTIONS BETWEEN MORTGAGOR AND MORTGAGEE.

1. Mortgagee may pursue all his remedies at once; but there may be cases of fraud or special circumstances in which he will be restrained.
2. Unless there be fraud or special contract, a mortgagee will not be restrained from selling under a power of sale.
3 & 4. Mortgagee with power of sale is a trustee of surplus.
5. Effect of mortgage of advowson.
6. Mortgagee in possession under an informal instrument. Court will not restrain mortgagor.
7. Rights of mortgagor of ship.
8. Injunctions at suit of equitable mortgagees.

1. As long as any thing remains due on the mortgage security, a mortgagee may pursue all his remedies concurrently. He may bring actions of covenant and ejectment, and may at the same time proceed to foreclose the mortgage (*g*). If he forecloses and afterwards sues on the covenant to pay, he thereby opens the foreclosure; but if he sues on the covenant and does not get fully paid, he may still go on and foreclose the mortgage. But if he has been fully paid by means of his personal remedy under the covenant, he cannot touch the estate, and is precluded from all proceedings afterwards: nor can he, if he obtains payment by means of his legal title, afterwards enforce his personal remedy (*h*). But there may be cases of fraud or special contract, or other peculiar circumstances which will deprive a mortgagee of his right to pursue all his remedies concurrently (*i*). Thus ejectment by a mortgagee was stayed (on security being given to redeem) by reason of intricate accounts, there being also a suit for an account pending against the mortgagee, and it being considered bene-

(*g*) Schoole *v.* Sall, 1 Sch. & Lef. 176; Drummond *v.* Pigou, 2 M. & K. 168; Taylor *v.* Waters, 1 M. & C. 266; Lockhart *v.* Hardy, 9 Beav. 349; Willes *v.* Levett, 1 De G. & S. 392; Cockell *v.* Bacon, 16 Beav. 158; Palmer *v.* Hendrie, 27 Beav. 349.

(*h*) Perry *v.* Barker, 8 Ves. 530, 13 Ves. 204; Taylor *v.* Waters, 1 M. & C. 266; Palmer *v.* Hendrie, 27 Beav. 349. See Herries *v.* Griffiths, 2 W. R. 72; Robinson *v.* Maguire, 9 Ir. Eq. 268.

(*i*) Cockell *v.* Bacon, 16 Beav. 158.

ficial to all parties to keep the possession in suspense in the mean time (*k*). So also where the vendor of land had taken a bond for the purchase-money, and afterwards sued at law on the bond, and insisted in equity on his equitable lien on the land, he was ordered to elect in which * court he * 192 would proceed (*l*). So also where it was doubtful whether under the terms of the contract a man was in fact a mortgagee or a purchaser instead of being a mortgagee, and the question was one properly for the determination of a court of equity, proceedings at law were restrained (*m*). So also, a mortgagee being bound in equity to reconvey the mortgaged estate to the mortgagor on full payment of the moneys due including interest and costs (*n*), a mortgagee will not be permitted to proceed at law if he has so dealt with the mortgaged estate as to render it impossible for him to reconvey it on full payment of all that is due. Thus where the mortgagor had transferred the equity of redemption, and the transferees and the mortgagees afterwards joined in a partial alienation of the property, the mortgagee was restrained from suing the mortgagor on his covenant to pay (*o*). So also where the mortgagee had lodged the title-deeds of the mortgaged estate with an attorney who claimed a lien on them for business done for him, he was restrained from proceeding at law upon the covenant until the deeds were secured, and a reconveyance could be had (*p*). In a case cited by Lord Redesdale (*q*), the executor of a mortgagee was restrained from enforcing payment where there was no heir of the mortgagee who could reconvey, and the moneys were ordered to be paid into court. Upon the same principle a mortgagee who has foreclosed and sold the estate for a less value than was due to him cannot proceed at law upon the covenant. Having by the sale put it out of his power to restore the estate upon full payment of the moneys due, he cannot be allowed to proceed on the personal securities.'

(*k*) Booth *v.* Booth, 2 Atk. 343. See Robinson *v.* Maguire, 9 Ir. Eq. 268.
(*l*) Barker *v.* Smark, 3 Beav. 64; *supra*, p. 106.
(*m*) Drummond *v.* Pigou, 2 M. & K. 172.
(*n*) See Lockhart *v.* Hardy, 9 Beav. 349; Paynter *v.* Carew, Kay, App. 36; Jenkins *v.* Jones, 2 Giff. 99; Walker *v.* Jones, 1 L. R. P. C. 50.
(*o*) Palmer *v.* Hendrie, 27 Beav. 349, 28 Beav. 341.
(*p*) Schoole *v.* Sall, 1 Sch. & Lef. 177.
(*q*) Ib.

The fact that the sale may have been a perfectly fair one makes no difference (*r*).

2. The court has no jurisdiction to restrain a mortgagee from selling under a power of sale, provided he keep *193 within the *terms of the power, and no case of fraud be made out (*s*). The allegation that he has not given due notice (*t*), or the fact that he may be acting harshly (*u*), is not a ground for the interference of the court (*x*). Unless there be fraud or special contract a mortgagee will not be restrained from selling under a power of sale (*y*). A mere offer unaccompanied by actual tender of the moneys actually due is not sufficient to prevent a sale (*z*). So long as he is acting *bonâ fide*, he can only be stopped by tender of the principal moneys due, interest and costs (*a*). A sale by a mortgagee under a power, even with stringent conditions, will not be stopped on light grounds (*b*). But pending a suit to redeem, a mortgagee will be restrained from transferring the legal estate or parting with the deeds (*c*). Where a special authority to sell has been given to a person, and it is alleged that it has been revoked at law, an injunction will not be granted to restrain a sale unless the power has been revoked in equity. Thus, in Harcourt *v.* Ramsbottom (*d*), an injunction to restrain the exercise of a power of sale given to secure a balance to be ascertained by an arbitrator was refused, although the award was made after the plaintiff had executed a deed for the purpose of revoking his authority.

3. A mortgagee with a power of sale is in the position of a trustee for the mortgagor, and those claiming under him of the surplus that may remain after the sale of the mortgaged prop-

---

(*r*) Lockhart *v.* Hardy, 9 Beav. 349. See Palmer *v.* Hendrie, 27 Beav. 351.

(*s*) See Jenkins *v.* Jones, 2 Giff. 99; Harding *v.* Tingey, 10 Jur. N. S. 872.

(*t*) Anon., 6 Madd. 10. See Metters *v.* Brown, 9 Jur. N. S. 959; Prichard *v.* Wilson, 10 Jur. N. S. 330.

(*u*) Matthie *v.* Edwards, 11 Jur. 761.

(*x*) See Ferrand *v.* Clay, 1 Jur. 165; Salaway *v.* Strawbridge, 7 D. M. & G. 594; Prichard *v.* Wilson, 10 Jur. N. S. 330; but comp. Jenkins *v.* Jones, 2 Giff. 99.

(*y*) Cockell *v.* Bacon, 16 Beav. 158;

Gill *v.* Newton, 12 Jur. N. S. 220. See Jenkins *v.* Jones, 2 Giff. 99; Harding *v.* Tingey, 10 Jur. N. S. 872.

(*z*) Matthie *v.* Edwards, 16 L. J. Ch. 405.

(*a*) Paynter *v.* Carew, Kay, App. 36. Comp. Paine *v.* Edwards, 8 Jur. N. S. 1200; Jenkins *v.* Jones, 2 Giff. 99.

(*b*) Kershaw *v.* Kalow, 1 Jur. N. S. 974.

(*c*) Rhodes *v.* Buckland, 16 Beav. 212. See Whitworth *v.* Rhodes, 20 L. J. Ch. 105.

(*d*) 1 J. & W. 505.

CH. XIV.]   MORTGAGOR AND MORTGAGEE.   * 194

erty (e). If judgments have been entered up against
the * mortgagee subsequently to the mortgage, the court   * 194
will, at the suit of the judgment creditors, restrain the
mortgagee who has sold under a power of sale from parting
with the surplus moneys (f).

4. The trustee of a chapel belonging to a public body, being
also a mortgagee of the chapel under an instrument executed
for the purposes of the trusts, will not be restrained from
exercising the rights of a mortgagee, although in opposition to
the trusts (g).

5. When an advowson is the subject of a mortgage, the
court will, upon the tender of the mortgage moneys by the
mortgagor, restrain the mortgagee from presenting, though a
bill for foreclosure has been instituted. The mortgagee does
not till after foreclosure acquire a right to present (h).

6. Where a first mortgagee had got possession under an
informal instrument, the court would not restrain proceedings
by the mortgagor, to recover possession, though he had disclaimed in a foreclosure suit (i).

7. A mortgagor of a ship remaining in possession retains
under the Merchant Shipping Act, 17 & 18 Vict. e. 104, s. 70, all
the rights and powers of ownership, and his contracts with regard to the ship will be valid and effectual, provided his dealings
do not materially impair the security of the mortgage. The
court will restrain the mortgagee from interfering with the
due execution of such contracts. When a mortgagor in possession had entered into a charter-party, the mortgagees were
restrained at the suit of the charterers from dealing with the
ship in derogation of the charter-party (k).

8. The mortgagee of an equity of redemption is precluded
by the nature of his security from taking proceedings at law,
but he may, on a proper case being made out, obtain an injunction to restrain the mortgagee or other person in possession

---

(e) Cholmondeley v. Clinton, 4 Bligh,
1, per Lord Eldon; Jenkins v. Jones, 2
Giff. 108.

(f) Robinson v. Hedge, 13 Jur. 846,
17 Sim. 183. See Brunton v. Neale,
14 L. J. Ch. 8.

(g) Att.-Gen. v.Hardy, 1 Sim. N.S.338.

(h) Amhurst v. Dawling, 2 Vern.
401. See Gardiner v. Griffith, 2 P.
Wms. 403.

(i) Stevens v. Lord, 2 Jur. 92.

(k) Collins v. Lamport, 34 L. J. Ch.
196.

of the legal estate from paying over to the mortgagor
* 195   the surplus * rents or moneys which remain after the
satisfaction of his own claim (*l*).   He may also have a
receiver appointed by whom the rents of the estate may be received and applied in satisfaction of his mortgage.   The court
will not, however, deprive of his legal remedy a prior incumbrancer, and give him an equitable remedy by receiver in lieu
of it, or at the instance of a puisne incumbrancer limit by injunction the elder incumbrancer in the assertion of his legal .
right.   A receiver will not be appointed if a prior legal incumbrancer is in possession, unless the applicant will pay off his
demand.   If the prior incumbrancer be not in possession, the
appointment may be made without prejudice to his right of applying for the possession.   A legal mortgagee cannot have a
receiver, but must take possession under his legal title (*m*).

An equitable mortgagee by deposit of deeds may obtain an
injunction for protection of his security (*n*).   So also may a
man who is possessed of an equitable lien (*o*).   The lien which
a solicitor has on the papers of his client will be protected by
injunction (*p*).

(*l*) Dalmer *v.* Dashwood, 2 Cox, 378;
Berney *v.* Sewell, 1 J. & W. 647; Parker *v.* Calcraft, 6 Madd. 11; Whitbread *v.* Jordan, 1 Y. & C. 303; Jenkins
v. Jones, 2 Giff. 99.

(*m*) Berney *v.* Sewell, 1 J. & W. 647;
Brookes *v.* Greathead, *ib.* 176.   See
Dalmer *v.* Dashwood, 2 Cox, 378;
Murtagh *v.* Grogan, 3 Moll. 117.

(*n*) Whitbread *v.* Jordan, 1 Y. & C.
303; Meux *v.* Bell, 7 Jur. 821.

(*o*) Holroyd *v.* Marshall, 10 H. L.
191; Middleton *v.* Magnay, 2 H. & M.
233; Gurnell *v.* Gardner, 4 Giff. 626;
but see, as to vendor's lien, Pell *v.* Northampton and Banbury Junction Railway
Co., 2 L. R. Ch. App. 100; Blakely *v.*
Dent, 15 W. R. 663.

(*p*) Stedman *v.* Webb, 4 M. & C. 346;
Richards *v.* Platel, Cr. & Ph. 79; Watson *v.* Lyon, 7 D. M. & G. 288.

* CHAPTER XV.   *196

INJUNCTIONS AGAINST THE VIOLATION OF COMMON LAW RIGHTS.

SECTION I. — THE PROTECTION OF LEGAL RIGHTS TO PROPERTY PENDING LITIGATION.

1. Court of equity will protect legal rights to property from damage pending litigation. Plaintiff must show *primâ facie* case in support of his title.
2. And a case of actual or threatened violation of the right should be made out.
3. Jurisdiction of court even in cases where there is no ground of action.
4. Right to relief not excluded by imposition of penalties.
5. Must show the court that irreparable damage is likely to ensue without its interference; what constitutes irreparable injury.
6. Conduct of the party who seeks the aid of the court must be free from blame.
7. Right to injunction lost by acquiescence.
8 & 9. What is necessary to constitute such acquiescence.
10. Rules respecting acquiescence do not apply with such strictness to corporations.
11. Conduct and dealings of a man with others than the party with whom the contest exists may constitute a case of acquiescence.
12. What conduct and circumstances are sufficient to exclude the consequences of acquiescence.
13. A less strong degree of acquiescence is sufficient to disentitle a party to an interlocutory injunction than is required to debar him from relief at the hearing of the cause.
14. Delay, though it may not amount to proof of acquiescence, may prevent interlocutory injunction.
15 & 16. The bill must state fully the entire case on which the claim to relief is founded, and be supported by affidavits.
17. The plaintiff must have a personal interest in the matter.
18. Defendant selling his interest after filing of bill does not prevent injunction.
19. Court may act for parties in their absence.
20. Practice of the court in dealing with the application.
21 & 22. Terms imposed on the defendant as the condition of not granting the injunction.
23. Terms imposed on plaintiff as a condition of granting an injunction.
24. Interim restraining order sometimes issued.
25. Order as to admissions to be made at the trial.
26. An injunction will not necessarily issue because a bill is not demurrable.
27. Bill will be dismissed unless court can form a favorable opinion as to the merits.
28. Court will grant an injunction pending an appeal, but with caution.
29. Practice when appeal is taken to the House of Lords.
30. Usual to order that the costs of an application for an injunction shall be costs in the cause.

1. THE jurisdiction of courts of equity is not confined to the protection of equitable rights, but extends to the protection of legal rights to property from damage pending litigation. The protection of legal rights to property from irreparable or at least from serious damage pending the trial of the legal right is part of the original and proper office of a court of equity (q). In exercising the jurisdiction the court does not pretend to determine legal rights to property, but merely keeps the property in its actual condition until the legal title can be established (r). The court interferes on the assumption that the party who seeks its interference has the legal right which he asserts, but needs the aid of the court for the protection of the property in question until the legal right can be ascertained (s). The office of the court to interfere being founded on the existence of the legal right, a man who seeks the aid of the court must be able to show a fair *primâ facie* case in support of the title which he asserts (t). He is not required to make out a clear legal title, but he must satisfy the court that he has a

* 197   fair question to * raise as to the existence of the legal right which he sets up (u), and that there are substantial grounds for doubting the existence of the alleged legal right, the exercise of which he seeks to prevent (x). The court must, before disturbing any man's legal right, or stripping him of any of the rights with which the law has clothed him, be satisfied that the probability is in favor of his case ultimately

(q) Hilton v. Lord Granville, Cr. & Ph. 283, 292; Caldwell v. Vanvlissengen, 9 Ha. 415, 424.

(r) Harman v. Jones, Cr. & Ph. 299, 301; Caldwell v. Vanvlissengen, 9 Ha. 415, 424.

(s) Ib.

(t) Saunders v. Smith, 3 M. & C. 714, 728; Bacon v. Jones, 4 ib. 436; Hilton v. Lord Granville, Cr. & Ph. 283, 292; Electric Telegraph Co. v. Nott, 2 Coop. C. C. 47; Shrewsbury and Chester Railway Co. v. Shrewsbury and Bir-

mingham Railway Co., 1 Sim. N. S. 410, 426; Att.-Gen. v. Sheffield Gas Co., 3 D. M. & G. 311, 326.

(u) Shrewsbury and Chester Railway Co. v. Shrewsbury and Birmingham Railway Co., 1 Sim. N. S. 410, 426.

(x) Sparrow v. Oxford, Worcester, and Wolverhampton Railway Co., 9 Ha. 436, 441. See Kemp v. London, Brighton, &c., Railway Co., 1 Ra. Ca. 506.

failing in the final issue of the suit (*y*). The mere existence of a doubt as to the title does not of itself constitute a sufficient ground for refusing an injunction, though it is always a circumstance which calls for the attention of the court (*z*). The court may grant an injunction, notwithstanding there has been an adverse decision upon the title in a court of law (*a*). Where a case for an injunction is under appeal, the court will not stay its hand in granting an injunction because the decision at law is under appeal, unless it has some grounds for doubting the correctness of the decision at law (*b*).

2. If the legal right is not disputed, but the fact of its violation is denied, a man who seeks the aid of the court must be able to show that the act complained of is an actual violation of the right (*c*), or is at least an act which must, if carried into effect, result necessarily or inevitably in a ground of action (*d*). The mere prospect or apprehension of injury, or the mere belief that the act complained of may or will be done, is not sufficient (*e*) ; *but if an intention to do *198 the act complained of can be shown to exist, or if a man insists on his right to do, or begins to do, or threatens to do, or gives notice of his intention to do an act which must, in the opinion of the court, if completed, give a ground of action, there is a foundation for the exercise of the jurisdiction (*f*). The mere denial by a man of his intention to do an act or to

<hr />

(*y*) Clayton *v.* Att.-Gen., 1 Coo. C. C. 120; Att.-Gen. *v.* Mayor of Wigan, 5 D. M. & G. 52.

(*z*) Ollendorf *v.* Black, 4 De G. & S. 211.

(*a*) *Ib.*

(*b*) Att.-Gen. *v.* Proprietors of Bradford Canal, 2 L. R. Eq. 71. See Mountcashell *v.* O'Neill, 3 Ir. Ch. 619; Earl of Shrewsbury *v.* Trappes, 2 D. F. & J. 172.

(*c*) Earl of Ripon *v.* Hobart, 3 M. & K. 169, 176; Electric Telegraph Co. *v.* Nott, 2 Coo. C. C. 55; Tipping *v.* Eckersley 2 K. & J. 264; Imperial Gas Co. *v.* Broadbent, 7 H. L. 600.

(*d*) Haines *v.* Taylor, 10 Beav. 471; 2 Ph. 209; Emperor of Austria *v.* Day, 3 D. F. & J. 217.

(*e*) Hanson *v.* Gardiner, 7 Ves. 307; Earl of Ripon *v.* Hobart, 3 M. & K.

169; Potts *v.* Potts, 3 L. J. Ch. 176; Haines *v.* Taylor, 10 Beav. 75, 2 Ph. 209; Campbell *v.* Allgood, 17 Beav. 628; Att.-Gen. *v.* Sheffield Gas Co., 3 D. M. & G. 304; Att.-Gen. *v.* Borough of Birmingham, 4 K. & J. 528, 546; Foster *v.* Birmingham, Wolverhampton, &c., Railway Co., 2 W. R. 378; Wicks *v.* Hunt, John. 372.

(*f*) Gibson *v.* Smith, 2 Atk. 182; Robinson *v.* Litton, *ib.* 209; Hanson *v.* Gardiner, 7 Ves. 305; Coffin *v.* Coffin, Jac. 71; Barry *v.* Barry, 1 J. & W. 651; Palmer *v.* Paul, 2 L. J. Ch. 154; Att.-Gen. *v.* Forbes, 2 M. & C. 123, 132; Haines *v.* Taylor, 10 Beav. 75, 2 Ph. 209; Campbell *v.* Allgood, 17 Beav. 628; Tipping *v.* Eckersley, 2 K. & J. 264, 270; Elliott *v.* North Eastern Railway Co., 1 J. & H. 145, 2 D. F. & J. 423, 10 H. L. 333.

14

infringe a right will not prevent the court from interfering (*g*);
but if a man asserts positively that it is not his intention to do
a certain act or to infringe a certain right, and there is no
evidence to show any intention on his part to do the act or
infringe the right, the court will not interfere (*h*).

3. The court has jurisdiction to interfere to restrain the
violation of a legal right, even though there be no ground of
action (*i*). The jurisdiction is not limited to cases where an
action at law can be maintained, but extends to cases where,
in consequence of the infirmity of legal process, there is
neither a right nor a remedy at law, but only what the law in
principle acknowledges to be a wrong (*k*).

4. In all cases where a civil right is given by statute, the
party to whom the right is given is entitled to all the benefits
known to the common law for the protection of that right, in
addition to those in the statute. The imposition of penalties
securing the right does not exclude the ordinary common law
remedies (*l*). When penalties are imposed by statute, a
*199   man who * seeks equitable relief will be required by the
court, as a condition of its assistance, to waive the
penalty or forfeiture (*m*).

5. The irreparable, or at least serious, nature of the mischief to which the property, the subject-matter in dispute, may
be exposed before a decision on the legal right can be had,
being the equity on which the interference of the court by
interlocutory injunction is founded (*n*), a man who seeks the
aid of the court must be able to satisfy the court that its interference is necessary to protect him from that species of injury

(*g*) Jackson *v.* Cator, 5 Ves. 688;
Potts *v.* Levy, 2 Drew. 272.

(*h*) Hanson *v.* Gardiner, 7 Ves. 305;
Potts *v.* Potts, 3 L. J. Ch. 176; Haines
v. Taylor, 10 Beav. 75, 2 Ph. 209;
Campbell *v.* Allgood, 17 Beav. 628;
Fooks *v.* Wilts, Somerset, and Wey-
mouth Railway Co., 5 Ha. 199; Wood-
man *v.* Robinson, 2 Sim. N. S. 204;
Kernot *v.* Potter, 3 D. F. & J. 447, 457;
Bell *v.* Wilson, 34 L. J. Ch. 572.

(*i*) Cory *v.* Yarmouth and Norwich
Railway Co., 3 Ha. 607.

(*k*) Emperor of Austria *v.* Day, 3 D.
F. & J. 55, 254.

(*l*) Cadell *v.* Robertson, 5 Pat. Sc.
Ap. 493, 503, *per* Lord Eldon. See
Cory *v.* Yarmouth and Norwich Rail-
way Co., 3 Ha. 607; Livingston *v.* Van
Ingen, 9 Johns. (Amer.) 507, 562;
Thompson *v.* New York and Harlem
Railroad Co., 3 Sandf. Ch. (Amer.)
626.

(*m*) 1 Atk. Mitf. Pl. 162; Colburn *v.*
Simms, 2 Ha. 554; Geary *v.* Norton, 1
De G. & S. 9.

(*n*) Att.-Gen. *v.* Sheffield Gas Co., 3
D. M. & G. 304; Johnson *v.* Shrewsbury and Birmingham Railway Co., *ib.*
931.

which the court calls irreparable, before the legal right can be established upon trial (*o*). By the term " irreparable injury " it is not meant that there must be no physical possibility of repairing the injury ; all that is meant is that the injury would be a grievous one, or at least a material one, and not adequately reparable by damages at law (*p*) ; and by the term " the inadequacy of the remedy by damages " is meant that the damages obtainable at law are not such a compensation as will in effect, though not *in specie*, place the parties in the position in which they formerly stood (*q*). If the act complained of threatens to destroy the subject-matter in question, the case may come within the principle, even though the damages may be capable of being accurately measured (*r*). The fact that the amount of damage cannot be accurately ascertained may constitute irreparable damage ; but if there be a reasonable means of approximating so nearly to the quantity of damage as to show on the whole that it will not be irreparable, * the case is different (*s*). Though * 200 the amount of damage may be difficult to ascertain, a man who has on a previous occasion compromised his rights against other parties by accepting a sum of money, may preclude himself from saying that the damage is irreparable, and cannot be compensated by money (*t*) ; but the argument that a man, by offering to accept a certain sum of money as the price of his abstaining from taking proceedings, has shown that the harm he anticipates is not irremediable, and that therefore he ought not to apply for an injunction, does not go far with the court (*u*). A man who has a full and complete

---

(*o*) Rigby *v*. Great Western Railway Co., 2 Ph. 50 ; Cory *v*. Yarmouth and Norwich Railway Co., 3 Ha. 605; Elmhirst *v*. Spencer, 2 Mac. & G. 50 ; Wood *v*. Sutcliffe, 2 Sim. N. S. 168 ; Child *v*. Douglas, 5 D. M. & G. 741 ; Att.-Gen. *v*. United Kingdom Telegraph Co., 30 Beav. 287 ; Dyke *v*. Taylor, 3 D. F. & J. 467.

(*p*) Pinchin *v*. London and Blackwall Railway Co., 5 D. M. & G. 860. See Earl of Ripon *v*. Hobart, 3 M. & K. 175 ; East Lancashire Railway Co. *v*. Hattersley, 8 Ha. 90 ; Att.-Gen. *v*.

Sheffield Gas Co., 3 D. M. & G. 304, 320.

(*q*) Wood *v*. Sutcliffe, 2 Sim. N. S. 165. See Ridgway *v*. Roberts, 4 Ha. 106, 116.

(*r*) Hilton *v*. Lord Granville, Cr. & Ph. 283, 292.

(*s*) Cory *v*. Yarmouth and Norwich Railway Co., 3 Ha. 603.

(*t*) Wood *v*. Sutcliffe, 2 Sim. N. S. 169; Paris Chocolate Co. *v*. Crystal Palace Co., 3 Sm. & G. 119 ; Dowling *v*. Betjeman, 2 J. & H. 544.

(*u*) Ainsworth *v*. Bentley, 14 W. R. 630.

remedy at law cannot be heard to say that the damage is irreparable (v). It is, however, no objection to the exercise of the jurisdiction by injunction that a man may have a legal remedy. The question in all cases is, whether the remedy at law is, under the circumstances of the case, full and complete. If the remedy at law does not fully come up to the requisitions of the case, the exercise of the jurisdiction may be proper and beneficial (x). Mere inconvenience, though the damage be slight, may, under the peculiar circumstances of the case, constitute irreparable damage within the rule of equity (y). In some cases, indeed, the court will not withhold its hand on the ground of the smallness of the damage, unless it be clear beyond all manner of doubt that the damage is inappreciable (z).[1]

6. The jurisdiction of the court to interfere by way of interlocutory injunction in support of a legal title being purely equitable, it is governed upon strict equitable principles. The court, where its summary interference is invoked, * 201   always looks * to the conduct of the party who makes the application, and will refuse to interfere, even in cases where it acknowledges a right, unless his conduct in the matter is free from blame (a). He must be able to satisfy the court that his own acts and dealings in the matter have been fair and honest, and free from any taint of fraud or illegality (b). A man who has by his conduct put himself in the wrong, or who has by his own conduct brought about the state of things of which he complains, cannot invoke the aid of the

(v) Kerrison v. Sparrow, 19 Ves. 449; Garstin v. Asplin, 1 Madd. 151; Jackson v. Stanhope, 15 L. J. Ch. 446; Cuddon v. Morley, 7 Ha. 206.

(x) Lumley v. Wagner, 1 D. M. & G. 616. See Att.-Gen. v. Aspinall, 2 M. & C. 613.

(y) Wandsworth Board of Works v. London and South Western Railway Co., 31 L. J. Ch. 854. See further, infra.

(z) Frewin v. Lewis, 4 M. & C. 254; Lloyd v. London, Chatham, and Dover Railway Co., 2 D. J. & S. 568. See infra.

(a) Blakemore v. Glamorganshire Railway Co., 1 M. & K. 168; Earl of Ripon v. Hobart, 3 M. & K. 180; Saunders v. Smith, 3 M. & C. 711, 730; Great Western Railway Co. v. Oxford, Worcester, and Wolverhampton Railway Co., 3 D. M. & G. 341, 359.

(b) Bateman v. Ramsay, Sau. & Sc. 459; Williams v. Roberts, 8 Ha. 325; Edelsten v. Edelsten, 1 D. J. & S. 185. See Ewing v. Osbaldistone, 2 M. & C. 53; Reynell v. Sprye, 1 D. M. & G. 679; supra, p 17.

[1] An injury not alleged to be continuing is no ground for an injunction. Coker v. Simpson, 7 Cal. 340.

court (c). If in his dealings with the person against whom he seeks relief, or with third parties, he has acted in an unfair or inequitable manner, he cannot have relief (d).

7. Parties who, possessing full knowledge of their rights, have lain by, and by their conduct have encouraged others to expend moneys or alter their condition in contravention of the rights for which they contend, cannot call upon the court for its summary interference (e).[1] Acquiescence by one of several co-plaintiffs in the act complained of precludes the interference of the court upon interlocutory application as much as upon decree; and the rule is the same although some of the plaintiffs are infants (f). The principle applies with peculiar force where the property on which the moneys are expended is mineral property (g), or property of a speculative character (h), or if the * act complained of is caused by a   * 202 public company in the execution and construction of their works (i). As the injury to a company in being stayed (if it shall ultimately turn out that they are acting lawfully) is great in proportion to the magnitude of their operations, the court will in general hold even slight acquiescence on the part of the complainant a bar to relief (i). The extent of the expenditure is to a certain degree the measure of the acquiescence (k).

8. In order to justify the application of the principle, it must clearly appear that the party against whom acquiescence is alleged should have full knowledge of his rights, and should

(c) Lloyd v. London, Chatham, and Dover Railway Co., 2 D. J. & S. 568; Dutton v. Furniss, 35 D. & J. Ch. 463.

(d) Nicholson v. Hooper, 4 M. & C. 179; Pope v. Lord Duncannon, 9 Sim. 179; Edelsten v. Vick, 11 Ha. 86. See infra.

(e) Birmingham Canal Co. v. Lloyd, 18 Ves. 515; Marker v. Marker, 9 Ha. 16; Great Western Railway Co. v. Oxford, Worcester and Wolverhampton Railway Co., 3 D. M. & G. 341, 354; Rochdale Canal Co. v. King, 2 Sim. N. S. 78, 16 Beav. 630; Pulling v. London, Chatham, and Dover Railway Co., 33 L. J. Ch. 505. See supra, p. 41.

(f) Marker v. Marker, 9 Ha. 1, 16.

(g) Hilton v. Lord Granville, Cr. & Ph. 283; Prendergast v. Turton, 1 Y.

& C. C. C. 98; 13 L. J. Ch. 268; Clegg v. Edmondson, 8 D M. & G. 808; Ernest v. Vivian, 33 L. J Ch. 513.

(h) See Crossley v Derby Gas Light Co., Webst. P. C. 120; Neilson v. Thompson, ib. 275.

(i) Greenhalgh v. Manchester and Birmingham Railway Co., 3 M. & C. 784; Semple v. London and Birmingham Railway Co., 1 Ra. Ca. 120; Ware v. Regent's Canal Co., 3 D. &. J. 212.

(k) Great Western Railway Co. v. Oxford, Worcester, &c., Railway Co., 3 D. M. & G. 341, 361.

[1] Morris and Essex R. Co. v. Prudden, 5 C. E. Green, 530; Goodin v. Cincinnati and Whitewater Canal Co., 18 Ohio St. 169.

by his conduct have encouraged the other party to alter his condition, and that the latter should have acted upon the faith of the encouragement so held out (*l*).[1] There is no acquiescence if the act has been permitted or the expenditure has been allowed to be made under an erroneous opinion and view, and in ignorance of the consequences (*m*). If both parties are equally ignorant of the consequences, or of the right which one of them, had he been aware of it, might have asserted, the one party cannot be made to suffer for his ignorance more than the other (*n*). Nor can there be acquiescence where there is no injury to acquiesce in (*o*).

9. The acquiescence of an agent, when acting within the scope of his authority, is binding on the principal; but in order that it should be binding, the agent must be acting within the scope of his authority (*p*).

10. A corporation or company may be bound by * 203 acquiescence as * well as an individual (*q*); but the rules respecting acquiescence which apply to an individual do not apply with the same strictness to a corporation or company (*r*).

(*l*) Dann *v*. Spurrier, 7 Ves. 230; Barnard *v*. Wallis, Cr. & Ph. 89; Greenhalgh *v*. Manchester and Birmingham Railway Co., 3 M. & C. 784; Marker *v*. Marker, 9 Ha. 16; Pentney *v*. Lynn Paving Commissioners, 13 W. R. 983; Ramsden *v*. Dyson, 1 L. R. H. L. 129; See *supra*, pp. 40–42.

(*m*) Bankart *v*. Houghton, 27 Beav. 425, 431; Johnson *v*. Wyatt, 2 D. J. & S. 18.

(*n*) Greenhalgh *v*. Manchester and Birmingham Railway Co., 3 M. & C. 784, 791; Bankart *v*. Houghton, 27 Beav. 425, 432.

(*o*) Haines *v*. Taylor, 2 Ph. 209.

(*p*) Att.-Gen. *v*. Briggs, 1 Jur. N. S. 1084.

(*q*) Laird *v*. Birkenhead Railway Co., John. 500; Curriers' Co. *v*. Corbett, 2 Dr. & Sm. 355; Hill *v*. South Staffordshire Railway Co., 11 Jur. N. S. 192.

(*r*) Curriers' Co. *v*. Corbett, 2 Dr. & Sm. 355.

[1] " The kind of acquiescence which will conclude a party has been defined by eminent equity judges as being something not well expressed by that term. 'Now acquiescence is not the term which ought to be used. If a party having a right stands by and sees another dealing with the property in a manner inconsistent with that right, and makes no objection while the act is in progress, he cannot afterwards complain. That is the proper sense of the word acquiescence.' " 2 Redfield on Railways, 354; Hentz *v*. Long Island R. Co., 13 Barb. 647.

Acquiescence, though not in the sense of conferring a right on the opposite party, but merely in the sense of depriving the complainant of his right to the interference of a court of equity, will, of course, defeat an application for an injunction. Grey *v*. Ohio and Pennsylvania R. Co., 1 Grant's Cases, 412. See also Swain *v*. Seamens, 9 Wallace, 254; Irvine *v*. Irvine, *ib*. 618. Where a party seeks an injunction to restrain a violation of a covenant under a lease, and such covenant is a continuing covenant running with the land, and its violation is of constant recurrence, his title to relief is not forfeited by long delay in making his application. The Society *v*. Low, 2 C. E. Green, 19.

11. The conduct and dealings of a man with others than the party with whom the contest exists may constitute a case of acquiescence, so as to preclude him from coming to the court for relief against a state of things to which his own conduct has led (*s*). Where accordingly the owners of a canal had permitted several persons to supply their mills with water for several purposes, the court would not restrain a man who had been allowed to lay down pipes to the canal from using the water in the same way as his neighbors (*t*). So also a landlord who had relaxed in favor of some of his tenants a covenant entered into for the benefit of all of them, was held not entitled to an injunction to restrain the other tenants from infringing the covenant (*u*).

12. The mere objection to, or a mere protest on the part of the plaintiff against, the act of the defendant, or a mere threat to take legal proceedings, is not in general sufficient to exclude the consequences of laches or acquiescence (*x*), though it may be sufficient under the peculiar circumstances of the case (*y*). Nor will the continual assertion of a claim unaccompanied by any act to give effect to it keep alive a right which would be otherwise precluded (*z*). But if moneys are expended on an undertaking after full and distinct notice that it is objected to, and that steps will be taken to prevent it (*a*), or with full * knowledge of the true condition of the title (*b*) ;   * 204 or if the acquiescence is satisfactorily accounted for

---

(*s*) Rundell *v.* Murray, Jac. 311; Saunders *v.* Smith, 3 M. & C. 730.

(*t*) Rochdale Canal Co. *v.* King, 2 Sim. N. S. 87.

(*u*) Roper *v.* Williams, T. & R. 18. See *infra*.

(*x*) Birmingham Canal Co. *v.* Lloyd, 18 Ves. 515; Prendergast *v.* Turton, 1 Y. & C. C. C. 98, 13 L. J. Ch. 268; Att.-Gen. *v.* Sheffield Gas Co., 3 D. M. & G. 304; Wicks *v.* Hunt, John. 374; Cooper *v.* Hubbuck, 30 Beav. 160. See Burrows *v.* Wall, 4 D. M. & G. 283.

(*y*) Buxton *v.* James, 5 De G. & S. 84; Att.-Gen. *v.* Sheffield Gas Co., 3 D. M. & G. 304; Patching *v.* Dubbins, Kay, 1; Coles *v.* Simms, 5 D. M. & G. 1; Scarisbrick *v.* Tunbridge, 3 Eq. Rep. 240. See Gordon *v.* Cheltenham Railway Co., 5 Beav. 229, 238.

(*z*) Clegg *v.* Edmondson, 8 D. M. & G. 808.

(*a*) Att.-Gen. *v.* Sheffield Gas Co., 3 D. M. & G. 304, 328; Rochdale Canal Co. *v.* King, 16 Beav 643; Coles *v.* Simms, 5 D. M. & G. 1; Att.-Gen. *v.* Luton Board of Health, 2 Jur. N. S. 180; Gale *v.* Abbott, 8 Jur. N. S. 987. See Manchester, Sheffield, and Lincolnshire Railway Co. *v.* Worksop Board of Health, 23 Beav. 207. See also, as to notice, Jones *v.* Royal Canal Co., 2 Moll. 319; Williams *v.* Earl of Jersey Cr. & Ph. 97; Illingworth *v.* Manchester and Leeds Railway Co., 2 Ra. Ca. 209.

(*b*) Rennie *v.* Young, 2 D. & J. 142; Ramsden *v.* Dyson, 1 L. R. H. L. 129.

and explained (c), as, for instance, that it has taken place upon the faith of a representation that no grievance would result from or be produced by the act (d), or upon the faith that negotiations were going on between the parties with a view to the settlement of the dispute on points in contest between them (e) ; or if the delay is while the acts done are preliminary to the acts against which he claims relief, and not such acts themselves (f), the consequences of acquiescence are excluded. Nor will a man be precluded from relief on the ground of acquiescence in what he was led to consider a mere temporary violation of his right (g). Nor does the acquiescence in a state of things which produces little injury warrant the subsequent extension of them to an extent productive of serious damage (h). "It is impossible to contend," said Lord Romilly, M. R. (i), "that because a man has acquiesced in the erection of certain works, which have produced little or no injury, he is not afterwards to have any remedy, if by the increase of the works at a subsequent period he sustains a serious injury. . . . I am unable to accede to the ar-

* 205   gument that he must be held to *have foreseen and assented, as a probable consequence, to the great and injurious additions which have been made to the works. He assented, it is true, to what was done and the consequences flowing necessarily therefrom, but no further. Those cases must be distinguished where the consequences of the act assented to are obvious and plain, and others where they are necessarily doubtful " (k).

(c) Goldsmid v. Tunbridge Wells Commissioners, 1 L. R. Ch. Ap. 349.

(d) Davies v. Marshall, 10 C. B. N. S. 711. See Rawlins v. Wickham, 3 D. & J. 304.

(e) Innocent v. Midland Railway Co., 1 Ra. Ca. 242; Lord Mexborough v. Bower, 2 L. T. 205; Earl of Lindsey v. Great Northern Railway Co., 10 Ha. 664; Foster v. Birm'ngham, Wolverhampton, &c., Railway Co., 2 W. R. 378.

(f) Northam Bridge and Roads Co. v. London and South Western Railway Co., 1 Ra. Ca. 653.

(g) Gordon v. Cheltenham Railway Co., 5 Beav. 229, 238; Innocent v. North Midland Railway Co., 1 Ra. Ca. 242; Att.-Gen. v. Luton Board of Health, 2 Jur. N. S. 182; Att.-Gen. v. Borough of Birmingham, 4 K. & J. 546.

(h) Bankart v. Houghton, 27 Beav. 425; Western v. M'Dermott, 2 L. R. Ch. Ap. 72.

(i) 27 Beav. 430.

(k) See Northam Bridge and Roads Co. v. London and South Western Railway Co., 1 Ra. Ca. 653; Swaine v. Great Northern Railway Co., 9 Jur. N. S. 1196, 33 L. J. Ch. 399; Child v. Douglas, 5 D. M. & G. 739; Goldsmid v. Tunbridge Wells Commissioners, 1 L. R. Ch. Ap. 349.

13. A less strong degree of acquiescence is sufficient to dis-entitle a party to an interlocutory injunction than is required to debar him from relief at the hearing of the cause. At the hearing of the cause it is the duty of the court to decide upon the right of parties, and the dismissal of the bill upon the ground of acquiescence amounts to a decision that a right which has once existed is absolutely and for ever lost. In dismissing a bill upon interlocutory application, the court does not conclude a right, but merely refuses, in the exercise of its discretion, to interfere summarily in favor of a party who has not shown due diligence in making the application (*l*). " A short acquiescence," said Lord Langdale, in Gordon *v.* Chel-tenham Railway Company (*m*), " may properly induce the court not to interfere *ex parte*. A longer acquiescence may, under the circumstances, throw serious doubt upon the right of the plaintiff, and induce the court not to interfere by inter-locutory order even when applied for on notice. But when acquiescence is used as an argument in support of a demurrer, there must, to make it effective, be such an acquiescence as wholly to disentitle the plaintiff to any relief. It must.be assumed that the plaintiff had originally a right, but that he has altogether deprived himself of it by acquiescence."

14. Delay, though it may not amount to proof of acquies-cence, may be sufficient to disentitle a man to the summary interference of the court by interlocutory injunction (*n*). But * delay in taking proceedings is not material so long   * 206 as matters remain *in statu quo* (*o*).

15. The bill must allege the substance of the ground of relief, and should state at once fully the entire case on which the claim to relief is founded (*p*). If the bill do not allege

---

(*l*) Patching *v.* Dubbins, Kay, 11; Imperial Gas Co. *v.* Broadbent, 7 H. L. 611; Pulling *v.* London, Chatham, and Dover Railway Co., 33 L. J. Ch. 505; Johnson *v.* Wyatt, 2 D. J. & S. 18, 25.
(*m*) 5 Beav. 233.
(*n*) Att.-Gen. *v.* Sheffield Gas Co., 3 D. M. & G. 304; Great Western Rail-way Co. *v.* Oxford, Worcester, &c., Railway Co., *ib.* 363; Pickford *v.* Grand Junction Railway Co., 3 Ra. Ca. 538, 559; Wicks *v.* Hunt, John. 872; Ware *v.* Regent's Canal Co., 3 D. & J. 230.

See Barker *v.* North Staffordshire Rail-way Co., 5 Ra. Ca. 401; Wintle *v.* Bristol and South Wales Railway Co., 10 W. R. 210.
(*o*) Rochdale Canal Co. *v.* King, 2 Sim. N. S. 78; Gale *v.* Abbott, 8 Jur. N. S. 987; Archbold *v.* Scully, 9 H. L. 388. See, as to waste, *infra*.
(*p*) Barker *v.* North Staffordshire Railway Co., 2 De G. & S. 55, 5 Ra. Ca. 401; Herz *v.* Union Bank of London, 1 Jur. N. S. 127; Nokes *v.* Fish, 3 Drew. 735.

the state of things on which the relief is founded, the relief prayed cannot be given, although the facts may appear by the evidence. Every minute fact need not be stated, but the substance of the ground for relief must appear on the bill (q). There must be such certainty in the averments of title upon which the bill is founded, that the defendant may be distinctly informed of the case which he is called upon to meet (r). Mere general allegations are not enough (s). A general allegation that the defendant admits the title of the plaintiff is too vague (t) ; nor can an allegation which states a material circumstance, not positively as a fact, but as an allegation made by another, be sustained (u). A statement that a party alleges a certain thing to be so and so cannot be considered as a positive statement that the thing is so and so (x) ; nor is a statement that the defendant alleges and the plaintiff believes the fact to be a sufficient allegation of a material fact (y). But a charge that the contrary of a pretence is the truth is equivalent to an allegation of the negative of the fact pretended (z).

* 207   16. * The allegations in the bill must be supported by affidavits, so as to show on the face of the evidence that they are well founded (a).

17. The application for an injunction must be made by a party having sufficient interest (b). A man who has no personal interest in the matter cannot move for an injunction, even though he may have been made a party to the suit (c). Nor can a man come into court to complain of an injury affecting the private property of another (d). Nor can relief be had if it can be satisfactorily shown that a suit has been instituted merely for the purposes of or at the instigation of

(q) Nokes v. Fish, 3 Drew. 735.
(r) Att.-Gen. v. Corporation of Norwich, 2 M. & C. 406 ; Banks v. Carter, 12 Jur. 366 ; Houghton v. Reynolds, 2 Ha. 264, Mitf. Pl. 45 ; Sheard v. Webb, 2 W. R. 343.
(s) Wormald v. De Lisle, 3 Beav. 18.
(t) Crowther v. Crowther, 23 Beav. 305.
(u) White v. Smale, 22 Beav. 72.
(x) Hammond v. Messenger, 9 Sim. 327.
(y) Egremont v. Cowell, 5 Beav. 620.

(z) Harrison v. Wiltshire, 4 L. J. Ch. N. S. 260 ; Mayor, &c., of Rochester v. Lee, 15 L. J. Ch. 97.
(a) Magnay v. Mines Royal Co., 3 Drew. 130, 133. See further, infra.
(b) Wynne v. Lord Newborough, 1 Ves. Jr. 164 ; Leake v. Beckett, 1 Y. & J. 339. See infra.
(c) Hunter v. Nockolds, 15 L. J. Ch. 320, 7 L. T. 41.
(d) Att.-Gen. v. United Kingdom Electric Telegraph, 30 Beav. 287.

another (e).   The court will not interfere on behalf of a man who claims relief not through direct equities of his own, but indirectly through the equities of other parties, on which equities those parties themselves do not insist (f).   If the act complained of affects the public interest, the suit should be instituted by the attorney-general at the instance of a relator (g).   If the act complained of affects the common right of a number of persons whose interest is identical in a judicial point of view, the suit should be instituted by one or more of them suing on behalf of the others (h).   The suit cannot be maintained against several persons for distinct and separate invasions of a right (i).   One tenant in common may, however, sue alone in respect of the wrong done to himself (k).

18. A man who has assigned or disposed of his interest in the subject-matter should not be made a party to the suit (l).   But *the parting by a defendant with his   *208 interest after the filing of the bill does not disentitle the plaintiff to an injunction (m).

19. Where there is a case for an injunction, and the injunction will operate for the benefit of parties not before the court, the absence of those parties, though a ground of demurrer to the bill, will not prevent the court from interfering.   It is enough that the property sought to be protected is really in danger (n).   In cases of injunction the court frequently acts for parties in their absence (o); but where the injunction would have the effect of injuring materially the rights of those

---

(e) Pentney v. Lynn Paving Commissioners, 13 W. R. 983.   See Forrest v. Manchester, Sheffield, and Lincolnshire Railway Co., 7 Jur. N. S. 887.

(f) Roberts v. Bozon, 3 L. J. Ch. 113.

(g) Att.-Gen. v. Compton, 1 Y. & C. C. C. 417; Soltau v. De Held, 2 Sim. N. S. 150.   See infra.

(h) Mozley v. Alston, 1 Ph. 790.   See infra.

(i) Dilly v. Doig, 2 Ves. Jr. 486; Hudson v. Maddison, 12 Sim. 416; Pollock v. Lester, 11 Ha. 274.

(k) Dent v. Turpin, 2 J. & H. 139; Batty v. Hill, 1 H. & M. 264.

(l) Sweet v. Maugham, 11 Sim. 51;

Hawkins v. Gardiner, 1 W. R. 345; Scarisbrick v. Tunbridge, 3 Eq. Rep. 240; Saunders v. Saunders, 3 Drew. 387; Clements v. Welles, 1 L. R. Eq. 200.   See Matthews v. King, 3 H. & C. 910.

(m) Bird v. Lake, 1 H. & M. 121.

(n) Const v. Harris, T. & R. 514; Evans v. Coventry, 5 D. M. & G. 911. See Walworth v. Holt, 4 M. & C. 619; Ackroyd v. Briggs, 14 W. R. 25.

(o) Const v. Harris, T. & R. 514; Evans v. Coventry, 5 D. M. & G. 911; Herries v. Griffiths, 2 W. R. 72.   See M'Beath v. Ravenscroft, 8 L. J. Ch. N. S. 208.

persons not before the court, the court will not ordinarily and without special necessity interfere (p).[1]

20. The court, upon the application for an interlocutory injunction in support of a legal right, will deal with the injunction upon the evidence before it, and will confine itself strictly to the immediate object sought, and as far as possible abstain from prejudging the question in the cause (q). If a fair *primâ facie* case be made out, and the case is free from objections of an equitable consideration, several courses are open to the court. Which of them will be adopted is always a matter for the discretion of the court, but, in the absence of special circumstances, the leading principle which is the rule of the court and limits its discretion is, that only such a restraint shall be imposed as may stop the mischief complained of, and keep the property in its actual condition until the hearing (r).

If the case, as made out, is plain and free from doubt, * 209   the court may, * in the exercise of its discretion, determine the question at once, and grant an injunction without putting the parties to any further expense and delay (s); but the case should be very clear for the court to adopt this course (t). If the defendant disputes the legal title of the plaintiff or denies the fact of its violation, the court will seldom, however clear the case may in its opinion be, grant an injunction without putting the plaintiff to establish his legal right (u). The court should even at times, for its own security, require the legal right to be established, whether it be asked or not, and not leave the matter to the option of

(p) Hartlepool Gas and Water Co. v. West Hartlepool Harbor and Railway Co., 12 L. T. N. S. 366. See M'Beath v. Ravenscroft, 8 L. J. Ch. N. S. 208.

(q) Skinners' Co. v. Irish Society, 1 M. & C. 162; Munro v. Wivenhoe, &c., Railway Co., 11 Jur. N. S. 614. Comp. Lister v. Leather, 3 Jur. N. S. 433.

(r) Blakemore v. Glamorganshire Railway Co., 1 M. & K. 154.

(s) Bacon v. Jones, 4 M. & C. 436; Smith v. Elger, 3 Jur. 790; Potts v. Levy, 2 Drew. 272; Eaden v. Frith, 1 H. & M. 573.

(t) Motley v. Downman, 3 M. & C. 17; Eaden v. Frith, 1 H. & M. 573.

(u) Bacon v. Jones, 4 M. & C. 436; Duke of Beaufort v. Morris, 6 Ha. 349; Campbell v. Scott, 11 Sim. 31; Norton v. Nicholls, 4 K. & J. 478; Mayor of Cardiff v. Cardiff Waterworks Co., 4 D. & J. 596; Eaden v. Frith, 1 H. & M. 573

[1] But an injunction will not be granted against a person who is not a party to the suit, and a person whose rights are acquired *pendente lite* may be bound by the decree; but it does not follow that he will be enjoined before decree without an opportunity of being heard. Schalk v. Schmidt, 1 McCarter, 268.

the defendant (x). In doubtful cases where the question as to the legal right is one on which the court is not prepared to pass an opinion (y), or the legal right being admitted the fact of its violation is denied (z), the course of the court is either to grant the injunction pending the trial of the legal right, or to order the motion to stand over until the legal right has been tried. In determining which of these two alternatives it shall adopt, the court is governed by the consideration as to the comparative mischief or inconvenience to the parties which may arise from granting or withholding the injunction (a), and will take care so to frame its order as not to deprive either party of the benefit he is entitled to, if in the event it turns out that the party in whose favor the order is made shall be in the wrong (b). If * upon the balance of conven-   * 210 ience and inconvenience it appear that greater damage would arise to the defendant by granting the injunction in the event of its turning out afterwards to have been wrongly granted, than to the plaintiff from withholding it in the event of the legal right proving to be in his favor, the injunction will not be granted, but the motion will be ordered to stand over until the hearing. If, on the other hand, it appear that greater damage would arise to the plaintiff by withholding the injunction in the event of the legal right proving to be in his favor, than to the defendant by granting the injunction in the event of the injunction proving afterwards to have been wrongly granted, the injunction will issue (c). The burden lies upon

(x) Harman v. Jones, Cr. & Ph. 301; Rigby v. Great Western Railway Co., 2 Ph. 49.

(y) Bramwell v. Halcomb, 3 M. & C. 739.

(z) Earl of Ripon v. Hobart, 3 M. & K. 177; Elmhirst v. Spencer, 2 Mac. & G. 50; Electric Telegraph Co. v. Nott, 2 Coop. C. C. 47; Imperial Gas Co. v. Broadbent, 7 H. L. 612.

(a) Bacon v. Jones, 4 M. & C. 436; Hilton v. Lord Granville, Cr. & Ph. 297; Cory v. Yarmouth and Norwich Railway Co., 3 Ha. 600; Shrewsbury and Chester Railway Co. v. Shrewsbury and Birmingham Railway Co., 1 Sim. N. S. 427; Ware v. Regent's Canal Co., 3 D. & J. 230; Munro v. Wivenhoe, &c., Railway Co., 11 Jur. N. S. 614.

(b) East Lancashire Railway Co. v. Hattersley, 8 Ha. 94.

(c) Att.-Gen. v. Mayor of Liverpool, 1 M. & C. 208; Greenhalgh v. Manchester and Birmingham Railway Co., 3 M. & C. 799; Saunders v. Smith, ib. 737; Hilton v. Lord Granville, Cr. & Ph. 297; Spottiswoode v. Clarke, 2 Ph. 157; Gordon v. Cheltenham Railway Co., 5 Beav. 289; Electric Telegraph Co. v. Nott, 2 Coop. C. C. 47; Cory v. Yarmouth and Norwich Railway Co., 3 Ha. 600; Shrewsbury and Chester Railway Co. v. Shrewsbury and Birmingham Railway Co., 1 Sim. N. S. 427; Beman v. Rufford, ib. 566; Coles v. Sims, 5 D. M. & G. 1.

the plaintiff, as the person applying for the injunction, of showing that his inconvenience exceeds that of the defendant. He
must make a comparative inconvenience entitling him to the
interference of the court (d).

21. In balancing the comparative convenience or inconvenience from granting or withholding an injunction, the court
will take into consideration what means it has of putting the
party who may be ultimately successful in the position he
would have stood if his legal rights had not been interfered
with (e). The court may often by imposing terms on the one
party, as the condition of either granting or withholding the
injunction, secure the other party from damage in the event of
his proving ultimately to have the legal right. If the court
feels that it can by imposing terms on the defendant secure the
plaintiff, in the event of the legal right being determined in his
favor, against damage from what may be done by the defendant
in the mean time, and the defendant is willing to accede
* 211   to the * terms required by the court, an injunction·will
not issue (f). The terms imposed on the defendant
as the condition of withholding the injunction vary with the
circumstances and the exigencies of the case (g). The defendant may be required to do such acts, or execute such
works, or to remove any works, or otherwise deal with the
same as the court shall direct (h), or to enter into an undertaking to refrain from doing in the mean time the acts complained of by the bill (i), or to abide by any order the court

(d) Child v. Douglas, 5 D. M. &
G. 741.
(e) Sanxter v. Foster, Cr. & Ph.
302; Rigby v. Great Western Railway
Co., 2 Ph. 44; East Lancashire Rail-
way Co. v. Hattersley, 8 Ha. 94.
(f) Bramwell v. Halcomb, 3 M. &
C. 737, 739; Rigby v. Great Western
Railway Co., 2 Ph. 44, 50; Swallow v.
Wallingford, 12 Jur. 403; Semple v.
London and Birmingham Railway Co.,
1 Ra. Ca. 134; Spencer v. London and
Birmingham Railway Co., ib. 159;
London and Birmingham Railway Co.
v. Grand Junction Canal Co., ib. 224;
Proprietors of Northam Bridge and
Roads v. London and Southampton
Railway Co., ib. 653, 9 L. J. Ch. N. S.
277; Cromford v. High Peak Rail-

way Co. v. Stockport, &c., Railway
Co., 1 D. & J. 326.
(g) Ib.; Clarence Railway Co. v.
Great North of England, &c., Railway
Co., 2 Ra. Ca. 763; Att.-Gen. v. Eastern Counties Railway Co., 3 Ra. Ca.
337; Bradbury v. Manchester, Sheffield,
&c., Railway Co., 15 Jur. 1167; Barker v. North Staffordshire Railway Co,
2 De G. & S. 55, 5 Ra. Ca. 401; Guion
v. Trask, 1 D. F. & J. 373; Freeman
v. Tottenham and Hampstead Junction
Railway Co., 11 Jur. N. S. 254. See
Bell v. Hull and Selby Railway Co., 1
Ra. Ca. 616.
(h) Att.-Gen. v. Manchester and
Leeds Railway Co., 1 Ra. Ca. 436;
Waterlow v. Bacon, 2 L. R. Eq. 514.
(i) Clarke v. Clarke, 13 W. R. 133.

may make as 'to damages or otherwise, in the event of the legal right being determined in favor of the plaintiff (*k*). If the permission to do the act complained of involves the making of profits, the terms imposed will be that the defendant shall keep an account of all profits made pending the trial of the right (*l*). An undertaking as to damages may be required as well as an undertaking to account (*m*).

22. Where an injunction is withheld upon the condition of the defendant entering into an undertaking as to terms, the court * may make it a part of the order that if default * 212 is made in complying with the order, the injunction shall issue (*n*).

23. As on the one hand the court may in doubtful cases, as a condition of withholding an injunction, require the defendant to enter into terms, so on the other hand it may, as a condition of granting an injunction, require the plaintiff to enter into an undertaking as to damages in the event of the right at law being determined in favor of the defendant, and the injunction proving to have been wrongly granted (*o*). The undertaking was formerly required only in cases where the application was *ex parte*, but the present course is to require the undertaking as well where the motion is on notice as where it is *ex parte* (*p*). Where the question at issue has reference to the payment of money, the court may, as a condition of granting an injunction, require the moneys to be paid into court (*q*).

24. Instead of issuing the writ of injunction in the first instance, the prohibition of the court is often issued and conveyed

(*k*) Jones *v.* Great Western Railway Co., 1 Ra. Ca. 685; M'Neill *v.* Williams, 11 Jur. 344; Ford *v.* Gye, 6 W. R. 235.

(*l*) Bramwell *v.* Halcomb, 3 M. & C. 737; Rigby *v.* Great Western Railway Co., 2 Ph. 44; Swallow *v.* Wallingford, 12 Jur. 403; Cory *v.* Yarmouth and Norwich Railway Co., 3 Ha. 603; Beman *v.* Rufford, 1 Sim. N. S. 566.

(*m*) Rigby *v.* Great Western Railway Co., 2 Ph. 44.

(*n*) Proprietors of Northam Bridge and Roads *v.* London and Southampton Railway Co., 1 Ra. Ca. 653; Spencer *v.* London and Birmingham Railway Co., *ib.* 159; London and Birmingham

Railway Co. *v.* Grand Junction Canal Co., *ib.* 224; Jones *v.* Great Western Railway Co., *ib.* 684; Att.-Gen. *v.* Eastern Counties Railway Co., 3 Ra. Ca. 337.

(*o*) Wombwell *v.* Bellasyse, 6 Ves. 110 n.; Marker *v.* Marker, 9 Ha. 22; Novello *v.* James, 5 D. M. & G. 876; Chappell *v.* Davidson, 8 D. M. & G. 1.

(*p*) Chappell *v.* Davidson, 8 D. M. & G. 1; Tuck *v.* Silver, John. 218; Wakefield *v.* Duke of Buccleugh, 11 Jur. N. S. 523, *infra.*

(*q*) Whitworth *v.* Rhodes, 20 L. J. Ch. 105; Garrett *v.* Salisbury and Dorset Railway Co., 2 L. R. Eq. 358. See *supra*, p. 19.

in the shape merely of an interim restraining order in the nature of an injunction, by which the defendant is restrained until after a particular day named, liberty being given to the plaintiff to serve notice of motion for an injunction for the day before such day (*r*). As the court treats the neglect and disobedience of its orders as a contempt, the object sought is equally attained by an order of this nature as by the writ. Where it is desired that the writ should not actually issue, the terms of the order should be that the defendant " be restrained," and not that " an injunction be granted to restrain " him (*s*).

* 213   25. * Upon granting or refusing an injunction, terms may be imposed as to making admissions at the trial (*t*). The subject-matter of the admission must not be a matter in issue in the cause. An admission on the pleadings must be quite clear and free from doubt before a party will be required to admit at the trial any thing which enters into the legal right of the opposite party (*u*).

26. If a plaintiff asking for equitable relief upon the ground of a legal title states upon his bill a title which cannot be supported at law, the defendant may take advantage of it by demurrer; but if the plaintiff states himself to stand in the position of having so far established his title at law as to give him at least a *primâ facie* title, the court will so far give credit to such circumstances as to afford him the aid of its jurisdiction until the suit shall be in such a state as to call upon the court for a decision, or to direct such proceedings as may be necessary to complete the investigation of the right at law (*x*). It is not, however, the law of the court that because a bill for an injunction is not demurrable, an injunction will issue. The court may refuse an injunction in many cases in which the facts, if stated upon the bill, would preclude a demurrer. Upon the demurrer the truth of the statements which appear on the face of the bill cannot be questioned, but upon

(*r*) See further *infra*.
(*s*) Goldsmid *v.* Croft, 4 W. R. 450. See Turner *v.* Turner, 15 Jur. 218.
(*t*) Hilton *v.* Lord Granville, Cr. & Ph. 283; Sweet *v.* Shaw, 8 L. J. N. S. Ch. 216; Sweet *v.* Cator, 11 Sim. 572;

Dickens *v.* Lee, 8 Jur. 186; Bohn *v.* Bogue, 10 Jur. 420.
(*u*) Duke of Beaufort *v.* Morris, 2 Ph. 683.
(*x*) Kay *v.* Marshall, 1 M. & C. 378, 387.

the application for the injunction the truth of these statements comes in question. It may also appear that from some equity which the defendant may disclose, the plaintiff is not entitled to an injunction (*y*).

27. If the plaintiff has not, in the opinion of the court, laid a sufficient foundation for his bill, the bill will be dismissed. The court will not order the motion to stand over or retain a bill, unless it has a favorable opinion on the merits of the case (*z*). Nor will the court, unless the circumstances of the case are * such as to lead it to form an opinion   * 214 as to the legality of the act complained of, or to put the case into a course of immediate investigation, allow the motion to stand over till the purpose has been so far executed as that its character may be judged of, but will refuse the motion (*a*). An injunction will not be granted on the principle that it will do no harm to the defendant, if he has not done the act complained of (*b*).

28. The mere fact that an appeal may be pending is not a ground for refusing an injunction to restrain the violation of a legal right. But the jurisdiction will be exercised with caution, the court rather inclining against the propriety of delaying the successful party, unless the circumstances of the case show that, consistently with a sound exercise of the discretion of the court, he ought not to be permitted to exercise his legal rights. The court may, however, interfere if there is danger of irreparable mischief being done in the mean time, or if the court has grounds for doubting the correctness of the decision at law (*c*).

29. If an appeal is dismissed by the court, the jurisdiction of the court is gone, and no order can be made to bind the parties pending an appeal to the House of Lords. Where a plaintiff whose bill is about to be dismissed intends to appeal to the House of Lords, he should ask that the decree dismiss-

---

(*y*) Kay *v.* Marshall, 1 M. & C. 373; Shrewsbury and Chester Railway Co. *v.* Shrewsbury and Birmingham Railway Co., 1 Sim. N. S. 410; Bowser *v.* Maclean, 2 D. F. & J. 415.

(*z*) Wicks *v.* Hunt, John. 372; Ware *v.* Regent's Canal Co., 3 D. & J. 231. See Coffin *v.* Coffin, Jac. 72.

(*a*) Haines *v.* Taylor, 2 Ph. 209.

(*b*) Coffin *v.* Coffin, Jac. 72.

(*c*) Earl of Mountcashell *v.* O'Neill, 3 Ir. Ch. 619; Att.-Gen. *v.* Proprietors of Bradford Canal, 2 L. R. Eq. 71.

15

ing the bill should be so framed as to keep alive the jurisdiction of the court (*d*). In Penn *v*. Bibby, 2 L. R. Eq. 305, a motion for a new trial having been refused by the Vice-Chancellor, and on appeal by the Lord Chancellor, the court declined to suspend the final order for an injunction pending an appeal to the House of Lords.

30. The court has full jurisdiction to deal at its discretion with the costs of a motion for an injunction upon notice at the time of the application (*e*). But inasmuch as it may ultimately turn out that the merits of the case may be very different from those which appear on the face of the matter at the time of the application, the usual course of the court is to order that the costs of the application shall be costs in the cause, and whoever gets the costs in the cause will have the

* 215 costs of the proceeding (*f*).[1] *No order for payment of costs will be made on an *ex parte* application (*g*).

31. The question as to the costs of a motion will be sometimes reserved until the hearing (*h*). When the costs are reserved they should be reserved till the hearing of the cause or further order, and not to the hearing simply: because, in the latter case, no order can be made relating to them, unless the cause is actually brought to a hearing (*i*). Sometimes the court will order the question whether the costs shall be costs in the cause to stand over till the hearing (*k*).

32. If no direction is given as to the costs of a motion at the time of the application, the court is generally guided by the following rules laid down by Sir J. Leach in 1 Sim. & St. 357 :

(*d*) Galloway *v*. Mayor, &c., of London, 3 D. J. & S. 59.

(*e*) Pearce *v*. Wycombe Railway Co., 17 Jur. 660.

(*f*) Maitland *v*. Backhouse, 17 L. J. Ch. 127, *per* Lord Cottenham. See M'Curdy *v*. Noak, *ib*. 165; Chilton *v*. Campbell, 20 Beav. 531. Coles *v*. Sims, 5 D. M. & G. 11.

(*g*) Nokes *v*. Gibbon, 3 Jur N S. 282, 5 W. R. 216; Cast *v*. Poyser, 26 L. J. Ch. 853.

(*h*) Waring *v*. Manchester. Sheffield, and Lincolnshire Railway Co., 18 L. J. Ch. 450; Rochdale Canal Co. *v*. King, 2 Sim. N. S. 78; Wilkinson *v*. Cummins, 11 Ha. 337; Felkin *v*. Lewis, 11 W. R. 981; Macdougall *v*. Jersey Imperial Hotel Co., 2 H. & M. 528; but see Lewis *v*. Smith, 1 Mac. & G. 417, 420.

(*i*) Rumbold *v*. Forteath, 4 Jur. N. S. 608. See Gardner *v*. Marshall, 14 Sim. 575; Jones *v*. Batten, 10 Ha. App. 11; Macdougall *v*. Jersey Imperial Hotel Co., 2 H. & M. 528, Dan. Ch. Pr. 1262. See further, Morg. and Davy on Costs, 34.

(*k*) M'Curdy *v*. Noak, 17 L. J. Ch. 165.

[1] Where a town treasurer was enjoined from paying out money raised by the town for an illegal purpose, he was held not liable to costs, being in no fault. Fiske *v*. Hazard, 7 R. I. 438.

1. That the party making a successful motion is entitled to his costs, as costs in the cause; but the party opposing it is not entitled to his costs, as costs in the cause. 2. That the party making a motion which fails is not entitled to his costs, as costs in the cause; but the party opposing it is entitled to his costs, as costs in the cause. 3. That where a motion is made by one party, and not opposed by the other, the costs of both parties are costs in the cause (*l*).

33. But there are several exceptions to these rules. If a defendant unsuccessfully resists a motion for an injunction but succeeds at the hearing and gets the costs of the suit, his costs of the motion will, notwithstanding the first of the above rules, be costs in the cause (*m*). So also where the motion for an injunction * stood over, and the bill was   * 216 ultimately dismissed with costs (*n*).

34. Other exceptions to Sir J. Leach's rule occur: — 1 Where the motion is rendered necessary by the default of the moving party, or for some other reason he is asking for an indulgence; 2. Where the motion is rendered necessary by the opposite party's default; or 3. Where the motion is irregular (*o*).

35. The respondent is entitled to the costs of an abandoned motion (*p*). The costs must, however, be applied for not later than the next seal after that for which the notice of motion was given, otherwise they will be refused (*q*).

36. If, on appeal from a motion, the Lord Chancellor is of opinion that the motion was improperly granted in the court below, he reverses the order made, with the costs incurred in the original motion (*r*).

37. The costs of the motion may be given, though they are

(*l*) See Marsack *v.* Reeves, 6 Madd. 108, 109; Great Western Railway Co. *v.* Oxford, Worcester, &c., Railway Co., 5 De G. & S. 439; Hind *v.* Whitmore, 2 K. & J. 463.

(*m*) Stevens *v.* Keating, 1 Mac. & G. 659; Finden *v.* Stephens, 17 L. J. Ch. 342. See Harding *v.* Tingey, 10 Jur. N. S. 873.

(*n*) Betts *v.* Clifford, 1 J. & H. 75.

(*o*) See Morg. and Davy on Costs,

32–47; see also as to costs of affidavits Camille *v.* Donato, 11 Jur. N. S. 27.

(*p*) Consol. Ord. XL. r. 23.

(*q*) Woodcock *v.* Oxford, &c., Railway Co., 17 Jur. 33; Eccles *v.* Liverpool Borough Bank, John. 402. See Smith, Ch. Pr. 248.

(*r*) Beardmer *v.* London and North Western Railway Co., 13 Jur. 327, H. & Tw. 161.

not asked for in the notice of motion (*s*) ; but not if the party served does not appear (*t*).

SECTION II. — TRIAL OF QUESTIONS OF LAW AND FACT ON WHICH TITLE TO RELIEF IN EQUITY DEPENDS. — DAMAGES.

1-3. Practice of the court in requiring the plaintiff to establish his right at law.
4. The findings of a judge sitting without a jury have the same effect as the verdict of a jury.
5. The trial of the question of fact and the hearing of the cause are separate and distinct matters, but they may by consent be taken together.
6. Trial not directed before the hearing.
7. Court may obtain the assistance of experts.
8, 9. Recent statute provisions as to direction of issues at law.
10. After determination of the legal right upon trial in his favor, the plaintiff has a strict right to an injunction until the hearing.
11. Practice as to costs of issues.
12-17. Recent statutes giving court power to assess damages in certain cases. Construction of same, and practice under them.

1. Parties seeking equitable relief could not formerly have their case wholly disposed of by the court, but were often obliged to go to a court of law to have other points determined upon which their rights depended (*u*). The course of the court upon the application for an injunction was either to * 217 grant the * injunction, putting the plaintiff to establish his right at law within a given time, or to retain the bill with liberty to bring an action (*x*). If an action at law could not, in the opinion of the court, be framed so as to meet the question, it was the course of the court to direct an issue, where it saw clearly what the issue in the case was (*y*). The legislature, with the view of meeting and diminishing the mischief arising from the division of an investigation which should be one and entire, and of extending the remedy, rendered it obligatory on the court of chancery, by 25 & 26 Vict. c. 42, to decide all questions of law or fact on the determination of

----

(*s*) Clarke *v.* Jaques, 11 Beav. 623 ; Powell *v.* Cockerell, 4 Ha. 572 ; Pearce *v.* Wycombe Railway Co., 17 Jur. 660.
(*t*) Pratt *v.* Walker, 19 Beav. 261.
(*u*) *Re* Hooper, 32 L. J. Ch. 55 ; Baylis *v.* Watkins, 8 Jur. N. S. 1165.
(*x*) Harman *v.* Jones, Cr. & Ph. 301 ; Stevens *v.* Keating, 2 Ph. 335 ; Chap-

pell *v.* Purday, *ib.* 228 ; Rodgers *v.* Nowill, 6 Ha. 351 ; Fernie *v.* Young, 1 L. R. H. L. 63.
(*y*) Earl of Ripon *v.* Hobart, 3 M. & K. 169 ; Cory *v.* Yarmouth and Norwich Railway Co., 3 Ha. 607. See Fernie *v.* Young, 1 L. R. H. L. 63.

which the title to relief or remedy in equity depends (z)
The court cannot accordingly now, except under exceptions
circumstances, require the plaintiff in an injunction suit t
establish his right at law, but must try the whole questio
before itself (a). The act, however, specially provides that i
is not obligatory on the court to grant relief in any suit cor
cerning any matter as to which a court of common law ha
concurrent jurisdiction, if it shall appear to the court that suc
matter has been improperly brought into equity, and that th
same ought to have been left to the sole determination of
court of law (b). Where accordingly an action at law ha
been commenced before the filing of the bill, the court is no
as a matter of course, bound to interfere (c). So also wher
an injunction was sought to restrain a man from interferin
with the plaintiff's right to real estate, the plaintiff's titl
being doubtful and depending on questions more suitable for
trial at law, and there being no danger of any material in
jury, the court refused to interfere (d). The court will
be * very careful not to invade the jurisdiction of courts   * 21
of common law in respect to titles to real estate, unless
its own jurisdiction is clearly and distinctly acquired (e). I
at the time of filing the bill the plaintiff has no ground fo
equitable relief, the suit is improperly brought into equit
within the meaning of the act (f).

2. The court must determine before itself, either with o
without a jury, any question of fact or law arising in th
suit (g). In a clear case the court may determine question
of fact at once, without taking the opinion of a jury upon th
point, although required by the defendant to do so (h). Bu
f it appear that there is really a question to be tried, the cour

---

(z) *Re* Hooper, 32 L. J. Ch. 55;
Baylis *v.* Watkins, 8 Jur. N. S. 1165;
Young *v.* Fernie, 1 D. J. & S. 353;
Egmont *v.* Darell, 1 H. & M. 563 ; Cope-
and *v.* Webb, 1 N. R. 119; Fernie *v.*
Young, 1 L. R. H. L. 63.

(a) *Re* Hooper, 32 L. J. Ch. 55;
Baylis *v.* Watkins, 8 Jur. N. S. 1165;
Davenport *v.* Jepson, 1 N. R. 173;
Fernie *v.* Young, 1 L. R. H. L. 63.

(b) Sec. 4.

(c) Curlewis *v.* Carter, 33 L. J. Ch
370.

(d) Ward *v.* Higgs, 12 W. R. 1074.
(e) *Ib.*

(f) Durell *v.* Pritchard, 1 L. R. Ch
Ap. 244.

(g) 25 & 26 Vict. c. 42, s. 3, embody
ing 21 & 22 Vict. c. 27, ss. 3–5; *infra*
p. 224.

(h) Eaden *v.* Frith, 1 H. & M. 574
See Robinson *v.* Anderson, 7 D. M. &
G. 239.

will not of itself decide the point, if either party desires a jury (i). On a trial before the court without a jury, the court does not require the same strictness in pleading as would be necessary in a trial by jury, but will follow that course of proceeding which it deems best, in order to diminish expense and hasten the determination of the suit (k).

3. The verdict of a jury summoned under the provisions of the Act 21 & 22 Vict. c. 27, s. 3, is a conclusive answer to any question of fact tried before that jury, and is binding on the court, unless there should be cause to set aside that verdict and to direct a new trial, or unless there should be some cause for entering up judgment upon matters of law *non obstante veredicto* (l). The motion for a new trial must be made in the first instance to the judge before whom the trial was had (m). There is the same right of appeal from any order made by the court on an application made for a new trial as from any other order of the court (n). Where the motion for a new trial is made before the court of appeal, the court will not consider whether the finding was proper, but merely whether there was sufficient evidence to warrant a verdict. Where the motion is grounded on the improper rejection of evidence, the evidence ought to have been formally tendered to the judge of the court below, and rejected by him (n).

* 219   4. * The findings of the judge sitting without a jury have the same effect as the verdict of a jury (o), and can only be questioned upon motion for a new trial, either to the judge before whom the trial was had or to the court of appeal in chancery (p). If not moved against in the proper course, the findings of the judge are final and irreversible (q). The proviso in s. 3, that there shall be the same right of appeal from any order made by the court upon an application made for a new trial as from any other order of the court, applies equally, whether the trial be had with or without a jury (r).

(i) Davenport *v.* Goldberg, 2 H. & M. 282; Tangye *v.* Stott, 14 W. R. 128.

(k) Renard *v.* Levinstein, 11 L. T. N. S. 505.

(l) Fernie *v.* Young, 1 L. R. H. L. 63; Simpson *v.* Holliday, *ib.* 315.

(m) See *ib.*

(n) 21 & 22 Vict. c. 27, s. 3; Simp-

son *v.* Holliday, 1 L. R. H. L. 315; Curtis *v.* Platt, *ib.* 337.

(o) 21 & 22 Vict. c. 27, s. 5.

(p) *Ib.*; Fernie *v.* Young, 1 L. R. H. L. 63; Curtis *v.* Platt, *ib.* 337.

(q) Fernie *v.* Young, 1 L. R. H. L. 63; Simpson *v.* Holliday, *ib.* 315.

(r) Curtis *v.* Platt 1 L. R. H. L. 337.

The court of appeal may, on application for a new trial, reverse an order or decree of the court below on questions of law arising on the evidence (s).

5. The trial of the question of fact and the hearing of the cause are separate and distinct matters, but they may by consent be taken together (t). If there be notice of motion for a new trial, the hearing of the cause will be ordered to stand over until the finding of the issues has been settled (u). After the discharge of the jury the court will not determine the question of fact without the concurrence of both sides (x).

6. A trial by jury before the court itself will not, unless by consent of counsel on both sides, be directed before the hearing (y). An interlocutory motion, therefore, that a jury might be summoned to try an issue upon which the cause depended, was refused (z).

7. The court may obtain the assistance of accountants, merchants, engineers, or other scientific persons, to enable it the better to determine any matters at issue in any cause or proceeding (a). * An inspector will not be appointed * 220 until an issue is before the court between the parties upon which to refer the matter to his opinion (b).

8. The 25 & 26 Vict. c. 42, s. 2, preserves to the court the power of directing issues to a court of law, where it is satisfied that a question of fact can be more conveniently tried in that way (c). But the court will not avail itself of the option thus left to it, except in exceptional cases and under special circumstances. It must be satisfied that the administration of justice in the particular case may be more conveniently exercised and promoted by directing such issue than by com-

---

(s) Ib.; Simpson v. Holliday, ib. 315.
(t) Fernie v. Young, 1 L. R. H. L. 63.
(u) Penn v. Jack, 14 W. R. 760, 14 L. T. N. S. 495. See Tangye v. Stott, 14 W. R. 386.
(x) Davenport v. Jepson, 1 N. R. 471.
(y) George v. Whitmore, 26 Beav. 557; Morrison v. Barrow, 1 D. F. & J. 633. See Edmunds v. Brougham, 12 Jur. N. S. 934.
(z) George v. Whitmore, 26 Beav. 557. Application for an order for the trial of an issue of fact can only be

made in chambers. Edmunds v. Brougham, 12 Jur. N. S. 934.
(a) 15 & 16 Vict. c. 80, s. 42.
(b) Stokes v. City Offices Co., 11 Jur. N. S. 560. See, as to weight to be attached to scientific evidence, Martin v. Headon, 2 L. R. Eq. 432.
(c) See Egmont v. Darell, 1 H. & M. 563; Eaden v. Frith, ib. 573; Bovill v. Goodier, 2 L. R. Eq. 195; Freeman v. Tottenham and Hampstead Railway Co., 11 Jur. N. S. 254. See, as to form of issue, Eaden v. Frith, 1 H. & M. 573.

pleting the hearing and inquiry before itself (*d*). As a general rule, the court will try the question before itself rather than direct an issue to a court of law (*e*). If an issue is directed to a court of law, the application for a new trial is to be made to the court which directed the issue (*f*).

9. The provisions of the Act 25 & 26 Vict. c. 42, do not apply to cases where the object of the suit is to recover or defend the possession of land under a legal title, or under a title which would have been legal but for some outstanding term, lease, or mortgage (and whether mesne profits or damages shall or shall not also be sought in such suit). Such relief shall only be given in equity in cases of the sort as would have been proper according to the rules and practice of the court if the act had not passed (*g*).

*221   10. *After the determination of the legal right upon trial in his favor, the plaintiff has a strict right to an injunction until the hearing. It is no answer to the application that the defendant volunteers to keep an account (*h*).

11. As a general rule, where a plaintiff's title to equitable relief depends on a legal right, and an issue is directed to a court of law, he is, if successful at law, entitled to his costs both at law and in equity (*i*). On the other hand, the bill will be dismissed with costs if he fails to establish his legal right (*k*). The same rules would appear to apply to issues tried before the court itself (*l*). In Weatherley *v.* Ross (*m*), where the issues were found partly for the plaintiff and partly for the defendant, no costs were given to the defendant. The costs of an issue are not strictly part of the costs of the suit,

---

(*d*) Young *v.* Fernie, 1 D. J. & S. 353.

(*e*) Egmont *v.* Darell, 1 H. & M. 563; Eaden *v.* Frith, *ib.* 573; Young *v.* Fernie, 4 Giff. 577. See Williams *v.* Williams, 33 Beav. 306; Cowgill *v.* Rhodes, *ib.* 310.

(*f*) Hope *v.* Hope, 10 Beav. 581; Swinfen *v.* Swinfen, 27 Beav. 148. See *ib.* as to rules in equity respecting new trials. See, as to principles on which a court of equity proceeds in directing and acting upon the result of an issue to a court of law, *Ex parte* Freeman and Stallingers of Sunder-

land, 1 Drew. 184. See also Stace *v.* Mabbott, 2 Ves. 552.

(*g*) Sec. 4.

(*h*) Renard *v.* Levinstein, 2 H. & M. 628.

(*i*) Corporation of Rochester *v.* Lee, 2 D. M. & G. 427. See Farina *v.* Silverlock, 4 K. & J. 650.

(*k*) Corporation of Rochester *v.* Lee, 2 D. M. & G. 427. See Chappell *v.* Purday, 2 Ph. 227.

(*l*) See Betts *v.* De Vitre, 34 L. J. Ch. 289.

(*m*) 1 H. & M. 349.

and may be disposed of after the issue is decided, before the hearing of the cause (*n*).

12. A court of equity has no inherent power to ascertain the amount of damages sustained by reason of tortious acts unattended with profits to the wrong-doer (*o*). But the jurisdiction to give and assess damages in respect of such acts has been lately conferred on the court by statute. It has been enacted by Statute 21 & 22 Vict. c. 27, s. 2, that in all cases in which the court has jurisdiction to entertain an application for an injunction against a breach of any covenant, contract, or agreement, or against the commission or continuance of any wrongful act, or for the specific performance of any covenant, contract, or agreement, the same court may award damages to the party injured, either in addition to or in substitution for such injunction or specific performance, and such damages may be assessed in such manner as the court shall direct (*p*).

The statute * does not transfer to the court the general * 222 jurisdiction of courts of common law by way of damages, or extend its jurisdiction to cases where previously to the statute it had no jurisdiction, or could not consistently with its rules and principles have interfered (*q*). The statute merely empowers the court to give damages in cases involving elements or ingredients of an equitable character. If the case as presented to the court is an equitable one, so that the subject-matter of the application is properly cognizable in equity, the court has jurisdiction under the statute to entertain the question of damages. If, on the other hand, the plaintiff has no equitable right at the time of filing the bill, so that the matter has been improperly brought into equity, the statute has no application (*r*). Damages may be awarded under the

(*n*) Duncan *v.* Varty, 2 Ph. 699; Rigby *v.* Great Western Railway Co., 19 L. J. Ch. 470; Betts *v.* De Vitre, 34 L. J. Ch. 289. See further on the subject, Morgan and Davy on Costs, 70–94.

(*o*) Powell *v.* Aikin, 4 K. & J. 343, 351. See Novello *v.* James, 5 D. M. & G. 876.

(*p*) Soames *v.* Edge, Johns. 669; Middleton *v.* Magnay, 2 H. & M. 233; Middleton *v.* Greenwood, 2 D. J. & S. 142.

(*q*) Wicks *v.* Hunt, Johns. 372;

Soames *v.* Edge, *ib.* 669; Rogers *v.* Challis, 27 Beav. 175; Collins *v.* Stuteley, 7 W. R. 710; Chinnock *v.* Sainsbury, 6 Jur. N. S. 1318; Norris *v.* Jackson, 1 J. & H. 319; Howe *v.* Hunt, 31 Beav. 420; Ferguson *v.* Wilson, 2 L. R. Ch. Ap. 77.

(*r*) Swaine *v.* Great Northern Railway Co., 33 L. J. Ch. 399; Hindley *v.* Emery, 1 L. R. Eq. 52; Durell *v.* Pritchard, 1 L. R. Ch. Ap. 244; Robson *v.* Whittingham, *ib.* 442; Ferguson *v.* Wilson, 2 L. R. Ch. Ap. 77.

statute if it appear that at the time of filing the bill there was
an equitable case, although the case for an injunction fails (*s*),
or although an injunction is not competent from circumstances
which have occurred since the filing of the bill (*t*). An inquiry as to damages may be directed in addition to the account (*u*).

13. The statute leaves it to the discretion of the court
whether it will award damages or leave the plaintiff to obtain
them at law (*x*). The exercise of the jurisdiction is not
rendered compulsory on the court by 25 & 26 Vict. c. 42 (*y*).
But the court, having regard to the spirit and intention of that
act, will entertain the question of damages in all cases where
it feels it would be well advised in doing so. Whether
*223   the court will go into *the question or not must de-
pend on the circumstances of each particular case. If
the court shall be of opinion that the question of damages can
be more effectually disposed of at law, it will not enter into
the question, but will dismiss the bill without prejudice to an
action at law. If, on the other hand, it feels that it can ad-
vantageously entertain the question, it will do so (*z*).

14. If the injury caused by the act complained of is of a
material nature, the court cannot give damages in substitution
for an injunction, but is bound to grant an injunction (*a*).
Where a tenant is plaintiff and the landlord is no party to
the suit, damages are out of the question, if material injury
may be caused to the reversion (*b*). The compensation which
is given under the statute is not such compensation as is to be
got at law where an action lies *toties quoties* for an injury, but
once for all the damage caused by the act complained of (*c*).
The damage must be in respect of any breach or default com-

(*s*) Wedmore *v.* Mayor of Bristol, 11
W. R. 136 ; Eastwood *v.* Lever, 33 L.
J. Ch. 355.

(*t*) Catton *v.* Wyld, 32 Beav. 266 ;
Davenport *v.* Ryland, 1 L. R. Eq.
302.

(*u*) Betts *v.* De Vitre, 34 L. J. Ch.
289 ; Southorn *v.* Reynolds, 12 L. T.
N. S. 75.

(*x*) Durell *v.* Pritchard, 1 L. R. Ch.
Ap. 244.

(*y*) *Ib.*; Johnson *v.* Wyatt, 2 D. J.
& S. 18.

(*z*) Jacomb *v.* Knight, 32 L. J. Ch.
601 ; Johnson *v.* Wyatt, 2 D. J. & S.
18 ; Curriers' Co. *v.* Corbett, 11 Jur.
N. S. 719 ; Swaine *v.* Great Northern
Railway Co., 33 L. J. Ch. 399 ; Durell
v. Pritchard, 1 L. R. Ch. Ap. 244.

(*a*) Stokes *v.* City Offices Co., 13 L.
T. N. S. 81.

(*b*) *Ib.*

(*c*) *Ib.*

mitted at the time of the suit. The court will not upon motion in the suit award damages in respect of acts which have since occurred (d). An inquiry as to damage will not be directed if the loss has arisen, not from the injunction, but from the pendency of the litigation (e).

15. The right to recover damages under the statute is not confined to cases where an action at law is maintainable (f). Nor is it necessary that damages should be specifically prayed by the bill. Damages may be had under the prayer for general relief (g). A man who has filed his bill for relief and damages * does not lose his right to damages because   * 224 performance has been obtained from the defendant before the suit comes to a hearing (h).

16. Damages may be assessed by a jury before the court, or by the court itself without a jury (i). If the case is a difficult one, the court will itself ascertain the damages. Where there is no difficulty in assessing damages, the question should be determined by a jury (k). The court may, if it is satisfied that the question may be more conveniently tried in that way, direct an issue to a court of law with reference to the amount of damages to be assessed (l).

17. On the dissolution of an *ex parte* injunction granted on the undertaking of the plaintiff as to damages, the defendant was entitled before the passing of the statute to have the damages ascertained as correctly as possible. The course was to refer the matter to the chief clerk, or to put the question in course of trial at law by a jury (m).

(d) Mayor, &c., of Hythe v. East, 35 L. J. Ch. 257.

(e) Bingley v. Marshall, 11 W. R. 1018. See, as to damages in case of pulling up a railway, Mold v. Wheatcroft, 30 L. J. Ch. 598. See, as to damages from not being allowed to use a vessel, De Mattos v. Gibson, 7 Jur. N. S. 282. See Cory v. Thames Iron, &c., Co., 11 W. R. 589. See, as to time for reference as to damages, Southworth v. Taylor, 28 Beav. 616 ; *supra*, p. 219.

(f) Eastwood v. Lever, 33 L. J. 355.

(g) Catton v. Wyld, 32 Beav. 266.

(h) Cory v. Thames Iron, &c., Co., 11 W. R. 589.

(i) 21 & 22 Vict. c. 27, ss. 3–5 ; Consol. Ord. XLI. 26–46 ; Morg. Ch. Ord. 272–274, 581–586 ; *supra*, p. 218, 219.

(k) Betts v. De Vitre, 34 L. J. Ch. 289.

(l) 21 & 22 Vict. c. 27, s. 6 ; 25 & 26 Vict. c. 42, s. 2 ; Cory v. Thames Iron, &c., Co., 11 W. R. 589.

(m) Novello v. James, 5 D. M. & G. 876.

SECTION III.—PERPETUAL INJUNCTIONS.—MANDATORY IN-
JUNCTIONS.

1. After the establishment of his legal right and the fact of its violation, plaintiff is
generally entitled as of course to a perpetual injunction.
2. Such injunction not refused merely because nominal damages only recovered at law.
3. Principles applied to interlocutory injunction in respect to acquiescence and delay
equally applicable to perpetual injunctions.
4. Suits for injunctions do not usually go to the hearing.
5. Perpetual injunctions not granted before the hearing.
6. Right to an account of profits is incidental to the right to an injunction.
7. Practice in reference thereto.
8—11. Practice in reference to costs.

Mandatory Injunctions.

12. Character of mandatory injunctions and principles upon which they are issued.
13. Due diligence should be used in making application for same.
14. Bill for mandatory injunction should not pray for preventive remedy.
15. Mandatory injunction seldom granted before hearing.

1. After the establishment of his legal right and the fact of
its violation, a man is in general entitled as of course to a perpetual injunction to prevent the recurrence of the wrong, unless
there be something special in the circumstances of the case (*n*).
The jurisdiction is founded on the equity of relieving a man
from the necessity of bringing action after action at law for
every violation of a common law right, and of finally quieting
the right, after a case has received such full decision as entitles
      a man to be protected against further trials of the
* 225   right (*o*).   * The award of an arbitrator is for the pur-
      poses of the injunction as good as a verdict (*p*). The
court will not in general grant a perpetual injunction until the
right and the violation of the right have been established
upon trial (*q*); but if a case be presented which satisfies the
mind of the judge that such a course would, if adopted, do
justice between the parties, the court may grant a perpetual
injunction without providing for a trial of the right (*r*).

(*n*) Wood *v.* Sutcliffe, 2 Sim. N. S.
166; Imperial Gas Co. *v.* Broadbent,
7 H. L. 612.
(*o*) *Ib.*; Lowndes *v.* Bettle, 33 L. J.
Ch. 451. See *supra*, pp. 132, 134.
(*p*) Imperial Gas Co. *v.* Broadbent, 7
H. L. 600.
(*q*) Duke of Beaufort *v.* Morris, 6
Ha. 340; Gray *v.* Liverpool and Bury
Railway Co., 4 Ra. Ca. 250; Imperial
Gas Co. *v.* Broadbent, 7 H. L. 600;
Potts *v.* Levy, 2 Drew. 272.
(*r*) Bacon *v.* Jones, 4 M. & C. 439;
Cuddon *v.* Morley, 7 Ha. 206; Potts *v.*
Levy, 2 Drew. 272.

2. The mere fact that trifling or merely nominal damages may have been recovered at law is not a ground for concluding that the right is not one which should be protected by perpetual injunction (s); but the minuteness of the damage may be a ground for the refusal of the court to interfere (t). The court will in general have regard not only to the dry strict rights of the plaintiff and defendant, but also to the surrounding circumstances, before it exercises the jurisdiction (u). The consideration of the balance of convenience and inconvenience in granting or withholding the injunction is not neglected by the court. If the granting the injunction would have the effect of inflicting serious damages upon the defendant without restoring or tending to restore the plaintiff to the position in which he originally stood, or doing him any real practical good (x), or if the mischief complained of can be properly, fully, and adequately compensated by a pecuniary sum (y), an injunction will not issue. If, on the other hand, the mischief complained of is of so material a nature that it cannot be properly, fully, and adequately compensated by a pecuniary sum, and the granting an injunction will restore or tend to restore the parties to the position in * which * 226 they formerly stood and have a right to stand, it is the duty of the court to interfere by perpetual injunction, notwithstanding the serious damage caused thereby to the defendant (z). The fact of an appeal pending at law is not a bar to an injunction, although it may influence the decision of the court as to the date at which the injunction should commence. The court will not hold its hand upon the ground of a decision being appealed from, unless it has some doubt of the justice of that decision (a). If a considerable time must necessarily

(s) Rochdale Canal Co. v. King, 2 Sim. N. S. 78, 16 Beav. 638.

(t) Wood v. Sutcliffe, 2 Sim. N. S. 166.

(u) Ib.; but see infra as to cases depending upon covenant or contract.

(x) Wood v. Sutcliffe, 2 Sim. N. S. 163; Bankart v. Houghton, 27 Beav. 431; but see infra as to cases depending on covenant or contract.

(y) Wood v. Sutcliffe, 2 Sim. N. S.

166. See Durell v. Pritchard, 1 L. R. Ch. Ap. 244.

(z) Wood v. Sutcliffe, 2 Sim. N. S. 166; Bankart v. Houghton, 27 Beav. 431; Imperial Gas Co. v. Broadbent, 7 H. L. 600; Tipping v. St. Helen's Smelting Co., 1 L. R. Ch. Ap. 66; Stokes v. City Offices Co., 13 L. T. N. S. 81; Att.-Gen. v. Proprietors of Bradford Canal, 2 L. R. Eq. 71.

(a) Att.-Gen. v. Proprietors of Bradford Canal, ib.

elapse to enable the parties to comply with an injunction without being put to grievous annoyance and expense, the court will order that the injunction do not commence until after the lapse of a certain stated period (b).

3. The principles of the court with respect to delay and acquiescence which apply to the case of applications for interlocutory injunctions are equally applicable to the case of applications for perpetual injunctions. To justify the court in refusing to interfere at the hearing, there must, it is true, be a stronger case of acquiescence than is sufficient to be a bar on the interlocutory application (c), but the same principle applies in both places. A man who, possessing a full knowledge of his rights, has lain by and has by his conduct encouraged others to expend moneys in contravention of the rights for which he afterwards contends, cannot come to the court for relief by perpetual injunction, however clear his right or whatever may be the value of the right, but must rest satisfied with such damages as a jury will give (d). A man may by acquiescence not only preclude himself from being able to dero-

* 227 gate from a state of * things which has been brought about by his own conduct, but may even give the adverse party a right to the interference of the court in the event of his complaining at law (e). But the court will not act upon light grounds against the legal rights of the parties. It requires a clear and strong case to lead the court to deprive a man of his right at law to prevent a particular act being done, or his right to recover damages if it be done. There must be fraud or such acquiescence as in the view of the court would make it a fraud in him afterwards to insist upon his legal right (f).

4. Suits for an injunction to restrain the violation of a common law right do not generally go to the hearing. The interlocu-

(b) Att.-Gen. v. Proprietors of Bradford Canal, 2 L. R. Eq. 71.

(c) Johnson v. Wyatt, 2 D. J. & S. 18; supra, 205.

(d) Dann v. Spurrier, 7 Ves. 231, 235; Rochdale Canal Co. v. King, 2 Sim. N. S. 78, 16 Beav. 630; Wood v. Sutcliffe, 2 Sim. N. S. 169; Davies v. Marshall, 10 C. B. N. S. 703, 1 Dr. & Sm. 557. See Imperial Gas Co. v. Broadbent, 7 H. L. 600; Gale v. Abbott, 8 Jur. N. S. 987; supra, p. 41–43, 205.

(e) Barrett v. Blagrave, 6 Ves. 104; Williams v. Earl of Jersey, Cr. & Ph. 97.

(f) Macher v. Foundling Hospital, 1 V. & B. 188; Gerrard v. O'Reilly, 3 Dr. & War. 414; Att.-Gen. v. Briggs, 1 Jur. N. S. 1084; Bankart v. Houghton, 27 Beav. 431; supra, p. 41–43, 205.

tory injunction is generally submitted to by the defendant, and the plaintiff is generally satisfied with the submission, and feels himself sufficiently protected. But he may, if he pleases, bring the suit to a hearing. He does not, however, usually do so unless he rules an account, or unless the plaintiff denies him some other relief to which he is entitled.

5. A perpetual injunction will not be granted before the hearing (*g*). But an injunction may by consent be made perpetual on motion (*h*). A man is not bound to apply by motion in the first instance. He may obtain a perpetual injunction at the hearing, although he has not applied for an injunction on interlocutory application (*i*). But he should take care to bring his case to the hearing in such a state as to enable the court to adjudicate upon it without delay. If he neglects to do so it is a mere matter of discretion how far the court will assist him at the hearing, or whether it will assist him at all (*k*).

6. If the act complained of involves the making of profits, the * right to an account of profits is incidental   * 228 to the right to an injunction. There can in general be no account if the case for an injunction fails, or if at the hearing there is nothing on which an injunction can operate (*l*). The account is limited to the profits actually made and the moneys actually received by the wrong-doer. There can be no account in respect of acts unattended with profit (*m*). The account is of all profits actually made for six years prior to the filing of the bill (*n*). An account will not be granted if there be delay in filing the bill (*o*).

(*g*) Day *v.* Snee, 3 V. & B. 171.
(*h*) Morrell *v.* Pearson, 12 Beav. 284.
(*i*) Bacon *v.* Jones, 4 M. & C. 436; Collins Co. *v.* Walker, 7 W. R. 222; Davies *v.* Marshall, 1 Dr. & Sm. 557; Gale *v.* Abbott, 8 Jur. N. S. 987.
(*k*) Bacon *v.* Jones, 4 M. & C. 436; Ward *v.* Key, 10 Jur. 792; Rodgers *v.* Nowill, 6 Ha. 331; Norton *v.* Nicholls, 4 K. & J. 475; Patent Type Founding Co. *v.* Walter, Johns. 731.
(*l*) Baily *v.* Taylor, 1 R. & M. 73; Price's Candle Co. *v.* Bauwen's Candle Co., 4 K. & J. 727. Comp. Garth *v.*

Cotton, 3 Atk. 751, 1 Ves. 524, 546. *Infra*, p. 284.
(*m*) Colburn *v.* Simms, 2 Ha. 560; Powell *v.* Aikin, 4 K. & J. 343, 351. *Infra*, p. 285.
(*n*) Crossley *v.* Derby Gas Light Co., 1 Webs. 119, 120; Dean *v.* Thwaite 21 Beav. 623. See further, *infra*, p. 286.
(*o*) Crossley *v.* Derby Gas Light Co., 4 L. J. Ch. N. S. 25, 1 Webs. 119, 120; Parrott *v.* Palmer, 3 M. & K. 643; Harrison *v.* Taylor, 11 Jur. N. S. 408. See Bagot *v.* Bagot, 32 Beav. 509. *Infra*, p. 286.

7. In consequence of the difficulty of working out a decree for an account of profits, such an account is usually taken. A reasonable compromise is generally found to be most for the benefit of the parties (*p*). If the amount of profits for which the defendant would have to account is small, the plaintiff usually waives the account (*q*), and if the defendant submits, the suit does not proceed to the hearing, but a decretal order is made, giving effect to the agreement between the parties. The plaintiff is entitled to discovery for the purposes of the account (*r*).

8. Suits for an injunction to restrain the violation of a legal right do not usually go to the hearing. The interlocutory injunction is generally submitted to by the defendant if upon trial the legal right is found to be in favor of the plaintiff, and the costs being paid by the defendant up to that time, the plaintiff is generally satisfied and feels himself sufficiently protected, but he has a right, if he thinks fit, to bring the cause to a hearing. If, however, the defendant offers to submit to the injunction with costs, and to give the plaintiff all the other relief to which he may be under the circumstances of
*229   * the case entitled, and no account is sought or the account is waived, the court, though it may give the plaintiff the decree, will not give him the costs of the subsequent prosecution of the suit up to the hearing (*s*). The tender must include the costs of the suit up to the time when the tender is made (*t*). If the defendant does not offer to submit to the injunction and pay all the costs up to that time (*u*), or if, although he offers to submit to the injunction, he refuses to pay the costs or to give the plaintiff any of the other relief to which he is entitled, the plaintiff is entitled to

---

(*p*) Crossley *v.* Derby Gas Light Co., 3 M. & C. 436.

(*q*) See Fradella *v.* Weller, 2 R. & M. 247.

(*r*) See *infra*.

(*s*) Millington *v.* Fox, 3 M. & C. 352; Colburn *v.* Simms, 2 Ha. 561; Chappell *v.* Davidson, 2 K. & J. 123; Nunn *v.* D'Albuquerque, 34 Beav. 595; Harvey *v.* Ferguson, 15 Ir. Ch. 277; Hudson *v.* Bennett, 12 Jur. N. S. 519. See Dan. Ch. Pr. 1277.

(*t*) Fradella *v.* Weller, 2 R. & M. 247; Geary *v.* Norton, 1 De G. & S. 12; Jamieson *v.* Teague, 3 Jur. N. S. 1206; Burgess *v.* Hill, 26 Beav. 244; Remnant *v.* Hood, 27 Beav. 74; M'Andrew *v.* Bassett, 33 L J. Ch. 561; Moet *v.* Couston, 33 Beav. 578; Nunn *v.* D'Albuquerque, 34 Beav. 595. See Dan. Ch. Pr. 1277.

(*u*) Potts *v.* Levy, 2 Drew. 272.

bring the suit to a hearing, and will have the costs of the suit (x). If both parties are in the wrong, the one claiming more than he is entitled to claim, and the other offering less than he was bound to offer, costs will not be given to either side (y).

9. A *bonâ fide* offer from the defendant before suit to give the plaintiff all the relief to which he is entitled, and which he ultimately obtains by the suit, may be a reason for depriving him of the costs of it (z). In Edelsten *v.* Edelsten (a), however, Lord Westbury said he could not take notice of negotiations antecedent to the suit, save in case of bad faith, unless they amounted to a release or binding agreement with respect to the cause of action. But in other cases it has been held * that a *bonâ fide* offer of the terms which are sub-   * 230 sequently imposed by the court is sufficient to deprive a plaintiff of the costs of the suit (b). A man, however, whose legal right has been invaded is under no obligation to make an application to the defendant before filing his bill for an injunction (c).

10. If the costs of the suit have been increased by an allegation in the bill which is untrue, such increased costs will have to be paid by the plaintiff, although his case may be substantially established (d).

11. The costs of the suit are often disposed of on interlocutory application before decree (e).[1]

(x) Fradella *v.* Weller, 2 R. & M. 247; Geary *v.* Norton, 1 De G. & S. 12; Kelley *v.* Hooper, 1 Y. & C. C. C. 197; Colburn *v.* Simms, 2 Ha. 561; Jamieson *v.* Teague, 8 Jur. N. S. 1206; Chappell *v.* Davidson, 2 K. & J. 123; Burgess *v.* Hill, 26 Beav. 244; Burgess *v.* Hateley, *ib.* 249; M'Andrew *v.* Bassett, 33 L. J. Ch. 561.

(y) Moet *v.* Couston, 33 Beav. 578. See Rochdale Canal Co. *v.* King, 16 Beav. 630; Pearce *v.* Wycombe Railway Co., 17 Jur. 660; Nunn *v.* D'Albuquerque, 34 Beav. 595; Ainsworth *v.* Walmesley, 1 L. R. Eq. 518.

(z) Millington *v.* Fox, 3 M. & C. 338; Colburn *v.* Simms, 2 Ha. 543, 561; Chappell *v.* Davidson, 2 K. & J. 123; Williams *v.* Thomas, 2 Dr. & Sm. 29, 37. See Woodman *v.* Robinson, 2 Sim. N. S. 204.

(a) 1 D. J. & S. 185, 203.

(b) Williams *v.* Thomas, 2 Dr. & Sm.

20, 37; Nesbitt *v.* Berridge, 32 Beav. 282.

(c) Burgess *v.* Hill, 26 Beav. 244; Burgess *v.* Hateley, *ib.* 249.

(d) Pierce *v.* Franks, 15 L. J. Ch. 122. See Dan. Ch. Pr. 1286.

(e) Morg. and Dav. on Costs, 47–62. As to the costs of motions see Mounsey *v.* Earl of Lonsdale, and Attorney-General *v.* Earl of Lonsdale, 10 Law Rep. Eq. Ca. 557. The old established rule, that the court of appeal will not give the costs of the appeal to a successful appellant, except under special circumstances, is still in force. If the court does not specially give the costs, the appellant is not entitled to them. 6 Law Rep. Ch. Ap. 138.

[1] Where a bill has been dismissed or demurrer allowed, and another bill is filed for the same matter, proceedings will be stayed in the second suit till the costs of the former are paid. Updike *v.* Bartles, 2 Beasley, 231.

Mandatory Injunctions.

12. Though a court of equity has no jurisdiction to compel the performance of a positive act tending to alter the existing state of things, such as the removal of a work already executed, it may, by framing the order in an indirect form, compel a defendant to restore things to their former condition, and so effectuate the same results as would be obtained by ordering a positive act to be done. The order when framed in such a form is called a mandatory injunction. The jurisdiction has been questioned (f), but its existence must be admitted as beyond all doubt (g).[1] It must, however, be exercised with caution, and is strictly confined to cases where the remedy at law is inadequate for the purposes of justice, and the restoring things to their former condition is the only remedy which will meet the requirements of the case.

* 231   If there is a full and complete remedy at * law, or if the injury done can be sufficiently estimated and properly compensated by a pecuniary sum, there is no case for a mandatory injunction (h). The court will not interfere by way of mandatory injunction without taking into consideration the

(f) Blakemore v. Glamorganshire Railway Co., 1 M. & K. 184.

(g) Robinson v. Lord Byron, 1 Bro. C. C. 588; Great North of England, &c., Railway Co. v. Clarence Railway Co., 1 Coll. 507; Hervey v. Smith, 1 K. & J. 392; Att.-Gen. v. Borough of Birmingham, 4 K. & J. 547. See Isenberg v. East India House Co., 33 L. J. Ch. 392.

(h) Deere v. Guest, 1 M. & C. 516; Wicks v. Hunt, John. 372; Att.-Gen. v. Conservators of Thames, 1 H. & M. 1; Isenberg v. East India House, &c., Co., 33 L. J. Ch. 392; Doran v. Carroll, 11 Ir. Ch. 379; Durell v. Pritchard, 1 L. R. Ch. Ap. 244.

[1] See Pierce v. New Orleans, 18 La. Ann. 242. A mandatory order is nothing more than a decree of specific performance, which is every day's practice in courts of equity, and which is seldom denied, unless where the remedy at law is perfectly adequate. 2 Redfield on Railways, 356; Sears v. Boston, 16 Pick. 357. The authorities upon the subject of mandatory injunctions are reviewed in The Rogers Locomotive and Machine Works v. Erie Railway Co., 5 C. E. Green, 387, and the conclusion reached by the chancellor that a mandatory injunction, or one which commands the defendant to do some positive act, will not be ordered except upon final hearing, and then only to execute the decree or judgment of the court, and never on a preliminary or interlocutory motion, or that if it ever does so issue, it is only in cases of obstruction to easements or rights of like nature, in which a structure erected and kept as the means of preventing such enjoyment will be ordered to be removed, as part of the means of restraining the defendant from interrupting the enjoyment of the right. In this case it was held, that an injunction will not be granted to compel a common carrier to transport goods at the rates fixed by law, but will lie to prevent a railway company bound by law to transport goods from entering into an agreement not to transport them at the rates fixed by law. Notice in this connection that a bill in equity does not lie at the instance of a private individual to enforce the performance of a public duty by a corporation in the absence of any special right or authority. Buck Mountain Coal Co. v. Lehigh Coal and Nav. Co., 50 Penn. St. 91.

comparative convenience and inconvenience which the granting or withholding the injunction would cause to the parties.
If the injury done is capable of being fully and abundantly
compensated by a pecuniary sum, while the inconvenience to
the other party from granting an injunction would be serious,
the court will not interpose by way of mandatory injunction,
but will either direct an inquiry before itself in order to ascertain the measure of damages that has been actually sustained,
or will, on dismissing the bill, reserve to the plaintiff his right
to proceed at law (*i*). If, on the other hand, the injury is of
so serious or material a character that the restoring things to
their former condition is the only remedy which will meet the
requirements of the case, or if the act complained of is in
breach of an express stipulation, the injunction will issue,
notwithstanding the amount of inconvenience to the other
party (*k*). If the act complained of is continued or carried
on after clear and distinct notice that it is objected to, the
jurisdiction will be exercised more freely than in cases where
complaint is not made until after it is completed (*l*) ; but the
mere fact that the act complained of has been continued or
carried on after notice of objection is not of itself a sufficient
ground for the exercise of the jurisdiction, if the injury done
can be amply, abundantly, and properly compensated by a
pecuniary sum (*m*). There is no rule which prevents the
court from granting a mandatory injunction where
* the injury sought to be restrained has been completed   * 232
before the filing of the bill (*n*).

13. A man who comes to the court for a mandatory injunction should use due diligence in making the application. Mere

(*i*) Jacomb *v.* Knight, 32 L. J. Ch.
602 ; Isenberg *v.* East India House,
&c., Co., 33 L. J. Ch. 392. See Low
v. Innes, 10 Jur. N. S. 1037.

(*k*) Isenberg *v.* East India House,
&c., Co., 33 L. J. Ch. 392 ; Durell *v.*
Pritchard, 1 L. R. Ch. Ap. 244. See
Low *v.* Innes, 10 Jur. N. S. 1037 ; Martin *v.* Headon, 2 L. R. Eq. 425, *infra*.

(*l*) Jacomb *v.* Knight, 32 L. J. Ch.
601 ; Hepburn *v.* Lordan, 2 H. & M.
345 ; Beadel *v.* Perry, 3 L. R. Eq. 465.

(*m*) Isenberg *v.* East India House,
&c., Co., 33 L. J. Ch. 392.

(*n*) Durell *v.* Pritchard, 1 L. R. Ch.
244. See Low *v.* Innes, 10 Jur. N. S.
1037 ; Curriers' Co. *v.* Corbett, 11 Jur.
N. S. 719 ; Martyr *v.* Lawrence, 2 D.
J. & S. 261 ; Martin *v.* Headon, 2 L.
R. Eq. 425. In Attorney-General *v.*
Mid-Kent Railway Co. and South Eastern Railway Co., 3 Law Rep. Ch. Ap.
100, the principles of the court as to
granting mandatory injunctions are
considered with reference to the difference between cases of nuisance and
cases of contract, and to the suit being
by an individual or by the Attorney-
General.

delay will not be fatal to the application if no mischief is caused thereby to the defendant, and the delay does not exceed a reasonable period (*o*); but the right to a mandatory injunction is gone if there has been unreasonable delay, and mischief would be caused thereby to the defendant (*p*).

14. A bill for a mandatory injunction should not pray for a preventive remedy. There can be no case for prevention where what is asked to be prevented has been actually done (*q*).

15. A mandatory injunction is seldom granted before the hearing (*r*), but it may be had upon interlocutory application (*s*). The application need not be made before the hearing (*t*).

SECTION IV. — INJUNCTIONS UNDER THE COMMON LAW PROCEDURE ACT, 1854.

1–4. Provisions and construction of statute conferring upon common law courts power to issue injunctions.

1. UNTIL recently the writ of injunction was the peculiar remedy of the court of chancery. But by the Common Law Procedure Act, 1854, it was enacted that in all cases of breach of contract or other injury, where the party injured is entitled to maintain and has brought an action, he may claim a writ of injunction against the repetition or continuance of such breach of contract or other injury, or the committal of any
* 233 breach of * contract, or injury of a like kind, arising out of the same contract relating to the same property or right; and he may also include in the same action a claim for damages or other redress (*u*); and judgment may be given that the writ of injunction do or do not issue, as justice may require, and in case of such disobedience such injunction may be enforced by attachment (*v*).

(*o*) Gale *v.* Abbott, 8 Jur. N. S. 987.
(*p*) Wicks *v.* Hunt, John. 372; Ward *v.* Higgs, 12 W. R. 1074. See Att.-Gen. *v.* Manchester and Leeds Railway Co., 1 Ra. Ca. 436; *supra*, p. 226.
(*q*) Curriers' Co. *v.* Corbett, 11 Jur. N. S. 719.
(*r*) Gale *v.* Abbott, 8 Jur. N. S. 987. See Child *v.* Douglas, Kay, 578.
(*s*) Lane *v.* Newdigate, 10 Ves. 192;

Robinson *v.* Lord Byron, 1 Bro. C. C. 588; Rankin *v.* Huskisson, 4 Sim. 13; Hervey *v.* Smith, 1 K. & J. 392; Att.-Gen. *v.* Metropolitan Board of Works, 1 H. & M. 312; Hepburn *v.* Lordan, 2 H. & M. 352.
(*t*) Gale *v.* Abbott, 8 Jur. N. S. 987.
(*u*) 17 & 18 Vict. c. 125, s. 79.
(*v*) *Ib.*, s. 81. See Jessell *v.* Chaplin, 2 Jur. N. S. 931.

2. The plaintiff may also, at any time after the commencement of the action, and whether before or after judgment, apply *ex parte* to the court or judge for a writ of injunction to restrain the defendant in such action from the repetition or continuance of the wrongful act or breach of contract complained of, or the committal of any breach of contract or injury of a like kind arising out of the same contract or relating to the same property or right, and such right may be granted or denied by the court or judge on such terms as to such court or judge shall seem reasonable and just, and may be enforced by attachment (x).

3. The act only confers úpon courts of law a concurrent jurisdiction with courts of equity by way of injunction in certain cases, and does not oust the jurisdiction of courts of equity in such matters (y). The act does not give courts of law power to grant an injunction against a threatened injury, but only in cases where the wrongful act has been actually commenced. The powers, moreover, given by the act can be used only against the defendant or defendants in the particular action, and can only affect them as to acts which they themselves do or authorize to be done. It must therefore in many cases fail entirely to provide the remedy sought by the injured party (z).

4. The rule for a writ of injunction under sec. 82 is a rule to show cause only in the first instance (a). The writ may be granted or denied upon such terms as to the duration of the * writ, keeping an account, giving security or * 234 otherwise, as to the court or a judge shall seem reasonable and just (b). An injunction under the clause is, unless the duration of the writ is expressly limited, a continuing injunction. If it is disobeyed at any time, the plaintiff may apply to the court, or, if the court be not sitting, to a judge, to enforce it by attachment (c).

(x) 17 & 18 Vict. c. 125, s. 82.
(y) Hodgson *v.* Duce, 4 W. R. 576.
(z) See Matthews *v.* King, 3 H. & C. 910, 12 Jur. N. S. App. 335. See, as to demurrers to the declaration, Bilke *v.*

London, Chatham, and Dover Railway Co., 3 H. & C. 95.
(a) Gittins *v.* Simes, 15 C. B. 362.
(b) *Ib.*
(c) De la Rue *v.* Fortescue, 2 H. & N. 324.

* 235   * CHAPTER XVI.

INJUNCTIONS AGAINST WASTE.

_____

SECTION I. — PRINCIPLES ON WHICH THE COURT ACTS IN
RESTRAINING WASTE.

1. Court proceeds on same principles as in other cases for protection of legal rights;
   not limited to cases where an action at law can be maintained.
2. Court will not interfere if waste be of a trivial nature, unless intent to commit
   further waste be shown.
3. Mere apprehension of waste not sufficient.
4. Requisites of plaintiff's pleadings.
5. He must waive all forfeitures, penalties, &c.
6. Absence of parties to be benefited will not prevent injunction.
7. Plaintiff should use diligence in making application, but delay is not so prejudicial
   as in some other cases.

1. THE jurisdiction of courts of equity in restraining waste
by injunction is founded upon the equity of protecting property
from irreparable injury. In cases of legal waste, or cases
which are cognizable at common law, the jurisdiction is in aid
of the legal right, and has been assumed for the purpose of
protecting the property pending the trial of the right. The
court interferes on the assumption that the plaintiff has a good
title at law to the right which he asserts, but needs the aid of
the court for the protection of his property until the right can
be established upon trial. The principles on which the court
interferes are the same as those upon which it proceeds in
other cases where its interposition is sought for the protection
of legal rights (_a_). The jurisdiction is not, however, limited
to cases where an action at law can be maintained, but extends
to cases where, in consequence of the infirmity of legal process, there is neither a right nor a remedy at law, but only
what the law in principle acknowledges to be a wrong (_b_).
Thus as early as the reign of King Richard the Second an

(_b_) 3 D. F. & J. 55, 254, _per_ Turner,   (_a_) _Supra_, p. 196, 208, 209.
L. J.

injunction was granted at the suit of a remainder-man to stay waste by a tenant for life or for years, although the existence of an intermediate life estate formed a temporary impediment to an action at law (c).¹ So also where there was a tenant for life, subject to waste, remainder for life, dispunishable of waste, * remainder in fee, the court would not permit   * 236 an agreement between the two tenants for life to commit waste to take effect against the remainder-man (d). So also where there is a tenant for life, remainder for life, with remainders over, the court will restrain the first tenant for life on the bill of the remainder-man for life (e), without making the owner of the inheritance a party (f). So also an injunction to stay waste has been granted on behalf of an infant *en ventre sa mère* (g).²

2. It is not necessary for a man to wait until a serious act of waste has been committed, before applying to the court for its interference by injunction (h). But the court will not interfere where the waste is trivial and of small extent (i), or where the person against whom relief is sought has stopped committing waste since the filing of the bill (k). If, however, an intention to commit further waste can be shown, the court

(c) Moore, 554; Roswell's case, 1 Roll. Ab. 377, pl. 13; Farrant v. Lovell, 3 Atk. 723.

(d) Lady Evelyn's case. cit. 2 Freem. 54, 1 Dick. 209; Fleming v. Bishop of Carlisle, cit. 1 Dick. 209; Abraham v. Bubb, 2 Freem. 52; Tracy v. Tracy 1 Vern. 23; Robinson v. Litton, 3 Atk. 210. See also Birch-Wolfe v. Birch, 9 Law Rep. Eq. Ca. 683.

(e) Tracy v. Tracy, 1 Vern. 23; Perrot v. Perrot, 3 Atk. 95.

(f) Dayrell v. Champneys, 1 Eq. Ca. Ab. 400, cit. 1 Dick. 197, 198. See Mollineux v. Powell, 3 P W. 268, n.

(g) Luttrel's case, cit. Prec. Ch. 50, 2 Vern. 710; Robinson v. Litton, 3 Atk. 211.

(h) Gibson v. Smith, 2 Atk. 182; Coffin v. Coffin, Jac. 71.

(i) Brace v. Taylor, 2 Atk. 253; Barry v. Barry, 1 J. & W. 653; Lambert v. Lambert, 2 Ir. Eq. 210; Doran v. Carroll, 11 Ir. Ch. 383.

(k) Barry v. Barry, 1 J. & W 653. Comp. Anon., 3 Atk. 485.

¹ In North Carolina it is held that a bill in equity cannot be maintained to restrain from committing waste one who is in exclusive possession, — claiming, colorably at least, the absolute estate, until the plaintiff has established his title at law, — or at all events an injunction will be granted only when the plaintiff is endeavoring to establish his title at law, and until he has a reasonable time allowed for that purpose. For the court of equity acts in such cases, not as superseding the jurisdiction of the courts of law over a legal title, but only in aid of a legal remedy, defective because dilatory. Bogey v. Shute, 4 Jones Eq. 174; Irwin v. Davidson, 3 Ired. Eq. 311; Smith v. Rome, 19 Geo. 89.

² Where an executory trust for the settlement of freehold estates "in strict settlement" directs either expressly or by reference to the trusts of other property that certain persons shall take life estates, the use of the words "in strict settlement" does not make the tenants for life dispunishable for waste. Stanley v. Coulthurst, 10 Law Rep. Eq. Ca. 259.

will interfere, though the first acts of waste may have been of a trivial nature (*l*) ; but where waste of one kind has been done or threatened, the injunction will not be extended to waste of another kind (*m*). If one act of waste be established as well in equitable as in legal waste, the court will restrain the equitable waste generally (*n*).

3. The court has jurisdiction, if a fair case of prospective injury can be made out, to interfere before waste has been actually committed (*o*). The mere apprehension or belief that waste will be committed is not sufficient (*p*) ; but if an intention to commit waste can be shown to exist, or if a

* 237 man insists on his * right or threatens to commit waste, there is a foundation for the exercise of the jurisdiction (*q*).

4. A man who applies for an injunction against waste is required to show a particular title. An affidavit generally that the plaintiff is entitled in fee-simple (*r*), or an affidavit as to information and belief, is not sufficient (*s*). Positive evidence of title is necessary (*t*). The plaintiff should also by his affidavit state some actual violation of his right, or a sufficient ground to apprehend it. An affidavit merely as to his apprehension that the defendant intends to commit waste, without stating any ground for it, is not sufficient. There must be some fact, like the marking of trees, sending a surveyor, or some threat (*u*).

5. A bill cannot be filed to restrain waste without waiving all forfeitures, penalties, &c. (*x*). The words " on pain of forfeiture" after a prohibition against the commission of waste does not take away the rights and remedies which arise from the prohibition itself, but will be regarded as having been in-

(*l*) Coffin *v.* Coffin, Jac. 71 ; Barry *v.* Barry, 1 J. & W. 653; Doran *v.* Carroll, 11 Ir. Ch. 383.

(*m*) Coffin *v.* Coffin, Jac. 72.

(*n*) Coffin *v.* Coffin, 6 Madd. 17

(*o*) See *supra*, p. 197.

(*p*) Hanson *v.* Gardiner, 7 Ves. 307 ; Potts *v.* Potts, 3 L. J. Ch. 176; Campbell *v.* Allgood, 17 Beav. 628.

(*q*) Gibson *v.* Smith, 2 Atk. 182; Robinson *v.* Litton, *ib.* 209 ; Hanson *v.* Gardiner, 7 Ves. 309 ; Coffin *v.* Coffin,

Jac. 71 ; Barry *v.* Barry, 1 J. & W. 650; Campbell *v.* Allgood, 17 Beav. 628 ; Doran *v.* Carroll, 11 Ir. Ch. 379.

(*r*) Whitelegg *v.* Whitelegg, 1 Bro. C. C. 57.

(*s*) Davies *v.* Leo, 6 Ves. 784.

(*t*) *Ib.* See *supra*, p. 206.

(*u*) Gibson *v.* Smith, 2 Atk. 182; Jackson *v.* Cater, 5 Ves. 688; Hanson *v.* Gardiner, 7 Ves. 309.

(*x*) 1 Atk. 451, Mitf. Pl. 162; *supra*, p. 198.

serted merely as a more effectual means of enforcing the obligation (y).

6. If there is a case for an injunction, and the injunction will operate for the benefit of parties not before the court, the absence of those parties will not prevent the court from interfering by injunction (z). The purchasers of timber wrongfully cut by a tenant for life are not necessary parties to a bill for an injunction to restrain him from selling the timber (a).

7. A man who comes to the court for an injunction against waste should use due diligence in making the application (b). * Delay, however, is not so prejudicial to the   * 238 plaintiff in cases of waste as in other applications for injunctions. In some cases, indeed, delay is not material. A man, for instance, who has been permitted to cut down half of the trees upon the land of another, can acquire no title from the negligence of the owner to cut down the remaining half (c). Nor can tenants who have been in the habit of cutting turf or working quarries for many years acquire a title as against their landlord to continue to do so (d). Nor is a man who buys land used by tenants for making bricks, or who purchases land with notice that the land was being converted into a burying-ground, precluded from complaining of waste committed after the purchase (e). The case, however, is different if the tenant for life or lessee has been encouraged by the acquiescence of the reversioner or lessee to expend moneys upon the property upon the faith and understanding that no obstacle will be afterwards thrown in the way of their enjoyment (f). In the case of mines the utmost promptitude in making the application is requisite (g).

(y) Blake v. Peters, 1 D. J. & S. 345.

(z) Const v. Harris, T. & R. 514; Ackroyd v. Briggs, 14 W. R. 25.

(a) Marker v. Marker, 9 Ha. 1. See further, as to parties, Wentworth v. Turner, 3 Ves. 3; Kingston v. Kingston, 2 Moll. 412; *supra*, pp. 207, 208.

(b) Barry v. Barry, 1 J. & W. 651. See Bagot v. Bagot, 32 Beav. 509.

(c) Att.-Gen. v. Eastlake, 11 Ha. 228, *per* Wood, V. C.

(d) Lord Courtown v. Ward, 1 Sch. & Lef. 8; Lord Waterpark v. Austin, 1 Jon. 627, n.

(e) Cregan v. Cullen, 16 Ir. Ch. 339.

(f) Barry v. Barry, 1 J. & W. 651. See *supra*, pp. 41–43, 201.

(g) Norway v. Rowe, 19 Ves. 159; Field v. Beaumont, 1 Sw. 204; Hilton v. Lord Granville, Cr. & Ph. 283; Parrott v. Palmer, 3 M. & K. 635; Clegg v. Edmondson, 8 D. M. & G. 808.

SECTION II. — LEGAL WASTE.

1. WASTE is a substantial injury to the inheritance done by one having a limited estate either of freehold or for years during the continuance of his estate (h). The essential character of waste is, that the party committing it is in rightful possession, and that there is a privity of title between the parties (i).

2. The consequences of waste do not attach unless substantial damage is done to the inheritance, which may be either, — 1st, by * diminishing the value of the estate; 2dly, by increasing the burdens upon it; or, 3dly, by

* 239

(h) Co. Litt. 53 a; 1 Cr. Dig. 115.   222; Lowndes v. Bettle, 33 L. J. Ch.
(i) Davenport v. Davenport, 7 Ha.   451.

impairing the evidence of title (*k*). An act which increases
the value of an estate may nevertheless be waste if it impairs
the evidence of title or increases the burdens on the property.
The owner of the inheritance has a right, if he pleases, to
require that the nature and character of the property shall not
be changed by the owner of the limited estate. The mere fact
that the evidence of title may be impaired by the alteration
renders it waste. Waste which increases the value of property
is called meliorating waste (*l*).

3. Waste is either voluntary or permissive. Voluntary
waste consists in the commission of acts which the owner of
the limited estate has no authority to do, such as cutting timber, pulling down buildings, opening mines, and the like.
Permissive waste arises from the omission of acts which it is
his duty to do, as, for example, permitting buildings to go to
decay by neglecting to repair them (*m*).

4. At common law waste was punishable only in the case of
tenant in dower, tenant by the curtesy, and guardian. These
estates being the creation of law, the law annexed to them the
condition that waste should be neither done nor permitted. A
tenant for life or for years was not at common law liable for
waste in the absence of an express stipulation to that effect in
the instrument by which his estate was created. An estate for
life being not the creation of the law, but of the parties to the
instrument, the law would not imply a condition against waste
in cases where no provision to that effect was made (*n*). This
defect in the law was remedied by the Statutes of Marlbridge,
52 Hen. 3, c. 23, and Gloucester, 6 Edw. 1, c. 5, which extended the protection of the writ of waste which lay at common law to tenants for life and tenants for years.

5. Timber trees are parcel of the inheritance. A
tenant for life * or years, or other owner of a limited   * 240
estate, has only a right to their shade and fruit during

(*k*) Doe *v.* Earl of Burlington, 5 B.
& Ad. 507, 517 ; Huntley *v.* Russell, 13
Q. B. 572, 588.

(*l*) 2 William Saund. 259 ; Simmons
v. Norton, 7 Bing. 649 ; Duke of Leeds

v. Amherst, 2 Ph. 123 ; Coppinger *v.*
Gubbins, 3 J. & L. 417.

(*m*) Co. Litt. 53 a ; White *v.* M'Cann,
1 Ir. C. L. 205.

(*n*) 2 Inst. 145, 299 ; Green *v.* Cole,
2 William Saund. 252.

the continuance of his estate (*o*).   It is waste if he cuts them down (*p*), or does any act to impair their value or cause them to decay, as if he lops or tops them (*q*). The cutting of timber which is over-ripe or in a state of decay is waste (*r*). Even if a lease be of land, trees, &c., expressly mentioning the trees, the lessee has no right to cut them (*s*).

6. Timber trees are such as are useful for the purpose of building.   Oak, ash, and elm, of the age of twenty years and upwards, are timber in all places (*t*), and by the custom of different counties, other trees, such as birch, beech, walnut, whitethorn, willow, blackthorn, hornbeam, &c., are timber (*u*).

7. The cutting of many sorts of trees, which are not other-wise timber, as hornbeams, hazels, willows, sallows, &c., &c., may, from the situation in which they are placed, be considered waste, as if they support a bank, or grow within the site of or shelter a house, or stand in a field, or are used as shelter by cattle (*x*).[1]

8. It is not waste to cut down trees which are not timber either by law or custom, or from the situation in which they are placed, unless some special prejudice arises thereby to the inheritance (*y*).   Nor is the proper and regular thinning of a wood for the purpose of improving the rest of the trees, waste, provided it be done in a reasonable and husbandlike
* 241   manner (*z*).   * But the destruction of germens or young plants destined to become trees, which destroys

---

(*o*) 4 Co. Rep. 62 b; 11 Co. Rep. 50 a; 1 Roll. Ab. 181; Berriman *v.* Peacock, 9 Bing. 384 ; Alexander *v.* Godley, 6 Ir. C. L. 458.

(*p*) Co. Litt. 53 a.

(*q*) *Ib.*

(*r*) Perrott *v.* Perrott, 3 Atk. 95. See now 19 & 20 Vict. c. 120, s. 11.

(*s*) Lifford's case, 11 Co. Rep. 46 b ; Dyer, 374, pl. 18 ; Shep. Touch. 95 ; Herring *v.* Dean and Chapter of St. Paul's, 3 Sw. 512.

(*t*) Co. Litt. 53 a ; 2 Roll. Ab. 814 ; Dyer, 65 a.

(*u*) Co. Litt. 53 a ; Barrett *v.* Barrett, Het. 36 ; Cook *v.* Cook, Cro. Car. 531 ; Duke of Chandos *v.* Talbot, 2 P. Wms. 606 ; Gordon *v.* Woodford, 27 Beav. 603 ; Cruise, Dig. tit. 3, ch. 2, ss.

5–7 ; Yool on Waste, 22 ; Craig on Trees, 11.

(*x*) Co. Litt. 53 a ; Darcy *v.* Askwith, Hob. 234 ; Philipps *v.* Smith, 14 M. & W. 593 ; Craig on Trees, 12.

(*y*) Co. Litt. 53 a ; Barrett *v.* Barrett, Het. 36 ; Philipps *v.* Smith, 14 M. & W. 589. See Pratt *v.* Brett, 2 Madd. 62.

(*z*) Pidgeley *v.* Rawling, 2 Coll. 275; Earl Cowley *v.* Wellesley, 1 L. R. Eq. 656.   See Bagot *v.* Bagot, 32 Beav. 509.

[1] It seems that in a case of sufficient importance the cutting of trees standing on the line between adjoining proprietors may be restrained by injunction. Relyea *v.* Beaver, 34 Barb. 547 ; and see cases cited.

the future timber, is waste (*a*). The turning of goats into a young wood is waste (*b*).

9. The general rules with respect to waste in timber are subject to exceptions in the case of what are called timber estates, where severed timber is for many purposes to be treated as annual rents and profits (*c*).

10. It is not waste to cut hedges, bushes, and underwood, and even oaks and ashes which have been usually cut as underwood, provided the cutting be done in a reasonable and husbandlike manner, and so as not to eradicate or destroy the germens or prevent their future growth (*d*). Nor is it waste to cut timber where the underwood is the most important part of the produce, and the cutting of timber is necessary for its growth (*e*).

11. It is not waste to fell trees which are completely dead and bear neither fruit nor leaves (*f*), and have not sufficient timber in them for buildings or posts (*g*).

12. Trees which have been excepted out of a demise may not be cut down by the tenant (*h*). An exception of trees generally applies only to timber trees, and not to apple or other fruit trees, or the like (*i*). Where the exception was of timber and * other trees, but not the annual * 242 fruit thereof, it was held that apple trees were not within it, because it was to be construed strictly against the lessor (*k*).

13. A tenant who has covenanted to deliver up all the trees

(*a*) Co. Litt. 53 a; Gage *v.* Smith, Godb. 210; Philipps *v.* Smith, 14 M. & W. 589.

(*b*) Rogers *v.* Price, 13 Jur. 820. See Doe *v.* Price, 8 C. B. 894.

(*c*) Ferrand *v.* Wilson, 4 Ha. 375; Briggs *v.* Lord Oxford, 1 D. M. & G. 363; Bridges *v.* Stephens, 2 Sw. 150, n.; Lord Lovat *v.* Duchess of Leeds, 2 Dr. & S. 75. See Oxenden *v.* Lord Compton, 2 Ves. Jr. 69.

(*d*) 2 Roll. Ab. 815; Co. Litt. 53 a; Darcy *v.* Askwith, Hob. 234; Gage *v.* Smith, Godb. 210; Pratt *v.* Brett, 2 Madd. 62; Brydges *v.* Stephens, 6 Madd. 279; Humphreys *v.* Harrison, 1 J. & W. 581; Pidgeley *v.* Rawling, 2 Coll. 275; Philipps *v.* Smith, 14 M. & W. 589; Bateman *v.* Hotchkin, 31

Beav. 486; Bagot *v.* Bagot, 32 Beav. 509; Earl Cowley *v.* Wellesley, 1 L. R. Eq. 656.

(*e*) Knight *v.* Duplessis, 2 Ves. 361. See 16 Ves. 179; Earl Cowley *v.* Wellesley, 1 L. R. Eq. 656.

(*f*) Co. Litt. 53 a; 2 Roll. Ab. 814.

(*g*) Manwood's case, Moor. 101; Dyer, 332; Gibbon on Dilap. 215.

(*h*) Heydon *v.* Smith, Godb. 173; Goodright *v.* Vivian, 8 East, 190. See Legh *v.* Heald, 1 B. & A. 622; Doe dem. Douglas *v.* Lock, 2 A. & E. 705; Pentland *v.* Somerville, 2 Ir. Ch. 289; Doe *v.* Price, 8 C. B. 894; Allen *v.* Carver, 15 Ir. C. L. 547.

(*i*) Wyndham *v.* Way, 4 Taunt. 316.

(*k*) Bullen *v.* Dunning, 5 B. & C. 842. See further Craig on Trees, 15.

standing in an orchard at the time of the demise, reasonable use and wear only excepted, is not precluded from removing trees decayed and past bearing from a part of the orchard which is too crowded (*l*) ; but if there be in the demise a covenant not to remove or grub up trees, the tenant cannot remove trees from one part of the premises to another, unless they are dead, even although he plants more trees than he removes (*m*). Where in a lease of a farm and the quarries upon the premises, with power for the tenant to open and work the quarries, all timber trees, trees likely to become timber, saplings, &c., were excepted, and there was also a covenant on the part of the tenant not to commit any waste by cutting down any timber trees or trees likely to become timber, saplings, &c., it was held that the effect of the covenant was that the tenant should not so cut any of the trees excepted, as that such cutting should amount to an excess of the right which it was intended he should exercise, and, therefore, that cutting trees in a manner necessary to a reasonable exercise of the power to get the stone was no breach of the covenant (*n*).

14. A copyholder, being considered in law to be a tenant at will, has in general the same possessory interest in the trees as he has in the land. He is equally as incapable of cutting down trees or doing any other act to the injury of the freehold except with the lord's concurrence, as a tenant for life or years of freehold land is without the concurrence of those in whom the remainder in fee-simple is vested (*o*). But by custom a copyholder of inheritance, or a copyholder for life, with power to renew and nominate his successor, may have *243 the right to fell * timber upon his tenement and retain the same for his own use (*p*). The custom could not be supported in the case of a copyholder for life or for years (*q*) ; but a copyholder of inheritance who has the right by custom may give the right to a particular tenant for life whose estate is carved out of his inheritance (*r*). The lord cannot, any more

(*l*) Doe dem. Jones *v.* Crouch, 2 Camp. 449.
(*m*) Doe *v.* Bird, 6 C. & P. 195.
(*n*) Doe *v.* Price, 8 C. B. 894. See Allen *v.* Carver, 15 Ir. C. L. 544.
(*o*) Scriven on Cop. 420.

(*p*) Blewett *v.* Jenkins, 12 C. B. N. S. 16. See Scriv. on Cop. 420.
(*q*) Scriv. on Cop. 420; 6 H. & N. 125, *per* Williams, J.
(*r*) Scriv. on Cop. 420; Denn *v.* Johnson, 10 East, 266.

than the copyholder, cut down trees upon the tenement of a copyholder, without a custom authorizing him to do so (s).

15. A tenant for life or for years has the right to cut timber by way of estovers for the necessary repairs of the house and principal buildings, the fences, gates, and agricultural implements. If there is no underwood, he may also cut, or at least lop, timber for the purpose of firewood (t). He has this privilege of common right, but the estovers must be reasonable (u). The right to estovers attaches as a right to the particular estate on which they have been taken. Estovers cut on one estate cannot be used on another (v). A tenant for life or for years may cut timber to repair houses which he is not strictly bound to repair (x) ; but he may not cut timber to make new fences or to build new houses, or to repair houses which he has wasted or suffered to be wasted (y). Nor can he cut timber for the purpose of working mines (z), or burning bricks (a), or generally for agricultural purposes (b). The cutting of timber which is not fit for repairs (c), or the cutting of more timber than is * necessary for repairs (d), is waste.   * 244 But if timber be cut down *bonâ fide* for the purpose of being used in repairs, the tenant is justified, though he may have over-calculated the quantity required (e). The timber cut must be applied specifically towards the actual repairs for which it has been cut. It cannot be sold for the purpose of raising money for the purchase of other timber (f), or for the purpose of defraying the expenses of past or contemplated repairs (g) ; nor can it be exchanged for other timber better

---

(s) Whitechurch *v.* Holworthy, 19 Ves. 212.

(t) Manwood's case, Moor. 101 ; 2 Roll. Ab. 823 ; Co. Litt. 41 b ; Vin. Ab. Waste ; Com. Dig. Waste ; Craig on Trees, 4. See Howley *v.* Jebb, 8 Ir. C. L. 435. See, as to covenant by lessee to repair, "having or taking sufficient housebote, and without committing waste." Dean. and Chapter of Bristol *v.* Jones, 1 El. & El. 484.

(u) Co. Litt. 41 b.

(v) Lee *v.* Alston, 1 Bro. C. C. 194, 3 Bro. C. C. 37, 1 Ves. Jr. 78 ; Nash *v.* Earl of Derby, 2 Vern. 537.

(x) Co. Litt. 54 b. See Sarles *v.* Sarles, 3 Sandf. Ch. (Amer.) 601.

(y) Co. Litt. 53 b ; 2 Roll. Ab. 815 ; Darcy *v.* Askwith, Hob. 234.

(z) Darcy *v.* Askwith, *ib.*, Hutt. 19.

(a) Livingston *v.* Reynolds, 26 Wend. (Amer.) 115.

(b) Jackson *v.* Brownson, 7 Johns. (Amer.) 228.

(c) Simmons *v.* Norton, 7 Bing. 648.

(d) Co. Litt. 53 b.

(e) East *v.* Harding, Cro. Eliz. 498 ; Doe *v.* Wilson, 11 East, 56.

(f) Co. Litt. 53 b ; Lewis Bowle's case, 11ˑ Co. Rep. 82 a ; Simmons *v.* Norton, 7 Bing. 648.

(g) Gorges *v.* Stanfield, Cro. Eliz. 593 ; Lee *v.* Alston, 1 Bro. C. C. 194, 3 Bro. C. C. 37 ; Gower *v.* Eyre, Coop. 156.

adapted for the repairs in question (*h*). It is waste even if the same wood which has been sold be bought back again (*i*).

16. Timber may not be cut for the purpose of firewood as long as there is any dry or decayed wood or underwood on the land (*k*). The right to firebote is limited to the taking of sufficient wood for the principal dwelling-house or mansion on the estate, and does not extend to firewood for farmers or laborers ; nor could a custom to that effect be supported (*l*).

17. A copyholder is entitled to estovers by custom, and it would appear that he is entitled to them of common right even without a custom (*m*).

18. The committee of a lunatic's estate may cut timber for repairs as a prudent owner would do (*n*).

19. The cutting of fruit trees growing in a garden or orchard is waste, unless they have been torn up by the wind (*o*). But it is not waste to cut fruit trees which do not grow in a garden or orchard, but grow scatteringly, on divers places of
* 245   the * land (*p*). The ploughing up a strawberry-bed before it is exhausted is waste (*q*).

20. It is waste if the tenant of a dove-house, warren, park, fish-pond, or the like, take so many of the animals that the perpetuity of succession is destroyed (*r*) ; or suffer the pale of the park to decay so that the deer escape, or permit the banks of the fish-pond to get out of repair so that the fish escape or the pond dries up (*s*). If the lessee of a warren by charter or prescription plough up the land, it is waste (*t*) ; but it is otherwise if it be only land stored with conies and not a legal warren ; and stopping up and digging cony burrows is not waste in a warren (*u*). Deer in a lawful park are part of the inheri-

---

(*h*) Att.-Gen. *v.* Stawell, 2 Anst. 601.
(*i*) Co. Litt. 53 b. See, as to wood cut for repairs by ecclesiastical persons, *infra.*
(*k*) 2 Roll. Ab. 820, pl. 9 ; Co. Litt. 53 b ; Cruise, Dig. 80 ; Cole *v.* Peyson, 1 Ch. Ca. 106 ; Jackson *v.* Brownson, 7 Johns. Ch. (Amer.) 228.
(*l*) Sarles *v.* Sarles, 3 Sand. Ch. (Amer.) 601.
(*m*) Heydon's case, 13 Co. Rep. 67 ; Scriven on Cop. 424, 425.
(*n*) *Ex parte* Ludlow, 2 Atk. 407.
(*o*) Co. Litt. 53 a ; Littler *v.* Thomp-

son, 2 Beav. 129. See Philipps *v.* Smith, 14 M. & W. 494.
(*p*) Bro. Ab. Waste, pl. 143.
(*q*) Watherell *v.* Howells, 1 Camp. 227.
(*r*) Co. Litt. 53 b ; Hob. 234 ; Vavasour's case, 2 Leon. 222 ; Anon., 4 Lev. 240 ; Kimpton *v.* Eve, 2 V. & B. 349 ; Ford *v.* Tynte, 2 J. & H. 150.
(*s*) Co. Litt. 53 a ; Hob. 234 ; Bathurst *v.* Burden, 2 Bro. C. C. 64.
(*t*) Co. Litt. 53 b ; Angerstein *v.* Hunt, 6 Ves. 487.
(*u*) Lurting *v.* Conn, 1 Ir. Ch. 278.

tance: it is waste in a tenant for life to do any thing to sever the deer from the inheritance; and it seems that reclaiming deer is an act of waste, because it makes them no longer venison in a park, but chattels like any other domesticated animals (x).

21. It is waste to suffer a wall of the sea to be in decay, so as by the flowing and reflowing of the sea the meadow or marsh be surrounded, whereby it becomes unprofitable; but if it be surrounded suddenly by the rage and violence of the sea, without any default of the tenant, it is not waste (y). So also it is waste if the tenant do not repair the banks or walls against rivers or other waters, whereby the meadows or marshes be surrounded and become rushy and unprofitable (z).

22. It is waste if a tenant for life or for years dig for clay, gravel, lime, brick-earth, minerals, stones, or the like (a). If there be a grant of lands, or of lands and mines expressly, he may dig and take the profits of mines, gravel-pits, or clay-pits, open at the time of the grant, or which a preceding tenant in tail under * the settlement, or other person * 246 rightfully entitled to open, may have opened, but he may not open new ones (b). Nor does a power to lease with the mines land on which there are both open and unopened mines authorize a lease of unopened mines (c). Lord Coke says that if there be no open mines, and a lease is made of the land with all mines therein, then the lessee may open and dig mines therein, otherwise the grant would be void (d); but the dictum is of doubtful authority (e).

23. As a tenant for life or years is entitled to continue the

(x) Ford v. Tynte, 2 J. & H. 153, per Wood, V. C. See Morgan v. Lord Abergavenny, 8 C. B. 768.
(y) Co. Litt. 53 b; Bro. Ab. Waste.
(z) Co. Litt. 53 b; Callis on Sewers, 146.
(a) Bro. Ab. Waste, pl. 93; Co. Litt. 53 b; 2 Roll. Ab. 816.
(b) Co. Litt. 54 b; Saunders' case, 5 Co. Rep. 12 a; Bishop of London v. Webb, 1 P. Wms. 528; Whitfield v. Bewit, 2 P. Wms. 240; Clavering v. Clavering, 2 P. Wms. 389; Sel. Ca. Ch. 79, Mose. 219; Plymouth v. Archer, 1 Bro. C. C. 159; Mitchell v. Dors, 6 Ves. 147; Grey v. Duke of Northum-

berland, 13 Ves. 236; Viner v. Vaughan, 2 Beav. 469; Huntley v. Russell, 13 Q. B. 591; Bagot v. Bagot, 32 Beav. 509; Earl Cowley v. Wellesley, 1 L. R. Eq. 656; Clegg v. Rowland, 2 L. R. Eq. 160.
(c) Clegg v. Rowland, 2 L. R. Eq. 160. Comp. Daly v. Beckett, 24 Beav. 114.
(d) Co. Litt. 54 b; Saunders' case, 5 Co. Rep. 12 a. See Darcy v. Askwith, Hob. 234.
(e) Whitfield v. Bewit, 2 P. Wms. 240. Comp. Coppinger v. Gubbins, 3 J. & L. 397. See Yool on Waste, 54.

working of mines which were open at the time he came in, so he may use all means necessary for working them. .He may, if it can be done without any special damage to the inheritance, sink new shafts and pits to follow the same vein of coal (*f*), or to reach new seams lying under the old seams (*g*). But it is doubtful whether he has a right to open pits or mines which have been abandoned, or the preparations for opening which have not been completed. The question must always depend on the circumstances of each particular case (*h*). There seems to be no authority on the question whether a new vein or bed may be worked by means of an old shaft (*i*).

24. When the Crown has only a bare reservation of royal mines without any right of entry, it cannot by prerogative grant a license to dig up the soil and search for mines; but if the mines are open, the Crown can restrain the owner of
* 247   the soil from * working them, and can work them itself or grant a license to others to work them (*k*).

25. A tenant for life or years has no right to minerals deposited on the land by mountain streams (*l*).

26. The rule that a tenant for life or years may continue the working of open mines, gravel or clay pits, does not, it would appear, extend to the case of quarries of limestone (*m*).

27. The words "mines and minerals" in an instrument include stone gotten by underground working, unless there is something in the nature or context of the deed to show that it was not intended to be included (*n*). As distinguished from a mine, a quarry refers to a place upon, or above, and not under the ground, whereas the word "mine" refers to underground workings (*o*).

28. The reservation of minerals includes all reasonable means of getting them (*p*).

(*f*) Whitfield *v.* Bewit, 2 P. Wms. 240; Clavering *v.* Clavering, *ib.* 388; Viner *v.* Vaughan, 2 Beav. 469.

(*g*) Spencer *v.* Scurr, 31 Beav. 334.

(*h*) Viner *v.* Vaughan, 2 Beav. 469; Bagot *v.* Bagot, 32 Beav. 509, 516.

(*i*) Yool on Waste, 55.

(*k*) Lyddall *v.* Weston, 2 Atk. 20, *per* Lord Hardwicke.

(*l*) Thomas *v.* Jones, 1 Y. & C.C.C. 520.

(*m*) Mansfield *v.* Crawford, 9 Ir. Eq. 271; Purcell *v.* Nash, 1 Jon. 625.

(*n*) Bell *v.* Wilson, 1 L. R. Ch. Ap. 303. Stone is a mineral. Every thing beyond the surface comes within the reservation of minerals in a grant of land. Midland Railway Co. *v.* Checkley, 15 W. R. 671.

(*o*) *Ib.*

(*p*) Earl of Cardigan *v.* Armitage, 2 B. & C. 197. See Harris *v.* Ryding, 5 M. & W. 60; Goold *v.* Great Western Deep Coal Co., 2 D. J. & S. 600.

29. A tenant for life or years may take reasonable estovers of gravel and clay for the repairs of buildings, although the pits were not open at the date of the grant or demise (*q*). There may be also estovers of brick-earth, lime, or the like, for the reparation of buildings or manuring the land (*r*). So also may there be estovers of coal (*s*). If there are open quarries of limestone on the land, the tenants may work them for estovers (*t*).

30. A tenant for life or years of land comprising turfs has a right to cut by way of estovers as many turfs as may be reasonably sufficient for consumption on the premises by way of firebote (*u*); but he may not cut turfs for the purposes of *sale (*x*), unless turfs have always been so *248 cut, or unless there is no other mode of enjoying the land (*y*).

31. The right of turbary only applies to turfs adapted for the purposes of fuel, and does not apply to turfs of grass (*z*).

32. By a recent statute any tenant for life, even though he may have incumbered his interest, may make, in certain cases, absolute or partial alienation of his mineral property (*a*).

33. A copyholder, whether of inheritance or for life, or for years only, has the same possessory interest in mines as he has in trees (*b*). By custom a copyholder of inheritance may have the right to break the surface and dig gravel, sand, and clay, without stint, from out of his own tenement for the purposes of sale off the manor (*c*). So also may a customary tenant have the right by custom to work mines for profit on his

(*q*) 2 Roll. Ab. 816.
(*r*) Co. Litt. 53 b, 54 b; Saunders' case, 5 Co. Rep. 12 a. See Livingston *v.* Reynolds, 20 Wend. (Amer.) 115, 2 Hill (Amer.), 157.
(*s*) 2 Roll. Ab. 816.
(*t*) Purcell *v.* Nash, 1 Jon. 625; Mansfield *v.* Crawford, 9 Ir. Eq. 271.
(*u*) De Salis *v.* Crossan, 1 Ba. & Be. 188; Lord Courtown *v.* Ward, 1 Sch. & Lef. 8; Howley *v.* Jebb, 8 Ir. C. L. 435.
(*x*) Chatterton *v.* White, 1 Ir. Eq. 200; White *v.* Walsh, 1 Jon. 626, n.; Lord Waterpark *v.* Austin, *ib.* 627, n.; Coppinger *v.* Gubbins, 3 J. & L. 410; Stevenson *v.* Moore, 7 Ir. Ch. 462; Howley *v.* Jebb, 8 Ir. C. L. 435.

(*y*) Coppinger *v.* Gubbins, 3 J. & L. 410; Stevenson *v.* Moore, 7 Ir. Ch. 462. See, as to grants of turbary, Hill *v.* Barry, Hay. & J. 688; Duggan *v.* Carey, 8 Ir. C. L. 210; Moore *v.* Orr, 8 Ir. C. L. 347; Hargrove *v.* Congleton, 12 Ir. C. L. 362, 868.
(*z*) See Wilson *v.* Willes, 7 East, 121; Wilkinson *v.* Haygarth, 12 Q. B. 837.
(*a*) 19 & 20 Vict. c. 120, ss. 32, 41; Rogers on Mines, 280–286.
(*b*) Scriv. on Cop. 427. See Bowser *v.* Maclean, 2 D. F. & J. 415.
(*c*) Marquis of Salisbury *v.* Gladstone, 9 H. L. 692; Hanmer *v.* Chance, 34 L. J. Ch. 413.

own copyhold tenement (*d*). But in the absence of custom the tenant cannot, without the leave of the lord, open or work new mines or work quarries upon his own tenement, nor on the other hand can the lord, in the absence of a custom, open and work mines upon the tenement of a copyholder (*e*).

34. By custom a copyholder may have a right to dig and take clay, limestone, marl, or gravel, for repairs or the *249 necessary *purposes of his occupation (*f*); and it is possible that such a privilege exists without reference to custom (*g*).

35. Any permanent alteration of the character of land, such as the conversion of meadow into arable land by ploughing it up (*h*), or arable land into wood, or a meadow into an orchard, is waste, even although the value of the land be increased, because it not only changes the course of husbandry, but affects the proof of title (*i*). But a mere temporary alteration in the ordinary and reasonable course of husbandry is not waste (*k*). The enclosure and cultivation of waste land is waste by reason of the injury to the evidence of title (*l*). So also the conversion of land into a burying-ground (*m*), and the breaking up of a bowling-green (*n*), are acts of waste.

36. By the general law a tenant for life or for years is under no obligation to cultivate land. It is not waste to suffer arable

(*d*) Bishop of Winchester *v.* Knight, 1 P. Wms. 406; Parrott *v.* Palmer, 3 M. & K. 632; Duke of Portland *v.* Hill, 2 L. R. Eq. 765.

(*e*) Bishop of Winchester *v.* Knight, 1 P. Wms. 406; Grey *v.* Duke of Northumberland, 13 Ves. 236, 17 Ves. 281; Bourne *v.* Taylor, 10 East, 189; Cuddon *v.* Morley, 7 Ha. 204; Duke of Portland *v.* Hill, 2 L. R. Eq. 765. See Bowser *v.* Maclean, 2 D. F. & J. 415.

(*f*) Bainbridge on Mines, 22; Gilb. Ten. 327.

(*g*) Heydon and Smith's case, 13 Co. Rep. 68.

(*h*) Co. Litt. 53 b; Lord Darcy *v.* Askwith, Hob. 234; Worsley *v.* Stewart, 4 Bro P. C. 377; Simmons *v.* Norton, 7 Bing. 647; Goring *v.* Goring, 3 Sw. 661; Pratt *v.* Brett, 2 Madd. 62; Martin *v.* Coggan, 1 Hog. 120; Morris *v.* Morris, *ib.* 238; Joley *v.* Stocley, *ib.* 248; Brophy *v.* Quarry, Hayes, 449;

Hunt *v.* Browne, Sau. & Sc. 179; Erpe *v.* Smith, Coop. C. C. 110; Duke of St. Albans *v.* Skipwith, 8 Beav. 357. See, as to what is ancient meadow, Hunt *v.* Browne, Sau. & Sc. 179; Martin *v.* Coggan, 1 Hog. 120; Morris *v.* Morris, *ib.* 238; Davies *v.* Davies, 2 Ir. Eq. 414; Murphy *v.* Daly, 13 Ir. C. L. 239.

(*i*) Co. Litt. 53 b; Lord Darcy *v.* Askwith, Hob. 234; Simmons *v.* Norton, 7 Bing. 647; Duke of St. Albans *v.* Skipwith, 8 Beav. 357. See French *v.* Macale, 2 Dr. & War. 269.

(*k*) 2 Roll. Ab. 814; Viner, Ab. tit. Waste; Malevrer *v.* Spinke, Dyer, 37 a; Simmons *v.* Norton, 7 Bing. 647; Cruise, Dig. tit. iii. c. 2, s. 19; Gibbon on Dilap. 198.

(*l*)) Queen's College *v.* Hallett, 14 East, 489.

(*m*) Hunt *v.* Browne, Sau. & Sc. 189; Cregan *v.* Cullen, 16 Ir. Ch. 339.

(*n*) City of London *v.* Pugh, 4 Bro. P. C. 395.

ground to lie fresh and not manured, so that it grows full of thorns: it is merely bad husbandry (o). To oblige a man to cultivate according to good husbandry, there must be either an express contract or a custom of the country (p). A custom of the country need not have existed from time immemorial, as * must a custom properly so called. It is * 250 sufficient if there be a general usage applicable to farms in the part of the country in which the land is situated (q). The mere relation of landlord and tenant creates an implied obligation on the part of the tenant to manage and use a farm in a husbandlike manner according to the custom of the country where the premises are situated (r), unless indeed the lease or agreement contains some express covenant or promise inconsistent with such custom and sufficient to exclude it (s). The removal of hay, straw, dung, crops, &c., from a farm is waste, where it is contrary to the custom of the country, and will be restrained by injunction (t). So also the sowing of land with pernicious crops, such as mustard, is waste, and will be restrained (u).

37. The obligation to cultivate lands according to the custom of the country does not apply to a garden or meadow let with a gentleman's residence (x)

38. Waste in houses or buildings consists either in pulling them down or in suffering them to go to decay (y). The law of waste extends not only to dwelling-houses, but to every description of buildings, such as outhouses and barns (z). An alteration of buildings which changes their nature and character is waste, even although the value of the premises be

(o) Bro. Ab. Waste, pl. 5, 2 Roll. Ab. 814; Hutton v. Warren, 1 M. & W. 472.

(p) Hutton v. Warren, 1 M. & W. 472, per Lord Wensleydale.

(q) Leigh v. Hewitt, 4 East, 154; Dalby v. Hirst, 1 B. & B. 224.

(r) Powley v. Walker, 5 T. R. 373; Halifax v. Chambers, 4 M. & W. 662; Beale v. Saunders, 3 Bing. N. C. 850.

(s) Hutton v. Warren, 1 M. & W. 466; Clark v. Royston, 13 M. & W. 752; Wilkins v. Wood, 17 L. J. Q. B. 319.

(t) Pulteney v. Shelton, 5 Ves. 147, 260, n.; —— v. Onslow, 16 Ves. 173;

Greenwood v. Bairston, 4 L. J. Ch. N. S. 245; Kimpton v. Eve, 2 V. & B. 349; Pratt v. Brett, 2 Madd. 62; Walton v. Johnson, 15 Sim. 352. See Johnson v. Goldswaine, 3 Anst. 749; Lathropp v. Marsh, 5 Ves. 259.

(u) Pratt v. Brett, 2 Madd. 62.

(x) Johnstone v. Symons, 9 L. T. 535; Gibbon on Dilap. 202. See as to cultivation of glebe land, Bird v. Relph, 4 B. & Ad. 826.

(y) Co. Litt. 53 a. See Kimpton v. Eve, 2 V. & B. 353; Pratt v. Brett, 2 Madd. 62.

(z) Doe v. Earl of Burlington, 5 B. & Ad. 507.

thereby increased. Thus, the converting two chambers into one, or *è converso*, or the converting a hand-mill into a horse-mill, or a corn-mill into a fulling-mill, or a malt-mill to a corn-mill, or a logwood-mill to a cotton-mill, have been held to be waste (*a*). So also the conversion * of a private house into a shop is waste (*b*). So also may the building of a new house, where there was one before, be waste, if it impair the evidence of title (*c*). In Smith *v.* Carter (*d*) the court restrained a man from pulling down a house and building another which the landlord objected to. "It is not sufficient," said Lord Romilly, M. R. (*e*), "that the house proposed to be built is a better one. The landlord has a right to exercise his own judgment and caprice, whether there shall be a change: if he objects, the court will not allow a tenant to pull down one house and build another in its place" (*f*).

39. A covenant to repair being positive as well as negative in its obligations, the tenant is thereby bound as well not to do an act amounting to voluntary waste as to repair dilapidations. An alteration of the demised premises may be a breach of the covenant to repair (*g*). The existence in a lease of a covenant to repair and to surrender up the buildings at the end of the term in good condition, does not preclude the court from granting an injunction to restrain the pulling down of buildings just before the end of the term (*h*). At common law it was waste when a house was burned down by negligence or mischance, but the landlord's action against the tenant in such cases has been taken away by statute (*i*). A lessee, however, who covenants generally to repair or to leave the premises in repair, is still bound to repair after a fire (*k*); and whether a

---

(*a*) Co. Litt. 53 a; Green *v.* Cole, 2 Willm. Saund. 228; City of London *v.* Graeme, Cro. Jac. 182; Brydges *v.* Kilburn, cit. 5 Ves. 689; Hunt *v.* Browne, Sau. & Sc. 191.

(*b*) Bonnett *v.* Sadler, 14 Ves. 526. See Douglas *v.* Wiggins, 1 Johns. Ch. (Amer.) 434; Gibbon on Dilap. 124.

(*c*) Co. Litt. 53 a; Cole *v.* Green, 1 Lev. 309; S. C., *nom.* Cole *v.* Forth, 1 Mod. 94. See Gibbon on Dilap. 125.

(*d*) 18 Beav. 78.

(*e*) *Ib.*

(*f*) See Bro. Ab. Waste; Cruise, Dig. tit. iii. c. 2, s. 12.

(*g*) Doe *v.* Jackson, 2 Stark. 293; Doe *v.* Bird, 6 Car. & P. 195; Gibbon on Dilap. 153.

(*h*) Mayor of London *v.* Hedger, 18 Ves. 356.

(*i*) Co. Litt. 53 b, 6 Anne, c. 31, 14 Geo. 3, c. 78. See *Re* Skingley, 3 Mac. & G. 221, 229; White *v.* M'Cann, 1 Ir. C. L. 205.

(*k*) Bullock *v.* Dommitt, 6 T. R. 650; Brecknock Co. *v.* Pritchard, *ib.* 750; Pym *v.* Blackburn, 3 Ves. 38.

lessee is bound to rebuild or not after a fire, he remains
liable to pay the rent if he has covenanted * generally   * 252
to do so (*l*). In *Re* Skingley (*m*), where a devisee
for life, with a condition against committing any manner of
waste and for keeping the premises in good and tenantable repair, became lunatic, and the premises were subsequently destroyed by an accidental fire, the court, in order to prevent the
risk of a forfeiture, held that the premises ought to be rebuilt
at the expense of the lunatic's estate (*n*).

40. The suffering houses, buildings, &c., to go to decay by
wrongfully neglecting to repair them is permissive waste (*o*).
A court of equity will not interfere with mere permissive
waste (*p*): nor will a suit be entertained in equity against a
tenant for life to compel him to repair (*q*), or against the executors of a deceased tenant for life for dilapidations (*r*).
Under special circumstances, however, a court of equity may
interfere either to prevent permissive waste (*s*), or to decree
an account for dilapidations against the estate of a deceased
tenant for life (*t*), or to order buildings to be repaired or
rebuilt by a tenant for life (*u*).

41. The general rule of law being that personal chattels
once annexed to the freehold become part of it, and may not
be again severed without the consent of the owner of the inheritance, it is waste if a tenant for life or years who has annexed
a personal chattel to the freehold afterwards takes it away (*v*).
But several exceptions have been engrafted on the general
rule. The most important of these exceptions is one in favor
of trade fixtures. Chattels which have been affixed to
the freehold for the * purposes of trade, and which re-   * 253

(*l*) Holtzapfel *v.* Baker, 18 Ves. 115;
Leeds *v.* Cheetham, 1 Sim. 146; Loffts
v. Dennis, 7 W. R. 199.
(*m*) 3 Mac. & G. 221.
(*n*) Powys *v.* Blagrave, Kay, 502, 4
D. M. & G. 448; Gregg *v.* Coates, 23
Beav. 33.
(*o*) See Gibbon on Dilap. 128.
(*p*) Lord Castlemaine *v.* Craven, 22
Vin. Ab. 523, 2 Eq. Ab. 758; Turner
v. Buck, 22 Vin. Ab. 522; Powys *v.*
Blagrave, Kay, 502, 4 D. M. & G.
448.
(*q*) Wood *v.* Gaynon, Amb. 395;
Warren *v.* Rudall, 1 J. & H. 1.

(*r*) Marquis of Lansdowne *v.* Marchioness of Lansdowne, 1 J. & W. 523;
Arkwright *v.* Colt, 2 Y. & C. C. C. 4;
Powys *v.* Blagrave, Kay, 495, 4 D. M.
& G. 448.
(*s*) Caldwell *v.* Baylis, 2 Mer. 408.
See Powys *v.* Blagrave, Kay, 495.
(*t*) Marsh *v.* Wells, 2 Sim. & St. 87;
Blake *v.* Peters, 1 D. J. & S. 345.
(*u*) *Re* Skingley, 3 Mac. & G. 221;
Gregg *v.* Coates, 23 Beav. 33; Cooke
v. Cholmondeley, 4 Jur. N. S. 827.
(*v*) Elwes *v.* Maw, 3 East, 38.

tain the general character of trade fixtures, may be re‑
moved by a tenant for years during his term (x). The ex‑
ception does not, however, extend to buildings which have
been let into the soil, although used for trading purposes. A
tenant for years, even under the most favorable circumstances,
has no right to remove any building which he has erected
merely because it is used only for the purposes of trade (y).
But by the 14 & 15 Vict, c. 25, s. 3, it is provided that if any
tenant of a farm or land shall, with the consent of the landlord,
erect at his own expense any farm building, or put up any
building, engine, or machinery, either for agricultural· purposes
or for the purposes of trade and agriculture, all such buildings
shall be removable, so as the tenant making such removal do
not in any wise injure the land or buildings belonging to the
landlord, or otherwise do put the same in like or as good plight
and condition as the same were in before the erection of the
things so removed. Before removal, however, the tenant must
give to the landlord or his agent a month's notice in writing of
his intention, and the landlord may thereupon elect to purchase
the things so proposed to be removed, whereupon the right to
remove them shall cease.

42. The tenant's privilege with respect to trade fixtures ex‑
tends to the case of nurserymen. An ordinary tenant may not
remove trees, ornamental hedges, or shrubs, or a border of box,
although planted by himself (z) : nor may a gardener who cul‑
tivates trees for their fruit remove them ; but a nurseryman
who rears trees, shrubs, and other produce of the soil for the
purposes of sale, has a right to remove, provided the
* 254　trees have not become of * larger growth than could
be dealt with by him in the ordinary way of his trade (a).

(x) Poole's case, Salk. 368 ; Lawton
v. Lawton, 3 Atk. 13 ; Lawton v. Salmon,
1 H. Bl. 259, n. ; Penton v. Robart, 2
East, 90 ; Dean v. Allaly, 3 Esp. 11 ;
Trappes v. Harter, 3 Tyrw. 603 ; Davis
v. Jones, 2 B. & Ald. 165 ; Elwes v.
Maw, 3 East, 38, 2 Smith, L. C. 141 ;
Foley v. Addenbroke, 13 M. & W. 174 ;
Whitehead v. Bennett, 27 L. J. Ch. 474.
See Shirreff v. Barnard, 8 Sim. 161 ;
Duke of Beaufort v. Bates, 3 D. F. &
J. 381.

(y) Penton v. Robart, 2 East, 90 ;

Elwes v. Maw, 3 East, 38, 2 Smith, L.
C. 141 ; Shinner v. Harman, 3 Ir. C.
L. 243 ; Whitehead v. Bennett, 27 L.
J. Ch. 474.

(z) Empson v. Soden, 4 B. & Ad.
655 ; Johnstone v. Symons, 9 L. T.
535. See Coffin v. Coffin, Jac. 71 ;
——— v. Copley, 3 Madd. 525, n. ;
Ferard on Fixt. 68, 69.

(a) Wyndham v. Way, 4 Taunt.
316 ; Wardell v. Ussher, 3 Scott, N. R.
508 ; Littler v. Thompson, 2 Beav. 129.
See Penton v. Robart, 2 East, 91.

The indulgence which exists with respect to trade fixtures extends also to many cases of fixtures put up by a tenant for years at his own expense for the purposes of ornament or domestic convenience, such as marble chimney-pieces, pier-glasses, wainscots fixed with screws, hangings nailed to the walls (*b*), stoves or grates fixed into the chimney with brickwork, and cupboards supported by holdfasts and the like (*c*). The privilege with respect to the removal of this class of fixtures must, however, be regarded as one of more limited extent than obtains in the case of trade fixtures. Trade fixtures are removable if the removal will not occasion serious prejudice to the freehold; but in the case of fixtures set up for ornament or domestic convenience, the rule is not only to take into consideration the injury to the freehold by severance, but also to consider the character, the use, the mode of attachment, the facility of severance, and the purpose for which the fixture may be reasonably regarded as having been set up (*d*). A fixture set up for the purposes of ornament or domestic convenience, which may be reasonably considered to have been put up by way of a substantial and permanent improvement, may not be removed, although the removal may be attended with no damage to the inheritance (*e*).

43. Chattels which have been annexed to the freehold by a tenant for years, if removable at all, should be removed by him before the expiration of the tenancy (*f*): but the right of removal *is not lost so long as the tenant continues   * 255 to occupy, although his term may have expired (*g*). A tenant whose interest is of an uncertain duration has, it would appear, a right to remove fixtures after it has expired, pro-

---

(*b*) Squier *v.* Mayer, Freem. Ch. 248, 2 Eq. Ab. 430; Beck *v.* Rebow, 1 P. Wms. 94; *Ex parte* Quincy, 1 Atk. 477; Lawton *v.* Lawton, 3 Atk. 15; Lee *v.* Risdon, 7 Taunt. 191, *per* Gibbs, C. J.

(*c*) Rex *v.* Inhabitants of St. Dunstan's, 4 B. & C. 686, *per* Bayley, J.; Lee *v.* Risdon, 7 Taunt. 191. See Colegrave *v.* Dios Santos, 1 B. & C. 77; Jenkins *v.* Gething, 2 J. & H. 520; Ferard on Fixt. 75; 2 Smith, L. C. 165–167.

(*d*) Buckland *v.* Butterfield, 2 B. & B. 54; Jenkins *v.* Gething, 2 J. & H. 520. See Kimpton *v.* Eve, 2 V. & B. 349; Bishop *v.* Elliott, 10 Exch. 496, 11 Exch. 113; Martin *v.* Roe, 7 E. & B. 237; Ferard on Fixt. 87–92.

(*e*) Buckland *v.* Butterfield, 2 B. & B. 54; Jenkins *v.* Gething, 2 J. & H. 520; Ferard on Fixt. 87–92.

(*f*) Lyde *v.* Russell, 1 B. & Ad. 394.

(*g*) Penton *v.* Robart, 2 East, 88. See 2 Smith, L. C. 169.

vided he does so within a reasonable time (*h*). The ordinary rule of law with respect to the removal of fixtures may, it must be remembered, be qualified by express agreement (*i*).

44. Questions respecting the right to fixtures may arise also between tenant for life and remainder-man, between heir and executor, between vendor and vendee, between mortgagor and mortgagee, and in some other cases (*j*). In cases between heir and executor the general rule of law obtains with the most rigor in favor of the inheritance and against the right to consider as a personal chattel any thing which has been annexed to the freehold (*k*). In cases between the executors of a tenant for life and the remainder-man, the right to fixtures is considered more favorably for the executor, but not so favorably as in favor of a tenant for years in cases between landlord and tenant (*l*). Successive incumbents of a benefice stand to each other somewhat in the relation of tenant for life and remainder-man, but in respect of the right to fixtures the law is much more liberal in favor of a deceased incumbent than in the ordinary case of tenant for life and remainder-man (*m*). In cases between vendor and vendee, or mortgagor and mortgagee, questions respecting the right to fixtures depend on the terms of the contract. If, however, the contract is silent on the subject, the general rule is against the right to consider as a personal chattel any thing which has been annexed to the freehold (*n*).

(*h*) See Weeton *v*. Woodcock, 7 M. & W. 14; Ombony *v*. Jones, 5 Smith (Amer.), 234 ; Ferard on Fixt. 106.

(*i*) 2 Smith, L. C. 169 ; Ferard on Fixt. 108–122 ; Sunderland *v*. Newton, 3 Sim. 450 ; Dumergue *v*. Rumsey, 2 H. & C. 777. See Sumner *v*. Bromilow, 34 L. J. Q. B. 130.

(*j*) 2 Smith, L. C. 176 ; Ferard on Fixt. 120–250 ; Haley *v*. Hammersley, 3 D. F. & J. 587.

(*k*) See 2 Smith, L. C. 172–175 ; Ferard on Fixt. 151–232 ; Farrar *v*. Chauffetete, 5 Denio (Amer.), 527 ;

Snedeker *v*. Warring, 2 Kern. (Amer.) 170 ; Murdoch *v*. Gifford, 4 Smith (Amer.), 28 ; Queen *v*. D'Eyn Court, 8 L. R. Eq. 382.

(*l*) 2 Smith, L. C. 171 ; Ferard on Fixt. 123–144.

(*m*) Martin *v*. Roe, 7 E. & B. 237. See Ferard on Fixt. 145–150.

(*n*) See 2 Smith, 172–175 ; Ferard on Fixt. 151–232 ; Haley *v*. Hammersley, 3 D. F. & J. 587 ; Farrar *v*. Chauffetete, 5 Denio (Amer.), 527 ; Snedeker *v*. Warring, 2 Kern. (Amer.) 170 ; Murdoch *v*. Gifford, 4 Smith (Amer.), 28.

1. An estate for life, whether it be given expressly by the ʒtrument which creates it, or whether it arises from equitable ɴsiderations, is always impeachable of waste, unless the conɪry be provided by express stipulation (*o*). The application ˙ an injunction to restrain a tenant for life or for years from ɴmitting waste is usually made by the owner of the inheriɪce, but the application may be made by a remainder-man life, as well as by the owner of the inheritance. The interɴtion of an intermediate estate for life does not deprive the ner of the inheritance or a remainder-man for life of his ʰt to an injunction (*p*). So, also, trustees to preserve con-

ɔ) Cole *v.* Peyson, 1 Ch. Rep. 57; ˌitfield *v.* Bewit, 2 P. Wms. 240; ight *v.* Atkyns, 17 Ves. 255, 19 ʒ. 299; 1 V. & B. 313; Turner *v.* ight, 2 D. F. & J. 234; Blake *v.* ers, 1 D. J. & S. 353.

ɔ) Roswell's case, 1 Roll. Ab. 377;

Tracy *v.* Tracy, 1 Vern. 23; Perrot *v.* Perrot, 3 Atk. 94; Robinson *v.* Litton, 3 Atk. 210; Farrant *v.* Lovell, *ib.* 728; Davies *v.* Leo, 6 Ves. 784. See Kingston *v.* Kingston, 2 Moll. 412; Blagrave *v.* Blagrave, 1 De G. & S. 252, *supra*, p. 235.

tingent remainders may bring a bill to stay waste against a tenant for life (*q*). In Garth *v.* Cotton (*r*) Lord Hardwicke held that trustees to preserve contingent remainders might have an injunction against a tenant for life and a remote remainder-man colluding to commit waste while the remainders were in expectancy (*s*). It would appear that trustees to preserve contingent remainders may not only bring a bill to stay waste, but are bound to do so for the benefit of the contingent remainders (*t*). If an estate of trustees to preserve

contingent remainders is omitted in copyholds, the estate
* 257 of freehold in the lord is sufficient to prevent * waste or
        the tortious destruction of the contingent estates until

the remainder-man comes into *esse.* (*u*).

2. If the legal estate is in trustees upon trust for a tenant for life, with remainders over, and the tenant for life commits waste, the trustees have a right to file a bill to stay the waste (*x*), and it is their duty to do so, if parties unborn are interested (*y*). A remainder-man, however, need not look to the trustees for protection, but has a right to apply for an injunction to restrain the tenant for life from committing waste (*z*).

3. The remainder-man of an undivided share of the inheritance may have an injunction and an account (*a*). When an estate for life is given with certain directions which impose an obligation on the tenant for life, not to be guilty of waste, either voluntary or permissive, the court will interpose to prevent either him or his alienee from doing any act which would be a breach of the condition or obligation (*b*).

4. A tenant in dower (*c*), and tenant by curtesy (*d*), being in the same position towards the owner of the inheritance as a tenant

---

(*q*) Perrot *v.* Perrot, 3 Atk. 94; Garth *v.* Cotton, *ib.* 751, 1 Dick. 183, 1 Ves. 524, 546.

(*r*) *Ib.*

(*s*) See Williams *v.* Duke of Bolton, 1 Cox, 72, 3 P. Wms. 268, n.

(*t*) Stansfield *v.* Habergham, 10 Ves. 278, *per* Lord Eldon.

(*u*) Gilb. Ten. 268; Habergham *v.* Vincent, 2 Ves. Jr. 204; Stansfield *v.* Habergham, 10 Ves. 281; see also Gale *v.* Gale, 2 Cox. 136.

(*x*) Denton *v.* Denton, 7 Beav. 388; Pugh *v.* Vaughan, 12 Beav. 517;

Powys *v.* Blagrave, Kay, 505, 4 D. M. & G. 448.

(*y*) *Ib.*

(*z*) Viner *v.* Vaughan, 2 Beav. 469.

(*a*) Co. Litt. 53 b; Whitfield *v.* Bewit, 2 P. W. 241.

(*b*) Kingham *v.* Lee, 15 Sim. 396. See Blagrave *v.* Blagrave, 1 De G. & S. 253.

(*c*) Bowle's case, 11 Co. Rep. 82 a, Co. Litt. 53 b; Dickin *v.* Hamer, 1 Dr. & S. 295.

(*d*) *Ib.*; Roberts *v.* Roberts, Hard. 96.

life, may not commit waste (e). Nor can a jointress com-
t waste upon the jointure estate (f).

5. As between coparceners, joint tenants, or tenants in
nmon, the court will not interpose to restrain waste (g),
less the wrong-doer is insolvent, or incapable of paying to
: other the excess of the value beyond his own share (h), or
occupying tenant to the other (i), or unless the waste
iounts to * destructive waste, or spoliation (j), or a * 258
rtition suit has been instituted (k).

6. Tenant in tail in possession, with successive estates tail
remainder, is dispunishable of both legal and equitable
iste, because he may at any time bar the entail, and acquire
: absolute fee-simple (l). It has been held that an infant
iant in tail in possession has the same right as one of full
e against the remainder-man, and that his guardians might
mmit waste, although by converting the nature of the property
m realty into personalty the next of kin of the infant would,
the event of his death, be benefited at the expense of the
nainder-man (m). In Saville's case (n), Lord King would
t restrain by injunction the guardians of an infant tenant
tail in possession from cutting timber, whilst the infant was
very bad health. After the death of the infant, which took
ice shortly afterwards, a bill by a remainder-man for an
:ount against his assets was dismissed (o). But it is doubt-
whether Saville's case would be followed at the present
j (p). An injunction may be had against the guardian of
infant tenant in tail, if the application be made on behalf
the infant (q). The right to be dispunishable of waste
:ends not only to the grantee of a tenant in tail, but also to

:) But see Carew v. Carew, 1 Eq. Ca.
221, 400, 14 Vin. Ab. 557
f) Aston v. Aston, 1 Ves. 267.
i) Goodwin v. Spray, 2 Dick. 667;
e v. Thomas, 7 Ves. 589; Twort v.
ort, 16 Ves. 129.
:) Smallman v. Onions, 3 Bro. C. C.

) Twort v. Twort, 16 Ves. 128.
j) Hole v. Thomas, 7 Ves. 589;
ham and Sunderland Railway Co.
Wawn, 3 Beav. 119; Arthur v.
ibe, 2 Dr. & Sm. 428; Ackroyd

v. Briggs, 14 W. R. 25. See Doe d.
Wawn v. Horn, 5 M. & W. 564.
(k) Hawley v. Clowes, 2 Johns. Ch.
(Amer.) 121.
(l) 3 Madd. 532, 2 D. F. & J. 246.
(m) Lyddall v. Clavering, cited Amb.
371.
(n) Cited Forr. 16, Mose. 224.
(o) See Tullitt v. Tullitt, Amb. 370;
Lyddall v. Clavering, ib. 371, n.
(p) See Craig on Trustees, 79–84.
(q) Hussey v. Hussey, 5 Madd. 44.
See Roberts v. Roberts, Hard. 96.

the grantee of such grantee (r). A tenant in tail must exercise his powers in respect to waste during the continuance of his estate, for at the instant of his death they cease (s).

7. A tenant in tail after possibility of issue extinct, who has been once in possession, is in respect of the estate * 259 of inheritance, * which has been once in him, as dispunishable of waste as a tenant for life, who is made so by express limitation (t); but he may not commit equitable waste (u). It may happen that a person is at the same time tenant for life and also tenant in tail after possibility of issue extinct of remainder expectant on his life estate; but there does not appear to be any distinction as far as waste is concerned between a person taking under such a limitation and a tenant in tail after possibility of issue extinct who has been once in possession (v).

8. The privileges of tenant in tail after possibility of issue extinct are in respect of the privity of his estate and of the inheritance that was once in him: if, therefore, he convey his estate to another, such person will be considered as a mere tenant for life (x).

9. A tenant in tail with the reversion in the Crown, and tenant in tail under an act of Parliament which precludes the barring of the entail, have all the legal rights and incidents which belong to a tenancy in tail, and are dispunishable of waste whether legal or equitable (y). But where the rights and incidents of the tenancy in tail are specially qualified by the provisions of the statute, the court may feel bound to interfere to prevent equitable waste (z).

10. A tenant in fee-simple, subject to an executory devise over, is within the principle of equitable waste, but he is dis-

(r) 8 Bac. Ab. 392.

(s) Roberts v. Roberts, Hard. 96; Cruise, Dig. tit. 2, ch. 1, s. 32.

(t) Lewis Bowle's case, 11 Co. Rep. 79 b; Williams v. Williams, 15 Ves. 480; Turner v. Wright, 2 D. F. & J. 247.

(u) Abraham v. Bubb, Freem. ch. 52, 2 Sw. 172 n.; Turner v. Wright, 2 D. F. & J. 247.

(v) See Williams v. Williams, 15 Ves. 423, 12 East, 209.

(x) Co. Litt. 28 a; Rice's case, 3 Leon. 241.

(y) Att.-Gen. v. Duke of Marlborough, 3 Madd. 540; Davis v. Duke of Marlborough, 2 Sw. 108; Turner v. Wright, 2 D. F. & J. 246.

(z) Att.-Gen. v. Duke of Marlborough, 3 Madd. 548; Turner v. Wright, 2 D. F. & J. 246.

ishable of legal waste (a), unless the testator has imposed
him a condition not to commit waste (b).

1. A tenant in fee-simple, holding under a devise to
ι and * his heirs for ever in the fullest confidence * 260
t he will devise the property among the members of
ertain class, has, during his life, all the rights and enjoy-
nts of a tenant in fee, and is dispunishable of waste (c).
he case," said Wood, V. C., in Turner v. Wright (d), is to
distinguished " from a gift of a fee with an executory devise
ιr. When such a gift takes effect, it does so altogether
ιors the tenant in fee, as if there had been no estate in him.
ιen, on the other hand, a person is interested with a power
distribution among the members of a class, he confers on
ιm the same estate which he held himself. It would be un-
sonable to assume that being endowed with a power of dis-
ιition of this kind, he should not have the same power
ιing his life which he could confer on his appointees after
death."

2. An heir taking by resulting trust until the happening of
contingency, is within the principle of equitable waste (e).

3. The well-known tenure so common in Ireland by lease
lives renewable for ever was considered by Lord Redesdale
much in the nature of a perpetuity, that he refused an
ιlication for an injunction to restrain the cutting of tim-
(f). But Lord St. Leonards, after a review of all the
horities, disapproved of this decision, and held that a lessee
lives renewable for ever is not at liberty to commit destruc-
ι waste. But he may, it would appear, commit meliorating
ιte (g). He may not, however, commit equitable waste,
ugh he has been made expressly unimpeachable of waste (h).

4. A bill for an injunction against waste will lie at the
ι of a copyholder against his lessee (i), of a copyholder in

) Turner v. Wright, John. 746, 2
ι. & J. 234, reviewing Robinson v.
ιn, 3 Atk. 209 ; Stansfield v. Haberg-
, 10 Ves. 273 ; Wright v. Atkyns,
ιes. 255, 19 Ves. 299, 1 V. & B.
T. & R. 143 ; Lord St. Leonards
ιeal Property, 376–387.
) Blake v. Peters, 1 D. J. & S. 345.
) Wright v. Atkyns ; Lord St. Leo-
s on Real Property, 383–387.

(d) John. 747
(e) Stansfield v. Habergham, 10 Ves.
273.
(f) Calvert v. Gason, 2 Sch. & L.
561.
(g) Coppinger v. Gubbins, 3 J. & L.
397.
(h) Pentland v. Somerville, 2 Ir. Ch.
289.
(i) Dalton v. Gill, Cary, 89, 90.

remainder against a copyholder for life (*k*), or of a copyholder
against the lord of the manor (*l*). So, also, a bill for an
* 261 injunction against * waste will lie at the suit of a lord
of a manor against his copyhold tenants (*m*), or their
under-tenants (*n*) ; and an interlocutory injunction has been
granted, although the answer denied that the lands were copyhold (*o*).

15. A mortgagee in possession with a sufficient security may
not commit waste (*p*), and he is bound to do necessary repairs (*q*). If, however, the security is insufficient, he is
entitled, so long as he is acting *bonâ fide*, to make the most of
the property for the purpose of discharging what is due to him.
He may cut timber, and open mines or quarries, but he does
so at his own risk and peril. If he incurs a loss, he cannot
charge it against the mortgagor, and if he obtains a profit, the
whole of that profit must go in discharge of the mortgage
debt (*r*). If the security is sufficient, and he has no authority
from the mortgagor (*s*), he will under similar circumstances
be charged with his receipts and disallowed his expenses (*t*).
If the mortgage be of an open mine, the mortgagee is entitled
to work it as a prudent owner would do, and he is not bound
to advance money for speculative-improvements (*u*).[1]

16. When a mortgagee in possession pending a redemption
suit committed waste, he was ordered on motion to deliver up

(*k*) Cornish *v.* New, Finch, 220;
Caldwell *v.* Baylis, 2 Mer. 408.

(*l*) Grey *v.* Duke of Northumberland,
17 Ves. 281 ; Bowser *v.* Maclean, 2 D.
F. & J. 415.

(*m*) Richards *v.* Noble, 3 Mer. 673 ;
Parrott *v.* Palmer, 3 M. & K. 632. See
Andrews *v.* Halse, 4 K. & J. 392.

(*n*) Cuddon *v.* Morley, 7 Ha. 202.

(*o*) Commissioners of Greenwich *v.*
Blackett, 12 Jur. 151.

(*p*) Farrant *v.* Lovell, 3 Atk. 723;
Hardy *v.* Reeves, 4 Ves. 479 ; Sandon
v. Hooper, 6 Beav. 246, 14 L. J. Ch.
120 ; Anon., 1 L. J. Ch. 119 ; Millett
v. Davey, 31 Beav. 470.

(*q*) Godfrey *v.* Watson, 3 Atk. 518 ;
Russell *v.* Smithies, 1 Anstr. 96 ; Lord
St. Leonards' Handy-Book, 117; 1 Seton
on Decrees, 398 ; Sandon *v.* Hooper, 6
Beav. 246, 14 L. J. Ch. 120. See Fisher
on Mortgages, 495.

(*r*) Witherington *v.* Banks, Sel. Ca.

Ch. 30; Millett *v.* Davey, 31 Beav
470 ; Lord St. Leonards Handy-Book,
117.

(*s*) Norton *v.* Cooper, 25 L. J. Ch.
121.

(*t*) Thorneycroft *v.* Crockett, 16 Sim.
445 ; Hood *v.* Easton, 2 Giff. 692. See
Hughes *v.* Williams, 12 Ves. 493.

(*u*) Rowe *v.* Wood, 2 J. & W. 555.
See Fisher on Mortgages, 499.

[1] In this country equity will restrain
the cutting and removing wood to the
injury of the mortgage security Moul-
ton *v.* Stowell, 16 N. H. 221 ; Robinson
v. Russell, 24 Cal. 467 ; Bunker *v.*
Locke, 15 Wis. 635 ; Natoma, &c., Co.
v. Clarkin, 14 Cal. 544 : or where the
wood and timber are necessary to the
enjoyment of the estate.   Davis *v.*
Reed, 14 Md. 152. So in Illinois an injunction will be issued to prevent waste
by mortgagor. Nelson *v.* Pinegar, 30
Ill. 473.

the premises to the mortgagor (x). Where a first mortgagee was in possession, he was restrained from paying over the surplus rents to the mortgagor instead of to the second mortgagee (y).

17. * The mortgagee of a burial-ground has notice   * 262 of the purposes to which it is devoted, and is bound by rights of burial, temporary or in perpetuity, granted by his mortgagor while left in possession (z).

18. The position of a mortgagor in possession of the mortgaged estate bears no analogy to that of a tenant for life. A mortgagor in possession is in equity the owner of the estate, and may exercise all acts of ownership and may commit waste, provided he does not diminish the security or render it insufficient (a); but if the security is insufficient he may not commit waste (b). In order that an injunction may go against a mortgagor in possession, it must appear on the affidavits that the security is insufficient, or will be rendered insufficient or scanty by the acts of waste complained of (c). The meaning of the term "insufficient" is thus explained by Wigram, V. C., in King v. Smith (d): "I think the question which must be tried is, whether the property the mortgagee takes as a security is sufficient in this sense — that the security is worth so much more than the money advanced — that the act of cutting timber is not to be considered as substantially impairing the value, which was the basis of the contract between the parties at the time it was entered into." In a case where the mortgagor in possession was bankrupt, but no assignees had as yet been chosen, he was restrained from committing waste (e), but in a case where he was merely in prison for debt the application for an injunction was refused (f).[1]

(x) Hanson v. Derby, 2 Vern. 392.

(y) Dalmer v. Dashwood, 2 Cox, 378.

(z) Moreland v.Richardson,24Beav.33.

(a) Kekewich v. Marker, 3 Mac. & G. 329.

(b) Robinson v. Litton, 3 Atk. 210; Farrant v. Lovell, ib. 723; Usborne v. Usborne, 1 Dick. 76; Hopkins v. Hopkins, cit. $ib.$; Uvedale v. Uvedale, cit. $ib.$; Cox v. Goodfellow, 8 Ves. 105, n.; Humphreys v. Harrison, 1 J. & W. 581; Hippesley v. Spencer, 5 Madd. 422; Ackroyd v. Mitchell, 3 L. T. N. S. 236.

(c) Cox v. Goodfellow, 8 Ves. 105, n.; Hippesley v. Spencer, 5 Madd. 422; Humphreys v. Harrison, 1 J. & W. 581; Leake v. Beckett, 1 Y. & J. 339; King v. Smith, 2 Ha. 244.

(d) 2 Ha. 244.

(e) Hampton v. Hodges, 8 Ves. 104.

(f) Humphreys v. Harrison, 1 J. & W. 582.

[1] Mortgagor of personal as well as real property restrained from committing waste. Parsons v. Hughes, 12 Md. 1. The severance of the engine and

19. A mortgagor who has sold the equity of redemption without taking any security as an indemnity against his
* 263   bond cannot * have an injunction against the purchaser to stay waste on the ground that the land may not be sufficient to satisfy the mortgage (*g*).

20. The same principles which apply in respect of waste by a mortgagor in possession are also applicable as between the heir or executor of a debtor in possession and a judgment creditor (*h*), and as between a purchaser who has obtained possession before the payment of the purchase-moneys and the vendor (*i*). So, also, where moneys due under a settlement are unpaid, the court has jurisdiction to prevent any waste which may tend to injure the security (*k*).

21. The obligations imposed by the common law upon a tenant for life or years, or existing by the custom of the country, apply as between landlord and tenant, except in so far as they may be excluded by the terms of the agreement which subsists between the parties (*l*). Acts contrary to the obligation of a tenant to deal with the premises according to the custom of the country or express agreement are not, properly speaking, acts of waste, unless they are also breaches of the common law, but being of a like mischief with acts of waste, they are restrained upon somewhat similar principles (*m*). There is, however, a distinction in the general principles upon which the court proceeds in restraining acts of waste done in violation of an express agreement from those on which it proceeds in restraining acts of pure waste at common law. In restraining pure waste, irrespectively of agreement, the court proceeds upon the ground of irreparable damage, and will not

---

machinery of a mill upon incumbered real estate is a fraud upon the prior judgment creditors of the debtor, such as a court of equity has jurisdiction to restrain by injunction ; but, *quære*, whether it will, at the suit of a mere judgment creditor, restrain such acts of a judgment debtor, in possession as owner, as would constitute waste at common law. Witmer's Appeal, 45 Penn. St. 455.

(*g*) Brumley *v.* Fanning, 1 Johns. Ch. (Amer.) 500.

(*h*) Leake *v.* Beckett, 1 Y. & J. 339.

(*i*) Crockford *v.* Alexander, 15 Ves. 138 ; Casamajor *v.* Strode, 1 Sim. & St. 381 ; Petley *v.* Eastern Counties Railway Co., 8 Sim. 483 ; Webster *v.* South Eastern Railway Co., 1 Sim. N. S. 272.

(*k*) Turkington *v.* Kearnan, Ll. & G. 45.

(*l*) Webb *v.* Plummer, 2 B. & Ald. 746 ; Philipps *v.* Smith, 14 M. & W. 589. See *supra*, p. 249, as to the custom of the country.

(*m*) Songhurst *v.* Dixey, Toth. 255 ; Kimpton *v.* Eve, 2 V. & B. 352.

interfere if the damage be small (*n*).   In restraining acts of
waste in breach of covenants the court proceeds upon
the principle that where a positive stipulation has * been   * 264
entered into between two parties, either party has a
right to insist upon its literal performance by the other irrespectively of the question of damage (*o*).

22. A termor who holds land at a ground rent is as much
entitled to an injunction to stay waste by his underlessee as if
he had an estate of inheritance (*p*).   So, also, may a receiver
have an injunction to restrain the tenants or undertenants
from committing waste (*q*).

23. As between landlord and tenant, no length of abuse will
give the tenant a right to commit waste.   The allowance of
the. abuse is only by the permission of the landlord, and can
never be turned against him by the tenant.   The rights of the
tenant are only to be ascertained by the lease (*r*).

24. At common law a dean and chapter, being a corporation
aggregate, could alienate their estates as fully and effectually
as a person seised in fee.   But bishops, deans, parsons, and
other corporations sole could not alienate their estates so as to
bind their successors without the consent of other parties.
Grants made by bishops required confirmation by the dean
and chapter, those made by deans required confirmation by
the bishop and chapter, and those made by parsons and vicars
required confirmation by the patron and ordinary (*s*).   By the
restraining statutes (*t*), however, all ecclesiastical persons are
disabled from alienating the possessions of the church for a
longer period than twenty-one years or three lives from the
making thereof (*u*).   It was not enacted expressly by these
statutes that the lessees should be made impeachable of
waste (*x*), but it has been long decided that ecclesiastical persons are restrained by the equity of the statute 13 Eliz. c. 10,
from making leases dispunishable of waste (*y*).

(*n*) Lambert *v.* Lambert, 2 Ir. Eq.
210; Doran *v.* Carroll, 11 Ir. Ch. 379;
Att.-Gen. *v.* Sheffield Gas Co., 3 D. M.
& G. 321; *supra*, p. 236.
(*o*) Kemp *v.* Sober, 1 Sim. N. S. 520,
on appeal, 19 L. T. 308; Tipping *v.*
Eckersley, 2 K. & J. 264.   See, further,
as to injunctions against breaches of
covenant, *infra.*
(*p*) Farrant *v.* Lovell, 3 Atk. 72.

(*q*) Mason *v.* Mason, Fl. & K. 429.
(*r*) Lord Courtown *v.* Ward, 1 Sch.
& L. 8.
(*s*) Cripps on the Clergy, 240.
(*t*) 1 Eliz. c. 19, s. 5, 13 Eliz. c. 10, s. 3.
(*u*) See also 14 Eliz. c. 11, 18 Eliz. c.
11.
(*x*) Co. Litt. 44 b.
(*y*) Dean and Chapter of Worcester's
case, 6 Co. Rep. 37 a; Herring *v.*

* 265   25. * A parson being at common law able to alienate his glebe land with the consent of the proper parties, might also with the consent of the same parties commit waste; but without such consent a parson has not at common law any more extensive privileges as to waste in general than an ordinary tenant for life (z). It seems, however, that in some respects a parson is more favorably situated than an ordinary tenant for life or years, and that some acts which are waste in ordinary cases are not necessarily waste in his case (a).

26. Timber growing on the estates of ecclesiastical persons is a fund for the benefit of the church, and may not be felled except for the repairs of the ecclesiastical buildings, the parsonage-house, the farms, and the barns and outhouses belonging to the parsonage (b). Timber growing in the church-yard may not be felled except for the necessary repairs of the chancel or the body of the church (c).

27. There has been some controversy whether an ecclesiastical person is bound specifically to apply the timber he has cut for the purposes of repairs towards the actual repairs for which it was wanted. From a passage in Ambler (d) it might appear that Lord Hardwicke was of opinion that a rector or vicar might cut and sell timber to any extent in order to provide a fund for general repairs; but the report of the case is too imperfect and too doubtful to give the weight of Lord Hardwicke's authority to such a proposition (e). The rule on the subject would appear to be that an ecclesiastical person may cut and sell timber for the purpose of providing other timber more suitable for the intended repairs, so long as no

* 266   more is cut than is necessary for the * purpose; but that he may not cut timber to defray the general expenses of his repairs (f).

Dean of St. Paul's, 3 Sw. 492; Wither v. Dean and Chapter of Winchester, 3 Mer. 421.

(z) Knight v. Moseley, Amb. 176; Strachey v. Francis, 2 Atk. 216; Duke of Marlborough v. St. John, 5 De G. & S. 178. See Hoskins v. Featherstone, 2 Bro. C. C. 552.

(a) Duke of St. Alban's v. Skipwith, 8 Beav. 355; Bird v. Ralph, 4 B. & A. 825, 2 A. & E. 773.

(b) Strachey v. Francis, 2 Atk. 216;

Jefferson v. Bishop of Durham, 1 B. & P. 129; Herring v. Dean and Chapter of St. Paul's, 3 Sw. 492; Wither v. Dean and Chapter of Winchester, 3 Mer. 421.

(c) Edw. 1, c. 35, stat. 2; Gibbon on Dilap. 54–56.

(d) 176.

(e) Wither v. Dean and Chapter of Winchester, 3 Mer. 421, 428, per Lord Eldon; Duke of Marlborough v. St. John, 5 De G. & S. 180, per V. C. Parker.

(f) Wither v. Dean and Chapter of

28. An ecclesiastical person may continue the working of mines or gravel-pits already open, and which have been lawfully opened, but he may not open new ones (*g*). Ecclesiastical persons, whether aggregate or sole, may grant leases for a long term of years for mining or other purposes with the sanction of the ecclesiastical commissioners (*h*). It is doubtful whether a parson could, without such sanction, make a lease of mines upon his glebe, even though with the consent of the patron and ordinary (*i*).

29. In the case of a parson the application for an injunction to stay waste should be made by the patron (*k*), or, if the patron is a consenting party to the waste, by the ordinary (*l*). The right to an injunction to restrain a bishop from wasting the property of the see resides in the Attorney-General, suing on behalf of the Crown, the patron of bishoprics (*m*), and possibly to some extent in the metropolitan (*n*). So a dean and chapter may be restrained at the suit of the Crown, but not at the suit of a lessee holding under them, except in so far as he may have derived any right or interest under the agreement (*o*).

30. The court of chancery has no jurisdiction to interfere at the suit of a parishioner to restrain the incumbent from making alterations in the church, church-yard, or other land in his possession in right of his church (*p*). But the court will act *as ancillary to the ecclesiastical court, and _* 267 grant an injunction where any act in the nature of

Winchester, 3 Mer. 421; Duke of Marlborough v. St. John, 5 De G. & S. 181. See Herring v. Dean and Chapter of St. Paul's, 2 Wills. Ch. 10, 3 Sw. 492.

(*g*) Knight v. Moseley, Amb. 176; Huntley v. Russell, 13 Q & B. 591.

(*h*) 5 & 6 Vict. c. 108, 21 & 22 Vict. c. 57.

(*i*) Holden v. Weeks, 1 J. & H. 283. See Doe v. Collinge, 7 C. B. 939; Bartlett v. Philipps, 4 D. & J. 414.

(*k*) 2 Roll. Ab. 813; Knight v. Moseley, Amb. 176, Bradley v. Strachey, Barnard, Ch. 399; Strachey v. Francis, 2 Atk. 216; Hoskins v. Featherstone, 2 Bro. C. C. 551; Acland v. Atwell, 3 Sw. 499, n.

(*l*) Holden v. Weeks, 1 J. & H. 285.

(*m*) Knight v. Moseley, Amb. 176; Jefferson v. Bishop of Durham, 1 B. & P. 116, 131; Wither v. Dean and Chapter of Winchester, 3 Mer. 427; Earl Fitzwilliam v. Moore, 3 Ir. Eq. 615.

(*n*) Wither v. Dean and Chapter of Winchester, 3 Mer. 427.

(*o*) Wither v. Dean and Chapter of Winchester, 3 Mer. 421; Herring v. Dean and Chapter of St. Paul's, 3 Sw. 492.

(*p*) Earl Fitzwilliam v. Moore, 3 Ir. Eq. 625; Cardinal v. Molyneux, 7 Jur. N. S. 854. See Woodman v. Robinson, 2 Sim. N. S. 204; and see, as to right of burial, Moreland v. Richardson, 24 Beav. 33.

waste is either threatened or committed (*q*). A suit accordingly by the church-wardens of a parish to restrain the vicar of the parish or any other person from pulling down the church-yard wall is maintainable (*r*). If the church-warden commences the suit whilst he is church-warden, he may continue it after his church-wardenship has ceased (*s*).

31. In Bartlett *v.* Philipps (*t*), the court was of opinion that the produce of waste of glebe land should be laid out in the permanent improvement of the living. In a subsequent case, however, Wood, V. C., held that a patron could not claim as of right an account and investment of the produce of past waste for the benefit of the living (*u*). But there is ground to believe that the dictum of Lord Hardwicke, in Knight *v.* Moseley (*v*), on which his decision was based, only meant that the patron could not claim such an account for his own benefit (*x*). At all events, on a proper application, the court may order timber growing on the glebe land to be cut, or mines under it to be worked, and the produce applied for the benefit of the living (*y*).

SECTION IV.—EQUITABLE WASTE.

1. Equitable waste by tenant for life without impeachment of waste.
2. Case of owner in fee settling his estate on himself for life with remainders over.
3. Equitable waste described.
4. Leading cases on subject.
5. When acts are of trivial nature court will not interpose.
6. Cutting of ornamental timber, equitable waste.
7-14. What are regarded as ornamental timber.
15. Measure of the obligation which attaches upon a tenant for life without impeachment of waste in reference to ornamental timber.
16. Cutting of young trees and saplings, equitable waste.
17. Cutting of underwood when equitable waste.
18. Tenancy for life without impeachment of waste may be qualified.

(*q*) Marriott *v.* Tarpley, 9 Sim. 279.
(*r*) Ib.
(*s*) Ib.
(*t*) 4 D. & J. 414.
(*u*) Holden *v.* Weeks, 1 J. & H. 278.

(*v*) Amb. 176.
(*x*) Yool on Waste, 80.
(*y*) Duke of Marlborough *v.* St. John, 5 De G. & S. 179; Holden *v.* Weekes, 1 J. & H. 278.

1. The estate of a tenant for life or years is often declared by the instrument which creates it to be " without impeachment of waste." The effect of the clause at law is not only to allow a tenant for life or years to commit waste, but it is a special power permitting him to appropriate the produce of the waste to his own use (z). A court of equity, however, considers the * excessive use of the legal power incident to   * 268 an estate unimpeachable of waste to be inequitable and unjust, and therefore controls it (a). " At law," said Turner, L. J., in Micklethwait v. Micklethwait (b), " a tenant for life without impeachment of waste has, during the continuance of his estate, the absolute power and dominion over the timber, &c., upon the estate ; but this court controls him in the exercise of that power upon this ground, that it will not permit an unconscientious use to be made of a legal power. When, therefore, the court is called upon to interfere in cases of this description, it is bound, in the first place, to consider whether there are any special circumstances to affect the conscience of the tenant for life, for in the absence of special circumstances it cannot be unconscientious in him to avail himself of the power which the testator has vested in him. In considering what are the special circumstances which the court will regard as affecting the conscience of a tenant for life, the intention of the settlor or devisor is principally to be regarded. If by his disposition or by his acts he has indicated an intention that there should be a continuous enjoyment in succession of that which he himself enjoyed, in the state in which he has himself enjoyed it, it is against conscience that a tenant for life,

(z) Lewis Bowle's case, 11 Co. Rep. 81 b; Aston v. Aston, 1 Ves. 264 ; Kekewich v. Marker, 3 Mac. & G. 327 ;

Clegg v. Rowland, 2 L. R. Eq. 160. See 2 Sw. 145–147, n.
(a) Marker v. Marker, 9 Ha. 1, 17.
(b) 1 D. & J. 504, 524.

claiming under his disposition, should by the exercise of a legal power defeat that intention " (*c*).

2. It appears that if an owner in fee settles his estate on himself for life with remainders over, he will not be allowed any larger privileges than he would have had if the settlor had been a stranger (*d*).

3. Waste which a court of equity will restrain as being an unconscientious exercise of a legal power, is called equitable waste. An act may amount to equitable waste although there is a total absence of malice. "The presence or ab-
* 269   sence," said Lord * Campbell, in Turner *v.* Wright (*e*),
" of a bad motive will not enable us to draw any satisfactory line between what is to be considered malicious and what is to be considered equitable waste, and no line to regulate the interposition of a court of equity by injunction can well be drawn other than the recognized and well-established line between legal and equitable waste" (*f*). If the restriction upon waste is connected with a trust, the court will act with greater readiness in restraining a legal power than in the absence of the trust (*g*).

4. The case which is frequently referred to as being the leading decision on the subject of equitable waste is well known by the name of Lord Barnard's case. It is, however, far from being the earliest decision on the subject, as it appears to have been a well-known branch of equitable jurisdiction in the time of Lord Nottingham. In Abraham *v.* Bubb (*h*), we find that great judge treating it as a settled point that if tenant for life does waste maliciously, a court of equity will restrain him, though he had an express power to commit waste. He cited the Bishop of Winchester's case and Lady Evelyn's case as instances in his recollection in which the court had so interposed. In several other cases about the same period the court declared that it would restrain both tenant for life without impeachment

---

(*c*) See Turner *v.* Wright, 2 D. F. & J. 245, *per* Lord Campbell.
(*d*) Vincent *v.* Spicer, 22 Beav. 380. See Vane *v.* Lord Barnard, 2 Vern. 738, Prec. Ch. 454; Barry *v.* Barry, 1 J. & W. 652; Coffin *v.* Coffin, Jac. 70; ———— *v.* Copley, 3 Madd. 525, n.

(*e*) 2 D. F. & J. 234, 245.
(*f*) See Aston *v.* Aston, 1 Ves. 265.
(*g*) Marker *v.* Marker, 9 Ha. 1, 18.
(*h*) 2 Eq. Ca. Ab. 757, Free. Ch. 53, 2 Show. 69.

of waste, and tenant in tail after possibility of issue extinct, from committing " wilful," " destructive," " malicious," " extravagant," or " humorous " waste (*i*).   These determinations led to the remarkable case of Vane *v.* Lord Barnard (*j*). Lord Barnard, who was tenant for life without impeachment of waste of Raby Castle under the marriage settlement of his son, with remainder to his son, in consequence of some displeasure which he had conceived against him, got workmen together and stripped the castle of the lead, iron, glass, &c., and was proceeding to pull it down, whereupon Lord Cowper granted an injunction and directed an inquiry as to the amount of damage actually done, and ordered it to be repaired at the expense of Lord Barnard.   * The ground upon which the * 270 doctrine was as yet founded was said to be the destruction of the inheritance, and upon this principle Lord Hardwicke said that if a tenant for life without impeachment of waste were to pull down farm-houses he would restrain him as much as if it were the case of a mansion-house (*k*).

5. If the acts complained of are of a trivial nature the court will not interpose.   Thus Lord Hardwicke observed that if the clause " without impeachment of waste " could be made use of to permit a son to call his father into a court of equity for every alteration he might make in pulling up the floor of the house, &c., it would be better for the public that Raby Castle had been pulled down than that such a precedent should have been set (*l*).

6. The cutting of timber planted or left standing for ornament comes within the principle of equitable waste.   " If," said Turner, L. J., in Micklethwait *v.* Micklethwait (*m*), " a devisor or settlor occupies a mansion-house with trees planted or left standing for ornament around or about it, or keeps such a mansion-house in a state of occupation, and devises or settles it so as to go in a course of succession, he may reasonably be presumed to anticipate that those who succeed him will occupy the mansion-house, and it cannot be presumed that he meant

---

(*i*) Williams *v.* Day, 2 Ch. Ca. 32; Cooke *v.* Whaley, 1 Eq. Ca. Ab. 400, Anon., Freem. Ch. 278.
(*j*) Prec. Ch. 454, 1 Salk. 161; 2 Vern. 738.

(*k*) 1 Ves. 265.   See Rolt *v.* Somerville, 2 Eq. Ca. Ab. tit. Waste, pl. 8.
(*l*) Peirs *v.* Peirs, 1 Ves. 521.
(*m*) 1 D. & J. 504, 524.

it to be denuded of that ornament which he has himself enjoyed " (*n*). The presumed will and intention of the settlor or devisor being the ground for the interference of the court, the court does, not proceed upon any fancied notions of its own as to whether or not timber may be ornamental (*o*), but confines its protection to trees which have been planted or left standing for ornament by him (*p*). However ornamental, in fact, trees may be, they will not be protected unless they have been dedi
* 271   cated in some way or other by the settlor or devisor to the purposes of ornament (*q*). * Trees, on the other hand, which have been treated as ornamental by him will be considered by the court to be ornamental, whether they are or are not, in point of fact, ornamental. The taste of the grantor is binding upon the tenant for life, and the court will not inquire as to what is beautiful or not. All it has to ascertain is the intention of the settlor or devisor (*r*).

7. Trees which have been planted or left standing for the purpose of excluding objects from view (*s*), or for the purpose of shelter and protection to a mansion-house (*t*), are regarded as ornamental timber. In Coffin *v.* Coffin (*u*), Lord Eldon refused that part of the order for an injunction which had been granted by the Vice-Chancellor, restraining a man from cutting trees which protected the premises from the effects of the sea. The reasons of his lordship are not given, and it is difficult to see why that part of the order was refused.

8. The protection of the court is confined to trees of a purely ornamental character. Trees which have been planted for profit as well as for ornament will not be protected (*x*).

9. The court has often much difficulty in determining

(*n*) See Turner *v.* Wright, 2 D. F. & J. 234, 245.
(*o*) Marker *v.* Marker, 9 Ha. 1, 17.
(*p*) Wombwell *v.* Bellasyse, 6 Ves. 110 n.; Marquis of Downshire *v.* Sandys, *ib.* 110; Marker *v.* Marker, 9 Ha. 1, 17; Halliwell *v.* Philipps, 4 Jur. N. S. 607; Ford *v.* Tynte, 2 D. J. & S. 127.
(*q*) *Ib.*; Williams *v.* Macnamara, 8 Ves. 70; Coffin *v.* Coffin, Jac. 71.
(*r*) Wombwell *v.* Bellasyse, 6 Ves. 110, n.; Marquis of Downshire *v.* Sandys, *ib.* 110; Coffin *v.* Coffin, Jac.
71; Lord Mahon *v.* Stanhope, 3 Madd. 523; Ford *v.* Tynte, 2 D. J. & S. 127.
(*s*) Day *v.* Merry, 16 Ves. 375; Campbell *v.* Allgood, 17 Beav. 627.
(*t*) Chamberlayne *v.* Dummer, 1 Bro. C. C. 166, 3 *ib.* 549; Aston *v.* Aston, 1 Ves. 265; Tamworth *v.* Lord Ferrers, 6 Ves. 419; Marquis of Downshire *v.* Sandys, *ib.* 107; Coffin *v.* Coffin, Jac. 71; Potts *v.* Potts, 3 L. J. Ch. 177; Campbell *v.* Allgood, 17 Beav. 626.
(*u*) Jac. 71.
(*x*) Halliwell *v.* Philipps, 4 Jur. N. S. 608. See Micklethwait *v.* Micklethwait, 1 D. & J. 527.

whether trees have been planted or left standing for ornament. The question in all cases of the sort is a question of fact, and the main difficulty lies in the evidence necessary to establish the fact (*y*). The existence of a mansion-house will, in many cases, supply the court with evidence on which to determine the point as to the ornamental character of timber, for trees when in the neighborhood of a mansion-house will be assumed to have been planted for ornament (*z*). If, however, a mansion-house * with which timber has been connected * 272 has been pulled down, or has gone to ruin or decay, and there is no evidence to show that the devisor or settlor contemplated that the house would be rebuilt and intended the trees to be preserved with that view, the timber will not be treated as ornamental. The mere fact that he may have thought that the house might possibly be rebuilt is not enough to make the timber ornamental timber (*a*). But if it appears to have been the contemplation of the settlor or devisor that the house should be rebuilt, or that the ground should be let on building leases, the timber will be treated as ornamental (*b*).

10. It is not, however, necessary that timber should be contiguous to a house or park in order to entitle it to the protection of the court as being ornamental (*c*). In Marquis of Downshire *v.* Sandys (*d*), Lord Eldon extended the protection of the court to timber planted for the ornament of the walks, rides, avenues, vistas, plantations, and pleasure-grounds of the estate ten miles round, as well as to clumps of trees which were planted for ornament on a common at a distance of at least two miles from the house, and separated from it by land belonging to other owners (*e*). A ride cut through a wood

(*y*) 9 Ha. 17.

(*z*) Micklethwait *v.* Micklethwait, 1 D. & J. 504, 526. See Wombwell *v.* Bellasyse, 6 Ves. 110, n.; Marker *v.* Marker, 9 Ha. 21.

(*a*) Newdigate *v.* Newdigate, 8 Bligh, N. S. 734; Micklethwait *v.* Micklethwait, 1 D. & J. 504, 527.

(*b*) Wellesley *v.* Wellesley, 6 Sim. 497; Morris *v.* Morris, 15 Sim. 507, 2 Ph.

206. See Micklethwait *v.* Micklethwait, 1 D. & J. 527.

(*c*) Wombwell *v.* Bellasyse, 6 Ves. 110, n.

(*d*) 6 Ves. 110.

(*e*) See Newdigate *v.* Newdigate, 1 Sim. 131, 2 Cl. & Fin. 601; Halliwell *v.* Philipps, 4 Jur. N. S. 606; Micklethwait *v.* Micklethwait, 1 D. & J. 504, 528; Ford *v.* Tynte, 2 D. J. & S. 127.

will not protect more of the wood than the part which is near the drive (*f*).

11. In a case where the owner of an estate with a residence purchased adjoining land with ornamental wood, the court would not, from the mere fact that he had not cut down any of the trees during his life, infer that he intended the woods to be regarded as standing for ornament (*g*). The case, however, would have been otherwise if there had been evi-

* 273   dence to show * that he had cut out vistas in the wood, or had cleared out trees and surrounded them by pleasure-walks and seats, or had erected statues, columns, or the like (*h*).

12. The court, it may be observed, has much greater difficulty in determining that trees have been left standing or preserved by the settlor or devisor for ornament, than it has in determining that trees have been planted for ornament; but the leaving trees standing beyond the usual and provident period of cutting, the clearing out of trees and surrounding them by pleasure-walks and seats, and other circumstances, from which an inference arises that the settlor or devisor regarded the trees with other views than as mere subjects of profit, may be considered as *primâ facie* evidence that trees were left standing for shelter or ornament (*i*). It is doubtful whether the court can ever go back beyond the time of an absolute owner of the estate for the purpose of ascertaining whether timber is to be treated as ornamental (*k*).

13. In a case where there was no evidence to show that there was any timber upon the estate which could fall within the description of ornamental timber contained in a deed of settlement, other than the timber in certain woods, the description was held to apply to that timber (*l*).

14. Although the court will, as a general rule, abstain from exercising a judgment upon matters of taste; yet where a

(*f*) Wombwell *v.* Bellasyse, 6 Ves. 110, n.; Halliwell *v.* Philipps, 4 Jur. N. S. 607. See Burgess *v.* Lamb, 16 Ves. 183; Marker *v.* Marker, 9 Ha. 1, 17.

(*g*) Halliwell *v.* Philipps, 4 Jur. N. S. 608.

(*h*) *Ib.*

(*i*) Lushington *v.* Boldero, 6 Madd. 149. See Halliwell *v.* Philipps, 4 Jur. N. S. 607.

(*k*) Micklethwait *v.* Micklethwait, 1 D. & J. 504, 513.

(*l*) Marker *v.* Marker, 9 Ha. 1. See Newdigate *v.* Newdigate, 1 Sim. 131, 2 Cl. & Fin. 601.

deed of settlement provided that enough of the most ornamental timber should always remain to leave the beauty of
the place unimpaired, and the deed evidently referred to the
state of the property at the time of its execution as the
standard of beauty, the court directed an inquiry whether
certain trees could be cut without impairing the beauty of the
place as it stood at the date of the settlement (*m*). " Although
there will be, no doubt," said L. J. Turner (*n*), " great difficulty
in executing a trust or enforcing an injunction to preserve
the property according to a * certain standard of beauty,   * 274
the difficulty is not such as it is beyond the power
of the court to grapple with."

15. The question what a prudent owner would do in the
proper and ordinary course of management of his property
can be no measure of the obligation which attaches in a court
of equity upon a tenant for life without impeachment of waste
with reference to timber planted or left standing for ornament.
If there be evidence to show that a wood planted or left standing for ornament had been resorted to by the absolute owner
for the supply of timber for repairs or sale, a tenant for life
without impeachment of waste may do the same, provided he
acts as a prudent owner in a due course of management would
do ; but if there be no evidence to show that the woods had
been resorted to by him for repairs or sale, the owner of ornamental timber may not cut for those purposes (*o*). He may,
however, thin trees planted or left standing for ornament (*p*).
So also when a tempest had produced gaps in a piece of
ornamental planting, by which unequal and discordant marks
and divisions were occasioned, the court would not restrain
the cutting a few trees, so as to produce a uniform and consistent appearance (*q*).

16. The cutting of saplings or young trees, not fit for the
purposes of timber, comes also within the principle of equitable
waste ; but a case of malicious waste must be made out,
amounting to a spoliation or destruction of the property. The

(*m*) Marker *v.* Marker, 9 Ha. 1.
(*n*) *Ib.* 18.
(*o*) Ford *v.* Tynte, 2 D. J. & S. 127.

(*p*) ———— *v.* Copley, 3 Madd. 525, n.
See Barry *v.* Barry, 1 J. & W. 654.
(*q*) Lord Mahon *v.* Lord Stanhope, 3
Madd. 523, n.

mere fact that he may be felling trees of younger growth than would be felled by a prudent owner in the course of a husbandlike management of the estate, is not enough to induce the court to interfere with the legal power of a tenant for life without impeachment of waste. To come within the principle of equitable waste, a case of spoliation or destruction must be made out (r). In Hole v. Thomas (s), Lord Eldon
* 275 considered the cutting saplings and * timber trees at unseasonable times to be a malicious destruction, and granted an injunction (t).

17. The cutting of underwood of an insufficient growth or at unseasonable times comes also within the principle of equitable waste, when it amounts to a destruction or spoliation of the property (u) ; and generally, it would appear, that the principle of equitable waste extends to any act which amounts to malicious waste, and goes to the wanton destruction and spoliation of the property (x).

18. If the tenant for life be expressly bound to keep certain buildings in repair, this qualifies the gift to him without impeachment of waste (y). The estate for life " without impeachment of waste" is sometimes qualified by the clause " except voluntary waste," or words to that effect. This was the case in Garth v. Cotton (z). In his judgment Lord Hardwicke said incidentally that timber could not be cut, but no relief was sought in that case against the tenant for life. In Vincent v. Spicer (a), Lord Romilly, M. R., considered the words " voluntary or permissive waste " qualifying an estate for life without impeachment of waste, as merely tantamount to " spoil and destroy," and held that the tenant for life or his assignee were entitled to cut such timber and other trees not

(r) O'Brien v. O'Brien, Amb. 106 ; Packington's case, 3 Atk. 216 ; Aston v. Aston, 1 Ves. 265 ; Peirs v. Peirs, ib. 521 ; Lady Strathmore v. Bowes, 2 Bro. C. C. 188 ; Smythe v. Smythe, 2 Sw. 252 ; Coffin v. Coffin, Jac. 71 ; Lord Tamworth v. Ferrers, 6 Ves. 419 ; Hole v. Thomas, 7 Ves. 589 ; Potts v. Potts, 3 L. J. Ch. 177 ; Pentland v. Somerville, 2 Ir. Ch. 289 ; Halliwell v. Philipps, 4 Jur. N. S. 608.
(s) 7 Ves. 589.
(t) See Chamberlayne v. Dummer, 1

Bro. C. C. 166, 3 ib. 549 ; Pentland v. Somerville, 2 Ir. Ch. 289.
(u) Hole v. Thomas, 7 Ves. 589 ; Brydges v. Stephens, 6 Madd. 279, 2 Sw. 150, n.
(x) See Aston v. Aston, 1 Ves. 264 ; Bishop of London v. Web, 1 P. Wms. 527.
(y) Caldwell v. Baylis, 2 Mer. 408.
(z) 3 Atk. 751, 1 Ves. 546, 1 Dick. 188.
(a) 22 Beav. 380.

planted or standing for ornament, as an owner of an estate in fee, having due regard to his present interest, and to the permanent advantage of the estate, might properly cut in a due course of management.

19. The terms " without impeachment of waste " as applied to trustees of a term for special purposes, have a different sense from that of the same words annexed to a tenancy for life. Trustees of a term without impeachment of waste are bound to a more provident execution of their powers than a tenant for life, and must act in their trust as the court itself would act (*b*).

20. * It probably makes no difference whether the es-   * 276 tate which is made unimpeachable of waste is freehold or a long term of years, determinable on the death of the lessee for life (*c*).   But it seems that if a long term of years be declared at its creation to be unimpeachable of waste, and be afterwards settled on one for life, with remainder over, although the life estate is not expressly declared to be unimpeachable of waste, it will be so treated as between itself and those claiming the rest of the term (*d*).

21. The limitation to a tenant for life without impeachment of waste is sometimes made by the settlement subject to a power in trustees for a term to enter and cut timber.   In a case where a discretionary power to this effect was vested in trustees for a term, the court protected them in the exercise of their power, there being an absence of all *mala fides* or of any wanton or unreasonable exercise of their discretion (*e*). So also where the limitation to a tenant for life without impeachment of waste was subject to the power in trustees with the consent of the tenant for life, to cut timber for the purpose of paying off a mortgage debt, the court, upon the construction of the settlement, restrained the tenant for life from cutting timber for his own benefit (*f*).

22. A tenant for life without impeachment of waste will not

_____

(*b*) Marquis of Downshire *v.* Sandys, 6 Ves. 107, 114.

(*c*) Garth *v.* Cotton, 3 Atk. 751; 1 Ves. 524, 546, 1 Dick. 183.

(*d*) Bridges *v.* Stephens, 2 Sw. 150, n.

See Lord Downshire *v.* Sandys, 6 Ves. 107; Craig on Trees, 50.

(*e*) Kekewich *v.* Marker, 3 Mac. & G. 311.

(*f*) Briggs *v.* Earl of Oxford, 5 De G. & S. 156.

be permitted to gain any undue advantage from the exercise of a power or trust for sale or exchange of the settled estates. Thus, in Lady Plymouth v. Archer (g), lands were devised upon trust for sale, the produce to be invested in other lands to be purchased and to be to the use of Lord Archer for life without impeachment of waste, with remainders over, and there was a declaration that the rents and profits of the lands, until sold, were to be to the use of the person entitled to the estate to be purchased. Lord Archer was held not entitled to cut timber on the lands devised, because, as he would have a right to cut timber on the estate to be bought, that would be * 277   giving him * double timber. In a case, Burgess v. Lamb (h), before Lord Eldon, trustees for the purchase of real estate were made successively tenants for life without impeachment of waste of the estate to be purchased. An estate having been purchased with a disproportionate quantity of timber upon it, the question was whether the moneys had been properly laid out, and whether an injunction could be sustained against the first tenant for life in cutting timber. This question Lord Eldon would not decide, the frame of the record not being such as to bring it properly before him ; but he said that if the timber bore a very considerable proportion to the value of the whole purchase, the tenant for life, who was one of the trustees, could not be permitted to cut it (i).

23. A tenant for life in remainder without impeachment of waste, may not commit waste before his own estate has fallen into possession by leave of a tenant for life in possession who is impeachable for waste (k). So also the court will interfere if the tenant for life and the remainder-man in fee, subject to contingent estates, are committing waste in collusion (l), or where waste is being committed by a tenant for life in possession, who has the next vested estate of inheritance in remainder, but subject to intermediate contingent estates (m).

(g) 1 Bro. C. C. 159.
(h) 16 Ves. 174.
(i) See Craig on Trees, 60–72.
(k) Lady Evelyn's case, cited 2 Freem. 55, 2 Sw. 172, & Dick. 209 ; Fleming v. Bishop of Carlisle, cited Dick. 209 ; comp. Davies v. Davies, 2 Ir. Eq. 415.

(l) Garth v. Cotton, 1 Dick. 183, 1 Ves. 524, 548, 3 Atk. 751 ; 6 Birch–Wolfe v. Birch, 9 L. R. Eq. 683.
(m) Williams v. Duke of Bolton, 1 Cox, 72. But see Aspinwall v. Leigh, 2 Vern. 218 ; Claxton v. Claxton, 2 Vern. 152.

SECTION V. — INTEREST AND PROPERTY IN SEVERED TIMBER,
ETC., ETC. — ACCOUNT.

1 & 2. Practice where timber is cut under order of the court.
3. Disposition to be made of the fund.
4. When an infant tenant in tail is in possession.
5. Jurisdiction of court on this general subject extended by statute.
6. Timber on glebe land ordered to be cut.
7. When court will order ornamental timber to be cut.
8. Who has property in severed timber.
9. Party to a wrongful cutting cannot derive any benefit from his wrongful act.
10. Disposition of timber cut from lunatic's estate.
11 & 12. Rule as to property in severed timber does not apply to old trees.
13 & 14. Same rule applies in cases of equitable waste as in legal waste.
15. Property in severed minerals vests in a manner similar to that of severed trees.
16. Other cases where same rule applies.
17. When injunction will lie to restrain future waste, account will be ordered.
18. Account always granted in cases of mines and collieries.
19. Pleading in cases to stay waste by incumbent of living, or by bishop.
20. Account between tenants in common.
21. Account limited to moneys actually received.
22. If a case for account be made out, the law will not inquire whether or not the act
    complained of was a sound exercise of discretion.
23. Remainder-man for life cannot have account.
24 & 25. Statute of Limitations.
26 & 27. Practice in cases of delay as to bringing suits to a hearing.

1. If there is any timber on the estate which is overripe or
in a state of decay, or which ought for any other reason to be
cut down, the court of chancery will, on the application
either of the tenant for life or the remainder-man, order it to
be cut down and sold, imposing at the same time such terms
with respect to the fund produced by the sale as are equitable
and proper (*n*).

2. * If the application is made by a remainder-man,   * 278
care will be taken that the tenant for life is not prejudiced by the taking of trees which are necessary for repairs (*o*).
The principle on which the court acts in cases of the sort,
being not the personal benefit of the parties, but the benefit of
the inheritance, the court will not order generally that those

(*n*) Bewick *v.* Whitfield, 3 P. W.   Ha. 457; Ferrand *v.* Wilson, 4 Ha.
268; Ormonde *v.* Kynnersley, 7 L. J. 382.
Ch. 155; Butler *v.* Kynnersley, 8 L. J.   (*o*) Bewick *v.* Whitfield, 3 P. W. 268.
Ch. 72; Tollemache *v.* Tollemache, 1

trees be cut down, which a provident owner might think fit
and proper to be cut down in a due course of management,
but will only order those trees to be cut down which are running to decay, or which it is beneficial should be cut down by
reason of being injurious to the other trees (*p*).

3. The fund arising from the sale of timber felled under the
order of the court will be ordered to be laid out either in the
purchase of lands, to be settled according to the uses to which
the estate is limited (*q*), or in other ways which may be beneficial to the estate (*r*), or will be ordered to remain in court,
or to be invested in consols. In an early case, Bewick *v.*
Whitfield (*s*), the court would not allow the tenant for life to
take any share in the interest of the fund (*t*); but it is now
the settled rule to allow the tenant for life to take the interest
of the proceeds for his life (*u*). In like manner a dowress
would receive one-third of the income (*v*). The fund
*279 itself produced * by the sale vests absolutely either in a
tenant for life without impeachment of waste, or in the
owner of the inheritance, whether in fee or in tail, whichever
estate comes first into possession after the death of the tenant
for life (*x*), and will, as between the claims of his real and
personal representatives, be considered in the nature of real
estate, unless something has been done in the mean time to
convert it into personalty (*y*).

(*p*) Hussey *v.* Hussey, 5 Madd. 44;
Tooker *v.* Annesley, 5 Sim. 237; Tollemache *v.* Tollemache, 1 Ha. 456; Ferrand *v.* Wilson, 4 Ha. 344. See, as to
the form of the order, Tooker *v.* Annesley, 5 Sim. 237; Consett *v.* Bell, 1 Y.
& C. C. C. 573; Tollemache *v.* Tollemache, 1 Ha. 456; Gent *v.* Harrison,
John. 523. See, when the tenant for
life is an infant, Consett *v.* Bell, 1 Y. &
C. C. C. 569.

(*q*) Mildmay *v.* Mildmay, 4 Bro. C. C.
76; Delapole *v.* Delapole, 17 Ves. 150;
Wickham *v.* Wickham, 19 Ves. 423.
See Powlett *v.* Duchess of Bolton, 3
Ves. 374.

(*r*) Osborne *v.* Osborne, cited 19 Ves.
422.

(*s*) 3 P. W. 268.
(*t*) But see Tooker *v.* Annesley, 5
Sim. 237; see also Osborne *v.* Osborne,
cited 19 Ves. 422.

(*u*) Tooker *v.* Annesley, 5 Sim. 237;
Waldo *v.* Waldo, 7 Sim. 262; Tollemache *v.* Tollemache, 1 Ha. 456; Ferrand *v.* Wilson, 4 Ha. 381; Gent *v.*
Harrison, John. 523; Field *v.* Brown,
27 Beav. 90. See Williams *v.* Duke of
Bolton, 1 Cox, 72; Bagot *v.* Bagot,
32 Beav. 509; Dyer *v.* Dyer, 34 Beav.
504.

(*v*) Dickin *v.* Hamer, 1 Dr. & S. 284;
Bishop *v.* Bishop, 10 L. J. Ch. N. S.
302.

(*x*) Tooker *v.* Annesley, 5 Sim. 237;
Waldo *v.* Waldo, 12 Sim. 107; Philipps
v. Barlow, 14 Sim. 263; Gent *v.* Harrison, John. 523; Field *v.* Brown, 27
Beav. 92.

(*y*) Field *v.* Brown, 27 Beav. 92.
See Tullitt *v.* Tullitt, Amb. 370; Dyer
v. Dyer, 34 Beav. 504.

4. Where there is an infant tenant in tail in possession, the court will authorize the cutting of all timber which is fit and proper to be felled in a due course of management of the property (z), and the produce arising from the sale will be considered as personal estate (a). If the infant has the fee, the produce arising from the sale of timber ordered by the court to be cut, seems to be real estate (b).

5. The jurisdiction of the court to direct the fall and sale of timber on settled estates, has been extended by the settled estates act (c). The court has been empowered by that act to authorize a sale of the whole or any part of the timber (except ornamental timber) growing on any settled estates. The manner of dealing with the purchase-moneys as presented in sec. 23 does not seem to be entirely in accordance with the rules previously existing.

6. The court, it has been said, will have no difficulty on a proper application in directing timber on glebe land to be cut down, and the produce applied for the benefit of the living (d).

7. The court will also order ornamental timber, or timber which forms a shelter or defence to a mansion-house, to be felled, where it is decaying or injurious to adjoining trees (e), or where it is necessary for the well-being, salubrity, and comfort of the * mansion-house that it should be * 280 cut, or where any other good reason can be shown why it should be cut (f). The property in ornamental timber cut under the authority of the court vests, it would appear, as well in equity as at law, in the tenant for life without impeachment of waste, as soon as it has been cut.

8. Timber which has been severed accidentally, as by a tempest (g), or has been wrongfully cut down by a trespasser, or

(z) Hussey v. Hussey, 5 Madd. 44.
(a) Tullitt v. Tullitt, Amb. 370, 1 Dick. 322.
(b) Tullitt v. Tullitt, Amb. 370. But see Dyer v. Dyer, 34 Beav. 504, comp. Ex parte Bromfield, 1 Ves. Jr. 462; Oxenden v. Lord Compton, 2 Ves. Jr. 69, 261. See also Ex parte Philipps, 19 Ves. 120.
(c) 19 & 20 Vict. c. 120, s. 11.
(d) Duke of Marlborough v. St. John, 5 De G. & S. 179.

(e) Lushington v. Boldero, 6 Madd.149.
(f) Campbell v. Allgood, 17 Beav. 637; Att.-Gen. v. Duke of Marlborough, 5 Madd. 280; Ormonde v. Kynnersley, 7 L. J. Ch. 155; Butler v. Kynnersley, 8 L. J. Ch. 67.
(g) Whitfield v. Bewit, 2 P. W. 241; Duke of Newcastle v. Vane, cited ib.; Bewick v. Whitfield, 3 P. W. 267, per Lord Talbot; Garth v. Cotton, 1 Ves. 524, 546, 1 Dick. 183, 3 Atk. 751; Lee v. Alston, 1 Bro. C. C. 196.

by a tenant for life or years, impeachable of waste, belongs to him who has, at the time of severance, the first estate of inheritance in *esse* whether in fee or tail (*h*), who may bring trover for it, notwithstanding the existence of intermediate estates and contingent remainders in tail that may afterwards arise and defeat his estate (*i*): but the owner of the inheritance may so adopt the acts of the person committing waste, as to prevent his obtaining the relief he would otherwise be entitled to (*k*). Lord Romilly, M. R., has in two or three cases held that the property in timber which has been severed either by accident, or by the act of a wrong-doer upon an estate in settlement, follows the uses of the settlement, the interest of the fund produced by the sale of the timber to be taken by the successive tenants for life (except the wrong-doer), and the fund itself, by the person who may happen to be owner * 281 of the inheritance at * the death of the last tenant for life (*l*). But the opinion of his lordship does not seem to be in accordance with the earlier authorities (*m*).

9. A man who has wrongfully cut timber, or been in any way party to the wrong, cannot derive any benefit from his wrongful act (*n*). Thus, where timber had been cut down under a collusive agreement between the tenant for life and the remainder-man in fee before the contingent estates came into *esse*, the latter was ordered to refund his share of the moneys produced by the sale of ˎthe timber (*o*). So, also,

---

(*h*) 4 Co. Rep. 62 a.; 5 Co. Rep. 76 b.; 11 Co. Rep. 46; Lewis Bowle's case, 11 Co. Rep. 79, 3 Lev. 209; Berry *v.* Heard, Cro. Car. 242; Udal *v.* Udal, Ab. 81; Whitfield *v.* Bewit, 2 P. W. 240; Lee *v.* Alston, 1 Bro. C. C. 194, 3 Bro. C. C. 37, 1 Ves. Jr 78; Williams *v.* Duke of Bolton, 3 P. W. 268 n.; Powlett *v.* Duchess of Bolton, 3 Ves. 374; Dare *v.* Hopkins, 2 Cox, 110; Pigot *v.* Bullock, 1 Ves. Jr. 479. See Bell *v.* Wilson, 1 L. R. Ch. Ap. 303. See Gent *v.* Harrison, John. 517, as to the relative rights of the heir and remainder-man for life without impeachment of waste in respect of timber wrongfully cut by a previous tenant for life. See also Rolt *v.* Lord Somerville, 2 Eq. Ca. Ab. 759.

(*i*) Lee *v.* Alston, 1 Bro. C. C. 37;

Dare *v.* Hopkins, 2 Cox, 110; Gent *v.* Harrison, John. 517.

(*k*) Gresley *v.* Monsley, 3 D. F. & J. 433.

(*l*) Bateman *v.* Hotchkin, 31 Beav. 486; Bagot *v.* Bagot, 32 Beav. 509. See Lushington *v.* Boldero, 15 Beav. 1.

(*m*) See also *Ex parte* Bromfield, 1 Ves. Jr. 459; Oxenden *v.* Lord Compton, 2 Ves. Jr. 264; Bell *v.* Wilson, 1 L. R. Ch. Ap. 303.

(*n*) Tooker *v.* Annesley, 5 Sim. 240. See Lushington *v.* Boldero, 15 Beav. 1; Bateman *v.* Hotchkin, 31 Beav. 486; Bagot *v.* Bagot, 32 Beav. 509.

(*o*) Garth *v.* Cotton, 1 Ves. 524, 546, 3 Atk. 751, 1 Dick. 183. See Stansfield *v.* Habergham, 10 Ves. 279; Lushington *v.* Boldero, 15 Beav. 1.

where a tenant for life of a settled estate with contingent remainders in tail, with remainder to himself in fee, wrongfully cut timber, while the contingent estates were in expectancy, he was not permitted to take any benefit from the produce of the sale of the timber (*p*). The rule that a man who has wrongfully cut timber cannot take any benefit from his wrongful act, applies also in the case of an unsettled estate. In Tullitt *v.* Tullitt (*q*), an infant being tenant in fee, his guardian, who was his mother, cut down trees as upon the part of the infant. The heir of the infant brought his bill to have the money which arose from the timber secured; and the court held that no benefit whatever should result to a person who might become the sole next of kin of the infant, but that the money should be reserved for the benefit of the inheritance (*r*).

10. The committee of a lunatic's estate in fee-simple may, it would appear, cut down timber fit and proper to be felled in a due course of management, and may after the death of the lunatic claim the proceeds as part of his personal estate, unless there is reason to believe that he has abused his trust, as * guardian, with the view of changing the quality of   * 282 the estate for his own interest (*s*). As between the heir and personal representatives of a lunatic, the proceeds of timber which have been cut upon an estate in fee-simple belonging to him are personal assets (*t*).

11. The rule with respect to property in severed timber does not apply to dotards or old trees, which have no timber in them, and which are either blown down, or felled by the tenant. They are the property of the tenant (*u*). So, also, are the proper and regular thinnings of trees in a wood, and the trimmings of hedges, the property of the tenant for life (*v*).

(*p*) Williams *v.* Duke of Bolton, 3 P. W. 268, 1 Cox, 72; Powlett *v.* Duchess of Bolton, 3 Ves. 374. See Dare *v.* Hopkins, 2 Cox, 112.

(*q*) Amb. 371.

(*r*) See Tooker *v.* Annesley, 5 Sim. 240; Craig on Trees, 110.

(*s*) *Ex parte* Bromfield, 1 Ves. Jr. 453; Oxenden *v.* Lord Compton, 2 Ves. Jr. 69, 261; Craig on Trees, 112; *Ex parte* Philipps, 19 Ves. 118. See also

ib. as to the distinction between the estates of lunatics and infants.

(*t*) *Ex parte* Bromfield, 1 Ves. Jr. 453; Oxenden *v.* Lord Compton, 2 Ves. Jr. 69, 261.

(*u*) Herlakenden's case, 4 Co. Rep. 63 b.; Countess of Cumberland's case, Moor. 812; Channon *v.* Patch, 5 B. & C. 897.

(*v*) Berriman *v.* Peacock, 9 Bing. 384; Pidgeley *v.* Rawling, 2 Coll. 275; Gordon *v.* Woodford 27 Beav. 603;

12. Where timber trees on copyhold lands are separated from the soil by whatever act or casualty in the absence of a special custom, the tenant's possessory right ends, and the landlord may take them. But as to pollards, dotards, bushes, &c., the law is otherwise; and if thrown down, they belong to the tenant (x).

13. The same principles with respect to property in severed timber which apply in cases of legal waste, are also generally applicable in cases of equitable waste. A tenant for life without impeachment of waste, who commits equitable waste by cutting ornamental timber, cannot be allowed to take any benefit from his wrongful act (y); but it would appear that if the timber cut by him is such as the court would upon a proper application have directed to be cut as for the benefit of the estate, the court may, at its discretion, allow the interest arising from the fund produced by the sale to be paid to the tenant for life (z). Whether the property in the timber, or the

* 283 fund *arising from the sale of the timber, belongs to the first owner of the inheritance, or follows the uses of the settlement, is a question which is not free from doubt. In Ormond v. Kynnersley (a); and Butler v. Kynnersley (b), Lord Lyndhurst was of opinion that no distinction could be made between legal and equitable waste in respect of the property in severed timber, and that the owner of the first vested estate of inheritance, who was not a wrong-doer, was entitled to it, as well in the one case as the other, notwithstanding the intervention of intermediate estates and contingent estates tail (c). But in three subsequent cases, — Wellesley v. Wellesley (d), Lushington v. Boldero (e), Duke of Leeds v. Amherst (f), — in none of which Butler v. Kynnersley appears to have been cited, it was assumed that the produce of ornamental timber, wrongfully cut, follows the uses of the settlement (g).

Bateman v. Hotchkin, 31 Beav. 486; Bagot v. Bagot, 32 Beav. 509; Earl Cowley v. Wellesley, 1 L. R. Eq. 656; comp. Craig on Trees, 59.
(x) Scriv. in Cop. 422, n. g.
(y) Wellesley v. Wellesley, 6 Sim. 497; Lushington v. Boldero, 15 Beav. 1.
(z) Bagot v. Bagot, 32 Beav. 509.
(a) 7 L. J. Ch. 155.
(b) 8 L. J. Ch. 71.

(c) See Rolt v. Somerville, 2 Eq. Ca. Ab. 759.
(d) 6 Sim. 497.
(e) 15 Beav. 1.
(f) 2 Ph. 120.
(g) See note to Lushington v. Boldero, 15 Beav. 9, 10; see, also, Bagot v. Bagot, 32 Beav. 509; Craig on Trees, 134.

14. In one case (*h*), an injunction was granted to restrain a person who had committed waste by cutting down timber, from carrying the timber away; but this cannot be considered sound law, though, perhaps, in a very exceptional case, an injunction might be granted on the ground of irreparable mischief. An injunction might, however, it appears, be granted to restrain the carrying away of timber standing at the time of process served (*i*).

15. The property in minerals severed from the inheritance vests in a manner similar to that of severed trees. The owner of the inheritance is entitled to the proceeds as against persons having estates in remainder prior to the ultimate limitation in fee vested in him (*j*). If a tenant for life impeachable of waste commits waste by opening mines, the minerals belong to the remainder-man in fee; but the latter may, by adopting the acts of the tenant for life, preclude himself from enforc-· ing his * rights (*k*). A tenant for life without impeach- * 284 ment of waste has of course a right to open new mines and to take the minerals for his own use (*l*).

16. Considerations of a similar nature apply in other cases of waste. Where, for instance, deer in a park have been reclaimed by a tenant for life, the property in the deer so reclaimed passes to the person entitled to the first estate of inheritance in remainder (*m*).

17. In all cases in which a bill for an injunction will lie to restrain future waste, a court of equity will, upon the principle of preventing a multiplicity of suits, give an account of past waste (*n*), but where from the determination of the estate of the wrong-doer, or some other reason, there is nothing on which the injunction can operate, and complete relief can be had in an action at law, a bill for an account will not, as a general rule, lie (*o*). But if the waste is of such a nature

(*h*) Anon., 1 Ves. Jr. 92.
(*i*) Watson *v.* Hunter, 5 Johns. Ch. (Amer.) 168.
(*j*) Bell *v.* Wilson, 1 L. R. Ch. Ap. 303.
(*k*) Gresley *v.* Monsley, 3 D. F. & J. 433. See Bagot *v.* Bagot, 32 Beav. 509.
(*l*) Countess of Plymouth *v.* Lady Archer, 1 Bro. C. C. 159.
(*m*) Ford *v.* Tynte, 2 J. & H. 150.

(*n*) Jesus College *v.* Bloom, 3 Atk. 263, Amb. 54; Parrott *v.* Palmer, 3 M. & K. 632.
(*o*) Jesus College *v.* Bloom, 3 Atk. 263, Amb. 54; Smith *v.* Cooke, 3 Atk. 381; Pulteney *v.* Warren, 6 Ves. 89; Grierson *v.* Eyre, 9 Ves. 346; Parrott *v.* Palmer, 3 M. & K. 632; Gent *v.* Harrison, John. 517. See Bailey *v.* Taylor, 1 R. & M. 73.

that there is no remedy at law, and a wrong will be sustained if equity does not interfere, a bill for an account will lie, although an injunction may not be competent. Thus, in Garth v. Cotton (*p*), a decree for an account of timber was made against the assets of a remainder-man in fee, who had colluded with the tenant for life in cutting timber before the birth of a contingent remainder-man (*q*). So, also, in cases of equitable waste, a bill for an account will lie against the assets of a deceased wrong-doer, though an injunction is not competent (*r*). So, also, a clerk after recovery in *quare impedit* is entitled to an account for waste (*s*).

* 285   18. * Mines and collieries, being a species of trade, an account of profits will in all cases be granted, without reference to the question whether or not an injunction will lie, or whether or not there is a remedy at law (*t*).

19. A bill for an injunction by the patron of a living to stay waste by an incumbent, or by the Attorney-General to stay waste by a bishop, should not pray for an account of the profits for their own benefit as patrons (*u*).

20. If one co-owner of land derives gain by committing destructive waste on the common property, he is liable to account to the other owners for their shares of the money so obtained (*x*). The tenant in common of a mine is accordingly entitled to an account of the moneys produced by working the mine (*y*). But a tenant in common in occupation of an estate is not liable to account for waste which falls short of destructive waste (*z*).

21. The account is limited to the moneys actually received and the profits actually made by the wrong-doer. There can

(*p*) 3 Atk. 751; 1 Ves. 524, 546; 1 Dick. 183.

(*q*) See Fishmongers' Co. v. Beresford, Beat. 607; Parrott v. Palmer, 3 M. & K. 632; Johnstone v. Hall, 2 K. & J. 422.

(*r*) Marquis of Lansdowne v. Marchioness of Lansdowne, 1 Madd. 116; Duke of Leeds v. Lord Amherst, 2 Ph. 117; Morris v. Morris, 3 D. & J. 323; Blake v. Peters, 1 D. J. & S. 345.

(*s*) Crampton v. Bishop of Meath, Sa. & Sc. 297.

(*t*) Bishop of Winchester v. Knight, 1 P. W. 406; Story v. Lord Windsor,

2 Atk. 630; Jesus College v. Bloom, 3 Atk. 263, Amb. 54; Pulteney v. Warren, 6 Ves. 89; Thomas v. Oakley, 18 Ves. 184; Jefferys v. Smith, 1 J. & W. 298; Parrott v. Palmer, 3 M. & K. 642.

(*u*) Knight v. Moseley, Amb. 176.

(*x*) Co. Litt. 200 b.; Martyn v. Knowlys, 8 T. R. 145. See Twort v. Twort, 16 Ves. 128.

(*y*) See Bentley v. Bates, 4 Y. & C. 182. See, also, Clegg v. Clegg, 3 Giff. 322.

(*z*) Griffies v. Griffies, 8 L. T. N. S. 758, 11 W. R. 943.

be no account in respect of acts unattended by profit (*a*). When, accordingly, equitable waste had been committed by a tenant for life without impeachment of waste in pulling down a mansion-house and building a new house with the materials of the old one on another part of the estate, but it did not appear that any profit had been derived from the sale of the materials, the court held that an account could not be had against the assets of the deceased tenant for life. The case would have been otherwise, if he had sold the materials and received the profits (*b*).

22. If a case for account be made out, the court cannot inquire, * whether the act complained of was or was   * 286 not a sound exercise of discretion with reference to the state of the property and to the interests of the family to which it belongs (*c*).

23. A mesne remainder-man for life, although entitled to an injunction to protect his enjoyment, has no interest to call for an account (*d*).

24. The statutory rule which gives a man twenty years from the time when his title accrues in possession for bringing a suit, applies to a claim for equitable waste, as well as to a claim for the land itself (*e*) ; but, if there has been acquiescence, relief will not be given, although the statutory period may not have run (*f*).

25. In the case of legal waste, the account in equity is confined within the same limits as the remedy at law (*g*). But if accounts have been rendered within six years before the filing of the bill of acts of waste committed during a period ending more than six years before the filing of the bill, the case is taken out of the statute of limitations (*h*). If a tenant for life impeachable of waste cuts timber and converts the produce

---

(*a*) Lee *v.* Alston, 1 Ves. Jr. 78, 1 Bro. C. C. 194, 3 Bro. C. C. 37 ; Colburn *v.* Simms, 2 Ha. 560 ; Powell *v.* Aikin, 4 K. & J. 343, 351 ; *supra*, p. 228.

(*b*) Morris *v.* Morris, 3 D. & J. 323.

(*c*) Duke of Leeds *v.* Lord Amherst, 2 Ph. 117.

(*d*) Pigot *v.* Bullock, 1 Ves. Jr. 479, 3 Bro. C. C. 538. See Gent *v.* Harrison, John. 524.

(*e*) Duke of Leeds *v.* Lord Amherst, 2 Ph. 117.

(*f*) Harcourt *v.* White, 28 Beav. 306. See Fishmongers' Co. *v.* Beresford, Beat. 613.

(*g*) *Supra*, p. 228.

(*h*) Hony *v.* Hony, 1 Sim. & St. 568. See, as to interest on produce of waste, Newdigate *v.* Newdigate, 1 Jur. 636.

to his own use, the statute of limitations begins to run against the remainder-man from the time of cutting, and not from the death of the tenant for life (*i*).

26. If there has been long delay in instituting the suit, the court will usually endeavor to deal liberally with the estate of the deceased tenant for life, inasmuch as, in many cases, it would not be for the benefit of the parties concerned to go into a long and expensive inquiry on the subject (*k*).

27. Suits for an injunction to stay waste should not be brought to a hearing when no account is sought, or the account is waived, and the defendant does not dispute the right of the plaintiff to have the injunction continued, or offers to submit to the injunction with costs (*l*).

(*i*) Seagram *v.* Knight, 3 L. R. Eq. 398.

(*k*) Bagot *v.* Bagot, 32 Beav. 509, 519. But see Duke of Leeds *v.* Lord Amherst, 20 Beav. 239. See, also, Bagot *v.* Bagot, 32 Beav. 509, 521, 522, as to accounts and inquiries in a case of waste, both in timber and mines, presenting a great complication of circumstances. See, also, Tooker *v.* Annesley, 5 Sim. 235, for the form of inquiry as to timber.

(*l*) Harvey *v.* Ferguson, 15 Ir. Ch. 277; Dunsany *v.* Dunne, *ib.* 279; *supra*, p. 228.

* CHAPTER XVII. * 287

INJUNCTIONS AGAINST TRESPASS.

1. THE jurisdiction of a court of equity to grant injunctions against trespass is comparatively of modern establishment (*a*). The court for a long time confined relief in equity to waste, founding its interference on the privity of title between the parties (*b*). The rigor of the old rule in confining relief in equity to waste, was relaxed for the first time by Lord Thurlow in a case where, the party complaining being in possession of a close, a wrong-doer was working into his minerals, and taking away the very substance of his estate (*c*). In relaxing the rule, Lord Thurlow acted with reluctance, and was influenced

---

(*a*) 3 Ra. Ca. 355.
(*b*) Davenport *v.* Davenport, 7 Ha. 217; Lowndes *v.* Bettle, 33 L. J. Ch. 451.

(*c*) Flamang's case, cit. 6 Ves. 147, 7 Ves. 308, 8 Ves. 90, 18 Ves. 186.

solely by the irreparable and destructive injury which would have followed the refusal (d). The principle established by Lord Thurlow in Flamang's case was approved by Lord Eldon, and followed by him in some cases; but the law on the subject was left by him in an unsatisfactory state. Succeeding judges have, on more than one occasion, pointed this out, and have felt much difficulty in finding the principle upon which to act in each case as it arose.[1]

2. The state of the law, and the various authorities, were reviewed with much care by Kindersley, V. C., in Lowndes $v.$ Bettle (e). "The proper mode," he said, "is to classify the cases under two heads: the one, where the party against whom the application for the injunction is made is in possession; and the other, where the plaintiff is in possession, and is asking the court to protect his estate. With respect to the cases where the defendant is in possession, the earliest is Hamilton $v.$ Worsefold, before Lord Thurlow, which is to be found in a note of Sir S. Romilly (f). That was a

* 288   case * in which it could hardly be considered that either party was actually in possession: perhaps the defendant was, but the plaintiff never recovered rent; and Lord Thur-

---

(d) 18 Ves. 186; 4 K. & J. 122.
(e) 33 L. J. Ch. 451.
(f) 10 Ves. 290, n.
[1] The interference of the court of equity by injunction in a case of trespass to land, and where an action at law will lie, is of modern origin, and the exercise of power to be justified only in a case of great and irreparable injury; and the petitioner should show at least a strong *primâ facie* case of a *right*. Falls Village Water Power Co. $v.$ Tibbetts, 31 Conn. 165. In Webber $v.$ Gage, 39 N. H. 186, it is said that where the injury is irreparable, not susceptible of being adequately compensated by damages, or such as, from its continuance or permanent mischief, must occasion a constantly recurring grievance, which cannot be otherwise prevented, as where loss of health, loss of trade or business, destruction of the means of subsistence, or permanent ruin to property, may or will ensue from the wrongful acts; in such case a court of equity will interfere by injunction in furtherance of justice and

the violated rights of the party. So where an easement or servitude is annexed by grant, or covenant, or otherwise to a private estate, the due and quiet enjoyment of it will be protected against encroachment by injunction. An application to restrain the commission of a trespass is addressed to the sound discretion of a court, and the irresponsibility of the defendant is one element to be weighed, and often of much importance, but by no means decisive. Morgan $v.$ Palmer, 48 N. H. 338.

Where property was bequeathed to the separate use of a *feme covert*, without any trustee being appointed by the will, and the property was about to be sold under an execution against the husband for his debt, it was held, that the legal estate being in the husband, and therefore there being no one to sue for the trespass, the court would interfere to protect the property by injunction. Smith $v.$ Bank of Wadesborough, 4 Jones, Eq. 303.

low, after some hesitation, granted an injunction, restraining not only the defendant, but the tenants from committing waste. Not much reliance can be placed upon that case, because there may have been collusion between the defendant and the tenants, and it may be that the defendant was not in possession. Lord Thurlow at first considered it as a trespass, but ultimately did restrain the defendant and the tenants (g). The next case was Pillsworth v. Hopton (h), in the year 1801. There the defendant being in possession, the plaintiff claimed under an adverse title, and Lord Eldon refused the injunction. The next case is Crockford v. Alexander (i), in 1808, a case of vendor and purchaser, a peculiar case, and hardly in point. The plaintiff had contracted to sell an estate to the defendant, who obtained possession and began to cut timber. It is difficult, therefore, to say that there might not have been privity. Jones v. Jones (k) was before Sir W. Grant. In that case a demurrer was filed by the defendant to a bill by an heir at law, seeking discovery and relief, including an injunction to stay waste and destruction pending litigation; Sir W. Grant allowed the demurrer. In that case it was held that an heir at law out of possession could not have an injunction against a devisee in possession. Sir W. Grant says, 'I cannot see a very good reason why the court, which interferes for the protection of property pending a suit in the ecclesiastical court, should not interfere to preserve real property pending a suit concerning the validity of the devise.' The next case is Haigh v. Jaggar (l). There there was a house and land, with coal under it. It did not appear that the plaintiffs were working, but the defendants were working out of their own mines into those of the plaintiffs. The latter parties brought two actions, and Knight Bruce, L. J., refused the injunction, expressing dissatisfaction with the state of the law. The next case is Davenport v. Davenport (m), in 1849, before Wigram, V. C. There, the defendant having been in possession *for nineteen years, the plaintiff, with a recently dis-   * 289 covered title, sought an injunction to restrain him from

(g) Reg. Book A., 1786, fol. 1.
(h) 6 Ves. 51.
(i) 15 Ves. 138.

(k) 3 Mer. 161.
(l) 2 Coll. 231.
(m) 7 Ha. 217.

cutting down ornamental timber; the Vice-Chancellor expressed his surprise at the state of the law, and said he was
compelled to allow the demurrer. The next case is Talbot *v.*
Hope (*n*). The court there stated how much more reluctant
it is to entertain a suit against a person in possession than
where he is not. The question which party is in possession is
therefore of great importance, and ought to be made the foundation of the distribution of the cases. In Neale *v.* Cripps (*o*),
an injunction was granted to restrain stripping timber off an
estate, on the ground that the acts done by the defendant
tended to the destruction of the estate. Sir A. Hart acted on
the same principle in Lord Fingal *v.* Blake (*p*) and Lloyd *v.*
Trimleston (*q*). The result of these cases is that where the
plaintiff is out of possession, the court will refuse to interfere
by granting an injunction, unless there be fraud or collusion,
or unless the acts perpetrated or threatened are so injurious as
to tend to the destruction of the estate (*r*)." He must also,
it would appear, be able to satisfy the court that there is an
action pending at law between him and the defendant in possession, which will try the right as between them (*s*).

3. "The cases where the plaintiff is in possession," said
Kindersley, V. C., in Lowndes *v.* Bettle (*t*), "may be divided
under two subordinate heads : first, where the defendant
claims under color of right ; and, secondly, where he is an
absolute stranger. Taking the second of these classes, we
have the case of Mogg *v.* Mogg (*u*), before Lord Thurlow, in
1786. There the injunction was refused on the ground that
the defendant was a mere trespasser, and an action would lie.
In Mortimer *v.* Cottrell (*v*), in 1789, where the defendant had
received from the plaintiff permission to dig to a certain depth,
but went beyond it, the injunction was refused, because
* 290   it was a * case of trespass, and the defendant might at
law have been turned out of possession immediately.

(*n*) 4 K. & J. 108.
(*o*) *Ib.* 472.
(*p*) 2 Moll. 50, 542.
(*q*) *Ib.* 81 ; see also Anwyl *v.* Owens,
22 L. J. Ch. 995.
(*r*) See Lancashire *v.* Lancashire, 9
Beav. 120.

(*s*) Talbot *v.* Hope, Scott, 4 K. & J.
96, 135, *per* Wood, V. C. See Vice *v.*
Thomas, 2 Coop. C. C. 122 ; Neale *v.*
Cripps, 4 K. & J. 472.
(*t*) 33 L. J. Ch. 451.
(*u*) 2 Dick. 670.
(*v*) 2 Cox, 205.

Mitchell v. Dors (x) was a case of coal-mines in work; there it was held to be trespass and not waste, and yet an injunction was granted, because, being coal-mines, the mischief was considered irreparable. I confess I cannot see why the mischief done in the case of coals is more irreparable mischief than in that of trees, for in both cases the injury, whether great or small, may be the subject of money compensation. Courthope v. Maplesden (y) was a case relating to timber, where the injunction was granted, the fact being that a stranger was colluding with the tenant. In Cowper v. Baker (z), a party was restrained from taking argillaceous stones under the sea. The case was also one of a stranger. In it the mischief was considered to be irreparable. The plaintiff was lord of the manor in possession, and his rights extended out beyond low-water mark. Lumps of argillaceous matter of great value were found within its limits. Great profit was derived from the sale of the article, and Lord Eldon considered the damage there done to the plaintiff to be irreparable, not because it was a destruction *simpliciter*, but because it was a taking away of the substance of the inheritance."

4. The other class into which Kindersley, V. C., subdivided the second head is where the trespass is under color of right. The meaning of the phrase under color of right or title has been thus explained by Wigram, V. C., in Davenport v. Davenport (a): "The party complaining has been in possession of property, and has complained that his possession was wrongfully invaded by some alleged trespasser. The alleged trespasser, on the other hand, has not admitted the possession of the plaintiff, nor claimed a right to invade such possession as he had, nor intended to do so, as in the case of underground workings of adjoining mines; and the court has distinguished these cases from ordinary cases of trespass, by saying the alleged wrong-doer claimed under color of title. The cases of railway companies taking lands under the compulsory powers given them by Parliament are of the same class. Neither party disputes the abstract right of * the other   * 291 to that which he claims. The dispute is as to the prac-

(x) 6 Ves. 147.   (z) 17 Ves. 128.
(y) 10 Ves. 289.   (a) 7 Ha. 217.

tical application of the law to the facts of the case. It has always appeared to me that the court was trying to get out of a technical rule with a view to the better protection of the property " (b). The first case in which the court interfered upon the ground of color of right, was, said Kindersley, V. C. (c), "a case before Lord Camden, not reported originally, but cited in Mogg v. Mogg (d). No name is there given to it, but it was a case where persons were cutting down timber under color of right to estovers. The plaintiff, who was lord of the manor, probably alleged the cutting to be beyond what was wanted for estovers. At all events, the injunction seems to have been granted. Lord Thurlow, however, said that the case did not apply to Mogg v. Mogg, for in that case there appeared to be a right to something in the defendants, though perhaps they carried it beyond what such right went to, and that, until such right was determined, it was very proper to stay them from doing an act which, if it turned out that they had no right to do, would be irreparable. But in Mogg v. Mogg the defendant had no interest; he was a mere trespasser. In the case of Robinson v. Lord Byron (e), the plaintiff was in possession of his own water-mill. The defendant was the owner of the water above the mill, and in order to vex the plaintiff sometimes kept back the water from the mill, and sometimes deluged it with water. In that case it was difficult to say which was in possession, but Lord Byron was restrained from so using the stream as to do mischief to the plaintiff's mills. In Smith v. Collyer (f), the injunction was refused by Lord Eldon because it was a case of trespass. There infants were in possession by their guardians, and defendant claimed as heir. Knight Bruce, L. J., in Haigh v. Jaggar (g), hesitated to say that Lord Eldon was wrong in Smith v. Collyer, but he was not satisfied that in the same circumstances the court would not now grant an injunction, and he referred to the change which had taken place in * 292 the law on the subject.   * Grey v. Duke of Northum-

(b) See Hattersley v. East Lancashire Railway Co., 8 Ha. 88; North Union Railway Co. v. Bolton and Preston Railway Co., 3 Ra. Ca. 345.
(c) 33 L. J. Ch. 456.

(d) 2 Dick. 670.
(e) 1 Bro. C. C. 588.
(f) 8 Ves. 89.
(g) 2 Coll. 231.

berland (*h*) was a case of copyhold, and there an *ex parte* injûnction was granted to restrain the opening of a mine. The defendant claimed as lord of a manor, and Lord Eldon, upon the motion to dissolve, said he would do so, unless some means of producing a speedy trial of the right at law could be insured. Kinder *v.* Jones (*i*) was also the case of a lord of a manor, the subject-matter of the suit being trees. There Sir W. Grant, sitting for the Lord Chancellor, granted the injunction. The next case on this head is Thomas Oakley (*k*). The defendant there, having the right of taking stone for building and other purposes from a quarry on a certain part of the estate of the plaintiff, took stone for the like purposes on other parts of his estate. The plaintiff filed his bill for an injunction and an account. The defendant demurred, and the demurrer was overruled on the ground that the defendant was subtracting from the inheritance. In all these cases (except Smith *v.* Collyer), where the plaintiff was in possession, and the motion was made for an injunction to restrain the defendant who claimed under an adverse title, the injunction was granted.

" Where, therefore, the plaintiff is in possession, and the person doing the acts complained of is an utter stranger, not claiming under color of right, the tendency of the court is not to grant an injunction, unless there are special circumstances, but to leave the plaintiff to his remedy at law, though where the acts tend to the destruction of the estate, the court will grant it. But where the party in possession seeks to restrain one who claims by adverse title, there the tendency will be to grant the injunction, at least where the acts done either did or might tend to the destruction of the estate."

5. There are two or three other cases on the subject, which Kindersley, V. C., did not mention. But the principle upon which they proceeded is in accordance with the general principles which he deduces from a survey of the cases. In Ryder *v.* Williams (*l*), an injunction was granted to restrain a person from pulling down posts and rails which the plaintiff had

---

(*h*) 13 Ves. 236.
(*i*) 17 Ves. 110.

(*k*) 18 Ves. 184.
(*l*) 4 L. J. Ch. N. S. 55.

erected round a plantation. So also, in Clowes *v.*
* 293 Beck (*m*), a trespasser * claiming under color of title
was restrained from taking away stones and shingle
from the sea-beach, so as to expose a mansion-house to the
encroachment of the sea. So also, where a receiver appointed
by the court was in possession, a man was restrained from
trespassing under an alleged claim of right, pending the trial
of the right (*n*). So also, in Hodgson *v.* Duce (*o*), a pauper
defendant, whose real and personal estate had been vested,
under an order of the Insolvent Debtor's Court, in an assignee
in insolvency, was restrained from committing trespass against
a man who had purchased from the assignee part of the premises so vested in him, and from annoying his tenants, on the
ground that the recovery of damages at law would not be a
sufficient remedy, and that the conduct of the defendant had
been vexatious in no ordinary degree (*p*).

6. In Lowndes *v.* Bettle (*q*), the plaintiff and his ancestors
had been in possession of an estate for eighty years, and the
defendant, claiming as heir-at-law, entered upon it, and exercised acts of ownership by cutting sods and felling timber,
with the view, as he alleged, of prosecuting his claim as heir
under the direction of the court. Kindersley, V. C., considering the acts of the defendant to be against conscience, and
that irremediable damage might result to the plaintiff in the
event of his refusing to interfere, granted an interim injunction, and afterwards made the injunction perpetual.

7. If the trespass does not amount to destructive trespass,
but is a case of mere ordinary naked trespass, the court will
not interfere, the courts of ordinary jurisdiction being competent to deal with the matter (*r*). Thus, where a claimant to
property had been nonsuited in ejectment, the court refused
to restrain him from vexatiously distraining on or otherwise
molesting the tenants (*s*). So also, where the owner of house-

(*m*) 13 Beav. 347.
(*n*) Blanchard *v.* Cawthorn, 6 Sim.
155, 1 Coop. t. B. 113. See Grand
Junction Canal Co. *v.* Dimes, 2 Jur.
1077.
(*o*) 2 Jur. N. S. 1014.
(*p*) See also Att.-Gen. *v.* Hallett, 16
M. & W. 569.

(*q*) 33 L. J. Ch. 451.
(*r*) Mogg *v.* Mogg, 2 Dick. 670;
Garstin *v.* Asplin, 1 Madd. 152; Jackson *v.* Stanhope, 15 L. J. Ch. 446.
(*s*) Best *v.* Drake, 11 Ha. 369; but
see Hodgson *v.* Duce, 2 Jur. N. S.
1014.

property filed a bill for an injunction against a defendant who had been his * lessee, but had forfeited his   * 294
lease, to restrain him from distraining on the tenants, a
demurrer for want of equity was allowed (*t*).

8. Cutting turf is not such a destructive trespass as the
court will, except under very special circumstances, restrain
by injunction (*u*).

9. The jurisdiction of a court of equity in cases of trespass
is in aid of the legal right. The court interferes on the
assumption that the party who makes the application has the
right which he asserts, but needs the interference of the court
for the protection of the property from irreparable damage
pending the trial of the right. If the right at law is clear,
and the breach of that right is clear, and serious damage is
likely to arise to the plaintiff if the defendant is allowed to
proceed with what he is doing or threatens to do, or has given
notice of doing, an injunction will be granted pending the trial
of the right (*x*). If the case is, in the opinion of the court,
free from doubt, the court may interfere at once without putting the plaintiff to establish his legal right, and grant a perpetual injunction (*y*). But if the right at law is not clear, or
the breach is doubtful, and no irreparable injury can arise to
the plaintiff pending the trial of the right, the case resolves
itself into a question of comparative convenience and inconvenience, whether the defendant will be more damnified by the
injunction being granted, or the plaintiff by its being withheld (*z*). An act of trespass, not in itself amounting to
serious damage, may, from its continuance, amount in the
opinion of the court to trespass attended by irreparable
damage (*a*).   * If the act complained of consists in the   * 295

(*t*) Aldis *v.* Fraser, 15 Beav. 220.
See Hanson *v.* Gardiner, 7 Ves. 308;
Sandys *v.* Murray, 1 Ir. Eq. 29; Wrixon
v. Condran, *ib.* 381; Congleton *v.*
Mitchell, 12 Ir. Eq. 34.

(*u*) Sandys *v.* Murray, 1 Ir. Eq. 29;
Wrixon *v.* Condran, *ib.* 380. See Dean
of Ely *v.* Warren, 2 Atk. 189.

(*x*) Clowes *v.* Beck, 13 Beav. 347;
North Union Railway Co. *v.* Bolton and
Preston Railway Co., 3 Ra. Ca. 345;
Barker *v.* North Staffordshire Railway
Co., 2 De G. & Sm. 55; *supra*, p. 209.

(*y*), Gray *v.* Liverpool and Bury Railway Co., 9 Beav. 391, 4 Ra. Ca. 235;
Lowndes *v.* Bettle, 33 L. J. Ch. 451;
supra, p. 209.

(*z*) Brocklebank *v.* Whitehaven Junction Railway Co., 5 Ra. Ca. 373, 379;
Gordon *v.* Cheltenham Railway Co., 5
Beav. 229; Sparrow *v.* Oxford, Worcester, and Wolverhampton Railway Co.,
9 Ha. 436; *supra*, 209–211.

(*a*) Hopkins *v.* Caddick, 18 L. T.
236.

erection of works or buildings on the land of the plaintiff, an injunction may be had as long as the works or buildings are in an incomplete state (*b*) ; but if the works or buildings have been completed, the court will not in general interfere, but will leave the plaintiff to his remedy at law by ejectment (*c*). If, however, the conduct of the defendant had been fraudulent, vexatious, or oppressive, and the trespass is of so serious a nature that the parties cannot be placed in the position in which they were before the acts of trespass were committed, without the interference of the court, the court will interpose, even though the act complained of has been completed. Thus, in Powell *v.* Aikin (*d*), the defendants were restrained from continuing to use air-courses and roads, which had been secretly and fraudulently made by the persons through whom they claimed title, through the minerals of the plaintiff. So also, in Bowser *v.* Maclean (*e*), the lessee of minerals in a copyhold manor was restrained, at the suit of a copyholder, from surreptitiously using a tramway through the subsoil of the plaintiff's land, for the purpose of carrying along it coals dug beyond the limits of the manor.

10. The principles upon which the court acts in restraining trespass on the part of companies or bodies of functionaries incorporated by act of Parliament, and having compulsory powers to take or enter lands, differ in some respects from those upon which it acts in restraining trespass by individuals. A private person who applies for an injunction to restrain a public incorporated company or body of functionaries from entering illegally on his land, is not required to make out a case of destructive trespass or irreparable damage. The inability of private persons to contend with these powerful bodies which have often large sums of money at their disposal, and are often too prone to act in an arbitrary and oppressive manner, raises an equity for the prompt interference of the court to
* 296   keep them * within the strict limits of their statutory

(*b*) Farrow *v.* Vansittart, 1 Ra. Ca. 602.

(*c*) Deere *v.* Guest, 1 M. & C. 516. See Moreland *v.* Richardson, 22 Beav. 604 ; Carnochan *v.* Norwich and Spalding Railway Co., 26 Beav. 171 ; Doran *v.* Carroll, 11 Ir. Ch. 379 ; Perks *v.* Wycombe Railway Co., 3 Giff. 662 ; Lind *v.* Isle of Wight Ferry Co., 7 L. T. N. S. 416.

(*d*) 4 K. & J. 343.
(*e*) 2 D. F. & J. 415.

powers, and prevent them from deviating in the smallest degree from the terms prescribed by the statute which gives them authority. If they enter upon a man's land without taking the steps required by the statute, the court will at once interfere. A man has a right to say that they shall not affect his land by stirring one step out of the exact limits prescribed by the statute. The principle upon which the court interferes in such cases is not so much the nature of the trespass as the necessity of keeping them within control (*f*). It is incumbent on them to prove clearly and distinctly from the statute the existence of the power which they claim a right to exercise. If there is any doubt with regard to the extent of the power claimed by them, that doubt must undoubtedly be for the benefit of the land-owner, and should not be solved in a manner to give to the company any power that is not clearly and expressly defined in the statute (*g*). The court has not only jurisdiction to interfere to restrain a company from affecting a man's land by stirring out of the exact limits prescribed by the statute which gives them authority, but is almost bound to interfere (*h*), and will, as a matter of course, interfere, unless the damage is so slight that no injury has arisen or is likely to arise, or unless the injury, if any has arisen, is so small as to be hardly capable of being appreciated by damages (*i*), or unless the remedy by damages at law is adequate and sufficient, or is, under the circumstances of the case, the proper remedy (*k*), or unless the trespass is one merely of a temporary nature (*l*). In. a case * where a company, acting *bonâ fide*, had taken possession of prop-   * 297

(*f*) Kemp *v.* London and Brighton Railway Co., 1 Ra. Ca. 495; Bell *v.* Hull and Selby Railway Co., *ib.* 635; Frewin *v.* Lewis, 4 M. & C. 254; Webster *v.* South Eastern Railway Co., 1 Sim. N. S. 272; Tawney *v.* Lynn and Ely Railway Co., 16 L. J. Ch. 282, 4 Ra. Ca. 619; Pinchin *v.* London and Blackwall Railway Co., 5 D. M. & G. 851; Sutton *v.* Mayor, &c., of Norwich, 27 L. J. Ch. 739; Tinkler *v.* Metropolitan Board of Works, 2 D. & J. 269.

(*g*) Simpson *v.* South Staffordshire Railway Co., 34 L. J. Ch. 380, 387.

(*h*) River Dun Navigation Co. *v.*

North Midland Railway Co., 1 Ra. Ca. 154.

(*i*) Warden of Dover Harbor *v.* South Eastern Railway Co., 9 Ha. 497; Ware *v.* Regent's Canal Co., 3 D. & J. 229; Wandsworth Board of Works *v.* London and South Western Railway Co., 31 L. J. Ch. 854.

(*k*) Turner *v.* Blamire, 1 Drew. 409. 1 Drew. 1. See 8 Vict. c. 20, ss. 32–42, as to the powers given to railway companies to take temporary possession of lands abutting on the intended railway for certain purposes.

(*l*) Standish *v.* Mayor of Liverpool,

erty by mistake, and the question at issue between the company and the land-owner was only a question of value, the
court would not interfere, there being no evidence to show any
culpable negligence on the part of the company (*m*).   Lord
Romilly, M. R., thought himself justified in taking into consideration in such a case the inconvenience which the public
would be exposed to from granting the injunction (*n*).

11. In cases where the contest lies between two incorporated
companies, the same principles apply as are applicable in ordinary cases (*o*).

12. In a suit against a company to restrain trespass, leave
must be had from the court, after a winding-up order under
25 & 26 Vict. c. 89 has been obtained, to proceed with the
suit (*p*).

13. If a company is in possession under a legal title, the
court will not interfere at the suit of a person alleging an
adverse legal title to restrain the company from continuing in
possession (*q*) ; but if land has been taken by a company improperly, or if the conduct of the company has been vexatious,
unreasonable, or oppressive, the court may restrain them from
continuing in possession until a proper compensation has been
made (*r*).

14. If the act complained of affects the public interest, the
remedy is by information at the suit of the Attorney-
*298 General (*s*).   * But a private person may sue alone,
even although the act complained of may affect the
public interest, if he can make out a case of special damage or
can show that greater damage is caused to him thereby than is
caused to the Queen's subjects in general (*t*).   There may in

(*m*) Wood *v.* Charing Cross Railway
Co., 33 Beav. 290.
(*n*) *Ib.*; but see *infra*.
(*o*) North Union Railway Co. *v.* Bolton and Preston Railway Co., 3 Ra.
Ca. 345; Manchester, Sheffield, and
Lincolnshire Railway Co. *v.* Great
Northern Railway Co., 9 Ha. 284.
(*p*) Wyley *v.* Exhall Coal Mining Co.,
33 Beav. 538.
(*q*) Webster *v.* South Eastern Railway Co., 1 Sim. N. S. 272; Pell *v.*
Northampton and Banbury Junction
Railway Co., 2 L. R. Ch. Ap. 100.

(*r*) Perks *v.* Wycombe Railway Co.,
3 Giff. 662.
(*s*) Att.-Gen. *v.* Cleaver, 18 Ves. 217 ;
Att.-Gen. *v.* Forbes, 2 M. & C. 133;
Thorne *v.* Taw Vale Railway Co., 13
Beav. 10 ; Att.-Gen. *v.* Sheffield Gas
Co., 3 D. M. & G. 304; Vestry of
Bermondsey *v.* Brown, 1 L. R. Eq. 204 ;
infra, p. 334.
(*t*) Semple *v.* London and Birmingham Railway Co., 9 Sim. 209 ; *infra*, p.
334.

such cases be both an information and a bill (*u*). The Metropolis Local Management Acts do not empower the commissioners or vestries named therein to maintain the suit except as relators (*x*).

15. A man who seeks the aid of the court to restrain trespass should show due diligence in making the application. Whatever may be the original equity of his case, if a man stands looking on while moneys are being expended by another, upon the faith that no objection will be afterwards made to his enjoyment of the property upon which the expenditure has been made, he will lose his right to the interference of the court by injunction (*y*).

16. In two cases before Lord Eldon, Agar's case (*z*), and Blakemore *v.* Glamorganshire Railway Co. (*a*), his lordship considered that acts of Parliament incorporating public companies were to be viewed in the light of contracts made by the legislature on behalf of every person interested in any thing to be done under them. In the first of these cases he said, " Where persons assume to satisfy the legislature that a certain sum is sufficient for the completion of a proposed undertaking, as a canal, if the owner of the estate through which the legislature has given to the speculators a right to carry the canal, can show that the persons so authorized are unable to complete their work, and is prompt in his application for relief, grounded on that fact, equity will not permit the farther prosecution of the undertaking." It may, however, be considered as established that the * language of Lord   * 299 Eldon in Agar's case and Blakemore's case is somewhat too extensive in its terms, and must be modified in accordance with the opinion of Alderson, B., in Lee *v.* Milner (*b*). " These acts of Parliament," said Alderson, B., " have been called parliamentary bargains made with each of

(*u*) Att.-Gen. *v.* Sheffield Gas Co., 3 D. M. & G. 304; Att.-Gen. *v.* United Kingdom Telegraph Co., 30 Beav. 287 ; *infra*, p. 335.

(*x*) Vestry of Bermondsey *v.* Brown, 1 L. R. Eq. 204; see also *supra*, p. 207, as to parties.

(*y*) Gordon *v.* Cheltenham Railway Co., 5 Beav. 229; Barker *v.* North

Staffordshire Railway Co., 5 Ra. Ca. 401; Hopkins *v.* Great Northern Railway Co., 11 L. T. 306 ; Wintle *v.* Bristol and South Wales Railway Co., 10 W. R. 210; *supra*, p. 201–205.

(*z*) Coop. 77, cit. 1 Sw. 250.

(*a*) 1 M. & K. 164.

(*b*) 2 Y. & C. 618.

the land-owners. Perhaps more correctly they ought to be treated as conditional powers given by Parliament to take the land of the different proprietors through whose estates the works are to proceed. Each land-owner, therefore, has a right to have the powers strictly and literally carried into effect as regards his own land, and has a right also to require that no variation shall be made to his prejudice in the carrying into effect the bargain between the undertakers and any one else. This I conceive to be the real view of the law by Lord Eldon in Blakemore's case (*c*). In Agar's case, one point, it was said, was that the Regent's Canal Company could not, for the sum which they had power to raise, complete their works, and if that were clearly made out, Lord Eldon said in the case before referred to that a court of equity would probably grant an injunction, and I fully accede to that proposition, in case the fact were clearly made out, and arose either out of circumstances occurring after the passing of the act, or from a failure to raise the sum contemplated by the act. For to take away any man's land where the whole work can never be performed is clearly injurious to him, and a substantial breach of the conditions on which the legislature granted the right to do it. So, again, if the *termini* were changed, and instead of proceeding to some great town or city, the canal or railway were to terminate in some obscure village, the same result would follow. But I cannot accede to the proposition that where the contract, so far as regards the land of the complaining land-owner is exactly performed, any variation made at a distant point and with the consent of the land-owner there, and producing no real injury to the complaining land-owner, ought to be the ground for an injunction in a court of equity to be
* 300   granted at his application." " In Agar's case," * said

Lord Cottenham in Salmon *v.* Randall (*d*), " I apprehend Lord Eldon must have gone upon this ground, that where acts of Parliament impose certain severe burdens upon individuals by interfering with their private rights and private property for the purpose of obtaining some great public good, if

(*c*) See Doe *v.* Bristol and Exeter   E. & B. 858; Ware *v.* Regent's Canal Railway Co., 6 M. & W. 320; York and   Co., 3 D. & J. 217. North Midland Railway Co. *v.* Reg., 1   (*d*) 3 M. & C. 439, 444.

the court sees that the undertaking cannot be completed, and therefore that the public cannot derive that benefit which was to be the equivalent for the sacrifice by the individual, the court will protect the individual from being compelled to make the sacrifice under the circumstances, and until it appears that the public will derive the proposed benefit from it. It is impossible to suppose Lord Eldon could have meant that after an act of Parliament has been passed, giving certain powers and authorizing a body of persons to carry on public works, those against whose rights such works are to be carried into effect are to come to this court and say, ' We will undertake to prove that you cannot, with the money which you have in hand, carry those works into effect,' and that therefore and immediately in that state of circumstances the court is to interfere." Lord Cottenham accordingly would not restrain commissioners appointed under a local act for the improvement of a town from taking the steps prescribed by the act for taking possession of certain land, merely because there was an allegation in the bill that they had not the means of paying for the premises, and because they had not produced satisfactory evidence to show that they had the means. So also, in Ware v. Regent's Canal Co. (e), Lord Chelmsford refused an injunction, though he admitted that the language of Lord Eldon appeared to sustain the proposition of the plaintiffs to its full extent. His lordship approved and adopted the language of Alderson, B., above cited, and added, " The words *to his prejudice*, in the judgment of Alderson, B., are emphatic, and mean not merely to his possible but to his actual prejudice " (f). Notwithstanding, therefore, the language of Lord Eldon in Agar's case and Blakemore's case, it may now be looked on as established, that a land-owner cannot maintain a suit to restrain a company from exercising their compulsory powers over his land on the ground either of the * resources of the   * 301 company being insufficient for the completion of the undertaking, or of a material variation being made or intended to be made in the construction of the works, unless he can prove to the satisfaction of the court that he will suffer actual

(e) 3 D. & J. 217.   (f) *Ib.* 225.

and material prejudice, either by the failure of the company to complete the undertaking, or by the variation, as the case may be (*g*).

17. Acts of Parliament are to be interpreted like contracts in general (*h*). The intention of the legislature must be gathered as far as possible from the words of the act as they stand (*i*). The words must be interpreted in their natural and ordinary sense. Full grammatical effect should be given, if possible, to every word used. If that is not possible, an endeavor should be made to give a meaning to the intention of the legislature after a consideration of the whole language (*k*). If an enactment be expressed in clear, positive, and explicit terms, its operation and effect are not to be cut down and restricted by the more limited tenor and scope of the preamble. But if the words of the enacting clause are not so clear and explicit as to admit of but one clear and distinct meaning, it is proper to resort to the preamble for the resolution of the doubt, and to put such construction on the enactment as will accord with the preamble (*l*).

18. Where a general act is incorporated with a special act, the general act must be looked at with reference to the powers conferred upon companies of dealing with the land when acquired, but the special act must be looked to for the purpose of ascertaining what is the contract between the land-owner and the company, and the power which the company has conferred upon it of taking the land of the land-owner (*m*).

* 302 A special act * of Parliament creating rights or imposing special duties is not repealed by a subsequent general act which makes no reference to it (*n*). Nor are the powers conferred upon certain persons by a special act con-

---

(*g*) Holyoake *v.* Shrewsbury and Birmingham Railway Co., 5 Ra. Ca. 421; Wintle *v.* Bristol and South Wales Union Railway Co., 10 W. R. 210.

(*h*) See *infra*.

(*i*) Att.-Gen. *v.* Corporation of London, 8 Beav. 286; Hughes *v.* Chester and Holyhead Railway Co., 1 Dr. & Sm. 524.

(*k*) Hughes *v.* Chester and Holyhead Railway Co., 1 Dr. & Sm. 524; *Re* Sussex Peerage case, 11 Cl. & Fin. 85,

143. See Dover Gas Co. *v.* Mayor of Dover, 7 D. M. & G. 545.

(*l*) Hughes *v.* Chester & Holyhead Railway Co., 1 Dr. & Sm. 524. See Dover Gas-light Co. *v.* Mayor of Dover, 7 D. M. & G. 545.

(*m*) Simpson *v.* South Staffordshire Water-works Co., 34 L. J. Ch. 387, *per* Lord Westbury.

(*n*) Trustees of Birkenhead Docks *v.* Laird, 4 D. M. & G. 742; Fitzgerald *v.* Champneys, 2 J. & H. 31

trolled by a subsequent statute, giving to other persons inconsistent powers in terms which, from their generality, would seem to overrule them (o). Powers to interfere with the rights and property of others will not be imported into an agreement, unless the court is able to collect, by necessary implication from the language of the instrument, that such was the intention of the legislature (p).

19. Where persons are empowered by the legislature to take lands compulsorily for the purposes of an undertaking, they are the proper judges of what land they need. They may take as much land as they shall deem necessary for the proper construction of the works which they are authorized to make, and of the works incidental to the main purpose of the undertaking, provided they act *bonâ fide;* but they cannot be allowed to exercise those powers for any purpose of a collateral kind, that is, for any purposes except those for which the legislature has invested them with extraordinary powers (q). A company accordingly having power to take land may not take it for the purposes of another company which have not power to take it (r). The case is different where a public body, such as the corporation of a city, is intrusted by the legislature with the duty of making public improvements in the city. The power thus intrusted to it for such a purpose will not be subject, as in the other case, to so strict and restricted a construction (s). Although a company, having power to take land, may not take * it for the purpose of another company which * 303 has not power to take it, a company, which has legally taken land, may enter into an agreement with another company for the joint use of it. The arrangement between the companies does not vitiate the title which the company has acquired to the land (t). If there is evidence to show that a company is taking land which is not *bonâ fide* required for the proper pur-

(o) London and Blackwall Railway Co. *v.* Limehouse Board of Works, 3 K. & J. 123.

(p) Dawson *v.* Paver, 5 Ha. 415.

(q) Webb *v.* Manchester and Leeds Railway Co., 4 M. & C. 118; Stockton and Darlington Railway Co. *v.* Brown, 9 H. L. 256; Richards *v.* Scarborough Market Co., 23 L. J. Ch. 110; Simpson *v.* South Staffordshire Water-works Co.,

34 L. J. Ch. 387; Galloway *v.* Mayor, &c., of London, 1 L. R. H. L. 34.

(r) Wood *v.* Epsom and Leatherhead Railway Co., 8 C. B. N. S. 731; Vane *v.* Cockermouth and Darlington Railway Co., 13 W. R. 1015.

(s) Galloway *v.* Mayor, &c., of London, 1 L. R. H. L. 34.

(t) Wood *v.* Epsom and Leatherhead Railway Co., 8 C. B. N. S. 731.

poses of the undertaking, it is not enough that the engineer of
the company may have made an affidavit that the land is or
would be wanted for the purposes of the undertaking. The
purposes must be specified so that the court may judge
whether the land is *bonâ fide* required (*u*). If there is no
ground to suspect *mala fides*, the court may give credit to the
testimony of the engineer, as to what would be a proper execution of the works (*x*). Whether land is necessary for
the purposes of the undertaking is a question of fact for a
jury (*y*).

20. Where an act of Parliament enables a proprietor in a
mineral district to make roads and railways over the lands of
other persons from his mines to a canal, he is not bound to
take the shortest practicable route, but may in the exercise
of his judgment adopt a more circuitous route, provided he
is acting *bonâ fide* and keeps within the provisions of the
act (*z*).

21. The Lands Clauses Act, 8 & 9 Vict. c. 18, is usually
incorporated with all acts giving companies power to take land.
Where the company is a railway company, the Railways
Clauses Consolidation Act, 8 & 9 Vict. c. 20, as well as the
Lands Clauses Act, is generally incorporated with the special
act in all cases where the special act has been obtained since
the enactment of the two general acts. These two acts, however, do not interfere with private contracts. They were intended only to apply where the parties have omitted, or are
unable, or could not be induced to determine their
* 304   rights by special agreement, and will not be * allowed
to override or control the provisions of a deed deliberately executed for the purpose of determining the rights of
parties and in which they are not referred to (*a*). If the
dealings between a land-owner and a company amount to a

(*u*) Flower *v.* London, Brighton, and
South Coast Railway Co., 2 Dr. & Sm.
330.   See Lund *v.* Midland Railway
Co., 34 L. J. Ch. 276.

(*x*) Selby *v.* Colne Valley and Halstead Junction Railway Co., 10 W. R.
661.

(*y*) Doe *v.* North Staffordshire Railway Co., 16 Q. B. 526; Wood *v.* Epsom

and Leatherhead Railway Co., 8 C. B.
N. S. 731.

(*z*) Richards *v.* Richards, John. 255.

(*a*) Sanderson *v.* Cockermouth and
Workington Railway Co., 19 L. J. Ch.
503; Clarke *v.* Manchester, Sheffield,
and Lincolnshire Railway Co., 1 J. &
H. 631; Newton *v.* Metropolitan Railway Co., 1 Dr. & Sm. 583.

contract, the case is withdrawn from the operation of the statute (*b*).

22. All companies incorporating these two acts with their own special act are bound to adhere strictly to the powers of taking land prescribed by these acts, and to proceed only in the mode and with the formalities required by them. The attempt to take or enter upon lands otherwise than in accordance with the mode pointed out by these acts, except in so far as they may be modified by the special act incorporating the company, is a trespass, and will be restrained by injunction (*c*).

23. By the 16th clause of 8 & 9 Vict. c. 18, the Lands Clauses Act, the compulsory powers cannot be put in force, unless the whole of the estimated capital of the company has been subscribed by them under a contract; and by clause 17 a certificate from two justices that the whole capital has been subscribed is sufficient evidence thereof. These clauses do not apply to the case of a branch railway made by an already existing company (*d*).

24. By the 18th clause a company, before taking or entering upon lands which they are authorized to take, must serve upon the land-owner or persons interested therein, or enabled by the act to sell and convey the same, a notice to treat, specifying the land which they require (*e*). Notice to treat must be served on the tenant in possession (*f*), and upon tenants who have an *interest in the land (*g*).   * 305
If after notice to treat has been served upon a tenant the tenancy expires, and another tenant enters into possession, notice to treat should be served on him (*h*). Notice upon the

<hr/>

(*b*) Newton *v.* Metropolitan Railway Co., 1 Dr. & Sm. 583. See Edinburgh and Glasgow Railway Co. *v.* Campbell, 4 Macq. 570.

(*c*) Birley *v.* Constables, &c., of Chorlton-upon-Medlock, 3 Beav. 503; Fooks *v.* Wilts, Somerset, and Weymouth Railway Co., 5 Ha. 199. See also Manchester, Sheffield, &c., Railway Co. *v.* Great Northern Railway Co., 9 Ha. 284; Stone *v.* Commercial Railway Co., 4 M. & C. 122; Schwinge *v.* London and Blackwall Railway Co., 3 Sm. & G. 30.

(*d*) Weld *v.* South Western Railway Co., 32 Beav. 340.

(*e*) See Martin *v.* London, Chatham, and Dover Railway Co., 1 L. R. Ch. App. 501. See, as to construction of Lands Clauses Act, Reg. *v.* Lord Mayor of London, 2 L. R. Q. B. 292.

(*f*) Carter *v.* Great Eastern Railway Co., 9 Jur. N. S. 618.

(*g*) Rogers *v.* Dock Company of Hull, 34 L. J. Ch. 165.

(*h*) Carter *v.* Great Eastern Railway Co., 9 Jur. N. S. 618.

next friend of an infant plaintiff and not on his guardian as required by the special act is insufficient (*i*). If the lands are in the possession of a receiver, or of the committee of a lunatic appointed by the court of chancery, the company should make a special application to the court. If they proceed, without the sanction of the court, to enforce the statutory powers, an injunction may be obtained to restrain them (*j*).

25. The notice to treat should state accurately the quantity and situation of the land required (*k*). Lands different in respect of boundaries from those included in the notice cannot be included in the precept to the sheriff to summon an assessing jury (*l*). A plan is generally annexed to the notice to treat. If any mistake is made on the face of the plan, the company will be unable to enter upon any land which may be omitted (*m*). Notice that land is wanted for the purposes of a railway is sufficient. The notice need not state that the land is wanted for the purposes of a station (*n*).

26. A company is not bound to comprise the whole of the land, which they may require, in the first notice, but may from time to time, until the compulsory powers expire, serve fresh notices to the same land-owner for taking any additional land which may be requisite for the works (*o*).

* 306   27. * After notice to treat once given neither party can get rid of the obligation. The relative situation of vendor and purchaser is to a certain extent, and for certain purposes, created by giving the notice (*p*). The land-owner to whom the notice is given (*q*), and the company giving the

---

(*i*) Earl of Harrington *v.* Metropolitan Railway Co., 13 L. T. N. S. 658.

(*j*) *Re* Taylor, 6 Ra. Ca. 741 : Tink *v.* Rundle, 10 Beav 318 : Richards *v.* Richards, John. 255.

(*k*) Stone *v.* Commercial Railway Co., 4 M. & C. 118.

(*l*) *Ib.*

(*m*) Kemp *v.* London, Brighton, &c., Railway Co., 1 Ra. Ca. 495. See, however, as to the correction of mistakes in the plans and books of reference of a railway company. 8 Vict. c. 20, s. 7; Kemp *v.* West End, &c., Railway Co., 1 K. & J. 689; Taylor *v.* Clemson, 2 Q. B. 978.

(*n*) Wood *v.* Epsom and Leatherhead Railway Co., 8 C. B. N. S. 731.

(*o*) Stamps *v.* Birmingham and Stour Valley Railway Co., 2 Ph. 673 ; Simpson *v.* Lancaster and Carlisle Railway Co., 15 Sim. 580, 4 Ra. Ca. 627 ; Sadd *v.* Maldon and Braintree Railway Co., 6 Exch. 143 ; Flower *v.* London, Brighton, &c., Railway Co., 2 Dr. & Sm. 330. See 26 & 27 Vict. c. 92, s. 8.

(*p*) Tawney *v.* Lynn and Ely Railway Co., 4 Ra. Ca. 619, 16 L. J. Ch. 282; Marquis of Salisbury *v.* Great Northern Railway Co., 17 Q. B. 840; Adams *v.* London and Blackwall Railway Co., 2 Mac. & G. 118; Haynes *v.* Haynes, 1 Dr. & Sm. 426.

(*q*) Metropolitan Railway Co. *v.* Wodehouse, 34 L. J. Ch. 297.

notice, are equally bound (*r*). The notice cannot be recalled or varied without the consent of the land-owner (*s*). It is no answer in general to say that there are no funds to go on with the undertaking (*t*). But commissioners appointed for a public purpose may recede from a notice to treat, on the ground of a deficiency of funds (*u*). Notice to treat will be considered as abandoned if there is great delay in proceeding under it (*x*). When the notice to treat is met by a counter-notice, under the 92d clause of the act, requiring the company to take the whole of the property, the company may recede from the notice and refuse to take any part (*y*). After notice under the 18th clause, and a counter-notice under the 92d clause, it is not necessary that there should be a second formal notice under the 18th clause before summoning a jury under the 23d clause, but under the 21st clause the company must give a reasonable opportunity to the land-owner to agree with them before causing a jury to be summoned (*z*). Where a land-owner has waived the service of notice, he cannot take an objection for want of it (*a*).

28. Inasmuch as the act applies only to corporeal hereditaments, the 18th clause does not apply to easements (*b*). It is not * necessary to serve the owner of a mere ease- * 307 ment, as a way-leave over the property (*c*).

29. There has been much difference of opinion whether, after the service of notice to treat, the land-owner and the company are brought within the ordinary jurisdiction of the court as to the specific performance of contracts. After an elaborate review of all the authorities, Kindersley, V. C., held that, though to a certain extent and for certain purposes, the notice to treat places the parties in the relation of vendor and

(*r*) Sparrow *v.* Oxford, Worcester, and Wolverhampton Railway Co., 9 Ha. 436.

(*s*) Tawney *v.* Lynn and Ely Railway Co., 4 Ra. Ca. 619, 16 L. J. Ch. 282.

(*t*) Rex *v.* Hungerford Market Co., 4 B. & Ad. 327 ; Reg. *v.* Commissioners of Woods and Forests, 15 Q. B. 773.

(*u*) Reg. *v.* Commissioners of Woods and Forests, *ib.*

(*x*) Hedges *v.* Metropolitan Railway Co., 28 Beav. 109.

(*y*) Reg. *v.* London and South Western Railway Co., 12 Q. B. 775, 5 Ra. Ca. 669 ; King *v.* Wycombe Railway Co., 28 Beav. 104.

(*z*) Schwinge *v.* London and Blackwall Railway Co., 3 Sm. & G. 30.

(*a*) Rex *v.* South Holland Drainage, 8 A. & E. 429.

(*b*) Pinchin *v.* London and Blackwall Railway Co., 5 D. M. & G. 862.

(*c*) Thicknesse *v.* Lancaster Canal Co., 4 M. & W. 472.

purchaser, and involves some of the consequences which flow from actual contract, it does not amount to a contract which a court of equity will enforce upon a bill for specific performance, even when filed by a land-owner against the company, still less that it constitutes a contract by the land-owner to sell his land (d). " The intention of the legislature," he said (e), " was not to create equitable rights or interests, but to give legal rights and impose legal obligations, such rights and obligations to be asserted and enforced by legal proceedings prescribed in the act " (f). But a notice to treat, followed by the subsequent fixing by arbitration of the purchase and compensation money, does create a contract enforceable at the suit of the vendor (g).

30. By the 84th clause the promoters of an undertaking are forbidden from taking possession of lands until after payment of the purchase-moneys in the mode prescribed in the act, provided always that they may, upon a certain notice therein specified, enter upon lands for the purpose of surveying the ground or setting out the line (h). The making a tunnel under a highway, without disturbing the surface, is an entry upon land within the clause (i). A company will be restrained from entering upon land until the moneys awarded have been paid or deposited, as required by the clause (k). The
* 308   clause will not, however, be * extended to enable a
land-owner to take advantage of the necessity which a company has for speedy occupation, and by reason of some accidental slip extort from the company a larger sum than the property is fairly worth (l). When a company enters upon land for the purposes of making a survey without giving the notice required by the clause, they may be restrained (m).

31. By the 85th clause, where a company is desirous of taking possession before any agreement has been entered into,

(d) Haynes v. Haynes, 1 Dr. & Sm. 426, 444.

(e) Ib. 436.

(f) Re Battersea Park Act; Re Arnold, 32 Beav. 591.

(g) Mason v. Stokes Bay Pier and Railway Co., 32 L. J. Ch. 110.

(h) See Rogers v. Dock Company at Hull, 34 L. J. Ch. 165.

(i) Ramsden v. Manchester, &c.,

Railway Co., 1 Exch. 723, 5 Ra. Ca. 552.

(k) Lee v. Milner, 2 Y. & C. 617.

(l) Wood v. Charing Cross Railway Co., 33 Beav. 290.

(m) Fooks v. Wilts, Somerset, and Weymouth Railway Co., 5 Ha. 199, 4 Ra. Ca. 210; but see Standish v. Mayor of Liverpool, 1 Drew. 1.

award made or verdict given, it is authorized to take possession upon payment into the bank of the sum claimed by any
party, who shall not consent, or such as shall be determined
by a surveyor, appointed by two justices, to be the value of
the property, and giving a bond with two sureties for payment
of the purchase-moneys, and compensation to be ascertained
under the provisions of the act. It is incumbent on those
who seek to avail themselves of the provisions of the clause
to show clearly and satisfactorily that they have fulfilled its
conditions and complied with its requisitions (n). Actual
payment is necessary before entry (o). Persons who proceed
under the clause cannot dispense with the notice to treat contained in the 18th clause (p) ; but they need not give notice
to the land-owner of their intention to make the deposit and
proceed under the provisions of the clause (q). Where there
has been a special contract with respect to the purchase of
land, the provisions of the clause do not apply. By the contract the matter is withdrawn from the operation of the act.
A company cannot enter upon land under the provisions of
the clause on payment of the money into the bank (r).

32. * If the first bond be informal or defective, a   * 309
second may be given. The court will not, after a valid
bond has been substituted, interfere on the ground that the
original possession taken under the defective bond is not a
taking possession under the act. An injunction which had
been granted on the ground of the informality of the bond was
held by Lord Cottenham to have been rightly dissolved upon
the substitution of a formal bond and the deposit of the sum
claimed by the plaintiff (s). The condition of the bond to be
given should adopt the very terms of the statute (t). A bond,

---

(n) Barker v. North Staffordshire
Railway Co., 2 De G. & S. 55, 5 Ra.
Ca. 401.

(o) Armstrong v. Waterford and
Limerick Railway Co., 10 Ir. Eq. 60.
Money paid into bank, under sec. 85, is
only a security for what shall be found
upon inquiry to be the value of the
interest taken. Martin v. London,
Chatham, and Dover Railway Co., 1
L. R. Ch. Ap. 501.

(p) Adams v. London and Blackwall

Railway Co., 2 Mac. & G. 118, 6 Ra.
Ca. 282.

(q) Bridges v. Wilts and Somerset
Railway Co., 4 Ra. Ca. 622, 16 L. J.
Ch. 335.

(r) Newton v. Metropolitan Railway
Co., 1 Dr. & Sm. 587.

(s) Willey v. South Eastern Railway
Co., 1 Mac. & G. 58, 6 Ra. Ca. 100.
See, also, Williams v. South Wales
Railway Co., 3 De G. & S. 354.

(t) Hoskins v. Philipps, 3 Exch. 168,

21

accordingly, conditioned not for payment absolutely, but on demand, is invalid (*u*). So, also, is a bond conditioned for payment "at any time hereafter" (*x*). A bond conditioned for
payment to land-owners jointly, where they are tenants in common, is bad (*y*). The bond should be given and the deposit
made in respect of all the land described in the notice to treat (*z*).

33. Two sureties are required to the bond as well where the
bond is given by a corporation as where it is given by an individual (*a*). The sureties may be appointed without notice to
the land-owner (*b*). They should be approved by two justices,
if the parties differ (*c*).

34. A company ought not to appoint as surveyor a person
who has been previously in their employment; but the
* 310   appointment * would not necessarily be invalid (*d*). If
the surveyor has made a valuation in such a way as to
enable him to do it fairly, the court will not disturb the valuation; but if it be not done in such a way, the court will interfere. The valuation of a house must not be made upon the
mere inspection of the exterior (*e*).

35. The proceedings under the clause were held not to be
invalid, although the money appeared to have been deposited
two days before the date of the valuation (*f*).

36. The clause applies only to lands taken, and not to lands
injuriously affected by the works (*g*).

5 Ra. Ca. 560; Poynder *v.* Great North-
ern Railway Co., 2 Ph. 330, 5 Ra. Ca.
202; Barker *v.* North Staffordshire
Railway Co., 2 De G. & S. 55, 5 Ra.
Ca. 401; Dakin *v.* London and North
Western Railway Co., 3 De G. & S.
414; Willey *v.* South Eastern Railway
Co., 1 Mac. & G. 58, 6 Ra. Ca. 100.

(*u*) Langham   *v.*   Great   Northern
Railway Co., 1 De G. & S. 486.

(*x*) Cotter *v.* Metropolitan Railway
Co., 10 Jur. N. S. 1014.

(*y*) Langham *v.* Great Northern Rail-
way Co., 1 De G. & S. 486. See, also,
Daubney *v.* Manchester, &c., Railway
Co., 10 L. T. 283.

(*z*) Barker *v.* North Staffordshire
Railway Co., 2 De G. & S. 55; Giles *v.*
London, Chatham, and Dover Railway
Co., 1 Dr. & Sm. 406.

(*a*) Barker *v.* North Staffordshire
Railway Co., 2 De G. & S. 55.

(*b*) Bridges *v.* Wilts, Somerset, and

Weymouth Railway Co., 16 L. J. Ch.
335, 4 Ra. Ca. 622; Langham *v.* Great
Northern Railway Co., 1 De G. & S.
486, 5 Ra. Ca. 263; Poynder *v.* Great
Northern Railway Co., 16 Sim. 3, 5
Ra. Ca. 196.

(*c*) Bridges *v.* Wilts, Somerset, and
Weymouth Railway Co., 16 L. J. Ch.
335, 4 Ra. Ca. 623.

(*d*) Langham   *v.*   Great   Northern
Railway Co., 1 De G. & S. 486; Barker
v. North Staffordshire Railway Co., 3
De G. & S. 55.

(*e*) Cotter *v.* Metropolitan Railway
Co., 10 Jur. N. S. 1014. See order,
ib.

(*f*) Stamps *v.* Birmingham and Stour
Valley Railway Co., 7 Ha. 251.

(*g*) Hutton *v.* London and South
Western Railway Co., 7 Ha. 262;
Lister *v.* Lobley, 7 A. & E. 124; Innocent *v.* North Midland Railway Co.,
1 Ra. Ca. 242.

37. The diversion of a stream is " a taking " within the meaning of the clause, the whole act having been incorporated with the Water-works Clauses Act, 10 & 11 Vict. c. 17. A corporation were accordingly restrained from making the diversion until compensation had been paid, or a bond given, as required by the clause (h).

38. Possession should not be taken by a company until a settlement has been come to with all parties interested. The taking possession after a settlement with the tenants in possession only is erroneous, and contrary to the provisions of the act (i). In cases of the sort, the court will usually, on the motion for an injunction, order it to stand over upon the terms of the company undertaking to lodge the money, and giving the usual bond under this section of the act (k).

39. * Persons who take lands which they are author-   * 311 ized to take, with the consent of owners or occupiers, cannot afterwards be treated as trespassers (l). Where a railway company had complied with the provisions of the clause, and had entered and taken land within the prescribed period for exercising the compulsory powers, their continuance in possession after the prescribed period without having the compensation assessed and the land conveyed to them, is not unlawful (m).

40. Whatever objections are made on the ground that the proceedings of a company are irregular, a land-owner who goes into equity to complain of the insufficiency of the bond, deposit, or other proceedings, under the statute, should state the whole of his first case in the first instance. He cannot in a later stage of the proceedings set up a new equity (n).

(h) Ferrand v. Corporation of Bradford, 21 Beav. 412.

(i) Inge v. Birmingham, Wolverhampton, and Stour Valley Railway Co., 3 D. M. & G. 666; Alston v. Eastern Counties Railway Co., 1 Jur. N. S. 1009; Ranken v. East and West India Docks Co., 12 Beav. 298; Martin v. London, Chatham, and Dover Railway Co., 1 L. R. Ch. App. 501. See Perks v. Great Wycombe Railway Co., 3 Giff. 662.

(k) Alston v. Eastern Counties Railway Co., 1 Jur. N. S. 1009; Armstrong v. Waterford and Limerick Railway Co., 10 Ir. Eq. 60; Carter v. Great Eastern Railway Co., 9 Jur. N. S. 618. See Perks v. Great Wycombe Railway Co., 3 Giff. 662.

(l) Doe v. North Staffordshire Railway Co., 16 Q. B. 526; Knapp v. London, Chatham, and Dover Railway Co., 2 H & C. 212.

(m) Doe v. North Staffordshire Railway Co., 16 Q. B. 526.

(n) Barker v. North Staffordshire Railway Co., 2 De G. & S. 55.

41. Provision is made in several clauses of the act for the manner in which, in cases of dispute, compensation shall be assessed for the interest in lands which the party is enabled to sell, or for any damage that may be sustained by him by reason of the execution of the works. In estimating the compensation, account must be had, not only of the value of the land to be purchased or taken, but also of the damage to be sustained by the owner by reason of the severing of the land taken from the other land of such owner, or otherwise injuriously affecting such other land by the exercise of the parliamentary powers (*o*).

42. The 68th clause further provides, that if any party shall be entitled to any compensation in respect of any lands or any interest therein, which shall have been taken for, or injuriously affected by, the execution of the works, or for which the promoters of the undertaking shall not have made satisfaction, the compensation shall be assessed in the mode therein prescribed. The clause refers to the taking of land as
* 312 authorized by the * 85th clause, and to land injuriously affected, where no adjoining lands of the same owner have been taken (*p*).

43. By the 92d clause it is enacted that " no party shall at any time be required to sell or convey to the promoters of the undertaking a part only of any house, or other building, or manufactory, if such party be willing and able to sell and convey the whole thereof." Owners under disability may avail themselves of the provisions of the clause (*q*). The clause applies, although the land-owner has only a leasehold interest (*r*), and holds the property in question under different demises (*s*). An owner who has been served with notice by a company to take part of his premises may, under the clause, refuse to sell less than the whole thereof; but he cannot by

(*o*) South Wales Railway Co. *v.* Richards, 18 L. J. Q. B. 310; Manning *v.* Eastern Counties Railway Co., 12 M. & W. 237; Grand Junction Railway Co. *v.* White, 2 Ra. Ca. 569; *Re* Duke of Beaufort, 6 Jur. N. S. 979.

(*p*) Doe *v.* North Staffordshire Railway Co., 16 Q. B. 526; Burkinshaw *v.* Birmingham and Grand Junction Rail-

way Co., 5 Exch. 475; Perks *v.* Great Wycombe Railway Co., 3 Giff. 662.

(*q*) St. Thomas' Hospital *v.* Charing Cross Railway Co., 1 J. & H. 406.

(*r*) Pulling *v.* London, Chatham, and Dover Railway Co., 33 L. J. Ch. 505.

(*s*) Macgregor *v.* Metropolitan Railway Co., 14 L. T. N. S. 354.

reason of such notice require that the whole be taken. The company may, on his refusal to sell less than the whole, abandon their notice, and refuse to take any part (*t*). The notice to treat is not reserved by the owner subsequently withdrawing his counter-notice on the company, requiring them to take the whole of his premises (*u*). The giving a counter-notice, under the clause, creates an equity against the land-owner, whether the original notice be valid or not. The court will not interfere to protect him, even after the compulsory powers have expired, except upon terms putting him to sell and convey the property which he has, by his counter-notice, offered to sell (*v*). A land-owner who did not give the counter-notice requiring the company to take the whole of his premises, until after the refusal of the company to give him what he asked for the part comprised in the notice, is not precluded from availing himself of the provisions of the clause (*x*). Where a company is required by the land-owner to take * the whole of his premises, under the provisions   * 313 of the clause the amount to be secured by deposit and bond, under s. 85, before taking possession, is the value of the whole of the premises, and not of the portion actually required by the company (*y*). The provisions of the clause apply, although the land may not fall within the limits of deviation (*z*).

44. The word " house " in the clause means all that would pass under the grant of a house in a conveyance, and will include the curtilage and garden (*a*). The word includes only

(*t*) Reg. *v*. London and South Western Railway Co., 12 Q. B. 775; King *v*. Wycombe Railway Co., 28 Beav. 104.

(*u*) *Ex parte* Quicke, 12 L. T. N. S. 580.

(*v*) Pinchin *v*. London and Blackwall Railway Co., 5 D. M. & G. 851.

(*x*) Gardner *v*. Charing Cross Railway Co., 2 J. & H. 248.

(*y*) Giles *v*. London, Chatham, and Dover Railway Co., 1 Dr. & Sm. 406; Gardner *v*. Charing Cross Railway Co., 2 J. & H. 258; Dadson *v*. East Kent Railway Co., 7 Jur. N. S. 941; Gibson *v*. Hammersmith and City Railway Co.,

2 Dr. & Sm. 603; Cotter *v*. Metropolitan Railway Co., 10 Jur. N. S. 1014.

(*z*) St. Thomas' Hospital *v*. Charing Cross Railway Co., 1 J. & H. 400.

(*a*) Grosvenor *v*. Hampstead Junction Railway Co., 1 D. & J. 446; Hewson *v*. London and South Western Railway Co., 8 W. R. 467; St. Thomas' Hospital *v*. Charing Cross Railway Co., 1 J. & H. 400; Cole *v*. West End and Crystal Palace Railway Co., 27 Beav. 242; King *v*. Wycombe Railway Co., 28 Beav. 105; Pulling *v*. London, Chatham, and Dover Railway Co., 33 L. J. Ch. 505.

what is necessary for the convenient use and occupation of the house, and not also what is subsidiary to, or necessary for, the convenience of the occupant of the house (*b*) : as, for instance, a field in front of the house, and separated from the house by a public road, and used as a pleasure-ground (*c*). The word "house" will apply to unfinished houses (*d*). A company will not, it would appear, be compelled to take less than the whole property constituting the house (*e*).

45. What is a "manufactory" within the meaning of the clause is in each case a question of fact. In Barker *v.* North Staffordshire Railway Company (*f*), two brine-pits were considered to be part of certain salt-works within the meaning of the clause. In Sparrow *v.* Oxford, Worcester, and Wolverhampton Railway Company (*g*), land included in the * 314 same wall with iron * and tin-plate works, but separated from them by a private road, over which a stranger had a right of way, and which was used for the deposit of ashes from the works, was held to be part of the manufactory. In another case cottages used as warehouses in connection with a manufactory situate on the opposite side of a public road, were held to be a part of the manufactory (*h*). In Reddin *v.* Metropolitan Board of Works (*i*), on the other hand, where the plaintiff carried on the business of a dust-contractor, which consists in collecting and sorting dust-heaps, and also, as a subsidiary business, worked up some of the components into plaster-powder and manure, the promoters of the undertaking having served a notice to take a "tot-shop" which was used only in connection with the sorting business, it was held that they could not be compelled to take the whole of the premises. The word "manufactory" includes trade fixtures (*j*).

(*b*) Steele *v.* Midland Railway Co., 1 L. R. Ch. Ap. 275.

(*c*) Fergusson *v.* London, Brighton, and South Coast Railway Co., 33 Beav. 103, 33 L. J. Ch. 29 ; Pulling *v.* London, Chatham, and Dover Railway Co., 33 L. J. Ch. 505. See Chambers *v.* London, Chatham, and Dover Railway Co., 1 N. R. 517.

(*d*) Alexander *v.* Crystal Palace Railway Co., 30 Beav. 556.

(*e*) Pulling *v.* London, Chatham, and Dover Railway Co., 33 L. J. Ch. 505.

(*f*) 2 De G. & S. 55.

(*g*) 9 Ha. 436, 2 D. M. & G. 94.

(*h*) Spackman *v.* Great Western Railway Co., 1 Jur. N. S. 790.

(*i*) 31 L. J. Ch. 660.

(*j*) Gibson *v.* Hammersmith and City Railway Co., 2 Dr. & Sm. 603 ; Cotter *v.* Metropolitan Railway Co., 10 Jur. N. S. 1014.

46. The following cases were decided on provisions somewhat similar to this clause in earlier statutes (*k*).

47. By the 93d clause owners may require a company to purchase small portions of intersected land. The expression "such land" in the 94th clause is not restricted to intersected lands situate in a town, but applies to all intersected lands whether so situate or not (*l*).

48. The promoters must satisfy mortgagees before taking possession. Where a company had entered into possession under the 85th clause, without making any provision for compensation for the mortgagees, the court restrained them from proceeding with their works, until the value of the interest of the mortgagees had been ascertained and secured (*m*).

49. Where the occupier of lands is a tenant at will, or from year *to year, his interest is to be assessed   * 315 summarily before two magistrates, and upon payment of the amount he must deliver up possession (*n*). If any lessee, on being required to do so, does not produce his lease or grant, or give the best evidence thereof, he may be treated as a tenant from year to year, and be dealt with accordingly under the provisions of the last section (*o*). The clause does not apply to a person who produces a lease which, though void at law, is equivalent in equity to a lease for a greater interest than a yearly tenancy (*p*).

50. Unless otherwise provided for in the special act, the powers for the compulsory purchase or taking of lands shall not be exercised after the expiration of three years from the passing of the special act (*q*). In a case, indeed, where the special act contained no limitation of time for the exercise of the compulsory powers of purchase, it was held that the period limited by the general act was applicable (*r*).

(*k*) Stone *v.* Commercial Railway Co., 4 M. & C. 122; Reg. *v.* London and Greenwich Railway Co., 3 Q. B. 166, 3 Ra. Ca. 138; Walker *v.* London and Blackwall Railway Co., 3 Q. B. 744.

(*l*) Eastern Counties Railway Co. *v.* Marriage, 9 H. L. 32.

(*m*) Ranken *v.* East and West India Dock Co., 12 Beav. 298; Martin *v.* London, Chatham, and Dover Railway Co., 1 L. R. Ch. App. 501. See Rogers *v.* Dock Company of Hull, 34 L. J. Ch. 165.

(*n*) Sec. 121.

(*o*) Sec. 122.

(*p*) Sweetman *v.* Metropolitan Railway Co., 1 H. & M. 543.

(*q*) Sec. 123.

(*r*) Seymour *v.* London and South Western Railway Co., 5 Jur. N. S. 753.

51. If the notice to take lands has been given within the period prescribed by the clause, any thing which remains to be done may be done subsequently, although the purchase may not be completed before the time limited by the clause (s). So, also, if a company give notice that the lands are required, and afterwards, even a day before the compulsory powers expire, give a bond and deposit money, in pursuance of the 85th clause, neither their power to purchase nor their power to enter upon the land is gone by the expiration of the prescribed period (t), the principle being that as soon as the company have given notice to take land they have exercised their powers of compulsory purchase, and that all the subsequent steps are not an exercise of the powers of compulsory purchase, but of powers which are intended to carry that purchase into
* 316 effect (u). Where the * promoters of a company gave notice a few days before the expiration of their compulsory powers to take part of a manufactory, and a counter-notice to take the whole was served on them after the expiration of that period, the court would not restrain them from taking steps to complete the purchase at the end of ten months after the expiration of their powers (y).

52. More delay on the part of the promoters after service of the notice does not raise any equity, because the land-owner has a remedy by mandamus, compelling the promoters to proceed (z). But if notice be given by a company immediately before the expiration of their compulsory powers, and there is great delay in completing the purchase, and the conduct of the promoters of the company is such as to lead the land-owner into the belief that the undertaking has been abandoned, they cannot be afterwards permitted to insist upon the notice (a).

(s) Reg. v. Birmingham and Oxford Railway Co., 15 Q. B. 634.

(t) Marquis of Salisbury v. Great Northern Railway Co., 17 Q. B. 840; Sparrow v. Oxford, Worcester, and Wolverhampton Railway Co., 9 Ha. 436. See Doe v. North Staffordshire Railway Co., 16 Q. B. 526; Worsley v. South Devon Railway Co., ib. 539.

(u) Sparrow v. Oxford, Worcester,

and Wolverhampton Railway Co., 9 Ha. 436.

(y) Pinchin v. London and Blackwall Railway Co., 5 D. M. & G. 851. See Schwinge v. London and Blackwall Railway, 3 De G. & S. 30.

(z) Reg. v. Birmingham and Oxford Junction Railway Co., 15 Q. B. 634; Pinchin v. London and Blackwall Railway Co., 5 D. M. & G. 864.

(a) Hedges v. Metropolitan Railway Co., 28 Beav. 109.

53. By the 124th clause provision is made for the purchase by promoters of companies of interests in lands, the purchase of which has been omitted by mistake (*b*).

54. Where the undertaking is a railway company, the special act usually enacts that it shall be lawful for the promoters of the undertaking to make and maintain the railway and works in the line and upon the land delineated in the plans and described in the books of reference, and to enter upon and take, and use such of the said land as shall be necessary for such purpose.

55. Plans deposited in compliance with the standing orders prior to the introduction of a bill into Parliament do not form any part of the act, except in so far as they may have been incorporated within its provisions ; nor can they be otherwise referred to for * the construction of the act (*c*).   * 317 The plans are only binding to the extent of determining the datum line and the line of railway measured with reference to that datum line, but not with reference to the surface levels, unless the act incorporates them within its provision (*d*). The particular works intended to be made need not appear on the deposited plan. It is enough that the land required shall be within the limits of deviation (*e*).

56. By the Railways Clauses Consolidation Act, 8 Vict. c. 20, ss. 11–15, a railway company may deviate a hundred yards from the datum line. The expression "deviation" is to be taken with reference to the line of railway only ; that is, the line of railway actually laid down shall not deviate more

---

(*b*) See Hyde *v.* Mayor of Manchester, 5 De G. & S. 249, affd. *ib.* 264 ; Doe *v.* Mayor of Manchester, 12 C. B. 474 ; Marquis of Salisbury *v.* Great Northern Railway Co., 5 C. B. N. S. 174 ; Jolly *v.* Wimbledon and Dorking Railway Co., 1 B. & S. 817 ; Martin *v.* London, Chatham, and Dover Railway Co., 1 L. R. Ch. Ap. 501.

(*c*) Feoffees of Heriot's Hospital *v.* Gibson, 2 Dow. 301 ; North British Railway Co. *v.* Todd, 12 Cl. & Fin. 722 ; R. *v.* Caledonian Railway Co., 16 Q. B. 19 ; Beardmer *v.* London and North Western Railway Co., 1 Mac. & G. 112, 1 H. & Tw. 161, 5 Ra. Ca. 728 ; Breynton *v.* London and North

Western Railway Co., 11 Jur. 28 ; Ware *v.* Regent's Canal Co., 3 D. & J. 212.

(*d*) North British Railway Co. *v.* Todd, 12 Cl. & Fin. 722 ; Beardmer *v.* London and North Western Railway Co., 1 Mac. & G. 112, 1 H. & Tw. 161, 5 Ra. Ca. 728 ; Ware *v.* Regent's Canal Co., 3 D. & J. 212.

(*e*) Weld *v.* South Eastern Railway Co., 32 Beav. 340, 33 L. J. Ch. 142. See, as to the rectification of mistakes in the plans and books of reference, 8 Vict. c. 20, s. 7 ; Taylor *v.* Clemson, 2 Q. B. 978, 11 Cl. & Fin. 610 ; Kemp *v.* West End of London and Crystal Palace Railway Co., 1 K. & J. 681.

than a hundred yards from the line delineated in the parliamentary plans, the *medium filum* of each being the commencement and termination in measuring the hundred yards (f). The word "levels" in the 11th section does not refer to surface levels (g).

57. When a viaduct or tunnel was marked on the plans deposited as intended to be made, no deviation could, under the Railways Clauses Consolidation Act, 8 & 9 Vict. c. 20, s. 13, be made except with the consent of the land-owner. It was necessary that the work, if made, should be made
* 318   accordingly (h). But under * 26 & 27 Vict. c. 92, s. 4, a railway company in the construction of the line may deviate from the line or level of any arch, tunnel, or viaduct described on the deposited plans or sections, so as the deviation be made within the limits of deviation shown on the plans, and so as the nature of the work described be not altered; and may also, with the consent of the board of trade, substitute any engineering work not shown on the deposited plans or sections for an arch, tunnel, or viaduct, as shown thereon. Memorandum of an intention to divert a road, however clearly expressed in the deposited plans, does not amount to a parliamentary license to divert or alter the road. Reg. *v.* Wycombe Railway Co., 2 L. R. Q. B. 310.

58. The words "other engineering works" contained in the 14th clause are referable to the general line and level of the railway, and not to the alteration of streets, roads, ways, &c., &c., mentioned in the 16th clause (i).

59. The promoters of a company must give notice of their intention to exercise their powers of deviation (k).

60. Land-owners who wish to prevent the promoters of a

(f) Doe *v.* Bristol and Exeter Railway Co., 6 M. & W. 320; Doe *v.* North Staffordshire Railway Co., 16 Q. B. 526.

(g) North British Railway Co. *v.* Todd, 12 Cl. & Fin. 722; Beardmer *v.* London and North Western Railway Co., 1 Mac. & G. 112, 1·H. & Tw. 161; Ware *v.* Regent's Canal Co., 3 D. & J. 212. See, as to meaning of word "town," in the 11th clause, Elliott *v.* South Devon Railway Co., 2 Exch. 725.

(h) Little *v.* Newport and Hereford Railway Co., 12 C. B. 752; Att.-Gen. *v.* Tewkesbury and Malvern Railway Co., 1 D. J. & S. 423.

(i) Beardmer *v.* London and North Western Railway Co., 1 Mac. & G. 112, 1 H. & Tw. 161. See, also, as to 14th clause, Att.-Gen. *v.* Tewkesbury and Malvern Railway Co., 1 D. J. & S. 423.

(k) 8 Vict. c. 20, s. 12. See Pearce *v.* Wycombe Railway Co., 1 Drew. 244, 17 Jur. 660.

railway company from using the powers of deviation reserved to them under 8 & 9 Vict. c. 20, ss. 11–15, should have appropriate clauses inserted in the special act (*l*). If there be nothing in the special act, or the matter in dispute having been referred to arbitration, there be nothing in the reference to arbitration, or in the award consequent thereon, to prevent them from doing so, a company may exercise the powers of deviation, as they think best within those limits (*m*).

61. A land-owner is not entitled to an injunction to restrain a railway company from proceeding with their works, although they are deviating to a greater extent than is authorized by * 8 & 9 Vict. c. 20, ss. 11–15, unless he can   * 319 show that he is substantially injured by the deviation (*n*).

62. Land which is necessary for the erection of stations and other conveniences for the proper working of the railway, or for the purpose of constructing the works authorized by 8 Vict. c. 20, s. 16, may be taken, though it is beyond the limits of deviation (*o*), provided such land be scheduled in the act and included in the plans and books of reference (*p*).

63. Land, on the other hand, not required for the purpose of enabling a company to construct their works in a proper and convenient manner may not be taken (*q*), even although it be within the limits of deviation. Thus, a railway company was restrained from taking a piece of land for the purpose of making an embankment and a greater slope on each side of a

(*l*) Eton College *v.* Great Western Railway Co., 1 Ra. Ca. 200; Gray *v.* Liverpool and Bury Railway Co., 9 Beav. 391; Sparrow *v.* Oxford, Worcester, and Wolverhampton Railway Co., 9 Ha. 436, 2 D. M. & G. 94; St. Thomas' Hospital *v.* Charing Cross Railway Co., 1 J. & H. 400. See Wood *v.* North Staffordshire Railway Co., 1 Mac. & G. 279; Leominster Canal Navigation Co. *v.* Shrewsbury and Hereford Railway Co., 3 K. & J. 654.

(*m*) Wood *v.* North Staffordshire Railway Co., 1 Mac. & G. 279; Selby *v.* Colne Valley and Halstead Railway Co., 10 W. R. 661.

(*n*) Holyoake *v.* Shrewsbury and Birmingham Railway Co., 5 Ra. Ca. 427. See Wintle *v.* Bristol and South Wales Union Railway Co., 10 W. R. 210.

(*o*) Cother *v.* Midland Railway Co., 2 Ph. 469; Crawford *v.* Chester and Holyhead Railway Co., 11 Jur. 918; Richards *v.* Scarborough Public Market Co., 23 L. J. Ch. 110; Midland Railway Co. *v.* Ambergate, &c., Railway Co., 10 Ha. 359; Sadd *v.* Maldon, Braintree, and Witham Railway Co., 6 Exch. 143; Doe *v.* North Staffordshire Railway Co., 16 Q. B. 526. See Wood *v.* Leatherhead Railway Co., 8 C. B. N. S. 731.

(*p*) Doe *v.* North Staffordshire Railway Co., 16 Q. B. 526. See Wrigley *v.* Lancashire and Yorkshire Railway Co., 4 Giff. 352. See, also, 26 & 27 Vict. c. 92, s. 8, as to power to take land for the purpose of erecting a lodge at a level crossing.

(*q*) See *supra*, p. 302.

cutting, and from claiming more land than was declared by a referee to be necessary for the purposes of the act (*r*). So a railway company was restrained from taking land for the purpose of excavating materials therefrom to be used in completing an embankment, though it was within the limits of deviation (*s*). So, also, a railway company was restrained from taking land not wanted for the purposes of the work, but for the purpose of digging out materials for their construction (*t*). So, also, a railway company was restrained from taking land for the purpose of altering a road, so as to be a convenience to a neighboring proprietor, though the
* 320   land lay within the limits * of deviation (*u*). Land, however, within the limits of deviation may be taken for the purpose of making a siding, so as to give local traffic an ingress on the main line (*x*). So, also, a company authorized to take land for the purposes of stations, works, and conveniences, may continue their line into the land so taken, and lay down such rails as may be required for the more convenient use of the station (*y*).

64. The court will not, on the ground of public inconvenience, restrain a railway company keeping within their powers of deviation from deviating from the plan, unless it can be shown that they are acting capriciously (*z*).

65. By the 16th and 19th clauses of the Railways Clauses Consolidation Act, 8 Vict. c. 20, railway companies are empowered to execute certain works in the mode and in the manner therein mentioned (*a*). By the 16th clause it is declared that they shall in the execution of such works do as little damage as can be. A railway company may erect buildings over streets in a town for the construction of stations, warehouses, &c., if it is necessary or reasonably convenient for the purposes of the line (*b*).

(*r*) Webb *v.* Manchester and Leeds Railway Co., 4 M. & C. 116.

(*s*) Eversfield *v.* Mid-Sussex Railway Co., 3 D. & J. 287.

(*t*) Bentinck *v.* Norfolk Estuary Co., 8 D. M. & G. 714.

(*u*) Dodd *v.* Salisbury and Yeovil Railway Co., 1 Giff. 161, aff. 33 L. T. 311.

(*x*) *Re* Yorkshire, Doncaster, and Goole Railway Co., 1 Jur. N. S. 975.

(*y*) Wood *v.* Epsom and Leatherhead Railway Co., 8 C. B. N. S. 731.

(*z*) Att.-Gen *v.* Great Western Railway Co., 14 W. R. 726.

(*a*) See, as to works in navigable rivers, Abraham *v.* Great Northern Railway Co., 16 Q. B. 586.

(*b*) Att.-Gen. *v.* Eastern Counties Railway Co., 2 Ra. Ca. 823.

66. By the 46th clause of the act provisions are made as to the carrying railways over roads (c).

67. By the 49th clause it is provided that bridges constructed to carry the line over a turnpike or other road shall be of the space and height provided according to the nature and width of the road (d). The descent into the road so as to carry the same * under the bridge is not to * 321 exceed certain specified gradients. It seems that no additional width is allowed for a foot-path (e), and that the company may lower the road without lowering the foot-path, if that be the more beneficial course (f).

68. The 50th clause provides for the width of the road and the ascent to bridges by which roads are constructed over railways (g). The company may not make the approaches to bridges nearer than the corresponding parts of the roads were before (h).

69. If the company find it necessary to interfere with any road, either public or private, so as to make it impassable for or dangerous or extraordinarily inconvenient to passengers or

(c) See Breynton v. London and North Western Railway Co., 4 Ra. Ca. 564; South Eastern Railway Co. v. Reg., 17 Q. B. 485, 1 H. L. 471, Warden of Dover Harbor v. London, Chatham, and Dover Railway Co., 3 D. F. & J. 559; Proprietors of Northam Bridge and Roads Co. v. London and Southampton Railway Co., 6 M. & W. 428, 1 Ra. Ca. 653; Trustees of Newcastle, &c., &c., Roads v. North Staffordshire Railway Co., 5 H. & N. 160; London and North Western Railway Co. v. Skerton, 5 B. & S. 559.

(d) Att.-Gen. v. London and Southampton Railway Co., 9 Sim. 78, 1 Ra. Ca. 383; Reg. v. Birmingham and Gloucester Railway Co., 2 Q. B. 47, 2 Ra. Ca. 694; Clarke v. Manchester, Sheffield, and Lincolnshire Railway Co., 1 J. & H. 631; Wintle v. Bristol and South Wales Railway Co., 10 W. R. 210; Wandsworth Board of Works v. London and South Western Railway Co., 31 L. J. Ch. 854; Att.-Gen. v. Tewkesbury and Malvern Railway Co., 1 D. J. & S. 425. See, as to special clauses to the same effect in a special act, Att.-Gen. v. Eastern Counties Railway Co., 3 Ra. Ca. 337; London and Brighton Railway Co. v.

Cooper, 2 Ra. Ca. 312. See, as to right to construct temporary bridges over roads during the progress of the works, London and Birmingham Railway Co. v. Grand Junction Railway Co., 1 Ra. Ca. 224; Priestley v. Manchester and Leeds Railway Co., 2 Ra. Ca. 134, 4 Y. & C. 63; Att.-Gen. v. Eastern Counties Railway Co., 3 Ra. Ca. 337. See, also, Clarke v. Manchester, Sheffield, and Lincolnshire Railway Co., 1 J. & H. 631, when there was an agreement to construct a suitable bridge over a street, but there was no reference to the general act.

(e) Reg. v. Rigby, 14 Q. B. 687.

(f) Reg. v. Manchester and Leeds Railway Co., 3 Q. B. 528.

(g) See Att.-Gen. v. London and Southampton Railway Co., 1 Ra. Ca. 283; Beardmer v. London and North Western Railway Co., 1 Mac. & G. 113; Reg. v. East and West India Docks and Railway Co., 2 E. & B. 466; South Eastern Railway Co. v. Reg., 20 L. J. Q. B. 428.

(h) See Reg. v. London and Birmingham Railway Co., 1 Ra. Ca. 317; Reg. v. Birmingham and Gloucester Railway Co., 2 Q. B. 47.

carriages, or to the persons entitled to the use thereof, they are first to provide a sufficient road in substitution for it (*i*), and unless the original road be restored, the substituted road or some other sufficient substituted road is to be put into a permanently substantial condition, equally convenient as the former road, or as near thereto as circumstances will allow (*k*).

* 322   70. * By 8 Vict. c. 20, s. 76, the owners or occupiers of lands adjoining a railway are empowered to lay down branches communicating with the railway, and the railway company is required to make openings in the line or sidings for the branches at places to be approved by the company. The assent of a company to an opening being made at a station is not in the nature of an easement, and cannot be revoked (*l*).

71. By 8 Vict. c. 20, s. 87, railway companies are empowered to enter into contracts with other railway companies for passing over each other's lines upon the payment of such tolls (*m*) and under such restrictions as may be mutually agreed upon (*n*), and to enter into a contract for the division

---

(*i*) A road already existing is not a substituted road within the meaning of the clause. Att.-Gen. *v.* Great Northern Railway Co., 4 De G. & S. 75; Reg. *v.* Scott, 3 Q. B. 543.

(*k*) Spencer *v.* London and Birmingham Railway Co., 8 Sim. 193, 1 Ra. Ca. 159; Att.-Gen. *v.* London and Southampton Railway Co., *ib.* 302; Reg. *v.* London and Birmingham Railway Co., *ib.* 317; Kemp *v.* London and Brighton Railway Co., *ib.* 495; Bell *v.* Hull and Selby Railway Co., 2 Ra. Ca. 279; London and Brighton Railway Co. *v.* Blake, *ib.* 332; Att.-Gen. *v.* Eastern Counties Railway Co., 3 Ra. Ca. 337; Att.-Gen. *v.* London and South Western Railway Co., 3 De G. & S. 439; Reg. *v.* Scott, 3 Q. B. 543; Att.-Gen. *v.* London and South Western Railway Co., 4 De G. & S. 75; Ellis *v.* London and South Western Railway Co., 2 H. & N. 424; Gawthern *v.* Stockport, Disley, and Whaleybridge Railway Co., 3 Jur. N. S. 573; Caledonian Railway Co. *v.* Colt, 3 Macq. 833; Att.-Gen. *v.* Dorset Central Railway Co., 9 W. R. 189; Marquis of Salisbury *v.* Great Northern Railway Co., 5 C. B. N. S. 174; Free-

man *v.* Tottenham, &c., &c., Railway Co., 11 Jur. N. S. 107, 254. The clause does not refer to the conversion of a road into a railway. Tanner *v.* South Wales Railway Co., 5 E. & B. 618. See, as to who is to be considered an "owner," Collinson *v.* Newcastle and Darlington Railway Co., 1 C. & K. 546; Mann *v.* Great Southern and Western Railway Co., 9 Ir. C. L. 105; Reg. *v.* Wycombe Railway Co., 2 L. R. Q. B. 310.

(*l*) Bell *v.* Midland Railway Co., 10 C. B. N. S. 287, 3 D. & J. 673.

(*m*) See, as to the meaning of the word "toll," Simpson *v.* Denison, 10 Ha. 51; Great Northern Railway Co. *v.* South Yorkshire Railway Co., 9 Exch. 644. See, also, South Yorkshire Railway Co. *v.* Great Northern Railway Co., 3 D. M. & G. 576.

(*n*) See, as to special conditions in agreements for the user of a railway, South Yorkshire Railway Co. *v.* Great Northern Railway Co., 3 D. M. & G. 576; Furness Railway Co. *v.* Smith, 1 De G. & G. 299. (User of a pier.) Shrewsbury and Birmingham Railway Co. *v.* Stour Valley Railway Co., 2 D.

or apportionment of the tolls with the view of carrying
out this object (*o*). The clause * does not authorize ＊ 323
an agreement which will amount in fact to a lease, or
to a transfer of the undertaking to another company (*p*), or
which will have the effect of enabling one company to carry
the whole of the traffic of another company, under color of
passing over the line of the other company (*q*), but merely
gives to one party a limited power to run a portion of its traffic
over the other line (*r*). An agreement between two railway
companies, giving one company the power to pass over the
line of the other on certain specified terms, confers rights of a
permanent nature, and is not a mere license determinable at
will, although it may not contain words of succession or reference as to time (*s*). The terms of the agreement are not
too vague, but will be held to concede a user consistent with
the proper enjoyment of the railway, the subject-matter of the
contract, and with the rights of the granting party (*t*).

72. Where an agreement has been entered into between
two companies as to the terms of passing over each other's
lines, the rights in respect of such passing depend upon the
terms of the agreement, and are no longer governed by the
Railways Consolidation Act, 8 Vict. c. 20, s. 87 (*u*).

73. The 92d clause of Railways Clauses Consolidation Act
seems intended to apply to the user of the line by the public
generally, and not to that under express agreements made
under the 87th clause. The intention appears clearly to be to
make railways public highways for engines and carriages properly constructed (*x*).

M. & G. 866; London, Brighton, and South Coast Railway Co. *v.* London and South Western Railway Co., 4 D. & J. 363. (User of a joint station.) Shrewsbury, &c., &c., Railway Co. *v.* Chester, &c., &c., Railway Co., 14 L. T. 433. (Interference with the user of a joint station.) Midland Railway Co. *v.* Ambergate, &c., &c., Railway Co., 10 Ha. 359. (User of a station.)

(*o*) See South Yorkshire Railway Co. *v.* Great Northern Railway Co., 3 D. M. & G. 583; East Lancashire Railway Co. *v.* Lancashire, &c., &c., Railway Co., 9 Exch. 591. See, also, Railway Traffic and Canal Act, 17 & 18 Vict. c. 31.

(*p*) Great Northern Railway Co. *v.* Eastern Counties Railway Co., 9 Ha. 306.

(*q*) Simpson *v.* Denison, 10 Ha. 51.

(*r*) Winch *v.* Birkenhead Railway Co., 5 De G. & S. 562; Simpson *v.* Denison, 10 Ha. 51.

(*s*) Great Northern Railway Co. *v.* Manchester, Sheffield, and Lincolnshire Railway Co., 5 De G. & S. 138.

(*t*) *Ib.*

(*u*) Great Northern Railway Co. *v.* Eastern Counties Railway Co., 9 Ha. 306.

(*x*) Midland Railway Co. *v.* Ambergate, &c., &c., Railway Co., 10 Ha. 359. See *ib.*, as to whether the right to use

74. Where a railway company is empowered by its act to form a junction with another line of railway, the latter * 324 company will * be restrained from interfering with the former company in making the junction (*y*). In making the junction a company may not take the land or interfere with the works of the company or person to whom the other railway belongs, or any of the works thereof, further than is necessary for making the junction (*z*). A railway which is empowered to use, enter upon, or take land necessary for the purposes of the junction, takes only an easement in the land of the other company (*a*), unless otherwise provided in the special act, or unless an agreement has been come to between the companies for the sale of the land (*b*).

75. The court will enforce by injunction the provisions of the 115th section of the Railways Clauses Consolidation Act, that no engine or other description of moving power shall be brought or used upon a railway, unless the same shall have been approved by the railway company as therein mentioned, notwithstanding that to enforce such right of inspection would occasion great inconvenience to the public traffic, and although it may appear that the provision is sought to be enforced, not from any apprehension of the use of improper engines, but for the purpose of impeding the traffic over the line of a competing company (*c*).

76. The court will enforce by injunction the provisions of the 117th section of the Railways Clauses Consolidation Act, that no carriage belonging to another company having the right to run over the line, shall pass along or be upon the railway unless it be at all times, so long as it shall be used or shall remain on the railway, of the construction and in the condition which the regulations of the company for the time being shall require. Parties whose right to use a railway is secured by act of Parliament cannot insist upon their right,

the railway includes the right to use the stations. Comp. Simpson *v.* Denison, 10 Ha. 51.

(*y*) Great Northern Railway Co. *v.* East and West India Docks, &c., &c., Railway Co., 7 Ra. Ca. 356.

(*z*) 26 & 27 Vict. c. 92, s. 11.

(*a*) Oxford, Worcester, and Wolverhampton Railway Co. *v.* South Staffordshire Railway Co., 1 Drew. 263.

(*b*) 26 & 27 Vict. c. 92, s. 10.

(*c*) Midland Railway Co. *v.* Ambergate, Nottingham, &c., &c., Railway Co., 10 Ha. 359.

and at the same time say that the rules and regulations made for the security of the line, the passengers, and the traffic, are unreasonable, unnecessary, and inapplicable to their particular traffic (*d*).

77. * Where an act of Parliament enables the owners   * 325 or occupiers of lands adjoining the railway to carry the line across the lands of a private person or another line of railway, the power is not confined to the owners or occupiers at the time the railway was made, but extends to persons who have become owners or occupiers since the passing of the act (*e*).

78. Where the special act prohibits a company from entering upon or taking lands without the consent of the owner, his consent must be obtained before the lands are taken. A rival company may, under the provisions of the clause, refuse to allow their railway to be crossed, although the effect of such a construction may be to prevent the undertaking from being carried into execution (*f*).

79. After a company have taken lands under their compulsory powers and paid the money, the owner of the land cannot restrain them in the mode of using the land (*g*). Nor can a man who has sold his land to a company and given them possession, have an injunction to restrain the company from continuing in possession of the land in default of payment of the purchase-money. His proper remedy is to enforce his lien or to have a receiver appointed (*h*).

80. The doctrine of part performance applies in the case of railway companies. Where a railway company had paid part of the purchase-moneys, and had taken possession, but retained the balance until a good title could be shown, the court held that they had purchased the right of possession, and would not restrain the company from continuing in possession

---

(*d*) See Rhymney Railway Co. *v.* Taff Vale Railway Co., 29 Beav. 153, affr. 9 W. R. 362, when the case turned upon a clause in a special act.

(*e*) Bishop *v.* North, 11 M. & W. 418; Monkland and Kirkintilloch Railway Co. *v.* Dixon, 3 Ra. Ca. 273; Bell *v.* Midland Railway Co., 3 D. & J. 673, 10 C. B. N. S. 287. See, also, Farrow *v.* Vansittart, 1 Ra. Ca. 602; Dand *v.* Kingscote, 2 Ra. Ca. 27.

(*f*) Clarence Railway Co. *v.* Great North of England, &c., &c., Railway Co., 4 Q. B. 46, 2 Ra. Ca. 763. See Gray *v.* Liverpool and Bury Railway Co., 9 Beav. 391.

(*g*) East and West India Docks, &c., &c., Railway Co. *v.* Dawes, 11 Ha. 363.

(*h*) Pell *v.* Northampton and Banbury Junction Railway Co., 2 L. R. Ch. App. 100.

22

of the land until payment of the balance into court (*i*).

* 326   81. * The lawfulness of the entry of a railway company upon land under the provisions of statutes earlier
in date than the Lands Clauses Act or Railways Clauses Consolidation Act, was disputed in several cases (*k*).

82. The commissioners of sewers, acting under 57 Geo. 3,
c. 29, cannot take compulsorily the whole of a house, unless
they have formally adjudged that possession of the whole is
necessary for the purpose of executing their powers (*l*). Under the Public Health Act, 11 & 12 Vict. c. 63, the powers of
local boards of health are confined to their own districts.
The Local Government Act, 21 & 22 Vict. c. 98, extends those
powers, but only for the purpose of distribution or outfall,
that is, cleansing the sewers, and does not give power to construct sewers out of the district (*m*). A local board has
power, under 11 & 12 Vict. c. 63, s. 45, to carry sewers
through land without the consent of the owners, but it has no
power, under s. 46, to enter upon land without the consent of
the owners, for the purpose of making reservoirs and deposit
beds for retaining the sewage (*n*).

83. Under the provisions of the Metropolis Local Management Act, 18 & 19 Vict. c. 120, works comprised within the
terms of the 135th section, may be constructed on making
compensation for damage without first acquiring the lands
under the provisions of the 150th–153d sections and the
Lands Clauses Act, notwithstanding that the works may be of
such a character as to involve an actual taking of land, and
may be within the powers of sections 150–153 (*o*).

84. The appeal given by the 211th section to the Metropolitan Board of Works, does not oust the jurisdiction of

* 327   the court where * any local board has exceeded its

(*i*) Capps *v.* Norwich and Spalding Railway Co., 9 Jur. N. S. 635.

(*k*) Doe *v.* Manchester, Bury, &c., Railway Co., 14 M. & W. 687; Jones *v.* Great Western Railway Co., 1 Ra. Ca. 684; Langford *v.* Brighton and Lewes Railway Co., 4 Ra. Ca. 69; Skerratt *v.* North Staffordshire Railway Co., 5 Ra. Ca. 166; South Western Railway Co. *v.* Coward, *ib.* 703; Doe *v.* Leeds and Bradford Railway Co., 15 Jur. 946.

(*l*) Thomas *v.* Daw, 2 L. R. Ch. App. 1.

(*m*) Haywood *v.* Lowndes, 4 Drew. 454.

(*n*) Sutton *v.* Mayor, &c., &c., of Norwich, 27 L. J. Ch. 739.

(*o*) North London Railway Co. *v.* Metropolitan Board of Works, John. 405; Hughes *v.* Metropolitan Railway Co., 7 Jur. N. S. 986. See Clarke *v.* Vestry of Paddington, 5 Jur. N. S. 138.

powers (p). The power of the board to require certain alterations to be made being a discretionary one in each particular
case, the board is bound to exercise its discretion in each particular case, and is acting *ultra vires*, if without exercising such
discretion it proceeds to make the alterations in pursuance of a
determination to require it to be made in all cases (q).

85. Under the Metropolitan Buildings Act, 18 & 19 Vict.
c. 122, if a party-wall is insufficient to bear a building about
to be laid on it, the builder has a right to pull down the party-
wall, even to the inconvenience of the adjoining owner (r). It
is required by the 143d section of 18 & 19 Vict. c. 120, that no
building is to be erected beyond the regular line of buildings
in the street in which the same is situate. This does not mean a
strict mathematical line, but a substantially regular line (s).

86. The Thames Embankment Act, 1862, 25 & 26 Vict.
c. 93, incorporates the Lands Clauses Act, with the additional
provision that the word "land" shall include easements and
interests in land. The owner of a wharf on the Thames had
a right of free access to the river, and also the right of load-
ing and unloading his barges at the wharf, but there was no
campshed or hard. The barges only rested at low water on
the mud of the foreshore. The court held that the filling up
the river in front of the wharf was not a taking or using for the
purposes of the undertaking any easement or interest, and
refused to restrain the defendants from proceeding with their
works until they had complied with the provisions of section
84 of the Lands Clauses Act (t).

87. The owner of a mine is often unable to obtain clear and
satisfactory proof that his neighbor is trespassing on his mine,
though he may have fair presumptive evidence of the fact.
The court will, in such cases, upon a fair *primâ facie* case
being made out, order the owner of the adjoining mine
to permit * an inspection to be made of his mine by   * 328
proper persons, named on behalf of the plaintiff (u), and

(p) Tinkler v. Wandsworth District
Board of Works, 2 D. & J. 261.
(q) Ib.
(r) Seawell v. Webster, 7 W. R. 691.
(s) Tear v. Freebody, 4 C. B. N. S.
228.
(t) Macey v. Metropolitan Board of
Works, 33 L. J. Ch. 377. See the
Temple Pier Co. v. Metropolitan Board
of Works, 34 L. J. Ch. 262.
(u) Lewis v. Marsh, 8 Ha. 97 ; Bennitt
v. Whitehouse, 28 Beav. 119. See
Ennor v. Barwell, 1 D. F. & J. 528.

will, as auxiliary to the inspection, order the removal, if necessary, of obstructions to the inspection, and that all steps be taken as are necessary to enable the inspector to make a complete inspection (*x*).

88. An order for inspection will be made on an interlocutory application (*y*). If a fair *primâ facie* case be made out, and an inspection is material, the mere denial of the defendant amounts to nothing. He must positively swear that injury will.be done him by being compelled to submit to the inspection (*z*). An order to inspect may be granted at the same time as an interim order for an injunction ; but if an undertaking is offered, and time is asked to answer affidavits, an inspection will not be ordered adversely, on the motion for an injunction (*a*). But if no affidavits be filed by the defendant before the time appointed, an inspection will, upon the renewal of the application, be ordered upon the undertaking of the plaintiff to answer such damage as the court will award (*b*).

89. It is not according to the course of the court to make, upon interlocutory application before the hearing, an order authorizing a man to break up the soil of another, for the purposes of inspection (*c*).

90. The court has jurisdiction, where apertures or roads have been made from one mine into the adjoining mine, to order that access be given to the mine, so as to enable the person whose mine has been encroached upon to block them up. This order was made in a case where the apertures and roads had been made by persons under whom the mine-owner claimed, and not by himself (*d*). The court did not feel that it could order the mine-owner to block them up, as he had not made them (*e*).

* 329   91. * A court of common law has now, under the Common Law Procedure Act, 1854, 17 & 18 Vict. c.

(*x*) East India Co. *v.* Kynaston, 3 Bligh, 153, 168 ; Earl of Lonsdale *v.* Curwen, *ib.* 168, n. ; Walker *v.* Fletcher, *ib.* 172, n. ; Att.-Gen. *v.* Chambers, 12 Beav. 159.

(*y*) Ennor *v.* Barwell, 1 D. F. & J. 528.

(*z*) Bennitt *v.* Whitehouse, 28 Beav. 119.

(*a*) Whaley *v.* Brancker, 10 Jur. N. S. 535

(*b*) *Ib.* ; 12 W. R. 595.

(*c*) Ennor *v.* Barwell, 1 D. F. & J. 528. See, as to order for inspection, Saul *v.* Metropolitan Railway Co., 16 L. T. N. S. 169.

(*d*) Powell *v.* Aikin, 4 K. & J. 360.

(*e*) *Ib.* 355 ; Clegg *v.* Dearden, 12 Q. B. 576.

125, s. 58, the same power of ordering things to be done that are necessary for inspection, which is exercised by courts of equity, as auxiliary to their power of ordering inspection (f). Where, accordingly, the defendant had erected a wall at the extremity of his mine, which prevented a proper inspection, the court ordered such a way to be made through the wall as was necessary for the purposes of inspection (g).

92. The account in cases of trespass for the underground working of mines will, as a general rule, be limited to minerals gotten within six years before the filing of the bill, unless it can be shown that the minerals have been abstracted intentionally, and that steps have been taken during the process to conceal and prevent the discovery (h). If the amount actually abstracted can be proved, the onus of proof will lie on the wrong-doer to show that it was not taken within the time during which the account is directed (i). In Powell $v.$ Aikin (k), one of the defendants had, for the purpose of better working his own mines, secretly worked into and made air-courses and roads through the mines of the plaintiff, and had, in doing so, fraudulently abstracted large quantities of coal. Subsequently, on his becoming embarrassed, his mortgagees, the other defendants, entered into possession, and, though not privy to his acts, continued to use the air-courses and the roads, and, as it was alleged, abstracted further quantities of the plaintiff's coals. Wood, V. C., held that the mortgagor and mortgagee were respectively accountable for the market value at the pit's mouth of all the coals removed or gotten, whilst they were respectively in possession, without prejudice to any question as to which of them was accountable for coal, the precise times of getting or removing which could not be ascertained. His Honor held that he could not throw upon the mortgagees the expense of filling up the air-courses or removing the roads, as they did not * make them (l), or decree * 330

(f) Bennett $v.$ Griffiths, 3 El. & El. 467.
(g) Ib.
(h) Dean $v.$ Thwaite, 21 Beav. 623; Hood $v.$ Easton, 2 Jur. N. S. 917; *supra*, p. 228.
(i) Ib.
(k) 4 K. & J. 343.
(l) See Clegg $v.$ Dearden, 12 Q. B. 576.

compensation to the plaintiff for the damage sustained by him in being obliged to leave additional barriers, or charge the defendants with a way-leave rent in respect of the air-courses and roads (m). The order directed all just allow-ances to be made to the parties chargeable in respect of the charges and expenses on account of the coals so gotten or removed (n). When a party out of possession of an estate claims an account, the right to which depends upon the right of possession, the court requires him to recover possession at law, before he files a bill for the consequential relief (o).

93. The court will interfere by mandatory injunction against trespass (p). If the trespass or damage is complete, and the title is a pure legal title, the court will not in general interfere by way of mandatory injunction, for there is a full remedy at law by ejectment (q). But if the damage is of a serious or irreparable character, or the trespass is of a continuing nature, the court may interfere by way of mandatory injunction, not-withstanding the existence of a remedy at law (r). In Rob-inson v. Lord Byron (s), the defendant having penned up the water of a stream which flowed through his park so as to pre-vent it flowing in its usual course to the plaintiff's mill, and at other times letting it on in such quantities as to endanger the mill of the plaintiff, he was restrained by mandatory in-junction. So also in a case where the plaintiffs had made out their right at law to build a bridge over the defendants' rail-way, and as a temporary easement to erect poles and other temporary obstructions upon land adjacent to the defendants' railway, and the defendants had, in order to prevent * 331 the plaintiffs from so * temporarily using their land, built up a wall which effectually prevented the plaintiffs

---

(m) But see now 21 & 22 Vict. c. 27, s. 2; *supra*, pp. 221–224.

(n) See Hood v. Easton, 2 Jur. N. S. 917; Millett v. Davey, 31 Beav. 470. See, also, account in waste, *supra*, pp. 284–286.

(o) Norton v. Frecker, 1 Atk. 523; Vice v. Thomas, 4 Y. & C. 538.

(p) See *supra*, p. 230–232, as to man-datory injunctions.

(q) Deere v. Guest, 1 M. & C. 516; Moreland v. Richardson, 22 Beav. 604; Doran v. Carroll, 11 Ir. Ch. 379. See

Att.-Gen. v. Manchester and Leeds Railway Co., 1 Ra. Ca. 436; Ward v. Higgs, 12 W. R. 1074.

(r) Martyr v. Lawrence, 2 D. J. & S. 261. See Great North of England, &c., Junction Railway Co. v. Clarence Rail-way Co., 1 Coll. 507; Ward v. Higgs, 12 W. R. 1074.

(s) 1 Bro. C. C. 588. To the same effect, London & N. W. Railway Co. v. Lancashire and Yorkshire Railway Co., 4 L. R. Eq. 174.

from carrying on their works, a mandatory injunction was granted restraining the defendants from continuing to use the wall, and from preventing the plaintiffs from making the bridge (*t*). So also where the lessees of a coal-mine had made apertures to ventilate the mine through the land of the plaintiff, and had mortgaged their interest in the mine to the defendants, who began to work the mine and continued to use the apertures, the court granted an injunction which was in some respects of a mandatory nature, restraining them from continuing to use the apertures, but declined to grant a mandatory injunction ordering them to fill up the apertures, inasmuch as they had not made them (*u*). So, also, in Manchester, Sheffield, and Lincolnshire Railway Co. *v.* Worksop Board of Health (*v*), a board of health was restrained by mandatory injunction from permitting a sewer to remain open (*x*). So also a man was restrained by mandatory injunction from permitting a building which he had erected on the roof of a neighbor's house to remain there (*y*). So also a man was restrained at the suit of his wife from continuing in possession of a house which formed part of her separate estate (*z*). So also the manager of a business was restrained from excluding the owner of the business from the business premises (*a*).

94. In a case where a wall had been knocked down, the court would not interfere by way of mandatory injunction, so as to order it to be built up again, but left the plaintiff to his remedy by damages at law (*b*).

95. After the establishment of his legal right and the fact of its violation, a man is entitled as of course to a perpetual injunction to restrain the recurrence of the wrong (*c*), unless there be something special in the circumstances of the case (*d*).

(*t*) Great North of England, &c., Junction Railway Co. *v.* Clarence Railway Co., 1 Coll. 507. See Philipps *v.* Treeby, 8 Jur. N. S. 999.

(*u*) Powell *v.* Aikin, 4 K. & J. 355.

(*v*) 23 Beav. 209.

(*x*) See Att.-Gen. *v.* Borough of Birmingham, 4 K. & J. 547.

(*y*) Martyr *v.* Lawrence, 3 D. J. & S. 261.

(*z*) Green *v.* Pledger, 5 Ha. 400, n.

(*a*) Eachus *v.* Moss, 14 W. R. 327.

(*b*) Doran *v.* Carroll, 11 Ir. Ch. 379.

(*c*) Imperial Gas-light Co. *v.* Broadbent, 7 H. L. 612 ; Lowndes *v.* Bettle, 33 L. J. Ch. 451.

(*d*) *Supra*, p. 225–228.

* 332   # * CHAPTER XVIII.

INJUNCTIONS AGAINST NUISANCE.

SECTION I. — PRINCIPLES ON WHICH THE COURT ACTS IN RESTRAINING NUISANCE.

1. THE jurisdiction of courts of equity over nuisance is in aid of the legal right, and has been assumed for the purpose of preserving and protecting property from irreparable or at least from substantial or material damage pending the trial of the right. If the case made out is such that the recovery of damages at law will give a full and adequate compensation for the injury, no foundation is laid for the interference of a court of equity.[1] If, on the other hand, the injury is of so material

---

[1] In the courts of the United States an objection that the plaintiff has a plain, complete, and adequate remedy at law goes to the jurisdiction of the forum, and may, therefore, be enforced by the judges *sua sponte*, though not raised by the pleadings or suggested by the counsel. Parker *v.* Winnipiseogee Lake Cotton and Woollen Co., 2 Black, 545.

a nature that it cannot be well or fully compensated by the recovery of damages at law, or be such as from its continuance and permanent mischief might occasion a constantly recurring grievance, a foundation is laid for the interference of the court (a). The jurisdiction was formerly exercised sparingly and with caution (b), but it is now fully established, and will be exercised as freely as in other cases in which the aid of the court is sought for the purpose of protecting legal rights from violation.[1]

2. A nuisance is an act unaccompanied by an act of trespass, which causes a substantial injury to the corporeal or incorporeal hereditaments of other persons. Where a man wrongfully disturbs another in the exclusive possession of property, he commits an act of trespass. Where the infringement of the right is the consequence of an act, which is not in itself an invasion * of property, the cause from which the   * 333 injury flows is termed a nuisance. In the one case it is the immediate act which causes the injury, in the other the injury is the consequence of an act done beyond the bounds of the property affected by it (c).

The jurisdiction of courts of equity over the subject-matter of nuisances does not arise from the fact that a nuisance exists, but results from the circumstance that the equitable power of the court is necessary to protect the party from an injury for which no adequate redress can be obtained by an action at law, or its interference is necessary to suppress interminable litigation for the recovery of damages for an actionable wrong. Carlisle v. Cooper, 6 C. E. Green, N. J. 576. See this case also, as to the conditions essential to the exercise of the power by the court. And as to the interference by injunction to prevent threatened mischief and injury without reparation, see Spooner v. McConnel, 1 McLean, C. C. 338; Mayor of Rochester v. Curtiss, 1 Clarke, Ch. 336; Bonaparte v. Camden and Amboy Railway, 1 Baldwin, 221; Gardner v. Newburgh, 2 Johns. Ch. 162; Amelung v. Seekamp, 9 Gill and J. 468; Browning v. Camden and Woodbury R. & T. Co., 3 Green, N. J., 47; Chapman v. Mad River and Lake Erie Railway, 6 Ohio, N. S. 119.

(a) Att.-Gen. v. Nicholl, 16 Ves. 338; Att.-Gen. v. Sheffield Gas Company, 3 D. M. & G. 319; Wilson v. Townend, 1 Dr. & Sm. 329.

(b) 3 M. & K. 180, per Lord Brougham.

(c) Reynolds v. Clarke, 2 Lord Raym. 1399; Scott v. Shepherd, 1 Smith, L. C. See, also, Weeton v. Woodcock, 5 M. & W. 594. As to the legal signification of the word "nuisance," see Harrison v. Good, 11 L. R. Eq. 338. Also Walker v. Brewster, 5 L. R. Eq. 25, where it is held that the collection of a crowd of noisy and disorderly people to the annoyance of the neighborhood outside grounds in which entertainments with music and fireworks are being given for profit, is a nuisance for which the giver of the entertainment is liable to an injunction; even though he has excluded all improper characters from the grounds, and the amusements within the grounds have been conducted in an orderly way to the satisfaction of the police. Also Crump v. Lambert, 3 L. R. Eq. 409; Inchbold v. Robinson, 4 L. R. Ch. Ap. 388.

[1] The powers of a court of equity are corrective as well as preventive. It may order them to be abated, as well as restrain them from being erected. State of Penn. v. Wheeling, &c., Bridge

3. Nuisances may be either of a private or a public nature. The only distinction between the two cases is, that a private nuisance is an injury to the property of an individual, while a public nuisance is an injury to the property of all persons who come within the sphere of its operation (*d*). The distinction between private and public nuisances was discussed in a singular case, Soltau *v.* De Held (*e*), where an injunction was sought to restrain the ringing of the bells of a Roman Catholic chapel close to the residence of the complaining party. " I conceive," said Kindersley, V. C., " that to constitute a public nuisance, the thing must be such as in its nature and consequences is a nuisance, an injury, or damage to all persons coming within the sphere of its operations, though it may be so in a greater degree to some than it is to others. For example, take the case of the operations of a manufactory, in the course of which operations volumes of smoke or of noxious effluvia are emitted. To all persons who are at all within the range of these operations, it is more or less objectionable, more or less a nuisance in the popular sense of the term. It is true that to those who are nearer to it, it may be a greater nuisance, a greater inconvenience, than it is to those who are more remote from it ; but still to all who are within the reach of it, it is more or less a nuisance or an inconvenience. Take another ordinary case, the most ordinary case of a public nuisance, the stopping of the king's highway, that is a nuisance to all who may have occasion to travel that highway. It may be a much greater nuisance to a person who has to travel it every day of his life, than it is to a person who has to travel it once a year or once in five years ; but it is more or less a nuisance to every one who has occasion to use it. If, however, the thing

Co., 13 Howard, 519 ; Van Bergen *v.* Van Bergen, 2 Johns. Ch. R. 272; Hammond *v.* Fuller, 1 Paige, 197; Earl *v.* De Hart, 1 Beas. 280 ; Del. & Rar. Canal Co. *v.* Rar. & Del. Bay R. Co., 1 C. E. Green, N. J. 378.

Equity will interfere by mandatory injunction to compel the restoration of running water to its natural channel, when wrongfully diverted therefrom, at the suit of the party whose lands include either the whole or a part of such channel. The grounds for equitable interpo-sition in such a case are twofold : first, the inadequacy of any legal remedy to secure the party in the enjoyment of his right to have the water flow in its natural channel ; second, to prevent a multiplicity of suits for damages accruing from the daily and continuous wrongful diversion of the stream. Corning *v.* Troy Iron and Nail Factory, 40 N. Y. 191.

(*d*) See Att.-Gen. *v.* Sheffield Gas Co., 3 D. M. & G. 320.

(*e*) 2 Sim. N. S. 142.

complained of is such that it is a great nuisance to those who are more immediately within * the sphere of * 334 its operations, but is no nuisance or inconvenience whatever, or is even advantageous or pleasurable to those who are more removed from it, then, I conceive, it does not come within the meaning of the term public nuisance (f). The case before me is a case in point. A peal of bells may be, and is, no doubt, an extreme nuisance to a person who lives within a very few feet or yards of them; but to a person who lives at a distance from them, although he is within the reach of their sound, it may be a positive pleasure, for I cannot assent to the proposition that in all circumstances and under all conditions the sound of bells must be a nuisance. . . . I may further say that it does not follow because a thing complained of is a nuisance to several individuals, that therefore it is a public nuisance. One may illustrate this very simply by supposing the case of a man building up a wall which has the effect of darkening the ancient lights of half a dozen dwelling-houses. It does not follow, because half a dozen persons or a dozen persons are suffering by the darkening of their ancient lights by the one wall, that therefore it is a public nuisance which can be indicted at the suit of the Crown, or for which the Attorney-General can file an information in this court. It is a private nuisance to each of the individuals aggrieved " (g).[1]

4. If the thing complained of is in its nature a public nuisance, the remedy is by information at the suit of the Attorney-General (h).[2] The circumstance, however, that the thing

(f) See Squire v. Campbell, 1 M. & C. 486.

(g) See Att.-Gen. v. Sheffield Gas Co., 3 D. M. & G. 325; Att.-Gen. v. Conservators of Thames, 1 H. & M. 1.

(h) Att.-Gen. v. Cleaver, 18 Ves. 211; Soltau v. De Held, 2 Sim. N. S. 150; Ware v. Regent's Canal Co., 3 D. & J. 228; Att.-Gen. v. Great Northern Railway Co., 1 Dr. & Sm. 161.

[1] " Hence it is not competent for one who suffers damage, in common with others only, to maintain a bill to enjoin a party from the continuance of a public nuisance, under color of legislative grant." 2 Redfield on Railways, 345; Bigelow v. Hartford Bridge Co., 14 Conn. 565; O'Brien v. Norwich and Worcester R. C., 17 Conn. 872; Delaware and Maryland R. v. Stump, 8 Gill & J. 479; Allen v. Board of Freeholders, 2 Beasley, 68; Zabriskie v. Jersey City and B. Railroad, ib. 314.

Though the jurisdiction of courts of equity to redress public nuisances by injunction is of ancient date, and seems clearly established, yet, as a general rule, equity will not interfere where the object sought can be as well attained in the ordinary tribunals. Jersey City v. City of Hudson, 2 Beasley 420.

[2] It is now settled that a court of equity may take jurisdiction in cases of public nuisance by an information filed by the Attorney-General. See

complained of may be a public nuisance, does not prevent an
individual who has sustained some special damage thereby,
over and above the general damage sustained by the rest of
the public, from applying to the court for protection by bill (i).[1]
There may, in such cases, be both an information and a bill.
The Attorney-General may file an information to restrain
* 335   the * thing complained of as a public nuisance, and the
individual who sustains a particular damage may join
as plaintiff, as well as relator, and have the remedy for himself
by bill (k).   In Attorney-General v. United Kingdom Electric
Telegraph Co. (l), the defendants having dug a trench along a
public foot-path, the Attorney-General filed an information to
restrain the public nuisance at the relation of the owner of the

People v. Davidson, 30 Cal. 379; Att.-
Gen. v. Utica Insurance Co., 2 Johns.
Ch. 382; Rowe v. Granite Bridge Co.,
21 Pick. 344; Att.-Gen. v. N. J. R. and
Trans. Co., 2 Green, Ch. R. 136.

But the remedy by indictment being
so efficacious, courts of equity entertain jurisdiction over public nuisances
with great reluctance, whether their intervention is invoked at the instance of
the Attorney-General, or of a private individual who suffers some injury therefrom distinct from that of the public.
Morris and Essex Railway Co. v. Prudden, 5 C. E. Green, 530; Higbee v.
Camden and Amboy Railroad, 4 C. E.
Green, 276.

(i) Crowder v. Tinkler, 19 Ves. 617;
Spencer v. London and Birmingham
Railway Co., 8 Sim. 193; Sampson v.
Smith, ib. 272; Soltau v. De Held, 2
Sim. N. S. 151.

(k) Att.-Gen. v. Johnson, 2 Wils. C.
C. 87; Att.-Gen. v. Forbes, 2 M. & C.
123; Soltau v. De Held, 2 Sim. N. S.
151; Att.-Gen. v. Sheffield Gas Co., 3
D. M. & G. 304.

(l) 30 Beav. 217.

[1] Some damage not common to the
public or large classes of people. Mil-
hau v. Sharp, 27 N. Y. Ct. Ap. 625;
Skiller v. Grandy, 13 Mich. 540; Hamilton v. Whittridge, 11 Md. 128. As
well as damage otherwise irreparable. Morris and Essex Railway Co.
v. Prudden, 5 C. E. Green, N. J. 530.

In Mississippi and Missouri Railroad
Co. v. Ward, 2 Black, 485, it is held that
a private individual who has sustained,
and is still sustaining individual injury
by a public nuisance, may maintain a

bill to restrain the same; nor need he
join his partners in the business affected any more than other individuals
similarly injured. It was also held
that where the suit is brought in a
federal court, the jurisdiction is determined by the value of the object to be
gained, to wit, the removal of the nuisance; and the suit is local, and must
be brought in the district where the
nuisance is situated.

A town cannot maintain a bill to
abate a nuisance upon the ground that
individual inhabitants are affected in
their private interests. As the owner
of property, a town has similar rights
with other owners; and such owners,
to maintain a bill for abatement, must
allege some particular grievance beyond that sustained by the public
generally. Perhaps the town might
be heard, in its corporate capacity,
where the health of the community was
endangered by a nuisance, or where
they might otherwise be subjected to
expense by reason of pauperism, and in
any other case involving corporate responsibility.

Where an erection is made under
color of authority of the state, if it be
a nuisance, it would seem that the
proper proceeding for its abatement
would be an information in the nature
of quo warranto, instituted by the Attorney-General, or an indictment by
the grand jury; or, if the state is
estopped by its grant, then by proceedings in the courts of the United States.
Dover v. Portsmouth Bridge, 17 N. H.
200.

soil, who also preferred a bill complaining of the same act as a trespass. The fact that an individual may be nearer a possible cause of injury, does not entitle him to maintain a bill for relief if he has not sustained any private damage, and there is no reason to apprehend that he will sustain any (*m*). Nor can an individual sue, though he may be more inconvenienced by the act complained of than the rest of the public, if it has been authorized by statute, and is one which from its nature must necessarily prove a nuisance, to some one or other of the public (*n*). A public company exceeding its legislative limits cannot be restrained by injunction at the suit of a rival company, which does not allege that it has sustained some private injury by such excess, though the act complained of may be injurious to the public interest (*o*).

5. The right of prosecution given to the Home Secretary by the Act 21 & 22 Vict. c. 104, s. 31, does not supersede the right of persons aggrieved by a nuisance to have an injunction (*p*).

6. The motives with which a suit is instituted are not generally to be regarded, but if it can be shown satisfactorily that the suit has been instituted by one man merely for the purposes of or at the instigation of another, the court will not relieve (*q*). The fact, however, that the suit may have been got up by a * third party is not enough to deprive a man of his * 336 right to have a nuisance discontinued (*r*). Nor is it wholly immaterial, where the public interest purports to be asserted, at least upon the interlocutory application, to look into the motives from which or under which the matter is brought forward (*s*). Where an injunction is sought on public grounds, the court will not interfere unless the public good

---

(*m*) Ware *v.* Regent's Canal Co., 3 D. & J. 212.

(*n*) Att.-Gen. *v.* Conservators of Thames, 1 H. & M. 1; Att.-Gen. *v.* Metropolitan Board of Works, *ib.* 313. See Biddulph *v.* St. George's Vestry, 33 L. J. Ch. 411.

(*o*) Stockport and District Waterworks Co. *v.* Mayor, &c., of Manchester, 9 Jur. N. S. 266.

(*p*) Att.-Gen. *v.* Metropolitan Board of Works, 1 H. & M. 298.

(*q*) Pentney *v.* Lynn Commissioners, 13 W. R. 983; *supra*, 207.

(*r*) Turner *v.* Mirfield, 34 Beav. 390.

(*s*) Att.-Gen. *v.* Sheffield Gas Co., 3 D. M. & G. 311, *per* Knight Bruce, L. J.; Felkin *v.* Herbert, 11 L. T. N. S. 173.

requires the issuing of the injunction, or unless proof of damage to individuals can be shown (t).

7. If the complaint is by an individual in respect of the injury done to his own comfort and enjoyment, the proper remedy is by bill. Two or more persons having distinct and separate tenements ought not to join as co-plaintiffs in a suit to restrain an act which, although a common injury to both or to all of them, is a separate nuisance to each of them, without making the Attorney-General a party (u).

8. The bill is usually brought by the occupier or by the lessee in possession, but the owner may sue on the ground of injury to his property, either alone or conjointly with the occupier (x). A lessee whose tenancy has expired during the establishment of the nuisance, but who has agreed for a renewal of the lease, may maintain the suit (y). So also may a tenant from year to year (z), even although he has received notice to quit, and the act complained of has been done by the assent of the landlord (a). In respect of mere personal inconvenience, a wife cannot sue alone (b).

9. In order that a reversioner should be able to sue at law for a nuisance, it is necessary that the wrong complained of should operate injuriously to the reversion, either by
* 337   being of a * permanent character or by operating as a denial of right (c). The rule in equity is the same (d).

10. As between a licensee and the owner of land who grants a license to him over the land, a right of action exists, but a licensee has no right of action in his own name against third parties who interfere with his enjoyment under the license (e).

(t) Ryde Commissioners v. Isle of Wight Ferry, 30 Beav. 616; Felkin v. Herbert, 30 L. J. Ch. 604, 4 L. T. N. S. 433, 11 L. T. N. S. 173.

(u) Hudson v. Maddison, 12 Sim. 416; Pollock v. Lester, 11 Ha. 274.

(x) Wilson v. Townend, 1 Dr. & S. 324; Cleeve v. Mahany, 9 W. R. 882; Radcliffe v. Duke of Portland, 3 Giff. 702; Jackson v. Duke of Newcastle, 33 L. J. Ch. 698.

(y) Gale v. Abbott, 8 Jur. N. S. 987.

(z) Simper v. Foley, 2 J. & H. 555.

(a) Jacomb v. Knight, 32 L. J. Ch. 601.

(b) White v. Cohen, 1 Drew. 312.

(c) Kidgill v. Moor, 9 C. B. 364; Dobson v. Blackmore, 9 Q. B. 991; Simpson v. Savage, 1 C. B. N. S. 347; Bell v. Midland Railway Co., 10 C. B. N. S. 306.

(d) Wilson v. Townend, 1 Dr. & Sm. 329; Johnstone v. Hall, 2 K. & J. 414; Jackson v. Duke of Newcastle, 33 L. J. Ch. 698.

(e) Ackroyd v. Smith, 10 C. B. 164; Whaley v. Laing, 3 H. & N. 675, 901; Hill v. Tupper, 2 H. & C. 121. See Calcraft v. West, 2 J. & L. 123.

Nor can an injunction be supported in any case where an action on the case for the act complained of cannot be maintained (f).

11. If the bill is brought by the occupier or lessee in possession, the landlord or reversioner need not be made a party (g). An uncertificated bankrupt may sue without making his assignees or other persons who have a common interest with him parties (h).

12. The interference of the court by interlocutory injunction being founded on the existence of the legal right, and having for its object the protection of property from irreparable injury pending the trial of the right, a man who comes to the court for an injunction to restrain nuisance must be able to satisfy the court that he has a good *primâ facie* title to the right which he asserts (i), and that there is danger of irreparable, or at least material, injury being done in the mean time, before the trial of the legal right can be had (k).[1] If the damage is so slight that no injury has arisen, or is likely to arise, or if the injury, if any has arisen, is adequately reparable by damages at law (l), or will be much more than compensated, in point of convenience, * to those who are injured by it, * 338 by the results which are to follow (m), the court will not entertain jurisdiction.[2] Nor will the court interfere if the damage is slight and the nuisance is merely of a temporary character (n) ; but a damage, though in itself slight, may from its continuance, or from delay in removing it, or from constant repe-

---

(f) Calcraft v. West, 2 J. & L. 123.

(g) Drayton v. Dale, 2 B. & C. 293; Semple v. London and Birmingham Railway Co., 9 Sim. 209.

(h) Semple v. London and Birmingham Railway Co., ib.

(i) Supra, p. 196.

(k) Earl of Ripon v. Hobart, 3 M. & K. 174; Att.-Gen. v. Sheffield Gas Co., 3 D. M. & G. 314; White v. Cohen, 1 Drew. 313; Wilson v. Townend, 1 Dr. & Sm. 329 ; Eaden v. Frith, 1 H. & M. 573; Inchbold v. Robinson, 4 L. R. Ch. Ap. 388. See, as to irreparable damage, supra, p. 199.

(l) Cory v. Yarmouth and Norwich Railway Co., 3 Ha. 604; Wintle v. Bristol and South Wales Railway Co., 10 W. R. 210.

(m) Att.-Gen. v. Sheffield Gas Co., 3 D. M. & G. 304.

(n) Att.-Gen. v. Sheffield Gas Co., 3 D. M. & G. 304; Cleeve v. Mahany, 9 W. R. 882; Swaine v. Great Northern Railway Co., 33 L. J. Ch. 399; Goldsmid v. Tunbridge Wells Commissioners, 1 L. R. Ch. Ap. 349. See Durrell v. Pritchard, 1 L. R. Ch. Ap. 244.

[1] See Carlisle v. Cooper, 6 C. E. Green, 576 ; and Mohawk Bridge Co. v. Utica and Schen. R., 6 Paige, 554; Bell v. O. and Penn. R., 25 Penn. St. 160 ; Hudson and Delaware Canal Co. v. New York and Erie R., 9 Paige, 323; Minturn v. Seymour, 4 Johns. Ch. 173.

[2] Harrison v. Brooks, 20 Geo. 537.

tition, become sufficiently substantial for the interference of the court (*o*). In estimating the injury the court has regard to all the consequences which may flow from the nuisance, not only to its present effect upon the comfort and convenience of the occupier, but also to any prospective increase of the nuisance and the probable detriment of the estate. If the court is satisfied that some degree of nuisance has been proved to exist, and to have been increasing, the court, in determining whether it should interfere, must have regard to its further continuance or increase: the interference of the court in cases of prospective injury must depend upon the nature and intent of the apprehended mischief, and upon the certainty or uncertainty of its increase or continuance; and the fact of the nuisance having commenced raises a presumption of its continuance (*p*). In determining whether the injury is serious or not, regard must be had to all the consequences which may flow from it (*q*). The mere fact that a certain act may cause a diminution in the value of property does not make that act a nuisance (*r*); but diminution in the value of property is often of great moment as evidence of the extent of a nuisance (*s*). In estimating the character of a nuisance, * more weight is due to the facts which are proved than to the conclusions drawn from scientific investigations. The conclusions to be drawn from scientific investigations are of value in aid or explanation and qualification of the facts which are proved; but it is upon the facts which are proved, and not upon such conclusions that the court ought mainly to rely (*t*).

13. The court will not in general interfere until an actual nuisance has been committed; but it may, by virtue of its jurisdiction to restrain acts which when completed will result

---

(*o*) Coulson *v.* White, 3 Atk. 21; Att.-Gen. *v.* Sheffield Gas Co., 3 D. M. & G. 304; Wandsworth Board of Works *v.* London and South Western Railway Co., 31 L. J. Ch. 854; Swaine *v.* Great Northern Railway Co., 33 L. J. Ch. 399.

(*p*) Goldsmid *v.* Tunbridge Wells Commissioners, 1 L. R. Ch. Ap. 349.

(*q*) Ib.

(*r*) Att.-Gen. *v.* Nicholl, 16 Ves. 338; Squire *v.* Campbell, 1 M. & C. 459, 486;

Soltau *v.* De Held, 2 Sim. N. S. 158. See Jackson *v.* Duke of Newcastle, 33 L. J. Ch. 698.

(*s*) Soltau *v.* De Held, 2 Sim. N. S. 158; White *v.* Cohen, 1 Drew. 318; Goldsmid *v.* Tunbridge Wells Commissioners, 1 L. R. Ch. Ap. 349. See Jackson *v.* Duke of Newcastle, 33 L. J. Ch. 698.

(*t*) Goldsmid *v.* Tunbridge Wells Commissioners, 1 L. R. Ch. Ap. 349.

in a ground of action, interfere before any actual nuisance has been committed, where it is satisfied that the act complained of will inevitably result in a nuisance (u).[1] So, also, where a man threatens or begins to do (x), or insists upon his right to do certain acts, the court will not hesitate to interfere, even though no nuisance may have been actually committed, where the circumstances of the case enable it to form an opinion as to the illegality of the acts complained of, and the irreparable injury which will ensue (y). But the mere fact that a man is commencing operations avowedly for a purpose which may be injurious to another is not enough, unless the circumstances of the case are sufficient to enable the court either to form its own opinion or to put the question into an immediate course of trial (z). The probability that the act complained of is only something which may, according to circumstances, or may at some considerable distance of time, prove a nuisance, is not sufficient (a). If there is no reason for supposing that there is any danger of mischief of a serious character being done suddenly before the interference of the court can be invoked, an injunction will not be granted (b). Where powers to do a certain * act are conferred by statute, the court * 340 will not assume that the exercise of them will create a nuisance (c).

14. If the defendant asserts positively that his acts will not cause a nuisance, or that it is his intention to guard against committing nuisance, and there is no reason to discredit the assertion, the court will not interfere (d).

(u) Haines v. Taylor, 2 Ph. 209; Dawson v. Paver, 5 Ha. 430; Potts v. Levy, 2 Drew. 272; Elwell v. Crowther, 31 Beav. 169; supra, p. 197.

(x) Palmer v. Paul, 2 L. J. Ch. 154.

(y) Elliott v. North Eastern Railway Co., 1 J. & H. 156, 2 D. F. & J. 423, 10 H. L. 333; North Eastern Railway Co. v. Crossland, 2 J. & H. 579; supra, p. 197.

(z) Haines v. Taylor, 2 Ph. 209.

(a) Earl of Ripon v. Hobart, 2 M. & K. 169; Att.-Gen. v. Mayor of Kingston, 34 L. J. Ch. 481.

(b) See Att.-Gen. v. Sheffield Gas Co., 3 D. M. & G. 304; Att.-Gen. v. Borough of Birmingham, 4 K. & J. 546; Wicks v. Hunt, John. 372.

(c) Biddulph v. St. George's Vestry 33 L. J. Ch. 411. See Att.-Gen. v. Conservators of Thames, 1 H. & M. 1.

(d) Warburton v. London and Blackwall Railway Co., 1 Ra. Ca. 558; Haines v. Taylor, 2 Ph. 209; Manchester, Sheffield, and Lincolnshire Railway Co. v. Worksop Board of Health, 23 Beav. 207; Wandsworth Board of Works v. London and South Western Railway Co., 31 L. J. Ch. 854; supra, p. 198.

[1] So an individual tax-payer has no right to file a bill to enjoin the proceedings of the assessors of taxes, in advance of the actual levy of the tax. Miller v. Grandy, 13 Mich. 540. Nor will an injunction be granted where the

15. If the right at law is clear or fairly made out, and the fact of its violation is also clear or fairly made out, it is the duty of the court to protect the property by injunction until the hearing.[1] In a strong case the court may, in the exercise of its discretion, determine the question at once without putting the parties to any further expense and delay (e) ; but, as a general rule, this course will not be adopted if the defendant disputes the right of the plaintiff or denies the fact of its violation (f). If the right at law or the fact of its violation is doubtful, the case resolves itself into a question of comparative injury, whether the defendant will be more damnified by the injunction being granted, or the plaintiff by its being withheld (g).[2] Terms may be imposed on the defendant as the condition of withholding an injunction; and, on the other hand, the plaintiff may be required, as the condition of the interference of the court in his favor, to give an undertaking as to damages in the event of the injunction proving to have been improperly granted (h).

16. If the title to the property sought to be protected has

consequences would be injurious to the corporation, and of no benefit to the complainants. Jones v. City of Newark, 3 Stockton, Ch. 452.

(e) Potts v. Levy, 2 Drew. 272; Eaden v. Frith, 1 H. & M. 573; supra, p. 209.

(f) Ib.; Duke of Beaufort v. Morris, 6 Ha. 349; supra, p. 209.

(g) Hilton v. Lord Granville, Cr. & Ph. 297; Cory v. Yarmouth and Norwich Railway Co., 3 Ha. 600; supra, p. 209, 210.

(h) Supra, p. 210–212.

[1] Where the right at law has not been first established, it must appear that there is danger of irreparable mischief, or the bill will be dismissed on general demurrer. Coe v. Winnipiseogee Lake Cotton and Woollen Manufac. Co., 37 N. H. 254; Burnham v. Kempton, 44 N. H. 78; Eastman v. Company, 47 N. H. 71; Bassett v. Company, ib. 426.

[2] A right to an injunction to suppress a nuisance does not necessarily follow from a right to an action at law for the injury, and an action at law need not precede it in many cases. Dana v. Valentine, 5 Met. 8; Curtis v. Winslow, 38 Vt. 690. See, also, this subject discussed in Aldrich v. Howard, 7 R. I. 87.

But where the nuisance apprehended is doubtful or contingent, equity will not interfere, but will leave the party to his remedy at law. Ellison v. Commissioners, 5 Jones, Eq. 57; Clark v. Lawrence, 6 ib. 83; St. James' Church v. Arrington, 36 Ala. 546; Hayden v. Tucker, 37 Mo. 214; Wolcott v. Mellick, 3 Stockt. 204; Parker v. Winnipiseogee Lake Cotton and Woollen Co., 2 Black, 552. Many cases will sustain an action at law which will not justify relief in equity. Parker v. Winnipiseogee Lake Cotton and Woollen Co., 2 Black, 545, and cases cited, ante, note 1, p. 337. Among the considerations which are stated to govern the court in such cases, are the character of the property which asks protection, as one slaughter-house would not be injured by another; priority of use by either party; relative loss to either party by reason of granting or withholding an injunction; and the character of the place in which the alleged nuisance exists. Curtis v. Winslow, 38 Vt. 690. See, also, for a full discussion of the subject, Wolcott v. Mellick, 3 Stockton, 204, and Parker v. Winnipiseogee Lake Cotton and Woollen Co., 2 Black, 552.

not been accepted by the plaintiff, he cannot seek the aid of the court (*i*).

17. Companies incorporated by act of Parliament, and having compulsory powers to take land and construct works, are bound * to act in strict accordance with the powers *341 which have been vested in them by statute. If they act in excess of their powers, and cause damage to the property of others, they are, like individuals, amenable to the process of the court by injunction (*k*). But as long as they keep within their statutory powers, no action at law or suit in equity can be maintained against them for any act done in the exercise of their statutory authority, however injurious it may be to the property of others. Although an act may amount to a nuisance, the unlawful character of the act is taken away if it has been sanctioned by the legislature (*l*). If, however, statutory powers are conferred under circumstances in which the powers may be exercised without in themselves causing a nuisance, and new and unforeseen circumstances render the exercise of the powers impossible without a breach of the law, these powers cannot be exercised without making the parties liable (*m*).

18. Equity, in restraining incorporated companies from committing nuisance in the construction of their works, follows the law. At law the rule is that if damage results from the construction of works not authorized by statute, or from the wrongful excess of its statutory powers by a public company, or from the negligent and unskilful construction of works which are authorized, the parties injured are left to their common-law right, and may maintain actions against the company, provided the injury is such as would support an action against an individual. If, on the other hand, the works are authorized by statute, and have been executed with proper skill and care, no action lies, however serious the damage may be, for the statutory authority is a bar (*n*). The party injured must

(*i*) Heath *v.* Maydew, 13 W. R. 199.
(*k*) Frewin *v.* Lewis, 4 M. &. C. 255; Oldaker *v.* Hunt, 6 D. M. & G. 389; Imperial Gas Co. *v.* Broadbent, 7 D. M. & G. 459, 7 H. L. 600; Ware *v.* Regent's Canal Co., 3 D. & J. 227.
(*l*) Rex *v.* Pease, 4 B. & A. 30.

(*m*) Queen *v.* Bradford Navigation Co., 6 B. & S. 681. See, as to construction of statutes, *supra*, p. 301.
(*n*) Lawrence *v.* Great Northern Railway Co., 16 Q. B. 643; Glover *v.* North Staffordshire Railway Co., *ib.* 912; *Re* Penny, 7 E. & B. 660; Broadbent *v.*

* 342   look for his remedy to the * proviso for compensation, if any, within the statute which authorizes the works. If there is no proviso to that effect in the statute, he is without a remedy (*o*). The right to statutory compensation does not arise unless in respect of damage which would have been the ground of an action if the act occasioning it had been done without the authority of the statute (*p*). The clauses as to compensation apply to the consequential damage done by a public body to lands lying without their district (*q*).[1]

19. Courts of equity, in conformity with the rule at law, will not interfere to restrain damage caused by a public company in the construction of their works, provided the injury done is the necessary and inevitable result of the exercise of the statutory powers, and provided the works have been executed with proper skill and care (*r*). The fact that the sum awarded by a jury under the clauses as to compensation may be no real compensation for the injury done, is not a ground for the interference of the court (*s*). If, however, the company, though keeping within the statutory powers, are constructing their works in so negligent and unskilful a manner as to cause injury to others, the court will interfere (*t*). Whether the works have been executed with proper skill and care is a question for the court to determine either with (*u*) or without the aid of a jury (*x*).

Imperial Gas Co., 7 D. M. & G. 459, 7 H. L. 600; Caledonian Railway Co. *v.* Colt, 3 Macq. 838; Brine *v.* Great Western Railway Co., 2 B. & S. 402; Queen *v.* Darlington Board of Health, 5 B. & S. 515, 6 B. & S. 562.

(*o*) Broadbent *v.* Imperial Gas Co., 7 D. M. & G. 459; Queen *v.* Darlington Board of Health, 5 B. & S. 515, 6 B. & S. 562.   See Barnsley Canal Co. *v.* Twibell, 7 Beav. 19.

(*p*) New River Co. *v.* Johnson, 2 El. & El. 435; Queen *v.* Metropolitan Board of Works, 3 B. & S. 710.

(*q*) Cator *v.* Lewisham Board of Works, 5 B. & S. 115.

(*r*) Hutton *v.* London and South Western Railway Co., 7 Ha. 259; Langham *v.* Great Northern Railway Co., 1 De G. & S. 485; Imperial Gas Co. *v.* Broadbent, 7 D. M. & G. 459, 7 H. L. 605; Ware *v.* Regent's Canal Co., 3 D. & J. 227; Stainton *v.* Woolrych, 23

Beav. 225; Att.-Gen. *v.* Borough of Birmingham, 4 K. & J. 528; Att.-Gen. *v.* Metropolitan Board of Works, 1 H. & M. 320.

(*s*) Stainton *v.* Woolrych, 23 Beav.234.

(*t*) Coats *v.* Clarence Railway Co., 1 R. & M. 181; Stainton *v.* Woolrych, 23 Beav. 225; Ware *v.* Regent's Canal Co., 3 D. & J. 227; Att.-Gen. *v.* Metropolitan Board of Works, 1 H. & M. 320.

(*u*) Ware *v.* Regent's Canal Co., 3 D. & J. 227.

(*x*) Stainton *v.* Woolrych, 23 Beav. 225.

[1] In Sandford *v.* The Railway Co., 24 Penn. St. 378, it is said: If railway corporations go beyond the powers which the legislature has given them, and, in a mistaken exercise of those powers, interfere with the property of individuals, the court is bound to interfere by bill, injunction, or otherwise, as the case may require. See, also, Mo-

20. Where the injury to lands from the works of a public company * is of so permanent a character as distin- *343 guished from mere damage as to amount to a permanent occupation of them, the provisions for compensation in respect of land injuriously affected, contained in the 68th section of the Lands Clauses Act, 8 Vict. c. 18, do not apply. The case becomes one of destructive trespass, and will be restrained as being such (*y*). The defendants in Ware *v.* Regent's Canal Company (*z*) having certain powers to construct a reservoir and raise the water to a certain height, the plaintiff applied for an injunction to restrain the company from doing damage to his land by flooding. Lord Chelmsford drew the distinction between works causing an occasional damage by flooding and works causing a permanent submerging of land. "The question," he said, "arises, what would be the rights and liabilities of the company in thus going to the extreme limits of their powers? The effect would be to permanently cover with water other lands than those which they have already purchased and taken, which they have the power to take under their act. If this had taken place during the period when the compulsory powers of the company could have been exercised, I apprehend that the plaintiff might have obtained relief through the aid of a court of equity, and have compelled the company to take these aditional lands. But if lands which they have no power to take, or, after the compulsory powers had ceased, lands which they had the power to take but had not taken, were permanently flooded, there can be no doubt that the plaintiff might have obtained an injunction to restrain the permanent occupation of his land." (*a*).

21. A public company, when acting in conformity with its statutory powers, need not, before commencing works which may injuriously affect lands, make or tender compensation for the conjectural damage (*b*); but it is bound to exercise in a *bonâ fide* manner the powers which have been conferred by

hawk and Hudson Railway *v.* Artcher, 6 Paige, 83 ; 2 Redfield on Railways, 309.

(*y*) Ware *v.* Regent's Canal Co., 3 D. & J. 227.

(*z*) *Ib.*

(*a*) See Imperial Gas Co. *v.* Broadbent, 7 D. M. & G. 459, 7 H. L. 600.

(*b*) Lister *v.* Lobley, 7 A. & E. 124; Hutton *v.* London and South Western Railway Co., 7 Ha. 259 ; Macey *v.* Metropolitan Board of Works, 33 L. J. Ch. 377. Comp. Att.-Gen. *v.* Conservators of Thames, 1 H. & M. 29.

statute, and may not cause by the construction of its
* 344   works more * damage than the necessity of the case
requires. Companies acting *bonâ fide* are, as a general
rule, the proper judges of the most convenient mode of executing their works (*c*). So long as there is no reason to suppose
that they are acting in an arbitrary or oppressive manner, or that
their conduct is other than *bonâ fide*, a court of equity will not
interfere with them in the fair exercise of their discretion ; but
if their conduct does not seem to be fair and *bonâ fide*, the court
will interfere. Thus, where a railway company was proceeding
to erect an arch of insufficient dimensions over a mill-race in
order to save themselves the expense of making a sufficient
one, the court, considering the conduct of the company not
bonâ fide, restrained them from making an arch of less than
certain specific dimensions (*d*). By the 16th clause of the
Railways Clauses Consolidation Act, 8 Vict. c. 20, railway
companies are required to do, in the exercise of their powers,
as little damage as can be. The proviso does not apply to
what is done, but to the manner of doing it (*e*).

22. By the 68th clause of the Lands Clauses Act, 8 Vict. c.
18, it is provided that if any party shall be entitled to compensation in respect of any lands, or of any interest therein, which
shall have been taken for or injuriously affected by the execution of the works, and for which the undertakers shall not have
made compensation, it shall be assessed in the manner therein
mentioned. In one case (*f*) Lord Cottenham held that all
persons who sought for compensation under the clause were
not only bound to prove damage, but must prove damage of
such a nature, before they could be permitted by a court of
equity to put in force the powers of the act, as would entitle
them to compensation under the clause, and he restrained,
accordingly, a land-owner from having compensation
* 345   assessed until he had established his * right at law to

(*c*) London and Birmingham Railway Co. *v.* Grand Junction Canal Co.,
1 Ra. Ca. 225 ; Priestley *v.* Manchester and Leeds Railway Co., 2 Ra. Ca.
134 ; Reg. *v.* Sharpe, 3 Ra. Ca. 33, n.
See Richards *v.* Richards, John. 255.
(*d*) Coats *v.* Clarence Railway Co., 1
R. & M. 181 ; Manser *v.* Northern and

Eastern Counties Railway Co., 2 Ra.
Ca. 380 ; Stainton *v.* Woolrych, 23
Beav. 234.
(*e*) Reg. *v.* East and West India
Docks Railway Co., 2 E. & B. 466 ;
supra, p. 320.
(*f*) London and North Western Railway Co. *v.* Smith, 1 Mac. & G. 216.

compensation : but this decision has been clearly over-ruled (*g*). The ground, indeed, on which Lord Cottenham proceeded no longer exists, for it has been lately held that the assessment of damages by the verdict of a jury under the clause is not conclusive as to the fact that lands have been damaged or injuriously affected, and does not, therefore, estop the company from denying in an action on the verdict and judgment thereon that there has been damage (*h*). If, however, there is an original equity affecting the claim, the court will interfere. "Where there is an original equity affecting the claim," said Turner, L. J., in Duke of Norfolk *v.* Tennant (*i*), "the statute does not take it away. It is, I think, as much the duty of this court to interpose by injunction in such cases as in the ordinary attempt to put in force the powers of the act for compulsory purchase, where the purchase has been the subject of contract." Where, accordingly, there had been some treaty for compensation for damage with a land-owner which had not been completed or carried out, but there was evidence to show that he had received consideration for an agreement, which he refused to perfect, the court restrained him from taking proceedings to obtain compensation under the clause (*k*).

23. The principles upon which the court proceeds in restraining nuisance on the part of incorporated companies are also applicable to nuisance on the part of public bodies, or boards of functionaries incorporated by act of Parliament for a public purpose, and for the promotion of the public benefit of the community (*l*). *Inasmuch as these *346 bodies are acting on behalf of the public interest, and have not any personal advantage to obtain from carrying out

(*g*) East and West India Docks, &c., Co. *v.* Gattke, 3 Mac. & G. 155; South Staffordshire Railway Co. *v.* Hall, 1 Sim. N. S. 388, 3 Mac. & G. 353; Sutton Harbor Co. *v.* Hitchens, 1 D. M. & G. 161; Duke of Norfolk *v.* Tennant, 9 Ha. 745; Bradford Local Board of Health *v.* Hopwood, 6 W. R. 818; Wallis *v.* Wallis, 4 Drew. 463. See Caledonian Railway Co. *v.* Ogilvy, 2 Macq. 245; Reg. *v.* London and North Western Railway Co., 3 E. & B. 470; Bradby *v.* Southampton Local Board of Health, 4 E. & B. 1014; Chapman *v.* Monmouthshire Railway Co., 2 H. & N. 277; Mortimer *v.* South Wales Railway Co., 1 El. & El. 375.

(*h*) Read *v.* Victoria and Pimlico Railway Co., 1 H. & C. 826.

(*i*) 9 Ha. 748.

(*k*) *Ib.* See London and South Western Railway Co. *v.* Coward, 5 Ra. Ca. 703; Maunsell *v.* Midland Great Western of Ireland Railway Co., 1 H. & M. 150.

(*l*) Frewin *v.* Lewis, 4 M. & C. 255.

the purposes for which they have been incorporated, the court is always disposed to assume that whatever they do, provided it be within the statutory powers, is a fair exercise of the discretion which has been reposed in them by the legislature (*m*), and will not interfere with them so long as they do not conduct themselves in an arbitrary or oppressive manner, and do not appear to be actuated by corrupt or improper motives (*n*). But if their conduct is, in the opinion of the court, arbitrary or oppressive, or does not appear to be a fair and *bonâ fide* exercise of the powers which have been conferred on them by the legislature, they will be restrained by injunction (*o*). The discretion reposed in them cannot be exercised by them in a mode not strictly within the statutory power. If a fair *primâ facie* case can be made out against them of breach of duty and a violation of the statute which gives them authority, the court will not hesitate to interfere, because there is a certain possible state of facts which would justify their conduct (*p*). The motives by which a man is actuated in seeking the aid of the court to keep them within the limits of their authority matter nothing (*q*). Nor can the fact that a large population may suffer unless the rights of an individual are invaded be taken into consideration by the court (*r*).

* 347   24. * The commissioners of sewers, under the statutes 23 Hen. 8, c. 5, and 3 & 4 Will. 4, c. 22, are a court of record. If they exceed their jurisdiction, there is a

---

(*m*) See Foster *v.* Hornsby, 2 Ir. Ch. 445; Dover Gas-light Co. *v.* Mayor of Dover, 7 D. M. & G. 545; Crossman *v.* Bristol and South Wales Railway Co., 1 H. & M. 531.

(*n*) Stainton *v.* Woolrych, 23 Beav. 236; Turner *v.* Blamire, 1 Drew. 409; Att.-Gen. *v.* Conservators of Thames, 1 H. & M. 1; Att.-Gen. *v.* Metropolitan Board of Works, *ib.* 315; Biddulph *v.* St. George's Vestry, 33 L. J. Ch. 411. See Austin *v.* Lambeth Vestry, 27 L. J. Ch. 388, 4 Jur. N. S. 1032.

(*o*) Coats *v.* Clarence Railway Co., 1 R. & M. 181; Att.-Gen. *v.* Metropolitan Board of Works, 1 H. & M. 298. See Foster *v.* Hornsby, 2 Ir. Ch. 426; Biddulph *v.* St. George's Vestry, 33 L. J. Ch. 411.

(*p*) Foster *v.* Hornsby, 2 Ir. Ch. 445.

See Armitstead *v.* Durham, 11 Beav. 556; Sutton *v.* Mayor, &c., of Norwich, 27 L. J. Ch. 739; Queen *v.* Bradford Navigation Co., 6 B. & S. 631.

(*q*) Sutton *v.* Mayor, &c., of Norwich, 27 L. J. Ch. 739; Wood *v.* Charing Cross Railway Co., 33 Beav. 290.

(*r*) Att.-Gen. *v.* Borough of Birmingham, 4 K. & J. 528; Spokes *v.* Bandbury Board of Health, 1 L. R. Eq. 42; Goldsmid *v.* Tunbridge Wells Improvement Commissioners, 1 L. R. Eq. 161, *ib.* Ch. App. 349. See Broadbent *v.* Imperial Gas Co., 7 D. M. & G. 462; Tipping *v.* St. Helen's Smelting Co.; 4 B. & S. 608; Raphael *v.* Thames Valley Railway Co., 2 L. R. Ch. Ap. 147. Comp. Wood *v.* Charing Cross Railway Co., 33 Beav. 290.

remedy in the Queen's Bench by *certiorari*. But the existence of the remedy at law does not exclude the jurisdiction of the court. If they exceed the due limits of their authority, and commit acts of nuisance, whether of a public (*s*) or a private (*t*) nature, the court has an undoubted right to interfere (*u*), unless the jurisdiction is expressly excluded (*x*). But the exercise of the jurisdiction is in every case a matter for the discretion of the court. In a case where there appeared to the court to be a shorter remedy at law by *certiorari*, an injunction which had been granted was dissolved (*y*).

25. The court will, on the other hand, on a proper case being made out, interfere by injunction at the suit of the commissioners of sewers. Thus, in Crossman *v*. Bristol and South Wales Railway Company (*z*), the court restrained parties from interfering with a natural deposit of beach protecting the country from the inundations of a navigable tidal river within the survey of the commissioners, notwithstanding the spot in question had been purchased by the parties under their parliamentary powers.

26. In Attorney-General *v*. Forbes (*a*) justices of peace were restrained from doing an act within their own county which would work a public nuisance out of their jurisdiction in the next county (*b*).

27. A board of health should not come to the court for an injunction unless a special case can be made out, inasmuch as * such bodies have a proper remedy under the   * 348 provisions of Act 11 & 12 Vict. c. 63 (*c*).

28. Bills to restrain nuisance have been entertained against the following public functionaries, in addition to those already mentioned: Drainage Commissioners (*d*); Commissioners of

(*s*) Box *v*. Allen, 1 Dick. 49; Birley *v*. Constables of Chorlton-on-Medlock, 3 Beav. 499.

(*t*) Box *v*. Allen, 1 Dick. 49.

(*u*) See Att.-Gen. *v*. Forbes, 2 M. & C. 133.

(*x*) See Birley *v*. Constables of Chorlton-on-Medlock, ·3 Beav. 499; Armitstead *v*. Durham, 11 Beav. 556.

(*y*) Kerrison *v*. Sparrow, 19 Ves. 449.

(*z*) 1 H. & M. 531.

(*a*) 2 M. & C. 123.

(*b*) See Birley *v*. Constables of Chorlton-on-Medlock, 3 Beav. 499; Armitstead *v*. Durham, 11 Beav. 556.

(*c*) Felkin *v*. Herbert, 11 L. T. N. S. 173.

(*d*) Earl of Ripon *v*. Hobart, 3 M. & K. 169; Dawson *v*. Paver, 5 Ha. 415.

Woods and Forests (*e*) ; Conservators of Thames (*f*) ; Boards of Health (*g*) ; Trustees of Turnpike Roads (*h*) ; the Secretary at War (*i*) ; the Metropolitan Board of Works (*k*) ; a highway board, constituted under 5 & 6 Will. 4, c. 50, acting as a local authority for carrying out the provisions of the Nuisances Removal Act, 18 & 19 Vict. c. 121 (*l*) ; a corporation acting under Local Government Act, 21 & 22 Vict. c. 98 (*m*).

29. The court has jurisdiction to restrain commissioners under a local drainage act, although the act gave jurisdiction to quarter sessions (*n*).

30. A man who comes to the court for relief by interlocutory injunction against nuisance must show due diligence in making the application. ＼Whatever may have been the original equity of his case, if he has by his conduct encouraged another to expend moneys or alter his condition in contravention of the rights for which he contends, he has deprived
* 349   himself of his * equity to the interference of the court (*o*). Accordingly, a lord of a manor claiming as against the tenants the right of property in the mines within the manor, who had stood by for a long period and allowed the tenants without objection to expend large sums of money in working the mines, was held precluded by his conduct from relief in equity (*p*). So, also, a man who had acquiesced for eighteen months in the deviation of part of a navigable river, and in the obstruction of a road by a railway company, was

---

(*e*) Squire *v.* Campbell, 1 M. & C. 459.

(*f*) Att.-Gen. *v.* Johnston, 2 Wils. C. C. 87 ; Att.-Gen. *v.* Conservators of Thames, 1 H. & M. 1.

(*g*) Oldaker *v.* Hunt, 6 D. M. & G. 376 ; Att.-Gen. *v.* Luton Board of Health, 2 Jur. N. S. 180; Manchester, Sheffield, and Lincolnshire Railway Co. *v.* Worksop Board of Health, 23 Beav. 198; Att.-Gen. *v.* Mayor, &c., of Kingston-upon-Thames, 34 L. J. Ch. 481.

(*h*) Weeks *v.* Heward, 10 W. R. 557. See Queen *v.* Darlington Board of Health, 5 B. & S. 515.

(*i*) Felkin *v.* Herbert, 4 L. T. N. S. 433, 30 L. J. Ch. 604, 11 L. T. N. S. 173.

(*k*) Att.-Gen. *v.* Metropolitan Board of Works, 1 H. & M. 320 ; Macey *v.* Metropolitan Board of Works, 33 L. J. Ch. 377.

(*l*) Att.-Gen. *v.* Richmond, 2 L. R. Eq. 306.

(*m*) Ellis *v.* Corporation of Bridgnorth, 2 J. & H. 67 See Queen *v.* Darlington Board of Health, 5 B. & S. 515. See, as to inclosure commissioners, Dawson *v.* Paver 5 Ha. 415; Turner *v.* Blamire, 1 Drew 409 ; Harris *v.* Jose, 14 W. R. 303 ; Earl Beauchamp *v.* Darby. 1 W N. 308.

(*n*) Armitstead *v.* Durham, 11 Beav. 556.

(*o*) *Supra*, pp. 201–205.

(*p*) Parrott *v.* Palmer 3 M. & K. 632.

held precluded from relief (q). So, also, a man who did not
file his bill until two years and a half after the works complained of as throwing flood-water over his lands were completed, was held precluded from relief (r). So, also, a man
who had permitted the owner of the adjoining premises to
rebuild them to a greater height than they were before, and
to alter his ancient lights and to open new ones, was held not
entitled to interrupt the lights after they were completed (s).

31. If the question as to nuisance is one which admits of a
determination prospectively, a man should not delay in coming
to the court. If he abstains from coming until the mischief is
actually done, he may be told he is too late (t).[1] If the act
complained of is caused by a public company in the execution
and construction of their works, it is more incumbent on the
party injured to apply without delay, than in ordinary cases (u).
Much, however, depends on the nature and character of the
nuisance. The allegation that a company has spent money
on the faith of a nuisance being allowed to go on increasing
indefinitely is not entitled to the same consideration as the fact
of such a permitted expenditure on buildings (x).

32. Though a stronger case of delay is required to affect
those who assert a public right, than when a private right
alone is in dispute, delay, even in such cases, is not
without * effect (y). In the case of a gradually increas-   * 350
ing nuisance the court will have regard to the nature of
the nuisance, and conclude that the relators have been waiting
to see whether the nuisance will continue to grow, or whether
circumstances may not of themselves arise which will check or

---

(q) Illingworth v. Manchester and
Leeds Railway Co., 2 Ra. Ca. 188.
(r) Wicks v. Hunt, John. 380.
(s) Cotching v. Bassett, 32 Beav.
101. See Davies v. Marshall, 10 C. B.
N. S. 703 ; 1 Dr. & Sm. 557.
(t) Dawson v. Paver, 5 Ha. 415.
(u) Supra, p. 202.
(x) Att.-Gen. v. Proprietors of Bradford Canal, 2 L. R. Eq. 71.
(y) Att.-Gen. v. Johnson, 2 Wils. C.
C. 87; Att.-Gen. v. Compton, 1 Y. &
C. C. C. 417; Att.-Gen. v. Sheffield
Gas Co., 3 D. M. & G. 311. But see
Att.-Gen. v. Mayor, &c., of Plymouth, 1
W. R. 445.

[1] "Mere delay in applying to the
court is frequently a ground for denying a preliminary injunction, and is
also a reason for courts of equity refusing to take cognizance of a case when
there is a remedy at law. But where
the legal right is settled, and the more
efficacious remedy of a court of equity
is necessary to complete relief, delay
is no ground for a denial of its aid,
unless it is coupled with such acquiescence as deprives the party of all
right to equitable relief." Carlisle v.
Cooper, 6 C. E. Green, 591.

diminish it (z). If the public have been slow in complaining, their delay is a proper subject for the consideration of the court in fixing the amount of time to be allowed for carrying the injunction into effect (a).

33. A general allegation that a defendant encouraged the erection of a nuisance while it was in progress is sufficient to let in evidence of such particular acts of encouragement as will sustain the equity, and is consequently sufficient to prevent a demurrer (b).

34. After the establishment of his right at law, and the fact of its violation, a man is entitled to a perpetual injunction to prevent the recurrence of the wrong, unless there be something special in the circumstances of the case (c).

SECTION II. — NUISANCE TO DWELLING-HOUSES AND HOUSES
OF BUSINESS.

(z) Att.-Gen. v. Proprietors of Bradford Canal, 2 L. R. Eq. 71.
(a) Ib.
(b) Williams v. Earl of Jersey, Cr.
& Ph. 91. See Smith v. Kay, 7 H. L. 750.
(c) Imperial Gas Co. v. Broadbent, 7 H. L. 612; Wood v. Sutcliffe, 2 Sim. N. S. 166; supra, pp. 224–227.

1. The foundation of the jurisdiction of courts of equity in the case of nuisance to dwelling-houses or houses of business is such a degree of injury to property as interferes materially with its comfort and enjoyment either for domestic purposes or for the purposes of business. If the house is a dwelling-house, the rule or standard of the amount of damage that calls for the exercise of the jurisdiction to grant preventive relief is the comfort and enjoyment in their abode to which the inmates are reasonably * entitled (d), and   * 351 this must be estimated according to the plain and simple notions entertained by persons in ordinary life, and not according to those held by persons accustomed to elegant and dainty habits of living (e). If the house is a manufactory or place of business, the rule or standard is damage of such an amount as to render it to a material extent less suitable for the purposes of business (f). The injury must be a present existing injury, and not one that may arise at some future period by reason of the premises being used for a different purpose. The fact that the property may be rendered thereby less fit for some other purposes to which it may by possibility be applied at a future time cannot be taken into consideration (g). The owner of vacant land which is intended for building-ground cannot have an injunction to restrain a nuisance in the vicinity thereof whereby the value of his property is diminished. The court cannot interfere, there being no certainty that a dwelling-house will be erected, or, if it should be, where the erection may be made. There cannot be an injunction unless the injury either actually exist, or the damage

---

(d) Jackson v. Duke of Newcastle, 33 L. J. Ch. 698, per Lord Westbury; Att.-Gen. v. Nicholl, 16 Ves. 338; Palmer v. Paul, 2 L. J. Ch. 154; Soltau v. De Held, 2 Sim. N. S. 159; Eaden v. Frith, 1 H. & M. 573.

(e) Walter v. Selfe, 4 De G. & S. 322, per Knight Bruce, L. J.; Soltau v. De Held, 2 Sim. N. S. 159.

(f) Jackson v. Duke of Newcastle, 33 L. J. Ch. 698, per Lord Westbury; Clarke v. Clark, 1 L. R. Ch. Ap. 16; Yates v. Jack, ib. 295; Martin v. Headon, 2 L. R. Eq. 425.

(g) Jackson v. Duke of Newcastle, 33 L. J. Ch. 698; Calcraft v. Thomson, 15 W. R. 387. Comp. Yates v. Jack, 1 L. R. Ch. Ap. 295.

appear to be certain and immediate, and not depending on a contingency (h).

2. The bill is usually brought by the occupier; but where the house is unoccupied, the owner may sue on the ground of damage to his property. If the house is inhabited, the owner may sue either alone or conjointly with the occupier (i). Where the house is inhabited, and the person suing is the owner, the court will in general look for evidence from the tenant in support of the allegation of nuisance (j).

* 352   3. * One of the nuisances to houses which most frequently calls for the interference of the court is the setting up by one man of erections on his land so as to obstruct the passage of light and air to the windows of his neighbor. It is not every impediment to the access of light and air which will warrant the interference of the court by injunction, or even entitle the party alleging himself to be injured to damages at law. In order to found a title to relief in equity, or even at law, in respect of such an impediment, some material or substantial injury must be established (k). The rule at law as to the amount of obstruction which is actionable has been thus laid down by Lord Wynford in Back v. Stacey (l): "To constitute an illegal obstruction of light by building it is not sufficient that the plaintiff has less light than before, or that the part of his house principally affected cannot be used for all the purposes to which it might otherwise have been applied. In order to give a right of action there must be a substantial privation of light sufficient to render the occupation of the house uncomfortable, or to prevent the plaintiff from carrying on his accustomed business on the premises as beneficially as he had formerly done. It may be difficult to draw the line, but a distinction must be drawn between a practical inconvenience and a real injury to the plaintiff in the enjoyment of the premises " (m).

(h) Dana v. Valentine, 5 Metc. (Amer.) 8.

(i) Sutton v. Lord Mountfort, 4 Sim. 559; Wilson v. Townend, 1 Dr. & Sm. 324; Cleeve v. Mahany, 9 W. R. 882; Jackson v. Duke of Newcastle, 33 L. J. Ch. 698. See supra, p. 336.

(j) Wilson v. Townend, 1 Dr. & Sm. 324; Cleeve v. Mahany, 9 W. R. 881.

See Radcliffe v. Duke of Portland, 3 Giff. 702.

(k) Johnson v. Wyatt, 2 D. J. & S. 18, 26; Curriers' Co. v. Corbett, 11 Jur. N. S. 719; Robson v. Whittingham, 1 L. R. Ch. Ap. 442; Dent v. Auction Mart Co., 2 L. R. Eq. 238.

(l) 2 Car. & P. 465.

(m) Parker v. Smith, 5 Car. & P.

4. It is not, however, in every case in which an action can be maintained at law for the obstruction of light that an injunction will be granted by a court of equity. Something more is required than that amount of injury for which damages can be recovered at law. Unless the abridgment of light is not only a substantial injury, but an injury not capable of being properly *and adequately compensated by *353 damages, the court will not interfere (n). Whether or not the injury complained of is substantial enough for the interference of the court, is a question which must in each case depend on the particular circumstances of the case. It is impossible to find any precise standard by which to determine the amount of light necessary to induce the court to exercise its protective jurisdiction. Each case must depend on evidence whether there has been a substantial reduction of the quantity of light which the owner of the house has a right to enjoy (o). In estimating the damage the court cannot consider whether the place in which the building is, is in the country or in a populous city (p). It is not necessary, in order to entitle a man to relief, that a present existing injury should be shown. The right conferred or recognized by the statute being an absolute or indefeasible right to the enjoyment of light, without reference to the purpose for which it has been used, a man who obstructs the light of his neighbor cannot be allowed to say that he has left him sufficient light for his present business. He must be able to show that for whatever purpose his neighbor may wish to employ the light, there would be no material interference with it (q). The quantity

438; Pringle v. Wernham, 7 Car. & P. 377; Wells v. Ody, ib. 410; Jacomb v. Knight, 32 L. J. Ch. 601; Johnson v. Wyatt, 2 D. J. & S. 18, 26; Isenberg v. East India House Estate Co., 33 L. J. Ch. 392; Dent v. Auction Mart Co., 2 L. R. Eq. 238. See Calcraft v. Thomson, 15 W. R. 387, per Lord Chelmsford.

(n) Att.-Gen. v. Nicholl, 16 Ves. 338; Gale v. Abbott, 8 Jur. N. S. 987; Jacomb v. Knight, 32 L. J. Ch. 601; Johnson v. Wyatt, 2 D. J. & S. 18, 26; Jackson v. Duke of Newcastle, 33 L. J. Ch. 698; Curriers' Co. v. Corbett, 11 Jur. N. S. 719; Dent v. Auction Mart Co., 2 L. R. Eq. 238. See Durell v. Pritchard, 1 L. R. Ch. Ap. 244.

(o) Calcraft v. Thomson, 15 W. R. 387. The court will not, under ordinary circumstances, restrain the erection of a building the height of which above an ancient light is not greater than the distance from the light. Beadel v. Perry, 3 L. R. Eq. 465.

(p) Yates v. Jack, 1 L. R. Ch. Ap. 295; Dent v. Auction Mart Co., 2 L. R. Eq. 238; Martin v. Headon, 2 L. R. Eq. 425.

(q) Yates v. Jack, 1 L. R. Ch. Ap. 295; Dent v. Auction Mart Co., 2 L. R. Eq. 238; Calcraft v. Thomson, 15 W. R. 387.

of light a man has a right to receive, is as much a part of his
property as his house, and requires equally the protection of
the court (*r*). A small degree of privation of light may, under
the special circumstances of the case, be a sufficient ground
for an injunction (*s*). The fact that the plaintiff may have
obscured in an insignificant degree his own windows,
* 354   does not deprive * him of the right to restrain another
person from erecting a building so as seriously to
diminish the supply of light (*t*).

5. The shutting out a pleasant prospect (*u*), the erection of
disagreeable objects in view (*v*), or the invasion of a man's
privacy by the opening of a window looking over his grounds (*x*),
or the erection of buildings which prevent goods displayed in a
shop from being seen from places where they would previously
have been seen (*y*), though they may not only annoy a neighbor, but may affect the value of his property, do not of themselves give a right of suit or action (*z*).

6. If the right at law, and the invasion of that right be clear
and free from doubt, the court may interfere at once, and grant
an injunction *simpliciter* (*a*), but if the right at law, or the
fact of its violation is denied, the court will not interfere without taking into consideration the comparative convenience or
inconvenience of granting or withholding the injunction. If
on the balance of convenience and inconvenience it appear that
the granting an injunction would be inflicting a great and disproportionate injury on the defendant, the injunction will not
issue, but the motion will be ordered to stand over upon defendant undertaking to alter the building or otherwise deal
with it, as the court shall direct, if the right at law should
prove to be in favor of the plaintiff (*b*).

(*r*) Martin *v.* Headon, 2 L. R. Eq.
425; Calcraft *v.* Thomson, 15 W. R.
387.

(*s*) Herz *v.* Union Bank of London,
2 Giff. 686, 24 L. T. 186. Lanfranchi
v. Mackenzie, 15 W. R. 614.

(*t*) Arcedeckne *v.* Kelk, 2 Giff. 513.

(*u*) Aldred's case, 9 Co. R. 58 a;
Att.-Gen. *v.* Doughty, 2 Ves. 453;
Bathurst *v.* Burden, 2 Bro. C. C. 64;
Fishmongers' Co. *v.* East India Co., 1
Dick. 163; Webb *v.* Bird, 10 C. B. N.
S. 276.

(*v*) Att.-Gen. *v.* Doughty, 2 Ves. 453.

(*x*) Jones *v.* Tapling, 12 C. B. N. S.
842, *per* Blackburn, J.

(*y*) Smith *v.* Owen, 35 L. J. Ch.
317; Butt *v.* Imperial Gas-light Co.,
2 L. R. Ch. Ap. 158.

(*z*) See Turner *v.* Shooner, 1 Dr. &
Sm. 467; Johnson *v.* Wyatt, 2 D. J. &
S. 18; Jackson *v.* Duke of Newcastle,
33 L. J. Ch. 698.

(*a*) Potts *v.* Levy, 2 Drew. 272.

(*b*) Smith *v.* Elger, 3 Jur. 790; *supra*,
p. 340.

7. A good title to the passage of light and air to windows may be given by grant or express agreement (c), or it may arise from proof of enjoyment for such time, and under such circumstances as will satisfy the provisions of the Prescription Act, 2 & 3 Will. 4, c. 71. Since the statute the right to light from enjoyment for the prescribed period does not rest upon any presumption * of grant or fiction of consent,   * 355 but is an absolute and indefeasible statutory right (d).

8. It being a settled rule of construction that the grant of a principal thing shall be held to carry with it all that is reasonably necessary for the enjoyment of the thing granted, for the purpose for which according to the obvious intent of the parties the grant was made (e), and that a grant is always to be taken strongly against the grantor (f), the right to light passes upon the sale of a house by the grant itself, even without any special word of conveyance. Where, accordingly, the same person possessing a house having the actual use and enjoyment of certain lights, and also possessing the adjoining land, sells the house, neither he, nor any person claiming under him, can build on the adjoining land so as to obstruct or interrupt the enjoyment of the lights, although the lights be new (g). The rule applies where the sales of both parts to different parties take place at one and the same time (h), and where two lessees derive interest under the same landlord; but if the estate which was originally prior in date becomes subsequent by operation of law, the privilege is gone, and attaches to the estate which has become prior by operation of law (i). The rule will not, however, apply where the buildings are in an unfinished and skeleton state, and it is uncertain whether the openings which have been left in the walls are intended for doors or windows (k).

(c) Morris v. Lord Berkeley, 2 Ves. 452; Att.-Gen. v. Doughty, ib. 453; East India Co. v. Vincent, 2 Atk. 83; Davies v. Marshall, 1 Dr. & Sm. 557.

(d) Tapling v. Jones, 11 H. L. 290.

(e) Pomfret v. Ricroft, 1 Saund. 322 e; Hall v. Lund, 1 H. & C. 676.

(f) Kooystra v. Lucas, 5 B. & Ald. 830.

(g) Swansborough v. Coventry, 9 Bing. 309; Palmer v. Fletcher, 1 Lev. 122; Cox v. Matthews, 1 Vent. 237;

Tenant v. Goldwin, 2 Lord Raym. 1093; Palmer v. Paul, 2 L. J. Ch. 154; Davies v. Marshall, 1 Dr. & Sm. 557; Herz v. Union Bank of London, 2 Giff. 686.

(h) Johnson v. Jordan, 2 Metc. (Amer.) 234; Swansborough v. Coventry, 9 Bing. 305. But see Collier v. Pierce, 7 Gray (Amer.), 18.

(i) Coutts v. Gorham, M. & M. 396.

(k) Glave v. Harding, 27 L. J. Exch 286.

9. There has been some difference of opinion as to whether the owner of two tenements, who sells and conveys one, retaining the other, does not, by implication of law, reserve a right to the enjoyment of light over the part granted in favor of the part retained in the form and condition in which it was * 356 at the time * of the conveyance (*l*). But it may be now considered as established, that no such reservation will be implied (*m*). It has accordingly been held that if a landowner sells any portion of his land, the purchaser has a right to build upon it so as to obstruct the ancient lights in a house on the remaining portion of the land (*n*). Where, however, houses have been built by the same person, as part of the same plan or scheme, and have been sold in an unfinished state to different persons, the openings of the windows being sufficiently visible (*o*), a mutual reservation of the right will be implied in favor of all the purchasers (*p*).

10. The law as to the acquisition of a legal right to the enjoyment of light from long user, depends upon the third and fourth clauses of the Prescription Act, 2 & 3 Will. 4, c. 71 (*q*). The actual and continuous enjoyment of light, as an easement (*r*), for twenty years next before the commencement of some suit or action, in which the claim is brought in question (*s*), without interruption, acquiesced in for a year (*t*), is made by those clauses to confer an absolute and indefeasible title, unless the enjoyment can be shown to have been by consent or agreement expressly given or made by deed or writing (*u*). An interruption after an enjoyment for nineteen years and a fraction is not such an interruption as will prevent the right from being established at the end of the twentieth

---

(*l*) Palmer *v.* Fletcher, 1 Lev. 122; Tenant *v.* Goldwin, 2 Lord Raym. 1093.

(*m*) White *v.* Bass, 7 H. & N. 722; Suffield *v.* Brown, 33 L. J. Ch. 249; Curriers' Co. *v.* Corbett, 2 Dr. & Sm. 355, 11 Jur. N. S. 719.

(*n*) White *v.* Bass, 7 H. & N. 722; but *quære* as to ancient lights. See Tapling *v.* Jones, 11 H. L. 290.

(*o*) Glave *v.* Harding, 27 L. J. Exch. 286.

(*p*) Compton *v.* Richards, 1 Price, 27. See Richards *v.* Rose, 9 Exch. 218; Pyer *v.* Carter, 1 H. & N. 916.

(*q*) See Truscott *v.* Merchant Tailors' Co., 11 Exch. 866; Gale *v.* Abbott, 8 Jur. N. S. 987.

(*r*) Harbidge *v.* Warwick, 3 Exch. 552.

(*s*) Cooper *v.* Hubbuck, 12 C. B. N. S. 456.

(*t*) See Onley *v.* Gardiner, 4 M. & W. 497; Harbidge *v.* Warwick, 3 Exch. 557.

(*u*) See Truscott *v.* Merchant Tailors' Co., 11 Exch. 863; Tapling *v.* Jones, 11 H. L. 290.

year (x). To constitute an interruption there must be a physical obstruction, or at least some overt act on the part of the owner of the servient tenement, indicating * that the claim is disputed (y). The question is in * 357 each case, whether the interruption has been really submitted to. It does not follow that an interruption is acquiesced in for a year, unless some suit or action has been brought within that time. Acquiescence may be negatived by evidence of any act showing a resistance to the obstruction (z). A promise given upon threat of legal proceedings is sufficient, but there is submission within the clause, if the person to whom the promise has been made allows twelve months to elapse from the date of the promise in taking legal proceedings, although he may have continued to complain (a).

11. The right, if acquired against a lessee, binds the inheritance (b). One of two lessees holding under the same reversion, may acquire the right against the other (c). A reversioner has no means of preventing the right being acquired against him, unless he can prevail on his lessee to interrupt the enjoyment, or get an acknowledgment in writing that the enjoyment is in writing (d). The third clause is retrospective, so that the right to light may be acquired by virtue of an enjoyment prior to the passing of the statute (e).

12. Where a title to light is shown under the statute, an obstruction cannot be justified by the custom of London, or any other local custom; but if no proceedings are taken until after the obstruction has lasted for a year, the custom will prevail (f).

(x) Flight v. Thomas, 8 Cl. & Fin. 231. See Eaton v. Swansea Waterworks Co., 17 Q. B. 272, per Lord Campbell.

(y) Carr v. Foster, 3 Q. B. 581; Onley v. Gardiner, 4 M. & W. 497; Plasterers' Co. v. Parish Clerks' Co., 6 Exch. 630.

(z) Bennison v. Cartwright, 5 B. & S. 1.

(a) Gale v. Abbott, 8 Jur. N. S. 987.

(b) Simper v. Foley, 2 J. & H. 555.

(c) Frewen v. Philipps, 11 C. B. N. S. 449.

(d) Ib.

(e) Simper v. Foley, 2 J. & H. 555.

(f) Salters' Co. v. Jay, 3 Q. B. 109; Truscott v. Merchant Tailors' Co., 11 Exch. 855; Cooper v. Hubbuck, 12 C. B. N. S. 456. See Yates v. Jack, 1 L. R. Ch. Ap. 295. Quære, Whether the custom of London still continues as to access of air. Curriers' Co. v. Corbett, 11 Jur. N. S. 719. The Metropolitan Buildings Act, 18 & 19 Vict. c. 122, s. 83, does not enable the building owner to raise or rebuild a party structure, so as to obstruct the ancient lights of the adjoining owner. Crofts v. Haldane, 2 L. R. Q. B. 194.

13. The right to the enjoyment of light by one tenement over another tenement, becomes, like other easements, extinguished upon unity of seisin and possession of both tenements in the same person, and merges in the general rights of property (*g*). If there be merely unity of possession with-
* 358 out unity of seisin, * the easement is suspended so long
as the unity of possession continues, and revives again upon the severance of the possession (*h*). Unity of ownership, for instance, of both tenements in leasehold for different estates, does not extinguish the right, but merely suspends it, so long as the ownership continues (*i*). So, also, where a man is seised in fee of one tenement and is either possessed for a term of years (*k*), or is seised for life (*l*), of the other, the right is merely suspended. There is no extinguishment where the title of a man to an easement is not so extensive as that of his title to the land charged with it (*m*).

14. The privilege of raising light through ancient windows may be lost by abandonment. In Lawrence *v.* Obee (*n*), where a window had been blocked up for nearly twenty years, Lord Ellenborough said the case stood as if it had never existed; but the better opinion is that the right is not destroyed by non-user of enjoyment for any definite period of years, but that the material inquiry in each case is, whether an intention to abandon the right permanently can, under the circumstances of the case, be reasonably presumed (*o*). The mere manifestation of an intention to abandon the right, or even an express notice to that effect, does not appear of itself to affect the right (*p*) ; but if an intention to abandon the right permanently can be reasonably presumed, and the owner of the servient tenement has upon the faith of such a belief been induced to

---

(*g*) Rex *v.* Inhabitants of Hermitage, Carth. 239; Canham *v.* Fisk, 2 Cr. & J. 126 ; Thomas *v.* Thomas, 2 Cr. M. & R. 34; James *v.* Plant, 4 A. & E. 766 ; Kavanagh *v.* Coal Mining Co., 14 Ir. C. L. 82; Ivimey *v.* Stocker, 1 L. R. Ch. Ap. 396.
(*h*) Rex *v.* Inhabitants of Hermitage, Carth. 239.
(*i*) Simper *v.* Foley, 2 J. & H. 555.
(*k*) Thomas *v.* Thomas, 2 Cr. M. & R. 34.

(*l*) Canham *v.* Fisk, 2 Cr. & J. 126; Warburton *v.* Parke, 2 H. & N. 64.
(*m*) Ivimey *v.* Stocker, 1 L. R. Ch. Ap. 396.
(*n*) 3 Camp. 514.
(*o*) Liggins *v.* Inge, 7 Bing. 693; Moore *v.* Rawson, 3 B. & C. 332; Hale *v.* Oldroyd, 14 M. & W. 789; Ward *v.* Ward, 7 Exch. 838.
(*p*) Moore *v.* Rawson, 3 B. & C. 332; Stokoe *v.* Singers, 8 E. & B. 31; but see *per* Erle, C. J., *ib.* 37.

incur expense or alter his condition, the owner of the dominant tenement will be held to have precluded himself by his conduct from afterwards setting up that the right has not been abandoned (*q*).

15. An owner of ancient lights, who, on rebuilding or altering his house, puts in new lights or enlarges the apertures of the old * ones, cannot as against an adjoin- * 359 ing proprietor acquire an absolute right to the increase of light except by an enjoyment for the prescribed period. He has no absolute right as against his neighbor to a greater amount of light than he had before. His neighbor may at any time before the lapse of the prescribed period build up and obstruct the access of light to the new windows, or to that portion which constitutes the enlargement of the old ones, so as to prevent the right to the new or increased lights from being acquired by enjoyment; but he may not in doing so abstract any portion of the light which ought to pass through the space occupied by the ancient windows. It is immaterial that he may not be able to obstruct the access of light to the new windows or to the increased apertures of the old ones without also obstructing the access of light to the ancient windows. He possesses no right of building so as to obstruct the ancient windows (*r*). The right when acquired under the statute is not lost by a temporary intermission of enjoyment not amounting to abandonment, nor can it be forfeited by any attempt to extend the right (*s*). A man, however, is not necessarily cut down to exactly the same quantity of light as has always been admitted through his windows. He may, if he can, by adopting modern improvements in the structure and glazing of his windows, or by replacing the old heavy sashes and frames by others of a lighter construction, let in more light and air than he had before, so long as he does not alter the original size of the apertures (*t*).

16. As it is extremely inconvenient to have questions of

(*q*) Reg. *v.* Chorley, 12 Q. B. 519; Stokoe *v.* Singers, 8 E. & B. 31; Jones *v.* Tapling, 12 C. B. N. S. 839, *per* Blackburn, J.; Tapling *v.* Jones, 11 H. L. 319, *per* Lord Chelmsford.

(*r*) Tapling *v.* Jones, 11 H. L. 290.
(*s*) *Ib.*
(*t*) Turner *v.* Spooner, 1 Dr. & Sm. 467.

light and air determined upon the motion for committal, the
court will not, if possible, grant an injunction in general
terms. But if the evidence does not enable it to come to any
satisfactory conclusion on a particular point, the court will,
with the view of freeing both parties from inconveniences, so
that the one will know previously what he may safely do, and
the other what he may properly object to, give liberty to the
parties on granting the injunction, to apply in chambers with
respect to the erection of buildings (u).

* 360   17. * Windows which have the privilege of receiving
light have also the privilege of receiving air, so that a
person may not obstruct the passage of air to the windows
of his neighbor (x). The passage of air to windows must be
distinguished from the passage of air for trade purposes, such
as drying timber (y), or serving a windmill (z). The right to
the passage of air for trade purposes is not an easement within
2 & 3 Will. 4, c. 71, nor can it arise from presumption of
lost grant, for the presumption of grant only arises where the
person against whom the right is claimed might have inter-
rupted the exercise of the supposed grant, and it would be
impossible in such a case to interrupt the acquisition of the
right without an unreasonable amount of labor and expense (a).

18. The enjoyment of pure and wholesome air is a right to
which the owners of land and the inmates of a dwelling-house
are of common right entitled. Any act which pollutes or
corrupts the air is strictly speaking a nuisance (b) ; but,
inasmuch as the business of life in cities and populous neigh-
borhoods renders it impossible that the air should retain its
natural state of purity, the law does not regard trifling inconveniences, but only regards inconveniences which sensibly
and materially diminish the comfort and enjoyment or value

(u) Stokes v. City Offices Co., 2 H.
& M. 650 ; Yates v. Jack, 1 L. R. Ch.
Ap. 293. See, as to value of scien-
tific evidence with respect to injury
to light and air, Webb v. Hunt, 14 W.
R. 725.

(x) Aldred's case, 9 Co. Rep. 58 a ;
Gale v. Abbott, 8 Jur. N. S. 987 ;
Radcliffe v. Duke of Portland, 3 Giff.

702. See Winter v. Brockwell, 8 East,
308.

(y) Roberts v. Macord, 1 M. & R.
230.

(z) Webb v. Bird, 13 C. B. N. S
841.

(a) Ib.

(b) Aldred's case, 9 Co. R. 58 b.

of property (c). In order to constitute an actionable nuisance, there must be not merely a nominal but a sensible and real damage. The pollution of the air must be of so sensible a nature as to diminish materially the value or interfere materially with the comfort and enjoyment of property which a reasonable man is entitled to expect, regard, however, being always had to the situation and mode of occupation of the property injuriously affected. That which is a sensible and real inconvenience to property in one place, and * occupied in one way, will be   * 361 none to property situate in another way. If a man lives in a town, he must of necessity submit himself to the consequences of the obligations of trade which may be carried on in his immediate locality, and are necessary for the purposes of commerce and for the benefit of the inhabitants of the town and the public at large. All that the law requires is that the business be carried on in a reasonable and proper manner, and that a man be not required to submit to greater personal inconvenience and discomfort than he may be reasonably required to do. The fact that the locality where a particular trade is carried on is one generally employed for the purpose of that and similar trades, will not exempt the person carrying it on from liability to an action in respect of injury created by it to property in the neighborhood. A man who by an act on his own land causes so much annoyance to another in the enjoyment of a neighboring tenement as to amount to a cause of action, cannot be heard to say that the place where the act was done was a proper and convenient one for the purpose (d).

19. Whether or not the pollution or corruption of air is substantial enough to induce the court to exercise its protective jurisdiction is a question which must depend on the particular circumstances of the case. It is impossible to find any precise standard by which to determine the question. Each case must depend on evidence as to the amount and nature of the nuisance. Injunctions will be granted, on a proper case being made out, to restrain persons from burning

(c) Tipping v. St. Helen's Smelting Co., 4 B. & S. 608; St. Helen's Smelting Co. v. Tipping, 11 H. L. 642.
(d) Ib.; Walter v. Selfe, 4 De G. &
S. 325; Cavey v. Ledbitter, 13 C. B. N. S. 470; Wanstead Board of Health v. Hill, ib. 479; Bamford v. Turnley, 3 B. & S. 62.

bricks (*e*), or discharging smoke (*f*), or other noxious or offensive vapors or gases (*g*), so as to affect substantially * 362 the * comfort and enjoyment in their home to which the inmates of a dwelling-house are entitled.[1] It is not necessary, in order to entitle a man to an injunction, that injury to vegetable life or vegetable health should be made out (*h*). Mere smoke or offensive odor alone, unaccompanied by noxious vapors, is a sufficient ground for the interference of the court (*i*). The fact that a man may have sold land with full knowledge that certain works were about to be erected thereon, does not disentitle him or those claiming under him to complain of any nuisance which the works may cause (*j*).

20. A lime-kiln (*k*), a dye-house (*l*), a tan-pit, a glass-house (*m*), a smelting-house, a tallow-furnace (*n*), a soap-boilery (*o*), a building for boiling whale-blubber (*p*), or for boiling horse-flesh for dogs (*q*), a tallow-chandler's shop (*r*), a varnish-maker's shop (*s*), a slaughter-house (*t*),[2] a brew-house (*u*), and a hog-stye (*v*) have all been held to be nuisances at common law (*x*). But a brew-house (*y*), or a

(*e*) Walter *v.* Selfe, 4 De G. & S. 325, on appeal, 19 L. T. 308 ; Pollock *v.* Lester, 11 Ha. 266, and Beardmore *v.* Treadwell, 3 Giff. 683 ; compromised on appeal, *ib.* 701. See Duke of Grafton *v.* Hilliard, cited, 1 Amb. 159, 18 Ves. 219, 19 L. J. 308 ; Barwell *v.* Brooks, 1 L. J. 75, 454, 15 Jur. 418 ; Cleeve *v.* Mahany, 9 W. R. 881.

(*f*) Sampson *v.* Smith, 8 Sim. 272 ; Crump *v.* Lambert, 3 L. R. Eq. 409. See Hudson *v.* Maddison, 12 Sim. 417 ; Semple *v.* London and Birmingham Railway Co., 1 Ra. Ca. 120.

(*g*) Broadbent *v.* Imperial Gas-light Co., 7 D. M. & G. 436, 7 H. L. 600 ; Tipping *v.* St. Helen's Smelting Co., 1 L. R. Ch. Ap. 66. See Semple *v.* London and Birmingham Railway Co., 1 Ra. Ca. 120.

(*h*) Walter *v.* Selfe, 4 De G. & S. 323 ; Crump *v.* Lambert, 3 L. R. Eq. 409.

(*i*) Crump *v.* Lambert, *ib.* See Swaine *v.* Great Northern Railway Co., 33 L. J. Ch. 399. It is no answer to a complaint by a manufacturer of a nuisance to his trade to say that the injury is felt only by reason of the delicate nature of the manufacture. Cooke *v.* Forbes, 5 L. R. Eq. 166.

(*j*) Tipping *v.* St. Helen's Smelting Co., 1 L. R. Ch. Ap. 66.

(*k*) 4 Ass. 3. See Aldred's case, 9 Co. R. 58 b.

(*l*) *Ib.*

(*m*) Jones *v.* Powell, Palm. 539.

(*n*) Morley *v.* Pragnell, Cro. Car. 510, 1 Roll. Ab. 88. See, as to candle-making being a nuisance, Arnot *v.* Brown, 1 Macq. 229.

(*o*) R. *v.* Pierce, Show. 327.

(*p*) Burntisland Whale Co. *v.* Trotter, 5 Wills. & Sh. Sc. Ap. 649.

(*q*) Grindley *v.* Booth, 3 H. & C. 669.

(*r*) Bliss *v.* Hall, 4 Bing. N. C. 183.

(*s*) R. *v.* Niel, 2 Car. & P. 485.

(*t*) R. *v.* Cross, 2 Car. & P. 484. See Pedie *v.* Swinton, Macl. & Rob. Sc. Ap. Ca. 1018.

(*u*) Jones *v.* Powell, Hut. 136.

(*v*) Aldred's case, 9 Co. R. 58 b.

(*x*) See Rex *v.* White, 1 Burr. 333.

(*y*) Att.-Gen. *v.* Cleaver, 18 Ves. 218 ; Gorton *v.* Smart, 1 Sim. & St. 66.

[1] And to restrain noises which disturb rest and prevent sleep. Rhodes *v.* Dunbar, 57 Penn. St. 274.

[2] Bishop *v.* Banks, 33 Conn. 118.

hospital for infectious diseases (z), are not necessarily nuisances at common law.[1]

21. The right to carry on an offensive trade so as to corrupt and pollute the air may be acquired against an individual by prescription or presumption of lost grant, but no length of time will legalize a public nuisance or enable a party to prescribe for its continuance. The public health, the welfare and safety of the community, are matters of permanent importance, to which all * the pursuits, occupations, and * 363 employments of individuals inconsistent with their preservation must yield (a).

22. The comfort and enjoyment in their home, to which the inmates of a dwelling-house are of right entitled, may be materially interfered with by the carrying on of noisy trades in the immediate neighborhood. The law does not, however, regard trifling inconveniences, but only regards inconveniences which sensibly and materially diminish the comfort and enjoyment of property. In order that a noisy trade may be an actionable nuisance, there must be not merely a nominal but such a sensible and real damage as a reasonable man would, if subjected to, find injurious, regard being had to the situation and mode of occupation of the property. That which is a

---

(z) Baines v. Baker, Amb. 158 ; Mutter v. Fyfe, 11 Dec. of Ct. of Sessn., 2d series, p. 303.

(a) Weld v. Hornby, 7 East, 199 ; R. v. Cross, 3 Camp. 227 ; Commonwealth v. Upton, 6 Gray (Amer.), 473.

[1] The keeping of a bawdy-house is a public nuisance, and any individual suffering a special damage therefrom is entitled to an injunction. Hamilton v. Whitridge, 11 Md. 132.

A lawful business may be carried on at unseasonable hours so as to become a nuisance, which will be restrained by injunction. Dennis v. Eckhardt, 3 Grant's Cases, 390. But if the business be lawful, and carried on reasonably, and does not affect the health, comfort, or ordinary uses and enjoyment of neighboring property, it cannot be a nuisance in fact or in anticipation, and the court cannot interfere with it. It is no ground for injunction, that the erection of a building will increase the rates of insurance of neighboring buildings. Rhodes v. Dunbar, 57 Penn. St.

274. Any business, however lawful in itself, which, as to those residing in the neighborhood where it is carried on, causes annoyances that materially interfere with the ordinary physical comfort of human existence, such as smoke, noise, and bad odors, even when not injurious to health, is a nuisance that a court of equity will restrain, but the discomfort must be physical, and not such as depends upon taste or imagination. It is usual and proper, where a building or works are being erected that can only be used for a purpose that is unlawful, to restrain the erection ; but when it is not made to appear that the business for which the building is intended, cannot possibly be carried on without becoming a nuisance, the injunction will be denied, and the defendant left at liberty to erect his building at the risk of being restrained in the use of it, if it prove a nuisance. Cleveland v. Citizens Gaslight Co., 5 C. E. Green, 201.

sensible and real inconvenience to property, situate in one place or occupied in one way, will be none to property situate in another place or occupied in another way. A man who lives in a town must, submit himself to the consequences of the obligations of trade which may be carried on in his immediate neighborhood, and which are actually necessary for commerce and for the benefit of the inhabitants of the town and the public at large. All that the law requires is, that the business be carried on in a fair and reasonable way, and that a man be not required to submit to greater personal inconvenience than he can, under the circumstances of the case, be reasonably required to do. A man who, in the exercise of a noisy trade, causes material damage to the property of a neighbor, cannot justify on the ground that the damage was caused by him in a reasonable and proper exercise of his trade in a reasonable and proper place $(b)^1$.

23. Mere noise alone will, on a proper case being made out, be a sufficient ground for an injunction (c). Injunctions have accordingly been granted to restrain persons from ring-

* 364 ing * bells (d), or carrying on a trade (e), so as to affect materially the comfort and enjoyment of property.

24. The doctrine of coming to a nuisance (f) may be looked on as exploded. A man is not precluded from maintaining an action or a suit by the fact that the business which creates the nuisance had been carried on before he took possession (g). " The plaintiff," said Tindal, C. J. (h), " came to his house

(b) Scott v. Frith, 4 F. & F. 349; Bradley v. Gill, 1 Lutw. 70; Salmon v. Bensley, R. & M. 189; Elliotson v. Feetham, 2 Bing. N. C. 137; Simpson v. Savage, 1 C. B. N. S. 347; Mumford v. Oxford, Worcester, and Wolverhampton Railway Co., 1 H. & N. 34.

(c) White v. Cohen, 1 Drew. 313; Eaden v. Firth, 1 H. & M. 573; Crump v. Lambert, 3 L. R. Eq. 409.

(d) Soltau v. De Held, 2 Sim. N. S. 133. See Ryder v. Williams, 4 L. J. Ch. N. S. 55.

(e) Crump v. Lambert, 3 L. R. Eq. 409.

(f) See 2 Bl. Comm. 402.

(g) Elliotson v. Feetham, 2 Bing. N. C. 134.

(h) Ib.

1 The fact that the neighborhood to be affected by the odors and offensive smell that will be caused by a business which the defendant is about to establish, and which complainant seeks to enjoin as a nuisance, already contains establishments devoted to noxious or disagreeable trades, is not enough to defeat the right to an injunction, unless such neighborhood has been by their continuance for years so wholly given up to such establishments that the addition of the one contemplated by the defendant will not add sensibly to the discomfort. Cleveland v. Citizens Gaslight Co., 5 C. E. Green, 201.

The considerations which would lead the court to enjoin the location of a cemetery near a dwelling are stated in Ellison v. Commissioners, 5 Jones, Eq. 57, and Clark v. Lawrence, 6 ib. 83.

clothed with all the rights appurtenant, one of which at common law is a right to wholesome untainted air, unless the business which creates the nuisance has been carried on for so great a length of time that the law will presume a grant from his neighbor in favor of the party who causes it." In Tipping v. St Helen's Smelting Company (i), the court held that the fact that a man had come to a nuisance did not disentitle him to relief by injunction.

25. An interference with the right of drain is a nuisance to a house. If the owner of a house, being also owner of land surrounding it, makes a drain or conduit through part of the land to his house and then sells the house with its appurtenants, the right to the conduit passes under the conveyance as a thing appertaining to the house. So, also, if he sells the land, reserving the house, the right to the drain or conduit is reserved, for the reservation of the house is a reservation of it with all its appurtenances (j). The doctrine as to the implication of a reservation of rights of drain in favor of the tenement retained as against the tenement granted, was carried further in the case of Pyer v. Carter (k). It was there held that, even in the absence of any reservation in the grant or conveyance, the right to a drain or conduit is reserved by implication of law over the part granted in favor of the part retained, if the actual existence of the drain or conduit at the time of the conveyance might have been found out upon inquiry by the grantor, although it was not * apparent,   * 365 and that it was immaterial that a drain or conduit might be made at a reasonable expense through the part retained. But the case has been expressly disapproved of by Lord Westbury, in Suffield v. Brown (l). "The true conclusion," he said (m), "is that the purchaser takes the house, as it is described in the conveyance, and not 'such as it is' at the time of the grant" (n). The doctrine of Pyer v. Carter was also disapproved of by the supreme court of Massachu-

---

(i) 1 L. R. Ch. Ap. 66.
(j) Nicholas v. Chamberlayne, Cro. Jac. 121. See Sury v. Pigott, Poph. 166; Hinchcliffe v. Lord Kinnoul, 5 Bing. N. C. 23; Suffield v. Brown, 33 L. J. Ch. 249; Ewart v. Cochrane, 4 Macq.

117; Dodd v. Burchell, 1 H. & C. 113.
(k) 1 H. & N. 916.
(l) 33 L. J. Ch. 249.
(m) Ib.
(n) See supra, p. 356.

setts, in Carbrey v. Willis (o) ; and the true rule was there laid down to be in accordance with an earlier decision of the same court, in Johnson v. Jordan (p), that if the owner of two adjoining messuages or lots of land sells one of them, retaining the other, no reservation of the right of drain will be taken as reserved by implication of law over the part of the granted in favor of the part retained, unless it is de facto annexed, and is in use at the time of the grant, and is necessary to the enjoyment of the part retained, and that a necessity cannot be deemed to exist, if a new drain can be made by reasonable labor and expense, without going through the land granted. In Johnson v. Jordan (q), the same rule was laid down where the two different messuages or lots were sold to different purchasers on the same day.

26. The same principles which apply to the right of drain are also applicable to the right of drip, or the right to the flow of water from the roof of one man's house on to the house or land of another. · The owner of the dominant tenement may lessen the burden of the servient tenement, but he cannot increase it without the consent of its proprietor. Without such consent he cannot increase the surface of his roof, or permit the water from neighboring roofs to increase that which naturally falls from his own (r).

27. Rights of drain and rights of drip are rights to artificial watercourses, and are, in respect of prescription and other circumstances of right, governed by the same principles and the same rules.

28. Other cases of nuisance to dwelling-houses,
* 366   where equitable * relief has been sought, are : a gunpowder manufactory (s) ; the storing of damp jute, or other highly combustible materials (t) ; the obstruction of a chimney (u) ; the erection of a public urinal in a street (v) ;

(o) 7 Allen (Amer.), 354.
(p) 2 Metc. (Amer.) 234.
(q) Ib.
(r) See Reynolds v. Clarke, 2 Lord Raym. 1399 ; Thomas v. Thomas, 2 Cr. M. & R. 34 ; Jack v. Lyall, 1 Sh. & Macl. Sc. Ap. 77 ; Fay v. Prentice, 1 C. B. 828 ; Battishill v. Reed, 18 C. B. 696 ; Martin v. Simpson, 6 Allen (Amer.), 102.

(s) Crowder v. Tinkler, 19 Ves. 617.
(t) Hepburn v. Lordan, 2 H. & M. 345. See Queen v. Lister, 1 Dear. and B. C. C. 209.
(u) Hervey v. Smith, 1 K. & J. 389, 22 Beav. 299.
(v) Biddulph v. Vestry of St. George's, 33 L. J. Ch. 411.

the establishment of a rifle-range in the neighborhood of a dwelling-house (*w*) ; the obstruction of a foot-path in front of a house (*x*) ; the breaking up a pavement (*y*) ; the holding a regatta with aquatic sports, and so bringing together large numbers of people (*z*).

29. Injunctions to restrain nuisance to a dwelling-house will, if required by the circumstances of the case, be in the mandatory form (*a*).

SECTION III.—NUISANCES TO SUPPORT.

1. The right to the support of land in its natural state, vertically by the subjacent strata, and laterally by the adjacent soil, is a right to which the owner of the surface is of common right entitled (*b*). The right is not in the nature of an easement, but is an incident to the right of the ordinary enjoyment of property (*c*). The right is not a right to have the whole or any part of the subjacent or adjacent soil left in its natural state, but is simply a right to have the surface supported in its natural state, so far as the subjacent or adjacent soil is naturally capable of affording support. The owner of the sub-

(*w*) Bannister *v.* Bigge, 34 Beav. 287.

(*x*) Wedmore *v.* Mayor of Bristol, 11 W. R. 136.

(*y*) Dover Gas-light Co. *v.* Mayor of Dover, 5 D. M. & G. 545. See Queen *v.* Longton Gas Co., 2 El. & El. 651.

(*z*) Bostock *v.* North Staffordshire Railway Co., 5 De G. & S. 584, 4 E. & B. 798, 3 Sm. & G. 283. See R. *v.* Moore, 3 B. & A. 186.

(*a*) Gale *v.* Abbott, 8 Jur. N. S. 987 ; Hervey *v.* Smith, 1 K. & J. 392 ; Hepburn *v.* Lordan, 2 H. & M. 345. See, as to the principles on which mandatory injunctions are granted, *supra*, p. 230–232. Where a plaintiff has proved his right to an injunction against a nuisance or other injury, it is no part of the duty of the court to inquire in what way the defendant can best remove it. The plaintiff is entitled to an injunction at once, unless the removal of the injury is physically impossible ; and it is the duty of the defendant to find his own way out of the difficulty, whatever inconvenience or expense it may put him to. Attorney-General *v.* Colney Hatch Lunatic Asylum, 4 L. R. Ch. Ap. 146.

(*b*) Humphries *v.* Brogden, 12 Q. B. 746 ; Hunt *v.* Peake, John. 710 ; Rowbotham *v.* Wilson, 8 H. L. 348, 355 ; Elliott *v.* North Eastern Railway Co., 10 H. L. 333.

(*c*) Bonomi *v.* Backhouse, 9 H. L. 512.

jacent or adjacent soil may work or dig on his own land in any
        way or to any extent he pleases, so long as he does not
* 367   cause the surface * of his neighbor's soil to subside or
        give way. He may, if an artificial support be substi-
tuted, excavate his land to such an extent as, but for the
artificial support, would cause a subsidence of the neighboring
land. Until actual damage be done, no cause of action arises;
but if damage result, neither the care and skill with which the
works may have been carried on, nor the unstable nature of
the soil, nor the difficulty of propping it up, will form any defence to an action (d). The right exists as well in the case
of lands which are not conterminous as of lands which are conterminous. Any land which depends mediately or immediately
on the support of other land, and is capable of being injured by
its removal, is for this purpose neighboring land (e). The right
to support may be qualified or waived by deed (f), but the
words of the deed must be express, and must show clearly and
distinctly that the right has been qualified or waived (g). A
custom or prescription to work mines without making compensation for any damage caused to dwelling-houses is unreasonable and bad (h).

2. The right to support from land being a right to support
from land in its natural state to land in its natural state, the
right includes only the right to such support as is furnished by
the permanent conditions of land, not by its accidental circumstances (i). The existence of water in a drowned mine being
obviously a circumstance of an accidental and temporary character, a mine-owner may drain it away, provided he works his
        mines in the ordinary and usual manner, although it
* 368   may contribute to the support of * the soil above. No

---

(d) Humphries v. Brogden, 12 Q. B.
746; Hunt v. Peake, John. 710; Bonomi v. Backhouse, 9 H. L. 512; Proud
v. Bates, 34 L. J. Ch. 407; Smith v.
Thackerah, 1 L. R. C. P. 564.

(e) Browne v. Robins, 4 H. & N. 186;
Bonomi v. Backhouse, 9 H. L. 503.
See Shaw v. Thackerah, 1 L.R.C.P.564.

(f) Rowbotham v. Wilson, 8 H. L.
360; Elliott v. North Eastern Railway
Co., 10 H. L. 333; Murchie v. Black,
19 C. B. N. S. 190.

(g) Smart v. Morton, 5 E. & B. 30;

Dugdale v. Robertson, 3 K. & J. 700;
Haines v. Roberts, 7 E. & B. 625;
Proud v. Bates, 34 L. J. Ch. 407;
Richards v. Harper, 12 Jur. N. S. 770.
See Goold v. Great Western Deep Coal
Co., 2 D. J. & S. 600.

(h) Hilton v. Lord Granville, 5 Q. B.
701, Cr. & Ph. 283. See Marquis of
Salisbury v. Gladstone, 9 H. L. 702;
but see Blackett v. Bradly, 1 B. & S. 940.

(i) North Eastern Railway Co. v.
Elliott, 1 J. & H. 145, 2 D. F. & J. 423,
10 H. L. 333.

right to resist the withdrawal of the water can be gained by prescription (*j*). If the support required is increased, either by increasing the weight of the supported land, or by diminishing its self-supporting power, no right exists to have this additional support supplied by the neighboring land, and no subsidence resulting from this cause gives a right of an action. If a man has so weakened his own soil by mining or other excavations under it that the surface requires more lateral support than before, the right to such additional support cannot be acquired by long enjoyment (*k*).

3. Houses and buildings are entitled to the same degree of support as the surface of the soil on which they stand, provided their extra weight is not such as to increase sensibly the tendency of the soil to subside (*l*), but if their additional weight has so loaded the soil that it requires more support than it did in its natural state, there is no right of support for the excess, and an action will not lie for damage against a neighbor or the owner of the subjacent strata, if the damage has been done without malice or negligence (*m*). There are dicta to the effect that a right to lateral support for heavy buildings may be acquired by twenty years' enjoyment (*n*). But the case does not come within the principle upon which presumption of grant from long enjoyment is founded; for presumption of grant only arises where the person against whom it is raised might have * prevented the　* 369 exercise of the subject of the presumed grant, and though it is quite true that the owner of the adjoining soil

---

(*j*) North Eastern Railway Co. *v.* Elliott, 1 J. & H. 145, 2 D. F. & J. 423, 10 H. L. 333.

(*k*) Partridge *v.* Scott, 3 M. & W. 220. See Webb *v.* Bird, 13 C. B. N. S. 843; Chasemore *v.* Richards, 7 H. L. 349.

(*l*) Roberts *v.* Haines, 6 E. & B. 643, 7 E. & B. 625; Brown *v.* Robins, 4 H. & N. 186; Stroyan *v.* Knowles, 6 H. & N. 454; Hunt *v.* Peake, John. 711.

(*m*) Wilde *v.* Minsterley, 2 Roll. Ab. 564; Palmer *v.* Fleshees, 1 Sid. 167; Wyatt *v.* Harrison, 3 B. & A. 871; Dodd *v.* Holme, 1 A. & E. 493; Partridge *v.* Scott, 3 M. & W. 220; Warburton *v.* London and Blackwall Railway Co., 1 Ra. Ca. 560; Gayford *v.* Nicholls, 9 Exch. 702; but see Rogers *v.* Taylor, 2 H. & N. 828.

(*n*) Wilde *v.* Minsterley, 2 Roll. Ab. 564; Palmer *v.* Fleshees, 1 Sid. 167; Wyatt *v.* Harrison, 3 B. & A. 871; Dodd *v.* Holme, 1 A. & E. 493; Partridge *v.* Scott, 3 M. & W. 220; Rogers *v.* Taylor, 2 H. & N. 828; Humphries *v.* Brogdén, 12 Q. B. 739; Gayford *v.* Nicholls, 9 Exch. 702; Bonomi *v.* Backhouse, El. Bl. & El. 654; Rowbotham *v.* Wilson, 8 E. & B. 140; Shaw *v.* Thackerah, 1 L. R. C. P. 564. See Brown *v.* Robins, 4 H. & N. 186; Solomon *v.* Vintners' Co., *ib.* 585; Hunt *v.* Peake, John. 710.

might dig a trench within his own boundary, so as to prevent the acquisition of the right, it would be going rather far to say that from his forbearance to do so a presumption of grant may be made (*o*). These considerations apply with much greater force to the case of vertical support.

4. A right to support of soil in excess of the ordinary common-law right, arises by implication of law, where the owner of land has granted the surface, reserving to himself the subjacent minerals, or has granted any part of his land, retaining the adjoining part. As a grant of property carries with it all legal incidents which are necessary for the reasonable enjoyment of the property in the state in which it was at the time of the grant, or which are necessary for the purposes for which, according to the obvious intent of the parties, the grant was made (*p*), such a measure of support, adjacent and subjacent, as is necessary for the land in the condition it was at the time of the grant or in the state for the purpose of putting it into which the grant was made, passes as an incident to the grant (*q*). A land-owner, accordingly, who has granted land to a railway company for the purposes of their line, reserving to himself the minerals and all liberties and privileges of working them, may not work them so as to let down the surface. In reserving mines the land-owner must be understood to have reserved them so far only as he can work them consistently with the grant he has made to the company. He cannot, by reason of his having reserved the mines, derogate from his own conveyance by removing the necessary support. Though the railway traffic on the line be much greater than on the line originally contemplated, so that the support contemplated could not have been so great as that which is afterwards * 370 required, the law as to support is the same; * for when a grant is made to a railway company, without any limitation as to its nature, the grantor must be understood to have warranted support, however the railway might be used, or to

(*o*) See Chasemore *v.* Richards, 7 H. L. 349; Webb *v.* Bird, 13 C. B. N. S. 843.
(*p*) *Supra*, p. 355.
(*q*) Harris *v.* Ryding, 5 M. & W. 60; Smart *v.* Morton, 5 E. & B. 30; Dugdale *v.* Robertson, 3 K. & J. 695; Caledonian Railway Co. *v.* Sprot, 2 Macq. 449; Caledonian Railway Co. *v.* Lord Belhaven, 3 Macq. 56; Elliott *v.* North Eastern Railway Co., 10 H. L. 333.

whatever purpose it might be applied (*r*). Whether the conveyance is by an ordinary private assurance, or takes place under the compulsory powers of an act of Parliament, the rule is the same (*s*). Nor does a proviso that any damage done by the working of the minerals shall be repaired at the expense of the mine-owner exclude the jurisdiction of the court, where the reservation of the minerals has been upon condition that no damage be caused by working them (*t*). "There is," said Wood, V. C. (*u*), "a positive prohibition of such working, and though a remedy is provided for damage done, the provisions for compensation cannot interfere with the jurisdiction of this court, and the company are entitled to an injunction to prevent the threatened injury" (*x*). The grantor of minerals is bound by the same obligations in respect of vertical and lateral support, as those by which the person through whom he claims was bound, and has the same rights (*y*).

5. When the proposed undertaking passes through a mineral district, provisions are often inserted in the act which authorizes the undertaking, excepting all minerals under the land taken by the company, but giving the company power, as soon as the workings of the minerals approach within a certain distance of the surface, to stop the workings on purchasing out the rights of the coal-owners, and paying them compensation for their loss in not being permitted to work them. If the option reserved to the company of purchasing out the minerals be declined, the mine-owner may proceed to win them, and will not be liable for any damage caused to the works of the company * provided his works be carried on in   * 371 the usual and ordinary manner. In Dudley Canal Company *v.* Grazebrook (*z*), the clause which empowered the mine-owner to proceed with the workings of the mines in the

---

(*r*) Caledonian Railway Co. *v.* Sprot, 2 Macq. 449 ; Caledonian Railway Co. *v.* Lord Belhaven, 3 Macq. 56 ; Proud *v.* Bates, 34 L. J. Ch. 407.

(*s*) Elliott *v.* North Eastern Railway Co., 10 H. L. 333.

(*t*) North Eastern Railway Co. *v.* Crossland, 2 J. & H. 565, aff'd., 32 L. J. Ch. 357.

(*u*) *Ib.*, 2 J. & H. 578.

(*x*) Caledonian Railway Co. *v.* Sprot,

2 Macq. 449 ; Elliott *v.* North Eastern Railway Co., 10 H. L. 333. See Goold *v.* Great Western Deep Coal Co., 2 D. J. & S. 600 ; Proud *v.* Bates, 34 L. J. Ch. 407.

(*y*) North Eastern Railway Co. *v.* Crossland, 32 L. J. Ch. 357.

(*z*) 1 B. & A. 59. See Great Western Railway Co. *v.* Bennett, 2 L. R. Ap. Ca. 27.

event of the option to purchase being declined, declared that
he might carry them on "provided no injury be done to the
navigation." The court said that the meaning of the proviso
could not be that the owners were to be responsible at all
events for any injury done to the canal, for then the company
would never purchase the minerals, that the reasonable mode
of reconciling the different parts of the act was to say " either
that the party working the mines was to do no unnecessary
damage or injury to the navigation, or no extraordinary damage or injury by working them out of the ordinary mode " (a).
In Stourbridge Canal Company v. Earl of Dudley (b), the
Exchequer Chamber, affirming a judgment of the Queen's
Bench, approved the principle laid down in Dudley Canal Company v. Grazebrook. The act provided that if the mine-
owner wished to work any minerals within a certain distance
from the canal, he was to give notice to the company, and the
company might then purchase, or otherwise the owner might
work such mines " provided no injury be done to the navigation." The company having omitted to purchase after the
notice required by the act had been given, the minerals were
worked within the specified distance in the usual and ordinary manner, but nevertheless damage was done to the
works of the company. The court held that the company
were not entitled to recover damages against the mine-
owner (c).

6. General provisions, defining the respective rights of mine-
owners and railway companies, have been inserted in the
Railways Clauses Consolidation Act, 8 Vict. c. 20. By the
77th clause all mines are excepted out of the conveyance to
the company, unless they shall have been expressly named
        therein and conveyed thereby. The 78th clause pro-
* 372   vides that * the mines under the line, or within forty
        yards therefrom, shall not be worked if the company
are willing to purchase them, and pay compensation to the
owner. Before proceeding to work them the owner is re-

(a) See Wyrley Canal Co. v. Bradley, 7 East, 368 ; Midland Railway Co.
v. Checkley, 15 W. R. 671.

(b) 3 El. & El. 409.

(c) See North Eastern Railway Co.
v. Elliott, 1 J. & H. 151 ; Birmingham
Canal Co. v. Earl of Dudley, 7 H. & N.
969.

quired to give thirty days' notice of his intention to do so to
the company, so as to give them the power of exercising the
option.   By the 79th clause it is enacted that if the company
do not within thirty days state their willingness to purchase
the minerals, the owner may work the mines " so that the
working be done in a manner proper and necessary for the
beneficial working thereof and according to the usual working
of such mines in the district where the same shall be situate."
It is also provided by the same clause that if any damage be
done to the railway by any improper working, it shall be repaired at the expense of the owner.

7. In construing these clauses, the Exchequer Chamber, in
Fletcher v. Great Western Railway Company (d), followed
the general principle laid down in Dudley Canal Company v.
Grazebrook, and held that a mine-owner was entitled to claim
compensation for such minerals lying within forty yards as he
might leave ungotten for the purpose of furnishing support to
the railway.   " All that the railway company requires," said
Cockburn, C. J., in delivering the judgment of the court (e),
" is the surface soil : it may be that the minerals will never be
worked by the land-owner, in which case the company ought
not to be subject to any expense ; and, therefore, the legislature interposes and says that the company shall be under no
obligation to pay the land-owner for that which may be required ; but if the mines come to be worked and the company
requires them as necessary for the support of the surface, they
must make compensation to the land-owner.   The very fact
that provision is made by the 78th section for possible injury
to the railway, shows that the legislature intended to reserve
the question of support and compensation.   The legislation
would be incomplete, if it were not applicable to the case of a
land-owner, who, having parted with the surface soil to be
used by a company for the purpose of putting an additional weight upon it, as a * railway company must   * 373
necessarily do, shall afterwards entertain an idea of
working the mines under or in the neighborhood of a railway.

(d) 5 H. & N. 689. Approved and   Great Western Railway Co. v. Bennett,
confirmed by the House of Lords.   2 L. R. Ap. Ca. 27.
(e) Ib.

The minerals are reserved to the land-owner, and the railway company is under no obligation of making any compensation in respect of them, until the necessity for it arises from his desire to work them. In such a case the company are to consider whether the working is liable to damage the railway, and then if they are willing to make such compensation for the mines, the owner is not to work them. The mines may never be worked, and it would be a great hardship on a railway company if, upon a speculative possibility, they were bound to make compensation for not working them. Such is the plain, intelligent, and equitable construction of these clauses, and one which is consistent with the scope of the act." In London and North Western Railway Company *v.* Ackroyd (*f*), accordingly, Wood, V. C., refused to restrain a mine-owner from working coal within forty yards of a tunnel of the plaintiffs, who endeavored to establish a right to support without making compensation. If the mine-owner proceeds to work his mines within the specified distance, without giving notice to the company of his intention to do so, as required either by special act, or by the 78th clause of the Railways Clauses Consolidation Act, he will be restrained by injunction (*g*).

8. The result of the authorities on the subject of the right of a public company to support for its line and works within a mineral district appears to be that where land with a reservation of the minerals has been conveyed by a private assurance (*h*), or has been taken under the compulsory powers of an act of Parliament (*i*), and there is a proviso in the assurance, or the act, that the minerals reserved shall not be worked so as to cause any damage to the works of the company, but no option is given to the company of purchasing out the minerals, when the working of the mines shall have advanced within a certain distance from the surface, the company are entitled to all subjacent and adjacent support which
* 374　* is given by the common law (*k*), and the mine-owner is not entitled to any compensation for not working, or

---

(*f*) 31 L. J. Ch. 588.
(*g*) Elliott *v.* North Eastern Railway Co., 10 H. L. 333.
(*h*) Caledonian Railway Co. *v.* Sprot, 2 Macq. 449.

(*i*) Elliott *v.* North Eastern Railway Co., 10 H. L. 333.
(*k*) *Ib.* See, as to the form of injunction in such cases, *ib.*

not being allowed to work his mines so near the works of the company so as to cause them damage (*l*). The claim for compensation ought to have been made at the time when the land was sold, or care ought to have been taken to insert a special clause in the act to that effect (*m*). Where, on the other hand, an option to purchase minerals lying within a certain distance from the works and line of the company has been reserved to the company either by special act, or by the Railways Clauses Consolidation Act, 8 Vict. c. 20, s. 78, but the company decline, after due notice, to exercise the option, the mine-owner may work within the specified distance without being answerable for any damage, provided the mines have been worked in the proper and ordinary manner. A court of equity will not restrain him from working them, except upon condition that compensation be made to him for his loss in not working them (*n*).

9. Where the minerals lie beyond the specified distance, and therefore within the proper bounds of the mine-owner, a company has an absolute right to support (*o*).

10. The Railways Clauses Consolidation Act, 8 Vict. c. 20, s. 78, applies to all owners of mines irrespectively of the fact whether any privity exists between them and the company.

11. The 81st clause of the Railways Clauses Consolidation Act, * 8 Vict. c. 20, enacts that the company   * 375 shall from time to time make compensation for any minerals not purchased by the company which cannot be obtained by reason of making and maintaining the railway. This clause may probably have been meant to apply to minerals lying beyond the specified distance, and within the

(*l*) Reg. *v.* Aire and Calder Navigation Co., 30 L. J. Q. B. 337.

(*m*) North Eastern Railway Co. *v.* Elliott, 1 J. & H. 154; Rex *v.* Leeds and Selby Railway Co., 3 A. & E. 683; Reg. *v.* Aire and Calder Navigation Co., 30 L. J. Q. B. 337.

(*n*) Wyrley Canal Co. *v.* Bradley, 7 East, 368; Dudley Canal Co. *v.* Grazebrook, 1 B. & A. 59; Stourbridge Canal Co. *v.* Earl of Dudley, 3 El. & El. 409; Fletcher *v.* Great Western Railway Co., 5 H. & N. 689; London and North Western Railway Co. *v.*

Ackroyd, 31 L. J. Ch. 588; Birmingham Canal Co. *v.* Earl of Dudley, 7 H. & N. 969; Bagnall *v.* London and North Western Railway Co., 1 H. & C. 544; Queen *v.* Fisher, 3 B. & S. 191. See, as to the mode in which compensation money is to be estimated, Barnsley Canal Co. *v.* Twibell, 13 L. J. Ch. 434; Great Western Railway Co. *v.* Bennett 2 L. R. Ap. Ca. 27.

(*o*) Caledonian Railway Co. *v.* Sprot, 2 Macq. 449; Elliott *v.* North Eastern Railway Co., 1 J. & H. 154, 2 D. F. & J. 423, 10 H. L. 333.

boundary of the mine-owner. If so the common-law right would be varied by the clause. The effect of the clause was not in any way considered either in Caledonian Railway Company v. Sprot, or Elliott v. North Eastern Railway Company.

12. As between two adjoining houses a right to lateral support cannot be acquired by long enjoyment (*p*). An alleged custom giving the right is unreasonable and void (*q*). Where, however, houses have been so constructed as to be mutually subservient to, and depending on each other, neither of them being capable of standing or being enjoyed without the support it derives from its neighbor, the alienation of one house by the owner of both does not estop him from claiming in respect of the house he retains that support from the house sold, which is at the same time afforded in return by the former to the latter tenement. "Where," said the court, in Richards v. Rose (*r*), "houses have been erected in common by the same owner upon a plot of ground; and therefore, necessarily requiring mutual support, there is either by a presumed grant, or by a presumed reservation, a right of mutual support, so that the owner who sells one of the houses, as against himself, grants such right and, on his own part also, reserves the right; and consequently the same mutual dependence on its neighbor still remains" (*s*). But the right to mutual easement exists only so long as the wall continues to be sufficient for the purpose, and the respective buildings remain in a condition to need and enjoy the support (*t*). If one of the buildings thus * 376 supported becomes so dilapidated * as to be unsafe and unfit for occupation, the owner may, upon giving reasonable notice to the owner of the adjoining house, take it down, notwithstanding the act of taking down would occasion the destruction of the whole wall, on condition of rebuilding it and completing the work with due speed (*u*). The right ceases upon the destruction of the buildings and the wall by fire, and

(*p*) Peyton v. Mayor of London, 9 B. & C. 736; Solomon v. Vintners' Co., 4 H. & N. 585; Kempston v. Butler, 12 Ir. C. L. 516.

(*q*) Kempston v. Butler, 12 Ir. C. L. 516.

(*r*) 9 Exch. 218, 221.

(*s*) Kempston v. Butler, 12 Ir. C. L. 516. See Suffield v. Brown, 33 L. J. Ch. 249.

(*t*) Sherred v. Cisco, 4 Sandf. (Amer.) 480; Partridge v. Gilbert, 1 Smith (Amer.), 601.

(*u*) Partridge v. Gilbert, *ib.*

the parties are remitted to their original and unqualified title to the division line (x).

13. A party-wall is a wall standing on the line between two estates owned by different owners for the use of both estates. The common use of a wall separating adjoining lots of land belonging to different owners is *primâ facie* evidence that the wall and the land on which it stands belong to both owners in equal undivided moieties as tenants in common (y). One of the tenants in common may take down the wall, if it be done with the intention of rebuilding it (z), but it must be with that intention (a). In Philipps v. Bordman (b), the owner of one-half of an ancient solid party-wall was restrained from cutting away a portion of its face and erecting a new wall upon his own land at a distance of two inches from the portion of the ancient wall which was left standing and connected with it by occasional projecting bricks and tiles.

14. Under the Party-Walls Act, 14 Geo. 3. c. 78, each owner of adjoining premises within the cities of London and Westminster having a common party-wall which stands partly on the land of each of them, owns that which is on his own land, and there is no tenancy, but each is entitled to certain easements in the wall of the other (c). This statute has been repealed and re-enacted in part by the Metropolitan Buildings Act, 18 & 19 Vict. c. 122, upon the provisions of which the law on the subject of party-walls within the metropolitan district now depends (d). The * nature of the property in party-   * 377 walls, as existing under the Party-Walls Act, does not seem to be altered by the later act (e).

(x) Sherred   v.   Cisco,   4   Sandf. (Amer.) 480.

(y) Matts v. Hawkins, 5 Taunt. 20; Cubitt v. Palmer, 8 B. & C. 257.

(z) Cubitt v. Palmer, *ib.*

(a) *Ib.*; Stedman v. Smith, 8 E. & B. 1.

(b) 4 Allen (Amer.), 147.

(c) Matts v. Hawkins, 5 Taunt. 20.

(d) See Wheeler v. Gray, 4 C. B. N. S. 584; Seawell v. Webster, 7 W. R. 691; Cowen v. Philipps, 33 Beav. 19.

(e) See, as to notice required by 83d and 85th sections of Metropolitan Buildings Act, 18 & 19 Vict. c. 122, Major v. Park Lane Co., 2 L. R. Eq. 453; Sims v. Estate Co., 14 W. R. 419.

SECTION IV.—NUISANCES RELATING TO WATER.

1. Acts which are nuisances in regard to water.
2. Proprietor of land on the margin of a stream, owns to the middle thread of the stream.
3. But has no right to use his property in the bed of the stream so as to interfere with the natural flow of the stream.
4 & 5. Rights in running water.
6. User of water for domestic purposes always reasonable; for agricultural or manufacturing whether or not reasonable a difficult question.
7. Diversion of water by riparian proprietor without returning it to its natural channel is an illegal user.
8. Use of stream at its source.
9. Principles applicable to use of streams flowing from under ground.
10. Pollution or fouling a stream a cause of action.
11. Statute on the subject.
12. New rights in water may be acquired by prescription.
13–15. Statute on the subject.
16. Easements in water, limits of and extinguishment of.
17. Alteration in the mode of use of water does not affect the right.
18. Interruption.
19. Abandonment of easement.
20. Right of riparian proprietors subject to all prescriptive rights.
21–24. Rights and liabilities of parties as to artificial streams and watercourses.
25. As to surface water.
6. Distinction between a watercourse and water of a casual character.
27. Same principles which apply to surface water applicable to subterraneous water of same casual description.
28. Land lying on a lower level is subject to the drainage of land on a higher level.
29. Mine-owners not responsible for damage done by flow of water from natural causes into adjoining mine.
30. Rights of proprietors on banks of rivers to protect themselves against flood water.
31. Rights to water may be created or modified by deed.
32. Right passes by implication.
33. Implication of reservation.
34. Injunctions will be granted to restrain diversion of water.
35. And to restrain fouling a stream.
36. And if necessary mandatory injunction will be issued.
37. Injunction will be issued to restrain damage to canals.
38. Also to a mill-race.

1. Another class of nuisances in which the interference of a court of equity by way of injunction is often sought, are nuisances relating to water. All acts done by a man on his own land, whereby the rights of his neighbor in water are injuriously affected, or whereby water becomes a cause of damage to the land of his neighbor, may be considered together as nuisances relating to water.

[392]

2. *Primâ facie*, every proprietor of land along the margin of a river or stream of running water above tide-water is the proprietor of the land covered by the water up to the middle thread of the stream. If the same person be the owner of the land on both sides of the river, he owns the bed of the whole river to the extent of the length of his land upon it (*f*). A grant of land bounded upon a stream or river above tide-water carries the soil up to the centre of the stream, unless there are expressions in the terms of the deed which limit the grant to the edge or margin of the river (*g*).

3. If from any cause the course of the stream should be permanently diverted, the proprietors on either side of the old channel have a right to use the soil of the *alveus*, each of them up to what was the *medium filum aquae* in the same way as they are entitled to the adjoining land: but no riparian proprietor is entitled to use his property in the *alveus* in such a manner as to interfere with the natural flow of the stream. An * encroachment on the *alveus* may be complained of * 378 without the necessity of proving that damage has been sustained, or is likely to be sustained (*h*).

4. A proprietor of land upon the banks of a river or stream of running water has no property in the water, but has merely a usufructuary interest in the water, as appurtenant to his land. He is entitled to the comfort, enjoyment, and benefit of the water in its natural state, as it flows past his land, as he is to all the other advantages belonging to the land of which he is owner. The right in no way depends upon prescription or presumed grant. It is a natural right incident to the ownership or possession of the adjacent soil (*i*). The right does not depend on the ownership of the soil covered by the water, but is appurtenant to the ownership of the bank (*k*). The rights

(*f*) Hargr. Tracts, 5; Wright *v.* Howard, 1 Sim. & St. 190; Bickett *v.* Morris, 1 L. R. Ap. Sc. Ca. 47. See Wishart *v.* Wyllie, 1 Macq. 389. See, as to soil of lakes, Marshall *v.* Ulleswater Co., 3 B. & S. 732, 6 *ib.*, 570.

(*g*) *Ex parte* Jennings, 6 Cow. (Amer.) 518; Howard *v.* Ingersoll, 13 How. (Amer.) 416; Lord *v.* Commissioners of Sidney, 12 Moo. P. C. 473;

Crossley *v.* Lightowler, 3 L. R. Eq. 295.

(*h*) Bickett *v.* Morris, 1 L. R. Sc. Ap. Ca. 47; Lord Norbury *v.* Kitchin, 15 L. T. N. S. 501.

(*i*) Mason *v.* Hill, 5 B. & A. 1; Chasemore *v.* Richards, 7 H. L. 349.

(*k*) Wood *v.* Waud, 3 Exch. 748; Lord *v.* Commissioners of Sidney, 12 Moo. P. C. 473; Stockport Waterworks Co. *v.* Potter, 3 H. & C. 300.

which a riparian proprietor has with respect to the water in a stream are derived from his possession of the land abutting on the water. He cannot grant away his water-rights apart from his estate so as to place the grantee in the possession of a riparian proprietor. The rights of a riparian proprietor with respect to the stream are limited only by those of persons in a similar or analogous position to himself with respect to it. If a riparian proprietor grants to one not a riparian proprietor a right to take water from the stream, the grantee cannot maintain an action in his own name against other riparian proprietors. He can only sue the grantor for any interference with him (l).

5. The right to the enjoyment of the stream in its natural state in flow, quantity and quality being a right, to which every proprietor of land on the banks of a river or stream of running water is of common right equally entitled, each proprietor is bound so to use the common right as not essentially to prevent or interfere with an equally beneficial enjoyment of it by all the other proprietors. No proprietor has a right to * 379 * use the water to the prejudice of his neighbor above or below him, unless he has a title to some exclusive enjoyment. He may use the water as it flows past his land, but he may not diminish materially the quantity, or corrupt sensibly the quality of the water, or unreasonably detain the water, or give it another direction, and he must return it to its ordinary channel where it leaves his land. He has a right to the fall and flow of the water and to the impelling force of the current for mill or other manufacturing purposes; and as incident thereto he has a right to erect dams, sluices, canals, and water-ways so as to fit the stream for the actual working of mills; but he may not, in doing so, accelerate the velocity of the current, so as to cause material injury or annoyance to his neighbor below him, who has an equal right to the subsequent use of the same water in its natural state, or retard the flow, or throw back the water so as to injuriously to affect the grounds, mills, or springs of his neighbor above him. Without the con-

(l) Stockport Waterworks Co. v. Bracewell, 2 L. R. Exch. 1; supra, p. Potter, 3 H. & C. 800; Nuttall v. 357; infra, p. 392.

sent of the adjoining proprietor, he may not divert or materially diminish the quantity of water which would otherwise descend to the proprietor below, or affect the fall or quality of the water, or run the water back upon the proprietor above (*m*). This is the clear and settled principle on the subject, but there is often difficulty in the application of it. A certain diminution in the quantity of the water, or an acceleration or retardation of the flow, is generally an implied element in the right of using the stream at all, but *de minimis non curat lex*, and unless the use be such as to affect materially the adjoining proprietor, a right of action will not arise. The test in all cases is whether the extent or mode of enjoyment has been such as to inflict a sensible injury upon other riparian proprietors, or to interfere in a substantial and perceptible degree with their common right to a like user of the same water (*n*). So long as a reasonable * user is made by a man of the water, and   * 380 no actual or perceptible damage arises to the right of another to a similar use of the same water, no action will lie (*o*). If, however, the user be unreasonable, an action will lie, although there be no actual present damage (*p*).

6. Whether the user of the water by an upper proprietor be reasonable is generally a question of fact depending on the particular circumstances of the case. Enjoyment of water for cattle or domestic purposes may be called the ordinary user. However small the stream, and however large the supply taken may be, user for these purposes is always reasonable, provided the enjoyment is *bonâ fide* and is had in the ordinary mode according to the common usage of the country. A proprietor lower down the stream has no ground of complaint against a proprietor higher up in case of a deficiency of the water (*q*).

(*m*) Luttrel's case, 4 Co., 86 b; Bealey *v.* Shaw, 6 East, 208; Wright *v.* Howard, 1 Sim. & St. 190; Mason *v.* Hill, 5 B. & A. 1; Embrey *v.* Owen, 6 Exch. 369; Webb *v.* Portland Manufacturing Co., 3 Sumn. (Amer.) 189. See, as to throwing back water, Cooper *v.* Barber, 3 Taunt. 99; Saunders *v.* Newman, 1 B. & Ald. 258.

(*n*) Tyler *v.* Wilkinson, 4 Mass. (Amer.) 397; Embrey *v.* Owen, 6 Exch. 353; Sampson *v.* Hoddinott, 1 C. B. N. S. 590; Miner *v.* Gilmour, 12

Moo. P. C. 131; Lingwood *v.* Stowmarket Co., 1 L. R. Eq. 77.

(*o*) Embrey *v.* Owen, 6 Exch. 353; Elliott *v.* Fitchburg Railway Co., 10 Cush. (Amer.) 191.

(*p*) Embrey *v.* Owen, 6 Exch. 353. See Rochdale Canal Co. *v.* King, 14 Q. B. 122.

(*q*) Miner *v.* Gilmour, 12 Moo. P. C. 131, as modified by Lord Norbury *v.* Kitchen, 9 Jur. N. S. 132. See Wood *v.* Waud, 3 Exch. 748; Nuttall *v.* Bracewell, 2 L. R. Exch. 1; Hood *v.*

The enjoyment of water for manufacturing or agricultural purposes may be called the extraordinary user. Whether the user in such cases has been just and reasonable may be often a difficult question. In determining the question a just regard must be had to the force and magnitude of the current, the volume of water, its height and velocity, the fall, the nature of the soil, the mode and duration of the user, the general usage of the country, and all other circumstances which may, in a particular case, bear upon the question. To take a large quantity of water from a large river for manufacturing or agricultural purposes would cause no sensible or perceptible diminution of the benefit to the prejudice of a lower proprietor; whereas taking the same quantity from a small stream passing a farm would be a great and manifest injury to those below who use it for domestic supply and watering cattle; and therefore it would be an unreasonable use of the water * 381 in the latter case, * and not in the former. The question in each case is entirely one of degree. It is impossible to define precisely the limits which separate the permitted use of a stream from its wrongful application (r).

7. The diversion by a riparian proprietor of any portion of the stream without returning the water to its natural channel before it leaves his land is an illegal user (s). As between two riparian proprietors, the proprietor on one side cannot carry off any portion of the water without the consent of the proprietor on the other side (t). Each of them is entitled to use one half of the water (u), but the stream itself is indivisible. The stream can be used by each only as an entire stream in its natural channel, and there can be no severance (x). If an

Williamson, 23 Dec. of Ct. of Sess., 2d series, p. 496; Lord Melville v. Denniston, 4 Dec. of Ct. of Sess., 2d series, p. 1231; Elliott v. Fitchburg Railway Co., 10 Cush. (Amer.) 191. But see 12 Jur. N. S. Ap. 354.

(r) Embrey v. Owen, 6 Exch. 369; Elliott v. Fitchburg Railway Co., 10 Cush. (Amer.) 191. See, as to the detention of water, Shears v. Wood, 7 Moo. 345; Williams v. Morland, 2 B. & C. 910; Sampson v. Hoddinott, 1 C. B. N. S. 590. See, as to the acceleration, Williams v. Morland, 2 B. & C. 910; or retardation of the flow, Cary v.

Daniels, 8 Metc. (Amer.) 466; Thurber v. Martin, 2 Gray (Amer.), 394; of a stream.

(s) Luttrel's case, 4 Co. Rep. 86 b; Bealey v. Shaw, 6 East, 208.

(t) Curtis v. Jackson, 13 Mass. (Amer.) 507; Arthur v. Case, 1 Paige, Ch. (Amer.) 448.

(u) Pratt v. Lamson, 2 Allen (Amer.), 275.

(x) Vanderbergh v. Van Bergen, 13 Johns. (Amer.) 212; Webb v. Portland Manufacturing Co., 3 Sumn. (Amer.) 189.

island divides the stream so that only a small portion of the stream descends on one side of the island and the residue on the other, the owner of the bank where the greater quantity of water flows is entitled to the use of the whole quantity flowing there, and the owner of the bank where the smaller quantity flows is entitled to no more of the water than naturally runs between his bank and the island, and has no right to place obstructions at the head of the island for the purpose of causing one half of the stream to descend on his side of the river (y).

8. Where a spring of water arises on a man's land, he may use it as he does any other property, which is the produce of his estate, without regard to the convenience or advantage of his neighbor, if the water is not at its source a watercourse. But if a stream begins to flow at the spring head in a defined channel, the rights incidental to streams of running water attach to it at the * source (z). The right to a * 382 natural stream includes a right to all accessions as soon as they have become actually part of a stream, from whatever source the water may have come (a).

9. The same principles which apply to natural streams flowing in a defined channel over the surface are also applicable to streams flowing from under the ground in a defined channel. The right in the latter case is equally a right ex jure naturae, and is incident to the adjacent land as a beneficial adjunct (b).

10. A riparian proprietor has a right to have the water of a natural stream run through his land in a natural state of purity (c). The pollution or fouling of a stream is a ground of action against a particular person, even although other persons may have so fouled the water, that the acts of the

(y) Crooker v. Bragg, 10 Wend. (Amer.) 260.

(z) Dudden v. Guardians of Clutton Union, 1 H. & N. 627; Gaved v. Martyn, 19 C. B. N. S. 732. See Ennor v. Barwell, 2 Giff. 410, in appeal, 4 L. T. N. S. 597.

(a) Broadbent v. Ramsbotham, 11 Exch. 617; Lord Blantyre v. Dunn, 10 Dec. of Ct. of Sess., 2d series, p. 509. See M'Clean v. Hamilton, 19 ib., p. 1006.

(b) Wood v. Waud, 3 Exch. 748; Dickenson v. Grand Junction Railway Co., 7 Exch. 300, per Pollock, C. B.; Chasemore v. Richards, 7 H. L. 384, per Lord Chelmsford; Hodgkinson v. Ennor, 4 B. & S. 229.

(c) Aldred's case, 9 Co. Rep. 58 b; Bealey v. Shaw, 6 East, 208; Wright v. Howard, 1 Sim. & St. 190; Mason v. Hill, 5 B. & A. 1.

defendant may not have rendered it less applicable to useful purposes than it was before. The damage is an injury to a right, and is therefore a damage in point of law (*d*). A man who has polluted a stream by discharging into it noxious matter cannot resist an action by showing that his trade was carried on in a proper manner and is a lawful trade (*e*).

11. A district board of works, constituted under the Metropolis Local Management Act, 18 & 19 Vict. c. 120, are not empowered by the act to pollute waters beyond the district over which the authority of the board extends (*f*).

12. After an adverse enjoyment for twenty years, a prescriptive right over and above the ordinary common-law right may be acquired to water, provided the person against whom * 383   the right * is asserted has had a reasonable opportunity of becoming acquainted with the state of the facts, and had it in his power to prevent the acquisition of the right (*g*). The mere omission by a riparian proprietor to use the water of the stream does not impair his title, or confer any right thereto upon another. The right exists whether he exercises it or not. He may begin to exercise it whenever he will. It is not the non-user by a man of his right, but the adverse enjoyment by another during twenty years which destroys the right (*h*). As between two opposite riparian proprietors, the user by the one of the whole or a greater part of the water by means of structures erected upon and within the limits of his own estate is not an adverse possession, which will raise the presumption of grant, for riparian proprietors on the opposite banks of a stream stand to each other in the relation and with substantially the rights of tenants in common (*i*). To consti-

(*d*) Wood *v.* Waud, 3 Exch. 748; Wood *v.* Sutcliffe, 2 Sim. N. S. 163; Crossley *v.* Lightowler, 3 L. R. Eq. 279. See, as to injunctions, *ib.*; *supra*, p. 225, 226.

(*e*) Stockport Waterworks Co. *v.* Potter, 7 H. & N. 160. See Hipkins *v.* Birmingham, &c., Gas Co., 5 H. & N. 74, 6 H. & N. 250; St. Helen's Smelting Co. *v.* Tipping, 11 H. & L. 642. For a consideration of the circumstances under which the court will interfere to prevent the pollution of a stream, see Att'y General *v.* Gee, 10 L. R. Eq. 131.

(*f*) Cator *v.* Lewisham Board of Works, 5 B. & S. 115.

(*g*) Bealey *v.* Shaw, 6 East, 208; Cooper *v.* Barber, 3 Taunt. 99; Daniel *v.* North, 11 East, 372; Wright *v.* Howard, 1 Sim. & St. 190; Saunders *v.* Newman, 1 B. & Ald. 258; Sampson *v.* Hoddinott, 1 C. B. N. S. 590; Chasemore *v.* Richards, 7 H. L. 349; Webb *v.* Bird, 13 C. B. N. S. 843.

(*h*) Bealey *v.* Shaw, 6 East, 208, Crooker *v.* Bragg, 10 Wend. (Amer.) 266; Crossley *v.* Lightowler, 3 L. R. Eq. 279.

(*i*) Pratt *v.* Lamson, 2 Allen (Amer.), 275; Beauman *v.* Kinsella, 8 Ir. C. L. 291.

tute adverse possession, the possession by the one must be so wholly inconsistent with the claim of the other as to amount to an actual ouster (j).

13. The acquisition of new rights to water by long user comes within the provisions of the Prescription Act, 2 & 3 Will. 4, c. 71. By the 2d and 4th clauses of that act the continuous enjoyment as of right of a watercourse, or the use of water as an easement, over or from any land or water for twenty years next before the commencement of some suit or action in which the claim has been brought in question (k) without interruption acquiesced in for a year (l), is evidence from which a jury is justified in presuming a right, if the claim be otherwise good at common law (m).

14. A right may be acquired under the statute to interfere with * the course of water either by damming   * 384 it up and forcing it back upon the land above, or by transmitting it altered in quality or quantity or velocity to the inferior proprietor (n). A claim to discharge a stream of water either in its natural state or changed in quality over land (o), or to foul a stream by throwing rubbish into it (p), or by discharging into it sewage water (q), or water fouled in the process of manufacture (r), or generally to interfere with its purity to such an extent as to cause damage to another (s), is within the statute. So also a claim to go on the soil of another to clear a mill-stream and repair its banks (t), or turn the water into an artificial watercourse (u), is within the statute.

15. Persons within the district where the custom of tin bounding prevails are not in a less favorable condition in

(j) *Ib.* See Stedman v. Smith, 8 E. & B. 1.

(k) Cooper v. Hubbuck, 12 C. B. N. S. 456.

(l) *Supra,* pp. 356–357 ; Ennor v. Barwell, 2 Giff. 420.

(m) Gaved v. Martyn, 19 C. B. N. S. 732.

(n) Wright v. Howard, 1 Sim. & St. 190 ; Sampson v. Hoddinott, 1 C. B. N. S. 590. See Cooper v. Barber, 3 Taunt. 99.

(o) Wright v. Williams, 1 M. & W. 77 ; Briscoe v. Drought, 11 Ir. C. L.

250. See Arkwright v. Gell, 5 M. & W. 203.

(p) Carlyon v. Lovering, 1 H. & N. 798 ; Gaved v. Martyn, 19 C. B. N. S. 732.

(q) Att.-Gen. v. Luton Board of Health, 2 Jur. N. S. 181.

(r) Moore v. Webb, I C. B. N. S. 673 ; Murgatroyd v. Robinson, 7 E. & B. 391.

(s) Weeks v. Heward, 10 W. R. 557.

(t) Peter v. Daniel, 5 C. B. 568 ; Beeston v. Weate, 5 E. & B. 996.

(u) Beeston v. Weate, 5 E. & B. 996.

reference to acquiring rights of water by prescription than in other parts of the country (x). The easement passes to the owner of the soil when the bounding comes to an end (y).

16. The right to affect the quality, the quantity, or the flow of water in a manner not justified by natural right is an easement, and is therefore subject to the general law of easements. The right becomes extinguished upon unity of seisin and possession of both tenements in the same person (z). The right when acquired by grant must be measured by the terms of the grant: when derived from prescription or under the statute, it must be measured by the actual enjoyment, and can only be commensurate with it. A man who has acquired a right by actual enjoyment is entitled to all which he has enjoyed during the prescribed period both to the same extent and * 385 in the same specific * manner, but to nothing more (a).[1]

If he has acquired the right to divert water in certain proportions, he cannot increase the proportions (b). So also if the enjoyment has been only upon certain days in the week, the water cannot be used on other days (c). The fact that the inhabitants of a town may have acquired a prescriptive right to drain their houses into a stream does not give a public board acting on behalf of the community a right to discharge the sewage of the town into the stream, so as to cause riparian

---

(x) Gaved v. Martyn, 19 C. B. N. S. 732; Ivimey v. Stocker, 1 L. R. Ch. Ap. 396.

(y) Ivimey v. Stocker, ib.

(z) Ewart v. Cochrane, 4 Macq. 117; Baird v. Fortune, ib. 141; supra, pp. 357, 358.

(a) Bealey v. Shaw, 6 East, 208; Davies v. Williams, 16 Q. B. 546; Moore v. Webb, 1 C. B. N. S. 676; Murgatroyd v. Robinson, 7 E. & B. 391; Stockport Waterworks Co. v. Potter, 7 H. & N. 160; Goldsmid v. Tunbridge Wells Commissioners, 1 L. R. Ch. Ap. 349.

(b) Brown v. Best, 1 Wils. 174.

(c) Strutt v. Bovingdon, 5 Esp. 56.

[1] As to restraining by injunction a nuisance caused by corrupting running water, and also acquiring a right to so corrupt the water by twenty years

adverse user, see Holsman v. Boiling Spring Bleaching Co., 1 McCarter, 335. See, also, upon this general subject, Crosby v. Bessey, 49 Maine, 539; Corning v. Troy Iron, &c., Factory, 39 Barb. 311; Jones v. Crow, 32 Penn. St. 398; Merrifield v. Lambert, 13 Allen, 17; Brown v. Ilkins, 25 Conn. 589; Wheatley v. Chrisman, 24 Penn. St. 298; Carlisle v. Cooper, 6 C. E. Green, 576.

An acquiescence by the plaintiff and his grantors for six years in the defendants' maintaining a dam under a claim of right to flow plaintiff's land, during which the defendants made expensive erections of mills and machinery to be operated by the power so gained, it was held, furnished good reason for refusing an injunction. Bassett v. Company, 47 N. H. 426.

proprietors a greater amount of inconvenience than they were exposed to before (*d*).

17. But although the extent of a prescriptive right is limited by the actual enjoyment, the mode and manner in which the right is exercised need not be the same. A change in the mode and object of the use of the water is justifiable, provided the quantity taken be not sensibly increased or the quality sensibly affected, or the alteration be not such as to cast a greater burden upon the other riparian proprietors. All that the law requires is that the rights of others be not sensibly or materially affected (*e*). Persons who have a right to navigate a canal are not limited to any mode of traction or propulsion. They may use steam power, provided it occasions no more than ordinary injury to the canal (*f*).

18. If a man having a limited right in water exercises the right in excess, the person against whom it is exercised may obstruct the whole flow, if he cannot obstruct the part in excess without obstructing the whole. An action will not lie for the obstruction * until the right has been * 386 reduced within its proper limits (*g*).

19. The right to an easement in water may be lost by abandonment, where the circumstances of the case are such that an intention to abandon the right permanently can be reasonably presumed (*h*.) The right, however, is not lost by a temporary interruption from natural causes (*i*).

20. The right of the other riparian proprietors to the water of a stream or river is subject to any prescriptive rights which any of them may have gained by enjoyment (*k*). On the other hand, a riparian proprietor who has acquired a prescriptive right to change the natural flow of a stream cannot after-

---

(*d*) Att.-Gen. *v.* Luton Board of Health, 2 Jur. N. S. 180; Att.-Gen. *v.* Borough of Birmingham, 4 K. & J. 528; Cawkwell *v.* Russell, 26 L. J. Exch. 34; Goldsmid *v.* Tunbridge Wells Commissioners, 1 L. R. Ch. Ap. 349.

(*e*) Luttrel's case, 4 Co. R. 86 b; Saunders *v.* Newman, 1 B. & Ald. 258; Thomas *v.* Thomas, 2 Cr. M. & R. 34; Hall *v.* Swift, 4 Bing. N. C. 381; Blanchard *v.* Baker, 8 Greenl. (Amer.) 253.

(*f*) Case *v.* Midland Railway Co., 27 Beav. 247.

(*g*) Cawkwell *v.* Russell, 26 L. J. Exch. 34; comp. Tapling *v.* Jones, 11 H. L. 290; *supra*, p. 359.

(*h*) *Supra*, p. 358; Crossley *v.* Lightowler, 3 L. R. Eq. 292. See, also, Drewett *v.* Sheard, 7 C. & P. 465.

(*i*) Hall *v.* Swift, 4 Bing. N. C. 381. See Carr *v.* Foster, 3 Q. B. 581.

(*k*) Bealey *v.* Shaw, 6 East, 208; Cary *v.* Daniels, 8 Metc. (Amer.) 466.

wards restore the water to the stream so as to injure the other
riparian proprietors (*l*).

21. The rights and liabilities of parties in respect of artificial
streams and watercourses are entirely distinct from the rights
and liabilities of riparian proprietors in respect of natural
streams and watercourses. The water in an artificial stream
is the property of the party by whom it is created or caused to
flow. If the stream so created is made to flow upon the land
of a neighbor without his consent, it is a wrong for which the
party causing the flow is liable ; but he may by long enjoyment
gain a right to continue the discharge. His neighbor, however, cannot gain by long enjoyment a right to insist on the
continuance of the discharge. The discharge of water for
twenty years from a mine by a mine-owner in the course of
his mining operations, or by a land-owner from his drainage
works, will give no right to a neighbor below who has enjoyed
the benefit of the water, so as to preclude the mine-owner from
ceasing to pump out his mine after the ore shall have been
        exhausted, or from sending the water off in a differ-
* 387 ent direction, or the land-owner * from altering the
        course or level of his drains (*m*). As between inter-
mediate proprietors below the one by whom the artificial
watercourse is created or caused to flow, the upper one may at
first intercept the water, but after twenty years' use the lower
proprietor gains a right to the flow as against the upper
one (*n*).

22. The circumstances, however, under which an artificial
watercourse has been made, and the manner in which it has
been used, may be such as to give the proprietors of land
adjacent all the rights which they would have been entitled to
claim as riparian proprietors, had it been a natural stream (*o*).

(*l*) Belknap *v.* Trimble, 3 Paige Ch.
(Amer.) 577.

(*m*) Arkwright *v.* Gell, 5 M. & W.
203 ; Wood *v.* Waud, 3 Exch. 748 ;
Greatrex *v.* Hayward, 8 Exch. 291 ;
Sampson *v.* Hoddinott, 1 C. B. N. S.
590 ; Rawstron *v.* Taylor, 11 Exch.
369 ; Briscoe *v.* Drought, 11 Ir. C. L.
250 ; Wardle *v.* Brocklehurst, 1 El. &
El. 1058 ; Gaved *v.* Martyn, 19 C. B.
N. S. 732.

(*n*) Arkwright *v.* Gell, 5 M. & W.

203 ; Wood *v.* Waud, 3 Exch. 748 ;
Briscoe *v.* Drought, 11 Ir. C. L. 250.

(*o*) Magor *v.* Chadwick, 11 A. & E.
571 ; Wood *v.* Waud, 3 Exch. 748 ;
Briscoe *v.* Drought, 11 Ir. C. L. 250 ;
Sutcliffe *v.* Booth, 32 L. J. Q. B. 136 ;
Ivimey *v.* Stocker, 1 L. R. Ch. Ap.
396 ; Nuttall *v.* Bracewell, 2 L. R.
Exch. 1 ; Lord Blantyre *v.* Dunn, 10
Dec. of Ct. of Sess., 2d series, p. 509 ;
M'Kenzie *v.* Wodrop, 16 *ib.* p. 381.

If it appear that the stream was originally intended to have a permanent flow, or to be of a permanent character, or if the party by whom, or in whose behalf it was caused to flow can be shown to have abandoned permanently the works by which the flow was caused without intention to resume them, and to have given up all right to and control over the stream, such stream may become subject to the law of prescription, and the other laws relating to natural streams (*p*).   Nor does a natural stream cease to be so by reason only of its flowing for a part of its course over an artificial bed (*q*).

23. The rule that the purpose for which the waters of an artificial watercourse have been collected or caused to flow, is to be regarded in determining whether rights or interests can be acquired in them by other persons than those who collected * them or caused them to flow, applies with   * 388 still greater force to the waters of canals than to artificial watercourses of an ordinary character (*r*).   A canal company having a duty imposed on it by the legislature to keep open the canal, the legislature must be taken at least *primâ facie* to have intended that the powers and control over the waters of the canal should be vested in the company (*s*). A canal company which has enjoyed for a number of years the flow of the surplus waters of another canal lying on a higher level, has no right to insist on the continuance of the flow (*t*).   Nor can the water of a canal be abstracted by the adjacent proprietors, without the consent of the company (*u*).

24. The fouling of the water of an artificial watercourse is a species of injury which does not stand upon the same footing as the abstraction of it.   Neither the party who originates the watercourse, nor the upper proprietors, nor the intermediate owners, may pollute the stream, so as to cast a greater burden

(*p*) Gaved *v.* Martyn, 19 C. B. N. S. 732; Ivimey *v.* Stocker, 1 L. R. Ch. Ap. 396.

(*q*) Beeston *v.* Weate, 5 E. & B. 986; Briscoe *v.* Drought, 11 Ir. C. L. 250; Gaved *v.* Martyn, 19 C. B. N. S. 732.

(*r*) Staffordshire and Worcestershire Canal Co. *v.* Birmingham Canal Co., 1 L. R. Ap. Ca. 254.

(*s*) *Ib.*

(*t*) *Ib.*   See Att.-Gen. *v.* Corporation of Plymouth, 9 Beav. 67.

(*u*) Rochdale Canal Co. *v.* King, 14 Q. B. 122; Rochdale Canal Co. *v.* Radcliffe, 18 Q. B. 287; Medway Navigation Co. *v.* Earl of Romney, 9 C. B. N. S. 586.

on the proprietors below (*x*). The right, however, may be acquired by long use (*y*).

25. The principles which apply to water flowing in a defined channel do not apply to water of a temporary and casual character, which does not flow in a regular channel, but merely squanders itself over the surface of land (*z*). Water of this character may be drained away or appropriated before it reaches any defined channel of water (*a*).

26. As distinguished from water of a casual and tem-
* 389 porary character, * a watercourse is a flow of water usually flowing in a certain direction, and by a regular channel, having a bed, banks, and sides, and possessing that unity of character by which the flow on one man's land can be identified with that on the land of his neighbor (*b*). It is not requisite that the stream should flow continuously; it may be dry at times, but it must have a well-defined and substantial existence (*c*). Water, though it may squander itself in flood-time over the surface, may nevertheless flow in a defined channel (*d*).

27. The same principles which apply to water of a casual and temporary character, which squanders itself over the surface, are equally, if not more strongly, applicable to subterraneous water of the same casual and undefined description, which does not flow in a defined channel, but merely percolates through the soil. A man may by operations on his own soil, or in the execution of works which he is authorized to make, intercept, drain away, and appropriate as much of such water as he pleases, notwithstanding the effect may be not only to prevent it reaching his neighbor's land, but even to cause the

---

(*x*) Magor *v.* Chadwick, 11 A. & E. 571; Wood *v.* Waud, 3 Exch. 748. See Manchester and Lincolnshire Railway Co. *v.* Worksop Board of Health, 23 Beav. 199; Whaley *v.* Laing, 3 H. & N. 675.

(*y*) Magor *v.* Chadwick, 11 A. & E. 571; Wood *v.* Waud, 3 Exch. 748.

(*z*) Broadbent *v.* Ramsbotham, 11 Exch. 602; Chasemore *v.* Richards, 7 H. L. 349.

(*a*) *Ib.*; Rawstron *v.* Taylor, 11 Exch. 375; Briscoe *v.* Drought, 11 Ir. C. L. 250. See Manchester, Shef-

field, and Lincolnshire Railway Co. *v.* Worksop Board of Health, 23 Beav. 198.

(*b*) Briscoe *v.* Drought, 11 Ir. C. L. 271, *per* Christian, J.   See Lord Blantyre *v.* Dunn, 10 Dec. of Ct. of Sess., 2d series, p. 509; Rex *v.* Inhabitants of Oxfordshire, 1 B. & A. 301.

(*c*) Luther *v.* Winnisimmet Co., 9 Cush. (Amer.) 171; Ashley *v.* Wolcott, 11 *ib.* 192.

(*d*) Briscoe *v.* Drought, 11 Ir. C. L. 250.

water already collected there in wells and ponds to percolate away, so as to leave his neighbor's land dry (*e*). The case is different where polluted water penetrates into the earth on one man's land, and percolates through to the wells and springs of his neighbor (*f*). In an American case, Brown *v.* Ilius (*g*), the court inclined to the opinion that if in the prosecution of a business, like that of the manufacture of gas, not a nuisance *per se*, a man uses materials upon his own land which penetrate into the earth, and corrupt underground sources of supply by percolating to a well * upon   * 390 his neighbor's land, he would not be liable for the damage done thereby. But the case cannot be considered sound law (*h*). In Hodgkinson *v.* Ennor (*i*), Blackburn, J., said there does not appear to be any distinction between the pollution of water in a state of percolation, and the pollution of water in a stream.

28. When land is so located that rain water naturally descends from the estate of the superior proprietor to the inferior estate, the owner of the latter cannot do any thing to prevent the course of such water. If he build a wall at the upper part of his estate so as to prevent the water from descending on it, whereby the land above is damaged, there is an actionable injury. The owner of land lying on a lower level is subject to the burden of receiving water which drains naturally from land on a higher level. The upper proprietor may drain his land, and the inferior proprietor must receive the water so drained; but the upper proprietor may not, by adopting a particular system of drainage, or by introducing alterations in the mode of drainage, cause the drainage water to flow on his neighbor's land in an injurious manner, or obstruct the drainage of other lands by overloading the ancient drains

(*e*) Acton *v.* Blundell, 12 M. & W. 324; Galgay *v.* Great Southern and Western Railway, 4 Ir. C. L. 456; Stainton *v.* Woolrych, 23 Beav. 225; Chasemore *v.* Richards, 7 H. L. 349; New River Co. *v.* Johnson, 2 El. & El. 435; Queen *v.* Metropolitan Board of Works, 3 B. & S. 710.

(*f*) See Turner *v.* Mirfield, 34 Beav. 390.

(*g*) 25 Conn. 583.

(*h*) See Tenant *v.* Goldwin, 2 Lord Raym. 1089, Salk. 21, 360; Turner *v.* Mirfield, 34 Beav. 390.

(*i*) 4 B. & S. 240.

with water (*k*).   The right may, however, be acquired by long use (*l*).

29. A mine-owner has a right to work his mines in the manner most convenient and beneficial to himself for the purpose of getting out any quantity of minerals from any part of the mine, and is not responsible for any damage occasioned by water which flows by gravitation or natural causes into an adjoining mine, provided the mines have been worked with due skill in the usual and ordinary manner (*m*).   But
* 391 he may not pump * water out of his mines into the adjoining mines, so as to increase the flow into them, or do any thing whereby water should be drained into the adjoining mines, which would not otherwise have arrived there by natural causes (*n*).   The owner of the lower mine must, if he wishes to guard against the natural flow of water from the mines of his neighbor, have a barrier in the upper part of his mine to pen back the water (*o*).   If the owner of the higher mine trespasses upon this barrier he is liable for the consequential damage, as well as for the value of the coal; but he is not bound to fill up the excavation which he has made (*p*). But in Lord Mexborough *v.* Bower (*q*), the tenant of a colliery was restrained from allowing a communication which he had opened with an adjoining mine in breach of covenant to remain open.

30. Proprietors on the banks of a river are entitled to protect their property from an invasion of water by building a bulwark, but they are not at liberty to conduct their operations so as to do any actual injury to the property on the opposite side of the river (*r*).   One riparian proprietor may not dam or pen

(*k*) Dawson *v.* Paver, 5 Ha. 415; Smith *v.* Kenrick, 7 C. B. 515; Dickinson *v.* City of Worcester, 7 Allen (Amer.), 19.   See Earl of Ripon *v.* Hobart, 3 M. & K. 169; Montgomerie *v.* Buchanan's Trustees, 15 Dec. of Ct. of Sess., 2d series, p. 853.

(*l*) Dickinson *v.* City of Worcester, 7 Allen (Amer.), 19.

(*m*) Walker *v.* Fletcher, 3 Bligh, 172; Smith *v.* Kenrick, 7 C. B. 564; Baird *v.* Williamson, 15 C. B. N. S. 376. See Duke of Beaufort *v.* Morris, 6 Ha. 341, 2 Ph. 683; Fletcher *v.* Rylands, 1 L. R.

Exch. 265; Baird *v.* Monkland Iron and Steel Co., 24 Dec. of Ct. of Sess., 2d series, p. 1418.

(*n*) Baird *v.* Williamson, 15 C. B. N. S. 376.

(*o*) Ib.; Baird *v.* Monkland Iron and Steel Co., 24 Dec. of Ct. of Sess., 2d series, p. 1418.

(*p*) Clegg *v.* Dearden, 12 Q. B. 576; Powell *v.* Aiken, 4 K. & J. 343.

(*q*) 7 Beav. 127.

(*r*) Bickett *v.* Morris, 1 L. R, Sc. Ap. 47.

up water so as to flood or otherwise injuriously affect the lands
of others (*s*), or by making embankments, or otherwise alter
the ancient course of flood water, so as to throw it in greater
quantity upon the land of his neighbor (*t*).

31. Rights to water may be created or modified by deed. If
there is a deed of grant, the nature and extent of the interest
and the rights and liabilities of the parties thereto are regulated wholly thereby, whether the water be a natural
stream (*u*), or * an artificial watercourse (*x*), or water * 392
of a casual and temporary character (*y*). The owner of
land cannot, however, create right in water unconnected with
the ordinary use and enjoyment of land, so as to constitute
property in the hands of the grantee. As between himself
and his grantee the grant is good, but as against third parties
it will not be enforced (*z*). A mere licensee of water, for
instance, cannot maintain an action against a third party by
whom the water has been polluted (*a*).

32. An easement in water being an easement of a continuous
nature, the right passes by implication of law and without any
general words of conveyance upon the grant of the land, house,
or mill to which the easement is annexed (*b*). Where, accordingly, the owner of two mills upon the same stream demised
the upper mill, he was held to have granted all such conveniences and rights over the lower mill as were necessary for
the reasonable enjoyment of the upper mill in the state in
which it was at the time of the demise (*c*). So, also, where a
man being the owner of a house or building, and of land surrounding it, through which a conduit or drain from the house
passed, sold the house or building, retaining the land, the

(*s*) Robinson *v.* Lord Byron, 1 Bro.
C. C. 588; Williams *v.* Morland, 2 B.
& C. 910; Ware *v.* Regent's Canal Co.,
3 D. & J. 212.

(*t*) Trafford *v.* Rex, 8 Bing. 204;
Menzies *v.* Lord Breadalbane, 3 Bligh,
N. S. 414; Wicks *v.* Hunt, John. 372;
Lawrence *v.* Great Northern Railway
Co., 16 Q. B. 643.

(*u*) Northam *v.* Hurley, 1 E. & B.
665; Whitehead *v.* Parks, 2 H. & N.
870; Sharp *v.* Waterhouse, 7 E. & B.
816; Walker *v.* Stewart, 2 Macq. 424.

(*x*) Lee *v.* Stevenson, El. Bl. & El.

512; Wardle *v.* Brocklehurst, 1 El. &
El. 1058. See Att.-Gen. *v.* Corporation
of Plymouth, 9 Beav. 67; Gaved *v.*
Martyn, 19 C. B. N. S. 732.

(*y*) Rawstron *v.* Taylor, 11 Exch.
369.

(*z*) Laing *v.* Whaley, 3 H. & N.
675, 901; Hill *v.* Tupper, 2 H. & C.
121; Stockport Waterworks Co. *v.*
Potter, 3 H. & C. 300.

(*a*) Laing *v.* Whaley, 3 H. & N. 675.

(*b*) See *supra*, 355.

(*c*) Hall *v.* Lund, 1 H. & C. 676.

right to use the drain or conduit was held to pass as a privilege annexed to the house or building, and necessary to its beneficial use (d).

33. There has been much difference of opinion as to whether the owner of two tenements who grants one of them, retaining the other, can be held by implication of law to have reserved to himself, in favor of the part retained, the benefit of an artificial watercourse which had, before severance, been enjoyed by the part retained over the part granted (e). In Pyer v. Carter (f), it was held that, if the owner of two tene-
* 393 ments * grants away one absolutely to a purchaser without any reservation, and then conveys the remaining one to another person, the grantee of the second tenement is entitled to the right of drain over the first tenement as it was used and enjoyed at the time of the grant to the first purchaser. But this decision has been expressly disapproved of by Lord Westbury in Suffield v. Brown (g), and the better opinion would appear to be that no such implication should be made except in the case of easements of necessity (h).

34. Injunctions will be granted by courts of equity to protect the legal right to the proper flow of water in a natural stream (i). In Ferrand v. Corporation of Bradford (j), a waterworks company acting under the Waterworks Clauses Act, 1847, was restrained from diverting a stream without paying compensation for the same or making a deposit and bond as required by the Lands Clauses Act, 8 Vict. c. 18, s. 85. Though merely nominal damages may have been recovered at law for the diversion of water, the court will interfere and vindicate the right by perpetual injunction, if the act complained of would cause irreparable mischief or permanent injury, or would destroy a right (k.)

(d) Nicholas v. Chamberlain, Cro. Jac. 121; Ewart v. Cochrane, 4 Macq. 117.
(e) See supra, p. 364.
(f) 1 H. & N. 916.
(g) 33 L. J. Ch. 249.
(h) Supra, p. 365.
(i) Cary, 36; Finch v. Resbridger, 2 Vern. 390; Bush v. Western, Prec. Ch. 530; Weller v. Smeaton, 1 Bro. C. C. 572; Robinson v. Lord Byron, 1 Bro.

C. C. 588; Dewhirst v. Wrigley, 1 C. P. C. 329; Lond v. Murray, 17 L. T. 248; William v. Heath, 1 L. T. N. S. 267; Tipping v. Eckersley, 2 K. & J. 264; Elwell v. Crowther, 31 Beav. 163. See Queen v. Darlington Board of Health, 5 B. & S. 515.
(j) 21 Beav. 412.
(k) Rochdale Canal Co. v. King, 2 Sim. N. S. 79, 16 Beav. 630.

35. Where substantial damage is shown, the court will restrain the fouling and pollution of water (*l*). If there is a house upon the property drawing its supply from the stream, the fouling of the stream so as to render the water unfit for domestic or culinary purposes is substantial damage (*m*). So, also, is the pollution of water to such an extent as to render it unfit for cattle * to drink (*n*), or for fish to live * 394 in (*o*), or for the purposes of manufacture (*p*). So also is the discharge of sewage matter into a stream so as to cause mud banks to be formed (*q*). So also may be the discharge of heated water into a stream (*r*). If the purity of a stream as claimed be in itself excessive, the court will not interfere unless a prescriptive right be shown. Thus an injunction was refused in the absence of a prescriptive right being shown to restrain a surveyor of roads from making a drain from a gravel-pit to a spring of water, which plaintiff had been in the habit of using for the purpose of supplying water to his beds of watercresses (*s*).

36. An injunction to restrain the fouling will, if required by the circumstances of the case, be in the mandatory form (*t*). In Spokes *v.* Banbury Board of Health (*u*), a local board of health was restrained from causing or permitting sewage matter or water polluted therewith to pass through drains or channels under their control into a river.

37. Other cases of nuisance to water which have been brought before the court are obstructions or damage to canals (*x*). A canal company, authorized but not ordered by

---

(*l*) Elmhirst *v.* Spencer, 2 Mac. & G. 45; Lingwood *v.* Stowmarket Co., 1 L. R. Eq. 77, 336. See, as to the form of the order for an injunction, Lingwood *v.* Stowmarket Co., 1 L. R. Eq. 77, 336.

(*m*) *Ib.*; Goldsmid *v.* Tunbridge Wells Commissioners, 1 L. R. Ch. Ap. 349.

(*n*) *Ib.*; Oldaker *v.* Hunt, 6 D. M. & G. 376; Att.-Gen. *v.* Luton Board of Health, 2 Jur. N. S. 181; Manchester, Sheffield, and Lincolnshire Railway Co. *v.* Worksop Board of Health, 23 Beav. 198; Att.-Gen. *v.* Borough of Birmingham, 4 K. & J. 528.

(*o*) Aldred's case, 9 Co. R. 59 a; Oldaker *v.* Hunt, 6 D. M. & G. 376;

Att.-Gen. *v.* Luton Board of Health, 2 Jur. N. S. 180; Att.-Gen. *v.* Borough of Birmingham, 4 K. & J. 528; Bidder *v.* Croydon Board of Health, 6 L. T. N. S. 778.

(*p*) Wood *v.* Sutcliffe, 2 Sim. N. S. 163; Tipping *v.* Eckersley, 2 K. & J. 264; Lingwood *v.* Stowmarket Co., 1 L. R. Eq. 77.

(*q*) Att.-Gen. *v.* Luton Board of Health, 2 Jur. N. S. 180.

(*r*) Tipping *v.* Eckersley, 2 K. & J. 264. See Mason *v.* Hill, 5 B. & Ad. 1.

(*s*) Weeks *v.* Heward, 10 W. R. 557.

(*t*) See *supra*, pp. 230–232, as to mandatory injunctions.

(*u*) 1 L. R. Eq. 42.

(*x*) Blakemore *v.* Glamorganshire

act of Parliament to supply their canal with water from a
 stream which was pure at the date of the act, cannot,
* 395 after the stream has been * made foul and polluted,
 though by the acts of others, go on supplying their
canal from its water, if they cause thereby a public nuisance (*y*).
It is no answer to an injunction to say that the company did
not pollute the water, they having the power to draw or not
to draw the water into their canal as they please ; or that by
restraining the canal company a worse nuisance would be
created ; or that the company may be obliged to close their
canal and expose themselves to an indictment on that
ground (*z*).

38. The court has also jurisdiction, on the ground of irreparable damage, to restrain a man through whose land an ancient
weir was constructed which turned the waters of a mill-stream
into a mill-race from preventing the mill-owner, who had a
prescriptive right to the mill-stream, from entering upon his
land for the purpose of repairing the weir (*a*).

SECTION V. — PURPRESTURES. — NUISANCE TO NAVIGABLE
TIDAL WATERS.

1. Purpresture defined; when restrained.
2. Fouling navigable tidal rivers, principles applicable to cases of.
3. Nuisance to a fishery restrained.
4. Right of Crown in navigable rivers, twofold: that of property and of conservation.
5. Powers and duties of commissioners of sewers.

1. An invasion of or encroachment on the soil of the sea-
shore or bed of an estuary or navigable tidal river, between
high and low water mark, while the same remains in the Crown,

---

Canal Co., 1 M. & K. 154 ; London and
Birmingham Railway Co. v. Grand
Junction Canal Co., 1 Ra. Ca. 224 ;
Priestley v. Manchester and Leeds
Railway Co., 2 Ra. Ca. 134, 4 Y. & C.
72 ; Manser v. Northern and Eastern
Counties Railway Co., 2 Ra. Ca. 381 ;
Case v. Midland Railway Co., 27 Beav.
247.
 (*y*) Att.-Gen. v. Proprietors of Brad-
ford Canal, 2 L. R. Eq. 71.

(*z*) *Ib.*
(*a*) M'Swiney v. Haines, 1 Ir. Eq.
323. See Peter v. Daniel, 5 C. B. 568 ;
Beeston v. Weate, 5 E. & B. 986 ;
Roberts v. Rose, 3 H. & C. 162. See
further, as to damage to a mill-race,
Coates v. Clarence Railway Co., 1 R. &
M. 182 ; Manser v. Northern and Eastern Counties Railway Co., 2 Ra. Ca.
380.

is a purpresture (*b*). There is a wide difference between a purpresture and a nuisance. Although they may both co-exist, either may exist without the other. If the act complained of be a purpresture, it may be restrained at the suit of the Attorney-General, whether it be a nuisance or not. Being an encroachment on the soil of the sovereign, like trespass on the soil of an individual, it will support an action irrespective of any damage which may accrue. But to constitute a public nuisance, damage to the public right of navigation or other public right must be shown to exist. If * the act   * 396 complained of be a mere purpresture without being at the same time a nuisance, the court will usually direct an inquiry to be made whether it is more beneficial to the Crown to abate the purpresture or to suffer the erection to remain and be arrested. But if the purpresture be also a public nuisance, this cannot be done, for the Crown cannot sanction a public nuisance (*c*).[1] It has no right to use its title to the soil so as to occasion a nuisance to its subjects, nor can it give any one a right to do so. Buildings or other erections which interfere with the public right of navigation over the water are nuisances at common law, whether made by the Crown or by a subject (*d*). The erection of a pier or embankment is not necessarily a nuisance. The true question in each case is, whether or not a damage accrues to the navigation in the particular locality. If an erection be a hindrance to the navigation, it is no defence that the public inconvenience is counterbalanced by the benefit to be afforded by it (*e*).

(*b*) See Att.-Gen. v. Chamberlaine, 4 K. & J. 292.

(*c*) Att.-Gen. v. Richards, 2 Anst. 603; Bristol Harbor case, cit. 18 Ves. 214; Att.-Gen. v. Burridge, 10 Price, 350; Att.-Gen. v. Parmeter, *ib.* 378; Parmeter v. Att.-Gen., *ib.* 412; Att.-Gen. v. Johnson, 2 Wills, Ch. 87.

(*d*) *Ib.*; Gann v. Free Fishers of Whitstable, 11 H. L. 192.

(*e*) Rex v. Ward, 4 A. & E. 386; Reg. v. Betts, 16 Q. B. 1023.

[1] People v. Vanderbilt, 26 N. Y. 287; same, 28 N. Y. 396.

In Mississippi and Missouri Railroad Co. v. Ward, 2 Black, 485, it is held that where a bridge over a navigable stream is erected for public purposes, and produces a public benefit, and leaves a reasonable space for the passage of vessels, it is not indictable, and that it must appear beyond a reasonable doubt to be a nuisance before it can be so decreed. In this case it was also held that the nuisance complained of, being a bridge across the Mississippi where that river divides the states of Illinois and Iowa, and the state line being in the middle of the river, the district court of the United States for Iowa had no power to abate the nuisance if it be a nuisance on the Illinois side. See the opinion of Nelson, J., dissenting; Wayne and Clifford, JJ., concurring with him.

2. The same principles apply with respect to nuisances arising from the discharge into navigable tidal rivers of matters
injurious to health, as are applicable in the case of ordinary
rivers (ƒ). The right of drainage into the sea and navigable
tidal rivers conferred by the Towns' Improvement Clauses
Act, 1847, is subject to the condition that no nuisance be
created (g).

3. In a case where a man had, by erecting an embankment
and enclosing the bed of a river, shut out and prevented the
tide from reaching a mussel-bed and breeding-ground, the
court granted an injunction on the principle of irreparable
damage, without deciding or entering upon the question as
to the ownership of the soil (h).

* 397   4. * The right of the Crown in navigable rivers is twofold: the right of property and the right of conservation.
These rights are perfectly distinct, and may both be transferred
and separated. The grant of the right of conservation does
not carry with it the soil or bed of the river. The right of
conservation, when retained by the Crown, is exercised by the
admiralty. No quay or encroachment can be made upon the
soil or bed of a navigable river below high-water mark, without
the license of the admiralty or other person in whom the
conservation is vested, and the Act 46 Geo. 3, c. 153, requires
that notice shall be given to the admiralty before any quay, &c.,
is erected on a tidal river, although the conservatorship shall
have been transferred. The Metropolitan Board of Works has
no power under their Acts, 18 & 19 Vict. c. 120, and 21 & 22
Vict. c. 104, to erect any works on the soil or bed of the river
Thames, without first obtaining the consent of the admiralty
and the conservators of the river (i).

5. The commissioners of sewers have long been invested with

(ƒ) Att.-Gen. v. Mayor, &c., of
Kingston-upon-Thames, 34 L. J. Ch.
481.

(g) Ib.

(h) Bridges v. Highton, 11 L. T. N.
S. 653. See, also, Allen v. Donnelly,
5 Ir. Ch. 229; Ashworth v. Browne, 10
Ir. Ch. 421.

(i) Brownlow v. Metropolitan Board
of Works, 13 C. B. N. S. 768, 16 C. B.
N. S. 546. See, as to the powers of the

Conservators of the Thames, the
Thames' Conservancy Act, 1861, 20 &
21 Vict. c. 147 (Local Act); Kearns v.
Cordwainers' Co., 6 C. B. N. S. 388;
Macey v. Metropolitan Board of Works,
33 L. J. Ch. 377; Att.-Gen. v. Conservators of Thames, 1 H. & M. 1. See,
also, as to Thames Embankment Act,
1862, Temple Pier Co. v. Metropolitan
Board of Works, 34 L. J. Ch. 262.

the power of determining where, and to what extent, public
convenience will justify an obstruction to any arm or inlet of
the sea or navigable river, and of otherwise controlling and
regulating them as the exigencies of the public will require (*k*).
Acting *bonâ fide* for the benefit of the levels, the commissioners
of sewers may erect defences against the inroads of the sea,
although they may cause the sea to flow with greater violence
against the adjoining land (*l*).

---

* SECTION VI. — VARIOUS NUISANCES.   * 398

1. Various nuisances which have been brought before the court.
2 & 3. Nuisances to churchyards cognizable by ecclesiastical courts.

1. Other cases of nuisance which have been brought before
the court are nuisances to a ferry (*m*) ; a highway (*n*) ; a
private right of way (*o*) [1] ; access to the sea shore or a navigable

(*k*) Callis on Sewers, 25.
(*l*) Rex *v.* Commissioners of Sewers,
&c., for Pagham, 5 B. & C. 355.
(*m*) Churchman *v.* Tunstall, Hard.
162, cited 2 Anst. 608 ; Cory *v.* Yarmouth and Norwich Railway Co., 3
Ha. 593 ; Letton *v.* Goodden, 2 L. R.
Eq. 123. See Huzzey *v.* Field, 2 Cr.
M. & R. 432 ; Peter *v* Kendall, 6 B. &
C. 703 ; Blacketer *v.* Gillett, 9 C. B.
26 ; North and South Shields Ferry
Co. *v.* Barker, 2 Exch. 136 ; Newton *v.*
Cubitt, 5 C. B. N. S. 627, 12 C. B. N.
S. 58, 13 C. B. N. S. 864 ; Leamy *v.*
Waterford and Limerick Railway
Co., 7 Ir. C. L. 27 ; Hemphill *v.*
M'Kenna, 3 Dr. & War. 183. See,
also, Campbell's Trustees *v.* Campbell,
6 Pat. Sc. Ap. 417.
(*n*) Squire *v.* Campbell, 1 M. & C.
459 ; Att.-Gen. *v.* Forbes, 2 M. & C.
123 ; Att.-Gen. *v.* Manchester and
Leeds Railway Co., 1 Ra. Ca. 436 ;
Spencer *v.* London and Birmingham
Railway Co., 8 Sim. 193, 1 Ra. Ca.
159 ; Semple *v.* London and Brighton
Railway Co., 9 Sim. 209, 1 Ra. Ca.
480 ; Thorne *v.* Taw Vale Railway and
Dock Co., 13 Beav. 10 ; Cunliffe *v.*
Whalley, *ib.* 411 ; Att.-Gen. *v.* Sheffield
Gas Co., 3 D. M. & G. 304 ; Dover Gas
Co. *v.* Mayor of Dover, 7 D. M. & G.

545 ; Att.-Gen. *v.* Conservators of
Thames, 1 H. & M. 32 ; Vestry of Bermondsey *v.* Brown, 1 L. R. Eq. 204 ;
supra, pp. 320, 321. See Reg. *v.* Train,
2 B. & S. 640. See, as to arches over
highways, Allen *v.* Provost of Rutherglen, 4 Pat. Sc. Ap. 270 ; Vestry of
Bermondsey *v.* Brown, 1 L. R. Eq.
204 ; Atkins *v.* Burdman, 2 Metc.
(Amer.) 457.
(*o*) Hadfield *v.* Manchester and South
Junction, &c., Railway Co., 12 Jur.
1083 ; Dorman *v.* Dorman, 3 Ir. Eq.
385.
[1] A bill alleging a prescriptive right
of way over the defendant's land to a
public road and market, and that the
complainant has no other outlet whereby to convey his produce to Baltimore
for sale, except by a circuitous and inconvenient route over the lands, and
by permission of persons who might,
at any time, withhold such permission,
makes out a case sufficient to warrant
an injunction restraining the defendant from further obstructing such
way. Shipley *v.* Caples, 17 Md. 179.
But the complainant's right should be
clear and undoubted, otherwise the
decree should be withheld until the
right is established at law. King *v.*
McCully, 38 Penn. St. 76.

river (*p*) ; a private siding to a railway (*q*) ; the entrance to a vault (*r*) ; a market (*s*) ; a right of stallage (*t*) ; ground dedicated to public recreation (*u*) ; the construction of a railway (*v*) ; and damage to crops (*x*).

2. A nuisance to a churchyard comes properly within the cognizance of the ecclesiastical courts (*y*).

* 399   3. * In Woodman *v.* Robinson (*z*), a bill was filed by a single parishioner against some of the churchwardens of a parish to restrain them from warming the church in a manner which he alleged to be injurious to health. Lord Cranworth considered it doubtful whether it was a public nuisance, and whether such a bill could be sustained by a single parishioner ; but it was not necessary to decide the point (*a*).

(*p*) Att.-Gen. *v.* Conservators of Thames, 1 H. & M. 1 ; Macey *v.* Metropolitan Board of Works, 33 L. J. Ch. 377 ; Att.-Gen. *v.* Boyle, 10 Jur. N. S. 309.

(*q*) Bell *v.* Midland Railway Co., 3 D. & J. 673, 10 C. B. N. S. 287.

(*r*) Daniel *v.* Anderson, 31 L. J. Ch. 610.

(*s*) Anon., 2 Ves. 414.

(*t*) Ellis *v.* Corporation of Bridgnorth, 2 J. & H. 67.

(*u*) Att.-Gen. *v.* Mayor of Southampton, 1 Giff. 363.

(*v*) Great North of England Railway Co. *v.* Clarence Railway Co., 1 Coll. 507 ; London and Birmingham Railway Co. *v.* Grand Junction Canal Co., 1 Ra. Ca. 224.

(*x*) Broadbent *v.* Imperial Gas Co., 7 D. M. & G. 436, 7 H. L. 600 ; Tipping *v.* St. Helen's Smelting Co., 1 L. R. Ch. Ap. 66 ; *supra*, pp. 360, 361.

(*y*) Large *v.* Alton, Cro. Jac. 462 ; Wenmouth *v.* Collins, 2 Lord Raym. 850 ; Quilter *v.* Newtown, Carth. 151 ; Wilson *v.* M'Math, 2 B. & Ald. 241, 3 Phill. 89 ; Buxton *v.* Calcote, Cade *v.* Newenham, 3 Phill. 91 ; Earl Fitzwilliam *v.* Moore, 3 Ir. Eq. 615.

(*z*) 2 Sim. N. S. 204.

(*a*) See as to acts in nature of waste in the churchyard, *supra*, pp. 262, 265–267

* CHAPTER XIX.   * 400

INJUNCTIONS TO RESTRAIN THE INFRINGEMENT OF PATENTS.

SECTION I.—PRINCIPLES ON WHICH THE COURT RESTRAINS THE INFRINGEMENT OF PATENTS.

1. Principles upon which court proceeds in restraining infringement of patent rights by interlocutory injunction.
2. When the court will interfere by injunction before trial at law.
3. In cases of recent patents.
4. No injunction when two parties have obtained patents for same invention.
5. Verdict at law not conclusive against person not party to the suit.
6. *Primâ facie* case of infringement as well as *primâ facie* title must be made out.
7. Practice when fact of infringement or validity of title is denied.
8. What the bill must allege.
9. Who must be made parties.
10. Affidavits to be made by plaintiff.
11. By defendant in opposition to injunction.
12. The defendant must answer fully the interrogatories which the plaintiff is entitled to make.
13. Effect of delay and acquiescence.
14. Admissions to be made at trial.

1. THE jurisdiction of courts of equity in restraining by interlocutory injunction the infringement of patent rights, is in aid of the legal right. The court proceeds on the assumption that the person who makes the application has the legal right which he asserts, but needs the aid of the court for the purpose of protecting his property from damage pending the trial of the legal right (a). The only remedy which a court of law could, till recently, give a patentee for the infringement of his patent rights, was the remedy by damages; but courts of law in which actions may be brought for the infringement of patents have been empowered by the 15 & 16 Vict. c. 83, to order an inspection, injunction, and account

(a) Bacon v. Jones, 4 M. & C. 436.

in patent cases. This enlargement of their jurisdiction has enabled courts of law of their own authority to do complete and final justice between the parties (*b*); but the original jurisdiction of courts of equity has not been in any way affected by the act.

2. It seems to have been formerly the opinion that a court of equity would not interfere by injunction to protect a patent right, until the right had been established at law (*c*);[1] but

(*b*) Holland *v.* Fox, 3 E. & B. 983; Vidi *v.* Smith, *ib.* 969.

(*c*) Millar *v.* Taylor, 4 Burr. 2303. See, also, 2 C. P. C. 61 n.

[1] The plaintiff will not be compelled to establish his right at law before injunction when a patent has been granted, and there has been an exclusive possession of some duration under it. "It is not possible to fix any precise term of years during which the exclusive possession must have continued. The reason of the presumption in favor of the validity of the grant is the acquiescence of the public in the exclusive right of the patentee, which it may reasonably be assumed would not exist unless the right was well founded. And it is obvious that this public acquiescence is entitled to more or less weight, according to the degree of the utility of the machine and the number of persons whose trade or business is affected by it." Curtis, J., Foster *v.* Moore, 1 Curtis, C. C. R. 286. And acquiescence in the claim of the patentee during the two years which he is permitted to sell his patented article before the date of the patent, is entitled to weight in considering his right to a temporary injunction. To make a *primâ facie* title without a judgment at law, the patentee must have had such an exclusive possession as, with his claim and the acquiescence of the public, lays a reasonable foundation for the presumption of the validity of his patent. An unsuccessful attempt to interrupt a possession, strengthens the presumption which arises from it. Sargent *v.* Seagrave, 2 Curt. 553; Orr *v.* Littlefield, 1 Wood. & M. 13; Grover and Baker Sewing Machine Co. *v.* Williams, 3 Fisher's Pat. Cases, 133; Sprague J., Motte *v.* Bennett, 2 Fisher's Pat. Cases, 642. The practice in the courts of the United States in respect to granting injunctions in patent cases, has always been that of the English Chancery.

Wayne, J., *ib.*; see also Nevins *v.* Johnson, 3 Blatch. 81. In the courts of the United States, in cases of waste and trespass, if the title of the complainant is denied, he must show that there are no facts to warrant the denial, or the injunction will be refused till the disputed questions of title are settled at law. Perry *v.* Parker, 1 Wood. & M. 280. Where, on a motion for a provisional injunction to restrain the infringement of letters-patent for a floating grain dryer and elevator, the patent was not attacked for want of novelty, and the infringement was clear, but the patent had never been tried or established at law or in equity, and no evidence was furnished as to its use, or as to the extent of its use, or as to acquiescence in the patent by the public, and the defendant showed that he had used his apparatus for about three years, and that no claim had been made against it under the patent until about six weeks previously, and the amount invested in the defendant's apparatus and business was large, and the business seemed to be precarious, and nothing appeared as to the defendant's responsibility, an injunction was withheld until the plaintiff should establish satisfactorily the point of acquiescence by the public, and show how the defendant's apparatus had been allowed to be used without interference; and leave was given to the plaintiff to renew his motion, on further papers, but the defendant was required to render sworn periodical accounts of the grain which should in future be treated by his apparatus, and to give satisfactory security by bond, with sureties to pay what might be recovered in the suit. Sykes *v.* Manhattan Elevator and Grain Drying Company, 6 Blatch. 496. But where the validity of a patent is fully established and its infringement is clear, the patentee has a right to protection by injunction, although great

this doctrine was denied by Lord Eldon in the case of the Universities of Oxford and Cambridge v. Richardson (d), and since that time the jurisdiction of the court to interfere in all cases where there is a clear color of title and assertion of right has not been disputed (e). The mere possession of a patent is not * of itself such color of title as will justify * 401 the court in protecting it by injunction; but if the possession is supported by a quiet and exclusive enjoyment of some duration (f), or if the title has been successfully as-

injury may thereby be caused to the infringer. Hodge v. Hudson River Railway Co., 6 Blatchf. 165. "A mere denial by an answer of the equity of the bill does not prevent the court from looking into the law and the facts of the case, when a special injunction is moved for, and granting or refusing it according to its discretion. And where the title to an injunction does not depend upon any controverted or doubtful facts, but upon the interpretation to be put by the court upon a written instrument, I consider it my duty to interpret it on such a motion, and grant or refuse the injunction according to the result of that interpretation. There may be cases in which there is so much doubt what the parties to an instrument intended to affect by it, that the court may think it proper to suspend its judgment until the surrounding circumstances can be more fully [and safely examined on a final hearing. It is possible, also, that where there are grave doubts concerning the legal effect of an instrument, the court might decline to interfere by special injunction, even though, if compelled to decide, their decision must be in favor of the complainant. Probably the circumstances of the case, and the degree of mischief which would be suffered by refusing the injunction, compared with the inconvenience and loss occasioned by granting it, would control the action of the court in the case supposed. But, in general, I apprehend that, if the title to a temporary injunction depends on the construction to a deed, the court will construe it and act accordingly, whatever view of that question the answer may have presented." Curtis, J., Clum v. Brewer, 2 Curtis, C. C. R. 506; Hodge v. Hudson River Railway Co., 6 Blatchf. 165. In the last case it also appeared that the defendant was willing to pay a reasonable sum for the use of the pat-

ented invention, and that the plaintiff had a fixed license fee for its use, and exercised the franchise solely by licensing, for fees, the use of the invention; and the court held, that the defendant ought to be enjoined only in case he should elect to be enjoined in preference to paying a reasonable license fee for the use of the invention to such extent as he might desire to use it during the unexpired term of the patent, such fee to be no greater than the regular fee, if any, established in such cases, and to be ascertained, as of the time of filing the bill, by a reference to a master on testimony to be produced before him. Also Smith v. Sharp's Rifle Manuf. Co., 3 Blatchf. 545; U. S. Annunciator Co. v. Sanderson, ib. 184. But see Howe v. Newton, 2 Fisher's Pat. Cas. 534; contra as to the practice in Mass. Dist. In such cases, Grier, J., says, injunction is not the proper remedy. Sanders v. Logan, 2 Fisher's Pat. Cas. 167. The application for temporary injunction may be granted or refused unconditionally, or terms may be imposed on either of the parties as conditions for making or refusing the order. Forbush v. Bradford, 11 Law Rep. 411, Curtis, J. One material question always is whether the defendant is responsible. Day v. Boston Belting Co., 6 Law Rep. 330, Sprague, J. See, also, Sickels v. Mitchell, 3 Blatchf. 552. See, also, as to general principles upon which injunction will be granted, Sickels v. Youngs, 3 Blatchf. 293.

(d) 6 Ves. 693.
(e) Mawman v. Tegg, 2 Russ. 385; Sheriff v. Coates, 1 R. & M. 166.
(f) Bouton v. Bull, 3 Ves. 140; Harmer v. Plane, 14 Ves. 130; Hill v. Thompson, 3 Mer. 622; Collard v. Allison, 4 M. & C. 487; Bickford v. Skewes, ib. 500; Stevens v. Keating, 2 Ph. 335; Caldwell v. Vanvlissengen, 9 Ha. 415.

27

serted in one or more actions at law, and the court has no
reason to be dissatisfied with the result (*g*), credit will be
given to the title, until its invalidity, if it be invalid, has been
established upon trial. Thus, in Newall *v.* Wilson (*h*), where
a patent had been in force for twelve years, and the title had
been maintained in two actions at law, and two other suits
had also terminated in favor of the patentee, an injunction
was granted pending the trial of the legal right, although a
fresh fact was brought forward impeaching the novelty of the
invention. But although a verdict at law may have been in
favor of a patent, the court will not in general grant an injunction unless the right is fully determined and the trial complete. Thus the court would not interfere after a trial at law
where the defendant had obtained a rule *nisi* for a new trial (*i*),
or had tendered a bill of exceptions to the verdict, there being
no reason to suppose that the course pursued by the defendant
in tendering the bill had been adopted for the purposes of
delay, or was otherwise than perfectly fair (*k*). But if the
result of the trial at law is, in the opinion of the court, satisfactory, the court may interfere at once, although the defendant is proceeding to take further steps at law (*l*). If the
defendant has failed in his motion for a new trial, or to get
the verdict set aside (*m*), and a nonsuit entered (*n*), it is a
            matter of course that an injunction should issue until
* 402 the hearing. An award in * favor of the validity of a
            patent made upon reference on a trial at law will be
treated by the court as a verdict at law (*o*).

3. If a patent be a recent one, and its validity be denied, the
court will not in general interfere by injunction until the legal
right has been established (*p*). But it is not a matter of course

(*g*) Hill *v.* Thompson, 3 Mer. 622;
Caldwell *v.* Vanvlissengen, 9 Ha. 424 ;
Davenport *v.* Goldberg, 2 H. & M. 282;
Bovill *v.* Goodier, 2 L. R. Eq. 195.
(*h*) 2 D. M. & G. 282.
(*i*) Hill *v.* Thompson, 3 Mer. 628.
(*k*) Collard *v.* Allison, 4 M. & C.
489; Bridson *v.* Macalpine, 8 Beav.
232.
(*l*) Boulton *v.* Bull, 3 Ves. 140; Neilson *v.* Harford, 1 Webs. 373; Bridson
v. Benecke, 12 Beav. 7; Lister *v.*

Leather, 3 Jur. N. S. 433; Baxter
v. Combe, 1 Ir. Ch. 284, 3 Ir. Ch. 245,
256.
(*m*) Neilson *v.* Harford, 1 Webs.
373.
(*n*) Russell *v.* Cowley, 2 C. P. C.
59 n.
(*o*) Lister *v.* Eastwood, 26 L. T. 4.
See Newall *v.* Elliott, 1 H. & C. 797.
(*p*) Hill *v.* Thompson, 3 Mer. 626.
Caldwell *v.* Vanvlissengen, 9 Ha. 424.

that a patentee should establish his right before applying to the court. If the question as to the validity of the patent be free from doubt and difficulty, or a fair *primâ facie* case be made out, the court may interfere, notwithstanding that the patent may be a recent one (*q*). The conduct or admissions of the defendant may amount to sufficient *primâ facie* evidence on which to grant an injunction, even in cases where there is a doubt as to the validity of the patent (*r*).

4. When two parties have obtained patents for the same invention, the court will not interfere by injunction, but will leave them to try their legal rights by *sci. fa.* (*s*)

5. Although a patentee may have obtained a verdict at law against a man for infringing his patent, another person who was not a party to the suit may contest the validity of the patent (*t*).

6. In order to warrant the interference of the court by injunction in support of a patent right, it is not enough that a good *primâ facie* title should be shown: it is also necessary that a fair *primâ facie* case of infringement be made out. However clear and undisputed the validity of a patent may be, the court will not interfere by injunction unless a fair *primâ facie* case of infringement can be shown (*u*).[1]

(*q*) Electric Telegraph Co. *v.* Nott, 2 Coo. C. C. 49, *per* Lord Cottenham ; Gardner *v.* Broadbent, 2 Jur. N. S. 1041; Clark *v.* Ferguson, 1 Giff. 184 ; Renard *v.* Levinstein, 10 L. T. N. S. 177.

(*r*) Muntz *v.* Grenfell, 7 Jur. 121, 2 Coo. C. C. 61 n. ; Betts *v.* Menzies, 3 Jur. N. S. 357.

(*s*) Basket *v.* Cunningham, 2 Ed. 137 ; Copeland *v.* Webb, 11 W. R. 134.

(*t*) Russell *v.* Barnsley, 1 Webs. 472; Crosskill *v.* Evory, 10 L. T. 459.

(*u*) Hill *v.* Thompson, 3 Mer. 626 ; Bridson *v.* Macalpine, 8 Beav. 230 ; Caldwell *v.* Vanvlissengen, 9 Ha. 424; Electric Telegraph Co. *v.* Nott, Coo. C. C. 41.

[1] If a defendant for a valuable consideration, covenants not further to infringe an existing patent, he will be enjoined by a court of equity from further infringing, unless he shows some equitable reason why he should not be bound by his covenant. Sargent *v.* Larned, 2 Curtis, C. C. R. 340.

But the circuit courts of the United States have no jurisdiction to enforce specific execution of a contract for the use of a patent right, where parties live in the state where suit is brought. Brooks *v.* Stolley, 3 McLean, 523.

Where an injunction restraining the infringement of a patent was issued on a final decree in a suit in equity, and a motion was afterwards made for an attachment against the defendant for violating the injunction by selling an article alleged to be an infringement of the patent, and it appeared that no such article had been sold by the defendant prior to the making of the decree, and it did not appear that such an article existed before the making of the decree, and an issue was fairly raised on the facts as to whether such article was an infringement of the patent, it was held that such issue could not be disposed of on a motion, on affidavits, but must be determined in a suit brought for the purpose. Liddle *v.* Cory, 7 Blatchf. 1.

7. If the court is satisfied that the patent is valid, and has
been infringed, it may interfere at once and grant an
* 403 injunction, * without putting the patentee to establish his
legal right; but if the validity of the patent or the fact of
its infringement is denied, the court will seldom, however clear
the case may be, grant an injunction without putting the plaintiff to establish his legal right.   The course of the court in
such cases is either to protect the right by injunction pending
the trial of the right, or to order the motion to stand over
until the legal right has been tried.   Which of these two
alternatives it shall adopt depends entirely on the discretion
of the court, according to the case made out.   In determining
the question, the court is governed by the consideration of the
comparative convenience or inconvenience from granting or
withholding the injunction (x).

8. The bill should allege the validity of the patent, the title
of the plaintiff to the relief prayed, and the infringement of the
patent by the defendant.   The bill need not set out the patent
at length, but may merely state the substance or effect of it,
and the proviso requiring specification.   After stating the
grant, the bill must show that the patentee has performed the
condition upon which he obtained his privilege, by enrolling a
specification within the time limited by the patent.   It is not
requisite that the specification should be set out at length.   It
is sufficient if the patentee alleges that he has done by his
specification all that is required by the patent (y).   If any part
of the title of the invention or specification has been disclaimed
or altered, the bill must show the nature of the disclaimer or
memorandum of alteration, and must set forth sufficient of both
documents to show the effect of the disclaimer, or the memorandum of alteration on the specification (z).[1]

(x) Bacon v. Jones, 4 M. & C. 436;
Electric Telegraph Co. v. Nott, 2 Coo.
C. C. 53; Wood v. Cockerell, ib. 58 n.;
Jones v. Pearce, ib.; Renard v. Levin-
stein, 2 H. & M. 628; $supra$, pp. 209,
210.

(y) Kay v. Marshall, 1 M. & C. 373;
Westhead v. Keene, 1 Beav. 287.

(z) Hindm. on Pat. 311. See Foxwell v. Bostock, 10 L. T. N. S. 144.

[1] In the United States courts an
injunction is not granted in any case
without reasonable previous notice to
the adverse party or his attorney, of
the time and place of moving for the
same. Sts. 2d March, 1793, c. 22, s. 5.
Hence all injunctions are special. Perry
v. Parker, 1 Woodbury & M. 280. But
the notice may be waived by an appearance.   Marsh v. Bennett, 5 McLean,
117.

An injunction granted on an original

9. If the patent privilege is vested in several persons, whether as grantees or assignees, they may be all joined as plaintiffs in the suit.   Any person to whom a part of a patent has been assigned may maintain the suit alone for the protection of his *own interest in the patent; but he must, in   *404 such a case, make his copartners defendants in the suit (a).   If a patent privilege has been infringed by several persons jointly, they ought to be all made defendants, and one bill is sufficient; but if several persons separately commit acts of infringement, a separate bill must be filed against each infringer (b).   Where numerous parties are alleged to be infringing the patent at the same time, the patentee should select that case of infringement which he may think best in order to try the question fairly, and proceed to obtain an interlocutory injunction, and should at the same time write to the others *in simili casu*, asking them whether they are willing to be bound by the determination in the cause, and if not, threatening to proceed against them all (c).   The directors of a company acting as its agents who have infringed a patent should be made parties (d).

10. A man who applies for an injunction *ex parte* to restrain the infringement of a patent-right must swear at the time of making the application that he believes that the invention was new, and had never been practised in the kingdom at the date of the patent.   It is not enough that it was believed to be new at the time the patent was taken out; for, although when he obtained the patent he might have very honestly sworn as to his belief of such being the fact, circumstances may have subsequently occurred, or information may have been since that time communicated to him, sufficient to convince him that it was not his original invention, and that he was under a mis-

---

bill before the surrender of a patent, cannot be maintained upon the new patent unless a supplemental bill be filed, founded thereon. Woodworth *v.* Stone, 3 Story, 749.

A writ of injunction, as a general rule, ought to contain a concise description of the particular acts or things in respect to which the party is enjoined, so that there may be no misapprehen-

sion on the subject. Whipple *v.* Hutchinson, 4 Blatchf. 192.

(a) See Westhead *v.* Keene, 1 Beav. 287.

(b) See Dilly *v.* Doig, 2 Ves. Jr. 486.

(c) Bovill *v.* Crate, 1 L. R. Eq. 388.

(d) Betts *v.* De Vitre, 34 L. J. Ch. 289, 11 Jur. N. S. 9, 217.

take when he made the application for the patent (e).¹ If the application is made by the patentee, he must verify all the material allegations of the bill. He must verify by affidavit the grant of the patent, its specification according to due form, and its due enrolment. If the application is made by an assignee of the patent, he must prove the assignment by the best evidence

he can procüre; and must also, if he can, procure
* 405   an affidavit from * the patentee (f). If the application

be made after the validity of the patent has been established at law, the affidavits must show the nature of the proceeding at law and the result (g). The affidavits must also show that an actual infringement has taken place, and must state the particulars in which the infringement consists (h), and must show that there has been no delay in making the application after knowledge of the infringement has been obtained (i).

11. The affidavits of the defendant in opposition to the application for an injunction, or in support of the motion to dissolve, should show either that the plaintiff was not the first and true inventor, or that the invention was not new, or that the specification was insufficient, or that no infringement has taken place, or he may state any other circumstance that would show the patent to be void. If he deny the novelty of the invention or the validity of the patent, an injunction will not be granted or supported, unless the plaintiff files a very clear and distinct affidavit as to the novelty of the invention or the validity of the patent. The motion may be allowed to stand over for that purpose (k).²

(e) Hill v. Thompson, 3 Mer. 624; Sturz v. De la Rive, 5 Russ. 329; Gardner v. Broadbent, 2 Jur. N. S. 1041; Mayer v. Spence, 1 J. & H. 87.

(f) Bickford v. Skewes, 4 M. & C. 500.

(g) Hill v. Thompson, 3 Mer. 624.

(h) Ib.; Mayer v. Spence, 1 J. & H. 87.

(i) Losh v. Hague, 1 Webs. 200.

(k) Whitton v. Jennings, 1 Dr. & Sm. 111.

¹ Rogers v. Abbott, 4 Wash. 514; Ogle v. Edge, ib. 584.

"And it is the usual practice, on moving for an injunction before the answer has been filed, to read such an affidavit, as well as others to the same purport." Curtis on Patents, s. 408.

On a motion, on affidavits, to dissolve an injunction in a patent suit, the defendants' proofs must overcome the equity of the bill, and the evidence in its support, or the motion will be denied. Sparkman v. Higgins, 1 Blatchf. 205.

As to course of practice on motions for temporary injunctions, see Day v. New Eng. Car Spring Co., 3 Blatchf. 154; and as to dissolution of same, see Poor v. Carleton, 3 Sumner, 70.

² In common cases, it is of course to dissolve an injunction, if the answer denies the whole merits; and the plain-

12. The defendant must answer fully the inquiries which the plaintiff is entitled to make. He cannot by denial of the plaintiff's title escape answering (*l*). He is bound, though he may deny the fact of infringement, to answer fully whether he uses in his process the materials mentioned in the specification; whether he uses any additional materials; and whether such additions, if any, make any difference in the process. But he is not, it would appear, bound to disclose the proportions in which he uses the specified materials, or what the additional materials are (*m*). If the subject of the patent be a machine, the patentee is entitled to have full information as to every variety of combination of machine used by the defendant by which the patent is infringed (*n*). A defendant is not excused from answering * fully on the ground that the * 406 validity of the patent has not been established (*o*). But a man who denies by his answer the fact of infringement is not bound to answer before the decree, interrogatories which assume the fact of infringement, and are immaterial to that question (*p*). A defendant seeking to protect himself from giving such discovery by answer is not bound to put in a plea denying infringement (*q*).

13. A man who seeks the aid of the court for the protection of his patent-rights must show proper diligence in making the application. If he has openly encouraged or silently acquiesced in the invasion of his right, or has allowed another to expend moneys or erect works upon the faith that no impediment will be placed in the way of his enjoyment, his equity to the extraordinary interference of the court is gone (*r*).[1] This doctrine is applicable not only to the case of the particular

---

tiff will not be permitted upon a motion to dissolve the injunction to read affidavits in contradiction to the answer. But in cases of special injunction it is otherwise; the continuance or dissolution of which, after the coming in of the answer, depends upon the sound discretion of the court. Poor *v.* Carleton, 3 Sumner, 70.

(*l*) Swinborne *v.* Nelson, 16 Beav. 416.

(*m*) Renard *v.* Levinstein, 3 N. R. 665, 10 L. T. N. S. 94.

(*n*) Foxwell *v.* Webster, 10 Jur. N. S. 137.

(*o*) Foxwell *v.* Webster, 10 Jur. N. S. 137, 3 N. R. 103.

(*p*) Delarue *v.* Dickenson, 3 K. & J. 388.

(*q*) *Ib.*

(*r*) Losh *v.* Hague, 1 Webs. 200; Neilson *v.* Thompson, *ib.* 275; Bacon *v.* Jones, 4 M. & C. 436; Bridson *v.* Benecke, 12 Beav. 1; Hancock *v.* Bewley, John. 601; Bovill *v.* Crate, 1 L. R. Eq. 388; *supra*, pp. 201–205.

[1] Smith *v.* Sharp's Rifle Manuf. Co., 3 Blatchf. 545.

conduct of the patentee towards the person with whom the controversy subsists, but also to cases where his conduct with others may influence the court in the exercise of its equitable jurisdiction (s). A man whose patent-rights are invaded by several persons should give distinct notice to each to discontinue the infringement. If he proceeds against one only, without giving notice to the others, and allows a considerable period to elapse before taking steps to enforce his rights against them, he may lose his right to the protection of the court (t). The omission to take active steps for the repeal of a subsequent patent by *scire facias* will not deprive a prior patentee of his right to the aid of the court, unless the subsequent patent has been put in practice (u).[1]

14. On directing an issue to try whether a patent has been infringed, the court may order the defendant to admit * 407   for the * purposes of the issue the title of the plaintiff as assignee or otherwise of the patent (x).

SECTION II.—TRIAL OF ISSUES.

1. Court may order separate issues to be tried before itself.
2. What particulars must be delivered by each party to the other before trial.
3. Evidence confined to the support of the particulars.
4. When no particulars will be required.
5. Defendant not allowed to add new issues of fact not suggested by his answer.
6. Course of proceeding where defendants are very numerous.
7. Order in which questions will be taken.
8. Practice as to evidence.

(s) Rundell v. Murray, Jac. 311; Saunders v. Smith, 3 M. & C. 711; *supra*, p. 203.

(t) Smith v. South Western Railway Co., Kay, 417.

(u) Newall v. Wilson, 2 D. M. & G. 290.

(x) Morgan v. Seaward, 1 Webs. 167. See Pidding v. Franks, 1 Mac. & G. 56. See, also, *supra*, p. 213.

[1] If a patentee has established his right to letters-patent, he is entitled to an interlocutory injunction under an extension of them without being put to a trial at law or proof of long possession. Clum v. Brewer, 2 Curtis, C. C. R. 506.

It is not a sufficient answer to an application for an injunction, that the infringement has been discontinued, unless compensation is made for such unlawful use. Sickels v. Mitchell, 3 Blatchf. 548.

1. The court may, if it shall think fit, direct separate issues to be tried before itself; but the practice of having separate issues should not be regarded as peremptory, but must be regarded merely as a convenient mode of arranging the questions to be decided before itself (y).

2. The plaintiff must deliver to the defendant before the trial the particulars.of the breaches complained of by him, and the defendant must deliver to the plaintiff particulars of any objections to the validity of the patent on which he means to rely at the trial (z). The particulars are sufficient if, taken together with the pleadings, they give the defendant a full and fair notice of the case made against him (a). A defendant stating the objections on which he means to rely at the trial as displacing the validity of the patent, must do so with precision, and should state exactly what case the plaintiff has to meet (b). The place or places in which, and the manner in which the invention is alleged to have been used prior to the date of the patent, should be stated (c).

3. No evidence can be given in support of any alleged infringement, or of any objections impeaching the validity of the patent, which shall not be contained in the particulars delivered (d). The * rule is applicable to trials before   * 408 the court in which particulars have been ordered to be delivered, as well as to trials at law (e). Evidence cannot be allowed in the course of the hearing before the court without a jury in respect of any matter affecting the validity of the patent not disclosed by the particulars of objections, although such evidence may have only come to the knowledge of the defendant since the delivery of particulars (f). But

(y) Curtis v. Platt, 11 L. T. N. S. 250, *per* Lord Westbury. See *supra*, 216–220, as to trial of issues. See, also, Addenda. See, as to forms of issues, Davenport v. Jepson, 1 N. R. 307; Spencer v. Jack, 8 Jur. N. S. 1165, 11 L. T. N. S. 242; Renard v. Levinstein, 11 L. T. N. S. 766; Penn v. Jack, 14 L. T. N. S. 495.

(z) 15 & 16 Vict. c. 83, s. 41; Renard v. Levinstein, 11 L. T. N. S. 505. See, as to order for delivery of particulars, Davenport v. Jepson, 1 N. R. 307.

(a) Needham v. Oxley, 1 H. & M. 248.

(b) Curtis v. Platt, 8 L. T. N. S. 657; Daw v. Eley, 1 L. R. Eq. 38; Penn v. Bibby, *ib.* 548.

(c) 15 & 16 Vict. c. 83, s. 41. See Palmer v. Wagstaff, 8 Exch. 840; Palmer v. Cooper, 9 Exch. 231; Penn v. Bibby, 1 L. R. Eq. 541; Morgan v. Fuller, 2 L. R. Eq. 297.

(d) 15 & 16 Vict. c. 83, s. 41.

(e) Curtis v. Platt, 8 L. T. N. S. 657.

(f) Daw v. Eley, 1 L. R. Eq. 38; Renard v. Levinstein, 13 W. R. 229.

leave will be given on short notice of motion to amend the particulars, so as to introduce such newly discovered evidence (*g*).

4. If replication has been filed and the court has refused to direct an issue, the defendant will not be required to deliver particulars (*h*). Nor, if the novelty of a patent is denied, has a plaintiff any right to the discovery of particulars, on which the plaintiff relies as showing a user of the thing patented prior to the date of the patent (*i*). The requirements of the statute as to the delivery of notice of objections is confined to questions affecting the validity of the patent, and does not extend to objections to the validity of the assignment (*k*).

5. A defendant will not be allowed to add new issues of fact not in any way suggested by his answer to the issues which have been already directed for trial (*l*).

6. In a case where a patentee had filed many bills against as many defendants for an alleged infringement of his patent, the court ordered the suit to be conducted by three of the defendants, representing three different classes of infringers, on behalf of the remainder, with liberty for any of the defendants to come in under the order (*m*).

7. The court may, in the exercise of its discretion, decline to consider the questions arising on the specification until the evidence on the whole case has been heard (*n*). At * 409 other * times the question as to the validity of the patent will be first tried (*o*).

8. Upon the trial of an issue the plaintiff is entitled to call witnesses in reply for the purpose of rebutting a case of prior user set up by the defendant. But after evidence has been summed up the defendant cannot adduce further evidence in answer to that given by the plaintiff (*p*).[1]

(*g*) Daw *v.* Eley, 1 L. R. Eq. 38; Penn *v.* Bibby, *ib.* 548.
(*h*) Bovill *v.* Goodier, *ib.* 35.
(*i*) Daw *v.* Eley, 2 H. & M. 725; Bovill *v.* Smith, 2 L. R. Eq. 459.
(*k*) Chollet *v.* Hoffman, 7 E. & B. 686.
(*l*) Morgan *v.* Fuller, 2 L. R. Eq. 296.
(*m*) Foxwell *v.* Webster, 10 Jur. N. S. 137, 9 L. T. N. S. 528. See Bovill *v.* Crate, 1 L. R. Eq. 388; *supra*, p. 39.

(*n*) Young *v.* Fernie, 4 N. R. 218.
(*o*) Foxwell *v.* Webster, 10 Jur. N. S. 137, 9 L. T. N. S. 528; Simpson *v.* Holliday, 1 L. R. Ap. Ca. 315.
(*p*) Penn *v.* Jack, 2 L. R. Eq. 315.
[1] Proceedings for the purpose of restraining the unlawful use of a machine are instituted against the owner or party concerned in the infringement, who is personally responsible for the violation. The offending machine is

SECTION III. — PATENT-RIGHTS.

1. The validity of a patent depends on two considerations. The species of manufacture for which the patent is claimed must be a proper subject for a patent privilege, and in the next place there must be a proper specification. What is the proper subject of a patent privilege is defined by the Statute of Monopolies, 21 Jac. 1, c. 3, s. 6. The statute did not create, but only controlled and defined the powers which the Crown has at all times exercised in the granting of patents. These grants

reached through the party legally accountable for the wrong, and without whose agency, directly or indirectly, there would have been no ground of complaint. But in cases where it becomes necessary to proceed directly against the machine itself, as it may be in extreme cases of contumacy, or fraudulent contrivance to evade an injunction, the proceedings must be instituted in the district in which the machine is located. Wilson *v.* Sherman, 1 Blatchf. 541.

And an injunction will not be granted in a district where the defendant neither resides nor carries on his business, as it would be inoperative and useless. Goodyear *v.* Chaffee, 3 Blatchf. 268.

of monopoly in respect of inventions are not by grant of the statute but by virtue of the prerogative. Patentees have always derived and still derive their rights not from the statute but from the grant of the Crown (*q*). By the 6th section of that statute it is provided that any declarations contained in the act " shall not extend to any letters-patent for the term of fourteen years for the sole working or making of any new manufactures within this realm to the true and first inventor of such manufactures which others at the time of working such letters-patent shall not use, so as also they be not contrary to the law nor mischievous to the State, or generally inconvenient." The granting of letters-patent does not preclude the Crown from the use of the invention protected by the patent, even without the assent of or compensation made to the patentee. The Crown is not bound unless it declares its intention to that effect (*r*).

* 410   2. * The word " manufacture " not only comprehends any thing made, but it also comprehends the mode, method, or process of making a thing, apart from its produce and results, such as a new machine, or a new combination of machinery, or a new process, or an improvement of an old process (*s*). A mere philosophical or abstract principle does not answer to the word " manufacture." The discovery of a principle or new property in matter, though it may form a valuable addition to the sum of human knowledge, is not within the policy of the patent law. Apart from its practical application in the arts or manufactures, a principle is not the subject-matter for a patent; but as soon as a principle becomes embodied with corporeal substances in some practical mode, so as to produce a new result in the arts or manufactures, there may be a patent. The patent is granted not for the principle but for the mode of carrying the principle into effect. Whether the inventor applies a well-known principle for the first time to produce a new result, or whether he has the additional merit of discovering the principle as well as its application, makes no

(*q*) Caldwell *v*. Vanvlissengen, 9 Ha. 426; Feather *v*. The Queen, 6 B. & S. 257.
(*r*) Feather *v*. The Queen, 6 B. & S. 257.
(*s*) Crane *v*. Price, 4 M. & G. 580; Morgan *v*. Seaward, 2 M. & W. 544. See Rex *v*. Wheeler, 2 B. & Ald. 345; Ralston *v*. Smith, 11 H. L. 223.

difference (t). What is called the principle of a machine in reference to the patent law is not a principle or an idea. The legal meaning of the principle of a machine is its mode of operation, or that peculiar device, or manner, or combination of devices, or parts in the structure of the machine, by which a certain effect is produced (u). A result or effect cannot, any more than a principle, be the subject of a patent. A patent must be for the mode of embodying the principle so as to produce a certain result or effect. It is for the discovery or invention of some practical method or means of producing a beneficial result or effect that a patent is granted. If the patent were for the result itself, all other persons would be prohibited * from making the same thing by any means *411 whatsoever (v). Two methods founded on the same principle may be good where the principle is applied by distinct methods and apparatus (x). The distinction between a machine and a process is that the term machine includes every mechanical device, or combination of mechanical powers or devices, to perform some function or produce a certain result; but where the result or effect is produced by chemical action, by the operation or application of some element or power of nature, or of one substance to another, such methods, modes, or operations are called processes. A new process is usually the result of discovery, a machine of invention (y).

3. To come within the statute of monopolies the "manufacture" must be "new." There cannot be a valid patent privilege for the new use of an old invention. The mere application of an old contrivance or an old process in the old way to an analogous subject, without any novelty or invention in the mode of applying the old contrivance or the old process

(t) Boulton v. Bull, 2 H. Bl. 463; Hornblower v. Boulton, 8 T. R. 95; Rex v. Cutter, 1 Stark. 353; Minter v. Wells, 1 Cr. M. & R. 505; Neilson v. Harford, 1 Webs. 342; Househill Co. v. Neilson, ib. 683; Baxter v. Combe, 1 Ir. Ch. 284; Crossley v. Potter, Macr. 244; Electric Telegraph Co. v. Brett, 10 C. B. 838.

(u) Barrett v. Hall, 1 Mass. (Amer.) 470, per Story, J.; Earl v. Sawyer, 4 Mass. (Amer.) 1; M'Cormick v. Tal-cott, 20 How. (Amer.) 402; Burr v. Duryee, 1 Wall. (Amer.) 531.

(v) Bean v. Smallwood, 2 Story (Amer.), 408; Leroy v. Tatham, 14 How. (Amer.) 174; O'Reilly v. Morse, 15 How. (Amer.) 62; Corning v. Burden, ib. 252; Baxter v. Combe, 1 Ir. Ch. 284.

(x) Hullett v. Hague, 2 B. & A. 370. See Seed v. Higgins, 8 H. L. 550.

(y) Corning v. Burden, 15 How. (Amer.) 267.

to the new purpose, is not a valid subject-matter for a patent (z) ;
but the new application of any means or contrivance may be
the subject of a patent, if it lies so much out of the track of the
former use as not naturally to suggest itself, but to require
some application of thought and study (a). If there is some
invention, skill, or ingenuity in the application, there may be
a patent for a new arrangement and combination of materials,
instruments, machinery, or processes formerly in use, whereby
a new and useful article, or a new effect, or a better effect than
before, is obtained (b). A cheaper way of using known
* 412   materials (c), * or a mere improvement in performing
an operation well known and long practised, not amounting to a new mode or process of performing it (d), or a mere
slight variation, if there be no invention (e), are not within the
protection of the statute; but a discovery by which part of
the machinery or one of the processes used in a manufacture
may be dispensed with (f), or an addition to or an improvement in a process or machinery already known and in use (g),
or a new process by which old materials can be applied for a
new purpose in the same manufacture (h), or an alteration in
the mode of manufacture (i), or a new means or contrivance
for effecting an old object or attaining a well-known result (k),
or an apparatus for carrying out a particular object (l), or a
discovery that two or more simple substances in certain definite

(z) Brook v. Aston, 8 E. & B. 478,
in error, 28 L. J. Q. B. 175; Patent
Bottle Co. v. Seymour, 5 C. B. N. S.
164; Horton v. Mabon, 12 C. B. N. S.
437, 16 C. B. N. S. 141; Harwood v.
Great Northern Railway Co., 11 H. L.
654; Ormson v. Clark, 14 C. B. N. S.
476; Thompson v. James, 32 Beav.
570; Jordan v. Moore, 1 L. R. C. P.
624.

(a) Penn v. Bibby, 2 L. R. Ch. Ap.
127.

(b) Huddart v. Grimshaw, Dav. P.
C. 265; Hill v. Thompson, 3 Mer. 629;
Gamble v. Kurtz, 3 C. B. 425; Newton
v. Grand Junction Railway Co., 5
Exch. 334 n.; Steiner v. Heald, 6
Exch. 607; Newton v. Vaucher, ib.
859; Lister v. Leather, 8 E. & B. 1004.

(c) Horton v. Mabon, 12 C. B. N. S.
448, per Willes, J., disapproving Crane
v. Price, 4 M. & G. 580.

(d) Ormson v. Clark, 14 C. B. N. S.
475.

(e) Dobbs v. Penn, 3 Exch. 427.

(f) Russell v. Cowley, 1 Webs.
463; Booth v. Kennard, 1 H. & N. 531.

(g) Boulton v. Bull, 2 H. Bl. 463;
Hill v. Thompson, 8 Taunt. 375, 3
Mer. 629; Minton v. Mower, 1 Webs.
142; Electric Telegraph Co. v. Brett,
10 C. B. 838; Lister v. Leather, 8 E. &
B. 1004.

(h) Hills v. Liverpool Gas-light Co.
9 Jur. N. S. 140. See Hills v. London
Gas-light Co., 5 H. & N. 313; Higgs
v. Goodwin, El. Bl. & El. 529.

(i) Beard v. Egerton, 3 C. B. 97.

(k) Losh v. Hague, 1 Webs. 202
Stevens v. Keating, 2 Webs. 183, per
Pollock, C. B.; Curtis v. Platt, 11 L.
T. N. S. 245.

(l) Newall v. Elliott, 10 Jur. N. S.
956

proportions will form a compound substance valuable for medical or other qualities (*m*), or a combination of two principles which had before been used separately in the same trade (*n*), or a combination of two or more old inventions (*o*), is a valid subject-matter for a patent (*p*).

4. The rule that the application to a substance of a process which has been previously applied to an analogous substance cannot be the subject-matter for a patent does not hold where * the process is a chemical process. The law *413 recognizes the right of an inventor who finds out and supplies for commercial purposes an article known previously only as a chemical curiosity (*q*).

5. To ascertain the novelty of an invention the entire invention must be taken ; and if, in all its parts taken together, it answer the purpose by the introduction of any new matter, by any new combination, or by a new application, it is a novelty within the meaning of the statute (*r*).

6. The novelty of a manufacture is a question of fact for the jury (*s*).

7. The law as declared by the statute of monopolies requires that the person to whom a patent privilege is granted should be the first and true inventor, and that the subject-matter of the patent should not be in use at the date of the patent. The publisher or introducer of a new invention into actual practice is the first and true inventor within the meaning of the statute. The source whence he may have derived his information is not a matter of which the law will take cognizance, unless there has been a fraud on the Crown (*t*), or unless the knowledge

(*m*) Bewley *v.* Hancock, 6 D. M. &. G. 391.

(*n*) Bovill *v.* Keyworth, 7 E. & B. 725.

(*o*) Smith *v.* London and North Western Railway Co., 2 E, & B. 69.

(*p*) See also Minter *v.* Wells, 1 Cr. M. & R. 505; Muntz *v.* Foster, 2 Webs. 93; Newton *v.* Vaucher, 6 Exch. 859; Wallington *v.* Dale, 7 Exch. 888; Oxley *v.* Holden, 8 C. B. N. S. 666.

(*q*) Young *v.* Fernie, 4 Giff. 577. See Sellers *v.* Dickinson, 5 Exch. 326; Stevens *v.* Keating, 2 Webs. 189, *per* Pollock, C. B.; Hills *v.* London Gaslight Co., 5 H. & N. 313; Bewley *v.* Hancock, 6 D. M. & G. 391.

(*r*) Newton *v.* Grand Junction Railway Co., 5 Exch. 331 n.

(*s*) Steiner *v.* Heald, 6 Exch. 607 ; Spencer *v.* Jack, 11 L. T. N. S. 242.

(*t*) Dollond's case, cited, 2 H. Bl. 470; Stead *v.* Anderson, 4 C. B. 813. But comp. Tennant's case, Dav. P. C. 429 ; Minter *v.* Wells, 1 Webs. 130; Cornish *v.* Keene, *ib.* 508; Bloxam *v.* Elsee, 1 C. & P. 558; Brunton *v.* Hawkes, 4 B. & Ald. 541 ; Lewis *v.* Marling, 10 B. & C. 22; Makepeace *v.* Jackson, 4 Taunt. 770; Gibson *v.* Brand, 1 Webs. 628; Beard *v.* Egerton, 3 C. B. 97; Smith *v.* Davidson, 19 Dec. of Ct. of Sess., 2d series, p. 691.

has been obtained from a person towards whom he stands in a confidential relation with respect to the subject of the patent (*u*). If the first inventor keeps his invention a secret and does not put it in practice until another makes the same invention and obtains a patent, the patent is valid and will prevail (*x*). The introducer of an invention from foreign parts is a true * 414 and first *inventor within the meaning of the statute (*y*). Whether the knowledge of the invention may have been derived from a foreigner or an Englishman resident abroad is immaterial (*z*).

8. If a person has discovered an improved principle and employs engineers, agents, or other persons to assist him in carrying out that principle, and they, in the course of experiments arising from that employment, make valuable discoveries accessory to the main principle, and tending to carry it out in a better manner, such experiments are the property of the employer and may be embodied in the patent (*a*).

9. If an invention goes into public use, or has been publicly employed in actual use, a man cannot afterwards have a patent, although he is the original inventor (*b*). Previous user or publication in any part of the realm will vitiate a subsequent patent in England (*c*). It is not necessary, in order to avoid a patent, to show that the invention was in general use at the date it was taken out. It is enough that the invention was publicly in actual use (*d*). A single instance of the prior sale of an article is a user sufficient to invalidate a subsequent patent (*e*). The manufacture even of an article for the pur-

(*u*) Milligan *v.* Marsh, 2 Jur. N. S. 1083.

(*x*) Dollond's case, cit. 2 H. Bl. 487; Smith *v.* Davidson, 19 Dec. of Ct. of Sess., 2d series, p. 691.

(*y*) Darcy *v.* Allin, Nov, 182, 183; Edgeberry *v.* Stephens, 2 Salk. 447; Beard *v.* Egerton, 3 C. B. 97; Nickels *v.* Ross, 8 C. B. 679.

(*z*) Nickels *v.* Ross, *ib.*; Steedman *v.* Marsh, 2 Jur. N. S. 391.

(*a*) Allen *v.* Rawson, 1 C. B. 551, 567; Hatton *v.* Kean, 7 C. B. N. S. 275, *per* Erle, C. J.

(*b*) Tennant's case, Dav. P. C. 429; Wood *v.* Zimmer, Holt, N. P. C. 82; Cornish *v.* Keene, 1 Webs. 501; House-

hill Co. *v.* Neilson, 9 Cl. & Fin. 788; Carpenter *v.* Smith, 9 M. & W. 300; Muntz *v.* Foster, 2 Webs. 93; Stead *v.* Anderson, 4 C. B. 813; Lang *v.* Gisborne, 31 Beav. 133.

(*c*) Brown *v.* Annandale, 8 Cl. & Fin. 437

(*d*) Wood *v.* Zimmer, Holt, N. P. C. 82; Losh *v.* Hague, 1 Webs. 202; Cornish *v.* Keene, *ib.* 508; Carpenter *v.* Smith, 9 M. & W. 300; Household Co. *v.* Neilson, 9 Cl. & Fin. 788, 807; Heath *v.* Smith, 3 E. & B. 256; *Re* Adamson, 6 D. M. & G. 420; *Re* Newall and Elliott, 4 C. B. N. S. 269.

(*e*) Morgan *v.* Seaward, 2 M. & W. 544; Minter *v.* Mower, 1 Webs. 142.

poses of sale, and the offer of it for sale, is sufficient, although
no sale has actually taken place, and it would appear to be
equally so if the article be made merely as a sample (f); but
user, in making an article which is sent abroad and not offered
for sale here, is not sufficient (g). Actual public user
will defeat a subsequent * patent, although the user be   * 415
merely for private purposes (h), or although the user be
by a foreigner, and the article be manufactured abroad (i). It
is doubtful whether a patent would be valid where another
man had, before the date of the patent, used the process, and
brought out articles for the purposes of profit, keeping the
method entirely secret (k). But the accidental use of a piece
of machinery (forming part of a mechanical contrivance which
may be afterwards applied to some ulterior purpose) without
any intention of producing the result, is not such a user
as will prevent a patent from being taken out by another person (l).

10. If an invention has been once in public actual use, it is
not necessary, in order to invalidate a subsequent patent, that
the use should come down to the time when the patent was
granted: the patent will not be valid, although the user may
have been long abandoned and discontinued, unless the recollection of the previous user has been altogether lost (m).
It is, on the other hand, no objection to the validity of a patent
that the invention has been previously made or discovered by
another person, if it has not been made public or openly used
before the date of the patent (n).

11. Previous user, in order to invalidate a subsequent patent, must be a user of the complete invention. If the invention is not complete, no experiments, however nearly they may

(f) Oxley v. Holden, 8 C. B. N. S.
666.
(g) Morgan v. Seaward, 2 M. & W.
544.
(h) Stead v. Williams, 7 M. & G. 818.
(i) Caldwell v. Vanvlissengen, 9 Ha.
415.
(k) Heath v. Smith, 3 E. & B. 273,
per Erle, C. J. But see Dollond's case,
cited, 2 H. Bl. 487.
(l) Harwood v. Great Northern Railway Co., 2 B. & S. 196; sed quære, ib.
231, per Exch. Ch. See Minter v.
Mower, 1 Webs. 140.

(m) Carpenter v. Smith, 9 M. & W.
300; Househill Co. v. Neilson, 9 Cl. &
Fin. 788. See Muntz v. Foster, 8 Jur.
206. But see Cornish v. Keene, 1
Webs. 44.
(n) Dollond's case, cited, 2 H. Bl.
470, 487; Hill v. Thompson, 3 Mer.
626; Forsyth v. Riviere, 1 Webs. 97;
Lewis v. Marling, 10 B. & C. 22; Gibson v. Brand, 4 M. & G. 198, 205, per
Erskine, J.; Smith v. Davidson, 19
Dec. of Ct. of Sess., 2d series, p. 691;
comp. Heath v. Smith, 3 E. & B. 256.

have approached to the discovery of the complete invention,
will be of avail (*o*) ; but it is often extremely difficult
* 416　to distinguish * accurately where the user of an invention for the mere purpose of experiment stops, and the
employment or user of it, as a completed invention, which the
inventor thinks cannot be made more perfect, begins (*p*).
The abandonment of an invention raises a strong presumption
that it was a mere experiment, was not complete, and had not
been reduced into beneficial practice (*q*).

12. A man, if he be the true and first inventor, may, notwithstanding publication, have a patent if he obtains his patent
before the invention gets into use (*r*).　But if a man be not
the true and first inventor, the mere fact of antecedent publication, so as to make the description of the article part of the
stock of public information, will vitiate a subsequent patent on
the ground of want of novelty (*s*).　A publication takes place
where a description of the invention is published in a book
and is offered publicly for sale in this country.　It is not at
all necessary to show that a single copy of the book has been
sold.　As soon as the public is informed of what the invention
consists, there is in point of law a complete publication of the
invention.　It is not necessary to show that the invention thus
publicly made known has been also put into actual use (*t*).
If the description has been published in a foreign country,
there is no publication in law here so long as it remains in a
foreign country ; but as soon as a description of the invention
is offered publicly for sale in this country, there is in law a
publication (*u*).　An antecedent publication will not, however,

<hr />

(*o*) Carpenter *v.* Smith, 9 M. & W.
300 ; Galloway *v.* Bleaden, 1 Webs.
521, 525 ; Jones *v.* Pearce, *ib.* 122 ;
Cornish *v.* Keene, *ib.* 511 ; Househill
Co. *v.* Neilson, 9 Cl. & Fin. 788 ; *Re*
Newall and Elliott, 4 C. B. N. S. 269 ;
Re Adamson, 6 D. M. & G. 420.

(*p*) Lang *v.* Gisborne, 31 Beav. 135,
per Lord Romilly, M. R.

(*q*) Minter *v.* Mower, 1 Webs. 142 ;
Jones *v.* Pearce, *ib.* 122 ; Lewis *v.*
Marling, 10 B. & C. 22 ; Househill Co.
v. Neilson, 9 Cl. & Fin. 788 ; Newton *v.*
Grand Junction Railway Co., 5 Exch.
331 n. ; Croll *v.* Edge, 9 C. B. 479 ;
Oxley *v.* Holden, 8 C. B. N. S. 666.

(*r*) Stead *v.* Anderson, 4 C. B. 813,

(*s*) *Ib.* The antecedent existence of
an invention not shown to have been
brought to any successful result, and
which was so far similar that, if subsequent in date to the patent, it would
have been held a colorable and clumsy
imitation for the purpose of effecting
the same result, does not invalidate the
patent by anticipation. Daw *v.* Eley,
3 L. R. Eq. 496.

(*t*) Househill Co. *v.* Neilson, 9 Cl. &
Fin. 788 ; Betts *v.* Menzies, 10 H. L. 117 ;
Lang *v.* Gisborne, 31 Beav. 133.

(*u*) Stead *v.* Williams, 7 M. & G. 818 ;
Lang *v.* Gisborne, 31 Beav. 133. See
Re Heurteloup, 1 Webs. 553 ; Stead *v.*
Anderson, 4 C. B. 813.

avoid a subsequent patent, unless it practically describes the invention. The nature of the antecedent statement must be such that a person of ordinary knowledge of the subject should at once perceive and * understand, and be able * 417 practically to apply the discovery without the necessity of making further experiments and gaining further information before the invention can be made useful. If something remains to be ascertained, which is necessary for the useful application of the discovery, that affords sufficient room for a subsequent patent. The information given in the publication must for the purposes of practical utility be equal to that given by the subsequent patent. Whatever is essential to the practical working and real utility of the invention must be read out of the prior publication. If specific details are necessary for the practical working and real utility of the alleged invention, they must be found substantially in the prior publication. Apparent generality or a proposition not true to its full extent will not prejudice a subsequent statement, which is limited and accurate, and a specific rule of application. If the prior publication neither forestalls, anticipates, nor renders unnecessary the invention, nor gives the public that peculiar benefit which they may derive from the discovery, the subject is a fit subject for a patent (v).

13. The specification of a patent amounts to a publication. A prior specification is not to be distinguished from any prior publication contained in a book published in the ordinary manner. An antecedent specification will not, however, amount to an anticipation of a subsequent discovery, unless it disclose a practical mode of producing the result, which is the effect of the subsequent discovery. The mere publication in a prior specification of a notion or mere suggestion that a particular article may be made, without any statement or proof how that object can be attained, and a practical result gained, is insufficient to show that a man has made a prior discovery which is in law an invention, and will not preclude a subsequent first discoverer of these means from taking out a patent (x). The

(v) Betts v. Menzies, 10 H. L. 117 ; Bett's Patent, 1 Moo. P. C. N. S. 49 ; Hills v. Evans, 31 L. J. Ch. 457 ; Young v. Fernie, 4 Giff. 577. See Househill Co. v. Neilson, 9 Cl. & Fin. 788.
(x) Huddart v. Grimshaw, 1 Webs.

filing of a provisional specification describing in part an
* 418   invention * which has been afterwards abandoned is not
such a publication as will render a subsequent patent
for the same invention void (*y*). Where two specifications of
different dates relating to the same external object contain
terms of art, their construction cannot be declared to be the
same, though the expressions used in both are identical, without the meaning and use of the terms of art employed therein
being first ascertained by evidence, and being shown to be the
same at the date of both the specifications (*z*).

14. The disclosure of an invention may be equivalent to a
publication. A necessary and unavoidable disclosure, if it be
only made in the course of mere experiments, is not a publication, although the same disclosure, if made in the cause of a
profitable user of an invention, previously ascertained to be useful, would be a publication (*a*). Nor is an experiment performed
in the presence of others, which not only turns out to be successful, but is actually beneficial in the particular instance,
necessarily a publication, so as to constitute a gift of an invention to the public (*b*). Nor is the disclosure of an invention
confidentially to another (*c*), or the loan of an invention to a
man for the purpose of having its qualities tested, and its use
for some time for that purpose, in a public work-room (*d*), or
the fact that a model or description of a machine may have
been shown to several persons, no machine, however, having
been made (*e*), such a publication as will vitiate a subsequent
patent.

15. Whether there has been a user or publication of an invention is a question of fact for the jury (*f*).

16. The condition of a patent privilege is that the person to

87 ; Dobbs *v.* Penn, 3 Exch. 427 ; Betts
v. Menzies, 10 H. L. 117 ; Hills *v.* Evans,
31 L. J. Ch. 457. See Rex *v.* Wheeler,
2 B. & Ald. 345 ; Stevens *v.* Keating, 2
Exch. 772 ; M'Cormick *v.* Gray, 7 H. &
N. 26.

(*y*) Oxley *v.* Holden, 8 C. B. N. S.
666.

(*z*) Betts *v.* Menzies, 10 H. L. 117 ;
Hills *v.* Evans, 31 L. J. Ch. 457.

(*a*) *Re* Adamson, 6 D. M. & G.
420.

(*b*) *Re* Newall and Elliott, 4 C. B. N.
S. 269.

(*c*) Smith *v.* Dickinson, 3 B. & P.
630 ; Bentley *v.* Fleming, 1 C. & K.
587 ; Morgan *v.* Seaward, 2 M. & W.
544.

(*d*) Bentley *v.* Fleming, 1 C. & K. 587,
per Cresswell, J.

(*e*) Lewis *v.* Marling, 10 B. & C.
22.

(*f*) Minter *v.* Wells, 1 Webs. 132;
Forsyth *v.* Riviere, *ib.* 97 ; Steiner *v.*
Heald, 6 Exch. 607.

whom the privilege has been granted, shall particularly describe and ascertain the nature of the invention, and show how the * invention is to be applied and carried into effect. * 419 The condition is introduced into letters-patent in order to prevent letters-patent from being granted for known things, and to secure to the public the benefit of the invention after the expiration of the time fixed for the duration of the monopoly (*g*). If the terms of the specification are equivocal, the consideration upon which the monopoly has been granted fails, and the patent is void. The specification must be in such terms as to be intelligible to a workman of ordinary skill and information on the subject. " The proper test," said Lord Campbell (*h*), " for a specification to show whether it is good or bad, is whether a workman of ordinary skill can, from merely reading it, make the thing of which it is the specification." The patentee must not only describe the invention, so as to enable a person who, reads it to use the invention, but must also disclose fully the best means within his knowledge of using the invention. The specification must so describe the invention, as to place the public on a footing of equality of knowledge with respect to it with the patentee (*i*). The whole of the patentee's knowledge (*k*), and every improvement in practice by him up to the time of the specification, must be given (*l*). If the specification omits any thing which the patentee knows to be useful or necessary (*m*), or does not communicate to the public the most beneficial mode known to him of exercising the subject of the patent privilege (*n*), or if it is calculated in any way to mislead (*o*), or is on* a * 420

(*g*) Hills *v*. London Gas-light Co., 5 H. & N. 340; Ralston *v*. Smith, 9 C. B. N. S. 117. See, also, *per* Jervis, C. J., Macr. 16.

(*h*) 8 E. & B. 937.

(*i*) Rex *v*. Wheeler, 2 B. & Ald. 345; Hastings *v*. Brown, 1 E. & B. 454.

(*k*) Crossley *v*. Beverley, 9 B. & C. 63.

(*l*) Turner *v*. Winter, 1 T. R. 602. Comp. Harmer *v*. Plane, 14 Ves. 430; Electric Telegraph Co. *v*. Brett, 10 C. B. 338.

(*m*) Neilson *v*. Harford, 8 M. & W.

806; Lewis *v*. Marling, 10 B. & C. 22; Muntz *v*. Foster, 2 Webs. 93.

(*n*) Bovill *v*. Moore, Dav. P. C. 361; Muntz *v*. Foster, 2 Webs. 93. Comp. Liardet *v*. Johnson, 1 Webs. 54 n.

(*o*) Bovill *v*. Moore, Dav. P. C. 361; Turner *v*. Winter, 1 T. R. 602; Savory *v*. Price, Ry. & M. 1; Sturz *v*. De la Rue, 5 Russ. 322; Lewis *v*. Marling, 10 B. & C. 22; Muntz *v*. Foster, 2 Webs. 93; Hastings *v*. Brown, 1 E. & B. 454; Hills *v*. Evans, 31 L. J. Ch. 457; Hills *v*. Liverpool United Gas-light Co., 32 L. J. Ch. 28; Simpson *v*. Holliday, 1 L. R. Ap. Ca. 315.

fair interpretation equivocal in its terms (p), or is too broad
and general (q), or if it leaves the public under the necessity of ascertaining the matter by experiment and further
inquiry (r), or does not show the public what they cannot do
without infringing the patent (s), or if the process described
in the specification does not produce that which the patent
professes to produce (t), the specification is bad and the patent
is altogether void. If two distinct processes are described as
being both efficient, and are both claimed as part of the invention, but one is found upon trial to be inefficient and useless, the patent is invalid (u). If a specification claims too
much it is immaterial that a skilled or practical workman
would not be misled. The mere inaccurate use, however, of
a word, if the sense be sufficiently clear, will not vitiate a
patent (x). Nor are errors material which appear on the face
of the specification or the drawings, and which, as they would
be immediately discovered in working out the instructions,
cannot possibly mislead (y). The specification of an invention which consists in the use of known materials in new proportions is not necessarily bad for uncertainty, though the
patentee does not limit himself to the · precise proportions
recommended (z).

17. If the patent be for an improvement, or a new arrangement, or combination of things formerly in use, the specification
must correctly describe the part, improvement, or combination,
which is claimed, and must define wherein the novelty
* 421   consists, so that * a person of ordinary understanding
and knowledge on the subject may, on reading the
specification see what is claimed as new and what is old. If

(p) Hastings v. Brown, 1 E. & B.
453; Spencer v. Jack, 11 L. T. N. S.
242.
(q) Stevens v. Keating, 2 Exch. 772,
2 Webs. 181; Booth v. Kennard, 2
H. & N. 95; Muntz v. Foster, 2 Webs.
93; Jordan v. Moore, 1 L. R. C. P.
624.
(r) Morgan v. Seaward, 2 M. & W.
544; Lewis v. Marling, 10 B. & C. 22;
Rex v. Cutler, 14 Q. B. 372; Stevens
v. Keating, 2 Exch. 772; Bovill v. Keyworth, 7 E. & B. 735; Hills v. Liverpool Gas-light Co., 32 L. J. Ch. 28;

Simpson v. Holliday, 1 L. R. Ap. Ca.
315.
(s) Morton v. Middleton, 1 Dec. of
Ct. of Sess., 3d series, p. 718.
(t) Turner v. Winter, 1 T. R. 602;
Crossley v. Potter, Macr. 244; Rex v.
Cutler, 14 Q. B. 372; Simpson v. Holli-
day, 1 L. R. Ap. Ca. 315.
(u) Simpson v. Holliday, ib.
(x) Minter v. Mower, 1 Webs. 138;
Derosne v. Fairie, ib. 157.
(y) Simpson v. Holliday, 13 W. R.
577.
(z) Patent Type Founding Co. v.
Richard, John. 381.

the specification does not ascertain and define the particular improvement, or the new arrangement or combination, which the patentee claims, but appears upon a fair reading to claim the whole and each particular part, the patent is void, if any particular part turns out to be old, or the combination itself proves to be not new (a). A claim, however, is not essential to a specification: that which appears to be part of the invention will be protected, although there be no express claim. A patent for an entire combination gives protection to each part that is new and material, without any express claim of particular parts (b). If an invention is partly original and partly communicated from a foreign country, the part communicated from the foreign country ought to be defined in the specification (c). Drawings or figures lodged with the specification may be so referred to as to be embodied in the description of the article claimed, and as to limit the claim or explain an ambiguity in a specification (d).

18. The specification constitutes no part of the patent itself, but must be read as if incorporated with it. If there be a material variance between the invention as specified and as described in the letters-patent, or if the patentee specifies for a more extensive and a different patent from that which has been granted, the patent is void (e). The novelty of every part of an invention * being the consideration on   * 422 which a patent is granted, the consideration fails and the patent is vitiated, if any part of that which is claimed as a new invention be not in fact new (f).

(a) Boulton v. Bull, 2 H. Bl. 463, 482; Harmer v. Plane, 14 Ves. 130; Hill v. Thompson, 3 Mer. 629, 8 Taunt. 375; M'Farlane v. Price, 1 Stark. 199; Carpenter v. Smith, 9 M. & W. 300; Kay v. Marshall, 8 Cl. & Fin. 245; Nickels v. Ross, 8 C. B. 679; Templeton v. M'Farlane, 1 H. L. 595; Holmes v. London and North Western Railway Co., 12 C. B. 831; Tetley v. Easton, 2 C. B. N. S. 706; Bush v. Fox, 5 H. L. 707.

(b) Lister v. Leather, 8 E. & B. 1004.
(c) Renard v. Levinstein, 10 L. T. N. S. 177.
(d) Hastings v. Brown, 1 E. & B. 454; Morton v. Middleton, 1 Dec. of Ct. of Sess., 3d series, p. 718.

(e) Hornblower v. Boulton, 8 T R. 95; Hill v. Thompson, 3 Mer. 629; Rex v. Metcalf, 2 Stark. 249; Crossley v. Beverley, 9 B. & C. 62, Morgan v. Seaward, 2 M. & W 544. Rex v. Wheeler, 2 B. & Ald. 345. Nickels v. Haslam, 7 M. & G. 378; Cook v. Pearce, 8 Q. B. 1044; Croll v. Edge, 9 C. B. 479; Oxley v. Holden, 8 C. B. N. S. 666.

(f) Hill v. Thompson, 3 Mer. 628, 8 Taunt. 375. Brunton v. Hawkes, 4 B. & Ald. 541; Morgan v. Seaward, 2 M. & W. 544; Kay v. Marshall, 8 Cl. & Fin. 245; Dobbs v. Penn, 3 Exch. 427; Holmes v. London and North Western Railway Co., 12 C. B. 831; Brook v. Aston, E. & B. 478.

19. The specification of a patent is required by a proviso in every grant to be enrolled in the court of chancery within a certain time. If it be not enrolled within the prescribed time, the patent is void. But a patent which has become void by non-enrolment within the prescribed time may be confirmed by statute. If a patent be confirmed unconditionally, a person who has taken out a patent for the same invention, after the avoidance, but before confirmation, will be precluded after confirmation from using his patent (*g*).

20. The provisional specification must describe generally and fairly the nature of the invention, but need not enter into all the minute details as to the manner in which the invention is to be carried into effect, which the complete specification is required to do (*h*). The complete specification must in all material matters agree with the provisional specification. No material addition or alteration ought to be made by which the nature of the invention as described in the complete specification can become in a material point different from the nature of the invention as described in the provisional specification (*i*). It is not competent to an inventor to pray in aid the provisional specification in order to explain or enlarge the meaning of the complete specification (*j*). The complete specification need not, however, extend to every thing included in the provisional specification (*k*). Any part of the provisional specification of a patent may be omitted in the complete specification, * 423 if there is no fraud, and the effect of * the remainder is not altered by the omission (*l*). In determining the priority of a patent, the filing of the provisional specification is the date of the patent (*m*).

21. The title of a patent must give a true idea, as far as it goes, of the nature of the invention, and should not include any thing more than what the patentee has actually invented (*n*). A variance between the invention as specified and as described

(*g*) Stead *v.* Carey, 1 C. B. 496.
(*h*) *Re* Newall and Elliott, 4 C. B. N. S. 269 ; Penn *v.* Bibby, 2 L. R. Ch. Ap. 127.   See 15 & 16 Vict. c. 83, ss. 6, 8, 9.
(*i*) Foxwell *v.* Bostock, 10 L. T. N. S. 144, 3 N. R. 546 ; Penn *v.* Bibby, 2 L. R. Ch. Ap. 127.   See Newall *v.* Elliott, 10 Jur. N. S. 954.

(*j*) Mackclean *v.* Rennie, 13 C. B. N. S. 52.
(*k*) Penn *v.* Bibby, 2 L. R. Ch. Ap. 127.
(*l*) Thomas *v.* Welch, 1 L. R. C. P. 192.
(*m*) Smith *v.* Davidson, 19 Dec. of Ct. of Sess., 2d series, p. 691.
(*n*) Sturz *v.* De la Rue, 5 Russ. 322.

is fatal to the patent, but if the title is not inconsistent with the specification, and no fraud is practised on the Crown or the subject, it is not a fatal objection that the title is so general as to be capable of comprising a different invention from that for which the patent is claimed (*o*). The specification may be referred to for the purpose of explaining the title of the patent (*p*). An ambiguous title will not vitiate a patent if the ambiguity is explained by the specification (*q*). The claim made in the specification will be construed with reference to the title (*r*).

22. Until entry of registration the original patentee is to be deemed and taken to be the sole and exclusive proprietor of the patent (*s*). The registration of a patent will complete an inchoate title. When the executors of a patentee assigned the patent and registered the assignment, but the probate of the will was not registered until afterwards, the title was held good (*t*).

23. The entirety, or a part, or share in a patent is assignable (*u*). The assignee takes the legal interest, and is not to be considered merely as a licensee. In the case of a patent belonging to several persons in common, each co-owner may assign his share, * and sue for an infringement with   * 424 out joining the other co-owners (*x*), and can also work the patent for his own benefit, and give, it would seem, licenses to work it (*y*). As between assignor and assignee, the former cannot be heard to say as against the latter that the patent is invalid (*z*).

24. A mere license to use a patent conveys no interest in the patent : it is an excuse for an infringement and nothing more (*a*).

(*o*) Cook *v.* Pearce, 8 Q. B. 1044; Sturz *v.* De la Rue, 5 Russ. 322; Nickels *v.* Haslam, 7 M. & G. 378; Neilson *v.* Harford, 8 M. & W. 806 ; Beard *v.* Egerton, 8 C. B. 165 ; Croll *v.* Edge, 9 C. B. 479 ; Stead *v.* Williams, 2 Webs. 137.

(*p*) Sturz *v.* De la Rue, 5 Russ. 322.

(*q*) Neilson *v.* Harford, 8 M. & W. 806.

(*r*) Oxley *v.* Holden, 8 C. B. N. S. 666.

(*s*) 15 & 16 Vict. c. 83, s. 35.

(*t*) Ellwood *v.* Christy, 18 C. B. N.

S. 494. See 15 & 16 Vict. c. 83, s. 35.

(*u*) 15 & 16 Vict. c. 83, s. 35.

(*x*) Dunnicliff *v.* Mallett, 7 C. B. N. S. 209 ; Walton *v.* Lavater, 8 C. B. N. S. 162. See Smith *v.* North Western Railway Co., 2 E. & B. 69.

(*y*) Mathers *v.* Green, 1 L. R. Ch. Ap. 29.

(*z*) Walton *v.* Lavater, 8 C. B. N. S. 162; Chambers *v.* Crichley, 33 Beav. 374.

(*a*) Bower *v.* Hodges, 13 C. B. 774, *per* Maule, J. See Lister *v.* Leather, 8 E. & B. 1004.

A mere licensee cannot sue for an infringement of the patent (*b*), but an exclusive licensee has a right to sue in the name of the patentee (*c*). A license to use a patent is in many respects analogous to a lease. As between a licensee and a patentee, a patentee who has assigned his interest in a patent, and has subsequently infringed the patent, is estopped from denying his title to convey (*d*). Past payments are irrecoverable, though the patent proves invalid (*e*) ; but future payments may be repudiated (*f*). A licensee is estopped from denying the validity of a patent during the continuance of the license (*g*), but an agreement to purchase a license will not in equity preclude a man from denying the validity of the patent (*h*) ; nor is a man who, upon an action for the infringement of a patent being brought against him, gave judgment by consent before declaration filed, and took a license to use the patent for a term, precluded after the expiration of the term either by the

* 425   license or the * judgment at law from denying the validity of the patent (*i*). Upon questions relating to the determination of a license by breach of covenant, the analogy to a lease prevails (*k*). A license to a man to manufacture a patent article is an authority to his vendee to vend it without the consent of the patentee (*l*).

25. The grantee or assignee of a patent is empowered by statute to enter a disclaimer or memorandum of alteration of part of the title or specification-(*m*). " The spirit of the act," said Maule, J., in Reg. *v.* Mill (*n*), " is this : that where there are objections that go only to a small and insignificant part of a patent, which if sustained would defeat it altogether, the patentee might relieve himself of the difficulty by a disclaimer."

(*b*) Derosne *v.* Fairie, 1 Webs. 154.
(*c*) Renard *v.* Levinstein, 2 H. & M. 628.
(*d*) Oldham *v.* Langmead, 1 Webs. 291.
(*e*) Taylor *v.* Hare, 1 B. & P. 260.
(*f*) Hayne *v.* Maltby, 3 T. R. 438; Pidding *v.* Franks, 1 Mac. & G. 56; Turner on Pat. 70.
(*g*) Bowman *v.* Taylor, 2 A. & E. 278; Baird *v.* Neilson, 8 Cl. & Fin. 726 ; Lawes *v.* Purser, 6 E. & B. 930; Hall *v.* Conder, 2 C. B. N. S. 22; Noton *v.* Brooks, 7 H. & N. 499; Grover and Baker Sewing Machine Co. *v.* Millard,

8 Jur. N. S. 713 ; Crossley *v.* Dixon, 10 H. L. 293. Comp. Haddan *v.* Smith, 16 Sim. 43 ; Trotman *v.* Wood, 16 C. B. N. S. 479.
(*h*) Pidding *v.* Franks, 1 Mac. & G. 45 ; Baxter *v.* Combe, 1 Ir. Ch. 284.
(*i*) Goucher *v.* Clayton, 34 L. J. Ch. 239.
(*k*) Warwick *v.* Hooper, 3 Mac. & G. 60.
(*l*) Thomas *v.* Hunt, 17 C. B. N. S. 183.
(*m*) 5 & 6 Will. 4, c. 83, 7 & 8 Vict. c. 69, s. 5, 15 & 16 Vict. c. 83, s. 39.
(*n*) 10 C. B. 379, 395.

The effect of a disclaimer is to strike out from the specification those parts which are disclaimed (o). A disclaimer when filed and enrolled is to be deemed and taken as part of the patent and specification (p), and operates as such as from the date of the original grant (q). The question whether a manufacture is or is not new within the statute must be judged upon the specification as reduced by the disclaimer (r). If the description contained in the specification as amended by the disclaimer does not amount to a new manufacture, there is no patent (s). The act requires a statement of the reasons for making the disclaimer (t).

26. A disclaimer is bad which seeks in effect to extend the specification, or to convert a bad specification into a good one by adding words. The patent must not be made by the operation of the disclaimer to include or comprehend something which was not originally contained in it. The invention claimed may be diminished or reduced, but must not be extended or enlarged, and the invention which remains after the disclaimer * must have been comprised in the original   * 426 specification (u). All the claiming clauses may be struck out of the specification by a disclaimer, if there remains in the body of the specification words sufficiently distinguishing what the invention is which the patentee claims (x). A thing may be disclaimed which leaves untouched a description which is in itself perfect, but a man cannot, under color of disclaiming, convert a bad specification into a good one by adding words that would convert a barren and unprofitable generality into a specific and definite and practical description, or convert that which, upon the description, is not applicable to any one definite form into a description applicable to a specific and definite mode of proceeding (y). The object of the act authorizing disclaimers is, that if there is in the specification a

(o) Tetley v. Easton, 2 C. B. N. S. 706.
(p) 5 & 6 Will. 4, c. 83, s. 1.
(q) Reg. v. Mill, 10 C. B. 379. Comp. Perry v. Skinner, 2 M. & W. 471; but see 15 & 16 Vict. c. 83, s. 39 ; see, also, Stocker v. Warner, 1 C. B. 148.
(r) Ralston v. Smith, 11 H. L. 223.
(s) Ib.

(t) 5 & 6 Will. 4, c. 83.
(u) Seed v. Higgins, 8 E. & B. 756, 8 H. L. 550; Foxwell v. Bostock, 10 L. T. N. S. 144.
(x) Thomas v. Welch, 1 L. R. C. P. 192.
(y) Ralston v. Smith, 11 H. L. 223. See Seed v. Higgins, 8 E. &. B. 755, 8 H. L. 550.

sufficient and good description of a useful invention, and that description is imperilled or hazarded by something being annexed to it which is capable of being severed, leaving the original description in its integrity good and sufficient without the necessity of addition, a patentee may, by the operation of the disclaimer, lop off the vicious matter, and leave the original invention as described in the specification untainted and uninjured by that vicious excess. But the statute did not contemplate that a patentee should have the power under the form of a disclaimer, of making material additions to the original specification, so as by the aid of the corrected form of words, and the additions so made, to introduce into the specification an accurate and perfect description of an invention which cannot be found in the original specification (z). It may, however, sometimes happen, that where something is cut out some few additions may be required to render intelligible that which remains, and to that extent there would be authority by the statute to make slight additions (a). What is to be the consequence if the disclaimer extends the right granted by the patent is not stated in the Statute 5 & 6 Will. c. 83. * 427 Probably * it may be held that the disclaimer is inoperative for the excess, where the wrong is clearly distinguishable, and not that it should be void for all purposes (b). A patentee may enter a disclaimer after he has assigned all his interest in the patent (c).

27. A patentee is not understood necessarily to claim every thing as new which he does not disclaim. It is enough if the extent of the claim be intelligible upon a fair reading of the document. Parts which manifestly form no part of the invention need not be disclaimed. (d).

28. The construction of a specification, as the construction of all other written instruments, belongs to the court, but the explanation of technical terms of art, or phrases used in commerce, are questions of fact upon which it is the province of a

(z) Ralston v. Smith, 11 H. L. 243, 244, per Lord Westbury.
(a) Ib. See Thomas v. Welch, 1 L. R. C. P. 192.
(b) Foxwell v. Bostock, 10 L. T. N. S. 144, per Lord Westbury.

(c) Wallington v. Dale, 7 Exch. 888.
(d) Lister v. Leather, 8 E. & B. 1004; Morton v. Middleton, 1 Dec. of Ct. of Sess., 3d series, p. 718. See Daw v. Eley, 3 L. R. Eq. 496.

jury to decide (e). If a specification contains no expressions
of art and commerce, but is expressed in plain and ordinary
language, so that the judge is sure he understands their
meaning, the construction of the specification is a pure question of law for the court. But if the specification contains
expressions of art and commerce, the explanation of such
terms is a question of fact for the jury, and it is for the court
to apply according to the rule of law what the jury finds to be
true (f). "The construction of all written instruments,"
said Lord Wensleydale, in Neilson v. Harford (g), "belongs
to the court, whose duty it is to construe all such instruments,
as soon as the true meaning of the words in which they are
couched and the surrounding circumstances, if any, have been
ascertained as facts by a jury; and it is the duty of the jury to
take the construction from the court either absolutely, if there
be no words to be construed, as words of art or phrases used
in commerce, and no surrounding circumstances to be ascertained : or conditionally, where these words or circumstances
are necessarily referred to them " (h). The same rule
applies where the question as to the validity of a * patent   * 428
depends on the comparison of two specifications. If
there are no expressions of art or phrases of commerce in the
specifications, but they are in plain and ordinary language,
the comparison of them is for the court, and the judge is
bound to construe them as he does other written instruments.
But if the specifications contain technical terms of art or
phrases of commerce, the duty of the court is confined to
giving the legal construction of the documents taken independently; but the work of comparing the two instruments
and ascertaining whether the words, as interpreted by the
court and contained in one specification, do or do not denote
the same external matter as the words, as interpreted and explained by the court, contained in the other specification, is a
matter of fact and within the province of a jury and not within
the function of the court (i). Whether or not a specification

(e) Hills v. Evans, 31 L. J. Ch. 459 ;
Betts v. Menzies, 10 H. L. 117.
  (f) Thomas v. Foxwell, 6 Jur. N. S.
271 ; Spencer v. Jack, 11 L. T. N. S.
242.

(g) 8 M. & W. 806.
(h) See Seed v. Higgins, 8 H. L.
565 ; Simpson v. Holliday, 1 L. R. Ch.
Ap. 320.
  (i) Bush v. Fox, 5 H. L. 707 ; Betts

contains a reasonably sufficient description of an invention (*k*), or whether drawings referred to in a specification are intelligible (*l*), is a question of fact for a jury.

29. Specifications are to be construed in a fair and candid spirit. The rules which govern the construction of specifications are the ordinary rules for the interpretation of written instruments. The words of a specification are to be construed according to their ordinary and proper meaning, unless it be shown by something in the context that a different construction ought to be adopted. The court looks at the language in the instrument, and interprets it fairly without any reference to the object of the inquiry. If any expressions are ambiguous, the court will look to the real intention of the patentee ; and if it can do so consistently with the language used, expound the patent favorably to the patentee. But the court will not violate the obvious meaning of the language, unless it is quite clear that the patentee intended something different from that which the expressions indicate (*m*).

*429   30. * To be a subject-matter for a patent privilege, an invention must be useful as well as new (*n*). The law does not look to the degree of utility ; it simply requires that the invention shall be capable of use, and that the use shall be such as sound morals and feelings do not discountenance. It is not necessary to establish that the invention is of such general use as to supersede all other means of accomplishing the same purpose (*o*). It is enough that it has no obnoxious or mischievous tendency, that it may be applied to practical use, and that so far as it is applied it is salutary (*p*). There is no reason indeed to hold that the question of utility is any thing more than a compendious mode introduced in comparatively modern times, of deciding the question whether the

v. Menzies, 10 H. L. 117 ; Thomas *v.* Foxwell, 6 Jur. N. S. 271 ; Hills *v.* Evans, 31 L. J. Ch. 457.

(*k*) Wallington *v.* Dale, 7 Exch. 888 ; Spencer *v.* Jack, 11 L. T. N. S. 242.

(*l*) Morton *v.* Middleton, 1 Dec. of Ct. of Sess., 3d series, p. 718.

(*m*) Palmer *v.* Wagstaffe, 9 Exch. 494 ; Elliott *v.* Turner, 2 C. B. 446 ; Thomas *v.* Foxwell, 6 Jur. N. S. 271. See Sellers *v.* Dickinson, 5 Exch. 312 ; Newton *v.* Grand Junction Railway Co.,

ib. 331 n. ; Betts *v.* Menzies, 10 H. L. 117 ; Simpson *v.* Holliday, 13 W. R. 578, *per* Lord Westbury. See Daw *v.* Eley, 3 L. R. Eq. 496.

(*n*) Manton *v.* Parker, Dav. P. C. 332 ; Bovill *v.* Moore, *ib.* 399 ; Hill *v.* Thompson, 8 Taunt. 375, 3 Mer. 626.

(*o*) Bedford *v.* Hunt, 1 Mass. (Amer.) 304, *per* Story, J. ; Tetley *v.* Easton, Macr. 63, *per* Pollock, C. B.

(*p*) Bedford *v.* Hunt, 1 Mass. (Amer.) 304, *per* Story, J.

patent is void under the statute of monopolies (q). The question of utility is for the jury (r).

SECTION IV.—INFRINGEMENT OF PATENTS.

1. What constitutes infringement.
2. The user of any new or material part of a patent for the purpose of effecting the object or part of the object proposed by the patentee is an infringement.
3 & 4. Patent for combination, how infringed.
5. Making a patented article though no sale is an infringement; so making and exporting to foreign country, or importing and selling here.
6. Intention not to infringe immaterial; so is ignorance.
7. Time covered by letters-patent.
8. Functions of the court and jury on the question as to infringement.
9. Right of patentee to an injunction does not depend on the exclusive privilege, but on the character of the patent as private property.

1. There is an infringement of a patent privilege when a man uses directly or indirectly the invention which is the subject of the privilege, or employs means only colorably different to produce the same result (s). Infringement involves substantial identity with the subject of the privilege. It is a copy of it either without variation, or with such variation as is consistent with its being in substance the same thing. If the invention be a machine, it will be infringed by a machine which incorporates in its structure and operation the substance of the invention, that is, by an arrangement of mechanism which performs * the same service or produces the same   * 430 effect in the same way or substantially the same way (t). The absence of one or more parts does not prevent a machine from being an infringement of another machine, if the two machines are in substance the same, and the principle in both is the same (u). But if a machine operates in a different manner there is no infringement, although the same gen-

---

(q) Morgan v. Seaward, 2 M. & W. 544, per Lord Wensleydale. See Lewis v. Marling, 10 B. & C. 22; Betts v. Walker, 14 Q. B. 363; Stead v. Williams, 2 Webs. 126.

(r) Bloxam v. Else, 1 C. & P. 565; Tetley v. Easton, Macr. 63.

(s) Crossley v. Beverley, 1 Webs. 106; Jupe v. Pratt, ib. 146; Muntz v. Foster, 2 Webs. 93; Stevens v. Keating, ib. 175; Bateman v. Moore, Macr.

102; Patent Type Founding Co. v. Richard, John. 381.

(t) Morgan v. Seaward, 2 M. & W. 544; Walton v. Potter, 1 Webst. 586; Newton v. Grand Junction Railway Co., 5 Exch 331 n.; Sellers v. Dickinson, 5 Exch. 326; Bateman v. Moore, Macr. 102, per Martin, B.; Stead v. Anderson, 4 C. B. 833.

(u) Jones v. Pearce, 1 Webs. 124; Russell v. Cowley, ib. 459.

eral principle be employed to get out the same result in both machines (x). The principle of two machines may be the same, although the forms or proportions may be different. They may substantially employ the same power in the same way, though the substantial mechanism be apparently different; on the other hand, the principle of two machines may be very different, although their external structure may have a great similarity in many respects (y).

2. The user of any new or material part of a patent for the purpose of affecting the object or part of the object proposed by the patentee, is an infringement (z). If the patent be for an entire combination, and part of the combination be new and part be old, the taking of a new or material part for a purpose similar or analogous to that which the patent was intended to effect, is an infringement, although the whole combination be not taken (a). But there is no infringement, although a new and material part may be taken, if it be taken for a different purpose from that for which it is used in * 431 the patent (b). Nor * is there an infringement, if it be taken not for the purpose of producing a profitable matter but for another purpose (c).

3. The patent for an entire combination is not infringed by a different combination for the same object of the same elements, or of equivalents for them, if not a mere colorable evasion or imitation (d). The principle which protects a patentee against the use by others of mechanical equivalents, is inapplicable to a case where the whole invention depends entirely on the particular machinery by means of which a well-known object is attained (e). If the patent be for a

---

(x) Seed v. Higgins, 8 H. L. 550; Bovill v. Pim, 11 Exch. 719; Curtis v. Platt, 11 L. T. N. S. 245, 35 L. J. Ch. 852. See Daw v. Eley, 3 L. R. Eq. 496.

(y) Barrett v. Hall, 1 Mass. (Amer.) 470; M'Cormick v. Talcott, 20 How. (Amer.) 402; Burr v. Duryee, 1 Wall. (Amer.) 531.

(z) Smith v. London and North Western Railway Co., 2 E. & B. 69; Sellers v. Dickinson, 5 Exch. 326; Newton v. Grand Junction Railway Co., ib. 331 n.; Bovill v. Keyworth, 7 E. & B. 728; De

la Rue v. Dickinson, ib. 739; M'Cormick v. Gray, 7 H. & N. 25.

(a) Lister v. Leather, 8 E. & B. 1004; Sellers v. Dickinson, 5 Exch. 312; Thomas v. Foxwell, 5 Jur. N. S. 37.

(b) Newton v. Vaucher, 6 Exch. 859; Thomas v. Foxwell, 5 Jur. N. S. 37; Lister v. Eastwood, 9 L. T. N. S. 766.

(c) Higgs v. Goodwin, El. Bl. & El. 529. See Caldwell v. Vanvlissengen, 9 Ha. 415.

(d) Curtis v. Platt, 11 L. T. N. S. 245, on appeal, 35 L. J. Ch. 852, 1 L. R Ap. Ca. 337. (e) Ib.

combination of two, three, or more old inventions, there is no infringement, unless the whole combination or all the parts of it have been substantially taken (*f*). A patent for a combination of three old inventions is not infringed by the user of any two of those parts only, or of two combined with a third, which is substantially different in form and in the manner of its arrangement and connection with the others, although serving the same purpose (*g*).

4. In Unwin *v.* Heath (*h*), a chemical patent for the use of a known substance described by its specific name, was held not to be infringed by the use of two other equally known substances, which according to the evidence of scientific witnesses, would go to produce the same effect (*i*).

5. The manufacture of a patented article for the purposes of sale, and the offer of it for sale is an infringement of the patent-right, though no sale has been actually effected. So, also, it would appear, is there an infringement, though the article has been made merely as a sample (*k*). The making of part of a patented article, and the exportation of that part to a foreign * country, is an infringement, if the part so made   * 432 and exported is new, and is claimed as new (*l*). So, also, is the sale in this country of a patented article made abroad and imported (*m*). So, also, is the enjoyment in this country of an advantage which is derived from the invention, although there is no intention of selling the article, and although the article is here only for a temporary purpose (*n*). It is sufficient to constitute user of a patented article that the same sort of benefit, however temporary and indirect, has been in fact derived from it as would arise from it in its ordinary use (*o*). There is an infringement, if a foreign vessel lawfully entering one of our ports has, and uses on board, a patented article (*p*). The user, however, on board an English vessel in

(*f*) Smith *v.* London and North Western Railway Co., 2 E. & B. 69; Newall *v.* Elliott, 10 Jur. N. S. 956; Finlay *v.* Allen, 19 Dec. of Ct. of Sess., 2d series, p. 1087.

(*g*) Prouty *v.* Ruggles, 16 Peters (Amer.), 336; Eames *v.* Godfrey, 1 Wall. (Amer.) 78.

(*h*) 5 H. L. 505.

(*i*) See Hills *v.* Liverpool Gas-light Co., 32 L. J. Ch. 28; Stevens *v.* Keating, 2 Webs. 181.

(*k*) Oxley *v.* Holden, 8 C. B. N. S. 666.

(*l*) Goucher *v.* Clayton, 34 L. J. Ch. 239.

(*m*) Wilson *v.* Lavater, 8 C. B. N. S. 162.

(*n*) Betts *v.* Neilson, 3 D. J. & S. 82.

(*o*) Ib.

(*p*) Caldwell *v.* Vanvlissengen, 9 Ha.

29

an English colony, of an article which is the subject of a patent for the United Kingdom, is not an infringement (*q*).

6. The intention not to infringe a patent is immaterial, if there has been an infringement (*r*). Nor is ignorance of the existence of a patent any answer to a charge of infringement (*s*).[1]

7. Letters-patent protect the patentee between the date of the provisional specification and the date of the patent, but the user of the patent by a person who has made the invention contemporaneously with the patentee between the date of the provisional specification and the granting of the patent will not subject him to an action as an infringer. After the granting of the patent, however, a man has no right to interfere with the monopoly of the patentee, although he may have made the discovery contemporaneously with the patentee (*t*).

* 433   8. * Where the question as to the infringement of a patent depends merely on the construction of the specification, it is a pure question of law for the judge; but when it depends on other circumstances, such as the degree of difference or similitude between two processes, it is a mixed question of law and fact. The question of fact is wholly for the jury, and it is for the judge to apply according to the rule of law what the jury finds to be true. This is generally done in summing up the case by the judge, he leaving the necessary facts to the jury, and giving conditionally the necessary directions in point of law. The opinion of scientific witnesses is only admissible in proof of facts. Their opinion as to whether or not there has been an infringement is not admissible (*u*).

415; but see now 15 & 16 Vict. c. 83, s. 26; see, also, Brown *v.* Duchesne, 19 How. (Amer.) 184, where the Supreme Court of the United States disapproved of the principle upon which Caldwell *v.* Vanvlissengen was decided, and declined to follow it as law.

(*q*) Newall *v.* Elliott, 10 Jur. N. S. 954.

(*r*) Heath *v.* Unwin, 15 Sim. 552; Stead *v.* Anderson, 4 C. B. 813; Unwin *v.* Heath, 5 H. L. 505; but see Stevens *v.* Keating, 2 Webs. 188.

(*s*) Curtis *v.* Platt, 11 L. T. N. S. 245. See Wilson *v.* Lavater, 8 C. B. N. S.

162; Nunn *v.* D'Albuquerque, 34 Beav. 595.

(*t*) Smith *v.* Davidson, 19 Dec. of Ct. of Sess., 2d series, p. 691.

(*u*) Seed *v.* Higgins, 8 H. L. 550. See Sellers *v.* Dickinson, 5 Exch. 323; Lister *v.* Leather, 8 E. & B. 1004.

[1] A bill will lie for an injunction, if the patent-right is admitted, or has been established, upon well-grounded proof of an apprehended intention of the defendant to violate the patent-right. A bill *quia timet* is an ordinary remedial process in equity. Story, J., Woodworth *v.* Stone, 3 Story, 752. See,

9. The right of a patentee to an injunction originates in the character of the patent as private property, and not in the mere exclusive privilege. A patent therefore to keep a theatre, which is a mere privilege granted to the party, gives him no right to an injunction against other parties who are infringing the law by keeping theatres without license (*v*).

SECTION V. — INSPECTION. — ACCOUNT. — DAMAGES, ETC.

1. When an inspection will be allowed.
2. Defendant may be ordered to deliver up samples for analysis.
3. Effect of laches.
4. Jurisdiction to order inspection enforced on courts of common law by statute.
5. When perpetual injunction is sought.
6. Right to account incident to right to injunction.
7. Right of tenant in common in patent.
8. Account how made up.
9. Unreasonable delay in application for account, fatal.
10. When account was only part of an agreement which the court could not wholly enforce it did not interfere.
11. Statute provision as to inquiry as to damages.
12. Discovery for the purposes of the account or inquiry as to damages.
13. Other relief which will be granted.
14. Account at common law by statute.
15 & 16. Costs of injunction allowed to complainant.

1. The owner of a patent is often unable to obtain clear and satisfactory proof that his patent is being infringed, though he may have fair presumptive evidence of the fact. In such cases a court of equity will, upon a fair *primâ facie* case being made out, order the defendant to permit an inspection to be made of his premises and machinery by proper persons named on behalf of the plaintiff (*x*). The order will not go to direct the alleged infringer to allow an inspection of all machines in his stock, but will direct * him to verify on affidavit the *434 several kinds of machines that he has sold or exposed for sale, and to produce one machine of each class for inspec-

also, Poppenhusen *v.* N. Y. G. P. Comb. Co., 4 Blatchf. 184.
(*v*) Calcraft *v.* West, 2 J. & L. 123.
(*x*) Morgan *v.* Seaward, 1 Webs. 169; Russell *v.* Cowley, *ib.* 458; Bovill *v.* Moore, 2 Coo. C. C. 56, n.; Amies *v.*

Kelsey, 22 L. J. Q. B. 84; Bennitt *v.* Whitehouse, 28 Beav. 121. See, as to the form of the order, Davenport *v.* Jepson, 1 N. R. 308. See further, as to inspection, *supra*, p. 328.

tion (*y*). An inspection will not be ordered unless it is material and really wanted for the purposes of the cause (*z*). If, however, a fair *primâ facie* case be made out, and an inspection is material for the purposes of the cause, the mere assertion of the defendant that there is no infringement goes for nothing. He must swear positively that injury will be done to him by his being compelled to submit to the inspection (*a*). The court will not, where it orders inspection, stop short of what is necessary to make the jurisdiction of the court effectual. If the defendant refuses to permit inspection, the court will then have to consider what ought to be done, whether it will compel inspection, and how. No such order has as yet been made, but the court can find the way to do complete justice (*b*). Where it is necessary, a similar inspection will be ordered to be made of the plaintiff's machinery and premises by persons named on behalf of the defendant (*c*).

2. An order for inspection will be made on interlocutory application (*d*). The court has also jurisdiction, on motion, to order a defendant tó deliver up samples for the purposes of analysis. Thus, where the plaintiffs were the owners of a patent for type-founding, and the defendant was a printer who used types alleged to be colorable imitations of the types patented by the plaintiffs, Wood, V. C., ordered the defendant to deliver up a sample for the purposes of analysis (*e*).

* 435   3. * Laches sufficient to defeat the right to an inter-locutory injunction is no bar to an order in the same matter for inspection or a sample (*f*).

4. The jurisdiction to order an inspection has been conferred on courts of common law by the 15 & 16 Vict. c. 83, s. 42 (*g*).

(*y*) Singer Manufacturing Co. *v.* Wilson, 13 W. R. 560, 5 N. R. 505. See Ellwood *v.* Christy, 18 C. B. N. S. 494.

(*z*) Amies *v.* Kelsey, 22 L. J. Q. B. 84; Shaw *v.* Bank of England, *ib.* Ex. 26, 210; Meadows *v.* Kirkman, 29 L. J. Ex. 205.

(*a*) Bennitt *v.* Whitehouse, 28 Beav. 121; *supra*, p. 328.

(*b*) East India Co. *v.* Kynaston, 3 Bligh, 153; Patent Type Founding Co. *v.* Walter, John. 727.

(*c*) Russell *v.* Cowley, 1 Webs. 459; Davenport *v.* Jepson, 1 N. R. 308. See,

as to the form of the order, Davenport *v.* Jepson, *ib.*

(*d*) Ennor *v.* Barwell, 1 D. F. & J. 529. See further, as to practice in cases of inspection, *supra*, p. 328.

(*e*) Patent Type Founding Co. *v.* Walter, John. 727. Comp. Patent Type Founding Co. *v.* Lloyd, 5 H. & N. 192. See, for a form of the order, Davenport *v.* Jepson, 1 N. R. 308.

(*f*) Patent Type Founding Co. *v.* Walter, John. 730.

(*g*) See Vidi *v.* Smith, 3 E. & B 969; Shaw *v.* Bank of England, 22 L. J.

A court of common law is not, it would appear, empowered by the clause to order a sample to be delivered up for the purposes of analysis (*h*).

5. Suits for an injunction to restrain the violation of patent-rights do not usually go to the hearing. If the interlocutory injunction is submitted to by the defendant, the plaintiff is generally satisfied with the submission, and feels himself sufficiently protected; but he may, if he pleases, bring the cause to a hearing, and is entitled to a perpetual injunction. He does not, however, usually bring the suit to a hearing unless he seeks an account, or unless the defendant denies him some other relief to which he is entitled (*i*).

6. The right to an account of profits in respect of articles manufactured or sold in violation of a patent privilege is incident to the right to an injunction to restrain future infringements. There can be no account if the case for an injunction fails, or if at the hearing there is nothing on which an injunction can operate (*k*). The rule applies even although it may appear that since the notice for an interim injunction the defendant has sold articles which the court would, upon that application, have restrained him from selling, had the facts and the law been at that time sufficiently ascertained (*l*).[1]

7. A tenant in common of a patent may work it for his own

Exch. 26, 210; Meadows *v.* Kirkman, 29 L. J. Ex. 205; Ellwood *v.* Christy, 18 C. B. N. S. 494.

(*h*) Patent Type Founding Co. *v.* Walter, 5 H. & N. 201.

(*i*) *Supra*, p. 227, 228.

(*k*) Baily *v.* Taylor, 1 R. & M. 73; Smith *v.* London and South Western Railway Co., Kay, 415; Price's Patent Candle Co. *v.* Bauwen's Candle Co., 4 K. & J. 727.

(*l*) Price's Patent Candle Co. *v.* Bauwen's Candle Co., 4 K. & J. 727.

[1] By the Act of Congress of July 8th, 1870, s. 55, it is provided, that in cases in equity "the claimant shall be entitled to recover, in addition to the profits to be accounted for by the defendant, the damages the complainant has sustained thereby, and the court shall assess the same or cause the same to be assessed under its direction, and the court shall have the same powers to increase the same in its discretion, that are given by

this act to increase the damages found by verdicts in actions upon the case, but all actions shall be brought during the term for which the letters-patent shall be granted or extended, or within six years after the expiration thereof." The power to increase the damages in actions on the case as provided in s. 59, same act, is that the court may enter judgment on the verdict for any sum above the amount found by the verdict as the actual damages sustained, according to the circumstances of the case, not exceeding three times the amount of such verdict, together with the costs. In Livingston *v.* Woodworth, 15 Howard, U. S. 546, it is held that in a suit in equity for an injunction and account of profits of a patented machine, the defendant is accountable only for what profits he actually made, not for what, by diligence and skill, he might have received. To same point, Dean *v.* Mason, 20 Howard, 198.

use, and keep what he can get, and is not liable to account to the other co-owners (*m*).[1]

* 436   8. * The account is of all the profits which the defendant has actually made by the infringement of the patent for six years prior to the filing of the bill (*n*). If the plaintiff be the assignee of a patent the account will only be taken from the date of the registration of the assignment (*o*).

9. There must be no unreasonable delay in making the application for an account. Unreasonable delay, if not satisfactorily accounted for, will be fatal to the application (*p*).

10. In a case where the account was only part of an agreement which the court could not wholly enforce, the court would not interfere, but left the plaintiff to his remedy at law (*q*).

11. An inquiry as to damages in addition to or in substitution for the account may be directed under the Chancery Regulation Act, 21 & 22 Vict. c. 27 (*r*). The plaintiff is entitled not only to an account against the manufacturer, but also to damages against the person using the patent article wherever it be found (*s*). Damages may be awarded under the act, although an injunction cannot be granted in consequence of the expiral of the patent pending the litigation, if it appear that at the time of filing the bill there was a case for an injunction (*t*). If the patentee prefer it, the court will allow him to proceed at law for damages, instead of the account (*u*).

12.' The defendant must, if required to do so for the purpose of the account or the inquiry as to damages, set out the price and profit and names of the purchasers of the patent articles (*v*), and the names and addresses of all persons

* 437   from whom he has * received sums of money in respect of royalties or licenses to use the patent article (*w*).

(*m*) Mathers *v.* Green, 1 L. R. Ch. Ap. 29.

(*n*) Crossley *v.* Derby Gas-light Co., 1 Webs. 119, 120, 4 L. J. Ch. N. S. 25; Ellwood *v.* Christy, 18 C. B. N. S. 494.

(*o*) Ellwood *v.* Christy, 18 C. B. N. S. 494. See, as to form of order for an injunction and account, Betts *v.* De Vitre, 34 L. J. Ch. 289.

(*p*) Crossley *v.* Derby Gas-light Co., 1 Webs. 119, 120, 4 L. J. Ch. N. S. 25.

(*q*) Kernot *v.* Potter, 3 D. F. & J. 447.

(*r*) Betts *v.* De Vitre, 34 L. J. Ch.

289. See Needham *v.* Oxley, 11 W. R. 852. See as to damages, pp. 221–224.

(*s*) Penn *v.* Bibby, 3 L. R. Eq. 308.

(*t*) Davenport *v.* Rylands, 1 L. R. Eq. 302. See Fox *v.* Dellestable, 15 W. R. 194.

(*u*) Hills *v.* Evans, 31 L. J. Ch. 457.

(*v*) Howe *v.* M'Kernan, 30 Beav. 547. See Delarue *v.* Dickinson, 3 K. & J. 388.

(*w*) Crossley *v.* Stewart, 1 N. R. 426, 7 L. T. N. S. 848.

[1] Clum *v.* Brewer, 2 Curtis, C. C. 506.

13. The protection which the court gives to a patentee by injunction is not limited to the prevention of the sale of articles in violation of the patent privilege during the term of the patent, but extends also to the prevention of the sale of articles which have been made during the continuance 'of the patent, after the expiration of the patent (*x*). The court will, if it is desired, grant a certificate in accordance with the 15 & 16 Vict. c. 83, s. 43, that the validity of the patent has come in question and has been determined in favor of the plaintiff (*y*). All articles in possession of the defendant made in violation of the patent may be ordered to be delivered up (*z*) or destroyed (*a*). But where a patent for a combination of machinery only has been infringed, the court will not order the machines to be broken, but will order them to be marked (*b*).

14. By the Patent Law Amendment Act, 15 & 16 Vict. c. 83, s. 42, courts of common law have been empowered to order an account in patent cases (*c*).

15. A man whose patent-right has been infringed is not bound to rest satisfied with the promise of the defendant not to commit any further infringement, but he has a right to have an injunction (*d*), and is entitled to the costs of the injunction (*e*).

16. The 43d section of the Patent Law Amendment Act, 15 & 16 Vict. c. 83, which empowers the court, at its discretion, to order the defendants to pay the costs of the plaintiff as between solicitor and client, does not apply to the costs of the first * trial (*f*). When the court considers the   * 438 plaintiff entitled to full costs as between solicitor and client, the decree or order should contain an express direction that the costs be so taxed (*g*).

(*x*) Crossley *v.* Beverley, 1 R. & M. 166, n. See Price's Patent Candle Co. *v.* Bauwen's Candle Co., 4 K. & J. 731.

(*y*) Needham *v.* Oxley, 2 N. R. 388, 11 W. R. 852.

(*z*) Tangye *v.* Stott, 14 W. R. 386. (*a*) Betts *v.* De Vitre, 34 L. J. Ch. 289.

(*b*) Needham *v.* Oxley, 11 W. R. 852. (*c*) See Holland *v.* Fox, 3 E. & B. 983; Vidi *v.* Smith, *ib.* 969; Lister *v.* Eastwood, 3 Comm. L. 1249; Ellwood *v.* Christy, 18 C. B. N. S. 494.

(*d*) Losh *v.* Hague, 1 Webs. 200, 2 Coo. C. C. 59, n.; Geary *v.* Norton, 1 De G. & S. 9.

(*e*) Geary *v.* Norton, 1 De G. & S. 9. See, as to costs of the motion, *supra*, pp. 214–216. See, as to costs of suit, *supra*, pp. 228, 229.

(*f*) Davenport *v.* Rylands, 1 L. R. Eq. 308; Penn *v.* Bibby, 3 *ib.* 308.

(*g*) Lister *v.* Leather, 4 K. & J. 425.

* 439   * CHAPTER XX.

INJUNCTIONS AGAINST THE INFRINGEMENT OF COPYRIGHT.

SECTION I. — PRINCIPLES ON WHICH THE COURT RESTRAINS
THE INFRINGEMENT OF COPYRIGHT.

1. Principles upon which court proceeds in granting injunction to restrain violation of copyright.
2. Pleading and affidavit.
3. Parties.
4. Delay and acquiescence.
5. Conduct of plaintiff.
6. Practice of the court in dealing with the application.
7. Waiver of penalties.
8. Extent of the injunction.
9. If pirated matter can be separated, injunction will issue only as to that.
10. Injunction not granted against whole of a book until quantity of pirated matter is ascertained.
11. Fraudulent intent not material if there has been an invasion of the right, but in doubtful cases intent material.
12. Defendant not allowed to sell copies except upon consent.

1. THE jurisdiction of courts of equity in restraining by interlocutory injunction the violation of copyright is in aid of the legal right, and is founded upon the necessity of protecting the property from irreparable damage pending the trial of the right (a).[1] The court proceeds on the assumption that the

---

(a) Saunders v. Smith, 3 M. & C. 728.

[1] The circuit courts of the United States, and any district court having the jurisdiction of a circuit court, have power upon a bill in equity filed by any party aggrieved, to grant injunctions to prevent the violation of any right secured by the copyright laws of the United States, according to the course and principles of courts of equity, on such terms as the court may deem reasonable. Act of Congress of July 8th, 1870, s. 106. At common law an author has a right to his unpublished manuscripts the same as to any other property he may possess. Little v. Hall, 18 How. U. S. 170; Wheaton v. Peters, 8 Peters, U. S. 591. And the ninth section of the act of July 8th, 1870, provides that any person who shall print or publish any manuscript whatever, without the consent of the author or proprietor first obtained (if such author or proprietor be a citizen of the United States, or resident therein), shall be liable to said author or proprietor for all damages occasioned by such injury, to be recovered by action on the case in any court of competent jurisdiction. As to what publication before copyright is taken out will render such copyright invalid, see Keene v. Wheatley, 9 Amer. Law Reg. 33.

person who makes the application has the right which he asserts, but needs the aid of the court for the purpose of protecting his property from damage pending the trial of the right (b). He is not required to make out a clear legal title. All that the court requires is that a case may be made out presenting a fair *primâ facie* title, whether legal or equitable, or a clear color of title with assertion of right (c).[1] An equitable interest, limited in point of time or extent, is sufficient (d).[2] But a mere agent to sell has not such a real interest in a work as will entitle him to relief (e). Where the plaintiff states circumstances showing a good equitable title, the court will, for the purpose of determining the fact of piracy, order the defendant to admit the legal title of the plaintiff (f).

2. If the author of the book is himself the plaintiff, he should *allege in his bill, or the affidavit accom-   * 440 panying it, his title by authorship. If the book, or an edition of the work containing new matter, has been published since 5 & 6 Vict. c. 45, he must show that the book, or the edition of the book which he seeks to protect, has been duly registered at Stationers' Hall (g). In the case of books published before that act, this is not necessary (h). If the plaintiff claims as assignee, he must by affidavit or otherwise show that the assignment to him has been in writing (i). He must make a particular title: it is not enough to say that he acquired the copyright, but he must trace his title to the author (k). But if he happens to be in the situation of assignee of an assignee, it is sufficient for him to show that the assignment to himself was in writing without tracing the title through the mesne assignees from the author. If he does

(b) Ib., supra, p. 196.
(c) Universities of Oxford and Cambridge v. Richardson, 6 Ves. 689 ; Mawman v. Tegg, 2 Russ. 391 ; Sheriff v. Coates, 1 R. & M. 167 ; Colburn v. Duncombe, 9 Sim. 151 ; Chappell v. Purday, 4 Y. & C. 485 ; Bohn v. Bogue, 10 Jur. 420.
(d) Sweet v. Cator, 11 Sim. 572.
(e) Nichol v. Stockdale, 3 Sw. 687.
(f) Sweet v. Shaw, 8 L. J. N. S. Ch. 216 ; Sweet v. Cator, 11 Sim. 572 ; Dickens v. Lee, 8 Jur. 183 ; Bohn v. Bogue, 10 Jur. 420. See, as to admissions, supra, p. 213.

(g) Sect. 24.
(h) Murray v. Bogue, 1 Drew. 353.
(i) Morris v. Kelly, 1 J. & W. 481. See Rundell v. Murray, Jac. 311.
(k) Gilliver v. Snaggs, 2 Eq. Ca. Ab. 522 ; Morris v. Kelly, 1 J. & W. 481.
[1] If there are reasonable doubts as to the validity of plaintiff's title, he will be required to try his title at law, and the injunction refused. Miller v. McElroy, 1 Amer. Law Reg. 205.
[2] Pierpont v. Fowle, 2 Wood. & M. 39 ; Little v. Gould, 2 Blatchf. 181.

so, the proof of want of title will be thrown on the defendant (*l*). It is not necessary that the plaintiff should specify
either in his bill or affidavits the parts of his work which have
been pirated. It is sufficient to allege generally that the work
of the defendant contains several passages which have been
pirated, and to verify them by affidavit (*m*).

3. If the plaintiff has merely an equitable title, the party in
possession of the legal title should be made a party (*n*). If
there has been a complete legal assignment, the assignor
should not be made a party (*o*). One suit cannot be maintained against several persons for distinct invasions of copyright (*p*).

4. A man who seeks the aid of the court for the protection
of his copyright from violation must show due diligence in
coming to the court. Delay or acquiescence will be
* 441   fatal to the application, * unless it can be satisfactorily
accounted for (*q*).[1] If the conduct of the party complaining has led to the state of things that occasions the application, he cannot have relief (*r*).[2] The doctrine applies not
only to the cases of his conduct towards the particular person
with whom the controversy subsists, but also to cases where
his conduct with others may influence the court in the exercise of its equitable jurisdiction (*s*). According to 5 & 6 Vict.
c. 45, s. 26, all suits and bills must be commenced within
twelve months of the offence.

5. The interference of the court by injunction being founded
on pure equitable principles, a man who comes to the court
must be able to show that his own conduct in the transaction
has been consistent with equity. A book accordingly which is
itself piratical cannot be protected from invasion (*t*): nor will

---

(*l*) Morris *v.* Kelly, 1 J. & W. 481.
(*m*) Sweet *v.* Maugham, 11 Sim. 51;
Hotten *v.* Arthur, 1 H. & M. 603.
(*n*) Colburn *v.* Duncombe, 9 Sim.
151.
(*o*) Sweet *v.* Maugham, 11 Sim. 51;
supra, p. 207.
(*p*) Dilly *v.* Doig, 2 Ves. Jr. 486.
See Hudson *v.* Maddison, 12 Sim. 416.
See further, as to parties, *supra*, pp. 207,
208.
(*q*) Mawman *v.* Tegg, 2 Russ. 393;
Baily *v.* Taylor, Taml. 295, 1 R. & M.

73; Campbell *v.* Scott, 11 Sim. 31;
Buxton *v.* James, 5 De G. & S. 84;
Tinsley *v.* Lacy, 1 H. & M. 747; *supra*,
pp. 201, 202.
(*r*) Rundell *v.* Murray, Jac. 311;
Saunders *v.* Smith, 3 M. & C. 711.
(*s*) Platt *v.* Button, 19 Ves. 447;
Rundell *v.* Murray, Jac. 311; Campbell
v. Scott, 11 Sim. 31.
(*t*) Cary *v.* Faden, 5 Ves. 24.
[1] See Webb *v.* Powers, 2 Wood. &
M. 521.
[2] Heine *v.* Appleton, 4 Blatchf. 125.

the court protect by injunction a work which is of an immoral, indecent, seditious, libellous, or irreligious nature (*u*).

6. If the court is satisfied that the alleged title is good, and that there has been a piracy, it may interfere at once, and restrain the piracy *simpliciter* by injunction; but this course will not be adopted except where the title and the fact of its violation are clearly made out. If the title is not clear, or the fact of its violation is denied, the course of the court is either to grant the injunction pending the trial of the legal right, or to direct the motion to stand over until the hearing, on the terms of the defendant keeping an account. Which of these alternations shall be adopted depends on the discretion of the court, according to the case made out (*x*). If irreparable damage would be caused to the property of the plaintiff by the refusal of the court to interfere, the injunction will be granted (*y*). If, * on the other hand, an injunction   * 442 would be an extreme hardship on the defendant as compared with the inconvenience to which the plaintiff would be put by being required in the first instance to establish his legal right, the other alternative will be adopted (*z*). Where the work is of a transitory or ephemeral character, greater caution is necessary in exercising the jurisdiction than when the book is of a more permanent character (*a*).

7. Where penalties are imposed by the Copyright Act, a man who seeks equitable relief will be required by the court, as a condition of its assistance, to waive the penalty or forfeiture (*b*).

8. If a case has been made out for an injunction, the court has also to determine whether the injunction shall be against the whole work or only against a part of it. The extent to which the injunction ought to go must depend in each case

---

(*u*) Southey *v.* Sherwood, 2 Mer. 435; Lawrence *v.* Smith, Jac. 471; *supra*, p. 186.

(*x*) Wilkins *v.* Aikin, 17 Ves. 424; Rundell *v.* Murray, Jac. 311; Sheriff *v.* Coates, 1 R. & M. 159; Bramhall *v.* Melcomb, 3 M. & C. 739; *supra*, p. 209.

(*y*) Sweet *v.* Shaw, 8 L. J. Ch. N. S. 216; Dickens *v.* Lee, 8 Jur. 185.

(*z*) Saunders *v.* Smith, 3 M. & C. 737; Bramhall *v.* Melcomb, *ib.* 739; Spottis-

wode *v.* Clark, 2 Ph. 157; M'Neil *v.* Williams, 11 Jur. 344; *supra*, pp. 209, 210.

(*a*) Matthewson *v.* Stockdale, 12 Ves. 275, *per* Lord Eldon; Spottiswode *v.* Clark, 2 Ph. 154, *per* Lord Cottenham. See Ainsworth *v.* Bentley, 14 W. R. 630. Comp. Ingram *v.* Stiff, John. 220, n.

(*b*) Colburn *v.* Simms, 2 Ha. 554. See Geary *v.* Norton, 1 De G. & S. 9.

upon the extent of the piracy and the nature of the work (*c*). If the pirated matter is considerable in amount, and is so intermixed with the original matter that it cannot be separated, the injunction will go against the whole work generally (*d*). Notwithstanding that the effect may be to destroy altogether the use and value of the original matter, the court will not refrain from granting an injunction. "If," said Lord Eldon (*e*), "the parts which have been copied cannot be separated from those which are original without destroying the use and value of the original matter, he who has made an improper use of that which did not belong to him must abide the consequence of so doing. If a man mixes up what belongs to him with what belongs to another, and the mixture be forbidden by law, he must again separate them, and he must bear all the *443 mischief and loss which the separation *may occasion.

If an individual chooses in any way to mix my literary work with his own, he must be restrained from publishing the literary work which belongs to me; and if the parts of the work cannot be separated, and if by that means the injunction which restrained the publication prevents also the publication of his literary matter, he has only himself to blame" (*f*). If, however, the pirated matter is not considerable in quantity or of much value in quality, or if, though considerable in value, it is very small in quantity, and quite out of proportion to the mass of original matter, the court will not, as a general rule, interfere, but will leave the plaintiff to his remedy by damages at law (*g*). In an American case (*h*) the pirated matter pervaded the whole work, and could not be separated from the rest of the work without destroying the whole work; but, as it was small both in quantity and value, the court would not interfere, on the ground that the remedy would be disproportionate to the injury. There may, however, be cases where the pirated matter, though small in quantity, is so material and of such value in

(*c*) Lewis *v.* Fullarton, 2 Beav. 6. See Ainsworth *v.* Bentley, 14 W. R. 630.

(*d*) Mawman *v.* Tegg, 2 Russ. 387; Lewis *v.* Fullarton, 2 Beav. 6; Sweet *v.* Maugham, 11 Sim. 51, 4 Jur. 479; Kelly *v.* Morris, 1 L. R. Eq. 697.

(*e*) Mawman *v.* Tegg, 2 Russ. 390.

(*f*) Lewis *v.* Fullarton, 2 Beav. 6; Kelley *v.* Morris, 1 L. R. Eq. 697.

(*g*) Mawman *v.* Tegg, 2 Russ. 394; Whittingham *v.* Wooler, 2 Sw. 428; Baily *v.* Taylor, Taml. 295, R. & M. 73; Sweet *v.* Cator, 11 Sim. 580; Bell *v.* Whitehead, 8 L. J. Ch. N. S. 141.

(*h*) Webb *v.* Powers, 2 Wood. & M. 498.

quality that the court may feel bound to interfere by injunction (*i*). In a case where the pirated matter formed a very small portion of the plaintiff's work, but constituted the bulk of the defendant's work, an injunction was granted (*j*). If an injunction has been granted against a work which is proposed to be published in successive numbers on the ground of piracy in the published numbers, the injunction will not be modified so as to permit the publication of the future numbers, while the question of piracy as to the others remains undetermined (*k*). In a case where to grant an injunction against the whole work would be a harsh step, the court will not suspend the publication altogether until the hearing of the cause (*l*).

9. * If the pirated matter can be separated from the   * 444 original matter, the injunction will issue only against that particular part (*m*).

10. The court will not grant an injunction against the whole of a book generally until it has ascertained by inspection or otherwise the quantity of the pirated matter (*n*). It was formerly the practice of the court either to refer it to the Master to report to what extent the one book was a copy of the other (*o*),[1] or to inspect the work itself (*p*). At the present day the court usually takes upon itself the inspection of the book (*q*). In Lewis *v.* Fullarton (*r*), a considerable quantity of matter having been shown to have been pirated, Lord Langdale considered himself justified in coming to the conclusion that other parts also of the work had been pirated, and granted an injunction in general terms without ascertaining the whole amount of the pirated matter. But in Jarrold *v.* Houlstone (*s*), Wood, V. C., said the court should grudge no labor in ascer-

(*i*) Bohn *v.* Bogue, 10 Jur. 420; Saunders *v.* Smith, 3 M. & C. 711; Bramhall *v.* Melcomb, *ib.* 739 ; Bell *v.* Whitehead, 8 L. J. Ch. N. S. 141. See Campbell *v.* Scott, 11 Sim. 51.

(*j*) Kelly *v.* Hooper, 4 Jur. 21.

(*k*) Barfield *v.* Nicholson, 2 L. J. Ch. 90.

(*l*) Ainsworth *v.* Bentley, 14 W.R. 630.

(*m*) Jarrold *v.* Houlstone, 3 K. & J. 708. See Emerson *v.* Davies, 3 Story (Amer.), 798; Webb *v.* Powers, 2 Wood. & M. 521.

(*n*) Mawman *v.* Tegg, 2 Russ. 398, *per* Lord Eldon.

(*o*) *Ib.* 400.

(*p*) Lewis *v.* Fullarton, 2 Beav. 6.

(*q*) Murray *v.* Bogue, 1 Drew. 368; Spiers *v.* Brown, 6 W. R. 352; Jarrold *v.* Houlstone, 3 K. & J. 708 ; Hotten *v.* Arthur, 1 H. & M. 603.

(*r*) 2 Beav. 6.

(*s*) 3 K. & J. 708.

[1] " Such a course is sometimes adopted upon the final hearing, but not when the question comes up on a motion for a preliminary injunction." Smith *v.* Johnson, 4 Blatchf. 252.

taining how far the injunction should extend. The court may leave it to the defendant to state in his affidavit exactly how much and what parts he has copied. If there is no reason to suppose a fraudulent intent on his part, this course may be adopted (*t*).

11. A man whose copyright has been invaded is entitled to sue either at law or in equity, although there may have been no fraudulent intention on the part of the defendant. It is enough that there has been an invasion of the right. The guilt, ignorance, or innocence of the party who invades the right is immaterial (*u*). But if it be doubtful whether or not there has been an invasion of the right, the intent be-
* 445 comes a material * consideration (*x*). If the defendant denies that he has made any use of the prior publication, but the court is of opinion, either from the occurrence of the same blunders or misprints in both publications (*y*), or from other causes, that the statement is false, the denial is evidence of a fraudulent intent, and an injunction will issue in cases in which it might not have gone had he admitted that he had made a fair use of, or been under obligation to, the prior publica-tion (*z*). A man who alleges that his work is a fair compila-tion and not the mere copy of another work should produce his original manuscript. The production of the manuscript is im-portant as evidence of *bona fides* (*a*).

12. Where an injunction is granted, the defendant will not be allowed to sell copies of a book already published upon terms of keeping an account, unless the plaintiff consent (*b*).

SECTION II. — COPYRIGHT IN GENERAL.

1. No copyright at common law.
2. Copyright defined.
3. Who are entitled to copyright.

(*t*) Mawman *v.* Tegg, 2 Russ. 395, 404; Jarrold *v.* Houlstone, 3 K. & J. 708.

(*u*) Reade *v.* Conquest, 11 C. B. N. S. 479; Murray *v.* Bogue, 1 Drew. 353; Reade *v.* Lacy, 1 J. & H. 524; Scott *v.* Stanford, 16 L. T. N. S. 51.

(*x*) See Webb *v.* Powers, 2 Wood. & M. (Amer.) 497.

(*y*) Longman *v.* Winchester, 16 Ves. 272; Mawman *v.* Tegg, 2 Russ. 394; Spiers *v.* Brown, 6 W. R. 352.

(*z*) Spiers *v.* Brown, 6 W. R. 352; Jarrold *v.* Houlstone, 3 K. & J. 722.

(*a*) Spiers *v.* Brown, 6 W. R. 352; Hotten *v.* Arthur, 1 H. & M. 603.

(*b*) Sweet *v.* Maugham, 11 Sim. 51.

1. The question has been the subject of much discussion (*c*), but it may be now considered as established that there is no copyright in a published work at common law, and that copyright exists only by statute (*d*).

2. Copyright within the meaning of the copyright statutes and according to the legal acceptation of the term is the exclusive right or monopoly of multiplying a work of literature or art after it has been published : the right, in other words, of preventing all others from copying, by printing or otherwise, a work of * literature or art which the * 446 author has published (*e*).   The right commences by publication (*f*).

3. The object of the copyright statutes being to encourage literature and art among British subjects, all persons who by residence within the British dominions at the time of publication owe the Crown a temporary allegiance, come within the description of British subjects for the purposes of copyright. An alien friend coming into one of the British colonies, and residing there during and at the time of publication in this country of a work first published in the United Kingdom, is entitled to copyright in the work so published, no matter where his work was composed, or whether he took up his residence solely with a view to publication (*g*).   But if at the time of publication a foreigner is not within the British dominions, he is not a person whom the ordinary copyright statutes are meant to protect (*h*).   A British author, however, need not be within the dominions at the time of the publication of his work.   If the work is first published within the dominions, he may have copyright in it, though he be resident abroad at the time of publication (*i*).   A work must be printed as well as published here, otherwise it will not be protected (*k*).

(*c*) See Millar *v.* Taylor, 4 Burr. 2303 ; Donaldson *v.* Beckett, *ib.* 2408, 2 Bro. P. C. 129 ; Cadell *v.* Robertson, 5 Pat. Sc. Ap. 493.

(*d*) Jefferys *v.* Boosey, 4 H. L. 833 ; Reade *v.* Conquest, 9 C. B. N. S. 768. See Wheaton *v.* Peters, 8 Pet. (Amer.) 591.

(*e*) Jefferys *v.* Boosey, 4 H. L. 920, *per* Lord Wensleydale.

(*f*) *Ib.* 815.

(*g*) Ollendorf *v.* Black, 4 De G. & S. 209 ; Low *v.* Routledge, 1 L. R. Ch. Ap. 42.

(*h*) See Jefferys *v.* Boosey, 4 H. L. 815 ; but see Low *v.* Routledge, 33 L. J. Ch. 717, *per* Kindersley, V. C.

(*i*) Jefferys *v.* Boosey, 4 H. L. 815. See Boucicault *v.* Delafield, 1 H. & M. 597.

(*k*) 4 H. L. 984, *per* Lord St. Leonards.

SECTION III. — LITERARY COPYRIGHT.

1. Copyright in literature depends upon the 5 & 6 Vict. c. 45.[1] By the second clause of the act the word " book " includes every volume, division of a volume, pamphlet, sheet of letterpress, sheet of music, map, chart, or plan separately published. The word " copyright " is defined to be the sole exclusive liberty of printing or otherwise multiplying * 447 copies of any subject to * which the said word is applied in the act. The act does not extend to prints or designs separately published ; but when prints and designs form part of a work in the text of which a man has copyright, the right extends to them as well as to the letterpress (*l*).

(*l*) Bogue *v.* Houlstone, 5 De G. & S. 275.　　　[1] Act of Congress of July 8, 1870.

2. Copyright in books published in the lifetime of the author is the property of the author or his assigns during the life of the author and seven years afterwards, or for forty-two years if the latter be the longer term. The copyright in books published after the death of the author lasts for forty-two years (m).[1]

3. The proprietor of a copyright in any book published since the 1st July, 1842, cannot maintain an action or suit in respect of the infringement of his right, unless he shall before commencing the action or suit have caused an entry of the book to be made in the register book at Stationers' Hall, pursuant to the Act 5 & 6 Vict. c. 45 (n). Under the former Copyright Acts this was not required (o). An entry must be made of the title of the first publication, and of the names and places of abode of the publisher and of the proprietor of the copyright (p). An entry is defective where the date of the publication is entered inaccurately, or the publishers are not entered accurately, either by their individual names or by the name of the firm (q). The address of his publishers is a sufficient description by an English author of his place of abode, so as to satisfy the provisions of s. 13 when he is out of England and has no place of abode there (r). Neglect on the part of the officials at Stationers' Hall to register the book may, it would seem, deprive an author of the benefit of the statute (s).

4. A separate article for a periodical is not a book to be registered within the clause (t). The protection afforded to the title of a newspaper or periodical by registration is not prospective, and only dates from the time of the first publication of such newspaper * or periodical (u). * 448 Copyright cannot be acquired in the mere title of a book by registration under the statute (v).

5. Any person associated by the proprietor of a copyright with himself in an entry in the register book has a *primâ facie*

(m) 5 & 6 Vict. c. 45, s. 3.
(n) Sect. 24.
(o) Murray v. Bogue, 1 Drew. 364.
(p) 5 & 6 Vict. c. 45, s. 13.
(q) Low v. Routledge,33 L. J. Ch. 717.
(r) Lover v. Davidson,1 C.B.N.S. 182.
(s) Cassell v. Stiff, 2 K. & J. 279.
(t) Murray v. Maxwell, 1 J. & H. 312.

(u) Correspondent Newspaper Co. v. Saunders, 13 W.R. 804, 11 Jur. N.S. 540
(v) Maxwell v. Hogg, 2 L. R. Ch Ap. 307.
   [1] In America copyright extends twenty-eight years, with continuance upon certain conditions for fourteen years more. Act of Congress of July 8, 1870, §§ 87, 88.

right to sue jointly with him in respect of an infringement (*x*).
Omission to register, when relied on as a defence to a suit for
infringement, should be distinctly pleaded (*y*).

6. The assignment of a copyright is not valid unless it be in
writing.[1] The rule is the same whether the assignment was
made before (*z*) or has been made since the Act 5 & 6 Vict.
c. 45 (*a*). If the assignment was made before the 5 & 6 Vict.
c. 45, attestation is not necessary (*b*); nor is attestation, it
would appear, necessary since the passing of the act (*c*).

7. A registered proprietor may assign his interest or any
portion of his interest in a copyright by making an entry in
the book of registry pursuant to the act (*d*). But the requisitions of the act must be strictly complied with. An assignee
by entry has no title to sue under the act, unless the requisitions of the act as to the entry of proprietorship have been duly
observed. If the entry of proprietorship is insufficient, there
is no valid assignment by subsequent entry (*e*).

8. It has been denied that there can be a partial assignment of a copyright (*f*); but a man may, under 5 & 6 Vict.
c. 45, s. 13, assign a portion of his interest in a copyright (*g*).

9. A foreign author resident abroad cannot, by assigning
a published work according to the law of his own
* 449   country, * give the assignee a title which will be recognized in this country (*h*).

(*x*) Stevens *v.* Wildy, 19 L. J. Ch. 190.
(*y*) Chappell *v.* Davidson, 18 C. B. 194.
(*z*) Power *v.* Walker, 3 M. & S. 7; Morris *v.* Kelly, 1 J. & W. 481; Clementi *v.* Walker, 2 B. & C. 861.
(*a*) Cassell *v.* Stiff, 2 K. & J. 279, 5 & 6 Vict. c. 45, s. 15.
(*b*) Cumberland *v.* Copeland, 1 H. & C. 194.
(*c*) See,— *ib.*—; but see 8 Jur. N. S. Ap. 148.
(*d*) Sect. 13. See Shepherd *v.* Conquest, 17 C. B. 441.
(*e*) Low *v.* Routledge, 33 L. J. Ch. 717.
(*f*) See Jefferys *v.* Boosey, 4 H. L. 815, *per* Lord St. Leonards; Lover *v.* Davidson, 1 C. B. N. S. 182; but see Sweet *v.* Cator, 11 Sim. 573.
(*g*) See Howitt *v.* Hall, 10 W. R. 381. In the absence of special contract to the contrary, the assignor of a copyright is entitled, after the assignment, to continue selling copies of the work printed before the assignment and remaining in his possession. Taylor *v.* Pillow, 7 L. R. Eq. 418.
(*h*) Jefferys *v.* Boosey, 4 H. L. 815.
[1] The provision of the United States statute is, "That copyrights shall be assignable in law, by any instrument of writing, and such assignment shall be recorded in the office of the Librarian of Congress within sixty days after its execution, in default of which it shall be void as against any subsequent purchaser or mortgagee for a valuable consideration without notice." Act of July 8, 1870, s. 89. In Stephens *v.* Cady, 14 How. N. S. 528, it was doubted by Nelson, J., whether a transfer of a copyright even by a sale, under a decree of a court of chancery, would pass the title so as to protect the purchaser, unless by a conveyance, in conformity with the requirement of the statute; and in this case it was held that the

10. An agreement between publishers and an author to print and publish a work at their own risk, on the terms of dividing equally with him half profits, and stipulating that if another edition should be required the author should make all necessary additions and alterations, is an agreement of a personal nature, and not an assignment of the copyright (*i*).

11. A license to publish is not an assignment of a copyright (*k*). The author or proprietor of a manuscript may, at common law, license another by parol to print and publish it, but the licensee cannot maintain an action against a third person, because he has not a legal title (*l*) ; but in equity a parol license to publish given by the author, and followed by his acquiescence, may deprive him of his right to an injunction to restrain the licensee from publishing the work (*m*).

12. An author who has sold one edition of his work to a publisher may not, until that edition has been sold off, publish another edition with passages identical with those to be found in the edition which has been sold (*n*).

13. Copyright is declared by the statute to be personal property (*o*). The right is not personal to the author or his assigns, but descends to his legal personal representatives. They may, after his death, acquire a copyright in writings or letters which the author or writer never intended to publish (*p*). Nor is the privilege confined to cases where there is a known author. A man who has found a manuscript in his * ancestor's repository, or got a gift * 450 of it, may have a copyright in it, although he cannot tell who was the author (*q*).

14. To come within the protection of the copyright statutes,

---

sale of a copperplate for a map, on an execution against the owner of the copyright of the map, does not pass to the purchaser a right to use the copperplate to print such maps.

(*i*) Stevens *v.* Benning, 6 D. M. & G. 223. See Reade *v.* Bentley, 3 K. & J. 271, 4 K. & J. 656.

(*k*) Reade *v.* Bentley, 4 K. & J. 656. See Power *v.* Walker, 3 M. & S. 7.

(*l*) Power *v.* Walker, 4 Camp. 9. See Curtis on Copyright, 224.

(*m*) Rundell *v.* Murray, Jac. 311;

Platt *v.* Button, 19 Ves. 447. See Folsom *v.* Marsh, 2 Story (Amer.), 109.

(*n*) Sweet *v.* Cator, 11 Sim. 572. See further, as to agreements between an author and a publisher, Colburn *v.* Simms, 2 Ha. 543; Reade *v.* Bentley, 3 K. & J. 271, 4 K. & J. 656; Cox *v.* Cox, 11 Ha. 118; Howitt *v.* Hall, 10 W. R. 381, 6 L. T. N. S. 348.

(*o*) 5 & 6 Vict. c. 45, s. 25.

(*p*) Dodsley *v.* M'Farquhar, Mor. Dict. of Dec., vols. 19, 20, p. 8308.

(*q*) Maclean *v.* Moody, 20 Dec. of Ct. of Sess., 2d series, p. 1154.

a work need not consist of new or original matter, nor is the privilege confined to works of literary merit. A mere compilation of old materials, or of materials which are common to all men, and are merely the result of inquiry and industry, may be the subject of copyright (*r*), such as a road or guide book (*s*), a book on chronology (*t*), a directory (*u*), a book of statistics (*v*), a trade (*x*) or shipping list (*y*), an analysis of acts of Parliament with appendices (*z*), a topographical dictionary (*a*), a court calendar (*b*), a spelling-book (*c*), a book of elementary lessons in arithmetic (*d*) or science (*e*), an annotated catalogue (*f*); additions, corrections, or original notes to an old work (*g*); reports of cases at law (*h*), marginal notes to reports of cases at law (*i*), or a collection of notes to a book (*k*), or of letters of a familiar description, or of letters of business (*l*).[1] A mere collection of receipts for cooking cannot, it has been said, be the

* 451   subject of * copyright, as it requires no mental labor (*m*); but the authorities do not support the *dictum*.

15. The translation of a foreign work which is not protected in this country may be the subject of copyright (*n*). But a work which has been previously published abroad cannot be afterwards the subject of a copyright in this country (*o*). There

(*r*) Barfield *v.* Nicholson, 2 Sim. & St. 7, 2 L. J. Ch. 90; Lewis *v.* Fullarton, 2 Beav. 6; Jarrold *v.* Houlstone, 3 K. & J. 708; Kelly *v.* Morris, 1 L. R. Eq. 697.

(*s*) Cary *v.* Longman, 1 East, 358.

(*t*) Trusler *v.* Murray, 1 East, 363, n.; Kelly *v.* Morris, 1 L. R. Eq. 697.

(*u*) Kelly *v.* Hooper, 4 Jur. 21.

(*v*) Scott *v.* Stanford, 3 L. R. Eq. 718; Cornish *v.* Upton, 4 L. T. N. S. 862.

(*x*) Cornish *v.* Upton, *ib.*

(*y*) Maclean *v.* Moody, 20 Dec. of Ct. of Sess., 2d series, p. 1154.

(*z*) Alexander *v.* M'Kenzie, 9 *ib.* p.748.

(*a*) Lewis *v.* Fullarton, 2 Beav. 6; Kelly *v.* Morris, 1 L. R. Eq. 697.

(*b*) Longman *v.* Winchester, 16 Ves. 269.

(*c*) Lennie *v.* Pillans, 5 Dec. of Ct. of Sess., 2d series, p. 417.

(*d*) Emerson *v.* Davies, 3 Story (Amer.), 768.

(*e*) Jarrold *v.* Houlstone, 3 K. & J. 708.

(*f*) Hotten *v.* Arthur, 1 H. & M. 603.

(*g*) Tonson *v.* Walker, 3 Sw. 672, cit.' 4 Burr. 2325; Cary *v.* Longman, 1 East, 358; Mason *v.* Murray, cit. *ib.*

(*h*) Sweet *v.* Shaw, 1 Jur. 917; Sweet *v.* Maugham, 11 Sim. 51; Saunders *v.* Smith, 3 M. & C. 729; Hodges *v.* Welsh, 2 Ir. Eq. 266.

(*i*) Stevens *v.* Wildy, 19 L. J. Ch. 190; Sweet *v.* Benning, 16 C. B. 459.

(*k*) Gray *v.* Russell, 1 Story (Amer.), 11.

(*l*) Pope *v.* Curl, 2 Atk. 341; Folsom *v.* Marsh, 2 Story (Amer.), 100.

(*m*) Rundell *v.* Murray, Jac. 314. See Wyatt *v.* Barnard, 3 V. & B. 77.

(*n*) Wyatt *v.* Barnard, 3 V. & B. 77.

(*o*) Clementi *v.* Walker, 2 B. & C. 861; Guichard *v.* Mori, 9 L. J. Ch. 227; Chappell *v.* Purday, 4 Y. & C. 485.

[1] This subject is discussed in Atwill *v.* Ferrett, 2 Blatchf. 39, and it is held that under the act of Feb. 3d, 1831, the author must, by his own intellectual labor applied to the materials of his composition, produce an arrangement or compilation new in itself. Gray *v.* Russell, to same point, 1 Story,11; Pierpont *v.* Fowle, 2 Wood. & M. 23; Emerson *v.* Davies, 3 Story, 778. As to an author's rights in letters, private or on business, see Folsom *v.* Marsh, 2 Story, 100.

may, however, be copyright if a work be published simultaneously here and abroad (*p*). To come within the statute the book must be published in this country (*q*).

16. If a publication be of an immoral, indecent, seditious, libellous, or irreligious nature, there can be no copyright (*r*). The labor expended on a work of this nature is not labor in respect of which a right of property can exist (*s*). Upon an analogous principle no copyright exists in a book, though its contents be innocent, which purports falsely to have been written by an author of reputation, and seeks under color of such a representation to impose on the public ; but the mere publication of a book with a false title-page or a false preface is not material if there be no intention to defraud the public and make a profit by the false representation (*t*).

17. The author of a book protected by copyright has the exclusive right to publish and sell every part of it. A subsequent writer may make a fair and legitimate use of a prior publication, but he may not copy or imitate it to such an extent as to damage the property of the author in his copyright. If so much is taken that the value of the original is sensibly diminished, or the labors of the original matter are substantially and to an injurious extent appropriated by another, that is sufficient in point of law to constitute a piracy (*u*).[1] To be a piracy it is not * necessary that   * 452 the later work should be a substitute for the original work (*v*). All that is necessary is that so much should be taken as to affect sensibly the property of the original writer (*x*). Whether the use which has been made of a prior work is a fair and legitimate use, or is substantially unlawful, is a question

(*p*) Boosey *v.* Purday, 4 Exch. 145 ; Cocks *v.* Purday, 5 C. B. 860.

(*b*) Clementi *v.* Walker, 2 B. & C. 861.

(*r*) Stockdale *v.* Onwhyn, 5 B. & C. 173 ; Walcot *v.* Walker, 7 Ves. 1 ; Southey *v.* Sherwood, 2 Mer. 435 ; Lawrence *v.* Smith, Jac. 471 ; Lord Byron *v.* Dugdale, 1 L. J. Ch. 239.

(*s*) Macaulay *v.* Shackell, 1 Bligh, N. S. 96, 127, *per* Lord Eldon. But see Curt. on Copyright, 169 ; 2 Story, Eq. Jur. 938.

(*t*) Wright *v.* Tallis, 1 C. B. 893.

(*u*) Folsom *v.* Marsh, 2 Story (Amer.), 115, *per* Story, J. ; Scott *v.* Stanford, 3 L. R. Eq. 718. See Campbell *v.* Scott, 11 Sim. 31 ; Lewis *v.* Fullarton, 2 Beav. 6 ; Jarrold *v.* Houlstone, 3 K. & J. 716. The extent of the use which may be rightfully made of a copyrighted book is discussed in Morris *v.* Wright, 5 L. R. Ch. Ap. 279.

(*v*) Bohn *v.* Bogue, 10 Jur. 420. See Sweet *v.* Shaw, 1 Jur. 917.

(*x*) *Ib.*

[1] Folsom *v.* Marsh, 2 Story, 115 ; Emerson *v.* Davies, 3 Story, 768.

not so much of kind as of degree, and depends upon the circumstances of each particular case (*y*). In many cases it is
extremely difficult to draw the line between what is a legitimate
and what is an unlawful and colorable use of a prior work (*z*).
The question of piracy turns most commonly upon the extent
or quantity of the materials taken, but it does not depend
necessarily upon the quantity. " We must often," said Story,
J., in Folsom *v.* Marsh (*a*), " in questions of the sort look to
the nature and objects of the selections made, the quantity and
value of the materials used, and the degree in which the use
may prejudice the sale, or diminish the profit, or supersede
the object of the original work. Many mixed ingredients enter
into the discussion of such questions. In some cases a considerable portion of the materials of the original work may be
fused into another work so as to be undistinguishable in the
mass of the latter which has other professed and obvious objects, and cannot fairly be deemed a piracy ; or they may be
inserted as a sort of distinct and mosaic work into the general
texture of the second work, and constitute the peculiar excel-
lence thereof, and then it may be a clear piracy. If a person
should, under color of publishing ' elegant extracts ' in poetry,
·include all the best pieces at large of a favorite poet whose
volume was secured by copyright, it would be difficult to say
why it was not an invasion of that right, since it might constitute the entire value of the volume." — " One writer," said
Lord Cottenham in Bramhall *v.* Melcomb (*b*), " might take all
        the vital parts of another's work, though it might be
* 453 but a small * proportion of the work in quantity. It
        is not always quantity but value that is looked
to " (*c*).

18. Extracts or quotations from a book which is protected
by copyright are not forbidden by the law. If they are taken
for the purposes of criticism, comment, or illustration, considerable license is allowed (*d*), for the selection of extracts for

(*y*) Sweet *v.* Benning, 16 C. B. 485,   Murray *v.* Bogue, 1 Drew. 369 ; Tins-
per Maule, J.   ley *v.* Lacy, 1 H. & M. 747 ; Gray *v.*
(*z*) *Ib.*   Russell, 1 Story (Amer.), 11 ; Scott *v.*
(*a*) 2 Story (Amer.), 100, 116.   Stanford, 3 L. R. Eq. 718.
(*b*) 3 M. & C. 738.   (*d*) Roworth *v.* Wilkes, 1 Camp. 94 ;
(*c*) Campbell *v.* Scott, 11 Sim. 31 ;   Whittingham *v.* Wooler, 2 Sw. 128.

such purposes, so far from being injurious, is often beneficial to the sale of the books from which they are taken (*e*). But there is a limit to the selection of passages even for the purposes of criticism or comment, though it is not easy to define that limit (*f*). If the selection is made fairly for the purpose of criticising or questioning the opinions expressed therein, or of explaining the criticism, passages of considerable length or of much value may be taken (*g*); but a reviewer may not, under the pretence of criticism, appropriate a large or vital part of the book of another. If the citations, though purporting to be made with a view to criticism, go in part to supersede the original work, and to substitute the review for it, such a use is deemed in law a piracy (*h*). Thus where a man had published a book giving specimens of modern English poetry, with an original essay and biographical notices, and inserted extracts from a poem written by Campbell, an injunction was granted against the publication (*i*).[1]

19. Extracts or quotations may be taken for other purposes than those of criticism, but the limit is much narrower than when they are taken for the purposes of criticism or comment. If so much is taken that the value of the original is sensibly diminished, or the labors of the author are substantially and to an injurious extent appropriated, that is sufficient in law to constitute a piracy (*j*). It is immaterial whether the quantity taken be small or large. * The question is * 454 whether substantial damage is caused to the property of the author (*k*). Where the proprietor of the Law Digest copied from the Jurist the head-notes of the reported cases, it was held to be an abuse of the right of extract (*l*). So also a man was restrained from copying reports of law cases from a work of the plaintiff (*m*). So also, in Dickens *v.* —— (*n*), the

(*e*) Bell *v.* Whitehead, 8 L. J. Ch. N. S. 141.
(*f*) Ib.
(*g*) Ib.; Roworth *v.* Wilkes, 1 Camp. 94; Folsom *v.* Marsh, 100, 113.
(*h*) Wilkins *v.* Aikin, 17 Ves. 422; Cary *v.* Kearsley, 4 Esp. 168; Folsom *v.* Marsh, 2 Story (Amer.), 100, 117.
(*i*) Campbell *v.* Scott, 11 Sim. 31.
(*j*) Folsom *v.* Marsh, 2 Story (Amer.), 100, 115; Bohn *v.* Bogue, 10 Jur. 420.

See Morris *v.* Wright, 5 L. R. Ch. Ap. 279.
(*k*) Curtis on Copyright, 252.
(*l*) Sweet *v.* Benning, 16 C. B. 459. See Tonson *v.* Walker 3 Sw. 672.
(*m*) Sweet *v.* Shaw, 1 Jur. 917.
(*n*) Cited 8 L. J. Ch. N. S. 141.
[1] See Gray *v.* Russell, 1 Story, 11, where this subject is discussed by Judge Story.

proprietor of a provincial newspaper was restrained from·
publishing large extracts from a novel unaccompanied by criticism (*o*). So also the printing and selling of a drama, large
passages of which were taken from a novel, was held to be an
infringement of the copyright in the novel (*p*). So also where
a man possessed a copyright in a play, and in a novel which ˈ
had been founded on the play, a dramatized version of the
novel containing scenes and passages which were common to
both play and novel was held to be an infringement of the
copyright in the play (*q*).

20. If the extracts are acknowledged, the acknowledgment
shows that the party did not intend to pass as his own what
belongs to another, but it does not justify or excuse the
piracy (*r*).

21. The most frequent form of piracy which comes before
the court is where the matter of a prior publication is adopted,
imitated, or transferred, with more or less colorable alteration,
to disguise the piracy. Where a book protected by copyright
is a historical or speculative work, or a work of invention or
imagination, or is generally a work of an original character, the
hand of the author can be followed without much difficulty ;
but where the work relates to a subject which cannot from its
very nature be entirely new, and in which the mode of expression and language are necessarily so common that two persons
must to a very great extent express themselves in identical
     terms in conveying the instruction or information which
* 455 they * are anxious to communicate, the difficulty is
     much increased (*s*). In certain cases of the sort, such
as mathematical tables, chronologies, almanacs, calendars,
maps, concordances, and similar publications, the result must
be nearly identical, and the only mode of determining whether
an unfair use of a prior publication has been made by a subsequent compiler is the copying of errors or misprints (*t*).

(*o*) See Campbell *v.* Scott, 11 Sim.
31. Comp. Dodsley *v.* Kinnersley, Amb.
403, which cannot, however, be considered law.
    (*p*) Tinsley *v.* Lacy, 1 H. & M. 747.
    (*q*) Reade *v.* Lacy, 1 J. & H. 524.
See Lewis *v.* Fullarton, 2 Beav. 6.
    (*r*) Bohn *v.* Bogue, 10 Jur. 420;

Scott *v.* Stanford, 3 L. R. Eq. 718. See
Campbell *v.* Scott, 11 Sim. 31 ; Tinsley
v. Lacy, 1 H. & M. 747.
    (*s*) Spiers *v.* Brown, 6 W. R. 352, *per*
Wood, V. C. ; Kelly *v.* Morris, 1 L. R.
Eq. 697. See Webb *v.* Powers, 2 Wood.
& M. (Amer.) 512.
    (*t*) *Ib.*

Dictionaries of all kinds, gazetteers, grammars, arithmetic, or other school-books, encyclopædias, itineraries, guide-books, and similar publications, are another class of cases in which much of the matter must be identical and no great novelty is practicable (*u*). In such cases, if there are no common errors in both, the recurrence of passages identically the same may be sufficient to be a conclusive proof of piracy (*v*). Where the resemblance does not amount to an identity of particular passages, the question becomes in substance whether there be such a conformity and similitude between the two works that the writer of the one must have copied or made an undue use of the other. What degree of resemblance will authorize the inference that one book is a copy or colorable imitation of another is often a question of great nicety, and depends on the circumstances of each particular case (*w*). A man is not debarred from consulting a prior work on the same subject. He may examine it to see whether it contains any thing which he has forgotten, or whether any reference is made there to some other work bearing on the subject (*x*). If he has bestowed much labor, and has honestly * exercised his   * 456 mind upon the work, he is not guilty of piracy, although he may have copied a good deal (*y*) : but if a man, instead of examining the original sources, or honestly exercising his mind on the work, avails himself of the labors of his predecessor, adopts his arrangement, borrows the materials which he has accumulated and combined together, or uses his language with colorable alterations or variations, he is guilty of piracy (*z*). "The true test of piracy," said Story, J., in

---

(*u*) Ib.; Webb *v.* Powers, 2 Wood & M. (Amer.) 512; Jarrold *v.* Houlstone, 3 K. & J. 708.

(*v*) Matthewson *v.* Stockdale, 12 Ves. 270; Wilkins *v.* Aikin, 17 Ves. 422; Mawman *v.* Tegg, 2 Russ. 385; Lewis *v.* Fullarton, 2 Beav. 6; Jarrold *v.* Houlstone, 3 K. & J. 708; Hotten *v.* Arthur, 1 H. & M. 603; Lennie *v.* Pillans, 5 Dec. of Ct. of Sess., 2d series, p. 417.

(*w*) Sayre *v.* Moore, 1 East, 361, n.; Trusler *v.* Murray, *ib.* 363, n.; Cary *v.* Kearsley, 4 Esp. 168; Matthewson *v.* Stockdale, 12 Ves. 270; Wilkins *v.* Aikin, 17 Ves. 422; Mawman *v.* Tegg,

2 Russ. 385; Stevens *v.* Wildy, 19 L. J. Ch. 190; Jarrold *v.* Houlstone, 3 K. & J. 708; Hotten *v.* Arthur, 1 H. & M. 603.

(*x*) Jarrold *v.* Houlstone, 3 K. & J. 716; Kelly *v.* Morris, 1 L. R. Eq. 697. See Murray *v.* Bogue, 1 Drew. 353.

(*y*) Hotten *v.* Arthur, 1 H. & M. 603; Spiers *v.* Brown, 6 W. R. 352; Murray *v.* Bogue, 1 Drew. 369.

(*z*) Jarrold *v.* Houlstone, 3 K. & J. 716, *per* Wood, V. C.; Lewis *v.* Fullarton, 2 Beav. 6; Hotten *v.* Arthur, 1 H. & M. 603; Kelly *v.* Morris, 1 L. R. Eq. 697; Gray *v.* Russell, 1 Story (Amer.), 11.

Emerson *v.* Davies (*a*), " is to ascertain whether the defendant has in fact used the plan, arrangement, or illustrations of the plaintiff as the model of his own book, with colorable alterations and variations only to disguise the use thereof; or whether his work is the result of his own labor, skill, and use of common materials and common sources of knowledge open to all men, and the resemblances are either accidental or arising from the nature of the subject. In other words, whether the defendant's book is a servile or evasive imitation of the plaintiff's work, or a *bonâ fide* compilation from other or independent sources " (*b*). The compiler of a dictionary or guide-book containing information derived from sources common to all, which must of necessity be identical in all cases, if correctly given, is not entitled to spare himself the labor and expense of original inquiry by adopting and republishing the information contained in previous works on the same subject. He must obtain and work at the information independently for himself, and the only legitimate use which he can make of previous works is for the purpose of verifying the correctness of his results (*c*). Where a number of passages are proved to have been copied by the copying of the blunders in them, other passages which are the same with passages in the original work will be presumed *primâ facie* to be likewise copied, though no blunders occur in them (*d*).

* 457   22. * A fair and *bonâ fide* abridgment of a book is not a piracy (*e*); but what constitutes a fair and *bonâ fide* abridgment in the sense of the law is by no means an easy question (*f*). In Dickens *v.* Lee (*g*), Knight Bruce, L. J., adopting the language of Lord Eldon in Wilkins *v.* Aikin (*h*), said the test was whether there has been a legitimate use of the original work in the fair exercise of a mental operation deserving the character of an original work. But as Story, J., has said (*i*), in commenting on the language of Lord Eldon in

---

(*a*) 3 Story (Amer.), 793.
(*b*) See Webb *v.* Powers, 2 Wood. & M. (Amer.) 497.
(*c*) Kelly *v.* Morris, 1 L. R. Eq. 697.
(*d*) Mawman *v.* Tegg, 2 Russ. 394, *per* Lord Eldon. See Lewis *v.* Fullarton, 2 Beav. 6; Jarrold *v.* Houlstone, 3 K. & J. 722. See, also, *supra*, p. 445.

(*e*) Newberry's case, Lofft. R. 775; Gyles *v.* Wilcox, 2 Atk. 141; Bell *v.* Walker, 1 Bro. C. C. 451.
(*f*) Folsom *v.* Marsh, 2 Story (Amer.), 107, *per* Story, J.
(*g*) 8 Jur. 184.
(*h*) 17 Ves. 422.
(*i*) Eq. Jur. 939.

Wilkins *v.* Aikin, this is another mode of stating the difficulty, rather than a test affording a clear criterion to discriminate between the cases. A mere colorable shortening of the original work by the omission of certain passages, or the mere selection or different arrangement of parts of the original work so as to bring the work into a smaller compass, is not a fair and *bonâ fide* abridgment (*k*). To be a fair and *bonâ fide* abridgment, there must be a substantial condensation of the material and intellectual labor and judgment bestowed thereon (*l*).[1] There is, however, much reason to doubt whether the doctrine that an abridgment is not a piracy can be considered sound. In his life of Lord Hardwicke, Lord Campbell (*m*) expressly disapproves of it; and in his treatise on Copyright, Mr. Curtis considers an abridgment to be on principle an invasion of copyright; and in a late case (*n*) Wood, V. C., said the cases as to abridgment had gone far enough, and expressed his disapproval of several of the dicta on the subject (*o*).

23. A digest made from the published reports, extracting the principle or the substance of the decision, and putting it into *new language, is a fair and *bonâ fide* abridg-   * 458
ment (*p*): but the copying from the reports the facts of cases and the judgments, and the arrangement of them in a different manner, is a piracy and not a fair abridgment (*q*).

24. The translation of a work not under the protection of copyright in the country where the translation is published infringes no right of property: but there is some doubt as to whether a translation is or is not an infringement when published in the country where the original work is protected. Certain *dicta* in Wyatt *v.* Barnard (*r*), Burnett *v.* Chetwood (*s*), and Prince Albert *v.* Strange (*t*), seem to be in favor of the opinion that a translation is not an infringement; but it is difficult to

---

(*k*) Gyles *v.* Wilcox, 2 Atk. 141; Butterworth *v.* Robinson, 5 Ves. 709; Dickens *v.* Lee, 8 Jur. 184; Sweet *v.* Shaw, 1 Jur. 917; Gray *v.* Russell, 1 Story (Amer.), 11.

(*l*) Folsom *v.* Marsh, 2 Story (Amer.), 107. See Webb *v.* Powers, 2 Wood. & M. (Amer.) 512.

(*m*) Page 56.

(*n*) Tinsley *v.* Lacy, 1 H. & M. 747.

(*o*) See also D'Almaine *v.* Boosey, 1

Y. & C. 288, *per* Lord Lyndhurst; Dickens *v.* Lee, 8 Jur. 184, *per* Knight Bruce, L. J.

(*p*) Sweet *v.* Benning, 16 C. B. 459.

(*q*) Butterworth *v.* Robinson, 5 Ves. 709.

(*r*) 3 V. & B. 77.

(*s*) 2 Mer. 441, n.

(*t*) 2 De G. & S. 693.

[1] Story's Executors *v.* Holcombe, 4 McLean, 311.

see upon what principle this doctrine can be upheld. A translation may, it is true, be a work of great labor, and may require the exercise of much industry and skill, but it does not follow that a translator should be able, by merely incorporating with the matter of the book the fruits of his own industry, to absorb the rights of the original author (*u*).[1] In Burnett *v.* Chetwood (*x*), Lord Macclesfield restrained a man from publishing the translation of a Latin work, but the ground on which he proceeded was, that it was not for the benefit of the public that a translation should be published. If a foreigner translates an English work, and an Englishman afterwards re-translates the foreign work into English, that would be an infringement of copyright (*y*). The translation of a foreign work may be the subject of copyright in this country. Any other man has an equal right to translate the original work, and to publish his translation, but he must not make an unfair use of the translation already published (*z*).

25. Under the International Copyright Act, 7 & 8 Vict. c. 12, the right of translation is reserved to foreign authors of books published abroad.

* 459   26. * There are dicta to be found in the reports to the effect that a subsequent writer may use the works of a previous writer, provided improvements, corrections, or additions are made (*a*); and in one case a verdict is reported to have been taken upon this principle under the direction of Lord Mansfield (*b*); but this cannot be considered to be a sound exposition of the law (*c*).

27. The extent to which music may be used by adaptation

(*u*) Curtis on Copyright, 291.

(*x*) 2 Mer. 441, n.

(*y*) Murray *v.* Bogue, 1 Drew. 353, *per* Kindersley, V. C.

(*z*) Wyatt *v.* Barnard, 3 V. & B. 77; Emerson *v.* Davies, 3 Story (Amer.), 780, *per* Story, J.

(*a*) See Cary *v.* Kearsley, 4 Esp. 168, 170; Matthewson *v.* Stockdale, 12 Ves. 275; Martin *v.* Wright, 6 Sim. 298.

(*b*) Sayre *v.* Moore, 1 East, 361, n.

(*c*) Curtis on Copyright, 263.

[1] In Stowe *v.* Thomas, 2 Amer. Law Reg. 210, it was held by Grier, J., that the translation into, and publication of, Mrs. Stowe's work called "Uncle Tom's Cabin," in German, was not an infringement of her copyright. It is said a "copy" of a book must be a transcript of the *language* in which the conceptions of the author are clothed; of something printed and embodied in a tangible shape; that in questions of infringement of copyright, the inquiry is not, whether the defendant has used the thoughts, conceptions, informations, or discoveries promulgated by the original, but whether his composition may be considered a *new work*, requiring invention, learning, and judgment, or only a mere transcript of the whole or parts of the original, with merely colorable variations. See this case for discussion of subject by counsel and court.

for a different kind of performance than that for which it was originally composed was considered in D'Almaine *v.* Boosey (*d*) ; and the doctrine was laid down that a piracy is committed where the appropriated music, though adapted to a different purpose than that of the original, may still be recognized by the ear, and that the adding variations makes no difference in the principle (*e*).

28. The privilege reserved to the author of a work, protected by copyright, is limited to the multiplication of copies. Any man may make what use he pleases of the work, so long as he does not multiply copies (*f*). The reading or recitation of it in public, or the representation on the stage of a play founded upon it, is not an infringement of the copyright (*g*) ; but copies may not, upon the occasion of the recitation or performance, be distributed among the audience (*h*). The multiplication of copies, though not for the purposes of sale, of a work which is the subject of copyright, is an infringement of the right (*i*).

29. Copies of a work which have been lawfully multiplied by a publisher during the term of his agreement for purchase with an author may be sold after the term has expired (*k*).

30. Copyright in articles contributed to an encyclopœdia, review, magazine, or other periodical publication, depends upon the 18th * section of 5 & 6 Vict. c. 45. The * 460 clause declares in substance, that where the proprietor, &c., of an encyclopædia, review, &c., employs a man to write articles for the purpose of publication therein, the copyright of the articles so expressly written for such encyclopædia, review, &c., shall, upon payment, be the property of the proprietor, &c., for the term of twenty-eight years; and that, after the term of twenty-eight years, the right of publishing, in a separate form, articles written for a review, &c., shall revert to the writer for the remainder of the term

---

(*d*) 1 Y. & C. 288.
(*e*) See Chappell *v.* Davidson, 2 K. & J. 131.
(*f*) See Reade *v.* Conquest, 9 C. B. N. S. 755; Tinsley *v.* Lacy, 1 H. & M. 747.
(*g*) Reade *v.* Conquest, 9 C. B. N.

S. 755; Tinsley *v.* Lacy, 1 H. & M. 747.
(*h*) *Ib.*
(*i*) Novello *v.* Sudlow, 12 C. B. 177 ; Tinsley *v.* Lacy, 1 H. & M. 747.
(*k*) Howitt *v.* Hall, 10 W. R. 381, 6 L. T. N. S. 848.

given by the act (*l*). There is a proviso in the clause declaring that the proprietor of an encyclopædia, review, &c., may not publish any such article, " separately or singly," without the consent of the author or his assigns, or otherwise than in the encyclopædia, review, &c., unless the article was written on the terms that the copyright therein should belong to the proprietor for all purposes (*m*). The meaning of the proviso, taken with the clause, is not to vest a copyright in the proprietors or publishers of a periodical work, but simply to give them a license to use the matter for a particular purpose (*n*). An author who has composed an article to be published in a certain periodical work is entitled to require that it be not published otherwise than as part of the periodical. The proprietors or publishers may not publish it as a single book, or separately from the periodical, in conjunction with any thing else, or in any other form than as part of the entire number of the periodical in which it first appeared (*o*). The republication in supplemental numbers of a selection of various tales previously published in a periodical is a separate publication within the meaning of the clause (*p*). The Christmas number of a serial must be treated as part of a periodical work (*q*). The author or his assigns may have an injunction to restrain the proprietor, &c., of an encyclopædia, review, &c., from publishing the article, " separately or singly," without first entering it at Stationers' Hall (*r*).

*461   31. *The reservation of the right of separate publication to the author of an article for a review or periodical publication for fourteen years after the expiration of the first twenty-eight years does not apply to an article written for an encyclopædia (*s*).

32. If the publisher of a magazine employs an editor, and the editor employs and pays a man for writing in the magazine, the copyright in the article does not, it would appear, vest in the publisher under the terms of the clause (*t*).

(*l*) See Sweet *v.* Benning, 16 C. B. 459.
(*m*) Bishop of Hereford *v.* Griffin, 16 Sim. 190.
(*n*) *Ib.*; Smith *v.* Johnson, 4 Giff. 632.
(*o*) Mayhew *v.* Maxwell, 1 J. & H. 312; Smith *v.* Johnson, 4 Giff. 632.
(*p*) Smith *v.* Johnson, 4 Giff. 632.
(*q*) Mayhew *v.* Maxwell, 1 J. & H. 312.
(*r*) *Ib.*
(*s*) Bishop of Hereford *v.* Griffin, 16 Sim. 190.
(*t*) Brown *v.* Cooke, 16 L. J. Ch. 141

33. Actual payment is a condition precedent to the vesting of the copyright in an article written for an encyclopædia, review, magazine, or other periodical work in the proprietor or publisher. A contract to pay is not sufficient (*u*). The pleadings should show that payment has been actually made (*x*).

34. A special statutory copyright exists in lectures, oral or written, by the 5 & 6 Will. 4, c. 65 (*y*).

35. Crown copyright is not, like ordinary copyright, the creation of statute. The Crown has, by virtue of its prerogative, the exclusive right to the publication of acts of Parliament, proclamations, orders of council, liturgies, books of divine service, the translation of the Bible, &c. (*z*). So long as there are separate subsisting patents for England and Scotland for the printing of Bibles, no other copies can be sold in either country, except those printed by the patentee in that country ; and so long as there is a subsisting patent for either country, no other copies can be sold except those printed by the patentee or patentees (*a*).

36. The Universities of England and Scotland, and the Colleges of Eton, Westminster, and Winchester, have, by Statute 15 Geo. 3, c. 53, a perpetual copyright in books given or bequeathed * to them for the advancement of *462 useful learning and other purposes of education. A similar privilege has been conferred on Trinity College, Dublin, by Stat. 41 Geo. 3, c. 27 (*b*).

37. The House of Lords claims the exclusive right to appoint a publisher of judicial proceedings before itself. This claim was recognized in Bathurst *v.* Kearsley (*c*) ; and an injunction was granted to restrain the publication of the trial of the Duchess of Kingston (*d*). On the authority of this precedent, Lord Erskine granted an injunction, until the hearing, to restrain the publication of Lord Melville's trial (*e*).

(*u*) Richardson *v.* Gilbert, 1 Sim. N. S. 337 ; Brown *v.* Cooke, 16 L. J. Ch. 141.
(*x*) Brown *v.* Cooke, *ib.*
(*y*) *Supra*, p. 190.
(*z*) Basket *v.* University of Cambridge, 1 W. Bl. 105 ; Basket *v.* Cunningham, 2 Eden, 137 ; Manners *v.* Bligh, 3 Bligh, N. S. 402.
(*a*) Universities of Oxford and Cambridge *v.* Richardson, 6 Ves. 689 ; Her Majesty's Printers *v.* Bell, Mor. Dict. of Dec., vols. 19, 20, p. 8316. See Curtis on Copyright, 120 ; Philipps on Copyright, 193.
(*b*) See 5 & 6 Vict. c. 45, s. 27.
(*c*) Cited 13 Ves. 504.
(*d*) *Ib.*
(*e*) Gurney *v.* Longman, 13 Ves. 504.

38. The Crown may, perhaps, by virtue of its prerogative, claim the exclusive right of publishing reports of judicial proceedings (f); but no such claim has been asserted for many years ; and in several cases individuals have been acknowledged by the court as proprietors of copyright in law reports (g). The copyright, however, in such cases is not in the actual judgments of the court, but in the diligence and skill that may be used in taking notes of what may fall from the judge, and in collecting the judgments and arranging the cases.

SECTION IV. — DRAMATIC AND MUSICAL COPYRIGHT.

1. Statutes giving copyright in dramatic pieces and musical compositions.
2. Construction of statute.
3. First public performance a publication.
4. The right is expressly given to author or his assignee.
5. Assignment of right to represent a dramatic piece must be in writing.
6. What may be an infringement.
7. Penalties.

1. Copyright in dramatic pieces and musical compositions depends upon 3 & 4 Will. 4, c. 15, and 5 & 6 Vict. c. 45. The literary copyright in this species of property, or the power of multiplying copies, is regulated by 5 & 6 Vict. c. 45, and is in all respects the same as the copyright in other published matter. With respect to the stage copyright in a drama and musical composition, these acts declare in substance that the author of a published dramatic piece or musical com-
* 463   position shall have * the sole liberty of representing and performing it at any place of dramatic entertainment (h).

2. A room may be a place of dramatic entertainment, though it be ordinarily used for other purposes (i). There is some doubt whether the protection of the statutes extends to musical compositions if they be not dramatic in their nature ; but a song which describes feelings in words of passion is dramatic

(f) See Millar $v.$ Taylor, 4 Burr. 2329; Curtis on Copyright, 129; Philipps on Copyright, 194.
(g) Butterworth $v.$ Robinson, 5 Ves. 709; Saunders $v.$ Smith, 3 M. & C. 711 ; Sweet $v.$ Shaw, 1 Jur. 917; Sweet $v.$ Benning, 16 C. B. 459; Hodges $v.$ Welsh, 2 Ir. Eq. 266.

(h) 3 & 4 Will. 4, c. 15, s. 1; 5 & 6 Vict. c. 45, ss. 20, 21. See Russell $v.$ Smith, 12 Q. B. 217. Comp. S. C., 15 Sim. 181; see, also, Reade $v.$ Conquest, 9 C. B. N. S. 758.
(i) Russell $v.$ Smith, 12 Q. B. 217.

in its nature (*j*). An introduction to a pantomime is within the statutes (*k*).

3. The first public representation or performance of a dramatic piece or musical composition is a publication (*l*).

4. The right is expressly given to the author or his assignee (*m*). An employer who merely suggests the subject, but has no share in the design or execution of the work, is not an author (*m*),[1] but an employer who forms the general design of an entertainment, and employs another to compose a musical composition as part of or as accessory to the entertainment, is the author of the whole entertainment within the meaning of the statute (*n*). A man, however, who adopts words of his own to an old air, and adds thereto a prelude and accompaniment also his own, acquires a copyright in the combination (*o*). So also does a man who arranges for the piano the music of an opera, containing no piano-forte score, acquire a copyright in the arrangement (*p*).

5. The assignment of the right to represent a dramatic piece or perform a musical composition must be in writing (*q*), but need not be by deed (*r*). The assignment of the copyright in a book containing a dramatic piece or musical composition does not carry with it the right to represent the dramatic piece or to * perform the musical composition, unless   * 464 some entry be made in the registry book that it was the intention of the parties that the assignment should have that effect (*s*). The proprietor, however, of the right of representing a dramatic piece or performing a musical composition is not bound to register (*t*).

(*j*) Russell *v.* Smith, 12 Q. B. 217.

(*k*) Lee *v.* Simpson, 3 C. B. 871.

(*l*) 5 & 6 Vict. c. 45, s. 20. See Macklin *v.* Richardson, Amb. 694; D'Almaine *v.* Boosey, 1 Y. & C. 299, *per* Lord Lyndhurst.

(*m*) See Shepherd *v.* Conquest, 17 C. B. 427.

(*n*) Hatton *v.* Kean, 7 C. B. N. S. 269.

(*o*) Lover *v.* Davidson, 1 C. B. N. S. 182. See Leader *v.* Purday, 7 C. B. 4.

(*p*) Wood *v.* Boosey, 15 W. R. 309; *infra*, p. 471.

(*q*) Shepherd *v.* Conquest, 17 C. B. 427.

(*r*) Marsh *v.* Conquest, 17 C. B. N. S. 418.

(*s*) 5 & 6 Vict. c. 45, s. 22. See Lacy *v.* Rhys, 4 B. & S. 873; Marsh *v.* Conquest, 17 C. B. N. S. 418.

(*t*) Russell *v.* Smith, 12 Q. B. 217. Lacy *v.* Rhys, 4 B. & S. 873; Marsh *v.* Conquest, 17 C. B. N. S. 418.

[1] A person cannot appropriate as his own, by copyright, alterations and improvements made in a musical composition by others at his procurement and for him. Atwill *v.* Ferrett, 2 Blatchf. 39.

6. The representation without the author's consent of the incidents of a published dramatic piece is an invasion of the stage copyright in the drama, although they may have been taken not from the drama but from a novel upon which the drama was founded (*u*).

7. Certain penalties are imposed by the 3 & 4 Will. 4, c. 15, for an infringement of the provisions of the act; but an injunction may nevertheless be obtained in equity to restrain the representation or performance of any dramatic piece or musical composition in violation of the provisions of the act (*x*).

SECTION V. — COPYRIGHT IN PRINTS, ENGRAVINGS, SCULPTURE, PHOTOGRAPHS, ETC.

1. Statutes giving copyright in prints, engravings, etchings, and lithographs.
2. When a copy is piratical.
3. Provision in place of registration.
4. Copyright only assigned by writing attested by two witnesses.
5. Prints, engravings, &c., in books protected without compliance with these statutes.
6 & 7. Prints engraved and struck off abroad, but published in England, not protected.
8. Knowledge of piracy by defendant not essential.
9. No copyright in immoral, obscene, or libellous prints.
10. Copyright in sculpture, photographs, drawings, and paintings.

1. Copyright in prints, engravings, and etchings depends upon 8 Geo. 2, c. 13, 7 Geo. 3, c. 38, and 17 Geo. 3, c. 57. These acts have been extended to Ireland by 6 & 7 Will. 4, c. 59. The protection of these acts has been extended to lithographs (*y*).

2. A copy is piratical within these acts if it comes so near the print, engraving, &c., &c., as to give every person seeing it the idea created by the original (*z*). The copy need not be exact: it is a piracy if it be substantially a copy (*a*). The copying an engraving by the process of photography is
* 465   a piracy (*b*). The * language of the statutes includes any copies made by any mechanical or chemical process,

---

(*u*) Reade *v.* Conquest, 11 C. B. N. S. 479; Reade *v.* Lacy, 1 J. & H. 524.
(*x*) Russell *v.* Smith, 15 Sim. 181; Reade *v.* Lacy, 1 J. & H. 524.
(*y*) 15 & 16 Vict. c. 12, s. 14.

(*z*) West *v.* Francis, 5 B. & Ald. 743. See Roworth *v.* Wilkes, 1 Camp. 94.
(*a*) Moore *v.* Clark, 9 M. & W. 692.
(*b*) Gambart *v.* Bull, 14 C. B. N. S. 306; Graves *v.* Ashford, 36 L. J. C. P. 139.

and capable of being multiplied indefinitely, but does not, it would appear, apply to copies made by hand, or to designs transferred to an article of manufacture (c).   An engraver is entitled to the protection of these statutes, although he may have copied from a drawing or a picture (d).

3. Registration is not requisite, but it is required by 8 Geo. 2, c. 13, s. 1, that the day of the first publication shall be truly engraved with the name of the proprietor on each plate, and printed on every copy.   The fulfilment of these requisitions is necessary to enable a man to recover the penalties imposed by the statute.   It was formerly doubted whether an action at law or a bill in equity could be maintained without a compliance with these requisitions (e).   It may, however, be considered as established, that no action or suit can be maintained, unless the date and name of the proprietor be engraved thereon according to statute (f).   It is not, however, necessary that the designation " proprietor " be added to the name (g).

4. The copyright in prints, &c., &c., can only be assigned by writing attested by two witnesses (h).   An assignee may maintain an action for piracy under the act (i).

5. Prints, engravings, &c., &c., forming part of a book, are protected by 5 & 6 Vict. c. 45, and need not comply with the requisitions of these statutes (k).

6. Prints engraved and struck off abroad, but published in this country, are not protected by these statutes (l).   But under the provisions of the International Copyright Act, 7 & 8 Vict. c. 12, s. 19, the inventor, designer, or engraver of a print first published * abroad may have protection on   *466 complying with the provisions of 8 Geo. 2, c. 13.   There can be no copyright in a foreign print or engraving, unless the

(c) Gambart v. Bull, 14 C. B. N. S. 306 ; Graves v. Ashford, 36 L. J. C. P. 139.
(d) Newton v. Cowie, 4 Bing. 234. See Sayre v. Moore, 1 East, 361, n.
(e) Blackwell v. Harper, 2 Atk. 93 ; Roworth v. Wilkes, 1 Camp. 94.
(f) Thompson v. Symonds, 5 T. R. 41 ; Harrison v. Hogg, 2 Ves. Jr. 323 ; Brooks v. Cock, 3 A. & E. 138 ; Colnaghi v. Ward, 12 L. J. Q. B. N. S. 1. See Bogue v. Houlstone, 5 De G. & S. 275 ; Avanzo v. Mudie, 10 Exch. 203 ;

Graves v. Ashford, 36 L. J. C. P. 139.
(g) Newton v. Cowie, 4 Bing. 234 ; Graves v. Ashford, 36 L. J. C. P. 139.
(h) See Curtis on Copyright, p. 112.
(i) Thompson v. Symonds, 5 T. R. 41.
(k) Bogue v. Houlstone, 5 De G. & S. 275.
(l) Clementi v. Walker, 2 B. & C. 861 ; Page v. Townsend, 5 Sim. 395. See Jefferys v. Boosey, 4 H. L. 959, per Lord Cranworth.

date of the publication and the name of the proprietor are engraved on the plate, and printed on the print, &c., &c., as required by that statute (*m*).

, 7. If the print, engraving, &c., &c., differs materially from the original in character, it is not a piracy within 17 Geo. 3, c. 57 (*n*).

8. An action may be maintained against a man for selling pirated copies of a print or engraving, though he may have no knowledge that they are piratical (*o*).

9. No action will lie to recover the value of immoral, obscene, or libellous prints (*p*). Nor can a copyright exist in an engraving of an immoral character (*q*).

10. Copyright in sculpture depends on the Statute 54 Geo. 3, c. 56 (*r*). Copyright in original drawings, paintings, and photographs depends on 25 & 26 Vict. c. 68 (*s*).

SECTION VI.— COPYRIGHT IN DESIGNS.

1. Copyright in designs.
2. Statutes regulating copyright in designs for ornament.
3. Duration of copyright.
4. Who is proprietor of a design within the meaning of the statutes.
5. Protection given whether application takes place within United Kingdom or elsewhere; whether inventor be or be not an alien.
6. Meaning of " design."
7 & 8. Requisites to entitle one to the benefit of the statutes.
9. After publication every article to which design is applied must be marked or labelled.
10. What constitutes infringement.
11. Ignorance of registration does not excuse piracy.
12. Proprietor of design entitled to injunction restraining manufacture.
13. Statutes regulating copyright in designs for utility.
14. Requisites in order to bring one within the protection of the statute.
15. Design both ornamental and useful may be registered under both acts.
16–19. Various statute provisions.

1. Copyright in the application of designs for ornament, and

(*m*) Avanzo *v.* Mudie, 10 Exch. 203.
(*n*) Martin *v.* Wright, 6 Sim. 297; Newton *v.* Cowie, 4 Bing. 234, *per* Lord Wynford.
(*o*) Gambart *v.* Sumner, 5 H. & N. 5.
(*p*) Fores *v.* Johnes, 4 Esp. 97.

(*q*) Du Bost *v.* Beresford, 2 Camp. 511.
(*r*) See Philipps on Copyright, 225.
(*s*) See Philipps on Copyright, pp. 218–224; Strahan *v.* Graham, 15 W. R. 487.

copyright in the application of designs for utility are distinct rights founded upon different statutes (*t*).

2. Copyright in designs for ornament is regulated by an act 5 & 6 Vict. c. 100, amended by Acts 6 & 7 Vict. c. 65 ; 13 & 14 Vict. c. 104 ; 21 & 22 Vict. c. 70 ; and 24 & 25 Vict. c. 73. Under these acts protection is given generally to new and original designs, whether in shape, or configuration, or otherwise applicable to the ornamentation of articles of manufacture (*u*).

3. * The duration of the copyright varies according * 467 to the different articles of manufacture (*x*).

4. The inventor or author of any new and original design is the proprietor of a design within the meaning of the acts, unless he may have executed the work on behalf of another person for a valuable consideration, in which case such person is considered the proprietor, and is entitled to be registered in the place of the inventor or author (*y*) ; and every person acquiring for a valuable consideration a new and original design, or the right to apply the same to the ornamentation of any article of manufacture, either exclusively of any other person or otherwise, and also every person upon whom the property in a design, or in the right to its application, has devolved, is considered the proprietor of the design in the respect in which the same has been so acquired and to that extent only (*z*).

5. Protection is given whether the application of the design takes place within the United Kingdom or elsewhere, or whether the inventor be or be not an alien (*a*).

6. The word "design" does not mean an invention, but means something in the nature of a drawing, diagram, or picture applicable to the ornamentation of some article of manufacture. There is no analogy between a patent for an invention and a copyright for a design. The mere combination of old materials in an old manner will be protected if there be a new design. It is not necessary that there should

---

(*t*) Harrison *v.* Taylor, 4 H. & N. 819 ; Windover *v.* Smith, 32 Beav. 200.

(*u*) Millingen *v.* Picken, 1. C. B. 799 ; Harrison *v.* Taylor, 4 H. & N. 819 ; Windover *v.* Smith, 32 Beav. 200.

(*x*) See Philipps on Copyright, 232.

(*y*) See Macrae *v.* Houldsworth, 2 De G. & S. 496.

(*z*) 5 & 6 Vict. c. 100, s. 4. See, as to mode of transfer of the right to a design, *ib.* s. 6.

(*a*) 24 & 25 Vict. c. 73, ss. 1, 2.

be invention. All that is required is that the design be new (b). But to be a new design, the combination of old materials must constitute one design, and must not be merely a multiplicity of old designs (c).

7. No person is entitled to the benefit of the statutes, unless the design or a description thereof has been registered before publication (d), or unless a pattern or portion of an * 468 article of * manufacture to which the design is applied, has been furnished to the registrar before publication (e). If there has been a publication of the design, it cannot be afterwards registered (f), but if the design has been provisionally registered, the exhibition of it at certain places specified in the act will not vitiate the copyright (g).

8. A design if described in the register must be accurately described. The nature and object of the design must appear in the certificate of registration. The court is bound to look at the purpose and object of the design which has been registered (h).

9. After publication, every article to which the design is applied should have certain marks upon it, or a label attached to it containing such marks (i). The proprietor of a duly registered design, whether he be a British subject or a foreign inventor, loses the benefit of the statutes, unless the proper registration marks are attached to all articles or substances to which the design is applied, whether the same are sold abroad or in the British dominions (j).

10. No person may, without the written consent of the proprietor, apply a design protected by the statutes, or any fraudulent imitation of it, for the purposes of sale to the ornamenting of any article, or substance, in respect of which the copyright in the design is in force; and no person may publish,

---

(b) Harrison v. Taylor, 4 H. & N. 815. See Perfect v. Shepard, 1 W. R. 213.

(c) Norton v. Nicholls, 1 El. & El. 761.

(d) 5 & 6 Vict. c. 100, s. 4; Norton v. Nicholls, 1 El. & El. 761. Comp. S. C., 4 K. & J. 475. See Lowndes v. Browne, 12 Ir. L. 293.

(e) 21 & 22 Vict. c. 70, s. 5; Macrae v. Houldsworth, 5 B. & S. 495.

(f) Dalglish v. Jarvie, 2 Mac. & G. 231.

(g) 13 & 14 Vict. c. 104, s. 3.

(h) Windover v. Smith, 32 Beav. 200. See, as to certificate of registration, 5 & 6 Vict. c. 100, s. 16.

(i) 5 & 6 Vict. c. 100, s. 4.

(j) Sarazin v. Hamel, 32 Beav. 151. See, as to registration marks, Heywood v. Potter, 1 E. & B. 439. But see now 21 & 22 Vict. c. 70, s. 4.

sell, or expose for sale, any article or substance, to which the design or any fraudulent imitation of it, has been so applied after knowledge from any source other than the proprietor of the design, that his consent has not been given to such application, or after having a written notice signed by him, or his agent to the same effect (*k*).

11. *Ignorance of the registration of a design does *469 not excuse a piracy of the right therein (*l*).

12. The proprietor of a design protected by statute is entitled to an injunction restraining not merely the sale, but the manufacture of any article to which the design is applied during the period of protection (*m*).

13. Copyright in designs having reference to some purpose of utility depends on 6 & 7 Vict. c. 65 and 13 & 14 Vict. c. 104. These statutes protect "any new or original design for any article of manufacture having reference to some purpose of utility, so far as such design shall be for the shape or configuration of such article, and that whether it be for the whole of such shape or configuration, or only a part thereof" (*n*). The statutes apply only to shape and configuration, and not to a combination of old designs (*o*), or to inventions, or new applications (*p*), however useful they may be: but if the new shape or configuration make an invention useful, it is within the protection of the statutes (*q*). The same article may be both the subject of a patent and of a registration under the statute, but in the former case the ·subject is the invention: in the latter the shape or configuration. If the shape or configuration be new, it is not necessary that there be invention (*r*).

14. In order to come within the protection of the statute, it is essential that the design should be new, and that it should be applied to some particular substance (*s*). Novelty must be

(*k*) 5 & 6 Vict. c. 100, s. 7. See De la Branchardiere *v.* Elvery, 4 Exch. 380; Norton *v.* Nicholls, 1 El. & El. 761.

(*l*) Macrae *v.* Houldsworth, 2 De G. & S. 497.

(*m*) Ib.

(*n*) 6 & 7 Vict. c. 65, s. 2. See Millingen *v.* Picken, 1 C. B. 799; Rogers *v.* Driver, 16 Q. B. 102; Windover *v.*

Smith, 32 Beav. 200; Mulloney *v.* Stevens, 10 L. T. N. S. 190.

(*o*) Reg. *v.* Bessell, 16 Q. B. 810; Mulloney *v.* Stevens, 10 L. T. N. S. 190.

(*p*) Millingen *v.* Picken, 1 C. B. 799; Margetson *v.* Wright, 2 De G. & S. 424.

(*q*) Rogers *v.* Driver, 16 Q. B. 102.

(*r*) Reg. *v.* Bessell, 16 Q. B. 810.

(*s*) Mulloney *v.* Stevens, 10 L. T. N. S. 190.

combined with utility, and the novelty must be substantial and not the mere extension of a well-known principle (t). The fact that some of the items claimed may not be conducive to some purpose of utility will not, it would appear, vitiate the registration if others of them are so (u).

*470   15. * A new and original design which is ornamental as well as useful, may be registered under both the Design Acts, but if it has been registered under 6 & 7 Vict. c. 65, and cannot be supported under that act, it cannot be protected under 5 & 6 Vict. c. 100, though it might have been supported under that act, if it had been registered under it (x).

16. The clauses as to the meaning of the word " proprietor," the transfer of designs, the piracy of designs, the certificate of registration, &c., &c., contained in 5 & 6 Vict. c. 100, have been incorporated with 6 & 7 Vict. c. 65 (y).

17. The registry of a design must be before publication, and every article made according to the design must bear thereon the word " registered " with the date of registration (z). The registration of any pattern or portion of an article of manufacture, to which a design is applied, instead of or in lieu of a copy, drawing, or description in writing is sufficient (a). The registration of an article protects the whole of the design shown upon it. It is the entire combination only, and no single part of it, although new, that is protected. There is no infringement, unless the entire combination be appropriated (b). The question of novelty and infringement is for the jury, but it is for the court, looking at the article registered, without the aid of a jury, to say whether the registration is sufficient (c).

18. An alien resident abroad may be proprietor of a design within the Act 24 & 25 Vict. c. 73 (d).

19. Designs embraced within the Acts 38 Geo. 3, c. 71, 54 Geo. 3, c. 56, 5 & 6 Vict. c. 100, are not included within 6 & 7 Vict. c. 65 (e).

(t) Windover v. Smith, 32 Beav. 200.
(u) Ib.
(x) Ib.
(y) Sect. 6; Windover v. Smith, 32 Beav. 200. See supra, pp. 467, 468.
(z) 6 & 7 Vict. c. 65, s. 3.

(a) 21 & 22 Vict. c. 70, s. 5.
(b) Macrae v. Houldsworth, 1 L. R. Q. B. 264.
(c) Ib.
(d) Sect. 1.
(e) 6 & 7 Vict. c. 65, s. 2.

SECTION VII.—INTERNATIONAL COPYRIGHT.

1–4. Statute provisions in relation to International Copyright.

1. The International Copyright Act, 7 & 8 Vict. c. 12, amended and explained by 15 & 16 Vict. c. 12, empowers the Queen, by order in council, to direct that authors, inventors, designers, * engravers, and makers of books, * 471 prints, articles of sculpture, and other works of art, first published abroad, shall have copyright here, and that authors of dramatic pieces and musical compositions first published and performed abroad shall have the sole liberty of representing or performing the same here. The protection given to translations of books published abroad depends on 15 & 16 Vict. c. 12, ss. 2–5 (f).

2. The 19th clause of the International Copyright Act, 7 & 8 Vict. c. 12, which enacts that no author of any book or dramatic piece, which shall be first published out of Her Majesty's dominions, shall have copyright therein, otherwise than under the provisions of the act, applies to British subjects first publishing in a country with which no international convention exists (g). A British author who first publishes in a country with which a convention has been made under the statute is entitled to protection. If no convention has been made with the country in which he first publishes he cannot be protected (h).

3. The right to sue depends on compliance with the conditions which the statute imposes on those who desire to reap the benefit of the act (i). The work which it is desired to protect must be duly registered within a certain time (j). The music of an opera which contained no piano-forte score, having been arranged for the piano by a musician, not the composer of the opera, it was held that the registration of the

(f) See Philipps on Copyright, 249. See, also, ib. 251, the Order in Council respecting international copyright with France.

(g) Boucicault v. Delafield, 1 H. & M. 597.
(h) Ib.
(i) Wood v. Boosey, 36 L. J. Q. B. 103.
(j) Ib.

name of the composer of the opera as the author was an undue registration, and that the name of the arranger should have been entered as the author (*k*). The proprietor of a foreign print, who claims copyright, must comply with the provisions of our own Engraving Acts. Nor can foreign authors claim any exception from the conditions affecting authors of works in this country (*l*). Neglect on the part of the * 472 officials * at Stationers' Hall to register a book, will deprive a foreign author of the benefit of the statute (*m*).

4. In Cassell *v.* Stiff (*n*), a motion was made to restrain the infringement of an alleged copyright in a French newspaper, but Wood, V. C., doubted whether the case came within the provisions of the Order in Council.

SECTION VIII.—ACCOUNT, COSTS, ETC.

1 & 2. Right to an account of profits incidental to right to an injunction.   Practice.
3. Plaintiff entitled to discovery.
4. Practice as to costs and perpetual injunction.

1. The right to an account of profits is incidental to the right to an injunction. If the cause is brought to a hearing, and a perpetual injunction is decreed, the plaintiff is entitled to the account as incidental to the relief by injunction (*o*). If the account is small, it is usually waived (*p*), but when it is not waived the court grants it upon principles which have been thus stated by Wigram, V. C., in Colburn *v.* Simms (*q*): "The court does not by an account accurately measure the damage sustained by the proprietor of an expensive work from the invasion of his copyright by the publication of a cheaper book. It is impossible to know how many copies of the dearer book are excluded from sale by the interposition of the cheaper one. The court by the account, as the nearest approximation which it can make to justice, takes from the wrong-doer all the

(*k*) Wood *v.* Boosey, 36 L. J. Q. B. 103.
(*l*) Avanzo *v.* Mudie, 10 Exch. 203.
(*m*) Cassell *v.* Stiff, 2 K. & J. 279.
(*n*) Ib.
(*o*) Baily *v.* Taylor, 1 R. & M. 73;
Sheriff *v.* Coates, *ib.* 159; Kelly *v.* Hooper, 1 Y. & C. C. C. 197.
(*p*) See Fradella *v.* Weller, 2 R. & M. 247.
(*q*) 2 Ha. 560.

profits he has made by his piracy, and gives them all to the party who has been injured. In doing that the court may give the injured party more in fact than he is entitled to, for *non constat* that a single additional copy of the more expensive work would have been sold, if the injury by the sale of the cheaper work had not been committed. The court does not give any thing more than the account " (*r*). The delivery up of the pirated copies depends entirely upon statute. There is not any common-law right on the subject (*s*). The 23d section of the Statute 5 & * 6 Vict. c. 45, which gives the   * 473
registered proprietor of copyright in literary matter the
right to have all the unsold copies of a pirated book delivered up, does not give him any right in a court of equity to more than the usual account of the net profits of all copies which may have been sold. He has no right in this court to an account of the gross proceeds. To recover the unsold copies he must proceed at law (*t*). At law he is entitled to have all the unsold copies delivered up to him for his own use without making any compensation for the cost of production and publication (*u*).

2. In a case within the Copyright of Designs Act, 5 & 6 Vict. c. 100, Knight Bruce, L. J., made an order for the delivery up to the plaintiff, for the purpose of being destroyed, of all drawings and cards used by the defendant in applying his design, and also of all articles manufactured by the defendants to which the plaintiff's design had been applied (*x*).

3. The defendant must, if required to do so for the purposes of the account or the inquiry as to damages, set out the number of copies containing pirated matter which have been sold by him (*y*). The plaintiff is entitled to continue the suit, until the discovery be given (*z*).

4. A man whose copyright is invaded is entitled to an injunction with costs (*a*). If the defendant do not, after injunction obtained, offer to pay the costs, and to give the plaintiff

(*r*) See, as to account in patent cases, *supra*, pp. 435, 436. See, as to inquiry as to damages, *supra*, pp. 221-224, 436.
(*s*) Colburn *v.* Simms, 2 Ha. 560.
(*t*) Delfe *v.* Delamotte, 3 K. &. J. 581.
(*u*) *Ib.*; 5 & 6 Vict. c. 45, s. 23.

(*x*) Macrae *v.* Houldsworth, 2 De G. & S. 497.
(*y*) Stevens *v.* Brett, 12 W. R. 572. See, also, *supra*, p. 436.
(*z*) See Colburn *v.* Simms, 2 Ha. 543; Kelly *v.* Hooper, 1 Y. & C. C. 197.
(*a*) *Supra*, pp. 214-216.

all the other relief to which he is entitled, the plaintiff may bring the suit to a hearing, and will be entitled to the costs of the suit, although at the hearing he may waive his right to the other relief (*b*). But if the defendant offers to submit to the injunction with costs, and to give the plaintiff all the relief to which he is entitled, the court will not give the plaintiff his costs of the subsequent prosecution of the suit to the hearing (*c*).

(*b*) Kelly *v*. Hooper, 1 Y. & C. C. C. 197; Colburn *v*. Simms, 2 Ha. 561; *supra*, pp. 227–230; *infra*, p. 490.   (*c*) *Supra*, p. 229.

*CHAPTER XXI.   *474

INJUNCTIONS TO RESTRAIN THE PIRACY OF TRADE-MARKS.

1. THE jurisdiction of courts of equity in restraining by interlocutory injunction the piracy of trade-marks is in aid of the legal right, and is founded on the equity of protecting

[493]

property from irreparable damage. The principles upon which a court of 'equity interferes, for the protection of trade-marks, are the same as those upon which it acts in other cases in protecting legal rights to property from violation (a).[1]

2. A trade-mark is a particular mark or symbol, used by a man for the purpose of denoting that the article to which it is affixed is sold or manufactured by him or by his authority, or that he carries on his business at a particular place. A trade-mark does not partake of the nature or character of a patent. A man has a right to manufacture the same article as an article made by another, unless the article be the subject of a patent, and to represent it as the same. If an article has acquired in the market a certain name, not as expressing the nature of a particular specimen, but as describing the nature of the article by whomsoever made, any man has a right to manufacture it and to call it by that name. No man, however, has a right to pass off his own goods as the goods of a rival trader. If a mark or symbol comes by use to be recognized in trade as the mark of the goods of a particular person, no other trader has a right to brand the same or a similar mark upon goods of a similar description, so as to induce a purchaser to believe that they are the goods of the person whose mark they bear. A man whose goods have obtained a reputation

* 475   in the market is entitled to * all the advantages of that reputation whether resulting from the greater demand for his goods or from the higher price which the public are willing to give for them rather than for the goods of other manufacturers whose reputation is not so high. No other trader has a right either directly or indirectly to represent that the article which he sells was manufactured by the person whose name or mark it bears as descriptive of quality or by any person to whom this person has assigned his business or his rights. He has no right to do this either by positive statements or by adopting the trade-mark of the person whose name it bears as descriptive of quality, or by using a trade-mark so nearly resembling it as to be calculated to mislead

(a) Leather Cloth Company v. American Cloth Company, 33 L. J. Ch. 200; supra, p. 196.

[1] Where it appears that the party infringing a trade-mark intends to continue the wrong, an injunction is the sole adequate remedy. Bradley v. Norton, 83 Conn. 157.

unwary and incautious purchasers (b).[1] A man whose mark or symbol as applied to goods of a particular description obtains currency in the market as an indication of superior value, or of some other circumstance that renders the articles to which it is applied acceptable to a purchaser, acquires the exclusive right to the use of the mark or symbol in connection with the sale of that particular class of goods. The right is limited to the use of the mark in connection with a particular class of goods. Apart from the particular use or application there is no right to the use of the symbol. The use of the same mark or symbol in connection with goods of a different class is not an infringement of the right (c).

3. The right to the exclusive use of a trade-mark is established, as soon as the particular article to which the mark or symbol is applied obtains acceptance and reputation in the market, and the mark or symbol gets currency as an indication of superior value, or of some other circumstance that renders the article to which it is applied acceptable to a purchaser. It is not necessary that there should have been such an antecedent user of the mark as to acquire for the article on which it is stamped a general notoriety and reputation in the market. The right *may be established as soon as *476 the article is actually in the market, but it cannot be acquired before that time (d).

4. A trade-mark may be either a local or a personal mark: the former indicating that the article so branded is made or sold at a particular place, the latter indicating that the article has been made or is sold by a particular person: but a mark, though it may in some respects indicate the person by whom goods are manufactured, may refer much more closely to the place of manufacture than to the person of the manufacturer. The mark though originally the name of the first maker of an article may in time, or from the mode in which it has been

(b) Perry v. Truefitt, 6 Beav. 66; Leather Cloth Co. v. American Cloth Co., 11 H. L. 523, 538, per Lord Kingsdown; Glenny v. Smith, 2 Dr. & Sm. 476; Seixo v. Provezende, 1 L. R. Ch. Ap. 192; Ainsworth v. Walmsley, 1 L. R. Eq. 508.

(c) Edelsten v. Edelsten, 1 D. J. & S. 185; Leather Cloth Co. v. American Cloth Co., 33 L. J. Ch. 199; Hall v.

Barrows, ib. 204; Macandrew v. Bassett, ib. 561; Braham v. Bustard, 1 H. & M. 447; Ainsworth v. Walmsley, 1 L. R. Eq. 508.

(d) Lawson v. Bank of London, 18 C. B. 84; Macandrew v. Bassett, 33 L. J. Ch. 561; Maxwell v. Hogg, 2 L. R. Ch. Ap. 307.

[1] Taylor v. Carpenter, 11 Paige, 292.

used, have become appropriated to goods manufactured at a particular place, or have become a sign of quality, or may have ceased to denote or be current as indicating that a particular person is the maker (e).

5. A name, symbol, or emblem, however unmeaning in itself, or even ridiculous, may be the subject of a trade-mark (f).[1]

6. A word or name which is merely descriptive of an article (g), or is the current name by which a particular article is known in the market (h), or is a name which merely denotes the general character of a business (i), cannot be the subject of a trade-mark.[2] But a name which is the ancient name of the country from which an article is procured may be adopted as a trade-mark in respect of the article (j). In Gout v. Aleploglu (k), the word "warranted" put on an article in Turkish letters was *held not to be a trade-mark,
* 477 because the Turkish word was to an Englishman wholly without meaning. So also may a system of numbers adopted and used by a man to designate his goods be the subject of the same protection as an ordinary trade-mark (l). A crest may be the subject of a trade-mark (m).

7. The principle which applies to the case of a man selling his own goods as the goods of another applies to the case of a man using the name of another for the purpose of reaping the

(e) Hall v. Barrows, 33 L. J. Ch. 204; Bury v. Bedford, ib. 465. See Canham v. Jones, 2 V. & B. 218. The original inventor of a new manufacture, and persons claiming under him, are alone entitled to designate such manufacture as "the original;" and if he or they have been in the habit of so designating their manufacture, an injunction will be granted to restrain another manufacturer from applying the designation to his goods. Cocks v. Chandler, 11 L. R. Eq. 446.

(f) Perry v. Truefitt, 6 Beav. 66; Braham v. Bustard, 1 H. & M. 447; Kinahan v. Bolton, 15 Ir. Ch. 75.

(g) Burgess v. Burgess, 3 D. M. & G. 896; Edelsten v. Vick, 11 Ha. 84. See Canham v. Jones, 2 V. & B. 218; Braham v. Bustard, 1 H. & M. 447.

(h) Braham v. Bustard, ib.; Young v. Macrae, 9 Jur. N. S. 322; Browne v. Freeman, 4 N. R. 476, 12 W. R. 305; Williams v. Osborne, 13 L. T. N. S. 948.

(i) London and Provincial Law As-

surance Society v. London and Provincial Joint Stock Life Assurance Co., 11 Jur 938; London Assurance v. London and Westminster Assurance Corporation, 32 L. J. Ch. 664; Colonial Life Assurance Co. v. Home and Colonial Life Assurance Co., 33 L. J. Ch. 741.

(j) Macandrew v. Bassett, 33 L. J. Ch. 561.

(k) 6 Beav. 69, n.

(l) Ainsworth v. Walmsley, 1 L. R. Eq. 518.

(m) Beard v. Turner, 13 L. T. N. S. 746; Standish v. Whitwell, 14 W. R. 512.

[1] Where the complainant had for many years manufactured steel pens, which had acquired a high reputation in the market, and marked them "303 extra fine," and with his name, the defendant was restrained from making similar pens with the same number and his own name. Gillott v. Esterbrook, 47 Barb. 455.

[2] Congress and Empire Spring Co. v. High Rock Congress Spring Co., 57 Barb. 526.

benefit of the reputation which that other has already acquired in the market. A man has a right to set up a shop anywhere for the sale of goods under his own name, although another may have been long selling the same class of goods under the same name, and although the goods, as associated with his name, may have acquired a reputation in the market. The mere user by a man of his own name is of itself no evidence of fraud, but there may be other elements in the case, showing that the name has been fraudulently used for the purpose of reaping the benefit of the reputation which another has already acquired. It is in each case a matter of evidence, whether or not the use of the name has been fraudulent (*n*). If a man changes his name and assumes another and sets up a business in the neighborhood of a person who has long carried on the same business under the name which he has assumed, fraud will be, as a general rule, presumed (*o*).

8. The same principles which apply to the right to use a name are also applicable to the case of the use of a partnership firm or style. If the use of a partnership firm or style be *bonâ fide*, the court will not interpose ; but if there be evidence to show that the name has been taken for the purpose of having the benefit of the reputation which another has acquired in the market, there is a case of fraud (*p*).

A man who has been in * the employment of a firm of   * 478 reputation has a right on setting up a business of a similar character to inform the public in any way he thinks fit that he has been in such employment ; but in so doing he must take especial care that it be not done in such a way as to mislead or lead to the belief that he is carrying on the business or a branch of the business of the firm whose name he uses (*q*). A man who has assigned the good-will of a business may, unless precluded by covenant, set up the same business in the immediate neighborhood, but he may not put himself forward as carrying on the same business, which he has assigned (*r*).

(*n*) Rodgers *v.* Nowill, 6 Ha. 325 ; Holloway *v.* Holloway, 13 Beav. 209 ; Burgess *v.* Burgess, 3 D. M. & G. 896 ; Taylor *v.* Taylor, 23 L. J. Ch. 255 ; Dent *v.* Turpin, 2 J. & H. 139 ; Churton *v.* Douglas, John. 174. See Sykes *v.* Sykes, 3 B. & C. 541 ; Foot *v.* Lee, 13 Ir. Eq. 490.

(*o*) Burgess *v.* Burgess, 3 D. M. & G. 896. See Croft *v.* Day, 7 Beav. 84 ; Southorn *v.* Reynolds, 12 L. T. N. S. 75.
(*p*) Croft *v.* Day, 7 Beav. 84.
(*q*) Glenny *v.* Smith, 2 Dr. & Sm. 476 ; Williams *v.* Osborne, 13 L. T. N. S. 498 ; *supra*, p. 167.
(*r*) Shackle *v.* Baker, 14 Ves. 468 ;

Upon the same principle a trader will be restrained from hold-ing himself out as being in business with another trader or from issuing circulars tending to lead the public to suppose that he has succeeded to the business of another trader. If the business of the latter suffers damage thereby, it is immate-rial that the words of the circular may be literally true (s).

9. A publisher or author has either in the title of his work or in the application of his name to the work, or in the par-ticular marks which designate it, a species of property similar to that which a trader has in his trade-mark, and may like a trader claim the protection of the court against such a use or imitation of the name, marks, or designation, as is likely in the opinion of the court to be a cause of damage to him in respect of that property (t). A man, however, has a full right to publish a similar work under the same title as that of another, if he represents it as distinct and original; but he may not with-out authority advertise his own work as the continuation of another (u).

*479   10. * A man cannot by advertising his intention of publishing a periodical under a certain name and making preparations for issuing it acquire a right to the exclusive use of the name, the periodical not having appeared before bill filed(x).

11. The name of the editor is not a necessary part of the title of a journal. In the absence of any special contract to that effect, the court will not restrain the owners of a journal from publishing it without the name of the editor (y).

12. If a trade-mark denotes the place or works where goods are made or denotes a particular business, the exclusive right to use the mark passes to a purchaser upon the sale and trans-fer of the place or works or the particular business (z). But

Cruttwell v. Lye, 17 Ves. 335; Churton v. Douglas, John. 174; *supra*, p. 167.

(s) Harper v. Pearson, 3 L. T. N. S. 547; Edgington v. Edgington, 11 L. T. N. S. 299; *supra*, pp. 169, 170.

(t) Hogg v. Kirby, 8 Ves. 215; Lord Byron v. Johnstone, 2 Mer. 29; Keene v. Harris, cited 17 Ves. 342; Seely v. Fisher, 11 Sim. 582; Spottiswoode v. Clark. 2 Ph. 154; Prowett v. Mortimer, 2 Jur. N. S. 414; Clement v. Maddick, 1 Giff. 98; Chappell v. Sheard, 2 K. & J. 117; Chappell v. Davidson, *ib.* 123, 8 D. M. & G. 1; Ingram v. Stiff, 5 Jur. N. S.

947; Maxwell v. Hogg, 2 L. R. Ch. Ap. 307.

(u) Hogg v. Kirby, 8 Ves. 215. See Archbold v. Sweet, 1 M. & R. 162.

(x) Maxwell v. Hogg, 2 L. R. Ch. Ap. 307.

(y) Crookes v. Petter, 6 Jur. N. S. 1131.

(z) Motley v. Downman, 3 M. & C. 1. See Hall v. Barrows, 33 L. J. Ch. 204; Bury v. Bedford, *ib.* 465; Leather Cloth Co. v. American Cloth Co., 11 H. L. 523; Banks v. Gibson, 34 Beav. 566; *supra*, p. 168.

a trade-mark which specially denotes the particular persons by whom goods are made is not assignable. A trade-mark, however, which, though it may in some respects indicate the persons by whom the goods are manufactured, refers more closely to the place of manufacture, or to the particular business, than to the person of the manufacturer, or has, though it may originally have denoted the persons by whom the goods are manufactured, become a sign of quality, and has ceased to denote that a particular person is the manufacturer, is assignable (a).[1]

13. Upon the formation of a partnership firm, a trade-mark to which one of the partners may be entitled becomes in the absence of any stipulation part of the partnership property (b).

14. The right to the use of a particular designation or partnership style passes, on the death of a partner, to the surviving partners or partner (c). On the death of a surviving partner it passes to his personal representatives (d). On the dissolution of a partnership, each of the partners has the right, in the absence of a stipulation to the contrary, to use it (e).[2]

15. * Two or more persons may be tenants in com-   * 480 mon in a trade-mark, and where such is the case, each of them has a right to sue alone in respect of the wrong done to himself (f).

16. The owner of a trade-mark and his agent cannot sue jointly, although the name of the agent appears on the trade-mark (g).

17. The right to a trade-mark being a personal right, the party complaining may proceed against the offending party in the country where he resides, wherever the injury-may have been done (h). An alien may sue without averring that the

---

(a) Bury v. Bedford, 33 L. J. Ch. 465.
(b) Ib. See Banks v. Gibson, 34 Beav. 566.
(c) Webster v. Webster, 3 Sw. 490, n.; Lewis v. Langdon, 7 Sim. 421; supra, p. 168.
(d) Hine v. Lart, 10 Jur. 107. See Dent v. Turpin, 2 J. & H. 139.
(e) Banks v. Gibson, 34 Beav. 566. See Smith v. Everett, 27 Beav. 446; Johnson v. Helleley, 2 D. J. & S. 446; supra, p. 167.
(f) Dent v. Turpin, 2 J. & H. 139; Batty v. Hill, 1 H. & M. 270; Southorn v. Reynolds, 12 L. T. N. S. 75.
(g) Delondre v. Shaw, 2 Sim. 237.

(h) Collins Co. v. Brown, 3 K. & J. 426; Collins Co. v. Cowen, ib. 430; Collins Co. v. Reeves, 4 Jur. N. S. 867
[1] The name established for a hotel is a trade-mark; and a tenant, by giving a particular name to a building, as a sign of the hotel business for which he uses it, does not thereby make the name a fixture of the building, and the property of the landlord upon the expiration of the lease. Woodward v. Lazar, 21 Cal. 448. See, also, Howe v. Searing, 19 How. Pr. Rep. 14.
[2] See Comstock v. Moore, 18 How. Pr. 421.

goods bearing the pirated mark have been actually sold in this country. It is sufficient that the counterfeit mark has been imposed on the goods in this country (i). A foreign sovereign or state may, like an individual, have an injunction to restrain the undue or unauthorized use of his or its name (j).

18. To entitle a person to sue it is not necessary to aver special damage ; it is sufficient to show that a general injury has been done to the plaintiff (k).

19. If other parties are necessary for any part of the relief prayed, that is sufficient to sustain a demurrer for want of parties, and it is no answer to such demurrer to say that that part of the relief may be waived at the hearing (l).

20. The interference of a court of equity to restrain the piracy of trade-marks being founded on pure equitable principles (m), a trader will not be protected in the exclusive use of a trade-mark, if the trade-mark contains misstate-
*481 ments of any *material fact calculated to deceive the public. A trader who falsely leads purchasers to believe that they are buying something different from that which in fact he is selling, or is guilty of any misrepresentation with respect to his goods as to amount to a fraud upon the public, disentitles himself as against a rival trader to that relief in a court of equity which he would have otherwise obtained (n). [1] If a trade-mark represents an article as protected by a patent, when in fact it is not so protected, such a statement amounts *primâ facie* to a misrepresentation of an important fact, which would disentitle the owner of the mark to relief in a court of equity against any man who pirated it (o). In the case of

(i) Collins Co. v. Brown, 3 K. & J. 426 ; Collins Co. v. Reeves, 4 Jur. N. S. 867. The rule as to the right of an alien to sue for the piracy of his trade-mark is the same in the State of New York. Taylor v. Carpenter, 2 Sandf. Ch. (Amer.) 603, 3 Story (Amer.), 463, 2 Wood. & Min. 1. It is not a bar to a suit there that a remedy is not reciprocally allowed to aliens in the country to which the alien who sues belongs. Ib. ; Coats v. Holbrook, 2 Sandf. Ch. (Amer.) 587.

(j) Emperor of Austria v. Day, 3 D. F. & J. 215, per Turner, L. J.

(k) Dent v. Turpin, 2 J. & H. 139. See Blofeld v. Payne, 4 B. & A. 410.

(l) Dent v. Turpin, 2 J. & H. 139. See, as to parties, supra, pp. 207, 208.

(m) See Maxwell v. Hogg, 2 L. R. Ch. Ap. 307 ; supra, pp. 17, 200, 201.

(n) Pidding v. How, 8 Sim. 477 ; Perry v. Truefitt, 6 Beav. 76 ; Edelsten v. Edelsten, 1 D. J. & S. 185 ; Collins Co. v. Reeves, 4 Jur. N. S. 865 ; Leather Cloth Co. v. American Cloth Co., 11 H. L. 523.

(o) Leather Cloth Co. v. American Cloth Co., 11 H. L. 543, per Lord Kingsdown ; Flavel v. Harrison, 10 Ha.

[1] Hobbs v. Francais, 19 How. Pr. Rep. 567 ; Fetridge v. Wells, 13 How. Pr. 385.

Edelsten *v.* Vick (*p*), Wood, V. C., doubted whether the rule
would be the same if there had been originally a patent, and
the statement in the trade-mark being true when first introduced, had been continued after it had ceased to be true. But
there can be no distinction between the cases. If the word
"patent" be not so used as to indicate the existing protection
of a patent, but merely as part of the designation of an article
thrown into the market, nobody is meant to be deceived, and
nobody is deceived. A patent may have expired and be known
to have expired fifty years ago, and yet the name of patent may
have become attached to the article, and be used in the trade
as designating it. But if the trade-mark represents the article
as protected by a patent, when in fact it is not so protected,
there is no difference whether the protection never existed or
has ceased to exist. If the true effect of the trade-mark or
label be to represent that the article stamped with it is protected by a patent, and it is not so protected, there is misrepresentation of a material fact, calculated to mislead the
public, and sufficient to debar the plaintiff from relief against
piracy in a court of equity (*q*). If a trade-mark is not only a
trade-mark properly so called, but contains statements
* materially affecting the value of the goods to which it   * 482
is affixed, these statements must be judged of like statements made in separate labels or advertisements (*r*).

21. The principle that a misstatement in a trade mark will
deprive a man of his right to apply to the court for relief, does
not apply to the case of the use of the name of a firm by any
but the original partners. The name of a firm may be used
long after all the original partners have died, or have ceased to
have any interest in the concern. By the usage of trade the
name of a firm is understood not to be confined to those who
first adopted it, but to extend to and include persons who have
been afterwards introduced as partners, or persons to whom
the original partners have transferred their business. The
use, therefore, of the old trade-mark of a firm by the new

467; Morgan *v.* M'Adam, 36 L. J. Ch.
228. But not when the goods have
from the usage of many years acquired
the designation in the trade generally
of patent. Marshall *v.* Ross, 8 L. R. Eq.
651.

(*p*) 11 Ha. 87.
(*q*) Leather Cloth Co. *v.* American
Cloth Co., 11 H. L. 523, 543.
(*r*) Leather Cloth Co. *v.* American
Cloth Co., 11 H. L. 523, 543, *per* Lord
Kingsdown.

partners or their successors is no fraud upon the public, but is merely a statement that they are carrying on the same business as was formerly carried on by the person or persons whose name constituted the trade-mark (*s*). The case, however, is different if a trade-mark be so completely personal in its nature, as necessarily to indicate that the goods to which it is affixed are the manufacture of a particular person. If an artist or artisan has acquired by his personal skill and ability a reputation which gives his works or goods in the market a higher value than those of other artists or artisans, there is an imposition on the public, if a man, to whom he has transferred his business, uses his name or trade-mark. A man may assign his business to another, but he cannot give him the right to use his name or mark, if the effect of the statement be necessarily to indicate that the goods to which it is affixed are the goods of the person whose name and mark they bear, and the value of the goods be materially affected by the statement (*t*). If, however, a trade-mark be a mark which refers more closely to the place of manufacture or to the particular business than to the firm of the manufacturer, although it may originally have denoted the person by whom the goods were manufactured, or has become a sign of quality, and ceased to denote that
* 483   a particular person * carries on the business, the assignee of the locality is not guilty of a misrepresentation to the public in making use of the mark (*u*).

22. It has not been determined whether a mere puffing exaggeration in labels, &c., is such a misstatement as will deprive a man of his right to the protection of the court. In Holloway *v.* Holloway (*x*), the owner of a patent medicine was protected, notwithstanding his profession to cure thereby all manner of diseases, on the ground that the medicine was stamped and protected by law. The general question was left undetermined, but the rule would appear to be, that a mere puffing exaggeration, by which no reasonable man ought to be deceived, goes for nothing (*y*).

(*s*) Leather Cloth Co. *v.* American Cloth Co., 11 H. L. 523.
(*t*) *Ib.*
(*u*) Bury *v.* Bedford, 33 L. J. Ch. 465. See Hall *v.* Burrows, *ib.* 204.

(*x*) 13 Beav. 209.
(*y*) *Ib.* See Perry *v.* Truefitt, 6 Beav. 76.

23. The owner of a trade-mark who seeks the aid of the court for the protection of his mark must use due diligence in making the application. Delay or acquiescence may deprive a man of his right to the protection of the court. The suit should be instituted without delay after the discovery of the fraud (z).[1] A protest however by the owner of the mark against the use of it by the other party (a), or advertisements cautioning the public against imposition (b), will disprove acquiescence, although there may have been for some time a colorable user. So, also, the consequences of delay may be excluded, if it can be shown that a man has continued to use the mark after being cautioned (c).

24. It is impossible to lay down any general rule as to what degree of resemblance is necessary to constitute the fraudulent or colorable imitation of a trade-mark. All that can be done is to ascertain in every case as it occurs, whether there is such a resemblance as that ordinary purchasers purchasing with ordinary caution are likely to be misled. There is no infringement, although there may be certain resemblances between two * trade-marks, if there be not such a gen- * 484 eral resemblance as to deceive an ordinary purchaser. The question in all cases of the sort is, not whether a careful and cautious purchaser, or a person conversant with the particular matter, or the public generally, or a majority of them, is likely to be deceived, but whether the unwary, the heedless, the incautious portion of the public would be likely to be deceived (d).[2] It is not necessary that the resemblance should be such as to deceive persons who should see the two marks placed side by side. If a purchaser looking at the

(z) Chappell v. Sheard, 2 K. & J. 117; Chappell v. Davidson, ib. 123; Kinahan v. Bolton, 15 Ir. Ch. 75; Beard v. Turner, 13 L. T. N. S. 746; Chubb v. Griffiths, 35 Beav. 127; supra, pp. 201-205.

(a) Motley v. Downman, 3 M. & C. 1.
(b) Kinahan v. Bolton, 15 Ir. Ch. 75.
(c) Harrison v. Taylor, 11 Jur. N. S. 408.

(d) Leather Cloth Co. v. American Cloth Co., 11 H. L. 523; Glenny v. Smith, 2 Dr. & Sm. 476; Seixo v. Provizende, 1 L. R. Ch. Ap. 192.

[1] Where the complainant, a manu-facturer of steel pens which were marked with his trade-mark, had placed upon his boxes a "caution" to the public to beware of pens similarly marked which were made by others, it was held that he had not thereby acquiesced in the use of this trade-mark by others. Gillott v. Esterbrook, 47 Barb. 455.

[2] Walton v. Crowley, 3 Blatchf. C. C. R. 440. Clark v. Clark, 25 Barb. 79; Brooklyn White L. Co. v. Masury, ib. 416. And the imitation of the manner of putting up articles will be enjoined. Williams v. Johnson, 2 Bosworth, 1.

article offered to him would naturally be led from the mark
impressed on it to suppose it to be the production of a rival
manufacturer, and would purchase it in that belief, the court
considers the use of such mark to be fraudulent. The actual
physical resemblance of the two marks is not the sole question
for consideration. If the goods of a manufacturer have from
the mark or device he has used become known in the market
by a particular name, the adoption by a rival trader of any
mark which will cause his goods to bear the same name in the
market may be as much a violation of the rights of that rival
as the actual copy of his device (e). If no one has in fact been
deceived the court may give the defendant the benefit of the
doubt (f), but the mere fact that no one has been deceived is
immaterial if the resemblance is calculated to deceive an ordinary purchaser, nor does it signify whether the defendant has
acted with a fraudulent intention or not. It is enough if even
without any unfair intention he has done that which is calculated to deceive (g).

25. Nor can a trader, even with some claim to use it, adopt
a brand the probable effect of which will be to lead the public
to suppose that they are buying the goods of a rival trader (h).

The fact that an article has been offered for sale to a
* 485   person * who asked for the plaintiff's article is sufficient
proof of fraud, though the article was not represented
to be the plaintiff's article (i). The express direction to a
manufacturer to imitate a man's way of making up his goods (j),
or to put upon goods the trade-mark of another (k), is always
a strong element of suspicion, but is not conclusive of fraud (l).
The change of one trade-mark for another, which resembles
closely the trade-mark of another, is strong evidence of
fraud (m).

(e) Seixo v. Provizende, 1 L. R. Ch. Ap. 192.

(f) Woollam v. Ratcliff, 1 H. & M. 259; Browne v. Freeman, 12 W. R. 305, 4 N. R. 476.

(g) Leather Cloth Co. v. American Cloth Co., 1 H. & M. 295, 11 H. L. 523; Glenny v. Smith, 2 Dr. & Sm. 476. See Edelsten v. Edelsten, 1 D. J. & S. 185.

(h) Seixo v. Provizende, 1 L. R. Ch. Ap. 192.

(i) Leather Cloth Co. v. American Cloth Co., 1 H. & M. 295; Edelsten v. Edelsten, 1 D. J. & S. 185.

(j) Woollam v. Ratcliff, 1 H. & M. 259.

(k) Collins Co. v. Reeves, 4 Jur. N. S. 865; Collins Co. v. Walker, 7 W. R. 222.

(l) See Farina v. Silverlock, 6 D. M. & G. 214; Taylor v. Taylor, 23 L. J. Ch. 255; Macandrew v. Bassett, 33 L. J. Ch. 561.

(m) Taylor v. Taylor, 23 L. J. Ch. 255.

26. Where there is no actual trade-mark, but the manufacturer merely employs certain symbols or indicia for the purpose of denoting his goods in the market, the more these symbols or indicia are employed by another, the more the suspicion increases that there is an intention to deceive (*n*). The fact that a trade-mark, or a name which accompanies the other symbols or indicia, may not have been taken (*o*), or that only a part of the mark has been taken (*p*), will not rebut the conclusion of fraud. It is no excuse that the person to whom the goods have been sold may be well aware, or may be informed, that they are not the manufacture of the person whose mark, or symbol, or indicia they bear, if they have been supplied for the purpose of being sold again in the market (*q*).

27. The making up of goods in a form so as to resemble the way in which another man makes up his goods (*r*), the use of wrappers for goods resembling those employed by another man (*s*), or of labels, resembling in shape, color, size, or general * appearance those imposed by another man   * 486 on his goods (*t*), the arrangement of type in such a way as to strike the eye and mislead the public (*u*), the use of similar words, letters, numbers or figures, or the arrangement of them in a similar mode (*x*), or other resemblances of a like nature (*y*), are always elements of a suspicious nature, and

---

(*n*) Knott *v.* Morgan, 2 Keen. 213; Woollam *v.* Ratcliff, 1 H. & M. 261; Leather Cloth Co. *v.* American Cloth Co., *ib.* 292. See Croft *v.* Day, 7 Beav. 88.

(*o*) Braham *v.* Bustard, 1 H. & M. 447; Kinahan *v.* Bolton, 15 Ir. Ch. 75.

(*p*) Kinahan *v.* Bolton, 15 Ir. Ch. 75.

(*q*) Sykes *v.* Sykes, 3 B. & C. 541; Chappell *v.* Davidson, 2 K. & J. 117.

(*r*) Holloway *v.* Holloway, 13 Beav. 209; Taylor *v.* Taylor, 23 L. J. Ch. 255; Woollam *v.* Ratcliff, 1 H. & M. 259; Braham *v.* Bustard, *ib.* 447.

(*s*) Blofield *v.* Payne, 4 B. & A. 410.

(*t*) Croft *v.* Day, 7 Beav. 84; Day *v.* Binning, 1 Coo. C. C. 489; Holloway *v.* Holloway, 13 Beav. 209; Shrimpton *v.* Laight, 18 Beav. 165; Taylor *v.* Taylor, 23 L. J. Ch. 255; Edelsten *v.* Vick, 11 Ha. 84; Burgess *v.* Burgess, 3 D. M.

& G. 896; Edelsten *v.* Edelsten, 1 D. J. & S. 185; Harrison *v.* Taylor, 11 Jur. N. S. 408.

(*u*) Day *v.* Binning, 1 Coo. C. C. 489; Burgess *v.* Burgess, 3 D. M. & G. 896; Taylor *v.* Taylor, 23 L. J. Ch. 255; Foot *v.* Lea, 13 Ir. Eq. 490; Glenny *v.* Smith, 2 Dr. & Sm. 476; Kinahan *v.* Bolton, 15 Ir. Eq. 75.

(*x*) Croft *v.* Day, 7 Beav. 84; Ransome *v.* Bentall, 3 L. J. Ch. N. S. 161; Purser *v.* Brain, 17 L. J. Ch. 141; Taylor *v.* Taylor, 23 L. J. Ch. 255; Kinahan *v.* Bolton, 15 Ir. Ch. 75; Glenny *v.* Smith, 2 Dr. & Sm. 476; Ainsworth *v.* Walmsley, 1 L. R. Eq. 518.

(*y*) Canham *v.* Jones, 2 V. & B. 220; Sedon *v.* Senate, cited *ib.*; Knott *v.* Morgan, 2 Keen. 219; Spottiswoode *v.* Clark, 2 Ph. 154; Gout *v.* Aleploglu, 6 Beav. 69, n.; Franks *v.* Weaver, 10 Beav. 297; Edelsten *v.* Edelsten, 1 D. J. & S. 185; Glenny *v.* Smith, 2 Dr. & Sm. 476.

will generally be enough to lead necessarily to the conclusion
of fraud. Fraud, however, will not be presumed unneces-
sarily (z). If the act may be innocent, the court will pause
before determining it to be fraudulent (a). In Farina v.
Silverlock (b), Lord Cranworth recognized the right of a
printer to print and sell generally labels to other persons than
the proprietor (c). As a general rule, however, a person
who, without the authority of the owner of the mark or brand,
stamps it upon goods and sells the goods so stamped to another,
lays himself open to the presumption that he is a party to the
fraud (d). If the acts complained of are likely to deceive, a
denial of intention is not sufficient (e).

28. In a case where goods were sold bearing the name
* 487 of a certain * man, but under a representation that they
were, in fact, the manufacture of another person, and
not of the man whose name they bore, Wood, V. C., held that
there was not such a representation given to the world of the
goods being the goods of the plaintiff as to justify the court in
interfering (f).

29. False statements with respect to goods and false representations which merely amount to a slander of the name or
goods of another must be carefully distinguished from false
representations, which hold out that goods made by one man
are, in fact, the manufacture of another. A false statement by
a man that his goods are the same as the goods of another,
when, in fact, they are inferior, or are even quite different, or
that he is the first inventor of a certain article, when, in fact, the
article made by him is merely a spurious imitation of an article
made by another, or that he has the means of using the same
processes which another uses by the employment of a person
who has been in his service, or that he has obtained a prize
medal from a particular sort of goods at an exhibition, goes for

(z) Motley v. Downman, 3 M. & C.
17; Spottiswoode v. Clark, 2 Ph. 156;
Welch v. Knott, 4 K. & J. 747; Chappell v. Davidson, 8 D. M. & G. 1;
Woollam v. Ratcliff, 1 H. & M. 259.

(a) Spottiswoode v. Clark, 2 Ph.
156; Farina v. Silverlock, 6 D. M. & G.
214; Welch v. Knott, 4 K. & J. 747;
Williams v. Osborne, 13 L. T. N. S.
498.

(b) 6 D. M. & G. 214.
(c) See Delondre v. Shaw, 2 Sim.
237.

(d) Pierce v. Franks, 15 L. J. Ch.
122; Collins Co. v. Reeves, 4 Jur. N.
S. 865; Collins Co. v. Walker, 7 W. R.
222.

(e) Edelsten v. Vick, 11 Ha. 84.
(f) Ainsworth v. Walmsley, 1 L. R.
Eq. 518.

nothing, so long as he does not represent that the goods which he makes or vends are in fact the manufacture of another, and there is not such a general resemblance between them as to deceive the public (*g*).

30. False representations which merely amount to the slander of the name or reputation of another, or are calculated to bring the name or reputation of another into contempt, do not furnish a ground for the interposition of a court of equity. The remedy, if any, is at law for a libel (*h*). A court of equity cannot interpose, unless a case of actual damage to property can be made out. Thus, in Clark *v.* Freeman (*i*), Lord Langdale would not restrain a man from selling pills, which he represented falsely to be the pills of an eminent physician, on the ground that, as the latter was not in the habit of selling his pills, no * actual damage had arisen to his * 488 property (*j*). So, also, in Martin *v.* Wright (*k*), Shadwell, V. C., would not restrain a man from exhibiting in a diorama an enlarged copy of the picture of an eminent artist (*l*). In Byron *v.* Johnstone (*m*), on the other hand, a man was restrained from publishing poems, which he falsely represented to be the poems of Lord Byron, on the ground that as Lord Byron was in the habit of publishing his poems for sale, the act of the defendant was an actual injury to his property. So, also, in Routh *v.* Webster (*n*), Lord Langdale restrained the directors of a company from publishing a prospectus of the company, falsely representing a man, as a trustee of the company, on the ground that the consequence might be to expose him to all sorts of liabilities and so be a cause of damage to his property.

31. At law the remedy for the piracy of a trade-mark is by an action on the case in the nature of a writ of deceit. Fraud

(*g*) Canham *v.* Jones, 2 V. & B. 218 ; Seely *v.* Fisher, 11 Sim. 582 ; Batty *v.* Hill, 1 H. & M. 270 ; Brown *v.* Freeman, 4 N. R. 476 ; Leather Cloth Co. *v.* American Cloth Co., 11 H. L. 523 ; but see, now, the Exhibition Medals Act, 1862, 26 & 27 Vict. c. 119. See, also, Morison *v.* Moat, 9 Ha. 241 ; Glenny *v.* Smith, 2 Dr. & Sm. 476.

(*h*) Clark *v.* Freeman, 11 Beav. 112 ; Martin *v.* Wright, 6 Sim. 297 ; Seely

v. Fisher, 11 Sim. 582. See Emperor of Austria *v.* Day, 3 D. F. & J. 240.

(*i*) 11 Beav. 112.

(*j*) But see *per* Lord Cairns, L. J., 2 L. R. Ch. Ap. 310.

(*k*) 6 Sim. 297.

(*l*) See, also, Seely *v.* Fisher, 11 Sim. 582.

(*m*) 2 Mer. 29.

(*n*) 10 Beav. 563.

is of the essence of the action.   Lord Cottenham held, in Millington v. Fox (o), that the remedy in equity does not, like the
remedy at law, depend on fraud; and that a man whose trade-
mark or symbol is used or appropriated by another may have
an injunction even although the user may have been innocent
and in ignorance of the prior appropriation of the mark (p).
There is room, however, to doubt whether the principle laid
down by Lord Cottenham in Millington v. Fox (q), can be
considered sound law.   The fundamental rule being, that no
man shall pass off his own goods as the goods of another, proof
of fraud would appear to be as necessary in equity as it is at
law.   A court of equity may, it is true, presume fraud in cases
in which the same inference could not be made at law; but
this circumstance does not justify the proposition, that the
          remedy in equity is not, like the remedy at law, founded
* 489   on fraud (r).   The doctrine, however, * laid down in
          Millington v. Fox, must be considered as law until the
question comes before a higher tribunal (s).

32. The owner of a trade-mark, whose mark has been illegally taken by another, is not bound to rely upon his assurance or promise not to repeat the illegal appropriation of the
mark, but is entitled to the protection of the court by injunction (t).   If a man at the desire of another imposes upon
goods a trade-mark which belongs to a third party, the court
will restrain them both by injunction (u).   Every man who
sells the goods lends himself to the perpetration of the fraud,
and may be restrained by injunction (v).   The owner of a
trade-mark may obtain an injunction to restrain a dock company or a wharfinger from parting with goods to which his

(o) 3 M. & C. 338.
(p) See Welch v. Knott, 4 K. & J.
747; Collins Co. v. Walker, 7 W. R.
222; Burgess v. Hills, 26 Beav. 244;
Burgess v. Hateley, ib. 249; Dixson v.
Fawcus, 3 El. & El. 537; Edelsten v.
Edelsten, 1 D. J. & S. 185; Macandrew
v. Bassett, 33 L. J. Ch. 561.
(q) 3 M. & C. 338.
(r) See Purser v. Brain, 17 L. J. Ch.
141; Leather Cloth Co. v. American
Cloth Co., 11 H. L. 523; Glenny v.
Smith, 2 Dr. & Sm. 476.

(s) Dixson v. Fawcus, 3 El. & El.
537; Edelsten v. Edelsten, 1 D. J. & S.
185.
(t) Routh v. Webster, 10 Beav. 561;
Millington v. Fox, 3 M. & C. 338;
Welch v. Knott, 4 K. & J. 747; Edelsten v. Edelsten, 1 D. J. & S. 185.
(u) Collins Co. v. Reeves, 4 Jur. N.
S. 865; Collins Co. v. Walker, 7 W. R.
222.
(v) Coats v. Holbrook, 2 Sandf. Ch.
(Amer.) 587; Chubb v. Griffiths, 35
Beav. 127.

mark has been fraudulently affixed (x). A man, however, who has innocently advanced moneys upon dock warrants for goods to which a certain trade-mark has been fraudulently affixed may, upon offering to remove the mark, have an injunction dissolved which has been granted to restrain the wharfinger from parting with the goods (y). In a case where a wharfinger who had received notice that certain goods in his possession were branded with a spurious mark, and that an injunction was about to be applied for to restrain him from parting with the goods, refused to deliver them up to the holder of the warrant, the court restrained an action of damage for the non-delivery (z).

33. A man whose trade-mark has been illegally taken by another is entitled to an account of profits in respect of the illegal user of the mark. A man who puts upon his goods the trade-mark of another cannot be heard to say that he did so innocently and without knowing to whom the mark belonged. Though he may not have known to whom the mark belonged, he must at least * have known that he had him- * 490 self no right to the mark, and this knowledge will make him liable to an account (a). A man, however, who innocently buys and afterwards sells goods bearing a spurious trade-mark is not liable to an account, unless in respect of sales made and profits acquired after knowledge of the spuriousness of the mark (b).

34. In taking the account, a man will not have to account for every species of profit made during the previous six years, but only for so much as is properly attributable to the user of the mark (c), nor will he be charged with bad debts as profits; but, on the other hand, he cannot charge the plaintiff with the cost of manufacturing the goods in respect of which the bad debts have been incurred (d).

35. When one of two persons entitled in common to the use of a trade-mark is suing alone, he should on praying for the

(x) Ponsardin v. Peto, 33 Beav. 642; Hunt v. Maniere, 34 Beav. 157.
(y) Ponsardin v. Peto, 33 Beav. 642.
(z) Hunt v. Maniere, 34 Beav. 157.
(a) Burgess v. Hills, 26 Beav. 244; Burgess v. Hateley, ib. 251; Collins Co. v. Walker, 7 W. R. 222; Welch v.

Knott, 4 K. & J. 747; Cartier v. Carlisle, 31 Beav. 292. See Harrison v. Taylor, 11 Jur. N. S. 408.
(b) Moet v. Couston, 33 Beav. 578.
(c) Cartier v. Carlisle, 31 Beav. 292.
(d) Edelsten v. Edelsten, 10 L. T. N. S. 780.

account pray for the payment to himself of such part of the profits as he may be entitled to (*e*).

36. On an inquiry as to what damage has accrued to a man from the unlawful use by another of his trade-mark the onus lies on him to prove special damage by loss of custom or otherwise, and it will not be assumed in the absence of evidence that the amount of goods sold by the defendant under the fraudulent trade-mark would have been sold by the plaintiff but for the defendant's unlawful user of the mark (*f*).

37. The defendant must, if required to do so for the purposes of the account or the inquiry as to damages, disclose the names of all persons to whom he has sold any goods with the mark imposed on them. If he be unable to do so, he may then be required to disclose the names of all persons to whom he has sold any goods which he will not swear positively were not stamped with the mark (*g*).

38. The question of costs turns upon the conduct
* 491 of the parties in * the matter. A man whose trade-mark has been taken by another is entitled to the costs of the injunction. If the defendant does not contest his right, but offers to submit to the injunction with costs, the plaintiff has obtained all he is entitled to, and should not bring the cause to a hearing. If he asks for something more, and brings his cause to a hearing but fails to make out his right, he loses his right to the costs of the suit. But if the defendant upon notice of the plaintiff's right and the fact of its violation, instead of submitting to the injunction with costs, contests the plaintiff's right or refuses any of the terms to which the plaintiff is entitled, the cause may be brought to a hearing and the plaintiff will have the costs of the suit (*h*). Infancy will not protect a man from paying the costs of the suit (*i*).

(*e*) Dent *v.* Turpin, 2 J. & H. 139.
(*f*) Leather Cloth Co. *v.* Hirschfield, 1 L. R. Eq. 299.
(*g*) *Ib.* 1 H. & M. 295. See *supra*, p. 473.
(*h*) Millington *v.* Fox, 3 M. & C. 338; Colburn *v.* Simms, 2 Ha. 561; Pierce *v.* Franks, 15 L. J. Ch. 122; Chappell *v.* Davidson, 2 K. & J. 123;

Farina *v.* Silverlock, 4 K. & J. 650; Burgess *v.* Hills, 26 Beav. 244; Burgess *v.* Hateley, *ib.* 251, Cartier *v.* Carlisle, 31 Beav. 292; Woollam *v.* Ratcliff, 1 H. & M. 259; Edelsten *v.* Edelsten, 1 D. J. & S. 185; Moet *v.* Couston, 33 Beav. 578; *supra*, p. 228.
(*i*) Chubb *v.* Griffiths, 35 Beav. 127.

39. A man who has *bonâ fide* advanced moneys before bill filed upon the security of goods bearing a counterfeit trade-mark has priority in respect of his advances and costs over the plaintiff's costs of suit (*k*).[1]

(*k*) Ponsardin *v*. Peto, 33 Beav. 642.
[1] The statute provisions in the United States in relation to trade-marks will be found in Act of Congress of July 8, 1870, ch. 230, §§ 77–84. -

*492   *CHAPTER XXII.

INJUNCTIONS IN RESPECT OF COVENANTS OR AGREEMENTS.

SECTION I.—INJUNCTIONS AGAINST BREACH OF COVENANT
OR AGREEMENT.

1 & 2. Jurisdiction of court and principles upon which it is exercised.
3. Terms on which court may order motion to stand over or may grant injunction.
4. Contract must be such that it may be specifically enforced.
5. Conduct of the party who makes the application will be taken into consideration.
6. Rights of other parties taken into consideration.
7. No equitable construction of a covenant distinct from its legal construction.
8–14. Rules of construction of covenants.
15 & 16. Implication of covenants.
17. Plan if referred to read along with the agreement.
18. Parties.
19. Reversioner may sue.
20. Varieties of covenants.
21. Certain negative covenants the breach of which is restrained by injunction.
22. Injunction will not be granted where covenant is uncertain.
23–25. Covenants in restraint of trade.
26. Restriction in point of time in such covenants.
27. On what the reasonableness or unreasonableness of the restriction depends.
28–31. Cases illustrating the subject.
32. Covenant not to make patented articles not in restraint of trade.
33. When restraint is limited in space, how the distance is measured.
34. Agreement in restraint of trade is divisible.
35. Consideration in contracts in restraint of trade.
36. Covenant in restraint of trade not implied, except in certain cases.
37. Contracts with a penalty. Liquidated damages.
38. Use of these terms in an instrument not conclusive.
39–42. How they are construed.
43. Court will not determine on interlocutory application whether sum reserved is a penalty or liquidated damages.
44. Injunctions not granted when damages are liquidated.
45. Violation of agreement not to apply to Parliament restrained.
46. But doubtful in case of covenant not to oppose a bill in Parliament.
47 & 48. Importation of a negative quality into an affirmative agreement.
49. Negative quality not imported into an agreement which cannot from its nature be specifically enforced.
50. May be imported where some of the stipulations are distinct and separate from the rest of the agreement.
51. Nor into a contract which is substantially affirmative.

1. THE jurisdiction of courts of equity by interlocutory injunction against breach of covenant or agreement, is in aid of the legal right, and has been assumed for the advancement of justice. The jurisdiction is exercised either by way of injunction or by way of specific performance (*a*). The consideration and principles upon which the court acts in restraining by injunction breaches of covenant differ in a material respect from those upon which it acts in decreeing specific performance. It is not the practice of the court to decree specific performance of part of an agreement, where there are other parts which it cannot carry out. Unless the whole agreement can be specifically enforced, and complete justice be done between the parties, the court will, as a general rule, decline to interfere (*b*). The court will not interpose partially, except in cases in which the parts of the agreement, which cannot be specifically enforced, are independent of those which may be specifically performed (*c*), or are subordinate provisions (*d*). The consideration and principles, upon which the court interferes by way of injunction, rest upon irreparable injury. The court does not look to the effect which may be ultimately produced by the restraint which is placed on the party who is disposed to break his contract, but gives all the relief in its power, and leaves nothing unperformed which it * can be ever called upon to perform. In all cases where * 493 specific performance can be decreed, the jurisdiction by injunction will attach as a matter of course, but it is not confined to such cases, but will be exercised in all cases where it can operate to bind men's consciences as far as they can be

(*a*) See Hunt *v.* Hunt, 8 Jur. N. S. 86.

(*b*) Gervais *v.* Edwards, 2 Dr. & War. 80; South Wales Co. *v.* Wythes, 5 D. M. & G. 880; Kernot *v.* Potter, 3 D. F. & J. 447; Ogden *v.* Fossick, 32 L. J. Ch. 73.

(*c*) Croome *v.* Lediard, 2 M. & K. 251; Gibson *v.* Goldsmid, 5 D. M. & G. 757; Kernot *v.* Potter, 3 D. F. & J. 447; Ogden *v.* Fossick, 32 L. J. Ch. 73.

(*d*) Blackett *v.* Bates, 2 H. & M. 270.

bound to a true and literal performance of their agreements. A court of equity will not suffer men to depart from their agreements at their pleasure, leaving the party with whom they have contracted to the mere chance of damages which a jury may give (e). The court will not refrain from granting an injunction only because there are other covenants to be performed which may be possibly broken hereafter (f). The interference of the court by way of injunction cannot however be had, unless the part of the agreement which is sought to be enforced is separable from, and forms a distinct part of the agreement (g).[1]

2. The jurisdiction of the court by way of interlocutory injunction against breach of covenant or contract being in aid of the legal right, and having for its object the protection of the property from irreparable damage pending the trial of the right, a man who seeks the aid of the court must be able to show a good *primâ facie* legal title to the right which he asserts (h). If the right at law under the covenant is clear or fairly made out, and the breach of it is clear or fairly made out, and serious injury is likely to arise from the breach, it is the duty of the court to interfere before the hearing to restrain the breach. But if the right at law under the covenant is not clear, or is not fairly made out, or the breach of it is doubtful and no irreparable injury can arise to the plaintiff, pending the trial of the right, the case resolves itself into a question of comparative injury, whether the defendant will be more damnified by the injunction being granted or the plaintiff by its being withheld (i). It is not necessary that the
* 494 breach in respect of which the interference * of the court is sought should have been actually committed: it is enough that the defendant claims and insists on his right to do the act complained of, although he may not have actually

---

(e) Lumley v. Wagner, 1 D. M. & G. 619; De Mattos v. Gibson, 4 D. & J. 282.

(f) Rigby v. Great Western Railway Co., 15 L. J. Ch. 271, *per* Wigram, V. C.

(g) Kernot v. Potter, 3 D. F. & J. 459.
(h) Capes v. Hutton, 2 Russ. 357; Sainter v. Ferguson, 1 Mac. & G. 289; *supra*, p. 196.

(i) Wilkinson v. Rogers, 2 D. J. & S. 62, 69; *supra*, pp. 208–210. See, as to irreparable injury, *supra*, p. 199.
[1] Where covenants, in form independent, are in fact part of the same transaction and mutual, equity will restrain the enforcement of one upon the failure of the other. King v. Lindsay, 3 Ired. Ch. 77.

done it (*k*). But the court will not interfere unless it is clear
that a breach is intended. The court will not assume that a
man means to violate his agreement (*l*).

3. The court may at its discretion, as a condition of ordering the motion to stand over, require the defendant to keep an
account and give an undertaking as to damages (*m*) ; or on
granting an injunction may require the plaintiff to give an undertaking as to damage or to submit to account, as the court may
direct (*n*). The circumstance that a lessor has the right of
re-entry for breach of a covenant does not preclude him from
coming to the court to restrain the breach (*o*).

4. But to warrant the interference of the court, it is not
enough that the right at law under the covenant or contract be
clear and the breach be clear. It is in all cases necessary that
the covenant or contract should be of such a nature that it can
consistently with the rules and principles of the court be specifically enforced. If the covenant or contract is from its nature
such that the court cannot enforce specifically its performance,
or if, from the nature of the act to be done or refrained from,
the remedy lies peculiarly, at law, and a full and adequate
compensation can be had there, the court will not interfere (*p*).
Thus, the court will not entertain jurisdiction where the claim
sought to be enforced is a mere money claim (*q*), or has
been * already treated between the parties as a proper   *495
subject for pecuniary compensation (*r*). Nor will the
court entertain jurisdiction in respect of contracts for building
or other work (*s*), unless a case of fraud can be made out (*t*),

(*k*) Tipping *v.* Eckersley, 2 K. & J.
264 ; *supra*, p. 198.
(*l*) Foster *v.* Birmingham, Wolverhampton, &c., Railway Co., 2 W. R.
378. See Moses *v.* Taylor, 11 W. R. 81.
(*m*) Rigby *v.* Great Western Railway
Co., 2 Ph. 44; Low *v.* Innes, 10 Jur.
N. S. 1037.
(*n*) East Lancashire Railway Co. *v.*
Hattersley, 8 Ha. 72 ; Ingram *v.* Stiff,
5 Jur. N. S. 947 ; *supra*, pp. 210–212.
(*o*) Parker *v.* Whyte, 32 L. J. Ch. 520.
(*p*) Collins *v.* Plumb, 16 Ves. 454 ;
Mann *v.* Stephens, 15 Sim. 379 ; Furness Railway Co. *v.* Smith, 1 De G. &
S. 299 ; Dollfus *v.* Pickford, 2 W. R.
220 ; Alexander *v.* Hammond, 3 W. R.
145 ; Holmes *v.* Eastern Counties Rail-

way Co., 3 K. & J. 675 ; Munro *v.* Wiv-
enhoe, &c., Railway Co., 11 Jur. N. S.
613 ; Fry on Specific Perform., 17–20.
(*q*) Todd *v.* Gee, 17 Ves. 273 ; Sains-
bury *v.* Jones, 2 Beav. 462 : Glennie *v.*
Imri, 3 Y. & C. 436 ; Coles *v.* Sims, 5
D. M. & G. 1.
(*r*) Paris Chocolate Co. *v.* Crystal
Palace Co., 3 Sm. & G. 119.   See
Wood *v.* Sutcliffe, 2 Sim. N. S. 168.
But see Ainsworth *v.* Bentley, 14 W.
R. 630 ; *supra*, p. 200.
(*s*) Ambrose *v.* Dunmow Union, 9
Beav. 508 ; Kirk *v.* Bromley Union, 2
Ph. 640 ; Paxton *v.* Newton, 2 Sm. &
G. 437 ; South Wales Railway Co. *v.*
Wythes, 1 K. & J. 186, 5 D. M. & G. 880.
(*t*) Waring *v.* Manchester Sheffield,

or unless it can be shown that the accounts arising out of the contract are so complicated that they cannot be satisfactorily taken at law (*u*) ; nor will the court entertain jurisdiction in the case of covenants or agreements for personal services, or involving duties of a personal and confidential character (*x*). Nor will the court interfere if the covenant is vague, indefinite, or uncertain in its terms (*y*), or if it appears in its form to be harsh and oppressive (*z*), or if the contract is of such a nature that one of the contracting parties would gain considerable advantage at the expense of the other from its enforcement, while the other would gain no corresponding benefit (*a*).

5. The conduct of the party who seeks the aid of the court will be taken into consideration upon the application for an injunction. A man who comes to the court to restrain the breach of a covenant or contract must be able to show that he comes with clean hands (*b*). He cannot have relief, unless

it appear that he has actually carried out, as far as in
*496 him lies, his own part of * the agreement (*c*), and un-
less he can show that he has used due diligence in making the application. Delay or acquiescence may disentitle him to relief (*d*). A covenantor who seeing a covenantee spend moneys upon property in doing acts which are inconsistent with the terms of the covenant, but upon the faith that no obstacle will be afterwards thrown in the way of his enjoyment, stands by and makes no objection while the moneys are being expended (*e*), or whose own acts have been inconsistent

and Lincolnshire Railway Co., 7 Ha. 482, 2 H. & Tw. 239 ; M'Intosh *v.* Great Western Railway Co., 2 De G. & S. 759.

(*u*) M'Intosh *v.* Great Western Railway Co., 3 Sm. & G. 146 ; *supra*, p. 58.

(*x*) Pickering *v.* Bishop of Ely, 2 Y. & C. C. C. 249 ; Johnson *v.* Shrewsbury and Birmingham Railway Co., 3 D. M. & G. 914 ; *supra*, pp. 50, 51.

(*y*) Mann *v.* Stephens, 15 Sim. 379 ; Paris Chocolate Co. *v.* Crystal Palace Co., 1 Sm. & G. 119 ; De Mattos *v.* Gibson, 4 D. & J. 276 ; Bernard *v.* Meara, 12 Ir. Ch. 389 ; Armstrong *v.* Courtney, 15 Ir. Ch. 138 ; Low *v.* Innes, 10 Jur. N. S. 1037.

(*z*) Kimberley *v.* Jennings, 6 Sim. 340 ; Talbot *v.* Ford, 13 Sim. 173 ; Croft *v.* Haw, 5 L. J. Ch. N. S. 305.

(*a*) Shrewsbury and Birmingham Railway Co. *v.* London and North Western Railway Co., 6 H. L. 113 ; Vivers *v.* Tuck, 1 Moo. P. C. N. S. 516.

(*b*) See Stiff *v.* Cassell, 2 Jur. N. S. 348 ; Maythorne *v.* Palmer, 11 Jur. N. S. 230 ; *supra*, pp. 17, 200, 201.

(*c*) Stocker *v.* Wedderburn, 3 K. & J. 405 ; De Mattos *v.* Gibson, 4 D. & J. 276 ; Peto *v.* Brighton, Uckfield, and Tunbridge Wells Railway Co., 1 H. & M. 468 ; Fechter *v.* Montgomery, 33 Beav. 22.

(*d*) Powell *v.* Allarton, 4 L. J. Ch. N. S. 91 ; Moses *v.* Taylor, 11 W. R. 81 ; Maythorne *v.* Palmer, 11 Jur. N. S. 230 ; Mitchell *v.* Steward, 1 L. R. Eq. 541 ; *supra*, p. 201.

(*e*) Barrett *v.* Blagrave, 6 Ves. 105 ;

with the covenant, or who has acquiesced in the doing of acts
which are inconsistent with it, cannot come to a court of equity
to have the covenant or contract enforced. Thus, where the
leases of an estate contained covenants by the lessees which
were intended to be for the general benefit of them all, *e.g.*,
a covenant to build on a uniform plan, and the landlord let
loose some of his tenants from the obligations of the covenants,
the court would not interfere to prevent a similar infringement
by others of the tenants (*f*). Nor would the court restrain the
erection of buildings contrary to a covenant, where the plaintiff
had himself erected buildings, the effect of which was to destroy those very advantages which the covenant was intended
to maintain (*g*). Nor will relief be given where there has
been for a considerable time a violation of the agreement
in respect of * which relief is sought both by defend-   *497
ant and plaintiff (*h*). But the case is different if the
covenant, though entered into by a landlord with all his
tenants, is only a covenant for the benefit of each tenant, and
not one for the benefit of all the other tenants (*i*), or if it is
left to the landlord himself to determine what tenants shall be
let loose from the obligations of the covenant (*k*). Nor is the
equity of a *cestui que trust* to require the due performance of a
covenant displaced by a breach of duty on the part of the trustees (*l*). Nor will the principle as to acquiescence be carried
so far as to hold a man who has permitted one infringement of
a covenant bound to permit another (*m*). Nor will passive
acquiescence in a breach of covenant attended with no damage,

---

Scarisbrick *v*. Tunbridge, 3 Eq. Rep.
240; Child *v*. Douglas, 5 D. M. & G.
739; Johnstone *v*. Hall, 2 K. & J. 414;
Eastwood *v*. Lever, 33 L. J. Ch. 355;
supra, pp. 201–203.   See Hudson *v*.
Bartram, 3 Madd. 40. Comp. Mitchell
v. Steward, 1 L. R. Eq. 541.

(*f*) Roper *v*. Williams, T. & R. 18;
Child *v*. Douglas, 5 D. M. & G. 739;
Whitehead *v*. Bennett, 9 W. R. 627.
See Schreiber *v*. Creed, 10 Sim. 9;
Whatman *v*. Gibson, 9 Sim. 196;
Scarisbrick *v*. Tunbridge, 3 Eq. Rep.
240. Comp. Eastwood *v*. Lever, 33
L. J. Ch. 357; Mitchell *v*. Steward, 1
L. R. Eq. 541; Western *v*. M'Dermott,
2 L. R. Ch. Ap. 72; Peek *v*. Matthews,
3 L. R. Eq. 409.

(*g*) Duke of Bedford *v*. Trustees of
British Museum, 2 M. & K. 552; Jack-
son *v*. Fenwick, 21 L. T. 223. Comp.
Kemp *v*. Sober, 1 Sim. N. S. 517;
Johnstone *v*. Hall, 2 K. & J. 414; West-
ern *v*. M'Dermott, 2 L. R. Ch. Ap.
72. See Shrewsbury and Birmingham
Railway Co. *v*. Stour Valley Railway
Co., 2 D. M. & G. 866, 882.

(*h*) Sheard *v*. Webb, 2 W. R. 343.

(*i*) Patching *v*. Dubbins, Kay, 1.

(*k*) Scarisbrick *v*. Tunbridge, 3 Eq.
Rep. 243. See Kemp *v*. Sober, 1 Sim.
N. S. 517.

(*l*) Eastwood *v*. Lever, 33 L. J. Ch.
355.

(*m*) Lloyd *v*. London, Chatham, and
Dover Railway Co., 2 D. J. & S. 568.

or at least with trifling damage, preclude a man from complaining of a breach whereby his enjoyment is directly and substantially affected (*n*).

6. The jurisdiction being discretionary, the court is bound to exercise it with a view to the way in which the granting relief will affect the rights of other persons (*o*).

7. The construction of a covenant or a contract is a pure question of law. There is no equitable construction of a covenant or contract as distinct from its legal construction. To construe is nothing more than to arrive at the meaning of the parties to the instrument (*p*).

8. The intention of the parties is to be collected from the language of the instrument, explained by reference to the circumstances under which it was made (*q*), the nature of the transaction (*r*), and the matters to which it relates (*s*).

*498 The * words of the instrument are to be interpreted in their ordinary grammatical sense and meaning, unless from the context of the instrument and the intention of the parties to be collected from it they appear to have been used in a different sense, or unless in their strict sense they are incapable of being carried into effect; subject, however, to this, that the meaning of a particular word may be shown by parol evidence to be different in some particular trade, place, or business from its proper and ordinary signification (*t*). It is not necessary, in order to render such evidence admissible, that there should be any ambiguity on the face of the instrument which has to be construed (*u*). If it appear that a term or phrase bears a peculiar meaning in the trade or business to which the contract relates, that meaning is *primâ facie* to be

(*n*) Western *v.* M'Dermott, 2 L. R. Ch. Ap. 72. See further, as to acquiescence, *supra*, pp. 201–205.

(*o*) Hope *v.* Corporation of Gloucester, 1 Jur. N. S. 320. See Maythorne *v.* Palmer, 11 Jur. N. S. 230.

(*p*) Iggulden *v.* May, 9 Ves. 333; Butcher *v.* Butcher, *ib.* 393; Shrewsbury and Birmingham Railway Co. *v.* London and North Western Railway Co., 3 Mac. & G. 70; Johnson *v.* Shrewsbury and Birmingham Railway Co., 3 D. M. & G. 931, 3 D. & J. 360, *per* Lord Chelmsford.

(*q*) Turner *v.* Evans, 2 E. & B. 512; Edinburgh, Perth, and Dundee Railway Co. *v.* Philipp, 2 Macq. 514, 526.

(*r*) Macintyre *v.* Belcher, 14 C. B. N. S. 663, *per* Erle, C. J.

(*s*) Rex *v.* Mashiter, 6 A. & E. 153.

(*t*) Mallan *v.* May, 13 M. & W. 511; Mercer *v.* Irving, El. Bl. & El. 563; Great Northern Railway Co. *v.* Harrison, 12 C. B. 576, 609; Edinburgh, Perth, and Dundee Railway Co. *v.* Philipp, 2 Macq. 514, 526.

(*u*) Myers *v.* Sarl, 3 El. & El. 306.

attributed to it, unless, upon the construction of the contract, enough appears either from express words or by necessary implication to show that the parties did not mean that meaning to prevail (x). Parol evidence is admissible for the purpose of identifying or ascertaining the subject-matter of a contract where the description of it in the instrument is so vague and indefinite as to be incapable of ascertainment without the aid of extrinsic evidence. But where this is not the case, and the writing is, on the face of it, capable of intelligible construction, that construction it should receive (y).

9. In construing a contract or a covenant the whole of the instrument is to be taken together, so as, if possible, to give effect to every part (z), and so that one of the provisions shall not be repugnant to another, if it can possibly be done (a). The recitals may be made use of to explain the operative part (b). * Where the words in the operative part are *499 clear and unambiguous, they cannot be controlled by the recitals or other parts of the instrument. But if those words are of doubtful meaning, the recitals and other parts of the instrument may be used as a test to discover the intention of the parties and to fix the meaning of those words (c).

10. Words in a contract which are wholly inconsistent with its nature (d), or with the main intention (e), are to be rejected.

11. Particular clauses of a contract are subordinate to its general provisions (f).

12. However broad may be the terms of a contract, it ex-

(x) Myers v. Sarl, 3 El. & El. 306. See James v. Plant, 4 A. & E. 749; Worthington v. Gimson, 2 El. & El. 618; Taylor v. Caldwell, 3 B. & S. 832.

(y) Ricketts v. Turquand, 1 H. L. 490; Evans v. Angell, 26 Beav. 202; Boyle v. Mullholland, 10 Ir. C. L. 150.

(z) Sicklemore v. Thissleton, 6 M. & S. 9; Rigby v. Great Western Railway Co., 14 M. & W. 811.

(a) Browning v. Wright, 2 Bos. & P. 13; Briggs v. Earl of Oxford, 5 De G. & S. 156.

(b) Bath & Montagu's case, 3 Ch. Ca. 106; Taggart v. Hewlett, 1 Mer. 502; Payler v. Homersham, 4 M. & S. 423; Lampon v. Corke, 5 B. & Ald. 606.

(c) Bath & Montagu's case, 3 Ch. Ca. 106; Cholmondeley v. Clinton, 2 J. & W 1, 99; Bailey v. Lloyd, 5 Russ. 330; Doe d. Timmis v. Steele, 4 Q. B. 663; Sorsbie v. Park, 12 M. & W. 146; Rooke v. Lord Kensington, 2 K. & J. 753; Walsh v. Trevanion, 15 Q. B. 733; Jenner v. Jenner, 35 L. J. Ch. 329; Young v. Smith, 1 L. R. Eq. 180.

(d) Mills v. Wright, 1 Freem. 247; Simpson v. Vaughan, 2 Atk. 32.

(e) Dallman v. King, 4 Bing. N. C. 105. See Rex v. Inhabitants of Exminster, 6 A. & E. 598.

(f) London Gas-light Co. v. Vestry of Chelsea, 8 C. B. N. S. 215. See Ringer v. Cann, 3 M. & W. 343.

tends only to those things concerning which it appears that the parties intended to contract (*g*).

13. If the terms of a contract are in any respect ambiguous or uncertain, it must be interpreted in the sense in which the promisor believed at the time of making it that the promisee understood it (*h*).

14. A contract must receive such a construction as will make it lawful (*i*), operative (*k*), reasonable (*l*), and capable of being carried into effect, if it can be done without violating the intention of the parties. But the language of a contract cannot be perverted in order to make it lawful (*m*) ; nor
* 500   can an unreasonable * stipulation be rejected if it was
     clearly the intention of the parties that it should form part of the contract (*n*).

15. Conditions not expressed will not be imported into an agreement unless there is something in the agreement which shows that the parties must have intended such conditions. There must be words in the instrument capable of sustaining the meaning which is sought to be implied from them (*o*). If the court is able to collect from the language of the whole instrument taken together an agreement between the parties that a certain thing shall be done, there is sufficient to enable the court to say that a covenant is created (*p*). It is not enough that the language may show that the parties contemplated that a particular thing might or might not be done. It must amount to a binding agreement between them that the

---

(*g*) Lyall *v.* Edwards, 6 H. & N. 337; Simons *v.* Johnson, 3 B. & A. 175; Payler *v.* Homersham, 4 M. & S. 423.

(*h*) See Mowatt *v.* Londesborough, 3 E. & B. 307, *per* Lord Campbell, C. J. ; Wheelton *v.* Hardisty, 8 *ib.* 284.

(*i*) Sterry *v.* Clifton, 9 C. B. 110; Harrington *v.* Kloprogge, 4 Doug. 5. See Shore *v.* Wilson, 9 Cl. & Fin. 397.

(*k*) Boyd *v.* Moyle, 2 C. B. 644; Russell *v.* Philipps, 14 Q. B. 891; Broom *v.* Batchelor, 1 H. & N. 255; Mare *v.* Charles, 5 E. & B. 978.

(*l*) Braunstein *v.* Accidental Death Insurance Co., 1 B. & S. 782; Jones *v.* Gibbons, 8 Exch. 922; Dallman *v.* King, 4 Bing. N. C. 105.

(*m*) See Mayor of Norwich *v.* Norfolk Railway Co., 4 E. & B. 397.

(*n*) Stadhard *v.* Lee, 3 B. & S. 364.

(*o*) Churchward *v.* Reg., 1 L. R. Q. B. 195, 211 ; Midland Railway Co. *v.* London and North Western Railway Co., 2 L. R. Eq. 525.

(*p*) Rigby *v.* Great Western Railway Co., 14 M. & W. 811; Aspdin *v.* Austin, 5 Q. B. 671, 683 ; James *v.* Cochrane, 7 Exch. 170, 177; Rashleigh *v.* South Eastern Railway Co., 10 C. B. 613 ; Great Northern Railway Co. *v.* Harrison, 12 C. B. 576, 609 ; Iven *v.* Elwes, 3 Drew. 25 ; Smith *v.* Mayor of Harwich, 2 C. B. N S. 651, 667 ; M'Intyre *v.* Belcher, 14 C. B. N. S. 654; Lay *v.* Mottram, 19 C. B. N. S. 479 ; Brooks *v.* Jennings, 1 L. R. C. P 476.

thing shall be done (*q*). It is not competent for the court to import a covenant which does not arise by necessary implication from the language of the instrument (*r*). When a man covenants to do a certain thing, it is necessarily implied that he will not wilfully incapacitate himself from doing it (*s*). If a man enters into an arrangement which can only take effect by the continuance of a certain existing state of circumstances, there is an implied engagement on his part that he shall do nothing of his own motion to put an end to that state of circumstances, under which alone the arrangement can be operative (*t*). But a man who has expressly covenanted to perform certain acts cannot be * held to have im-   * 501 pliedly covenanted for every act convenient or even necessary for the perfect performance of his express covenant (*u*).

16. Stipulations which are necessary to make a contract reasonable (*x*), or conformable to usage (*y*), are implied in respect of matters concerning which the contract manifests no contrary intention (*z*).

17. A plan, if referred to by an instrument, must be read along with it and be looked to for the purpose of explaining it (*a*). But the mere exhibition of a plan does not amount to a representation or warranty that all the ground exhibited in the plan shall be put or shall continue in the same state in which it was exhibited upon the plan (*b*). The case, however, is different, if the plan has been made distinctly and expressly a part of the agreement (*c*).

(*q*) Aspdin *v*. Austin, 5 Q. B. 671, 683 ; Rashleigh *v*. South Eastern Railway Co., 10 C. B. 612; James *v*. Cochrane, 7 Exch. 170, 177; Smith *v*. Mayor of Harwich, 2 C. B. N. S. 651, 667.

(*r*) *Ib.*; Iven *v*. Elwes, 3 Drew. 25.

(*s*) M'Intyre *v*. Belcher, 14 C. B. N. S. 654. See Hooper *v*. Brodrick, 11 Sim. 47; Piggott *v*. Stratton, 1 D. F. & J. 33 ; Iven *v*. Elwes, 3 Drew. 25.

(*t*) Stirling *v*. Maitland, 5 B. & S. 840.

(*u*) Aspdin *v*. Austin, 5 Q. B. 671, 683; Rashleigh *v*. South Eastern Railway Co., 10 C. B. 612; Smith *v*. Mayor of Harwich, 2 C. B. N. S. 651, 667.

(*x*) Jones *v*. Gibbons, 8 Exch. 922.

(*y*) Field *v*. Lelean, 6 H. & N. 617;

Pollock *v*. Stables, 12 Q. B. 765; Bayliffe *v*. Butterworth, 1 Exch. 425 ; Syers *v*. Jonas, 2 Exch. 111; Dale *v*. Humfrey, El. Bl. & El. 1004.

(*z*) Hutton *v*. Warren, 1 M. & W. 475. See Suse *v*. Pompe, 8 C. B. N. S. 538.

(*a*) Clarke *v*. Manchester, Sheffield, and Lincolnshire Railway Co., 1 J. & H. 631; Nicholson *v*. Rose, 4 D. & J. 10. See Tulk *v*. Moxhay, 18 L. J. Ch. 85.

(*b*) Feoffees of Heriot's Hospital *v*. Gibson, 2 Dow. 301; Squire *v*. Campbell, 1 M. & C. 459, 486 ; Fewster *v*. Turner, 11 L. J. Ch. 161; Tulk *v*. Moxhay, 18 L. J. Ch. 85. See Eastwood *v*. Lever, 33 L. J. Ch. 355.

(*c*) Rankin *v*. Huskisson, 4 Sim. 15; Slee *v*. Corporation of Bradford, 4 Giff. 262.

18. The original covenantor is not a proper party to a suit to restrain an assignee of the lease from violating a covenant in the lease, if he has parted with all interest in the property and is not in any way in fault (*d*). Nor can a man who has parted with all his interest under an agreement sue for the violation of it without making the assignee a party (*e*). Although several persons may be entitled to complain of a breach of covenant, one alone of such persons may maintain the suit: the others need not be parties to or be repre-

* 502 sented in a suit to maintain * it (*f*). Trustees who have sold land for building plots, subject to restrictive covenants, are necessary parties to a suit to enforce the cov-enants. The remaining purchasers should also be represented in the record (*g*). Tenants in common assignees of the rever-sion of a lease may join in suing or be jointly sued in covenants therein (*h*).

19. The assignee of a lessee was at common law liable in covenant and entitled to bring covenant, but the assignee of a lessor was not. The 32 Hen. 8, c. 34, has however placed the assignee of a reversioner on the same footing in this respect as the assignee of a lessee, and gives to reversioners the benefit of covenants entered into with their predecessors in title. The successive reversioners, as they become entitled to the estate, have a right to insist upon the performance of the covenants irrespectively of the damage which may accrue from the breach (*i*). But reversioners entitled in remainder are pre-cluded from suing, unless they can prove special damage to themselves in respect of the interest in the reversion (*k*). Courts of equity in interfering at the suit of reversioners in remainder to restrain breaches of covenant, follow the analogy of the rule at law, and will not grant injunctions unless mate-rial damage has been shown (*l*). Thus in the case where the

(*d*) Scarisbrick *v.* Tunbridge, 3 Eq. Rep. 243; Clements *v.* Welles, 1 L. R. Eq. 200. See *supra*, 207, as to par-ties.

(*e*) Thorne *v.* Taw Vale Railway and Dock Co., 13 Beav. 10.

(*f*) Western *v.* M'Dermott, 2 L. R. Ch. Ap. 72.

(*g*) Eastwood *v.* Lever, 33 L. J. Ch. 355.

(*h*) Womersley *v.* Daley, 26 L. J. Exch. 219.

(*i*) Isherwood *v.* Oldknow, 3 M. & S. 382.

(*k*) Jackson *v.* Pesked, 1 M. & S. 234; Baxter *v.* Taylor, 4 B. & Ad. 72; Mumford *v.* Oxford, &c., Railway Co., 1 H. & N. 34; Simpson *v.* Savage, 1 C. B. N. S. 349.

(*l*) Johnstone *v.* Hall, 2 K. & J. 423.

reversioner of a leasehold house held under a lease for 999 years (the tenant for life not being a plaintiff) sought to restrain the lessee from keeping a school contrary to a covenant in the lease, which stipulated that no trade or business whatever should be carried on in the house, but that it should be used simply as a dwelling-house, Wood, V. C., refused to grant an injunction on the ground that the damage was too minute for the court to interfere at the suit of a reversioner. The case would have been different had the lessee been carrying on a noxious or offensive trade (m).

20. * Covenants are either of an affirmative or nega-　*503 tive nature. Where a man covenants that something has been done or shall be done hereafter, the covenant is affirmative. Where a man covenants that a thing has not been done or shall not be done hereafter, the covenant is a negative one. In cases where the covenant is affirmative, the remedy in equity is by way of specific performance. If it is a negative one, the remedy is by way of injunction.

21. In restraining by injunction the breach of a negative covenant, the interference of the court is in effect an order for specific performance. " An agreement," said Lord St. Leonards in Lumley v. Wagner (n), " may be as effectually performed in this way as by an order for the performance of the thing to be done." Persons accordingly who had entered into a covenant not to ring church bells at stated periods and had accepted the benefits of the covenant were restrained from violating its obligations (o). So also an author who, on the sale of a work had covenanted with the purchaser not to do any thing which might be detrimental to the sale or publication of that work, was restrained from publishing a rival work on the same subject (p). So also an agreement between a publisher and an author that the latter should write a tale for the former and should not during the continuance of the agreement write for any other publication, was enforced by injunction. The injunction went to restrain another publisher from employing

(m) Johnstone v. Hall, 2 K. & J. 423.
(n) 1 D. M. & G. 615.
(o) Martin v. Nutkin, 2 P. W. 266.
(p) Barfield v. Nicholson, 2 Sim. & St. 1, 2 L. J. Ch. 90 ; Ingram v. Stiff, 5 Jur. N. S. 947 ; Ainsworth v. Bentley, 14 W. R. 630. See Fullarton v. M'-Phun, 13 Dec. of Ct. of Sess., N.S. 219.

him (*q*). So also tenants were restrained from having more
than two grain crops in any five years of the term (*r*), and
from breaking up pasture-land (*s*), contrary to covenants
in their lease (*t*). So also a man who had covenanted
not to perform or write for any other than a particular
theatre was restrained according to the terms of the
* 504   * covenant (*u*). So also a public board of functionaries
was restrained from erecting buildings on a plot of land,
opposite a club-house, contrary to covenant (*x*). So also the
lessee of a mine who had covenanted not to remove machinery
from a mine was restrained according to the terms of the covenant (*y*). So also a railway company which had bought land
from a man, and had covenanted with him in the purchase deed
not to erect any building upon it to a greater height than
eighteen feet within the distance of eighty feet from certain
other property of his, was restrained according to the terms of
the covenant (*z*). So also a railway company was restrained
from removing from the railway carriages placards and advertisements of the plaintiff, and from removing from the stations
the book-stalls of the plaintiff, contrary to covenant (*a*). So
also a man who had purchased land under a condition prohibiting building thereon except after permission obtained, was
restrained from building before obtaining the permission required (*b*). So also the lessee of a house who had covenanted
not to carry on any business or trade on the demised premises,
was restrained from setting up a school (*c*), from carrying on
the trade or business of a baker, confectioner, beershop-
* 505   keeper (*d*), hairdresser (*e*), or auctioneer (*f*).   * So

(*q*) Stiff *v.* Cassell, 2 Jur. N. S. 348.
(*r*) Fleming *v.* Snook, 5 Beav. 252.
(*s*) Grey de Wilton *v.* Saxon, 6 Ves. 106; Pulteney *v.* Shelton, 5 Ves. 260, n.
(*t*) See, as to covenants in a farm-ing lease, Gale *v.* Bates, 3 H. & C. 84.
(*u*) Morris *v.* Colman, 18 Ves. 437.
(*x*) Rankin *v.* Huskisson, 4 Sim. 13.
(*y*) Hamilton *v.* Dunsford, 6 Ir. Ch. 412.
(*z*) Lloyd *v.* London, Chatham, and Dover Railway Co., 2 D. J. & S. 568. See Foster *v.* Birmingham, Wolver-hampton, and Dudley Railway Co., 2 W. R. 378.

(*a*) Holmes *v.* Eastern Counties Rail-way Co., 3 K. & J. 675.
(*b*) Att.-Gen. *v.* Briggs, 1 Jur. N. S. 1084.
(*c*) Kemp *v.* Sober, 1 Sim. N. S. 520, on appeal, 19 L. T. 308; Johnstone *v.* Hall, 2 K. & J. 423; Wickenden *v.* Web-ster, 6 E. & B. 387.
(*d*) Hodson *v.* Coppard, 29 Beav. 4.
(*e*) Clements *v.* Welles, 1 L. R. Eq. 200.
(*f*) Parker *v.* Whyte, 1 H. & M. 167. See Moses *v.* Taylor, 11 W. R. 81. A covenant not to use a house as a shop may be broken by user of it for the sale of goods without any structu-ral or architectural alteration of the

also where the lease of a shop contained a covenant that it should be occupied for the business of a shop and no other, the court restrained the lessee from carrying on the business of an auctioneer (*g*). So also the under-lessee of a man who had covenanted not to carry on a particular trade on the demised premises will be restrained from carrying it on, although such covenant was not contained in the original lease, but only in an assignment thereof (*h*). So also a man who had covenanted not to let any house as an hotel or to let any land for the erection of any house to be used as an hotel or inn within certain limits, was restrained from selling any land for such a purpose or from doing any act that might aid in the violation of the covenant (*i*). So also the court will enforce by injunction a covenant in a lease not to assign without license (*k*). So also a man who had *covenanted in a   *506 separation deed not to molest his wife, was restrained according to the terms of his covenant (*l*). So also a man who

house. Wilkinson *v.* Rogers, 2 D. J. & S. 62. A covenant not to carry on the trade of a butcher is broken by selling raw meat, though it was not exposed in the shop windows, but was visible to passengers if they looked in, and was not killed there. Doe *v.* Spry, 1 B. & Ald. 617. A covenant not to carry on the business of a common brewer or retailer of beer is broken by the carrying on the business of a retail brewer. Simons *v.* Farren, 1 Bing. N. C. 128. But a covenant not to use a "public house for sale of beer, wine, malt liquor, or spirits," is not broken by taking out an ordinary excise license for the sale of beer not to be drunk on the premises. Pease *v.* Coats, 2 L. R. Eq. 688. See Marks *v.* Benjamin, 5 M. & W. 565. A covenant not to carry on the business of a horse-hair manufacturer is not broken by merely dealing in horse-hair. Harms *v.* Parsons, 32 Beav. 328. The trade of a coachmaker does not fall within the provisions of a covenant against carrying on an offensive trade. Bonnett *v.* Sadler, 14 Ves. 526. See Moses *v.* Taylor, 11 W. R. 81, as to whether the setting up a mock auction is an offensive trade within the meaning of the covenant. Nor is the opening a house as a public house a breach of covenant not to carry on a trade or business that might be offen-

sive, or an annoyance, or disturbance, to any of the tenants of the lessor or any part of the neighborhood. Jones *v.* Thorne, 1 B. & C. 716. See Gorton *v.* Smart, 1 Sim. & St. 66; Hickman *v.* Isaacs, 4 L. T. N. S. 285. The keeping a lunatic asylum is not carrying on an offensive trade. Doe d. Wetherell *v.* Bird, 2 A. & E. 161. See Moses *v.* Taylor, 11 W. R. 81. See also, as to offensive trades, Barrow *v.* Richard, 8 Paige, Ch. (Amer.) 357; Seymour *v.* M'Donald, 4 Sandf. Ch. (Amer.) 503. See, as to breach of condition against sub-letting, Browne *v.* Lord Sligo, 10 Ir. Ch. 1. See, as to what amounts to a breach of covenant in a building lease, Schreiber *v.* Creed, 10 Sim. 9; Patching *v.* Dubbins, Kay, 1; Child *v.* Douglas, *ib.* 560. A covenant is broken by permitting acts of a third party in contravention of it. It is not necessary to show any act of commission on the part of the defendant. Borgins *v.* Edwards, 2 F. & F. 111.

(*g*) Steward *v.* Winter, 4 Sandf. Ch. (Amer.) 587.

(*h*) Clements *v.* Welles, 1 L. R. Eq. 200.

(*i*) Jay *v.* Richardson, 30 Beav. 563. See Clarkson *v.* Edge, 33 Beav. 227.

(*k*) Dyke *v.* Taylor, 3 D. F. & J. 467.

(*l*) Sanders *v.* Rodway, 16 Beav. 211.

had covenanted in a separation deed not to take any legal proceedings against his wife with the view of forcing her to cohabit
with him, was restrained from commencing a suit for restitution of conjugal rights against her (*m*). So also a married
woman who has by a formal act of acceptance acquiesced in a
separation deed, containing a covenant that she should not endeavor to compel her husband to allow her "any further or
greater support, maintenance, or alimony" than a certain
annuity, will be restrained from taking proceedings in the
divorce court to obtain an allowance for alimony, as incident
to her petition for a judicial separation on the ground of
adultery (*n*). So also the court restrained the publication of
facts, agreed not to be published if a certain sum of money
were paid, although the plaintiff was not prepared to pay the
whole sum (*o*). So also an injunction was granted to restrain
the publication of the recovery of a judgment debt against a
man contrary to agreement, where the threat to sell the judgment debt by auction was not *bonâ fide* but for the purpose of
getting better terms (*p*).

22. If the covenant is vague or uncertain in its terms, or of
such a nature that the court cannot, consistently with its rules
and principles, enforce it, an injunction will not be granted (*q*).
Thus the court would not enforce by injunction a covenant not
to build, except so as to be an ornament rather than otherwise
to the adjoining property (*r*).

23. A class of negative covenants which the court will enforce by injunction are covenants in partial restraint of trade,
where the limitation is reasonable. Covenants in total restraint
       of trade are absolutely void upon grounds of public
* 507   policy (*s*). "The *law," said Lord Wynford, in Homer
      v. Ashford (*t*), "will not permit any one to restrain a
man from doing what his own interest and the public welfare
require that he should do. Any deed therefore by which a man

(*m*) Hunt *v.* Hunt, 8 Jur. N. S. 86;
but see Wilson *v.* Wilson, 5 H. L. 40.

(*n*) See Williams *v.* Baily, 2 L. R.
Eq. 731.

(*o*) Anon., 3 Jur. N. S. 685.

(*p*) Jamieson *v.* Teague, 3 Jur. N. S.
1206.

(*q*) *Supra*, p. 495.

(*r*) Mann *v.* Stephens, 15 Sim. 379.

(*s*) Mitchell *v.* Reynolds, 1 P. Wms.
181; Chesman *v.* Nainby, 2 Stra. 739,
S. C., 2 Lord Raym. 1456; Wickens *v.*
Evans, 3 Y. & J. 318; Mallan *v.* May,
11 M. & W. 653.

(*t*) 3 Bing. 328.

binds himself not to employ his talents, his industry, or his capital, in any useful undertaking in the kingdom, would be void." If the restraint is general, the shortness of time for which it may be imposed will not render it good. Thus, where a coal-merchant's clerk or traveller bound himself not to follow or be employed in the business of a coal-merchant for the space of nine months after he should have left the service of his employers, the bond was held void (*u*). In a previous case, Whittaker *v.* Howe (*x*), Lord Langdale enforced by injunction a covenant on the part of an attorney not to practise within Great Britain for twenty years. The case cannot, however, be considered sound law. It is quite inconsistent with Ward *v.* Byrne, which was decided after mature deliberation (*y*).[1] According to Bryson *v.* Whitehead (*z*), a trader may sell a secret and restrain himself generally from using it; but, as Lord Wensleydale pointed out in Ward *v.* Byrne (*a*), a limit of space was introduced by consent of the parties. In Avery *v.* Langford (*b*), a covenant not to set up a trading establishment within a district of considerable extent was enforced, as the court did not consider it too general in its terms. "I think," said Wood, V. C. (*c*), "that a court of law would not hold such a bond to be invalid because the terms of the condition were too large, but would construe that condition with respect to the nature of the trading establishment which was the subject of the sale, and would take it to mean that the defendant was not to set up within this district any trading establishment which would interfere with that of the plaintiff."

24. Covenants in restraint of trade, though only partial, if nothing shows them to be reasonable, are presumed to be void upon * grounds of public policy (*d*) ; but cov-   * 508 enants in partial restraint of trade, where there is a fair and reasonable ground for the restriction, are good and valid.

(*u*) Ward *v.* Byrne, 5 M. & W. 548; Hinde *v.* Gray, 1 M. & G. 195.
(*x*) 3 Beav. 383.
(*y*) See Nicholls *v.* Stretton, 10 Q. B. 346; Mumford *v.* Gething, 7 C. B. N. S. 305.
(*z*) 1 Sim. & St. 77.
(*a*) 5 M. & W. 548.
(*b*) Kay, 663.
(*c*) *Ib.*

(*d*) Mitchell *v.* Reynolds, 1 P. Wms. 181; Mallan *v.* May, 11 M. & W. 665.
[1] In McClurg's Appeal, 58 Penn. St., an agreement for a valuable consideration not to practise medicine within twelve miles of a particular locality, was held not unreasonable, and breach of it restrained by injunction. Butler *v.* Burleson, 16 Vt. 176 ; Beard *v.* Dennis, 6 Ind. 200.

They are upheld, not because they are advantageous to the individual with whom the contract is made, and a sacrifice *pro tanto* of the rights of the community, but because it is for the benefit of the public at large that they should be enforced. Such restraints upon trade, so far from being injurious to trade, are in many cases necessary for the protection of those who are engaged in it. Instead of cramping, they encourage the employment of capital, and the promotion of industry (*e*). Such is the case of the disposal or sale of the good-will of a trade or business, carried on in a particular locality, where the vendor covenants and agrees not to carry on the same business in the same place (*f*) ; or the taking an apprentice, clerk, traveller, or servant upon the terms that he shall not, during or after the termination of his engagement, solicit custom from his master's customers (*g*), or set up the same trade, business, or profession in opposition to his employer, in his immediate neighborhood, or in the district over which the master's business extends (*h*) ; or the dissolution of a partnership on the retirement of one of the partners of a firm upon the terms and subject to an agreement that he will not at any time set up business in opposition to the remaining partners, or any new partners, or their assignees, in the district where the business is carried on (*i*).

* 509   25. * A man who has covenanted not to carry on business in his own name, or for his own benefit, or in the name of or for the benefit of any other person within a certain district, is not prevented from soliciting orders within the district for a third person who is carrying on business

---

(*e*) Homer *v.* Ashford, 3 Bing. 326 ; Mallan *v.* May, 11 M. & W. 665 ; Tallis *v.* Tallis, 1 E. & B. 391 ; Mumford *v.* Gething, 7 C. B. N. S. 305.

(*f*) Mitchell *v.* Reynolds, 1 P. Wms. 181 ; Archer *v.* Marsh, 6 A. & E. 959 ; Wallis *v.* Day, 2 M. & W. 273 ; Jones *v.* Lees, 1 H. & N. 189.

(*g*) Rannie *v.* Irvine, 7 M. & G. 969 ; Homer *v.* Ashford, 3 Bing. 328 ; Nicholls *v.* Stretton, 7 Beav. 42, 10 Q. B. 346 ; Mumford *v.* Gething, 7 C. B. N. S. 305.

(*h*) Chesham   *v.* Nainby, 2 Lord Raym. 1456 ; Nicholls *v.* Stretton, 7 Beav. 42, 10 Q. B. 346 ; Mallan *v.* May, 11 M. & W. 668 ; Sainter *v.*

Ferguson, 7 C. B. 716, 1 Mac. & G. 286 ; Dendy *v.* Henderson, 11 Exch. 194 ; Benwell *v.* Inns, 24 Beav. 310 ; Edmonds *v.* Plews, 6 Jur. N. S. 1091. Comp. King *v.* Hansell, 5 H. & N. 106.

(*i*) Gale *v.* Reed, 8 East, 80 ; Leighton *v.* Wales, 3 M. & W. 545 ; Price *v.* Green, 16 M. & W. 346 ; Tallis *v.* Tallis, 1 E. & B. 391 ; Burrows *v.* Foster, cited Clark *v.* Leach, 32 Beav. 18 ; Clarkson *v.* Edge, 33 L. J. Ch. 443. See also, as to covenants not being too general, Gale *v.* Reed, 8 East, 80 ; Wickens *v.* Evans, 3 Y. & J. 318 ; Jones *v.* Lees, 1 H. & N. 189.

beyond the district (*k*), but he may not solicit orders for his own benefit within the prescribed limits, though he has no residence, shop, or place of business within them (*l*), or send goods to places within them from a place beyond them, where he is carrying on business (*m*). A covenant not to be engaged in a specified trade or " in any way, matter, or thing whatsoever, in anywise relating thereto," within a given district, does not prevent the covenantor from lending money to a person engaged in such trade within the district, upon mortgage of his trade premises, although he may know that the mortgagor has no means of paying the debt, except out of the profits of the business, but he may not retain any direct hold on the profits of the business (*n*). There is nothing in such a covenant, it would appear, to prevent the covenantor from buying any number of houses within the district, fitting them up, or selling them for the purposes of the trade in question, provided he has no direct interest in the business carried on in them after such sales. A mortgage expressly charging the debt upon the profits of a business would be probably a breach of the covenant (*o*).

26. A restraint on trade is not good unless it is reasonable. Whether it is so or not, is a question to determine (*p*). In respect of time the restriction may be unlimited (*q*). The death or discontinuance from business of the covenantee does not release the covenantor from the obligations of the covenant (*r*). *According to Benwell *v*. Inns (*s*), the *510 benefit of the covenant passes to an assign of the covenantee. But in respect of space, the restraint must be confined within reasonable limits. If the area of exclusion is larger and wider than the protection of the party with whom the contract is made can possibly require, it is unreasonable,

(*k*) Clarke *v*. Watkins, 9 Jur. N. S. 142.
(*l*) Turner *v*. Evans, 2 E. & B. 512, 2 D. M. & G. 740.
(*m*) Brampton *v*. Beddoes, 13 C. B. N. S. 538.
(*n*) Bird *v*. Lake, 1 H. & M. 338.
(*o*) Ib.
(*p*) Mallan *v*. May, 11 M. & W 653; Tallis *v*. Tallis, 1 E. & B. 391.
(*q*) Hitchcock *v*. Coker, 6 A. & E.

438; Pemberton *v*. Vaughan, 10 Q. B. 87; Elves *v*. Crofts, 10 C.B. 241; Tallis *v*. Tallis, 1 E. & B. 391.
(*r*) Hitchcock *v*. Coker, 6 A. & E. 438; Sainter *v*. Ferguson, 7 C. B. 718; Elves *v*. Crofts, 10 C. B. 241; Mumford *v*. Gething, 7 C. B. N. S. 305; Hastings *v*. Whittey, 2 Exch. 615, *per* Lord Wensleydale; Atkyns *v*. Kinneir, 4 Exch. 776.
(*s*) 24 Beav. 307.

34   [529]

and the contract, which would enforce it, is void (*t*). The rule upon the subject has been thus laid down by Tindal, C. J., in Horner *v.* Graves (*u*) : " We do not see how a better test can be applied to the questions, whether reasonable or not, than by considering whether the restraint is such only as to afford a fair protection to the interests of the party in favor of whom it is given, and not so large as to interfere with the interests of the public." The fact that the area of exclusion may be apparently larger than the area of the business of the party insisting on the contract, is not a reason for avoiding it (*x*). Unless the restraint is such as to be plainly and obviously unnecessary, the restraint is good (*y*). In Mallan *v.* May (*z*), Lord Wensleydale, in delivering the judgment of the court, doubted whether the comparative populousness of particular districts ought to be taken into consideration, and said : " We think it would be better to lay down such a limit as, under any circumstances, would be sufficient protection to the interests of the contracting party, and if the limit stipulated for does not exceed that, to pronounce the contract to be valid." And in Tallis *v.* Tallis (*a*), where the business was that of canvassing publishers, and the area of exclusion was very large, the court held, that unless the defendant could make it obviously and plainly clear, that the plaintiff's interest did not require the defendant's exclusion, or that the public interest would be sacrificed if the defendant's intended

*511   * publications were excluded, the contract would not be held void.

27. The reasonableness or unreasonableness of the restriction in respect of space depends in a great measure on the nature of the business and the mode in which it is usually carried on (*b*). No certain and precise boundary can be laid down within which the restraint would be reasonable, and beyond which it would be excessive. Some trades and professions require a limit of a much larger range than others.

(*t*) Hitchcock *v.* Coker, 6 A. & E. 438; Avery *v.* Langford, Kay, 663 ; Dendy *v.* Henderson, 11 Exch. 194.

(*u*) 7 Bing. 743.
(*x*) Tallis *v.* Tallis, 1 E. & B. 391. See Dendy *v.* Harrison, 11 Exch. 194.

(*y*) Horner *v.* Graves, 7 Bing. 743.
(*z*) 11 M. & W. 667.
(*a*) 1 E. & B. 391.
(*b*) Horner *v.* Graves, 7 Bing. 743 ; Hitchcock *v.* Coker, 6 A. & E. 439; Avery *v.* Langford, Kay, 663.

An area of exclusion which would be unreasonable in one trade or profession is in another necessary for the protection of the business. Businesses, such as those of attorneys, bankers, publishers, &c., &c., which can be carried on by agents and correspondence, fill up and occupy a much wider district than those which depend for their success and proper management upon personal superintendence (c).

28. In Davis v. Mason (d), the borough of Thetford and ten miles round; in Hayward v. Young (e), twenty miles round a place; in Sainter v. Ferguson (f), a district comprising the populous town of Macclesfield and seven miles round; and in Atkyns v. Kinneir (g), a district comprising a radius of two and a half miles from a certain house in London, were held reasonable limits in the case of a surgeon (h).

29. In Hitchcock v. Coker (i), Taunton and three miles round was held a reasonable limit in the case of a druggist. In Mallan v. May (k), London was held to be a reasonable limit (l); but in Horner v. Graves (m), York and one hundred miles round was held to be an unreasonable limit in the case of a dentist.

30. In the case of an attorney, London and one hundred and fifty miles round was * held a reasonable limit (n). * 512 In Whittaker v. Howe (o), Lord Langdale enforced by injunction a covenant on the part of an attorney not to practise in Great Britain for the space of twenty years (p).

31. In the case of a perfumer, toyman, and hair-merchant, London and Westminster was held a reasonable, but London and Westminster and six hundred miles round was held an unreasonable limit (q). In the case of a horse-hair manufacturer, Birmingham and two hundred miles round was held a

(c) Horner v. Graves, 7 Bing. 743; Mallan v. May, 11 M. & W. 653; Dendy v. Henderson, 11 Exch. 194; Tallis v. Tallis, 1 E. & B. 391.
(d) 5 T. R. 118.
(e) 2 Chitt. 407.
(f) 7 C. B. 716.
(g) 4 Exch. 776.
(h) See Giles v. Hart, 5 Jur. N. S. 1381; Carnes v. Nesbitt, 7 H. & N. 778; Fox v. Scard, 33 Beav. 327.
(i) 6 A. & E. 438.
(k) 11 M. & W. 653.

(l) See, as to meaning of London, ib. 13 M. & W. 511; but see Wallace v. Att.-Gen., 33 L. J. Ch. 314.
(m) 7 Bing. 735.
(n) Bunn v. Guy, 4 East, 190. See Howard v. Woodward, 34 L. J. Ch. 47.
(o) 3 Beav. 383.
(p) But see Nicholls v. Stretton, 10 Q. B. 346; and supra, p. 507.
(q) Price v. Green, 16 M. & W. 346.

reasonable limit (r). In the case of a tailor, twenty miles from a certain house in Cornhill was held a reasonable limit (s). In the case of a milkman, five miles from Northampton Square, in the County of Middlesex (t), and three miles from Charles Street, Grosvenor Square (u), were held reasonable limits. In the case of a wine and spirit merchant a limit comprising the three counties of Carnarvon, Anglesey, and Merioneth, was held reasonable (x). In the case of the trade of a general merchant in a country district, a limit comprising a considerable section of the county of Cornwall was held reasonable (y). In the case of canvassing publishers, London and one hundred and fifty miles from the Post Office, Dublin, Edinburgh, and any other town in which the covenantees might have had an establishment within six months previous to the date of the covenant, were held not unreasonable limits (z). In the case of a coaching business, a covenant not to run any coach from Reading to London was enforced by injunction (a). In the case of a carrier, a covenant not to carry goods between London and numerous towns in Norfolk was held reasonable (b); and

in the case of a butcher, a limit of five miles was held
* 513   reasonable (c). *A covenant, however, which restrains
a man from carrying on business not merely at such place or places as the plaintiff might be practising in at the expiration of the service, but at any place where he might have been practising before, though for ever so short a space of time, is unreasonable (d).

32. A covenant by the licensee of a patent not to make any of the articles, which are the subject of the patent, without the invention applied to them, is not void as in restraint of trade (e).

33. When the restraint is limited in point of space, the distance in question is to be measured in a straight line upon a horizontal plane, unless it is expressly, or by necessary im-

(r) Harms v. Parsons, 32 Beav. 328.
(s) Rolfe v. Rolfe, 15 Sim. 88.
(t) Proctor v. Sargent, 2 M. & G. 20.
(u) Benwell v. Inns, 24 Beav. 307.
(x) Turner v. Evans, 2 D. M. & G. 740.
(y) Avery v. Langford, Kay, 663.

(z) Tallis v. Tallis, 1 E. & B. 391. See Mallan v. May, 11 M. & W. 653.
(a) Williams v. Williams, 2 Sw. 253. See Leighton v. Wales, 3 M. & W. 545.
(b) Archer v. Marsh, 6 A. & E. 959.
(c) Elves v. Crofts, 10 C. B. 241.
(d) Mallan v. May, 11 M. & W. 653.
(e) Jones v. Lees, 1 H. & N. 189.

plication directed to be measured by the most practicable mode of access (*f*).

34. An agreement in restraint of trade is divisible. Where an agreement of the sort contains a stipulation which is capable of being construed divisibly, and one part is void, as being unreasonable, while the other is not, the latter will be upheld, and the contract will not be held void altogether (*g*).

35. According to the earlier cases a covenant in restraint of trade was void, unless the consideration was adequate to the restriction ; but, since Hitchcock *v.* Coker (*h*), it may be considered as settled at law that the adequacy of the consideration will not be inquired into, and that if there be a legal consideration of value the contract will be upheld without reference to the amount of value (*i*). A court of equity may, however, at its discretion, decline to interfere where the disproportion between the restriction and the consideration is so great as to render the agreement a hard bargain and oppressive (*k*).

36. There is not any implied covenant or promise on the part of * the vendor or assignor of a business not   * 514 to set up the same trade in opposition to the purchaser in the neighborhood of the spot where the business is carried on (*l*) ; but where the lease of a house and the good will of a trade had been sold and assigned upon an understanding by word of mouth that the vendor should not set up the same trade in the same street, he was restrained by injunction from infringing the oral contract (*m*). If the business of a firm has been carried on under an adopted name, a man who sells the good will of the business cannot set up the same business under the same name or style, but he cannot be prevented from using his own name (*n*).

(*f*) Leigh *v.* Hind, 9 B. & C. 776; Atkyns *v.* Kinneir, 4 Exch. 776 ; Duignan *v.* Walker, John, 446. See 1 Smith, L. C. 355.

(*g*) Chesman *v.* Nainby, 2 Lord Raym. 1456; Mallan *v.* May, 11 M. & W. 664 ; Price *v.* Green, 13 M. & W. 696, 16 M. & W. 346.

(*h*) 6 A. & E. 438.

(*i*) Archer *v.* Marsh, *ib.* 959 ; Leighton *v.* Wales, 3 M. & W. 551 ; Pilkington *v.* Scott, 15 M. & W. 657 ; Sainter

v. Ferguson, 7 C. B. 716 ; Tallis *v.* Tallis, 1 E. & B. 391.

(*k*) See Kimberley *v.* Jennings, 6 Sim. 340 ; Croft *v.* Haw, 5 L. J. Ch. N. S. 305; Parkin *v.* Thorold, 16 Beav. 59 ; Falcke *v.* Grey, 4 Drew. 659 ; Vivers *v.* Tuck, 1 Moo. P. C. N. S. 516.

(*l*) Cruttwell *v.* Lye, 17 Ves. 346 ; *supra*, p. 167.

(*m*) Harrison *v.* Gardner, 2 Madd. 198 ; *supra*, p. 41.

(*n*) Churton *v.* Douglas, John. 174 ; *supra*, p. 167.

37. A sum of money is sometimes named in an instrument
as payable upon the breach of a covenant. In such cases the
court has to determine whether the contract will be satisfied by
the payment of the sum named in the instrument, or whether
it will not; whether, in other words, the sum named was inserted by way of penalty to secure the performance of the
agreement, or whether it was the intention of the parties that
the act might be done on the payment of the sum named as an
equivalent. If the covenant is an absolute one, and the sum
named as payable upon breach has been inserted by way of
penalty to secure the performance of the covenant, the payment of the penalty does not oust the court of its jurisdiction
to prevent the doing of the act stipulated not to be done (*o*).
" A penalty," said Lord Loughborough, in Hardy *v.* Martin (*p*),
" is never considered in this court as the price of doing a thing
which a man has expressly agreed not to do " (*q*). But if the
real intent and meaning of the contract is that a man should
have the power, if he chooses, to do a particular act upon the
payment of a certain specified sum, the power to do the act
      upon the payment of the sum agreed on is part of the
* 515 express contract between the * parties; and a court of
      equity will neither compel him to abstain from doing
it nor relieve him, if he does do it, from the payment of the
sum agreed on as an equivalent (*r*).

38. The mere use of the terms " penalty " or " liquidated
damages " in a covenant is not conclusive as to the meaning
of the instrument, and does not determine the intention of the
parties. Like any other question of construction, the intention is to be gathered from the nature of the agreement, and
the language of the whole instrument taken together (*s*). If
it appear from the agreement, taken as a whole, that the sum

(*o*) Howard *v.* Hopkyns, 2 Atk. 371; Sloman *v.* Walter, 1 Bro. C. C. 418; French *v.* Macale, 2 Dr. & War. 276; Bird *v.* Lake, 1 H. & M. 111; Fox *v.* Scard, 33 Beav. 327; Howard *v.* Woodward, 84 L. J. Ch. 47; *supra,* pp. 80, 81.

(*p*) 1 Cox, 26.
(*q*) Comp. Stration *v.* Graham, 3 Pat. Sc. Ap. 119; Craigie *v.* M'Kenzie, 6 Pat. Sc. Ap. 117.

(*r*) Lowe *v.* Peers, 4 Burr. 2225, 2228; Street *v.* Rigby, 6 Ves. 818; French *v.* Macale, 2 Dr. & War. 276; Sainter *v.* Ferguson, 1 Mac. & G. 289; Gerrard *v.* O'Reilly, 3 Dr. & War. 414; Coles *v.* Sims, 5 D. M. & G. 1; Ranger *v.* Great Western Railway Co., 5 H. L. 94; Carnes *v.* Nesbitt, 7 H. & N. 778; *supra,* pp. 80, 81.
(*s*) Mercer *v.* Irving, El. Bl. & El. 563.

specified was not intended by the parties to be liquidated damages, it will be treated as a penalty, although the words " liquidated damages " may have been used (*t*). On the other hand, if the sum is not a penal sum, it will not be treated as a penalty merely because it is called so in the agreement (*u*). It is not material that the contract may be alternative in its form, if it appear clearly that there is essentially an agreement to do one of the alternatives (*x*).

39. Where the payment of a smaller sum is secured by a larger (*y*), or where the damages to arise from the breach are not uncertain, but are capable of being ascertained, as where there is a particular sum to be paid which is less than the sum named as payable upon breach, the last-named sum will be considered as a penalty (*z*). So, also, where an agreement * contains several stipulations of various degrees   * 516 of importance, the breach of all or any of which gives rise to an amount of damage which may be accurately measured, and a disproportionate sum is annexed as payable generally upon breach of all or any of the stipulations, the latter sum will be considered as a penalty, and not as liquidated damages (*a*). But if a contract, consisting of one or more stipulations, provides for the payment of a specified sum by way of compensation in case of the non-performance of all or of any of the things stipulated to be done, and the damages in each case of non-performance are in their nature altogether indefinite and uncertain, the sum named will be regarded as liquidated damages, and not as a penalty. Thus, where a surgeon had covenanted not to practise within a certain dis-

(*t*) Coles *v.* Sims, 5 D. M. & G. 1; Bird *v.* Lake, 1 H. & M. 111; Howard *v.* Woodward, 34 L. J. Ch. 47.

(*u*) Astley *v.* Weldon, 2 Bos. & P. 346; Kemble *v.* Farren, 6 Bing. 141; Jones *v.* Green, 3 Y. & J. 304; Green *v.* Price, 13 M. & W. 701; Gerrard *v.* O'Reilly, 2 Dr. & War. 414; Sainter *v.* Ferguson, 7 C. B. 728; Coles *v.* Sims, 5 D. M. & G. 1; Ranger *v.* Great Western Railway Co., 5 H. L. 72; Betts *v.* Burch, 4 H. & N. 506; Carnes *v.* Nesbitt, 7 H. & N. 778; Sparrow *v.* Paris, *ib.* 594; Dimech *v.* Corlett, 12 Moo. P. C. 229.

(*x*) Finch *v.* Earl of Salisbury, Finch. 212.

(*y*) Astley *v.* Weldon, 2 Bos. & P. 346; Aylett *v.* Dodd, 2 Atk. 238; Seton *v.* Slade, 7 Ves. 273.

(*z*) Reynolds *v.* Bridge, 6 E. & B. 541, *per* Coleridge, J.

(*a*) Kemble *v.* Farren, 6 Bing. 141; Davies *v.* Penton, 6 B. & C. 223; Horner *v.* Flintoff, 9 M. & W. 680; Green *v.* Price, 13 M. & W. 701; S. C. as Price *v.* Green, 16 M. & W. 346; Galsworthy *v.* Strutt, 1 Exch. 667; Atkyns *v.* Kinneir, 4 Exch. 781; Reynolds *v.* Bridge, 6 E. & B. 541; Ranger *v.* Great Western Railway Co., 5 H. L. 119; Dimech *v.* Corlett, 12 Moo. P. C. 229.

trict, or interfere with the patients of the plaintiff within that district, or induce them to employ any other medical man, &c., and to pay as liquidated damages, in the event of any infringement of any of the stipulations of the covenant, the sum of £1000, it was held that, as the damages arising from the breach of these different stipulations were altogether uncertain and difficult to ascertain, the parties had a right to measure them for themselves and settle the amount to be paid for a breach of all or any one of the stipulations (*b*). So, also, where an attorney had covenanted not to carry on business within a certain district, or solicit or influence the clients of another attorney, and that if he in any way infringed that covenant he should pay £1000 as liquidated damages, it was held to be liquidated damages in the event of either of the things being done which were stipulated not to be done (*c*).

So, also, where a man had covenanted not to carry on a
* 517   certain trade within London or * 600 miles thereof, and

for the observance of the covenant bound himself in the sum of £5000, as liquidated damages, it was held that the whole sum was recoverable in the event of either of the things being done which he had covenanted not to do (*d*). The fact that the sum agreed on is made payable upon one event only is evidence to show that it was intended to be liquidated damages (*e*).

40. When the amount of the penalty is small, as compared with the value of the subject of the agreement, the sum reserved will be treated as a mere penalty, and not as an alternative argument (*f*).

41. The fact that a sum named in a lease as payable upon breach of the covenants therein contained, may greatly exceed the actual damage, does not render the sum so reserved a penalty. The court looks on it as an increased rent agreed

---

(*b*) Atkyns *v.* Kinneir, 4 Exch. 781; Sainter *v.* Ferguson, 7 C. B. 716; Reynolds *v.* Bridge, 6 E. & B. 528; Mercer *v.* Irving, El. Bl. & El. 563. See, also, Leighton *v.* Wales, 3 M. & W. 545; Cass *v.* Thompson, 5 W. R. 289; Ranger *v.* Great Western Railway Co., 5 H. L. 73; Sparrow *v.* Paris, 7 H. & N. 594.

(*c*) Galsworthy *v.* Strutt, 1 Exch. 663.

(*d*) Price *v.* Green, 16 M. & W. 346.

(*e*) Sainter *v.* Ferguson, 7 C. B. 716; Cass *v.* Thompson, 5 W. R. 289; comp. Fox *v.* Scard, 33 Beav. 327.

(*f*) Chilliner *v.* Chilliner, 2 Ves. 528; Hobson *v.* Trevor, 2 P. Wm. 191; Howard *v.* Hopkyns, 2 Atk. 371; Logan *v.* Wienholt, 1 Cl. & Fin. 611. See Fry on Specific Performance, p. 28.

upon between the parties to be paid during the rest of the
term. Thus in Woodward v. Gyles (g), where the agreement
was that the defendant should not plough up any part of the
land, and that if he did plough up any part of it he should
pay at the rate of 20s. per acre per annum, the court held
that the parties had fixed a price for the ploughing and refused
an injunction. " The reservation of the reserved rent in this
case," said Lord St. Leonards in French v. Macale (h), " during the whole term shows that the parties contemplated the
payment of one rent in one event, and of another rent in
another state of circumstances." So also in Rolfe v. Peter-
son (i), where a certain sum was reserved, and the lessee
covenanted that, in case any part of the land which had been
in tillage for the last twenty years should be broken up, he
would pay the further sum of £5 per acre for every acre so
broken up over the rent reserved and upon the same days of
payment, the court held this a case for liquidated damages, fixed and agreed upon between the * parties (k). * 518
So also in Farrant v. Olmius (l), the reservation of an
additional sum of £50 for every acre of meadow land, which
shall be ploughed up or converted into tillage, was held to be
liquidated damages. " There is nothing unreasonable," said
Lord Tenterden (m), " in a landlord stipulating that particular
lands shall be converted into tillage, and that in case that be
done a larger sum shall be paid by way of stipulated damages " (n). So also in a case where there was a covenant
against erecting a weir under double the yearly rent, therein-
after reserved, to be recovered by distress, the sum so reserved
was held to be liquidated damages, notwithstanding it was called
a penalty in the instrument. The power of distress reserved
in an instrument is strong evidence that the sum so reserved
is liquidated damages (o).

42. But where in addition to the increased rent there is also
a stipulation that the doing of the act provided against shall

(g) 2 Vern. 119.
(h) 2 Dr. & War. 276.
(i) 2 Bro. P. C. 436.
(k) Per Lord St. Leonards, French
v. Macale, 2 Dr. & War. 277. See
Jones v. Green, 3 Y. & J. 298.

(l) 3 B. & Ald. 692.
(m) Ib.
(n) Smith v. Ryan, 9 Ir. L. 235.
(o) Gerrard v. O'Reilly, 3 Dr. & War.
414. See French v. Macale, 2 Dr. &
War. 269.

be attended with a forfeiture of the interest of the covenantor, the sum is a penalty and not liquidated damages (*p*). Where, too, the covenant is in its nature continuing, the sum reserved as payable upon breach will be regarded as a penalty and not as liquidated damages. Thus, where a lessee had covenanted not to burn the demised premises, part of which was ancient meadow, under the penalty of £10 per acre to be recovered in the reserved rent for every acre so burned, he was restrained by Lord St. Leonards from burning part of the premises (*q*).

43. A court of equity will not determine upon interlocutory application to dissolve an injunction whether a sum reserved is a penalty or liquidated damages, but will only consider whether there is a good *primâ facie* case for an injunction and whether more mischief will be done by granting than by withholding it (*r*).

*519   44. *After a court of law has determined that the word " penalty " in an agreement not to do a certain act under a certain penalty means liquidated damages, a man cannot come to the court for an injunction to restrain the further breach of the agreement after obtaining damages at law: the fact that owing to the bankruptcy of the defendant after judgment in the action the plaintiff has not recovered the sum stipulated by way of damages does not give him any equity to an injunction (*s*). So also where a man had commenced an action to recover a penalty as and for liquidated damages for the breach of an agreement on the part of the defendant not to practise as a surgeon within a certain district, it was held he was not entitled to an injunction also to restrain him from so practising (*t*). If a man after obtaining an injunction brings an action for damages, the defendant may come to the court and will have the injunction dissolved (*u*).

45. A court of equity has jurisdiction on a proper case being made out to restrain parties from violating an agreement not

(*p*) French *v.* Macale, 2 Dr. & War. 269.

(*q*) French *v.* Macale, 2 Dr. & War. 269. See Howard *v.* Hopkyns, 2 Atk. 371; City of London *v.* Pugh, 4 Bro. P. C. 395; Carden *v.* Butler, 1 Hay & J. 112; Thornton *v.* Kendall, 11 W. R. 352.

(*r*) Coles *v.* Sims, 5 D. M. & G. 1.

(*s*) Sainter *v.* Ferguson, 1 Mac. & G. 286. See Fox *v.* Scard, 33 Beav. 327.

(*t*) Carnes *v.* Nesbitt, 7 H. & N. 158, 778; Mayall *v.* Higby, 1 H. & C. 152. See Bird *v.* Lake, 1 H. & M. 111.

(*u*) Fox *v.* Scard, 33 Beav. 327.

to apply to Parliament. In exercising the jurisdiction the court, as in other cases when it interposes by way of injunction, acts merely upon the person, and does not in any way interfere with the privileges of Parliament (x) ; it simply says that it is not competent for a given party to apply to Parliament (y). What is a proper case for the interference of the court is a question of much difficulty. The fact that the intended application to Parliament will abrogate existing rights and create new ones can give no right to an injunction, for every man has a right to apply to Parliament for a special law to supersede the rules of property by which he is bound (z). Nor will the court interfere, even when an agreement not to apply to Parliament has been entered into for the purpose of protecting private interests, * if the party who * 520 makes the application to the legislature can urge it upon grounds of public policy, for such questions are subjects for the discussion of the legislature and are beyond the province of a court of equity (a). The only case in which the court will interfere is where the matter complained of is connected solely with private property (b). Accordingly, Lord Cottenham refused to restrain a railway company from applying to Parliament for leave to abandon a part of their railway in contravention of an agreement entered into with the plaintiff, who had withdrawn his opposition to a bill in a previous session of Parliament upon consideration of the company agreeing to carry the railway in the direction which they proposed by their bill to abandon (c). So also Wood, V. C., refused to restrain a railway company from applying to Parliament for powers to make a new line in contravention of an agreement entered into with the plaintiff company, on the faith of which the plaintiff company had withdrawn all opposition to the bill presented by the defendant company in a previous session of

(x) Heathcoate v. North Staffordshire Railway Co., 2 Mac. & G. 109.

(y) Lancaster and Carlisle Railway Co. v. North Western Railway Co., 2 K. & J. 304.

(z) Ware v. Grand Junction Canal Co., 2 R. & M. 470, 483 ; Heathcoate v. North Staffordshire Railway Co., 2 Mac. & G. 109 ; Steele v. Midland Railway Co., 2 L. R. Ch. Ap. 237.

(a) Lancaster and Carlisle Railway Co. v. North Western Railway Co., 2 K. & J. 304. See Stockton and Hartlepool Railway Co. v. Leeds and Thirsk Railway Co., 2 Ph. 666.

(b) Lancaster and Carlisle Railway Co. v. North Western Railway Co., 2 K. & J. 303.

(c) Heathcoate v. North Staffordshire Railway Co., 2 Mac. & G. 100.

Parliament (d). So also in Attorney-General v. Manchester and Leeds Railway Co. (e), there having been a motion pending before the Lord Chancellor with reference to a particular bridge, which was to be made over the road in a way which was supposed to be injurious to the public, the parties had undertaken that nothing should be done until the hearing of the cause to interfere with the existing state of things, and notwithstanding the undertaking they had taken the opportunity of inserting in a bill before Parliament a clause to liberate them from that undertaking entirely, and 'to enable them to do that which they had undertaken not to do, Lord Cottenham, though he expressed himself in the strongest terms as to the conduct of the railway company, said he saw very great difficulty in preventing an application to Parliament, and
* 521 that unless a strong authority * were adduced he should not assume that particular jurisdiction (f).

46. Whether a court of equity will interfere to restrain parties from violating a covenant not to oppose a bill in Parliament is doubtful (g). But in a case where the bill would, if passed into an act, have had the effect of depriving a minority of the shareholders of a railway company of the protection of the Wharncliffe order, the court would not enforce a covenant not to oppose it (h).

47. The mode in which contracts or covenants, when affirmative in form, are, as a general rule, enforced by courts of equity, is by decree for specific performance. But contracts and covenants, though affirmative in form, may often involve a negative in substance. When the importation of a negative quality into an affirmative agreement is not against the meaning of the agreement, a court of equity will import the negative quality and restrain the doing of acts which are inconsistent with the agreement (i). Thus in Webster v. Dillon (k), where

(d) Lancaster and Carlisle Railway Co. v. North West. Rail. Co., 2 K. & J. 293.
(e) 1 Ra. Ca. 436.
(f) 2 K. & J. 304, per Wood, V. C.
(g) Parker v. River Dun Navigation Co., 1 De G. & S. 192; Maunsell v. Midland Great Western Railway Co. of Ireland, 1 H. & M. 162.
(h) Maunsell v. Midland Great West. Rail. Co. of Ireland, 1 H. & M. 162.

(i) Lumley v. Wagner, 1 D. M. & G. 604; Holmes v. Eastern Counties Railway Co., 3 K. & J. 675; Storer v. Great Western Railway Co., 2 Y. & C. C. C. 48; De Mattos v. Gibson, 4 D. & J. 299; Seawell v. Webster, 7 W. R. 691; Peto v. Brighton, Uckfield, and Tunbridge Wells Railway Co., 1 H. & M. 468; Blackett v. Bates, 2 H. & M. 270.
(k) 3 Jur. N. S. 432.

an actor had agreed to perform at Sadler's Wells Theatre, but the agreement did not contain a stipulation that he would not perform elsewhere, Wood, V. C., restrained him from performing at any other place than the plaintiff's theatre on the nights on which he had by his agreement covenanted to act there. So also a man, who in a demise of land has entered into a covenant for quiet enjoyment, will be restrained from doing acts which are in violation of the covenant (*l*). So also lessees who had covenanted to manage land or cultivate a farm in a husband-like *manner have been restrained from   *522 ploughing up pasture (*m*) or meadow land (*n*), from carrying off the farm hay, straw, dung, crops, &c., except according to the custom of the country (*o*), and the usual course of husbandry (*p*), from sowing the land with pernicious crops (*q*), and turning young goats into a wood (*r*). So also persons who had covenanted to keep the banks of rivers and ponds in repair were restrained from destroying or injuring them (*s*). So also a man who had covenanted to keep and preserve trees from waste and damage was restrained from felling or injuring the timber (*t*). So also a railway company which had obtained the ownership of land under an agreement with the land-owners as to the mode in which a bridge or a road was to be constructed on the land, was not allowed to depart from the terms of the agreement. Another company claiming under the former is equally bound (*u*). So also a man who

---

(*l*) Tipping *v.* Eckersley, 2 K. & J. 270. See Shaw *v.* Stenton, 2 H. & N. 858; Rolleston *v.* New, 4 K. & J. 640; Great Northern Railway Co. *v.* Lancashire and Yorkshire Railway Co., 1 Sm. & G. 81.

(*m*) Drury *v.* Molins, 6 Ves. 328; Pratt *v.* Brett, 2 Madd. 62.

(*n*) Pratt *v.* Brett, *ib.*

(*o*) Pulteney *v.* Shelton, 5 Ves. 260, n.; Kimpton *v.* Eve, 2 V. & B. 349; Pratt *v.* Brett, 2 Madd. 62; Walton *v.* Johnson, 15 Sim. 352. See Johnson *v.* Goldswaine, 3 Anstr. 750; citing Geast *v.* Lord Belfast. See, also, 2 Bro. C. C. 64, n.

(*p*) Onslow *v.* ——, 16 Ves. 173. See, as to covenants to cultivate according to the custom of the country, Webb *v.* Plummer, 2 B. & Ald. 746; Womersley *v.* Dally, 26 L. J Exch. 219; *supra,*

pp. 249, 250. See also, as to covenants in a farming lease, Gale *v.* Bates, 3 H. & C. 84. In Pratt *v.* Brett, 2 Madd. 62, and Onslow *v.* ——, 16 Ves. 173, the tenant was tenant from year to year. In Onslow *v.* ——, *ib.*, there appears to have been no express covenant to cultivate in a husband-like manner: the covenant seems to have been implied by the court. But see Lathropp *v.* Marsh, 5 Ves. 260; Johnson *v.* Goldswaine, 3 Anstr. 749.

(*q*) Pratt *v.* Brett, 2 Madd. 62.

(*r*) Rogers *v.* Price, 13 Jur. 820.

(*s*) Lord Bathurst *v.* Burden, 2 Bro. C. C. 64; Lord Kilmorey *v.* Thackeray, cited *ib.*

(*t*) Bernard *v.* Meara, 12 Ir. Ch. 389. See also, as to covenants as to trees, *supra,* p. 242.

(*u*) Edinburgh, &c., Railway Co. *v.*

has covenanted to carry on a certain business will be restrained from doing or causing any thing to be done, which would put it out of his power or the power of any other person to carry on the business (*x*). So also a lessor who has entered into a direct,

specific, and express covenant with a lessee to perform
* 523   all the covenants in the original lease, under * which he

holds from his own lessor, may not by any surrender of the lease derogate from the rights which his own lessee has acquired from him under the lease, and he will be restrained by injunction from acting in violation of the covenants, under which he became bound to his own lessee (*y*). So also railway companies have been restrained from entering into agreements which are in violation of or are inconsistent with a subsisting agreement (*z*) So also where the lessee of a mill with engines, boilers, and other machinery attached thereto, who had covenanted to keep the same in good repair, reasonable tear and wear excepted, had pulled down part of the machinery and put up in its place more powerful machinery, his assignees in bankruptcy were restrained from removing the new machinery (*a*). So also where a plan has been approved between parties for the erection of a building, one of them will be restrained from afterwards interfering with the mode of building approved (*b*). So also where a husband had stipulated by deed that a child should be under the sole care and protection of his wife, the court will, if it can be shown that the control of the father would be injurious to the child, restrain him from removing or prosecuting any proceedings to obtain the child from the custody of his wife or from interfering with her in the management, care, and protection of the child (*c*).

48. In Mayor of London *v.* Hedger (*d*), it was decreed upon

Campbell, 4 Macq. 578. See Foster *v.* Birmingham, Wolverhampton, &c., Railway Co., 2 W. R. 378.

(*x*) Hooper *v.* Brodrick, 11 Sim. 47. See Lumley *v.* Wagner, 1 D. M. & G. 604.

(*y*) Piggott *v.* Stratton, 1 D. F. & J. 33.

(*z*) Shrewsbury and Chester Railway Co. *v.* Shrewsbury and Birmingham Railway Co., 1 Sim. N. S. 410; Great

Western Railway Co. *v.* Birmingham and Oxford Junction Railway Co., 2 Ph. 597.

(*a*) Sunderland *v.* Newton, 3 Sim. 450.

(*b*) Slee *v.* Corporation of Bradford, 4 Giff. 262.

(*c*) Swift *v.* Swift, 34 Beav. 266; comp. Vansittart *v.* Vansittart, 2 D. & J. 249.

(*d*) 18 Ves. 355.

demurrer that a covenant by a lessee to deliver up at the end of the term the premises in good repair has not the effect of preventing him from being restrained during the term from pulling down the premises and carrying away the materials (*e*).

49. * But if an agreement affirmative in form is of   * 524 such a nature that it cannot be specifically enforced, and the application for an injunction is in effect and spirit an application for a decree for specific performance, the court will not import a negative quality into the agreement, but will leave the plaintiff to his remedy by damages at law (*f*). Thus, in Clarke *v.* Price (*g*), where the defendant had agreed to take notes of cases in court, and compose reports for the plaintiff, and had failed to do so, Lord Eldon refused to restrain him from making reports for other persons (*h*). So, also, where a grant had been made to the plaintiff of an office involving duties of a personal and confidential character, the court refused to restrain the defendant from employing any other person than the plaintiff in the office, as the case was one where, from its very nature, specific performance could not be decreed (*i*). So, also, where the plaintiff had contracted with a railway company for a stipulated sum to work the line of the railway, and to keep the engines and rolling stock in repair, the court, upon the ground that the agreement was one which from its very nature could not be specifically enforced, refused to restrain the company from employing any other person than the plaintiff in the duties for which he had been engaged (*j*). So, also, where a company had engaged to employ the plaintiff as

(*e*) See Ward *v.* Duke of Buckingham, cited 10 Ves. 161, as to the enforcement of covenants, affirmative in character, which, as appeared from defendant's conduct, he was going to perform. See also, as to importing a negative character into an affirmative covenant, Newmarch *v.* Brandling, 3 Sw. 99 ; Frogley *v.* Lord Lovelace, John. 333 ; Lady Andover *v.* Robertson, 26 L. T. 23 ; Philipps *v.* Treeby, 8 Jur. N. S. 999.

(*f*) Lumley *v.* Wagner, 1 D. M. & G. 622; De Mattos *v.* Gibson, 4 D. & J. 299 ; Peto *v.* Brighton, Uckfield, and Tunbridge Wells Railway Co., 1 H. & M. 468.   See Heathcoate *v.* North Staffordshire Railway Co., 2 Mac. & G.

112; Stevens *v.* Benning, 6 D. M. & G. 223 ; Knight *v.* Burgess, 10 Jur. N. S. 166.

(*g*) 2 Wils. C. C. 157.
(*h*) See Baldwin *v.* Society of Useful Knowledge, 9 Sim. 393 ; Hope *v.* Hope, 22 Beav. 351.
(*i*) Pickering *v.* Bishop of Ely, 2 Y. & C. C. C. 249.   See Firth *v.* Ridley, 33 Beav. 518 ; comp. Thornton *v.* Kendall, 11 W. R. 352.
(*j*) Johnson *v.* Shrewsbury and Birmingham Railway Co., 3 D. M. & G. 914.   See Horne *v.* North Western Railway Co., 10 W. R. 170; Chaplin *v.* North Western Railway Co., 5 L. T. N. S. 601.

a broker for engaging freights, effecting charter-parties, &c., and it was stipulated that his name should appear jointly with that of the secretary in all the advertisements of the company, the court would not restrain the company from issuing
* 525   any advertisement, unless the name of the * plaintiff was therein inserted (k). So, also, the court would not restrain the directors of a company from acting upon and enforcing the resignation of an agent (l). So, also, where an indenture was held to constitute the relation of master and servant and not that of partner, Lord Truro dissolved an injunction which had been granted restraining the defendant from excluding the plaintiff from the management of the business (m). So, where a man had covenanted to use and keep open the demised premises as an inn, the court would not restrain him from discontinuing to use them and keep them open as an inn (n). So, also, where a contract is vague, indefinite, or uncertain in its terms, the court will not import a negative into it and enforce it by way of injunction (o). So, also, in a case where there was a proviso in the lease of a mine that the lessor might at the end of the term purchase the machinery in the mine at a certain valuation to be made by arbitrators, one of them to be nominated by the lessee, the court would not restrain the lessee from removing the machinery at the end of the term, as it could not compel him to name an arbitrator (p). So, also, the court would not restrain a man from disclosing a secret which he had agreed to keep (q), or from selling certain medicines, made from a secret receipt, to any other person than the plaintiff (r). Nor, where the stipulations sought to be enforced are subsidiary to the whole agreement, will a negative be imported so as to be a foundation for an injunction, unless the whole agreement is capable of being specifically enforced (s).

(k) Brett v. East India and London Shipping Co., 2 H. & M. 404.

(l) Mair v. Himalaya Tea Co., 1 L. R. Eq. 411.

(m) Stocker v. Brocklebank, 3 Mac. & G. 267.

(n) Hooper v. Brodrick, 11 Sim. 47.

(o) Paris Chocolate Co. v. Crystal Palace Co., 3 Sm. & G. 119; De Mattos v. Gibson, 4 D. & J. 276; Bernard v. Meara, 12 Ir. Ch. 389; Armstrong v.

Courtenay, 15 Ir. Ch. 138; Low v. Innes, 10 Jur. N. S. 1037.

(p) Hamilton v. Dunsford, 6 Ir. Ch. 412.

(q) Newberry v. James, 2 Mer. 446; Williams v. Williams, 3 Mer. 157; supra, p. 181.

(r) Newberry v. James, 2 Mer. 446; but see Williams v. Williams, 3 Mer. 157; supra, p. 181.

(s) Paris Chocolate Co. v. Crystal

50. *But though the agreement may be one which *526 cannot from its very nature be specifically enforced as a whole, the court will, where parts of the agreement are distinct and separable from the rest, import a negative and interfere by way of injunction (t). Where, therefore, a railway company had granted to certain lessees a license to publish advertisements in the company's carriages, and the sole license of selling books, &c., at their stations, the court restrained the company from removing the advertisements, and from evicting the plaintiff from the bookstalls at the stations, though there were other parts of the agreement which the court could not enter into (u).

51. If the contract is substantially an affirmative one, a negative will not be imported into it so as to form a foundation for an injunction. Thus, where the contract was to sell " all the coal, &c.," to the plaintiff, the court did not think it could be maintained that a negative was involved in the contract so as to disable the defendant from supplying other persons with coals, &c., he having covenanted to sell *all* to the plaintiff (x). " The contract," said Wood, V. C. (y), " is a substantial one, not a mere negative contract, designed to prevent the defendant from dealing with other parties to the prejudice of one who wishes to exercise a monopoly."

52. The contract of charter-party is, from the peculiar nature of the subject of the contract, an exception to the rule that a negative quality will not be imported into an affirmative agreement, unless the agreement is of such a nature that a decree for specific performance can be made (z). " I think," said Lord Chelmsford, in De Mattos v. Gibson (a), " that a vessel under a charter-party ought to be regarded as a chattel of peculiar value to the charterer, and that although a court of equity cannot compel a specific performance of the contract which it contains, yet that it will restrain the employment of

---

Palace Co., 3 Sm. & G. 119; Scottish North Eastern Railway Co. v. Stewart, 3 Macq. 382. See Brett v. East India and London Shipping Co., 2 H. & M. 404.

(t) Holmes v. Eastern Counties Railway Co., 3 K. & J. 675.

(u) Ib.

(x) Pollard v. Clayton, 1 K. & J. 474.

(y) Ib.

(z) De Mattos v. Gibson, 4 D. & J. 276; Sevin v. Deslandes, 30 L. J. Ch. 457; Messageries Impériales v. Baines 11 W. R. 322.

(a) 4 D. & J. 276, 298.

the vessel in a different manner, whether such employ-
* 527   ment is * expressly or impliedly forbidden according to
the principle expressed in Lumley *v.* Wagner." If a
charter-party is *bonâ fide* entered into between the owner of
a vessel and the charterer, either party is entitled to an injunction to restrain the other from doing any thing inconsistent
with the agreement (*b*).

53. If the agreement consists of two or more stipulations,
and is one which cannot from its very nature be specifically
enforced as a whole, the court will not import a negative
quality into the agreement so as to be a foundation for an
injunction, unless the person who makes the application has
actually performed his own part of the agreement. The mere
assertion on his part that it is his intention to perform his part
of the agreement is not sufficient, unless the court can decree
specific performance against him (*c*). Thus, where an agreement had been entered into between a railway company and a
contractor, whereby the contractor agreed to complete the line
of railway, and the company agreed to pay him in shares
and debentures as the works progressed, but the company
repudiated the contract, the court refused to restrain the
company from dealing with the debentures and shares in a
manner inconsistent with the agreement, on the ground that
it was beyond the power of the court to make him perform his
part of the contract (*d*). So, also, in Fechter *v.* Montgomery (*e*), the manager of a London theatre engaged a provincial
actor, desirous of appearing on a London stage for two years.
Though there was nothing express on the subject, the court
enforced an engagement on the part of the manager to employ the actor for a reasonable time, and on the part of
the actor not to perform elsewhere. The manager having
delayed the appearance of the actor for five months, the court
considered that his conduct was in spirit a breach of the engagement, and would not restrain the actor from acting else-

(*b*) Sevin *v.* Deslandes, 30 L. J. Ch.
457 ; Messageries Impériales *v.* Baines,
11 W. R. 322; Heriot *v.* Nicholas, 12
W. R. 844. See, as to the measure of
damages in such a case, De Mattos *v.*
Gibson, 1 J. & H. 79 ; S. C., 7 Jur. N. S.
282.

(*c*) Peto *v.* Brighton, Uckfield, and
Tunbridge Wells Railway Co., 1 H. &
M. 468.
(*d*) *Ib.* See Rigby *v.* Great Western
Railway Co., 15 L. J. Ch. 266 ; Ogden
v. Fossick, 32 L. J. Ch. 73.
(*e*) 33 Beav. 22.

where.   In Holmes *v.* Eastern Counties Railway (*f*),
the conduct of the * plaintiff in respect to his part of   * 528
the agreement had not been strictly honorable, but the
damage to which he would have been exposed, had the injunction been refused, was so serious and irreparable, that the court
imported a negative quality into the agreement and granted an
injunction.   The court, however, acted unwillingly (*g*).

54. There was till recently much doubt upon the authorities
whether the court would enforce by injunction the negative part
of an agreement containing both affirmative and negative stipulations, unless the affirmative part of the agreement was of such
a nature that it could be specifically enforced by decree.   The
authorities on the subject were not uniform.   In some cases
it had been held that the negative part could not be enforced
by injunction, unless the agreement could be enforced as a
whole (*h*) ; but in other cases the negative part had been enforced, although the court had no power to decree specific
performance of the whole agreement (*i*).   The authorities
were reviewed by Lord St. Leonards in Lumley *v.* Wagner (*k*),
and the principle was fully established by him that the court
may enforce the negative part of an agreement by injunction,
although the affirmative part is of such a nature that it cannot
be specifically enforced by decree.   The defendant had there
entered into an engagement with the plaintiff to sing at his
theatre and not to sing at any other theatre.   Lord St. Leonards restrained her from singing at any other theatre than the
plaintiff's, though it was beyond all doubt that he had not the
power to decree specific performance of the affirmative part of
the agreement.   " The case," he said (*l*), " is a mixed one,
consisting not of two correlatives to be done, one by the plaintiff and the other by the defendant, but of an act to be done by
the defendant alone, to which is superadded a negative stipulation on her part to abstain from the commission of any act
which will break in upon her affirmative covenant, the one

(*f*) 3 K. & J. 675.
(*g*) See Hamilton *v.* Dunsford, 6 Ir. Ch. 412.
(*h*) Kemble *v.* Kean, 6 Sim. 333 ; Kimberley *v.* Jennings, 6 Sim. 340.
(*i*) Rolfe *v.* Rolfe, 15 Sim. 88 ; Diet-richsen *v.* Cabburn, 2 Ph. 52 ; Great Northern Railway Co. *v.* Manchester, Sheffield, and Lincolnshire Railway Co., 5 De G. & S. 149.
(*k*) 1 D. M. & G. 604.
(*l*) *Ib.* 618.

being auxiliary to, concurrent and operating with the
* 529 * other. The agreement to sing for the plaintiff during
three months at his theatre, and during that term not to
sing for anybody else, is not a correlative contract; it is in
effect one contract. The engagement to perform at one theatre
must necessarily exclude the right to perform at the same time
at another theatre " (m). The negative part, however, of an
agreement will not be enforced, unless it constitute a distinct,
separate, and substantive part of the agreement. If the negative part is merely subsidiary or incidental to the affirmative
part, or if the affirmative and negative stipulations are merely
correlative to and not capable of being separated from each
other, the court will not enforce the negative part by injunction, unless the affirmative part is of such a nature that it can
be specifically enforced (n). Thus, in Hills v. Croll (o), Lord
Lyndhurst refused to restrain the violation of a negative covenant. " It was," said Lord St. Leonards (p), " a case in which
A. had given B. a sum of money, and B. had covenanted that
he would buy all the acids he wanted from the manufactory of
A., who covenanted that he would supply the acids, and B.
also covenanted that he would buy his acids from no other
person. Lord Lyndhurst refused to prohibit B. from obtaining
acids from any other quarter, both because the covenants were
correlative, and because he could not compel A. to supply B.
with acids ; and if, therefore, he had restrained B. from taking
acids from any other quarter, he might have ruined him in the
event of A. breaking his affirmative covenant to supply the
acids."

55. A man who seeks the aid of the court to enforce by
injunction the negative part of an agreement, which contains
also affirmative stipulations, is required to show that he has
performed his own part of the agreement. If he has not

(m) Webster v. Dillon, 3 Jur. N. S. 433.
(n) Hills v. Croll, 2 Ph. 60, 1 D. M. & G. 627, n.; South Wales Railway Co. v. Wythes, 5 D. M. & G. 889; Hamilton v. Dunsford, 6 Ir. Ch. 412; Peto v. Brighton, Uckfield, and Tunbridge Wells Railway Co., 1 H. & M. 468; Brett v. East India and London Shipping Co., 2 H. & M. 404; Kernot v. Potter, 3 D. F. & J. 459. See Lumley v. Wagner, 1 D. M. & G. 604; Ogden v. Fossick, 32 L. J. Ch. 73; Green v. Low, 22 Beav. 627; Paris Chocolate Co. v. Crystal Palace Co., 3 Sm. & G. 119.
(o) 2 Ph. 60, 1 D. M. & G. 627, n.
(p) 1 D. M. & G. 626.

actually done all that the contract required on his part,
the court will * not interfere (q). The mere assertion   * 530
on his part that it is his intention to complete his own
part of the agreement is not sufficient, unless the court can
decree specific performance against him (r). But if the damage to the plaintiff from refusing the injunction would be serious, the court may interpose, although his conduct in respect
to his own part of the agreement has not been strictly honorable (s).

56. The jurisdiction of courts of equity over contracts and
covenants is not confined to cases where an action at law can
be maintained, but extends to cases where an action at law is
not maintainable. It is in many cases a matter of much doubt
whether a covenant with respect to the use and occupation of
land runs with the land, so as to bind at law an assignee,
although assigns be expressly named in the covenant; but
covenants controlling the enjoyment of land, though not binding at law, will be enforced in equity, provided the person into
whose hands the land passes has taken it with notice of the
covenants (t). " The question," said Lord Cottenham (u), " is
not whether the covenant runs with the land, but whether a
party shall be permitted to use the land in a manner inconsistent with the contract entered into by his vendor, and with
notice of which he purchased " (x). Where, accordingly, the
owner of the fee had granted leases restricting the lessees from
erecting a hotel without the consent of himself, his heirs,
or * assigns, which restriction was required in conse-   * 531
quence of the lessor having covenanted with another
lessee not to let any land or house for that purpose, a pur-

(q) Stocker v. Wedderburn, 3 K. &
J. 405 ; De Mattos v. Gibson, 4 D. & J.
276 ; Fechter v. Montgomery, 33 Beav.
22. See Rigby v. Great Western Railway Co., 15 L. J. Ch. 266; Hope v.
Hope, 22 Beav. 351 ; but see S. C. on
appeal, 8 D. M. & G. 781.

(r) Peto v. Brighton, Uckfield, and
Tunbridge Wells Railway Co., 1 H. &
M. 468.

(s) Holmes v. Eastern Counties Railway Co., 3 K. & J. 675; supra, p.
527.

(t) Tulk v. Moxhay, 2 Ph. 774, 1 H.
& Tw. 105, 18 L. J. Ch. 83.

(u) Ib.
(x) Whatman v. Gibson, 9 Sim. 196 ;
Mann v. Stephens, 15 Sim. 377. ; Patching v. Dubbins, Kay, 1, affi'd. 23 L. J.
Ch. 45 ; Coles v. Sims, 5 D. M. & G. 1 ;
Child v. Douglas, Kay, 560, 5 D. M. &
G. 739; Jackson v. Fenwick, 21 L. T.
223 ; Johnstone v. Hall, 2 K. & J. 414 ;
Hodson v. Coppard, 29 Beav. 4 ; Herbert v. Maclean, 12 Ir. Ch. 84 ; Parker
v. Whyte, 1 H. & M. 167 ; Eastwood v.
Lever, 33 L. J. Ch. 357 ; Clements v.
Welles, 1 L. R. Eq. 200 ; Wilson v. Hart,
1 L. R. Ch. Ap. 463 ; Western v. M'Der-
mott, 2 L. R. Ch. Ap. 72.

chaser of the reversion in fee of one of the plots leased subject to the restriction, who subsequently purchased the lease of
the same lot, was restrained from building a hotel on the
land (*y*). If land is vested in trustees who sell building lots,
subject to restrictive covenants, each purchaser has an equity
against the other purchaser to compel the observance of the
covenants (*z*). Where land in settlement is sold, the purchaser's covenants are analogous to a reservation, and enure
to the benefit of all parties interested under the settlement (*a*).
Subsequent purchasers of the estate may enforce them, although they bought in ignorance of their existence (*b*).

57. The jurisdiction in granting relief against the breach of
covenants, which do not run with the land, by persons who
take with notice, is not limited to cases where the covenant is
in respect of the use and occupation of land. The court has
jurisdiction on a proper case being made out to enjoin against
the breach of collateral or personal covenants by persons who
take with notice. The remedy by damages at law being, as a
general rule, adequate in such cases for the purpose of justice,
no case is to be found in the books in which the jurisdiction
has been exercised, but there seems to be no doubt of its
existence. A contrary doctrine was laid down by Lord
Brougham in Keppell *v.* Bailey (*c*), but that case can be no
longer considered as an authority (*d*).

58. The principle of the court with respect to notice in its
application to the case of persons taking with notice of a previous contract, has been thus generalized by Knight Bruce, L. J.,
in De Mattos *v.* Gibson (*e*) : " It may be stated at least as a
general rule that where a man by gift or purchase acquires
property from another, with knowledge of a previous contract
lawfully, and for valuable consideration, made by him
* 532 * with a third person to use and employ the property
for a particular purpose in a specified manner, the
acquirer shall not, to the material damage of the third person
in opposition to the contract, and inconsistently with it, use and
employ the property in a manner not allowable to the giver or

(*y*) Jay *v.* Richardson, 30 Beav. 567.   (*b*) *Ib.*
(*z*) Eastwood *v.* Lever, 33 L. J. Ch.   (*c*) 2 M. & K. 517.
357.   (*d*) Sug. V. & P. App. 801–803.
  (*a*) Child *v.* Douglas, Kay, 560.   (*e*) 4 D. & J. 282.

seller " (*f*). Accordingly, the mortgagee of a charter-party, or the purchaser of a ship, with notice of a charter-party previously entered into, was restrained from doing any act which would have the effect of interfering with the due performance of the charter-party (*g*).

59. If the right at law under the covenant is clearly established and the breach is clear, and the covenant is of such a nature that it can consistently with the rules and principles of the court be specifically enforced, the court will not, unless under very exceptional circumstances, take into consideration at the hearing the comparative injury to the parties from granting or withholding the injunction (*h*). There may be cases in which it is clear that the damage to arise from the breach would be inappreciable, and in which the court would refuse to interfere. But the case must be free from all possibility of doubt. It must be clear that there is no appreciable or at all events no substantial damage before the court will refuse, upon the ground of smallness of damage, to withhold its hand from enforcing the execution (*i*). The mere fact that there has been a breach of covenant is a sufficient ground for the interference of the court by injunction. A covenantee has the right to have the actual enjoyment of property *modo et formâ* as stipulated for by him (*k*). It is no answer to say that the act complained of will inflict no injury on the plaintiff, or will be even beneficial to him. It is for the plaintiff to judge whether * the agreement shall be preserved as far as he   * 533 is concerned, or whether he shall permit it to be violated. It is not necessary that he should show that any damage has been done. It being established that the acts of the defendant are a violation of the contract entered into by him, the court will protect the plaintiff in the enjoyment of the right which

(*f*) See Barfield *v.* Nicholson, 2 L. J. Ch. 90; Hoare *v.* Dresser, 7 H. L. 317.

(*g*) De Mattos *v.* Gibson, 4 D. & J. 276 ; Messageries Impériales *v.* Baines, 11 W. R. 322.

(*h*) Tipping *v.* Eckersley, 2 K. & J. 270; Johnstone *v.* Hall, *ib.* 420 ; Dickenson *v.* Grand Junction Canal Co., 15 Beav. 270.

(*i*) Lloyd *v.* London, Chatham, and Dover Railway Co., 2 D. J. & S. 568.

See Rigby *v.* Great Western Railway Co., 15 L. J. Ch. 266; Lady Andover *v.* Robertson, 26 L. T. 23 ; Warden of Dover Harbor *v.* South Eastern Railway Co., 9 Ha. 493 ; Western *v.* M'Dermott, 2 L. R. Ch. Ap. 72.

(*k*) Tipping *v.* Eckersley, 2 K. &. J. 270; Johnstone *v.* Hall, *ib.* 420 ; Pigott *v.* Stratton, John. 354, 1 D. F. & J. 33; Western *v.* M'Dermott, 2 L. R. Ch. Ap. 72.

he has purchased (*l*). The circumstance that a work undertaken in breach of contract is one of great public importance, cannot be taken into consideration (*m*).

60. In exercising the jurisdiction by way of mandatory injunction against acts in violation of contract, covenant, or agreement, the court looks to the express stipulation of the agreement, and is not, as in cases of trespass or nuisance, influenced by considerations as to the nature or extent of the damage, or the comparative convenience or inconvenience of granting or withholding the injunction. A man who enters into an agreement is bound in equity to a true and literal performance of it. He cannot be suffered to depart from it at his pleasure, leaving the other party to his remedy by damages at law (*n*). There may be cases in which it is so clear that the mischief to arise from a breach of covenant would be inappreciable, that the court may decline to interfere on the ground that a mandatory injunction would be out of all proportion to the requirements of the case, and would operate with extreme harshness on the defendant (*o*). But, as a general rule, the inconvenience to the defendant will not be taken into consideration (*p*). Nor can the defendant be permitted to set up the inconvenience to the public which would arise from his being compelled to perform his agreement (*q*).

* 534   61. * The case of Lane *v.* Newdigate (*r*) is the first instance to be found in the books in which an order for a mandatory injunction was made against a breach of agreement. The plaintiff was assignee of a lease granted by the defendant for the purpose of erecting mills, and the defendant was bound

---

(*l*) Dickenson *v.* Grand Junction Railway Co., 15 Beav. 270 ; Piggott *v.* Stratton, John. 341. See Rigby *v.* Great Western Railway Co., 15 L. J. Ch. 266 ; Lady Andover *v.* Robertson, 26 L. T. 23 ; Ingram *v.* Morecraft, 33 Beav. 49.

(*m*) Lloyd *v.* London, Chatham, and Dover Railway Co., 2 D. J. & S. 568.

(*n*) Storer *v.* Great Western Railway Co., 2 Y. & C. C. C. 48. See Lumley *v.* Wagner, 1 D. M. & G. 619 ; Lloyd *v.* London, Chatham, and Dover Railway Co., 2 D. J. & S. 568.

(*o*) Warden of Dover Harbor *v.* South Eastern Railway Co., 9 Ha. 493. See Lloyd *v.* London, Chatham, and Dover Railway Co., 2 D. J. & S. 568.

(*p*) *Supra*, p. 231. See, as to mandatory injunctions, *supra*, p. 280.

(*q*) Raphael *v.* Thames Valley Railway Co., 2 L. R. Ch. Ap. 147 ; Foster *v.* Birmingham, Wolverhampton, and Dudley Railway Co., 2 W. R. 378 ; see, also, Att.-Gen. *v.* Borough of Birmingham, 4 K. & J. 528 ; Goldsmid *v.* Commissioners of Tunbridge Wells, 1 L. R. Ch. Ap. 349.

(*r*) 10 Ves. 192.

by covenant to supply water for canals and reservoirs on his own estate to work the plaintiff's mills. The plaintiff brought his suit to enforce the doing of repairs by the defendant, and the restoring a cut and stop-gate in existence at the date of the lease, and the removing a lock which had been made since the date of the lease. Lord Eldon doubted whether he could order repairs to be done, or the works to be restored, but arrived at the same end by restraining the defendant from hindering the enjoyment of the plaintiff by keeping the works out of repair, or by the use of the lock, or by continuing the removal of the stop-gates (s). So also an agreement to grant a right of way was carried into effect by an injunction to restrain the removal of the materials and the destruction of the way (t). So also a man was restrained from continuing to keep up a wall on his land which obstructed a right which the plaintiff had under an agreement with him to use a certain road (u). So also the commissioners of woods and forests, who had granted a lease of ground to the plaintiff as a site for a club-house, and had covenanted in the lease that part of the land adjoining the ground so let should be laid out as an ornamental garden, and that no buildings should be erected thereon, were restrained from permitting such buildings as had already been erected from continuing on the ground (x). So also a solicitor who had sold his business to the plaintiff, but kept possession of the books contrary to his covenant, was restrained from keeping the books away from the possession of the plaintiff, and from permitting the same to * remain away   * 535 from the office of the plaintiff (y). So also a partner who had taken away one of the partnership books from the counting-house of the firm in breach of a covenant in the partnership deed, was restrained from continuing to violate the covenant (z), and from keeping it at any other place than the partnership premises (a). So also a mine-owner who had

(s) See Lord Kilmorey v. Thackeray, cited 2 Bro. C. C. 64. Comp. Blakemore v. Glamorganshire Railway Co., 1 M. & K. 185.
(t) Newmarch v. Brandling, 3 Sw. 99.
(u) Philipps v. Treeby, 8 Jur. N. S. 999.

(x) Rankin v. Huskisson, 4 Sim. 13.
(y) Whittaker v. Howe, 3 Beav. 383.
(z) Taylor v. Davis, 4 L. J. Ch. N. S. 18, 7 L. J. Ch. N. S. 178, 3 Beav. 388, n.
(a) Greatrex v. Greatrex, 1 De G. & S. 692.

covenanted to leave sufficient barriers against the adjoining
collieries, but had broken his covenant, was restrained from
permitting a communication with an adjoining mine to remain
open and water to flow therefrom (*b*). So also a railway company who had agreed with a man to make a road at a certain
level, were restrained from making a road at a lower level
than they had agreed to do (*c*). So also where a building has
been erected in a form that is in violation of a contract or an
act of Parliament, the court may restrain the defendant from
using the building (*d*), or may compel him to alter the elevation or form of the building so as to be in conformity with the
terms of the contract or the act of Parliament, as the case
may be (*e*).

SECTION II. — INJUNCTIONS IN AID OF SPECIFIC PER-
FORMANCE.

1. Pending suit for specific performance, defendant may be restrained from alienating, &c., subject-matter.
2. Relief may be given even against third parties.
3. But defendant cannot be restrained from buying second estate.
4. Purchaser will be restrained, pending bill for specific performance, from bringing action at law for his deposit.
5. But deposit must be paid into court.
6. Injunction will be granted if *primâ facie* case be made out.
7. Cases of injunction against ejectment.
8. Practice where the legal title to the thing agreed upon remains in one of the con-tracting parties while an equitable right passes to the other.
9. Instrument may be supported as an agreement in equity which has no effect at law.
10. Injunction to restrain actions at law after dismissal of bill for specific performance.
11. To restrain proceedings at law after decree for specific performance.

1. A court of equity has jurisdiction pending a suit for
specific performance to restrain the vendor from alienating or
affecting by other acts the subject-matter in litigation. Whether
or not the jurisdiction will be exercised depends on the special
circumstances of the case.[1] If there is a clear, undisputed

(*b*) Lord Mexborough *v.* Bower, 7 Beav. 127, affi'd. 2 L. T. 205. See Powell *v.* Aiken, 4 K. & J. 355.
(*c*) Foster *v.* Birmingham, Wolver-hampton, and Dudley Railway Co., 2 W. R. 378. See Raphael *v.* Thames Valley Railway Co., 2 L. R. Ch. Ap. 147.
(*d*) Warden of Dover Harbor *v.*

South Eastern Railway Co., 9 Ha. 493.
(*e*) Franklyn *v.* Tuton, 5 Madd. 469. See Sanderson *v.* Cockermouth Rail-way Co., 11 Beav. 497; Storer *v.* Great Western Railway Co., 2 Y. & C. C. C. 48; Child *v.* Douglas, Kay, 577.
[1] The ground of the jurisdiction of a court of equity is, that a court of law

contract, the court will not permit the vendor to transfer the legal estate to * a third person (ƒ). But if the   * 536
validity of the contract is open to doubt, the question
whether the vendor shall be permitted to transfer the legal estate
to a third person, pending a suit for specific performance,
becomes a question of comparative convenience or inconvenience. If, on the one hand, greater inconvenience would
arise to the plaintiff from withholding the injunction than to the
defendant from granting it, an injunction will be granted (g).
If, on the other hand, greater inconvenience would arise to the
defendant from granting the injunction than to the plaintiff
from withholding it, an injunction will not be granted (h).[1]

is inadequate to decree a specific performance, and can relieve the injured
party only by a compensation in damages, which, in many cases, would fall
far short of the redress which his situation might require. "Whenever, therefore, the party wants the thing *in specie*,
and he cannot otherwise be fully compensated, courts of equity will grant
him a specific performance. They will
decree the specific performance of a
contract for the sale of lands, not because of the peculiar nature of land, but
because a party cannot be adequately
compensated in damages. So in respect to personal estate : the general
rule that courts of equity will not entertain jurisdiction for a specific performance of agreements respecting goods,
chattels, stocks, *choses in action*, and
other things of a merely personal nature,
is limited to cases where a compensation in damages furnishes a complete
and satisfactory remedy. Corbin v.
Tracy, 34 Conn. 325 ; 2 Story's Eq.
Jur. ss. 717, 718. In Connecticut, a
parol contract for the sale of lands will
be enforced in equity, where possession
has been delivered and held, and especially if the vendee has paid a part or
all of the purchase-money, and has made
improvements on the estate. Green v.
Finin, 35 Conn. 178. A court of equity
will also decree the specific performance
of a contract for the sale of stock in an
incorporated company, but not for the
transfer of stock, such as stock in the
consolidated funds of England, as one
may always obtain that in the market.
Duncuft v. Albrecht, 12 Sim. 189 ; Shaw
v. Fisher, 2 De G. & S. 11 ; Todd v.
Taft, 7 Allen, 371 ; Leach v. Fobes, 11
Gray, 506.   There has been the most

controversy in the English courts of
equity as bearing upon the question of
decreeing specific performance of contracts, to transfer shares in joint-stock
companies, upon the point of the sufficiency of the proof. 1 Redfield on Railways, 132, n. Courts of equity will
interpose and give relief by injunction or
specific performance, when rights growing out of contracts as to personal property can only be protected otherwise
by numerous and expensive law-suits.
Penn. Coal Co. v. Del. & H. Canal Co.,
31 N. Y. 91.
  (ƒ) Hadley v. London Bank of Scotland, 3 D. J. & S. 63. See Spiller v.
Spiller, 3 Sw. 556 ; Curtis v. Marquis
of Buckingham, 3 V. & B. 168.
  (g) Hadley v. London Bank of Scotland, 3 D. J. & S. 63. See Echcliff v.
Baldwin, 16 Ves. 267 ; Shrewsbury
and Chester Railway Co. v. Shrewsbury
and Birmingham Railway Co., 1 Sim.
N. S. 425.
  (h) Hadley v. London Bank of Scotland, 3 D. J. & S. 63. See Wheatley
v. Slade, 4 Sim. 126 ; Great Western
Railway Co. v. Birmingham and Oxford Junction Railway Co., 2 Ph. 597 ;
Turner v. Wright, 4 Beav. 40 ; Shrewsbury and Chester Railway Co. v.
Shrewsbury and Birmingham Railway
Co., 1 Sim. N. S. 425.
  [1] And a court of equity will never,
it seems, decree specific performance
of a contract which is impossible on the
part of the defendant, although the
inability be the result of defendant's
own fault. Nor will specific performance be decreed against one party in
favor of another who has disregarded
his own reciprocal obligations in the
matter ; as, *e.g.*, against a grantee of

2. Relief may be given even against parties whose rights are independent of the contract. Thus, where the suit related to an agreement for the sale of a next presentation to a living, the bishop of the diocese was restrained from instituting, or in the case of a lapse taking place pending the suit, from collating to the living any clerk nominated by the plaintiff (*i*).

3. A vendor has no equity to prevent his purchaser from buying a second estate from some one else pending the transaction, on the ground that by making such second purchase he may be rendered unable to complete the first (*k*).

4. In cases where the court entertains jurisdiction by way of specific performance, it is not the course of the court to permit an action at law in respect of the same subject-matter (*l*). Upon this principle the court will, as a general rule, after a bill for specific performance has been filed, restrain the purchaser from bringing an action at law to recover his

* 537   deposit (*m*). So * also in Duke of Beaufort *v.* Glyn (*n*), where the demurrer to a bill for specific performance had been overruled, the court restrained an action at law for the deposit (*o*). But the court may, under the circumstances of the case, decline to exercise the jurisdiction (*p*). An injunc-

---

land charged with certain duties in regard to it, in favor of a grantor who has made a re-entry both unlawful and fraudulent. Nor where the duties to be fulfilled by the grantee are continuous and involve the exercise of skill, personal labor, and cultivated judgment; as, *e.g.*, to deliver marble of certain kinds, and in blocks of a kind that the court is incapable of determining whether they accord with the contract or not. Nor where there is a want of mutuality in the contract; as, *e.g.*, where it is stipulated that one of the parties may abandon the contract at any time on giving a year's notice. Nor where the party, a grantor, has a complete remedy at law; as, *e.g.*, in a grant of quarry land, the grantee agreeing to quarry and deliver to the grantor certain sorts of marble from it, and the grantor reserving a right of re-entry in case of non-performance in order to supply himself, and having, moreover, a remedy by an ordinary suit at law upon the contract. Marble Company *v.* Ripley, 10 Wallace, U. S. 339. See, also, Willard *v.* Tayloe, 8 Wallace, U. S. 557.

There is a settled distinction in equity between enforcing specifically and rescinding a contract. An agreement may not be entitled to be enforced, and yet not be so objectionable as to call for the exercise of equity jurisdiction to rescind it. Seymour *v.* Delancy, 9 Johns. Ch. 222. Nor unless the contract is so certain as to enable the court to arrive at the clear result of what is meant by all the terms contained in it, will it be specifically enforced. B. & M. Railroad *v.* Babcock, 3 Cush. 228.

(*i*) Nicholson *v.* Knapp, 9 Sim. 326.

(*k*) Syers *v.* Brighton Brewery Co., 13 W. R. 220.

(*l*) Prothero *v.* Phelps, 7 D. M. & G. 734.

(*m*) Levy *v.* Lindo, 3 Mer. 82; Johnson *v.* Smart, 2 Giff. 156; Kell *v.* Nokes, 32 L. J. Ch. 785.

(*n*) 3 Sm. & G. 213.

(*o*) Simmons *v.* Haseltine, 5 Jur. N. S. 270.

(*p*) Lloyd *v.* Collett, 4 Bro. C. C. 469; Stewart *v.* Alliston, 1 Mer. 26; Tanner *v.* Smith, 4 Jur. 810. See Pincke *v.*

tion to restrain an action at law for the deposit may be granted against the agents of the parties. In one case an injunction against the purchaser proceeding at law to recover the deposit from the seller's attorney, who was not a party, was refused with costs (q); but in a later case an injunction was granted to restrain the purchaser from proceeding in an action against the auctioneer who was not a party $(r.)$.

5. Upon restraining an action at law for the deposit, the court, as a general rule, exercises the jurisdiction only upon the terms of the deposit being paid into court (s). But a vendor will not be compelled to pay the deposit into court where it is the fault of the purchaser that he retains both the deposit and the estate (t). In Duke of Beaufort v. Glyn (u), where a demurrer by a purchaser to a bill for specific performance had been overruled, the deposit was not ordered to be paid into court.

6. When the interference of the court is sought in aid of specific performance, it is sufficient for the plaintiff to show a *primâ facie* case for specific performance to induce the court to interfere by injunction (x). It is not necessary that it should be clear that the plaintiff will succeed at the hearing; it is enough if there is ground for supposing that relief may be given (y). If the bill states a substantial question between the * parties, the title to the injunction may be   * 538 good, although the title to the relief prayed for may ultimately fail (z). On this motion the court will not decide delicate points (a), nor allow it to be resisted on points such as delay, which can only be decided at the hearing (b).

7. If it appear to be doubtful whether a tenant will be entitled to a decree for specific performance, the court will either refuse to grant an injunction to restrain the landlord from

Curteis, 4 Bro. C. C. 330; Morley v. Cook, 2 Ha. 106.

(q) Brown v. Frost, E. T. 1818. MSS.; Sug. V. & P. 229, n.

(r) Ib.

(s) Annesley v. Muggridge, 1 Madd. 593; Levy v. Lindo, 3 Mer. 82; Lawson v. Paddon, 5 L. T. 170.

(t) Wynne v. Griffith, 1 Sim. & St. 147.

(u) 3 Sm. & G. 213.

(x) Powell v. Lloyd, 1 Y. & J. 427.

(y) Hudson v. Bartram, 3 Madd. 440; Attwood v. Barham, 2 Russ. 186; Crosbie v. Tooke, 1 M. & K. 433. See Morgan v. Rhodes, ib. 435; supra, p. 14.

(z) Great Western Railway Co. v. Birmingham and Oxford Junction Railway Co., 2 Ph. 603.

(a) Price v. Assheton, 1 Y. & C. Exch. 82.

(b) Levy v. Lindo, 3 Mer. 81.

pursuing his legal right, or if it restrain him, it will put the
tenant upon terms which would secure to the landlord, if it
should turn out at the hearing that the tenant was not entitled
to specific performance, the whole benefit he could have if the
injunction had not been granted (c). In one case an injunction was refused upon the ground of the insolvency of the tenant,
and the fact of his having injured the premises (d). But the
bankruptcy of the person with whom a landlord has contracted
is no defence to a bill for specific performance of an agreement
by a person to whom the benefit of the agreement has been
assigned, provided the assignee is solvent and in a condition to
enter into the usual covenants, and there is no evidence to
show that the contract was entered into upon considerations
personal to the assignor. In such a case the landlord was
restrained from bringing ejectment (e).

8. Upon agreements for the purchase of interests in lands
and tenements or other agreements, it often happens that the
legal title to the thing agreed for remains in one of the contracting parties, while an equitable right passes to the other.
In such cases the court will, as a general rule, restrain the
party in possession of the legal title from proceeding upon it
at law, to disturb the other party in his enjoyment of the thing
agreed for, at least until the hearing, unless the party
* 539   who has the * equitable right has by his conduct deprived himself of his equity (f). If the plaintiff in
equity has by tortuous means got into possession of property
pending a suit to establish his legal title, the court will not
stay proceedings at law against him for recovery of possession (g).[1]

9. The court will sometimes interfere by injunction to support as an agreement in equity an instrument which has no

(c) Attwood v. Barham, 2 Russ. 186 ;
Sanxter v. Foster, Cr. & Ph. 302 ; Pyke
v. Northwood, 1 Beav. 152 ; Paris
Chocolate Co. v. Crystal Palace Co.,
3 Sm. & G. 120. See Boardman v.
Mostyn, 6 Ves. 471 ; supra, pp. 18, 19,
94.
(d) Buckland v. Hall, 8 Ves. 92 ; but
see Boardman v. Mostyn, 6 ib. 471.
(e) Crosbie v. Tooke, 1 M. & K. 431.
See Morgan v. Rhodes, ib. 435.

(f) Shannon v. Bradstreet, 1 Sch. &
Lef. 53 ; Green v. Green, 2 Mer. 86 ;
supra, p. 91.
(g) Grafton v. Griffin, 1 R. & M. 336 ;
supra, p. 105.
[1] A court will not by an ex parte order
or process, turn even a wrongdoer out
of possession. People v. Simonson, 10
Mich. 335.

effect at law, and will even under special circumstances give effect to an executory agreement against the legal effect of a legal instrument (*h*).

10. The dismissal of the bill of the vendor for specific performance does not, as a general rule, interfere with his right to bring an action for breach of the agreement; nor is it necessary, though it is usual, to state in the decree that the dismissal is without prejudice to the legal right (*i*). But an action at law will be restrained where the bill has been dismissed for want of title (*k*), or where the decree in equity proceeded on the ground that the literal performance of the thing for which the action at law is brought had been waived (*l*)

11. The court will, on decreeing specific performance, grant a perpetual injunction to restrain proceedings at law (*m*). Claims for damages arising out of or connected with the decree must be submitted to the court, and should not be prosecuted at law (*n*).

SECTION III. — INJUNCTIONS AGAINST ACTIONS AT LAW UPON COVENANTS.

1. Injunctions granted where questions connected with the conduct of the parties are involved in the construction to be put upon the covenants.

1. A court of equity will restrain actions at law upon a covenant, where the matters involve questions connected with the * conduct of the parties in relation to the   * 540 construction to be put upon the covenants which are clearly unfit for a court of law. The court will not refuse its jurisdiction upon questions of contract, where considerations of conduct are involved, and where in order to arrive at the proper construction of the terms of an instrument more than

---

(*h*) Brown *v.* Warner, 14 Ves. 156; Dally *v.* Catchlowe, 4 Pr. 147.

(*i*) Macnamara *v.* Arthur, 2 B. & B. 349, Sug. V. & P. 235.

(*k*) Macnamara *v.* Arthur, 2 B. & B. 349.

(*l*) Reynolds *v.* Nelson, 6 Madd. 290.

See Prothero *v.* Phelps, 7 D. M. & G. 722.

(*m*) Green *v.* Low, 22 Beav. 625; Frank *v.* Basnett, 2 M. & K. 618; Prothero *v.* Phelps, 7 D. M. & G. 734.

(*n*) Prothero *v.* Phelps, 7 D. M. & G. 734; *supra*, p. 104.

proceedings at law will be necessary (*o*). The court accordingly under very peculiar circumstances involving the conduct of parties restrained by perpetual injunction an action for rent and insurance (*p*).

(*o*) Leather Cloth Co. *v.* Bressey, 3 Giff. 474.   (*p*) *Ib.*

* CHAPTER XXIII.   * 541

INJUNCTIONS AGAINST INCORPORATED AND OTHER COMPANIES.

1. Courts of equity will, on a proper case being made out, restrain companies, whether incorporated by statute or constituted under deeds of settlement from doing illegal acts, or violating the duties which attach in equity to the relation of shareholders and directors, *inter se.*

2. The principles on which the court interferes in restraining a company from doing illegal acts are the same as those on which it interferes in other cases. If the right at law is clear and the breach is clear, and serious injury is likely to arise from the breach, the court will interfere at once and protect the right by injunction. But if the right at law is not clear or the breach is doubtful, the court, in determining whether or not it shall interfere by injunction, is guided by the balance of convenience and inconvenience likely to arise to the parties from granting or withholding the injunction (*a*).

3. Acts on the part of a company incorporated by statute, may be illegal, either as against the public, or as against third parties, or as against individual members of the company, or as against the general body of the members, or they may be in violation of the duties which bind in equity the .directors and shareholders, *inter se* (*b*).

4. Rights arising under acts of Parliament are legal rights and are dealt with by the court according to ordinary rules and principles (*c*). Companies incorporated by statute * 542 are bound * to confine themselves within the limits of the jurisdiction, which has been intrusted to them by the legislature, and to proceed in the mode which the legisla-

(*a*) Fielden *v.* Lancashire and Yorkshire Railway Co., 2 De G. & S. 531; Bullock *v.* Chapman, *ib.* 211; Norman *v.* Mitchell, 5 D. M. & G. 673; *supra,* p. 208–210.
(*b*) Browne *v.* Monmouthshire Canal Co., 13 Beav. 45.

(*c*) Weale *v.* West Middlesex Waterworks Co., 1 J. & W. 371; Att.-Gen. *v.* Corporation of Liverpool, 1 M. & C. 171; Att.-Gen. *v.* Borough of Birmingham, 4 K. & J. 528.

ture has pointed out. If a company goes beyond the line of its authority, and violates the rights of others, it becomes amenable to the jurisdiction of the court by injunction (d).[1]

5. Companies incorporated for a special purpose exist for those purposes only for which they have been incorporated, and for no other purpose whatever (e). The agency of the company, the course of action, and the sphere of action of the company, are limited entirely to that which is defined by the legislature. What it is empowered to do it has a right to do, and what it is not empowered to do it must be considered as having no right to do (f). Courts of equity will restrain a company, which has been incorporated for a special purpose, from going beyond or exceeding the scope of the purposes for which it has been incorporated. Thus, a railway company was restrained at the suit of the Attorney-General on the relation of a stranger to the company from carrying on the business of coal merchants (g). "It is," said Wood, V. C. (h), "a principle of public policy that where Parliament has authorized a company to raise a large capital for a specific purpose, the privilege confers no right upon the company to employ their capital in competition with the general public upon speculations of a different kind" (i). Although the act may contain no prohibition in express terms against the company engaging in any business except to construct and maintain the railway, there is in every such act an implied contract (k).

6. The suit should be instituted by the Attorney-General.

(d) Frewin v. Lewis, 4 M. & C. 254 ; Mayor of Liverpool v. Chorley Waterworks Co., 2 D. M. & G. 860 ; supra, p. 296.

(e) Rochdale Canal Co. v. Radcliffe, 18 Q. B. 287 ; National Manure Co. v. Donald, 4 H. & N. 8.

(f) Stockport District Waterworks Co. v. Mayor, &c., of Manchester, 9 Jur. N. S. 266.

(g) Att.-Gen. v. Great Northern Railway Co., 1 Dr. & Sm. 154.

(h) Ib.

(i) Hare v. London and North Western Railway Co., 2 J. & H. 109.

(k) Att.-Gen. v. Great Northern Railway Co., 1 Dr. & Sm. 154.

[1] Delaware and Rar. Canal et al. v. Rar. and Del. Bay Railway Co., 1 C. E. Green, (N. J.) 378, and cases cited ; Sandford v. Railroad Co., 24 Penn. St. 378. An injunction is the proper remedy to secure to a party the enjoyment of a statute privilege of which he is in the actual possession, and when his legal title is not put in doubt. Livingston v. Van Ingen, 9 Johns. 506 ; Croton Turnpike Co. v. Ryder, 1 Johns. Ch. 615 ; Boston and Lowell Railroad v. Salem and Lowell Railroad Co., 2 Gray, 1 ; Del. and Rar. Canal et al. v. Rar. and Del. Bay Railway Co., 1 C. E. Green, (N. J.) 378. But an injunction will not lie to restrain officers from entering upon official duties under an illegal appointment. The remedy is at law by quo warranto, and to be invoked after entry into or exercise of authority under their appointment. Updegraff v. Crans, 47 Penn. St. 103.

A rival company is not qualified to represent the rights and interests of the public (*l*). Whether the suit can be
* 543 maintained * by an individual, a stranger to the company, appears to be doubtful (*m*). To support an information, no substantial damage or definite injury to the public need be shown. It is enough that the company has not strictly followed, or is about to transgress the powers which have been vested in it by the legislature (*n*) ; but the court will not, as a general rule, entertain jurisdiction, unless it is clear that the interest of the public calls for its interference (*o*).[1]

7. If a railway company, authorized by special act to construct a main line with a branch, complete the one and take no steps to complete the other, the remedy is by mandamus, and not by injunction (*p*).

8. If an act has been declared to be illegal by a competent authority, the court will interfere without considering the grounds on which the act has been declared illegal (*q*). A railway company accordingly has been restrained from opening their line without the sanction of the Board of Trade (*r*).

(*l*) Stockport Waterworks Co. *v.* Mayor, &c., of Manchester, 9 Jur. N. S. 266.

(*m*) See Att.-Gen. *v.* Great Northern Railway Co., 1 Dr. & Sm. 159 ; Hare *v.* London and North Western Railway Co., 2 J. & H. 109.

(*n*) Att.-Gen. *v.* Oxford, Worcester, and Wolverhampton Railway Co., 2 W. R. 330 ; Mayor of Liverpool *v.* Chorley Waterworks Co., 2 D. M. & G. 860; Ware *v.* Regent's Canal Co , 3 D. & J. 228 ; Hare *v.* London and North Western Railway Co., 2 J. & H. 111.

(*o*) Att.-Gen. *v.* Birmingham, &c., Derby Railway Co., 2 Ra. Ca. 125 ; Att.-Gen. *v.* Birmingham and Oxford Railway Co., 15 Jur. 1024, 3 Mac. & G. 453 ; Att.-Gen. *v.* Oxford, Worcester, and Wolverhampton Railway Co., 2 W. R. 330.

(*p*) Att.-Gen. *v.* Birmingham and Oxford Junction Railway Co., 4 De G. & S. 490.

(*q*) Att.-Gen. *v.* Oxford, Worcester, and Wolverhampton Railway Co., 2 W. R. 330.

(*r*) *Ib.* See, as to sanction of Board of Trade, Pearce *v.* Wycombe Railway Co., 1 Drew. 244 ; Att.-Gen. *v.* Great Northern Railway Co., 1 Dr. & Sm. 154.

[1] "But courts of equity are far more ready, upon a bill properly framed, to interpose to enforce a public duty of a railway company, than a mere private duty." 2 Redfield on Railways, 325. In Buck Mountain Coal Co. *v.* Lehigh Coal and Nav. Co., 50 Penn. St. 91, it was held, that a bill in equity to enforce the performance of a public duty by a corporation cannot be maintained by a private party, in the absence of any special right or authority. In this case where the slackwater navigation of the Lehigh Coal and Navigation Company, with dams, locks, and other appliances, were damaged, broken, and swept away by a flood, it was held that a bill in equity could not be maintained by another company to enjoin the said corporation from neglecting to repair and put in operation their navigation ; and that the complainants had no right to a decree compensating them for damages sustained in consequence of the non-repair. The court intimate, however, that a bill might probably be maintained in behalf of the commonwealth by the Attorney-General. Equity will not interfere by injunction to redress public nuisances, when the object sought can be obtained by ordinary legal methods. Jersey *v.* Hudson, 2 Beasley, 420.

9. Courts of equity will not restrain a railway company from making certain charges (s), or from charging the plaintiff for the carriage of his goods otherwise than equally with other persons (t). But by the Railway Traffic and Canal Act, 1854, 17 & 18 Vict. c. 34, ss. 2, 3, power is given to the Court of Common Pleas to grant an injunction against railway and canal companies, who, by their traffic arrangements, give any undue * or unreasonable preference to, or * 544 advantage to, or in favor of any particular person or company in any particular description of traffic, in any respect whatever (u). In Barrett v. Great Northern Railway Co. (x), it was held that the court will not interfere, unless a case of public inconvenience be made out (y).[1]

10. A private person who applies for an injunction to restrain a company from violating the provisions of an act of Parliament, must be able to satisfy the court that he will suffer substantial injury from the act complained of (z). As a general principle, where the statute prohibits the doing of a particular act, affecting the public, no person has a right of action against another merely because he has done the prohibited act. It is incumbent on the party complaining to allege and prove that the doing of the act prohibited has caused him some special damage, some peculiar injury beyond that which he may be supposed to sustain in common with the rest of the Queen's subjects, by an infringement of the law. But when the act prohibited is obviously prohibited for the pro-

(s) Pickford v. Grand Junction Railway Co., 3 Ra. Ca. 538, 558.

(t) Sutton v. South Eastern Railway Co., 1 L. R. Exch. 32.

(u) Garton v. Bristol and Exeter Railway Co., 6 C. B. N. S. 639 ; Ransome v. Eastern Counties Railway Co., 8 C. B. N. S. 709.

(x) 1 C. B. N. S. 423.

(y) Comp. Att. Gen. v. Great Northern Railway Co., 1 Dr. & Sm. 154. See Palmer v. London and South Western Railway Co., 1 L. R. C. P 588, as to the principles in which the jurisdiction under the act will be exercised.

(z) Holyoake v. Shrewsbury and Birmingham Railway Co., 5 Ra. Ca. 421 ; Mayor of Liverpool v. Chorley Waterworks Co., 2 D. M. & G. 860 ; Cromford and High Peak Railway Co. v. Stockport, &c., Railway Co., 1 D. & J. 326 ; Wintle v. Bristol and South Wales Railway Co., 10 W. R. 210 ; Stockport District Waterworks Co. v. Mayor, &c., of Manchester, 9 Jur. N. S. 266.

[1] Until the provisions of a railroad charter in relation to compensation for property taken are complied with, the company may be restrained by injunction from taking the property. People v. Law, 34 Barb. 494. See also, to same effect, Anderson v. Commissioners, 12 Ohio St. 635; Horton v. Hoyt, 11 Iowa, 496.

tection of a particular party, then it is not necessary to allege special damage (a).

11. The cases in which the aid of a court of equity is sought for the purpose of restraining a company from infringing the legal rights of private persons, are generally either cases of trespass or nuisance (b); but there are other cases in which the aid of the courts is sought which cannot properly be arranged under either of those heads.

* 545   12. * In Bostock v. North Staffordshire Railway Co. (c), the right of a land-owner to insist that a company incorporated by statute shall be restricted in their exercise of the ownership of land, taken from him under their compulsory powers, by the terms of the Act of Incorporation, was maintained. The plaintiff was the representative of the owner, and was the actual occupier of a mansion-house and estate, part of which had been acquired by a company of persons, who were by act of Parliament incorporated and authorized to make a canal and form a reservoir, in order to supply their canal with water, and "for no other purpose whatsoever." Parker, V. C., to whom an application had been made for an injunction to restrain the defendants, in whom the canal company had vested, from making use of the reservoir to the injury of the plaintiff, by letting out pleasure-boats upon it, &c., &c. (d), had directed a case for the opinion of a court of law · upon two questions: — first, whether the defendants could lawfully let out boats for hire on the lake and reservoir; and secondly, whether the company could lawfully use the lake or reservoir for any other purpose than for supplying the canal with water. A majority of the judges of the Queen's Bench answered the questions in the negative, and held that the company under the act had no right against the representatives of those from whom the lands were originally purchased to use the lands in any other way than for the purposes of the navigation, if such use was prejudicial to those persons. Erle, C. J., differed from the majority of the court, holding that the creation of a corporation for a specific purpose, gave it all the

(a) 1 Exch. 877, per Lord Wensley-dale.
(b) See supra, pp. 294, 341–345.

(c) 4 E. & B. 798.
(d) Ib.; 5 De G. & S. 584.

rights incident to a corporation, with a superadded duty to fulfil that specific purpose, but without restrictions other than those expressly or by necessary implication imposed by the legislature, and that there being nothing in the use of pleasure-boats inconsistent with the duty of keeping up the navigation, there was nothing to take away from the defendant's right to use them, that right being incident at common law to their tenancy in fee-simple of the land covered with water.   Stuart, V. C., upon the authority of the majority of the court, restrained the company from using * the reservoir to   *546 the injury of the plaintiff, or for any other purposes than those authorized by the act.   " The right of ownership," he said, " conferred on public companies, must be restricted and qualified by the terms of the legislative act.   The subscriber, whose money is given to compensate the land-owner, has a right to confine the exercise of the ownership to the specified purpose.   The land-owner has also an equal right " (e).   A case somewhat similar came before the court in Warden of Dover Harbor v. South Eastern Railway Co. (f).   There land had been sold to the company, and there was a provision in the act " that the whole of the land so sold should be appropriated to and solely for the purposes of the railway and other build-ings connected therewith."   The court held it was not a breach on the part of the company to erect a building used chiefly for passengers on the railway, with a room appropriated as a cus-tom-house to which persons not travelling by the railway occa-sionally resorted, but had some doubts as to whether the letting out of bedrooms in the building might not be a violation of the act.   However, in Astley v. Sheffield and Lincolnshire Railway Co. (g), where a railway company had taken lands of the plaintiff under their compulsory powers for the purpose of making a railway, the court refused upon the abandonment of the railway to restrain the company from a user of the land not shown to be productive of irreparable injury to the plaintiff (h).

13. The acts of a company may be illegal as against an

(e) Ib.; 3 Sm. & G. 283. See Mayor of Norwich v. Norfolk Railway Co., 4 E. & B. 414 ; Hill v. Tupper, 2 H. & C. 121.

(f) 9 Ha. 489.
(g) 2 D. & J. 463.
(h) See East and West India Docks, &c., Railway Co. v. Dawes, 11 Ha. 363.

individual member of the company. The court will, upon a
proper case being made out, interfere by injunction in aid of
the legal right. Injunctions have accordingly been granted to
restrain the illegal forfeiture of shares (*i*) ; the insertion and
continuance of a man's name on the register of share-
*547 holders (*k*) ; the illegal suspension * of a shareholder
from his rights (*l*) ; and the permitting a man to execute the deed of settlement and the registering shares (*m*).
If an equitable case can be made to appear, a company will be
restrained by injunction from making calls upon one of its
members (*n*). The court will not, however, interfere by injunction to restrain an action at law for calls, if the plaintiff
in equity has a good defence at law (*o*).

14. A member of a body corporate may be a creditor of, or
debtor to, the company, just as if he were not a member. He
may not only sue the company at law, but, having obtained
judgment against it, he may execute that judgment against his
co-shareholders, if they were liable to be proceeded against in
that way by ordinary creditors. A court of equity will not
interfere at the instance of the shareholders proceeded against,
and stay execution against them, either on the ground that the
plaintiff is himself a member of the company, and therefore
bound to contribute to his own payment, or upon the ground
that the rights of the parties cannot be ascertained without
taking the accounts of the company (*p*). The court will not,
however, permit an unfair or inequitable use to be made by a
company of a creditor's name in an action against a shareholder (*q*). If judgment has been obtained through concert

<hr/>

(*i*) Naylor *v.* South Devon Railway
Co., 1 De G. & S. 32 ; Watson *v.* Eales,
23 Beav. 300 ; Norman *v.* Mitchell, 5 D.
M. & G. 648. See Barton's case, 4 D.
& J. 46. See, also, Harris *v.* North
Devon Railway Co., 20 Beav. 384 ;
Playfair *v.* Birmingham, Bristol, &c.,
Railway Co., 1 Ra. Ca. 640.

(*k*) Taylor *v.* Hughes, 2 J. & L. 24 ;
Bargate *v.* Shortridge, 5 H. L. 297. See
Bullock *v.* Chapman, 2 De G. & S. 212 ;
comp. Taft *v.* Harrison, 10 Ha. 489.

(*l*) Adley *v* Whitstable Co., 17 Ves.
315, 19 Ves. 304.

(*m*) Fyfe *v.* Swaby, 16 Jur. 49 ; Norman *v.* Mitchell, 5 D. M. & G. 648.

(*n*) Taft *v.* Harrison, 10 Ha. 489 ;
Smith *v.* Reese River Co., 2 L. R. Eq.
264 ; comp. Norman *v.* Mitchell, 5 D.
M. & G. 648. See *supra*, pp. 15, 16, 33.

(*o*) Mangles *v.* Grand Dock Co., 10
Sim. 540 ; Macbride *v.* Lindsay, 9 Ha.
574 ; *supra*, pp. 15, 32. See Ornamental,
&c., Co. *v.* Brown, 2 H. & C. 63.

(*p*) Rheam *v.* Smith, 2 Ph. 726 ; Hammond *v.* Ward, 3 Drew. 103 ; Hardinge
v. Webster, 1 Dr. & Sm. 101 ; Lindley
on Partnership, 719.

(*q*) Taylor *v.* Hughes, 2 J. & L. 24 ;
Lewis *v.* Billing, 4 Ra. Ca. 414 ; *supra*,
p. 49.

or collusion between the directors of the company and the
creditor with the view of being used against certain shareholders or for the purpose of enforcing contributions from
them (*r*), or if the creditor proceeds after judgment at
the instigation of the directors * against certain share-   * 548
holders pointed out by the directors (*s*), the proceedings
at law will be restrained (*t*).

15. Companies formed for a special purpose, and whether
constituted under deed of settlement or incorporated by act
of Parliament, by charter, letters-patent or registration, are
looked upon in equity as analogous to a partnership, and the
members of the company in their individual capacity are considered to have rights *inter se*, analogous to those of partners
inter se (*u*). The shareholders may by general consent depart
from the contract which they have entered into with each other
and enter into a new contract, but they cannot do so without
the consent of every individual member comprising the company (*x*). Any single shareholder has a right to say that
the business of the company shall be carried on according
to the agreement which united the shareholders together
at the time he embarked his moneys in the undertaking,
and may require the company to abstain from applying the
funds of the company to any other purpose than the proper
purposes of the concern, in which he was induced to engage (*y*).
Though every other shareholder may be opposed to him, any
single shareholder has a right to institute a suit on behalf of
himself and all other shareholders who have a common interest
with himself to restrain the application of the common funds

(*r*) Taylor *v*. Hughes, 2 J. & L. 24;
Fernihough *v*. Leader, 4 Ra. Ca. 373,
15 L. J. Ch. 458; Horn *v*. Kilkenny,
&c., Railway Co., 1 K. & J. 399; *supra*,
p. 49.

(*s*) Bargate *v*. Shortridge, 5 H. L.
247; *supra*, p. 49.

(*t*) See Lund *v*. Blanshard, 4 Ha. 290;
Woodhams *v*. Anglo-Australian, &c.,
Co., 2 D. J. & S. 162. See Gillespie *v*.
Barnwall, 10 L. T. 263, as to case in a
club.

(*u*) Simpson *v*. Denison, 10 Ha. 51;
Bostock *v*. North Staffordshire Railway
Co., 4 E. & B. 814, *per* Erle, C. J.;
Fraser *v*. Whalley, 2 H. & M. 10, 28.

(*x*) *Ex parte* Morgan, 1 Mac. & G.

236; Bennett's case, 5 D. M. & G. 297;
Ernest *v*. Nicholls, 6 H. L. 401. See, as
to companies formed on the cost-book
principle, Thomas *v*. Hobler, 8 Jur. N.
S. 125.

(*y*) Natusch *v*. Irving, Gow on Part.
App. 398, 3d edition; Const *v*. Harris,
T. & R. 496; Simpson *v*. Denison, 10
Ha. 51; Simpson *v*. Westminster Palace
Hotel Co., 8 H. L. 717; Maunsell *v*.
Midland Great Western Railway Co. of
Ireland, 1 H. & M. 130; Filder *v*. Lon-
don, Brighton, &c., Railway Co., *ib*.
489; Macdougall *v*. Jersey Imperial
Hotel Co., 2 H. & M. 528; Featherston-
haugh *v*. Lee Moor Porcelain Clay Co.,
1 L. R. Eq. 318.

of the company to any other purpose than the proper purposes
of the concern, and a court of equity will interpose on
* 549 his behalf by injunction (z). The amount of * interest
of the complaining shareholder will not be taken into
consideration (a).

16. A holder of scrip certificates may maintain the suit (b).
So also may the shareholder of an old company which was
afterwards incorporated with a new company sue in respect of
the funds of the new company, although he has not complied
with all the formalities required to make him a shareholder of
the new company (c). A railway company which has taken
shares in another railway company (d), or is the equitable
owner of shares in another railway company, may also maintain
the suit, the trustees in whom the shares are vested being
made in the latter case defendants (e). A shareholder may in
respect of any matter in which he has a common interest with
the other members of the society to which he belongs, instead
of suing on behalf of himself and all others similarly interested, sue the directors and the company, as a body, making
the shareholders parties and pray for relief common to all (f).

17. A shareholder in a rival company may maintain the
suit (g), provided the suit is a *bonâ fide* one, instituted
honestly, sincerely, and really for the benefit and common
interest of the shareholders whom he claims to represent (h).
The fact that the suit may not have been instituted from the
best of motives is not sufficient to debar him from suing; but

(z) Mozley v. Alston, 1 Ph. 798;
Beman v. Rufford, 1 Sim. N. S. 564;
M'Donnell v. Grand Canal Co., 3 Ir. Ch.
578; Macbride v. Lindsay, 9 Ha. 585;
Carlisle v. South Eastern Railway Co.,
1 Mac. & G. 699; Burt v. British Nation
Life Assurance Association, 4 D. & J.
174; Fawcett v. Laurie, 1 Dr. & Sm.
192; Hare v. London and North Western Railway Co., 2 J. & H. 80; Simpson v. Westminster Palace Hotel Co., 8
H. L. 717.
(a) M'Donnell v. Grand Canal Co.,
3 Ir. Ch. 578.
(b) Bagshaw v. Eastern Union Railway Co., 2 Mac. & G. 389.
(c) Spackman v Lattimore, 3 Giff. 16.
(d) Great Western Railway Co. v. Oxford, Worcester, and Wolverhampton
Railway Co., 3 D. M. & G. 341.

(e) Great Western Railway Co. v.
Rushout, 5 De G. & S. 306.
(f) Fawcett v. Laurie, 1 Dr. & Sm.
192.
(g) Colman v. Eastern Counties Railway Co., 10 Beav. 1; Salomons v.
Laing, 12 Beav. 353; Munt v. Shrewsbury and Chester Railway Co., 13
Beav. 1; Winch v. Birkenhead, Lancashire, &c. Railway Co., 5 De G. & S.
581; Hare v. London and North Western Railway Co., 2 J. & H. 80; Att.-
Gen. v. Great Northern Railway Co., 1
Dr. & Sm. 159.
(h) Forrest v. Manchester, Sheffield,
and Lincolnshire Railway Co., 7 Jur.
N. S. 887; Thomas v. Hobler, 8 Jur.
N. S. 125; Fraser v. Whalley, 2 H. &
M. 10.

if he appears to be the mere puppet and nominee of the
rival company, and the suit *appears to be instituted in   *550
reality on behalf of the rival company, it is illusory, and
relief will not be given (*i*).

18. A shareholder cannot, however, institute a suit on
behalf of himself and all other shareholders unless for a purpose in which his interest is identical in a judicial point of
view with that of those whom he professes to represent (*k*).
If he has a distinct and separate interest from that of the rest
of the shareholders, he cannot sue on behalf of himself and
them (*l*). Thus, although the court may in a suit so framed
restrain the directors of a company from declaring a future
dividend, it cannot upon an application in this form restrain
the payment of a dividend already declared, because, as soon
as a dividend has been declared, each shareholder acquires a
separate right to his share of the dividend (*m*). Even though
the dividend may have been improperly declared, each individual shareholder is entitled to sue for as much of the dividend
as he may be entitled to (*n*). A man who by his conduct has
personally precluded himself from suing cannot maintain the
suit (*o*): nor should a suit be instituted by a shareholder
on behalf of himself and all other shareholders, complaining
of transactions in which some of them have acquiesced (*p*).
A purchaser of shares is bound by the acquiescence of his
vendor (*q*).

(*i*) Forrest *v.* Manchester, Sheffield,
and Lincolnshire Railway Co., 7 Jur.
N. S. 887; Hattersley *v.* Lord Shel-
burne, 31 L. J. Ch. 873; Filder *v.* Lon-
don, Brighton, &c., Railway Co., 1 H.
& M. 489. See Rogers *v.* Oxford,
Worcester, and Wolverhampton Rail-
way Co., 2 D. & J. 674, *per* Knight
Bruce, L. J.; Ffooks *v.* South Western
Railway Co., 1 Sm. & G. 166, *per* Stuart,
V. C.; Hare *v.* London and North
Western Railway Co., 2 J. & H. 119,
per Wood, V. C.

(*k*) Mozley *v.* Alston, 1 Ph. 790;
Clay *v.* Rufford, 8 Ha. 281; Williams
v. Salmon, 2 K. & J. 463. See Apperly
v. Page, 1 Ph. 779; Sharp *v.* Day, *ib.*
771; Macbride *v.* Lindsay, 9 Ha. 574;
Doyle *v.* Muntz, 4 Ra. 422, 10 Jur. 914;
Moseley *v.* Cressey's Co., 1 L. R. Eq.
405.

(*l*) Macbride *v.* Lindsay, 9 Ha. 574;

Syers *v.* Brighton Brewery Co., 13 W.
R. 220.

(*m*) Carlisle *v.* South Eastern Railway Co., 1 Mac. & G. 689.

(*n*) Fawcett *v.* Laurie, 1 Dr. & Sm.
199.

(*o*) Burt *v.* British Nation Life Assurance Association, 4 D. & J. 158. See
Sharp *v.* Taylor, 2 Ph. 801; Sheppard
v. Oxenford, 1 K. & J. 491, 3 W. R. 397.

(*p*) Kent *v.* Jackson, 14 Beav. 367, 2
D. M. & G. 49; Ffooks *v.* South West-
ern Railway Co., 1 Sm. & G. 142;
Sturge *v.* Eastern Union Railway Co.,
7 D. M. & G. 180, *per* Turner, L. J.;
Stupart *v.* Arrowsmith, 3 Sm. & G. 176.
But see White *v.* Carmarthen, &c.,
Railway Co., 1 H. & M. 786.

(*q*) Ffooks *v.* South Western Railway Co., 1 Sm. & G. 142. See, however, now, 15 & 16 Vict. c. 86, s. 49;
Clements *v.* Bowes, 1 Drew. 684.

* 551   19. * Persons on whom separate and distinct frauds have been committed cannot join in suing together with respect to those frauds (r); but if several persons have been induced by misrepresentation, by which all were alike deceived, to concur in advancing moneys for a common purpose, one or more may sue on behalf of himself or themselves and all the others (s).[1]

20. If a man sues on behalf of himself and all other shareholders, he must confine his prayer to such relief as is really for the benefit of the shareholders whom he represents. He cannot pray alternative relief, one branch of which is a benefit to himself but antagonistic to the interests of the other shareholders (t).

21. The directors should be made parties to a bill to restrain the doing of an unlawful act by the company (u). If the object of the bill is to restrain the carrying out of an agreement with other companies, all the companies are necessary parties (x). A company may, under the circumstances of the case, not be a necessary party to a suit to impeach the acts of the directors (y).

22. A shareholder who seeks to restrain the application of the funds of a company to purposes unconnected with the proper business of the company or corporation must use due diligence in making the application. Laches in instituting the suit may prove fatal to the application. Shareholders cannot lie by, sanctioning or by their silence at least acquiescing in an arrangement which is *ultra vires* of the company to which they belong, watching the result: if it be favorable and profitable to themselves to abide by it and insist on its validity; but if it

---

(r) Jones v. Garcia del Rio, T. & R. 297; Crosskey v. Bank of Wales, 4 Giff. 314.

(s) Beeching v. Lloyd, 3 Drew. 227; Macbride v. Lindsay, 9 Ha. 574; Hallows v. Fernie, 3 L. R. Eq. 520.

(t) Thomas v. Hobler, 8 Jur. N. S. 125.

(u) Ferguson v. Wilson, 2 L. R. Ch. Ap. 90, *per* Lord Cairns, L. J.

(x) Hare v. London and North Western Railway Co., 1 J. & H. 253. See 2 J. & H. 80; Parker v. River Dun Navigation Co., 1 De G. & S. 192;

Maunsell v. Midland Great Western Railway Co. of Ireland, 1 H. & M. 130.

(y) Gregory v. Patchett, 33 Beav. 595.

[1] Persons who are citizens, voters, and tax-payers of a county may be parties plaintiff in an action to restrain by an injunction the expenditures of county moneys by the county judge, in the erection of a court-house at a place which is not the county seat of a county. Rice v. Smith, 9 Iowa, 570. See also Smith v. Myers, 15 Cal. 33.

prove unfavorable and disastrous, then to institute proceedings to set it aside (z). In Graham v. Birkenhead, Lancashire, and Cheshire * Junction Railway Co. (a), the suit   *552 was instituted by a shareholder to restrain the completion of part only of the company's works. There had been several suits for the same purpose, instituted by other shareholders, but for reasons to which it is not material to advert these suits were never effectively prosecuted. It had been known for a considerable time that it was not intended by the directors to complete the company's works, as originally contemplated, and that in fact there were not sufficient funds for that purpose. It was also well known that the directors had for some time completed part of the works. The court refused to interfere on the ground of the acquiescence of the plaintiff and the other shareholders in the acts complained of for eighteen months (b). So also in Ffooks v. South Western Railway Co. (c), the court refused to restrain a railway company from completing works after the parliamentary powers had expired, which had been acquiesced in for twelve months before those powers had expired (d). So also where shareholders complained of acts *ultra vires* which they had acquiesced in for six years, relief was refused (e).

23. Whether the court should, in cases where there has been acquiescence, interfere at the suit of a shareholder to restrain the application of the funds of the company in a manner not authorized by the Act of Incorporation or the deed of settlement, or should decline to interfere on the ground of acquiescence is often a question of much delicacy. In determining the question the court looks to the peculiar circumstances of each case, and will, as a general rule, adopt that course which is most for the advantage of the whole body of the share-

(z) Gregory v. Patchett, 33 Beav. 595, 602. See also, as to acquiescence by shareholders in irregular transactions, Walford v. Adie, 5 Ha. 112, Richmond's case, 4 K. & J. 305; *Re* Magdalena Steam Navigation Co., John. 690; *Re* Norwich Yarn Co., 22 Beav. 165; Burt v. British Nation Life Assurance Association, 4 D. & J. 158; Brotherhood's case, 31 Beav. 365, 8 Jur. N. S. 926; Grady's case, 1 D. J. & S. 493; Lane's case, *ib.* 513; Stewart's case, 1 L. R. Ch. Ap. 513.

(a) 2 Mac. & G. 159.

(b) See Gray v. Chaplin, 2 Russ. 126; Kent v. Jackson, 14 Beav. 367, 2 D. M. & G. 49; Ellis v. Henderson, 3 Bell. Sc. App. 1; Stupart v. Arrowsmith, 3 Sm. & G. 176.

(c) 1 Sm. & G. 142.

(d) See Hare v. London and North Western Railway Co., 2 J. & H. 80.

(e) Gregory v. Patchett, 33 Beav. 595.

*553 holders (*f*). Shareholders *in a company will not be held debarred from relief on the ground of acquiescence, if being aware that an illegal agreement has been entered into, they delay taking proceedings until an attempt is made to carry it out (*g*). So also where parties seek to restrain the directors of a railway company from devoting part of the funds of the company towards paying the expenses of an application to Parliament, it is no answer to say they are disentitled by delay in not making the application sooner. The members of the company have a right to suppose that a proper application of the funds will be made. Till the money is in fact being wrongfully, applied no grounds exist for the interference of the court (*h*). An application by directors to Parliament does not necessarily give notice of an intention to apply the funds of the company improperly (*i*). In a case where the guaranteed shareholders in a railway company did not assert their rights in 1854, when a construction adverse to them was put forward by the directors of the company, they were held not bound on the ground of acquiescence from filing a bill in 1859 to restrain the directors from paying the other shareholders, till the arrears of the guaranteed shares had been paid, but they were held precluded by their acquiescence from claiming the dividends that had been wrongly paid to the other shareholders between 1856 and the time of filing the bill (*k*).

24. In interfering by injunction at the suit of a shareholder suing on behalf of himself and all other members of the company to restrain a company, formed for a special purpose, from doing acts or entering into engagements, which are not within the proper purposes for which it was established, the court not only enforces the equitable relations which subsist between the members *inter se*, but acts in aid of the legal right.

(*f*) Graham *v.* Birkenhead, Lancashire, and Cheshire Junction Railway Co., 2 Mac. & G. 160 ; Cooper *v.* Earl Powis, 3 De G. & S. 688 ; Hodgson *v.* Earl of Powis, 1 D. M. & G. 6 ; Webb *v.* Direct London and Portsmouth Railway Co., 1 D. M. & G. 521 ; Stuart *v.* London and North Western Railway Co., *ib.* 721 ; Ffooks *v.* London and South Western Railway Co., 1 Sm. & G. 161. See *Re* Era Assurance Co., 2 J. & H. 400 ; *Re* Phœnix Life Assurance Co., *ib.* 441 ; White *v.* Carmarthen, &c., Railway Co., 1 H. & M. 786.

(*g*) Charlton *v.* Newcastle and Carlisle Railway Co., 5 Jur. N. S. 1100.

(*h*) Att.-Gen. *v.* Eastlake, 11 Ha. 22. See White *v.* Carmarthen, &c., Railway Co., 1 H. & M. 786.

(*i*) Great Western Railway Co. *v.* Rushout, 5 De G. & S. 290 ; Green *v.* Nixon, 23 Beav. 530.

(*k*) Matthews *v.* Great Northern Railway Co., 5 Jur. N. S. 284.

The * suit by a shareholder to restrain a company from   * 554
doing illegal acts or entering into engagements which
are beyond the proper purposes of the company, must be in
form on behalf of all the shareholders. It is immaterial that
some of the shareholders may be opposed to the suit (*p*).

25. Injunctions have been granted at the suit of a shareholder suing on behalf of himself and all other shareholders to
restrain a railway company from applying the funds of the
company towards the establishment of a steam packet company
in connection with the railway (*q*); or in the purchase of
shares in another railway company (*r*). So also railway companies have been restrained from applying moneys raised for
the purpose of completing a particular branch, to the purposes
of any part of the main line (*s*), and from applying the corporate funds in the construction of part only of the line or
otherwise, than with the view and purpose of completing the
whole (*t*). Where, however, in a somewhat similar case, it
appeared that greater mischief would arise from granting than
withholding the injunction, the court refused to interfere (*u*).

26. The application of the funds of a company in making
presents to the directors, or in discounting their bills (*v*), in
bribing a land-owner to buy off his opposition in Parliament (*x*); in the * purchase of the shares of a retiring   * 555
shareholder (*y*); or in the payment of interest to the

(*p*) Beman *v.* Rufford, 1 Sim. N. S.
564; White *v.* Carmarthen, &c., Railway Co., 1 H. & M. 786. See also Mills
v. Northern Railway of Buenos Ayres
Co., 5 L. R. Ch. Ap. 621.

(*q*) Colman *v.* Eastern Counties Railway Co., 10 Beav. 1. Comp. Forrest
v. Manchester, Sheffield, and Lincolnshire Railway Co., 30 Beav. 40, aff'd.
on other grounds, 7 Jur. N. S. 887;
South Wales Railway Co. *v.* Redmond,
10 C. B. N. S. 675.

(*r*) Salomons *v.* Laing, 12 Beav. 339.
See Maunsell *v.* Midland Great Western
Railway Co. of Ireland, 1 H. & M. 130.
It appears to be doubtful whether it is
ultra vires in a railway company, who
being empowered to take shares in
another railway company, have taken
shares to the full extent of their powers
to take new shares allotted to the holders of old shares. Great Western

Railway Co. *v.* Metropolitan Railway
Co., 32 L. J. Ch. 382.

(*s*) Bagshaw *v.* Eastern Union Railway Co., 2 Mac. & G. 389. See 6 H.
L. 137.

(*t*) Cohen *v.* Wilkinson, 12 Beav. 134,
1 Mac. & G. 486. See Logan *v.* Courtown, 13 Beav. 22.

(*u*) Hodgson *v.* Earl of Powis, 1 D.
M. & G. 14. See Caledonian and Dumbartonshire Railway Co. *v.* Magistrates
of Helensburgh, 2 Macq. 418.

(*v*) York and North Midland Railway Co. *v.* Hudson, 16 Beav. 485;
Bluck *v.* Mallalue, 27 Beav. 404.

(*x*) Scottish North Eastern Railway
Co. *v.* Stewart, 3 Macq. 382, *per* Lord
Cranworth. See Leominster Canal
Navigation Co. *v.* Shrewsbury and
Hereford Railway Co., 3 K. & J. 654.

(*y*) Hodgkinson *v.* National Live
Stock Insurance Co., 4 D. & J. 423.

shareholders before any profits have been realized out of capital or borrowed moneys (z) ; or generally in a way not provided for by the act which regulates the business of the company (a), is an improper application of them, and will be restrained by injunction (b).

27. The payment of dividends on the ordinary stock of a company until the arrears of dividend on preference shares, created under the provisions of an act of Parliament, shall have been successively paid according to their priorities (c), out of the profits accruing subsequently to the date of the arrears (d), is improper, and will be restrained by injunction (e). The fact that the owner of preference shares may have in former years acquiesced in the declaration of a dividend on the ordinary shares, whilst there was an arrear of dividend due on the preference shares, will not deprive him of his right in respect of subsequent arrears, though it will preclude him from making any claim in respect of these particular arrears (f). A preferential shareholder may file a bill to restrain a company from making a dividend prejudicial to his interests without waiting till there are funds to make a dividend (g).

* 556   28. * The application of the funds of a company in paying the expenses of a bill in Parliament is improper, unless specially authorized by the act or any acts incorporated therewith (h). "The intended application," said Turner, L. J., in Simpson v. Denison (i), "is for another and a differ-

See *Ex parte* Morgan, 1 Mac. & G. 225 ; Kent v. Jackson, 14 Beav. 382.

(z) Macdougall v. Jersey Imperial Hotel Co., 2 H. & M. 528. See Allen v. Talbot, 30 L. T. 316.

(a) *Re* St. George's Steam Packet Co., 21 L. J. Ch. 593 ; *Ex parte* Cropper, 1 D. M. & G. 147.

(b) See Grimes v. Harrison, 26 Beav. 435 ; Simpson v. Westminster Palace Hotel Co., 8 H. L. 712 ; *Re* Kent Building Society, 1 Dr. & Sm. 417 ; Macdougall v. Jersey Hotel Co., 2 H. & M. 528 ; Crewer and Wheal Abraham Mining Co. v. Williams, 14 W. R. 1003 ; Joint Stock Discount Co. v. Brown, 12 Jur. N. S. 899.

(c) Crawford v. North Eastern Railway Co., 3 K. & J. 733.

(d) Stevens v. South Devon Rail-

way Co., 9 Ha. 325 ; Henry v. Great Northern Railway Co., 1 D. & J. 607 ; Matthews v. Great Northern Railway Co., 28 L. J. Ch. 375 ; Corry v. Londonderry and Enniskillen Railway Co., 29 Beav. 263. See Coates v. Nottingham Waterworks Co., 30 Beav. 86. See, as to interest on the arrears, Corry v. Londonderry and Enniskillen Railway Co., 29 Beav. 263.

(e) See *ib.*, as to the manner in which profits are to be ascertained for the purpose of making a dividend.

(f) Matthews v. Great Northern Railway Co., 28 L. J. Ch. 373.

(g) Sturge v. Eastern Union Railway Co., 7 D. M. & G. 158.

(h) See 8 & 9 Vict. c. 16.

(i) 10 Ha. 62.

ent purpose from that which is described in the act under which the company is formed, and which constitutes the partnership deed of the company " (k).   Accordingly railway companies have been restrained from applying any part of their funds towards the expenses incident to an application to Parliament for the promotion of a branch line (l), or a new line in extension of the existing one (m), for the improvement of the navigation of a river communicating by means of a branch line with the main line (n), or for the purpose of bringing about an alteration in the constitution of the company (o), or for the purpose of carrying out an arrangement with another company (p).   The application of the funds of a company towards making up the Parliamentary deposit required for bills in Parliament promoted by another company (q), or towards repaying moneys borrowed by the promoters, and subscribed by them in conformity with the standing orders of Parliament (r), is improper.

29. In Bell v. Sierra Nevada Co., Limited (s), the directors of a foreign company resident in England were restrained from applying the funds of the company in defraying the expenses of an intended application to a foreign legislature.

30. The rule is different where expenses have been incurred in opposing a bill in Parliament which would, if sanctioned, be injurious to the undertaking.   In such cases the funds of the * company may be applied in meeting the expenses * 557 so incurred (t).

31. The distinction between going to Parliament for an alteration of the constitution, or a variation or extension of the powers of a company, and applying the funds of the company towards the payment of the expenses of going to Parliament

---

(k) Vance v. East Lancashire Railway Co., 3 K. & J. 50; East Anglian Railway Co. v. Eastern Counties Railway Co., 11 C. B. 775.

(l) Great Western Railway Co. v. Rushout, 5 De G. & S. 309.

(m) Vance v. East Lancashire Railway Co., 3 K. & J. 50.

(n) Munt v. Shrewsbury and Chester Railway Co., 13 Beav. 1.

(o) Stevens v. South Devon Railway Co., ib. 59.

(p) Simpson v. Denison, 10 Ha. 51.

See Parker v. River Dun Navigation Co., 1 De G. & S. 192.

(q) Maunsell v. Midland Great Western Railway Co. of Ireland, 1 H. & M. 130.

(r) Spackman v. Lattimore, 3 Giff. 16.

(s) 1 D. F. & J. 183.

(t) Bright v. North, 2 Ph. 216; Att.-Gen. v. Andrews, 2 Mac. & G. 230; Att.-Gen. v. Mayor of Wigan, 5 D. M. & G. 54.

is a well defined one (*u*). Every company acting in its corporate capacity has full power to make an application to Parliament for these or other purposes. There is no ground on
which a court of equity can interfere (*v*). In Bell *v.* Sierra
Nevada Co. (*x*), the court would not restrain a company from
applying to the legislature of a foreign country, even though
nearly all the shareholders were resident in England, there
appearing to be no intention on the part of the company to act
except with the sanction of the foreign legislature. In Astley
v. Manchester, Sheffield, and Lincolnshire Railway Co. (*y*),
the court refused to restrain a railway company, which had
taken lands of the plaintiff under their compulsory powers for
the purpose of making a railway, from making an application
to Parliament upon the abandonment of the railway to enable
them to use the land for a different purpose and in a different
undertaking. In one instance, indeed (*z*), the majority of a
chartered society was restrained from surrendering the existing
charter with a view to procure a new one materially differing
from it, but the authority of the case must be now considered
very questionable (*a*).

32. When a public company incorporated by statute is
engaging in a transaction which is *ultra vires*, the court can
only deal with the case as it exists, and will not take into consideration the possibility of further powers being obtained by
the company (*b*).

* 558   33. * Companies formed for a special purpose may
          not enter into contracts or engagements which are not
within the proper purposes for which they are established, or
are not authorized either by the deed of settlement or the act
of Parliament, as the case may be. Where a contract is one
which, from the nature and object of incorporation, the corporate body is by necessary or reasonable inference from the pro- *

(*u*) Simpson *v.* Denison, 10 Ha. 61.
(*v*) Ware *v.* Grand Junction Waterworks Co., 2 R. & M. 470; Great Western Railway Co. *v.* Rushout, 5 De G. &
S. 311; Vance *v.* East Lancashire Railway Co., 3 K. & J. 57; Stevens *v.*
South Devon Railway Co., 13 Beav.
49; Hattersley *v.* Lord Shelburne, 31
L. J. Ch. 873.
(*x*) 1 D. F. & J. 188.

(*y*) 2 D. & J. 463.
(*z*) Ward *v.* Society of Attorneys, 1
Coll. 370.
(*a*) See as to the Wharncliffe Order,
Maunsell *v.* Midland Great Western
Railway Company of Ireland, 1 H. &
M. 162.
(*b*) Great Western Railway Co. *v.*
Metropolitan Railway Co., 32 L. J. Ch.
382.

visions of the deed of settlement or the act prohibited from making, it is *ultra vires* at law and void (*c*). "Where," said Lord Wensleydale, in South Yorkshire Railway Company and River Dun Navigation Company *v.* Great Northern Railway Company (*d*), "a corporation is created by act of Parliament for particular purposes with special powers, their deed, though under their corporate seal, does not bind them, if it appear by the express provisions of the statute creating the corporation, or by necessary or reasonable inference from its enactments, that the deed is *ultra vires ;* that is, that the legislature meant that such a deed should not be made " (*e*). Contracts frustrating or necessarily inconsistent with or for a purpose wholly inconsistent with the objects for which a company is established, are impliedly forbidden by the act (*f*).

34. One company may not purchase the business of another company (*g*), or transfer its business and delegate its powers to another company (*h*), or amalgamate with another company (*i*), unless specially authorized to do so either by the deed of settlement * or the act of incorporation. * 559 General powers of management or powers to enter into contracts or arrangements with other companies do not authorize an amalgamation (*k*). In Charlton *v.* Newcastle and Carlisle Railway Company (*l*), two railway companies had entered into two illegal agreements for an amalgamation, and after bill filed had entered into a third agreement, in the place of the two others, with the intent of carrying out the same object, as

---

(*c*) South Yorkshire, &c., Railway Co. *v.* Great Northern Railway Co., 9 Exch. 55, 84 ; Shrewsbury and Birmingham Railway Co. *v.* London and North Western Railway Co., 6 H. L. 136 ; Scottish North Eastern Railway Co. *v.* Stewart, 3 Macq. 382.

(*d*) 9 Exch. 55, 84.

(*e*) Chambers *v.* Manchester and Milford Railway Co., 5 B. & S. 588.

(*f*) South Wales Railway Co. *v.* Redmond, 10 C. B. N. S. 682. See Mayor of Norwich *v.* Norfolk Railway Co., 4 E. & B. 416, *per* Erle, C. J.

(*g*) Ernest *v.* Nicholls, 6 H. L. 401.

(*h*) Beman *v.* Rufford, 1 Sim. N. S. 566 ; Great Northern Railway Co. *v.* Eastern Counties Railway Co., 9 Ha. 306 ; Winch *v.* Birkenhead, &c., Railway Co., 5 De G. & S. 562 ; Kearns *v.* Leaf, 1 H. & M. 681. See Gregory *v.* Patchett, 33 Beav. 595.

(*i*) Gilbert *v.* Cooper, 10 Jur. 580 ; Lewis *v.* Cooper, 4 Ra. Ca. 413 ; *Re* Era Insurance Co., 2 J. & H. 400 ; Kearns *v.* Leaf, 1 H. & M. 681.

(*k*) Gilbert *v.* Cooper, 10 Jur. 580, 4 Ra. Ca. 396 ; *Re* Era Insurance Co., 2 J. & H. 400. Comp. Anglo-Australian Insurance Co. *v.* British Provincial Insurance Society, 3 Giff. 521, on appeal, 8 Jur. N. S. 628 ; *Re* Bank of Hindustan, Higgs' case, 2 H. & M. 657. See now, as to amalgamation of railway companies, 26 & 27 Vict. c. 92, ss. 36–55.

(*l*) 5 Jur. N. S. 1097.

far as law would allow. The court, without determining the
validity of the third agreement, granted an injunction against
carrying out the two others.

35. Companies cannot borrow moneys on bonds except in
the way authorized by the acts under which they are incorporated (*m*) ; nor can a railway company draw, accept, or indorse
bills of exchange (*n*) ; but there is nothing to prevent a railway or other company from issuing bonds to a contractor for a
debt really due (*o*). Nor is a man employed by the directors
of a company bound to inquire whether they are acting within
the limits of their powers, but can enforce against the company
claims in respect of matters in which he has been employed,
even although he may have had knowledge that the funds of
the company are being applied to an unauthorized purpose (*p*).

36. Directors of a shipping company with limited liability
under the Joint-Stock Companies Act have power to borrow
money by mortgage of the company's ships (*q*).

37. A company has no right, unless authorized by the deed
of settlement, or the act of Parliament incorporating it, to
      issue preference shares (*r*).   Railway companies cannot
* 560 create preference * shares under the general powers con-
      tained in ordinary railway acts (*s*), nor can a general
meeting of the shareholders of a company under powers of
Companies Act, 1862, s. 50, create them, unless authorized to
do so by the deed of settlement (*t*).

38. An agreement by one railway company to take a lease
of the line of another railway company, is *ultra vires* and void,
unless specially authorized by statute (*u*).

39. The 112th clause of the Railways Clauses Consolidation

(*m*) Chambers *v.* Manchester and
Milford Railway Co., 5 B. & S. 588;
Rashdall *v.* Ford, 2 L. R. Eq. 750.
See Bryon *v.* Metropolitan Saloon Om-
nibus Co., 3 D. & J. 123.

(*n*) Bateman *v.* Mid Wales Railway
Co., 1 L. R. C. P. 499.

(*o*) White *v.* Carmarthen Railway
Co., 1 H. & M. 786.

(*p*) Green *v.* Nixon, 23 Beav. 530.

(*q*) Australian, &c., Co: *v.* Mounsey,
4 K. & J. 733.

(*r*) Moss *v.* Syers, 32 L. J. Ch. 711;
Hutton *v.* Scarborough Cliff Hotel Co., 2
Dr. & Sm. 514, affi'd. 34 L. J. Ch. 643.

(*s*) Sturge *v.* Eastern Union Railway Co., 7 D. M. & G. 158. See 26 &
27 Vict. c. 118, ss. 13–15, as to general
powers given to railway companies to
create preference shares.

(*t*) Hutton *v.* Scarborough Cliff Hotel
Co., 2 Dr. & Sm. 521.

(*u*) East Anglian Railway Co. *v.*
Eastern Counties Railway Co., 11 C. B.
775; Macgregor *v.* Dover and Deal Railway Co., 18 Q. B. 618. See Shrewsbury and Birmingham Railway Co. *v.*
London and North Western Railway
Co., 6 H. L. 113.

Act, 8 & 9 Vict. c. 20, which prescribes the covenants which shall be contained in the lease of a railway to any person or company, does not authorize the lease of a railway, but merely points out the covenants to be inserted in every lease. A railway company may not accept or grant a lease, sale, or transfer of its own or any other line of railway except under express powers conferred by statute (v). In Exeter and Crediton Railway Company v. Buller (w), where the special act authorized a lease of the line " to the Bristol and Exeter, or any other company," and negotiations had been going on with the sanction of the shareholders, for leasing the line to the Bristol and Exeter Railway Company, the directors were restrained from leasing it to that company at the suit of the majority of the shareholders, who were desirous of leasing it to another line.

40. A railway company which has been empowered by statute to purchase a canal company, does not act *ultra vires* by availing itself of the powers given to canal companies by 8 & 9 Vict. c. 42, " An act to enable companies to become carriers of goods upon their canal," and taking a lease of * the tolls of another canal (x). A canal company is * 561 not empowered by the act to transfer its property to another company (y).

41. A working agreement between two railway companies for 99 years (z), or one which stipulates that the profits shall be so shared as to give a certain percentage to each (a), is *ultra vires* and will be restrained (b). But a traffic agreement between two railway companies for a certain number of years to divide the profits of the whole traffic in certain fixed proportions calculated on the past course of traffic, and entered into *bonâ fide* for the purpose of avoiding competition, is not *ultra vires* (c). The managing body of a railway company, however, have no power to enter into a contract fixing and regulating the future

---

(v) 8 & 9 Vict. c. 96. See also 21 & 22 Vict. c. 75, s. 3, and 23 & 24 Vict. c. 41, as to canal and navigation companies.

(w) 5 Ra. Ca. 211.

(x) Rogers v. Oxford, Worcester, and Wolverhampton Railway Co., 2 D. & J. 662.

(y) M'Donnell v. Grand Canal Co., 3 Ir. Ch. 578.

(z) Winch v. Birkenhead, &c., Railway Co., 5 De G. & S. 562.

(a) Charlton v. Newcastle Railway Co., 5 Jur. N. S. 1097.

(b) See now, as to working agreements, 26 & 27 Vict. c. 92, ss. 22–29.

(c) Hare v. London and North Western Railway Co., 2 J. & H. 80.

traffic which may be carried upon a line of railway, which the company may thereafter be empowered to construct, so as to give another company an interest in such traffic and profit (*d*).

42. An agreement between two railway companies to make an application to Parliament for the necessary powers to carry out certain heads of agreement between them, which are not to be acted on until the necessary powers have been obtained, is not illegal (*e*) ; but any attempt to act upon the agreement before the necessary powers have been obtained is illegal (*f*).

43. An agreement cannot be considered legal, though some of the terms involve acts which may be lawfully done, if the purpose of the agreement be to work out something illegal. Therefore where railway companies agree to do acts which they have power to do, as well as others which they have no power to do, a court of equity will restrain them from
*562 acting on the agreement * at all, where the purpose of the company is to carry out an illegal scheme (*g*).

44. Where the shareholders of a company had by resolutions authorized acts partly within and partly beyond their powers, such acts being distinct and capable of being carried out alone, an injunction was granted at the suit of a shareholder before notice of any attempt to carry out the illegal part of the scheme (*h*). A shareholder is not excluded from relief by injunction against the provisions of an agreement which are illegal, because the same instrument contains, in addition to the illegal provisions, other matters and things over which he has no control (*i*). An agreement between two railway companies containing clauses *ultra vires* and clauses for referring all disputes arising under the agreement

(*d*) Midland Railway Co. *v.* London and North Western Railway Co., 2 L. R. Eq. 525. In Att.-Gen. *v.* Ely, H. & S. Railway Co., 6 L. R. Eq. 106, it is held by Lord Romilly, M. R. that it is not the province of a court of equity to interfere to compel defendants who have done something *ultra vires*, but *bonâ fide* with the view of accommodating the public to do something other than they have done which would be *intra vires* and therefore legal, but would be more inconvenient to the public, or the persons complaining than that which exists.

(*e*) Winch *v.* Birkenhead, &c., Railway Co., 5 De G. & S. 562; Maunsell *v.* Midland Great Western Railway Co. of Ireland, 1 H. & M. 130; Hattersley *v.* Lord Shelburne, 31 L. J. Ch. 873.

(*f*) Hattersley *v.* Lord Shelburne, 31 L. J. Ch. 873.

(*g*) Hattersley *v.* Lord Shelburne, 31 L. J. Ch. 873. See M'Donnell *v.* Grand Canal Co., 3 Ir. Ch. 578.

(*h*) Charlton *v.* Newcastle and Carlisle Railway Co., 5 Jur. N. S. 1097.

(*i*) Maunsell *v.* Midland Great Western Railway Co. of Ireland, 1 H. & M. 133.

is void, and the companies will be restrained, at the suit of a shareholder, from proceeding to arbitration (*k*).

45. How far engagements entered into by the promoters of a company before the Act of Incorporation has been obtained are binding upon the company after incorporation, is a subject which has led to much difference of opinion. Lord Cottenham decided distinctly in three cases that the contracts of the promoters are or may be binding on the company after incorporation (*l*). These decisions have not been expressly overruled, but their propriety has been more than once questioned, and has indeed been expressly denied in the House of Lords. In a carefully considered judgment, Lord Cranworth expressed himself strongly in favor of the rule that a company should not be held bound by the contracts of the promoters unsanctioned by the legislature, and doubted whether he should not advise their lordships to declare that these decisions of Lord Cottenham were no longer to be considered law. But he hesitated to * do so, as it was not necessary in that case to * 563 call upon their lordships to pronounce a decision one way or the other upon the abstract question, inasmuch as the particular contract in that case was beyond the power of the company (*m*). In Thomas *v.* Hobler (*n*), Lord Westbury held that a company formed on the cost-book principle is only bound by the rules and regulations entered in the cost-book, and is not bound by a preliminary contract entered into before the formation of the company.

46. Companies may, however, after incorporation, ratify and adopt agreements which have been entered into by the projectors. Thus, where a land-owner withdrew his opposition in Parliament to a railway bill upon an agreement with the projectors that the company would take his land upon certain terms, and the company after incorporation allowed judgment in an action upon the agreement to be entered up against itself,

(*k*) Maunsell *v.* Midland Great West. Railway Co. of Ireland, 1 H. & M. 133.

(*l*) Edwards *v.* Grand Junction Railway Co., 1 M. & C. 650; Stanley *v.* Chester and Birkenhead Railway Co., 3 M. & C. 773; Petre *v.* Eastern Counties Railway Co., 1 Ra. Ca. 462. See Earl of Shrewsbury *v.* North Staffordshire Railway Co., L. R. Eq. 593, 616.

(*m*) Caledonian and Dumbartonshire Railway Co. *v.* Magistrates of Helensburgh, 2 Macq. 391; Preston *v.* Liverpool and Manchester Railway Co., 5 H. L. 605; Scottish North Eastern Railway Co. *v.* Stewart, 3 Macq. 382; Earl of Shrewsbury *v.* North Staffordshire Railway Co., 1 L. R. Eq. 593.

(*n*) 8 Jur. N. S. 125.

the court held the recognition of the contract sufficient to render it binding on the company, whatever might have been the case, had there been no such recognition (o). From the observations of Wood, V. C., in Bedford and Cambridge Railway Company v. Stanley (p), it may be concluded that agreements on the part of the promoters of a company may be adopted by the company after incorporation, where the purpose for which they have been entered into is within the powers of the incorporated body, and where the agreement is in itself fair and reasonable (q).

47. An agreement by a land-owner with the promoters of a railway company to sell them, in the event of their obtaining an act of Parliament, as much land as they may require at a fixed rate, is binding upon him, although the company has no existence at the time of the contract. It is no objection
* 564   on the * ground of mutuality that the company is not bound to take the land (r).

48. If it appears from the contract that the vendor is not to be paid the stipulated price unless the company, when incorporated, require and actually take the land, the contract is considered to be conditional on taking the land (s).

49. An agreement entered into and drawn up with all due formalities, between the directors of an incorporated company and a land-owner, to take land in the event of an application to Parliament for an alteration of the line or for permission to make a branch, being granted, is valid (t).

(o) Williams v. St. George's Harbor Co., 2 D. & J. 547.

(p) 2 J. & H. 746.

(q) See Leominster Canal Navigation Co. v. Shrewsbury and Hereford Railway Co., 3 K. & J. 668, per Wood, V. C., explaining Caledonian and Dumbartonshire Railway Co. v. Magistrates of Helensburgh, 2 Macq. 391.

(r) Bedford and Cambridge Railway Co. v. Stanley, 2 J. & H. 746. A railway company, by agreement with a land-owner, were let into possession of land which they required for part of their line, and made their railway over it, giving a bond for payment of the purchase money on a future day, but made default in payment of the bond, and it was held that the land-owner was not entitled to an injunction to restrain the company from continuing in possession until the purchase-money was paid, and whether the land-owner might not be entitled to a receiver, or to have the purchase money paid into court, quære. Pell v. Northampton & B. Junction Railway Co., 2 L. R. Ch. Ap. 100.

(s) Webb v. Direct London and Portsmouth Railway Co., 1 D. M. & G. 521; Stuart v. London and North Western Railway Co., ib. 721; Gage v. Newmarket Railway Co., 18 Q. B. 457; Edinburgh, Perth, and Dundee Railway Co. v. Philip, 2 Macq. 514; Scottish North Eastern Railway Co. v. Stewart, 3 Macq. 382.

(t) Gooday v. Colchester Railway Co., 17 Beav. 133; Eastern Counties Railway Co. v. Hawkes, 5 H. L. 331; Leominster Canal Navigation Co. v.

50. If a contract between two companies is illegal, the court will not assist either of the parties in obtaining a collateral benefit which the agreement would give, or aid them in any manner which would promote the object of the agreement (*u*).

51. The application of the funds of a company to a purpose not falling properly within the objects of the company must be carefully distinguished from cases where the application is to a purpose legitimately connected with the purpose for which the company was formed, and which is in furtherance of or conducive to the welfare of the concern. The application of the funds of the company to such a purpose is not improper. Thus, a company incorporated for the purpose of keeping a hotel was held entitled to lease part of the hotel for a short term of years to the head of a government department (*x*). So also a railway and steam ferry company may lend out its ferry-boats on excursion trips, when not wanted for the ferry (*y*). So also * a contract between a railway company and an * 565 individual to run a steamer between the terminus of the railway in England and the coast of Ireland was held valid, as being in furtherance of the object for which the company was formed and incorporated, viz., the facilitation of communication between England and Ireland (*z*). So also the directors of a fire insurance company may, in the exercise of their discretion, make payments to persons insured in respect of losses not falling strictly within the terms of the policies, if such payments are conducive to the welfare of the company and calculated to promote its interest, or if the payment of such losses is in accordance with the usual custom of other insurance companies (*a*).

52. In a case where the directors of a projected company,

Shrewsbury and Hereford Railway Co., 3 K. & J. 669; Scottish North Eastern Railway Co. *v.* Stewart, 3 Macq. 382.

(*u*) Great Northern Railway Co. *v.* Eastern Counties Railway Co., 9 Ha. 306.

(*x*) Simpson *v.* Westminster Palace Hotel Co., 8 H. L. 712. See Featherstonhaugh *v.* Lee Moor Porcelain Co., 1 L. R. Eq. 318.

(*y*) Forrest *v.* Manchester, Sheffield, and Lincolnshire Railway Co., 30 Beav. 40, affirmed on other grounds, 7 Jur. N. S. 887.

(*z*) South Wales Railway Co. *v.* Redmond, 10 C. B. N. S. 675. See Wilby *v.* West Cornwall Railway Co., 2 H. & N. 703; Young *v.* Brompton Waterworks Co., 1 B. & S. 675. See, also, Mayor of Norwich *v.* Norfolk Railway Co., 4 E. & B. 414, *per* Erle, C. J.; Eastern Countries Railway Co. *v.* Hawkes, 5 H. L. 372, *per* Lord St. Leonards; Warden of Dover Harbor *v.* South Eastern Railway Co., 9 Ha. 489. Comp. Simpson *v.* Denison, 10 Ha. 62.

(*a*) Taunton *v.* Royal Insurance Co., 2 H. & M. 135. See Ellis *v.* Henderson, 3 Bell, Sc. Ap. 1.

being unable to carry out the project to its full extent, determined upon winding up the affairs and returning to the applicants for shares the full amount of the deposits made by them, and deposits amounting to two-thirds of the amount deposited had been returned to the depositors and the remainder was in course of payment, the court held they were justified in the course they had taken, it being morally impossible that the payment could have been carried out in its integrity from the events which had happened (*b*).

53. An act, although it may be beyond the powers of the directors or managing body of a company, may be capable of being adopted and confirmed at a meeting of the shareholders as a body. If so, the question is properly a subject of internal regulation and management, and the court will not interfere until all reasonable attempts have been made to take the sense of the general body of the shareholders on the matters *566 in question. *Before applying to the court, all the means provided by the articles, the deed of settlement, or the Act of Incorporation, as the case may be, for the purpose of bringing the matter before the general body of the shareholders, must be resorted to and exhausted (*c*). Accordingly where two members of an incorporated company had filed a bill against the directors and others, charging them with fraudulent and illegal acts and praying for the appointment of a receiver, the court refused to interfere on the ground that the acts complained of were capable of confirmation at the option of the shareholders, and that it did not appear that any attempt had been made to bring the matter before the general body of the shareholders (*d*). So also, and upon the same grounds, the court refused to restrain persons, who were alleged to have been improperly or illegally appointed directors, from acting as such (*e*). So also, and upon the same grounds, the court has refused to restrain —

(*b*) Bank of Switzerland *v.* Bank of Turkey, 5 L. T. N. S. 549.
(*c*) Carlen *v.* Drury, 1 V. & B. 154; Ellison *v.* Bignold, 2 J. & W. 503; Foss *v.* Harbottle, 2 Ha. 461; Mozley *v.* Alston, 1 Ph. 800; Lord *v.* Copper Mining Co., 2 Ph. 740; Browne *v.* Monmouthshire, &c., Canal Co., 13 Beav. 32; Orr *v.* Glasgow, &c., Railway Co., 3 Macq. 799; Davidson *v.* Tulloch, *ib.* 796, *per* Lord Cranworth; Fraser *v.* Whalley, 2 H. & M. 10; Macdougall *v.* Jersey Hotel Co., *ib.* 528; Gregory *v.* Patchett, 33 Beav. 595.
(*d*) Foss *v.* Harbottle, 2 Ha. 461.
(*e*) Mozley *v.* Alston, 1 Ph. 790; Hattersley *v.* Lord Shelburne, 31 L. J. Ch. 873.

(1) The payment of a dividend by a company before its own works were completed (f), or before its own unsecured debts were paid (g), or the payment of a dividend not justified by the pecuniary condition of the company (h).

(2) The issuing of preference shares, there being a power in the act to create them (i).

(3) The making a call, if made in a proper form and for a proper purpose (k), there being no equity upon which the court can interfere to restrain a company from making calls, or can *inquire into the propriety or necessity of making   * 567 a call (l) ; the making of necessary calls by directors who have been guilty of improper conduct (m) ; the making of a call, alleged to be unfair and unnecessary on one set of shareholders in an amalgamated company (n) ; actions for calls on improperly relinquished shares (o) ; or actions for calls where the moneys raised by the calls have been improperly applied (p).

(4) The application of moneys raised by the issue of new shares to a purpose different from that for which they were raised (q) ; the borrowing moneys on debentures (r) ; the return of deposits to subscribers (s) ; and the continuance in office of the directors appointed in the place of others removed (t).

(5) The application of profits in the repayment of contributed capital, there being no express prohibition in the deed of

(f) Browne v. Monmouthshire Railway Co., 13 Beav. 32.

(g) Stevens v. South Devon Railway Co., 9 Ha. 313.

(h) Gregory v. Patchett, 33 Beav. 595, 606, per Lord Romilly, M. R. Comp. Macdougall v. Jersey Hotel Co., 2 H. & M. 528.

(i) Edwards v. Shrewsbury and Birmingham Railway Co., 2 De G. & S. 537 ; Hutton v. Scarborough Cliff Hotel Co., 2 Dr. & Sm. 514.

(k) Cooper v. Shropshire Union Railway Co., 6 Ra. Ca. 136. Comp. Hodgkinson v. National Live Stock Insurance Co., 4 D. & J. 422.

(l) Macbride v. Lindsay, 9 Ha. 574.

(m) Logan v. Courtown, 13 Beav. 22.

(n) Bailey v. Birkenhead, Lancashire and Cheshire Junction Railway Co., 12 Beav. 433. Comp. Hodgkinson v. National Live Stock Insurance Co., 4 D. & J. 422 ; Orr v. Glasgow, &c., Railway Co., 3 Macq. 799.

(o) Harris v. North Devon Railway Co., 20 Beav. 384 ; Playfair v. Birmingham, Bristol, &c., Railway Co., 1 Ra. Ca. 640. Comp. Hodgkinson v. National Live Stock Insurance Co., 4 D. & J. 422 ; Orr v. Glasgow, &c., Railway Co., 3 Macq. 799.

(p) Orr v. Glasgow &c., Railway Co., 3 Macq. 799.

(q) Yetts v. Norfolk Railway Co., 3 De G. & S. 293.

(r) Bryon v. Metropolitan Saloon Omnibus Co., 3 D & J. 123.

(s) Kent v. Jackson, 14 Beav. 367. 2 D. M. & G. 49.

(t) Inderwick v. Snell, 2 Mac. & G. 216. See Lord v. Copper Mines Co., 2 Ph. 740 ; Exeter and Crediton Railway Co. v. Buller, 5 Ra. Ca. 211.

settlement, although the deed seems to contemplate a continuing capital as in an ordinary partnership (u).

(6) The commencement of business by a company constituted under the Joint-Stock Companies Act, 1862, on the ground that all the nominal capital has not been subscribed, or on the ground that the business actually commenced is on a much smaller scale than that contemplated by the prospectus (x).

54. But if it is absolutely necessary that the court should interfere to prevent irreparable mischief from being done before the time for taking the necessary steps to call a general meeting of the shareholders can arrive (y), or if the directors
* 568 are adopting * a particular course for the express purpose of preventing the free action of the shareholders (z), the court will interfere (a).

55. If the measures adopted by the directors or managing body are plainly beyond the powers of the company, and are plainly inconsistent with the objects for which the company was constituted, the court will, at the instance of the minority, interfere to prevent the performance of the act complained of, whether or not an appeal has been made by the minority to the body of the shareholders generally (b). But even in such cases it may often be better to have recourse to such extra-judicial remedies as may be open before applying to the court (c).

56. When a factious minority is illegally resisting the majority, the court has jurisdiction to interfere.

57. A general meeting, though it has power to alter those regulations of the company which relate to management, has no power to alter the regulations which relate to the constitution of the company (d).

(u) Binney v. Ince Hall Coal and Canal Co., 35 L. J. Ch. 363.

(x) Macdougall v. Jersey Imperial Hotel Co., 2 H. & M. 528.

(y) Great Western Railway Co. v. Rushout, 5 De G. & S. 310. Comp. Gregory v. Patchett, 33 Beav. 595, 606.

(z) Fraser v. Whalley, 2 H. & M. 10.

(a) See Re London Mercantile Discount Co., 35 L. J. Ch. 229; Re Imperial Mercantile Credit Association, 12 Jur. N. S. 739.

(b) Gregory v. Patchett, 33 Beav. 595, 606.

(c) Bailey v. Birkenhead, Lancashire, and Cheshire Junction Railway Co., 13 Beav. 433; Edwards v. Shrewsbury, &c., Railway Co., 2 De G. & S. 537; Exeter and Crediton Railway Co. v. Buller, 5 Ra. Ca. 211, 16 L. J. Ch. 449.

(d) Hutton v. Scarborough Cliff Hotel

58. Where an association is formed, the members of which have bound themselves by certain rules, they are bound by their rules, and the court will not interfere except in cases of breach of trust or oppression (e). The court is not the proper forum for litigation of disputes between the members of a benefit building society. The case being one which depends on the construction of the rules, the court will not interfere (f). A benefit building * society is not pre-   * 569 cluded from investing its funds in the purchase of a real estate (g).

59. Where the court interferes by injunction, at the suit of a shareholder suing on behalf of himself and all the other share-holders, to restrain a company from doing improper or illegal acts, it will also to the extent of its powers redress what has been done and give relief to persons injured thereby, although it be not called upon to dissolve the company and wind up its affairs (h).

60. In a suit by a shareholder on behalf of himself and all other shareholders to restrain an illegal payment of dividends, the plaintiff is not entitled to costs as between solicitor and client (i).[1]

Co., 2 Dr. & Sm. 521, 34 L. J. Ch. 643. See Yeates v. Roberts, 3 Drew. 170 ; Bryon v. Metropolitan Saloon Omnibus Co., 3 D. & J. 123 ; Macdougall v. Jersey Hotel Co., 2 H. & M. 528 ; Gregory v. Patchett, 33 Beav. 595. See Joint-stock Discount Co. v. Brown, 12 Jur. N. S. 899.

(e) See Clough v. Ratcliffe, 1 De G. & S. 164; Yeates v. Roberts, 3 Drew. 170, 7 D. M. & G. 227 ; Pare v. Clegg, 29 Beav. 589.   See Bank of Turkey v. Ottoman Co., 14 L. T. N. S. 545.

(f) Trott v. Hughes, 16 L. T. 260.

(g) Mullock v. Jenkins, 14 Beav. 628. See Grimes v. Harrison, 26 Beav. 435 ; Queen v. D'Eyncourt, 4 B. & S. 820. See also, as to injunctions against trus-tees of a benefit society, Evans v. Coven-try, 5 D. M. & G. 911. See ib., as to parties.

(h) Gregory v. Patchett, 33 Beav. 595, 607.

(i) Morgan v. Great Eastern Railway Co., 1 H. & M. 560.

[1] Equity will interfere by injunction to restrain the infringement of corpo-rate franchises. "It is considered that this interference is solely in aid of the legal right, that if the legal right is free from doubt equity may assume to decide it, or to act definitely upon its acknowledged existence. If it is con-sidered conjectural, and altogether problematical, equity ordinarily will not interfere until the legal right is established by the judgment of the appropriate legal tribunal. But, in their discretion, courts of equity will interfere by injunction during the pendency of the trial at law to prevent irreparable injury, to avoid multiplicity of suits, and in some cases where there is given no adequate legal redress." 2 Redfield on Railways, 341, and cases cited.

* 570   * CHAPTER XXIV.

INJUNCTIONS AGAINST CORPORATIONS.

1. Power of corporations to alienate their property.
2. Court will not interfere at suit of a member of corporation to prevent forfeiture of charter.
3. Parties to suit.
4. Provisions of English statute.
5. Public functionaries or bodies restrained from going beyond their authority.
6 & 7. Misapplication of funds by municipal corporations restrained.
8. Effect of delay in making application for injunction.
9 & 10. Constitution of eleemosynary corporations.
11. Trustees of a charity restrained from misapplication of funds.
12–14. Authority of court over spiritual or ecclesiastical corporations.

1. CORPORATIONS, civil, ecclesiastical, or of any nature what-ever, have, like individuals, full power at common law to dispose of all the property of which they are seised in fee (a). Unless a trust can be established (b), or unless the corporation itself comes forward to complain of a fraud practised in the management of its own affairs (c), a court of equity has no jurisdiction to interfere. The application of the property of the corporation to other than corporate purposes is not a ground for the interference of the court unless a breach of trust can be shown (d). But if corporate property be affected by a trust, the power and jurisdiction of the court to enforce and execute the trust attaches equally as it does upon other property similarly circumstanced (e).[1] The burden of proof

(a) Mayor, &c., of Colchester v. Lowten, 1 V. & B. 226 ; Evan v. Corporation of Avon, 29 Beav. 144 ; Att.-Gen. v. St. John's Hospital, Bedford, 2 D. J. & S. 621.

(b) Ib.; Att.-Gen. v. Corporation of Cashel, 3 Dr. & War. 314.

(c) Att.-Gen. v. Corporation of Belfast, 4 Ir. Ch. 119.

(d) Att.-Gen. v. Corporation of Carmarthen, Coop. 30 ; Mayor, &c., of Colchester v. Lowten, 1 V. & B. 226 ; Parr v. Att.-Gen., 8 Cl. & Fin. 409 ;

Att.-Gen. v. Portreeve of Avon, 33 L. J. Ch. 172.

(e) Att.-Gen. v. Mayor, &c., of Dublin, 1 Bligh, N. S. 312 ; Dummer v. Corporation of Chippenham, 14 Ves. 245 ; Mayor, &c., of Colchester v. Lowten, 1 V. & B. 226 ; Att.-Gen. v. St. John's Hospital, 2 D. J. & S. 621.

[1] But the courts of equity very often interfere to restrain corporations from making use of their funds for a purpose wholly aside of the general object of their incorporation, and this will be done at the suit of shareholders, although a

lies on the party who seeks to establish the trust (*f*). In Attorney-General *v.* Corporation of Cashel (*g*), where the mem-

majority may have sanctioned by their votes the act complained of. 2 Redfield on Railways, 326. See Grand Trunk Railway *v.* Cook, 29 Ill. 237; Kean *v.* Johnson, 1 Stockt. Ch. 401; Winebrenner *v.* Colder, 43 Penn. St. 244; March *v.* Eastern Railway, 40 N. H. 548. In the last case it is held the suit should be in form in behalf of all the stockholders; and in Nazro *v.* Merchants Mutual Ins. Co., 14 Wis. 295, it is said the capital stock of an incorporated company is a trust fund over which the court has jurisdiction as over other trusts. But a majority may expend surplus funds in the hands of the company, to extend its business within its chartered powers, and to kindred enterprises beyond its original powers if sanctioned by express legislative grant. Pratt *v.* Pratt, 33 Conn. 446; Durfee *v.* Old Colony and F. R. R., 5 Allen, 230; Sturges *v.* Knapp, 31 Vt. 1. As an individual stockholder cannot maintain an action at law against the directors of a corporation for mismanaging its affairs or defrauding it, such directors being the agents of the corporation and liable only to it, their principal, for their acts, an individual stockholder may maintain a suit in equity against the directors of a corporation for misconduct in office: where the corporation is unable to bring a suit at law, or where, through collusion or fraud, it neglects to seek redress, and an application has been made to the directors for the use of the corporate name to bring suit and refused, such suit should proceed in behalf of all the stockholders, and make the directors and corporation parties, and should allege the neglect of the corporation to seek redress and the demand refused of the use of the corporate name. Allen *v.* Curtis, 26 Conn. 456; Peabody *v.* Flint, 6 Allen, 52. See this last case as to what delay in bringing the bill will defeat the plaintiff's right. As to the duties of directors, see Richards *v.* New Hamp. Ins. Co., 43 N. H. 263; Hall *v.* Vt. and Mass. Railway, 28 Vt. 401; Smith *v.* Prattville Man. Co., 29 Ala. 503. In the last case it was held that the directors of a corporation would not be compelled to declare dividends out of the surplus earnings of the company unless it was shown that they refused from a wilful abuse of their discretion. In Dodge *v.* Woolsey, 18 How. U. S. 341, it is stated

that courts of equity have a jurisdiction over corporations, at the instance of one or more of their members, to apply preventive remedies by injunction, to restrain those who administer them from doing acts which would amount to a violation of charters, or to prevent any misapplication of their capitals or profits which might result in lessening the dividends of stockholders, or the value of their shares, as either may be protected by the franchises of a corporation, if the acts intended to be done create what is in the law denominated a breach of trust. And the jurisdiction extends to inquire into and to enjoin, as the case may require that to be done, any proceedings by individuals, in whatever character they may profess to act, if the subject of complaint is an imputed violation of a corporate franchise, or the denial of a right growing out of it, for which there is not an adequate remedy at law. In this case the directors of a bank refused to take the proper measures to resist the collection of a tax upon the bank which they believed to have been imposed upon it in violation of its charter, and it was held to be a breach of trust which entitled a stockholder to maintain a bill against them, asking for such relief as the case might require. The court say, the "refusal upon the part of the directors, by their own showing, partakes more of disregard of duty than of an error of judgment. It was a non-performance of a confessed official obligation, amounting to what the law considers a breach of trust, though it may not involve intentional moral delinquency. It was a mistake, it is true, of what their duty required from them, according to their own sense of it, but being a duty by their own confession, their refusal was an act outside of the obligation which the charter imposed upon them to protect what they conscientiously believed to be the franchises of the bank. A sense of duty and conduct contrary to it, is not 'an error of judgment merely,' and cannot be so called in any case. It amounted to an illegal application of the profits due to the stockholders of the bank into which a court of equity will inquire to prevent its being made."

(*f*) Evan *v.* Corporation of Avon, 29 Beav. 144.

(*g*) 3 Dr. & War. 314.

bers of the corporation had to take an oath against alienation generally, Lord St. Leonards held that a trust not to alienate must be inferred ; but in Evan *v.* Corporation of Avon (*h*), where the oath which the members of the corporation had to take was against alienation so as to prejudice the corpora-

* 571   tion, the court held that no trust was created, and * that the corporation itself had the power of determining whether a sale was prejudicial or not, and overruled a demurrer to a bill for an injunction to restrain a corporation from selling part of the corporate property, there being no evidence of fraud on the part of the corporation.

2. The court will interfere at the suit of a member of the corporation to prevent the destruction of the corporation (*i*), or to prevent a forfeiture of the charter (*k*).

3. If there be a trust and the trust be for public purposes, or the act complained of affects the revenues of the corporation, the suit should be instituted by the Attorney-General at the instance of a relator, who, if he has any interest in the matter, may join as plaintiff (*l*). If the Attorney-General declines to interfere, and the parties differ among themselves as to the proper mode of administering the trust, a certain number may file a bill on behalf of themselves and others, making some of the dissentients and the Attorney-General defendants (*m*). If the trust be of a private nature, or the act complained of does not affect the revenues of the corporation, the suit must be by bill (*n*), and the Attorney-General should not be made a party (*o*). A corporation may itself institute the suit, although the transactions complained of may have been carried into effect in its name by the members of the governing body (*p*). Where a corporation had not been kept up for a long series of

---

(*h*) 29 Beav. 144.
(*i*) Ward *v.* Society of Attorneys, 1 Coll. 370.
(*k*) Rendall *v.* Crystal Palace Co., 4 K. & J. 327.
(*l*) Att.-Gen. *v.* Mayor of Dublin, 1 Bligh, N. S. 347; Skinners' Co. *v.* Irish Society, 12 Cl. & Fin. 425 ; Evan *v.* Corporation of Avon, 29 Beav. 144; Att.-Gen. *v.* Portreeve of Avon, 33 L. J. Ch. 172; Lang *v.* Purves, 8 Jur. N. S. 524.

(*m*) Lang *v.* Purves, 8 Jur. N. S. 524.
(*n*) Att.-Gen. *v.* Forster, 10 Ves. 335; Att.-Gen. *v.* Newcombe, 14 Ves. 1; Davis *v.* Jenkins, 3 V. & B. 157; Carter *v.* Cropley, 8 D. M. & G. 681 ; *supra,* p. 175.
(*o*) Att.-Gen. *v.* Newcombe, 14 Ves. 1; Davis *v.* Jenkins, 3 V. & B. 157; Att.-Gen. *v.* Portreeve of Avon, 33 L. J. Ch. 172.
(*p*) Att.-Gen. *v.* Wilson, Cr. & Ph. 1.

years to its proper numbers, the court held the corporation itself was not a necessary party (*q*).

4. The funds and property of all corporations which are within the Municipal Corporation Act, 5 & 6 Will. 4, c. 76, have been impressed by that act with the character of a trust. The *corporation has been constituted by the   *572 act a trustee for public purposes of the borough fund and property, and is as such subject to the jurisdiction of the court. Although the act contains provisions for correcting abuses in respect of the borough property, there is nothing to exclude the ordinary jurisdiction of the court to prevent breach of trust (*r*). In Attorney-General *v.* Corporation of Yarmouth (*s*), a corporation was restrained from granting a lease at an undervalue and for a fine, contrary to the provisions of the 95th clause of the act. The court has, it would appear, jurisdiction, upon a proper case being made out, to restrain a municipal corporation from making a rate (*t*); but the proper remedy is to apply to a court of law, either to quash the rate under the provisions of the act, or to apply by *certiorari* to the Queen's Bench under 7 Will. 4 and 1 Vict. c. 78 (*u*).

5. Public functionaries or bodies, incorporated by statute for a public purpose or the promotion of a public benefit, may not exceed the jurisdiction which has been intrusted to them by the legislature. So long as they strictly confine themselves within the limits of their jurisdiction, and proceed in the mode which the legislature has pointed out, the court will not interfere to see whether any regulation or alteration which they make is good or bad; but if, under pretence of an authority which the law does give them to a certain extent, they go beyond the line of their authority, and assume to themselves a power which the law does not give them, the court no longer considers them as acting under the authority

---

(*q*) Daugars *v.* Rivaz, 28 Beav. 233.
(*r*) Att.-Gen. *v.* Corporation of Liverpool, 1 M. & C. 201; Att.-Gen. *v.* Aspinall, 2 M. & C. 613; Att.-Gen. *v.* Corporation of Poole, 4 M. & C. 17; Att.-Gen. *v.* Wilson, Cr. & Ph. 1; Parr *v.* Att.-Gen., 8 Cl. & Fin. 409.

(*s*) 21 Beav. 625.
(*t*) Att.-Gen. *v.* Corporation of Lichfield, 11 Beav. 121.
(*u*) Att.-Gen. *v.* Mayor, &c., of Wigan, Kay, 268.

of their commission, but treats them as persons acting without legal authority (*x*).[1]

6. Municipal corporations dealing with borough funds,
*573   and * acting under a general or some local statute, and

public bodies or functionaries, incorporated by statute for carrying into effect certain works, are bound to apply the corporate funds for the purposes directed, and in the mode pointed out, by the act which gives them authority, and for no other purpose whatsoever (*y*).[2] The application of the corporate funds to any other purpose than the proper purposes of the act, however desirable it may be, is improper, and will be

(*x*) Frewin *v.* Lewis, 4 M. & C. 254. See Speer *v.* Carter, 17 Ves. 216; Armitstead *v.* Durham, 11 Beav. 556; Tinkler *v.* Wandsworth District Board of Works, 2 D. & J. 261; Austin *v.* Lambeth Vestry, 27 L. J. Ch. 388. See, as to injunctions against trespass and nuisance by public bodies of functionaries, *supra*, pp. 295, 345.

(*y*) Att.-Gen. *v.* Mayor of Wigan, Kay, 268, 5 D. M. & G. 54; Att.-Gen. *v.* Corporation of Belfast, 4 Ir. Ch. 119.

[1] The passing of a resolution, by the common council of a municipal corporation, directing one of the departments to give a contract for work and labor to specified persons, is a legislative act, and cannot be restrained by injunction. But after such resolution has been passed, on a proper case being shown for relief, an injunction may issue to prevent the resolution from being carried into effect. People *v.* Mayor, &c., of New York, 32 Barb. 35. And the imposition of any tax or burden on the tax-payers of a city contrary to law will be restrained on a complaint filed by any tax-payer, on his own behalf, as well as on behalf of others similarly situated, or on behalf of any corporator of the city, having an interest in the corporate property thereof, on a similar complaint showing an illegal division or application of the corporate property. Wood *v.* Draper, 24 Barb. 187. But see, in this connection, Greene *v.* Mumford, 5 R. I. 472. It is a general principle that the court of chancery is not the proper tribunal to correct the irregularities or errors of inferior tribunals, and that in ordinary cases it should not interfere with the ordinance of a municipal corporation; but there are

exceptions, such as to prevent a multiplicity of suits, or where irreparable damage is the consequence of their execution, or where extrinsic facts are necessary in order to show, not the illegality or informality of the ordinance, but the illegality of its execution against the individual who seeks the protection of this court, and in all cases of fraud. Morris Canal and Banking Co. *v.* Jersey City, 1 Beasley, 252; Vanoren *v.* Mayor of New York, 9 Paige, 388; Oakley *v.* Trustees of Williamsburg, 6 Paige, 262; Baldwin *v.* City of Buffalo, 29 Barb. 396.

[2] The passing of a resolution by the common council of a city granting the right which they were forbidden by the injunction to grant, on condition that the grantees should accept the terms of the resolution, was a violation of the injunction by those who voted for it, whether the terms were accepted or not, the resolution itself doing all that the council could do on their part to make the grant effectual. Such an act was not one of municipal legislation, but in substance a grant upon condition, and the effect of the injunction could not be avoided by giving to an act not legislative in its character, the form of an ordinance or resolution. So far as such resolution was an executive act, by actually making the grant, it was a clear violation of the injunction, even though the legislative powers of the board could not be arrested by the order of the court. In the exercise of its conceded powers, it was the duty of the board to see that it did not go beyond them and do an act which had been lawfully forbidden. People *v.* Sturtevant, 9 N. Y. 263.

restrained by injunction (z). " By the proper purposes of the act," said Wood, V. C. (a), " the legislature does not mean some further extension of the powers already obtained. No application of the money to that which did not exist when the act passed can in any sense whatever be a purpose of the act. . . . Persons having in their hands funds which have been appropriated by an act of Parliament to certain purposes cannot, without the previous consent of the court, apply them for an extension of those purposes, although it is purely a *bonâ fide* extension, or a more enlarged application of the fund to those purposes which the legislature has regarded as good and beneficial." The application accordingly of corporate or borough funds towards the payment of the expenses of an act of Parliament for increased powers is, unless it be made with the previous consent of the court, or unless it is sanctioned by the legislature, improper, and a breach of trust. Where parties have presented a bill to Parliament which has been rejected, and they have not previously taken the precaution to obtain the sanction of the court to the application, any attempt to apply the corporate funds to the payment of the expenses will be restrained by the court (b). So, also, commissioners under a local act for draining and lighting a town, " with powers to pay all costs incident to the purposes of the act, and to carry the intents and purposes of the act into full and complete execution in other respects," were restrained from * applying any part of the rates raised under the act in * 574 paying the expenses of an application to Parliament (c).

A corporation, however, is justified in applying the corporate funds in the payment of expenses incurred in opposing a bill in Parliament which would, if sanctioned, be injurious to the property of the corporation (d), but not in obtaining a new act for the purpose of remedying the injury which had resulted to

(z) Att.-Gen. v. Mayor of Wigan, Kay, 274.
(a) Ib.
(b) Att.-Gen. v. Corporation of Norwich, 16 Sim. 225, affi'd. 21 L. J. Ch. 139; Att.-Gen. v. Guardians of Poor of Southampton, 17 Sim. 6; Att.-Gen. v. Compton, 1 Y. & C. C. C. 417; Att.-Gen. v. Mayor, &c., of Plymouth, 1 W.

R. 445; Trevillian v. Mayor, &c., of Exeter, 24 L. J. Ch. 157.
(c) Att.-Gen. v. Eastlake, 11 Ha. 205; Att.-Gen. v. Andrews, 2 Mac. & G. 223.
(d) Att.-Gen. v. Andrews, 2 Mac. & G. 223; Att.-Gen. v Mayor of Wigan, 5 D. M. & G. 54; Att.-Gen. v. Mayor, &c., of Plymouth, 1 W. R. 445. See Bright v. North, 2 Ph. 216.

the corporate property from the effects of an act which had not been opposed during its progress in Parliament (e).

7. In Attorney-General v. Daniel (f), where a vestry, authorized by act of Parliament to levy rates for certain purposes, had mixed the moneys arising from distinct rates into one fund for the purpose of meeting the general expenditure of the parish, the court restrained them from applying any portion of one class of rates and receipts in supplying the deficiencies in any other class of rates, and generally from applying the moneys recovered by them for any other purposes than those for which they were authorized by the act to be collected (g). Where a body of persons are by statute constituted trustees for certain public purposes, and powers are conferred on them to levy rates upon the district to a certain limited amount, they are authorized (if not expressly prohibited) to apply the rates of any one year in the payment of debts properly incurred in a previous year in the execution of those trusts. It is otherwise, however, if the power of rating be unlimited in amount. Where one of the purposes of the trust is such that it can only be properly carried out by raising a sum of money larger than the current rates can supply, the trustees are justified in raising this sum by way of loan, and paying the same with interest out of future rates (h).

8. Delay in making the application to restrain a cor-
* 575 poration from * applying the corporate funds to other
purposes than the proper purposes of the act is not material (i).

9. Eleemosynary corporations, or corporations for charity purposes, are subject to the rules, laws, statutes, and ordinances ordained by the founder or the visitor whom he has appointed (k). To all eleemosynary corporations the right of visitation is incident. Where the king is founder, the king and his successors are the visitors: if a private person has been the founder, his heirs and assigns are the visitors. If the heirs of

(e) Att. - Gen. v. Eastlake, 11 Ha. 205.
(f) 9 L. J. Ch. N. S. 394.
(g) See Att.-Gen. v. Corporation of Thetford, 8 W. R. 467.
(h) Att.-Gen. v. Church, 2 H. & M.

697. See Harrison v. Stickney, 2 H. L. 108.
(i) Att. - Gen. v. Eastlake, 11 Ha. 205; Att.-Gen. v. Mayor, &c., of Plymouth, 1 W. R. 445.
(k) Philipps v. Bury, 2 T. R. 346, 1 Lord Raym. 5.

a founder fail, and no visitor has been appointed, the right of visitation devolves on the Crown, and is exercised on behalf of the Crown by the court of chancery (*l*). The visitor has an exclusive jurisdiction over all matters which come within the scope of his authority (*m*). Whatever relates to the internal management and regulation of the charity rests within the exclusive jurisdiction of the visitor. The decisions of the visitor, so long as he keeps within his jurisdiction, are final, and not examinable at law (*n*) or in equity (*o*). If the visitor has not acted, or has declined to act in a case where he ought to act, or is about to interfere in a case where he has no jurisdiction, application must be made to the court of Queen's Bench for a *mandamus* or a prohibition, as the case may be, and not to the court of chancery (*p*). The court has no jurisdiction to interfere with the visitorial power, unless it finds a breach of trust (*q*); but where there is a breach of trust the court will interfere to see the trusts properly performed, notwithstanding there may be a general or a special visitor (*r*). Thus, where a French Protestant * Church had been estab- * 576 lished by letters-patent from the Crown, and the governing body had, apart from the charter of incorporation, funds impressed with a trust in favor of the pastor, who, when elected, was presented, approved, and instituted by the Crown, the court, notwithstanding the visitorship of the Crown, restrained the governing body from hindering the pastor in the duties of his office (*s*). Where the duties of the visitor are not confined to overlooking the character of the institution, but extend to the management of the property, he is, so far as there is a trust, subject to the jurisdiction of the court (*t*).

10. Eleemosynary corporations are either hospitals, colleges,

(*l*) Eden *v.* Foster, 2 P. Wms. 326; Att.-Gen. *v.* Gaunt, 3 Swn. 148; R. *v.* Catherine Hall, 4 T. R. 233.

(*m*) King *v.* Bishop of Ely, 2 T. R. 290; Green *v.* Rutherforth, 1 Ves. 462.

(*n*) Philipps *v.* Bury, 2 T. R. 346; St. John's College *v.* Toddington, 1 Burr. 200.

(*o*) Att.-Gen. *v.* Smythies, 2 M. & C. 135; Whiston *v.* Dean and Chapter of Rochester, 7 Ha. 532; Thompson *v.* University of London, 33 L. J. Ch. 625.

(*p*) Whiston *v.* Dean and Chapter of Rochester, 7 Ha. 532.

(*q*) Att.-Gen. *v.* Foundling Hospital, 2 Ves. J. 43; *Re* Berkhampstead School, 2 V. & B. 134; Thompson *v.* University of London, 33 L. J. Ch. 625.

(*r*) Att.-Gen. *v.* St. Cross Hospital, 17 Beav. 435.

(*s*) Daugars *v.* Rivaz, 28 Beav. 233.

(*t*) Att.-Gen. *v.* Lock, 3 Atk. 165; Att.-Gen. *v.* Foundling Hospital, 2 Ves. J. 47; Att.-Gen. *v.* Smythies, 2 M. & C. 135.

or free grammar schools incorporated for the teaching of children (*u*). Protestant dissenting chapels, incorporated by charter or letters-patent for religious purposes, may be also classed under this head (*x*).

11. Trustees of a charity, whether they be a corporation or individuals, having in their hands funds devoted to certain charitable purposes, must devote the funds of the charity to those purposes. The application of the funds to other than such purposes is a breach of trust, and will be restrained (*y*).

12. The visitor of a spiritual or ecclesiastical corporation has the same exclusive right over all matters which come within the scope of his authority as the visitor of an eleemosynary one (*z*). The court of chancery has no jurisdiction over the visitorial power unless it finds a trust (*a*); but where there is a trust the court will interfere to see the trust properly performed, notwithstanding there may be a visitor (*b*).

* 577 The relationship in * the ordinary sense of trustee and *cestui que trust* does not exist between the dean and chapter of a cathedral, and the head-master of a grammar school attached to it, where both the cathedral and the school are governed by the statutes of the founder and are subject to the jurisdiction of a special visitor, and where the head-master is paid out of the common fund of the endowment. Where, accordingly, the Dean and Chapter of Rochester, in exercise of a power vested in them by the statutes of their founder, summarily dismissed the head-master of the grammar school attached to the cathedral from his office without hearing him in his defence, the court refused to interfere by injunction either *durante lite*, or otherwise, to restrain the dean and chapter from removing him from his office, or from appointing another head-master in his stead (*c*).

(*u*) Att.-Gen. *v.* Price, 3 Atk. 108; *Ex parte* Berkhampstead School, 2 V. & B. 144; Att.-Gen. *v.* Brazenose College, 2 Cl. & Fin. 296.

(*x*) Att.-Gen. *v.* Cock, 2 Ves. 273; Att.-Gen. *v.* Lord Dudley, Coop. 146; Att.-Gen. *v.* Fowler, 15 Ves. 85; Att.-Gen. *v.* Molland, 1 Younge, 562; Daugars *v.* Rivaz, 28 Beav. 233.

(*y*) Att.-Gen. *v.* Compton, 1 Y. & C. C. 417; Att.-Gen. *v.* Brandreth, *ib.* 200; Att.-Gen. *v.* Corporation of New-

bury, C. P. C. 72; Att.-Gen. *v.* Sherborne School, 18 Beav. 256.

(*z*) Reg. *v.* Dean and Chapter of Chester, 15 Q. B. 513; Reg. *v.* Dean and Chapter of Rochester, 17 Q. B. 1.

(*a*) Whiston *v.* Dean and Chapter of Rochester, 7 Ha. 532.

(*b*) Att.-Gen. *v.* St. Cross Hospital, 17 Beav. 435.

(*c*) Whiston *v.* Dean and Chapter of Rochester, 7 Ha. 532.

13. Pending a suit respecting the right of nomination to a benefice, a bishop will be restrained from taking advantage of the lapse and exercising the presentation (*d*). So, also, where an improper appointment has been made of a chaplain or vicar by persons in whom the appointment is vested, the court will restrain a bishop from instituting the person so appointed (*e*).

14. By the restraining statutes all ecclesiastical persons are restrained from alienating the possessions of the church for a longer period than twenty-one years from the making thereof (*f*).

(*d*) Edenborough *v.* Archbishop of Canterbury, 2 Russ. 93; Att.-Gen. *v.* Cuming, 2 Y. & C. C. C. 139; Nicholson *v.* Knapp, 9 Sim. 326; Daly *v.* Archbishop of Dublin, Fl. & K. 263.

(*e*) Att.-Gen. *v.* Bishop of Lichfield, 5 Ves. 825; Att.-Gen. *v.* Earl of Powis, Kay, 186.

(*f*) See further, *supra*, pp. 264–267.

* 578 * CHAPTER XXV.

INJUNCTIONS FOR OR AGAINST JUDGMENT CREDITORS.

1. A COURT of equity will, on a proper case being made out, interfere by injunction either at the suit of a judgment creditor (*a*), or for the purpose of restraining a judgment creditor from executing his judgment (*b*).

2. The rights of judgment creditors are purely legal rights, and the interposition of the court in their favor rests upon the principle of aiding the legal right (*c*). The court will interpose its aid for the purpose of removing out of the way any impediments which may exist to the exercise by judgment creditors of their legal rights, or it may interfere for the preservation of property pending disputes at law as to the rights of judgment creditors (*d*), or for the protection of property charged by the judgment from injury or destruction until such time as the judgment creditor can have the benefit of his charge (*e*). The court may also in the exercise of its original jurisdiction in the administration of assets have occasion to deal with the legal rights of judgment creditors (*f*).

3. A creditor does not under the statute of Westminster

<hr>

(*a*) Smith *v.* Hurst, 10 Ha. 30.
(*b*) Whitworth *v.* Gaugain, 1 Ph. 735; Langton *v.* Horton, 1 Ha. 549; Earl of Shrewsbury *v.* Trappes, 2 D. F. & J. 172; *supra*, pp. 21–25.
(*c*) Smith *v.* Hurst, 10 Ha. 30. See Benham *v.* Keane, 3 D. F. & J. 333.

(*d*) Neate *v.* Duke of Marlborough, 3 M. & C. 421; Smith *v.* Hurst, 10 Ha. 30.
(*e*) Godfrey *v.* Tucker, 33 Beav. 280; Partridge *v.* Foster, 34 Beav. 1.
(*f*) Smith *v.* Hurst, 10 Ha. 30.

obtain a charge or lien on the land of his debtor by virtue
of his judgment. The statute only gives him the option of
obtaining one by issuing an *elegit*. Until he has exercised his
option and sued out an *elegit*, he has not a complete legal title
and cannot come to the court to have the benefit of his charge
or lien against the land of his debtor (*g*). The court
will, it is true, recognize a * title by the judgment in a   * 579
suit for redemption or in a suit to administer an estate.
But the jurisdiction in such cases is founded upon this, that
inasmuch as the court finds the creditor in a condition to
acquire a charge on the estate, it cannot deal with the estate
without regarding the interest of the person who by issuing an
elegit has a right to obtain a charge on it (*h*).

4. The Statute 1 & 2 Vict. c. 100, s. 13, makes a judgment
duly registered an immediate charge on the lands of a debtor,
but declares that the creditor cannot have the benefit of the
charge until after the expiration of twelve months from the
time of entering up the judgment (*i*). But in all cases in
which the judgment debtor's interest is an expiring interest, or
where the judgment debtor is destroying or getting rid of the
property charged by the judgment, the creditor can come in
the mean time to the court to prevent the thing charged from
being diminished or destroyed (*k*). A judgment creditor, however, who has sued out an *elegit* is, notwithstanding 1 & 2 Vict.
c. 110, entitled to relief under Edward I. c. 18, though the
year from entering up judgment has not expired (*l*).

5. A judgment creditor is not required by 1 & 2 Vict. c.
100, to issue execution on his judgment, but by 23 & 24 Vict.
c. 38, s. 1, it is declared that a judgment shall not be a charge
upon land so as to affect purchasers, unless the judgment creditor shall issue execution and duly register the writ of execution (*m*). By a later act, 27 & 28 Vict. c. 112, s. 1, it is

(*g*) Barnwall *v.* Barnwall, 3 Ridg. 59;
Neate *v.* Duke of Marlborough, 3 M. &
C. 421; Smith *v.* Hurst, 1 Coll. 705, 10
Ha. 30; Godfrey *v.* Tucker, 33 Beav.
280.

(*h*) Neate *v.* Duke of Marlborough,
3 M. & C. 421; Godfrey *v.* Tucker, 33
Beav. 280.

(*i*) Smith *v.* Hurst, 10 Ha. 30. See
Derbyshire and Staffordshire Railway

Co. *v.* Bainbrigge, 15 Beav. 146; Harrison *v.* Pennell, 4 Jur. N. S. 683.

(*k*) Bristed *v.* Wilkins, 3 Ha. 235;
Watts *v.* Jefferyes, 3 Mac. & G. 372;
Yescombe *v.* Landon, 28 Beav. 80. See
Partridge *v.* Foster, 34 Beav. 1.

(*l*) Partridge *v.* Foster, 34 Beav. 1.
See Smith *v.* Hurst, 10 Ha. 30; Godfrey *v.* Tucker, 33 Beav. 280.

(*m*) Wallis *v.* Morris, 10 Jur. N. S. 741.

declared that no judgment entered up thereafter shall affect
any land, until such land shall have been actually delivered in
execution by virtue of a writ of *elegit*, and the writ shall have
been duly registered, but that the judgment creditor to whom
land has been actually delivered in execution shall be
* 580 entitled forthwith to have the benefit of his *judgment (*n*). The act does not, however, deprive a judgment creditor of his charge who is unable to have the land
delivered to him. Where, therefore, mortgagees were about to
sell under a power contained in the instrument, the court at
the suit of a judgment creditor of the mortgagor, who had sued
out an *elegit* but could not obtain possession of the land under
the writ, the legal estate and possession being in the hands of
the mortgagees, restrained the mortgagees from paying the
surplus to the mortgagor (*o*).

6. A judgment creditor who seeks the aid of the court, must,
where it is required by the act under which he sues, show that
he has sued out the writ of *elegit* or *fi. fa.*, the execution of
which is avoided, and has registered the same, or the defendant may demur (*p*).

7. A creditor under an execution takes all that belongs to
the debtor and nothing more. The judgment operates as a
charge upon the beneficial interest of the debtor, and only
attaches upon what is at the time it is entered up or afterwards
becomes his property. The creditor takes the property subject
to every incumbrance to which it was subject in the hands of
the debtor. If the debtor has a legal estate, subject to an
equity, the judgment will be a charge upon the estate, subject
to the same equity. In the case of an equitable estate, it will
be a charge upon the equitable estate. A judgment creditor
does not by giving notice or taking out a stop-order acquire
priority over a prior mortgagee or assignee who has not done
so (*q*). A judgment creditor, accordingly, will be restrained

(*n*) See *Re* Isle of Wight Ferry Co., 34 L. J. Ch. 194; *Re* Hull and Hornsea Railway Co., 35 L. J. Ch. 838.
(*o*) Thornton *v.* Finch, 4 Giff. 515.
(*p*) Mitf. Plead. 101.
(*q*) Whitworth *v.* Gaugain, 3 Ha. 425, 1 Ph. 735; Brearcliff *v.* Dorring-ton, 4 De G. & S. 124; Abbott *v.* Strat-ten, 3 J. & L. 603; Anderson *v.* Kems-head, 16 Beav. 339; Scott *v.* Hastings, 4 K. & J. 633; Kinderley *v.* Jervis, 22 Beav. 1. See Seymour *v.* Lucas, 1 Dr. & Sm. 177; Wickham *v.* New Bruns-wick, &c., Railway Co., 1 L. R. P. C. 64.

from executing his judgment against an equitable mortgagee by deposit, although he had not notice of the mortgage at the time he obtained his judgment (r).

8. As between debenture holders of a railway company and judgment creditors, a debenture holder cannot obtain an injunction * to restrain a judgment creditor from suing ＊581 out an *elegit* (s). He may obtain the appointment of a receiver of the tolls of the railway, but he has no charge on the land, estate, and effects of the company. His security is only a charge on the tolls of the undertaking as a living and going concern (t). The right of the receiver to the rates and tolls is paramount to the claims of a judgment creditor under an *elegit*. But the latter has a right to have such possession of the land as may avail him subject to the right and interest of the receiver and collector of rates, tolls, and dues, and to the provisions of the act of Parliament as to the user of the undertaking for the public (u). He may, under his *elegit*, take the rolling stock and chattels of the company (x), but he will be restrained by injunction from taking up the rails or the fixtures (y).

9. The garnishee clauses of the Common Law Procedure Act, 1854, do not give a right of coming into equity in respect of an equitable charge when the debt was not in existence at the time when the order on which the proceeding is founded was made by the common law judge (z).

10. After notice of the filing and registration of a trust deed for creditors, or an inspectorship, or composition deed under the Bankruptcy Act, 1861 (a), or after a winding-up order, &c., &c. (b), a judgment creditor may not proceed to execution without leave of the court.

11. By 13 Eliz. c. 20, a beneficed clergyman is prohibited and disabled from charging or contracting to charge the fruits of his living, or any part of them, even as against himself.

(r) Whitworth v. Gaugain, 3 Ha. 425, 1 Ph. 735.
(s) Russell v. East Anglian Railway Co., 3 Mac. & G. 104.
(t) Gardner v. London, Chatham, and Dover Railway Co., 2 L. R. Ch. Ap. 201.
(u) Potts v. Warwick and Birmingham Canal Co., Kay, 142.

(x) See Gardner v. London, Chatham, and Dover Railway Co., 2 L. R. Ch. Ap. 201.
(y) Legg v. Mathieson, 2 Giff. 71.
(z) Clark v. Perry, 1 Jur. N. S. 992.
(a) *Supra*, p. 107.
(b) *Supra*, p. 106.

The disabilities imposed by the Statute of Elizabeth are not removed by 1 & 2 Vict. c. 110. The judgment creditor of a beneficed clergyman is not entitled to the appointment of a receiver, and an injunction to restrain another judgment creditor subsequent to him in date, who has sued out a writ of *sequestrari facias* upon his judgment, from proceeding *582 to execution on his sequestration (c). *In White *v.* Bishop of Peterborough (d), where a third incumbrancer on a rectory had obtained a sequestration, a receiver was appointed at the instance of the second incumbrancer, and an injunction granted to restrain the party in possession under the sequestration from collecting the rents and profits of the rectory; but the incumbrance in this case had been created during the years 1803 and 1817, a period during which the Statute of Elizabeth was not put in force (e).

(c) Bates *v.* Brothers, 2 Sm. & G. 522; Hawkins *v.* Gathercole, 6 D. M. & G.

(d) 3 Sw. 109.
(e) See Bates *v.* Brothers, 2 Sm. & G. 522.

*CHAPTER XXVI.   *583

INJUNCTIONS IN MATTERS OF BANKRUPTCY.

1. Where bankruptcy statutes are silent, application must be made to court of equity.
2. Injunctions granted in aid of court of bankruptcy.
3. Division of jurisdiction in bankruptcy matters.
4–7. Injunctions by court of bankruptcy.
8. Injunctions against proceedings in bankruptcy.
9 & 10. When court of chancery will restrain sale of bankrupt's property.
11. Injunction against assignees.

1. THE court of bankruptcy has to a certain extent an equitable as well as a legal jurisdiction (*a*). But the equitable jurisdiction of the court of bankruptcy has always been a matter of uncertainty, so far as it is not expressed in the statutes relating to bankruptcy (*b*). In matters, therefore, connected with bankruptcy, where the bankrupt statutes are silent, application for injunctions should be made to the court of chancery (*c*). The application to the court of chancery must be made by bill and motion in the ordinary way.

2. If an equitable case be made out, the court of chancery will interfere in aid of the court of bankruptcy; but in the absence of equitable circumstances to found its jurisdiction, a court of equity as distinguished from the chancellor sitting in bankruptcy, will not interfere in aid of the bankruptcy jurisdiction (*d*).

3. What shall be deemed the bankrupt's estate is often a question in which the aid of courts of other jurisdiction than those in bankruptcy is required. It is in, many cases impossible to arrive at any safe conclusion upon the question of debt or no debt by any other means than a bill in equity.

(*a*) *Ex parte* Stephens, 11 Ves. 27 ; *Ex parte* Hanson, 12 Ves. 347 ; *Ex parte* Dewdney, 15 Ves. 496 ; *Ex parte* Roffey, 19 Ves. 469; *Ex parte* Hilton, 1 J. & W. 470; *Ex parte* Van Sandau, 1 Ph. 445.

(*b*) *Ex parte* Boucer, Fonb. 158.
(*c*) Pennell *v.* Roy, 3 D. M. & G. 135.
(*d*) Pennell *v.* Roy, 3 D. M. & G. 137.

What, too, is joint or separate estate, whether or not specific property is part of the bankrupt's estate, or whether the assignees are about to give to one class of creditors property which belongs to another, or whether the creditors are not entitled to proceed in equity to prove that they are creditors upon the estate, are questions that must often be
* 584   * decided by other courts (e). When, accordingly, an action at law was brought by assignees in bankruptcy against parties who claimed an equitable lien by deposit of deeds on a lease forming part of the bankrupt's estate, the court restrained the action (f). But as soon as it has been determined what is the bankrupt's estate, the whole administration of it falls under the jurisdiction of the court of bankruptcy. A court of equity has no jurisdiction to interfere in the mere distribution of the estate of a bankrupt, either on the ground of trust or otherwise (g). The court, accordingly, would not interfere at the suit of persons who claimed to be admitted as creditors in respect of a breach of trust which was the subject of a suit in equity to restrain the assignees in bankruptcy from paying any dividend which might be declared until the cause in equity was heard, without reserving a sufficient dividend to secure plaintiff's demand (h).

4. Where a party after the proof of a debt brought an action for the same debt, the court of review had jurisdiction to grant an injunction restraining the action (i); but in *Ex parte* Boucer (j) the court of bankruptcy refused to restrain a creditor who had proved from proceeding at law for the same debt. In such a case there can be no doubt that a court of equity would interfere (k).

5. Injunctions were granted by the court of review to restrain assignees from proceeding in an action, where there was a good legal defence to the action (l), or where they had not

(e) Thompson v. Derham, 1 Ha. 373.
(f) Meux v. Smith, 1 M. D. & D. 396, 2 M. D. & D. 789.
(g) Thompson v. Derham, 1 Ha. 358; Halford v. Gillow, 13 Sim. 44. Comp. Cook v. Sturgis, 3 D. & J. 506, 4 Jur. N. S. 1070. Comp. Atkinson v. Plummer, Eden on Inj. 298.
(h) Thompson v. Derham, 1 Ha. 358.

(i) Ex parte Diack, 2 Mont. & A. 675; Ex parte Flower, De Gex, 503.
(j) Fonb. 157.
(k) See 12 Ves. 346.
(l) Ex parte Pearce, 2 M. D. & D. 142; Ex parte Clegg, 3 Dea. & Ch. 505. But see Bankruptcy Consolidation Act, 1849.

an equitable as well as a legal right (*m*). The court of bankruptcy has, perhaps, still jurisdiction to restrain the assignees from suing on a legal title where the assertion of the title would * be against conscience, but there can be *585 no doubt that a court of equity would in such a case interfere.

6. It seems to be doubtful whether the court of review had jurisdiction to restrain a party whom it had committed for contempt from suing the party who obtained the order for commitment in an action for false imprisonment (*n*).

7. Injunctions have been granted by the court of bankruptcy to restrain vexatious litigation (*o*), to prevent the improper or improvident sale or disposition of the bankrupt's property (*p*), and to restrain the advertisement of bankruptcy in the Gazette (*q*).

8. The court of chancery will not in general interfere with proceedings in the court of bankruptcy, for that court has, to a certain extent, an equitable jurisdiction, and is therefore capable of doing justice between the parties in matters of equity. But the court will interfere if a special case for its interference be made out (*r*).

9. The court of chancery will, on a proper case being made out, restrain by injunction a sale of the bankrupt's property (*s*). Assignees under a separate bankruptcy are entitled to deal with the joint property as the solvent partner might himself have dealt with it. Under special circumstances, however, an injunction may be applied for by the solvent partner against the sale of the property by the assignees on his offering to account (*t*). But the application will, it is apprehended, be only granted where a sacrifice is about to be made of the property ; or there is some irregularity in the sale ; or where the

(*m*) *Ex parte* Booth, 4 Dea. & Ch. 211.
(*n*) *Ex parte* Van Sandau, 1 Ph. 448.
(*o*) Flower *v.* Herbert, 2 Ves. 326 ; *Ex parte* White, 4 Dea. & Ch. 279 ; *Ex parte* Davy, *ib.* 322 ; Thorpe *v.* Goodall, 17 Ves. 393 ; *Ex parte* Grant, Buck. 90 ; *Re* Delahoyd, 11 Ir. Ch. 404. See Kirkpatrick *v.* Dennett, 1 Sim. & St. 408.
(*p*) *Ex parte* Figes, 1 Gl. & Ja. 122. See *Ex parte* Montgomery, *ib.* 339 ; *Re*

Atkinson, 1 Mont. D. & D. 238. Comp. *Re* Walsh, 9 Ir. Ch. 16 ; Pike *v.* Martin, 7 Jur. N. S. 251.
(*q*) *Ex parte* Fletcher, 1 V. & B. 350 ; *Ex parte* Lavender, 1 Mont. & A. 699 ; *Ex parte* Wood, 4 Jur. 251 ; *Ex parte* Bowers, 1 D. M. & G. 468.
(*r*) *Supra*, p. 153.
(*s*) Allen *v.* Kilbre, 4 Madd. 464. Comp. *Re* Walsh, 9 Ir. Ch. 16 ; Pike *v.* Martin, 7 Jur. N. S. 251.
(*t*) Allen *v.* Kilbre, 4 Madd. 464.

solvent partner engages to pay over to the assignees the value of the shares of the bankrupt partner in the property offered for sale (*u*).

* 586   10. * The order by the court of bankruptcy for sale of goods as in the reputed ownership of a bankrupt is *ex parte*, and cannot be discharged upon appeal. The court of chancery has jurisdiction notwithstanding such order to restrain a sale and determine the rights of parties (*x*). An application by the true owner to the court of bankruptcy to stay proceedings is not a bar to a bill for an injunction to stay a sale (*y*).

11. Assignees in bankruptcy will be restrained at the suit of a judgment creditor whose judgment was entered up previously to the bankruptcy from parting with moneys paid into a bank in the names of the bankrupt and the assignees (*z*).

(*u*) Deac. Bank, 817.
(*x*) Mather *v.* Lay, 2 J. & H. 374.
(*y*) *Ib.*
(*z*) Robinson *v.* Hedger, 13 Jur. 846.

* CHAPTER XXVII.   * 587

INJUNCTIONS TO RESTRAIN SETTING UP TERMS OR OTHER IMPEDI-
MENTS TO THE FAIR TRIAL OF A RIGHT.

1. Cases in which the court have prevented the setting up of impediments to a trial at
law, against conscience.
2. But interference of the court depends on what is called good conscience.
3 & 4. Pleading and parties.
5. Injunction not granted on motion.

1. COURTS of equity in many cases act as auxiliary to the
administration of justice in other courts by removing impediments to the fair decision of a question, and preventing a man
who possesses an advantage at law from using it against conscience as an impediment to the fair trial of the right. Thus,
if an ejectment is brought to try a right to land in a court of
common law, a court of equity will restrain the party in possession from setting up any title (as, for instance, a term of
years or other interest in a trustee, lessee, or mortgagee) which
may prevent the fair trial of the right (a). So, also, where a
landlord against whom ejectment had been brought had by
negligence suffered judgment to go by default, and the tenant
had thereupon attorned to the person who had recovered in
ejectment, Lord Eldon, upon bill filed by the landlord, restrained the tenant and the person who had recovered in ejectment from setting up the lease in any ejectment which the
landlord might bring (b). So, also, the court restrained a man
from setting up at law a release which was impeachable on
equitable grounds as an impediment to the plaintiff's recovering a fair compensation for injuries which he had received (c).
So, also, in a case where the Statute of Limitations had

(a) Bond v. Hopkins, 1 Sch. & Lef.
430; D'Arcy v. Blake, 2 Sch. & Lef.
387; Strickland v. Strickland, 6 Beav.
81; Blomfield v. Eyre, 8 Beav. 250;
Thornton v. Court, 3 D. M. & G. 293;
Quin v. Ratcliff, 6 Jur. N. S. 1327.

(b) Baker v. Mellish, 10 Ves. 544.
See Griffith v. Edwards, 2 Jur. N. S.
584.
(c) Stewart v. Great Western Railway Co., 2 D. J. & S. 319.

taken effect between the filing of the bill and the decree, the court restrained a man from insisting on the benefit of it at law (*d*). So, also, a man was restrained from setting
* 588 * up in bar to an action of ejectment a non-claim on a fine which had been levied pending a suit in equity (*e*). So, also, the court will remove out of the way any impediment which may exist to the exercise by judgment creditors of their legal rights (*f*).

2. But this species of relief will not be granted in every case. The question as to whether the court will interfere to take from one man in favor of another that which would be a good defence at law depends on what is called good conscience (*g*). If the parties stand on equal equities, the court will not prevent the party in possession of a legal advantage from making use of it to defend his title (*h*). A purchaser, for instance, for valuable consideration without notice will not be deprived by a court of equity of any advantage at law which he may have fairly obtained for his protection. If there be several incumbrancers or purchasers, each claiming in equity by a good title without notice, and one who is later in time succeeds in obtaining an outstanding legal estate not held upon express trusts, or a judgment, or other legal advantage, the possession of which may be a protection to himself or an embarrassment to other claimants, he will not be deprived of this advantage by a court of equity (*i*). A man may, moreover, by acquiescence, raise such difficulties as to prevent the court from interfering to remove temporary bars (*k*). Nor will the court interpose without being satisfied that the party claiming its assistance has a better substantial legal right. In Fraund *v.* Turner (*l*)

(*d*) Sirdefield *v.* Price, 2 Y. & J. 73. See Pulteney *v.* Warren, 6 Ves. 73 ; Brown *v.* Newall, 2 M. & C. 558, 573.

(*e*) Pincke *v.* Thornycroft, 4 Bro. P. C. 92. See O'Donel *v.* Brown, 1 Ba. & Be. 262.

(*f*) Smith *v.* Hurst, 10 Ha. 30, *per* Turner, L. J.

(*g*) Bond *v.* Hopkins, 1 Sch. & Lef. 413, 430 ; Hovenden *v.* Annesley, 2 Sch. & Lef. 607 ; Blennerhasset *v.* Day, 2 Ba. & Be. 137. See Archbold *v.* Scully, 9 H. L. 387.

(*h*) *Ib.*; Maundrell *v.* Maundrell, 10 Ves. 246 ; Golebourn *v.* Alcock, 2 Sim.
552. See Brackenbury *v.* Brackenbury, 2 J. & W. 391.

(*i*) Bassett *v.* Nosworthy, Finch. 102 ; Jerrard *v.* Saunders, 2 Ves. Jr. 457 ; Maundrell *v.* Maundrell, 7 Ves. 567 ; S. C. 10 Ves. 246 ; Golebourn *v.* Alcock, 2 Sim. 552 ; Philipps *v.* Philipps, 8 Jur. N. S. 145 ; Eyre *v.* Burmester, 10 H. L. 90, 103. See Saunders *v.* Dehew, 2 Vern. 271 ; *Ex parte* Knott, 11 Ves. 609 ; Carter *v.* Carter, 3 K. & J. 618.

(*k*) Blennerhasset *v.* Day, 2 Ba. & Be. 137

(*l*) Fitz. 105.

it was said that in the case of voluntary instruments equity will not * take away any defence which a party may have at law, but that in the case of instruments founded on valuable consideration a man will be restrained from making use at law of an advantage which he cannot in conscience set up.

   * 589

3. A man who seeks the interference of a court of equity to restrain a man from setting up at law an instrument which is impeachable on equitable grounds is not bound, as the price of its interference, to bring the whole matter into equity (*m*).

4. A bill to prevent the setting up of an outstanding term or estate should allege that there is such a term or estate, and should state what sort of a term or estate it is. The mere allegation that the defendant threatens to set up some outstanding term or other legal estate will not do (*n*). But an allegation that there are some outstanding terms which, if set up by way of defence, would defeat the ejectment, and that the defendant threatens to set up those terms, is sufficient (*o*). The person in whom the term is vested is not a necessary party to a suit praying that defendant at law may be restrained from setting it up (*p*).

5. An injunction to restrain the setting up of outstanding terms will not be granted on a motion prior to a decree or decretal order, except by consent, as the principle of such a bill is that the court directs the mode of proceeding at law under the decree, and that in general till the decree the court must suppose the parties to be litigating upon questionable rights (*q*).

(*m*) Stewart *v.* Great Western Railway Co., 2 D. J. & S. 319.

(*n*) Jones *v.* Jones, 3 Mer. 161 ; Wingate *v.* Roberts, 2 L. J. Ch. 164 ; Stansbury *v.* Arkwright, 6 Sim. 481 ; Rumbold *v.* Forteath, 3 K. & J. 44.

(*o*) Baker *v.* Harwood, 7 Sim. 373 ; Neale *v.* Postlethwaite, 6 L. J. Ch. N. S. 293. See, also, Houghton *v.* Reynolds, 2 Ha. 265.

(*p*) Brookes *v.* Burt, 1 Beav. 106.

(*q*) Hylton *v.* Morgan, 6 Ves. 293 ; Byrne *v.* Byrne, 2 Sch. & Lef. 537 ; Barney *v.* Luckett, 1 Sim. & St. 419 ; Northey *v.* Pearce, *ib.* 420. But comp. Ringer *v.* Blake, 3 Y. & C. 593.

* 590   * CHAPTER XXVIII.

INJUNCTIONS TO STAY WRONGFUL ACTS OF A SPECIAL NATURE.

1. (1) THE court of chancery will, upon a proper case being made out, restrain an improper transfer of stock. Thus the

[612]

wife of a bankrupt having an absolute power of appointment over stock standing in the English funds died abroad, having disposed by will of those funds to her sister who resided abroad, and became her administratrix. The husband being at the time in insolvent circumstances had before the death of the wife sold property in this country, remitted the proceeds to France, and invested them in the wife's name. These funds had, on the death of the wife, come into the hands of the administratrix, and could not be reached. Under these circumstances the assignees of the bankrupt obtained an injunction to restrain the transfer of the stock standing in the English funds (a). So, also, an injunction was granted to restrain the transfer of stock standing in the name of a steward, there being evidence to show that it was in a great measure the produce of his master's property (b). In Barry v. Donnellan (c), the trustee of a debtor who was out of the jurisdiction, and had been outlawed, was restrained at the suit of a creditor who was taking steps to clothe himself with a legal grant from the Crown from selling the stock, until the plaintiff had obtained the grant (d). When a transfer is about to be made of stock to wrong persons through mistake, the court will not grant an injunction *ex parte* against the defendant * to restrain * 591 the transfer, unless the plaintiff swears that he believes the defendant will avail himself of the error, and refuse to make a re-transfer (e).

2. An injunction may be had to restrain the Bank of England from permitting the transfer of stock or paying dividends (f). The bank may be made parties (g), but it is not necessary to make them so (h). The application may be made upon notice, or *ex parte* on affidavit verifying the urgency of the case (i). The filing of the bill, with service of notice of

<hr />

(a) Stead v. Clay, 4 Russ. 550. See Glasse v. Marshall, 15 Sim. 71.

(b) Lord Chedworth v. Edwards, 8 Ves. 46. See Pennell v. Deffell, 4 D. M. & G. 390.

(c) 1 Hog. 339.

(d) See Goldsmith v. Russell, 5 D. M. & G. 547.

(e) Arkwright v. Gryles, 13 L. J. Ch. N. S. 303.

(f) Ross v. Sherer, 5 Madd. 458, 6 Madd. 1; *Ex parte* Hertford, 1 Ph. 129, 203.

(g) Temple v. Bank of England, 6 Ves. 770; but see Edridge v. Edridge, 3 Madd. 386; Hammond v. Neame, 1 Sw. 38.

(h) 39 & 40 Geo. 3, c. 36.

(i) Hammond v. Maundrell, 6 Ves. 772 a, n.; Doolittle v. Walton, 2 Dick. 442.

motion, upon the bank operates itself as an injunction against the bank; but if, after giving notice to the bank, the plaintiff does not apply for an injunction, or take further proceedings, the defendant may obtain an order that the bank permit the transfer on a given day, unless in the mean time an injunction shall be granted (*k*).

3. By 5 Vict. c. 5, s. 4, the court may upon motion or petition of the party interested, without bill filed, restrain the bank or any public company from permitting the transfer of stock in the public funds, or any stock or shares in any public company, standing in any names in their books, or from paying any dividends due or to become due thereon; and the order is to specify the amount of the stock or the particular shares, and the names in which the same may be standing (*l*). A restraining order under the clause operates as an injunction, and is in force until discharged (*m*). The fact that a party has obtained a *distringas* under the 5th section does not prevent him from applying for an injunction under section 4 (*n*). The *distringas* under section 5 will not be indefinitely continued if no bill be filed (*o*).

4. When a transfer of stock in the Bank of England is sought to be restrained, the usual mode is to obtain a *592 *distringas* against * the bank, which will restrain the transfer for eight days after a request for that purpose by or on behalf of the party in whose name the stock is standing (*p*).

5. The East India Company need not be made party to a suit to restrain the transfer of stock or payment of dividends (*q*).

6. The Bank of England is not bound to look beyond the legal title to stock. If it looks beyond the legal title and takes notice of the contents of a will, it must do so throughout. It cannot take notice so far and no farther. The bank cannot,

---

(*k*) Ross *v.* Sherer, 5 Madd. 458, 6 Madd. 1. See, as to form of order, Set. on Decr. 920.

(*l*) See, as to affidavit, *Ex parte* Field, 1 Y. & C. C. C. 1.

(*m*) *Ex parte* Hertford, 1 Ph. 203.

(*n*) *Ib.* 129, 203.

(*o*) S. C. 1 Ha. 584. See Set. on Decr. 921.

(*p*) Consol. Ord. 27, rr. 1–4; Morg. Ch. Ord. 491.

(*q*) 39 & 40 Geo. 3, c. 36, s. 4. See, as to East India Co.'s Bonds, issued under 51 Geo. 3, c. 64, s. 4, Glasse *v.* Marshall, 15 Sim. 71.

therefore, restrain an executor from selling out stock and transferring it into his own name (*r*). When it is doubtful whether a bequest of stock vests in the legatees as a specific bequest, or whether it vests in the executor, and the bank refuses to transfer it to the executors without proof of the death of the legatees, the executors will not be restrained from bringing an action against the bank, for if the executor cannot maintain an action against the bank, the bank does not want the protection of a court of equity; if he can maintain an action, then the true construction of the Act 1 Geo. 1, c. 19, ss. 11 & 12, authorizes or does not prevent the action, and there is no equity (*s*).

7. (2) The court will, on a proper case being made, interfere to prevent a sale. Thus, trustees have been, under the circumstances of the case, restrained from selling until it should have been ascertained what would be most for the benefit and welfare of the *cestuis que trustent* (*t*). So also where a vendor had power to sell, but it was questionable whether the sale was being made properly in pursuance of the power, the sale was stayed (*u*). So also where a foreign vessel was driven into Plymouth by stress of weather, Lord Eldon, at the instance of the supercargo and part-owner, granted an injunction to prevent the master from selling the cargo (*x*). So also where the representatives of a mortgagor had obtained the mortgage deeds * from the mortgagee by fraud, Lord Eldon   * 593 granted an injunction to restrain the defendants from selling or mortgaging the estate (*y*). So also any vexatious alienations during the progress of a suit will be restrained (*z*). Pending an appeal the court will sometimes stay the sale of property directed by the decree to be sold, but if the property consists of personal chattels remaining in the possession of the appellant, he must give ample security for the value (*a*).

(*r*) Bank of England *v.* Parsons, 5 Ves. 669; Franklin *v.* Bank of England, 1 Russ. 575.

(*s*) Bank of England *v.* Lunn, 15 Ves. 569.

(*t*) Wiles *v.* Gresham, 1 Eq. Rep. 348.

(*u*) Hawes *v.* James, 1 Wils. Ch. 2.

(*x*) Delafield *v.* Guanabens, Dan. Ch. Pr. 1507.

(*y*) Wallis *v.* Willis, *ib.*

(*z*) *Per* Lord Eldon, 4 Dow, 440; Curtis *v.* Marquis of Buckingham, 3 V. & B. 168; Turner *v.* Wright, 4 Beav. 40; Powell *v.* Wright, 7 Beav. 444; *supra*, p. 535.

(*a*) Nerot *v.* Burnand, 2 Russ. 56; Jenkins *v.* Herries, Sug. V. & P. 63.

8. Every trust deed for sale is on the implied condition that the trustees will in the execution of the trust pay equal and fair attention to the interest of all parties concerned, and take care to procure an advantageous sale (b). When trustees for sale had not apprised the owner of their intention to sell, and were about to proceed precipitately to a sale, the court restrained the sale (c). If a bill is filed for the execution of a trust, a sale cannot be made without the leave of the court (d). Trustees for sale will not be restrained from selling because they cannot show a good title (e). A trustee for sale may not avoid a fair and unobjectionable contract by entering into a subsequent contract for a higher price. When a vendor sells to A., and then sells to B. with notice, and B. does some act to interfere with A.'s right, the court will restrain B. as well as the vendor (f).

9. The court has no jurisdiction to restrain a mortgagee from selling under his power of sale, provided he keeps within the terms of the power, and no case of fraud can be made out. Unless there be fraud or special contract, a mortgagee will not be restrained from selling (g).

10. When the thing about to be sold is in the nature of a specific chattel, which cannot be the subject of compen-
* 594 sation by damages, * as where the defendant was about to sell diamonds to which the plaintiff claimed title, he was restrained by injunction (h). So also when a chattel necessary for conducting a particular business is in the possession of persons who claim a lien upon it, and threaten an immediate sale, the court has jurisdiction to interfere by injunction and prevent irreparable injury to the debtor by giving him an opportunity of redeeming it (i). A man, however, who has put a fixed price on a specific chattel, cannot be heard to say that damages at law would not be a sufficient remedy (k).

(b) Anon., 6 Madd. 10; Roberts v. Bozon, 3 L. J. Ch. 113.
(c) Anon., 6 Madd. 10.
(d) Walker v. Smallwood, Amb. 676.
(e) Roberts v. Bozon, 3 L. J. Ch. 113.
(f) Goodwin v. Fielding, 4 D. M. & G. 90.
(g) Cockell v. Bacon, 16 Beav. 158; supra, pp. 191–192.

(h) Tonnins v. Prout, 1 Dick. 387. See Fells v. Read, 3 Ves. 70; Lady Arundell v. Phipps, 10 Ves. 140; Ridgway v. Roberts, 4 Ha. 106; Falcke v. Gray, 4 Drew. 651.
(i) North v. Great Northern Railway Co., 2 Giff. 69.
(k) Dowling v. Betjemann, 2 J. & H. 544.

If a fiduciary relation exists between the parties, the right of a man who intrusts goods to another to be protected in the beneficial enjoyment of his property *in specie* is not confined to articles possessing any peculiar or intrinsic value. Whatever the description of the chattels may be, the court will interfere to prevent a sale either by the party intrusted with the goods, or by a person claiming under him through an alleged abuse of power (*l*). An agent, accordingly, was restrained from parting with the possession of furniture and household effects by which the plaintiff's title would be embarrassed (*m*).

11. The court will not, unless a trust can be made out, restrain the sheriff from selling the goods of a man found upon the land of a person against whom execution had issued upon a judgment at law (*n*).

12. Neither will an injunction be granted to restrain a voluntary settlor of freehold, copyhold, or leasehold estate from affecting the settlement by a subsequent sale (*o*).

13. Where a vessel has become unable to proceed on her voyage without repairs, the owners of goods shipped on board the * vessel may obtain the assistance of the * 595 court to restrain the captain from selling the cargo. But before the court will grant such assistance, the plaintiffs must show their title to the goods, and must settle with the captain for what is due to him, and must exonerate the captain from his contract to deliver the goods at the place of destination, and from all liability on the bills of lading (*p*).

14. Where the judicial sale of a mortgaged estate has been effected under the process and judgment of a court of competent jurisdiction in a colony, and no case of fraud is made out, equity has no jurisdiction to interfere by injunction (*q*).

15. (3) If there is danger that a negotiable instrument fraudulently, or improperly, or illegally obtained, or which ought

(*l*) Wood *v*. Rowcliffe, 3 Ha. 306, 2 Ph. 382. See Pooley *v*. Budd, 14 Beav. 34; Pollard *v*. Clayton, 1 K. & J. 462.

(*m*) Wood *v*. Rowcliffe, 3 Ha. 306, 2 Ph. 382.

(*n*) Garstin *v*. Asplin, 1 Madd. 151; Jackson *v*. Stanhope, 15 L. J. Ch. 446.

(*o*) Pulvertoft *v*. Pulvertoft, 18 Ves. 84. Comp. Bill *v*. Cureton, 2 M. & K.

503; *supra*, p. 172. If a case of equitable lien can be shown, the court will restrain the sale of the property until the hearing. Blakeley *v*. Dent, 15 W. R. 663.

(*p*) Rayne *v*. Benedict, 10 L. J. Ch. 297.

(*q*) White *v*. Hall, 12 Ves. 321. Comp. Lord Cranstown *v*. Johnstone, 3 Ves. 182, 5 Ves. 277.

not to be negotiated, will get into the hands of a *bonâ fide* holder without notice, and for valuable consideration to the prejudice of the maker or acceptor, or persons interested in it, the court will interfere to restrain the negotiation, assignment, or indorsement of the instrument, and will order it to be delivered up (*r*).

16. In Bank of England *v.* Anderson (*s*), an injunction was granted at the suit of the bank to restrain a banking company, carrying on the business within the distance of sixty-five miles from London, from accepting a bill of exchange payable at less than six months from the time of giving such acceptance (*t*).

17. (4) The court will, upon a proper case being made out, restrain a man from parting with property and appropriating it to his own use (*u*); from parting with bills of lading (*x*) or moneys (*y*); from parting with documents in his pos-
* 596 session belonging to the * plaintiff, and from preventing the plaintiff and his solicitor from having access to the documents at reasonable times after reasonable notice (*z*); from preventing the delivery of deeds (*a*); from delivering up goods to another (*b*); from paying moneys (*c*); and from receiving (*d*), applying for (*e*), or executing any power of attorney enabling a person to receive moneys (*f*). A debtor who is colluding with the executor will be restrained from paying his debt to him (*g*). So, also, upon bill filed by a creditor against the executors, heir and purchaser of real estate, charged with the payment of debts, an injunction was granted to restrain the

---

(*r*) Smith *v.* Haytwell, Amb. 66, 3 Atk. 566; Patrick *v.* Harrison, 3 Bro. C. C. 476; Lloyd *v.* Gurdon, 2 Sw. 180; Hood *v.* Aston, 1 Russ. 412; ——— *v.* Bozon, 3 L. J. Ch. 57; Sharp *v.* Arbuthnot, 13 Jur. 219; Green *v.* Pledger, 3 Ha. 165; Simons *v.* Cridland, 5 L. T. N. S. 523.

(*s*) 2 Keen, 328.
(*t*) See Bank of England *v.* Booth, *ib.* 466, 7 Cl. & Fin. 509.
(*u*) Malcolm *v.* Scott, 3 Ha. 39; Zulueta *v.* Sieveking, 11 L. T. 449.
(*x*) Lidgett *v.* Williams, 4 Ha. 456; United States *v.* Prioleau, 11 Jur. N. S. 793.
(*y*) Marsh *v.* Peacocke, 9 Jur. N. S. 789.
(*z*) Goodale *v.* Goodale, 16 Sim. 316.
(*a*) Constable *v.* Rogers, 3 L. T. 261.
(*b*) Manlove *v.* Carter, 12 L. T. 169;

United States *v.* Prioleau, 11 Jur. N. S. 792. See, as to stoppage *in transitu*, Goodhart *v.* Lowe, 2 J. & W 349; Meletopulo *v.* Ranking, 6 Jur 1095; Newton *v.* Hubback, 2 W. R. 339; Straker *v.* Ewing, 34 Beav. 147; Schotsman *v.* Lancashire and Yorkshire Railway, 2 L. R. Ch. Ap. 332.

(*c*) Dalmer *v.* Dashwood, 2 Cox, 378; Hawkshaw *v.* Parkins, 2 Sw. 549.
(*d*) Knight *v.* Knight, 4 W. R. 771; Lloyd *v.* Eagle. 28 L. J Ch. 389; Knight *v.* Bulkeley, 27 L. J. Ch. 592.
(*e*) Lloyd *v.* Eagle, 28 L. J. Ch. 389.
(*f*) Knight *v.* Bulkeley, 27 L. J. Ch. 592; Lloyd *v.* Eagle, 28 L. J. Ch. 389.
(*g*) See Benfield *v.* Solomons, 9 Ves. 77; Saxton *v.* Davies, 18 Ves. 72; Lancaster *v.* Evors, 4 Beav. 158; Burrowes *v.* Gore, 6 H. L. 925.

purchaser from paying the purchase-moneys to the heir upon whom the estate had descended (*h*). Upon the same principle it is probable that a purchaser would be restrained from paying the purchase-moneys to a devisee, for the statute of fraudulent devises places the devisee and the heir in the same situation, making them personally responsible after alienation of the estate, and discharging *bonâ fide* purchasers without notice from liability (*i*). In Glasse *v.* Marshall (*k*), the East India Company were restrained from paying over the principal and interest secured upon East India bonds to a person who had wrongfully obtained possession of them, or to any other person than the lawful owner of them.

18. Although the court has no jurisdiction to interfere with the sovereign acts of a foreign government, or to make a decree against a foreign ambassador who does not submit to the jurisdiction (*l*), * an injunction may be had restrain- *597 ing a third party from handing over to a foreign ambassador a fund, the right to which is in dispute (*m*).

19. A husband will, on a proper case being made out, be restrained from transferring property in fraud of the equitable rights of his wife (*n*).

20. (5) The court will, upon a proper case being made out, restrain commissioners from enrolling an award (*o*). So also, it is a well-settled head of equitable jurisdiction to interfere so as to remove the effect of a void instrument, or the registration of an affidavit which appears to create a cloud upon title (*p*).[1]

21. (6) The court will, upon a proper case being made out, restrain a husband from preventing his wife from seeing a person whom she wishes to consult (*q*); from disposing of or

(*h*) Green *v.* Lowes, 3 Bro. C. C. 217.
(*i*) Matthews *v.* Jones, 2 Anst. 506, Sug. V. & P. 656.
(*k*) 15 Sim. 71.
(*l*) *Supra*, p. 3.
(*m*) Gladstone *v.* Musurus Bey, 1 H. & M. 495.
(*n*) Anon., 9 Mod. 43; Roberts *v.* Roberts, 2 Cox, 422; Flight *v.* Cook, 2 Ves. 619; Cadogan *v.* Kennett, Cowp. 432, 436.
(*o*) Foster *v.* Hornsby, 2 Ir. Ch. 426.
(*p*) Davis *v.* Duke of Marlborough, 2 Sw. 157; Hone *v.* O'Flahertie, 9 Ir. Ch. 119, Story, Eq. Jur. 700.
(*q*) Middleton *v.* Middleton, 1 J. & W. 94.
[1] Sullivan *v.* Finnegan, 101 Mass. 447; Clousten *v.* Shearer, 99 Mass. 209; Williams *v.* Fitzhugh, 37 N. Y. 448. For the citation of authorities settling the question that courts of equity have jurisdiction to remove a title or claim which may operate as a cloud upon the title of the owner, and from which an injury to him might reasonably be feared, see Tucker *v.* Kenniston, 47 N. H. 270.

intermeddling with the wife's separate estate (*r*); from assigning, transferring, or in any way disposing of any part of her property which falls under the dominion of the court during the coverture, until a proper settlement should be made on her (*s*), or pending a suit instituted by her in the Divorce Court for declaration of nullity of marriage (*t*). Where personal chattels were bequeathed to a single woman for life for her separate use, without the intervention of a trustee, upon their being seized in execution by a judgment creditor of an after-acquired husband, who was, in fact, at law entitled to such chattels, but in equity only as a trustee for his wife, an injunction was granted to restrain a sale (*u*). But equity will not interpose in prejudice of the legal rights of a husband over his wife's property, if such property can be made available without resorting to a court of equity (*v*).

* 598   22. * The court will not interfere at the suit of a creditor of a wife divorced from her husband, and entitled to alimony under a sentence of the court, to restrain the husband from paying over her alimony to her (*x*).

23. (7) Where it appears that an infant ward is about to make a marriage without the consent of the court, an injunction will be granted not only to restrain the marriage, but also all communication with the infant, and all intercourse, either personal or by letter; and if the guardian is suspected of countenancing the intended marriage, he will be restrained from permitting the marriage or giving his consent without the leave of the court (*y*). If the infant about to contract an improper marriage has no property, or is not a ward of court, his parent may, by settling a small sum of money for his or her benefit, in order to give the court jurisdiction, and filing a bill for the execution of the trusts of the settlement, obtain an injunction to restrain the other party, with whom marriage is

(*r*) Green *v*. Green, 5 Ha. 400, n.
(*s*) Roberts *v*. Roberts, 2 Cox, 422; Ellis *v*. Ellis, 2 Coo. C. C. 234. See Osborne *v*. Morgan, 9 Ha. 432.
(*t*) Sealey *v*. Gaston, 13 W. R. 577. See Caldicott *v*. Baker, *ib*. 449.
(*u*) Newlands *v*. Paynter, 4 M. & C. 408.
(*v*) 1 Roper on Husb. and Wife, 257; Osborne *v*. Morgan, 9 Ha. 432.

(*x*) Vandergucht *v*. De Blaquiere, 8 Sim. 315.
(*y*) Lord Raymond's case, Ca. T. Talb. 58; Smith *v*. Smith, 3 Atk. 307; Beard *v*. Travers, 1 Ves. 313; Roach *v*. Garvan, 1 Dick. 88, 1 Ves. 157; Pearce *v*. Crutchfield, 14 Ves. 206; Warter *v*. York, 19 Ves. 454.

contemplated, from marrying the plaintiff, or having any communication with him or her, as the case may be (z).

24. (8) The court may also, on a proper case being made out, deprive a father in cases of immorality, cruelty, ill treatment, &c., of his legal right to the custody of his children (a). Children will not be removed from their father merely because he is poor, or unable to maintain them (b), or on the ground that it would be most for their welfare and benefit (c). , Mere acts of harshness or severity of a father, such as are injurious to the health of the children, or the fact of a somewhat passionate temper, are not sufficient ground for removing the children from his custody. To warrant the removal of children from the custody of their * father, a case must be made * 599 out either of moral turpitude, or such a degree of cruelty as to render him unfit to have the management of them (d). The fact that a father is living in adultery with a woman is not a sufficient ground to induce the court to deprive him of the custody of his children, where no misconduct on his part is shown with reference to the management and education of the child (e). Parents have in several cases been restrained from taking their children abroad, or interfering in any manner with their education (f). The court will not interfere with the discretion of a foreign guardian who has been appointed by a court of competent jurisdiction (g).

25. (9) Although the court has no jurisdiction to interfere with the public duties of any of the departments of government, it will, on a proper case being made out, restrain a department of government from doing a merely ministerial act. Thus, the lords of the treasury were restrained by injunction from paying over certain moneys to a man, there being a doubt as to

(z) Dawson v. Thompson, 12 L. T. N. S. 178. See Gynn v. Gilbard, 1 Dr. & Sm. 356; Biddle v. Jackson, 26 Beav. 282.

(a) Wilcox v. Drake, 2 Dick. 631; Powel v. Cleaver, 2 Bro. C. C. 499; Whitfield v. Hales, 12 Ves. 492; Shelley v. Westbrooke, Jac. 266, n.; Re England, 1 R. & M. 499; Anon., 2 Sim. N. S. 69.

(b) Re Fynn, 2 De G. & S. 457; Re Curtis, 28 L. J. Ch. 458.

(c) Re Curtis, ib.

(d) Ib.; Blake v. Wallscourt, 7 L. T. 545.

(e) Ball v. Ball, 2 Sim. 35.

(f) Ex parte Warner, 4 Bro. C. C. 101; Creuze v. Hunter, 2 Cox, 242; De Manneville v. De Manneville, 10 Ves. 52. See Biggs v. Terry, 1 M. & C. 675; Campbell v. Mackay, 2 M. & C. 31.

(g) Nugent v. Vetzera, 2 L. R. Eq. 704.

the persons who were really entitled to them (*h*). So, also, it was held that the court had jurisdiction to examine and enforce the equities with which a man receiving moneys under an adjudication by the commissioners for the settlement of French claims might be affected (*i*). So, also, the jurisdiction has been sustained against the secretary for war (*k*).[1]

26. (10) Where a sequestration has been issued by the court of chancery for non-performance of a decree or order, and the defendant refuses to deliver possession to the sequestrator, an injunction will be awarded to cause possession to be delivered up (*l*). The order that an injunction shall
* 600   issue is of course (*m*).   * If the order for delivery of possession be disobeyed, a writ of assistance will be issued to the sheriff to put the sequestrator in possession (*n*). The affidavit in support of an application for a writ of assistance need not show an existing non-compliance with the order to be enforced (*o*).

27. (11) The court has jurisdiction upon a proper case being made out to restrain the sailing of a ship. If the shares in the vessel are ascertained, and the only point in question is whether the majority of the part-owners should take the ship away without giving security to the minority for the value of their shares, the court will not interfere, for the court of admiralty can do justice in the matter (*p*). The fact that a part-owner may be entitled to an account of the part-earnings of the vessel is not a sufficient ground for the interference of the court (*q*). But if the shares are unascertained and their respective amount is a subject of dispute between the parties, the court will entertain jurisdiction on the ground of the defi-

(*h*) Ellis *v.* Grey, 6 Sim. 214. See Rankin *v.* Huskisson, 4 Sim. 13.

(*i*) Hill *v.* Reardon, Jac. 84, 2 Russ. 630.

(*k*) Felkin *v.* Herbert, 30 L. J. Ch. 604; *supra*, p. 348.

(*l*) Bird *v.* Littlehales, 3 Sw. 300, n. See East India Co. *v.* Kynaston, 3 Bligh, 153, 165.

(*m*) Huguenin *v.* Baseley, 15 Ves. 180. See, as to writ of sequestration, Tatham *v.* Parker, 1 Sm. & G. 506.

(*n*) Bird *v.* Littlehales, 3 Sw. 299, n.; Huguenin *v.* Baseley, 15 Ves. 180; Barkley *v.* Barkley, Set. on Decr. 1229,

Consol. Ord. XXIX. r. 5. See Empringham *v.* Short, 3 Ha. 461; East India Co. *v.* Kynaston, 3 Bligh, 153, 165.

(*o*) Webster *v.* Taylor, 18 Jur. 869. See, as to form of writ, Seton on Decr. 1228; as to practice, see Ayck. Ch. Pr. 223; Morgan, Ch. Ord. 497.

(*p*) Castelli *v.* Cook, 7 Ha. 89; Hallaran *v.* Donal, 9 Ir. Eq. 219.

(*q*) Castelli *v.* Cook, 7 Ha. 89.

[1] A state comptroller was restrained from selling a railroad to the prejudice of bond-holders. Darby *v.* Wright, 3 Blatchf. C. C. R. 170.

ciency of the powers of the court of admiralty to ascertain what the shares of the parties are, and will restrain the sailing of the vessel until the share of the party complaining shall be ascertained and security be given for the amount of it (r). So also the court will at the suit of a shipper of goods, the delivery of which is not complete, restrain the vessel from sailing with the goods on board (s). The court will be much disinclined to grant an injunction to restrain a man from taking his ship to any other than a certain port, thereby in effect compelling him to proceed to such port (t). A party who seeks to restrain a vessel from sailing must use due diligence in making the application. Where the application was made the day before she was to sail, and there were no circumstances * shown to account for the delay, the court * 601 would not interfere (u).

28. The owner of a vessel will be restrained from doing any act inconsistent with the charter-party (x).

29. The legal right to receive the freight of a vessel being in the captain, the court will not in the absence of an allegation, and proof that he was about to misapply it, restrain him from receiving it (y).

30. The 17 & 18 Vict. c. 104, s. 65, does not prevent the court from protecting the property in a ship during litigation (z). There are many cases in which the owners of a vessel may be entitled to the assistance of the court; as, for instance, where the ship is under engagements of which the threatened conduct of parties would prevent the fulfilment, or where damages would not be an adequate compensation, and in which justice would not be done except by protecting *in specie* the interests of the owner of the chattel (a).

(r) Haly v. Goodson, 2 Mer. 79; Castelli v. Cook, 7 Ha. 89. See Ridgway v. Roberts, 4 Ha. 106.

(s) Newton v. Hubback, 2 W. R. 339; but see Goodhart v. Lowe, 2 J. & W. 349.

(t) Lidgett v. Williams, 4 Ha. 465.

(u) Christie v. Craig, 2 Mer. 137; Hallaran v. Donal, 9 Ir. Eq. 219.

(x) De Mattos v. Gibson, 4 D. & J. 276; Sevin v. Deslandes, 30 L. J. Ch. 457; Messageries Impériales v. Baines, 11 W. R. 322. See further, *supra*, pp. 526, 527.

(y) Guion v. Trask, 1 D. F. & J. 373.

(z) Orr v. Dickinson, John. 1. See *supra*, pp. 96, 150, as to the Merchant Shipping Acts.

(a) *Per* Wigram, V. C., 4 Ha. 116. See, as to the duty of a mortgagee of a vessel in dealing with it, Marriott v. Anchor Reversionary Co., 3 D. F. & J. 177; see, also, as to injunction to restrain the captain from selling the cargo, *supra*, p. 595.

31. (12) The court has jurisdiction upon a proper case being made out to restrain presentation or induction to an ecclesiastical benefice (*b*). Lord Eldon said incidentally that he should not hesitate to interfere by injunction and appointment of a receiver in a case where it was clear that a party had obtained an estate comprehending an advowson by fraud (*c*). So also, where an advowson is the subject of a mortgage, the court would probably restrain the mortgagee from presenting, upon the same principle that it compels the mortgagee to nominate such person as the mortgagor shall appoint (*d*). In

* 602 Nicholson *v.* * Knapp (*e*), a patron was restrained from presenting, and the bishop of the diocese from instituting, or in the case of a lapse taking place from collating to the living any clerk pending a suit for specific performance. So also an archbishop was restrained from collating by way of lapse to a deanery pending a suit in the ecclesiastical court respecting the presentment by the chapter (*f*). So also upon the principle of preserving property pending litigation, the court will, in a suit to impeach the conveyance of an advowson, restrain the institution of a clerk even as against a defendant claiming to be a purchaser for value without notice (*g*). In a case where the presentation of a living was vested in trustees, but by neglect the number of trustees was not filled up at the time of avoidance, the court would not restrain the heir-at-law of the surviving trustee from presenting (*h*).

32. (13) It is doubtful whether the court has jurisdiction to enjoin against an extent (*i*).

33. (14) The court will, on a proper case being made out, restrain the managing committee of a railway company from acting on an order for payment out to them of a sum deposited by them in the name of the said company in the bank in com-

(*b*) Potter *v.* Chapman, Amb. 98.
(*c*) 16 Ves. 70.
(*d*) Amhurst *v.* Dawling, 2 Vern. 401; Gardiner *v.* Griffith, 2 P. W. 404; Mackenzie *v.* Robinson, 3 Atk. 559; Gubbins *v.* Creed, 2 Sch. & Lef. 214, 218.
(*e*) 9 Sim. 326; *supra*, p. 577.
(*f*) Daly *v.* Archbishop of Dublin, Fl. & K. 263.
(*g*) Greenslade *v.* Dare, 17 Beav. 503. See Wyvill *v.* Bishop of Exeter, 1 Price,

292; Dowling *v.* Maguire, Ll. & G. temp. Plunk. 1.
(*h*) Att.-Gen. *v.* Bishop of Lichfield, 5 Ves. 824. See, as to advowsons vested in trustees, Edenborough *v.* Archbishop of Canterbury, 2 Russ. 93; Att.-Gen. *v.* Cuming, 2 Y. & C. C. C. 139; *supra*, p. 173. See, as to advowsons vested in tenants in common, Johnston *v.* Baber, 25 L. J. Ch. 899.
(*i*) Whitehouse *v.* Partridge, 3 Sw. 376.

pliance with the standing orders of the House of Commons (*k*). The injunction may be granted by a different judge than the one by whom the order was made (*l*).

34. (15) When by the rules of a society a salaried officer is bound to pay moneys received by him by virtue of his office to the treasurer of the society and he retains moneys in discharge of the arrears of his salary alleged by him to be due, the court will restrain him from further acting as such salaried officer (*m*).

35. * (16) An injunction may be had to restrain a man * 603 from opening letters addressed to another (*n*). *Primâ facie* all letters must be taken to be intended for the person to whom they are addressed, but if the person to whom they are addressed is the secretary of a company, the company may open such letters as appear from some other indication than the mere address to be intended for them. Letters not bearing any such indications may not be opened by the company except in the presence of the person to whom they are addressed (*o*).

36. The court has no jurisdiction to restrain the Postmaster-General from delivering letters at a certain address (*p*).

37. (17) A court of law or equity has the power to prohibit the publication of proceedings which are pending in all cases where the interests of justice are likely to be injuriously affected by their publication (*q*). But it is in each case a matter for the discretion of the court whether or not it will interfere. The court will not restrain every report in the columns of a newspaper which may appear to be unfair in any respect (*r*). If however the case is one in which the court feels it ought to interfere, it is no excuse that the publication may have been by defence, and in answer to similar publications by the other side, although it may excuse the party sought to be restrained from the costs of the motion for that purpose (*s*).

(*k*) Goodman *v.* De Beauvoir, 4 Ra. Ca. 381 ; Castendieck *v.* De Burgh, *ib.* 386, 15 L. J. Ch. 425.

(*l*) Castendieck *v.* De Burgh, *ib.*

(*m*) Shaw *v.* Hill, 9 Jur. 821.

(*n*) Scheile *v.* Brakell, 11 W. R. 796 ; Edgington *v.* Edgington, 11 L. T. N. S. 299.

(*o*) Stapleton *v.* Foreign Vineyard Association, 12 W. R. 976.

(*p*) *Ib.*

(*q*) Anon., 2 Ves. 520 ; R. *v.* Clement, 4 B. & Ald. 219 ; Brook *v.* Evans, 29 L. J. Ch. 616 ; Coleman *v.* West Hartlepool Railway Co., 8 W. R. 734.

(*r*) Brook *v.* Evans, 29 L. J. Ch. 616.

(*s*) Coleman *v.* West Hartlepool Railway Co., 8 W. R. 734.

38. (18) There was formerly a practice of granting injunctions to quiet the possession until the hearing. The object of this species of motion was to restrain the party against whom the application was made from taking forcible possession of the premises pending the litigation; or if forcible possession had been taken to avoid it. To obtain this order it was required by analogy to the statutes of forcible entry that the party applying should have had peaceable possession of the premises for
* 604 the space of * three years before the filing of the bill (*t*).

The practice has fallen entirely into disuse in England. There has been no instance of such an injunction since the case of Hughes *v.* Trustees of Modern College (*u*). In that case Lord Hardwicke granted an injunction to restrain the commissioners of a turnpike road from forcibly entering upon garden ground and digging gravel. His lordship treated it as a case of destructive trespass, and expressly said that " there was a remedy at law, but that would be only for the wrong done, and not equal to the remedy in equity." The establishment of the jurisdiction of the court in cases of destructive trespass seems to have been the cause of the disuse into which this practice has fallen (*x*).[1]

(*t*) Hawkes *v.* Champion, Cary, 51; Dowche *v.* Perrott, *ib.* 63; Sapcote *v.* Newport, *ib.* 66.

(*u*) 1 Ves. 187.

(*x*) See further on the subject, Eden on Injunctions, pp. 332–335.

[1] In Texas it is held that a party who has held adverse possession of land for the period prescribed by the statute of limitations, may maintain an action founded on the title thereby acquired to be quieted in the possession and to remove clouds from such title. Moody *v.* Holcomb, 26 Texas, 714. As to injunctions to remove a cloud from a title, see Walker *v.* Peay, 22 Ark. 103; Standish *v.* Dow, 21 Iowa, 363; Butler *v.* Rutledge, 2 Cold. (Tenn.) 4; Stout *v.* Cook, 37 Ill. 283. A city may maintain a suit in equity to quiet its title to land alleged to have been dedicated by the defendant as a public square. Pella *v.* Scholte, 21 Iowa, 463. As to the possession of the complainant necessary in order to maintain a bill to quiet title, see Apperson *v.* Ford, 23 Ark. 746; Low *v.* Staples, 2 Nev. 209. It is proper, if not absolutely necessary, that the defendant should specially plead all matters in confession and avoidance of the complaint. Bunch *v.* Bunch, 26 Ind. 400. Where a widow knowingly permits a purchaser to part with his money for real estate, under the assurance that the land is free from her claim of dower therein, and she accepts and enjoys the use of the whole purchase-money as a bequest under the will of her husband, such acts on her part constitute an *estoppel en pais,* and she will not be permitted to set up a claim to dower in said premises, and she will be enjoined from proceeding to obtain possession of the premises. Wood *v.* Seely, 32 N. Y. 105. It has been held that a grantee can maintain a suit to enjoin the sale of the granted premises on execution against the grantor, because such sale, though invalid, would cloud his title. England *v.* Lewis, 25 Cal. 337.

* CHAPTER XXIX.   * 605

PRACTICE.

SECTION I. — IN WHAT MANNER INJUNCTIONS ARE OBTAINED.

[627]

1. THE writ of injunction issues pursuant to order, and will not in general be granted except upon bill filed (*a*), and except the party against whom it is prayed is a party to the suit (*b*). Thus where a bill was filed by a seller for specific performance, and an injunction was moved for to restrain the purchaser from proceeding at law to recover the deposit from the seller's attorney, to whom it was paid, the motion was refused with costs, the attorney not being a party to the suit (*c*).

2. There are, however, certain exceptions to the general rule. Where, for instance, a decree has been made against an executor for the administration of assets, an injunction may be had on motion in the suit at the application either of the executor, or of the heir, or of a creditor, to restrain another creditor from proceeding at law (*d*). So also after the court is in full possession of a cause, a man will be restrained upon motion in the suit from proceeding at law in respect of the same matter (*e*).

So also a man who has purchased under a decree will * 606 be restrained * from acting contrary to the spirit of the decree, although not a party to the suit (*f*). So also a tenant holding under a receiver will be restrained on motion, though not a party to the suit (*g*). The attorneys, agents, servants, and workmen of a party enjoined may be enjoined although the bill and notice of motion may only ask for an

(*a*) Savory *v.* Dyer, Amb. 70; Wright *v.* Atkyns, 1 V. & B. 313; Wood *v.* Beadell, 3 Sim. 273; Blomfield *v.* Eyre, 8 Beav. 250; Russell *v.* London, Chatham, and Dover Railroad Co., 4 Giff. 404. See *Re* Xeres Wine Co., 14 W. R. 43; Smith and Fleming's case, 1 L. R. Ch. Ap. 538; but see Kingham *v.* Maisey, 2 Sim. 41; Edgcumbe *v.* Carpenter, 1 Beav. 171.

(*b*) Dawson *v.* Princeps, 2 Anst. 521; Iveson *v.* Harris, 7 Ves. 256; Armitstead *v.* Durham, 11 Beav. 556; Lord Norbury *v.* Alleyne, 1 Dr. & Wal. 337; Lund *v.* Blanshard, 4 Ha. 290; Hodson *v.* Coppard, 29 Beav. 4. Comp. Hammond *v.* Maundrell, 6 Ves, 772 a, n.; Cholmondeley *v.* Clinton, 19 Ves. 261.

(*c*) Brown *v.* Frost, Sug. V. & P. 229, n.

(*d*) Carron Iron Co. *v.* Maclaren, 5 H. L. 416, 440. See further, *supra*, pp. 108–110, 160.

(*e*) *Supra*, pp. 105, 160.

(*f*) Casamajor *v.* Strode, 1 Sim. & St. 381.

(*g*) Walton *v.* Johnson, 15 Sim. 352. See Att.-Gen. *v.* Duke of Ancaster, Dick. 68; Mogg *v.* Mogg, *ib.* 670; Williams *v.* Morris, 13 Ir. Eq. 149

injunction against the defendant (*h*), but the injunction will nòt be extended to his tenants (*i*).

3. Another case in which an injunction will be granted without bill filed for the express purpose is where a plaintiff is proceeding against the defendant both at law and in equity at the same time and for the same matter. In such a case the defendant may call on him to elect in which court he will proceed, and if he elects to' proceed in equity he is restrained from proceeding at law by the order which directs him to elect (*k*).

4. Another class of cases in which an injunction may be obtained without a bill being filed for that purpose is where an action has been brought against one of the officers of the court for damages for illegal acts done in the execution of its process (*l*).

5. There are also instances where, under special circumstances, an injunction has been granted without bill filed upon the undertaking of the party applying to file a bill immediately (*m*). In a case in Ireland this indulgence was carried to a considerable length. A bill for the specific performance of an agreement had been dismissed with costs, the plaintiff not having been able to make a good title. He then brought an action upon the agreement, and upon a motion made by the defendant to restrain him from proceeding at law, Lord Manners granted * an injunction upon the defendant's   * 607 undertaking to file a bill forthwith (*n*).

6. It is also necessary that an injunction should be specifically prayed by the bill. If the bill does not pray for an injunction, the plaintiff cannot move for one under the prayer for general relief (*o*). But leave will be given to amend by adding a prayer for an injunction (*p*). At the hearing, however, an in-

---

(*h*) Freeman *v.* Burke, 7 Ir. Eq. 282; Humphreys *v.* Roberts, Set. on Decr. 869; Hodson *v.* Coppard, 29 Beav. 4; *infra*, p. 624.

(*i*) Hodson *v.* Coppard, *ib.*; but see Att.-Gen. *v.* Duke of Ancaster, Dick. 68.

(*k*) Consol. Ord. XLII. rr. 5–7. See further, *supra*, p. 103.

(*l*) Frowd *v.* Laurence, 1 J. & W. 655; Walker *v.* Micklethwait, 1 Dr. & Sm. 149. See *Re* Weaver, 2 M. & C. 441.

(*m*) Acherley *v.* Vernon, cit. 2 Eq. Ab. 527; Duke of Buckingham *v.* Duchess of Buckingham, 2 Eq. Ab. 527, Eden on Inj. 47.

(*n*) Macnamara *v.* Arthur, 2 B. & B. 349, Mitf. Plead. 55, n.; but see Russell *v.* London, Chatham, and Dover Railway Co., 4 Giff. 404.

(*o*) Savory *v.* Dyer, Amb. 70; Wright' *v.* Atkyns, 1 V. & B. 314.

(*p*) Jacob *v.* Hall, 12 Ves. 458; Wood *v.* Beadell, 3 Sim. 273.

junction may be granted although not prayed by the bill (*q*). So also after decree parties to the suit, or persons who have come in, or may come in under the decree, will be restrained from violating the spirit of, or taking proceedings that are contrary to the decree, although an injunction be not prayed by the bill (*r*). The court will, also, under similar circumstances, interfere to prevent injury to the property, either by the parties litigant or others. Thus, if after a decree to account, the mortgagor attempts to cut timber, the court will enjoin him, though there was no prayer for an injunction in the bill (*s*).

7. An injunction may be obtained in a suit by bill or information (*t*), or on an administration summons (*u*).

8. Injunctions are generally obtained on motion, but they may be obtained on petition. Several cases are to be found in the books in which injunctions have been obtained on petition (*x*). But inasmuch as the reasons for granting injunctions upon petition without bill filed no longer exist (*y*), the practice has become obsolete.

* 608   9. * An injunction may be applied for at any stage of the proceedings (*z*), and as well in vacation as in term, or whether the court is sitting or not (*a*). It was formerly the rule that a petition should be presented if the court had risen for the long vacation, but this is not in accordance with the present practice.

10. If the application be *ex parte*, the bill must fully and fairly state the case within the knowledge of the plaintiff, so that the court may see that *primâ facie* the thing is fair in the aspect in which it is presented to the court. All the facts must be

(*q*) Reynell *v.* Sprye, 1 D. M. & G. 660. See Blomfield *v.* Eyre, 8 Beav. 250.

(*r*) Paxton *v.* Douglas, 8 Ves. 520; Wright *v.* Atkyns, 1 V. & B. 314; Casamajor *v.* Strode, 1 Sim. & St. 381; Wedderburn *v.* Wedderburn, 2 Beav. 209; Goodman *v.* Kine, 8 Beav. 379; Flight *v.* Chambre, 14 Jur. 123; Grand Junction Canal Co. *v.* Dimes, 17 Sim. 38; Turner *v.* Turner, 19 L. J. Ch. 352.

(*s*) Wright *v.* Atkyns, 1 V. & B. 313.

(*t*) Att.-Gen. *v.* Sheffield Gas Co., 3 D. M. & G. 312.

(*u*) Brooker *v.* Brooker, 3 Sm. & G.

475. See further, *supra*, pp. 108, 109, 110.

(*x*) Smith *v.* Smith, 3 Atk. 304; Smith *v.* Clark, Dick. 455; Nichols *v.* Kearsley, *ib.* 645; Mayor, &c., of London *v.* Bolt, 5 Ves. 129; *Re* Creagh, 1 B. & B. 108; *Re* Weaver, 2 M. & C. 441; Turner *v.* Turner, 19 L. J. Ch. 352.

(*y*) Stead *v.* Glay, 2 Coop. C. C. 173, n.

(*z*) Bacon *v.* Jones, 4 M. & C. 433.

(*a*) Temple *v.* Bank of England, 6 Ves. 770; Lane *v.* Barton, 1 Ph. 363; Hammond *v.* Smith, 15 L. J. Ch. 40; Chappell *v.* Davidson, 2 K. & J. 125.

brought before the court which are material to be brought forward. There must be no concealment or misrepresentation. All the *res gestæ* must be represented as they actually are (*b*).

11. The bill having been filed, a printed copy properly stamped and indorsed must be served on the defendant (*c*). A written copy of the bill may be filed upon the personal undertaking of the plaintiff or his solicitor to file a printed copy within fourteen days ; and a written copy properly stamped and indorsed may be served on the defendant, and such service has the same effect as the service of a printed copy (*d*). In very pressing cases leave may be had to file an unstamped copy of a written bill (*e*). If a written copy has been filed with a proper stamp, the requisite printed copy may be filed without a stamp (*f*). Leave may be had, upon a proper case being made out, to file a printed copy after the expiration of fourteen days (*g*).

12. Service is effected by serving a copy on the defendant personally, * or by leaving the same with his servant, * 609 or some member of his family, at his dwelling-house or usual place of abode (*h*). If it be made to appear that ordinary service cannot be effected upon the defendant, the court will direct substituted service to be made on his agent or solicitor (*i*). The jurisdiction of the court to order substituted service is discretionary (*k*), and will only be exercised where there is reason to believe that the service will come to the knowledge of the defendant (*l*). A man who applies for an order for substituted service must state what steps have been taken to effect personal service, and that all means to do so have been exhausted. The court is very vigilant in directing

---

(*b*) Att.-Gen. *v.* Mayor, &c., of Liverpool, 1 M. & C. 210 ; Stedman *v.* Webb, 4 M. & C. 346 ; Goodman *v.* De Beauvoir, 4 Ra. Ca. 381, 384 ; Barker *v.* North Staffordshire Railway Co., 5 Ra. Ca. 401 ; Hemphill *v.* M'Kenna, 3 Dr. & War. 183 ; Castelli *v.* Cook, 7 Ha. 89 ; Dalglish *v.* Jarvie, 2 Mac. & G. 231 ; Maclaren *v.* Stainton, 16 Beav. 290.

(*c*) 15 & 16 Vict. c. 86, s. 5.

(*d*) 15 & 16 Vict. c. 86, s. 6. See Dan. Ch. Pr. 361, 362. See, also, Falkland Islands Co. *v.* Lafone, 3 W. R. 561 ; Garland *v.* Riordan, 33 Beav. 448.

(*e*) Kershaw *v.* Kalow, 1 Jur. N. S. 974.

(*f*) Jones *v.* Batten, 2 D. M. & G. 111.

(*g*) Ferrand *v.* Corporation of Bradford, 8 D. M. & G. 93 ; Moss *v.* Syers, 9 Jur. N. S. 1220. See, also, Lord Abingdon *v.* Thornhill, 24 L. J. Ch. 536.

(*h*) Ord. X. r. 1. See Daniel Ch. Pr. 402, 404 ; Morgan Ch. Ord. 389.

(*i*) Sergison *v.* Beavan, 9 Ha. App. 29 ; Hamond *v.* Walker, 3 Jur. N. S. 686 ; Hope *v.* Carnegie, 1 L. R. Eq. 126, Daniel Ch. Pr. 404–408, Morgan Ch. Ord. 390–392.

(*k*) Maclean *v.* Dawson, 4 D. & J. 150.

(*l*) Hope *v.* Hope, 4 D. M. & G. 328.

substituted service, and will never order it unless personal service is impracticable (*m*).

13. Before the name of any person shall be used in a suit as next friend of any infant, married woman, or other party, or as relator in an information, he is required to sign a written authority to the solicitor for that purpose, and such authority shall be filed with the bill or information (*n*). In very pressing cases, however, an order will be granted to file an information without the written authority of the relator (*o*).

14. The bill having been filed, and a copy having been served on the defendant, notice of motion for an injunction should be served on him. The notice may be served on any defendant, who, having been duly served with a copy of the bill, shall not have caused appearance to be entered within the time limited for that purpose (*p*). If the motion concerns only one interested party, he alone should be served. If other parties are interested in the question raised by the motion, they should all be served (*q*). The notice is served either personally on the party or at his dwelling-house, and sometimes substi-

* 610　tuted service * is ordered. The service is ordered to be substituted where it can be made out to the satisfaction of the court that the usual service cannot be effected (*r*). The service is on the solicitor or town agent after the appearance of the party to the suit (*s*).[1]

15. Service of notice of motion upon a defendant before he has appeared is irregular, but special leave may be sometimes obtained to serve a party to the cause before he has appeared (*t*). The leave must be stated in the notice (*u*). Leave given to serve notice of motion before appearance does not also include

---

(*m*) Firth *v.* Bush, 9 Jur. N. S. 481.

(*n*) 15 & 16 Vict. c. 86, s. 11.

(*o*) Att.-Gen. *v.* Murray, 13 W. R. 65.

(*p*) Ord. III. r. 8.

(*q*) See Service *v.* Castaneda, 9 Jur. 367; Moseley *v.* Moseley, 9 W. R. 531.

(*r*) *Supra*, p. 609.

(*s*) Ord. III. r. 5.

(*t*) Hill *v.* Rimmell, 2 M. & C. 641; Jacklin *v.* Wilkins, 6 Beav. 608; Hewitt *v.* Price, 2 Coop. C. C. 168, n.

(*u*) Cooke *v.* ———, 4 L. J. Ch. 141; Hill *v.* Rimmell, 8 Sim. 632; Jacklin *v.* Wilkins, 6 Beav. 608.

[1] And there are many cases where it has been decided that strictly regular service of the injunction is not necessary to enable the injured party to prosecute, in order to be restored to his legal rights, lost by a violation of the injunction. Ramstock *v.* Roth, 18 Wis. 522; Livingston *v.* Swift, 23 How. Pr. R. 1; Hull *v.* Thomas, 3 Edw. Ch. 236; People *v.* Brower, 4 Paige, 405; People *v.* Compton, 1 Duer, 563; People *v.* Sturtevant, 5 Seld. 278.

leave to serve short notice. If that is required it must be expressly ordered (*x*). If defendant file affidavits in answer to a motion for an injunction, he waives the irregularity of giving notice of motion before appearance (*y*).

16. In very pressing cases, where the mischief sought to be restrained is serious, imminent, or irremediable, or where the mere act of giving notice to the defendant of the intention to make the application might be of itself productive of the mischief apprehended by inducing him to accelerate the act, in order that it might be complete before the time for making the application should have arrived, an injunction may be applied for *ex parte* as soon as the bill is filed upon certificate of the bill having been filed, without serving the defendant with a copy of the bill, or notice of motion for an injunction. In cases of less urgency, where the injury, though serious, is not so serious as to require the immediate interference of the court, leave may be had to serve notice of motion, or short notice of motion along with the bill, but not before the bill has been filed (*z*). Leave has been given to serve notice of motion before bill filed on the undertaking that the bill shall be on the file when service is effected (*a*). If leave has been given to serve notice of motion * or short notice of mo- * 611 tion along with the bill, the notice must state that it is served by leave, otherwise the defendant may disregard it (*b*).

17. If, upon an application *ex parte*, the court thinks that the case is not so urgent as to require its immediate interference, it will order notice of the application to be served on the defendant (*c*).

18. If the defendant has appeared, he must, as a general rule, be served (*d*). But in cases of extreme urgency the court may grant an injunction without notice even after appearance (*e*).

(*x*) Hart *v.* Tulk, 6 Ha. 611; Newton *v.* Chorlton, 10 Ha. App. 31.
(*y*) Fitzgerald *v.* Bult, 9 Ha. App. 65.
(*z*) Simmonds *v.* Heaviside, 22 Beav. 412; Chambers *v.* Toynbee, 12 W. R. 1100. See, *contra*, Fosbrook *v.* Woodcock, 12 Jur. 956; Parker *v.* Great Northern Railway Co., 4 De G. & S. 138.
(*a*) Maynard *v.* Fraser, 26 L. T. 88.
(*b*) Moggridge *v.* Thomas, 2 Coop.

C. C. 166; Chambers *v.* Toynbee, 12 W. R. 1100.
(*c*) See Lord Byron *v.* Johnston, 2 Mer. 29.
(*d*) Marasco *v.* Boiton, 2 Ves. 112; Collard *v.* Cooper, 6 Madd. 190; Perry *v.* Weller, 3 Russ. 519; Mansfield *v.* Short, 2 Coop. C. C. 169, n.; Langham *v.* Great Northern Railway Co., 1 De G. & S. 486.
(*e*) Allard *v.* Jones, 15 Ves. 605; Harrison *v.* Cockerell, 3 Mer. 1; Col-

The affidavit in support of the application should state the fact of appearance, otherwise it is irregular (f).

19. A notice of motion must be properly entitled in the cause in which it is made (g), and must express before what judge the motion is intended to be made (h), and should state on whose behalf the motion is to be made. If notice of motion be given in an information, it must be on behalf of the Attorney-General, and not on behalf of the relator (i).

20. The notice of motion must state the day on which the motion is to be made. If notice of motion be served for a day not appropriated for the hearing of motions, and the notice does not purport to be with leave of the court, the defendant may disregard it (k). Unless the court gives special leave to the contrary, there must be at least two clear days between * 612 the * service of a notice of motion and the day named in the notice for hearing the motion; and in the computation of such two clear days, Sundays and other days on which the offices are closed, except Monday and Tuesday in Easter week, are not to be reckoned (l). If a proper case can be made out, leave may be had to serve short notice of motion. The leave must be stated in the notice (m).

21. The notice should state clearly the terms of the order asked for (n). If it is intended to ask for the costs of the application, the notice should so express it, otherwise if the defendant neglects to appear, the costs of the motion cannot be given (o). But where the defendant appears on the motion, costs may be given though not asked for by the notice (p).

22. An *ex parte* application for an injunction may be made at any time according to the urgency of the case. If the motion

lard v. Cooper, 6 Madd. 190; Petley v. Eastern Counties Railway Co., 8 Sim. 483; Acraman v. Bristol Dock Co., 1 R. & M. 321; Bell v. Hull and Selby Railway Co., 1 Ra. Ca. 623; Lewis v. Langham, 2 Coop. C. C. 170, n.; Randall v. Commercial Railway Co., ib. 169, n.

(f) Harrison v. Cockerell, 3 Mer. 1; Randall v. Commercial Railway Co., 8 L. J. Ch. N. S. 252, 2 Coop. C. C. 169, n.; Sutton v. Mumford, ib. 171, n. See Betts v. Barton, 3 Jur. N. S. 154.

(g) Rowlatt v. Cattell, 2 Ha. 186, Dan. Ch. Pr. 1442.

(h) Ord. XXXIII. r. 1. See Dan. Ch. Pr. 1443.

(i) Att.-Gen. v. Wright, 3 Beav. 447.

(k) Hill v. Rimmell, 8 Sim. 632; Lloyd v. Gordon, 2 Coop. C. C. 171, n.

(l) Ord. XXXVII. rr. 11, 12.

(m) Harris v. Lewis, 8 Jur. 1063; Hart v. Tulk, 6 Ha. 611; Newton v. Chorlton, 10 Ha. App. 31; Chambers v. Toynbee, 12 W. R. 1100.

(n) Brown v. Robertson, 2 Ph. 173. See Dan. Ch. Pr. 1443, 1448.

(o) Pratt v. Walker, 19 Beav. 261.

(p) Clark v. Jaques, 11 Beav. 623; Butler v. Gardener, 12 Beav. 525.

be upon notice, it must be made upon one of the days appropriated for the hearing of motions.   Every day in term is, strictly speaking, a motion day ; but it is not the practice of the court to hear motions except on seal days.   If a man desires that a motion should be heard on a day not appropriated to the hearing of motions, he must obtain leave of the court and then give notice to the other party (q).

23. Every application for an injunction, except in an interpleader suit, must be supported by affidavits verifying the material allegations of the bill, so as to show that on the face of the evidence they are well founded (r).   The affidavits should contain no allegation not inserted in the bill.   Facts not founded on allegations in the bill must not be introduced into the affidavits.   Affidavits are to be considered only as evidence of the allegations made in the bill, and cannot be attended to as laying a foundation for equities not otherwise claimed (s).   There *must be no variance between the   * 613 allegations in the bill or the aid thereby sought and the affidavits in support of it (t).[1]

24. The affidavits are usually made by the plaintiff himself (u), but they may be made by any person acquainted with the facts (x).   An affidavit, however, made by the solicitor of the plaintiff, or by any other person than the plaintiff himself, is not sufficient, unless a good reason can be given for its not being made by the plaintiff himself (y).   The affidavits must not be sworn until after the bill has been filed (z).   No matter what the merits may be, an injunction founded on affidavits sworn before the filing of the bill cannot stand (a).

(q) Anon., 4 L. J. Ch. 204 ; Chaffers v. Baker, 2 W. R. 546.

(r) See Magnay v. Mines Royal Co., 3 Drew. 130, 133.

(s) Dawson v. Yates, 1 Beav. 301 ; Burgess v. Horne, 14 L. T. 461.

(t) Wattleworth v. Pitcher, 2 Pri. 189 ; Stocking v. Llewellyn, 3 L. T. 33.

(u) Mollett v. Enequist, 25 Beav. 609.

(x) Kenworthy v. Accunor, 3 Madd. 550 ; Lord Byron v. Johnstone, 2 Mer. 29 ; Hamilton v. Board, 1 N. R. 379.

(y) Lord Byron v. Johnstone, 2 Mer. 29 ; Spalding v. Keely, 7 Sim. 377 ; Scotson v. Gaury, 1 Ha. 99.

(z) Francome v. Francome, 11 Jur. N. S. 123.

(a) Williams v. Davies, 2 Coop. C. C. 172, n.

[1] As to the American practice in reference to affidavits, see Youngblood v. Schamp, 2 McCarter, 42. The usage and practice in Maryland do not require other affidavits than that of the complainant to procure an injunction before answer where the facts are in pais. Myers v. Amey, 21 Md. 302. But an injunction will not be granted on facts stated on information and belief only. Armstrong v. Sanford, 7 Minn. 49. As to giving notice before granting an injunction, see Dinehart v. La Fayette, 19 Wis. 677.

25. An affidavit must be correctly intituled in the cause or matter in which it is made. It is, however, sufficient if it was correctly intituled when it was sworn, although the title of the cause may have been subsequently altered by amendment (*b*).

26. All affidavits are to be taken and expressed in the first person of the deponent (*c*). The affidavit must commence by stating that the party " makes oath and says," for even though the *jurat* express that the party was sworn, it will not be sufficient unless the affidavit also state that the party makes oath (*d*).

27. Every statement in an affidavit must be divided into paragraphs, and every paragraph numbered consecutively and as nearly as may be confined to a distinct portion of the subject (*e*) ; and each statement must show the means of knowledge of the person making such statement (*f*). If the statement is made merely on belief, the deponent must state the grounds of his belief, so as to show that he has some reasonable and proper cause for making the statement, and has not sworn merely to raise an issue. Hearsay evidence, though not
* 614   admissible at the * hearing of a cause, is admissible on interlocutory applications as putting the opposite party to answer it, and if not expressly denied is to be assumed for the purposes of the application to be in accordance with the facts. Hearsay evidence may be introduced as a ground of belief, though it consists of conversations with third persons who may be, but are not produced (*g*).

28. The fact that an affidavit may depart from the common form is a circumstance to excite jealousy, and the court will so regard it, unless a reason is shown for such departure. But if a sufficient reason is shown the affidavit will not be rejected (*h*).

29. The affidavits in support of an *ex parte* injunction should always state the precise time at which the plaintiff, or those

(*b*) Hawes *v.* Bamford, 9 Sim. 653. See further, Daniel Ch. Pr. 826.
(*c*) Ord. XVIII. rr. 1, 2.
(*d*) Philipps *v.* Prentice, 2 Ha. 542 ; *Re* Newton, 2 D. F. & J. 3.
(*e*) 15 & 16 Vict. c. 86, s. 37.
(*f*) Ord. 5th Feb. 1861, r. 23.
(*g*) Bird *v.* Lake, 1 H. & M. 118. See

Scott *v.* Becher, 4 Pri. 346 ; Woodhatch *v.* Freeland, 11 W. R. 398. But see Stamps *v.* Birmingham, Wolverhampton, and Stour Valley Railway Co., 7 Ha. 251, 255.
(*h*) Woodhatch *v.* Freeland, 11 W. R. 398.

acting for him, became aware of the threatened injury (*i*). They must show either that notice to the defendant would be mischievous, or that the mischief is so urgent, that it would be done, if notice were served on the defendant before the injunction could be obtained. If the affidavits fall short of this point, the motion will be ordered to stand over, and notice of it must be served on the defendant (*k*).

30. An affidavit cannot be produced in court or otherwise for the purpose of grounding any order, writ, process, or proceeding thereon, unless duly filed in the office of the clerks of writs and records (*l*). The office copy of the affidavit must be in court at the time of making the motion (*m*). Sometimes, however, in vacation, when the matter has been pressing, the court has taken the affidavits into its own hands and then considered them as filed (*n*).

31. Affidavits cannot be read on the hearing of a motion unless filed before ten o'clock of the day for which the notice was given (*o*). There does not however appear to be any rule that * they must be filed any particular time before * 615 the hearing of the motion (*p*). If the affidavit be such as by the practice of the court admits of no denial, the late time at which it is filed cannot be objected to (*q*). But the court will not allow a party to gain an advantage from filing affidavits at the last moment (*r*). If, on the motion coming on to be heard, a proper case can be made out, the motion will be ordered to stand over to enable the defendant to answer the affidavits (*s*). If the application appears to be a reasonable one, it will be granted on the application of counsel without more (*t*). In cases where the reasonableness of the application is not so clear, the court may require an affidavit that the party applying has a defence but needs further time to answer the affidavits.

(*i*) Calvert *v.* Gray, 2 Coop. C. C. 171, n.
(*k*) Anon., 1 L. J. Ch. 4.
(*l*) Ord. XVIII. r. 5.
(*m*) Jackson *v.* Cassidy, 10 Sim. 326; Elsey *v.* Adams, 4 Giff. 398.
(*n*) Att.-Gen. *v.* Lewis, 8 Beav. 179.
(*o*) Anon., 10 Sim. 50.
(*p*) *Ex parte* Leicester, 6 Ves. 432; Munro *v.* Wivenhoe, &c., Railway Co., 13 W. R. 880.

(*q*) Jones *v.* ——, 8 Ves. 46.
(*r*) Carew *v.* Yates, 1 W. R. 11.
(*s*) *Ib.*; Electric Telegraph Co. *v.* Nott, 11 Jur. 273; Besemeres *v.* Besemeres, Kay, App. 17.
(*t*) Carew *v.* Yates, 1 W. R. 11; Electric Telegraph Co. *v.* Nott, 11 Jur. 273; Besemeres *v.* Besemeres, Kay, App. 17.

32. An affidavit in support of a notice of motion should not be filed prior to the date of the notice of motion, as the opposite party is not bound to search for affidavits filed prior to the date of the notice. If it is intended to use an affidavit previously filed in the cause, notice of such intention should be served on the opposite party (*u*). But if the other party files an affidavit in answer to such affidavit, it is a waiver of any objection on the ground of want of notice (*x*).

33. An affidavit of service of notice of motion is not available unless filed at the latest before the rising of the court on the day on which the application is made (*y*).

34. If the application for an injunction is *ex parté*, the party applying must deliver copies of the affidavits upon which it was granted upon payment of the proper charges, immediately upon the receipt of the usual request and undertaking, or within the time specified in the request as directed by the court (*z*).

35. After the motion is opened no new evidence can be
* 616   offered * except with the leave of the court (*a*). The court may, however, admit affidavits after the case is opened, if a failure of justice is likely to occur by reason of their rejection or if great inconvenience would ensue (*b*). The court may take notice of matters given in evidence in previous proceedings in the cause and may refer to notes made by the court on such occasions (*c*).

36. Upon motion by appeal from an order granting or refusing an injunction, fresh evidence may be adduced in support of or to discharge the injunction (*d*). The rule that no new evidence can be adduced on a motion after it is opened extends to the case of documents which it is proposed to verify *vivâ voce* by the attesting witness (*e*).

(*u*) Clement *v.* Griffith, C. P. C. 470. See Bowdler *v.* Bowdler, 9 L. J. Ch. N. S. 394. Comp. Lister *v.* Leather, 3 Jur. N. S. 433.

(*x*) Blackmore *v.* Glamorganshire Railway Co., 5 Russ. 151.

(*y*) Lord Milltown *v.* Stewart, 8 Sim. 34 ; Marshall *v.* Colehill, 2 Coop. C. C. 172, n.

(*z*) Ord. XXXVI. r. 9.

(*a*) Electric Telegraph Co. *v.* Nott, 11 Jur. 273 ; Smith *v.* Swansea Dock Co., 9 Ha. App. 20 ; Bird *v.* Lake, 1 H. & M. 118.

(*b*) East Lancashire Railway Co. *v.* Hattersley, 8 Ha. 86 ; Anderton *v.* Yates, 15 Jur. 833 ; Munro *v.* Wivenhoe, &c., Railway Co., 13 W. R. 880. See Glover *v.* Daubney, 32 L. J. Ch. 547.

(*c*) Lister *v.* Leather, 3 Jur. N. S. 433.

(*d*) Const *v.* Barr, 2 Russ. 163 ; Pole *v.* Joel, 2 D. & J. 285.

(*e*) Bird *v.* Lake, 1 H. & M. 111.

37. Application for *ex parte* injunctions and writs of *ne exeat regno* must be made at the commencement of the sittings of the court instead of at the rising: such motions take precedence of all other motions (*f*). Where several counsel state that they have respectively pressing motions to make, the court calls on the senior counsel (*g*). Where notice of motion has been given for a certain day, that motion does not thereby obtain precedence on that day (*h*).

38. The amendment of the bill pending notice of motion for an injunction operates as a waiver of the notice (*i*). A fresh notice is necessary on the amended bill (*k*). If the plaintiff desires to amend his bill pending notice of motion, he should apply specially by summons to amend without prejudice to the notice of motion (*l*). Leave may be had to amend even where a general demurrer to the bill was allowed (*m*).

39. * If the sole plaintiff or (if there are more than   * 617 one) all the plaintiffs are resident out of the jurisdiction, any defendant to the bill may before he takes any proceedings in the suit require the plaintiff or plaintiffs to give security for costs (*n*). But a plaintiff resident abroad will not be compelled to give security for costs when the bill is filed by way of defence to an action at law (*o*), though the bill seeks other relief (*p*).

40. If the application for an injunction be made on notice, the parties may proceed on affidavits on both sides (*q*). Formerly affidavits could not except under special circumstances be read against the answer of the defendant (*r*). He was bound to rest his case on the merits confessed in the answer (*s*). But under the new practice in applications for an injunction or to dissolve an injunction, the answer of the defendant is for

(*f*) 1 L. J. Ch. 60.
(*g*) Soltau *v.* De Held, 15 Jur. 1151.
(*h*) Ib.
(*i*) Martin *v.* Fust, 8 Sim. 199; Gouthwaite *v.* Rippon, 1 Beav. 54; Monypenny *v.* ——, 1 W. R. 99.
(*k*) London and Blackwall Railway Co. *v.* Limehouse Board of Works, 3 K. & J. 123.
(*l*) Martin *v.* Fust, 8 Sim. 199; Child *v.* Douglas, Kay, 560.
(*m*) Smith *v.* Dixon, 12 W. R. 934. See Rawlings *v.* Lambert, 1 J. & H. 458.
(*n*) Morg. & Dav. on Costs, 3.

(*o*) Watteeu *v.* Billam, 3 De G. & S. 516.
(*p*) Wilkinson *v.* Lewis, 3 Giff. 394. See Morg. & Dav. on Costs, 12.
(*q*) Magnay *v.* Mines Royal Co., 3 Drew. 130.
(*r*) See Norway *v.* Rowe, 19 Ves. 155; Rock *v.* Matthews, 2 De G. & S. 227, 234; Custance *v.* Cunningham, 13 Beav. 363.
(*s*) Magnay *v.* Mines Royal Co., 3 Drew. 130. See Bentinck *v.* Willink, 2 Ha. 1.

the purpose of evidence on such application to be regarded merely as an affidavit, and affidavits may be received and read in opposition thereto (t).[1]

41. Whether or not the court will grant the application depends on the merits as collected from the affidavits. If a sufficient *primâ facie* case be made out, the court will consider the case sufficiently proved, unless the defendant files an affidavit denying it (u). The affidavit must traverse all the facts on which the plaintiff's equity depends. A mere general denial is not sufficient (x). If the affidavits of the plaintiff and the defendant are altogether conflicting (y), or if the balance of evidence is in favor of the defendant, the motion will be

* 618   dismissed or ordered * to stand over. Either party may require the attendance of any witness before an examiner of the court or before an examiner specially appointed for the purpose, and may examine such witness orally for the purpose of using his evidence upon the motion; and any party having made an affidavit is bound, on being duly required to

---

(t) 15 & 16 Vict. c. 86, s. 59. See Wightman v. Wheelton, 23 Beav. 397.

(u) Potts v. Potts, 3 L. J. Ch. 176; Bell v. Wilson, 34 L. J. Ch. 572.

(x) Pyecroft v. Pyecroft, 2 Sm. & G. 326. See Scott v. Becher, 4 Pri. 346; Denys v. Locock, 3 M. & C. 205; Palin v. Gathercole, 1 Coll. 565.

(y) De Tastet v. Bordenave, Jac. 516; Sanxter v. Foster, Cr. & Ph. 302; M'Curdy v. Noak, 17 L. J. Ch. 165.

[1] Where the allegations of the bill are fully and specifically controverted by the defendant's affidavit, an injunction *pendente lite* will be refused. Gagliardo v. Crippen, 22 Cal. 362. But to dissolve an injunction the denial must be of the same positive character as the averment. Smith v. Appleton, 19 Wis. 468; Horner v. Jobs, 2 Beasley, 19; Brown v. Fuller, 2 Beasley, 271. See, also, Morris Canal, &c., Co. v. Jersey City, 3 Stockton, 13. Where the defendant sets up entirely new matter to avoid the complainant's equity, although it is a good defence and a good answer to the equity, the court will not dissolve the injunction as a general rule. Carson v. Coleman, 3 Stockton, 106; Brewster v. Newark, ib. 114; Morris Canal Co. v. Jersey City, 1 Beasley, 227. See Hargraves v. Jones, 27 Geo.

233. As to the exception to the rule, that upon a denial of the equity the defendant is entitled to a dissolution of an injunction, see Leigh v. Clark, 3 Stockton, 110. Where in such case there is shown a strong probability that the ends of justice will be better answered by its continuance, it will be continued. Furman v. Clark, 3 Stockton, 135. Although the equity of the bill is not answered, if the continuation of the injunction is a material injury to the defendant, and its dissolution is no present injury to the complainant, or cannot prejudice his right, the court may, in its discretion, dissolve the injunction. Bechtel v. Carslake, 3 Stockton, 244. Where the defendant, who has been restrained, denies the equity, but the others most interested in the subject-matter admit all the material allegations, the injunction must stand. Zabriskie v. Vreeland, 1 Beasley, 179. An injunction will not be issued upon facts stated on information and belief only. Bank of Orleans v. Skinner, 9 Paige, 305; Armstrong v. Sanford, 8 Minn. 49. The proper filing of such an answer as would dissolve an injunction, if granted, will prevent one from issuing. Bell v. Purvis, 15 Md. 22.

do so, to attend before an examiner for the purpose of being cross-examined (*z*).

42. But the court has a discretionary power of acting upon such evidence as may be before it at the time of the application, and as may appear necessary to meet the justice of the case (*a*). The court will not allow a motion to stand over in order to allow witnesses to be examined, if it is satisfied that the application is made for the purpose of creating delay (*b*), or that the evidence is sufficient to enable it to deal satisfactorily with the motion (*c*). A witness cannot be cross-examined in open court upon an interlocutory application, but only at the hearing, and in cases in which issue has been joined by filing replication (*d*).

43. The case made out must correspond with the allegations in the bill (*e*). If a man brings prominently forward and relies upon a given case, the court will not allow him, if he should fail in that case, to spell out another and say he might have framed his case so as to show a title to the relief asked (*f*). A man who complains of injury of a peculiar and special kind cannot be allowed to give evidence of another injury of a special and peculiar kind (*g*). An injunction is only granted on a * specific case. The court never grants injunc- * 619 tions on general complaints (*h*). The relief prayed must be consistent with the case made out (*i*), and be such as may be asked for upon the frame of the bill (*k*). An injunction granted on motion must be such as is prayed by the bill.

(*z*) 15 & 16 Vict. c. 86, s. 40; Besemeres *v.* Besemeres, Kay, App. 17; Clarke *v.* Law, 2 K. & J. 28; Lloyd *v.* Whitty, 19 Beav. 57; Nicholls *v.* Ibbetson, 7 W. R. 430; Edwards *v.* Spaight, 2 J. & H. 617; Singer Sewing Machine Manufacturing Co. *v.* Wilson, 2 H. & M. 584; Morg. Ch. Ord. p. 192.

(*a*) 15 & 16 Vict. c. 86, s. 40.

(*b*) Normanville *v.* Stanning, 10 Ha. App. 20.

(*c*) Mayer *v.* Spence, 1 J. & H. 87. But see Wightman *v.* Wheelton, 23 Beav. 397; Braithwaite *v.* Kearns, 34 Beav. 202.

(*d*) Ord. 5th Feb. 1861, rr. 7, 19, 21. See Bodger *v.* Bodger, 11 W. R. 80. Comp. Nichols *v.* Ibbetson, 7 W. R. 430.

(*e*) Butts *v.* Matthews, 5 L. J. Ch. N. S. 134; Burton *v.* Blakemore, 2 Jur. 1062; Hertz *v.* Union Bank of London, 1 Jur. N. S. 127.

(*f*) Whitworth *v.* Gaugain, Cr. & Ph. 325; Castelli *v.* Cook, 7 Ha. 89; Barker *v.* North Staffordshire Railway Co., 2 De G. & S. 55, 5 Ra. Ca. 401. See Pentney *v.* Lynn Paving Commissioners, 13 W. R. 983.

(*g*) Hertz *v.* Union Bank of London, 1 Jur. N. S. 127.

(*h*) Ib.

(*i*) Att.-Gen. *v.* Grocers' Co., 1 Keen, 506; Jones *v.* Latimer, 1 Jur. 980. See Hill *v.* Great Northern Railway Co., 5 D. M. & G. 66.

(*k*) Castelli *v.* Cook, 7 Ha. 89.

It is not competent to the court to grant an injunction in terms not prayed by the bill (*l*).

44. An injunction will not be granted pending a demurrer; but the court will upon application, where the matter is pressing, order the demurrer to be argued immediately (*m*). If the demurrer is overruled the plaintiff may then move for an injunction (*n*). The usual course now is for the demurrer to be brought on and argued with the motion for an injunction (*o*). It does not follow that because a bill for an injunction is not demurrable an injunction will issue. An injunction may be refused in many cases where the facts stated upon the bill would preclude a demurrer (*p*). Though an injunction will not be usually granted pending a demurrer, the pendency of a demurrer does not prevent a plaintiff from serving the defendant with notice of motion, and it would seem that when justice requires it an injunction will be granted pending a demurrer (*q*).

45. Nor will an injunction be granted pending a plea; but an early day will be appointed for the argument (*r*). Nor can a motion be made for an injunction where the bill has been found to contain scandalous matter, until the scandalous matter is expunged (*s*).

46. Instead of issuing the writ of injunction in the first instance the court will often grant an interim order in the nature of an *injunction, by which the defendant is * 620 restrained until after a particular day named, liberty being given to the plaintiff to serve notice of motion for an injunction for the day before such day. The usual practice is to extend the order over the whole of the next motion day, in order that the plaintiff may serve, by leave of the court, the defendant with notice of motion for an injunction for that day. There is, however, no fixed rule on the subject. If it appear that the defendant would be oppressed by extending the order

(*l*) Burdett *v.* Hay, 33 L. J. Ch. 41.
(*m*) Cousins *v.* Smith, 13 Ves. 164; Jones *v.* Taylor, 2 Madd. 181; Const *v.* Harris, T. & R. 510, n.; Anon. *v.* Bridgewater Canal Co., 9 Sim. 378.
(*n*) Rashleigh *v.* Buller, Dick. 153; Franklyn *v.* Thomas, 3 Mer. 225, 234; Claughton *v.* Hadwell, 6 Madd. 299; Farquharson *v.* Pitcher, 2 Russ. 81.

(*o*) Seton, 872.
(*p*) Kay *v.* Marshall, 1 M. & C. 373. See *supra*, p. 213.
(*q*) Wardle *v.* Claxton, 9 Sim. 412.
(*r*) Humphreys *v.* Humphreys, 3 P. W. 395; Anon., 2 Atk. 113.
(*s*) Davenport *v.* Davenport, 6 Madd. 251.

over the whole of the next motion day, the court will either name a day short of that day, giving the plaintiff leave to serve the defendant with notice of motion for an injunction for that day, or will extend the order over the whole of the next motion day, giving the defendant leave to move sooner to discharge the order on notice, with liberty to the plaintiff to move simultaneously for an injunction in the event of the defendant electing to advance the motion (*t*). In many respects there is a convenience in proceeding by interim order instead of granting an injunction. Among other conveniences the defendant is not put to the necessity of coming to the court to discharge the order (*u*). Interim orders are generally granted upon *ex parte* application, but they may be granted where the motion is upon notice, or the pleadings show issues raised which must be discussed at the hearing (*x*). Where the application is *ex parte* it is necessary that the court should be informed of all material facts. The court does not, perhaps, upon an application for an interim order, require the same special mention of all particulars which it requires where the application is for an *ex parte* injunction, but it is the duty of the party who makes the application to bring all material facts before the notice of the court (*y*).

47. Where an interim order has been obtained, and simultaneous applications are made on the part of the plaintiff for an injunction in the terms of the order, and on the part of the defendant to discharge the order, the plaintiff has a right to begin (*z*).

48. The motion, if not brought on the day or during the seal for * which notice has been given, should be * 621 saved. If it be not saved it will be treated as abandoned (*a*). A counsel for the motion on being afterwards instructed cannot subsequently save the motion to the next seal (*b*). But if counsel has been instructed to move on the seal day mentioned in the notice of motion and neglects to do so, the court may not treat the motion as abandoned (*c*). The

(*t*) Fraser *v.* Whalley, 2 H. & M. 10.
(*u*) Fuller *v.* Taylor, 32 L. J. Ch. 376.
(*x*) Coleman *v.* West Hartlepool Railway Co., 3 L. T. N. S. 847
(*y*) Fuller *v.* Taylor, 32 L. J. Ch. 376.
(*z*) Fraser *v.* Whalley, 2 H. & M. 10.

(*a*) Cuthbert *v.* Fane, 1 Jur. 890; Turner *v.* Turner, 15 Jur. 1165; *Re* Banwen Iron Co., 17 Jur. 127.
(*b*) *Re* Smith, 23 Beav. 284.
(*c*) See Wedderburn *v.* Llewellyn, 13 W. R. 939.

motion may be saved at any time before the court rises, although the motions may have been finished (*d*).

49. Upon the motion being made, if counsel does not appear in opposition to the motion, it is granted on affidavit of service (*e*). The office copy of the affidavit must be produced in court on the day the motion is made before the court rises (*f*). * If the affidavit of service is imperfect or irregular the service cannot be subsequently verified, but a new notice of motion must be given (*g*). The order which is made on affidavit of service is in the terms of the notice. An order made on affidavit of service is liable to be discharged if there be any irregularity in the notice (*h*) or affidavit (*i*) on which it is founded, or if it adds to (*k*) or departs from the terms of the notice (*l*).

50. In doubtful cases where damage may be occasioned to the defendant, in the event of an injunction or interim restraining order proving to have been wrongly granted, the court will require the plaintiff, as a condition of its interference in his favor, to enter into an undertaking to abide by any order it may make as to damages. The undertaking was formerly required only in cases where the application was *ex parte*, but the present practice is to require the undertaking as well, where the motion is on notice, as where it is *ex parte* (*m*). If
* 622   the * plaintiff is not within the jurisdiction (*n*), or is a limited company (*o*), the undertaking of some responsible person within the jurisdiction is required. An undertaking as to damages will be required from a married woman in respect of her separate estate (*p*).

51. In cases where the equity of the plaintiff is perfectly clear, or where the damage, if any, which might accrue is of a

---

(*d*) Cass *v.* Bailey, Smith, Ch. Pr. 248, n.
(*e*) Davidson *v.* Leslie, 9 Beav. 104; Angier *v.* May, 3 W. R. 330.
(*f*) Smith, Ch. Pr. 249.
(*g*) Barton *v.* Chambers, 4 Beav. 547; Angier *v.* May, 3 W. R. 330. See Salomon *v.* Stalman, 4 Beav. 243.
(*h*) Moody *v.* Hebberd, 11 Jur. 941.
(*i*) Salomon *v.* Stalman, 4 Beav. 243.
(*k*) Pratt *v.* Walker, 19 Beav. 261; *Ex parte* Carew, 23 L. J. Ch. 761.
(*l*) Hutton *v.* Hepworth, 6 Ha. 315. See Dan. Ch. Pr. 1448.

(*m*) Chappell *v.* Davidson, 8 D. M. & G. 1; Tuck *v.* Silver, John. 218; De Mattos *v.* Gibson, 5 Jur. N. S. 347; Ingram *v.* Stiff, *ib.* 947; Adamson *v.* Wilson, 3 N. R. 368; Wakefield *v.* Duke of Buccleugh, 11 Jur. N. S. 523, Seton, 870; *supra*, p. 212.
(*n*) Hamilton *v.* Board, 1 N. R. 379.
(*o*) Anglo - Danubian, &c., Co. *v.* Rogerson, 10 Jur. N. S. 87.
(*p*) Holden *v.* Waterlow, 15 W. R. 139.

vague and uncertain nature, the undertaking will not be required (q).[1]

52. The undertaking is ordinarily given through counsel, and forms part of the order; but where the order is granted in vacation without the attendance of counsel, the undertaking is inserted in the registrar's book, and signed by the plaintiff or his solicitor (r). If the undertaking is entered into by a man who is a stranger to the cause he is required to sign the registrar's book (s). The court may, however, upon a proper application, allow the undertaking to be sent by post and filed instead of the party signing the registrar's book (t).

53. Security for payment of any damage which may be awarded in pursuance of the undertaking is sometimes required (u).

54. The undertaking remains in force notwithstanding the dismissal of the bill (x).

55. If the question at issue between the parties has reference to the payment of moneys, the court will, generally, as a condition of granting an injunction, require the moneys to be paid into court (y).

56. As, on the one hand, the court may in doubtful cases require the plaintiff to enter into an undertaking as to damages, as the condition of its interference, in his favor; so, on the other *hand, it may require the defendant to *623 enter into terms as a condition of withholding an injunction (z).[2]

57. A motion for an injunction may by consent be turned into a motion for decree, a time being fixed for the plaintiff to file any affidavits he may desire, and also for defendant to file affi-

---

(q) Adamson v. Wilson, 3 N. R. 368.
(r) Seton, 870.
(s) Gurney v. Behrends, 9 Ha. App. 89.
(t) Pacific Steam Navigation Co. v. Gibbs, 14 W. R. 218.
(u) Seton, 864.
(x) Newby v. Harrison, 3 D. F. & J. 290.
(y) Supra, pp. 19, 20, 212.
(z) Supra, pp. 210, 211.
[1] If no order is made that the party seeking the injunction shall pay to the party enjoined such damages as he shall sustain, or no bond required, no damages can be recovered by the party enjoined; and when a bond is required and given, no greater damages can be recovered than the penalty. Sturgis v. Knapp, 33 Vt. 486. And when the damages to the different parties are clearly several, it seems the bond will be held to be several, though its language would indicate a joint obligation. Ib. See, also, Browner v. Davis, 15 Cal. 9; Corner v. Zuntz, 14 La. An. 861.
[2] Ewing v. Filley, 43 Penn. St. 384.

davits in answer, and either party being at liberty after the cause has been set down to expedite the hearing (a). The plaintiff may obtain an enlargement of the time for filing affidavits, but he may not by amendment, after the time for filing affidavits has elapsed, raise a new case (b).

58. In cases where an injunction is granted application may be made by the defendant to have the cause advanced as soon as it is ready for trial; not so where it is refused (c).

59. If the question in the suit is distinctly raised on the motion for the injunction, and is ripe for decision, the order on the motion ought to declare the rights of parties. The terms of the order should be specific, and should define the limits of the right. If the language of the order should be in itself vague, ambiguous, uncertain, or indefinite, giving no clear line of conduct, the order cannot be maintained. The language of the order should be such that it is quite plain what it permits and what it prohibits. An order which merely prohibits a man from doing what he has no authority to do, without showing him what are the limits of his authority, and leaves him to find out what is forbidden and what is allowed, is irregular (d). If, however, as sometimes happens, it is impossible for the court to define exactly the limits of the right, an order which merely amounts to a declaration of right is not irregu-
* 624 lar (e). If the court can only restrain a man * from doing what it thinks not right, it will, where it can point out what ought to be done, state the reasons by which it has come to its conclusion, or the manner in which it appears to the court that what seems an evil may be remedied (f).

60. The orders pronounced by the court upon applications for

(a) Green v. Low, 22 Beav. 395; Wilkinson v. Cummins, 11 Ha. 343; Att.-Gen. v. Charles, 11 W. R. 253; Clarke v. Clark, 13 W. R. 133, Dan. Ch. Pr. 1449.

(b) Clarke v. Clark, 13 W. R. 133. See 15 & 16 Vict. c. 86, ss. 15, 16, Ord. XXXIII. rr. 4–8, Morg. Ch. Ord. pp. 165–168, 514–516.

(c) Maunsell v. Midland Great Western Railway Co. of Ireland, 1 H. & M. 152. See Att.-Gen. v. Charles, 11 W. R. 253.

(d) Earl of Ripon v. Hobart, 3 M. & K. 173; Cother v. Midland Railway Co.,

2 Ph. 472; Dalglish v. Jarvie, 2 Mac. & G. 239; Warden of Dover Harbor v. London, Chatham, and Dover Railway Co., 3 D. F. & J. 559; Bird v. Lake, 1 H. & M. 122; Jay v. Richardson, 30 Beav. 563; Low v. Innes, 10 Jur. N. S. 1037.

(e) Elliott v. North Eastern Railway Co., 10 H. & L. 333; North Eastern Railway Co. v. Crossland, 2 J. & H. 565, 32 L. J. Ch. 353.

(f) Att.-Gen. v. London and South Western Railway Co., 3 De G. & S. 439.

interlocutory injunctions have varied at different times. The form most frequently adopted enjoined the party " till further order " (g). In some cases the injunction has been till " appearance and further order " (h) ; in others till " answer and further order " (i). The form now usually adopted is, " until the hearing of the cause, or until further order " (k). In the case of a bill of discovery, however, the form is " until answer or further order " (l).

61. If the object of the suit is to restrain proceedings in another court, the injunction will be awarded against the defendant, his attorneys and agents. If it is to restrain the commission of an illegal act, such as waste, trespass, nuisance, &c., it is awarded against the defendant, his servants, workmen, and agents ; and these words will be inserted in the order, although the bill and notice of motion only ask for an injunction against the defendant (m).

62. When a plaintiff sues on behalf of himself and others to stay proceedings at law, it seems that an injunction to stay proceedings against the plaintiff only will be granted, and not against the other persons on behalf of whom he sues (n).

63. An order for an injunction having been obtained, it should be drawn up, passed, and entered without delay (o).[1] In cases

(g) Lane v. Newdigate, 10 Ves. 192.
(h) Lord Grey de Wilton v. Saxon, 6 Ves. 106.
(i) Potter v. Chapman, 1 Dick. 146 ; Robinson v. Lord Byron, 1 Bro. C. C. 588; Drewry v. Molins, 6 Ves. 328, Dan. Ch. Pr. 1511.
(k) Seton, 870.
(l) Senior v. Pritchard, 16 Beav. 473 ; Lovell v. Galloway, 17 Beav. 1 ; Ooddeen v. Oakley, 2 D. F. & J. 158.
(m) Seton, 869. See Lord Wellesley v. Earl of Mornington, 11 Beav. 180. See, for form of order, Seton, 867, No. 1.
(n) Armitstead v. Durham, 11 Beav. 556, 561, n.
(o) See Bateman v. Wiatt, 11 Beav. 587.
[1] Where an injunction was ordered in April but not tested till June, and not served till June of the next year, a writ of attachment against the defendant for disobeying the injunction was refused. After such lapse of time the plaintiff should have applied to the court for permission to use it. Mc-

Cormick v. Jerome, 3 Blatchf. C. C. R. 486. An injunction should not be broader than is necessary ; that is, it should not, in enjoining a defendant against doing what he has no right to do, enjoin him in such a way as may possibly prevent his doing that which he may properly do. Marble Company v. Ripley, 10 Wallace, 339. Where a party is in court, and hears an order of injunction pronounced, he is as much bound as if he had been actually served with the writ. Milne v. Van Buskirk, 9 Iowa, 558; and in The People v. Sturtevant, 9 N. Y. 278, Johnson, J., says, in reference to the service of an injunction and the liability of the defendant to punishment for contempt in disobeying it : " In administering the law in respect to the violation of injunctions, the court of chancery never lost sight of the principle that it was the disobedience to the order of the court which constituted the contempt ; and, therefore, although it required of the party availing himself of its order a substantial compliance with the rules

where the matter is so urgent that the object of the
* 625 injunction * might be defeated if the party were bound
to wait till the order could be passed, and the writ
issued upon it, the practice is to serve the party personally
with notice in writing that the injunction has been ordered,
and that it will be sealed and served as soon as it can be
passed through the offices, or else to procure a transcript of
the minutes of the order signed by the registrar, and to serve
the same personally by delivering a copy of it, showing at the
same time the original transcript so signed (p).

64. The writ of injunction is prepared by the solicitor of the
party (q). It must be signed by one of the clerks of records
and writs, and sealed with the seal of that office (r). At the
time the writ is presented for sealing, either a full or an
abridged copy of the writ, written on brief paper, and called
a docket, must be left; and the order awardihg the injunction, or an office copy thereof, must be produced (s). The
writ must be indorsed with the name and place of business
of the plaintiff's solicitor, and of his agent, if any; or with the
name and place of residence of the plaintiff, where he acts in
person; and in either case with the address for service, if
any (t).

65. The service of the injunction or restraining order should
be personal (u), and is effected by leaving with the person served

of practice upon the subject, it would
not usually allow the effect of its orders
to be wholly lost, when the party
sought to be bound by the order had
actual knowledge, or notice of its existence, although there might have occurred some slip in the formal method
of bringing it home to him." Hull v.
Thomas, 3 Edw. Ch. R. 236; People
v. Brower, 4 Paige, 405; and in People
v. Sturtevant, supra, it was held that an
injunction against a corporate body is
binding upon all individuals acting for
the corporation, to whose knowledge
the injunction comes. But a court of
equity will not restrain a municipal
corporation from passing a resolution
or ordinance giving permission to a
railroad corporation to run steam-en-
gines on particular streets or avenues of
the city, unless in a case where it
appears that the mere voting on, and
formal passage of, such resolution or
ordinance, would instantly, without any
action or attempt to enforce any right
or privilege under it, effect an irremediable private injury.

(p) Kimpton v. Eve, 2 V. & B. 349;
Scott v. Becher, 4 Pri. 346; Van Sandau v. Rose, 2 J. & W. 264; Rattray v.
Bishop, 3 Madd. 220; M'Neill v. Garratt, Cr. & Ph. 98; Chuck v. Cremer,
2 Ph. 113; Gooch v. Marshall, 8 W. R.
410, Dan. Ch. Pr. 1513. In country
cases the terms of an injunction are
often communicated as soon as it is
granted by telegraph to an agent, who
prepares therefrom and serves the
formal notice mentioned in the text.
Dan. Ch. Pr. 1513.

(q) Ord. III. 1.
(r) Ord. I. 37, Dan. Ch. Pr. 1513.
(s) Dan. Ch. Pr. 1513.
(t) Ord. III. 2, 5, Dan. Ch. Pr. 1513.
(u) Woodward v. King, 2 Ch. Ca. 203,
2 Dick. 797; Van Sandau v. Rose, 2 J.
& W. 264; Gooch v. Marshall, 8 W. R.
410.

a true copy of the writ or order, and at the same time showing him the original writ as duly issued, or the restraining order as duly passed and entered (x). If it can be satisfactorily made to appear that the defendant is keeping out of the way, substituted service will be ordered (y).

---

*SECTION II. — DISSOLUTION OF INJUNCTION.   * 626

1. Interlocutory injunction may be dissolved at any time before hearing of the cause.
2. Practice where interim order has been obtained.
3. Plaintiff cannot on motion to dissolve make a new case.
4. Dissolution must generally be on motion in open court.
5. Practice in case of *ex parte* injunctions.
6. Motion to dissolve should be made before the court granting the injunction.
7. Evidence on motion to dissolve.
8 & 9. Misrepresentation sufficient ground for dissolving *ex parte* injunction.
10. Plaintiff may make another application.
11. Practice on dissolution of injunctions to stay proceedings at law until discovery.
12. Motion to dissolve pending application for production of documents refused.
13–16. Who shall move to dissolve.
17. Where order for injunction is irregular, motion should be made to discharge the order.
18. Irregularity of injunction may be waived.
19. After long acquiescence, application for dissolution not readily entertained.
20. Delay may deprive one of right to dissolution.

1. An interlocutory injunction may be dissolved at any time before the hearing of the cause. If the allegations which constitute the equity of the bill are falsified by affidavits on the other side, or if the court shall be of opinion that the injunction was improperly granted, it will order the injunction to be dissolved (z). A defendant who wishes to have an injunction dissolved must serve the plaintiff's solicitor with notice of motion for that purpose. If other parties are interested with him as co-defendants, it may be necessary to serve them also with notice of motion (a). The motion may be made by the defendant either on affidavits in opposition to those filed

(x) Woodward v. King, 2 Ch. Ca. 203, 2 Dick. 797, Dan. Ch. Pr. 1514.

(y) Pearce v. Crutchfield, 14 Ves. 206; Williams v. Johns, 1 Mer. 303, n.; Lord Portarlington v. Graham, 5 Sim. 418; Kirkman v. Honnor, 6 Beav. 400; Skegg v. Simpson, 2 De G. & S. 454;

Pycroft v. Williams, 5 W. R. 464; Heald v. Hay, 9 W. R. 369, Morg. Ch. Ord. 472, Dan. Ch. Pr. 940, 1514.

(z) Sanxter v. Foster, Cr. & Ph. 302.

(a) Service v. Castaneda, 9 Jur. 367; *supra*, p. 609; *infra*, p. 631.

by the plaintiff, or he may wait until he has filed his answer, and then move to dissolve the injunction, using his answer as an affidavit, the plaintiff being entitled to file counter-affidavits to contradict either the answer or the affidavits of the defendant. The injunction will either be continued or dissolved according to the merits as disclosed by the pleadings and the preponderance of the evidence. A defendant who has good ground for demurring is not under any obligation to demur; but may, instead of demurring, meet the case by affidavit, and rely on the same objections as would have formed a good ground for demurring to the bill (b).

2. Where an interim order has been obtained, and simultaneous applications have been made for an injunction, and to discharge the order, the plaintiff is entitled to begin (c).

3. An injunction cannot, on the motion to dissolve, be sustained on grounds not raised by the bill (d). Nor is * 627 it competent * for the plaintiff, on the motion to dissolve, to make a new case (e).

4. An injunction cannot be dissolved unless upon motion in open court. In pressing cases, however, the Lord Chancellor has occasionally appointed a special hearing at his house for that purpose (f). Unless the court gives special leave to the contrary, there must be at least two clear days between the service of notice of motion to dissolve, and the day named in the notice for hearing the motion (g). If special leave be given by the court, the leave must be stated in the notice (h). The notice should be given for one of the days appropriated to the hearing of motions (i); but if a case of urgency be made out, leave may be had from the court to give notice of motion for a day not appropriated to the hearing of motions. The notice should state that the motion is with leave (k). The plaintiff is sometimes required by the interim order to undertake that he will accept short notice to discharge the order (l).

(b) Jones v. Garcia Del Rio, T. & R. 297; Hudson v. Maddison, 12 Sim. 416; Barnsley Canal Co. v. Twibell, 7 Beav. 19.

(c) Fraser v. Whalley, 2 H. & M. 10.

(d) Cresy v. Beavan, 13 Sim. 99; Burdett v. Hay, 33 L. J. Ch. 41; supra, pp. 618, 619.

(e) Barker v. North Staffordshire Railway Co., 5 Ra. Ca. 401.

(f) Eden on Inj. 326.

(g) Consol Ord. XXXIII. r. 2. See p. 611.

(h) Hill v. Rimmell, 2 M. & C. 641.

(i) Steedman v. Poole, 11 Jur. 555.

(k) Hill v. Rimmell, 2 Jur. 45.

(l) Seton, 867.

5. In cases where an injunction has been obtained *ex parte*, the court will, where an application is made on counter-affidavits to dissolve the injunction, entertain the application immediately, and will not give the plaintiff time to file affidavits in reply, unless it shall be of opinion that justice requires that he should have time allowed him for replying to the affidavits. With a view to the determination of the question, the court will hear as much of the case as is sufficient to enable it to form a judgment in the matter (*m*).

6. The motion to dissolve should be made before the court by which the injunction was granted (*n*). But if the cause has been transferred to another branch of the court the application may be made to that branch of the court to which the cause * has become attached (*o*). If leave be reserved * 628 a Vice-Chancellor may vary an order, or dissolve an injunction, granted by the Lord Chancellor (*p*).

7. Upon motion to dissolve, the plaintiff in equity has no right to insist that the motion shall stand over in order to give him time to cross-examine witnesses who have made affidavits for the defendant (*q*) : affidavits filed in·support of statements introduced into the bill by amendment after injunction granted, and tending to support the injunction, cannot be read on motion to dissolve that injunction (*r*).

8. If, on the motion to dissolve an *ex parte* injunction, it appear that the plaintiff has misstated his case, either by misrepresentation, or by the suppression of material facts, so that an injunction has been obtained which would not have been obtained if a more accurate statement of the case had been made, the injunction will be dissolved on that ground alone (*s*).[1] The

(*m*) Anon.

(*n*) George *v.* Watmouth, 4 L. J. Ch. N. S. 61; Bell *v.* Hull and Selby Railway Co., 1 Ra. Ca. 616; Paredes *v.* Lizardi, 9 Beav. 490. See Hammond *v.* Smith, 15 L. J. Ch. 40; Castendieck *v.* De Burgh, *ib.*, 425, 4 Ra. Ca. 386.

(*o*) Sturgeon *v.* Hooker, 1 De G. & S. 484.

(*p*) George *v.* Watmouth, 4 L. J. Ch. N. S. 61 ; Pinchin *v.* London and Blackwall Railway Co., 5 D. M. & G. 865.

(*q*) Normanville *v.* Stanning, 10 Ha. App. 20. See *supra*, p. 618.

(*r*) Prince Albert *v.* Strange, 1 Mac. & G. 25, 47.

(*s*) Brown *v.* Newall, 2 M. & C. 558, 570; Semple *v.* London and Birmingham Railway Co., 1 Ra. Ca. 493; Bell *v.* Hull and Selby Railway Co., *ib.* 616; Greenhalgh *v.* Manchester and Birmingham Railway Co., 3 M. & C. 799; Stedman *v.* Webb, 4 M. & C. 346, 351; Castelli *v.* Cook, 7 Ha. 89, 94; Dalglish *v.* Jarvie, 2 Mac. & G. 238; Philipps *v.* Prichard, 1 Jur. N. S. 750; Fitch *v.* Rochfort, 18 L. J. Ch. 458.

[1] And upon motion to dissolve the

plaintiff will not be allowed to maintain it on the merits then disclosed (*t*). Nor can he be heard to say that he was not aware of the importance of the facts so misstated or concealed (*u*), or that he had forgotten them (*x*).

9. But even though the affidavits on which the injunction was obtained may not have stated all the facts, there may not have been such misstatement or suppression as to lead the court to grant the injunction. In order that a misstatement may be material, there must have been a degree of misrepre-
* 629 sentation or * suppression presenting a case different from the case which really existed, and having a tendency to lead the court to issue the injunction (*y*). If the case has been properly brought forward, and there has been no concealment, the court, if any consideration has been overlooked, will say it has itself to blame for not having looked more carefully into the case (*z*). The plaintiff is only bound by the facts which he states, and not by his statements of the legal consequences arising from the facts stated (*a*). Nor, indeed, may his ignorance of the fact, that the act of which he

injunction the court will dismiss the bill where it appears from the answer that the cause is in possession of another court of concurrent jurisdiction. Withers *v.* Denmead, 22 Md. 135. A want of due diligence in prosecuting a suit in equity is cause for dissolving an injunction. Hoagland *v.* Titus, 1 McCarter, (N. J.)81; Schalk *v.* Schmidt, *ib.* 268. Although the answer denies all the equity of the bill, yet if the case made by the bill seems to require investigation, and irreparable injury would be sustained by a dissolution of the injunction, it will be retained. *Ib.,* and see McKibbin *v.* Brown, 1 McCarter, (N. J.) 13; Dubois *v.* Budlong, 10 Bosw. (N. Y.) 700; Mimes *v.* McLean, 6 Jones Eq. (N. C.) 200; Gardner *v.* Perkins, 9 Cal. 553; Scott *v.* Ames, 3 Stockt. 261. See Johnson *v.* Wide West, &c., Co., 22 Cal. 479. Where new matter is introduced in an answer, in avoidance of the plaintiff's equity, it will not be considered on a motion to dissolve the injunction. Allen *v.* Pearce, 6 Jones, Eq. (N. C.) 309. The rule that a motion to dissolve an injunction before answer must be supported by affidavit, is a rule of practice for the relief of the court, and not for protection of complainant. Kneedler *v.* Lane, 3 Grant, 523. A complainant may properly make every one a party who is a participator in the fraud. He has a right to do this for the purpose of discovery, and the general rule is, that he has a right to hold his injunction until he obtains that discovery. Robinson *v.* Davis, 3 Stockt. 302. But although the general rule is that an injunction properly granted will not be dissolved until all the defendants have answered, there are many exceptions to it. Baltimore and Ohio Railroad *v.* Wheeling, 13 Gratt. 40.

(*t*) Att.-Gen. *v.* Corporation of Liverpool, 1 M. & C. 211; Hilton *v.* Lord Granville, 4 Beav. 131; De Fencheres *v.* Dawes, 11 Beav. 46; Castelli *v.* Cook, 7 Ha. 89, 94; Dalglish *v.* Jarvie, 2 Mac. & G. 238; Fitch *v.* Rochfort, 18 L. J. Ch. 458.

(*u*) Att.-Gen. *v.* Corporation of Liverpool, 1 M. & C. 210, 211; Dalglish *v.* Jarvie, 2 Mac. & G. 241.

(*x*) Clifton *v.* Robinson, 16 Beav. 355; Sheard *v.* Webb, 2 W. R. 343.

(*y*) Brown *v.* Newall, 2 M. & C. 558, 571.

(*z*) Castelli *v.* Cook, 7 Ha. 89, 94.

(*a*) Brown *v.* Newall, 2 M. & C. 558.

complained was being put a stop to at the time when he applied for the injunction, amount to such a misrepresentation as to lead the court to hold that the injunction was improperly obtained. It is enough if the facts were stated as they were shortly before the filing of the bill, and that the plaintiff was not aware of the fact at the time of the application (*b*). The court does not deal with the same severity and strictness in the case of an injunction obtained on motion, as with an injunction obtained *ex parte;* but the circumstances of the case may be such as to call upon the court to visit the plaintiff with the same severity (*c*).

10. A man who has obtained an *ex parte* injunction which was afterwards dissolved on the ground of concealment of material facts, is not precluded from making an application for another injunction on the merits (*d*).

11. Under the old law, if the injunction were to restrain proceedings at law until answer, the defendant was entitled, after a sufficient answer had been put in by him, to move at once to dissolve, which was also a question of course, unless the plaintiff undertook to except to the answer, or to show cause on the merits confessed by the answer that there was sufficient equity to continue the injunction (*e*). The recent changes in the practice of the court not having entirely assimilated the * practice on applications to stay proceedings at law   * 630 with the practice in special injunctions, but " so far only as the nature of the case will admit," some parts of the former practice are still in force (*f*). Accordingly, where injunctions have been granted to restrain proceedings at law " until answer," or " until answer or further order," or " until answer with liberty to apply," or any similar terms, the purpose of the injunction being the discovery to be got by the answer, the defendant is still, as under the old practice, not entitled to move to dissolve until a sufficient answer has been put in (*g*) ; but as soon as

---

(*b*) Semple *v.* London and Birmingham Railway Co., 1 Ra. Ca. 493.

(*c*) Maclaren *v.* Stainton, 16 Beav. 279, 290.

(*d*) Fitch *v.* Rochfort, 18 L. J. Ch. 458. See Philipps *v.* Prichard, 1 Jur. N. S. 750.

(*e*) 3 Drew. 133, *per* Kindersley, V.

C. See King *v.* Abbotson, 7 L. J. Exch. N. S. 6.

(*f*) Lovell *v.* Galloway, 17 Beav. 1.

(*g*) Mollett *v.* Enequist, 26 Beav. 467; Ooddeen *v.* Oakley, 2 D. F. & J. 161. See Howes *v.* Howes, 1 Beav. 197.

an answer, the sufficiency of which is not denied, has been
filed within the prescribed time (*h*), or as soon as the plaintiff
has allowed the time for excepting to expire (*i*), he is entitled
as of course to have an injunction granted for the purpose of
discovery dissolved.[1] The plaintiff cannot have it continued
upon a case made by amendment (*j*). He must file a fresh
bill if he wishes further discovery (*k*), or if an injunction on
the merits is desired after a full answer has been put in (*l*).
The filing a plea does not entitle a defendant to have an injunction until answer dissolved (*m*). The application to dissolve must be upon notice (*n*).

12. The court has refused to entertain a motion to dissolve
an injunction pending an application for the production of
documents (*o*).

13. If an injunction has been granted against two or more
persons, each of them must move to dissolve. As to the party
who applies, an injunction will be dissolved, but not as against
the others who have not applied (*p*). Where there are several
defendants to a bill for an injunction restraining proceedings at
law until answer, the general rule is that the injunction
* 631 is not * to be dissolved until all have answered (*q*);

(*h*) See Fox *v.* Hill, 2 D. & J. 353;
Ooddeen *v.* Oakley, 2 D. F. & J. 158.
(*i*) Mollett *v.* Enequist, 25 Beav. 609,
26 Beav. 466.
(*j*) Mollett *v.* Enequist, 25 Beav.
609, 26 Beav. 466.
(*k*) *Ib.*
(*l*) Magnay *v.* Mines Royal Co., 3
Drew. 130, 133.
(*m*) Wroe *v.* Clayton, 10 Sim. 185.
(*n*) Ooddeen *v.* Oakley, 2 D.F. & J.161.
(*o*) Storer *v.* Jackson, 12 Sim. 503.
(*p*) Bramwell *v.* Halcomb, 3 M. & C.
737. A plaintiff cannot without giving
notice read the answer of a defendant
against a co-defendant. Feilden *v.* Sla-
ter, 7 L. R. Eq. 523.
(*q*) White *v.* Steinwacks, 19 Ves. 84;
Nanney *v.* Vaughan, 8 Sim. 439; Bowles
v. Orr, 1 Y. & C. 474. See Lewis *v.*
Smith, 7 Beav. 470.
[1] Filing exceptions to an answer constitutes no objection to the dissolution
of the injunction, if the equity of the
bill on which the injunction rests has
been fully answered. Roberts *v.* Hodges,
1 C. E. Green, (N. J.) 299; McGee *v.*
Smith, *ib.* 462. And an injunction may be

dissolved before the answers of merely
nominal defendants are filed. Shricker
v. Field, 9 Iowa, 366. To dissolve an
injunction, the denial of the answer
must be of facts within the knowledge
of the party denying under oath. But
when the answer is by a corporation,
and the facts are not alleged to be, and
from their nature could hardly be
within the knowledge of the person
making oath, or of the corporation, it is
immaterial whether the denial of the
corporation under seal is equivalent
to a denial under oath, for the purpose
of dissolving injunction. Higbee *v.*
Camden and Am. Railroad, 4 C. E.
Green, 276. See, also, Morris Canal *v.*
Fagan, 3 C. E. Green, 215; Suffern *v.*
Butler, *ib.* 220. But whether or not to
dissolve an injunction even upon a full
denial of the equity of the bill is a
matter within the discretion of the
court. Camden and Am. Railroad *v.*
Stewart, 3 C. E. Green, 489; Irick *v.*
Black, 2 *ib.* 190. Injunction will not
be dissolved upon new matter alone
set up in the answer. The Society *v.*
Low, 2 C. E. Green, 19.

but there are exceptions to the rule, and an injunction may often be dissolved as to those who have answered without waiting until all have answered (*r*). If all the defendants have answered, some of them may move to dissolve as against all (*s*).

14. In an interpleader suit the notice to dissolve the injunction must be served on all the defendants (*t*). In other cases one may move to dissolve in the absence of the rest (*u*).

15. A man who, since the granting the injunction, has become bankrupt, may move to dissolve without making his assignees parties. If the court shall be of opinion that it is necessary to protect the interest of the assignees, and that injustice would be done to them by allowing the injunction to continue, it will dissolve the injunction at the application of the bankrupt, although the assignees are not before the court (*v*).

16. If the application to dissolve be made by a stranger to the suit in which an injunction has been obtained, he may properly proceed by petition to set aside the injunction (*w*).

17. In cases where the order for an injunction is irregular, a motion should be made to discharge the order, not to dissolve the injunction. By moving to dissolve the injunction the irregularity is waived (*x*).[1] The court will not, on an application to discharge an order for irregularity, sustain it on the merits (*y*). Where an order has been made on motion, and affidavit of service in the absence of parties, the court will, on proper * application, give the absent party leave   *632 to move to discharge (*z*).

(*r*) Joseph *v.* Doubleday, 1 V. & B. 497; Caird *v.* Campbell, 2 Moll. 399; Kilby *v.* Stanton, 2 Y. & J. 75; Imperial Gas-light Co. *v.* Clarke, Younge, 580; Glascott *v.* Copper Mines Co., 11 Sim. 314; Lewis *v.* Smith, 7 Beav 470; Money *v.* Jordan, 13 Beav. 229. See Prince *v.* Haydin, 3 Y. & J. 190.

(*s*) Macgregor *v.*Cunningham, 16 Sim. 365. See Montague *v.* Hill, 4 Russ. 128.

(*t*) Masterman *v.* Lewin, 2 Ph. 182, 186; *supra*, p. 130.

(*u*) Joseph *v.* Doubleday, 1 V. & B. 497; Money *v.* Jordan, 13 Beav. 229. See, however, Thompson *v.* Geary, 5 Beav. 131.

(*v*) M'Beath *v.* Ravenscroft, 8 L. J. Ch. N. S. 208.

(*w*) Bourbaud *v.* Bourbaud, 12 W. R. 1024.

(*x*) Vipan *v.* Mortlock, 2 Mer. 476; Angier *v.* May, 3 W. R. 330.

(*y*) Brooks *v.* Purton, 4 Beav. 494; St. Victor *v.* Devereux, 6 Beav. 584.

(*z*) Mapp *v.* Elcock, 22 L. J. Ch. 707.

[1] An injunction granted in a case in which the court has jurisdiction, if erroneously granted, is voidable only, not void; and until set aside it is entitled to obedience. The People *v.* Sturtevant, 9 N. Y. 263. An injunction may always be vacated on motion, when the reasons for granting it have ceased to exist; as when a railroad company enjoined by reason of the want of legislative authority have since obtained such authority. Wetmore *v.* Law, 34 Barb. 515.

18. Although an injunction may have issued irregularly, the irregularity may be waived by any act of the defendant, affirming the subsistence of a regular injunction (*a*). The question whether there has been a misrepresentation or concealment of material facts upon the application for an *ex parte* injunction cannot be taken into consideration on appeal from an order made by the court in which the injunction was granted, or by which it was continued (*b*).

19. After long acquiescence under an order for an injunction, an application for dissolving it will not be readily entertained (*c*). Where an order for an injunction had been made in a case where the court had no jurisdiction, Lord Westbury would not disturb the order on the ground of the acquiescence of the defendant, but allowed it to stand over on the undertaking of the plaintiff (*d*).

20. Delay in moving to dissolve an injunction may deprive a man of his right to have an injunction dissolved (*e*). So, also, on the other hand, delay in appealing from the refusal of a motion for an injunction may be a bar to the application (*f*).

SECTION III.—EFFECT OF CERTAIN PROCEEDINGS ON INJUNCTIONS.

1. Effect of abatement of suit, on injunction.
2. Practice where relators to an information are dead.
3. Effect on injunction of bankruptcy of sole plaintiff.
4. Injunction granted "until answer or further order," &c., not dissolved *ipso facto* by putting in answer.
5. Effect of allowance of demurrer.
6. Allowance of a plea does not dissolve injunction.
7 & 8. Effect of amendment on injunction.
9. Supplemental bill does not put an end to the injunction.
10 & 11. Effect of dismissal of bill.

1. An injunction is not dissolved by the abatement of the suit in which it has been granted. The abatement of the suit by

(*a*) Travers *v.* Lord Stafford, 2 Ves. 20; Vipan *v.* Mortlock, 2 Mer. 476.
(*b*) Bell *v.* Hull and Selby Railway Co., 1 Ra. Ca. 616.
(*c*) Glascott *v.* Lang, 3 M. & C. 451; Bickford *v.* Skewes, 4 M. & C. 500; Feistel *v.* King's College, Cambridge, 10 Beav. 491; Great Western Railway Co. *v.* Oxford, Worcester, &c., Railway Co., 3 D. M. & G. 341.

(*d*) Cardinall *v.* Molyneux, 7 Jur. N. S. 854.
(*e*) Bell *v.* Hull and Selby Railway Co., 1 Ra. Ca. 616.
(*f*) Williams *v.* St. George's Harbor Co., 2 D. & J. 547. See South Staffordshire Railway Co. *v.* Hall, 16 Jur. 39.

the death of a sole plaintiff, or of a defendant, does not
of itself * dissolve an injunction (*g*). If a sole plaintiff * 633
dies, the defendant may before decree serve a motion on
his representatives that they may revive within a given time,
or in default that the injunction should be dissolved (*h*).
After a decree continuing an injunction, such an application is
irregular (*i*), for the injunction is untouched and remains in
force (*k*). If one of many plaintiffs dies, a similar notice is
served on the solicitors of the surviving plaintiffs (*l*). When
an injunction has been obtained in a cause which afterwards
abates by the death of the defendant, the practice is to move
on the part of the defendant's representative that the plaintiff
may revive within a limited time, or that the injunction
be dissolved (*m*). Upon the revival of the suit against his
personal representatives the injunction stands without further
order (*n*).

2. Where relators to an information are all dead the court
will restrain proceedings until a new relator is appointed (*o*).

3. The bankruptcy of a sole plaintiff, though it renders the
suit defective, does not dissolve an injunction which has been
granted in the suit, but the defendant may serve notice of
motion on the assignees to revive the suit within a given time,
or that the bill may be dismissed (*p*). The bankruptcy of
one of many plaintiffs does not affect an injunction, or prevent
the defendant from moving to dismiss in due time for want of
prosecution (*q*).

4. An injunction which has been granted " until answer or
further order," or " until answer with liberty to apply,"
is not * dissolved *ipso facto* by the putting in of a suf- * 634

(*g*) Ferrand *v.* Hamer, 4 M. & C. 147.

(*h*) Wheeler *v.* Malins, 4 Madd. 171, Consol Ord. XXXII. r. 4. See Lee *v.* Lee, 1 Ha. 622; Fisher *v.* Fisher, 4 Ha. 196; Price *v.* Berrington, 11 Beav. 90.

(*i*) Oldfield *v.* Cobbett, 20 Beav. 563. See Askew *v.* Townsend, 2 Dick. 471.

(*k*) *Ib.*

(*l*) Adamson *v.* Hall, T. & R. 258.

(*m*) Stuart *v.* Ancell, 1 Cox, 411; Hill *v.* Hoare, 2 Cox, 50. See 15 & 16 Vict. c. 86, s. 52.

(*n*) Kennedy *v.* Lloyd, 8 Ir. Eq. 581.

(*o*) Att.-Gen. *v.* Haberdashers' Co., 16 Jur. 717.

(*p*) Randall *v.* Mumford, 18 Ves. 424; Caird *v.* Campbell, 1 Moll. 484; Wheeler *v.* Malins, 4 Madd. 171. See Lord Huntingtower *v.* Sherborne, 5 Beav. 380; Lee *v.* Lee, 1 Ha. 621; Fisher *v.* Fisher, 4 Ha. 196; M'Beath *v.* Ravenscroft, 8 L. J. Ch. N. S. 208; Meiklam *v.* Elmore, 4 D. & J. 208; Jackson *v.* Riga Railway Co., 28 Beav. 75. See, also, Bourbaud *v.* Bourbaud, 12 W. R. 1024, where the plaintiff was a foreigner.

(*q*) Caddick *v.* Masson, 1 Sim. 501.

ficient answer, but remains in force until it is discharged by the order of the court (r).

5. The allowance of a demurrer to the whole bill puts an end to an injunction which had been previously obtained (s). But leave will be given to amend without prejudice to an injunction, where a demurrer has been allowed to the bill on a technical ground alone (t).

6. The allowance of a plea does not dissolve an injunction. There may be some equity shown to continue it. An order for its dissolution must be obtained (u).

7. A plaintiff may, after obtaining an injunction, obtain an order to amend without prejudice to the injunction. Under the old practice an order to amend the bill without prejudice to the injunction might, in the case of special injunctions (x), or in cases where an injunction to restrain proceedings at law had been obtained on the merits (y), be obtained of course (z). It was not necessary to save the injunction by inserting the words "without prejudice" in the order (a). Whether, under the old practice, an order to amend after the common injunction had been obtained, and before answer without prejudice to the injunction was an order of course, or to be moved for specially, does not appear to have been clearly settled (b). Nor, indeed, does it seem to have been clear whether it was necessary under the old practice to save the injunction by inserting the words "without prejudice" in the order (c). But the practice

* 635 as to common and special * injunctions having been assimilated by 15 & 16 Vict. c. 86, s. 38, there can be no doubt that, under the present practice, an order to amend

(r) Ooddeen v. Oakley, 2 D. F. & J. 161.
(s) Schneider v. Ligardi, 9 Beav. 468.
(t) Rawlings v. Lambert, 1 J. & H. 458; Harding v. Tingey, 10 Jur. N. S. 872; Low v. Routledge, 35 L. J. Ch. 717.
(u) Philipps v. Langhorn, Dick. 148; Ferrand v. Hamer, 4 M. & C. 143, 147.
(x) Pickering v. Hanson, 2 Sim. 488, correcting report in Pratt v. Archer, 1 Sm. & St. 433; Warburton v. London and Blackwall Railway Co., 2 Beav. 253.
(y) King v. Turner, 6 Madd. 255; Woodroffe v. Daniel, 9 Sim. 410.

(z) See Ferrand v. Hamer, 4 M. & C. 143.
(a) Warburton v. London and Blackwall Railway Co., 2 Beav. 253. See Harvey v. Hall, 11 L. R. Eq. 31.
(b) Mason v. Murray, Dick. 536; Bliss v. Boscawen, 2 V. & B. 102; Sharp v. Ashton, 3 V. & B. 144; Davis v. Davis, 2 Sim. 515; Warburton v. London and Blackwall Railway Co., 2 Beav. 253; Ferrand v. Hamer, 4 M. & C. 143; Brooks v. Purton, 1 Y. & C. C. C. 271.
(c) Bliss v. Boscawen, 2 V. & B. 102; contra, Davis v. Davis, 2 Sim. 515; Warburton v. London and Blackwall Railway Co., 2 Beav. 253.

is in all cases of course, and that the injunction whether expressly saved or not is unaffected, unless the record is changed, or the equity on which the injunction was obtained is displaced or materially altered by the amendments (*d*). Although a demurrer is filed a plaintiff is at liberty, before it is argued, to obtain an order of course, to amend his bill, and the amendment will not prejudice the injunction (*e*).

8. After an answer has been put in displacing the plaintiff's equity, and entitling the defendant to dissolve the injunction, leave to amend without prejudice to the injunction will not be given (*f*), but in a case where the answer stated facts which were a surprise on the plaintiff leave was given (*g*).

9. A supplemental bill does not put an end to an injunction (*h*).

10. If the bill is dismissed the injunction goes of course whether it was granted on the merits or otherwise (*i*). A motion or order for its dissolution is not necessary. But the dismissal of the bill does not prevent the plaintiff from filing another for the same purpose under a different state of circumstances (*k*), or upon new facts (*l*). If the dismissal has been with costs a second motion for the same object cannot be made until those costs have been either paid or secured by payment (*m*).

11. An order for an injunction (*n*), or cause shown against dissolving an injunction (*o*), does not prevent a defendant from * moving to dismiss if otherwise entitled to do * 636 so (*p*). Nor does notice to dissolve prevent a defendant from moving pending the notice to dismiss for want of prosecution (*q*). A plaintiff may, notwithstanding the pendency of a

---

(*d*) Att.-Gen. *v.* Marsh, 16 Sim. 572. See Sharp *v.* Ashton, 3 V. & B. 144; Davis *v.* Davis, 2 Sim. 515.

(*e*) Warburton *v.* London and Blackwall Railway Co., 2 Beav. 253.

(*f*) Penfold *v.* Stoveld, 3 Madd. 471; Mollett *v.* Enequist, 25 Beav. 609, 26 *ib.* 466.

(*g*) Vesey *v.* Wilks, 3 Madd. 475. See further, as to amendment of bills, Consol Ord. IX., rr. 8–24, Morg. Ch. Ord. 381–388, Daniel Ch. Pr. 366–388.

(*h*) D'Arcy *v.* Sumner, 2 Moll. 359.

(*i*) Hannam *v.* South London Waterworks Co., 2 Mer. 63; Day *v.* Snee, 3 V. & B. 171; Green *v.* Pulsford, 2 Beav. 70.

(*k*) Mayor of Liverpool *v.* Chorley Waterworks Co., 2 D. M. & G. 852; Castelli *v.* Cook, 7 Ha. 89, 99.

(*l*) Att.-Gen. *v.* Sheffield Gas Co., 3 D. M. & G. 304, 341.

(*m*) Oldfield *v.* Cobbett, 12 Beav. 91; Burdell *v.* Hay, 33 Beav. 189.

(*n*) Day *v.* Snee, 3 V. & B. 171; Naylor *v.* Taylor, 16 Ves. 127; James *v.* Biou, 3 Sw. 244; Stagg *v.* Knowles, 3 Ha. 241.

(*o*) Earl of Warwick *v.* Duke of Beaufort, 1 Cox, 111.

(*p*) See Baker *v.* M'Clellan, 27 L. J. Ch. 57.

(*q*) Farquharson *v.* Pitcher, 3 Russ. 383.

motion for an injunction, obtain an order dismissing his bill (r).[1]

SECTION IV. — CONTINUING OR GRANTING INJUNCTIONS AT THE HEARING.

1. Practice as to continuing injunctions at the hearing.
2. As to extending injunctions at the hearing.
3. When perpetual injunctions will be granted.
4. When injunction will be granted at the hearing, although not prayed for.
5. Injunction may be made perpetual on motion by consent.
6. Perpetual injunction granted at hearing though no interlocutory application be made.
7. Plaintiff has right to hearing for perpetual injunction.
8. Perpetual injunction in effect a decree.

1. An injunction which has been granted upon an interlocutory is superseded by the decree made at the hearing of the cause. If it is intended that it should remain in force it must be expressly continued (s). Injunctions are continued at the hearing either provisionally or permanently. They may be continued provisionally pending inquiries or accounts which are preparatory to a final adjudication upon further consideration (t). Injunctions may be permanently continued or made perpetual by the decree where the party enjoined is in possession of some instrument conferring a legal right which it is

(r) Markwick v. Pawson, 33 L. J. Ch. 703.

(s) Seton, 944.

(t) Old v. Old, Seton, 105, No. 3.

[1] An appeal from an order dissolving an injunction cannot affect the validity of the order, or revive the process and give it force and effect. Chancellor Kent says : "An appeal only stays future proceedings in the court ; but here are no further proceedings. The order is perfect and finished eo instanti that it is entered : and if the injunction could be revived by the mere act of the party in filing an appeal, it would be giving to him not only a power of control over the orders of the court, but of creating an injunction. The supreme court of this state in Hoyt v. Gelston, 13 Johns. 139, held that an injunction was not revived by an appeal so as to operate as a stay of proceedings at law ; and the supreme court of the United States, in Young v. Grundy, 6 Cranch, 51, held that no appeal would ever lie upon an interlocutory order dissolving an injunction. Whether an appeal can be sustained is a question for the court of errors ; but supposing it can be sustained, it is impossible that a process that is duly discharged, and functus officio, can be revived by the mere act of the party. How could this court undertake to enforce the process and punish contempts of it, in the very face of the order dissolving it ? When a process is once discharged and dead, it is gone for ever ; and it can never be revived but by a new exertion of judicial power." Wood v. Dwight, 7 Johns, Ch. 295 ; Hicks v. Michael, 15 Cal. 107. And an injunction is not affected by an appeal from it. Merced Mining Co. v. Fremont, 7 Cal. 130. It is the duty of the party holding an injunction to prosecute his claim with all diligence. Huffman v. Hummer, 2 C. E. Green, 263 ; Dodd v. Flavell, ib. 255.

contrary to equity that he should be permitted to exercise to the detriment of the plaintiff (*u*). The general course of the court, however, where a party is in possession of a security or other instrument which it is against conscience that he should use against the defendant, is to direct it to be delivered up and cancelled. This course may be adopted even where the instrument is void at law (*x*).

2. The practice of extending injunctions at the hearing, so as to render them perpetual, is also applied to prevent the continuance or repetition of the violation of a common-law right (*y*).

3. Perpetual injunctions will also be decreed where the same question has been frequently litigated between the parties, or where it is likely to be contested in a multiplicity of suits (*z*).

4. *An injunction will be granted at the hearing *637 whenever it is necessary for the purposes of complete justice (*a*), although it is not prayed by the bill (*b*).

5. As a general rule an injunction can only be made perpetual at the hearing of the cause (*c*). But an injunction may by consent be made perpetual on motion (*d*).

6. In order to entitle a man to an injunction at the hearing it is not absolutely necessary that he should previously have made an interlocutory application for one (*e*) ; and he is at liberty to claim an injunction, although he may have previously failed to obtain one, or to support it when obtained (*f*).

7. A man has a right to bring the cause to a hearing for the purpose of obtaining a perpetual injunction, although the defendant may have submitted to the interlocutory injunction (*g*).

8. An injunction which has been made perpetual is in effect a decree. It remains in force notwithstanding the abatement of the suit (*h*).

(*u*) Chennell *v.* Churchman, 3 Bro. C. C. 16, n.; Minshaw *v.* Jordan, *ib.* 17, n.; Hanington *v.* Du Chatel, 1 Bro. C. C. 124, 2 Sw. 158, n.; *supra*, p. 132.

(*x*) *Supra*, pp. 16, 33.
(*y*) *Supra*, pp. 224–227.
(*z*) *Supra*, pp. 134–137.
(*a*) Dickenson *v.* Grand Junction Canal Co., 15 Beav. 260.

(*b*) Blomfield *v.* Eyre, 8 Beav. 259 ; Reynell *v.* Sprye, 1 D. M. & G. 660.
(*c*) Day *v.* Snee, 3 V. & B. 171.
(*d*) Morrell *v.* Pearson, 12 Beav. 284; *supra*, p. 227.
(*e*) Bacon *v.* Jones, 4 M. & C. 436; *supra*, p. 227.
(*f*) Baily *v.* Taylor, 1 R. & M. 73.
(*g*) *Supra*, pp. 227–229.
(*h*) Askew *v.* Townsend, 2 Dick. 471 ; *supra*, p. 133.

SECTION V.—CONSEQUENCES OF THE BREACH OF AN INJUNC-
TION OR RESTRAINING ORDER.

1. Injunction or restraining order must be implicitly observed.
2. Court will not punish for contempt unless party knew order had been passed.
3. Enough to show that the party had notice of the order.
4–8. Order for committal how obtained. How service is made. May move to commit one of the defendants only.
9. Breach of injunction or order must be clearly shown.
10. Obtaining injunction by misrepresentation, a contempt.
11 & 12. Threatening letters, &c., to plaintiff or his witnesses, a contempt.
13–17. Other acts which are a contempt.
18. Persons not named in the writ of injunction not liable to be committed.
19. Party not committed for acts of servants.
20. Injunction protects whom.
21–24. Defences to charge of contempt.
25 & 26. Practice upon hearing on charge of contempt.

1. An order for an injunction, or interim restraining order, must be implicitly observed, and every diligence must be exercised to obey it to the letter (*i*). However erroneously or irregularly obtained, the order must be implicitly observed so long as it exists. A party affected by it cannot disregard it or treat it as a nullity, but must have it discharged on a proper application (*k*). * A man who does not obey it to the letter so long as it exists is guilty of contempt, unless there be something to mislead upon the plain reading of the order (*l*). An undertaking entered into with the court is equivalent to, and will have the effect of an injunction so far that any infringement thereof may be made the subject of an application to the court (*m*).

2. The court will not punish for a breach of injunction or restraining order, unless it be clear that the party alleged to be in contempt knew that the injunction had issued, or that the

* 638

(*i*) Harding *v.* Tingey, 12 W. R. 684; Spokes *v.* Banbury Board of Health, 1 L. R. Eq. 42.

(*k*) Woodward *v.* Earl of Lincoln, 3 Sw. 626. See Partington *v.* Booth, 3 Mer. 149; Fennings *v.* Humphery, 4 Beav. 1; Blake *v.* Blake, 7 Beav. 514; Chuck *v.* Cremer, 2 Ph. 113; South Staffordshire Railway Co. *v.* Hall, 16 Jur. 93; Russell *v.* East Anglian Railway Co., 3 Mac. & G. 104. Comp. Daw *v.* Eley, 3 L. R. Eq. 496.

(*l*) Spokes *v.* Banbury Board of Health, 1 L. R. Eq. 42. See Russell *v.* East Anglian Railway Co., 3 Mac. & G. 104.

(*m*) London and Birmingham Railway Co. *v.* Grand Junction Canal Co., 1 Ra. Ca. 224; Att.-Gen. *v.* Manchester and Leeds Railway Co., *ib.* 436; Lawford *v.* Spicer, 2 Jur. N. S. 564; Att.-Gen. *v.* Boyle, 10 Jur. N. S. 309.

order had been made. He ought, strictly speaking, to be served with the writ or order itself in the manner already pointed out (*n*). But if the matter is pressing, and there is not time to procure it, the service of the writ or order itself will be dispensed with, and service of a copy of the minutes of the order, or of a notice of its having been obtained, will be sufficient. An injunction operates from the date of the order, and not from the time of sealing. If, after service of the notice or the copy of the minutes, the defendant or other party in contempt acts in opposition to the order, he is guilty of a contempt, and may be committed (*o*).[1]

3. A committal may, indeed, be ordered where neither the writ nor the minutes of the order have been served, nor any personal notice given. It is enough if a man can be shown to have had notice of the order; as, for instance, if he were in court at the time the order was made (*p*). If, indeed, a man remains in court until the order is about to be made, he cannot, by leaving before the order is actually pronounced, avoid its consequences (*q*). In one case (*r*) Lord Eldon observed that if the party admitted that he believed the order was made, the principle was the same as if * his belief was formed * 639 from information, short of actual notice, and that there would be authority enough to apply the practice, if the defendant would not swear that he did not believe the order was pronounced. There must, however, be no unnecessary delay in getting the order drawn up, or the writ under seal, and in serving it when obtained (*s*). In a case where the plaintiff had delayed in getting the order drawn up and served, the court

(*n*) *Supra*, p. 625.
(*o*) M'Neill *v.* Garratt, Cr. & Ph. 98; Gooch *v.* Marshall, 8 W. R. 410; *supra*, p. 625.
(*p*) Anon., 3 Atk. 567 ; Skip *v.* Harwood, *ib.* 564.
(*q*) Hearn *v.* Tennant, 14 Ves. 136.
(*r*) Kimpton *v.* Eve, 2 V. & B. 351.
(*s*) *Ib.*; Van Sandau *v.* Rose, 2 J. & W. 264. See Bateman *v.* Wiatt, 11 Beav. 587.
1 A party is guilty of contempt if he stand by and quietly suffer an injunction to be violated. Proceedings for contempt are to punish the guilty party, and to compel restitution to the party injured. Stimpson *v.* Putnam, 41 Vt.

246. Failure to have service made of the original *subpœna* with the bill and injunction seasonably for the term to which the *subpœna* was made returnable, does not operate a discontinuance of the proceedings, so that the order of the chancellor and the injunction issued in pursuance of it become vacated and void. If the defendant is apprised of the existence of the injunction it is operative upon him, and he may not disregard and violate it, though service may have been improperly delayed so far as to afford adequate ground for a dissolution. Howe *v.* Willard, 40 Vt. 655; Stimpson *v.* Putnam, 41 Vt. 238.

would not treat the defendant as in contempt, although he was present in court at the hearing of the motion (*t*).

4. The order for committal is obtained upon motion, notice of which must be duly served personally upon the party committing the contempt (*u*). The terms of the notice should be that the party "may stand committed" to Whitecross prison for breach of the injunction (*x*). If the breach has been committed by a person not named in the writ or order, the notice of motion must be that he may be committed for his contempt in knowingly assisting in the breach (*y*). The plaintiff may obtain an order *ex parte* that the defendant may stand committed on a certain day, unless he shows cause against it. The order must be served personally on the defendant (*z*). An *ex parte* order, however, for immediate committal is not irregular (*a*).

5. If there has been personal service of motion, or of the order *nisi*, service on defendant's solicitor is not necessary (*b*). If it can be satisfactorily shown that personal service cannot be effected, the plaintiff may, on a proper case being made out, obtain an order that substituted service may be made, and upon an affidavit of such service an order for his commitment may be made (*c*).

6. A motion to commit can only be made on a seal day (*d*). The motion must be supported by affidavits (*e*). The affidavits in support of the application should specify the particu-
* 640　lar acts constituting * the breach. A general allegation that the defendant has violated the order is not sufficient (*f*). Affidavits filed originally to obtain an injunction may be used to show that the contempt charged has been committed (*g*). There must be an affidavit of personal service (*h*).

7. The breach of an injunction being in the nature of a

(*t*) James *v.* Downes, 18 Ves. 522.
(*u*) Angerstein *v.* Hunt, 6 Ves. 488.
(*x*) Dan. Ch. Pr. 1523.
(*y*) Lord Wellesley *v.* Earl of Mornington, 11 Beav. 180, 181.
(*z*) Durant *v.* Moore, 2 R. & M. 33; Lechmere-Charlton's case, 2 M. & C. 316.
(*a*) *Ex parte* Clarke, 1 R. & M. 563.

(*b*) Bowdler *v.* Bowdler, 9 L. J. Ch. N. S. 394.
(*c*) Pulteney *v.* Shelton, 5 Ves. 147.
(*d*) Saxby *v.* Saxby, 7 Sim. 140.
(*e*) *Ib.*
(*f*) Morris *v.* Morris, 1 Hog. 238.
(*g*) Thornhill *v.* Thornhill, 1 Jur. N. S. 73.
(*h*) Van Sandau *v.* Rose, 2 J. & W. 264; Gooch *v.* Marshall, 8 W. R. 410.

wrong, it is no objection that the plaintiff has moved to commit one of the defendants only (*i*).

8. Lord Eldon is reported to have said that a motion to commit for breach of an injunction could not be made without a production of the writ (*j*). But in a case before Lord Cottenham, he held that if a party having notice of an injunction is guilty of a breach of it, he may be committed without the production of the writ (*k*).

9. An order for commitment is *strictissimi juris*, and cannot be sustained, unless it can be shown upon the clearest evidence that there has been an actual breach of the injunction or the order (*l*). If the injunction be in general terms restraining a man from doing acts which shall be attended with certain specified effects, and not from doing certain specified acts, the court must be satisfied upon the clearest evidence that the acts complained of have resulted from the cause assigned (*m*). The general terms of an injunction will not, however, be restricted by reference to the particular injury complained of, if it has been in spirit violated (*n*). In determining whether there has been a breach, the court must have regard to the circumstances under which, and the objects for which, the injunction was obtained (*o*). In a case where an injunction had been obtained for the purpose of restraining a man from pulling down houses, the * court held the injunction not broken by * 641 defendant obtaining an entry into the house by breaking a window and the lock of one of the doors, the plaintiff having excluded the defendant by shutting the doors and windows (*p*). An intention to violate an injunction is immaterial, unless the breach be actually carried into effect (*q*). Thus, where an injunction was granted restraining a man and his servants from stopping, impeding and obstructing the passage of boats, &c., along a canal, the placing of a bar which was capable of being

(*i*) Newman *v.* Ring, 10 Jur. 463.
(*j*) Ellerton *v.* Thirsk, 1 J. & W. 376.
(*k*) M'Neill *v.* Garratt, Cr. & Ph. 98.
(*l*) Mann *v.* Stephens, 15 Sim. 377; Dawson *v.* Paver, 5 Ha. 424; Grand Junction Canal Co. *v.* Dimes, 17 Sim. 38; Harding *v.* Tingey, 12 W. R. 684; Daugars *v.* Rivaz, 1 W. N. 301.

(*m*) Dawson *v.* Paver, 5 Ha. 424.
(*n*) Att.-Gen. *v.* Great Northern Railway Co., 4 De G. & S. 75.
(*o*) Loder *v.* Arnold, 15 Jur. 117. See Russell *v.* East Anglian Railway Co., 3 Mac. & G. 104.
(*p*) Loder *v.* Arnold, 15 Jur. 117.
(*q*) Grand Junction Canal Co. *v.* Dimes, 17 Sim. 38.

easily moved across the canal, and the stationing of persons at a bridge on the canal to give notice to persons passing along that they were trespassing, without, however, attempting to stop them, or bringing actions of trespass, is not a breach (r).

10. The obtaining an injunction *ex parte* upon misrepresentation or suppression of facts is not a contempt of court which will be punished by attachment (s). If a plaintiff who has obtained an injunction misrepresents to the public what has been done by the court, and the defendant, to correct that misrepresentation, does an act which in strictness is a breach of the injunction, the court will not entertain any complaint against him on the part of the plaintiff for such a breach (t).

11. The publication of attacks on the plaintiff or his witnesses, or the sending threatening letters addressed to him or them pending a suit, is a contempt of court upon which to found an order for commitment (u).

12. It is a contempt of court to publish in a newspaper, after the affidavits in a cause have been filed, but before the hearing, an article holding up to ignominy, or attributing falsehood to the person making the application, or his witnesses (v). In order to purge his contempt, the publisher must express his
* 642 regret and * contrition to the court, and is not obliged to apologize to the persons to whom the falsehood was attributed (x). Although the court will punish as a contempt any publication of its proceedings which may tend to prepossess the public mind, or disturb the free course of justice, it is not every unfair proceeding or advertisement, or other publication containing erroneous statements, that it will punish by committal (y).

13. It is a breach of an injunction, restraining an action at law, to obtain a judge's order to change the venue in the action (z),

(r) Grand Junction Canal Co. v. Dimes, 17 Sim. 38.

(s) M'Carthy v. Maguire, 1 Moll. 47; Brown v. Newall, 2 M. & C. 558.

(t) Barfield v. Nicholson, 2 L. J. Ch. 90.

(u) Anon., 2 Atk. 469; Lechmere-Charlton's case, 2 M. & C. 316; Littler v. Thompson, 2 Beav. 129; *Ex parte* Van Sandau, 1 Ph. 455; Birch v. Walsh, 10 Ir. Eq. 93; Smith v. Lakeman, 26 L. J. Ch. 305; Brook v. Evans, 6 Jur.

N. S. 1026; Coleman v. West Hartlepool Railway Co., 8 W. R. 734.

(v) Littler v. Thompson, 2 Beav. 129; Felkin v. Herbert, 10 Jur. N. S. 62.

(x) Felkin v. Herbert, 10 Jur. N. S. 62.

(y) Matthews v. Smith, 3 Ha. 331; Brook v. Evans, 6 Jur. N. S. 1025.

(z) Pariente v. Bensusan, 13 Sim. 522.

to give notice of trial (*a*), or to deliver a declaration (*b*). If an injunction has been granted staying execution, the taking a single step towards execution beyond the completion of the judgment is a breach of the injunction (*c*). Where an injunction has been obtained even after execution executed, it is a breach to call upon the sheriff to pay over the money, but if the sheriff has voluntarily paid over the money it seems there would be no breach (*d*).

14. It is a breach of an injunction restraining proceedings at law to lodge with the sheriff an attachment for non-payment of costs, although such costs may have been actually taxed before the issuing of the injunction (*e*). So, also, where legal process had been put into the sheriff's hands before the issuing of the injunction, and the plaintiff at law did not, on being applied to by the sheriff for further instructions, stop the process, it was held that the refusal to countermand the writ was an actual continuance of the order previously given by the plaintiff at law to the sheriff, and was a contempt (*f*).

15. If an injunction is obtained by a defendant at law who has * given bail, the proceeding against the bail is   * 643 a breach (*g*); but where an injunction to restrain proceedings at law has been obtained by an obligor in a joint and several bond upon a bill to which the co-obligor was not a party, a proceeding at law against the co-obligor is a breach of the injunction (*h*).

16. If an injunction has been granted against three plaintiffs at law, and dissolved only as against two, it is a contempt of court for the three afterwards to go on with the action; but if the injunction has been dissolved generally, and not as against two only, it is not a contempt for the two to proceed in the name of the three (*i*). Nor is the assignee of a *chose in action* guilty

---

(*a*) Bird *v.* Brancker, 2 Sm. & St. 186.

(*b*) Mills *v.* Cobby, 1 Mer. 3. See, also, 3 P. W. 147.

(*c*) Bullen *v.* Ovey, 16 Ves. 141; Mills *v.* Cobby, 1 Mer. 3; Franklyn *v.* Thomas, 3 Mer. 225; Brooks *v.* Purton, 1 Y. & C. C. C. 275; Burbidge *v.* Robinson, 14 Jur. 473. See Marsack *v.* Bailey, 2 Sm. & St. 577. Comp. Hankey *v.* Morris, 2 Eq. Ca. Ab. 528.

(*d*) Axe *v.* Clarke, 2 Dick. 549. But see, *per* Lord Eldon, Franklyn *v.* Thomas, 3 Mer. 234; Hawkshaw *v.* Parkins, 2 Sw. 539.

(*e*) Partington *v.* Booth, 3 Mer. 148.

(*f*) Woodley *v.* Boddington, 9 Sim. 214.

(*g*) 1 V. & B. 19; Leonard *v.* Attwell, 17 Ves. 386.

(*h*) Chaplin *v.* Cooper, 1 V. & B. 19.

(*i*) Money *v.* Jordan, 13 Beav. 229.

of a breach of injunction by taking proceedings at law after the dissolution of the injunction against himself, though the injunction has not been dissolved as against the assignor (*k*).

17. Where a creditor proceeds against an executor after notice of a decree to account, or after decree in an administration suit, it is so far a contempt that he will be deprived of all costs after receipt of notice of the decree (*l*).

18. Persons not named in the order or writ of injunction are not liable to be committed for the breach of an injunction by which they are enjoined (*m*). Thus, where an injunction restrained only A. B., but did not extend to "his servants and agents," the court declined to commit an agent of A. B. for breach of the injunction, inasmuch as he was not expressly enjoined in terms (*n*). So, also, an injunction restraining a defendant, his servants and agents, does extend to his tenants (*o*). The agents, however, of a man against whom an injunction has been awarded will be committed for contempt, if having knowledge of the injunction they act in contravention of the order of the court (*p*).

19. If no blame can be attached to a man personally, * 644   the court * will not commit him for contempt because his servants may have violated the injunction (*q*). But a man may be guilty of a breach of injunction by aiding and abetting those who are committing an act inconsistent with it, although he may not actually have taken part in such an act. Thus, where an injunction had been granted to restrain A., his servants and workmen, from cutting wood, it was held a breach of the injunction in A. to be present and be acting as leader where a number of poor people drove away the servants of the plaintiff and cut wood, although A. did not actually assist, but dissuaded the people from using violence, the ground being that remaining and acting as a leader, and not actually inter-

(*k*) Imperial Gas-light Co. *v.* Clarke, Younge, 584.

(*l*) Curre *v.* Bowyer, 3 Madd. 456; *supra*, p. 118.

(*m*) Iveson *v.* Harris, 7 Ves. 256.

(*n*) Lord Wellesley *v.* Lord Morning- ton, 11 Beav. 180. See Montague *v.* Hill, 4 Russ. 128.

(*o*) Hodson *v.* Coppard, 29 Beav. 4.

(*p*) Lord Wellesley *v.* Lord Morning- ton, 11 Beav. 181. See Powel *v.* Follet, Dick. 116; Lewes *v.* Morgan, 5 Pri. 518.

(*q*) Rantzen *v.* Rothschild, 14 W. R. 96.

fering to prevent the act complained of, he was, in the opinion of the court, inferentially assisting and aiding them (*r*).

20. An injunction protects only those named in the record, but if those named in the record can procure other parties equally interested with themselves to submit to the same terms as the plaintiffs on the record submit to, the court will give them the same relief or protection as to the plaintiffs on the record (*s*).

21. It is open to a man who is charged with having committed a breach of an injunction to show that the order carried on its face the period of its duration, and that, as that period has expired, there is no order which he has been guilty of infringing (*t*).

22. If there has been long delay in executing a warrant of commitment, the court will not entertain an *ex parte* application having for its object the enforcement of the order under which the warrant was issued. The plaintiff must get a new order on a motion to commit, or move on motion that cause may be shown why a new warrant should not issue (*u*).

23. The plaintiff may by acquiescence in the breach of an injunction deprive himself of the right to move for the commitment of the defendant, but there must, in order to deprive the party who has obtained the order of the right to move for commitment * upon breach, be a case made out *645 almost amounting to such a license to the party enjoined to do the act enjoined against, as would entitle him to maintain a bill against others from doing that act. The party enjoined must show such acquiescence as would be sufficient to create a new right in him. In a case where the court had granted an injunction to restrain the use of a trade-mark, and a breach had taken place, the court held that unless the defendant could show satisfactorily that he intended to use, and unless he undertook to use a particular mark which would not interfere with the plaintiff's mark, there must be an order for his committal (*v*).

(*r*) St. John's College *v.* Carter, 4 M. & C. 497. See Woodward *v.* Earl of Lincoln, 3 Sw. 626.

(*s*) Lund *v.* Blanshard, 4 Ha. 290.

(*t*) Daw *v.* Eley, 3 L. R. Eq. 496.

(*u*) St. John's College *v.* Carter, 8 Jur. 1036.

(*v*) Rodgers *v.* Nowill, 3 D. M. & G. 619.

24. If the party guilty of a breach of injunction is a peer or a member of Parliament (x), or a corporate body (y), or a company, or a person against whom process of contempt cannot issue, whether from his being out of the jurisdiction (z) or otherwise (a), the proper course is to move that a writ of sequestration shall issue (b).

25. If, upon hearing the affidavits on both sides, the court shall be of opinion that the party is guilty of a breach of injunction, it makes an order for his commitment, and he will not be discharged unless he pays the adverse party his costs (c). But where the breach is not wilful or contemptuous, or if the defendant has endeavored to set himself right, or expresses his regret for what he has done, the court is generally satisfied by merely making him pay the costs of the application of bringing the breach under the notice of the court (d).

* 646   26. * An order for commitment for breach of an injunction must state the affidavit of service of the restraining order or injunction, and either the affidavit of service of the notice of motion to commit, or the appearance of counsel for the defendant upon the motion (e). The order ought in strictness to be prefaced by an express adjudication that the act complained of is a contempt, but the absence of such adjudication is not a ground for discharging such an order for irregularity. It is not irregular to engraft upon the order an order that the party committed shall pay the costs of his contempt; but, if the order extends to charges and expenses as well as costs, it is to that extent irregular (f).[1]

(x) Rantzen $v.$ Rothschild, 14 W. R. 96. Comp. Lechmere-Charlton's case, 2 M. & C. 316.

(y) Att.-Gen. $v.$ Great Northern Railway Co., 4 De G. & S. 75; Spokes $v.$ Banbury Board of Health, 1 L. R. Eq. 42. See East India Co. $v.$ Kynaston, 3 Bligh, 153, 163.

(z) Re East of England Bank, 2 Dr. & Sm. 284.

(a) See Storer $v.$ Great Western Railway Co., 1 Y. & C. C. C. 180.

(b) See as to writ of sequestration, Empringham $v.$ Short, 3 Ha. 461; Tatham $v.$ Parker, 1 Sm. & G. 513.

(c) Harr. Ch. Pr.

(d) Bullen $v.$ Ovey, 16 Ves. 141; Leonard $v.$ Attwell, 17 Ves. 385; Par-

tington $v.$ Booth, 3 Mer. 149; Marsack $v.$ Bailey, 2 Sim. & St. 577; Woodley $v.$ Boddington, 9 Sim. 214; Littler $v.$ Thompson, 2 Beav. 129; Brooks $v.$ Purton, 1 Y. & C. C. C. 277; Newman $v.$ Ring, 10 Jur. 463; Lawford $v.$ Spicer, 2 Jur. N. S. 564; Lane $v.$ Sterne, 3 Giff. 629; Harding $v.$ Tingey, 12 W. R. 684; Rantzen $v.$ Rothschild, 14 W. R. 96.

(e) Stephens $v.$ Workman, 11 W. R. 503.

(f) Ex parte Van Sandau, 1 Ph. 605.
[1] Where the principal defendant had filed his bill in equity, and obtained a temporary injunction to stay plaintiffs' action at law against him, and had also, agreeably to the rule of court in such cases, filed his bond of indemnity

with sureties ; and where the principal defendant had failed to maintain his said bill, and thereby become liable on his bond of indemnity, as the reasonable damages which plaintiffs should recover under such bond, it was held that during the time plaintiffs were delayed by said injunction they should be allowed to recover their legal taxable costs, both in the suit at law and the bill in equity ; provided the plaintiff has not and cannot realize the same on the original proceedings against the principal defendant ; also plaintiffs' reasonable counsel fees, which they are liable to pay in both of the original cases for the same time, — but not interest accruing on the original note in the suit at law, unless plaintiff can show that the original defendant has become insolvent since the injunction, or that the plaintiff has suffered some damage equal to such interest, without fault. Derry Bank *v.* Heath, 45 N. H. 524. But a *liability* to pay money as for counsel fees, if it has not been actually paid, will not entitle the plaintiff to a judgment for damages. Prader *v.* Grimm, 28 Cal. 11. See, also, *ib.* 539, as to amount of damages and that several suits may be brought by joint obligees. Where a party was restrained by injunction from taking possession of a farm from March to September, he was allowed, in an action on the injunction bond, to show not only the value of the use of the land during that period, but that he lost the crops for the season by being kept out of the land. Edwards *v.* Edwards, 31 Ill. 474. A dissolution of an injunction is a technical breach of the bond, for which nominal damages may be recovered. Stone *v.* Cason, 1 Oregon, 100. But it is held that where the suit in which the injunction is obtained is dismissed by the action of the party who obtained it, this constitutes no admission that it was improperly sued out, which must be proved before damages can be recovered. Gelston *v.* Whitesides, 3 Cal. 309. A bond given on the issuing of an injunction is for the benefit of all the defendants that are enjoined, whether served with the process of injunction or not. Hence, if a party, without service of the injunction, obeys the injunction, he may, without any appearance, recover damages sustained by reason of the injunction. It has been held that it is the duty of the defendant to obey an injunction if he knows it has been granted, although it has not been served ; and if he disobeys it, he will be liable to an attachment. Cumberland Coal Co. *v.* Hoffman Steam Coal Co., 39 Barb. 16. To effect a regular service of an injunction, the writ itself, under the seal of the court, must be shown to the party against whom it issues, and a true copy thereof delivered to him. Personal service will be dispensed with where the party is out of the state or cannot be found. The modern practice is for the court, by special order, to dispense with personal service where the defendant avoids the service of the writ, or other circumstances as render such order necessary or proper. Haring *v.* Kauffman, 2 Beasley, 398, and cases cited. Upon a bond conditioned for the payment of all costs and damages arising from the obligors obtaining an injunction, money paid by the obligee for counsel fees is recoverable. Corcoran *v.* Judson, 24 N. Y. 106 ; Edwards *v.* Bodine, 11 Paige, 224 ; Coates *v.* Coates, 1 Duer, 664 ; McRae *v.* Brown, 12 La. An. 181 ; Thaie *v.* Quan Wan, 3 Cal. 216. Damages for injury to the defendant's credit by reason of the injunction, are not recoverable in suit on the bond. Hibbard *v.* McKindley, 28 Ill. 240. And where the injunction was to stay a suit at law, the plaintiff was allowed to allege and show, as a breach of the condition of the bond, that, by reason of the delay in obtaining judgment and execution, occasioned by the injunction, the property of the defendant in the suit at law was so wasted, sold, incumbered, and disposed of, that the plaintiff lost his debt. Tryon *v.* Robenson, 10 Richardson's Law, (S. C.) 160.

INDEX.

Abandonment, 358, 386A.

ABATEMENT OF SUIT,

    injunction not dissolved by, 632, 633.

ABRIDGMENT,

    copyright in, 457.

    whether or not a piracy, 457.

ACCESS,

    of light and air to windows, 352, 353.

    to the sea-shore or a navigable river, 398.

    order to permit, 328.

ACCEPTANCE,

    of bill of exchange, injunction against the, 595.

ACCIDENT,

    general doctrine as to, 55, 56.

    no equity on ground of, where there is negligence, 23, 57.

        or when a man fails to observe a covenant, 56, 85.

    timber severed by, 280.

ACCOUNT,

    general doctrine as to, 57–61.

        complicated accounts, 58–61.

        mutual accounts, 59.

        stated account, 60–62.

        settled account, 62.

    injunctions against actions at law for, 62, 63.

        pleading and parties, 63.

    injunctions against proceedings at law against executors after order for, 108, 109.

    as incident to an injunction to restrain the violation of a common-law right, 228, 284, 472.

        no account in general unless injunction be competent, 228, 284, 435.

            exceptions, 284, 285.

43

ACCOUNT — *continued.*

limited to moneys actually received, and profits actually made, 228, 285.

no account, if acts be unattended by profit, 228, 285, 472.

limited to profits for six years before bill filed, 228, 286, 329, 436.
exception, 329.

delay and acquiescence, as a bar to the application, 228, 286, 436.

discovery for purposes of, 228, 473, 490.

of waste, 284–286.

in timber, 278–281.

in trespass, 329, 330.

in patent cases, 435–437.

in copyright cases, 472, 473.

in trade-mark cases, 489, 490.

account not usually taken, 228, 435.

ACQUIESCENCE, *see Delay.*

principle of, 41, 201.

on what founded, 40, 41.

what is necessary to constitute, 42, 202.

application of the principle, 17, 40, 201.

extent of the principle, 40–42.

cases in which principle does not apply, 42, 43, 202–204.

as a bar to an interlocutory injunction, 17, 201, 205, 298, 348, 349, 406, 440, 483, 496.

as a bar to relief at the hearing, 205, 226.

cases in which the principle applies most strongly, 201, 202, 349.

extent of expenditure to a certain degree the measure of, 202.

may give a man an equity to restrain another from seeking damages at law, 226, 227.

of agent binds the principal, 202.

binding on corporation as well as individual, 42, 203.

circumstances, &c., excluding, 203, 204, 483.

conduct with others may constitute, 203, 496.

under order for an injunction, effect of, 632.

ACTING,

not a publication, 184.

injunction to restrain a player from, 521, 527.

ACTS OF PARLIAMENT,

special railway act, 316, 325, 326.

construction of, 301–303.

rights arising under, are legal rights, 541.

ADDITION,

copyright in, 459.

ADMINISTRATION OF ASSETS. See *Decree for Administration of Assets.*

ATTORNEY-GENERAL,

must sue, if act complained of affects the public interest, 297, 334, 542, 571.

injunctions at suit of, to restrain trespass, 297.

injunctions at suit of, to restrain nuisance, 334, 396.

purprestures, 395.

a company from going beyond the purposes for which it was incorporated, 542.

injunctions at suit of, to restrain a corporation or public body from misapplying its funds, 571–573.

not a party if act complained of do not affect the public interest, 174.

AWARD,

jurisdiction of equity over, 140.

no injunction to restrain arbitrator from making, 142.

injunction to restrain parties from proceeding before arbitrator for an, 142, 143.

no injunction when under statute of Will. 3, 140.

no injunction if made a rule of court of common law, 141.

under Benefit Building Act, 142.

injunction to restrain commissioners from enrolling, 597.

B.

BANK OF ENGLAND. See *Transfer of Stock.*

injunctions at suit of, to restrain a banking company from accepting a bill of exchange, 595.

restrained by injunction, 591.

restraining order against, 591.

BANKER,

bill of interpleader by, 130.

BANKRUPT,

may move to dissolve, without making assignees parties, 631.

injunctions to restrain sale of property of, 585, 586.

BANKRUPTCY,

injunctions in matters of, 583.

of plaintiff does not dissolve an injunction, 633.

injunctions against action at law, after filing a trust deed, &c., in, 107.

BANKRUPTCY COURT,

injunctions in aid of, 583, 584.

injunctions by, 584, 585.

injunctions against proceedings in, 153, 585.

injunction to stay sale of goods ordered to be sold by the, 586.

BANKS OF A RIVER,

not to repair, is waste, 245.

BARRIERS IN MINES, 391.

BELL RINGING,
injunctions against, 363, 364, 503.

BENEFIT BUILDING SOCIETY,
members bound by rules, 568.
no interference of equity with, 568.
may invest funds in real estate, 569.
award, 142.

BIBLES,
copyright in, 461.

BILL OF EXCHANGE,
injunctions against negotiation of, 595.
injunctions against acceptance of, 595.

BILL OF LADING,
interpleader by captain against parties claiming, one paramount to and
the other under a, 123.

BILL OF PEACE, 134–136, *Addenda.*

BISHOP. See *Ecclesiastical Persons.*
may not open mines, 266.
injunctions against, 266.
restrained from presenting, instituting, or collating, 577, 601, 602.

BOARDS OF HEALTH, 326.
injunctions against, 326, 348, 393, 394.
injunctions at suit of, 347.

BOND,
given under Lands Clauses Act, 308, 309.
given as a reward for exercising influence over another, 49.

BOOK. See *Copyright.*
within the meaning of the Copyright Act, 446.
of an immoral, indecent, seditious, &c., nature, no copyright in, 451.
a separate article for a periodical is not a, 447.
of chronology, copyright in, 450, 455.
of statistics, copyright in, 450.
elementary lessons in science, arithmetic, &c., coypright in, 450.

BREACH,
of covenant or agreement. See *Agreement ; Covenant.*
of injunction, 637, 638.
what constitutes, 641–643.
acquiescence in, 644–646.
committal for, 638, 639, 645.
sequestration for, 645.
costs, 645.

BREWHOUSE,
not necessarily a nuisance, 362.

CHILD,

general doctrine with respect to dealings between father and, 45–47.

injunctions against father with respect to custody of, 598, 599.

CHIMNEY,

injunctions against obstructing a, 366.

CHURCH, *see minister*

altering the fittings in a, 266.

warming a, 399.

injunctions to restrain a man, improperly appointed minister, from performing divine service in a, 173.

CHURCHYARD,

timber in a, 265.

nuisance in a, 398.

injunctions against waste in a, 266, 267.

rights of burial in a, 262.

CLAY,

waste by digging, 245, 248.

estovers of, 247, 248.

clean hands right of copyholder of inheritance by custom to dig, 248. *complainant must have 2 oo.*

CLERK,

restrained from communicating, or making public papers, documents, &c., of his employer, 177, 178.

CLOUD UPON TITLE,

injunctions to remove the effect of an instrument, which operates as a, 597.

COLLUSION,

waste by, 277.

between directors of a company and creditor to enforce his debt against a particular shareholder, 547.

COLOR OF TITLE,

trespass under, 290, 291.

COLORABLE IMITATION,

of a work protected by copyright, 454–456.

of a trade-mark, 483–485.

COMMISSION,

injunctions to enforce the assignment by an officer in the army of the proceeds of his, 102.

COMMISSIONERS,

ecclesiastical, 266.

drainage,

restrained by injunction, 348.

of sewers, 347.

restrained by injunction, 347.

injunctions at suit of, 347.

COMPANIES — *continued.*

 who may sue, 549–551.

 pleading, 551.

 defendants to suit, 551.

 delay and acquiescence as a bar to the suit, 551–553.

 costs, 569.

may apply corporate funds to a purpose legitimately connected with the objects of the company, 564, 565.

not interfered with in matters of internal regulation, 565–567.

 • unless in exceptional cases, 567, 568.

powers of a general meeting of, 568.

forfeiture of shares in, 94, 95.

COMPENSATION,

 under Lands Clauses Act, 311, 343, 344.

 for land taken, 311, 343.

 for lands injuriously affected, 341, 342.

 for severance, 311.

 for minerals, 372, 373.

 land-owner not bound to prove damage before seeking, 344.

 need not be tendered before commencing works, 343.

 injunction to restrain a man from seeking, 345. *Complainant must be without fault* 200

COMPLETE JUSTICE,

 as understood in equity, 3, 4.

COMPOSITION DEED,

 fraud upon a, 49.

CONCEALMENT. See *Fraud.*

 in a specification renders a patent void, 419.

CONCURRENT JURISDICTION,

 meaning of, 3. *Condition of granting or refusing* 210

CONDITION PRECEDENT, 98.

 must be literally performed, 98.

 no relief in equity except there be fraud, 98.

CONDITION SUBSEQUENT, 97.

 forfeiture for breach of, 97.

  relief against, 97, 98.

CONFIDENCE. See *Fiduciary Relation, Trustees.*

 injunctions against acts in breach of, 177, 183.

CONFIDENTIAL COMMUNICATIONS,

 injunctions against the disclosure of, 177–179.

 not protected from disclosure, if there be fraud or an illegal purpose, 177–179. *What are Confidential 178*

CONSERVATION,

 right of, in navigable tidal waters, 397.

COVENANTS — *continued.*

    rights of other parties taken into consideration, 497.

    negative, enforced by injunction, 503–506.

    negative quality imported into affirmative, 521–523.

    negative quality not imported into affirmative, 524–526.

    containing affirmative and negative stipulations, 528, 529.

    enforcement of, against persons taking with notice, 530–532.

    injunctions against actions at law upon, 539, 540.

    forfeiture for breach of, 85–90.

        no relief against, except under special circumstances, 85, 91.

    to insure, relief against forfeiture for breach, 87.

    mandatory injunctions against breach of, 533–535.

    perpetual injunctions against breach of, 532, 533.

CREDITORS. See *Decree for Administration of Assets.*

    injunctions against actions at law by, after decree for administration, 107.

    transactions in fraud of, 49. *5 7 9*

CRIMINAL PROCEEDINGS,

    no injunction to restrain, 2.

CROPS,

    damage to, 398.

CROWN COPYRIGHT, 461.

CURTESY,

    tenant by, may not commit waste, 239, 257.

CUSTOM,

    of London, 357.

    of the country, 249, 250.

    of a manor, forfeiture according to, 97.

        no relief against, 97.

D.

DAMAGE,

    irreparable, 199, 200, 225, 350.

    prospective or threatened, 197, 198, 236, 339.

    special, 298, 334, 544.

    temporary, 338.

    substantial, 238, 300, 301, 544.

    from repetition may be substantial, 338.

    to rights in water, 378–380, 382, 393, 394.

    in the construction of works, rightfully and properly done, 341, 342.

        wrongfully or improperly done, 341, 342.

DAMAGES,

    courts of equity have no inherent power to give, 221.

    effect and meaning of Statute 21 & 22 Vict. c. 27, as to, 221, 222.

    exercise of jurisdiction as to, is discretionary, 222.

DELAY. See *Acquiescence*.

may disentitle a man to an interlocutory injunction, 205, 206, 298, 349, 406, 551.

in applying to court to restrain proceedings at law, 30, 94.

in cases of waste, not so material as in other cases, 238.

not material, so long as things remain *in statu quo*, 206, 574.

in coming for an account, 228, 286.

DELIVERY,

of deeds, goods, &c., to another, injunctions against the, 596.

up of possession, injunctions to stay, 21.

DEMURRER, *In interpleader 126*

injunction not granted pending, 619.

exception in special cases, 213, 619.

and motion for injunction argued together, 619.

injunction not necessarily granted on overruling, 213, 619.

injunction put an end to by allowance of, 634.

except, allowance be on technical grounds, 634. *Do to not lie by one deft because another improperly joined 127*

DESIGNS,

copyright in, 466–470.

DEVIATION,

limits of, under Railways Clauses Act, 317–320.

land necessary for the proper purposes of the company may be taken, though beyond the, 319.

land may not be taken, except for the proper purposes of the act, although within, 319.

injunction to restrain a railway company from exercising their powers of, 318, 320.

DICTIONARIES,

copyright in, 450.

piracy of, 455.

DILAPIDATIONS, 252.

DIRECTORY,

copyright in a, 450.

piracy of, 455.

DISCLAIMER,

in reference to the patent law, 425–427.

DISCLOSURE,

of confidential communications, papers, &c., restrained, 177, 178.

no injunction, if there be fraud, &c., 177–179.

of trade secrets not restrained, 181.

unless there be breach of confidence, 181.

DISCOVERY,

injunctions to restrain proceedings at law until, 27, 28.

pleading and affidavits, 28–30.

ELECTION,

between action and suit, 103.

injunctions to stay proceedings at law after, to sue in equity, 103–105.

ELECTRIC TELEGRAPH COMPANY,

injunctions against, 335.

ENDORSEMENT,

of securities, injunctions against, 595.

ENGRAVINGS,

copyright in, 464–466.

piracy of, 464–466.

no copyright in immoral, &c., 466.

printed abroad, copyright in, 465, 466, 471.

ENTRY,

on land, 326.

under the Lands Clauses Act, 307–316.

clauses prohibiting, without consent of land-owner, 325.

under Public Health Act, 326.

under Metropolis Local Management Act, 326.

under Thames Embankment Act, 327.

in the register book, 447.

EQUITABLE ASSIGNMENT,

what constitutes an, 99, 100.

notice of the assignment necessary as against purchasers for value, 100, 101.

future property may be the subject of, 100.

cases in which there can be no valid, 101, 102.

by an officer in the army of the proceeds of his commission, 102.

injunctions to enforce, 99, 100.

EQUITABLE GROUNDS FOR RESTRAINING PROCEEDINGS AT LAW,

accident, 55.   See *Accident.*

lost bond or other security, 56.

as distinguished from negligence, 22, 23, 57.

no equity in favor of lessee upon destruction of house by fire, 56, 57.

or of a man who having entered into a covenant fails to perform it, *ib.* 85.

account, 57–63.   See *Account.*

as distinguished from set-off, 59.

complicated accounts, 58–61.

mutual accounts, 59.

stated or settled impeached for fraud, 61, 62.

in case of fiduciary relationship, 57, 58.

injunctions against actions for account, 62, 63.

fraud, 31–33.   See *Fraud.*

G.

GAMING TRANSACTIONS, 50.

GARDENS,
waste in, 244.

GAS COMPANY,
restrained from committing nuisance, 361, 362.

GENERAL MEETING,
of a company, limits of powers of a, 568.

GIVING JUDGMENT, 18, 19.

GENERAL RELIEF,
injunction not obtained under prayer for, 607.
damages may be had under prayer for, 223.

GLEBE,
timber on, 265, 267. *Good will 574, 167*

GOVERNMENT,
no interference with the public duties of a department of the, 3, 599.
no interference with the sovereign acts of a foreign, 3.
department of, restrained from doing a ministerial act, 599.

GRAMMARS,
copyright in, 450, 455.
piracy of, 455.

GRANT,
construction of a, 355, 392.
of lands and mines, 246.

GRAVEL,
waste by digging, 245–247.
estovers in, 247, 248.
right of copyholder of inheritance by custom to dig, 248.

GUARDIAN AND WARD. See *Infant.*
general doctrine with respect to dealings between, 45, 46.
injunction to restrain intercourse between, 598.
injunction to restrain guardian from permitting marriage of ward, 598.
no interference with discretion of foreign guardian, 599.

GUIDE BOOK,
copyright in a, 450.
piracy of, 455.

H.

HARBORS,
nuisance to, 396. *Harm injunction not granted because will do no 114*

HEALTH,
boards of, restrained by injunction, 348, 394.

HEIR,
by resulting trust within principle of equitable waste, 260.

INFORMATION — *continued.*

to restrain corporations from misapplying the corporate funds, 571–573.

name of person not to be used as relator in an, without written authority, 609.

INFRINGEMENT,

of copyright, 451.

in books, 451–459.

in dramatic pieces and musical compositions, 459, 463, 464.

in prints, &c., 464–466.

in designs, 468, 469.

of patents, 429–432.

functions of judge and jury on questions as to the, 433.

intention immaterial, if there has been an, 432, 444.

INJUNCTION. See *Motion, Writ of Injunction.*

meaning of interlocutory, 11, 12, 196.

general principles on which granted, 12, 14, 196, 208–210.

not in general granted, except on bill filed, 605.

exceptions, 605–607.

should be specifically prayed by bill, 607.

not in general granted, except against a party to the bill, 605–607.

exceptions, 605–607, 624.

generally obtained on motion, 607, 608.

may be obtained at any stage of the proceedings, 608.

may be obtained during vacation, 608.

obtained on *ex parte* application, 608, 610.

not granted, pending demurrer, plea, &c., 619.

prayed must be consistent with case made out, 619.

ordered on affidavit of service, if defendant does not appear, 621.

terms of order for, 624.

order for, should be specific and should declare the rights, 623.

waiver of irregular, 632.

acquiescence under order for, 632.

service of notice of order for, 625, 638.

operates from date of order, 625, 637, 638.

effect of amendment on, 634.

goes of course on dismissal of bill, 635.

dissolution of, 626.

discharge of order for, 631.

not dissolved by abatement of suit, 632.

until answer, not dissolved by putting in a sufficient answer, 633.

continuing, at the hearing, 637.

perpetual, 11, 225.

not granted before the hearing, 227.

granted though not prayed by the bill, 607, 637.

is in effect a decree, 133, 637.

mandatory, 230.

MINISTER — *continued.*

of a chapel, improperly dismissed, injunction from hindering in the discharge of his office, 173.

injunction to restrain a, from preaching, 173.

MISAPPLICATION,

of corporate or other funds, restrained by injunction, 548, 554, 572, 573.

MISREPRESENTATION. See *Fraud.*

MISTAKE,

in law, 52, *Addenda.*

when relieved against, 52.

in fact, 53.

when relieved against, 53, 54.

in pleading or conduct of a cause, &c., 22, 54.

rectification of instrument on ground of, 55.

in books of reference of a railway company, 305.

MONEYS,

injunctions to restrain the receipt, payment, &c., of, 595–597.

injunctions to restrain a man from applying for, 596.

or executing a power of attorney enabling another to receive, 596.

payment of, into court, on obtaining an injunction, 19, 20, 212, 622.

MORTGAGEE,

may in general pursue all his remedies, concurrently, 105, 106, 191.

may, on a proper case being made out, be restrained from pursuing all his remedies concurrently, 191, 192.

restrained from suing mortgagor on his covenant to pay, 192.

restrained from exercising power of sale, 193.

from parting with surplus moneys, 193, 261.

from presenting to a benefice, 194.

from dealing with a ship in derogation of a charter-party, 194, 532.]

may not commit waste, if security be sufficient, 261.

may commit waste, if security be not sufficient, 261.

of burial-ground may not commit waste, 262.

committing waste, pending redemption suit, 261.

injunctions at suit of equitable, 194, 195, 261.

interest of, in lands taken under Lands Clauses Act, 314.

MORTGAGOR IN POSSESSION,

may not commit waste, if security be insufficient, 262.

pleading on application for injunction, 262.

may not commit waste if bankrupt, 262.

MOTION.

injunctions obtained on, 607, 608.

form of notice of, 611.

service of notice of, 609–611.

time for making, 612?

MOTION — *continued.*

    saving, 620, 621.

    hearing, on affidavits, 617, 618.

    evidence on the, 615, 616, 618.

    declaration of the rights of parties on the, 623, 624.

    for injunction turned into motion for decree, 623.

    to advance the cause, 623.

    to dissolve, 626, 627.

        ex parte injunctions, 628, 629.

        injunctions until discovery, 629, 630.

        who should move, 630, 631.

        in interpleader suits, 130.

        effect of delay, 632.

    to discharge an irregular order, 631, 632.

    for a new trial, 218–220, *Addenda.*

    to commit for breach of injunction, 639.

        notice of, 639.

        form of, 639.

MOTIONS,

    order of taking the, 616.

MOTIVES,

    of instituting a suit sometimes regarded, 207, 335, 336, 549.

MULTIPLICITY OF SUITS,

    bill to restrain, 134–136.

MUSICAL COMPOSITION,

    copyright in, 462, 464.

        what constitutes piracy of, 459.

N.

NAVIGABLE TIDAL RIVER,

    rights of Crown to soil of, 395, 397.

    purpresture, 395.

        injunction to restrain, 395.

    right of conservation, 397.

    nuisance to public right of navigation, 396.

        injunctions against, 396.

    fouling a, 396.

    private rights of fishing in a, 136, 396.

        injunctions to protect, 136, 396.

    access to,

        injunctions against obstructing, 398.

NAVIGATION,

    nuisance to, 395, 396.

NEGOTIATION OF SECURITIES,

    injunctions against the, 595.

NUISANCE — *continued.*

    to dwelling-houses and houses of business, 350, 351, 365, 366.

        standard of damage required by the court as a condition of its interference by injunction, 351.

        who may sue, 351.

        obstructing of light and air, 352–360.

        pollution of air, 360–362.

        noise and noisy trades, 363, 364.

        interference with right of drain and drip, 364, 365.

        various nuisances, 365, 366.

        mandatory injunctions against, 366.

    to support, 366–377.

    relating to water, 377–395.

        injunctions against, 393–395.

    to navigable tidal waters, 395, 396.

    perpetual injunction against, 350.

NUISANCES REMOVAL ACT,

    persons acting under, restrained by injunction, 348.

Officer to Removal of 175

O.

OFFICER OF A COMPANY,

    man restrained from acting as, 602.

OFFICER OF THE COURT,

    injunctions to restrain proceedings at law against an, 144.

        receivers, 145.

        sequestrators, 146.

    injunction, to restrain proceedings at law by an, 147.

    sheriff not an, 147.

ORCHARDS,

    waste in, 244.

ORNAMENTAL TIMBER. See *Equitable Waste, Timber, Trees.*

OUTLAWRY,

    injunctions to stay process in, 21.

P.

PAINTINGS,

    copyright in, 466.

PARENT AND CHILD,

    rule in equity as to dealings between, 45, 46.

    parent restrained from custody of child, 598, 599.

PARK,

    waste in a, 245.

        reclaiming deer, 245.

PARLIAMENT,

construction of acts of, 301, 302.

no injunction in general to restrain a man from applying to, 9, 557.

court may, however, restrain a man from applying to, 519, 520.

agreement not to apply to, may be enforced, 519, 520.

injunction to restrain a company from applying the corporate funds in paying the expenses of an application to, 556, 573, 574.

PARLIAMENTARY POWERS.

to take land, nature of, 298–300.

persons having, may take what they deem necessary, if there be *bona fides*, 302, 303.

PARTICEPS CRIMINIS,

the aid of the court may be sometimes given to a, 51.

PARTICULARS,

delivery of, 407, 408.

PARTIES,

absence of, not material, if property be in danger, 208, 237.

in suits to restrain the violation of a common-law right, 207, 208, 440.

one suit cannot be maintained against several persons for distinct invasions of a right, 207, 336, 404, 440, 550, 551.

misjoinder of, 336, 480, 551.

demurrer for want of, 480. *action against Corporation 570*

PARTING,

with property, documents, &c., injunctions to restrain the, 489, 595, 596.

PARTNER, *Both may carry on business in old name 167*

injunctions to restrain a man from holding out another as, 169, 170.

injunctions to restrain an action at law by one, against another, 169.

may, in the absence of agreement, carry on business after dissolution, 167, 478.

restrained from carrying on business after dissolution contrary to agreement, 167.

who seeks equity must do equity, 170.

misconduct of, quarrels, &c., 168.

protection of partnership property from creditors of a deceased or bankrupt, 169.

PARTNERSHIP,

effect of appointment of a receiver of a, 170.

injunctions during or after dissolution of, 166.

injunction, though dissolution not sought, 164, 165.

injunction to restrain a man from holding out that he is in, with another trader, 478.

PARTNERSHIP STYLE. See *Trade-Mark.*

right to, after dissolution, 167, 168, 477–479.

after decease of partner, 168, 479.

passes on the assignment of the business, 168, 479.

PETITION,
    injunction granted on, 607, 608.
PHOTOGRAPHS,
    copyright in, 466.
PIRACY,
    of copyright in books, 451–455.
    of copyright in prints, engravings, &c., 464, 465.
    of copyright in musical compositions, 459.
    of trade-marks, 483, 484.
PISCARY,
    drying up, 245.
PLANS,
    of a projected railway, 305, 316, 317.
    if referred to, read along with agreement, 501.
    mere exhibition of, not a warranty, 501.
PLEA,
    injunction not granted pending a, 619.
    effect of allowance of, on injunction, 634.
PLEA ON EQUITABLE GROUND. See *Equitable Plea.*
PLEADING,
    in bills to restrain actions at law, 16, 17.
                until discovery, 29, 30.
    in interpleader suits, 126, 127.
    in bills for the protection of legal rights pending the trial of the right, 206, 237.
    in bills to restrain the infringement of patents, 403–405.
    in bills to restrain the infringement of copyright, 439, 440.
    acquiescence in a nuisance, 350.
    damage in trade-mark cases, 480.
    in suits to restrain setting up terms, 589.
    in suits by judgment creditors, 580.
    in suits by a shareholder against a company, 551.
    parties seeking equitable relief must waive penalties, 237, 442.
POSSESSION,
    taken under Lands Clauses Act, 304–310.
    no injunction against parties continuing in, 311, 325.
    ordered to be delivered up to sequestrator, 599, 600.
    injunction to quiet, until the hearing, 603, 604.
    injunction to stay delivery up of, 21.
    of a cause by the court,
        injunctions against proceedings at law after, 103–105.
PREFERENCE SHARES, 559, 560.
    injunction against issuing, 566.
PRESCRIPTION ACT, 354, 356, 383, 384.
    cases in which it does not apply, 360, 362.

RAILWAY COMPANY — *continued.*
restrained from doing improper acts, 559.
restrained from issuing preference shares, 559, 560.
working agreements of, with another company, 560–562.
power of, to pass over another line, 322–324.
agreement of, as to passing over another line, 322, 323.
powers of, to effect a junction with another line, 323, 324.

RAILWAY TRAFFIC AND CANAL ACT, 543.
injunctions under, 543, 544. *Reason none required if has power of removal 175*

RECEIVER, *Cannot be interfered with 145, 146*
pending suit respecting probate, 162.
in partnership cases, 170.
of rents of land, 195.
promoters of a company taking land in possession of a, 305.
proceedings at law against, restrained, 145, 146.
may have an injunction against waste by tenants for years, 264.
effect of appointment of, 170.

RECREATION,
ground dedicated to public, 398.

RECTIFICATION,
of instruments on ground of mistake, 55.

REFERENCE,
books of, 316, 317. *Reformation of Contracts 54*

REGATTA,
holding a, 366.

REGISTRATION. See *Copyright.*

REGISTRY,
injunction to stay indorsement of certificate of, 96.

RELATOR,
name of person not to be used as, without written authority, 609.
unless in very pressing cases, 609. *Religious Societies See "Church" Minister*

REMAINDER-MAN. See *Copyholder, Reversioner.*
may not commit waste, 277.
may not join in waste for his own benefit, 256, 277.
may have an injunction against waste by tenant for life, 235.
for life may have an injunction against waste, 236, 256.
mesne, may have an injunction against waste, 256.
but not an account, 286.
of equitable estate may have an injunction against waste, 257.
of part of the inheritance may have an injunction against waste, 257.
relief in equity against sale by, of his interest in remainder, 48. *Removal where is transferred to/not 175*

RENEWABLE LEASES. See *Lessee, Tenant for Lives renewable for ever.*

RENEWAL,
covenant for perpetual, forfeiture for breach of, 90.

RENT,
   relief against forfeiture for non-payment of, 83, 84.
REPAIRS. See *Estovers, Covenant, Forfeiture, Permissive Waste.*
REPORTS,
   of cases at law, copyright in, 450, 462.
RESTRAINT OF TRADE,
   covenants in, 506–508.
      when valid, 508–511.
      enforceable by injunction, 504–507, 512, 513.
REVERSIONER,
   may have an injunction against nuisance, 336, 337, 351.
   may have an injunction against breach of covenant, 502.
   bound, if right to light is acquired against lessee, 357.
   sale by, set aside, 48.
REVIEW,
   copyright in articles contributed to a, 459–461.
REVIVOR,
   not necessary in perpetual injunction, 133.
RIDE,
   protection to timber given by a, 272.
RIGHT OF COMMON,
   bill of peace in respect of, 135, 136.
RIGHT OF WAY,
   nuisance to a, 398.
   obstruction of a, 534.
RIPARIAN PROPRIETORS,
   rights and liabilities of, 378–381, 391.
   injunctions against, 330, 393, 394.
   cannot grant their water-rights apart from their estate in the land, 378.
RIVER. See *Stream, Water, Watercourse.*
   rights of riparian proprietors in the bed of a, 377.
   rights of riparian proprietors in the water of a, 378, 379.
   user of water of, for domestic purposes, 380.
   user of water of, for manufacturing or agricultural purposes, 380.
   banks of a, getting out of repair, 522.
   navigable tidal, nuisance to a, 396, 397.
      rights of Crown in a, 395–397.
      right of conservation, 397.
      powers of commissioners of sewers as to a, 397.
      private or exclusive right of fishery in a, 136, 396.
ROAD, *allowing walls &c. 245.*
   power to mineral proprietor to make a, over land of others, 303.
   public interference with or obstruction of a, 320, 321, 534.
   construction of railways over, 320, 321.

SECRETS,
    of trade, injunctions against the disclosure of, 181.
    no injunction against disclosing, contrary to agreement, 525.
SECURITIES,
    marshalling, 69, 70.
    right of surety to, in hands of the creditor, 77.
    injunction against the negotiation, assignment, &c., of, 595.
SEEDS,
    sowing land with pernicious, 250.
SEPARATION DEED,
    covenants in a, enforced by injunction, 506.
SEQUESTRATION
    injunctions in matters of, 599, 600.
    writ of, for breach of injunction, 645.
SEQUESTRATOR,
    injunctions to restrain proceedings against, 146.
    forcibly dispossessed, injunction to restore possession of, 146.
    writ of assistance to put, in possession, 147, 600.
SERVICE,
    of bill, 608, 609.
    of notice of motion, 609, 610.
    of short notice of motion, 610.
    of notice of injunction, 624, 638.
    of order for injunction, 624, 625.
    substituted, 609, 625.
    affidavit of, 621.
        order for injunction made on, if defendant do not appear, 621.
    of notice of motion to commit, 639.
SET–OFF. See *Equitable Set-Off.*
    general doctrine as to, 63, 64.
SETTING UP IMPEDIMENTS. See *Setting up Terms.*
    at law, parties restrained from, 587–589.
        purchaser for value without notice, not restrained, 588.
SETTING UP TERMS,
    parties restrained from, 587.
        pleading, 589; parties, 589.
        not done upon motion, 589.
    purchaser for value without notice not restrained from, 588.
SETTLOR,
    waste by the, 268.
    voluntary,
        of real estate may defeat the settlement by sale, 172, 594.
        of personal chattels not restrained from defeating the settlement,
        172.

SURETY — *continued.*

not discharged by taking further security, 75.

    by passive inactivity of debtor, 75, 76.

    by assignment of debt, 75.

reservation of rights against, on giving time, 73.

entitled to benefit of securities in hands of creditor, 77.

creditor not bound to proceed against the debtor before proceeding against, 76.

cannot put an end to liability, 76.

indorsee of accommodation bill is in the position of a, 71.

notice that a man appearing as a joint debtor is a, is binding on creditor from date of notice, 78.

T.

TENANT. See *Landlord and Tenant.*

TENANT BY THE CURTESY OR DOWER,
liable for waste at common law, 239, 257.

TENANT FOR LIFE. See *Estovers.*

liable for waste by statute, 239, 256.

property of, in timber, &c., 239–241, 280.

may not fell timber, except for special purposes, 240, 241, 243.

may take estovers of timber, 243, 244.

may not open mines, 246.

may work open mines, 245, 246.

may not work open limestone quarries, 247.

may take estovers of minerals, clay, &c., 247.

may cut turfs for estovers, 247.

in remainder may have an injunction, 235, 236, 257.

TENANT FOR LIFE WITHOUT IMPEACHMENT OF WASTE, 267, 268.

may not commit equitable waste, 268, 282.

pulling down mansion-house, buildings, &c., 269.

cutting ornamental timber, 270–274, 282, 283.

    trees planted for shelter, 271.

may thin ornamental timber, &c., 274.

may not cut young trees or saplings, 274.

    or underwood of insufficient growth, 275.

may open and work mines, 284.

may not derive an undue advantage from a power of sale or exchange, 276.

receiving price of growing timber on a sale, 279.

may not commit waste by collusion, 277.

may not authorize waste before his estate comes into possession, 277.

made subject to trustee of a term, 276.

qualified by clause " except voluntary waste," &c., 275.

TERMS. See *Setting up Terms*.
 imposed as a condition of granting or withholding an injunction, 18, 19, 210, 211, 621–623.
 of order for injunction, 624.

TIMBER,
 what trees are, 239–241.
 property in growing, 240.
 rights of copyholder in, 242.
 rights of copyholder of inheritance by custom in, 242, 243.
 waste in, 240, 241.
 on ecclesiastical estates, 265.
 property in, severed accidentally or wrongfully, 280, 282, 283.
  wrongdoer can derive no benefit, 281, 282.
  proper thinnings of trees, &c., in a wood, 282.
 cut under the direction of the court, 277–279.
  application of produce, 278, 279.
  on estate of infant, 279.
  on ecclesiastical estates, 267, 279, 285.
  Settled Estates Act, 279.
 property in, severed on estate of infant, 258, 279.
  severed on lunatic's estate, 244, 281.
 ornamental, what is to be considered, 270–274.
  property in, severed wrongfully, 282.
   cut under direction of the court, 279.
  may be thinned, 274.

TIMBER ESTATES, 241.

TITLE, *Property to be acquired 1 &c.*
 color of, 290, 291.
 of a book, right of author in the, 478, 479.
 of a journal, name of editor not a necessary part of, 479.
 of a patent, 423.

TRADE,
 fixtures set up for, 253.
 trees planted for the purpose of, 253.
 covenants in restraint of, 505–513.
  restraint in point of time, 509.
  restraint as to space, 510–513.
 injunctions to restrain setting up a, 167, 504, 505, 507, 513.

TRADE LIST,
 copyright in, 450.

TRADE-MARK,
 nature of a, 474, 475.
 may be either local or personal, 476.
 subject of a, 476.
 name may be a, 476.

TRESPASS — *continued.*

 naked trespass, 293.

 principles on which the court interferes, 294, 295.

  pleading, 311.

  no injunction in general, if act is complete, 295.

   exceptions, 295.

 trespass by companies or bodies, incorporated by statute, 295.

  principles on which the court interferes, 296, 297, 304.

   no injunction to restrain a company in possession under a legal or equitable title from continuing in possession, 297, 311, 325.

   after winding-up order, leave must be had, 297.

  if there be public damage, the Attorney-General should sue, 297.

  private persons may sue, if specially injured, 298, 300, 318.

 delay and acquiescence as a bar to an injunction, 201–205, 298.

 account as incident to injunctions against, 329.

  limited to six years before bill filed, 329.

   exception, if there be fraud, 329.

  of minerals, charges, allowances, &c., 330.

 perpetual injunctions against, 331.

 mandatory injunctions against, 330, 331.

TRIAL OF ISSUES, 217.

 not directed before hearing, 219.

 mode of, 218, 224.

 scientific evidence on, 219.

 in a patent suit, 407–409.

 verdict of jury, 218.

 findings of the judge, 219.

 verdict or findings may be questioned, 219.

 motion for new, 218–220, *Addenda.*

 costs, 221.

TRUE AND FIRST INVENTOR, 413, 414.

TRUSTEES,

 injunctions against, 171, 172, 592.

 for public purposes, injunctions against misapplication of trust funds by, 571–574, 576.

  who should sue, 174, 571.

  parties to the suit, 174, 571.

 under trust deeds for religious bodies, injunctions against, 173, 174.

  who should sue, 174. ·

  parties, 174.

 under trust deeds for the purposes of education, injunctions against, 173, 175, 176.

 of the fee, right and duty of, in respect to waste, 257.

 for purchase, also tenants for life, 277.

 of a term of years without impeachment of waste, 275, 276.

Cambridge: Press of John Wilson and Son.

18639295R00469

Printed in Great Britain
by Amazon